# Texas

**Published by AAA Publishing**
1000 AAA Drive, Heathrow, FL 32746-5063
Copyright AAA 2013, All rights reserved

**Advertising Rate and Circulation Information: (407) 444-8280**

**Printed in the USA by Quad/Graphics**

**This book is printed on paper certified by third-party standards for sustainably managed forestry and production.**

Printed on recyclable paper.
Please recycle whenever possible.

**Stock #4621**

# CONTENTS

Attractions, hotels, restaurants and other travel experience information are all grouped under the alphabetical listing of the city in which those experiences are physically located—or the nearest recognized city.

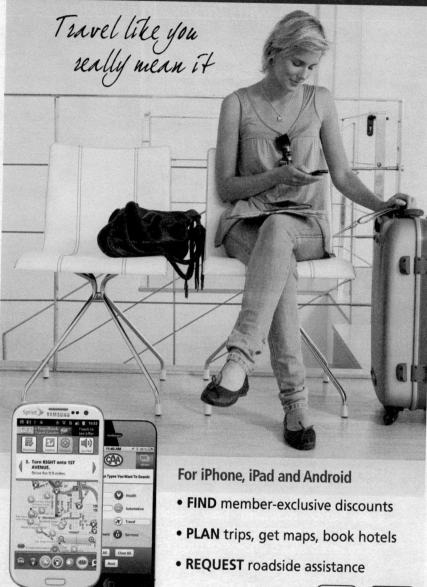

# Go. With AAA Mobile

*Travel like you really mean it*

For iPhone, iPad and Android

- **FIND** member-exclusive discounts
- **PLAN** trips, get maps, book hotels
- **REQUEST** roadside assistance

Download it at your app store

## AAA.com/mobile or CAA.ca/mobile

# BEHIND-THE-SCENES
## SNEAK PEEK

### *AAA Inspectors:*
### *On the Job for Members*

Curious about the experts behind AAA's reliable travel information? Get an inside look at the AAA professionals who inspect some 70,000 hotels, restaurants and attractions every year.

AAA inspectors travel anonymously to ensure a guest experience similar to yours—sometimes glamorous, occasionally awful and, often, just right for a particular travel experience.

That's where AAA's detailed guidelines and reliable ratings come in—ensuring the places you select provide the environment you expect… from simple to family friendly to world-class.

**Scan to view an entertaining video.**

## A to Z City Listings

Cities and places are listed alphabetically within each state or province. Attractions, hotels and restaurants are listed once — under the city in which they are physically located.

Cities that are considered part of a larger destination city or area have an expanded city header. The header identifies the larger region and cross-references pages that contain shared trip planning resources:

- Destination map – outline map of the cities that comprise a destination city or area
- Attraction spotting map – regional street map marked with attraction locations
- Hotel/restaurant spotting map and index – regional street map numbered with hotel and restaurant locations identified in an accompanying index

Cities that are not considered part of a larger destination city or area but have a significant number of listings may have these resources within the individual city section:

- Attraction spotting map
- Hotel/restaurant spotting map and index

## About Listed Establishments

AAA/CAA Approved attractions, hotels and restaurants are listed on the basis of merit alone after careful evaluation and approval by full-time, professionally trained AAA/CAA inspectors. An establishment's decision to advertise in the TourBook guide has no bearing on its evaluation or rating; nor does inclusion of advertising imply AAA endorsement of products and services.

Information in this guide was believed accurate at the time of publication. However, since changes inevitably occur between annual editions, please contact your AAA travel professional or visit AAA.com to confirm prices and schedules.

## Location Abbreviations

Directions are from the center of town unless otherwise specified, using these highway abbreviations:

**Bus. Rte.**=business route
**CR**=county road
**FM**=farm to market
**FR**=forest road
**Hwy.**=Canadian highway
**I**=interstate highway
**LR**=legislative route
**R.R.**=rural route
**SR/PR**=state or provincial route
**US**=federal highway

## Atlas Section

The Atlas Section provides navigable road maps from the AAA Road Atlas series. The overview map displays the entire coverage area. Corresponding, numbered detail maps offer a closer view for route planning and navigation.

## Mobile Tags

Look for Microsoft Tags or QR codes throughout the TourBook guide and scan them with your smartphone to access special online offers, menus, videos and more.

To scan Microsoft Tags or QR codes:

- Download AAA's recommended scanning app to your smartphone at http://gettag.mobi.
- Start scanning Tags or QR codes.
- Link to featured content.

Some advertisers may use bar codes other than Microsoft Tags or QR codes. In those cases, please note any accompanying text that indicates where to download the required reader.

# Attraction Listings

 **SAVE** **ATTRACTION NAME**, 3 mi. n. off SR 20A (Main Ave.), consists of 250 acres with Olmsted-designed gardens, a 205-foot marble and coquina bell tower and a Mediterranean-style mansion. One of the state's oldest attractions, the tower and gardens were dedicated to the American people in 1929 by President Calvin Coolidge on behalf of their founder, a Dutch immigrant.

Other features include daily concerts from the 60-bell carillon, a nature observatory and Nature Preserve Trail. The visitor center presents art exhibits, an orientation film and exhibits about the family legacy, the carillon and endangered plants and animals found on the property.

**Hours:** Gardens daily 8-6. Last admission 1 hour before closing. Visitor center daily 9-5. Estate tours are given at noon and 2. Carillon concerts are given at 1 and 3. Phone ahead to confirm schedule. **Cost:** $10; $3 (ages 5-12). Gardens and estate $16; $8 (ages 5-12). **Phone:** (555) 555-5555.

🔌 🍴 🏕 🚇 Dupont Circle, 13

AAA/CAA inspectors may designate an attraction of exceptional interest and quality as a AAA GEM — a *Great Experience for Members®.* See GEM Attraction Index (listed on CONTENTS page) for complete list of locations.

## Adventure Travel

Activities such as air tours, hiking, skiing and white-water rafting are listed to provide member information and do not imply AAA/CAA endorsement. For your safety, be aware of inherent risks and adhere to all safety instructions.

## Cost

Prices are quoted without sales tax in the local currency (U.S. or Canadian dollars). Children under the lowest age specified are admitted free when accompanied by an adult. Most establishments accept credit cards, but a small number require cash, so please call ahead to verify.

## Icons

**SAVE** Show Your Card & Save® member discount

🔌 Electric vehicle charging station on premises. Domestic station information provided by the U.S. Department of Energy. Canadian station information provided by Plug'n Drive Ontario.

🏕 Camping facilities

🍴 Food on premises

🏃 Recreational activities

🐕 Pets on leash allowed

🧺 Picnicking allowed

In select cities only:

🚇 Mass transit station within 1 mile. Icon is followed by station name and AAA/CAA designated station number within listing.

## Information-Only Attraction Listings

Bulleted listings, which include the following categories, are listed for informational purposes as a service to members:

- **Gambling establishments** (even if located in a AAA/CAA Approved hotel)
- **Guided food tours**
- **Participatory recreational activities** (those requiring physical exertion or special skills)
- **Wineries that offer tours and tastings**

# Hotel and Restaurant Listings

**1 Diamond Rating** – AAA/CAA Approved hotels and restaurants are assigned a rating of one to five Diamonds. Red Diamonds distinguish establishments that participate in the AAA/CAA logo licensing program. For details, see p. 11 or AAA.com/Diamonds.

**fyi** indicates hotels and restaurants that are not AAA/CAA Approved and/or Diamond Rated but are listed to provide additional choices for members:

- **Hotels** may be unrated if they are too new to rate, under construction, under major renovation or not evaluated; or if they do not meet all AAA requirements. Hotels that do not meet all AAA requirements may be included if they offer member value or are the only option; details are noted in the listing.
- **Restaurants** may be unrated if they have not yet been evaluated by AAA.

**2 Classification or Cuisine Type** – Noted after the Diamond Rating.

- **Hotel Classifications** indicate the style of operation, overall concept and service level. Subclassifications may also be added. (See p. 12 list.)
- **Restaurant Cuisine Types** identify the food concept from more than 100 categories. If applicable, a classification may also be added. (See p. 13 list.)

**3 Dollar Amounts** – Quoted without sales tax in the local currency (U.S. or Canadian dollars), rounded up to the nearest dollar. Most establishments accept credit cards, but a small number require cash, so please call ahead to verify.

- **Hotel Rates** indicate the publicly available two-person rate or rate range for a standard room, applicable all year.
- **Restaurant Prices** represent the minimum and maximum entrée cost per person. Exceptions may include one-of-a-kind or special market priced items.

**4 Spotting Symbol** – Ovals containing numbers correspond with numbered location markings on hotel and restaurant spotting maps.

**5 Parking** – Unless otherwise noted, parking is free, on-site self parking.

**6 Hotel Value Nationwide** – Blue boxes highlight member benefits available at AAA/CAA Approved locations across a hotel chain. (See Just For Members section for details.)

**7 Hotel Unit Limited Availability** – Unit types, amenities and room features preceded by "some" are available on a limited basis, potentially as few as one.

**8 Hotel Terms** – Cancellation and minimum stay policies are listed. Unless otherwise noted, most properties offer a full deposit refund with cancellations received at least 48 hours before standard check-in. Properties that require advance payment may not refund the difference for early departures. "Resort fee" indicates a charge may apply above and beyond the quoted room rate.

**9 Hotel Check-in/Check-out** – Unless otherwise noted, check-in is after 3 p.m. and check-out is before 10 a.m.

**10 Restaurant Dress Code** – Unless otherwise noted, dress is casual or dressy casual.

**11 Restaurant Menu** – Where indicated, menus may be viewed in a secure online environment at AAA.com or, if a mobile tag is provided, via the restaurant's website.

**12 Hotel Icons** – May be preceded by CALL and/or SOME UNITS.

*Member Information:*

**SAVE** Rate guarantee: discounted standard room rate or lowest public rate available at time of booking for dates of stay.

**ECO** Eco-certified by government or private organization. Visit AAA.com/eco for details.

Electric vehicle charging station on premises. Domestic station information provided by the U.S. Department of Energy. Canadian station information provided by Plug'n Drive Ontario.

**X** Smoke-free premises

In select cities only:

Mass transit station within 1 mile. Icon is followed by station name and AAA/CAA designated station number within listing.

*Services:*

Airport transportation

Pets allowed (Call property for restrictions.)

Pets allowed (Call property for restrictions and fees.)

Restaurant on premises

Restaurant off premises

Room service for 2 or more meals

Full bar

Child care

## HOTEL LISTING

**HOTEL NAME**

(555)555-5555  **50**

**1**
**2**
**3**

Hotel
$109-$199

**LOGO** AAA Benefit: Members save a minimum 5% off the best available rate.

**4**

**6**

**5**
**9**

**Address:** 300 Main St 55555 **Location:** I-275 exit 31 southbound; exit 30 northbound. 1.6 mi w on SR 688 (Oak Rd). Dupont Circle, 13. **Facility:** 149 units, some efficiencies. 3 stories, interior corridors. **Parking:** on-site (fee). **Terms:** check-in 4 pm, cancellation fee imposed, resort fee. **Amenities:** video games. **Pool(s):** heated outdoor. **Activities:** hot tub, exercise room. **Guest Services:** valet and coin laundry. **Featured Amenity: continental breakfast.**

**7**
**8**

**12**

## RESTAURANT LISTING

**RESTAURANT NAME**

555/555-5555

**1**
**2**
**3**

Continental
Steak Seafood
Fine Dining
$15-$35

**AAA Inspector Notes:** *Historic.* A romantic aura punctuates the modern and casual dining room, which is accented with floral arrangements and dramatic, freshly cut branches. The seasonal menu centers on Tuscan-American cuisine. The pastry chef's decadent creations are popular. Semiformal attire. **Features:** full bar, patio dining, happy hour. **Address:** 26 N Main St 55555 **Location:** SR A1A southbound, 2.7 mi s of jct SR 520. Dupont Circle, 13.
*Menu on AAA.com*

**10**

**11**

**13**

---

**BIZ** Business area

**⚿M** Accessible features (Call property for available services and amenities.)

*Activities:*

🎰 Full-service casino

🏊 Pool

💪 Health club on premises

*In-Room Amenities:*

**HS** High-speed Internet service

**SHS** High-speed Internet service
(Call property for fees.)

📶 Wireless Internet service

📶 Wireless Internet service
(Call property for fees.)

📶 No wireless Internet service

📺 Pay movies

🧊 Refrigerator

🔲 Microwave

☕ Coffee maker

**📺** No air conditioning

📺 No TV

☎ No telephones

**13** **Restaurant Icons**

**SAVE** Show Your Card & Save® member discount

**ECO** Eco-certified by government or private organization. Visit AAA.com/eco for details.

⚡ Electric vehicle charging station on premises. Domestic station information provided by the U.S. Department of Energy. Canadian station information provided by Plug'n Drive Ontario.

**🅰** No air conditioning

**⚿M** Accessible features (Call property for available services and amenities.)

🚭 Designated smoking section

B Breakfast

L Lunch

D Dinner

**24** Open 24 hours

**LATE** Open after 11 p.m.

🐾 Pet-friendly (Call property for restrictions.)

In select cities only:

🚉 Mass transit station within 1 mile. Icon is followed by station name and AAA/CAA designated station number within listing.

# Just For Members

## Understanding the Diamond Ratings

Hotel and restaurant evaluations are unscheduled to ensure our professionally trained inspectors encounter the same experience members do.

- When an establishment is Diamond Rated, it means members can expect a good fit with their needs. The inspector assigns a rating that indicates the type of experience to expect.

- While establishments at high levels must offer increasingly complex personalized services, establishments at every level are subject to the same basic requirements for cleanliness, comfort and hospitality. Learn more at AAA.com/Diamonds.

## Hotels

Budget-oriented, offering basic comfort and hospitality.

Affordable, with modestly enhanced facilities, décor and amenities.

Distinguished, multi-faceted with enhanced physical attributes, amenities and guest comforts.

Refined, stylish with upscale physical attributes, extensive amenities and high degree of hospitality, service and attention to detail.

Ultimate luxury, sophistication and comfort with extraordinary physical attributes, meticulous personalized service, extensive amenities and impeccable standards of excellence.

## Restaurants

Simple, familiar specialty food at an economical price. Often self-service, basic surroundings.

Familiar, family-oriented experience. Home-style foods and family favorites, often cooked to order, modestly enhanced and reasonably priced. Relaxed service, casual surroundings.

Fine dining, often adult-oriented. Latest cooking trends and/or traditional cuisine, expanded beverage offerings. Professional service staff and comfortable, well-coordinated ambience.

Distinctive fine-dining, typically expensive. Highly creative chefs, imaginative presentations and fresh, top-quality ingredients. Proficient service staff, upscale surroundings. Wine steward may offer menu-specific knowledge.

Luxurious and consistently world-class. Highly acclaimed chefs, artistic and imaginative menu selections using the finest ingredients. Maitre d' and unobtrusive, expert service staff.

### What's the difference?

- Red Diamonds mark establishments that participate in the AAA/CAA logo licensing program for increased visibility to members.

- Black Diamonds identify all other AAA/CAA Approved and Diamond Rated establishments.

# Hotel Classifications

Quality and comfort are usually consistent across each Diamond Rating level, but décor, facilities and service levels vary by classification.

1884 Paxton House Inn
Thomasville, GA

**Bed & Breakfast –** Typically owner-operated with a high degree of personal touches. Guests are encouraged to interact during evening and breakfast hours. A continental or full, hot breakfast is included in the room rate.

Barkwells
Mills River, NC

**Cabin –** Often located in wooded, rural or waterfront locations. Free-standing units are typically rustic and of basic design. As a rule, essential cleaning supplies, kitchen utensils and complete bed and bath linens are supplied.

Camelot by the Sea
Myrtle Beach, SC

**Condominium –** Apartment-style accommodations of varying design or décor, units often contain one or more bedrooms, a living room, a full kitchen and an eating area. As a rule, essential cleaning supplies, kitchen utensils and complete bed and bath linens are supplied.

The Red Horse Inn Cottages
Landrum, SC

**Cottage –** Often located in wooded, rural or waterfront locations. Free-standing units are typically home-style in design and décor. As a rule, essential cleaning supplies, kitchen utensils and complete bed and bath linens are supplied.

The Lodge at Moosehead
Lake, Greenville, ME

**Country Inn –** Although similar in definition to a bed and breakfast, country inns are usually larger in scale with spacious public areas and offer a dining facility that serves breakfast and dinner.

Grand America Hotel
Salt Lake City, UT

**Hotel –** Typically a multistory property with interior room entrances and a variety of guest unit styles. The magnitude of the public areas is determined by the overall theme, location and service level, but may include a variety of facilities such as a restaurant, shops, a fitness center, a spa, a business center and meeting rooms.

Windsor Palms Vacation
Rentals-All Star Vacation
Homes, Kissimmee, FL

**House –** Free-standing units of varying home-style design. Typically larger scale, often containing two or more bedrooms, a living room, a full kitchen, a dining room and multiple bathrooms. As a rule, essential cleaning supplies, kitchen utensils and complete bed and bath linens are supplied.

BEST WESTERN Bryson Inn
Mount Airy, NC

**Motel –** A one- or two-story roadside property with exterior room entrances and drive-up parking. Public areas and facilities are often limited in size and/or availability.

Lost Valley Ranch
Deckers, CO

**Ranch –** Typically a working ranch featuring an obvious rustic, Western theme, equestrian-related activities and a variety of guest unit styles.

# Hotel Subclassifications

These additional descriptives may be added to the classification for more information:

- **Boutique** – Often thematic, typically informal yet highly personalized; may have a luxurious or quirky style that is fashionable or unique.
- **Casino** – Extensive gambling facilities are available, such as blackjack, craps, keno and slot machines.
- **Classic** – Renowned and landmark properties, older than 50 years, well known for their unique style and ambience.
- **Contemporary** – Overall theme reflects characteristics of present mainstream trends.
- **Extended Stay** – Offers a predominance of long-term accommodations with a designated full-service kitchen area within each unit.
- **Historic** – Over 75 years old with one of the following documented historical features: maintains the integrity of the historical nature, listed on the National Register of Historic Places, designated a National Historic Landmark or located in a National Register Historic District.

- **Resort** – Extensive recreational facilities and programs may include golf, tennis, skiing, fishing, water sports, spa treatments or professionally guided activities.
- **Retro** – Overall theme reflects a contemporary design that reinterprets styles from a past era.
- **Vacation Rental** – Typically houses, condos, cottages or cabins; these properties are "home away from home" self-catering accommodations.
- **Vintage** – Overall theme reflects upon and maintains the authentic traits and experience of a past era.

## Restaurant Classifications

If applicable, in addition to the cuisine type noted under the Diamond Rating, restaurant listings may also include one or both classifications:

- **Classic** – Renowned and landmark operation in business for 25 plus years; unique style and ambience.
- **Historic** – Meets one of the following: Listed on National Register of Historic Places, designated a National Historic Landmark or located in a National Register Historic District.

## Service Animals

Under the Americans with Disabilities Act (ADA), U.S. businesses that serve the public must allow people with disabilities to bring their service animals into all areas of the facility where customers are normally allowed to go.

Businesses may ask if an animal is a service animal and what tasks the animal has been trained to perform. Businesses may not ask about the person's disability, require special identification for the animal or request removal of the animal from the premises except in limited cases that require alternate assistance. Businesses may not charge extra fees for service animals, including standard pet fees, but may charge for damage caused by service animals if guests are normally charged for damage they cause.

Call the U.S. Department of Justice ADA Information Line: (800) 514-0301 or TTY (800) 514-0383, or visit ada.gov. Regulations may differ in Canada.

## AAA/CAA Approved Hotels

For members, AAA/CAA Approved means quality assured.

- Only properties that meet basic requirements for cleanliness, comfort and hospitality pass inspection.
- Approved hotels receive a Diamond Rating that tells members the type of experience to expect.

### Guest Safety

Inspectors view a sampling of rooms during evaluations and, therefore, AAA/CAA cannot guarantee the presence of working locks and operational fire safety equipment in every guest unit.

### Member Rates

AAA/CAA members can generally expect to pay no more than the maximum TourBook listed rate for a standard room. Member discounts apply to rates quoted within the rate range and are applicable at the time of booking. Listed rates are usually based on last standard room availability. Within the range, rates may vary by season and room type. Obtain current AAA/CAA member rates and make reservations at AAA.com.

#### Exceptions

- Rates for properties operating as concessionaires for the U.S. National Park Service are not guaranteed due to governing regulations.
- Special advertised rates and short-term promotional rates below the rate range are not subject to additional member discounts.
- During special events, hotels may temporarily increase room rates, not recognize discounts or modify pricing policies. Special events may include Mardi Gras, the Kentucky Derby (including pre-Derby events), college football games, holidays, holiday periods and state fairs. Although some special events are listed in the TourBook guides and on AAA.com, it's always wise to check in advance with AAA travel professionals for specific dates.

**If you are charged more than the maximum TourBook listed rate,** question the additional charge. If an exception is not in effect and management refuses to adhere to the published rate, pay for the room and contact AAA/CAA. The amount paid above the stated maximum will be refunded if our investigation indicates an unjustified charge.

## Reservations and Cancellations

When making your reservation, identify yourself as a AAA/CAA member and request written confirmation of your room type, rate, dates of stay, and cancellation and refund policies. At registration, show your membership card.

To cancel, contact the hotel or your AAA/CAA club office, depending on how you booked your reservation. Request a cancellation number or proof of cancellation.

**If your room is not as specified and you have written confirmation of your reservation for a specific room type,** you should be given the option of choosing a different room or receiving a refund. If management refuses to issue a refund, contact AAA/CAA.

### Contacting AAA/CAA About Approved Properties

If your visit to a AAA/CAA Approved attraction, hotel or restaurant doesn't meet your expectations, please tell us about it — *during your visit or within 30 days*. Be sure to save your receipts and other documentation for reference.

Use the easy online form at AAA.com/TourBookComments to send us the details.

Alternatively, you can email your comments to: memberrelations@national.aaa.com or submit them via postal mail to: AAA Member Comments, 1000 AAA Dr., Box 61, Heathrow, FL 32746.

## AAA/CAA Preferred Hotels

All AAA/CAA Approved hotels are committed to providing quality, value and member service. In addition, those designated as AAA/CAA Preferred Hotels also offer these extra values at Approved locations nationwide. Valid AAA/CAA membership required.

- **Best AAA/CAA member rates for your dates of stay.**
- **Seasonal promotions and special member offers.** Visit AAA.com to view current offers.
- **Member benefit.** See the blue boxes in hotel listings for the chains shown in the right-hand column below to find values offered at AAA/CAA Approved locations nationwide. Details valid at the time of publication may change without notice.

- **Total satisfaction guarantee.** If you book your stay with AAA/CAA Travel and your stay fails to meet your expectations, you can apply for a full refund. Bring the complaint to the hotel's attention during the stay and request resolution; if the complaint is not resolved by the hotel, ask your AAA/CAA travel agent to request resolution through the AAA/CAA Assured Stay program.

**Preferred Hotels**

Total Satisfaction Guarantee

Best Western, Best Western Plus and Best Western Premier

TEN DISTINCT HOTEL BRANDS

Waldorf Astoria Hotels & Resorts, Conrad Hotels & Resorts, Hilton Hotels & Resorts, DoubleTree, Embassy Suites Hotels, Hilton Garden Inn, Hampton Hotels, Homewood Suites, Home2 Suites and Hilton Grand Vacations

Park Hyatt, Andaz, Grand Hyatt, Hyatt Regency, Hyatt Hotels & Resorts, Hyatt Place and Hyatt House

MARRIOTT

JW Marriott Hotels, EDITION, Autograph Collection Hotels, Renaissance Hotels, AC Hotels, Marriott Hotels & Resorts, Courtyard, SpringHill Suites, Fairfield Inn & Suites, Residence Inn, TownePlace Suites and Gaylord Hotels

**starwood**
Hotels and Resorts

Aloft, Element, Four Points, Le Meridien, Sheraton, St. Regis, The Luxury Collection, W Hotels and Westin

# Show Your Card & Save® Member Discounts

Visit AAA.com/searchfordiscounts to find local Show Your Card & Save discounts. Your AAA/CAA club may offer even greater discounts on theme park tickets. Amtrak, Gray Line and theme park discounts may be used for up to six tickets; restaurant savings may be used for up to six patrons. Other restrictions may apply. All offers subject to change. For complete restrictions, visit your AAA office or AAA.com/restrictions.

## ATTRACTIONS

### SeaWorld, Busch Gardens, Sesame Place

- Save on admission at the gate, participating AAA/CAA offices or AAA.com/SeaWorld.
- Save 10% on up-close dining; visit Guest Relations for details.

### Six Flags

- Save on admission at the gate, participating AAA/CAA offices or AAA.com/SixFlags.
- Save 10% on merchandise of $15 or more at in-park stores.

### Universal Orlando Resort and Universal Studios Hollywood

- Save on admission at the gate, participating AAA/CAA offices or AAA.com/Universal.
- Save on Blue Man Group tickets and at select food and merchandise venues in-park and at Universal CityWalk®.

## DINING & SHOPPING

### Hard Rock Cafe

- Save 10% on food, nonalcoholic beverages and merchandise at all locations in the U.S. and Canada and select international locations.

### Landry's Seafood House, The Crab House, Chart House, Oceanaire, Saltgrass Steak House, Muer Seafood Restaurants and Aquarium Restaurants

- Save 10% on food and nonalcoholic beverages at all of the above restaurants.
- Save 10% on merchandise at Aquarium and Downtown Aquarium restaurants.
- Location information: AAA.com/Discounts.

### Tanger Outlet Centers

- Simple present your AAA card in any Tanger Shopper Services Center or Management Office, and you'll receive a FREE coupon booklet filled with hundreds of dollars in savings from top brand names and designer outlet stores (a $5 value). Visit AAA.com/searchfordiscounts for locations.

## TRANSPORTATION & TOURS

### Amtrak

- Save 10% on rail fare booked at least 3 days in advance of travel date at AAA.com/Amtrak.

### Gray Line

- Save 10% on sightseeing tours of 1 day or less worldwide at AAA.com/GrayLine.

### Hertz

- Save on daily, weekend, weekly and monthly rentals at AAA.com/hertz or 1-800-654-3080.

17

Pack your bags with
# UNLIMITED AAA TRAVEL REWARDS
Take your travel farther with the AAA Member Rewards Visa® credit card

**EXCLUSIVE OFFER FOR AAA MEMBERS!**

## Redeem unlimited rewards toward your next AAA vacation*

- **3X POINTS** on qualifying AAA and travel purchases
- **2X POINTS** on gas, grocery and drug store purchases
- **1 POINT PER $1** on purchases everywhere else
- **GET AAA BRANCH VOUCHERS FOR TRAVEL** worth up to 40% more than cash rewards"

**VISIT** AAA.com/creditcard | **STOP BY** any AAA branch

For information on the rates, fees, other costs and benefits of this credit card, visit the website listed above or your AAA branch.
* Earn 1 point per dollar of new net retail purchase transactions (qualifying purchases less credits, returns, and adjustments) charged to the card each billing cycle. Earn 2 points per dollar for purchases made with the card at any eligible gas, grocery or pharmacy retail merchant categories as designated by us. Earn 3 points per dollar for purchases made with the card through any participating AAA Club when AAA is the merchant of record, or at eligible retail travel merchant categories as designated by us. Details accompany new account materials.
** 50,000 points can be redeemed for a $700 AAA Voucher compared to $500 in cash rewards. The redemption value for AAA vouchers varies based on the number of points redeemed.
This credit card program issued and administered by FIA Card Services, N.A. Visa and Visa Signature are registered trademarks of Visa International Service Association and are used by the Issuer pursuant to license from Visa U.S.A. Inc. AAA is a trademark of American Automobile Association, Inc.
©2013 Bank of America Corporation

ARA2FE54

South Padre Island

# Texas

If you're fixin' to head to Texas, you'd best study up on what it means to be tough. The quickest way to round up respect in the Lone Star State is to demonstrate that you've got true grit.

The state's pioneers had gumption galore. Initially *conquistadores*, Estevanico and Álvar Núñez Cabeza de Vaca took a lesson from the Native Americans and transformed themselves into healers and savvy traders. And although most of the rest of his expedition had returned to Mexico after finding no trace of treasure, Francisco Vázquez de Coronado plugged on despite mounting disappointments.

René-Robert Cavelier, Sieur de La Salle, survived a perilous journey from France and established a promising settlement, only to be killed shortly thereafter at the hands of his own men. Stephen F. Austin's unassuming presence gained him widespread regard, thereby allowing him to greatly advance the Americans' cause during the Texas Revolution.

Chili packs a strong wallop

## Don't Mess with Texas

Almost everything about Texas reveals some trademark of an iron will.

Plants are hardy. Tumbleweeds roll across the landscape, seemingly oblivious to the searing sun, coarse sand and swirling winds. Wildflowers, most notably the ubiquitous bluebonnet and Indian paintbrush, spread out like colorful carpets across fields. The prickly pear cactus gives a painful poke to anyone who wanders too close.

With one sting, scorpions and tarantulas can take down an enemy many times larger than themselves. The distinctive horns of longhorn cattle contributed significantly to the breed's longevity. And rattlesnakes have the upper hand in nearly any confrontation.

You've got to have pluck and a stomach of steel just to tackle the food for which the state is known. Tamales sear away layers from the lining of the digestive tract. Jalapeños bring the most strapping of men to tears.

Chili packs a wallop stronger than a spurned lover sending a four-knuckle message to his romantic rival. If Texas had a state condiment, it would no doubt be Tabasco.

And what better to wash it all down than a sinus-clearing, throat-torching prairie fire—a shot of tequila blended with a minimum of three drops of hot sauce and garnished with a dash of black pepper?

## Recreation

The variety of ways in which you can play in Texas is as vast as the acreage on which you can do it.

Boating, swimming and other water sports abound on the immense Toledo Bend Reservoir, on the Louisiana border; Lake Texoma, on the Oklahoma border; Sam Rayburn Reservoir, north of Jasper; Lake Tawakoni, south of Greenville; and Lake Livingston, west of Livingston.

For a varied canoeing run that offers shallow floats, long pools and sporadic, turbulent rapids, visit Devil's River, north of Del Rio. To really unwind, go tubing on the Guadalupe or Frio rivers.

Scuba diving is but one way to enjoy the sparkling waters of Lake Travis, the southernmost body of water in the Highland Lakes chain, a 150-mile-long stretch of reservoirs on the Colorado River northwest of Austin. Offshore diving is spectacular at Flower Garden National Marine Sanctuary, 110 miles south of the Texas-Louisiana border.

Thumbing their noses at the notion that you can't catch a wave in Texas, surfing enthusiasts head to the short jetties between Flagship Pier and 61st Street in Galveston; J.P. Luby Surf Park in Corpus Christi; or the South Padre Island jetty.

You'll find excellent fishing just about anywhere you drop a line. You can hook catfish, white and striped bass and crappie at Amistad Reservoir, on the Mexican border west of Del Rio. Caddo Lake, east of Jefferson, is noted for its pickerel and sunfish. Trophy largemouth bass inhabit the depths of Lake Fork, east of Emory.

For a saltwater battle, pick your spot along the Gulf Coast and hope your bait catches the eye of a wahoo, red drum bonito, mackerel, marlin or pompano; boats can be chartered at nearly every coastal town.

Before you head off with your tackle box in tow, phone (512) 389-4800 or (800) 792-1112 to learn about regulations and required licenses, stamps and tags.

Hiking trails of varied difficulty wind through East Texas' four national forests—the Angelina, Davy Crockett, Sabine and Sam Houston. Breathtaking vistas reward hikers who navigate the rugged gorge in Pedernales Falls State Park, east of Johnson City. No less majestic is the colorful mountain and desert scenery of Big Bend and Guadalupe Mountains national parks in West Texas.

For a tough bicycling ride with plenty of roots, branches and tight wooded stretches, take on the terrain at Jack Brooks Park, southeast of Houston. If you'd rather pass on Mother Nature's surprises, pedal the paved trail at McKinney Falls State Park, southeast of Austin.

To view the countryside from high in the saddle, visit Hill Country State Natural Area, southwest of Bandera, where 40 miles of multiuse trails are prime real estate for horseback riding. Several adjacent ranches offer horse rentals. Trails through the semi-rough terrain of Palo Duro Canyon State Park, southeast of Amarillo, also are worth exploring; you can rent horses from stables on the canyon floor.

Most state parks let you pitch a tent for a camping adventure. If you're prepared to rough it, hop on a private or charter boat in Port O'Connor and head to Matagorda Island Wildlife Management Area, a richly historical area with a widely diverse animal population. The park has no electricity, drinking water, concessions or telephones.

Shake out your sails and go windsurfing at Windsurf Bay Park on Lake Ray Hubbard, northeast of Dallas. Face the challenge of a climbing excursion at Enchanted Rock, north of Fredericksburg; or Mineral Wells, west of Weatherford. Or take to the sky from South Padre Island for a parasailing thrill.

Palo Duro Canyon State Park, Canyon

# Historic Timeline

|  |  |
|---|---|
| 1519 | Spanish explorer Alonso Álvarez de Piñeda is the first European to reach Texan shores. |
| 1685 | René-Robert Cavelier, Sieur de La Salle, founds a French colony at Matagorda Bay. |
| 1716 | Spaniards establish Catholic missions in the region. |
| 1823 | Stephen F. Austin builds an American colony on the Brazos River. |
| **1836** | Texas wins its independence from Mexico at the Battle of San Jacinto; statehood is granted in 1845. |
| 1900 | The deadliest hurricane in U.S. history strikes Galveston, killing about 8,000 people. |
| 1901 | Oil is discovered in the Spindletop field near Beaumont. |
| 1962 | NASA's Johnson Space Center opens in Houston. |
| **1963** | President Kennedy is assassinated in Dallas. |
| 2001 | The collapse of Houston-based Enron is the largest bankruptcy in U.S. history to date. |
| 2005 | Former Texas governor George W. Bush is sworn in for a second term as president. |

# What To Pack

| Temperature Averages Maximum/Minimum | JANUARY | FEBRUARY | MARCH | APRIL | MAY | JUNE | JULY | AUGUST | SEPTEMBER | OCTOBER | NOVEMBER | DECEMBER |
|---|---|---|---|---|---|---|---|---|---|---|---|---|
| Amarillo | 49/23 | 54/27 | 62/34 | 71/42 | 79/52 | 87/61 | 91/65 | 89/64 | 82/56 | 72/45 | 58/32 | 50/24 |
| Corpus Christi | 66/46 | 70/49 | 76/56 | 81/62 | 86/69 | 90/74 | 93/74 | 93/75 | 90/72 | 84/64 | 75/55 | 68/48 |
| Dallas | 55/36 | 61/41 | 69/49 | 77/56 | 84/65 | 92/73 | 96/77 | 96/76 | 89/69 | 79/58 | 66/47 | 57/39 |
| El Paso | 57/33 | 63/38 | 70/44 | 78/51 | 87/61 | 95/69 | 94/72 | 92/70 | 87/64 | 78/52 | 66/40 | 57/33 |
| Houston | 63/45 | 67/48 | 74/55 | 79/61 | 86/68 | 91/74 | 94/75 | 93/75 | 89/72 | 82/62 | 73/53 | 65/47 |
| San Antonio | 62/39 | 67/43 | 74/50 | 80/57 | 86/66 | 91/72 | 95/74 | 95/74 | 90/69 | 82/59 | 71/49 | 64/41 |

**From the records of The Weather Channel Interactive, Inc.**

# Good Facts To Know

## ABOUT THE STATE

**POPULATION:** 25,145,561.

**AREA:** 261,797 square miles; ranks 2nd.

**CAPITAL:** Austin.

**HIGHEST POINT:** 8,749 ft., Guadalupe Peak.

**LOWEST POINT:** Sea level, Gulf of Mexico.

**TIME ZONE(S):** Central/Mountain. DST.

## REGULATIONS

**TEEN DRIVING LAWS:** The minimum age for an unrestricted driver's license is 18. During the provisional licensure period, no more than one passenger under age 21 is permitted (family members are exempt) and driving is not permitted midnight-5 a.m. Phone (512) 424-2600 for more information about Texas driver's license regulations.

**SEAT BELT/CHILD RESTRAINT LAWS:** Seat belts are required for driver and all passengers ages 8 and over. Child restraints are required for children under age 8 and under 57 inches. AAA recommends the use of seat belts and appropriate child restraints for the driver and all passengers.

**CELL PHONE RESTRICTIONS:** All drivers are prohibited from using handheld cell phones and text messaging while driving in school crossing zones. Drivers under age 18 are not permitted to use cell phones while driving for 12 months after a driver's license is obtained. Drivers in El Paso are prohibited from using handheld cell phones and text messaging while driving. Drivers in Arlington, Austin, Galveston, McAllen, Missouri City, San Antonio and Stephenville are prohibited from text messaging while driving.

**HELMETS FOR MOTORCYCLISTS:** Required for all riders under age 21. Optional for ages 21 and over with sanctioned training safety course or proof of medical insurance (minimum $10,000 coverage).

**RADAR DETECTORS:** Permitted.

**MOVE OVER LAW:** Driver is required to slow down and vacate the lane nearest stopped police, fire and rescue vehicles using audible or flashing signals. The law also applies to recovery vehicles, such as tow trucks.

**FIREARMS LAWS:** Vary by state and/or county. Contact the Texas Department of Public Safety, 5805 North Lamar Blvd., P.O. Box 4087, Austin, TX 78752; phone (512) 424-2000.

## HOLIDAYS

**HOLIDAYS:** Jan. 1 ■ Martin Luther King Jr. Day, Jan. (3rd Mon.) ■ Confederate Heroes' Day, Jan. 19 ■ Washington's Birthday/Presidents Day, Feb. (3rd Mon.) ■ Texas Independence Day, Mar. 2 ■ San Jacinto Day, Apr. 21 ■ Memorial Day, May (last Mon.) ■ Emancipation Day, June 19 ■ July 4 ■ Lyndon Baines Johnson Day, Aug. 27 ■ Labor Day, Sept. (1st Mon.) ■ Veterans Day, Nov. 11 ■ Thanksgiving, Nov. (4th Thurs.) ■ day after Thanksgiving, Nov. (4th Fri.) ■ Christmas Eve, Dec. 24 ■ Christmas, Dec. 25 ■ Boxing Day, Dec. 26.

## MONEY

**TAXES:** Texas' statewide sales tax is 6.25 percent. Cities and/or counties may impose additional rates up to 2 percent for a maximum rate of 8.25 percent. The state hotel tax rate is 6 percent; cities and some counties can each levy local hotel taxes, generally at rates varying up to 7 percent. A 10 percent tax is levied on car rentals.

## VISITOR INFORMATION

**INFORMATION CENTERS:** State welcome centers are on I-40 in Amarillo ■ on I-10W in Anthony ■ in the Capitol complex in Austin ■ on US 75/69 in Denison ■ on I-35 at US 77 in Gainesville ■ on US 90W Loop 25 in Langtry ■ on I-35 at US 83 in Laredo ■ on I-10E in Orange ■ on I-30 in Texarkana ■ off US 77 in the Rio Grande Valley ■ on I-20E in Waskom ■ and on Central Freeway in Wichita Falls. The Capitol complex center is open daily 9-5. All others are open daily 8-6, Memorial Day-Labor Day, and daily 8-5, rest of year. All centers are closed Jan. 1, Easter, Thanksgiving, Christmas Eve and Christmas. Phone (512) 463-8586 or (800) 452-9292.

**FURTHER INFORMATION FOR VISITORS:**
Travel Information Division
200 E. Riverside Dr., Bldg. 150
Austin, TX 78701
(512) 486-5800
(800) 452-9292 (tourist information and road conditions)

**NATIONAL FOREST INFORMATION:**
U.S. Forest Service Supervisor's Office
2221 N. Raguet St.
Lufkin, TX 75904
(936) 639-8501

**FISHING AND HUNTING REGULATIONS:**
Texas Parks & Wildlife Department
4200 Smith School Rd.
Austin, TX 78744
(512) 389-4820 (licenses and permits)
(800) 792-1112

# Texas Annual Events
Please call ahead to confirm event details.

| JANUARY | FEBRUARY | MARCH |
|---|---|---|
| ■ Fort Worth Stock Show and Rodeo / Fort Worth 817-877-2420<br>■ Texas Citrus Fiesta Mission 956-585-9724<br>■ MLK Grande Parade Houston 713-953-1633 | ■ San Antonio Stock Show & Rodeo / San Antonio 210-225-5851<br>■ Charro Days Fiesta Brownsville 956-542-4245<br>■ Texas Cowboy Poetry Gathering / Alpine 423-837-2326 | ■ North Texas Irish Festival Dallas 214-821-4173<br>■ South by Southwest (SXSW) / Austin 512-467-7979<br>■ Houston Livestock Show and Rodeo / Houston 832-667-1000 |

| APRIL | MAY | JUNE |
|---|---|---|
| ■ Buccaneer Days Corpus Christi 361-882-3242<br>■ Mauriceville Crawfish Festival / Orange 409-782-3488<br>■ Fiesta San Antonio San Antonio 210-227-5191 | ■ Old Pecan Street Spring Arts Festival / Austin 512-485-3190<br>■ Western Heritage Classic Abilene 325-677-4376<br>■ Tejano Conjunto Festival en San Antonio / San Antonio 210-271-3151 | ■ International Festival Round Top 979-249-3129<br>■ Texas Folklife Festival San Antonio 210-458-2224<br>■ Mesquite ProRodeo Mesquite 972-285-8777 |

| JULY | AUGUST | SEPTEMBER |
|---|---|---|
| ■ Kaboom Town / Addison 800-233-4766<br>■ Great Texas Mosquito Festival / Clute 979-265-8392<br>■ Freedom Fest / San Antonio 210-207-8605 | ■ XIT Rodeo and Reunion Dalhart 806-244-5646<br>■ Festival of Glass and Antique Show and Sale Rosenberg 281-240-0382<br>■ Celebrate Bandera Bandera 830-796-4447 | ■ Plano Balloon Festival Plano 972-867-7566<br>■ GrapeFest / Grapevine 817-410-3185<br>■ Autumn at the Arboretum: The Great Pumpkin Festival / Dallas 214-515-6500 |

| OCTOBER | NOVEMBER | DECEMBER |
|---|---|---|
| ■ State Fair of Texas / Dallas 214-565-9931<br>■ Texas Rose Festival / Tyler 903-597-3130<br>■ Heart O' Texas Fair and Rodeo / Waco 254-776-1660 | ■ International Quilt Festival Houston 713-781-6864<br>■ Wurstfest / New Braunfels 830-625-9167<br>■ World Championship Ranch Rodeo / Amarillo 806-378-3096 | ■ Tropical Christmas Celebration / Rockport 361-729-2213<br>■ Dickens on the Strand Galveston 409-765-7834<br>■ Armadillo Christmas Bazaar / Austin 512-447-1605 |

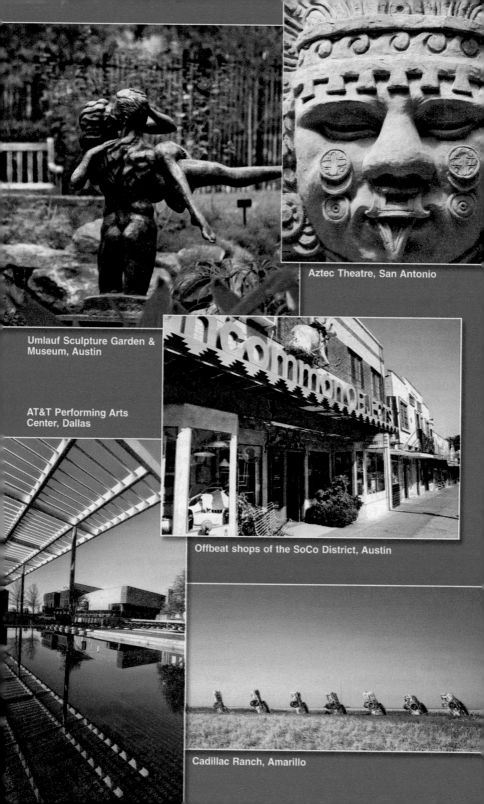

Aztec Theatre, San Antonio

Umlauf Sculpture Garden & Museum, Austin

AT&T Performing Arts Center, Dallas

Offbeat shops of the SoCo District, Austin

Cadillac Ranch, Amarillo

# Index: Great Experience for Members

## AAA editor's picks of exceptional note

Big Bend National Park

Witte Museum

National Museum of the Pacific War

Moody Gardens

# Texas Atlas Section

## ROADS/HIGHWAYS

- INTERSTATE
- CONTROLLED ACCESS
- CONTROLLED ACCESS TOLL
- TOLL ROAD
- PRIMARY DIVIDED
- PRIMARY UNDIVIDED
- SECONDARY DIVIDED
- SECONDARY UNDIVIDED
- LOCAL DIVIDED
- LOCAL UNDIVIDED
- UNPAVED ROAD
- UNDER CONSTRUCTION
- TUNNEL
- PEDESTRIAN ONLY
- AUTO FERRY
- PASSENGER FERRY
- SCENIC BYWAY
- 10 DISTANCE BETWEEN MARKERS
- EXIT NUMBER-FREE/TOLL
- INTERCHANGE FULL/PARTIAL
- WELCOME CENTER
- REST AREA/ SERVICE CENTER

## BOUNDARIES

- INTERNATIONAL
- STATE
- COUNTY
- TIME ZONE
- CONTINENTAL DIVIDE

## ROAD SHIELDS

- 95 95 INTERSTATE/BUSINESS
- 22 22 22 U.S./STATE/COUNTY
- 127 127 FOREST/INDIAN
- TRANS- CANADA
- 1 PROVINCIAL AUTOROUTE
- 1 MEXICO
- 66 HISTORIC ROUTE 66
- VT 41 REFERENCE PAGE INDICATOR

## AREAS OF INTEREST

- INDIAN
- MILITARY
- PARK
- FOREST
- GRASSLANDS
- HISTORIC
- INT'L/REGIONAL AIRPORT
- INCORPORATED CITY

## POINTS OF INTEREST

- ○ TOWN
- NATIONAL CAPITAL
- STATE/PROVINCIAL CAPITAL
- AAA/CAA CLUB LOCATION
- FEATURE OF INTEREST
- COLLEGE/UNIVERSITY
- CAMPGROUND INFORMATION PROVIDED BY WOODALL'S®
- CUSTOMS STATION
- HISTORIC
- LIGHTHOUSE
- MONUMENT/MEMORIAL
- STATE/PROVINCIAL PARK
- NATIONAL WILDLIFE REFUGE
- SKI AREA
- SPORTS COMPLEX
- DAM

**CITIES/TOWNS** are color-coded by size, showing where to find AAA Approved and Diamond rated lodgings or restaurants listed in the AAA TourBook guides and on AAA.com:

- ● Red - major destinations and capitals; many listings
- ● Black - destinations; some listings
- ● Grey - no listings

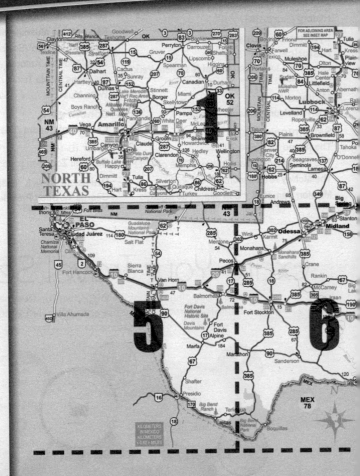

**TEXAS**

*Gulf of Mexico*

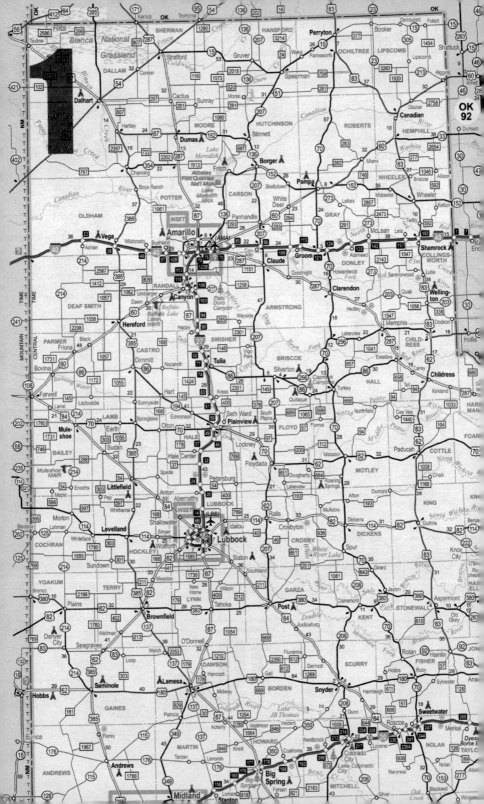

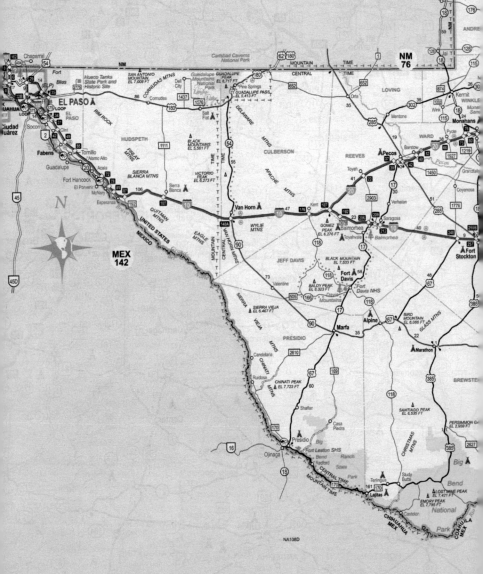

# Western TEXAS

1:2,027,520
Scale in Miles
20    0    20
20    0    20
Scale in Kilometers

**9**

ZAVALA

Pearsall
101

Charlotte
Christine
37
92
KARN

83
34
85
97
11
140
Campbellton
31
88
Peggy
99

Crystal City
FRIO
Dilley
ATASCOSA
32
Whitsett
83
76

44
84
35
16
Choke Canyon Reservoir
99
Choke Canyon
72

Brundage
Big Wells
85
LA SALLE
68/69
18
31
97
Fowlerton
Tilden
Calliham
23
Three Rivers
69
281
11

21
277
El Indio
1644
Carrizo Springs
Asherton
83
65
Catarina
Cotulla
George West
281

1021
DIMMIT
83
57
27
MCMULLEN
LIVE OAK

COAHUILA
624
41
16
624
44
59
281

2
39
44
12
Nueces
44
44
3
Freer
40
JIM WELLS

Encinal
25
San Diego
8

COAHUILA
NUEVO LEON
Hidalgo
15
15
44
339
359

NUEVO LEON
255
19
3
24
WEBB
56
16
2295
Benavides
2295

Columbia
1472
19
4
18
14
35
?
59
41
2295
43
37

Nuevo Laredo
INSET
(LRD)
10
Laredo
DUVAL
Oilton
Realitos
Concepcion
716

20
LOOP
359
55
Mirando City
Bruni
359
359
339
Falfurrias

2
85
83
48
649
Hebbronville
285
34
281

MEX
USA
ZAPATA
51
JIM HOGG
281

85
San Ygnacio
16
649
16
BROOKS

Zapata
2687
Guerra
1017

Presa Falcon
Lopeno
International Falcon Reservoir
Falcon
649
Santa Elena
755
72

2
Nueva Ciudad Guerrero
Falcon Heights
55
2686
San Isidro
281

STARR
649
755
1017
Line

54
Ciudad Miguel Aleman
Roma
Rio Grande City
490
HIDALGO
69C

Camargo
83
Sullivan City
Edinburg

TAMAULIPAS
83
Palmview
39
Mission
McA
5
Presa Marte R Gomez
Bentsen-Rio Grande Valley
MFE
Pharr
10

TAMAULIPAS
Hidalgo
Reynosa

NUEVO LEON
40

40D
97
Santa Ana NWR

MEX 142
**KILOMETERS IN MEXICO KILOMETERS x 0.62 = MILES**
109

NA110D

# Make the Most of Your Trip
## with AAA eTourBook® Guides

Maximize your travel experience when you take along AAA eTourBook guides for your ereader or smartphone. Each of the more than 100 available digital titles is packed with:

- Destination details
- AAA Approved and Diamond Rated hotel and restaurant listings
- Attraction and event information
- Preplanned itineraries
- Editor's don't-miss picks

Download now at
AAA.com/ebooks

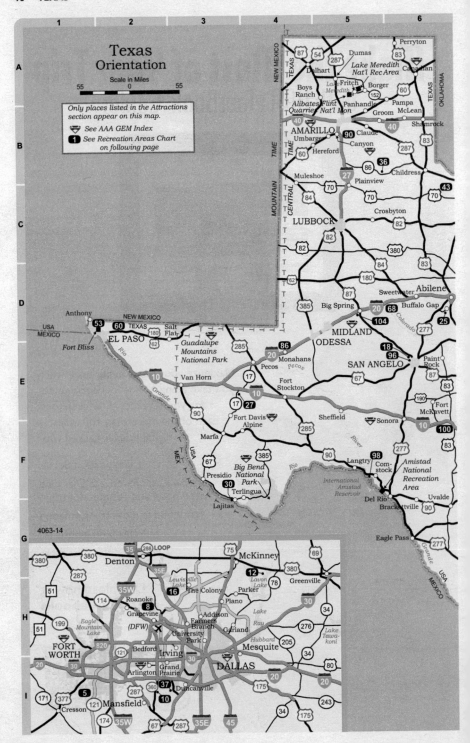

## Texas
### Orientation

Scale in Miles

55    0    55

Only places listed in the Attractions
section appear on this map.

See AAA GEM Index

**1** See Recreation Areas Chart
on following page

4063-14

© AAA

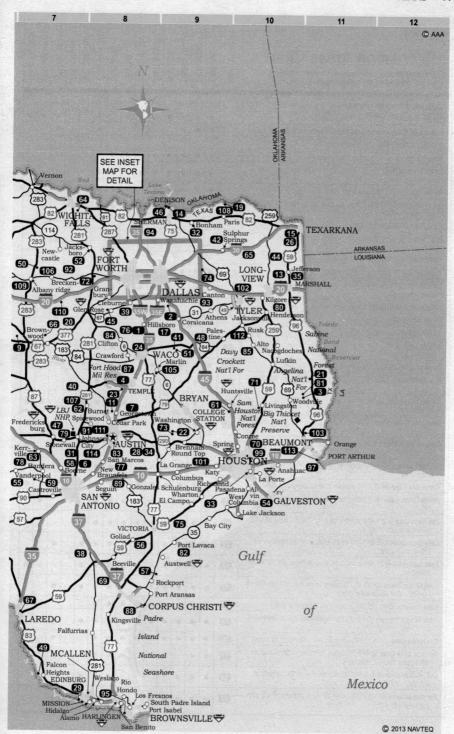

© 2013 NAVTEQ

# Recreation Areas Chart

The map location numerals in column 2 show an area's location on the preceding map.

| | Map Location | Camping | Picnicking | Hiking Trails | Boating | Boat Ramp | Boat Rental | Fishing | Swimming | Pets on Leash | Bicycle Trails | Skin/Scuba | Visitor Center | Lodge/Cabins | Food Service |
|---|---|---|---|---|---|---|---|---|---|---|---|---|---|---|---|
| **NATIONAL PARKS** (See place listings.) | | | | | | | | | | | | | | | |
| **Big Bend (F-3)** 801,163 acres. Horse rental. | | • | • | • | • | | | • | | • | | | • | • | • |
| **Guadalupe Mountains (E-3)** 86,416 acres. Horseback riding trails. | | • | • | • | | | | | | • | | | • | | |
| **NATIONAL FORESTS** (See place listings.) | | | | | | | | | | | | | | | |
| **Angelina (E-10)** 153,179 acres. East Texas. | | • | • | • | • | • | | • | • | • | | | | | |
| **Davy Crockett (E-9)** 161,500 acres. East Texas. Hunting; horseback riding trails. | | • | • | • | • | • | • | • | • | • | | | | | |
| **Sabine (D-11)** 160,798 acres. East Texas. Hunting. | | • | • | • | • | • | | • | • | • | | | | | |
| **Sam Houston (E-10)** 163,037 acres. East Texas. Hunting; horseback riding trails. | | • | • | • | • | • | | • | • | • | • | | | | |
| **NATIONAL PRESERVES** (See place listings.) | | | | | | | | | | | | | | | |
| **Big Thicket (E-10)** 105,684 acres. Canoeing, hunting, kayaking; horseback riding trails. | | • | • | • | | | | • | • | | | • | • | | |
| **NATIONAL RECREATION AREAS** (See place listings.) | | | | | | | | | | | | | | | |
| **Amistad (F-6)** 67,000 acres. Pictographs. | | • | • | • | • | • | • | • | • | • | | • | | | |
| **Lake Meredith (A-5)** 16,504 acres. Hunting, water skiing; horseback riding trails. | | • | • | | • | • | | • | • | | | • | | | |
| **NATIONAL SEASHORES** (See place listings.) | | | | | | | | | | | | | | | |
| **Padre Island (H-8)** 130,697 acres. | | • | • | • | • | | | • | • | • | | | • | | • |
| **ARMY CORPS OF ENGINEERS** | | | | | | | | | | | | | | | |
| **Aquilla Lake (D-8)** 3,280 acres 9.5 mi. s.w. of Hillsboro via I-35 and FM 310. | **1** | | | | • | • | | • | • | | | | | | |
| **Bardwell Lake (D-9)** 3,570 acres 4 mi. s.w. of Ennis via SR 34. | **2** | • | • | • | • | • | | • | • | • | • | | | | |
| **B.A. Steinhagen Lake (E-11)** 13,700 acres 15 mi. e. of Woodville via US 190. | **3** | • | • | • | • | • | | • | • | • | • | | | | |
| **Belton Lake (E-8)** 12,300 acres 4 mi. n.w. of Belton via SR 317 and FM 439. | **4** | • | • | • | • | • | | • | • | • | | | | • | • |
| **Benbrook Lake (I-1)** 3,770 acres 12 mi. s.w. of Fort Worth on US 377. | **5** | • | • | • | • | • | | • | • | • | | | | | |
| **Canyon Lake (F-8)** 8,240 acres 16 mi. n.w. of New Braunfels via SR 306. | **6** | • | • | • | • | • | | • | • | • | • | | • | | • |
| **Granger Lake (E-8)** 4,400 acres 10 mi. n.e. of Taylor via SR 95 and FM 971. | **7** | • | • | • | • | • | | • | • | • | | | | • | |
| **Grapevine Lake (H-2)** 7,280 acres n.e. of Grapevine on SR 121. | **8** | • | • | • | • | • | • | • | • | • | • | | • | • | • |
| **Hords Creek Lake (E-7)** 510 acres 8 mi. w. of Coleman on FM 153. | **9** | • | • | • | • | • | | • | • | • | | | | • | |
| **Joe Pool Lake (I-2)** 7,470 acres 2 mi. s. of Grand Prairie off I-20 on Great South Pkwy. | **10** | • | • | • | • | • | • | • | • | • | | | • | | • |
| **Lake Georgetown (E-8)** 1,310 acres 4 mi. w. of Georgetown via I-35 and CR 2338. | **11** | • | • | • | • | • | | • | • | • | • | | • | | |
| **Lake Lavon (G-4)** 21,400 acres 3 mi. e. of Wylie on SR 78. Water skiing. | **12** | • | • | • | • | • | | • | • | • | | | | | • |
| **Lake O' the Pines (D-10)** 19,780 acres 25 mi. n.e. of Longview off FM 726. (See Longview p. 399.) | **13** | • | • | • | • | • | | • | • | • | • | | • | | |
| **Lake Texoma (C-9)** 195,326 acres. (See Denison p. 225.) | **14** | • | • | • | • | • | | • | • | • | | | | | |
| **Lake Wright Patman (C-10)** 33,750 acres 9 mi. s.w. of Texarkana on US 59. | **15** | • | • | • | • | • | | • | • | • | | | • | | |
| **Lewisville Lake (H-2)** 28,980 acres in Lewisville. Golf (18 holes). | **16** | • | • | • | • | • | • | • | • | • | | | • | | • |
| **Navarro Mills Lake (D-9)** 5,070 acres 18 mi. w. of Corsicana via SR 31 and FM 667. Hunting. | **17** | • | • | | • | • | | • | • | • | | | | | |
| **O.C. Fisher Lake (E-5)** 5,440 acres 3 mi. n.w. of San Angelo off FM 853. | **18** | • | • | • | | | | • | • | • | | | | | |
| **Pat Mayse Lake (C-10)** 8,000 acres 12 mi. n. of Paris off US 271. (See Paris p. 432.) | **19** | • | • | • | • | • | | • | • | • | | | • | | |

# Recreation Areas Chart

The map location numerals in column 2 show an area's location on the preceding map.

| | MAP LOCATION | CAMPING | PICNICKING | HIKING TRAILS | BOATING | BOAT RAMP | BOAT RENTAL | FISHING | SWIMMING | PETS ON LEASH | BICYCLE TRAILS | SKIN/SCUBA | VISITOR CENTER | LODGE/CABINS | FOOD SERVICE |
|---|---|---|---|---|---|---|---|---|---|---|---|---|---|---|---|
| Proctor Lake (D-7) 4,610 acres 3.5 from Hasse via US 377 and FM 2861. | 20 | • | • | • | • | • | • | • | • | • | • | | | | |
| Sam Rayburn Reservoir (E-11) 114,500 acres 20 mi. n. of Jasper via US 96 and FM 1007. (See Angelina National Forest p. 65.) | 21 | • | • | • | • | • | • | • | • | • | | | | • | • |
| Somerville Lake (F-9) 11,460 acres w. of Somerville. | 22 | • | • | • | • | • | • | • | • | • | | | • | • | • |
| Stillhouse Hollow Lake (E-8) 6,430 acres 4 mi. s.w. of Belton via US 190 and FM 1670. | 23 | • | • | • | • | • | • | • | • | • | | | | | • |
| Waco Lake (E-8) 7,270 acres in Waco. Horseback riding trails. | 24 | • | • | • | • | • | | • | • | • | | | • | | |
| **STATE** | | | | | | | | | | | | | | | |
| Abilene (D-6) 621 acres 16 mi. s.w. of Abilene via FM 89 near Buffalo Gap. (See Abilene p. 47.) | 25 | • | • | • | | | | • | • | • | | | • | | |
| Atlanta (C-10) 1,500 acres 12 mi. n.w. of Atlanta off US 59. | 26 | • | • | • | • | • | | • | • | • | | | | | |
| Balmorhea (E-4) 43 acres .1 mi. n.e. of Balmorhea on SR 17S. Spring-fed swimming pool. | 27 | • | • | | | | | | • | • | | • | • | | |
| Bastrop (F-8) 3,500 acres 1 mi. n.e. of Bastrop off SR 21. Scenic. Canoeing, golf (18 holes). | 28 | • | • | • | | • | | • | • | • | | | • | • | |
| Bentsen-Rio Grande Valley (I-7) 588 acres 6 mi. s.w. of Mission off US 83. Scenic. (See Mission p. 420.) | 29 | • | • | • | | | | • | | • | | | • | | |
| Big Bend Ranch (F-3) 287,000 acres 4 miles s.e. of Presidio on River Road (FM 170). Historic. (See Presidio p. 445.) | 30 | • | • | • | | | | • | | • | | | • | | |
| Blanco (F-7) 105 acres 1 mi. s. of Blanco off US 281. Boats with electric motors only. | 31 | • | • | • | • | • | | • | • | • | | | | | |
| Bonham (C-9) 261 acres 3.5 mi. s.e. of Bonham on FM 271. | 32 | • | • | • | • | • | | • | • | • | | | • | | |
| Brazos Bend (G-9) 4,897 acres 20 mi. s.w. of Richmond on FM 762. (See Richmond p. 448.) | 33 | • | • | • | | | | • | | • | | | • | | |
| Buescher (F-8) 1,016 acres 3 mi. n.w. of Smithville off SR 71. Scenic. | 34 | • | • | • | | • | | • | | • | | | | • | |
| Caddo Lake (D-10) 484 acres 15 mi. n.e. of Marshall off SR 43. Historic. Scenic. (See Longview p. 399.) | 35 | • | • | • | • | • | • | • | • | • | | | • | • | • |
| Caprock Canyons (B-5) 13,960 acres 3.5 mi. n. of SR 86, then n. on FM 1065 in Quitaque. Rock climbing; horseback riding trails. Bison herd. | 36 | • | • | • | • | | | • | • | • | | | • | | |
| Cedar Hill (I-2) 1,810 acres on FM 1382 near Cedar Hill. Bird-watching. | 37 | • | • | • | • | • | | • | • | • | | | | | • |
| Choke Canyon (G-7) e. of Calliham on SR 72. | 38 | • | • | • | • | • | | • | • | • | | | | | |
| Cleburne (D-8) 529 acres 12 mi. s. of Cleburne via US 67 and Park Rd. 21. (See Cleburne p. 139.) | 39 | • | • | • | • | • | • | • | • | • | | | | | |
| Colorado Bend (E-7) s. of Bend on FM 501. Cave tours. | 40 | • | • | • | | • | | • | • | • | | | | | |
| Confederate Reunion Grounds (D-9) 7 mi. s.w. of Mexia on SR 14. Historic. | 41 | | • | • | • | • | | • | • | • | | | • | | |
| Cooper Lake (C-9) s. of Cooper off SR 24. Horseback riding trails. | 42 | • | • | • | • | • | • | • | • | • | | | | • | |
| Copper Breaks (C-6) 1,889 acres 12 mi. s. of Quanah on SR 6. Horseback riding trails. | 43 | • | • | • | • | • | | • | • | • | | | | | |
| Daingerfield (C-10) 551 acres 2 mi. s.e. of Daingerfield on SR 49. | 44 | • | • | • | • | • | • | • | • | • | | • | • | • | • |
| Dinosaur Valley (D-8) 1,274 acres 5 mi. w. of Glen Rose off US 67. Historic. Horseback riding trails. (See Glen Rose p. 285.) | 45 | • | • | • | | | | • | | • | | | | | |
| Eisenhower (C-9) 423 acres off US 75, 2 mi. n. on FM 1310 at Lake Texoma. (See Denison p. 225.) | 46 | • | • | • | • | • | • | • | • | • | | | • | | |
| Enchanted Rock (F-7) 18 mi. n. of Fredericksburg on FM 965. Rock climbing. (See Fredericksburg p. 268.) | 47 | • | • | • | | | | | | • | | | • | | |
| Fairfield Lake (D-9) 1,460 acres 4.5 mi. n. of Fairfield off FM 2570. | 48 | • | • | • | • | • | • | • | • | • | | | • | • | • |
| Falcon (H-7) 572 acres s. of Falcon Heights on Park Rd. 46. (See Falcon Heights p. 245.) | 49 | • | • | • | • | • | • | • | • | • | | | | | |
| Fort Griffin (D-7) 506 acres 15 mi. n. of Albany on US 283. Historic. Horseback riding trails. (See Albany p. 54.) | 50 | • | • | • | | | | • | | • | | | • | | |

# Recreation Areas Chart

The map location numerals in column 2 show an area's location on the preceding map.

| | MAP LOCATION | CAMPING | PICNICKING | HIKING TRAILS | BOATING | BOAT RAMP | BOAT RENTAL | FISHING | SWIMMING | PETS ON LEASH | BICYCLE TRAILS | SKIN/SCUBA | VISITOR CENTER | LODGE/CABINS | FOOD SERVICE |
|---|---|---|---|---|---|---|---|---|---|---|---|---|---|---|---|
| **Fort Parker (E-9)** 1,459 acres 7 mi. s. of Mexia on SR 14. | 51 | • | • | • | • | • | • | • | • | • | • | • | • | | |
| **Fort Richardson (D-7)** 396 acres 1 mi. s. of Jacksboro off US 281. Historic. *(See Jacksboro p. 380.)* | 52 | • | • | • | | | | • | • | • | • | | • | | |
| **Franklin Mountains (D-1)** 24,000 acres 3.8 mi. e. of El Paso on I-10 at McKelligon Canyon Rd. *(See El Paso p. 234.)* | 53 | • | • | • | | | | | | • | • | | • | | |
| **Galveston Island (G-10)** 1,950 acres. Historic. *(See Galveston p. 275.)* | 54 | • | • | • | • | • | | • | • | • | | | • | | |
| **Garner (F-7)** 1,700 acres 8 mi. n. of Concan on FM 1050. | 55 | • | • | • | | | | • | • | • | • | | • | | |
| **Goliad (G-8)** 188 acres .2 mi. s. on US 77A/183. Historic. *(See Goliad p. 286.)* | 56 | • | • | • | | | | • | • | • | | | • | | |
| **Goose Island (G-8)** 314 acres 12 mi. n.e. of Rockport off SR 35. *(See Rockport p. 449.)* | 57 | • | • | • | • | • | | • | | • | | | • | | |
| **Guadalupe River/Honey Creek (F-7)** 1,938 acres 13 mi. e. of Boerne on SR 46. Nature programs. Children's center, horseback riding trails. | 58 | • | • | • | | | | • | • | • | | | • | | |
| **Hill Country (F-7)** 5,369 acres 4 mi. n.e. of Tarpley on FM 1077. Horseback riding trails. *(See Bandera p. 114.)* | 59 | • | • | • | | | | • | • | • | • | | | | |
| **Hueco Tanks (D-2)** e. of El Paso on US 180/62, then 8 mi. n. on FM 2775. Rock climbing. *(See El Paso p. 235.)* | 60 | • | • | • | | | | | | • | | | | | |
| **Huntsville (E-9)** 2,083 acres 6 mi. s. of Huntsville off I-45. Horseback riding trails (no personal horses permitted; horses are provided by park stables), playground. | 61 | • | • | • | • | • | • | • | • | • | | | • | • | |
| **Inks Lake (E-7)** 1,200 acres 9 mi. w. of Burnet off SR 29. Canoeing, water skiing. *(See Burnet p. 132.)* | 62 | • | • | • | | | | • | • | • | | | • | • | • |
| **Kerrville-Schreiner (F-7)** 517 acres 3 mi. s.w. of Kerrville off SR 16 on FM 173. | 63 | • | • | • | • | • | | • | • | • | • | | • | | |
| **Lake Arrowhead (C-7)** 524 acres 15 mi. s.e. of Wichita Falls via US 281 and FM 1954. Horseback riding trails. *(See Wichita Falls p. 569.)* | 64 | • | • | • | • | • | | • | | • | • | | | | |
| **Lake Bob Sandlin (C-10)** 9 mi. w. of Mount Pleasant on FM 127. | 65 | • | • | • | | | | • | • | • | • | | | | |
| **Lake Brownwood (D-7)** 537 acres 16 mi. n.w. of Brownwood off SR 279. | 66 | • | • | • | | | | • | • | • | | | | • | |
| **Lake Casa Blanca (H-7)** 371 acres e. of Laredo off US 59 to Loop 20. | 67 | • | • | • | | | | • | • | • | • | | | | • |
| **Lake Colorado City (D-6)** 500 acres 10 mi. w. of Colorado City on I-20. | 68 | • | • | • | | | | • | • | • | | | • | • | |
| **Lake Corpus Christi (H-8)** 288 acres 4.5 mi. s. of Mathis on SR 359, then 2 mi. n.w. on Park Rd. 25. *(See Corpus Christi p. 147.)* | 69 | • | • | • | | | | • | • | • | | | | | |
| **Lake Houston (F-10)** 3 mi. e. of New Caney on FM 1485. Horseback riding trails. | 70 | • | • | • | | | | • | • | | | | • | | |
| **Lake Livingston (E-10)** 82,600 acres 5 mi. s.w. of Livingston off US 190. Horseback riding trails. | 71 | • | • | • | • | • | • | • | • | • | • | | • | • | • |
| **Lake Mineral Wells (D-7)** 3,004 acres 4 mi. e. of Mineral Wells on US 180. Rock climbing; horseback riding trails. | 72 | • | • | • | • | • | | • | • | • | • | | | | |
| **Lake Somerville (F-9)** 2,600 acres 15 mi. n.w. of Brenham on SR 36. Horseback riding trails. | 73 | • | • | • | • | • | | • | • | • | • | | | | |
| **Lake Tawakoni (D-9)** 376 acres 4 mi. n. of Wills Point on FM 2475. | 74 | • | • | • | | | | • | • | • | • | | | | • |
| **Lake Texana (G-9)** 575 acres 6 mi. s.e. of Edna on SR 111. Water skiing. | 75 | • | • | • | • | • | | • | • | • | | | | | |
| **Lake Whitney (D-8)** 23,560 acres 4 mi. w. of Whitney on SR 22. | 76 | • | • | | | | | • | • | • | | • | | | |
| **Lockhart (F-8)** 263 acres 45 mi. s. of Austin off US 183. Golf. | 77 | • | • | • | | | | • | • | • | | | | | |
| **Lost Maples (F-7)** 2,200 acres 5 mi. n. of Vanderpool on FM 187. Natural area. *(See Bandera p. 114.)* | 78 | • | • | • | | | | • | • | • | | | • | | |
| **Lyndon B. Johnson (F-7)** 733 acres e. of Stonewall on US 290. Historic. *(See Stonewall p. 543.)* | 79 | | • | • | | | | • | • | • | | | • | | |

# Recreation Areas Chart

The map location numerals in column 2 show an area's location on the preceding map.

| | MAP LOCATION | CAMPING | PICNICKING | HIKING TRAILS | BOATING | BOAT RAMP | BOAT RENTAL | FISHING | SWIMMING | PETS ON LEASH | BICYCLE TRAILS | SKIN/SCUBA | VISITOR CENTER | LODGE/CABINS | FOOD SERVICE |
|---|---|---|---|---|---|---|---|---|---|---|---|---|---|---|---|
| Martin Creek Lake (D-10) 287 acres 8 mi. n.e. of Henderson off SR 43. *(See Longview p. 399.)* | 80 | • | • | • | • | • | • | • | • | • | • | • | | • | |
| Martin Dies Jr. (E-11) 705 acres 15 mi. e. of Woodville on US 190. | 81 | • | • | • | • | • | • | • | • | • | • | • | | • | • |
| Matagorda Island (G-9) 7,325 acres in Matagorda Island Wildlife Management Area, accessed by private or charter boat from Port O'Connor. | 82 | • | • | | | | | • | • | • | • | | | | |
| McKinney Falls (F-8) 641 acres 7 mi. s.e. of Austin off US 183. *(See Austin p. 81.)* | 83 | • | • | • | | | | • | • | • | | | • | | |
| Meridian (D-8) 503 acres 3 mi. s.w. of Meridian off SR 22. | 84 | • | • | • | • | | | • | • | • | | | | | |
| Mission Tejas (E-10) 363 acres just n. of Weches on Park Rd. 44. Historic. *(See Davy Crockett National Forest p. 223.)* | 85 | • | • | • | | | | • | • | | | | | | |
| Monahans Sandhills (E-4) 3,840 acres 5 mi. e. of Monahans off I-20 to Park Rd. 41. Horseback riding trails. *(See Monahans p. 421.)* | 86 | • | • | • | | | | | | • | | | • | | |
| Mother Neff (E-8) 259 acres 9 mi. w. of Moody on SR 236. | 87 | • | • | • | • | | | • | • | • | | | | | |
| Mustang Island (H-8) 3,954 acres 14 mi. s. of Port Aransas on SR 361. *(See Port Aransas p. 441.)* | 88 | • | • | | | | | • | • | • | • | | | | |
| Palmetto (F-8) 265 acres 6 mi. s.e. of Luling off US 183. | 89 | • | • | • | | • | • | • | • | • | | | | | |
| Palo Duro Canyon (B-5) 16,402 acres 12 mi. e. of Canyon on SR 217. Scenic. Horse rental, outdoor drama. *(See Canyon p. 134.)* | 90 | • | • | • | • | | | • | • | • | • | | • | • | |
| Pedernales Falls (F-8) 5,212 acres 9 mi. e. of Johnson City via FM 2766. Horseback riding trails. *(See Johnson City p. 382.)* | 91 | • | • | • | | | | • | • | • | | | | | |
| Possum Kingdom (D-7) 1,528 acres 17 mi. n.e. of Caddo via Park Rd. 33. | 92 | • | • | | | | | • | | | | | | • | • |
| Purtis Creek (D-9) 1,533 acres 4 mi. n. of Eustace on FM 316. | 93 | • | • | • | • | • | • | • | • | • | • | | | | |
| Ray Roberts Lake (C-8) 29,350 acres 15 mi. n. of Denton via I-35 and FM 455. Horseback riding trails. | 94 | • | • | • | • | • | • | • | • | • | | | • | | |
| Resaca de la Palma (I-8) 8 mi. n. of Brownsville off FM 1732. Nature programs. Bird-watching; nature trails. *(See Brownsville p. 128.)* | 95 | | • | • | | | | | | • | • | | • | | |
| San Angelo (E-6) 7,677 acres n. of San Angelo on US 87 to FM 2288. | 96 | • | • | • | • | | | • | | • | • | | | | |
| Sea Rim (F-11) 15,109 acres 10 mi. s. of Sabine Pass off SR 87. Water skiing; canoe trails. | 97 | • | • | • | • | • | | • | • | • | | | | | |
| Seminole Canyon (F-5) 2,172 acres 8 mi. w. of Comstock on US 90. Historic. *(See Comstock p. 145.)* | 98 | • | • | • | | | | | | • | • | | • | | |
| Sheldon Lake (F-10) w. of Sheldon on US 90 Bus. Rte. | 99 | | • | • | • | • | | • | | | | | • | | |
| South Llano River (F-6) 2,640 acres 5.5 mi. s. of Junction on Park Rd. 73. | 100 | • | • | • | | | | • | • | • | • | | | | |
| Stephen F. Austin (F-9) 667 acres 6 mi. e. of Sealy via I-10 and FM 1458. Historic. | 101 | • | • | • | | | | • | | • | • | | | | |
| Tyler (D-10) 986 acres 2 mi. n. of Tyler off FM 14. | 102 | • | • | • | • | | | • | • | • | | | | • | • |
| Village Creek (F-11) 2,005 acres in Lumberton. Playground. | 103 | • | • | | | | | • | • | • | | | • | • | |
| **OTHER** | | | | | | | | | | | | | | | |
| Comanche Trail (D-5) 400 acres s. of Big Spring via US 87 or FM 700. Golf (18 holes), RV camping, tennis; amphitheater, nature trails, playgrounds. *(See Big Spring p. 121.)* | 104 | • | • | • | | | | | | | | • | | | |
| Falls on the Brazos (E-9) 22 acres 3 mi. s. of Marlin on FM 712. *(See Marlin p. 410.)* | 105 | • | • | • | | | | • | • | • | | | • | | |
| Hubbard Creek Lake (D-7) 15,250 acres 4 mi. w. of Breckenridge on US 180. Water skiing. | 106 | • | • | • | • | • | | • | • | | | | | | |
| Lake Buchanan (E-7) 10 acres 9 mi. w. of Burnet on SR 29 and 15 mi. e. of Llano. *(See Burnet p. 132.)* | 107 | • | • | • | | | | • | • | • | | | | • | |
| Lake Crook (C-9) 2,717 acres about 5 mi. n.w. of Paris off US 271. | 108 | • | • | | • | • | | • | • | | | | | | |

## Recreation Areas Chart

The map location numerals in column 2 show an area's location on the preceding map.

| | MAP LOCATION | CAMPING | PICNICKING | HIKING TRAILS | BOATING | BOAT RAMP | BOAT RENTAL | FISHING | SWIMMING | PETS ON LEASH | BICYCLE TRAILS | SKIN/SCUBA | VISITOR CENTER | LODGE/CABINS | FOOD SERVICE |
|---|---|---|---|---|---|---|---|---|---|---|---|---|---|---|---|
| **Lake Fort Phantom Hill (D-7)** 4,246 acres about 10 mi. n.e. of Abilene via FM 600. | 109 | • | • | | • | • | | • | • | | | | | | |
| **Lake Leon (D-7)** 50 acres 6 mi. s. of Ranger off FM 2461. | 110 | • | • | | • | • | | • | • | | | | | • | • |
| **Pace Bend (F-8)** 1,400 acres 27 mi. n.w. of Austin via SR 71. | 111 | • | • | • | • | • | | • | • | • | • | | | | |
| **Rusk (D-10)** 100 acres 3 mi. w. of Rusk on US 84. Basketball, tennis. *(See Rusk p. 454.)* | 112 | • | • | • | • | | | • | | | • | | | | • |
| **Sabine Lake (F-10)** e. of Port Arthur via SR 82 and Martin Luther King, Jr. Bridge. Water skiing. *(See Port Arthur p. 442.)* | 113 | • | • | • | • | • | | • | • | • | • | | | | |
| **Zilker (F-8)** 351 acres 1.5 mi. s.w. of Austin on Barton Springs Rd. *(See Austin p. 82.)* | 114 | | • | • | • | | | • | • | • | | | • | | |

# Explore. Excite. Experience.

**Get the travel information that turns vacations into extraordinary experiences.**

· Descriptive destination details
· Don't-miss things to see and do
· Insider tips from AAA travel experts
· Member rates and convenient hotel booking

  **Explore AAA.com and CAA.ca today.**

**ABILENE** (D-6) pop. 117,063, elev. 1,726'
• Restaurants p. 49

For centuries the Central Plains around Abilene were filled only with buffalo. In the late 1870s cattle replaced the buffalo, and a tent city soon took shape. The efforts of Col. C.W. Merchant convinced Jay Gould's Texas and Pacific Railway to route its tracks through the settlement, which was named Abilene after the Kansas cattle boomtown. Abilene soon became a major shipping point for cattle.

Livestock still plays a role in the economy of this city, which has grown into an urban center supporting such diverse industries as petroleum refining, manufacturing and the production of musical instruments. The city also has three universities, a symphony orchestra and a theater.

Nearby recreation and historic areas include the ruins of Fort Phantom Hill, 10 miles northeast on FM 600, and 621-acre Abilene State Park, 16 miles southwest via FM 89 *(see Recreation Areas Chart)*. The guardhouse, commissary, powder magazine and several chimneys are all that remain of Fort Phantom Hill, once part of a string of forts along the Texas frontier.

**Abilene Convention and Visitors Bureau:** 1101 N. 1st St., Abilene, TX 79601. **Phone:** (325) 676-2556 or (800) 727-7704.

**12TH ARMORED DIVISION MEMORIAL MUSEUM** is at 1289 N. Second St. Organized in 1942, the 12th Armored Division trained at Camp Barkeley and fought in France, Austria and Germany during World War II. The museum describes the division's history along with that of the Second World War through displays of armored vehicles, period weapons, flags, uniforms and photographs. A seven-part diorama depicts the 1945 Herrlisheim battle, and veterans describe their experiences in video presentations.

**Time:** Allow 30 minutes minimum. **Hours:** Tues.-Sat. 10-5. Last ticket sales 1 hour before closing. Closed major holidays. **Cost:** $5; $4 (ages 60+, military and students with ID); $2 (ages 7-12); free (World War II veterans). **Phone:** (325) 677-6515.

**ABILENE ZOO** is at 2070 Zoo Ln. in Nelson Park. Animals of the North American Plains are compared to those of similar habitats in Africa, Asia and Australia. The zoo houses more than 500 amphibians, birds, mammals and reptiles. **Time:** Allow 1 hour minimum. **Hours:** Daily 9-5 (also Thurs. 5-9, Memorial Day-Labor Day). Last admission 30 minutes before closing. Closed Jan. 1, Thanksgiving and Christmas. **Cost:** $5; $4 (ages 60+); $2.50 (ages 3-12). **Phone:** (325) 676-6085.

**FRONTIER TEXAS!**, 625 N. First St., offers a look at frontier life through audiovisual and interactive exhibits. A surround-sound theater allows visitors to experience a buffalo stampede and a shootout, while a holographic presentation introduces frontier folk, settlers and Native Americans. Interactive exhibits include a stagecoach and a saloon; life-size buffalo replicas may be seen.

**Time:** Allow 30 minutes minimum. **Hours:** Mon.-Sat. 9-6, Sun. 1-5. Closed Jan. 1, Thanksgiving and Christmas. **Cost:** $8; $6 (ages 60+ and military with ID); $5 (students and teachers with ID); $4 (ages 3-12). **Phone:** (325) 437-2800.

**THE GRACE MUSEUM** is at 102 Cypress St. Art, history and children's museums are housed in this historic building. Features include fine arts collections, a photography gallery, local history exhibits and hands-on activities for children. **Hours:** Tues.-Sat. 10-5 (also Thurs. 5-8). Closed major holidays. **Cost:** $8; $4 (ages 55+ and military, teachers and college students with ID); $3 (ages 4-12); free (Thurs. 5-8). **Phone:** (325) 673-4587.

**NATIONAL CENTER FOR CHILDREN'S ILLUSTRATED LITERATURE,** 102 Cedar St., displays original art created for children's literature. Traveling exhibits enhance the permanent collection. **Time:** Allow 30 minutes minimum. **Hours:** Tues.-Sat. 10-4. Closed Thanksgiving and Christmas. **Cost:** Free. **Phone:** (325) 673-4586.

 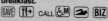 

Plan complete trip routings with the TripTik® Travel Planner on AAA.com/CAA.ca

## BEST WESTERN WHITTEN SOUTH          (325)695-1262

Hotel
$99-$119

**AAA Benefit:** Members save 10% or more with Best Western!

**Address:** 3950 Ridgemont Dr 79606 **Location:** US 83/84 exit Buffalo Gap Rd to Ridgemont Dr, just w. Adjacent to Mall of Abilene. **Facility:** 61 units. 2 stories (no elevator), exterior corridors. **Pool(s):** outdoor. **Guest Services:** valet and coin laundry, area transportation. **Featured Amenity: full hot breakfast.**

## COMFORT INN & SUITES          (325)232-8801

Hotel $79-$114 **Address:** 6350 Directors Pkwy 79606 **Location:** US 83/84 S exit Antilley Rd, just w. Across from Abilene Regional Medical Center. **Facility:** 73 units. 4 stories, interior corridors. **Pool(s):** heated outdoor. **Activities:** hot tub, exercise room. **Guest Services:** valet and coin laundry.

## COMFORT SUITES UNIVERSITY          (325)672-0338

Hotel
$99-$299

**Address:** 1902 E Overland Tr 79601 **Location:** I-20 exit 288; on N Frontage Rd. **Facility:** 68 units, some two bedrooms. 4 stories, interior corridors. **Pool(s):** heated indoor. **Activities:** hot tub, exercise room. **Guest Services:** valet and coin laundry. **Featured Amenity: continental breakfast.**

## COURTYARD BY MARRIOTT          (325)695-9600

Hotel $103-$129 **Address:** 4350 Ridgemont Dr 79606 **Location:** US 83/84 exit Buffalo Gap Rd, 1 mi s on W Frontage Rd to Ridgemont Dr, then 0.5 mi w. **Facility:** 100 units. 3 stories, interior corridors. **Pool(s):** heated outdoor. **Activities:** exercise room. **Guest Services:** complimentary laundry.

**AAA Benefit:** Members save 5% or more!

## FAIRFIELD INN & SUITES BY MARRIOTT ABILENE          (325)695-2448

Hotel $90-$160 **Address:** 3902 Turner Plaza 79606 **Location:** US 83/84 exit Buffalo Gap Rd, 1 mi s on W Frontage Rd to Ridgemont Dr, then just w. **Facility:** 71 units. 4 stories, interior corridors. **Pool(s):** heated indoor. **Activities:** hot tub, exercise room. **Guest Services:** valet and coin laundry.

**AAA Benefit:** Members save 5% or more!

## HAMPTON INN BY HILTON          (325)695-0044

Hotel $89-$135 **Address:** 3917 Ridgemont Dr 79606 **Location:** US 83/84 S exit Buffalo Gap Rd to Ridgemont Dr, just w. **Facility:** 63 units. 4 stories, interior corridors. **Terms:** 3-night minimum stay, cancellation fee imposed. **Pool(s):** heated indoor. **Activities:** hot tub, exercise room. **Guest Services:** valet laundry.

**AAA Benefit:** Members save up to 10%!

## HILTON GARDEN INN ABILENE          (325)690-6432

Hotel $99-$179 **Address:** 4449 Ridgemont Dr 79606 **Location:** US 83/84 S exit Buffalo Gap Rd, 1 mi s on W Frontage Rd to Ridgemont Dr, then 1 mi w. **Facility:** 123 units. 4 stories, interior corridors. **Terms:** 1-7 night minimum stay, cancellation fee imposed. **Amenities:** video games. **Pool(s):** heated indoor. **Activities:** hot tub, exercise room. **Guest Services:** valet and coin laundry.

**AAA Benefit:** Members save up to 10%!

## HOLIDAY INN EXPRESS & SUITES          (325)675-9800

Hotel $104-$119 **Address:** 1802 E Overland Tr 79601 **Location:** I-20 exit 288; on N Frontage Rd. **Facility:** 66 units. 3 stories, interior corridors. **Activities:** exercise room. **Guest Services:** valet and coin laundry.

## HOLIDAY INN EXPRESS MALL SOUTH          325/695-0500

Hotel. Rates not provided. **Address:** 3112 S Clack St 79606 **Location:** US 83/277 and Southwest Dr, just e to Catclaw Dr, then just n. **Facility:** 66 units. 3 stories, interior corridors. **Pool(s):** outdoor. **Activities:** hot tub, exercise room. **Guest Services:** valet and coin laundry.

## MCM ELEGANTE SUITES          (325)698-1234

Hotel $129-$349 **Address:** 4250 Ridgemont Dr 79606 **Location:** US 83/84 exit Buffalo Gap Rd, 1 mi s of W Frontage Rd to Ridgemont Dr, then 0.5 mi w. Adjacent to Mall of Abilene. **Facility:** 175 units. 3 stories, interior/exterior corridors. **Terms:** cancellation fee imposed. **Amenities:** video games. **Pool(s):** heated indoor. **Activities:** hot tub, exercise room. **Guest Services:** valet and coin laundry.

## RESIDENCE INN BY MARRIOTT          (325)677-8700

Extended Stay Contemporary Hotel $129-$179 **Address:** 1641 Musgrave Blvd 79601 **Location:** I-20 exit 288; on N Frontage Rd. **Facility:** 117 kitchen units, some two bedrooms. 4 stories, interior corridors. **Pool(s):** heated outdoor. **Activities:** hot tub, exercise room. **Guest Services:** valet and coin laundry.

**AAA Benefit:** Members save 5% or more!

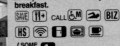

## SLEEP INN & SUITES UNIVERSITY    (325)437-9601

Hotel
$75-$150

**Address:** 250 Killough Cove 79601 **Location:** I-20 exit 286C, just s. **Facility:** 55 units. 3 stories, interior corridors. **Pool(s):** outdoor. **Activities:** exercise room. **Guest Services:** valet and coin laundry.

SAVE CALL &M 🏊 BIZ HS
🛜 📶 🍽 📺 /SOME UNITS 🛏️

SLEEP INN
BY CHOICE HOTELS

**Brand new hotel. Free hot breakfast, WIFI, business & fitness ctr, pet friendly, close to ACU & HSU.**

## SUPER 8    (325)701-4779

Hotel
$79-$109

**Address:** 4397 Sayles Blvd 79605 **Location:** US 83/84 exit Buffalo Gap Rd southbound, just e to Industrial Blvd, 0.5 mi e to Sayles Blvd, then just s; exit Buffalo Gap Rd northbound, just e. **Facility:** 54 units. 3 stories, interior corridors. **Pool(s):** outdoor. **Guest Services:** valet and coin laundry. **Featured Amenity:** continental breakfast.

SAVE 🍴 🏊 HS 🛜 📶 🍽
📺 /SOME UNITS 🛏️

## WINGATE BY WYNDHAM    (325)690-6400

Hotel
$79-$299

**Address:** 3010 Catclaw Dr 79606 **Location:** US 83/277 and Southwest Dr, just e to Catclaw Dr, then just n. **Facility:** 66 units. 3 stories, interior corridors. **Amenities:** safes. **Pool(s):** outdoor. **Activities:** hot tub, exercise room. **Guest Services:** coin laundry. **Featured Amenity:** full hot breakfast.

SAVE 🍴 CALL &M 🏊 BIZ HS
🛜 ❌ 📶 🍽 📺

### WHERE TO EAT

## ABILENE SEAFOOD TAVERN    325/695-1770

Seafood. Casual Dining. $7-$36 **AAA Inspector Notes:** Seafood dominates the menu, but a nice selection of steaks also is available at this English Tudor-designed restaurant. **Features:** full bar, patio dining, happy hour. **Address:** 1882 S Clack St 79605 **Location:** US 83/84/277 exit S 14th St, 1 mi s on W Frontage Rd. L D

## ABUELO'S THE FLAVOR OF MEXICO    325/692-4776

Mexican. Casual Dining. $9-$20 **AAA Inspector Notes:** Many traditional Mexican dishes are served in this upscale and spacious dining area. The adult beverages reflect an inventive spirit. **Features:** full bar. **Address:** 4782 S 14th St 79605 **Location:** Jct US 83/84 and S 14th St; on northeast corner; in Woodhaven Center. L D CALL &M

## BEEHIVE RESTAURANT    325/675-0600

Steak. Casual Dining. $6-$30 **AAA Inspector Notes:** Locals love this place for its large and comfortable bar, well-made Angus steaks and friendly staff. **Features:** full bar. **Address:** 442 Cedar St 79601 **Location:** Center. **Parking:** street only. L D

## COPPER CREEK RESTAURANT    325/692-4424

Steak Seafood. Fine Dining. $8-$37 **AAA Inspector Notes:** An upscale western lodge theme provides the ambience for this restaurant, which features steaks, chops and seafood selections. Homemade desserts are excellent and change on a regular basis. The 16-ounce prime rib is a favorite of mine. **Features:** full bar, patio dining. **Address:** 4401 Loop 322 79602 **Location:** Loop 322 exit Industrial Blvd, 0.5 mi n on E Frontage Rd. L D CALL &M

## EL CHICO    325/695-2875

Tex-Mex
Casual Dining
$8-$15

**AAA Inspector Notes:** Inside and out, the decor of the popular Mexican restaurant is inviting. The menu features traditional favorites such as enchiladas, tacos, burritos and fajitas. The broad menu also lists a few American classics. **Features:** full bar. **Reservations:** suggested. **Address:** 4310 Buffalo Gap Rd 79606 **Location:** Just se of jct US 83 and Buffalo Gap Rd. L D

## GRANDY'S RESTAURANT

American. Quick Serve. $4-$8 **AAA Inspector Notes:** Fried chicken and country-fried steak are menu standbys at the restaurant, a regional franchise. They also offer a family-style dining menu. The décor is a step up from that of most quick-serve eateries and more resembles that of a conventional restaurant. Some elements of increased service include additional rolls, iced tea refills and tray removal. B L D

*For additional information, visit AAA.com*

**LOCATIONS:**
**Address:** 4134 Buffalo Gap Rd 79605 **Location:** Just ne of jct US 83 and Buffalo Gap Rd. **Phone:** 325/692-6192
**Address:** 401 Westwood Dr 79603 **Location:** Jct N 1st St and Westwood Dr, just n. **Phone:** 325/676-4397

## LYTLE LAND AND CATTLE CO.    325/677-1925

Steak. Casual Dining. $7-$30 **AAA Inspector Notes:** Steaks are the name of the game at this ranch house-style restaurant that is a favorite among the local residents. **Features:** full bar. **Address:** 1150 E South 11th St 79602 **Location:** Jct E South 11th St and Judge Ely Blvd. L D 🚬

## ADDISON (H-3) pop. 13,056, elev. 636'

On July 3 crowds gather downtown for the Kaboom Town celebration's family-friendly activities and sensational fireworks show.

**CAVANAUGH FLIGHT MUSEUM** is at 4572 Claire Chennault. Exhibits are housed in several hangars and chronicle the history of American, British, German and Polish military aircraft from World War I through the Cold War. **Tours:** Guided tours are available. **Time:** Allow 1 hour minimum. **Hours:** Mon.-Sat. 9-5, Sun. 11-5. **Cost:** $10; $7 (ages 65+ and students and military with ID); $5 (ages 4-12). **Phone:** (972) 380-8800. 🍴

**THE MARY KAY MUSEUM** is at 16251 Dallas Pkwy. Located inside the Mary Kay World Headquarters, the museum pays homage to its founder Mary Kay Ash. Awards, books, cosmetics, jewelry, photographs and other memorabilia highlight the evolution of Mary Kay products.

**Time:** Allow 30 minutes minimum. **Hours:** Mon.-Fri. 9-5. Closed major holidays. Phone ahead to confirm schedule. **Cost:** Free. Under 10 must be with an adult. **Phone:** (972) 687-6300.

(See map & index p. 184.)

## ADDISON QUORUM COURTYARD BY MARRIOTT
(972)404-1555 **54**

Hotel
$50-$179

**AAA Benefit:** Members save 5% or more!

**Address:** 15160 Quorum Dr 75001 **Location:** Just n of jct Belt Line Rd. **Facility:** 176 units. 7 stories, interior corridors. **Pool(s):** outdoor. **Activities:** hot tub, exercise room. **Guest Services:** valet and coin laundry, boarding pass kiosk.

## BEST WESTERN PLUS ADDISON GALLERIA HOTEL
(972)701-0881 **62**

Hotel
$59-$129

**AAA Benefit:** Members save 10% or more with Best Western!

**Address:** 14975 Landmark Blvd 75254 **Location:** Dallas North Tollway exit Belt Line Rd, just w, then just s. **Facility:** 80 units. 2 stories, interior corridors. **Pool(s):** outdoor. **Activities:** hot tub, exercise room. **Guest Services:** coin laundry.

AAA/CAA travel information:
Available online, on the go
and in print!

## COMFORT SUITES BY CHOICE HOTELS
(972)503-6500 **56**

Hotel
$69-$149

**Address:** 4555 Belt Line Rd 75001 **Location:** Just w of Addison Rd; behind Macaroni Grill. **Facility:** 78 units. 3 stories, interior corridors. **Pool(s):** heated indoor. **Activities:** exercise room. **Guest Services:** valet and coin laundry. **Featured Amenity:** full hot breakfast.

## COURTYARD BY MARRIOTT-DALLAS ADDISON/MIDWAY
(972)490-7390 **65**

Hotel $54-$209 **Address:** 4165 Proton Dr 75001 **Location:** 0.8 mi s of jct Belt Line and Midway rds, just w. **Facility:** 145 units. 2 stories (no elevator), interior corridors. **Pool(s):** outdoor. **Activities:** hot tub, exercise room. **Guest Services:** valet and coin laundry.

**AAA Benefit:** Members save 5% or more!

## CROWNE PLAZA NORTH DALLAS/NEAR THE GALLERIA
(972)980-8877 **66**

Hotel
$109-$219

**Address:** 14315 Midway Rd 75001 **Location:** I-635 exit 23 (Midway Rd), 1.5 mi n. **Facility:** 429 units. 4 stories, interior corridors. **Terms:** cancellation fee imposed. **Amenities:** *Some:* safes. **Pool(s):** heated outdoor. **Activities:** hot tub, exercise room. **Guest Services:** valet and coin laundry, area transportation. *(See ad this page.)*

▼ See AAA listing this page ▼

(See map & index p. 184.)

## DALLAS ADDISON MARRIOTT QUORUM BY THE GALLERIA
(972)661-2800  **63**

Hotel $99-$259 **Address:** 14901 Dallas Pkwy 75254 **Location:** I-635 exit 22D, 2 mi n of jct I-635 and Dallas North Tollway; west side. **Facility:** 547 units. 12 stories, interior corridors. **Parking:** on-site (fee) and valet. **Amenities:** *Some:* safes. **Pool(s):** outdoor, indoor. **Activities:** sauna, hot tub, tennis, exercise room. **Guest Services:** complimentary and valet laundry, boarding pass kiosk, area transportation.

**AAA Benefit:** Members save 5% or more!

## HAMPTON INN
(972)991-2800  **59**

Hotel $62-$129 **Address:** 4505 Beltway Dr 75001 **Location:** Jct Beltway Dr and Midway Rd, just s, then just e. Located in a business park. **Facility:** 158 units. 4 stories, interior corridors. **Terms:** 1-7 night minimum stay, cancellation fee imposed. **Pool(s):** outdoor. **Activities:** exercise room. **Guest Services:** valet laundry, area transportation.

**AAA Benefit:** Members save up to 10%!

## HAWTHORN SUITES BY WYNDHAM
(972)386-4800  **53**

Extended Stay Hotel $76-$110

**Address:** 15200 Addison Rd 75001 **Location:** Just n of Belt Line Rd. **Facility:** 70 efficiencies. 3 stories, interior corridors. **Pool(s):** outdoor. **Activities:** exercise room. **Guest Services:** valet and coin laundry, area transportation. **Featured Amenity: full hot breakfast.**

## HILTON GARDEN INN-ADDISON
(972)233-8000  **57**

Hotel $99-$159 **Address:** 4090 Belt Line Rd 75001 **Location:** Just e of jct Belt Line Rd and Marsh Ln; set back on south side of road. **Facility:** 96 units. 3 stories, interior corridors. **Terms:** 1-7 night minimum stay, cancellation fee imposed. **Pool(s):** outdoor. **Activities:** hot tub, exercise room. **Guest Services:** valet and coin laundry, area transportation.

**AAA Benefit:** Members save up to 10%!

## HOLIDAY INN-ADDISON/NORTH DALLAS  (972)490-1212  **50**

Hotel $59-$299 **Address:** 4960 Arapaho Rd 75001 **Location:** Dallas North Tollway exit Arapaho Rd, just w. **Facility:** 101 units. 4 stories, interior corridors. **Amenities:** *Some:* safes. **Pool(s):** outdoor. **Activities:** exercise room. **Guest Services:** valet and coin laundry, area transportation.

## HOLIDAY INN EXPRESS HOTEL & SUITES
972/503-7800  **60**

Hotel. Rates not provided. **Address:** 4355 Beltway Dr 75001 **Location:** Jct Beltway Dr and Midway Rd, just s, then just e. **Facility:** 102 units. 4 stories, interior corridors. **Pool(s):** outdoor. **Activities:** exercise room. **Guest Services:** valet and coin laundry, area transportation.

## HOMEWOOD SUITES BY HILTON
(972)788-1342  **58**

Extended Stay Hotel $99-$159 **Address:** 4451 Belt Line Rd 75001 **Location:** Just e of jct Belt Line and Midway rds. **Facility:** 120 efficiencies, some two bedrooms. 3 stories, interior/exterior corridors. **Terms:** 1-7 night minimum stay, cancellation fee imposed. **Amenities:** video games. **Pool(s):** heated outdoor. **Activities:** hot tub, exercise room. **Guest Services:** valet and coin laundry, area transportation.

**AAA Benefit:** Members save up to 10%!

## HYATT HOUSE DALLAS/ADDISON
(972)661-3113  **52**

Extended Stay Hotel $64-$169

HYATT house

**AAA Benefit:** Members save 10%!

**Address:** 4900 Edwin Lewis Dr 75001 **Location:** Just n of jct Belt Line Rd and Quorum Dr to Edwin Lewis Dr, just w. **Facility:** 132 units, some two bedrooms, efficiencies and kitchens. 2-3 stories (no elevator), exterior corridors. **Terms:** cancellation fee imposed. **Pool(s):** outdoor. **Activities:** hot tub, exercise room. **Guest Services:** valet and coin laundry, area transportation. **Featured Amenity:** breakfast buffet.

## LA QUINTA INN & SUITES DALLAS ADDISON GALLERIA
(972)404-0004  **64**

Hotel $75-$120 **Address:** 14925 Landmark Blvd 75254 **Location:** Jct Belt Line Rd and Landmark Blvd, just s. **Facility:** 152 units. 3 stories, interior corridors. **Pool(s):** outdoor. **Activities:** hot tub, exercise room. **Guest Services:** valet and coin laundry, area transportation.

## QUALITY INN & SUITES
(972)991-8888  **55**

Hotel $60-$150 **Address:** 4103 Belt Line Rd 75001 **Location:** Between Midway Rd and Marsh Ln. **Facility:** 105 units. 2 stories (no elevator), exterior corridors. **Pool(s):** outdoor. **Activities:** hot tub. **Guest Services:** valet and coin laundry.

## RESIDENCE INN BY MARRIOTT-ADDISON
(972)866-9933  **61**

Extended Stay Hotel $99-$169 **Address:** 14975 Quorum Dr 75254 **Location:** Just s of jct Belt Line Rd and Quorum Dr. **Facility:** 150 units, some two bedrooms, efficiencies and kitchens. 3 stories, interior corridors. **Pool(s):** heated outdoor. **Activities:** hot tub, exercise room. **Guest Services:** valet and coin laundry, area transportation.

**AAA Benefit:** Members save 5% or more!

Learn about inspections

and Diamond Ratings at

AAA.com/Diamonds

(See map & index p. 184.)

## SPRINGHILL SUITES BY MARRIOTT DALLAS/ADDISON
(972)774-1010 **51**

**Hotel**
**$61-$179**

SPRINGHILL SUITES° *Marriott*

**AAA Benefit:** Members save 5% or more!

**Address:** 15255 Quorum Dr 75001 **Location:** Jct Belt Line Rd and Quorum Dr, just n. **Facility:** 159 units. 5 stories, interior corridors. **Pool(s):** outdoor. **Activities:** hot tub, exercise room. **Guest Services:** valet and coin laundry, area transportation.

SAVE ECO CALL &M ⛵ HS 📶 ✕ 🍴 🖥 💻

## WHERE TO EAT

### ADDISON CAFE
972/991-8824 **61**

▼▼▼ Northern French. Fine Dining. $10-$27 **AAA Inspector Notes:** Glass walls and sleek black and white tones are contrasted by colorful artwork and lush greenery in this romantic bistro setting. Upscale Northern French fare features entrées like veal and smoked salmon, all pleasingly presented and very well prepared. **Features:** full bar. **Reservations:** suggested, weekends. **Address:** 5290 Belt Line Rd 75254 **Location:** Just e of Dallas North Tollway; corner of Montfort Dr and Belt Line Rd. [L] [D]

### ANDIAMO ITALIAN RESTAURANT
972/233-1515 **44**

▼▼▼ Italian. Fine Dining. $10-$30 **AAA Inspector Notes:** In business for more than 20 years, the dining room at this eatery has a semiformal look and the Italian specialties will definitely please. The cuisine is Tuscan, with diverse selections of pasta, seafood, chicken and veal. Try the chicken marsala—it is exceptional. The cappuccino pie is an ideal dessert. **Features:** full bar. **Reservations:** suggested. **Address:** 4151 Belt Line Rd, Suite 101 75001 **Location:** Jct Belt Line and Midway rds; northwest corner. [L] [D]

### ANTONIO RISTORANTE
972/458-1010 **42**

▼▼ Italian. Casual Dining. $14-$29 **AAA Inspector Notes:** This small restaurant is located just off Addison Circle. The entrées feature veal, chicken, seafood and pasta. They are especially proud of their cioppino and have been recognized for their pizzas. **Features:** full bar. **Address:** 4985 Addison Cir 75001 **Location:** Jct Quorum Dr and Addison Rd; northwest corner. **Parking:** valet and street only. [L] [D] [N]

### BENEDICT'S RESTAURANT
972/490-0500 **52**

▼▼ Breakfast. Casual Dining. $5-$13 **AAA Inspector Notes:** This homey restaurant has served the Addison area for years. Locals flock here for breakfast, lunch and brunch—unfortunately, no dinner. You can get omelets and frittatas with an Italian, Mexican or American flair to suit your taste. And as the name would suggest, this place specializes in eggs Benedict which rival those from Brennan's in New Orleans. **Address:** 4800 Belt Line Rd 75240 **Location:** Just w of jct Dallas North Tollway. [B] [L]

### BEST THAI
972/239-6334 **45**

▼▼ Thai. Casual Dining. $9-$16 **AAA Inspector Notes:** The small family-owned and -operated restaurant offers a small dining room with richly decorated walls and a menu mix of both traditional and updated Thai recipes. With a diverse menu of curry, noodle, stir-fry, seafood and even vegan dishes available, there is something for everyone. **Features:** beer & wine. **Address:** 4135 Belt Line Rd, Suite 112 75001 **Location:** Just w of jct Midway and Belt Line rds. [L] [D]

### THE BLUE GOOSE CANTINA
972/726-8771 **68**

▼▼ Tex-Mex. Casual Dining. $10-$18 **AAA Inspector Notes:** Guests can sample a best-selling margarita, grandma's favorite recipe, as they relax in a Mexican cantina setting. Sour cream enchiladas—rice, beans and chicken in sour cream sauce rolled in a fresh tortilla—are a top selection. Patio seating is a treat in the evenings most of the year. Parking can be a challenge on weekends. **Features:** full bar, patio dining, Sunday brunch. **Address:** 14920 Midway Rd 75001 **Location:** Jct Belt Line and Midway rds, just s. [L] [D]

### BLUE MESA GRILL
972/934-0165 **54**

▼▼▼ Southwestern. Casual Dining. $10-$17 **AAA Inspector Notes:** Glazed saltillo tiles, boveda ceilings and a focal fireplace invoke the Southwest theme of this café. The menu features New Mexican flair and a generous tequila selection. Crunch on blue corn and sweet potato chips in the airy dining room before diving into one of the sampler plates that include an original tamale pie and mesquite-grilled skewers of meat. For dessert, try the dark chocolate empanadas. **Features:** full bar, patio dining, Sunday brunch, happy hour. **Address:** 5100 Belt Line Rd, Suite 500 75254 **Location:** Jct Dallas North Tollway; in Village on the Parkway. [L] [D] [N]

### CANARY BY GORJI
972/503-7080 **58**

▼▼▼ Mediterranean. Fine Dining. $23-$36 **AAA Inspector Notes:** This place can get quite loud when it fills up. Maybe it's because everyone is raving about the food. The innovative Mediterranean menu includes such items as beef tips in pomegranate cream sauce, deep-fried polenta with shrimp, pan-seared rainbow trout and a selection of steaks. The chef will likely stop by your table to say hello. The intimate spot with close-set tables is located in a shopping center with plenty of other dining options, but this place stands out. **Features:** beer & wine. **Reservations:** suggested. **Address:** 5100 Belt Line Rd, Suite 402 75254 **Location:** Jct Dallas North Tollway; in Village on the Parkway. [D]

### CANTINA LAREDO
972/458-0962 **50**

▼▼ Tex-Mex Casual Dining $10-$26

**AAA Inspector Notes:** Modern yet relaxed, this restaurant features creative Mexican fare. A great starter of top-shelf guacamole, which is prepared tableside, primes the palate for an entree of enchiladas, tacos, fajitas and chiles rellenos. **Features:** full bar, Sunday brunch. **Address:** 4546 Belt Line Rd 75244 **Location:** 0.3 mi e of jct Midway and Belt Line rds. [L] [D] [N]

**Gourmet Mexican food, fresh-squeezed lime margaritas**

### CHAMBERLAIN'S STEAK & CHOP HOUSE
972/934-2467 **59**

▼▼▼ Steak. Fine Dining. $23-$38 **AAA Inspector Notes:** This chef-owned establishment offers a selection of 21-day-aged beef, chicken, pork, veal and lamb chops, and even venison. Be sure to make a reservation, as this is a popular location for many of the locals to gather for a sophisticated night on the town. **Features:** full bar. **Reservations:** suggested. **Address:** 5330 Belt Line Rd 75254 **Location:** Dallas North Tollway exit Belt Line Rd, just e. **Parking:** on-site and valet. [D] CALL &M [N]

### FERRARI'S ITALIAN VILLA
972/980-9898 **70**

▼▼▼ Italian. Fine Dining. $11-$30 **AAA Inspector Notes:** This charming villa makes you believe you have entered into another world with all its charisma. Everything is made from scratch, and you can watch your food being made in the open kitchen's traditional stone oven. The chef is from Sardinia and provides a menu that is well representative of all Italy. Enjoy pasta dishes, cioppino, crab claws, filet mignon and Chilean sea bass. **Features:** full bar, patio dining, happy hour. **Reservations:** suggested. **Address:** 14831 Midway Rd 75001 **Location:** Dallas North Tollway exit Belt Line Rd, 1.4 mi w, then 0.5 mi s. [L] [D] CALL &M

### FOGO DE CHAO
972/503-7300 **47**

▼▼▼ Brazilian. Casual Dining. $32-$49 **AAA Inspector Notes:** The smokehouse ambience taken from the styles of southern Brazil comes from the large pit at the entrance and the staff in gaucho dress. There is no menu, just one price for all you care to enjoy of 12 slow-roasted cuts of meat, salad, fried bananas and mashed potatoes. Those who don't enjoy meat as much can opt for a salad bar meal only. **Features:** full bar. **Reservations:** suggested. **Address:** 4300 Belt Line Rd 75001 **Location:** Just e of jct Midway Rd. **Parking:** on-site and valet. [L] [D]

(See map & index p. 184.)

## GLORIA'S LATIN CUISINE   972/387-8442   67

◆◆ Latin American. Casual Dining. $10-$17 **AAA Inspector Notes:** Latin American recipes with eye-catching presentations are served in a relaxing, colorful atmosphere. Options include regional specialty dishes such as plantain pupusa, tamales wrapped in banana leaves, fajitas, pollo asado and black beans with rice. This location features a Cuban band on Friday and Saturday nights, when a dress code comes into place and guests abandon their tables to salsa. **Features:** full bar, patio dining, Sunday brunch. **Address:** 5100 Belt Line Rd, Suite 852 75254 **Location:** Just e of Dallas North Tollway; at Village on the Parkway.  L   D

## HOUSTON'S   972/960-1752   57

◆◆◆ American. Casual Dining. $15-$37 **AAA Inspector Notes:** This popular, spacious restaurant features leather booths and an open kitchen. On the menu you will find tasty burgers, steaks and salads. Portions are large, the fresh grilled fish selection changes daily, and there is a small wine list. **Features:** full bar. **Address:** 5318 Belt Line Rd 75240 **Location:** 0.8 mi w of Preston Rd.

L   D

## INDIA WEST BY ROSS DUGGAL   972/503-5000   55

◆◆◆ Indian. Fine Dining. $11-$32 **AAA Inspector Notes:** This eatery has a very upscale and modern approach to Indian fare, offering both traditional favorites and creative options. The dining room is awash in earthy tones, dimly lit and perfect for a date or special occasion, but it's not the place for families. **Features:** full bar, patio dining. **Address:** 5290 Belt Line Rd #114 75254 **Location:** Just e of Dallas North Tollway.  L   D

## JASMINE RESTAURANT   972/991-6867   53

◆◆ Chinese. Casual Dining. $10-$25 **AAA Inspector Notes:** Dark wood set off by bright colors envelopes you in a casual supper club atmosphere as you enjoy delicious, traditional favorites. Egg and shrimp rolls, soups and many reliable choices like the tasty lemon chicken combine to create a satisfying meal. **Features:** full bar. **Address:** 4002 Belt Line Rd, Unit 200 75001 **Location:** I-635 exit 23 (Midway Rd), 2 mi n to Belt Line Rd, then 0.3 mi w.

L   D

## JAXX STEAKHOUSE   972/458-7888   65

◆◆◆ Steak. Casual Dining. $13-$35 **AAA Inspector Notes:** A local favorite since 1992, the restaurant specializes in steaks and seafood. Don't let the name fool you, very nice wood-trimmed décor and waiters with ties make for a more upscale experience. According to the bartender, this was a favorite "hangout" of Mickey Mantle when he was in the area. **Features:** full bar, happy hour. **Address:** 14925 Midway Rd, Suite 101 75001 **Location:** Just s of jct Belt Line and Midway rds.  L   D   ◣

## KENNY'S ITALIAN KITCHEN   972/661-9380   56

◆◆ Italian. Casual Dining. $10-$30 **AAA Inspector Notes:** Although this restaurant may be traditional in both its décor and menu selections, the attitude here is quite refreshing. At Kenny's they aim to please, so go ahead and make any special request—they'll do it. Find two dishes tempting? They'll split the plate for you. This makes it simple to try delicious portions of Northern Italian cuisine such as veal osso buco, mushroom ravioli or eggplant parmigiana. Lunch is not served on the weekends. **Features:** full bar, happy hour. **Address:** 5100 Beltline Rd 75254 **Location:** Dallas North Tollway exit Belt Line Rd, just e, then just s. **Parking:** on-site and valet.

L   D

## LA MADELEINE COUNTRY FRENCH CAFE   972/239-9051

◆ Traditional French. Quick Serve. $6-$12 **AAA Inspector Notes:** A fireplace creates the focal point at this cozy European style café where you can always get a quiche or savory stuffed puffed pastry on the go or stick around for a chicken crêpe or French dip sandwich. Heartier entrées are offered and every season promises menu surprises. Whatever you decide on you probably will not get out the door without enjoying one of their tempting sweet pastries. **Features:** wine only. **Address:** 5290 Belt Line Rd, Suite 112 75240 **Location:** Dallas North Tollway, north of Dallas.  B   L   D

## LEFTY'S LOBSTER & CHOWDER HOUSE   972/774-9518   46

◆◆ Seafood. Casual Dining. $6-$57 **AAA Inspector Notes:** With décor that succeeds in taking you to the shore, this family-owned and -operated restaurant doesn't just do seafood. They also offer steaks, chicken, pasta dishes and regional favorites like po'boys and Cajun-spiced trout. But don't ignore the obvious; do make sure you try the chowder. **Features:** full bar. **Address:** 4021 Belt Line Rd, Unit 101 75001 **Location:** Jct Belt Line and Runyan rds; northwest corner; in strip center.  L   D   ◣

## THE LONDONER   972/458-2444   63

◆◆ English. Casual Dining. $7-$12 **AAA Inspector Notes:** The restaurant is a good representation of an Old English eatery, with darts and pool tables on the pub side and rustic wood and brick décor enhancements. Traditional British delicacies include shepherd's pie, fish and chips and bangers and mash, which match well with the many ales and beers. While there are lots of choices in Addison for this type of pub experience, this one is more unique and manages to take you across the pond. **Features:** full bar, patio dining, Sunday brunch. **Address:** 14930 Midway Rd 75001 **Location:** Just s of jct Midway and Belt Line rds.

L   D   LATE   ◣   ◢

## LOVING HUT   972/980-1840   66

◆ Vegan. Casual Dining. $8-$17 **AAA Inspector Notes:** Do away with what you may think vegan food needs to be because the menu here will please those looking for sandwiches, wraps, stir-fries or noodle and fried rice dishes. Soy-based items are combined with an array of vegetables and sauces to create items that may seem familiar but provide a higher nutritional benefit. **Address:** 14925 Midway Rd, Suite 102 75001 **Location:** I-635 exit 23 (Midway Rd), 1.5 mi n.  L   D

## MAGIC TIME MACHINE   972/980-1903   49

◆◆◆ American. Casual Dining. $12-$29 **AAA Inspector Notes:** Ever have Snow White or Willy Wonka take your family's drink order? That fanciful event is commonplace at this fun restaurant filled with themed seating and costumed waitstaff. You may be waited on by Super Mario or Cinderella, you never know! The original building was a school and the exterior remains pretty much the same. **Features:** full bar. **Address:** 5003 Belt Line Rd 75254 **Location:** Just w of Dallas North Tollway.  D   ◣

## MI PIACI   972/934-8424   64

◆◆◆ Italian. Fine Dining. $14-$38 **AAA Inspector Notes:** Your choices for dining in this area are many, but you don't want to miss out on Mi Piaci. The open and airy dining rooms are decorated in a sophisticated Italian style, and diners can see their pasta being made the moment they walk in the door. Risotto with bay scallops, unusual pastas, spice-rubbed pork tenderloin and a long list of enticing desserts are just a few of the items to be enjoyed. **Features:** full bar. **Reservations:** suggested. **Address:** 14854 Montfort Dr 75240 **Location:** Jct Dallas North Tollway and Belt Line Rd, just e to Montfort Dr, then just s. **Parking:** on-site and valet.

L   D

## NATE'S SEAFOOD & STEAKHOUSE   972/701-9622   62

◆◆ Regional Seafood. Casual Dining. $9-$30 **AAA Inspector Notes:** The family-owned and -operated restaurant prepares seafood and steak with a Louisiana flair. An excellent selection of combination plates might appeal to those who can't make up their mind. Redfish on the half-shell is a customer favorite. Live music is featured on Thursdays. **Features:** full bar, patio dining, happy hour. **Address:** 14951 Midway Rd 75001 **Location:** Just s of jct Belt Line and Midway rds. **Parking:** valet and street only.  L   D   ◣

## REMINGTON'S SEAFOOD GRILL   972/386-0122   51

◆◆ Seafood. Casual Dining. $12-$30 **AAA Inspector Notes:** Fresh New England-style seafood has been consistently served for the past 20 years among artsy nautical décor. Enjoy grilled, blackened or sautéed red snapper, oysters on the half shell and hearty chowder, all served in a casual split-level dining area. The staff does well here with the busy crowd. **Features:** full bar. **Address:** 4580 Belt Line Rd 75001 **Location:** I-635 exit 23 (Midway Rd), 1.5 mi n to Belt Line Rd, then just e.  L   D   CALL  ◢M

(See map & index p. 184.)

### THE SAFFRON HOUSE
972/239-1800   60

▼▼▼ Indian. Casual Dining. $9-$22 **AAA Inspector Notes:** The delicate flavors of the East are featured in the restaurant's Mughlai cuisine, with curries, fragrant herbs and rich sauces. The eggplant masala is excellent. Lamb in a cashew gravy and chicken dosai also are nice options. The dining room is like a little jewel box with brick colored roof, sparkling mini chandeliers, jewel-toned glass pendants and the intimate feel of the cozy dining room. **Features:** full bar, patio dining. **Address:** 5100 Belt Line Rd, Unit 728 75254 **Location:** Dallas North Tollway exit Belt Line Rd, just e to Montfort Dr, then just s; in Village on the Parkway. L D

### SHERLOCK'S BAKER ST. PUB
972/726-6100

▼▼ English. Casual Dining. $8-$19 **AAA Inspector Notes:** The English-style public house invites gaming with such attractions as darts, chess, pool and some arcade games. Examples of British fare include bangers and mash, fish and chips and shepherd's pie. Diners find it easy to entertain themselves between courses. **Features:** full bar. **Address:** 5100 Belt Line Rd, Suite 776 75254 **Location:** Jct Dallas North Tollway and Belt Line Rd; in Village on the Parkway. L D LATE 🖊

### SNUFFER'S
972/991-8811   69

▼ American. Casual Dining. $8-$12 **AAA Inspector Notes:** This burger joint is perfect for getting together with friends and sipping margaritas. Kick back with the classic sounds of Motown and chow down! It's rustic, noisy and crowded but very popular and has been serving the Dallas area for the past 20 years. **Features:** full bar, happy hour. **Address:** 14910 Midway Rd 75244 **Location:** I-635 exit 23 (Midway Rd), 1.5 mi n. L D 🖊

### SPRING CREEK BBQ
972/385-0970

▼ Barbecue. Casual Dining. $8-$13 **AAA Inspector Notes:** Expect Texas-Style barbecue at its simple, homey best. Hickory smoked ribs, beef, pork and turkey lace the air with a spicy aroma that mingles with the scent of freshly baked rolls and cold ice cream slowly melting over a dish of homemade peach cobbler. Plates often are loaded with all the coleslaw, potato salad and corn on the cob they can support. Part of a small chain, this barbecue restaurant displays a rustic décor that gives patrons the impression they are "at the ranch." **Features:** beer only. **Address:** 14941 Midway Rd 75001 **Location:** Jct Belt Line and Midway rds, just s. L D

### TEXAS DE BRAZIL
972/385-1000   43

▼▼▼ Brazilian. Fine Dining. $20-$45 **AAA Inspector Notes:** "Gauchos" bring skewered meat selections directly to the table at the Brazilian-style steakhouse, and diners use a small colored coaster to let the server know when they are ready for another selection of beef, chicken, pork or lamb. The extensive salad bar gets meals off to the right start. Desserts are worthy of serious consideration. **Features:** full bar, Sunday brunch, happy hour. **Reservations:** suggested. **Address:** 15101 Addison Rd 75001 **Location:** Jct Belt Line and Addison rds; northeast corner. L D

### THAI ORCHID RESTAURANT
972/720-8424

▼▼ Thai. Casual Dining. $7-$18 **AAA Inspector Notes:** Patrons can enjoy fresh, flavorful Thai food with no added monosodium glutamate at this restaurant. The varied menu includes salads, soups, stir-fried dishes, distinctive curries, seafood and noodles. **Features:** beer & wine. **Address:** 4930 Belt Line Rd, Suite 190 75254 **Location:** Jct Belt Line Rd and Landmark Blvd, just s. L D

### TOKYO ONE JAPANESE RESTAURANT
972/386-8899   48

▼▼ Japanese. Casual Dining. $17-$28 **AAA Inspector Notes:** For lunch and dinner, the restaurant lays out an extensive buffet of Japanese food. Chefs eagerly grill teriyaki bowls and prepare selections of fresh sushi. Although pricey, the multiple items and quality justify the cost. You will find crab legs, oysters, sashimi and sushi, exotic salads, stir-frys and a variety of desserts like chocolate-dipped strawberries—all very attractively presented. **Features:** full bar, happy hour. **Address:** 4350 Belt Line Rd 75001 **Location:** 0.3 mi e of jct Midway and Belt Line rds. L D

## ALAMO (I-8) pop. 18,353, elev. 101'

Incorporated in 1924 and named for the Alamo Land and Sugar Co., this Rio Grande Valley town produces vegetables and citrus.

**SANTA ANA NATIONAL WILDLIFE REFUGE** is 7 mi. s. on FM 907, then .25 mi. e. on US 281. This 2,088-acre refuge harbors birds found only in southern Texas, including the great kiskadee, hook-billed kite and green jay. Twelve miles of walking trails weave through the refuge, and an interpretive 90-minute tram ride is offered. **Hours:** Visitor center daily 8-4. Trails dawn-dusk. Tram runs three times daily, mid-Dec. to mid-Apr. Closed Jan. 1, Thanksgiving and Christmas. **Cost:** $3 (per private vehicle). Tram fare $4; $3.50 (ages 65+); $2 (ages 0-11). **Phone:** (956) 784-7500.

### LA QUINTA INN & SUITES ALAMO AT EAST MCALLEN
(956)783-6955

▼▼▼ Hotel $85-$120 **Address:** 909 E Frontage Rd 78516 **Location:** US 83 exit Alamo Rd. **Facility:** 61 units. 3 stories, interior corridors. **Amenities:** safes. **Pool(s):** indoor. **Activities:** hot tub, exercise room. **Guest Services:** coin laundry.
🖥 CALL 🗗M 🛁 BIZ HS 🛜 ✕ 🛏 🍽 🖥
/ SOME UNITS 🐾

## ALBANY (D-7) pop. 2,034, elev. 1,412'

Settled on the north fork of Hubbard Creek, Albany was a supply point on the Western Trail to Dodge City. The surrounding area is known as the home of the Herefords. The town also is home to the *Albany News*, which was established in 1883 and contains a frontier news file open for public inspection.

The 1883 courthouse is the oldest still in use in Texas. Ledbetter Picket House, 24 S. Main St., is a dog-run cabin that was a site for supplying salt to the Confederacy. Nearby Fort Griffin *(see attraction listing)* is one of eight surviving frontier posts on the 650-mile Texas Forts Trail in west central Texas.

During the last two weekends in June, the Prairie Theatre on CR 1084 holds the outdoor play Fort Griffin Fandangle, which recalls the history of Fort Griffin and the founding of Albany; phone (325) 762-3838.

**Albany Chamber of Commerce:** 2 Railroad St., P.O. Box 2047, Albany, TX 76430. **Phone:** (325) 762-2525.

**FORT GRIFFIN STATE HISTORIC SITE** is 15 mi. n. on US 283. Built in 1867, Fort Griffin was a major U.S. Army base. The town that grew around the fort became one of the most notorious places on the frontier. Ruins of the fort, including barracks, a mess hall and living quarters, are visible. A herd of Texas longhorn grazes in the 506-acre park. The visitor center houses interactive exhibits. *See Recreation Areas Chart.*

**Hours:** Daily 8-5. Visitor center daily 8-4:30. Campground daily 24 hours. Closed Jan. 1, Thanksgiving, Christmas Eve and Christmas. **Cost:** $4; $3 (ages 6-18 and students with ID); free (ages 0-5). **Phone:** (325) 762-3592. 🅰 🎒 🎋

**THE OLD JAIL ART CENTER** is at 201 S. Second St. Housed in a former 1877 jail, the center features pre-Columbian displays, an Asian collection, American and European pieces and contemporary

Texas art. **Time:** Allow 1 hour minimum. **Hours:** Tues.-Sat. 10-5, Sun. 2-5. Closed major holidays. **Cost:** Free. **Phone:** (325) 762-2269.

## ALIBATES FLINT QUARRIES NATIONAL MONUMENT (B-4)

Alibates Flint Quarries National Monument is 34 miles northeast of Amarillo off SR 136 on the south shore of Lake Meredith *(see Lake Meredith National Recreation Area place listing p. 391)*. The land at this 1,370-acre site is rich in flint, which occurs in a variety of colors and was used for toolmaking and barter by prehistoric cultures up to 12,000 years ago. The area around the monument was the source of many ancient implements discovered throughout the Southwest and Great Plains.

Park headquarters near Fritch is open daily 9-4. Phone ahead to confirm hours and holiday closures. Flint quarries can be visited only on a 1-mile ranger-guided walking tour offered daily at 10 and 2; reservations are required. Grounds closed Jan. 1, Thanksgiving and Christmas. Free. For more information contact Alibates Flint Quarries National Monument, 419 E. Broadway, P.O. Box 1460, Fritch, TX 79036; phone (806) 857-3151.

## ALICE pop. 19,104

**BEST WESTERN EXECUTIVE INN**   (361)664-2133

Motel
$109-$139

**AAA Benefit:** Members save 10% or more with Best Western!

**Address:** 1350 S US 281 Business Rt 78332 **Location:** On US 281 business route, just s of Cecilia St. Located in a quiet rural area. **Facility:** 41 units. 1 story, exterior corridors. **Pool(s):** outdoor. **Guest Services:** coin laundry.

Free full hot breakfast, WIFI, pool/hot tub, laundry. All rooms w/microfridge. Dining & golf nearby.

HAMPTON INN ALICE   (361)664-1111

Hotel $109-$189 **Address:** 3135 E Main St 78332 **Location:** On SR 44, 4.8 mi e; jct US 281. **Facility:** 61 units. 3 stories, interior corridors. **Terms:** 1-7 night minimum stay, cancellation fee imposed. **Pool(s):** outdoor. **Activities:** hot tub, exercise room. **Guest Services:** valet and coin laundry.

**AAA Benefit:** Members save up to 10%!

HOLIDAY INN EXPRESS & SUITES ALICE   (361)664-7111

Hotel $79-$209 **Address:** 2965 E Main St 78332 **Location:** On SR 44, 4.8 mi e; jct US 281. **Facility:** 69 units. 3 stories, interior corridors. **Terms:** cancellation fee imposed. **Amenities:** safes. **Pool(s):** outdoor. **Activities:** hot tub, exercise room. **Guest Services:** valet and coin laundry.

LA QUINTA INN & SUITES ALICE   (361)661-1777

Hotel $109-$204 **Address:** 2400 E Main St 78332 **Location:** 0.8 mi e of downtown. Located in a modern commercial area. **Facility:** 65 units. 3 stories, interior corridors. **Pool(s):** outdoor. **Activities:** hot tub, exercise room. **Guest Services:** coin laundry.

### WHERE TO EAT

EL JALICIENCE MEXICAN RESTAURANT   361/661-0911

Tex-Mex. Casual Dining. $6-$10 **AAA Inspector Notes:** Enjoy large portions of Tex-Mex favorites, like cheesy enchiladas, fajitas and carne guisada. There's plenty of combination plates available, too. Fresh-baked pastries and Mexican cookies wrap up the meal nicely. **Features:** beer & wine. **Address:** 1915 E Main St 78332 **Location:** Just e of Sunset Dr.

## ALLEN pop. 84,246

- **Hotels & Restaurants map & index p. 179**
- **Part of Dallas area — see map p. 161**

HAMPTON INN & SUITES DALLAS/ALLEN   (214)495-7667

Hotel $109-$169 **Address:** 830 W Stacy Rd 75013 **Location:** US 75 exit 37 (Stacy Rd), just w. **Facility:** 103 units. 5 stories, interior corridors. **Terms:** 1-7 night minimum stay, cancellation fee imposed. **Amenities:** video games. **Pool(s):** heated indoor. **Activities:** hot tub, exercise room. **Guest Services:** valet laundry.

**AAA Benefit:** Members save up to 10%!

HILTON GARDEN INN DALLAS/ALLEN   (214)547-1700   20

Hotel $94-$189 **Address:** 705 Central Expwy S 75013 **Location:** US 75 exit 33 (Bethany Dr), just n on frontage road. **Facility:** 150 units. 6 stories, interior corridors. **Terms:** 1-7 night minimum stay, cancellation fee imposed. **Pool(s):** heated outdoor. **Activities:** hot tub, exercise room. **Guest Services:** valet and coin laundry.

**AAA Benefit:** Members save up to 10%!

HOLIDAY INN EXPRESS & SUITES ALLEN/DALLAS   (972)727-2000   18

Hotel $95-$129 **Address:** 205 Central Expwy N 75013 **Location:** US 75 exit 35; on southbound frontage road. **Facility:** 87 units. 4 stories, interior corridors. **Terms:** cancellation fee imposed. **Amenities:** safes. **Pool(s):** heated outdoor. **Activities:** hot tub, exercise room. **Guest Services:** valet and coin laundry.

PYRAMIDS HOTEL   (972)396-9494   19

Hotel $89-$149 **Address:** 407 Central Expwy S 75013 **Location:** US 75 exit 33 (Bethany Dr), just n on frontage road. **Facility:** 59 units. 2 stories (no elevator), interior corridors. **Terms:** cancellation fee imposed. **Amenities:** safes. **Pool(s):** heated indoor. **Activities:** sauna, hot tub, exercise room. **Guest Services:** valet laundry.

### WHERE TO EAT

GRIMALDI'S PIZZERIA   214/383-9703   10

Pizza. Casual Dining. $9-$18 **AAA Inspector Notes:** Located in a charming retail center, this pizzeria pays homage to New York with its menu dedicated solely to crispy pizza. Coal-fired ovens, fresh handmade mozzarella and secret sauce combine to make a delicious pie and the engaging staff makes this a great stop anytime. **Features:** full bar, patio dining. **Address:** 836 Market St 75013 **Location:** US 75 exit 33 (Bethany Dr), just w, then just s; in Watters Creek Shopping Center. **Parking:** street only.

(See map & index p. 179.)

### THE LONDONER
214/383-2500 [11]

💎💎 English. Casual Dining. $8-$14 **AAA Inspector Notes:** This isn't a small cozy pub—it's cavernous. But that allows lots of space for dining, enjoying the bar, sitting by a fire, playing pool or trying your luck at darts. This may be the best of all pubs in one great location. Although they are most proud of their fish and chips, the menu offers the English classics of bangers and mash and shepherd's pie but also some American classics, sandwiches and of course good bar food to go with the beers. **Features:** full bar, patio dining, Sunday brunch. **Address:** 932 Garden Park 75013 **Location:** US 75 exit 33 (Bethany Dr), just w, then just s; in Watters Creek Shopping Center. [L] [D] CALL 🅶M

### SILVER THAI CUISINE
972/747-7452 [9]

💎💎 Thai. Casual Dining. $9-$28 **AAA Inspector Notes:** Curries, noodle dishes, seafood, big-bowl soups and a variety of specialty dishes are served in a modern dining room with an active bar scene. You'll find it at the far end of the shopping center. **Features:** full bar. **Reservations:** suggested. **Address:** 906 W McDermott Rd, Suite 104 75013 **Location:** US 75 exit 34 (McDermott Rd), just w; in Twin Creeks Shopping Center. [L] [D]

## ALPINE (F-3) pop. 5,905, elev. 4,481'

Alpine, with its valley location in the heart of Big Bend, resembles the towns and villages dotting European mountain regions. The Texas Alps, like their namesake, attract throngs of outdoor enthusiasts who use Alpine as a base for mountain and desert exploration. Recreational opportunities range from hiking in the area's large parks to hunting in nearby canyons.

Kokernot Springs, on the Kokernot Lodge grounds, is the site of the Burgess Water Hole, which was used by pioneers, immigrants, stagecoach passengers and others to quench their thirst during desert passages.

**Alpine Chamber of Commerce:** 106 N. 3rd St., Alpine, TX 79830. **Phone:** (432) 837-2326 or (800) 561-3712.

**MUSEUM OF THE BIG BEND** is on the Sul Ross State University campus facing US 90. Exhibits present the artifacts and history of the Big Bend region, including a reconstructed general store and a Native American exhibit. **Hours:** Tues.-Sat. 9-5, Sun. 1-5. **Cost:** Donations. **Phone:** (432) 837-8143.

### BEST WESTERN ALPINE CLASSIC INN
(432)837-1530

💎💎 Hotel $86-$96

**AAA Benefit:** Members save 10% or more with Best Western!

**Address:** 2401 E Hwy 90 79830 **Location:** Jct SR 118 and US 67/90, 1.5 mi e. **Facility:** 63 units. 2 stories, interior corridors. **Pool(s):** outdoor. **Activities:** hot tub. **Guest Services:** coin laundry.

SAVE [YI+] CALL 🅶M 🔁 [BIZ] 📶 ✕ 🗎 📷 💻 / SOME UNITS 🐾

**Get pet travel tips and enter the photo contest at AAA.com/PetBook**

### HAMPTON INN
(432)837-7344

💎💎💎 Hotel $125-$169

**AAA Benefit:** Members save up to 10%!

**Address:** 2607 W Hwy 90 79830 **Location:** On US 90, 2 mi w. **Facility:** 64 units. 3 stories, interior corridors. **Terms:** 1-7 night minimum stay, cancellation fee imposed. **Amenities:** safes. **Pool(s):** heated indoor. **Activities:** hot tub, exercise room. **Guest Services:** coin laundry. **Featured Amenity:** breakfast buffet.

SAVE [YI+] CALL 🅶M 🔁 [BIZ] [HS] 📶 🗎 📷 💻

### HOLIDAY INN EXPRESS & SUITES
(432)837-9597

💎💎💎 Hotel $119

**Address:** 2004 E Hwy 90 79830 **Location:** On US 90, 2 mi e of downtown. **Facility:** 71 units. 3 stories, interior corridors. **Amenities:** safes. **Pool(s):** heated indoor. **Activities:** hot tub, exercise room. **Guest Services:** coin laundry.

SAVE [YI+] CALL 🅶M 🔁 [BIZ] [HS] 📶 ✕ 🗎 📷 💻

### THE HOLLAND HOTEL
(432)837-2800

💎💎💎 Classic Historic Hotel $115-$225 **Address:** 209 W Holland Ave 79830 **Location:** On US 90 eastbound and 6th St. **Facility:** This delightful historic hotel in downtown offers all the modern conveniences. Rooms are spacious with comfortable décor. 24 units, some two bedrooms. 4 stories, interior corridors. **Terms:** 3 day cancellation notice-fee imposed. **Dining:** The Century Bar and Grill, see separate listing. **Activities:** game room. **Guest Services:** complimentary laundry.

[YI] [Y] [BIZ] 📶 ✕ ☎ 🗎 📷 💻 / SOME UNITS 🐾

### THE MAVERICK INN
432/837-0628

💎💎 Hotel $85-$105 **Address:** 1200 E Holland Ave 79830 **Location:** Just e of downtown. Across from university. **Facility:** 21 units, some efficiencies. 1 story, exterior corridors. **Terms:** cancellation fee imposed. **Pool(s):** outdoor. **Guest Services:** complimentary laundry.

[YI+] 🔁 [BIZ] [HS] 📶 ✕ ☎ 🗎 📷 💻 / SOME UNITS 🐾

### OAK TREE INN
(432)837-5711

💎💎 Hotel $59-$77 **Address:** 2407 E Holland Ave (Hwy 90/67) 79830 **Location:** On US 90, 2 mi e. **Facility:** 40 units. 2 stories (no elevator), interior corridors. **Activities:** exercise room. **Guest Services:** coin laundry.

[YI] CALL 🅶M 📶 ✕ 🗎 📷 / SOME UNITS 🐾 🐾 💻

### WHERE TO EAT

### THE CENTURY BAR AND GRILL
432/837-1922

💎💎💎 Regional International. Fine Dining. $13-$30 **AAA Inspector Notes:** Creative interpretation of regional cuisine is the specialty of this restaurant's talented chef. The seasonal menu features a variety of aged beef, wild game, fowl and seafood prepared in appetizers, salads and entrées. The in-house desserts are luscious and the caramel cheesecake is especially decadent. The upscale atmosphere and well-presented wine list in addition to the knowledgeable personable servers make for a great dining experience. **Features:** full bar, patio dining. **Reservations:** suggested. **Address:** 209 W Holland Ave 79830 **Location:** On US 90 eastbound and 6th St; in The Holland Hotel. **Parking:** street only. [D]

LA TRATTORIA 432/837-2200

Italian. Casual Dining. $7-$22 **AAA Inspector Notes:** This casual eatery offers a wide variety of hand-tossed pizzas, sandwiches, salads and pasta dishes. Also on the menu is a selection of fresh fruit smoothies and espresso drinks. **Features:** beer & wine. **Address:** 901 E Holland Ave 79830 **Location:** Downtown.

L D

REATA 432/837-9232

Western American. Casual Dining. $9-$34 **AAA Inspector Notes:** The menu lists such choices as beef, seafood and Mexican entrees. Food is moderately priced and prepared with fresh ingredients. **Features:** full bar. **Reservations:** suggested. **Address:** 203 N 5th St 79830 **Location:** US 90, just n. **Parking:** street only.

L D

THE SADDLE CLUB 432/837-9770

Small Plates. Casual Dining. $8-$14 **AAA Inspector Notes:** Interesting eclectic décor makes for a fun experience at this favorite local watering hole. The seasonal tapas menu features creative interpretations of local ranch cuisine. **Features:** full bar, patio dining, happy hour. **Address:** 211 E Holland Ave 79830 **Location:** Between 3rd and 4th sts; downtown. **Parking:** street only. D

## ALTO (E-10) pop. 1,225, elev. 433'

In the heart of the tomato-growing redland belt, Alto, derived from the Spanish word for "high," is the highest point between the Angelina and Neches rivers.

**CADDO MOUNDS STATE HISTORIC SITE** is 6 mi. w. on SR 21W. The southwesternmost ceremonial center of the Moundbuilder culture, this settlement was occupied by Caddo Indians approximately A.D. 800-1300. A museum features artifacts from the site. An interpretive trail guides visitors to the burial and temple mounds; another trail leads to a segment of the historic El Camino Real. **Time:** Allow 1 hour, 30 minutes minimum. **Hours:** Tues.-Sun. 8:30-4:30. Closed Jan. 1, Thanksgiving, Christmas Eve and Christmas. **Cost:** $4; $3 (ages 6-18 and students with ID); free (ages 0-5). **Phone:** (936) 858-3218.

## ALVARADO pop. 3,785

COMFORT INN & SUITES (817)783-2900

Hotel $79-$89 **Address:** 400 Village Park Dr 76009 **Location:** I-35W exit 26B, just e. **Facility:** 68 units. 3 stories, interior corridors. **Pool(s):** outdoor. **Activities:** hot tub, exercise room. **Guest Services:** valet and coin laundry.

LA QUINTA INN & SUITES ALVARADO (817)783-8700

Hotel $79-$114 **Address:** 1165 Hwy 67 W 76009 **Location:** I-35W exit 26B, just e. **Facility:** 65 units. 3 stories, interior corridors. **Pool(s):** outdoor. **Activities:** hot tub, exercise room. **Guest Services:** coin laundry.

SUPER 8 (817)790-7378

Hotel $50-$120

**Address:** 5445 S I-35W 76009 **Location:** I-35W exit 27A (US 67), just e to 1st traffic light, then 0.4 mi n on access road. **Facility:** 48 units. 3 stories, interior corridors. **Pool(s):** outdoor. **Activities:** hot tub, exercise room. **Guest Services:** coin laundry. **Featured Amenity:** continental breakfast.

GRANDY'S RESTAURANT 817/790-5200

American. Quick Serve. $4-$8 **AAA Inspector Notes:** Fried chicken and country-fried steak are menu standbys at the restaurant, a regional franchise. They also offer a family-style dining menu. The décor is a step up from that of most quick-serve eateries and more resembles that of a conventional restaurant. Some elements of increased service include additional rolls, iced tea refills and tray removal. **Address:** 1203 S Parkway Dr 76009 **Location:** I-35W exit 24. B L D

## ALVIN (F-10) pop. 24,236, elev. 51'
- **Restaurants p. 58**
- **Hotels & Restaurants map & index p. 324**

Founded in 1876 as a stop along the railroad route connecting Galveston and Richmond, Alvin was named for founder Alvin Morgan. It was here that Major League Baseball pitcher Nolan Ryan spent his childhood. The city survived despite hurricanes in 1900 and 1915 and a devastating fire in 1902.

**Alvin Convention and Visitors Bureau:** 200 Historic Depot Center Blvd., Alvin, TX 77511. **Phone:** (281) 585-3359.

**BAYOU WILDLIFE PARK** is 3 mi. e. of SR 35 on FM 517. The 86-acre park features a tram ride that lets visitors view and feed rare and endangered animals in natural settings. A petting zoo and picnic facilities are on the grounds. **Time:** Allow 2 hours minimum. **Hours:** Daily 10-4, Mar.-July; Tues.-Sun. 10-3, rest of year. Last tram leaves 30 minutes before closing. Closed Easter, Thanksgiving and Christmas. **Cost:** $18; $9 (ages 2-11). Prices may vary; phone ahead. **Phone:** (281) 337-6376.

**THE NOLAN RYAN EXHIBIT CENTER** is at 2925 S. Bypass 35 on the campus of Alvin Community College. Photographs, memorabilia, videos and an illustrated chronology highlight the Major League Baseball career of Nolan Ryan. An interactive exhibit simulates the sensation of the celebrated pitcher's fastball hitting a catcher's mitt. **Note:** Backpacks and baby strollers are not permitted. **Time:** Allow 45 minutes minimum. **Hours:** Mon.-Fri. 9-4. Closed major holidays. **Cost:** $5; $2.50 (ages 6-12 and 65+). Under 12 must be with an adult. **Phone:** (281) 388-1134.

AMERICAS BEST VALUE INN & SUITES (281)331-0335 160

Motel $56-$66 **Address:** 1588 S Hwy 35 Loop 77511 **Location:** SR 35 Bypass, 0.5 mi sw of SR 6. Located in a commercial area. **Facility:** 40 units. 2 stories (no elevator), exterior corridors. **Terms:** cancellation fee imposed. **Pool(s):** outdoor. **Guest Services:** coin laundry.

(See map & index p. 324.)

**BEST WESTERN ALVIN INN**                    (281)331-4545

Hotel
$75-$110

**AAA Benefit:** Members save 10% or more with Best Western!

**Address:** 1470 S Loop 35 77511 **Location:** Jct SR 35 and 6, 0.5 mi sw. **Facility:** 40 units. 2 stories (no elevator), exterior corridors. **Pool(s):** outdoor. **Guest Services:** coin laundry.

---

### WHERE TO EAT

**JOE'S BARBEQUE COMPANY**                    281/331-9626

Barbecue. Casual Dining. $6-$26 **AAA Inspector Notes:** On the edge of town, this restaurant accommodates crowds of people with large shade trees and a huge parking lot. Texas barbecue is at the heart of a menu that also includes hamburgers and po'boys. While someone may be available to fill tea glasses before they go dry, this is a fast-paced, counter-service eatery. **Features:** beer only. **Address:** 1400 E Hwy 6 77511 **Location:** Just e of jct SR 6 and 35.

---

## AMARILLO (B-5) pop. 190,695, elev. 3,672'

- Hotels p. 62 • Restaurants p. 64
- Hotels & Restaurants map & index p. 60

Originally called Oneida, the town was established in 1887 and renamed shortly thereafter by majority rule. The name Amarillo, which means "yellow" in Spanish, likely came from the gold-colored soil surrounding Amarillo Creek and the lustrous wildflowers that thrive in season. In celebration of the name change many residents painted their homes a yellow hue.

Located at the intersection of the Fort Worth & Denver Railroad and the Atchison, Topeka and Santa Fe, Amarillo was a railhead for the late 19th-century cattle drives and remains a major cattle-feeding and shipping town. Every Monday you can mingle with cattlemen and catch a whiff of Amarillo at one of the nation's largest livestock auctions, the Amarillo Livestock Auction.

Unless you're the *yellow* type, be sure to check out reputedly haunted The Nat, 604 S. Georgia St. Formerly an indoor swimming pool that opened in 1922, the building was converted to a dance hall in 1926. Guests boogied to the live tunes of Louis Armstrong, Duke Ellington, Buddy Holly and Roy Orbison. The Nat was closed to public dancing in the 1960s and the historical landmark is now an antique mall.

Discover the area's quirky side by heading west on I-40 to Cadillac Ranch, where you'll behold 10 graffiti-covered vintage Cadillacs half-buried nose-down in a field. Dubbed "Hood Ornament of Route 66," this unusual roadside attraction is a popular stop for locals and visitors armed with spray paint and cameras.

**Amarillo Convention & Visitor Council:** 1000 S. Polk St., P.O. Box 9480, Amarillo, TX 79101. **Phone:** (806) 374-1497 or (800) 692-1338.

**Shopping areas:** Major shopping centers include Westgate Mall, off I-40W on the west side of the city between Coulter and Soncy streets; and Wolflin Village and Wolflin Square, both at the southeast corner of I-40W and Georgia Street. Antiques can be found along historic Route 66 and Sixth Street between Georgia and Western streets.

**AMARILLO BOTANICAL GARDENS** is off I-40 exit 65 (Coulter St.) at 1400 Streit Dr. Four acres include such themed gardens as a butterfly, fragrance and Japanese garden. A tropical conservatory features a waterfall, tropical plantings and seasonal displays. Blooming season is mid-May to late October. Special exhibits and events are offered seasonally.

**Hours:** Tues.-Sat. 9-5, Sun. 1-5, Apr.-Nov.; Tues.-Fri. 9-5, Sat. 1-5, rest of year. Closed major holidays. Phone ahead to confirm schedule. **Cost:** $5; $4 (ages 60+); free (ages 0-12). **Phone:** (806) 352-6513.

**AMARILLO MUSEUM OF ART** is at 2200 S. Van Buren St. on the Amarillo College campus. Six galleries are devoted to changing exhibits of the visual arts spanning the 1st to the 21st century. **Hours:** Tues.-Fri. 10-5, Sat.-Sun. 1-5. Closed major holidays. **Cost:** Free. **Phone:** (806) 371-5050.

**AMERICAN QUARTER HORSE HALL OF FAME & MUSEUM** is off I-40 exit 72A to Quarter Horse Dr. Interactive exhibits, artwork and multimedia presentations tell the story of the American Quarter Horse from its early racing days in Colonial Virginia to modern ranching in the Southwest. The equine champions, as well as the people who helped them reach their potential, are honored in the Hall of Fame.

**Time:** Allow 1 hour minimum. **Hours:** Mon.-Sat. 9-5. Closed Jan. 1, Thanksgiving, Christmas Eve and Christmas. **Cost:** $6; $5 (ages 55+); $2 (ages 6-18). **Phone:** (806) 376-5181 or (888) 209-8322.

**DON HARRINGTON DISCOVERY CENTER AND SPACE THEATER** is off I-40 exit 65 (Coulter St.) in Harrington Regional Medical Center Park at 1200 Streit Dr. This kid-geared science center has interactive, hands-on exhibits that will entertain and educate visitors of all ages. You'll learn about birds of prey, the human body, the solar system and more. Changing exhibits are displayed, and the Space Theater features changing astronomy-related presentations.

**Time:** Allow 1 hour, 30 minutes minimum. **Hours:** Tues.-Sat. 9:30-4:30 (also Mon. 9:30-4:30, May-Sept.), Sun. noon-4:30. Phone ahead for theater show schedule. Closed Easter, Thanksgiving, Christmas Eve and Christmas. **Cost:** (Includes theater) $10; $7 (ages 3-12 and 60+). **Phone:** (806) 355-9547 or (800) 784-9548.

**International Helium Centennial Time Columns Monument** is at 1200 Streit Dr., on the grounds of the Don Harrington Discovery Center and Space Theater. This 60-foot stainless steel monument commemorates the discovery of helium in 1868.

(See map & index p. 60.)

Erected in 1968, the monument contains sealed time capsules filled with data related to helium as well as a $10 savings account deposit that will be worth $1 quintillion when the capsule is opened in the year 2968. **Cost:** Free.

**KWAHADI MUSEUM OF THE AMERICAN INDIAN** is off I-40 exit 76 (Tiltrotor Dr.), then .5 mi. w. on frontage road along the n. side of I-40 to 9151 I-40E. The museum houses a collection of paintings and exhibits that illustrate the Pueblo and Plains Indian cultures. During the summer the museum also features dance performances.

**Time:** Allow 30 minutes minimum. **Hours:** Wed.-Sun. 1-5, June-Aug.; Sat.-Sun. 1-5, rest of year. Closed Jan. 1, Easter, Thanksgiving, Christmas Eve and Christmas. **Cost:** $5; $4 (ages 55+); $3 (ages 3-17). **Phone:** (806) 335-3175.

 **PALO DURO CANYON STATE PARK**—see Canyon p. 134.

 **PANHANDLE-PLAINS HISTORICAL MUSEUM**—see Canyon p. 134.

**SPLASH AMARILLO** is off I-40 exit 74 (Whittaker Rd.), then .3 mi w. to 1415 Sunrise Dr. Visitors to this 14-acre park can race down Sensational Sidewinder and Speed Slides, surf at Whitewater Waves, float down the Lazy River and play in the interactive Kiddie Pool. The Bucket Dump Tower holds 750 gallons of water. Beach volleyball courts also are on the grounds.

**Time:** Allow 5 hours minimum. **Hours:** Mon.-Sat. noon-7, Sun. noon-6, early June-late Aug. **Cost:** $22; $18 (under 48 inches tall); $15 (ages 65+ and military with ID); free (ages 0-2). After 3:30 p.m. $17; $15 (ages 65+ and military with ID); free (ages 0-2). **Phone:** (806) 376-4477. 🍴 🛝

**THOMPSON PARK** is off US 287N exit 24th Ave. to 2401 Dumas Dr. Encompassing 610 acres, the park includes a zoo, an amusement park, a 36-hole golf course, two small lakes, picnic areas, bike trails, ball parks, a dog park and sections for flying model airplanes and playing disc golf. **Time:** Allow 2 hours minimum. **Hours:** Dawn-5:30. **Phone:** (806) 378-3036.

**Amarillo Zoo** is at N. 24th Ave. and Dumas Dr. in Thompson Park. A herd of bison grazes on a 14-acre range in the zoo, which displays animals indigenous to the area. Wallabies, bears, lions, tigers and spider monkeys also may be seen. A small playground is at the center of the zoo. **Hours:** Daily 9:30-5. Closed Jan. 1, Thanksgiving and Christmas. **Cost:** $4; $3 (ages 62+); $2 (ages 3-12); free (Mon.). **Phone:** (806) 381-7911.

**Wonderland Park** is at 2601 Dumas Dr. in Thompson Park. More than 30 rides and attractions are featured, including the Texas Tornado double-loop roller coaster and the Shoot the Chute water ride. Other amusements include an 18-hole miniature golf course, arcades, children's rides, a pirate ship and the Fantastic Journey haunted house.

**Hours:** Tues.-Thurs. 7 p.m.-10 p.m., Fri. 5-10, Sat.-Sun. 1-10, June-Aug.; schedule varies, Apr.-May. **Cost:** Ride tickets $1.50 each (Drop of Fear, Fantastic Journey, Texas Tornado, Texas Intimidator and Shoot the Chute require two tickets); all other rides require one ticket). Miniature golf $5. Semi-inclusive admission (excluding Drop of Fear, Fantastic Journey, Texas Tornado and miniature golf) Tues.-Thurs. $16.95; $13.95 (under 42 inches tall); Fri. $18.95, $15.95 (under 42 inches tall ); Sat.-Sun. $24.95; $19.95 (under 42 inches tall). Spectator admission $5 (must be under 36 inches tall or ages 21+). **Phone:** (806) 383-3344 or (800) 383-4712. 🍴

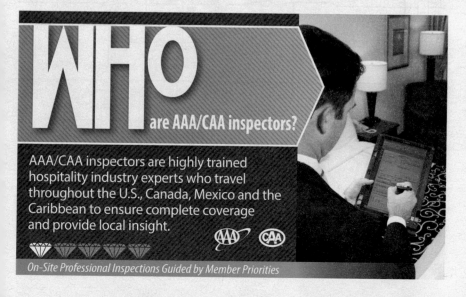

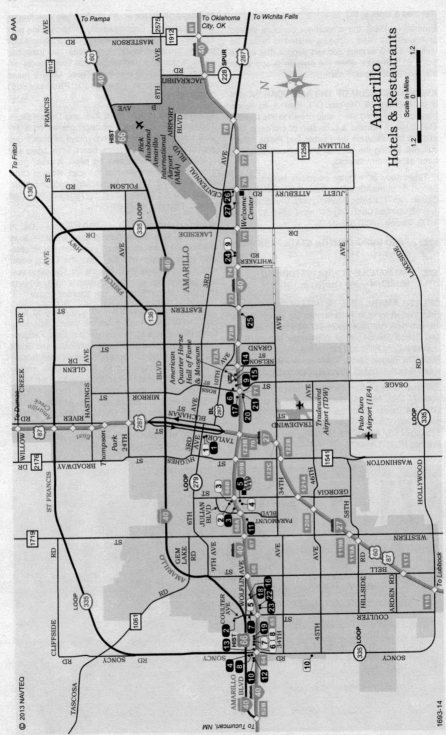

Amarillo
Hotels & Restaurants

Scale in Miles

© AAA

© 2013 NAVTEQ

1693-14

# Amarillo

This index helps you "spot" where approved hotels and restaurants are located on the corresponding detailed maps. Hotel daily rate range is for comparison only. Restaurant price range is a combination of lunch and/or dinner. Turn to the listing page for more detailed rate and price information and consult display ads for special promotions.

## AMARILLO

| Map Page | Hotels | Diamond Rated | Rate Range | Page |
|---|---|---|---|---|
| ① p. 60 | Courtyard by Marriott Amarillo Downtown | ▽▽▽ | $119-$149 | 63 |
| ② p. 60 | **BEST WESTERN Medical Center Inn** | ▽▽▽ | $60-$130 (SAVE) | 62 |
| ③ p. 60 | Magnuson Grand Hotel Amarillo | ▽▽▽ | $89-$139 | 63 |
| ④ p. 60 | Country Inn & Suites By Carlson, I-40 West | ▽▽▽ | $79-$229 | 62 |
| ⑤ p. 60 | Holiday Inn Express & Suites | ▽▽▽ | $109-$199 | 63 |
| ⑥ p. 60 | **Microtel Inn & Suites by Wyndham Amarillo** | ▽▽ | $70-$100 (SAVE) | 64 |
| ⑦ p. 60 | **Days Inn** | ▽▽ | $49-$59 (SAVE) | 63 |
| ⑧ p. 60 | Comfort Inn & Suites Amarillo | ▽▽▽ | $69-$159 | 62 |
| ⑨ p. 60 | **Comfort Inn & Suites** | ▽▽▽ | $74-$169 (SAVE) | 62 |
| ⑩ p. 60 | Hilton Garden Inn | ▽▽▽ | $101-$159 | 63 |
| ⑪ p. 60 | **Baymont Inn & Suites** | ▽▽▽ | $59-$99 (SAVE) | 62 |
| ⑫ p. 60 | Homewood Suites by Hilton | ▽▽▽ | $109-$189 | 63 |
| ⑬ p. 60 | Drury Inn & Suites-Amarillo | ▽▽▽ | $110-$169 | 63 |
| ⑭ p. 60 | **Sleep Inn Amarillo** | ▽▽ | $60-$99 (SAVE) | 64 |
| ⑮ p. 60 | **Ashmore Inn & Suites** | ▽▽▽ | $90-$159 (SAVE) | 62 |
| ⑯ p. 60 | Fairfield Inn & Suites by Marriott West Amarillo | ▽▽▽ | $100-$140 | 63 |
| ⑰ p. 60 | **Days Inn East Amarillo** | ▽▽ | $69-$79 (SAVE) | 63 |
| ⑱ p. 60 | Residence Inn by Marriott | ▽▽▽ | $130-$210 | 64 |
| ⑲ p. 60 | Courtyard by Marriott | ▽▽▽ | $89-$119 | 62 |
| ⑳ p. 60 | **Baymont Inn & Suites** | ▽▽▽ | $59-$89 (SAVE) | 62 |
| ㉑ p. 60 | La Quinta Inn Amarillo East Airport Area | ▽▽ | $75-$114 | 63 |
| ㉒ p. 60 | Hampton Inn & Suites Amarillo West | ▽▽▽ | $99-$159 | 63 |
| ㉓ p. 60 | Sleep Inn & Suites | ▽▽▽ | $80-$210 | 64 |
| ㉔ p. 60 | **Big Texan Inn** | ▽▽ | $79-$99 (SAVE) | 62 |
| ㉕ p. 60 | **BEST WESTERN Santa Fe** | ▽▽ | $80-$130 (SAVE) | 62 |
| ㉖ p. 60 | Fairfield Inn & Suites by Marriott Amarillo Airport | ▽▽▽ | $119-$149 | 63 |
| ㉗ p. 60 | Holiday Inn Express & Suites | ▽▽▽ | Rates not provided | 63 |

| Map Page | Restaurants | Diamond Rated | Cuisine | Price Range | Page |
|---|---|---|---|---|---|
| ① p. 60 | O.H.M.S. Cafe & Bar | ▽▽ | International | $8-$34 | 64 |
| ② p. 60 | Dyer's Bar-B-Que | ▽▽ | Barbecue | $7-$19 | 64 |
| ③ p. 60 | Macaroni Joe's | ▽▽▽ | Italian | $8-$26 | 64 |
| ④ p. 60 | 575 Pizzeria | ▽▽ | Pizza | $7-$16 | 64 |
| ⑤ p. 60 | My Thai | ▽▽ | Thai | $6-$9 | 64 |
| ⑥ p. 60 | Saltgrass Steakhouse | ▽▽ | Western Steak | $9-$31 (SAVE) | 65 |
| ⑦ p. 60 | Country Barn Steakhouse | ▽▽ | Steak Barbecue | $7-$28 | 64 |

| Map Page | Restaurants (cont'd) | Diamond Rated | Cuisine | Price Range | Page |
|----------|---------------------|---------------|---------|-------------|------|
| ⑧ p. 60 | Kabuki Romanza | ▼▼ | Japanese | $10-$42 | 64 |
| ⑨ p. 60 | Big Texan Steak Ranch | ▼▼ | Steak | $9-$40 | 64 |
| ⑩ p. 60 | Sakura Japanese Steakhouse & Sushi Bar | ▼▼ | Japanese | $8-$37 | 65 |

## ASHMORE INN & SUITES     (806)374-0033  ⑮

▼▼▼▼
Hotel
$90-$159

**Address:** 2301 I-40 E 79104 **Location:** I-40 exit 72A (Nelson St), just nw. **Facility:** 138 units, some efficiencies. 4 stories, interior corridors. **Terms:** cancellation fee imposed. **Pool(s):** heated indoor. **Activities:** hot tub, exercise room. **Guest Services:** valet and coin laundry.

## BAYMONT INN & SUITES     (806)372-1425  ⑳

▼▼▼
Hotel
$59-$89

**Address:** 1700 I-40 E 79103 **Location:** I-40 exit 71 (Ross-Osage), just e on south frontage road. **Facility:** 114 units. 2 stories (no elevator), interior corridors. **Terms:** 1-7 night minimum stay, cancellation fee imposed. **Amenities:** video games. **Pool(s):** heated outdoor. **Guest Services:** valet laundry. **Featured Amenity: continental breakfast.**

## BAYMONT INN & SUITES     (806)356-6800  ⑪

▼▼▼
Hotel
$59-$99

**Address:** 3411 I-40 W 79109 **Location:** I-40 exit 67, just e on south frontage road. **Facility:** 96 units. 2 stories (no elevator), interior corridors. **Pool(s):** heated outdoor. **Activities:** exercise room. **Guest Services:** valet and coin laundry. **Featured Amenity: continental breakfast.**

## BEST WESTERN MEDICAL CENTER INN
     (806)358-7861  ②

▼▼▼
Hotel
$60-$130

**Best Western**
**AAA Benefit:** Members save 10% or more with Best Western!

**Address:** 1610 Coulter St 79106 **Location:** I-40 exit 65 (Coulter St), 0.6 mi n. Adjacent to Amarillo Medical Center. **Facility:** 103 units. 2 stories (no elevator), interior/exterior corridors. **Terms:** 2-3 night minimum stay - seasonal. **Pool(s):** heated indoor. **Activities:** hot tub, exercise room. **Guest Services:** coin laundry. **Featured Amenity: full hot breakfast.**

## BEST WESTERN SANTA FE     (806)372-1885  ㉕

▼▼▼
Hotel
$80-$130

**Best Western**
**AAA Benefit:** Members save 10% or more with Best Western!

**Address:** 4600 I-40 E 79103 **Location:** I-40 exit 73 (Eastern St) eastbound; exit Bolton St westbound, U-turn on south frontage road. **Facility:** 55 units. 2 stories (no elevator), interior corridors. **Pool(s):** heated outdoor. **Featured Amenity: breakfast buffet.**

## BIG TEXAN INN     806/372-5000  ㉔

▼▼▼
Motel
$79-$99

**Address:** 7701 I-40 E 79118 **Location:** I-40 exit 75 (Lakeside Dr), just w on north frontage road. **Facility:** 54 units. 2 stories (no elevator), interior corridors. **Terms:** 14 day cancellation notice. **Dining:** Big Texan Steak Ranch, see separate listing. **Pool(s):** outdoor. **Guest Services:** coin laundry.

 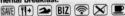    

## COMFORT INN & SUITES     (806)331-7829  ⑨

▼▼▼
Hotel
$74-$169

**Address:** 2101 I-40 E 79102 **Location:** I-40 exit 72A (Nelson St), just n. **Facility:** 94 units. 3 stories, interior corridors. **Amenities:** safes. **Pool(s):** heated indoor. **Activities:** hot tub, exercise room. **Guest Services:** valet and coin laundry. **Featured Amenity: full hot breakfast.**

## COMFORT INN & SUITES AMARILLO     (806)457-9100  ⑧

▼▼▼ Hotel $69-$159 **Address:** 2300 Soncy Rd 79124 **Location:** I-40 exit 64 (Soncy Rd), just w. **Facility:** 71 units. 3 stories, interior corridors. **Pool(s):** heated indoor. **Activities:** hot tub, exercise room. **Guest Services:** valet and coin laundry.

## COUNTRY INN & SUITES BY CARLSON, I-40 WEST
     (806)356-9977  ④

▼▼▼ Hotel $79-$229 **Address:** 2000 Soncy Rd 79121 **Location:** I-40 exit 64 (Soncy Rd), just n. **Facility:** 82 units. 3 stories, interior corridors. **Pool(s):** heated indoor. **Activities:** hot tub, exercise room. **Guest Services:** valet and coin laundry.

## COURTYARD BY MARRIOTT     (806)467-8954  ⑲

▼▼▼ Hotel $89-$119 **Address:** 8006 I-40 W 79106 **Location:** I-40 exit 65 (Coulter St), 0.5 mi w on north frontage road. **Facility:** 89 units. 3 stories, interior corridors. **Pool(s):** heated indoor. **Activities:** hot tub, exercise room. **Guest Services:** valet and coin laundry.

**AAA Benefit:** Members save 5% or more!

(See map & index p. 60.)

## COURTYARD BY MARRIOTT AMARILLO DOWNTOWN
(806)553-4500 **1**

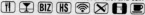 **Historic Hotel** $119-$149 **Address:** 724 S Polk St 79101 **Location:** Jct 8th and S Polk sts; on northwest corner; downtown. **Facility:** Despite a full renovation in 2010, this 1927 property maintained its beautiful exterior architectural details to provide a taste of yesteryear. 107 units. 10 stories, interior corridors. **Activities:** exercise room. **Guest Services:** valet and coin laundry.

**AAA Benefit:** Members save 5% or more!

## DAYS INN
(806)359-9393 **7**

Hotel
$49-$59

**Address:** 2102 S Coulter St 79106 **Location:** I-40 exit 65 (Coulter St), just n. **Facility:** 50 units. 2 stories (no elevator), exterior corridors. **Parking:** winter plug-ins. **Terms:** cancellation fee imposed. **Amenities:** safes. **Pool(s):** heated indoor. **Activities:** hot tub, limited exercise equipment. **Guest Services:** coin laundry. **Featured Amenity:** full hot breakfast.

## DAYS INN EAST AMARILLO
(806)379-6255 **17**

Hotel
$69-$79

**Address:** 1701 I-40 E 79102 **Location:** I-40 exit 71 (Ross-Osage), just w on north frontage road. **Facility:** 119 units. 5 stories, interior corridors. **Terms:** cancellation fee imposed. **Pool(s):** heated outdoor. **Activities:** exercise room. **Guest Services:** coin laundry. **Featured Amenity:** breakfast buffet.

## DRURY INN & SUITES-AMARILLO
(806)351-1111 **13**

**Hotel** $110-$169 **Address:** 8540 W I-40 79106 **Location:** I-40 exit 65 (Coulter St), 0.8 mi w on north service road. **Facility:** 163 units. 6 stories, interior corridors. **Terms:** cancellation fee imposed. **Pool(s):** heated indoor. **Activities:** hot tub, exercise room. **Guest Services:** valet and coin laundry.

## FAIRFIELD INN & SUITES BY MARRIOTT AMARILLO AIRPORT
(806)322-6777 **26**

**Hotel** $119-$149 **Address:** 1740 Airport Blvd 79118 **Location:** I-40 exit 76 (Airport Blvd), just n. **Facility:** 79 units. 4 stories, interior corridors. **Pool(s):** heated indoor. **Activities:** hot tub, exercise room. **Guest Services:** valet and coin laundry.

**AAA Benefit:** Members save 5% or more!

## FAIRFIELD INN & SUITES BY MARRIOTT WEST AMARILLO
(806)351-0172 **16**

**Hotel** $100-$140 **Address:** 6600 I-40 W 79106 **Location:** I-40 exit 66 (Bell St), 0.5 mi w on north frontage road. **Facility:** 74 units. 3 stories, interior corridors. **Pool(s):** heated indoor. **Activities:** hot tub, exercise room. **Guest Services:** valet and coin laundry.

**AAA Benefit:** Members save 5% or more!

## HAMPTON INN & SUITES AMARILLO WEST
(806)467-9997 **22**

**Hotel** $99-$159 **Address:** 6901 I-40 W 79106 **Location:** I-40 exit 65 (Coulter St), just e on south frontage road. **Facility:** 64 units. 3 stories, interior corridors. **Terms:** 1-7 night minimum stay, cancellation fee imposed. **Amenities:** video games. **Pool(s):** heated indoor. **Activities:** sauna, hot tub, exercise room. **Guest Services:** valet and coin laundry.

**AAA Benefit:** Members save up to 10%!

## HILTON GARDEN INN
(806)355-4400 **10**

**Hotel** $101-$159 **Address:** 9000 I-40 W 79159 **Location:** I-40 exit 64 (Soncy Rd), just w. **Facility:** 90 units. 4 stories, interior corridors. **Terms:** 1-7 night minimum stay, cancellation fee imposed. **Pool(s):** heated indoor. **Activities:** hot tub, exercise room. **Guest Services:** valet and coin laundry.

**AAA Benefit:** Members save up to 10%!

## HOLIDAY INN EXPRESS & SUITES
(806)322-3050 **5**

**Hotel** $109-$199 **Address:** 2806 Wolflin Ave 79109 **Location:** I-40 exit 68B, just s. **Facility:** 90 units. 3 stories, interior corridors. **Terms:** cancellation fee imposed. **Amenities:** safes. **Pool(s):** heated indoor. **Activities:** hot tub, exercise room. **Guest Services:** valet and coin laundry.

## HOLIDAY INN EXPRESS & SUITES
806/335-2500 **27**

**Hotel.** Rates not provided. **Address:** 9401 I-40 E 79118 **Location:** I-40 exit 76 (Airport Blvd), just w on north frontage road. **Facility:** 69 units. 3 stories, interior corridors. **Pool(s):** heated indoor. **Activities:** hot tub, exercise room. **Guest Services:** coin laundry.

## HOMEWOOD SUITES BY HILTON
(806)355-2222 **12**

**Extended Stay Contemporary Hotel** $109-$189 **Address:** 8800 I-40 W 79124 **Location:** I-40 exit 64 (Soncy Rd), just w. **Facility:** 92 units, some two bedrooms and efficiencies. 3 stories, interior corridors. **Terms:** 1-7 night minimum stay, cancellation fee imposed. **Amenities:** video games. **Pool(s):** outdoor. **Activities:** exercise room. **Guest Services:** valet and coin laundry.

**AAA Benefit:** Members save up to 10%!

## LA QUINTA INN AMARILLO EAST AIRPORT AREA
(806)373-7486 **21**

**Hotel** $75-$114 **Address:** 1708 I-40 E 79103 **Location:** I-40 exit 71 (Ross-Osage), just e on south frontage road. **Facility:** 130 units. 2 stories (no elevator), exterior corridors. **Amenities:** video games. **Pool(s):** heated outdoor. **Guest Services:** valet and coin laundry.

## MAGNUSON GRAND HOTEL AMARILLO
(806)358-6161 **3**

**Hotel** $89-$139 **Address:** 3100 I-40 W 79102 **Location:** I-40 exit 68 (Georgia St), just w on north frontage road. **Facility:** 263 units, some two bedrooms. 10 stories, interior corridors. **Terms:** 21 day cancellation notice-fee imposed. **Dining:** 2 restaurants. **Pool(s):** heated indoor. **Activities:** hot tub, exercise room, massage. **Guest Services:** valet laundry, area transportation.

(See map & index p. 60.)

## MICROTEL INN & SUITES BY WYNDHAM AMARILLO
(806)372-8373

◆◆ Hotel $70-$100

**Address:** 1501 S Ross St 79102 **Location:** I-40 exit 71 (Ross-Osage), just n. **Facility:** 45 units. 2 stories, interior corridors. **Terms:** cancellation fee imposed. **Pool(s):** heated indoor. **Activities:** hot tub, exercise room. **Guest Services:** coin laundry. **Featured Amenity:** continental breakfast.

SAVE ⓘ CALL ✆M ➦ BIZ HS 🛜 🖥 📷 / SOME UNITS 🐾 🖵

---

## RESIDENCE INN BY MARRIOTT
(806)354-2978 ⓲

◆◆◆ Extended Stay Contemporary Hotel $130-$210 **Address:** 6700 I-40 W 79106 **Location:** I-40 exit 66 (Bell St), 0.5 mi w on north frontage road. **Facility:** 78 units, some two bedrooms, efficiencies and kitchens. 3 stories, interior corridors. **Terms:** resort fee. **Pool(s):** heated indoor. **Activities:** hot tub, exercise room. **Guest Services:** valet and coin laundry.

**AAA Benefit:** Members save 5% or more!

CALL ✆M ➦ BIZ 🛜 ✕ 🖥 📷 🖵 / SOME UNITS 🐾

---

## SLEEP INN AMARILLO
(806)372-6200 ⓮

◆◆ Hotel $60-$99

**Address:** 2401 I-40 E 79104 **Location:** I-40 exit 72A (Nelson St), just w on north frontage road. **Facility:** 55 units. 2 stories (no elevator), interior corridors. **Pool(s):** heated indoor. **Activities:** hot tub. **Guest Services:** valet laundry. **Featured Amenity:** full hot breakfast.

SAVE ⓘ CALL ✆M ➦ BIZ HS 🛜 🖥 📷 / SOME UNITS 🖵

**Recently Renovated. Easy I-40 access. Walking distance from Cracker Barrel. Free Wifi and Cable.**

SLEEP INN BY CHOICE HOTELS

---

## SLEEP INN & SUITES
(806)242-7777 ㉓

◆◆◆ Motel $80-$210 **Address:** 6915 I-40 W 79106 **Location:** I-40 exit 65 (Coulter St); on south frontage road. **Facility:** 63 units. 3 stories, interior corridors. **Pool(s):** heated indoor. **Activities:** hot tub, exercise room. **Guest Services:** valet and coin laundry.

ⓘ CALL ✆M ➦ BIZ HS 🛜 ✕ 🖥 📷 🖵

---

 **WHERE TO EAT**

## 575 PIZZERIA
806/331-4900 ④

◆◆ Pizza. Casual Dining. $7-$16 **AAA Inspector Notes:** Build your own pizza from a selection of 32 very fresh items or choose from one of the 25 red or white specialty gourmet pizzas at this popular establishment. **Features:** beer & wine. **Address:** 2803 Civic Cir 79109 **Location:** I-40 exit 68B (Georgia St), 1 blk s to Wolflin Ave, then 1 blk w to Civic Cir; in Civic Circle Shopping Center. L D

## ABUELO'S THE FLAVOR OF MEXICO
806/354-8294

◆◆ Mexican. Casual Dining. $7-$19 **AAA Inspector Notes:** A very nice selection of many traditional dishes served in an upscale and spacious dining area. Inventive adult beverages are available. **Features:** full bar. **Reservations:** suggested. **Address:** 3501 45th Ave 79109 **Location:** I-127 exit 120B (45th Ave), just w. L D CALL ✆M ✕

## BIG TEXAN STEAK RANCH
806/372-6000 ⑨

◆◆◆ Steak. Casual Dining. $9-$40 **AAA Inspector Notes:** Saturated with Western style, the restaurant employs servers dressed in cowboy hats and boots. Beef, chicken and seafood entrees are hearty. Diners who can polish off the enormous, 72-ounce steak in an hour receive it free. **Features:** full bar. **Address:** 7701 I-40 E 79118 **Location:** I-40 exit 75 (Lakeside Dr), just w on north frontage road; in Big Texan Inn. B L D CALL ✆M ✕

## COUNTRY BARN STEAKHOUSE
806/335-2325 ⑦

◆◆◆ Steak Barbecue. Casual Dining. $7-$28 **AAA Inspector Notes:** Featuring Bonsmara Beef, the restaurant has many steaks to choose from, as well as nicely smoked prime rib, seafood, lamb chops, barbecue and Mexican dishes. Lighter-fare sandwiches and burgers also are offered. **Features:** full bar. **Address:** 8200 I-40 W 79106 **Location:** I-40 exit 65 (Coulter St), 0.5 mi w on north frontage road. L D LATE CALL ✆M

## DYER'S BAR-B-QUE
806/358-7104 ②

◆◆◆ Barbecue. Casual Dining. $7-$19 **AAA Inspector Notes:** The eatery serves delicious barbecue dishes in a rustic, Western-style atmosphere. Finger foods are favorites, as are preparations of Delta Dyer's Mississippi farm-raised catfish. Dyer's Bar-B-Que is just minutes away from the Westgate Mall and downtown. You might also try the mouthwatering slow-cooked barbecue. Be sure to save room for their delicious desserts. **Features:** full bar. **Address:** 1619 Kentucky St, Bldg E, Suite 526 79102 **Location:** I-40 exit 68 (Georgia St), just nw; in Wellington Square. L D CALL ✆M ✕

## HOFFBRAU STEAKHOUSE
806/358-6595

◆◆ Steak. Casual Dining. $7-$25 **AAA Inspector Notes:** The varied menu incorporates many steak choices. In the dining room, the feel is comfortable and relaxed. Don't miss tasty pecan cobbler for dessert. **Features:** full bar. **Address:** 7203 I-40 W 79106 **Location:** I-40 exit 65 (Coulter St), just e on south frontage road. L D ✕

## KABUKI ROMANZA
806/353-4242 ⑧

◆◆ Japanese. Casual Dining. $10-$42 **AAA Inspector Notes:** The interesting and unusual dining room theme includes hibachi tables on a platform that resembles a large boat. The bar has water cascading over a glass wall. A variety of sushi dishes, steak and seafood are offered, including Kobe beef and lobster. **Features:** full bar, patio dining. **Address:** 8130 I-40 W 79121 **Location:** I-40 exit 65 (Coulter St), 0.5 mi w on north frontage road. L D

## MACARONI JOE'S
806/358-8990 ③

◆◆◆ Italian. Fine Dining. $8-$26 **AAA Inspector Notes:** This fine-dining experience includes very nice presentations of steaks, seafood, pasta dishes, chicken, duck and even elk chops, all served with savory sauces. Service is attentive and pleasant. **Features:** full bar. **Address:** 1619 S Kentucky St 79102 **Location:** I-40 exit 68 (Georgia St), just w on westbound frontage road; in Wellington Square. L D

## MY THAI
806/355-9541 ⑤

◆◆ Thai. Casual Dining. $6-$9 **AAA Inspector Notes:** The good variety of offerings includes several spicy selections and a few vegetarian entrées. The open dining area and lack of background music when combined with a large crowd of diners makes for a somewhat noisy experience. Generous portions of freshly prepared dishes have kept the restaurant a local favorite for many years. **Address:** 2029 Coulter St 79106 **Location:** I-40 exit 65 (Coulter St), just n. L D

## O.H.M.S. CAFE & BAR
806/373-3233 ①

◆◆ International. Casual Dining. $8-$34 **AAA Inspector Notes:** Buffet luncheons and full-service dinners highlight the offerings at this downtown location. Closed for lunch on Saturday. **Features:** full bar. **Address:** 619 S Tyler St 79101 **Location:** On northeast corner of Tyler and 7th sts; downtown. **Parking:** on-site and street. L D

(See map & index p. 60.)

SAKURA JAPANESE STEAKHOUSE & SUSHI BAR
806/358-8148   10

◆◆ Japanese. Casual Dining. $8-$37 AAA Inspector Notes: The rectangular sushi bar is centrally located with a lounge area on one side and traditional seating on the other. A hibachi grilling area has separation from other diners. Colorful Japanese wall murals, lighting and décor create an ambiance fitting the cuisine. Features: full bar, patio dining. Address: 4000 Soncy Rd 79121 Location: I-40 exit 64 (Soncy Rd), 1.5 mi s. ⌊L⌋ ⌊D⌋

SALTGRASS STEAKHOUSE   806/351-0349   6

◆◆ Western Steak. Casual Dining. $9-$31 AAA Inspector Notes: Those looking for something different should try the comfortable steakhouse, which never says no to a special request. Born from the spirit of Texas cattle drives, the restaurant resembles a Texas lodge, with high ceilings and mounted animal heads. Baby back ribs are so tender the meat falls off the bone. Also on the menu are hearty steaks, prime rib, chicken, seafood and yummy desserts. Features: full bar. Address: 8300 I-40 W 79106 Location: I-40 exit 65 (Coulter St), 0.7 mi w on north frontage road.
⌊SAVE⌋ ⌊L⌋ ⌊D⌋ CALL ⌊&M⌋

# AMISTAD NATIONAL RECREATION AREA (F-6)

Amistad National Recreation Area is northwest of Del Rio via US 90. The 64,860-acre reservoir is an outgrowth of the Amistad Dam water-storage project, a joint venture of the United States and Mexico. The boundaries of the area extend 74 miles up the Rio Grande and portions of the Pecos and Devils rivers. More than 6 miles long, the dam creates 86-mile-long Lake Amistad.

This tract of land and water was the prehistoric home of Native Americans. Excavations have uncovered more than 300 sites. Primitive campsites are at San Pedro Flats on Spur 454, Governor's Landing on Spur 349 and at two other points, one along US 277N and one along Spur 406. Houseboats can be rented from Southwest Lakes Resort; phone (830) 774-4157.

Popular activities include picnicking, swimming and hiking. Fishing is possible all year. A Mexican license must be obtained for fishing in Mexican waters. Hunting is permitted only in designated areas. Shotgun hunting for dove, quail, ducks and other waterfowl is permitted. Other hunting is only by bow and arrow and is restricted to deer, rabbits, javelinas and turkeys. Rifles and pistols are not permitted.

The recreation area is open all year. The Visitor Information Center at 9685 US 90, west of Del Rio, is open daily 8-5; closed Jan. 1, Thanksgiving and Christmas. For further information write the Superintendent, Amistad National Recreation Area, National Park Service, 4121 Veterans Blvd., Del Rio, TX 78840; phone (830) 775-7491. See Recreation Areas Chart.

# ANAHUAC (F-10) pop. 2,243, elev. 21'
• Part of Houston area — see map p. 301

Atakapan Indians were among the first inhabitants of the Anahuac region. By the 19th century, the bluff above the Trinity River was known as Perry's Point. A fort was built there in 1830 by a Mexican garrison under the command of Col. John Davis Bradburn, who named the installation after the ancient capital of the Aztecs. The first armed confrontation between Anglo-American and Mexican troops occurred at Anahuac in 1832, and the fort was left in ruins.

ANAHUAC NATIONAL WILDLIFE REFUGE is e. on Belton Lane to FM 562, s. to FM 1985, then 4 mi. e. The 34,000-acre coastal marsh refuge is important for waterfowl and other migrating birds. Wildlife watching, fishing, hunting, photography and educational programs are available. Hours: Public use areas daily 1 hour before dawn-1 hour after dusk. Designated areas daily 24 hours. Cost: Free. Phone: (409) 267-3337.

# ANDREWS pop. 11,088

HOLIDAY INN EXPRESS   (432)524-4800
◆◆◆ Hotel $169-$249 Address: 1100 S Main St 79714 Location: US 385, 1 mi s. Facility: 67 units. 3 stories, interior corridors. Terms: cancellation fee imposed. Pool(s): outdoor. Activities: exercise room. Guest Services: coin laundry.
⌊¶↑⌋ CALL ⌊&M⌋ ⌊≋⌋ ⌊BIZ⌋ ⌊HS⌋ ⌊⇱⌋ ⌊✕⌋ ⌊▤⌋ ⌊▦⌋ ⌊▥⌋

# ANGELINA NATIONAL FOREST (E-10)

Elevations in the forest range from 100 ft. on the Neches River below the Sam Rayburn Reservoir Dam to 406 ft. at Moss Hill. Refer to AAA maps for additional elevation information.

Angelina National Forest surrounds Sam Rayburn Reservoir in East Texas, off US 69 east of Lufkin. The forest's 153,160 acres encompass fragments of the "Pineywoods" region, which was heavily logged early in the 20th century. Towering pines and hardwoods have returned, sheltering deer, squirrels and occasional turkeys.

Sam Rayburn Reservoir is the largest reservoir wholly within the state, and its 560-mile shoreline is dotted with campgrounds and marinas. Plentiful bass and catfish make it popular with anglers. Two notable wilderness areas within the forest are Turkey Hill and Upland Island.

Relics of the region's logging days can be seen along the 5.5-mile Sawmill Trail. The trail consists of two loops: one extending from Bouton Lake Recreation Area and the other from Boykin Springs Recreation Area and the Aldridge Sawmill. Portions of each loop follow the Neches River past vestiges of an old tram line, logging camps and ruined bridges.

For information contact the district ranger station; phone (936) 897-1068, or write the Forest Supervisor, 2221 N. Raguet St., Lufkin, TX 75901. See Recreation Areas Chart.

Contact us about AAA/CAA

Approved properties at

AAA.com/TourBookComments

## ANGLETON pop. 18,862

### BEST WESTERN ANGLETON INN    (979)849-5822

Hotel
$79-$86

**AAA Benefit:** Members save 10% or more with Best Western!

**Address:** 1809 N Velasco St 77515 **Location:** Jct SR 35 and Business Rt SR 288, 1 mi n. **Facility:** 45 units. 2 stories (no elevator), exterior corridors. **Pool(s):** outdoor. **Featured Amenity:** full hot breakfast.

---

### LA QUINTA INN & SUITES ANGLETON    (979)864-3383

Hotel $109-$144 **Address:** 2400 W Mulberry St 77515 **Location:** Jct SR 35 and 288; on northwest corner. **Facility:** 57 units. 3 stories, interior corridors. **Pool(s):** outdoor. **Activities:** hot tub, exercise room. **Guest Services:** coin laundry.

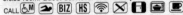

## ANTHONY (D-1) pop. 5,011, elev. 1,578'

**WET N' WILD WATERWORLD** is at 8804 S. Desert Blvd. More than 200 trees provide shade for a variety of water attractions. Among the highlights are Alien Vortex, a steep vertical slide; The Old Woman & the Shoe, a double slide for infants and toddlers; the Raging Rapids bumper ride; and Wild Island Wave Pool. The park hosts concerts and special events and allows guests to bring in food and beverages.

**Time:** Allow 6 hours minimum. **Hours:** Mon.-Fri. 11-6, Sat.-Sun. 10-7, June 1-Labor Day; Sat.-Sun. 10-7, in May. **Cost:** $21.99; $19.99 (ages 4-12); $15.99 (ages 65+); $2.99 (ages 1-3). **Parking:** $2. **Phone:** (915) 886-2222.

---

### BEST WESTERN OASIS OF THE SUN    (915)886-3333

Hotel
$83-$94

**AAA Benefit:** Members save 10% or more with Best Western!

**Address:** 9401 S Desert Blvd 79821 **Location:** I-10 exit 0, just s. **Facility:** 62 units. 2 stories, exterior corridors. **Pool(s):** outdoor. **Activities:** sauna, hot tub, exercise room. **Guest Services:** valet and coin laundry. **Featured Amenity:** full hot breakfast.

---

## ARANSAS PASS pop. 8,204

### HAWTHORN SUITES BY WYNDHAM    (361)758-1774

Extended Stay Hotel
$85-$140

**Address:** 501 E Goodnight Ave 78336 **Location:** On SR 361. **Facility:** 86 kitchen units. 3 stories, interior corridors. **Terms:** cancellation fee imposed. **Pool(s):** outdoor. **Activities:** hot tub, exercise room. **Guest Services:** coin laundry. **Featured Amenity:** full hot breakfast.

---

**WHERE TO EAT**

### PEPITO'S MEXICAN RESTAURANT    361/758-5562

Tex-Mex. Casual Dining. $8-$12 **AAA Inspector Notes:** This small and casual restaurant with friendly service has specialty plates like chiles relleno and shrimp fajitas. The very spicy side salad is garnished with specks of hot serrano peppers. **Features:** beer & wine. **Address:** 1212 N State Hwy 35 78336 **Location:** Just n of city limits. B L D

## ARLINGTON (I-2) pop. 365,438, elev. 617'

• Hotels p. 70 • Restaurants p. 72
• Hotels & Restaurants map & index p. 68, 257

The city of Arlington grew out of a trading post established at Marrow Bone Springs in accordance with the Indian Peace Council of 1843. Originally named Hayter, the town was renamed for Robert E. Lee's hometown in Virginia. Upon the arrival of the Texas and Pacific Railway in 1876, Arlington became a market center for surrounding communities, remaining an agricultural community until after World War II. The construction of a General Motors assembly plant in 1951 spurred commercial expansion; city population increased by more than 75 percent during the 1970s.

**Arlington Convention and Visitors Bureau:** 1905 E. Randol Mill Rd., Arlington, TX 76011-8214. **Phone:** (817) 461-3888 or (800) 433-5374.

**AT&T STADIUM** is at 1 Legends Way. The home of the Dallas Cowboys and venue for the 2011 Super Bowl XLV and annual AT&T Cotton Bowl Classic boasts 80,000 seats and a retractable roof. Visitors on guided 1.5-hour walking tours can explore several areas, including the field, post-game interview room, press boxes and players' and cheerleaders' locker rooms. Self-guiding tours allow access to the field, post-game interview room, locker rooms and field club. Guided and self-guiding tours highlighting the stadium's 21 contemporary art pieces also are available.

**Note:** Food, beverages, camcorders, and cameras with a lens length of 3 or more inches are not permitted. **Time:** Allow 1 hour, 30 minutes minimum. **Hours:** Stadium tours depart every 30 minutes Mon.-Sat. 10-4:30, Sun. 11-3:30. Guided art tour departs Tues and Thurs. at 10, noon and 2. Self-guiding art tour (includes iPod Touch rental) departs Mon. and Wed. at 10, noon and 2. Phone for holiday

(See maps & indexes p. 68, 257.)

schedules. Last tour departs 1 hour, 30 minutes before closing. Tour schedule varies the day before special event days; no tours are conducted on special event days. Phone ahead to confirm schedule.

**Cost:** Guided stadium tour (includes a photograph of the visitor's experience) $27.50; $22.50 (ages 5-12 and 66+). Self-guiding stadium tour $17.50; $14.50 (ages 5-12 and 66+). Guided art tour $22. Self-guiding art tour with iPod Touch rental $16. Self-guiding art tour with personal device $14. Reservations are recommended. **Phone:** (817) 892-4161 or (817) 892-4000. [T]

**INTERNATIONAL BOWLING MUSEUM AND HALL OF FAME,** 621 Six Flags Dr., spotlights the past, present and future of bowling. Visitors learn about the sport's 5,000-year history through interactive exhibits, films and video games and also explore modern coaching trends and test their skills on a string-pin bowling lane. **Time:** Allow 1 hour minimum. **Hours:** Tues.-Sat. 9:30-5. Closed Thanksgiving and Christmas. **Cost:** $9.50; $7.50 (ages 4-18 and 65+). **Phone:** (817) 649-5105.

**RANGERS BALLPARK IN ARLINGTON** is at 1000 Ballpark Way. A behind-the-scenes look at the home of the Texas Rangers includes a visit to the press box, City of Arlington suite, batting cages and Rangers' dugout.

**Time:** Allow 1 hour minimum. **Hours:** Guided 50-minute field tours are offered Mon.-Sat. 9-4, Sun. 11-4 on non-game days and Mon.-Sat. 9-2, Sun. 11-2 on evening game days, Apr.-Sept. Tours also are offered Tues.-Sat. 10-4, rest of year. No tours are offered on days with afternoon games. **Cost:** $12; $10 (ages 62+ and students with ID); $6 (ages 4-14). **Phone:** (817) 273-5099.

**RIVER LEGACY LIVING SCIENCE CENTER** is 1.5 mi. n. of I-30 on Cooper St. to 703 N.W. Green Oaks Blvd. The center features an interactive exhibit hall, terraria, aquariums and outdoor education programs for all ages. The 1,300-acre River Legacy Parks include paved and unpaved nature trails and picnic facilities.

**Time:** Allow 1 hour, 30 minutes minimum. **Hours:** Center Mon.-Sat. 9-5; closed major holidays. Park daily 5 a.m.-10 p.m. **Cost:** Free. **Phone:** (817) 860-6752. [T]

[SAVE] **SIX FLAGS HURRICANE HARBOR** is at 1800 E. Lamar Blvd., just n. of I-30 between exits SR 360 and FM 157. This 47-acre water theme park features a wave pool and numerous waterslides, such as Black Hole, Sea Wolf and Shotgun Falls. Visitors can ride the funnel-shaped Tornado; explore the treasures of Hooks Lagoon, a five-story interactive tree house; catch a wave on Surf Rider, a bodyboard experience in the Boogie Beach area; or float down the Lazy River.

Outside food and beverages are prohibited. **Time:** Allow 6 hours minimum. **Hours:** Park open daily, Memorial Day to mid-Aug.; Sat.-Sun., mid-Aug. through Sept. 30. Hours vary. Phone ahead to confirm schedule. **Cost:** $29.99; $24.99 (under 48 inches tall); free (ages 0-2). Rates may vary; phone ahead. **Parking:** $14; $19 (preferred). **Phone:** (817) 640-8900. [T]

[GEM] **SIX FLAGS OVER TEXAS** is at 2201 Road to Six Flags. The 205-acre theme park depicts Texas under the flags of France, Mexico, the Republic of Texas, the Old South, Spain and the United States.

More than 100 rides, attractions and shows include the Texas Giant, a coaster made of wood and steel; Titan, a steel coaster reaching speeds up to 85 mph as the trains zip through spirals, plunges, helixes and a 120-foot-long tunnel; Mr. Freeze, which thrills riders in forward and reverse; a 200-foot parachute drop; Roaring Rapids, a river-rafting adventure; and Runaway Mountain, a coaster that travels in the dark.

Superheroes, including Batman and Robin, the Green Lantern, Flash and Wonder Woman, patrol the park. Two superheroes have their own rides: Gotham City is the appropriate home of the Batman the Ride coaster, and Superman Tower of Power has a 325-foot free fall.

Music Mill Amphitheatre has big-name entertainment in season. Looney Tunes USA is devoted to children and their parents. The park can be seen via a turn-of-the-20th-century-style train, and a 300-foot oil derrick tower provides a good view.

Picnic facilities (adjacent to the parking lot) are available. Lockers, strollers and air-conditioned kennels can be rented. **Time:** Allow 8 hours minimum. **Hours:** Daily, late May-early Aug.; Sat.-Sun., Mar. 1-late May, mid-Aug. through Oct. 31 and day after Thanksgiving-Dec. 31. Hours vary. Phone ahead to confirm schedule.

**Cost:** $59.99; $42.99 (under 48 inches tall); free (ages 0-2). Rates may vary; phone ahead. AAA members save on select services and merchandise. See guest relations for details. **Parking:** $17; $22 (preferred). **Phone:** (817) 530-6000, or (817) 607-6150 for schedule information. [T]

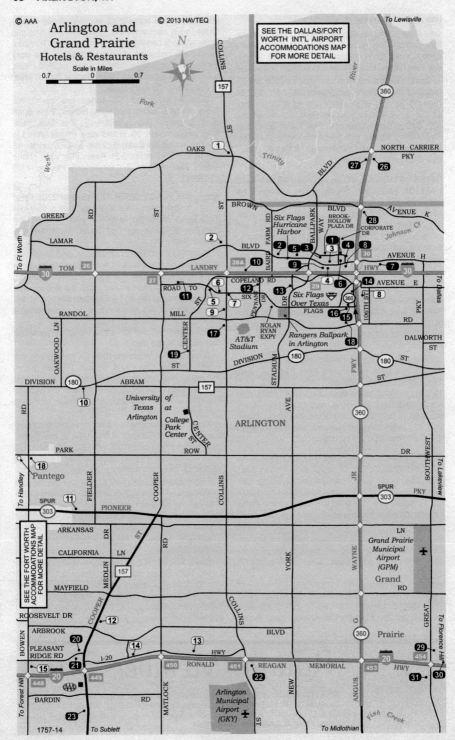

© AAA

© 2013 NAVTEQ

## Arlington and Grand Prairie
### Hotels & Restaurants

Scale in Miles
0.7    0    0.7

N

SEE THE DALLAS/FORT WORTH INT'L AIRPORT ACCOMMODATIONS MAP FOR MORE DETAIL

SEE THE FORT WORTH ACCOMMODATIONS MAP FOR MORE DETAIL

To Lewisville
To Ft Worth
To Handley
To Forest Hill
To Sublett
To Midlothian
To Dallas
To Lakeview
To Florence Hill

Six Flags Hurricane Harbor
Six Flags Over Texas
Rangers Ballpark in Arlington
AT&T Stadium
University of Texas at Arlington
College Park Center
Nolan Ryan Expy
Brook-Hollow Plaza Dr
Corporate Dr

ARLINGTON
Pantego
Grand Prairie
Grand Prairie Municipal Airport (GPM)
Arlington Municipal Airport (GKY)

1757-14

# Arlington and Grand Prairie

This index helps you "spot" where approved hotels and restaurants are located on the corresponding detailed maps. Hotel daily rate range is for comparison only. Restaurant price range is a combination of lunch and/or dinner. Turn to the listing page for more detailed rate and price information and consult display ads for special promotions.

## ARLINGTON

| Map Page | Hotels | Diamond Rated | Rate Range | Page |
|---|---|---|---|---|
| 1 p. 68 | **Hawthorn Suites by Wyndham** | ◆◆◆ | $89-$269 SAVE | 71 |
| 2 p. 68 | TownePlace Suites by Marriott Arlington Near Six Flags | ◆◆ | $75-$499 | 72 |
| 3 p. 68 | Hampton Inn & Suites Arlington North Entertainment District | ◆◆◆ | $99-$229 | 71 |
| 4 p. 68 | **Wingate by Wyndham** | ◆◆◆ | $89-$179 SAVE | 72 |
| 5 p. 68 | SpringHill Suites by Marriott Arlington Near Six Flags | ◆◆◆ | $98-$129 | 72 |
| 6 p. 68 | **Hilton Arlington** | ◆◆◆ | $109-$299 SAVE | 71 |
| 7 p. 68 | **Crowne Plaza Arlington Suites** | ◆◆◆ | Rates not provided SAVE | 70 |
| 8 p. 68 | Fairfield Inn & Suites by Marriott Arlington Near Six Flags | ◆◆ | $79-$329 | 70 |
| 9 p. 68 | Hilton Garden Inn Dallas /Arlington | ◆◆◆ | $129-$409 | 71 |
| 10 p. 68 | **Holiday Inn Arlington NE- Rangers Ballpark** | ◆◆◆ | Rates not provided SAVE | 71 |
| 11 p. 68 | Comfort Suites Six Flags in Arlington | ◆◆◆ | $90-$150 | 70 |
| 12 p. 68 | Courtyard by Marriott Dallas/Arlington by the Ballpark | ◆◆◆ | $99-$299 | 70 |
| 13 p. 68 | **Sheraton Arlington Hotel** | ◆◆◆ | $109-$449 SAVE | 72 |
| 14 p. 68 | La Quinta Inn & Suites Dallas/Arlington 6 Flags Dr | ◆◆◆ | $115-$174 | 71 |
| 15 p. 68 | Homewood Suites by Hilton | ◆◆◆ | $132-$159 | 71 |
| 16 p. 68 | **Hyatt Place Dallas/Arlington** | ◆◆◆ | $79-$299 SAVE | 71 |
| 17 p. 68 | **Days Inn Six Flags/Ballpark/Cowboys Stadium** | ◆◆ | $55-$219 SAVE | 70 |
| 18 p. 68 | Holiday Inn Express Hotel & Suites Arlington Six Flags Area | ◆◆ | $89-$199 | 71 |
| 19 p. 68 | The Sanford House Inn & Spa | ◆◆◆ | $149-$299 | 72 |
| 20 p. 68 | **BEST WESTERN Cooper Inn & Suites** | ◆◆ | $80-$100 SAVE | 70 |
| 21 p. 68 | Holiday Inn Express Hotel & Suites | ◆◆◆ | $109-$189 | 71 |
| 22 p. 68 | Hampton Inn & Suites of Arlington South | ◆◆◆ | $104-$154 | 71 |
| 23 p. 68 | **Microtel Inn by Wyndham Arlington/Dallas Area** | ◆◆ | $59-$79 SAVE | 72 |

| Map Page | Restaurants | Diamond Rated | Cuisine | Price Range | Page |
|---|---|---|---|---|---|
| 1 p. 68 | Piranha Killer Sushi | ◆◆ | Sushi | $11-$23 | 74 |
| 2 p. 68 | **Piccolo Mondo Italian Restaurant** | ◆◆ | Italian | $10-$34 | 73 |
| 3 p. 68 | Cacharel | ◆◆◆ | French | $14-$60 | 73 |
| 4 p. 68 | Saltgrass Steakhouse | ◆◆ | Steak | $9-$30 SAVE | 74 |
| 5 p. 68 | Olenjack's Grille | ◆◆ | New American | $10-$46 | 73 |
| 6 p. 68 | Birra Poretti's | ◆◆ | Italian | $8-$18 | 72 |
| 7 p. 68 | **El Chico** | ◆◆ | Tex-Mex | $7-$16 | 73 |
| 8 p. 68 | Mariano's Mexican Cuisine | ◆◆ | Mexican | $8-$20 | 73 |

| Map Page | Restaurants (cont'd) | Diamond Rated | Cuisine | Price Range | Page |
|---|---|---|---|---|---|
| ⑨ p. 68 | Airways Hamburgers | ▼ | Burgers | $3-$6 | 72 |
| ⑩ p. 68 | Arlington Steakhouse | ▼ | Steak | $8-$18 | 72 |
| ⑪ p. 68 | Taste of Europe | ▼▼ | Russian | $9-$14 | 74 |
| ⑫ p. 68 | Thai House Restaurant | ▼▼ | Thai | $7-$16 | 74 |
| ⑬ p. 68 | Chuy's | ▼▼ | Tex-Mex | $6-$10 | 73 |
| ⑭ p. 68 | Saltgrass Steakhouse | ▼▼ | Steak | $9-$30 [SAVE] | 74 |
| ⑮ p. 68 | Bobby V's | ▼ | American | $6-$10 | 72 |

## GRAND PRAIRIE

| Map Page | Hotels | Diamond Rated | Rate Range | Page |
|---|---|---|---|---|
| 26 p. 68 | Hampton Inn Arlington/DFW Airport Area | ▼▼ | $89-$169 | 288 |
| 27 p. 68 | BEST WESTERN PLUS Arlington North Hotel & Suites | ▼▼▼ | $99-$399 [SAVE] | 288 |
| 28 p. 68 | Hyatt Place Dallas/North Arlington/Grand Prairie | ▼▼▼ | $69-$279 [SAVE] | 288 |
| 29 p. 68 | Quality Inn & Suites | ▼▼ | $81-$100 [SAVE] | 288 |
| 30 p. 68 | Comfort Suites | ▼▼▼ | $79-$175 | 288 |
| 31 p. 68 | Super 8 | ▼▼ | $59-$99 [SAVE] | 288 |

## PANTEGO

| Map Page | Restaurant | Diamond Rated | Cuisine | Price Range | Page |
|---|---|---|---|---|---|
| 18 p. 68 | El Chico | ▼▼ | Tex-Mex | $7-$16 | 432 |

## BEST WESTERN COOPER INN & SUITES
(817)784-9490  20

▼▼ Hotel
$80-$100

AAA Benefit: Members save 10% or more with Best Western!

**Address:** 4024 Melear Dr 76015 **Location:** I-20 exit 449B (Cooper St), just n, then just w. **Facility:** 66 units. 2 stories (no elevator), exterior corridors. **Pool(s):** outdoor. **Activities:** exercise room. **Guest Services:** coin laundry. **Featured Amenity:** full hot breakfast.

[SAVE] [↕️] [🏊] [📶] [🍴] [📺] [🖥️] /SOME UNITS [🔒]

## COMFORT SUITES SIX FLAGS IN ARLINGTON
(817)460-8700  11

▼▼▼ Hotel $90-$150 **Address:** 411 W Road To Six Flags St 76011 **Location:** I-30 exit 27 (Cooper St) eastbound; exit 28 (Collins St) westbound, just s, then just e. **Facility:** 108 units. 4 stories, interior corridors. **Pool(s):** outdoor. **Activities:** playground, exercise room. **Guest Services:** coin laundry, area transportation.

[↕️] CALL [&M] [🏊] [BIZ] [HS] [📶] [✖️] [🍴] [🖥️] [📺] /SOME UNITS [🔒]

## COURTYARD BY MARRIOTT DALLAS/ARLINGTON BY THE BALLPARK
(817)277-2774  12

▼▼▼ Hotel $99-$299 **Address:** 1500 Nolan Ryan 76011 **Location:** I-30 exit 28 (Collins St) westbound; exit 28B eastbound, just s to Copeland Rd, 0.4 mi e, then just s. **Facility:** 147 units. 3 stories, interior corridors. **Pool(s):** outdoor. **Activities:** hot tub, exercise room. **Guest Services:** valet and coin laundry.

AAA Benefit: Members save 5% or more!

[ECO] [↕️] [🏊] [BIZ] [📶] [✖️] [🖥️] /SOME UNITS [🍴] [📺]

## CROWNE PLAZA ARLINGTON SUITES
817/394-5000  7

▼▼▼ Hotel
Rates not provided

**Address:** 700 Ave H E 76011 **Location:** I-30 exit 30 (SR 360), just n to exit Lamar Blvd/Ave H, then just e. **Facility:** 200 units. 7 stories, interior corridors. **Pool(s):** heated indoor. **Activities:** sauna, hot tub, exercise room. **Guest Services:** valet and coin laundry, area transportation.

[SAVE] [✈️] [🍴] [📶] [🍸] [🏊] [BIZ] [📶] [↕️] [🖥️] /SOME UNITS [HS]

## DAYS INN SIX FLAGS/BALLPARK/COWBOYS STADIUM
(817)261-8444  17

▼▼ Hotel
$55-$219

**Address:** 910 N Collins St 76011 **Location:** I-30 exit 28 (Collins St), 1 mi s. **Facility:** 92 units. 4 stories, interior corridors. **Terms:** 3 day cancellation notice-fee imposed. **Pool(s):** outdoor. **Featured Amenity:** continental breakfast.

[SAVE] [↕️] [🏊] [📶] [✖️] [🖥️] /SOME UNITS [🍴] [📺]

## FAIRFIELD INN & SUITES BY MARRIOTT ARLINGTON NEAR SIX FLAGS
(817)649-5800  8

▼▼ Hotel $79-$329 **Address:** 2500 E Lamar Blvd 76006 **Location:** SR 360 exit Ave H/Lamar Blvd, just w. **Facility:** 101 units. 3 stories, interior corridors. **Pool(s):** outdoor. **Activities:** exercise room. **Guest Services:** valet and coin laundry.

AAA Benefit: Members save 5% or more!

[↕️] CALL [&M] [🏊] [📶] [✖️] [🖥️] [🍴] [📺]

(See maps & indexes p. 68, 257.)

## HAMPTON INN & SUITES ARLINGTON NORTH
ENTERTAINMENT DISTRICT
(817)652-9562 **3**

Hotel $99-$229 **Address:** 2200 Brookhollow Plaza 76006 **Location:** SR 360 exit Ave H/Lamar Blvd, 0.5 mi w. **Facility:** 103 units. 5 stories, interior corridors. **Terms:** 1-7 night minimum stay, cancellation fee imposed. **Pool(s):** heated indoor. **Activities:** exercise room. **Guest Services:** valet and coin laundry.

**AAA Benefit:** Members save up to 10%!

## HAMPTON INN & SUITES OF ARLINGTON SOUTH
(817)419-3700 **22**

Hotel $104-$154 **Address:** 1100 E I-20 76018 **Location:** I-20 exit 451 (Collins St); on eastbound frontage road. **Facility:** 98 units. 4 stories, interior corridors. **Amenities:** video games. **Pool(s):** outdoor. **Activities:** exercise room. **Guest Services:** valet and coin laundry, area transportation.

**AAA Benefit:** Members save up to 10%!

## HAWTHORN SUITES BY WYNDHAM
(817)640-1188 **1**

Hotel $89-$269

**Address:** 2401 Brookhollow Plaza Dr 76006 **Location:** I-30 exit 30 (SR 360), just n to Lamar Blvd, just w to Brookhollow Plaza Dr, then just n. **Facility:** 129 units, some kitchens. 3 stories, exterior corridors. **Pool(s):** outdoor. **Activities:** hot tub, exercise room. **Guest Services:** valet and coin laundry. **Featured Amenity:** full hot breakfast.

## HILTON ARLINGTON
(817)640-3322 **6**

Hotel $109-$299

Hilton
HOTELS & RESORTS

**AAA Benefit:** Members save 5% or more!

**Address:** 2401 E Lamar Blvd 76006 **Location:** Just w of SR 360 exit Ave H/Lamar Blvd; just nw of I-30 exit 30 (SR 360). **Facility:** 308 units. 15 stories, interior corridors. **Terms:** 1-7 night minimum stay, cancellation fee imposed. **Amenities:** video games, safes. **Pool(s):** heated outdoor, heated indoor. **Activities:** hot tub, exercise room. **Guest Services:** valet laundry, area transportation.

## HILTON GARDEN INN DALLAS /ARLINGTON
(817)274-6644 **9**

Hotel $129-$409 **Address:** 2190 E Lamar Blvd 76006 **Location:** I-30 exit 28 (Collins St) eastbound, just n, then just e; exit 29 (Ballpark Way) westbound. **Facility:** 132 units. 4 stories, interior corridors. **Terms:** 1-7 night minimum stay, cancellation fee imposed. **Pool(s):** heated outdoor. **Activities:** hot tub, exercise room. **Guest Services:** valet and coin laundry.

**AAA Benefit:** Members save up to 10%!

## HOLIDAY INN ARLINGTON NE- RANGERS BALLPARK
817/460-2500 **10**

Hotel
Rates not provided

**Address:** 1311 Wet N Wild Way 76011 **Location:** I-30 exit 29 (Ballpark Way); on westbound service road. **Facility:** 147 units. 4 stories, interior corridors. **Pool(s):** heated indoor. **Activities:** hot tub, exercise room. **Guest Services:** valet and coin laundry, area transportation.

## HOLIDAY INN EXPRESS HOTEL & SUITES
(817)784-8750 **21**

Hotel $109-$189 **Address:** 1721 Pleasant Pl 76015 **Location:** I-20 exit 449 (Cooper St) westbound; exit 449B (Cooper St N) eastbound, just n, then just e. **Facility:** 101 units. 3 stories, interior corridors. **Pool(s):** outdoor. **Activities:** hot tub, exercise room. **Guest Services:** complimentary and valet laundry.

## HOLIDAY INN EXPRESS HOTEL & SUITES ARLINGTON SIX FLAGS AREA
(817)640-5454 **18**

Hotel $89-$199 **Address:** 2451 E Randol Mill Rd 76011 **Location:** I-30 exit 30 (SR 360), 0.4 mi s, then just w. **Facility:** 103 units. 3 stories, interior corridors. **Pool(s):** outdoor. **Activities:** hot tub, exercise room. **Guest Services:** valet and coin laundry, area transportation.

## HOMEWOOD SUITES BY HILTON
(817)633-1594 **15**

**Extended Stay Hotel** $132-$159 **Address:** 2401 Road to Six Flags St E 76011 **Location:** I-30 exit 30 (SR 360), 0.5 mi s on southbound frontage road, then just w. **Facility:** 89 efficiencies, some two bedrooms. 4 stories, interior corridors. **Terms:** 1-7 night minimum stay, cancellation fee imposed. **Pool(s):** heated indoor. **Activities:** hot tub, exercise room. **Guest Services:** valet and coin laundry.

**AAA Benefit:** Members save up to 10%!

## HYATT PLACE DALLAS/ARLINGTON
(817)649-7676 **16**

Hotel $79-$299

**HYATT PLACE**
**AAA Benefit:** Members save 10%!

**Address:** 2380 Road to Six Flags St E 76011 **Location:** I-30 exit 30 (SR 360), 0.5 mi s on southbound frontage road, then just w. **Facility:** 127 units. 6 stories, interior corridors. **Terms:** cancellation fee imposed. **Pool(s):** heated outdoor. **Activities:** exercise room. **Guest Services:** valet laundry, area transportation. **Featured Amenity:** breakfast buffet.

## LA QUINTA INN & SUITES DALLAS/ARLINGTON 6 FLAGS DR
(817)640-4142 **14**

Hotel $115-$174 **Address:** 825 N Watson Rd 76011 **Location:** SR 360 exit Six Flags Dr northbound; exit Ave H/Lamar Blvd southbound; on southbound frontage road. **Facility:** 178 units. 6 stories, interior corridors. **Pool(s):** heated outdoor. **Activities:** hot tub, exercise room. **Guest Services:** valet and coin laundry, area transportation.

(See maps & indexes p. 68, 257.)

## MICROTEL INN BY WYNDHAM ARLINGTON/DALLAS AREA
(817)557-8400 [23]

Hotel
$59-$79

**Address:** 1740 Oak Village Blvd 76017 **Location:** I-20 exit 449B (Cooper St) westbound; exit 449A (Cooper St) eastbound; just s, then just w. **Facility:** 42 units. 2 stories (no elevator), interior corridors. **Pool(s):** outdoor. **Guest Services:** coin laundry. **Featured Amenity:** continental breakfast.

## THE SANFORD HOUSE INN & SPA
(817)861-2129 [19]

Boutique Hotel $149-$299 **Address:** 506 N Center St 76011 **Location:** I-30 exit 28A (Collins St/FM 157), 0.7 mi s to Randol Mill Rd, 0.4 mi w to N Center St, then 0.5 mi s. **Facility:** The property is located in a quiet residential neighborhood and offers well-manicured grounds and rooms that are spacious and beautifully appointed with original artwork and comfortable seating. 12 units, some cottages. 2 stories (no elevator), interior/exterior corridors. **Terms:** cancellation fee imposed. **Activities:** spa.

## SHERATON ARLINGTON HOTEL
(817)261-8200 [13]

Hotel
$109-$449

Sheraton
HOTELS & RESORTS

**AAA Benefit:** Members get up to 20% off, plus Starwood Preferred Guest® bonuses!

**Address:** 1500 Convention Center Dr 76011 **Location:** I-30 exit 29 (Ballpark Way), 0.4 mi e on Copeland Rd to Convention Center Dr, then just s. Next to Arlington Convention Center & Cowboy Stadium. **Facility:** 311 units. 19 stories, interior corridors. **Parking:** on-site and valet. **Terms:** cancellation fee imposed, resort fee. **Dining:** 2 restaurants. **Pool(s):** outdoor. **Activities:** hot tub, exercise room. **Guest Services:** valet and coin laundry, area transportation.

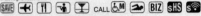

## SPRINGHILL SUITES BY MARRIOTT ARLINGTON NEAR SIX FLAGS
(817)860-2737 [5]

Hotel $98-$129 **Address:** 1975 E Lamar Blvd 76006 **Location:** I-30 exit 29 (Ballpark Way), 0.4 mi n to Lamar Blvd, then just w. **Facility:** 121 units. 3 stories, interior corridors. **Pool(s):** heated outdoor. **Activities:** hot tub, exercise room. **Guest Services:** valet and coin laundry, area transportation.

**AAA Benefit:** Members save 5% or more!

## TOWNEPLACE SUITES BY MARRIOTT ARLINGTON NEAR SIX FLAGS
(817)861-8728 [2]

Extended Stay Hotel $75-$499 **Address:** 1709 E Lamar Blvd 76006 **Location:** 2 mi w of SR 360. Opposite entrance to Six Flags Hurricane Harbor Waterpark. **Facility:** 94 kitchen units, some two bedrooms. 3 stories, interior corridors. **Pool(s):** outdoor. **Guest Services:** complimentary and valet laundry.

**AAA Benefit:** Members save 5% or more!

## WINGATE BY WYNDHAM
(817)640-8686 [4]

Hotel
$89-$179

**Address:** 1024 Brookhollow Plaza Dr 76006 **Location:** SR 360 exit Ave H/Lamar Blvd, 0.3 mi w to Brookhollow Plaza Dr, then 0.3 mi n. **Facility:** 92 units. 4 stories, interior corridors. **Amenities:** safes. **Pool(s):** outdoor. **Activities:** hot tub, exercise room. **Guest Services:** valet laundry, area transportation. **Featured Amenity:** full hot breakfast.

## WHERE TO EAT

### ABUELO'S THE FLAVOR OF MEXICO
817/468-2622

Tex-Mex. Casual Dining. $9-$20 **AAA Inspector Notes:** Just off I-20 in south Arlington, the restaurant feels like an escape to a Mexican villa. Elaborate pillars, large palm trees and even a fountain with a life-size sculpture in the center surround the dining room courtyard. The cuisine is standard Tex-Mex, with several more upscale selections of seafood, beef and chicken. Outdoor seating is available on the fenced patio. **Features:** full bar. **Address:** 1041 W I-20 76017 **Location:** I-20 exit 450 (Matlock Rd), just w; on westbound access road. [L] [D]

### AIRWAYS HAMBURGERS
817/461-1601 [9]

Burgers. Quick Serve. $3-$6 **AAA Inspector Notes:** Sports fans and locals alike frequent this conveniently located burger joint. Charbroiled hamburgers are the signature offering, but sandwiches, hot dogs and traditional sides like onion rings and french fries also are available. Lunch rush can be hectic, but if you get there a little later you can probably get a seat with a view of Cowboy Stadium, which is an architectural feat no matter who you root for. **Features:** beer only, patio dining. **Address:** 1106 N Collins St 76011 **Location:** I-30 exit 28 (Collins St) westbound; exit 28A (Collins St/FM 157) eastbound, 0.5 mi s. [L] [D]

### ARLINGTON STEAKHOUSE
817/275-7881 [10]

Steak. Casual Dining. $8-$18 **AAA Inspector Notes:** The modest building next to the railroad tracks may not seem like much from the outside, but it has been serving Arlington-area residents since 1931. The friendly, folksy restaurant dishes up steaks, prime rib, pork chops, chicken-fried steak and huge yeast rolls in a simple but welcoming atmosphere. A local favorite. **Features:** beer only. **Address:** 1724 W Division St 76012 **Location:** I-30 exit 26 (Fielder Rd), 1.5 mi s, then just w. [L] [D]

### BIRRA PORETTI'S
817/265-0555 [6]

Italian. Casual Dining. $8-$18 **AAA Inspector Notes:** This Arlington institution combines elements of an Italian restaurant and Irish pub. On the menu is traditional Italian cuisine, including pizzas cooked in a stone oven. The Sunday brunch is a hit. The center of the facility is a lounge designed as an Irish pub with a large bar. It's convenient to shopping, Cowboy Stadium and The Ballpark. **Features:** full bar, patio dining, Sunday brunch, happy hour. **Address:** 668 Lincoln Square 76011 **Location:** I-30 exit 28 (Collins St), just s to Road to Six Flags St, then just w. [L] [D]

### BOBBY V'S
817/467-9922 [15]

American. Casual Dining. $6-$10 **AAA Inspector Notes:** Sports memorabilia, TVs for catching the big game and even a boxing ring are all part of the fun sports bar atmosphere. Munch on tasty burgers and sandwiches and test your game savvy with live sports trivia every Sunday night. This place is a must for sports fans. The staff makes every effort to make your meal enjoyable, but you may have a bit of a wait depending on the particular sports events that are playing on TV. **Features:** full bar. **Address:** 4301 S Bowen Rd 76016 **Location:** I-20 exit 448 (Bowen Rd), just n. [L] [D] [LATE]

(See maps & indexes p. 68, 257.)

**CACHAREL**   817/640-9981   3

French. Fine Dining. $14-$60 **AAA Inspector Notes:** In addition to panoramic, ninth-floor views of the city, guests can enjoy beautiful paintings on the dining room walls of this elegant eatery. Representative of the French-inspired cuisine are choices such as roasted breast of duck, swordfish piccata and rack of lamb. Desserts veer from the usual suspects and are a nice ending to any meal. **Features:** full bar. **Reservations:** suggested. **Address:** 2221 E Lamar Blvd, 9th Floor 76006 **Location:** I-30 exit 30 (SR 360), just n to Ave H/Lamar Blvd, then just w. L D

**CHUY'S**   817/557-2489   13

Tex-Mex. Casual Dining. $6-$10 **AAA Inspector Notes:** Delicious fare is served in a funky atmosphere where you might sit in a dining room adorned with fake palm trees, hubcaps on the ceiling or Mexican retablos on the wall. No matter where you sit the food is super savory, the salsas pack heat, the tortillas are always hand made and the service is consistently friendly. The menu is not extensive but offers tacos, enchiladas, burritos and combo platters. Kids are always welcome. **Features:** full bar, patio dining, happy hour. **Address:** 4001 Bagpiper Way, Suite 199 76018 **Location:** I-20 exit 450 (Matlock Rd); on westbound frontage road; in Highlands Shopping Center. L D

**CORKY'S BRICK OVEN PIZZERIA**   817/561-2675   49

Pizza. Casual Dining. $5-$12 **AAA Inspector Notes:** With a rich history that dates back to 1937 when the first Corky's was established in Connecticut, this family-run operation proudly serves Neapolitan-style pizza. A wood-burning oven assures a crispy crust, charred just a little—as it's supposed to be, the owners will gladly tell you. A few pasta dishes, calzones and panini round out the menu, and BYOB is permissible. **Address:** 4760 Little Rd 76017 **Location:** I-20 exit 445 westbound, just s; exit 444 eastbound to US 287 exit Little Rd, just n. L D

**EL CHICO**   817/265-2127   7

**Tex-Mex
Casual Dining
$7-$16**

**AAA Inspector Notes:** Inside and out, the decor of the popular Mexican restaurant is inviting. The menu features traditional favorites such as enchiladas, tacos, burritos and fajitas. The broad menu also lists a few American classics. **Features:** full bar. **Address:** 1315 N Collins St 76011 **Location:** I-30 exit 28 (Collins St) westbound; exit 28A (Collins St/FM 157) eastbound, 0.3 mi s. L D

**GRANDY'S RESTAURANT**

American. Quick Serve. $4-$8 **AAA Inspector Notes:** Fried chicken and country-fried steak are menu standbys at the restaurant, a regional franchise. They also offer a family-style dining menu. The décor is a step up from that of most quick-serve eateries and more resembles that of a conventional restaurant. Some elements of increased service include additional rolls, iced tea refills and tray removal. B L D

*For additional information, visit AAA.com*

**LOCATIONS:**
**Address:** 4180 S Cooper St 76015 **Location:** I-20 exit 450 westbound, 1.1 mi w to S Cooper St, then just n; exit 449A eastbound to S Cooper St, then just n. **Phone:** 817/472-5345

**Address:** 2450 SE Green Oaks Blvd 76018 **Location:** Just w of jct SE Green Oaks Blvd and SR 360 (S Watson Rd).
**Phone:** 817/466-4776

**LA MADELEINE COUNTRY FRENCH CAFE**

Traditional French. Quick Serve. $6-$12 **AAA Inspector Notes:** A fireplace creates the focal point at this cozy European style café where you can always get a quiche or savory stuffed puffed pastry on the go or stick around for a chicken crêpe or French dip sandwich. Heartier entrées like rotisserie chicken are offered and every season promises menu surprises. Whatever you decide on you probably will not get out the door without enjoying one of their tempting sweet pastries. **Bar:** wine only. B L D

*For additional information, visit AAA.com*

**LOCATIONS:**
**Address:** 2101 N Collins St 76011 **Location:** Jct Lamar Blvd and Collins St. **Phone:** 817/461-3634

**Address:** 4201 S Cooper St, Suite 731 76015 **Location:** I-20 exit 449 (Cooper St), just ne; at entry to Parks at Arlington Mall.
**Phone:** 817/417-5100

**MARIANO'S MEXICAN CUISINE**   817/640-5118   8

Mexican. Casual Dining. $8-$20 **AAA Inspector Notes:** You can hardly go wrong at Mariano's; after all he did invent the frozen margarita machine. Forty years later his food is going just as strong as the drink. Fajitas, enchiladas, fish tacos and chile rellenos are served alongside a tempting margarita menu. Its proximity to Arlington's attractions makes this a no-brainer for families wanting a crowd-pleasing menu and an easy commute back to the hotel or parks. **Features:** full bar, happy hour. **Address:** 2614 Majesty Dr 76011 **Location:** SR 360 exit Ave H/Lamar Blvd southbound, 0.9 mi s to Randol Mill Rd, U-turn under highway, just n to Majesty Dr, then just e; exit Randol Mill Rd northbound; n on frontage road. L D

**MERCADO JUAREZ CAFE**   817/557-9776

Tex-Mex. Casual Dining. $7-$15 **AAA Inspector Notes:** This small local chain has been serving classic Tex-Mex cuisine in the area for more than 20 years. Fajitas, tacos al carbon and plenty of crunchy nachos are accompanied by handmade tortillas and salsa. Brightly painted frescoes, window frames and doors enliven the Mexican cantina. **Features:** full bar, patio dining. **Address:** 125 E I-20 76018 **Location:** I-20 exit 450 (Matlock Rd), just nw. L D

**OLENJACK'S GRILLE**   817/226-2600   5

New American. Casual Dining. $10-$46 **AAA Inspector Notes:** A welcome find among a sea of chain restaurants, this place excels at presenting contemporary American cuisine with a Texas flair. The signature dish is shrimp and grits, but steak, swordfish and chicken-fried steak are just a few of the other items offered on the menu. Small plates for noshing also are offered. This is a popular pre- or post-Cowboy game stop. A covered patio is available. **Features:** full bar, Sunday brunch. **Address:** 770 Road to Six Flags St E, Suite 100 76011 **Location:** I-30 exit 28 (Collins St), just s, then just w; in Lincoln Square Shopping Center. L D CALL &M

**PAPPADEAUX SEAFOOD KITCHEN**   817/543-0545

Cajun Seafood. Casual Dining. $10-$45 **AAA Inspector Notes:** A seafood lover's delight, the restaurant taps into a little bit of New Orleans with its Cajun dishes and elaborate menu selections. Patrons might start off with a creative choice of blackened oyster and shrimp fondeaux with crayfish and let the feast begin. While music plays in the background, patrons can dig into dirty rice or spicy gumbo loaded with seafood. Well-seasoned shrimp and fish are prepared in varied ways. **Features:** full bar, patio dining, happy hour. **Address:** 1304 E Copeland Rd 76011 **Location:** I-30 exit 28 (Collins St) westbound; exit 28A (Collins St/FM 157) eastbound; on eastbound frontage road. L D

**PAPPASITO'S CANTINA**   817/795-3535

Tex-Mex. Casual Dining. $8-$40 **AAA Inspector Notes:** Fine traditional offerings are served in an upscale cantina atmosphere. Often crowded during peak hours, the immensely popular stop dishes up generous portions of sizzling fajitas, enchiladas and other traditional Mexican favorites, including some shrimp specialties. The terrific days begin. Well-seasoned shrimp and fish are prepared in varied ways. Tables in the large dining room are closely spaced. Ice cream with cinnamon on chocolate bread pudding shouldn't be missed. **Features:** full bar. **Address:** 321 Road to Six Flags St W 76011 **Location:** I-30 exit 28A (Collins St/FM 157), just s to center, just sw to Road to Six Flags St, then just w. L D

**PICCOLO MONDO ITALIAN RESTAURANT**
817/265-9174   2

**Italian
Casual Dining
$10-$34**

**AAA Inspector Notes:** This popular business lunch spot is cozy and prepares a mixture of traditional favorites such as veal parmigiana, lasagna and fettuccine Alfredo. Warm, crusty Italian bread enhances any selection. Try the chocolate profiterole: a tasty puffy pastry dessert with chocolate sauce. **Features:** full bar. **Reservations:** suggested. **Address:** 829 E Lamar Blvd 76011 **Location:** I-30 exit 28 (Collins St), just n. *Menu on AAA.com* L D

**(See maps & indexes p. 68, 257.)**

PIRANHA KILLER SUSHI      817/261-1636   ①

▼▼ Sushi. Casual Dining. $11-$23 **AAA Inspector Notes:** Don't let its location in a strip mall deter you from eating at this unexpected surprise that serves a lot more than sushi. It also offers a long list of starters and hot entrées, including crab cakes, grilled salmon, udon and pad thai. That said, the sushi is artfully and creatively prepared and deserves more than a little consideration. The décor is contemporary, with a sushi bar focal point and lots of hard surfaces that can make for a loud dinner experience. **Features:** full bar, patio dining, happy hour. **Address:** 859 NE Green Oaks Blvd 76006 **Location:** I-30 exit 28 (Collins St), 2 mi n.

Ⓛ   Ⓓ

ROCKFISH SEAFOOD GRILL      817/419-9988

▼▼ Seafood. Casual Dining. $7-$20 **AAA Inspector Notes:** Patrons shuffle through peanut shells on the floor as they make their way to their seats and are easily distracted by the numerous pieces of hunting and fishing memorabilia adorning the walls and ceiling. Although guests kick back in a log cabin-style interior, the freshly caught fish gets more sophisticated preparation than campfire roasting. The chef uses an array of sauces and cooking styles, and soups are hearty and fresh. **Features:** full bar. **Address:** 3785 S Cooper St 76015 **Location:** I-20 exit 449 (Cooper St) westbound; exit 449A eastbound, 1 mi n.   Ⓛ   Ⓓ

SALTGRASS STEAKHOUSE

▼▼ Steak. Casual Dining. $9-$30 **AAA Inspector Notes:** Those looking for something different should try the comfortable steakhouse, which never says no to a special request. Born from the spirit of Texas cattle drives, the restaurant resembles a Texas lodge, with high ceilings and mounted animal heads. Baby back ribs are so tender the meat falls off the bone. Also on the menu are hearty steaks, prime rib, chicken, seafood and yummy desserts. **Bar:** full bar. (SAVE) Ⓛ   Ⓓ

*For additional information, visit AAA.com*

**LOCATIONS:**
**Address:** 2200 E Lamar Blvd 76006 **Location:** SR 360 exit Ave H/Lamar Blvd, 0.5 mi w. **Phone:** 817/640-3880     ④
**Address:** 1051 W I-20 76015 **Location:** I-20 exit 450 (Matlock Rd); on westbound service road. **Phone:** 817/417-7171     ⑭

SHERLOCK'S BAKER ST. PUB      817/226-2300

▼▼ English. Casual Dining. $8-$19 **AAA Inspector Notes:** The English-style public house encourages such gaming as darts, chess, pool and some arcade games. Among the specialties are such favorites as bangers and mash, fish and chips and shepherd's pie. This is a good place to dine and stay entertained between courses. **Features:** full bar, happy hour. **Address:** 254 Lincoln Square Center, Suite 254 76011 **Location:** I-30 exit 28 (Collins St) eastbound; exit 28B (Collins St) westbound.   Ⓛ   Ⓓ   (LATE)

THE SPAGHETTI WAREHOUSE      817/557-0321

▼▼ Italian. Casual Dining. $7-$17 **AAA Inspector Notes:** The Italian-style restaurant chain sustains a festive family atmosphere. All entrees include bottomless tossed salad or soup. Patrons enjoy plentiful portions of such classic dishes as ravioli, lasagna, baked penne or the richly flavored cannelloni Florentine. Splurging on one of the many desserts, such as tiramisu, espresso mousse cake or carrot cake, is worthwhile. **Features:** full bar. **Address:** 1255 W I-20 76017 **Location:** I-20 exit 450 (Matlock Rd); on westbound frontage road.

Ⓛ   Ⓓ

SPRING CREEK BBQ      817/465-0553

▼ Barbecue. Casual Dining. $8-$11 **AAA Inspector Notes:** Expect Texas-Style barbecue at its simple, homey best. Hickory smoked ribs, beef, pork and turkey lace the air with a spicy aroma that mingles with the scent of freshly baked rolls and cold ice cream slowly melting over a dish of homemade peach cobbler. Plates often are loaded with all the coleslaw, potato salad and corn on the cob they can support. Part of a small chain, this barbecue restaurant displays a rustic décor that gives patrons the impression they are "at the ranch." **Features:** beer only. **Address:** 3608 S Cooper St 76015 **Location:** I-20 exit 449 (Cooper St) westbound; exit 449A eastbound, 0.5 mi n.   Ⓛ   Ⓓ

TASTE OF EUROPE      817/275-5530   ⑪

▼▼ Russian. Casual Dining. $9-$14 **AAA Inspector Notes:** The quaint restaurant harbors a wide selection of Eastern European dishes and exotic Russian food. Borscht, cabbage rolls, blintzes, potato pancakes and crêpes are just some of the items offered at this family-run restaurant. Take home some Russian delicacies from the on-site market or nesting dolls from the gift shop. **Address:** 1901 W Pioneer Pkwy 76013 **Location:** Between Fielder and Bowen rds.

Ⓛ   Ⓓ

TEXAS LAND AND CATTLE STEAKHOUSE      817/461-1500

▼▼ Steak. Casual Dining. $7-$27 **AAA Inspector Notes:** A variety of large Prime steaks, delicious salads and scrumptious desserts await you at the friendly Texas ranch-style restaurant. Try the signature slow-smoked sirloin, which never fails to please, or the Caesar salad, another favorite. A Texas steakhouse means everything is bigger, from large cuts and oversize salads to potatoes and side dishes. Those not in the mood for beef can opt for chicken, quail or seafood. Dessert is an occasion. **Features:** full bar. **Address:** 2009 E Copeland Rd 76011 **Location:** I-30 exit 29 (Ballpark Way); southwest corner of I-30 and Ballpark Way.   Ⓛ   Ⓓ

THAI HOUSE RESTAURANT      817/375-0441   ⑫

▼▼ Thai. Casual Dining. $7-$16 **AAA Inspector Notes:** Although Thai House is a quick jaunt from the interstate, it can be a little hard to find. Once you find it, don't let the shopping center's appearance deter you, because the food here does not disappoint. They serve traditional preparations of noodle dishes, curries and stir-fries done with artful attention to presentation. **Address:** 3701 S Cooper St, Suite 131 76015 **Location:** I-20 exit 449B (Cooper St), 0.7 mi n.

Ⓛ   Ⓓ

## ATHENS (D-9) pop. 12,710, elev. 492'
• Part of Dallas area — see map p. 161

   Chosen as the seat of Henderson County in 1850, Athens was so named because it was expected to become the cultural center of the state, as was its namesake in Greece. A century later it was discovered that Athens, like its namesake, had been established on seven major hills.

**City of Athens Department of Tourism:** 201 W. Corsicana St., Athens, TX 75751. **Phone:** (903) 677-0775 or (888) 294-2847.

**EAST TEXAS ARBORETUM & BOTANICAL SOCIETY** is off I-27 exit 3, then .8 mi. e. to 1601 Patterson Rd. These 104 acres encompass lush botanical gardens, an arboretum and a 2-mile hiking trail with a suspension bridge and two other bridges. The restored 1851 home of Bushrod J.W. Wofford includes furniture, a spinning wheel and cooking utensils common to the mid-1800s. **Time:** Allow 1 hour minimum. **Hours:** Grounds daily dawn-dusk. House Mon.-Fri. 9-4. **Cost:** $2; free (ages 0-12). **Phone:** (903) 675-5630.

**TEXAS FRESHWATER FISHERIES CENTER** is 4 mi. e. of SR 31 on FM 2495. More than 300,000 gallons of aquarium exhibits display every major species of freshwater fish found in Texas. The center includes a dive show auditorium, a fishing museum, an angler's pavilion, wetland trails and a casting pond. Catch-and-release fishing equipment is provided. A 15-minute tram ride takes visitors on a tour of the outdoor hatchery.

   **Hours:** Tues.-Sat. 9-4, Sun. 1-4. Dive show and tram tour offered Tues.-Fri. at 11, Sat. at 11 and 2,

Sun. at 2. Closed Jan. 1, Easter, Thanksgiving, Christmas Eve and Christmas. **Cost:** (Includes fishing) $5.50; $4.50 (ages 65+); $3.50 (ages 4-12). **Phone:** (903) 676-2277.

## RECREATIONAL ACTIVITIES

### Scuba Diving

- **Athens Scuba Park** is 6 blks. e. on SR 31, then 1 blk. n. to 500 N. Murchison St. **Hours:** Wed.-Fri. 10-5, Sat.-Sun. 8-6, Apr.-Oct. Phone ahead to confirm schedule. **Phone:** (903) 675-5762.

**BEST WESTERN PLUS ROYAL MOUNTAIN INN & SUITES**                              (903)292-1750

Hotel
$90-$150

**AAA Benefit:** Members save 10% or more with Best Western!

**Address:** 1814 State Hwy 31 E 75751 **Location:** 1 mi sw of jct Loop 7. **Facility:** 61 units. 3 stories, interior corridors. **Pool(s):** heated outdoor. **Activities:** hot tub, exercise room. **Guest Services:** valet and coin laundry.

### WHERE TO EAT

OLE WEST STEAKHOUSE                              903/675-8200

Steak. Casual Dining. $7-$21 **AAA Inspector Notes:** Located on the east side of town, this steakhouse has been in business for 30 years. The Western theme is enforced with cowboy paraphernalia on walls and on shelves, and an extensive buffet is served for both lunch and dinner. It includes salads, vegetables and regional favorites like tacos and enchiladas. A la carte items include steaks, chicken and seafood. **Address:** 1502 E Tyler St (SR 31 E) 75751 **Location:** 1.9 mi e of jct SR 19 and 31.  L  D

## ATLANTA  pop. 5,675

**BEST WESTERN PINEYWOODS INN**                              (903)799-8500

Motel
$100-$110

**AAA Benefit:** Members save 10% or more with Best Western!

**Address:** 306 Loop Hwy 59 N 75551 **Location:** 0.6 mi n of jct US 59 and SR 77. **Facility:** 42 units. 2 stories (no elevator), interior corridors. **Pool(s):** outdoor. **Guest Services:** valet and coin laundry. **Featured Amenity: full hot breakfast.**

### WHERE TO EAT

GRANDY'S RESTAURANT                              903/796-5577

American. Quick Serve. $4-$8 **AAA Inspector Notes:** Fried chicken and country-fried steak are menu standbys at the restaurant, a regional franchise. They also offer a family-style dining menu. The décor is a step up from that of most quick-serve eateries and more resembles that of a conventional restaurant. Some elements of increased service include additional rolls, iced tea refills and tray removal. **Address:** 2005 W Main St 75551 **Location:** Just sw of jct US 59 (Main St) and SR 77.  B  L  D

## AUSTIN  (F-8) pop. 790,390, elev. 511'
- **Hotels p. 93 • Restaurants p. 97**
- **Attractions map p. 79**
- **Hotels & Restaurants map & index p. 83, 86**

Austin combines the grandeur and air of consequence of a state capital, the youthful energy and Bohemian vibe of a college town and the economic optimism of a fast-growing Sun Belt city. You can see it all in the city's skyline: the graceful dome of the Texas Capitol, taller even than the U.S. Capitol; the gilt-edged clock faces adorning University of Texas Tower; and the shiny new office and residential high rises springing up like wildflowers along Congress Avenue and the shores of Lady Bird Lake. Add to this eclectic mix some old-fashioned Western individualism and cowboy style, and you've got a city with a personality all its own.

While the Capitol and surrounding government office buildings form the heart of downtown Austin, it's the more than 50,000-student University of Texas at Austin *(see attraction listing p. 82)* that provides the highly educated employees coveted by such computer companies as IBM, Hewlett-Packard and Dell, Inc., founded by former UT student Michael Dell. So many high-tech corporations have opened up shop locally that the region's been dubbed the "Silicon Hills."

Austin's skilled labor pool—along with its sunny weather, diverse scenery and very supportive film commission—has also attracted filmmakers, who have made it Texas's most important movie and television production center. More than 350 feature films, television shows and major commercials have been filmed here in the past two decades. If you have seen "Alamo," "Spy Kids," "Waiting for Guffman," "Dazed and Confused," "Slacker," "Miss Congeniality," "Sin City" or "Friday Night Lights," you've seen an Austin-made film.

The city's economic growth hasn't been without consequences. Odds are you've heard of the popular "Keep Austin Weird" slogan. Appearing on bumper stickers and T-shirts, it not only sums up the city's affinity for the unconventional but also the concern that its quirkiness may be slipping away. Since 1980 the population has more than doubled and with downtown real estate prices soaring and affluence on the upswing, gentrification has made incursions into some of Austin's most famously offbeat neighborhoods. But the city hasn't quite lost its counter-culture credentials yet thanks to the pride many Austinites take in their hippie past. And with each UT freshman class comes a regular infusion of youthful thinking and innovative ideas that are destined to keep Austin original, vibrant and with any luck, weird, for years to come.

UT also played a big role in Austin's genesis as "Live Music Capital of the World" in the 1960s and '70s. Back then, singer Willie Nelson helped popularize Austin's country music scene, and former UT student Clifford Antone opened Antone's, his legendary "Home of the Blues," and one of the first music clubs along now club-crowded 6th Street. In 1975 Austin's reputation for live music soared when

(See maps & indexes p. 83, 86.)

the "Austin City Limits" show first aired on PBS, recorded live at KLRU on UT's campus. Ever since then the nationally broadcast show has introduced audiences to local musical groups as well as national and international acts.

Today young musicians flock to the city, eager to launch their careers in a community known for fostering new talent. And with nearly 200 live venues, including stages at Austin-Bergstrom International Airport, and major music events like the 🎸 South by Southwest (SXSW) festival and the 🎸 Austin City Limits Music Festival, Austin continues to welcome musicians and music lovers alike, justifying its "live music capital" claim.

Of course, Austin is literally a capital, and reminders of its long history at the center of Texas politics are everywhere. Strolling down Austin's Congress Avenue, for example, you can't miss a bronze statue of a woman heroically poised to light a cannon, her dress flowing backward as if in a strong wind, her face twisted in a defiant grimace. Meet Angelina Eberly, a fiery innkeeper who in 1842 helped thwart Sam Houston, President of the Republic of Texas, in his plans to relocate the new nation's capital (Texas won its independence from Mexico in 1836 but didn't become a U.S. state until 1845) from Austin to a site he argued was less vulnerable to Mexican incursions.

Despite opposition from the legislature, Houston ordered a detachment of Texas Rangers to remove the government archives from Austin, which citizens feared would bring their town closer to permanently losing its capital status. When Eberly discovered Houston's men loading wagons with the documents, she fired the town cannon, alerting her fellow citizens. They recovered the documents, entrusted them to the formidable Mrs. Eberly, and the episode known as the Archive War ended without bloodshed. Austin became the capital again in 1844 and has remained so ever since.

One feature of the city that hasn't remained the same is the Colorado River, on the banks of which Austin, then known as Waterloo, was founded in the 1830s. Several dams have been built over the years, forming the Highland Lakes, a chain of reservoirs that stretches west 163 miles and includes lakes Austin, Travis, Marble Falls, LBJ, Inks and Buchanan.

In 2007, the Austin City Council renamed downtown's Town Lake to honor Lady Bird Johnson, who had championed restoration of its natural beauty years before. Dividing Austin in half, Lady Bird Lake features a popular 10-mile-long recreation trail lined with lush vegetation, benches, shelters and water fountains; it even has its own pedestrian bridge. On weekday evenings, joggers and bikers enjoying their post-workday workout crowd the path, and collegiate crews in training scull across the lake.

Whether on foot or riding a bike, visitors can veer off the Lady Bird Lake Trail in Zilker Metropolitan Park (see attraction listing p. 82) to reach Barton Creek Greenbelt, an additional 7.2 miles of pathway that twists and turns alongside a rocky creek past sheer cliff walls and abundant greenery. Another Zilker Park activity locals frequently recommend is a dip in Barton Springs Pool, which remains a constant 68 degrees even on the hottest summer day.

During the 🎸 Statesman Capitol 10K in late March or April, more than 22,000 people traverse a 6.2-mile course from Barton Springs Road to Riverside Drive. Highlights include a timed run and a wheelchair race. In October, 🎸 LIVESTRONG Challenge Ride for the Roses draws more than 6,000 bicyclists of varying experience levels participating in 20- to 100-mile courses.

For views of the city, mansion-lined Lake Austin and the surrounding Hill Country, Mount Bonnell (see attraction listing p. 81), a mile past the west end of 35th Street, can't be beat. But be prepared for a bit of a climb: it takes 99 steps to reach the top. Another view of Austin that visitors shouldn't miss is the Ann W. Richards Congress Avenue Bridge (see attraction listing p. 79), or more specifically, the underside of the bridge. From early April through late September, spectators assemble at sunset to witness more than a million Mexican free-tailed bats flood out from crevices beneath the bridge for their nightly insect feast.

Austin Visitor Center: 209 E. 6th St., Austin, TX 78701. Phone: (512) 478-0098 or (866) 462-8784.

## Self-guiding Tours

Brochures outlining historic areas are available from the Austin Visitor Center.

## Shopping

Finding stores that live up to the city's "Keep Austin Weird" motto means heading downtown where chain stores are the exception and not the rule. You'll discover Austin's best collection of offbeat shops in the SoCo District, an area along busy Congress Avenue south of Lady Bird Lake between Academy and Oltorf streets. Park along the west side of Congress where the majority of stores are; there are spaces on Congress and along side streets.

Standing tall among the health food stores, novelty shops, vintage clothing stores, folk art galleries and funky home furnishing emporiums is one of Austin's venerable institutions, Allen's Boots. Step beneath the big red boot above the door and come inside if only to breathe in the sweet smell of leather from all the shiny, beautifully crafted cowboy boots. And if you want to dress Western from toe to head, Allen's Boots sells an assortment of cowboy hats as well.

Other SoCo landmarks you'll want to poke your head into: Mi Casa Gallery, chock-full of high-end Mexican folk art including multiple images of Our Lady of Guadalupe as well as a few pieces by local artists; Tesoros Trading Co., an importer of international arts and crafts; and Monkey See, Monkey Do!, which sells diverse novelty items including retro toys, figurines representing obscure Japanese cartoon characters, joke books and scathing political commentary delivered in the form of refrigerator magnets.

(See maps & indexes p. 83, 86.)

On the first Thursday of each month, SoCo stores stay open until 10 p.m. On these nights galleries host art shows, street vendors sell crafts and bands jam out on improvised stages. Just be aware that parking on first Thursday nights can be a real pain. Your best bet is to park at the free garage at 505 Barton Springs Rd. and ride the Congress Avenue 'Dillo trolley bus south to where the stores are.

Among SoCo's bohemian businesses, you'll notice a couple relatively new shopping plazas with stores offering higher-end merchandise. Such retailers are the rule, not the exception, in the 2nd Street District just on the other side of Lady Bird Lake. Centered around Austin's low-slung, copper-sheathed city hall, which opened in 2004 at 2nd and Lavaca streets, the district boasts several upscale boutiques, and as more of the planned high-rise developments are completed, that number will no doubt increase.

Along with 2nd Street's outdoor cafes and fashionable restaurants, you'll find shops selling all sorts of trendy clothing, pricey knick-knacks and stylish jewelry to Austin's well-heeled professional class. Look for designer home furnishings, linens and bedding at The Home Retreat.

The nearby Market District takes its name from the flagship store of Whole Foods Market, the national natural food supermarket chain established in Austin more than 25 years ago. You'll find several interesting shopping plazas adjacent to Whole Foods, near the intersection of N. Lamar Boulevard and W. 6th Street. Local landmark Waterloo Records occupies the corner diagonally across from the supermarket. Inside is just about every genre of music you'd care to name along with a comprehensive collection of local recording artists as well as videos, used CDs and even an assortment of vinyl records.

Book People, on the same side of Lamar as Whole Foods, is Austin's answer to the bookstore megachains although it doesn't have anything close to the local character of its record store counterpart across the street. Whole Foods itself is worth a stop, if not for a quick snack then at least to see its outdoor café complete with shade-creating metal sculptures and a brook trickling through a rock-filled channel set in the flagstones at your feet.

The Congress Avenue District, centered about the same street as SoCo but on the north side of Lady Bird Lake, caters to a very different crowd than its funky south-of-the-lake counterpart. Here clothing stores selling suits and conservative casual wear are sprinkled in among the restaurants and art galleries. Legislators have to buy their power ties somewhere, right? What more convenient place than along the street leading to the Capitol? And at nearby souvenir shops along E. 6th Street you can buy an almost painfully colorful red tie-dye shirt with the words "Keep Austin Weird" printed across it.

Anything but stodgy, the district on the western edge of the University of Texas along Guadalupe Street is affectionately called "The Drag." Naturally, businesses here sell stuff college undergrads would buy, and foremost among these is the University Co-Op, where students can stock up on T-shirts, mouse pads, beer cozies, key chains, pens, notebooks, etc., all emblazoned with the Texas Longhorns logo. But you don't have to be in the market for a used textbook to enjoy a stroll along the Drag; there's also sporting goods stores, independent booksellers, vintage clothing shops and retailers boasting all sorts of environmentally friendly goods, including the Whole Earth Provision Co.

Shopping malls outside Austin's downtown area offer the usual mix of nationally recognized department, clothing and specialty stores, but one outlying retail center stands out: The Domain at US 183 and MoPac Expressway North. This lovely Main Street-style shopping village has a Macy's and a Neiman Marcus on opposite ends of a curving road lined with whimsical sculptures, colorful mosaics, rustic stonework and oak-shaded parks. Among The Domain's specialty stores are an Apple store, Louis Vuitton, Sur La Table and Tiffany & Co.

## Nightlife

Austin squeezes a surprising number of bars, lounges and restaurants into its compact and walkable downtown. Most feature live entertainment at some point during the week while a few never take a night off. Musical styles on tap range from country and western to blues to rock to punk with just about everything in between. Austinites don't call their hometown the "Live Music Capital of the World" for nothing.

You'll find the heaviest concentration of clubs, pubs and watering holes along 6th Street east of Congress in the shadow of Austin's historic Driskill Hotel. The dignified landmark with its solemn white-columned porticos and arched windows contrasts starkly with the raucous carnival atmosphere prevailing here. Amplified music blares from speakers while barkers stationed at each entrance call out to passersby, announcing the night's drink specials and featured acts. Walls of these 19th-century commercial buildings are typically brick and do nothing to dampen sound, which seems just fine with the throngs of revelers, who are for the most part under 30.

Maggie Mae's has been a 6th Street institution for more than 25 years, and with its decent cover bands and large beer selection, this rowdy hangout continues to draw hordes of both tourists and locals. And you don't have to leave the premises when you need a break: Maggie Mae's has a rooftop deck where you can have a conversation and enjoy a nice breeze. A long, narrow room at street level serves as the main performance space, but if that gets too crowded, you can step into the adjacent open-air courtyard and still hear the music.

With its weathered brick and stone walls and venerable neon sign, Stubb's Bar-B-Q, 801 Red River St., looks every bit the Red River Street institution that it is. Stubb's books an impressive lineup of hip-hop, rock, alternative and country acts at both its indoor stage and its popular outdoor amphitheater. Performers who have played Stubb's include Willie Nelson, Joan Jett,

(See maps & indexes p. 83, 86.)

Death Cab for Cutie, Spoon, Dwight Yoakam and Ludacris. The barbecue served here gets rave reviews, and Stubb's combines a barbecue buffet with live music during its Sunday Gospel Brunch. Nearby, Elysium, 705 Red River St., specializes in goth and industrial with an '80s alternative night thrown in. Elysium is more of a dance club, but it usually features live bands Thursday and Friday nights.

If hanging with the goth crowd at Elysium isn't your style, try Barcelona, 209 E. 6th St., a dance club that maintains its low profile on 6th Street by a) announcing itself to the world with only a low-key awning stamped in diminutive letters and b) being in a basement. Look for the huge neon sign over the visitor center next door and you can't miss this literally underground club. House and techno music dominate, but other musical styles find a ready home here depending on the night and the DJ. With enough mood lighting for two bars its size, Barcelona creates an ambience that's more stylish and sophisticated than what you'll find at most places on 6th Street.

Following 6th Street west across Congress Avenue brings you into the Warehouse District, distinguished by the stairs you'll have to climb as you navigate its sidewalks. It's easy to see that the raised entrances here once facilitated the unloading and loading of goods. The crowds here tend to be over 30 in contrast to the 6th Street and Red River districts, and restaurants are both more numerous and more upscale.

If the evening is mild and rain-free, visit Cedar Street Courtyard, 208 W. 4th St., a brick-paved space nestled between two buildings. Trees and vine-covered walls make this a pleasant, shaded niche during the day, and jazz bands provide entertainment on the courtyard stage. There's also an indoor area where patrons retreat during inclement weather and sample from among the bar's two dozen flavored martinis.

Thanks to a redevelopment project launched in the early 2000s, once-drowsy Rainey Street—a mixed-use historic district sandwiched between I-35 and Lady Bird Lake on downtown's southeastern edge—has emerged as a favorite nightborhood for in-the-know Austinites. Dilapidated bungalows have been renovated into cozy, come-as-you-are bars with backyards, porches and a whole lot of character. Best-loved spots include Bar 96 (96 Rainey St.), a tin-ceilinged sports pub; Lustre Pearl (97 Rainey St.), where patrons unite (or fight) over ping-pong games, brush up on their Hula-Hooping skills and chat it up in Adirondack chairs; and Clive Bar (609 Davis St.), whose dark wood paneling and white vinyl chairs help create a vintage vibe.

On the south side of Lady Bird Lake is the offbeat enclave centered around South Congress called, appropriately enough, SoCo. Better known for consignment shops, health food stores and folk art galleries, SoCo is where you'll also find the Continental Club, 1315 S. Congress Ave., another bright star in

Austin's constellation of live music locales. This intimate establishment opened as a supper club in 1957, but since the 1970s its red-velvet curtained stage has seen all manner of country, rock, rockabilly and swing bands.

Just a little ways down the road and across the street is Güero's Taco Bar, 1412 S. Congress Ave. Not only is Güero's a fun spot to people watch while enjoying Tex-Mex cuisine that includes a salsa bar, fresh-made tortillas and savory fish tacos, but the restaurant's oak-shaded, picnic-table-filled outdoor area is the scene of concerts Thursday through Sunday, too.

The name of the restaurant and music venue just around the corner at 301 W. Riverside Dr.—Threadgill's World Headquarters—might sound a bit grandiose, but it's a tribute to two legendary sites from Austin's music history. In the 1930s, Kenneth Threadgill opened a bar in his gas station just north of the city limits, and musicians came from all over for the beer and late-night jam sessions until it closed in the 1970s.

The 1970s also happens to have been the heyday of the Armadillo World Headquarters, one of Austin's most important music clubs, where an "Austin sound" emerged that was somewhere between country and rock 'n' roll and where performers as diverse as Ray Charles, Willie Nelson, Frank Zappa, B.B. King, Bruce Springsteen, The Charlie Daniels Band and hundreds of others played. The "'Dillo" was torn down in 1981, but Threadgill's World Headquarters sits next door to the storied music hall's former site, serving down-home Southern cooking and hosting bands in its beer garden most nights of the week.

Antone's, 2015 E. Riverside Dr., is the kind of no-frills place where drinks are served in plastic cups and concert posters and autographed photos serve as interior decor. Ever since Antone's was founded in 1975 by the late Clifford Antone, this relatively unadorned space has been all about the music. Known for showcasing acts throughout the week, Austin's "Home of the Blues" has hosted blues greats Muddy Waters, John Lee Hooker, Fats Domino, Buddy Guy, Junior Wells and B.B. King as well as lesser known and local talents. Sharing the complex with Antone's is the edgier Emo's Austin. Since it's open to all ages and has a reputation for cheap beer and the latest and greatest punk and alternative bands, the average age at Emo's skews toward the early 20s.

You could easily miss the Broken Spoke at 3201 S. Lamar Blvd., which looks more like a rural grocery and feed store than one of Austin's—and indeed Texas's—best-known country music dance halls. A gravel parking lot, an old oil pump jack and a rusty vintage streamline bus advertising Lone Star beer greet visitors to this decidedly unpretentious honky-tonk. Yet despite the humble setting, a sign at the entrance proudly declares, "Through this door pass the best country music dancers in the world." The restaurant in front serves diner fare, including deliciously juicy hamburgers, and a couple small

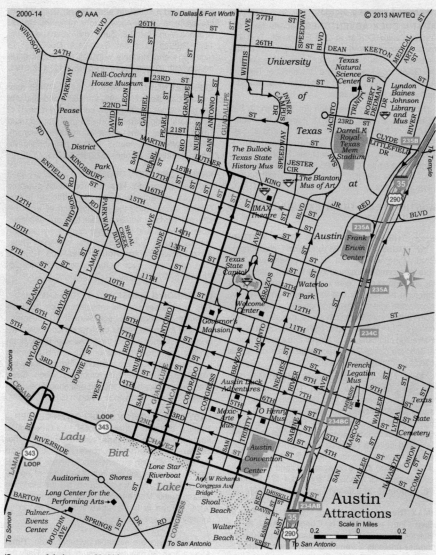

(See maps & indexes p. 83, 86.)

rooms have been given over to mementos—concert posters, signed photos, album covers and sundry other items—representing the Broken Spoke's 40-plus years as a music venue. Of course, the country music tradition continues with bands scheduled every Tuesday through Saturday nights.

## ANN W. RICHARDS CONGRESS AVENUE BRIDGE

spans Lady Bird Lake between Cesar Chavez St. and Barton Springs Rd. When engineers refurbished the bridge in 1980, they inadvertently created an ideal roost for migrating Mexican free-tailed bats. Today the underside of the bridge is home to what's been called "the world's largest urban bat colony," which at its annual peak in August numbers as many as 1.5 million of the creatures.

Shortly after dusk each evening, swarms of bats flood out from the narrow crevices beneath the bridge to hunt for insects, a sight that attracts hundreds of spectators. A great spot for bat watching is the grassy area at the bridge's southeast corner where visitors will also find several signs describing bat anatomy and why the bridge offers the perfect seasonal home for them. **Time:** Allow 30 minutes minimum. **Hours:** Daily 24 hours. Bats emerge daily shortly after dusk, early Mar.-late Sept. **Cost:** Free. **Phone:** (512) 416-5700, ext. 3636.

(See maps & indexes p. 83, 86.)

**AUSTIN DUCK ADVENTURES** departs from the Austin Visitor Center at 209 E. 6th St. This 75-minute narrated tour aboard a Hydra Terra amphibious vehicle includes the Texas State Capitol, the Governor's Mansion, The University of Texas at Austin, 6th Street, historic Congress Avenue and a splashdown in Lake Austin.

**Hours:** Tours are given Mon.-Fri. at 11 and 2, Sat. at 10, noon, 2 and 4, Sun. at 11, 2 and 4, June-Labor Day; Mon.-Tues. at 2, Wed.-Fri. at 11 and 2, Sat.-Sun. at 11, 2 and 4, rest of year. Closed Jan. 1, Easter, Thanksgiving and Christmas. Phone ahead to confirm schedule. **Cost:** $25.95; $23.95 (ages 55+ and students with ID); $15.95 (ages 3-12). **Phone:** (512) 477-5274.

**AUSTIN STEAM TRAIN EXCURSIONS**—see Cedar Park p. 136.

**THE BULLOCK TEXAS STATE HISTORY MUSEUM** is off I-35 exit Martin Luther King Jr. Blvd., then w. to 1800 N. Congress Ave. This sprawling complex explores three themes: Land, Identity and Opportunity. Three floors of interactive exhibits chronicle the region's first inhabitants and early explorers; the fight for independence and statehood; and 20th-century contributions to space, industry and technology. The Texas Spirit Theater re-creates the Galveston hurricane, an oil gusher and a rocket launch at Johnson Space Center, complete with such special effects as moving seats, wind and smoke.

**Time:** Allow 3 hours minimum. **Hours:** Mon.-Sat. 9-6, Sun. noon-6. Closed Jan. 1, Easter, Thanksgiving, Christmas Eve and Christmas. **Cost:** Museum $9; $8 (college students with ID); $7 (ages 65+ and military with ID); $4 (ages 4-17). Texas Spirit Theater $5; $4 (ages 4-17, ages 65+, and military and college students with ID). Combination ticket (includes museum, Texas Spirit Theater and IMAX Theatre) $22; $18 (ages 65+, and military and college students with ID); $16 (ages 4-17). **Parking:** $8. **Phone:** (512) 936-4649 or (866) 369-7108. ⓘ

**IMAX Theatre** is off I-35 exit Martin Luther King Jr. Blvd., then w. to 1800 N. Congress Ave., at The Bullock Texas State History Museum. This 400-seat theater presents a variety of large-format films, including "Texas: The Big Picture" and select Hollywood feature-length releases. **Note:** Seating is not permitted after show starts. **Time:** Allow 1 hour minimum. **Hours:** Films are shown daily; phone ahead for show schedule. **Cost:** $8; $7 (ages 65+, and military and college students with ID); $6 (ages 4-17). A combination ticket with The Bullock Texas State History Museum is available. Ticket prices for feature-length films may vary; phone ahead. **Phone:** (512) 936-8746 or (866) 369-7108.

**THE CONTEMPORARY AUSTIN—LAGUNA GLORIA** is at 3809 W. 35th St. Visitors can tour Driscoll Villa, the 1916 Italianate-style estate that was once the home of Clara Driscoll. The 12-acre grounds overlooking Lake Austin include historic gardens and a sculpture park. **Tours:** Guided tours are available. **Time:** Allow 1 hour minimum. **Hours:** Grounds Mon.-Sat. 9-5, Sun. 10-5. Villa Tues.-Sun. 10-4. Guided tours Sat.-Sun. at 1. **Cost:** $5; $3 (ages 65+ and students with ID); free (ages 0-18, military with ID and Tues.). **Phone:** (512) 458-8191.

**ELISABET NEY MUSEUM** is at 304 E. 44th St. near Ave. H. Established in 1892, the home and studio of the 19th-century sculptor now contains collections of her plaster and marble portraits of European and Texas notables. **Time:** Allow 30 minutes minimum. **Hours:** Wed.-Sun. noon-5. Closed major holidays. **Cost:** Donations. **Phone:** (512) 458-2255.

**FRENCH LEGATION MUSEUM** is 1 blk. e. of I-35 at 802 San Marcos St. This restored 1840s structure features artifacts from the Republic of Texas. Guided tours inside the legation and of a reconstructed carriage house and kitchen are available. **Note:** Strollers and bulky child carriers are not permitted. **Tours:** Guided tours are available. **Time:** Allow 1 hour minimum. **Hours:** Tues.-Sun. 1-5. Last tour departs 1 hour before closing. **Cost:** $5. **Phone:** (512) 472-8180.

**GOVERNOR'S MANSION** is at 1010 Colorado St. This 1856 Greek Revival mansion, which occupies an entire city block, has been home to 40 governors. It is said to be the oldest continuously occupied executive residence west of the Mississippi River. Noteworthy paintings, period antiques and Stephen Austin's writing desk are displayed. **Hours:** Tours depart Tues.-Thurs. every 20 minutes 10-noon. **Cost:** Free. Reservations are required and should be made at least 2 weeks in advance. **Phone:** (512) 305-8524.

**LADY BIRD JOHNSON WILDFLOWER CENTER** is 10 mi. s. on Loop 1, then e. to 4801 La Crosse Ave. Featuring display gardens, nature trails, a visitor center, an observation tower and a rooftop rainwater-collection system, this 279-acre botanical garden encourages the increased use of native plants. Flowers bloom year-round, but the blooming season peaks March through May. An open-air butterfly garden is landscaped with 300 butterfly-friendly plant species.

Guided tours are available by reservation. **Time:** Allow 1 hour, 30 minutes minimum. **Hours:** Daily 9-5 (also Thurs. 5-8), Jan.-May; Tues.-Sat. 9-5, Sun. noon-5, rest of year. Visitor center closes at 4. Closed July 4 and Thanksgiving. Phone ahead to confirm schedule. **Cost:** $9; $7 (ages 60+ and students ages 13+ with ID); $3 (ages 5-12). **Phone:** (512) 232-0100. ⓘ ⓕ

**LONE STAR RIVERBOAT** departs from the dock under the south end of the First Street Bridge; parking is available for a fee at the Hyatt Regency Austin hotel, 208 Barton Springs Rd. On the 1-hour narrated sunset/bat-watching cruise, passengers aboard a pontoon boat can observe a horde of bats emerging from the underside of the Ann W. Richards Congress Avenue Bridge. **Time:** Allow 1 hour

(See maps & indexes p. 83, 86.)

minimum. **Hours:** Cruises depart daily approximately 30 minutes before dusk (also Sat. and Sun. at 3), Mar.-Oct. Boats begin loading 45 minutes prior to departure. **Cost:** $10; $8 (ages 60+); $7 (ages 3-12). Cash only. **Phone:** (512) 327-1388. 🏧

**McKINNEY FALLS STATE PARK** is at 5808 McKinney Falls Pkwy. The park has 10 miles of well-marked trails, including a 2.8-mile paved stretch for bicycling. Sights along the trails include waterfalls, the remains of original owner Thomas McKinney's homestead and gristmill, the ruins of McKinney's horse trainer's cabin, and a rock shelter that once served as a dwelling for Native Americans.

For day-trippers there are 120 picnic sites; for overnight visitors there are 89 campsites, 81 of which have hookups. Visitors can learn about the park's natural and historical features in the visitor center and participate in seasonal interpretive programs. *See Recreation Areas Chart.* **Time:** Allow 2 hours minimum. **Hours:** Park daily 8 a.m.-10 p.m. Visitor center Fri.-Sun. 10-4. **Cost:** $6; free (ages 0-12). **Phone:** (512) 243-1643. 🏕 🚫 🍴 🏧

**MEXIC-ARTE MUSEUM** is at 419 Congress Ave. Exhibits feature contemporary and traditional works by Mexican, Latin American and U.S.-born Latino artists. Changing exhibits offering photography, paintings and sculpture highlight both established and emerging artists. **Time:** Allow 1 hour minimum. **Hours:** Mon.-Thurs. 10-6, Fri.-Sat. 10-5, Sun. noon-5. **Cost:** $5; $4 (ages 65+ and students with ID); $1 (ages 0-12); free (Sun.). **Phone:** (512) 480-9373.

**MOUNT BONNELL PARK** is at 3800 Mount Bonnell Rd. This 5-acre park overlooking Lake Austin offers wonderful views of the surrounding countryside including Austin's skyline. Mansions crowd the shoreline immediately below the park's vantage point, which has an elevation of 781 feet. A long series of stone stairs lead from the parking area up to the top, although a gently sloping trail follows the ridgeline back to the roadway farther north, offering an alternative route. **Time:** Allow 30 minutes minimum. **Hours:** Daily 5 a.m.-10 p.m. **Cost:** Free. **Phone:** (512) 974-6700. 🏧

**NEILL-COCHRAN HOUSE MUSEUM** is at 2310 San Gabriel St. The furniture in this restored 1855 Greek Revival house reflects 19th century eclectic tastes. Designed by architect/master builder Abner Cook, who also designed the Texas Governor's mansion, the building has been a private residence, a hospital for Union soldiers during Reconstruction, and the first home of the Texas Institute for the Blind. **Time:** Allow 30 minutes minimum. **Hours:** Tues.-Sat. 2-5. Closed Thanksgiving and Christmas Eve-Jan. 2. **Cost:** $5; $1 (ages 0-15). **Phone:** (512) 478-2335.

**O. HENRY MUSEUM,** 3 blks. w. of I-35 at 409 E. 5th St., chronicles the life of William Sydney Porter during the years he lived in Austin. The short-story writer, better known as O. Henry, authored such classics as "The Gift of the Magi," "The Ransom of Red Chief" and "The Cop and the Anthem." On display in this Queen Anne-style cottage, where he lived in the 1890s with his wife and daughter, are many of the author's personal effects, including a copy of "The Rolling Stone," his Austin-published newspaper. **Time:** Allow 30 minutes minimum. **Hours:** Wed.-Sun. noon-5. Closed Jan. 1, July 4, Thanksgiving, day after Thanksgiving and Christmas. Phone ahead to confirm schedule. **Cost:** Free. **Phone:** (512) 472-1903. 🏧

**TEXAS MILITARY FORCES MUSEUM** is at 2200 W. 35th St., Bldg. 6, on Camp Mabry. Exhibits highlight the history of state military forces from the Texas Revolution to the present. Dioramas and an abundance of equipment including jets, helicopters, small aircraft, track and wheeled vehicles and artillery pieces also are displayed. **Note:** A photo ID is required to enter the base. **Time:** Allow 1 hour, 30 minutes minimum. **Hours:** Tues.-Sun. 10-4. Closed Thanksgiving, Christmas Eve and Christmas. **Cost:** Free. **Phone:** (512) 782-5659.

**TEXAS STATE CAPITOL** is on Congress Ave. at 11th St. Completed in 1888, the Renaissance Revival-style Capitol is clad in Texas "sunset red" granite and features an impressive dome crowned by "Goddess of Liberty," a nearly 16-foot-tall statue of a woman holding up a gilded five-pointed star. Several monuments are scattered throughout the Capitol's extensive park-like grounds. Housed within the 1856-57 General Land Office Building on 11th Street, the Capitol Visitors Center features interactive exhibits, theaters, maps and visitor information.

**Time:** Allow 1 hour minimum. **Hours:** Capitol building open Mon.-Fri. 7 a.m.-10 p.m., Sat.-Sun. 9-8. Guided tours are given Mon.-Fri. 8:30-4:30, Sat. 9:30-3:30, Sun. noon-3:30. Capitol Visitors Center open Mon.-Sat. 9-5, Sun. noon-5. Closed Jan. 1, Easter, Thanksgiving, Christmas Eve and Christmas. **Cost:** Free. **Phone:** (512) 463-0063 or (512) 305-8400.

**TEXAS STATE CEMETERY** is at 909 Navasota St. The graves of notable Texan politicians and veterans, including Stephen F. Austin, who brought the first settlers to Texas in 1821, are on the grounds. Monuments by such Texas sculptors as Elisabet Ney dot the property. The limestone visitors center, inspired by the Alamo and the San Jose Mission Granary, houses a museum detailing the history of the cemetery. **Time:** Allow 1 hour minimum. **Hours:** Grounds daily 8-5. Visitors center and museum Mon.-Fri. 8-5. **Cost:** Free. **Phone:** (512) 463-0605.

**THE THINKERY,** 1830 Simond Ave., is a hands-on museum for youngsters through age 11. Activity galleries like Innovators' Workshop, Spark Shop, Currents and Let's Grow introduce them to science, technology, engineering, arts and math. Watch a fun demonstration in the Kitchen Lab and explore Our Backyard—an outdoor exhibit—featuring a climbing

## 82   AUSTIN, TX

(See maps & indexes p. 83, 86.)

structure and places to rest and enjoy a gentle stream and a native elm tree. Programs designed for specific age groups are offered as well.

**Hours:** Tues.-Sat. 10-5 (also Wed. 5-8), Sun. noon-5. Closed Jan. 1, Memorial Day, July 4, Labor Day, Thanksgiving and Christmas. **Cost:** $6.50; $4.50 (age 1); donations (Wed. 5-8); free (under 1 and Sun. 4-5). **Phone:** (512) 472-2499.

**UMLAUF SCULPTURE GARDEN & MUSEUM** is 1.5 mi. n.w. on Barton Springs Rd., then s. to 605 Robert E. Lee Rd. More than 100 sculptures by internationally known sculptor Charles Umlauf and other contemporary sculptors belong to the museum collection. Ranging from detailed realism to lyrical abstractions, sculptures of different mediums are situated throughout a wood and water hillside setting as well as inside the museum.

**Time:** Allow 1 hour minimum. **Hours:** Wed.-Fri. 10-4, Sat.-Sun. noon-4. Closed Jan. 1, July 4, Thanksgiving, Christmas Eve, Christmas and Dec. 31. **Cost:** $3.50; $2.50 (ages 60+); $1 (students with ID); free (ages 0-5). **Phone:** (512) 445-5582.

**UNIVERSITY OF TEXAS AT AUSTIN** is bounded by Martin Luther King Jr. Blvd., Guadalupe and Red River sts. Chartered in 1883, the Austin campus is the keystone of the statewide university system. It boasts one of the largest endowments of any public university and is a noted national research center with several internationally renowned scholars on its faculty, including a Nobel laureate.

Campus walking tours are offered daily through the visitor center on the second floor of Walter Webb Hall at 405 W. 25th St.; tours of the U.T. Tower are available by reservation. **Hours:** Tours depart Mon.-Fri. at 10 and 2, Sat. at 10. **Cost:** Tower tours $6. **Phone:** (512) 471-1000, or (512) 475-7348 for walking tours.

**The Blanton Museum of Art** is at jct. Congress Ave. and Martin Luther King Jr. Blvd. at 200 E. Martin Luther King Jr. Blvd. The museum features changing exhibitions and a 17,000-piece permanent collection that includes European paintings, an encyclopedic collection of prints and drawings, and modern and contemporary American and Latin-American art.

**Time:** Allow 1 hour, 30 minutes minimum. **Hours:** Tues.-Fri. 10-5 (also third Thurs. of the month 5-9), Sat. 11-5, Sun. 1-5. Closed major holidays. **Cost:** $9; $7 (ages 65+); $5 (ages 13-21 and college students with ID); free (Thurs.). **Phone:** (512) 471-7324.

**Lyndon Baines Johnson Library and Museum** is at 2313 Red River St. Papers of the Johnson presidency are preserved at the complex, which also includes sculptures of President and Mrs. Johnson, interactive exhibits featuring historic films and telephone recordings, gifts from foreign heads of state, Johnson's 1968 Lincoln limousine, a collection of American political memorabilia and changing displays depicting American history.

Displays chronicle Johnson's life, from his boyhood along the Pedernales River to his retirement at his ranch. A 7/8-scale replica allows visitors to enter the Oval Office of Johnson's administration (1963-69). An 11-minute multimedia program about Johnson's life is shown throughout the day. The First Lady's Gallery highlights Lady Bird Johnson's life from the time she met Lyndon Johnson to the present. **Time:** Allow 1 hour minimum. **Hours:** Museum daily 9-5; closed Christmas. Library reading room Mon.-Fri. 9-5; closed federal holidays. **Cost:** $8; $5 (ages 65+); $3 (ages 13-17). **Phone:** (512) 721-0200.

**Texas Natural Science Center** is at 2400 Trinity St. The center houses the Texas Memorial Museum and contains skeletons of dinosaurs, collections of fossils, gems, rocks and minerals and several dioramas of preserved Texas animals. Paleontologists are available to answer questions. **Time:** Allow 1 hour minimum. **Hours:** Mon.-Thurs. 9-5, Fri. 9-4:45, Sat. 10-4:45, Sun. 1-4:45. Closed major holidays. **Cost:** Free. **Phone:** (512) 471-1604.

**ZILKER METROPOLITAN PARK** is 1.5 mi. s.w. on Barton Springs Rd. bordering Lady Bird Lake. The centerpiece of the 351-acre park is Barton Springs, a spring-fed 1,000-foot-long swimming pool with a constant temperature of 68 F. Opportunities for bicycling, canoeing, hiking and picnicking are available *(see Recreation Areas Chart).* A museum and an outdoor theater also are on the grounds. A 20-minute train ride aboard the Zilker Zephyr is offered.

**Time:** Allow 4 hours minimum. **Hours:** Park open daily 5 a.m.-10 p.m. Barton Springs open Fri.-Wed. 5 a.m.-10 p.m., Thurs. 5-9 a.m. and 7-10 p.m. (weather permitting). Train operates daily 10-6. **Cost:** Park admission $5 (per private vehicle), mid-Mar. through Labor Day weekend; $5 (Sat.-Sun. and holidays), free (Mon.-Fri.), rest of year. Barton Springs $3; $2 (ages 12-17); $1 (ages 0-11 and 65+). Train $3; $2 (ages 1-11 and 65+). **Phone:** (512) 974-6700 for the park, or (512) 476-9044 for Barton Springs.

**Austin Nature & Science Center** is off Stratford Dr. at 301 Nature Center Dr. Visitors can explore the animals, plants and geology of central Texas through interactive outdoor exhibits and nature trails. The Dino Pit features reproductions of local fossils, dinosaur tracks and archeological finds. Wildlife exhibits include native Texas mammals, birds and reptiles that have been injured or orphaned. **Time:** Allow 1 hour minimum. **Hours:** Mon.-Sat. 9-5, Sun. noon-5. Closed Jan. 1, July 4, Thanksgiving and Christmas. **Cost:** Donations. **Phone:** (512) 974-3888.

**Zilker Botanical Gardens** is at 2220 Barton Springs Rd. Oriental, rose, butterfly, cactus, herb and native plant gardens are featured. The Hartman Prehistoric Garden re-creates a local dinosaur habitat with ponds, a waterfall and re-creations of plants from prehistoric times. The Austin Area Garden Center also is on the grounds. **Time:** Allow 1 hour minimum. **Hours:** Daily 7-7, Mar.-Oct.; 7-5, rest of year. Phone ahead to confirm schedule. **Cost:** $2; $1 (ages 3-12 and 62+). **Phone:** (512) 477-8672.

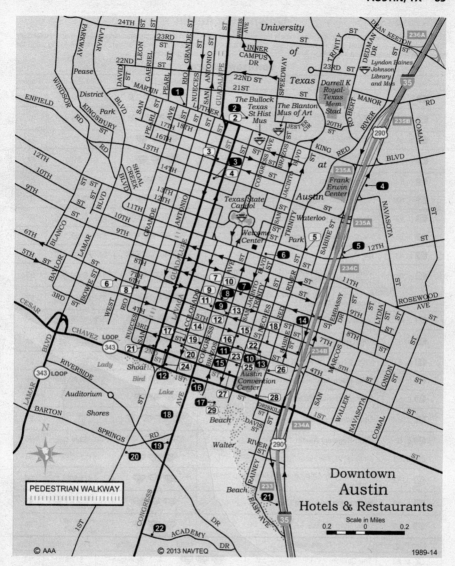

Downtown
Austin
Hotels & Restaurants

# Downtown Austin

This index helps you "spot" where approved hotels and restaurants are located on the corresponding detailed maps. Hotel daily rate range is for comparison only. Restaurant price range is a combination of lunch and/or dinner. Turn to the listing page for more detailed rate and price information and consult display ads for special promotions.

## DOWNTOWN AUSTIN

| Map Page | Hotels | Diamond Rated | Rate Range | Page |
|---|---|---|---|---|
| ❶ p. 83 | Hotel Ella | ◆◆◆◆ | $229-$499 SAVE | 95 |
| ❷ p. 83 | The AT&T Executive Education and Conference Center | ◆◆◆◆ | $159-$329 SAVE | 93 |
| ❸ p. 83 | DoubleTree Suites by Hilton Hotel Austin | ◆◆◆ | $169-$399 | 94 |
| ❹ p. 83 | DoubleTree by Hilton Hotel Austin - University Area | ◆◆◆ | $99-$179 | 94 |
| ❺ p. 83 | Super 8 Central | ◆◆ | $79-$205 SAVE | 97 |
| ❻ p. 83 | La Quinta Inn Austin Capitol | ◆◆◆ | $119-$224 | 97 |
| ❼ p. 83 | Omni Austin Hotel Downtown | ◆◆◆◆ | $169-$649 SAVE | 97 |
| ❽ p. 83 | InterContinental Stephen F. Austin Hotel | ◆◆◆◆ | $159-$599 SAVE | 97 |
| ❾ p. 83 | The Driskill | ◆◆◆◆ | $179-$649 SAVE | 94 |
| ❿ p. 83 | Courtyard by Marriott Austin Downtown/Convention Center | ◆◆◆ | $160-$500 SAVE | 93 |
| ⓫ p. 83 | Residence Inn by Marriott Austin/Downtown/Convention Center | ◆◆◆ | $170-$500 SAVE | 97 |
| ⓬ p. 83 | W Austin (See ad p. 96.) | ◆◆◆◆ | $299-$609 SAVE | 97 |
| ⓭ p. 83 | Hilton Austin | ◆◆◆◆ | Rates not provided SAVE | 94 |
| ⓮ p. 83 | Hilton Garden Inn Austin Downtown | ◆◆◆ | $109-$299 | 94 |
| ⓯ p. 83 | Hyatt Place Austin Downtown | ◆◆◆ | $179-$799 SAVE | 95 |
| ⓰ p. 83 | Radisson Hotel & Suites-Austin | ◆◆◆ | $159-$609 | 97 |
| ⓱ p. 83 | Four Seasons Hotel | ◆◆◆◆ | Rates not provided SAVE | 94 |
| ⓲ p. 83 | Hyatt Regency Austin | ◆◆◆◆ | $99-$399 SAVE | 95 |
| ⓳ p. 83 | Embassy Suites Hotel-Downtown | ◆◆◆ | $132-$284 | 94 |
| ⓴ p. 83 | Extended Stay America-Austin/Downtown/Town Lake | ◆◆◆ | $74-$99 | 94 |
| ㉑ p. 83 | Holiday Inn Lady Bird Lake | ◆◆◆ | Rates not provided SAVE | 95 |
| ㉒ p. 83 | Hotel Saint Cecelia | ◆◆◆ | Rates not provided | 95 |

| Map Page | Restaurants | Diamond Rated | Cuisine | Price Range | Page |
|---|---|---|---|---|---|
| ② p. 83 | The Carillon | ◆◆◆ | American | $17-$70 | 98 |
| ③ p. 83 | Clay Pit | ◆◆◆ | Indian | $8-$20 | 98 |
| ④ p. 83 | 15th Street Cafe | ◆◆ | American | $7-$26 | 97 |
| ⑤ p. 83 | Brick Oven Restaurant | ◆◆ | Italian | $8-$20 | 98 |
| ⑥ p. 83 | Hut's Hamburgers | ◆◆ | Burgers Sandwiches | $5-$9 | 98 |
| ⑦ p. 83 | Hickory Street | ◆◆ | Comfort Food | $7-$13 | 98 |
| ⑧ p. 83 | The Hoffbrau | ◆ | Steak | $8-$19 | 98 |
| ⑨ p. 83 | Perry's Steakhouse & Grille | ◆◆◆ | Steak | $24-$55 | 99 |
| ⑩ p. 83 | Roaring Fork | ◆◆◆ | Steak | $10-$36 | 99 |
| ⑪ p. 83 | Thai Passion | ◆◆ | Thai | $9-$17 | 99 |

| Map Page | Restaurants (cont'd) | Diamond Rated | Cuisine | Price Range | Page |
|---|---|---|---|---|---|
| ⑫ p. 83 | **The Driskill Grill** | ◈◈◈◈ | New American | $32-$85 | 98 |
| ⑬ p. 83 | 1886 Cafe and Bakery | ◈◈◈ | American | $10-$18 | 97 |
| ⑭ p. 83 | Truluck's | ◈◈◈ | Seafood Steak | $12-$45 | 99 |
| ⑮ p. 83 | The Old Pecan Street Cafe | ◈◈ | American | $8-$15 | 99 |
| ⑯ p. 83 | Eddie V's Edgewater Grill-Downtown | ◈◈◈ | Steak Seafood | $19-$48 | 98 |
| ⑰ p. 83 | Sullivan's Steakhouse | ◈◈◈ | Steak | $24-$55 | 99 |
| ⑱ p. 83 | Carmelo's Ristorante | ◈◈◈ | Northern Italian | $14-$42 | 98 |
| ⑲ p. 83 | Manuel's Downtown | ◈◈ | Mexican | $10-$26 | 99 |
| ⑳ p. 83 | **Cantina Laredo** | ◈◈ | Mexican | $9-$26 | 98 |
| ㉑ p. 83 | La Condesa | ◈◈ | Mexican | $10-$38 | 98 |
| ㉒ p. 83 | Finn & Porter | ◈◈◈ | Steak | $24-$48 | 98 |
| ㉓ p. 83 | Vince Young Steakhouse | ◈◈◈ | Steak | $21-$50 | 99 |
| ㉔ p. 83 | **III Forks** | ◈◈◈ | Steak Seafood | $25-$60 | 97 |
| ㉕ p. 83 | Fogo De Chao | ◈◈◈ | Brazilian Steak | $27-$46 | 98 |
| ㉖ p. 83 | Moonshine Patio Bar & Grill | ◈◈ | American | $10-$22 | 99 |
| ㉗ p. 83 | Fleming's Prime Steakhouse & Wine Bar | ◈◈◈ | American | $16-$46 | 98 |
| ㉘ p. 83 | Ironworks Barbeque | ◈ | Barbecue | $6-$14 | 98 |
| ㉙ p. 83 | Trio | ◈◈◈◈ | Steak Seafood | $23-$45 | 99 |

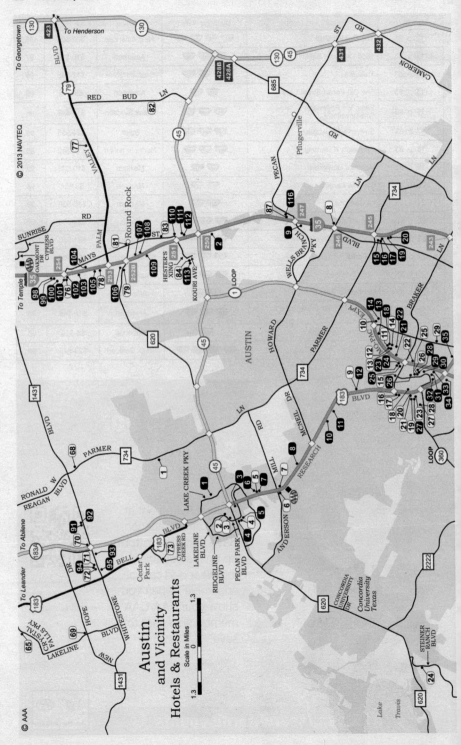

Austin
and Vicinity
Hotels & Restaurants

© AAA

© 2013 NAVTEQ

Scale in Miles

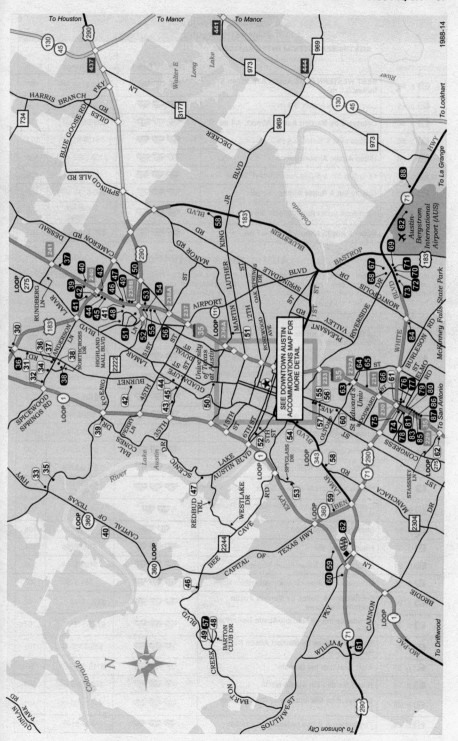

## ✈ Airport Hotels

| Map Page | AUSTIN-BERGSTROM INTERNATIONAL (Maximum driving distance from airport: 4.7 mi) | Diamond Rated | Rate Range | Page |
|---|---|---|---|---|
| 68 p. 86 | BEST WESTERN PLUS Austin Airport Inn & Suites, 3.5 mi | ◆◆◆ | $110-$150 SAVE | 100 |
| 73 p. 86 | Comfort Suites Airport, 3.9 mi | ◆◆◆ | $99-$199 | 100 |
| 69 p. 86 | Courtyard by Marriott Austin Airport, 3.4 mi | ◆◆◆ | $99-$599 SAVE | 101 |
| 71 p. 86 | Hampton Inn & Suites, 3.9 mi | ◆◆◆ | $139-$189 | 103 |
| 82 p. 86 | Hilton Austin Airport, 1.0 mi | ◆◆◆ | $109-$269 SAVE | 104 |
| 70 p. 86 | La Quinta Inn & Suites Austin Airport, 3.3 mi | ◆◆◆ | $115-$160 | 106 |
| 88 p. 86 | Quality Inn & Suites Airport, 1.5 mi | ◆◆◆ | $80-$130 SAVE | 107 |
| 67 p. 86 | Staybridge Suites Austin Airport, 3.6 mi | ◆◆◆ | Rates not provided | 108 |
| 84 p. 86 | Super 8 Austin Airport South, 4.7 mi | ◆◆◆ | $99-$360 SAVE | 108 |

# Austin and Vicinity

This index helps you "spot" where approved hotels and restaurants are located on the corresponding detailed maps. Hotel daily rate range is for comparison only. Restaurant price range is a combination of lunch and/or dinner. Turn to the listing page for more detailed rate and price information and consult display ads for special promotions.

## AUSTIN

| Map Page | Hotels | Diamond Rated | Rate Range | Page |
|---|---|---|---|---|
| 1 p. 86 | La Quinta Inn & Suites-Austin/Cedar Park-Lakeline | ◆◆◆ | $109-$144 SAVE | 106 |
| 2 p. 86 | La Quinta Inn & Suites Round Rock South | ◆◆◆ | $89-$144 | 106 |
| 3 p. 86 | Extended Stay America Austin Northwest Lakeline Mall | ◆◆ | $54-$69 | 102 |
| 4 p. 86 | Holiday Inn Express Hotel & Suites | ◆◆◆ | $125-$205 | 105 |
| 5 p. 86 | Hampton Inn & Suites Austin/Cedar Park-Lakeline | ◆◆◆ | $99-$149 | 103 |
| 6 p. 86 | Crossland Economy Studios Austin West | ◆ | $39-$49 | 101 |
| 7 p. 86 | Comfort Suites Northwest | ◆◆◆ | $119-$169 | 100 |
| 8 p. 86 | Staybridge Suites Austin Northwest | ◆◆◆ | $129-$259 | 108 |
| 9 p. 86 | Holiday Inn Express Hotel & Suites | ◆◆◆ | Rates not provided | 105 |
| 10 p. 86 | Extended Stay Deluxe (Austin/Northwest/Research Park) | ◆◆ | $64-$74 | 102 |
| 11 p. 86 | Studio 6-Northwest #6032 | ◆◆ | $63-$83 | 108 |
| 12 p. 86 | Hilton Garden Inn | ◆◆◆ | $109-$209 | 104 |
| 13 p. 86 | La Quinta Inn & Suites Austin Mopac North | ◆◆◆ | $109-$184 | 106 |
| 14 p. 86 | Extended Stay America Austin-Arboretum-North | ◆◆◆ | $64-$79 | 102 |
| 15 p. 86 | Fairfield Inn & Suites by Marriott Austin North/Parmer Lane | ◆◆◆ | $127-$142 SAVE | 103 |
| 16 p. 86 | Residence Inn by Marriott-Austin North/Parmer Lane | ◆◆◆ | $125-$171 SAVE | 107 |
| 17 p. 86 | SpringHill Suites by Marriott Austin North/Parmer Lane | ◆◆◆ | $89-$349 SAVE | 107 |
| 18 p. 86 | Aloft Austin at the Domain | ◆◆◆ | $119-$299 SAVE | 99 |
| 19 p. 86 | Hilton Garden Inn Austin North | ◆◆◆ | $99-$399 SAVE | 104 |
| 20 p. 86 | Courtyard by Marriott Austin North/Parmer Lane | ◆◆◆ | $99-$399 SAVE | 101 |
| 21 p. 86 | Fairfield Inn & Suites by Marriott Austin NW | ◆◆◆ | $99-$199 | 103 |

## AUSTIN (cont'd)

| Map Page | Hotels (cont'd) | Diamond Rated | Rate Range | Page |
|---|---|---|---|---|
| 22 p. 86 | **Westin Austin at the Domain** | ◆◆◆◆ | $159-$369 (SAVE) | 109 |
| 23 p. 86 | Homewood Suites by Hilton Arboretum NW | ◆◆◆ | $189-$399 | 105 |
| 24 p. 86 | SpringHill Suites by Marriott Austin NW | ◆◆◆ | $89-$169 | 108 |
| 25 p. 86 | Hampton Inn Northwest | ◆◆◆ | $169-$399 | 103 |
| 26 p. 86 | Staybridge Suites Austin Arboretum | ◆◆◆ | $169-$199 | 108 |
| 27 p. 86 | **Renaissance Austin Hotel** | ◆◆◆◆ | $129-$319 (SAVE) | 107 |
| 28 p. 86 | Extended Stay America Austin Arboretum | ◆◆ | $64-$79 | 102 |
| 29 p. 86 | **HYATT house Austin/Arboretum** | ◆◆◆ | $79-$410 (SAVE) | 105 |
| 30 p. 86 | Candlewood Suites Austin Northwest | ◆◆◆ | Rates not provided | 100 |
| 31 p. 86 | **Embassy Suites Austin Arboretum** | ◆◆◆ | $139-$209 (SAVE) | 102 |
| 32 p. 86 | **Courtyard by Marriott-Austin Northwest/ Arboretum** | ◆◆◆ | $99-$199 (SAVE) | 101 |
| 33 p. 86 | **Hyatt Place Austin/Arboretum** | ◆◆◆ | $89-$449 (SAVE) | 105 |
| 34 p. 86 | Holiday Inn Austin Northwest/Arboretum | ◆◆◆ | Rates not provided | 105 |
| 35 p. 86 | Extended Stay America Austin Arboretum South | ◆◆ | $54-$64 | 102 |
| 36 p. 86 | Econo Lodge | ◆◆ | $60-$149 | 101 |
| 37 p. 86 | Orangewood Inn & Suites Austin-North | ◆◆ | Rates not provided | 107 |
| 38 p. 86 | Hotel Allandale | ◆◆◆ | Rates not provided | 105 |
| 39 p. 86 | **Super 8 Austin North** | ◆◆ | $64-$209 (SAVE) | 108 |
| 40 p. 86 | Extended Stay America Austin-North Central | ◆◆ | $54-$59 | 102 |
| 41 p. 86 | **BEST WESTERN Atrium North** | ◆◆ | $89-$249 (SAVE) | 100 |
| 43 p. 86 | Hampton Inn Austin-North | ◆◆◆ | $99-$149 | 103 |
| 44 p. 86 | **Hyatt Place Austin - North Central** | ◆◆◆ | $79-$219 (SAVE) | 106 |
| 45 p. 86 | **Country Inn & Suites By Carlson North** | ◆◆◆ | Rates not provided (SAVE) | 100 |
| 46 p. 86 | Quality Inn North Austin | ◆◆ | $51-$219 | 107 |
| 47 p. 86 | Drury Inn & Suites-Austin North | ◆◆◆ | $100-$179 | 101 |
| 48 p. 86 | Habitat Suites Hotel | ◆◆◆ | Rates not provided | 103 |
| 49 p. 86 | **DoubleTree by Hilton Austin** | ◆◆◆ | $109-$209 (SAVE) | 101 |
| 50 p. 86 | Crowne Plaza | ◆◆◆ | $129-$299 | 101 |
| 51 p. 86 | **Holiday Inn Austin Midtown** | ◆◆◆ | $99-$239 (SAVE) | 104 |
| 52 p. 86 | La Quinta Inn Austin Highland Mall | ◆◆ | $75-$154 | 106 |
| 53 p. 86 | Embassy Suites Austin Central | ◆◆◆ | $116-$151 | 102 |
| 54 p. 86 | **Fairfield Inn & Suites by Marriott-Austin Central** | ◆◆◆ | $89-$299 (SAVE) | 103 |
| 55 p. 86 | **Courtyard by Marriott Austin-University Area** | ◆◆◆ | $89-$299 (SAVE) | 101 |
| 56 p. 86 | **Super 8 University Austin** | ◆◆ | $85-$410 (SAVE) | 108 |
| 57 p. 86 | **Omni Barton Creek Resort & Spa** | ◆◆◆◆ | $149-$499 (SAVE) | 107 |
| 58 p. 86 | **Super 8-183/Airport** | ◆◆◆ | $79-$360 (SAVE) | 108 |
| 59 p. 86 | La Quinta Inn & Suites Austin Southwest at Mopac | ◆◆◆ | $119-$214 | 106 |

## AUSTIN (cont'd)

| Map Page | Hotels (cont'd) | Diamond Rated | Rate Range | Page |
|---|---|---|---|---|
| **60** p. 86 | Extended Stay America Austin Southwest | ♦♦ | $64-$74 | 102 |
| **61** p. 86 | Hampton Inn Austin/Oak Hill | ♦♦♦ | $99-$169 | 103 |
| **62** p. 86 | **Holiday Inn Express Sunset Valley** | ♦♦♦ | $129-$139 (SAVE) | 105 |
| **63** p. 86 | **BEST WESTERN PLUS Austin City Hotel** | ♦♦♦ | $120-$180 (SAVE) | 100 |
| **64** p. 86 | La Quinta Inn Austin Oltorf | ♦♦ | $85-$154 | 106 |
| **65** p. 86 | **Howard Johnson** | ♦♦ | $55-$100 (SAVE) | 105 |
| **66** p. 86 | **Wyndham Garden Hotel** | ♦♦♦ | $89-$169 (SAVE) | 109 |
| **67** p. 86 | Staybridge Suites Austin Airport | ♦♦♦ | Rates not provided | 108 |
| **68** p. 86 | **BEST WESTERN PLUS Austin Airport Inn & Suites** | ♦♦♦ | $110-$150 (SAVE) | 100 |
| **69** p. 86 | **Courtyard by Marriott Austin Airport** | ♦♦♦ | $99-$599 (SAVE) | 101 |
| **70** p. 86 | La Quinta Inn & Suites Austin Airport | ♦♦♦ | $115-$160 | 106 |
| **71** p. 86 | Hampton Inn & Suites | ♦♦♦ | $139-$189 | 103 |
| **72** p. 86 | Holiday Inn Express & Suites Austin Airport | ♦♦♦ | $90-$299 | 105 |
| **73** p. 86 | Comfort Suites Airport | ♦♦♦ | $99-$199 | 100 |
| **74** p. 86 | La Quinta Inn Austin South/IH-35 | ♦♦ | $79-$154 | 106 |
| **75** p. 86 | **Omni Austin Hotel Southpark** | ♦♦♦♦ | $109-$799 (SAVE) | 106 |
| **76** p. 86 | Hampton Inn Austin-South | ♦♦♦ | Rates not provided | 103 |
| **77** p. 86 | **Homewood Suites-Austin South/Airport** | ♦♦♦ | $139-$349 (SAVE) | 105 |
| **78** p. 86 | Candlewood Suites-South | ♦♦♦ | $69-$159 | 100 |
| **79** p. 86 | **Comfort Suites-South** | ♦♦♦ | $100-$400 (SAVE) | 100 |
| **80** p. 86 | **Baymont Inn & Suites Austin** | ♦♦ | $59-$159 (SAVE) | 100 |
| **81** p. 86 | Austin Airport Marriott South | ♦♦♦ | $119-$599 | 99 |
| **82** p. 86 | **Hilton Austin Airport** (See ad p. 104.) | ♦♦♦ | $109-$269 (SAVE) | 104 |
| **83** p. 86 | **SpringHill Suites by Marriott Austin Airport/South** | ♦♦♦ | $99-$459 (SAVE) | 107 |
| **84** p. 86 | **Super 8 Austin Airport South** | ♦♦♦ | $99-$360 (SAVE) | 108 |
| **85** p. 86 | **Fairfield Inn & Suites by Marriott Austin Airport/South** | ♦♦♦ | $79-$399 (SAVE) | 103 |
| **86** p. 86 | **Courtyard by Marriott Austin Airport/South** | ♦♦♦ | $99-$499 (SAVE) | 101 |
| **87** p. 86 | **Residence Inn by Marriott Austin Airport/South** | ♦♦♦ | $110-$800 (SAVE) | 107 |
| **88** p. 86 | **Quality Inn & Suites Airport** | ♦♦♦ | $80-$130 (SAVE) | 107 |

| Map Page | Restaurants | Diamond Rated | Cuisine | Price Range | Page |
|---|---|---|---|---|---|
| **1** p. 86 | Z'Tejas Southwestern Grill | ♦♦♦ | Southwestern | $10-$26 | 114 |
| **2** p. 86 | Texican Cafe-Lakeline | ♦♦ | Tex-Mex | $8-$25 | 113 |
| **3** p. 86 | Plucker's Lakeline | ♦♦ | Wings | $8-$20 | 112 |
| **4** p. 86 | Freda's Seafood Grill | ♦♦♦ | Seafood Steak | $10-$30 | 110 |
| **5** p. 86 | Cover 2 | ♦♦ | American | $7-$15 | 110 |
| **6** p. 86 | Reale's Pizza and Cafe | ♦♦ | Southern Italian | $8-$20 | 112 |
| **7** p. 86 | Kerbey Lane Cafe--Northwest | ♦ | Breakfast Comfort Food | $7-$13 | 111 |
| **8** p. 86 | Wings 'n More | ♦♦ | Wings | $6-$28 | 114 |

| Map Page | Restaurants (cont'd) | Diamond Rated | Cuisine | Price Range | Page |
|---|---|---|---|---|---|
| ⑨ p. 86 | Bone Daddy's House of Smoke | ▽▽ | American | $9-$22 | 109 |
| ⑩ p. 86 | Tacodeli Northwest | ▽ | Mexican | $3-$7 | 113 |
| ⑪ p. 86 | Fleming's Prime Steakhouse & Wine Bar | ▽▽▽ | American | $16-$46 | 110 |
| ⑫ p. 86 | Jasper's | ▽▽▽ | Steak Seafood | $10-$42 | 111 |
| ⑬ p. 86 | Kona Grill | ▽▽▽ | Fusion | $10-$30 | 111 |
| ⑭ p. 86 | Urban, An American Grill | ▽▽▽ | American | $10-$29 | 114 |
| ⑮ p. 86 | Roaring Fork Stonelake | ▽▽▽ | Steak | $10-$36 | 112 |
| ⑯ p. 86 | Brick Oven--Arboretum | ▽▽ | Italian Pizza | $7-$22 | 109 |
| ⑰ p. 86 | Saltgrass Steakhouse | ▽▽ | Western Steak | $9-$30 SAVE | 112 |
| ⑱ p. 86 | Truluck's | ▽▽▽ | Seafood Steak | $26-$50 | 113 |
| ⑲ p. 86 | Banderas | ▽▽▽ | American | $13-$30 | 109 |
| ⑳ p. 86 | The Cheesecake Factory | ▽▽▽ | American | $9-$30 | 110 |
| ㉑ p. 86 | Estancia Churrascaria Arboretum | ▽▽▽ | Brazilian Steak | $22-$36 | 110 |
| ㉒ p. 86 | Mighty Fine | ▽ | Burgers | $4-$6 | 111 |
| ㉓ p. 86 | Blue Baker | ▽ | American | $6-$11 | 109 |
| ㉔ p. 86 | Steiner Ranch Steakhouse | ▽▽▽ | Steak | $19-$48 | 113 |
| ㉕ p. 86 | Iron Cactus Southwestern Grill | ▽▽▽ | Southwestern | $7-$25 | 111 |
| ㉖ p. 86 | North by Northwest Restaurant and Brewery | ▽▽▽ | American | $8-$24 | 111 |
| ㉗ p. 86 | Z'Tejas Southwestern Grill | ▽▽▽ | Southwestern | $10-$26 | 114 |
| ㉘ p. 86 | Eddie V's Edgewater Grille-Arboretum | ▽▽▽ | Steak Seafood | $19-$48 | 110 |
| ㉙ p. 86 | Andiamo Ristorante | ▽▽▽ | Italian | $10-$30 | 109 |
| ㉚ p. 86 | Mikado Ryotei | ▽▽▽ | Japanese Small Plates Sushi | $9-$32 | 111 |
| ㉛ p. 86 | Waterloo Ice House Northwest | ▽▽ | American | $8-$15 | 114 |
| ㉜ p. 86 | Satay Restaurant | ▽▽ | Thai | $10-$22 | 112 |
| ㉝ p. 86 | Siena Ristorante Toscano | ▽▽▽ | Northern Italian | $10-$49 | 113 |
| ㉞ p. 86 | Cover 3 | ▽▽▽ | American | $10-$36 | 110 |
| ㉟ p. 86 | County Line On The Lake | ▽▽ | Barbecue | $9-$23 | 110 |
| ㊱ p. 86 | Hopdoddy Burger Bar | ▽ | Burgers | $6-$12 | 111 |
| ㊲ p. 86 | Bartlett's | ▽▽▽ | American | $10-$34 | 109 |
| ㊳ p. 86 | Tarka Indian Kitchen | ▽ | Indian | $7-$9 | 113 |
| ㊴ p. 86 | Chez Zee American Bistro | ▽▽ | American | $9-$29 | 110 |
| ㊵ p. 86 | Trento | ▽▽ | Italian | $9-$24 | 113 |
| ㊶ p. 86 | Taj Palace Indian Restaurant & Bar | ▽▽ | Indian | $10-$20 | 113 |
| ㊷ p. 86 | Fonda San Miguel | ▽▽▽ | Mexican | $17-$40 | 110 |
| ㊸ p. 86 | Kerbey Lane Cafe-Central | ▽▽ | Breakfast Comfort Food | $7-$13 | 111 |
| ㊹ p. 86 | Central Market Cafe | ▽ | American | $7-$15 | 109 |
| ㊺ p. 86 | Waterloo Ice House Avery Ranch | ▽▽ | American | $6-$15 | 114 |
| ㊻ p. 86 | County Line On The Hill | ▽▽ | Regional Barbecue | $9-$23 | 110 |

| Map Page | Restaurants (cont'd) | Diamond Rated | Cuisine | Price Range | Page |
|---|---|---|---|---|---|
| ㊼ p. 86 | Mozart's Coffee Roasters | ◆ | Coffee/Tea Breads/Pastries | $2-$6 | 111 |
| ㊽ p. 86 | **Hill Country Dining Room** | ◆◆◆ | American | $23-$45 | 110 |
| ㊾ p. 86 | 8212 Wine Bar & Grill | ◆◆◆ | American | $13-$24 | 109 |
| ㊿ p. 86 | Kerbey Lane Cafe-UT | ◆◆ | Breakfast Comfort Food | $7-$13 | 111 |
| 51 p. 86 | Eastside Cafe | ◆◆◆ | Continental | $10-$24 | 110 |
| 52 p. 86 | Beets Cafe | ◆◆ | Vegan | $8-$14 | 109 |
| 53 p. 86 | Tacodeli Central | ◆ | Mexican | $3-$7 | 113 |
| 54 p. 86 | Uchi | ◆◆ | Japanese Sushi Small Plates | $10-$42 | 113 |
| 55 p. 86 | Perla's Seafood & Oyster Bar | ◆◆◆ | Regional Seafood | $10-$38 | 112 |
| 56 p. 86 | Hopdoddy Burger Bar | ◆ | Burgers | $6-$12 | 111 |
| 57 p. 86 | Vespaio | ◆◆◆ | Italian | $17-$32 | 114 |
| 58 p. 86 | Matt's El Rancho | ◆◆ | Tex-Mex | $7-$33 | 111 |
| 59 p. 86 | Texican Cafe Brodie Oaks | ◆◆ | Tex-Mex | $8-$25 | 113 |
| 60 p. 86 | Nueva Onda | ◆ | Mexican | $2-$9 | 112 |
| 61 p. 86 | Onion Creek Grill | ◆◆◆ | American | $8-$31 | 112 |
| 62 p. 86 | Twin Peaks | ◆◆ | Comfort Food Sandwiches | $7-$16 | 113 |

## CEDAR PARK

| Map Page | Hotels | Diamond Rated | Rate Range | Page |
|---|---|---|---|---|
| 91 p. 86 | Candlewood Suites | ◆◆◆ | $89-$159 | 137 |
| 92 p. 86 | Holiday Inn Express Hotel & Suites | ◆◆◆ | $89-$169 | 137 |
| 93 p. 86 | La Quinta Inn & Suites Austin - Cedar Park | ◆◆◆ | $102-$164 | 137 |
| 94 p. 86 | **BEST WESTERN Cedar Inn** | ◆◆ | $85-$119 SAVE | 137 |
| 95 p. 86 | **Comfort Inn** | ◆◆ | $65-$200 SAVE | 137 |

| Map Page | Restaurants | Diamond Rated | Cuisine | Price Range | Page |
|---|---|---|---|---|---|
| 68 p. 86 | Bellini's Texas Grill | ◆◆ | Comfort Food | $6-$14 | 137 |
| 69 p. 86 | Reunion Grille | ◆◆ | Comfort Food | $9-$19 | 137 |
| 70 p. 86 | Mighty Fine | ◆ | Burgers | $4-$6 | 137 |
| 71 p. 86 | C. R. Surf and Turf | ◆◆ | Seafood Steak | $7-$34 | 137 |
| 72 p. 86 | 1431 Cafe | ◆◆ | Breakfast Comfort Food | $5-$10 | 137 |
| 73 p. 86 | Hemingway Restaurant and Bar | ◆◆ | American | $7-$17 | 137 |

## ROUND ROCK

| Map Page | Hotels | Diamond Rated | Rate Range | Page |
|---|---|---|---|---|
| 98 p. 86 | SpringHill Suites by Marriott | ◆◆◆ | $83-$139 | 452 |
| 99 p. 86 | Courtyard by Marriott Austin Round Rock | ◆◆◆ | $89-$139 | 452 |
| 100 p. 86 | **Holiday Inn Austin North Round Rock** | ◆◆◆ | Rates not provided SAVE | 452 |
| 101 p. 86 | Holiday Inn Express & Suites | ◆◆◆ | $105-$119 | 452 |
| 102 p. 86 | Hilton Garden Inn | ◆◆◆ | $99-$149 | 452 |
| 103 p. 86 | La Quinta Inn & Suites Austin Round Rock North | ◆◆◆ | $89-$144 | 452 |

## ROUND ROCK (cont'd)

| Map Page | Hotels (cont'd) | Diamond Rated | Rate Range | Page |
|---|---|---|---|---|
| 104 p. 86 | **BEST WESTERN Executive Inn** | ◈◈ | $87-$129 SAVE | 451 |
| 105 p. 86 | **Country Inn & Suites By Carlson** | ◈◈◈ | $89-$109 SAVE | 452 |
| 106 p. 86 | Comfort Suites | ◈◈◈ | $89-$299 | 452 |
| 107 p. 86 | Candlewood Suites | ◈◈◈ | Rates not provided | 451 |
| 108 p. 86 | Extended Stay America Austin-Round Rock-N | ◈◈ | $49-$59 | 452 |
| 109 p. 86 | Staybridge Suites Austin-Round Rock | ◈◈◈ | $104-$189 | 453 |
| 110 p. 86 | Homewood Suites by Hilton | ◈◈◈ | $129-$179 | 452 |
| 111 p. 86 | Hampton Inn Austin-Round Rock | ◈◈◈ | $109-$199 | 452 |
| 112 p. 86 | **Residence Inn by Marriott Austin Round Rock** | ◈◈◈ | $89-$319 SAVE | 452 |
| 113 p. 86 | Austin Marriott North | ◈◈◈ | $100-$300 | 451 |

| Map Page | Restaurants | Diamond Rated | Cuisine | Price Range | Page |
|---|---|---|---|---|---|
| 76 p. 86 | Saltgrass Steakhouse | ◈◈ | Steak | $9-$31 SAVE | 453 |
| 77 p. 86 | The Salt Lick Bar-B-Que | ◈◈ | Barbecue | $9-$23 | 453 |
| 78 p. 86 | La Margarita | ◈◈ | Mexican | $7-$16 | 453 |
| 79 p. 86 | French Quarter | ◈◈◈ | Southern American | $10-$36 | 453 |
| 81 p. 86 | Main Street Grill | ◈◈◈ | American | $9-$35 | 453 |
| 82 p. 86 | Thai Spoon Restaurant | ◈◈ | Thai | $6-$7 | 453 |
| 83 p. 86 | Gino's Italian Restaurant | ◈◈ | Italian | $8-$22 | 453 |
| 84 p. 86 | River City Grill | ◈◈ | American | $9-$32 | 453 |

## PFLUGERVILLE

| Map Page | Hotel | Diamond Rated | Rate Range | Page |
|---|---|---|---|---|
| 116 p. 86 | **Comfort Suites Austin (Pflugerville)** | ◈◈◈ | $100-$300 SAVE | 436 |

| Map Page | Restaurant | Diamond Rated | Cuisine | Price Range | Page |
|---|---|---|---|---|---|
| 87 p. 86 | Fish Daddy's Grill House | ◈◈ | American | $7-$15 | 436 |

## LEANDER

| Map Page | Restaurant | Diamond Rated | Cuisine | Price Range | Page |
|---|---|---|---|---|---|
| 65 p. 86 | Luigi's Ristorante Italiano | ◈◈ | Italian | $7-$16 | 395 |

# DOWNTOWN AUSTIN

• Restaurants p. 97
• Hotels & Restaurants map & index p. 83

## THE AT&T EXECUTIVE EDUCATION AND CONFERENCE CENTER
(512)404-1900 **2**

Hotel
$159-$329

**Address:** 1900 University Ave 78705 **Location:** Jct Martin Luther King Jr Blvd and University Ave; uptown. **Facility:** Adjacent to the University of Texas, this hotel offers upscale lodging and conference facilities. 297 units. 7 stories, interior corridors. **Terms:** 2-3 night minimum stay, cancellation fee imposed. **Amenities:** safes. **Dining:** 2 restaurants. **Pool(s):** heated outdoor. **Activities:** massage. **Guest Services:** valet laundry.

## COURTYARD BY MARRIOTT AUSTIN DOWNTOWN/ CONVENTION CENTER
(512)236-8008 **10**

Hotel
$160-$500

COURTYARD Marriott  **AAA Benefit:** Members save 5% or more!

**Address:** 300 E 4th St 78701 **Location:** Between Trinity St and San Jacinto Blvd. **Facility:** 270 units. 11 stories, interior corridors. **Parking:** on-site (fee) and valet. **Pool(s):** heated indoor. **Activities:** hot tub, exercise room. **Guest Services:** valet and coin laundry.

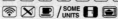

(See map & index p. 83.)

## DOUBLETREE BY HILTON HOTEL AUSTIN - UNIVERSITY AREA
(512)479-4000 **4**

WWW Hotel $99-$179 **Address:** 1617 I-35 N 78702 **Location:** I-35 exit Martin Luther King Jr Blvd, just n on northbound frontage road. **Facility:** 149 units. 6 stories, interior corridors. **Terms:** 1-7 night minimum stay, cancellation fee imposed. **Pool(s):** outdoor. **Activities:** exercise room. **Guest Services:** valet and coin laundry.

**AAA Benefit:** Members save 5% or more!

[icons]

## DOUBLETREE SUITES BY HILTON HOTEL AUSTIN
(512)478-7000 **3**

WWW Hotel $169-$399 **Address:** 303 W 15th St 78701 **Location:** Just nw of state capitol building. **Facility:** 188 kitchen units, some two bedrooms. 15 stories, interior corridors. **Parking:** on-site (fee) and valet. **Terms:** 1-7 night minimum stay, cancellation fee imposed. **Dining:** 15th Street Cafe, see separate listing. **Pool(s):** heated outdoor. **Activities:** hot tub, exercise room. **Guest Services:** valet and coin laundry, area transportation.

**AAA Benefit:** Members save 5% or more!

[icons]

## THE DRISKILL
(512)474-5911 **9**

WWW
Classic Historic Hotel
$179-$649

**HYATT**

**AAA Benefit:** Members save 10%!

**Address:** 604 Brazos St 78701 **Location:** Jct 6th St. **Facility:** Named after cattle baron Colonel Jesse Driskill, this landmark has been a grand dame of Austin hotels since it was built in 1886. Displays of historic artwork and artifacts are featured. 189 units, some two bedrooms. 5-12 stories, interior corridors. **Parking:** valet only. **Terms:** cancellation fee imposed. **Amenities:** safes. **Dining:** 1886 Cafe and Bakery, The Driskill Grill, see separate listings, entertainment. **Activities:** steamroom, massage. **Guest Services:** valet laundry.

[icons]

## EMBASSY SUITES HOTEL-DOWNTOWN
(512)469-9000 **19**

WWW Hotel $132-$284 **Address:** 300 S Congress Ave 78704 **Location:** Just s of Congress Avenue Bridge. **Facility:** 261 units, some two bedrooms. 9 stories, interior corridors. **Terms:** 1-7 night minimum stay, cancellation fee imposed. **Pool(s):** heated indoor. **Activities:** hot tub, exercise room. **Guest Services:** valet and coin laundry, area transportation.

**AAA Benefit:** Members save 5% or more!

[icons]

## EXTENDED STAY AMERICA-AUSTIN/DOWNTOWN/TOWN LAKE
(512)476-1818 **20**

WWW **Extended Stay Hotel** $74-$99 **Address:** 507 S 1st St 78704 **Location:** I-35 exit 234B southbound; exit 234A northbound, 1.8 mi w on Cesar Chavez St/E 1st St, then 0.5 mi s. **Facility:** 130 units, some efficiencies. 3 stories, interior corridors. **Terms:** cancellation fee imposed. **Guest Services:** coin laundry.

[icons]

## FOUR SEASONS HOTEL
512/478-4500 **17**

WWW WWW
Hotel
Rates not provided

**Address:** 98 San Jacinto Blvd 78701 **Location:** Jct Congress Ave and Cesar Chavez St; 2 blks e on Lady Bird Lake Tr. **Facility:** This luxury hotel features a scenic lakeside setting; guest rooms are decorated in a sophisticated Southwestern style. 291 units, some two bedrooms. 9 stories, interior corridors. **Parking:** valet only. **Amenities:** safes. **Dining:** Trio, see separate listing, entertainment. **Pool(s):** heated outdoor. **Activities:** steamroom, bicycles, spa. **Guest Services:** valet laundry.

[icons]

## HILTON AUSTIN
512/482-8000 **13**

WWW WWW
Hotel
Rates not provided

**Hilton**
HOTELS & RESORTS

**AAA Benefit:** Members save 5% or more!

**Address:** 500 E 4th St 78701 **Location:** Jct 4th and Neches sts. **Facility:** Upscale accommodations and services are the rule at this hotel conveniently located next to the convention center. 800 units. 31 stories, interior corridors. **Parking:** on-site and valet. **Amenities:** safes. **Dining:** Finn & Porter, see separate listing. **Pool(s):** heated outdoor. **Activities:** sauna, hot tub, steamroom, spa. **Guest Services:** valet laundry.

[icons]

## HILTON GARDEN INN AUSTIN DOWNTOWN
(512)480-8181 **14**

WWW Hotel $109-$299 **Address:** 500 N I-35 78701 **Location:** I-35 exit 234B southbound; exit 234C northbound; on southbound frontage road. **Facility:** 254 units. 18 stories, interior corridors. **Parking:** on-site (fee) and valet. **Terms:** 1-7 night minimum stay, cancellation fee imposed. **Pool(s):** outdoor. **Activities:** hot tub, exercise room. **Guest Services:** valet and coin laundry.

**AAA Benefit:** Members save up to 10%!

[icons]

(See map & index p. 83.)

**HOLIDAY INN LADY BIRD LAKE**   512/472-8211  **21**

Hotel
Rates not provided

**Address:** 20 N I-35 78701 **Location:** I-35 exit 233. **Facility:** 322 units. 11-14 stories, interior corridors. **Pool(s):** heated outdoor. **Activities:** bicycles, game room, exercise room. **Guest Services:** valet and coin laundry, area transportation.

**HOTEL ELLA**   (512)495-1800  **1**

Classic Boutique Hotel
$229-$499

**Address:** 1900 Rio Grande St 78705 **Location:** Jct Rio Grande St and Martin Luther King Jr Blvd. **Facility:** This boutique hotel with distinctive architecture and upscale ambience is in a historic area convenient to downtown destinations. 48 units. 2-3 stories, interior corridors. **Terms:** 3 day cancellation notice-fee imposed. **Activities:** massage.

**HOTEL SAINT CECELIA**   512/852-2400  **22**

Boutique Hotel. Rates not provided. **Address:** 112 Academy Dr 78704 **Location:** Jct S Congress Ave and Riverside Dr, 2 blks s. **Facility:** In a quiet residential neighborhood just one block from the South Congress Avenue social scene, the beautiful property offers upscale accommodations. 14 units. 2-3 stories (no elevator), exterior corridors. **Pool(s):** heated outdoor. **Guest Services:** valet laundry.

**HYATT PLACE AUSTIN DOWNTOWN**   (512)476-4440  **15**

Hotel
$179-$799

**HYATT PLACE**
**AAA Benefit:** Members save 10%!

**Address:** 211 E 3rd St 78701 **Location:** Corner of Brazos and 3rd sts. **Facility:** 296 units. 18 stories, interior corridors. **Parking:** on-site (fee) and valet. **Terms:** cancellation fee imposed. **Pool(s):** heated indoor. **Activities:** exercise room. **Guest Services:** valet laundry. **Featured Amenity:** breakfast buffet.

**HYATT REGENCY AUSTIN**   (512)477-1234  **18**

Hotel
$99-$399

**HYATT REGENCY**
**AAA Benefit:** Members save 10%!

**Address:** 208 Barton Springs Rd 78704 **Location:** At south end of Congress Avenue Bridge; on south bank of Town Lake. **Facility:** Well-appointed accommodations await travelers at this hotel set on the Colorado River with excellent views of downtown. 448 units, some two bedrooms. 17 stories, interior corridors. **Parking:** on-site (fee) and valet. **Terms:** check-in 4 pm, cancellation fee imposed. **Amenities:** safes. **Pool(s):** outdoor. **Activities:** hot tub, bicycles, exercise room, massage. **Guest Services:** valet and coin laundry.

▼ See AAA listing p. 97 ▼

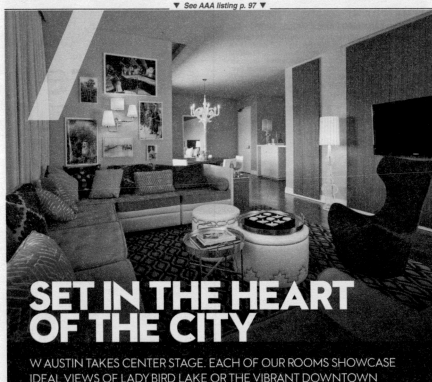

# SET IN THE HEART OF THE CITY

W AUSTIN TAKES CENTER STAGE. EACH OF OUR ROOMS SHOWCASE IDEAL VIEWS OF LADY BIRD LAKE OR THE VIBRANT DOWNTOWN SKYLINE. WHEN IT'S TIME FOR A BITE, INDULGE IN TRACE, SERVING LOCALLY SOURCED PLATES FROM SURROUNDING FARMS. IF IT'S ALONE TIME YOU'RE AFTER, DISAPPEAR TO AWAY® SPA, WHERE CUSTOM TREATMENTS AWAIT.

CONTEMPORARY IN DESIGN, WITH WHATEVER/WHENEVER® SERVICE, W AUSTIN IS A TRUE RETREAT.

200 LAVACA STREET AUSTIN, TEXAS 78701  512.542.3600

**WHOTELS.COM/AUSTIN**

**W**

AUSTIN

# Make the Most of Your Trip

## Download eTourBook® Guides at
## AAA.com/ebooks

(See map & index p. 83.)

## INTERCONTINENTAL STEPHEN F. AUSTIN HOTEL
(512)457-8800  8

Classic Hotel
$159-$599

**Address:** 701 Congress Ave 78701 **Location:** Northeast corner of 7th St and Congress Ave. **Facility:** Located in a building dating from 1924 and centered in the midst of all downtown destinations, this hotel offers a historic stay with modern conveniences and amenities expected in today's marketplace. 190 units. 16 stories, interior corridors. **Parking:** valet only. **Terms:** cancellation fee imposed. **Amenities:** safes. **Dining:** Roaring Fork, see separate listing. **Pool(s):** heated indoor. **Activities:** hot tub, exercise room. **Guest Services:** valet laundry.

## LA QUINTA INN AUSTIN CAPITOL
(512)476-1166  6

 Hotel $119-$224 **Address:** 300 E 11th St 78701 **Location:** Just e of state capitol building. **Facility:** 150 units. 4 stories, interior/exterior corridors. **Parking:** valet only. **Pool(s):** outdoor. **Activities:** exercise room. **Guest Services:** valet laundry.

## OMNI AUSTIN HOTEL DOWNTOWN  (512)476-3700  7

Hotel
$169-$649

**Address:** 700 San Jacinto Blvd 78701 **Location:** At 8th St and San Jacinto Blvd. **Facility:** This hotel offers large accommodations and is within walking distance of many of Austin's attractions. 392 units, some two bedrooms and kitchens. 20 stories, interior corridors. **Parking:** on-site (fee) and valet. **Terms:** cancellation fee imposed. **Amenities:** safes. **Pool(s):** heated outdoor. **Activities:** hot tub, exercise room, massage. **Guest Services:** valet laundry.

## RADISSON HOTEL & SUITES-AUSTIN  (512)478-9611  16

Hotel $159-$609 **Address:** 111 E Cesar Chavez St 78701 **Location:** At 1st St and Congress Ave. **Facility:** 413 units. 12 stories, interior corridors. **Parking:** on-site (fee) and valet. **Terms:** cancellation fee imposed. **Amenities:** safes. **Pool(s):** outdoor. **Activities:** bicycles, exercise room, massage. **Guest Services:** valet laundry.

## RESIDENCE INN BY MARRIOTT AUSTIN/DOWNTOWN/CONVENTION CENTER
(512)472-5553  11

Extended Stay
Contemporary
Hotel
$170-$500

**AAA Benefit:** Members save 5% or more!

**Address:** 300 E 4th St 78701 **Location:** Between Trinity St and San Jacinto Blvd. **Facility:** 179 efficiencies, some two bedrooms. 12 stories, interior corridors. **Parking:** on-site (fee) and valet. **Pool(s):** heated indoor. **Activities:** hot tub, exercise room. **Guest Services:** valet and coin laundry. **Featured Amenity:** breakfast buffet.

## SUPER 8 CENTRAL
(512)472-8331  5

Motel
$79-$205

**Address:** 1201 N I-35 78702 **Location:** I-35 exit 234; at 12th St. **Facility:** 60 units, some two bedrooms. 2 stories (no elevator), exterior corridors. **Terms:** cancellation fee imposed. **Pool(s):** outdoor. **Guest Services:** coin laundry. **Featured Amenity:** continental breakfast.

## W AUSTIN
(512)542-3600  12

 Contemporary Hotel $299-$609

**AAA Benefit:** Special member room rates, plus Starwood Preferred Guest® bonuses!

**Address:** 200 Lavaca St 78701 **Location:** At Lavaca and 2nd sts. **Facility:** The hotel offers upscale, contemporary accommodations in the heart of downtown with easy access to dining and the entertainment district. A professional staff provides exceptional guest services. 251 units, some two bedrooms. 11 stories, interior corridors. **Parking:** valet only. **Terms:** cancellation fee imposed. **Amenities:** safes. **Pool(s):** heated outdoor. **Activities:** bicycles, exercise room, spa. **Guest Services:** valet laundry, area transportation. *(See ad p. 96.)*

## WHERE TO EAT

### 15TH STREET CAFE
512/478-7000  4

American. Casual Dining. $7-$26 **AAA Inspector Notes:** Steaks, chicken and seafood selections, as well as daily special meals, can be sampled in a contemporary setting. **Features:** full bar. **Address:** 303 W 15th St 78701 **Location:** Just nw of state capitol building; in DoubleTree Suites by Hilton Hotel Austin. **Parking:** on-site (fee). B  L  D

### 1886 CAFE AND BAKERY
512/474-5911  13

American. Casual Dining. $10-$18 **AAA Inspector Notes:** *Classic Historic.* In a historically renovated area of the famous hotel, the upscale restaurant serves distinctive breakfasts; lighter lunches of burgers, gourmet pizza and sandwiches; and full dinners such as steaks, seafood and chicken. Desserts, including the specialty sundaes, are prepared fresh on site. A children's menu is available. **Features:** full bar. **Address:** 604 Brazos St 78701 **Location:** Jct 6th St; In The Driskill. **Parking:** valet and street only. B  L  D  CALL

### III FORKS
512/474-1776  24

 Steak Seafood Fine Dining $25-$60

**AAA Inspector Notes:** All beef products served here are USDA Prime and include favorites such as filet mignon, bone-in-rib-eye, New York Strip, prime rib, burgers and pork chops. Seafood delicacies feature ahi tuna, shrimp, scallops and crab. The menu also offers Australian lobster, Chilean sea bass, lamb and Atlantic salmon. Staff members peruse the dining room serving fresh sliced and seasoned scallions and tomatoes. Finish off with homemade desserts which include a delectable bread pudding. **Features:** full bar. **Reservations:** suggested. **Address:** 111 Lavaca St 78701 **Location:** Jct Lavaca and Caesar Chavez sts. **Parking:** valet and street only. D

**USDA Prime beef, fresh fish, cold-water lobster tails**

**(See map & index p. 83.)**

BRICK OVEN RESTAURANT          512/477-7006  **5**
♦♦ ♦♦ Italian. Casual Dining. $8-$20 **AAA Inspector Notes:** Menu highlights include Italian favorites such as calzones, stromboli, pizza and pasta dishes. **Features:** full bar. **Address:** 1209 Red River St 78701 **Location:** Jct 12th and Red River sts. L  D

---

**CANTINA LAREDO**          512/542-9670  **20**

♦♦ ♦♦

Mexican
Casual Dining
$9-$26

**AAA Inspector Notes:** Modern yet relaxed, this restaurant features creative Mexican fare. A great starter of top-shelf guacamole, which is prepared tableside, primes the palate for an entree of enchiladas, tacos, fajitas and chiles rellenos. **Features:** full bar, Sunday brunch. **Address:** 201 W 3rd St 78701 **Location:** 1 blk w of Congress Ave. L  D

**Gourmet Mexican food,
fresh-squeezed lime margaritas**

---

THE CARILLON          512/404-3655  **2**
♦♦♦ American. Casual Dining. $17-$70 **AAA Inspector Notes:** Evening selections feature seafood, steaks and lamb, while luncheons are themed buffets. I particularly enjoyed the Cajun offerings during my visit. **Features:** full bar. **Address:** 1900 University Ave 78705 **Location:** Jct Martin Luther King Jr Blvd and University Ave; uptown. **Parking:** on-site and valet. B  L  D  CALL ♿M

CARMELO'S RISTORANTE          512/477-7497  **18**
♦♦♦ Northern Italian. Fine Dining. $14-$42 **AAA Inspector Notes:** *Historic.* Built in 1872, the oldest standing train depot in Texas has become home to one of the area's most romantic eateries. An Italian patio with a garden and fountain makes a lovely scene in which to enjoy pasta, seafood, beef and chicken dishes. **Features:** full bar. **Reservations:** suggested, weekends. **Address:** 504 E 5th St 78701 **Location:** I-35 exit 3rd and 8th sts, just w. **Parking:** valet only. L  D

CLAY PIT          512/322-5131  **3**
♦♦♦ Indian. Casual Dining. $8-$20 **AAA Inspector Notes:** A contemporary Indian-fusion style characterizes preparations of chicken, steak, lamb, prawns and mixed-grill ingredients. The establishment occupies a late 1800s mercantile. **Features:** full bar. **Address:** 1601 Guadalupe St 78701 **Location:** I-35 exit 15th St, 7 blks w to Guadalupe St, then 1 blk n on southbound lanes. L  D

---

**THE DRISKILL GRILL**          512/474-5911  **12**

♦♦♦ ♦♦♦

New
American
Fine Dining
$32-$85

**AAA Inspector Notes:** *Classic Historic.* Attentive, discreet service accents the experience at the intimate, elegant restaurant. Innovative preparations of seafood, steak, lamb and specialty items are pleasingly presented in an elegant manner. I particularly enjoyed the rib-eye steak served with Peruvian purple potatoes, but don't shy away from the quail, lobster, duck or lamb chops. Menus vary each day, with only the freshest ingredients presented for your dining enjoyment. **Features:** full bar. **Reservations:** suggested. **Address:** 604 Brazos St 78701 **Location:** Jct 6th St; in The Driskill. **Parking:** valet only. D  CALL ♿M

EDDIE V'S EDGEWATER GRILL-DOWNTOWN
512/472-1860  **16**
♦♦♦ Steak Seafood. Fine Dining. $19-$48 **AAA Inspector Notes:** A nice variety of appetizers and a good wine list complement the many seafood and prime steak entrées. The atmosphere is definitely upscale. **Features:** full bar, happy hour. **Address:** 301 E 5th 78701 **Location:** At San Jacinto Blvd. **Parking:** on-site and valet. D  CALL ♿M

FINN & PORTER          512/482-8000  **22**
♦♦♦ ♦♦♦ Steak. Fine Dining. $24-$48 **AAA Inspector Notes:** Excellent presentations are delivered in the modern, upscale restaurant, which projects a relaxed ambience. Selections of lamb, beef, veal and chicken, as well as a multitude of seafood entrees, tempt the customer. **Features:** full bar. **Reservations:** suggested. **Address:** 500 E 4th St 78701 **Location:** Jct 4th and Neches sts; in Hilton Austin. **Parking:** valet and street only. D

FLEMING'S PRIME STEAKHOUSE & WINE BAR
512/457-1500  **27**
♦♦♦ ♦♦♦ American. Fine Dining. $16-$46 **AAA Inspector Notes:** The warm, clubby atmosphere is the ideal setting for perfectly grilled steaks and seafood. Side dishes come in hearty portions, and salads are fresh and crisp. More than 100 wine selections are available. **Features:** full bar. **Reservations:** suggested. **Address:** 320 E 2nd St 78701 **Location:** I-35 exit Cesar Chavez St, 3 blks w to Trinity St, then 1 blk n; across from convention center. **Parking:** valet and street only. D

FOGO DE CHAO          512/472-0220  **25**
♦♦♦ Brazilian Steak. Casual Dining. $27-$46 **AAA Inspector Notes:** With 15 entrée choices to mix and match, beef rules the house, but delicious cuts of chicken, pork and flavorful sausages also are presented at this fixed-price restaurant where attentive servers make sure your plate is never empty. I sampled about half of the selections, and all were excellent; the other half will have to wait until my next visit. **Features:** full bar. **Reservations:** suggested. **Address:** 309 E 3rd St 78701 **Location:** At Trinity and 3rd sts; next to convention center. **Parking:** valet and street only. L  D  CALL ♿M

HICKORY STREET          512/477-8968  **7**
♦♦ ♦♦ Comfort Food. Casual Dining. $7-$13 **AAA Inspector Notes:** On this spacious patio spot, soups, salads, sandwiches and daily specials are served. **Features:** full bar, patio dining, Sunday brunch, happy hour. **Address:** 800 Congress Ave 78701 **Location:** Jct 8th St and Congress Ave; northwest corner. **Parking:** street only. L  D  CALL ♿M  🐕

THE HOFFBRAU          512/472-0822  **8**
♦♦ ♦♦ Steak. Casual Dining. $8-$19 **AAA Inspector Notes:** Steaks are the name of the game at the restaurant, which has existed in its original location since 1934. **Features:** beer only. **Address:** 613 W 6th St 78701 **Location:** Corner of 6th and Nueces sts. L  D

HUT'S HAMBURGERS          512/472-0693  **6**
♦♦ ♦♦ Burgers Sandwiches. Casual Dining. $5-$9 **AAA Inspector Notes:** Established in 1939 and now housed in a former drive-in that featured carhop service, this landmark offers 20 different types of burgers, including the Wolfman Jack and the Alley-Oop. Soups, salads, sandwiches and such Southern favorites as fried chicken, chicken-fried steaks, ham steaks and meatloaf also are offered. **Features:** beer & wine. **Address:** 807 W 6th St 78703 **Location:** Just w of jct West Ave. **Parking:** on-site and street. L  D  CALL ♿M

IRONWORKS BARBEQUE          512/478-4855  **28**
♦♦ Barbecue. Quick Serve. $6-$14 **AAA Inspector Notes:** Overlooking Waller Creek from a converted ironworks building, the eatery features a fine range of beef, pork and chicken barbecue dishes generously served with fresh sides of beans and potato salad. Luscious desserts are prepared in house daily. **Features:** beer only. **Address:** 100 Red River St 78701 **Location:** Just w of I-35; corner of E 1st and Red River sts; next to convention center. L  D  🅰️🅲

LA CONDESA          512/499-0300  **21**
♦♦ ♦♦ Mexican. Casual Dining. $10-$38 **AAA Inspector Notes:** The flavors of Central Mexico are featured at this contemporary restaurant with a nicely varied menu. I treated myself to some excellent ribs. **Features:** full bar, Sunday brunch. **Reservations:** required. **Address:** 400A W 2nd St 78701 **Location:** Northwest corner of Guadalupe and 2nd sts. **Parking:** street only. ECO  L  D

(See map & index p. 83.)

### MANUEL'S DOWNTOWN
512/472-7555  (19)

▼▼ Mexican. Casual Dining. $10-$26 **AAA Inspector Notes:** Designed in shades of black with columns and well-spaced tables, the dining room doesn't adopt the decor of a typical Mexican kitchen. An extensive tequila list complements such menu highlights as grilled fajitas and vegetarian chiles rellenos. A jazz brunch adds spice on Sundays. **Features:** full bar, patio dining, Sunday brunch. **Address:** 310 Congress Ave 78701 **Location:** Jct 3rd St and Congress Ave. **Parking:** street only. [L] [D]

### MOONSHINE PATIO BAR & GRILL
512/236-9599  (26)

▼▼ American. Casual Dining. $10-$22 **AAA Inspector Notes:** This downtown restaurant's straightforward comfort food includes steak, chicken and seafood entrées as well as such specialty items as buffalo meatloaf. **Features:** full bar, patio dining, Sunday brunch, happy hour. **Address:** 303 Red River St 78701 **Location:** Jct E 3rd and Red River sts. **Parking:** valet and street only. [L] [D] [🐕]

### THE OLD PECAN STREET CAFE
512/478-2491  (15)

▼▼ American. Casual Dining. $8-$15 **AAA Inspector Notes:** Conveniently close to the convention center, four different types of Benedicts are served as part of a breakfast menu that is presented until 5 pm each afternoon. **Features:** full bar, patio dining, Sunday brunch. **Address:** 504 Trinity St 78701 **Location:** Northwest corner of Trinity and 5th sts. **Parking:** street only. [B] [L] [D]

### PERRY'S STEAKHOUSE & GRILLE
512/474-6300  (9)

▼▼▼ Steak. Fine Dining. $24-$55 **AAA Inspector Notes:** An excellent selection of prime steaks, lamb and pork chops are served at this professional, upscale establishment. **Features:** full bar. **Reservations:** suggested. **Address:** 114 W 7th St 78701 **Location:** Jct 7th and Colorado sts. **Parking:** valet and street only. [D] CALL [🅼]

### ROARING FORK
512/583-0000  (10)

▼▼▼ Steak. Fine Dining. $10-$36 **AAA Inspector Notes:** Steak, seafood, chicken, duck and pork entrees are presented in an upscale environment with an overall Western atmosphere. **Features:** full bar, Sunday brunch. **Reservations:** suggested. **Address:** 701 Congress Ave 78701 **Location:** Northeast corner of 7th St and Congress Ave; in InterContinental Stephen F. Austin Hotel. **Parking:** valet and street only. [L] [D] CALL [🅼]

### SERRANO'S
512/322-9080

▼▼ Tex-Mex. Casual Dining. $8-$17 **AAA Inspector Notes:** *Historic.* The Tex-Mex cafe is known for its stuffed jalapenos, which tempt those with a taste for something spicy (and a nearby water glass). Among good choices are crunchy flautas and sizzling fajitas. **Features:** full bar. **Address:** 1111 Red River St 78701 **Location:** Corner of 11th and Red River sts. **Parking:** street only. [L] [D]

### SULLIVAN'S STEAKHOUSE
512/495-6504  (17)

▼▼▼ Steak. Fine Dining. $24-$55 **AAA Inspector Notes:** Named for John L. Sullivan, heavyweight champion of the world in the 1880s, the upscale steakhouse prepares a wide selection of steaks, chops and seafood. Decorated with black-and-white photographs of Sullivan, Jack Dempsey and other boxing legends. **Features:** full bar. **Reservations:** suggested. **Address:** 300 Colorado St 78701 **Location:** Corner of 3rd and Colorado sts. **Parking:** valet only. [L] [D] CALL [🅼]

### TEXADELPHIA

▼ Sandwiches. Quick Serve. $6-$9 **AAA Inspector Notes:** Texas cheese steak and beer are the name of the game at the laid-back eatery. While catching up on sports statistics, guests can wash down customized sandwiches and juicy burgers with a selection from an encyclopedia of brews. **Bar:** beer only. [L] [D]

*For additional information, visit AAA.com*

**LOCATIONS:**

**Address:** 501 W 15th St 78701 **Location:** Southwest corner of 15th and San Antonio sts. **Phone:** 512/391-9189

**Address:** 2422 Guadalupe St 78705 **Location:** Across from University of Texas; on The Drag. **Phone:** 512/480-0107

### THAI PASSION
512/472-1244  (11)

▼▼ Thai. Casual Dining. $9-$17 **AAA Inspector Notes:** The expertly prepared authentic Thai cuisine features noteworthy culinary creations daily. **Features:** beer & wine. **Address:** 620 Congress Ave, Suite 105 78701 **Location:** Between Congress Ave and Colorado St; entrance on 7th St. [L] [D] [LATE]

### TRIO
512/685-8300  (29)

▼▼▼ Steak Seafood. Fine Dining. $23-$45 **AAA Inspector Notes:** The peaceful terrace overlooks a lake and beautifully landscaped grounds. An excellent choice is focaccia-encrusted pork medallions with mashed potatoes and grilled asparagus. The star over Texas dessert layers chocolate mousse and sponge cake. **Features:** full bar, Sunday brunch. **Reservations:** suggested. **Address:** 98 San Jacinto Blvd 78701 **Location:** Jct Congress Ave and Cesar Chavez St; 2 blks e on Lady Bird Lake Tr; in Four Seasons Hotel. **Parking:** on-site and valet. [L] [D]

### TRULUCK'S
512/482-9000  (14)

▼▼▼ Seafood Steak. Fine Dining. $12-$45 **AAA Inspector Notes:** The chef's daily creations include jumbo fresh Florida stone crab claws, live Maine lobster, Australian cold water lobster tail, sesame-crusted ahi tuna, miso-glazed organic totem black cod, oysters Rockefeller, sautéed super-lump crab cake, juicy and flavorful Niman Ranch aged beef and a variety of delicious steamed sides including their signature Parmesan mashed potatoes. **Features:** full bar. **Address:** 400 Colorado St 78701 **Location:** Jct 4th and Colorado sts. **Parking:** valet and street only. [D] CALL [🅼]

### VINCE YOUNG STEAKHOUSE
512/457-8325  (23)

▼▼▼ Steak. Fine Dining. $21-$50 **AAA Inspector Notes:** Upscale steakhouse serving prime cuts of beef in a convenient downtown location. I had a fabulous bone-in rib-eye steak that you could cut with your fork. **Features:** full bar. **Reservations:** suggested. **Address:** 301 San Jacinto Blvd 78701 **Location:** Jct 3rd St and San Jacinto Blvd. **Parking:** valet and street only. [D] CALL [🅼]

### FRANKLIN BBQ
512/653-1187

[fyi] Not evaluated. Expect waiting in line for several hours before being able to place your order at this rustic location while having many items already sold out at this very popular 2010 Bon Appétit winner of Best Barbecue in the USA! **Address:** 900 E 11th St 78702 **Location:** 1 blk e of I-35.

## AUSTIN (F-8)
* Restaurants p. 109
* Hotels & Restaurants map & index p. 86

### ALOFT AUSTIN AT THE DOMAIN
(512)491-0777  (18)

▼▼▼ Hotel $119-$299

**AAA Benefit:** Enjoy the new twist, get up to 20% off + Starwood Preferred Guest® bonuses!

**Address:** 11601 Domain Dr 78758 **Location:** Loop 1 (Mo-Pac Expwy) exit Burnett Rd/Duval Rd, just e; in The Domain. **Facility:** 140 units. 6 stories, interior corridors. *Bath:* shower only. **Amenities:** safes. **Pool(s):** outdoor. **Activities:** exercise room. **Guest Services:** valet and coin laundry.

### AUSTIN AIRPORT MARRIOTT SOUTH
(512)441-7900  (81)

▼▼▼ Hotel $119-$599 **Address:** 4415 S I-35 78744 **Location:** I-35 N exit 228; on northbound frontage road. **Facility:** 211 units. 5 stories, interior corridors. **Amenities:** safes. **Pool(s):** heated indoor. **Activities:** hot tub, exercise room. **Guest Services:** valet and coin laundry.

**AAA Benefit:** Members save 5% or more!

(See map & index p. 86.)

## BAYMONT INN & SUITES AUSTIN    (512)447-5511 **80**

Hotel
$59-$159

**Address:** 4323 I-35 S 78744 **Location:** I-35 exit 230A (Stassney Rd) southbound; exit 230 (Ben White Blvd/SR 71) northbound. **Facility:** 95 units, some kitchens. 4 stories, interior corridors. **Terms:** 2 night minimum stay - seasonal and/or weekends. **Pool(s):** outdoor. **Activities:** exercise room. **Guest Services:** valet and coin laundry. **Featured Amenity:** continental breakfast.

## BEST WESTERN ATRIUM NORTH    (512)339-7311 **41**

Hotel
$89-$249

**AAA Benefit:** Members save 10% or more with Best Western!

**Address:** 7928 Gessner Dr 78753 **Location:** I-35 exit 240A, 0.4 mi w on US 183. **Facility:** 118 units. 4 stories, interior corridors. **Terms:** 2-3 night minimum stay - seasonal. **Pool(s):** heated indoor. **Activities:** sauna, exercise room.

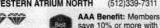

## BEST WESTERN PLUS AUSTIN AIRPORT INN & SUITES
(512)386-5455 **68**

Hotel
$110-$150

Best Western
PLUS

**AAA Benefit:** Members save 10% or more with Best Western!

**Address:** 1805 Airport Commerce Dr 78741 **Location:** Jct SR 71 (E Ben White Blvd) and Riverside Dr, just n; in Airport Commerce Park. **Facility:** 75 units. 3 stories, interior corridors. **Pool(s):** outdoor. **Activities:** exercise room. **Guest Services:** coin laundry.

---

## BEST WESTERN PLUS AUSTIN CITY HOTEL
(512)444-0561 **63**

Hotel
$120-$180

**AAA Benefit:** Members save 10% or more with Best Western!

**Address:** 2200 S I-35 78704 **Location:** I-35 exit 232A (Oltorf Blvd); on west side access road. **Facility:** 155 units. 3 stories, interior/exterior corridors. **Terms:** 2-3 night minimum stay - seasonal. **Pool(s):** outdoor. **Activities:** hot tub, exercise room. **Guest Services:** coin laundry. **Featured Amenity:** full hot breakfast.

Best Western
PLUS

**Located on I-35 just minutes from downtown, 6th St & SOCO, Austin's trendy shopping & eating district.**

---

## CANDLEWOOD SUITES AUSTIN NORTHWEST
512/338-1611 **30**

Extended Stay Hotel. Rates not provided. **Address:** 9701 Stonelake Blvd 78759 **Location:** Jct Capital of Texas Hwy (SR 360) and Stonelake Blvd, just s. **Facility:** 125 efficiencies. 4 stories, interior corridors. **Activities:** exercise room. **Guest Services:** valet and coin laundry.

## CANDLEWOOD SUITES-SOUTH    (512)444-8882 **78**

Extended Stay Hotel $69-$159 **Address:** 4320 S I-35 78745 **Location:** I-35 exit 230 (Ben White Blvd/SR 71) northbound; exit 231 (Woodward Rd) southbound; on southbound frontage road. **Facility:** 122 efficiencies. 3 stories, interior corridors. **Terms:** cancellation fee imposed. **Activities:** exercise room. **Guest Services:** complimentary and valet laundry.

## COMFORT SUITES AIRPORT    (512)386-6000 **73**

Hotel $99-$199 **Address:** 7501 E Ben White Blvd 78741 **Location:** I-35 exit 230B (Ben White Blvd/SR 71), 3.6 mi e. **Facility:** 84 units. 4 stories, interior corridors. **Activities:** exercise room. **Guest Services:** valet and coin laundry.

## COMFORT SUITES NORTHWEST    (512)219-1800 **7**

Hotel $119-$169 **Address:** 13681 N Hwy 183 78750 **Location:** Jct US 183 and SR 620, just s. **Facility:** 65 units. 3 stories, interior corridors. **Pool(s):** outdoor. **Activities:** hot tub, exercise room. **Guest Services:** coin laundry.

## COMFORT SUITES-SOUTH    (512)444-6630 **79**

Hotel
$100-$400

**Address:** 1701 E St. Elmo Rd 78744 **Location:** I-35 exit 228 northbound, just n on east frontage road. **Facility:** 50 units. 3 stories, interior corridors. **Pool(s):** heated indoor. **Activities:** hot tub, exercise room. **Guest Services:** valet and coin laundry. **Featured Amenity:** breakfast buffet.

## COUNTRY INN & SUITES BY CARLSON NORTH
512/380-0008 **45**

Hotel
Rates not provided

**Address:** 7400 I-35 N 78752 **Location:** I-35 exit 240A, just s on west frontage road. **Facility:** 75 units. 3 stories, interior corridors. **Pool(s):** outdoor. **Activities:** hot tub, exercise room. **Guest Services:** coin laundry. **Featured Amenity:** full hot breakfast.

(See map & index p. 86.)

## COURTYARD BY MARRIOTT AUSTIN AIRPORT
(512)386-7464   **69**

Hotel
$99-$599

**AAA Benefit:** Members save 5% or more!

**Address:** 7809 E Ben White Blvd 78741 **Location:** Jct SR 71 (E Ben White Blvd) and Riverside Dr. **Facility:** 150 units. 5 stories, interior corridors. **Pool(s):** heated indoor. **Activities:** hot tub, exercise room. **Guest Services:** valet and coin laundry.

## COURTYARD BY MARRIOTT AUSTIN AIRPORT/SOUTH
(512)912-1122  **86**

Hotel
$99-$499

**AAA Benefit:** Members save 5% or more!

**Address:** 4533 S I-35 78744 **Location:** I-35 exit 229 (Stassney Rd) southbound; exit 230B (Ben White Blvd/SR 71) northbound. **Facility:** 110 units. 4 stories, interior corridors. **Pool(s):** heated indoor. **Activities:** hot tub, exercise room. **Guest Services:** valet and coin laundry.

## COURTYARD BY MARRIOTT AUSTIN NORTH/PARMER LANE
(512)339-8374  **20**

Hotel
$99-$399

**AAA Benefit:** Members save 5% or more!

**Address:** 12330 N IH-35 78753 **Location:** I-35 exit 245, just s on west frontage road. **Facility:** 145 units. 5 stories, interior corridors. **Pool(s):** heated indoor. **Activities:** exercise room. **Guest Services:** valet and coin laundry.

## COURTYARD BY MARRIOTT-AUSTIN NORTHWEST/ARBORETUM
(512)502-8100  **32**

Hotel
$99-$199

**AAA Benefit:** Members save 5% or more!

**Address:** 9409 Stonelake Blvd 78759 **Location:** Jct Capital of Texas Hwy (SR 360) and Stonelake Blvd, 1 mi s. **Facility:** 102 units. 4 stories, interior corridors. **Amenities:** video games. **Pool(s):** heated indoor. **Activities:** hot tub, exercise room. **Guest Services:** valet and coin laundry.

## COURTYARD BY MARRIOTT AUSTIN-UNIVERSITY AREA
(512)458-2340  **55**

Hotel
$89-$299

**AAA Benefit:** Members save 5% or more!

**Address:** 5660 N I-35 78751 **Location:** I-35 exit 238A; on west frontage road. **Facility:** 198 units. 9 stories, interior corridors. **Amenities:** video games. **Pool(s):** outdoor. **Activities:** hot tub, exercise room. **Guest Services:** valet and coin laundry.

### CROSSLAND ECONOMY STUDIOS AUSTIN WEST
(512)331-4747  **6**

**Extended Stay Hotel** $39-$49 **Address:** 12621 Hymeadow Rd 78729 **Location:** US 183 N exit Lake Creek Pkwy, just n, then just e. **Facility:** 139 efficiencies. 3 stories, exterior corridors. **Bath:** shower only. **Terms:** cancellation fee imposed. **Guest Services:** coin laundry.

### CROWNE PLAZA
(512)323-5466  **50**

**Hotel** $129-$299 **Address:** 6121 I-35 N 78752 **Location:** I-35 exit 238A; on east frontage road. **Facility:** 293 units. 7 stories, interior corridors. **Terms:** cancellation fee imposed. **Pool(s):** outdoor. **Activities:** hot tub, exercise room. **Guest Services:** valet laundry.

### DOUBLETREE BY HILTON AUSTIN
(512)454-3737  **49**

Hotel
$109-$209

**AAA Benefit:** Members save 5% or more!

**Address:** 6505 I-35 N 78752 **Location:** I-35 exit 238A; on east frontage road. **Facility:** 350 units, some two bedrooms. 6 stories, interior corridors. **Parking:** onsite (fee) and valet. **Terms:** 1-7 night minimum stay, cancellation fee imposed. **Pool(s):** outdoor. **Activities:** hot tub, exercise room. **Guest Services:** valet laundry, area transportation.

### DRURY INN & SUITES-AUSTIN NORTH
(512)467-9500  **47**

**Hotel** $100-$179 **Address:** 6711 I-35 N 78752 **Location:** I-35 exit 238A; on east frontage road. **Facility:** 224 units. 4 stories, interior corridors. **Terms:** cancellation fee imposed. **Pool(s):** outdoor. **Activities:** exercise room. **Guest Services:** valet and coin laundry.

### ECONO LODGE
(512)835-7070  **36**

**Hotel** $60-$149 **Address:** 9102 Burnet Rd 78758 **Location:** US 183 and Burnet Rd; on northeast corner. **Facility:** 39 units. 2 stories (no elevator), exterior corridors.

## 102   AUSTIN, TX

(See map & index p. 86.)

### EMBASSY SUITES AUSTIN ARBORETUM
(512)372-8771 **31**

Hotel
$139-$209

 **AAA Benefit:**
Members save 5%
or more!

**Address:** 9505 Stonelake Blvd 78759 **Location:** Jct Capital of Texas Hwy (SR 360) and Stonelake Blvd, 0.5 mi s. **Facility:** 150 units. 6 stories, interior corridors. **Terms:** 1-7 night minimum stay, cancellation fee imposed. **Pool(s):** heated indoor. **Activities:** hot tub, exercise room. **Guest Services:** valet laundry, area transportation. **Featured Amenity: full hot breakfast.**

### EMBASSY SUITES AUSTIN CENTRAL   (512)454-8004 **53**

Hotel $116-$151 **Address:** 5901 I-35 N 78723 **Location:** I-35 exit 238A; on east frontage road. **Facility:** 260 units. 10 stories, interior corridors. **Terms:** 1-7 night minimum stay, cancellation fee imposed. **Amenities:** video games. **Pool(s):** heated indoor. **Activities:** hot tub, exercise room. **Guest Services:** valet and coin laundry, area transportation.

**AAA Benefit:**
Members save 5%
or more!

### EXTENDED STAY AMERICA AUSTIN ARBORETUM   (512)231-1520 **28**

Extended Stay Hotel $64-$79 **Address:** 10100 Capital of Texas Hwy 78759 **Location:** Jct Loop 1 (Mo-Pac Expwy) and Capital of Texas Hwy (SR 360), just w. **Facility:** 102 efficiencies. 4 stories, interior corridors. **Terms:** 3 day cancellation notice. **Guest Services:** coin laundry.

### EXTENDED STAY AMERICA AUSTIN-ARBORETUM-NORTH   (512)833-0898 **14**

Extended Stay Hotel $64-$79 **Address:** 2700 Gracy Farms Ln 78758 **Location:** 2 mi n of US 183 on Loop 1 (Mo-Pac Expwy) exit Burnet Rd. **Facility:** 113 efficiencies. 2 stories (no elevator), interior corridors. **Terms:** cancellation fee imposed. **Pool(s):** heated outdoor. **Activities:** limited exercise equipment. **Guest Services:** coin laundry.

### EXTENDED STAY AMERICA AUSTIN ARBORETUM SOUTH   (512)837-6677 **35**

Extended Stay Hotel $54-$64 **Address:** 9100 Waterford Centre Blvd 78758 **Location:** US 183 exit Burnet Rd; on westbound frontage road. **Facility:** 124 units, some efficiencies. 2 stories (no elevator), exterior corridors. **Terms:** cancellation fee imposed. **Guest Services:** coin laundry.

### EXTENDED STAY AMERICA AUSTIN-NORTH CENTRAL   (512)339-6005 **40**

Extended Stay Hotel $54-$59 **Address:** 8221 N I-35 78753 **Location:** I-35 exit 241; on east frontage road. **Facility:** 118 efficiencies, some two bedrooms. 3 stories, interior corridors. **Terms:** cancellation fee imposed. **Pool(s):** outdoor. **Activities:** exercise room. **Guest Services:** coin laundry.

### EXTENDED STAY AMERICA AUSTIN NORTHWEST LAKELINE MALL   (512)258-3365 **3**

Extended Stay Hotel $54-$69 **Address:** 13858 US Hwy 183 N 78750 **Location:** Jct US 183 and SR 620; on southwest corner. **Facility:** 101 efficiencies. 4 stories, interior corridors. **Terms:** cancellation fee imposed. **Guest Services:** coin laundry.

### EXTENDED STAY AMERICA AUSTIN SOUTHWEST   (512)892-4272 **60**

Extended Stay Hotel $64-$74 **Address:** 5100 US Hwy 290 W 78735 **Location:** I-35 exit 230; US 290 W exit Brodie Ln, 1 mi w. **Facility:** 117 efficiencies. 4 stories, interior corridors. **Terms:** cancellation fee imposed. **Guest Services:** coin laundry.

### EXTENDED STAY DELUXE (AUSTIN/NORTHWEST/RESEARCH PARK)   (512)219-6500 **10**

Extended Stay Hotel $64-$74 **Address:** 12424 Research Blvd 78759 **Location:** US 183 exit Oak Knoll Dr; on eastbound frontage road. **Facility:** 120 efficiencies, some two bedrooms. 3 stories, interior corridors. **Pool(s):** outdoor. **Activities:** exercise room. **Guest Services:** coin laundry.

(See map & index p. 86.)

## FAIRFIELD INN & SUITES BY MARRIOTT AUSTIN AIRPORT/SOUTH
(512)707-8899  **85**

Hotel
$79-$399

**AAA Benefit:** Members save 5% or more!

**Address:** 4525 S I-35 78744 **Location:** I-35 exit 230 (Ben White Blvd/SR 71) northbound; exit 229 (Stassney Rd) southbound. **Facility:** 63 units. 3 stories, interior corridors. **Pool(s):** heated indoor. **Activities:** hot tub, exercise room. **Guest Services:** valet and coin laundry. **Featured Amenity:** full hot breakfast.

## FAIRFIELD INN & SUITES BY MARRIOTT-AUSTIN CENTRAL
(512)302-5550  **54**

Hotel
$89-$299

**AAA Benefit:** Members save 5% or more!

**Address:** 959 Reinli St 78751 **Location:** I-35 exit 238A. On west frontage road. **Facility:** 63 units. 3 stories, interior corridors. **Amenities:** video games. **Pool(s):** heated indoor. **Activities:** hot tub, exercise room. **Guest Services:** valet and coin laundry. **Featured Amenity:** full hot breakfast.

## FAIRFIELD INN & SUITES BY MARRIOTT AUSTIN NORTH/PARMER LANE
(512)821-0376  **15**

Hotel
$127-$142

**AAA Benefit:** Members save 5% or more!

**Address:** 12536 N IH-35 78753 **Location:** I-35 exit 245, just w. **Facility:** 150 units. 5 stories, interior corridors. **Pool(s):** heated indoor. **Activities:** exercise room. **Guest Services:** valet and coin laundry, area transportation. **Featured Amenity:** full hot breakfast.

## FAIRFIELD INN & SUITES BY MARRIOTT AUSTIN NW
(512)527-0734  **21**

Hotel $99-$199 **Address:** 11201 N Mo-Pac Expwy 78759 **Location:** US 183 N, 1.5 mi n on Loop 1 (Mo-Pac Expwy) exit Braker Ln; on east frontage road. **Facility:** 134 units. 4 stories, interior corridors. **Pool(s):** heated outdoor. **Activities:** hot tub, exercise room. **Guest Services:** valet and coin laundry, area transportation.

**AAA Benefit:** Members save 5% or more!

---

Explore on-the-go travel tools at AAA.com/mobile or CAA.ca/mobile

## HABITAT SUITES HOTEL
512/467-6000  **48**

Hotel. Rates not provided. **Address:** 500 E Highland Mall Blvd 78752 **Location:** I-35 exit 238A, just w on CR 2222 to Airport Blvd, 0.6 mi n to Highland Mall Blvd, then 0.4 mi e. **Facility:** 96 efficiencies, some two bedrooms. 2 stories, exterior corridors. **Pool(s):** outdoor. **Activities:** hot tub. **Guest Services:** valet and coin laundry.

## HAMPTON INN & SUITES
(512)389-1616  **71**

Hotel $139-$189 **Address:** 7712 E Riverside Dr 78744 **Location:** I-35 exit 230B (Ben White Blvd/SR 71), 3.2 mi e on SR 71. **Facility:** 102 units. 5 stories, interior corridors. **Terms:** 1-7 night minimum stay, cancellation fee imposed. **Pool(s):** outdoor. **Activities:** tennis, exercise room. **Guest Services:** valet and coin laundry.

**AAA Benefit:** Members save up to 10%!

## HAMPTON INN & SUITES AUSTIN/CEDAR PARK-LAKELINE
(512)249-0045  **5**

Hotel $99-$149 **Address:** 10811 Pecan Park Blvd 78750 **Location:** Jct US 183 and SR 620; just w to Pecan Park Blvd. **Facility:** 71 units. 3 stories, interior corridors. **Terms:** 1-7 night minimum stay, cancellation fee imposed. **Amenities:** video games. **Pool(s):** outdoor. **Activities:** hot tub, exercise room. **Guest Services:** valet and coin laundry.

**AAA Benefit:** Members save up to 10%!

## HAMPTON INN AUSTIN-NORTH
(512)452-3300  **43**

Hotel $99-$149 **Address:** 7619 I-35 N 78752 **Location:** I-35 exit 240A; on east frontage road. **Facility:** 121 units. 4 stories, interior corridors. **Terms:** 1-7 night minimum stay, cancellation fee imposed. **Pool(s):** heated outdoor. **Activities:** exercise room. **Guest Services:** valet laundry.

**AAA Benefit:** Members save up to 10%!

## HAMPTON INN AUSTIN/OAK HILL
(512)891-7474  **61**

Hotel $99-$169 **Address:** 6401 US Hwy 290 W 78735 **Location:** US 290 W, just e of William Cannon Dr; on south side of road. **Facility:** 106 units. 3 stories, interior corridors. **Terms:** 1-7 night minimum stay, cancellation fee imposed. **Pool(s):** outdoor. **Activities:** exercise room. **Guest Services:** valet and coin laundry.

**AAA Benefit:** Members save up to 10%!

## HAMPTON INN AUSTIN-SOUTH
512/442-4040  **76**

Hotel. Rates not provided. **Address:** 4141 Governor's Row 78744 **Location:** I-35 exit 231 (Ben White Blvd/SR 71), just e. **Facility:** 123 units. 6 stories, interior corridors. **Pool(s):** outdoor. **Activities:** exercise room. **Guest Services:** valet laundry.

**AAA Benefit:** Members save up to 10%!

## HAMPTON INN NORTHWEST
(512)349-9898  **25**

Hotel $169-$399 **Address:** 3908 W Braker Ln 78759 **Location:** 1 mi n of US 183 on Loop 1 (Mo-Pac Expwy) exit W Braker Ln. **Facility:** 124 units. 6 stories, interior corridors. **Terms:** 1-7 night minimum stay, cancellation fee imposed. **Pool(s):** outdoor. **Activities:** exercise room. **Guest Services:** valet laundry.

**AAA Benefit:** Members save up to 10%!

(See map & index p. 86.)

## HILTON AUSTIN AIRPORT
(512)385-6767

Hotel
$109-$269

**AAA Benefit:** Members save 5% or more!

**Address:** 9515 Hotel Dr 78719 **Location:** SR 71; service road exit at airport. **Facility:** 262 units. 4 stories, interior corridors. **Parking:** on-site (fee) and valet. **Terms:** 1-7 night minimum stay, cancellation fee imposed. **Amenities:** safes. **Pool(s):** heated outdoor. **Activities:** hot tub, exercise room. **Guest Services:** valet and coin laundry. *(See ad this page.)*

     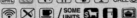  

## HILTON GARDEN INN
(512)241-1600

Hotel $109-$209 **Address:** 11617 Research Blvd 78759 **Location:** US 183 N exit Duval Rd, just n; on east frontage road. **Facility:** 138 units. 5 stories, interior corridors. **Terms:** 1-7 night minimum stay, cancellation fee imposed. **Pool(s):** heated indoor. **Activities:** hot tub, exercise room. **Guest Services:** valet and coin laundry.

**AAA Benefit:** Members save up to 10%!

## HILTON GARDEN INN AUSTIN NORTH
(512)339-3626

Hotel
$99-$399

**AAA Benefit:** Members save up to 10%!

**Address:** 12400 N 1H-35, Building C 78761 **Location:** I-35 exit 245; on west frontage road. **Facility:** 117 units. 5 stories, interior corridors. **Terms:** 1-7 night minimum stay, cancellation fee imposed. **Pool(s):** outdoor. **Activities:** hot tub, exercise room. **Guest Services:** valet and coin laundry.

## HOLIDAY INN AUSTIN MIDTOWN
(512)451-5757

Hotel
$99-$239

**Address:** 6000 Middle Fiskville Rd 78752 **Location:** I-35 exit 238A; just off west frontage road. **Facility:** 189 units. 9 stories, interior corridors. **Terms:** 3 day cancellation notice-fee imposed. **Amenities:** *Some:* safes. **Pool(s):** outdoor. **Activities:** exercise room. **Guest Services:** valet and coin laundry.

---

▼ See AAA listing this page ▼

## Complimentary wireless internet in all guest rooms

- 24 hour complimentary shuttle to Austin Bergstrom Airport
- Creeks Restaurant & Lounge
- 24 hour In-Room Dining
- Resort style salt water pool
- Hill Country inspired open-air atrium

 Approved

 Hilton AUSTIN AIRPORT

## Hilton Austin Airport
9515 Hotel Dr., Austin, TX 78719 | RESERVATIONS: 800-HILTONS | 512.385.6767
austinairport.hilton.com

---

Discover free apps for mapping and more

at AAA.com/mobile or CAA.ca/mobile

**(See map & index p. 86.)**

## HOLIDAY INN AUSTIN NORTHWEST/ARBORETUM
512/343-0888 **34**

▼▼▼ **Hotel.** Rates not provided. **Address:** 8901 Business Park Dr 78759 **Location:** Jct US 183 and Loop 1 (Mo-Pac Expwy); on southwest corner. **Facility:** 194 units. 4 stories, interior corridors. **Amenities:** video games. **Dining:** 2 restaurants. **Pool(s):** heated outdoor, heated indoor. **Activities:** hot tub, exercise room. **Guest Services:** valet and coin laundry.

## HOLIDAY INN EXPRESS & SUITES AUSTIN AIRPORT
(512)386-7600 **72**

▼▼▼ **Hotel** $90-$299 **Address:** 7601 E Ben White Blvd 78741 **Location:** I-35 exit 230B (Ben White Blvd/SR 71), 3.2 mi e. **Facility:** 80 units. 4 stories, interior corridors. **Terms:** cancellation fee imposed. **Pool(s):** outdoor. **Activities:** hot tub, exercise room. **Guest Services:** valet and coin laundry.

## HOLIDAY INN EXPRESS HOTEL & SUITES
512/251-9110 **9**

▼▼▼ **Hotel.** Rates not provided. **Address:** 14620 N I-35 78728 **Location:** I-35 exit 247; on west frontage road. **Facility:** 84 units. 3 stories, interior corridors. **Pool(s):** outdoor. **Activities:** exercise room. **Guest Services:** coin laundry.

## HOLIDAY INN EXPRESS HOTEL & SUITES
(512)249-8166 **4**

▼▼▼ **Hotel** $125-$205 **Address:** 12703 Ranch Rd 620 N 78750 **Location:** US 183, 0.5 mi w. **Facility:** 65 units, some two bedrooms. 3 stories, interior corridors. **Pool(s):** outdoor. **Activities:** hot tub, exercise room. **Guest Services:** valet and coin laundry.

## HOLIDAY INN EXPRESS SUNSET VALLEY
(512)891-9500 **62**

◆◆◆ Hotel $129-$139

**Address:** 4892 Hwy 290 W 78735 **Location:** I-35 exit 230 (Ben White Blvd/SR 71), 2.5 mi w to Westgate Blvd, then 1.5 mi w on north frontage road. **Facility:** 99 units. 3 stories, interior corridors. **Featured Amenity: full hot breakfast.**

## HOMEWOOD SUITES-AUSTIN SOUTH/AIRPORT
(512)445-5050 **77**

◆◆◆ Extended Stay Contemporary Hotel $139-$349

HOMEWOOD SUITES BY HILTON **AAA Benefit:** Members save up to 10%!

**Address:** 4143 Governor's Row 78744 **Location:** I-35 exit 231 (Ben White Blvd/SR 71) southbound; exit 229 northbound; at Ben White Blvd. **Facility:** 96 efficiencies, some two bedrooms. 5 stories, interior corridors. **Terms:** 1-7 night minimum stay, cancellation fee imposed. **Pool(s):** outdoor. **Activities:** exercise room. **Guest Services:** valet and coin laundry. **Featured Amenity: full hot breakfast.**

## HOMEWOOD SUITES BY HILTON ARBORETUM NW
(512)349-9966 **23**

▼▼▼ **Extended Stay Hotel** $189-$399 **Address:** 10925 Stonelake Blvd 78759 **Location:** US 183 N to Loop 1 (Mo-Pac Expwy) exit Anderson Rd, just e to Braker Ln; on northwest corner. **Facility:** 97 efficiencies, some two bedrooms. 4 stories, interior corridors. **Terms:** 1-7 night minimum stay, cancellation fee imposed. **Pool(s):** outdoor. **Activities:** exercise room. **Guest Services:** valet and coin laundry.

**AAA Benefit:** Members save up to 10%!

## HOTEL ALLANDALE
512/452-9391 **38**

▼▼▼ **Hotel.** Rates not provided. **Address:** 7685 Northcross Dr 78757 **Location:** Loop 1 (Mo-Pac Expwy), 1.5 mi n to Northcross Dr, then just s; behind Northcross Mall. **Facility:** 68 kitchen units, some two bedrooms. 2 stories (no elevator), exterior corridors. **Terms:** check-in 4 pm. **Amenities:** safes. **Pool(s):** outdoor. **Activities:** hot tub, exercise room. **Guest Services:** valet and coin laundry.

## HOWARD JOHNSON
(512)462-9201 **65**

◆◆◆ Hotel $55-$100

**Address:** 2711 I-35 S 78741 **Location:** I-35 exit 231 (Woodward Ave) southbound; exit 232A (Oltorf St) northbound; on northbound frontage road; just n of jct I-35 and US 290/SR 71. **Facility:** 87 units. 3 stories, interior corridors. **Activities:** exercise room. **Guest Services:** coin laundry. **Featured Amenity: continental breakfast.**

## HYATT HOUSE AUSTIN/ARBORETUM
(512)342-8080 **29**

◆◆◆ Extended Stay Contemporary Hotel $79-$410

H HYATT house

**AAA Benefit:** Members save 10%!

**Address:** 10001 N Capital of Texas Hwy 78759 **Location:** US 183, N Capital of Texas Hwy (SR 360), just e. **Facility:** 130 efficiencies, some two bedrooms. 3 stories, interior corridors. **Terms:** cancellation fee imposed. **Pool(s):** outdoor. **Activities:** hot tub, exercise room. **Guest Services:** valet and coin laundry. **Featured Amenity: breakfast buffet.**

## HYATT PLACE AUSTIN/ARBORETUM
(512)231-8491 **33**

◆◆◆ Hotel $89-$449

HYATT PLACE

**AAA Benefit:** Members save 10%!

**Address:** 3612 Tudor Blvd 78759 **Location:** Jct US 183 and N Capital of Texas Hwy (SR 360), 1 blk e to Stonelake Blvd, 0.5 mi s to Tudor Blvd, then just e. **Facility:** 127 units. 6 stories, interior corridors. **Terms:** cancellation fee imposed. **Pool(s):** heated outdoor. **Activities:** exercise room. **Guest Services:** valet laundry, area transportation. **Featured Amenity: breakfast buffet.**

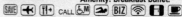

(See map & index p. 86.)

## HYATT PLACE AUSTIN - NORTH CENTRAL
(512)323-2121  **44**

Hotel
$79-$219

**HYATT PLACE**
**AAA Benefit:** Members save 10%!

**Address:** 7522 N I-35 78752 **Location:** I-35 exit 240A; on west frontage road. **Facility:** 120 units. 5 stories, interior corridors. **Terms:** cancellation fee imposed. **Pool(s):** heated outdoor. **Activities:** exercise room. **Guest Services:** valet laundry. **Featured Amenity:** breakfast buffet.

SAVE 〔↑〕 CALL &M 🏊 BIZ 📶 ⊠ ⊟ 💻 / SOME UNITS HS

## HYATT REGENCY LOST PINES RESORT AND SPA
(512)308-1234  

Resort Hotel
$129-$519

**HYATT REGENCY**
**AAA Benefit:** Members save 10%!

**Address:** 575 Hyatt Lost Pines Rd 78612 **Location:** SR 71, 13 mi e of Austin-Bergstrom International Airport; 9 mi w of Bastrop. **Facility:** The large full-service resort is conveniently located east of the airport and offers ideal activities for couples, families and business-related interests. 491 units. 3-4 stories, interior corridors. **Parking:** on-site and valet. **Terms:** check-in 4 pm, 3 day cancellation notice-fee imposed, resort fee. **Amenities:** safes. **Dining:** 9 restaurants, also, Firewheel Cafe, see separate listing. **Pool(s):** heated outdoor. **Activities:** sauna, hot tub, steamroom, fishing, regulation golf, tennis, recreation programs, bicycles, playground, spa. **Guest Services:** valet and coin laundry.

SAVE ECO ⊕ 〔↑〕 🍴 🛋 ⌇ CALL &M 🏊 🔧 BIZ HS 📶 ⊠ ⊟ 💻 / SOME UNITS 🛒

## LA QUINTA INN & SUITES AUSTIN AIRPORT
(512)386-6800  **70**

WWW Hotel $115-$160 **Address:** 7625 E Ben White Blvd 78741 **Location:** I-35 exit 230B (Ben White Blvd/SR 71), 8.8 mi e. **Facility:** 142 units. 5 stories, interior corridors. **Pool(s):** outdoor. **Activities:** hot tub, exercise room. **Guest Services:** valet and coin laundry.

⊕ 〔↑〕 CALL &M 🏊 BIZ 📶 / SOME UNITS 🛒 ⊟ 💻

## LA QUINTA INN & SUITES-AUSTIN/CEDAR PARK-LAKELINE
(512)568-3538  **1**

WWW Hotel $109-$144

**Address:** 10701 Lakeline Mall Dr 78717 **Location:** Jct US 183 and Lakeline Dr, 0.5 mi e, then just s on Lake Creek Dr. **Facility:** 80 units. 3 stories, interior corridors. **Pool(s):** outdoor. **Activities:** hot tub, exercise room. **Guest Services:** coin laundry. **Featured Amenity:** full hot breakfast.

SAVE CALL &M 🏊 HS 📶 ⊠ ⊟ 💻 💻 / SOME UNITS 🛒

## LA QUINTA INN & SUITES AUSTIN MOPAC NORTH
(512)832-2121  **13**

WWW Hotel $109-$184 **Address:** 11901 N Mo-Pac Expwy 78759 **Location:** US 183, 2 mi n on Loop 1 (Mo-Pac Expwy) exit Duval Rd. **Facility:** 149 units. 3 stories, interior corridors. **Pool(s):** heated outdoor. **Activities:** hot tub, exercise room. **Guest Services:** valet and coin laundry.

⊕ CALL &M 🏊 📶 💻 / SOME UNITS 🛒 ⊟ 💻

## LA QUINTA INN & SUITES AUSTIN SOUTHWEST AT MOPAC
(512)899-3000  **59**

WWWW Hotel $119-$214 **Address:** 4424 S Loop 1 (Mo-Pac Expwy) 78735 **Location:** Jct Loop 1 (Mo-Pac Expwy), US 290 and SR 71 E; on southbound frontage road. **Facility:** 128 units. 5 stories, interior corridors. **Pool(s):** heated outdoor. **Activities:** hot tub, exercise room. **Guest Services:** valet and coin laundry.

CALL &M 🏊 HS 📶 💻 / UNITS 🛒 ⊟ 💻

## LA QUINTA INN & SUITES ROUND ROCK SOUTH
(512)246-2800  **2**

WWW Hotel $89-$144 **Address:** 150 Parker Dr 78728 **Location:** I-35 exit 250; on west frontage road. **Facility:** 86 units. 4 stories, interior corridors. **Pool(s):** outdoor. **Activities:** hot tub, exercise room. **Guest Services:** valet and coin laundry.

⊕ 〔↑〕 CALL &M 🏊 📶 💻 ⊟ 💻 / SOME UNITS 🛒

## LA QUINTA INN AUSTIN HIGHLAND MALL
(512)459-4381  **52**

WW Hotel $75-$154 **Address:** 5812 I-35 N 78751 **Location:** I-35 exit 238A; on west frontage road. **Facility:** 122 units. 2 stories (no elevator), exterior corridors. **Pool(s):** outdoor.

⊕ 〔↑〕 🏊 📶 💻 / SOME UNITS 🛒 HS ⊟ 💻

## LA QUINTA INN AUSTIN OLTORF
(512)447-6661  **64**

WW Hotel $85-$154 **Address:** 1603 E Oltorf Blvd 78741 **Location:** I-35 exit 232A (Oltorf Blvd), just s. **Facility:** 133 units. 2 stories, interior/exterior corridors. **Pool(s):** outdoor.

〔↑〕 🏊 📶 💻 / SOME UNITS 🛒 ⊟ 💻

## LA QUINTA INN AUSTIN SOUTH/IH-35
(512)443-1774  **74**

WW Hotel $79-$154 **Address:** 4200 I-35 S 78745 **Location:** I-35 exit 231 southbound; exit 230 northbound, just s of jct US 290 and SR 71; on north frontage road. **Facility:** 129 units. 2 stories (no elevator), exterior corridors. **Pool(s):** outdoor.

〔↑〕 CALL &M 🏊 📶 💻 / SOME UNITS 🛒 HS ⊟ 💻

## OMNI AUSTIN HOTEL SOUTHPARK
(512)448-2222  **75**

Hotel
$109-$799

**Address:** 4140 Governor's Row 78744 **Location:** I-35 exit 230B (Ben White Blvd/SR 71) southbound; exit 230 northbound; on east frontage road. **Facility:** Spacious rooms, upscale amenities and refined public areas can be experienced at this hotel in southern Austin. 312 units, some two bedrooms. 14 stories, interior corridors. **Terms:** cancellation fee imposed. **Amenities:** safes. **Dining:** Onion Creek Grill, see separate listing. **Pool(s):** heated outdoor, heated indoor. **Activities:** sauna, hot tub, exercise room, massage. **Guest Services:** valet laundry, area transportation.

SAVE ⊕ 〔↑〕 🍴 🛋 CALL &M 🏊 BIZ 📶 ⊠ 💻 / SOME UNITS 🛒 ⊟ 💻

(See map & index p. 86.)

## OMNI BARTON CREEK RESORT & SPA
(512)329-4000

Resort Hotel
$149-$499

**Address:** 8212 Barton Club Dr 78735 **Location:** Jct Capital of Texas Hwy (SR 360) and FM 2244 (Bee Caves Rd), 1 mi w to Barton Creek Blvd, 1.7 mi s. **Facility:** A full-service resort with tennis, a spa and championship golf, this property offers upscale surroundings and sweeping Hill Country views. A professional staff attends to every guest need. 318 units, some two bedrooms. 9 stories, interior corridors. **Parking:** on-site and valet. **Terms:** check-in 4 pm, 3 day cancellation notice-fee imposed, resort fee. **Amenities:** video games, safes. **Dining:** 8212 Wine Bar & Grill, Hill Country Dining Room, see separate listings. **Pool(s):** heated outdoor, heated indoor. **Activities:** hot tub, steamroom, regulation golf, miniature golf, tennis, recreation programs, playground, spa. **Guest Services:** valet laundry.

## ORANGEWOOD INN & SUITES AUSTIN-NORTH
512/836-0079

 **Hotel.** Rates not provided. **Address:** 9121 N I-35 78753 **Location:** I-35 exit 241 northbound; exit 240A southbound; on east frontage road. **Facility:** 150 units. 3 stories, interior corridors. **Pool(s):** outdoor.

## QUALITY INN & SUITES AIRPORT   (512)385-1000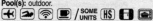

Hotel
$80-$130

**Address:** 2751 Hwy 71 E 78617 **Location:** On SR 71, 0.5 mi e of airport. **Facility:** 112 units. 3 stories, interior corridors. **Pool(s):** outdoor. **Activities:** exercise room. **Guest Services:** coin laundry. **Featured Amenity:** full hot breakfast.

## QUALITY INN NORTH AUSTIN   (512)617-4900

 **Hotel** $51-$219 **Address:** 6911 I-35 N 78752 **Location:** I-35 exit 238A; on east frontage road. **Facility:** 291 units. 2 stories (no elevator), exterior corridors. **Pool(s):** outdoor. **Activities:** exercise room. **Guest Services:** coin laundry.

## RENAISSANCE AUSTIN HOTEL   (512)343-2626

Hotel
$129-$319

**R**
RENAISSANCE HOTELS

**AAA Benefit:** Members save 5% or more!

**Address:** 9721 Arboretum Blvd 78759 **Location:** Jct US 183 and N Capital of Texas Hwy (SR 360); southwest corner. **Facility:** The full-service hotel offers upscale accommodations and services. It is located in the trendy Arboretum shopping district. 492 units. 10 stories, interior corridors. **Parking:** on-site and valet. **Amenities:** safes. **Dining:** Banderas, see separate listing. **Pool(s):** heated outdoor, heated indoor. **Activities:** sauna, hot tub, exercise room, massage. **Guest Services:** valet laundry.

## RESIDENCE INN BY MARRIOTT AUSTIN AIRPORT/SOUTH
(512)912-1100

Extended Stay Contemporary Hotel
$110-$800

**Residence** Inn Marriott.

**AAA Benefit:** Members save 5% or more!

**Address:** 4537 S I-35 78744 **Location:** I-35 exit 229 (Stassney Rd) southbound; exit 230 (Ben White Blvd/SR 71) northbound; on northbound frontage road. **Facility:** 66 units, some two bedrooms, efficiencies and kitchens. 3 stories, interior corridors. **Amenities:** video games. **Pool(s):** heated outdoor. **Activities:** hot tub, exercise room. **Guest Services:** valet and coin laundry. **Featured Amenity:** full hot breakfast.

## RESIDENCE INN BY MARRIOTT-AUSTIN NORTH/PARMER LANE
(512)977-0544

Extended Stay Contemporary Hotel
$125-$171

**Residence** Inn Marriott.

**AAA Benefit:** Members save 5% or more!

**Address:** 12401 N Lamar Blvd 78753 **Location:** I-35 exit 245, just w. **Facility:** 88 kitchen units, some two bedrooms. 4 stories, interior corridors. **Pool(s):** outdoor. **Activities:** hot tub, exercise room. **Guest Services:** valet and coin laundry. **Featured Amenity:** full hot breakfast.

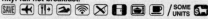

## SPRINGHILL SUITES BY MARRIOTT AUSTIN AIRPORT/SOUTH
(512)441-8270

Hotel
$99-$459

SPRINGHILL SUITES Marriott.

**AAA Benefit:** Members save 5% or more!

**Address:** 4501 S I-35 78744 **Location:** I-35 exit 228; on northbound frontage road. **Facility:** 152 units. 6 stories, interior corridors. **Pool(s):** heated indoor. **Activities:** hot tub, exercise room. **Guest Services:** valet and coin laundry. **Featured Amenity:** continental breakfast.

## SPRINGHILL SUITES BY MARRIOTT AUSTIN NORTH/PARMER LANE
(512)833-8100

Hotel
$89-$349

SPRINGHILL SUITES Marriott.

**AAA Benefit:** Members save 5% or more!

**Address:** 12520 N I-35 78753 **Location:** I-35 exit 245, just w. **Facility:** 132 units. 5 stories, interior corridors. **Pool(s):** heated indoor. **Activities:** hot tub, exercise room. **Guest Services:** valet and coin laundry. **Featured Amenity:** full hot breakfast.

(See map & index p. 86.)

## SPRINGHILL SUITES BY MARRIOTT AUSTIN NW
(512)349-0444  **24**

▼▼▼ **Hotel** $89-$169 **Address:** 10936 Stonelake Blvd 78759 **Location:** 1 mi n of US 183 on Loop 1 (Mo-Pac Expwy). **Facility:** 99 units. 5 stories, interior corridors. **Pool(s):** heated indoor. **Activities:** hot tub, exercise room. **Guest Services:** valet and coin laundry.

**AAA Benefit:** Members save 5% or more!

🛫 🍴 CALL 🔆M 🏊 BIZ 📶 ✕ 🗄 📷 📺

## STAYBRIDGE SUITES AUSTIN AIRPORT   512/389-9767  **67**

▼▼▼ **Extended Stay Contemporary Hotel.** Rates not provided. **Address:** 1611 Airport Commerce Dr 78741 **Location:** Jct SR 71 (E Ben White Blvd) and Riverside Dr, just n. Located in Airport Commerce Park. **Facility:** 161 efficiencies, some two bedrooms. 4 stories, interior corridors. **Pool(s):** outdoor. **Activities:** exercise room. **Guest Services:** valet and coin laundry.

🛫 CALL 🔆M 🏊 BIZ HS 📶 🗄 📷 📺 / SOME UNITS 🛏

## STAYBRIDGE SUITES AUSTIN ARBORETUM
(512)349-0888  **26**

▼▼▼ **Extended Stay Hotel** $169-$199 **Address:** 10201 Stonelake Blvd 78759 **Location:** Jct N Capital of Texas Hwy (SR 360) and Stonelake Blvd, 1 blk n. **Facility:** 121 efficiencies, some two bedrooms. 4 stories, interior corridors. **Terms:** cancellation fee imposed. **Pool(s):** heated outdoor. **Activities:** exercise room. **Guest Services:** complimentary and valet laundry.

🛫 🍴 CALL 🔆M 🏊 BIZ HS 📶 ✕ 🗄 📷 📺 / SOME UNITS 🛏

## STAYBRIDGE SUITES AUSTIN NORTHWEST
(512)336-7829  **8**

▼▼▼ **Extended Stay Hotel** $129-$259 **Address:** 13087 Hwy 183 N, Lot 3 78750 **Location:** US 183 N exit Anderson Mill Rd, just n of exit on east frontage road; s of Anderson Mill Rd. **Facility:** 80 efficiencies, some two bedrooms. 4 stories, interior corridors. **Terms:** cancellation fee imposed. **Pool(s):** heated outdoor. **Activities:** exercise room. **Guest Services:** complimentary and valet laundry.

🍴 CALL 🔆M 🏊 BIZ HS 📶 ✕ 🗄 📷 📺 / SOME UNITS 🛏

## STUDIO 6-NORTHWEST #6032
(512)258-3556  **11**

▼ ▼ **Extended Stay Motel** $63-$83 **Address:** 11901 Pavilion Blvd 78759 **Location:** US 183 exit Oak Knoll Dr westbound; exit Duval Rd/Balcones Woods Dr eastbound; on eastbound frontage road. **Facility:** 133 units. 2 stories (no elevator), exterior corridors. **Guest Services:** coin laundry.

🛫 📶 🗄 📷 📺 / SOME UNITS 🛏

## SUPER 8-183/AIRPORT
(512)926-5100  **58**

▼▼▼ **Hotel** $79-$360 **Address:** 5606 E 51st St 78723 **Location:** Jct US 183 S and 51st St. **Facility:** 62 units, some efficiencies. 3 stories, interior corridors. **Terms:** cancellation fee imposed. **Pool(s):** outdoor. **Activities:** hot tub, exercise room. **Guest Services:** valet and coin laundry. **Featured Amenity: continental breakfast.**

SAVE ECO CALL 🔆M 🏊 HS 📶 ✕ 🗄 📷 📺

## SUPER 8 AUSTIN AIRPORT SOUTH   (512)334-4130  **84**

▼▼▼ **Hotel** $99-$360 **Address:** 3120 Montopolis Dr 78744 **Location:** Jct Ben White Blvd/SR 71 and Montopolis Dr; on southwest corner. **Facility:** 37 units, some kitchens. 3 stories, interior corridors. **Amenities:** safes. **Activities:** exercise room. **Guest Services:** valet and coin laundry. **Featured Amenity: continental breakfast.**

SAVE ECO 🛫 🍴 BIZ HS 📶 ✕ 🗄 📷 📺

## SUPER 8 AUSTIN NORTH
(512)339-1300  **39**

▼▼▼ **Hotel** $64-$209 **Address:** 8128 N I-35 78753 **Location:** I-35 exit 241; on west frontage road. **Facility:** 123 units. 4 stories, interior corridors. **Amenities:** safes. **Pool(s):** outdoor. **Activities:** hot tub, exercise room. **Guest Services:** coin laundry. **Featured Amenity: continental breakfast.**

SAVE 🛫 🍴 🏊 BIZ 📶 🗄 📷 📺 / SOME UNITS 🛏

### 6 mi to Downtown, UT, museums. Free hot breakfast Free WIFI. All rooms w/microfridge. Pool/Gym/Spa.

## SUPER 8 UNIVERSITY AUSTIN   (512)451-7001  **56**

▼ ▼ **Hotel** $85-$410 **Address:** 5526 I-35 N 78751 **Location:** I-35 exit 238A southbound; exit 238B northbound; on southbound frontage road. **Facility:** 140 units. 3 stories, exterior corridors. **Pool(s):** outdoor. **Activities:** hot tub. **Guest Services:** coin laundry. **Featured Amenity: continental breakfast.**

SAVE 🛫 🍴 🏊 BIZ 📶 🗄 📷 📺 / SOME UNITS 🛏

(See map & index p. 86.)

**VINTAGE VILLAS HOTEL AND EVENTS**     (512)266-9333
▼▼▼ **Boutique Hotel** $129-$299 **Address:** 4209 Eck Ln 78734 **Location:** Jct CR 2222 and SR 620, 5 mi w to Eck Ln, 0.6 mi n. **Facility:** You may be in the company of newlyweds, as this is a local favorite spot for weddings. Distinctive décor, Texas artwork and handmade furniture sport a Texas flair. 44 units, some kitchens. 3 stories (no elevator), interior corridors. **Terms:** check-in 4 pm, 3 day cancellation notice-fee imposed. 🛎 📶 🖥 📷 💻

---

**WESTIN AUSTIN AT THE DOMAIN**     (512)832-4197  ㉒

▼▼ ▼▼
Hotel
$159-$369

**WESTIN**
HOTELS & RESORTS
**AAA Benefit:** Enjoy up to 20% off your next stay, plus Starwood Preferred Guest® bonuses!

**Address:** 11301 Domain Dr 78758 **Location:** Jct Braker and Burnet rds; on northwest corner; in The Domain. **Facility:** Located in an upscale enclave, this property fits perfectly with the overall ambience of the area. 341 units. 8 stories, interior corridors. **Parking:** on-site and valet. **Terms:** resort fee. **Amenities:** safes. **Dining:** Urban, An American Grill, see separate listing. **Pool(s):** heated outdoor. **Activities:** hot tub, exercise room. **Guest Services:** valet laundry.

[SAVE] 🍴 🏋 🍸 CALL 🖐M 🏊 📶 BIZ $HS 📶 ✕ 🖥 💻 / SOME UNITS 🛏

---

**WYNDHAM GARDEN HOTEL**     (512)448-2444  ㉖㉖

▼▼▼
Hotel
$89-$169

**Address:** 3401 I-35 S 78741 **Location:** I-35 exit 231 (Woodward St) southbound; exit 230 (Ben White Blvd/SR 71) northbound; on northbound frontage road. **Facility:** 210 units. 5 stories, interior/exterior corridors. **Amenities:** safes. **Pool(s):** outdoor. **Activities:** hot tub, exercise room. **Guest Services:** valet and coin laundry, area transportation.

[SAVE] 🛗 🍴 🍸 CALL 🖐M 🏊 BIZ HS 📶 ✕ 💻 / SOME UNITS S🏊 🖥 📷

---

**LAKE AUSTIN SPA RESORT**     512/372-7300
[fyi] Not evaluated. **Address:** 1705 S Quinlan Park Rd 78732 **Location:** Jct SR 620 and Quinlan Park Rd, 5.2 mi s. Facilities, services, and décor characterize a mid-scale property.

---

**WHERE TO EAT**

**8212 WINE BAR & GRILL**     512/329-4000  ㊾
▼▼▼ American. Casual Dining. $13-$24 **AAA Inspector Notes:** Hill Country views accentuate the meals at the contemporary restaurant. The menu comprises soups, sandwiches, salads, steak, seafood, ribs and other delicious choices. **Features:** full bar. **Address:** 8212 Barton Club Dr 78735 **Location:** Jct Capital of Texas Hwy (SR 360) and FM 2244 (Bee Caves Rd), 1.7 mi s; in Omni Barton Creek Resort & Spa. **Parking:** on-site and valet. L D CALL 🖐M

**ABUELO'S THE FLAVOR OF MEXICO**     512/306-0857
▼▼ Mexican. Casual Dining. $8-$20 **AAA Inspector Notes:** A very nice selection of many traditional Mexican dishes is served in an upscale and spacious dining area. Inventive adult beverages are available. **Features:** full bar. **Address:** 2901 S Capital of Texas Hwy 78746 **Location:** Jct Loop 1 (Mo-Pac Expwy) and Capital of Texas Hwy (SR 360); in Barton Creek Square Mall. L D CALL 🖐M

**ANDIAMO RISTORANTE**     512/719-3377  ㉙
▼▼▼ Italian. Casual Dining. $10-$30 **AAA Inspector Notes:** Upscale Italian dishes are found at this very nice restaurant. I really enjoyed the fennel potato soup, a salad with apple strips and a homemade dressing, and the veal ravioli with Italian sausage. Seasonal menus prevail. **Features:** beer & wine. **Address:** 2521 Rutland Dr 78758 **Location:** Jct Burnet Rd and Rutland Dr; on southeast corner. L D

**BANDERAS**     512/795-6100  ⑲
▼▼▼ American. Fine Dining. $13-$30 **AAA Inspector Notes:** The upscale restaurant prepares interesting tapas, in addition to seafood, steaks and chicken, not to mention fine desserts. **Features:** full bar. **Address:** 9721 Arboretum Blvd 78759 **Location:** Jct US 183 and N Capital of Texas Hwy (SR 360); southwest corner; in Renaissance Austin Hotel. **Parking:** on-site and valet. B L D CALL 🖐M

**BARTLETT'S**     512/451-7333  ㊲
▼▼▼ American. Casual Dining. $10-$34 **AAA Inspector Notes:** The popular restaurant's menu lists à la carte selections of prime rib, steaks, fish and pork chops, as well as lighter fare offerings of salads and hamburgers, and club, chicken and outstanding French dip sandwiches, which are a favorite of mine. **Features:** full bar. **Reservations:** required. **Address:** 2408 W Anderson Ln 78757 **Location:** Jct Burnet Rd and W Anderson Ln; on northwest corner. L D CALL 🖐M

**BEETS CAFE**     512/477-2338  ㊾㉒
▼ Vegan. Casual Dining. $8-$14 **AAA Inspector Notes:** "Living foods" are featured at this restaurant where distinct flavors come from the creative pairings of ingredients. **Features:** wine only. **Address:** 1611 W 5th St, Suite 165 78703 **Location:** Just e of Loop 1 (Mo-Pac Expwy). **Parking:** street only. B L D

**BERRYHILL BAJA GRILL**     512/327-9033
▼ Mexican. Casual Dining. $6-$12 **AAA Inspector Notes:** This place is known for its fish tacos, but the tamales and burritos deserve a second look. There are varied Mexican treats; the chunky tomato salsa is reason enough to stop in. **Features:** full bar. **Address:** 3600 N Capital of Texas Hwy, Bldg A, Suite 110 78746 **Location:** Capital of Texas Hwy (SR 360), 0.5 mi s of Colorado River Bridge. L D CALL 🖐M

**BLUE BAKER**     512/346-2583  ㉓
▼ American. Quick Serve. $6-$11 **AAA Inspector Notes:** Prepared-on-site breads, pastries, soups, salads, sandwiches and pizzas. I had the "B.B." sandwich, which was tasty and paired with the tomato-basil bisque. **Features:** patio dining. **Address:** 10000 Research Blvd 78759 **Location:** Jct US 183 and Great Hills Tr; on southwest corner; in The Shops at Arboretum. B L D CALL 🖐M

**BONE DADDY'S HOUSE OF SMOKE**     512/346-3025  ⑨
▼▼ American. Casual Dining. $9-$22 **AAA Inspector Notes:** Guests appreciate the relaxed atmosphere and diverse menu of smokehouse favorites. Also available is lighter fare, including sandwiches and salads. During my last meal, I had the BLT salad with some baby back ribs and whole chicken wings and enjoyed every bit of it. For sharing, the beer can chicken is an excellent choice. **Features:** full bar. **Address:** 11617 Research Blvd 78759 **Location:** Jct I-35 and US 183; US 183 N exit Duval Rd, just n. L D LATE CALL 🖐M

**BRICK OVEN--ARBORETUM**     512/345-6181  ⑯
▼▼ Italian Pizza. Casual Dining. $7-$22 **AAA Inspector Notes:** Favorite Italian dishes, including calzones, stromboli, pasta and pizza, highlight the menu. I treat myself to any of the specialty pizzas on the menu. **Features:** beer & wine. **Address:** 10710 Research Blvd 78759 **Location:** Jct Braker Ln and US 183; southwest corner. L D

**CENTRAL MARKET CAFE**     512/206-1020  ㊵
▼ American. Quick Serve. $7-$15 **AAA Inspector Notes:** The fun, energetic bistro prepares large portions of such imaginative dishes as steak or chicken fajitas salad with pico de gallo, sour cream and margarita dressing. This self-serve eatery is located in a local supermarket, which is situated in a shopping plaza and park area. **Features:** beer & wine. **Address:** 4001 N Lamar Blvd 78756 **Location:** Jct Lamar Blvd and 38th St, just n. L D

(See map & index p. 86.)

### THE CHEESECAKE FACTORY        512/241-0777  20
▼▼▼ American. Casual Dining. $9-$30 **AAA Inspector Notes:** A display case of mouthwatering cheesecakes is the first thing visitors see as they walk through the door. The extensive menu incorporates many types of cuisine, including Asian, Italian, Greek and Spanish. **Features:** full bar, Sunday brunch. **Address:** 10000 Research Blvd 78759 **Location:** Jct US 183 and Great Hills Tr; in Arboretum Shopping Center. **Parking:** on-site and valet.
L  D

### CHEZ ZEE AMERICAN BISTRO        512/454-2666  39
▼▼ ▼ American. Casual Dining. $9-$29 **AAA Inspector Notes:** A family restaurant specializing in Southwest cuisine. Try the interesting mixed grill of filet mignon, a lamb chop and a Maryland crab cake, but leave plenty of room for the wonderful homemade desserts. **Features:** full bar, Sunday brunch, happy hour. **Address:** 5406 Balcones Dr 78731 **Location:** Loop 1 (Mo-Pac Expwy) exit CR 2222, 2 blks w. L  D

### COUNTY LINE ON THE HILL        512/327-1742  46
▼▼ Regional Barbecue. Family Dining. $9-$23 **AAA Inspector Notes:** Guests can enjoy a favorite beverage on the stone patio overlooking the Hill Country before savoring the slow-smoked meats the popular barbecue restaurant turns out. **Features:** full bar, patio dining. **Address:** 6500 W Bee Caves Rd 78746 **Location:** Jct Capital of Texas Hwy (SR 360) and FM 2244 (Bee Caves Rd), 0.3 mi w. L  D

### COUNTY LINE ON THE LAKE        512/346-3664  35
▼▼ Barbecue. Casual Dining. $9-$23 **AAA Inspector Notes:** With a view overlooking Mount Bonnell, the 1940s-style restaurant near the river serves barbecue specialties. Diners can feast on all-you-can-eat ribs, potato salad and vegetables. A jukebox fills the dining room with old standards. I always enjoy the smoked prime rib. **Features:** full bar, patio dining, happy hour. **Address:** 5204 CR 2222 78731 **Location:** 9.5 mi nw; 0.3 mi e of jct Capital of Texas Hwy (SR 360). L  D  CALL &M

### COVER 2        512/506-9953  5
▼▼ American. Casual Dining. $7-$15 **AAA Inspector Notes:** Soups, salads, excellent burgers and a nice assortment of sandwiches and specialty items are available at this upscale and contemporary restaurant. I really enjoyed the flatbread choices. **Features:** full bar. **Address:** 13701 Research Blvd 78750 **Location:** US 183 exit Anderson Mill; on E Frontage Rd; on south end of Lake Creek Shopping Center. L  D

### COVER 3        512/374-1121  34
▼▼▼ American. Casual Dining. $10-$36 **AAA Inspector Notes:** Classic salads, burgers, sandwiches and entrées of chicken, seafood and steaks in a contemporary setting. Patio dining is available. The brick chicken macaroni 'n cheese was outstanding, as was the peach pudding cake. **Features:** full bar, patio dining, happy hour. **Address:** 2700 W Anderson Ln 78757 **Location:** Jct Burnet Rd and Anderson Ln, 0.5 mi w. L  D

### DAILY GRILL        512/836-4200
▼▼ American. Casual Dining. $11-$32 **AAA Inspector Notes:** In the fashionable Domain, the restaurant presents a menu of steaks, chops, seafood and chicken, not to mention featured home-style favorites. **Features:** full bar, patio dining. **Address:** 11506 Century Oaks Terr 78758 **Location:** Jct Loop 1 (Mo-Pac Expwy) and Braker Ln; in The Domain. **Parking:** on-site and valet.
L  D  CALL &M  🍴

### EASTSIDE CAFE        512/476-5858  51
▼▼▼▼ Continental. Casual Dining. $10-$24 **AAA Inspector Notes:** In a 1928 bungalow, the cafe is adorned with pictures and lush foliage. Diners can opt for patio seating. The menu centers on sophisticated fare, including tempting desserts. **Features:** beer & wine, Sunday brunch. **Reservations:** suggested. **Address:** 2113 Manor Rd 78722 **Location:** I-35 exit Manor Rd, 0.5 mi e.
L  D

### EDDIE V'S EDGEWATER GRILLE-ARBORETUM        512/342-2642  28
▼▼▼ Steak Seafood. Fine Dining. $19-$48 **AAA Inspector Notes:** A generous selection of seafood and prime steak entrees is complemented by appetizers that include offerings from the oyster bar. The atmosphere is upscale. **Features:** full bar, happy hour. **Address:** 9400-B Arboretum Blvd 78759 **Location:** US 183 to Capital of Texas Hwy (SR 360), 0.5 mi w to Arboretum Blvd, then just n. **Parking:** on-site and valet. D  CALL &M

### ESTANCIA CHURRASCARIA ARBORETUM        512/345-5600  21
▼▼▼ Brazilian Steak. Fine Dining. $22-$36 **AAA Inspector Notes:** A generous selection of salad bar items accompanies the never-ending presentation of at least 12 different cuts of meat at this really fun dining spot. **Features:** full bar. **Reservations:** suggested. **Address:** 10000 Research Blvd 78759 **Location:** Jct US 183 and Great Hills Blvd; southwest corner. D  D  CALL &M

### FIREWHEEL CAFE        512/308-1234
▼▼▼ American. Casual Dining. $12-$30 **AAA Inspector Notes:** Casual resort dining with many upscale amenities awaits patrons of this restaurant. Choices range from soups and salads to sandwiches and entrees of steak, pasta and seafood. **Features:** full bar. **Address:** 575 Hyatt Lost Pines Rd 78612 **Location:** SR 71, 13 mi e of Austin-Bergstrom International Airport; 9 mi w of Bastrop; in Hyatt Regency Lost Pines Resort and Spa. **Parking:** on-site and valet. B  L  D  CALL &M

### FLEMING'S PRIME STEAKHOUSE & WINE BAR        512/835-9463  11
▼▼▼ American. Fine Dining. $16-$46 **AAA Inspector Notes:** The warm, clubby atmosphere is the ideal setting for perfectly grilled steaks and seafood. Side dishes come in hearty portions, and salads are fresh and crisp. More than 100 wine selections are available. **Features:** full bar. **Reservations:** suggested. **Address:** 11600 Century Oaks Terr 78758 **Location:** Jct W Braker Ln and Loop 1 (Mo-Pac Expwy); in Domain Shopping Enclave. D  CALL &M

### FONDA SAN MIGUEL        512/459-4121  42
▼▼▼ Mexican. Casual Dining. $17-$40 **AAA Inspector Notes:** The charming Mexican inn decor comes complete with colorful paintings, pottery and other wares. Tex-Mex entrees, plus culinary delights from various regions in Mexico, fill an excellent menu that includes chicken, seafood and beef dishes. Lush greenery and a fountain that melds nicely with the decor scheme enhances the waiting area at the entry. **Features:** full bar, Sunday brunch. **Reservations:** suggested. **Address:** 2330 W North Loop Blvd 78756 **Location:** Just w of Burnet Rd. D

### FREDA'S SEAFOOD GRILL        512/506-8700  4
▼▼▼ Seafood Steak. Casual Dining. $10-$30 **AAA Inspector Notes:** Included in a nice selection of entrées are seafood, steak, chicken and pasta dishes. The northwest Austin restaurant also serves rich desserts. The pecan tilapia is one of the house favorites. **Features:** full bar, Sunday brunch. **Address:** 10903 Pecan Park Blvd 78750 **Location:** Jct US 183 and SR 620, 0.5 mi w to Pecan Park Blvd, then just s. L  D

### HILL COUNTRY DINING ROOM        512/329-4000  48
▼▼▼ ◆◆◆◆

**American Fine Dining $23-$45**

**AAA Inspector Notes:** On the menu at the fine-dining establishment is a wide selection of beef, veal, lamb, chicken and seafood entrees. The resort setting affords expansive views of the golf courses and Hill Country. **Features:** full bar. **Address:** 8212 Barton Club Dr 78735 **Location:** Jct Capital of Texas Hwy (SR 360) and FM 2244 (Bee Caves Rd), 1 mi w to Barton Creek Blvd, 1.7 mi s; in Omni Barton Creek Resort & Spa. **Parking:** valet only. B  D  CALL &M

### HILL COUNTRY PASTA HOUSE        512/266-9445
▼▼ Italian. Casual Dining. $10-$25 **AAA Inspector Notes:** Traditional pasta dishes--as well as seafood, beef, veal and chicken entrees--are wonderfully prepared in this restaurant in the Lake Travis area. Pecan wood-fired gourmet pizzas are also tempting. **Features:** full bar. **Address:** 3519 SR 620 N (Lake Travis) 78734 **Location:** Jct SR 620 and CR 2222, 5.6 mi w. L  D  CALL &M

(See map & index p. 86.)

## HOPDODDY BURGER BAR 512/467-2337 ③⑥
Burgers. Casual Dining. $6-$12 **AAA Inspector Notes:** You can match your imaginative burger made from beef, bison or lamb with your favorite beer, wine or margarita at this popular new eatery. **Features:** beer & wine. **Address:** 2438 W Anderson Ln 78757 **Location:** Jct Burnet Rd and Anderson Ln, just w. L D

## HOPDODDY BURGER BAR 512/243-7505 ⑤⑥
Burgers. Casual Dining. $6-$12 **AAA Inspector Notes:** Expect long lines at this very popular and trendy spot featuring handcrafted burgers and some salad selections. **Features:** full bar, patio dining, happy hour. **Address:** 1400 S Congress Ave 78704 **Location:** At S Congress Ave and Gibson St. **Parking:** street only. L D

## HUDSON'S ON THE BEND 512/266-1369
Regional Southwestern. Fine Dining. $20-$49 **AAA Inspector Notes:** Preparations on the nicely varied menu include exotic dishes like rattlesnake, kangaroo, elk and a mixed grill of venison, rabbit and quail. Veal, beef and seafood entrées also are offered. **Features:** full bar. **Reservations:** suggested. **Address:** 3509 SR 620 N 78734 **Location:** Jct SR 620 and CR 2222, 5.6 mi w. D

## IRON CACTUS SOUTHWESTERN GRILL 512/794-8778 ②⑤
Southwestern. Casual Dining. $7-$25 **AAA Inspector Notes:** Distinctive Southwestern flavorings enhance entrées of steak, chicken, pork, pot roast and Mexican fare at the contemporary restaurant. Sunday offers a lunch buffet. Do not pass on the Mexican mousse. **Features:** full bar, patio dining, Sunday brunch, happy hour. **Address:** 10001 Stonelake Blvd 78759 **Location:** US 183 N to Capital of Texas Hwy (SR 360), 2 blks e; on northeast corner. L D CALL M

## JASPER'S 512/834-4111 ⑫
Steak Seafood. Fine Dining. $10-$42 **AAA Inspector Notes:** The casual yet upscale and contemporary restaurant offers delicious choices to please everyone with its inventive appetizers, steaks, chops, chicken, seafood and pork. I really enjoyed the selection of mini desserts the last time I visited, not to mention the excellent prime rib of beef. **Features:** full bar, Sunday brunch. **Address:** 11506 Century Oaks Terr, Suite 128 78758 **Location:** Jct Loop 1 (Mo-Pac Expwy) and Braker Ln; in The Domain. **Parking:** on-site and valet. D CALL M

## KERBEY LANE CAFE-CENTRAL 512/451-1436 ④③
Breakfast Comfort Food. Casual Dining. $7-$13 **AAA Inspector Notes:** Gingerbread pancakes and eggs with tortillas are served all day. Separate dining rooms are built in the sleeping quarters of the renovated home. Wooden floors and floral-patterned walls add pleasant touches. **Features:** full bar. **Address:** 3704 Kerbey Ln 78731 **Location:** W of Lamar Blvd off W 38th St and Kerbey Ln. **Parking:** street only. B L D ㉔

## KERBEY LANE CAFE--NORTHWEST 512/258-7757 ⑦
Breakfast Comfort Food. Casual Dining. $7-$13 **AAA Inspector Notes:** Natural ingredients factor into many of the popular restaurant's preparations of American comfort food. **Features:** full bar, patio dining. **Reservations:** suggested. **Address:** 13435 Research Blvd 78750 **Location:** Jct US 183 N and Anderson Mill Rd; on east frontage road. B L D ㉔

## KERBEY LANE CAFE-UT 512/477-5717 ⑤⓪
Breakfast Comfort Food. Casual Dining. $7-$13 **AAA Inspector Notes:** Patrons can have table service or sit at the counter to enjoy soups, salads, sandwiches, Mexican dishes or items from the full breakfast menu at this popular local restaurant. It's located just north of the University of Texas campus. **Features:** full bar. **Address:** 2606 Guadalupe St 78705 **Location:** Between 26th and 27th sts; uptown. B L D ㉔

## KONA GRILL 512/835-5900 ⑬
Fusion. Fine Dining. $10-$30 **AAA Inspector Notes:** The eclectic menu reflects Pacific influences. In addition to noodle dishes and sushi, it lists specialties of macadamia nut chicken and lemon grass-encrusted swordfish. The dining room has a large aquarium, a private area and a sushi bar. The patio opens during warm weather. **Features:** full bar, patio dining, happy hour. **Reservations:** required. **Address:** 11410 Century Oaks Terr 78758 **Location:** Loop 1 (Mo-Pac Expwy) and Braker Ln, just n; in The Domain. L D CALL M

## LA MADELEINE COUNTRY FRENCH CAFE
Traditional French Breakfast Sandwiches. Casual Dining. $7-$15 **AAA Inspector Notes:** A fireplace creates the focal point at this cozy European style café where you can always get a quiche or savory stuffed puffed pastry on the go or stick around for a chicken crêpe or French dip sandwich. Heartier entrées like rotisserie chicken are offered and every season promises menu surprises. Whatever you decide on you probably will not get out the door without enjoying one of their tempting sweet pastries. B L D

*For additional information, visit AAA.com*

**LOCATIONS:**
**Address:** 9828 Great Hills Tr, Suite 650 78759 **Location:** Jct US 183 and Great Hills Tr; on northwest corner. **Phone:** 512/502-2474
**Address:** 701 Capital of Texas Hwy 78746 **Location:** Capital of Texas Hwy (SR 360) and FM 2244 (Bee Caves Rd), just s; in Westlake Hills Shopping Center. **Phone:** 512/306-1998
**Address:** 5493 Brodie Ln 78745 **Location:** Jct US 290, just s. **Phone:** 512/287-4081

## MATT'S EL RANCHO 512/462-9333 ⑤⑧
Tex-Mex. Casual Dining. $7-$33 **AAA Inspector Notes:** Surrounded by beautiful oak trees, this family restaurant has a quaint patio for al fresco dining. All items, including the delicious desserts, are prepared from scratch. Try shrimp or steak, or something a little different. **Features:** full bar, patio dining. **Address:** 2613 S Lamar Blvd 78704 **Location:** 0.5 mi s of jct Oltorf St and Lamar Blvd. L D

## MIGHTY FINE 512/418-0444 ㉒
Burgers. Quick Serve. $4-$6 **AAA Inspector Notes:** All-American fare of large juicy burgers, generous portions of fries and hand-made premium milk shakes satisfy patrons of this restaurant near Arboretum and The Domain in the Arborwalk Shopping Mall. **Features:** beer only. **Address:** 10515 N Mo-Pac Expwy 78759 **Location:** Jct Loop 1 (Mo-Pac Expwy) and Braker Ln; in Arborwalk Center. L D

## MIKADO RYOTEI 512/833-8188 ㉚
Japanese Small Plates Sushi. Fine Dining. $9-$32 **AAA Inspector Notes:** Patrons can select among nicely varied sushi-bar offerings or have a complete entrée of steak, duck, seafood or chicken. Small plates are also available. Dishes are prepared in a traditional Japanese manner. **Address:** 9033 Research Blvd 78758 **Location:** Jct US 183 and Burnet Rd; on northeast corner. L D CALL M

## MOZART'S COFFEE ROASTERS 512/477-2900 ㊼
Coffee/Tea Breads/Pastries. Quick Serve. $2-$6 **AAA Inspector Notes:** Guests can sip coffee imported from any of 20 countries or any of 23 flavors of tea while noshing on homemade pastries, specialty cheesecakes and fruit tarts. The specialty shop, which sits on the banks of Lake Austin, offers indoor or outdoor seating. **Address:** 3825 Lake Austin Blvd 78703 **Location:** Loop 1 (Mo-Pac Expwy) exit Lake Austin Blvd, 2 mi w. B L D LATE CALL M

## NORTH BY NORTHWEST RESTAURANT AND BREWERY 512/467-6969 ㉖
American. Gastropub. $8-$24 **AAA Inspector Notes:** An upscale manner prevails at the restaurant, where chicken, beef, pork, seafood and daily specials highlight the varied menu. The hand-crafted beers and ales. The tenderloin steak sandwich was very tasty, as was the bleu cheese tomato bisque. For dessert, the peanut butter mousse was really fun. **Features:** full bar, patio dining, Sunday brunch, happy hour. **Address:** 10010 Capital of Texas Hwy N 78759 **Location:** US 183 N to Capital of Texas Hwy (SR 360), 2 blks e; on northeast corner. L D CALL M

(See map & index p. 86.)

**NUEVA ONDA**  512/447-5063  60

Mexican. Quick Serve. $2-$9 **AAA Inspector Notes:** The outdoor patio is a colorful and popular spot to enjoy some quick and fresh Tex-Mex favorites at this southside outpost. **Features:** beer & wine. **Address:** 2218 College Ave 78704 **Location:** Jct College and Congress aves. B L

**ONION CREEK GRILL**  512/448-2222  61

American. Casual Dining. $8-$31 **AAA Inspector Notes:** Steaks, chops, seafood and pasta entrees make up the menu. A professional flair is evident in the dining room. **Features:** full bar. **Address:** 4140 Governor's Row 78744 **Location:** I-35 exit 230B (Ben White Blvd/SR 71) southbound; exit 230 northbound; on east frontage road; in Omni Austin Hotel Southpark. B L D

**PAPPADEAUX SEAFOOD KITCHEN**  512/452-9363

Regional Cajun Seafood. Casual Dining. $9-$40 **AAA Inspector Notes:** A seafood lover's delight, the restaurant taps into a little bit of New Orleans with its Cajun dishes and elaborate menu selections. Patrons might start off with a creative choice of blackened oyster and shrimp fondeaux with crayfish and let the feast begin. While music plays in the background, patrons can dig into dirty rice or spicy gumbo loaded with seafood. Well-seasoned shrimp and fish are prepared in varied ways. **Features:** full bar, patio dining, happy hour. **Address:** 6319 I-35 N 78752 **Location:** I-35 exit 239 northbound; exit 238B southbound; on east frontage road.

L D CALL M

**PAPPASITO'S CANTINA**  512/459-9214

Mexican. Casual Dining. $13-$44 **AAA Inspector Notes:** Fine traditional offerings are served in an upscale cantina atmosphere. Often crowded during peak hours, the immensely popular stop dishes up generous portions of sizzling fajitas, enchiladas and other traditional Mexican favorites, including some shrimp specialties. The terrific margaritas are guaranteed to get attention. Tables in the large dining room are closely spaced. Ice cream with cinnamon on chocolate bread pudding shouldn't be missed. **Features:** full bar, happy hour. **Address:** 6513 I-35 N 78752 **Location:** I-35 exit 238A; on east frontage road. L D CALL M

**PERLA'S SEAFOOD & OYSTER BAR**  512/291-7300  55

Regional Seafood. Casual Dining. $10-$38 **AAA Inspector Notes:** Choose between contemporary indoor dining or a relaxing misted patio environment in the trendy South Congress district and select from many wonderful seafood delicacies at this restaurant featuring professional service. **Features:** full bar. **Reservations:** required. **Address:** 1400 S Congress Ave 78704 **Location:** S Congress Ave and Elizabeth St, 1 blk n. **Parking:** on-site and street. L D

**PLUCKER'S LAKELINE**  512/258-9464  3

Wings. Casual Dining. $8-$20 **AAA Inspector Notes:** Large and moist chicken wings with a choice of several sauces is the specialty here. Enjoy the sports-bar atmosphere while dining. I tried the spicy lemon-pepper sauce for my wings and they were great! **Features:** full bar, happy hour. **Address:** 11066 Pecan Park Blvd 78613 **Location:** Jct SR 620 and Pecan Park Blvd, just n. L D

**POK-E-JO'S SMOKEHOUSE**

Barbecue. Quick Serve. $4-$12 **AAA Inspector Notes:** This popular and relaxed spot slow-smokes delicious barbecue meats, which guests can order with a selection of tasty side dishes. **Bar:** beer only. L D

*For additional information, visit AAA.com*

**LOCATIONS:**
**Address:** 9828 Great Hills Tr 78759 **Location:** US 183 and Great Hills Tr; on northwest corner. **Phone:** 512/338-1990

**Address:** 2121 W Parmer Ln 78727 **Location:** Jct Loop 1 (Mo-Pac Expwy) and Parmer Ln, just e. **Phone:** 512/491-0434

**Address:** 4109 SR 360 (Capital of Texas Hwy) 78704 **Location:** Jct Capital of Texas Hwy (SR 360) and S Lamar Blvd, just nw; in Brodie Oaks Shopping Center. **Phone:** 512/440-0447

**Address:** 1000 E 41st St 78751 **Location:** Jct 41st St and I-35. **Phone:** 512/302-1200

**REALE'S PIZZA AND CAFE**  512/335-5115  6

Southern Italian. Casual Dining. $8-$20 **AAA Inspector Notes:** Steaks, chicken, veal, seafood and traditional pasta are prepared in the Southern Italian manner. In addition to a nice selection of appetizers, the menu lists pizzas, sub sandwiches and calzones. The atmosphere is warm. In my opinion, they serve some of the best pizza to be found anywhere. **Features:** full bar. **Address:** 13450 Research Blvd 78750 **Location:** Jct US 183 and Anderson Mill Rd; in The Plaza 183 Center. L D CALL M

**ROARING FORK STONELAKE**  512/342-2700  15

Steak. Casual Dining. $10-$36 **AAA Inspector Notes:** Upscale contemporary dining in the Arboretum district northwest of the city is what you'll find here. The wide array of choices on the menu, including inventive appetizers and a mixed grill of filet mignon, sausage, lamb chops and baby back ribs, is guaranteed to please everyone. The Yucatan shrimp appetizer was beautifully presented. **Features:** full bar, Sunday brunch. **Address:** 10850 Stonelake Blvd 78759 **Location:** Jct US 183 and Braker Ln, just e, then just n. L D CALL M

**RUDY'S COUNTRY STORE AND BAR-B-QUE**  512/250-8002

Barbecue. Quick Serve. $4-$12 **AAA Inspector Notes:** This small, informal barbecue chain has a twist: The tasty food is ordered by the pound. Guests can mix and match and order three-quarters of a pound of beef with a half-pound of turkey or pork, for example. Desserts and coleslaw are prepackaged, and precooked beans accompany the meat. A drive-through window is available at most locations. **Features:** beer & wine. **Address:** 7709 FM 620 N 78726 **Location:** Jct SR 620 and CR 2222, 0.5 mi e. B L D

**SALTGRASS STEAKHOUSE**  512/340-0040  17

Western Steak. Casual Dining. $9-$30 **AAA Inspector Notes:** Those looking for something different should try the comfortable steakhouse, which never says no to a special request. Born from the spirit of Texas cattle drives, the restaurant resembles a Texas lodge, with high ceilings and mounted animal heads. Baby back ribs are so tender the meat falls off the bone. Also on the menu are hearty steaks, prime rib, chicken, seafood and yummy desserts. **Features:** full bar. **Address:** 10614 Research Blvd 78759 **Location:** US 183 exit Braker Ln, just s on southbound frontage road.

SAVE L D

**SATAY RESTAURANT**  512/467-6731  32

Thai. Casual Dining. $10-$22 **AAA Inspector Notes:** Specialties include coconut-based soup and skewer meats with steamed rice and peanut sauce. Yam cakes and fried egg rolls are particularly tasty. Natural lighting fills the large, open dining room, which features attractive Asian decor. **Features:** full bar. **Reservations:** suggested. **Address:** 3202 W Anderson Ln 78757 **Location:** Northwest corner of Shoal Creek and Anderson Ln, just e of Loop 1 (Mo-Pac Expwy). L D

**SERRANO'S**

Tex-Mex. Casual Dining. $8-$17 **AAA Inspector Notes:** The Tex-Mex cafe is known for its stuffed jalapenos, which tempt those with a taste for something spicy (and a nearby water glass). Among good choices are crunchy flautas and sizzling fajitas. **Bar:** full bar. L D

*For additional information, visit AAA.com*

**LOCATIONS:**
**Address:** 11100 Pecan Park Blvd 78613 **Location:** Jct US 183 and SR 620, 1 blk n to Lakeline Mall Dr, then just w. **Phone:** 512/258-3441

**Address:** 5030 US 290 W 78735 **Location:** Jct US 290/Southwest Pkwy/Loop 1 (Mo-Pac Expwy); on northeast corner; in shopping center. **Phone:** 512/891-7592

**SHERLOCK'S BAKER ST. PUB**  512/380-9443

English. Casual Dining. $7-$14 **AAA Inspector Notes:** Scotch eggs, bangers and mash, shepherd's pie and fish 'n chips are among the palate-pleasing entrees at this English pub. Steak and seafood dishes and sandwiches and burgers also are available. **Features:** full bar. **Address:** 9012 Research Blvd 78758 **Location:** US 183 and Burnet Rd; on southwest corner. L D CALL M

(See map & index p. 86.)

## SIENA RISTORANTE TOSCANO  512/349-7667  (33)

▼▼▼▼ Northern Italian. Fine Dining. $10-$49 **AAA Inspector Notes:** Steaks, lamb, veal, pork tenderloin and seafood pastas adorn the menu of the upscale Tuscan villa. The mixed grill is exceptionally interesting. Patio seating is an option. **Features:** full bar, patio dining, happy hour. **Reservations:** suggested. **Address:** 6203 N Capital of Texas Hwy, Bldg B 78731 **Location:** Jct Capital of Texas Hwy (SR 360) and CR 2222; on southeast corner.

L  D  CALL  &M

## STEINER RANCH STEAKHOUSE  512/381-0800  (24)

▼▼▼▼ Steak. Casual Dining. $19-$48 **AAA Inspector Notes:** The multi-story, upscale restaurant provides fabulous views of Lake Travis and the Hill Country. Enjoy beverages on the spacious patios or by the large firepit before dining on Prime cuts of beef, lamb, elk, pork, seafood or pasta dishes. A bone-in filet mignon is often found as a specialty of the night. I had the rack of lamb the last time I visited and it was excellent. **Features:** full bar, Sunday brunch. **Reservations:** suggested. **Address:** 5424 Steiner Ranch Blvd 78732 **Location:** Jct SR 620 and Steiner Ranch Blvd, 0.5 mi w.

D  CALL  &M

## TACODELI CENTRAL  512/732-0303  (53)

▼ Mexican. Quick Serve. $3-$7 **AAA Inspector Notes:** A nice selection of favorite tacos, including those of the breakfast variety, are on the menu. **Features:** patio dining. **Address:** 1500 Spyglass Dr 78705 **Location:** Loop 1 (Mo-Pac Expwy) exit Barton Skyway, 0.5 mi e to Spyglass Dr; on northwest corner.  B  L  D

## TACODELI NORTHWEST  512/339-1700  (10)

▼ Mexican. Quick Serve. $3-$7 **AAA Inspector Notes:** A nice selection of favorite tacos, including breakfast tacos for the early crowd, are available. **Features:** patio dining. **Address:** 12001 Burnet Rd 78705 **Location:** Jct Burnet Rd and Gracie Farms.

B  L

## TAJ PALACE INDIAN RESTAURANT & BAR
512/452-9959  (41)

▼ Indian. Casual Dining. $10-$20 **AAA Inspector Notes:** The exotic scene is filled with Indian trinkets, wall hangings, brass, Taj Mahal marble, silk and beads. From curries to tandoori chicken, traditional entrees are well-prepared. Many choices line the Monday buffet and the Tuesday vegetarian buffet. **Features:** beer & wine. **Address:** 6700 Middle Fiskville Rd 78752 **Location:** I-35 exit 239/240 southbound; exit 239 northbound, just off west frontage road.

L  D

## TARKA INDIAN KITCHEN  512/323-0955  (38)

▼ Indian. Quick Serve. $7-$9 **AAA Inspector Notes:** This fast-casual version of Indian cuisine does not sacrifice freshness or flavor with its menu of biryanis, curries, kebabs and numerous vegetarian selections. The earthy tones effuse a warm glow over both the young families and young urbanites that patronize this Green Certified restaurant. **Features:** beer & wine, patio dining. **Address:** 2525 W Anderson Ln 78757 **Location:** Loop 1 (Mo-Pac Expwy) exit Anderson Ln, 0.6 mi e; in Walmart Shopping Center.  L  D

## TEXADELPHIA

▼ Sandwiches. Quick Serve. $6-$9 **AAA Inspector Notes:** Texas cheese steak and beer are the name of the game at the laid-back eatery. While catching up on sports statistics, guests can wash down customized sandwiches and juicy burgers with a selection from an encyclopedia of brews. **Bar:** beer only.  L  D

*For additional information, visit AAA.com*
**LOCATIONS:**
**Address:** 14010 N US 183, Suite 500 78717 **Location:** Jct US 183 and SR 620, just n. **Phone:** 512/249-0249
**Address:** 5400 Brodie Ln, Suite 230 78745 **Location:** Jct US 290/SR 71 and Brodie Ln, 0.5 mi s. **Phone:** 512/891-6464
**Address:** 5510 S I-35, Suite E-410 78745 **Location:** I-35 exit 229 (Stassney Rd), just n on west frontage road. **Phone:** 512/804-0804
**Address:** 9828 Great Hills Tr 78759 **Location:** Jct US 183 N and Great Hills Tr; on northwest corner. **Phone:** 512/338-1338

## TEXAS LAND AND CATTLE STEAKHOUSE

▼▼ Steak. Casual Dining. $9-$28 **AAA Inspector Notes:** A variety of large Prime steaks, delicious salads and scrumptious desserts await you at the friendly Texas ranch-style restaurant. Try the signature slow-smoked sirloin, which never fails to please, or the Caesar salad, another favorite. A Texas steakhouse means everything is bigger, from large cuts and oversize salads to potatoes and side dishes. Those not in the mood for beef can opt for chicken, quail or seafood. Dessert is an occasion. **Bar:** full bar.  L  D  CALL  &M

*For additional information, visit AAA.com*
**LOCATIONS:**
**Address:** 14010 N Hwy 183 78717 **Location:** US 183 and SR 620, just n. **Phone:** 512/258-3733
**Address:** 6007 I-35 N 78752 **Location:** I-35 exit 238, jct I-35 and US 290; southeast corner. **Phone:** 512/451-6555
**Address:** 1101 S Mo-Pac Hwy 78746 **Location:** Jct Loop 1 (Mo-Pac Expwy) and CR 2244. **Phone:** 512/330-0030
**Address:** 5510 S I-35 78745 **Location:** I-35 exit 229 (Stassney Rd), on northwest corner of west frontage road and Stassney Ln.
**Phone:** 512/442-6448

## TEXICAN CAFE BRODIE OAKS  512/707-1733  (59)

▼▼ Tex-Mex. Casual Dining. $8-$25 **AAA Inspector Notes:** Guests of the festive restaurant are treated to generous portions of El Paso-inspired Tex-Mex dishes. **Features:** full bar, patio dining, happy hour. **Address:** 4141 Capital of Texas Hwy 78704 **Location:** Jct SR 71 and Lamar Blvd; in Brodie Oaks Shopping Center.

L  D  CALL  &M

## TEXICAN CAFE-LAKELINE  512/506-9900  (2)

▼▼ Tex-Mex. Casual Dining. $8-$25 **AAA Inspector Notes:** Guests of the festive restaurant are treated to generous portions of El Paso-inspired Tex-Mex dishes. **Features:** full bar, patio dining, happy hour. **Address:** 11066 Pecan Park Blvd 78613 **Location:** Jct US 183 and SR 620, 1 blk n, 1 blk w.  L  D  CALL  &M

## TEXICAN CAFE-SOUTH  512/282-9094

▼▼ Tex-Mex. Casual Dining. $8-$25 **AAA Inspector Notes:** Guests of the festive restaurant are treated to generous portions of El Paso-inspired Tex-Mex dishes. **Features:** full bar, happy hour. **Address:** 11940 Manchaca Rd 78748 **Location:** I-35 exit 227, 2.4 mi w to Manchaca Rd, then 2 mi s.  L  D

## TRENTO  512/328-7555  (40)

▼ Italian. Casual Dining. $9-$24 **AAA Inspector Notes:** Italian favorites are presented in an upscale manner at this contemporary restaurant. **Features:** full bar, Sunday brunch, happy hour. **Address:** 3600 N Capital of Texas Hwy 78746 **Location:** Jct Capital of Texas Hwy (SR 360) and Colorado River, just s; across from Davenport Ranch.  L  D

## TRULUCK'S  512/794-8300  (18)

▼▼▼ Seafood Steak. Fine Dining. $26-$50 **AAA Inspector Notes:** The chef's daily creations include jumbo fresh Florida stone crab claws, live Maine lobster, Australian cold water lobster tail, sesame-crusted ahi tuna, miso-glazed organic totem black cod, oysters Rockefeller, sautéed super-lump crab cake, juicy and flavorful Niman Ranch aged beef and a variety of delicious steamed sides including their signature Parmesan mashed potatoes. **Features:** full bar, patio dining. **Address:** 10225 Research Blvd 78759 **Location:** Jct US 183 and Great Hills Tr.  D  CALL  &M

## TWIN PEAKS  512/383-9699  (62)

▼ Comfort Food Sandwiches. Casual Dining. $7-$16 **AAA Inspector Notes:** Sporting events are broadcast on 10 screens inside the lodge-style restaurant, where the menu lists chili, sandwiches and dinner plates of beef, chicken, ribs or shrimp. **Features:** full bar. **Address:** 701 E Stassney Ln 78745 **Location:** I-35 exit 229; on southwest corner.  L  D

## UCHI  512/916-4808  (54)

▼▼▼ Japanese Sushi Small Plates. Casual Dining. $10-$42 **AAA Inspector Notes:** This fashionable sushi restaurant uses local, seasonal ingredients to complement seafood that's flown in daily from the well-known Tsukiji Fish Market in Tokyo. I particularly enjoyed the tiger shrimp tempura and the Wagyu beef you prepare at the table on a hot rock. **Features:** full bar. **Address:** 801 S Lamar Blvd 78704 **Location:** 0.3 mi s of Barton Springs Rd. **Parking:** on-site and valet.

D  CALL  &M  ✎

(See map & index p. 86.)

URBAN, AN AMERICAN GRILL     512/832-4197   14
▼▼▼ American. Fine Dining. $10-$29 **AAA Inspector Notes:** Chops, seafood, chicken and steaks are offered during the dinner hours with lighter fare of salads, sandwiches and personal-size pizzas for lunch, all served in an upscale environment. **Features:** full bar. **Address:** 11301 Domain Dr 78759 **Location:** Jct Braker and Burnet rds; on northwest corner; in The Domain; in Westin Austin at the Domain. **Parking:** on-site and valet.
B L D CALL M

VESPAIO     512/441-6100   57
▼▼▼ Italian. Casual Dining. $17-$32 **AAA Inspector Notes:** Upscale dishes show an accent on Northern Italian flavors. Nice presentations enhance the overall dining experience. A generous array of daily specials complements the standard menu, which is well-varied. **Features:** full bar. **Reservations:** suggested. **Address:** 1610 S Congress Ave 78704 **Location:** Between Riverside Dr and Oltorf St. **Parking:** on-site and street. D

WATERLOO ICE HOUSE AVERY RANCH     512/255-4873   45
▼▼ ◆◆ American. Casual Dining. $6-$15 **AAA Inspector Notes:** The relaxed establishment gives patrons the option to eat outside. Choices range from salads and sandwiches to burgers and specialty dishes. **Features:** full bar, patio dining. **Address:** 14900 Avery Ranch Rd 78613 **Location:** Jct W Parmer Ln and Avery Ranch Rd; on northwest corner. L D

WATERLOO ICE HOUSE NORTHWEST     512/418-9700   31
▼▼ ◆◆ American. Casual Dining. $8-$15 **AAA Inspector Notes:** The relaxed establishment gives patrons the option to eat outside. Choices range from salads and sandwiches to burgers and specialty dishes. **Features:** full bar. **Address:** 6203 N Capital of Texas Hwy 78731 **Location:** Jct Capital of Texas Hwy (SR 360) and FM 2222; on northeast corner. B L D

WINGS 'N MORE     512/981-6673   8
▼▼ Wings. Casual Dining. $6-$28 **AAA Inspector Notes:** Buffalo-style chicken wings are the featured item on a menu that also lines up baby back ribs, chicken, chicken-fried steak, seafood selections, soups and salads. **Features:** full bar. **Address:** 1200 W Howard Ln 78753 **Location:** I-35 exit 246, just e. L D CALL M

Z'TEJAS SOUTHWESTERN GRILL     512/346-3506   27
▼▼▼ Southwestern. Casual Dining. $10-$26 **AAA Inspector Notes:** Separate lunch and dinner menus offer fish, chicken, beef and pork entrees prepared in a Southwestern style. **Features:** full bar, patio dining, Sunday brunch, happy hour. **Address:** 9400 Arboretum Blvd 78759 **Location:** US 183 N to Capital of Texas Hwy (SR 360), 0.5 mi w to Arboretum Blvd, then just n. L D CALL M

Z'TEJAS SOUTHWESTERN GRILL     512/388-7772   1
▼▼ ◆◆ Southwestern. Casual Dining. $10-$26 **AAA Inspector Notes:** Separate lunch and dinner menus offer fish, chicken, beef and pork entrées prepared in a Southwestern style. The rib-eye chicken-fried steak is always great. **Features:** full bar, patio dining. **Address:** 10525 W Parmer Ln 78717 **Location:** Jct W Parmer Ln and Avery Ranch Rd. L D CALL M

WINK     512/482-8868
fyi Not evaluated. With a changing menu showcasing everything from striped bass to blackbuck antelope, this upscale eatery offers an intimate, unpretentious dining experience. **Address:** 1014 N Lamar Blvd 78703 **Location:** Just sw of W 11th St.

## AUSTWELL (G-9) pop. 147, elev. 24'

Austwell was founded in 1911 by Preston Rose Austin, a cotton grower and land developer who owned 20,000 acres along the lower Guadalupe River. Austin combined his name and business partner Jesse McDowell's to create a town designation. Hotels, stores, lumberyards and cotton gins were among Austin's financial stakes in the community; he also donated a school, a church and land for a train station. In 1914, he dredged Hynes Bay to create a shipping channel. Five years later, the town was badly damaged by a storm, and it never recovered from a second deluge in 1942.

**ARANSAS NATIONAL WILDLIFE REFUGE COMPLEX** is 6 mi. s.e. on FM 2040. At more than 115,000 acres, this refuge encompasses the tidal flats and salt marshes of the Blackjack Peninsula on San Antonio Bay. Inhabitants of the refuge include alligators, armadillos, white-tailed deer, raccoons and javelinas. Among the more than 400 species of birds are roseate spoonbill, crested caracara, sora rail, a variety of ducks and endangered whooping cranes. The best viewing times year-round are early morning and late afternoon; whooping cranes are best viewed from late October to early April.

The visitor center features mounted specimens, wildlife literature and a whooping crane video. The refuge includes a 40-foot observation tower, several miles of walking trails and a self-guiding, 16-mile auto tour; register at the center. **Hours:** Refuge daily 30 minutes before dawn-30 minutes after dusk. Visitor center daily 8:30-4:30; closed Thanksgiving and Christmas. **Cost:** $5 (per private vehicle with two or more occupants); $3 (per private vehicle with single occupant); free (ages 0-17). **Phone:** (361) 286-3559.

## BALCH SPRINGS pop. 23,728
• Part of Dallas area — see map p. 161

GRANDY'S RESTAURANT     972/557-3622
▼ American. Quick Serve. $4-$8 **AAA Inspector Notes:** Fried chicken and country-fried steak are menu standbys at the restaurant, a regional franchise. They also offer a family-style dining menu. The décor is a step up from that of most quick-serve eateries and resembles that of a conventional restaurant. Some elements of increased service include additional rolls, iced tea refills and tray removal. **Address:** 12011 Elam Rd 75180 **Location:** I-635 exit 1B, just w. B L D

## BALCONES HEIGHTS pop. 2,941
• Hotels & Restaurants map & index p. 484
• Part of San Antonio area — see map p. 458

GRADY'S BAR-B-QUE     210/732-3636   93
▼ Barbecue. Quick Serve. $7-$10 **AAA Inspector Notes:** A city favorite for more than 30 years. **Features:** beer only. **Address:** 4109 Fredericksburg Rd 78201 **Location:** Between Vance Jackson Rd and Loop 410. L D

## BANDERA (F-7) pop. 857, elev. 1,258'

The cypress trees that line the Medina River lured settlers to Bandera in 1853 to establish a lumber mill. In the 1870s the town was a staging area for large cattle drives through Bandera Pass and along the Western Trail to Montana and Kansas, earning the town the title of "Cowboy Capital of the World."

Modern Bandera is surrounded by dude ranches, and the cypress trees shade visitors canoeing, kayaking or tubing down the Medina River. Nearby Medina Lake offers water sports and excellent year-round fishing. Hill Country State Natural Area, west near Tarpley, is popular with equestrians, while Lost Maples State Natural Area, northwest near Vanderpool, offers exceptional wildlife viewing and autumn foliage. *See Recreation Areas Chart.*

**Bandera County Convention and Visitors Bureau:** 126 SR 16S, P.O. Box 171, Bandera, TX 78003. **Phone:** (830) 796-3045 or (800) 364-3833.

## RECREATIONAL ACTIVITIES
### Horseback Riding
- **Rancho Cortez** is at 872 Hay Hollar Rd. **Hours:** One-hour, half-day and day trips are offered; phone ahead for schedule. **Phone:** (830) 796-9339 in Texas, or (866) 797-9339 outside of Texas.
- **Twin Elm Guest Ranch** is at 810 FM 470. **Hours:** One-hour rides are offered by appointment Mon.-Sat. at 9:30, 11, 2 and 3:30, Sun. at 9:30 and 11. **Phone:** (830) 796-3628 or (888) 567-3049.

---

O S T RESTAURANT                              830/796-3836

Regional American. Casual Dining. $5-$15 **AAA Inspector Notes:** Atop the Old Spanish Trail, the decidedly Western dinette boasts fast, Texas-friendly service and plenty of feel-good, downhome food. **Address:** 305 Main St 78003 **Location:** On SR 173, just e of SR 16; downtown. **Parking:** street only. [B] [L] [D]

## BASTROP pop. 7,218

BASTROP INN MOTEL                             512/321-3949

Motel $55-$90 **Address:** 102 Childers Dr 78602 **Location:** Just e at SR 71/21 and Loop 150. **Facility:** 32 units. 2 stories (no elevator), exterior corridors. **Terms:** cancellation fee imposed. **Pool(s):** outdoor. **Guest Services:** coin laundry.

---

BEST WESTERN BASTROP PINES INN      (512)321-0900

Hotel
$99-$169

**AAA Benefit:** Members save 10% or more with Best Western!

**Address:** 107 Hunters Crossing Blvd 78602 **Location:** SR 71 exit Ed Burleson Blvd, just w on south access road. **Facility:** 60 units. 3 stories, interior corridors. **Pool(s):** outdoor. **Activities:** hot tub, exercise room. **Guest Services:** coin laundry.

---

COMFORT SUITES                               (512)321-3377

Hotel $69-$149 **Address:** 505 Agnes St 78602 **Location:** SR 71 exit Hasler Blvd; on south frontage road. **Facility:** 69 units. 3 stories, interior corridors. **Pool(s):** heated indoor. **Activities:** hot tub, exercise room. **Guest Services:** coin laundry.

 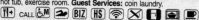   

---

Trust your vehicle to AAA/CAA
Approved Auto Repair facilities

---

HAMPTON INN & SUITES                        (512)321-2898

Hotel
$119-$199

**AAA Benefit:** Members save up to 10%!

**Address:** 240 S Hasler Blvd 78602 **Location:** SR 71 exit Hasler Blvd, 2 blks s. **Facility:** 89 units. 4 stories, interior corridors. **Terms:** 1-7 night minimum stay, cancellation fee imposed. **Pool(s):** indoor. **Activities:** hot tub, exercise room. **Guest Services:** coin laundry. **Featured Amenity:** full hot breakfast.

---

HOLIDAY INN EXPRESS HOTEL & SUITES       (512)321-1900

Hotel $99-$399 **Address:** 491 Agnes St 78602 **Location:** Jct SR 71/95, 2 mi w. **Facility:** 56 units. 3 stories, interior corridors. **Terms:** cancellation fee imposed. **Pool(s):** outdoor. **Activities:** hot tub, exercise room. **Guest Services:** coin laundry.

---

QUALITY INN                                  (512)321-3303

Hotel $59-$400 **Address:** 106 Hasler Blvd 78602 **Location:** Jct SR 71. **Facility:** 42 units. 2 stories (no elevator), interior corridors. **Pool(s):** outdoor.

---

SUPER 8                                      (512)321-6000

Motel
$64-$200

**Address:** 3110 Hwy 71 E 78602 **Location:** On SR 71, 3 mi e. **Facility:** 37 units. 2 stories (no elevator), exterior corridors. **Pool(s):** outdoor. **Activities:** hot tub. **Featured Amenity:** continental breakfast.

---

### WHERE TO EAT

NANCY'S STEAKHOUSE                           512/321-0700

Steak Seafood. Casual Dining. $8-$25 **AAA Inspector Notes:** The Western-themed steak house's menu lists a wide variety of Angus steaks, seafood, chicken and pasta entrées, along with some lighter fare. **Features:** full bar. **Address:** 696 Hwy 71 W 78602 **Location:** Jct SR 71 and 304; on south frontage road.

---

## BAY CITY (G-9) pop. 17,614, elev. 56'
• Hotels p. 116

Established in 1894, Bay City is a commercial center for farming, ranching, oil and nuclear energy.

**MATAGORDA COUNTY MUSEUM** is at jct. SRs 35 and 60 (Ave. F) at 2100 Ave. F. Built in 1917, the site operated as a post office for more than 70 years. An exhibit highlights explorer René-Robert Cavelier, Sieur de La Salle's ship, *La Belle*, which sank near Matagorda Bay. A replica of the ship and artifacts are featured. A children's museum has hands-on activities.

An additional exhibit explains the history of the Karankawa Indians. **Time:** Allow 30 minutes minimum. **Hours:** Wed.-Sat. 1-5. Closed major holidays. **Cost:** $4; $3 (ages 50+); $2 (ages 3-18). **Phone:** (979) 245-7502.

**COMFORT SUITES**                                    (979)245-9300

◆◆◆ **Hotel** $90-$120 **Address:** 5100 7th St 77414 **Location:** On SR 35 (7th St), 2.2 mi e. **Facility:** 68 units. 3 stories, interior corridors. **Pool(s):** outdoor. **Activities:** hot tub, exercise room. **Guest Services:** valet and coin laundry.

[icons] / SOME UNITS

**HAMPTON INN & SUITES BAY CITY**                     (979)245-7100

◆◆◆ **Hotel** $99-$139 **Address:** 4617 7th St 77414 **Location:** On SR 35 (7th St), 3 mi e. **Facility:** 86 units. 4 stories, interior corridors. **Terms:** 1-7 night minimum stay, cancellation fee imposed. **Pool(s):** outdoor. **Activities:** hot tub, exercise room. **Guest Services:** valet and coin laundry.

**AAA Benefit:** Members save up to 10%!

[icons]

**LA QUINTA INN & SUITES BAY CITY**                   (979)323-9095

◆◆◆ **Hotel** $119-$154 **Address:** 5300 7th St 77414 **Location:** On SR 35 (7th St), 3 mi e of downtown. **Facility:** 57 units. 3 stories, interior corridors. **Pool(s):** outdoor. **Activities:** exercise room. **Guest Services:** coin laundry.

[icons] / SOME UNITS

## BAYTOWN   pop. 71,802
### • Part of Houston area — see map p. 301

**BAYMONT INN & SUITES BY WYNDHAM**   (281)839-1400

◆◆◆
Extended Stay Hotel
$79-$159

**Address:** 7212 E Point Blvd 77521 **Location:** I-10 exit 792 (Garth Rd), just n. **Facility:** 82 efficiencies. 3 stories, interior corridors. **Amenities:** safes. **Pool(s):** outdoor. **Activities:** hot tub, exercise room. **Guest Services:** valet and coin laundry. **Featured Amenity: continental breakfast.**

[icons] / SOME UNITS

**COMFORT SUITES**                                    (281)421-9764

◆◆◆ **Hotel** $90-$180 **Address:** 7209 Garth Rd 77521 **Location:** I-10 exit 792 (Garth Rd), just n. **Facility:** 61 units. 3 stories, interior corridors. **Amenities:** safes. **Pool(s):** outdoor. **Activities:** hot tub, exercise room. **Guest Services:** valet and coin laundry.

[icons] / SOME UNITS

**DAYS INN BAYTOWN**                                  (281)421-2233

◆◆
Hotel
$60-$120

**Address:** 5021 East Frwy 77521 **Location:** I-10 exit 792 (Garth Rd). **Facility:** 50 units. 2 stories (no elevator), exterior corridors. **Pool(s):** outdoor. **Activities:** exercise room. **Guest Services:** coin laundry. **Featured Amenity: continental breakfast.**

[icons]

**HAMPTON INN**                                       (281)421-1234

◆◆◆ **Hotel** $99-$189 **Address:** 7211 Garth Rd 77521 **Location:** I-10 exit 792 (Garth Rd). **Facility:** 70 units. 3 stories, interior corridors. **Terms:** 1-7 night minimum stay, cancellation fee imposed. **Pool(s):** outdoor. **Activities:** exercise room. **Guest Services:** valet and coin laundry.

**AAA Benefit:** Members save up to 10%!

[icons] / SOME UNITS

---

**LA QUINTA INN & SUITES BAYTOWN EAST**     (281)421-5566

◆◆◆ **Hotel** $72-$107 **Address:** 5215 I-10 E 77521 **Location:** I-10 exit 792 (Garth Rd), just ne. **Facility:** 103 units, some kitchens. 4 stories, interior corridors. **Pool(s):** outdoor. **Activities:** exercise room. **Guest Services:** coin laundry.

[icons]

**SPRINGHILL SUITES BY MARRIOTT HOUSTON BAYTOWN**
(281)421-1200

◆◆◆ **Hotel** $99-$239 **Address:** 5169 I-10 E 77521 **Location:** I-10 exit 792 (Garth Rd), just n. **Facility:** 101 units. 4 stories, interior corridors. **Pool(s):** heated indoor. **Activities:** hot tub, exercise room. **Guest Services:** valet and coin laundry.

**AAA Benefit:** Members save 5% or more!

[icons]

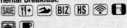
### WHERE TO EAT

**GOING'S BARBEQUE & STEAK CO.**                      281/422-4600

◆ Barbecue. Casual Dining. $4-$19 **AAA Inspector Notes:** The cafeteria-style barbecue eatery offers everything from prime rib, steaks and chicken-fried steak to barbecue beef sandwiches. Expect no frills, just plenty of choices, generous portions and big drinks to wash it all down. A kids' menu is available, and dinner on Thursday features all-you-can-eat barbecue, while dinner on Friday offers buy one steak and get the second at half-price. **Features:** beer only. **Address:** 1007 N Main St 77520 **Location:** I-10 exit 793 (Main St), 4.7 mi s. [L] [D]

**LUBY'S**                                            281/422-6178

◆◆ American. Casual Dining. $7-$12 **AAA Inspector Notes:** First opened in 1947 in south Texas, this cafeteria with over 100 outlets features a wide variety of salads, fresh fruits, seafood...including crunchy shrimp...pastas, meat, poultry and just baked cakes and pies. Ask about the kids specials and Lu Ann platters...an entrée with choice of 2 vegetables and a roll. Many locations offer drive-thru service. **Address:** 1201 W Baker Rd 77521 **Location:** I-10 exit 792 (Garth Rd), 2.4 mi s. [L] [D]

## BEAUMONT   (F-11) pop. 118,296, elev. 21'
### • Restaurants p. 118

The early economy of Beaumont, which was settled around 1824, was based on cattle, lumber and rice. Then on Jan. 10, 1901, in the nearby Spindletop field, the first great Texas oil well blew. The Beaumont area currently forms one of the largest concentrations of petroleum refineries in the nation. Agriculture also contributes to the economy of this thriving deep-water Neches River port.

Visitor information is available at the Babe Didrikson Zaharias Museum and Visitors Center *(see attraction listing).*

**Beaumont Convention and Visitors Bureau:** 505 Willow St., P.O. Box 3827, Beaumont, TX 77704. **Phone:** (409) 880-3749 or (800) 392-4401.

**Shopping areas:** Parkdale Mall, off Eastex Freeway at Dowlen Rd., counts Dillard's, JCPenney, Macy's and Sears among its 140 stores.

**ART MUSEUM OF SOUTHEAST TEXAS** is at 500 Main St. Permanent and changing exhibits are offered at the museum, which displays American paintings, graphics, drawings, decorative arts and photography as well as contemporary folk art. **Time:**

Allow 1 hour minimum. **Hours:** Mon.-Fri. 9-5, Sat. 10-5, Sun. noon-5. Closed major holidays. **Cost:** Donations. **Phone:** (409) 832-3432.

## BABE DIDRIKSON ZAHARIAS MUSEUM AND VISITORS CENTER is at 1750 I-10E (off exit 854).
This museum displays golfing trophies, Olympic medals, artifacts and memorabilia honoring Babe Zaharias, a woman considered to be one of the great athletes of the 20th century. **Time:** Allow 30 minutes minimum. **Hours:** Daily 9-5. Closed Thanksgiving and Christmas. **Cost:** Free. **Phone:** (409) 833-4622 or (800) 392-4401.

## BEAUMONT BOTANICAL GARDENS is s. off I-10
Walden Rd. exit to 6088 Babe Zaharias Dr. in Tyrrell Park. Numerous azaleas, orchids and other plants native to the area surround fountains and ponds. Bird-watching opportunities are abundant throughout the gardens. **Time:** Allow 30 minutes minimum. **Hours:** Daily dawn-dusk. Closed major holidays. **Cost:** Free. **Phone:** (409) 842-3135.

## CLIFTON STEAMBOAT MUSEUM is at 8727 Fannett Rd.
Exhibits highlight the steamboat era, the Battle of San Jacinto, the Civil War and its significance to southeast Texas and southwest Louisiana, and the republic of Texas and its statehood. An art gallery and exhibits about World War II and the Boy Scouts also are available. **Time:** Allow 30 minutes minimum. **Hours:** Mon.-Fri. 9-4:30 by appointment. Closed major holidays. **Cost:** $5; $4 (ages 6-15 and 55+). **Phone:** (409) 842-3162.

## EDISON MUSEUM is at 350 Pine St.
In the 1929 Travis Street Substation, the museum features interactive exhibits that highlight the inventions and innovations of Thomas Alva Edison. More than 60 artifacts explain Edison's role in the many uses of electricity, recorded music, motion pictures and the light bulb. **Time:** Allow 30 minutes minimum. **Hours:** Mon.-Fri. 9-5. Closed major holidays. **Phone:** (409) 981-3089.

## FIRE MUSEUM OF TEXAS is at Walnut and Mulberry sts.
in the Beaumont Fire Headquarters Station. A 24-foot-tall fire hydrant greets visitors to this museum, which displays the State of Texas Firefighter Memorial and such firefighting paraphernalia as hats, extinguishers, alarm systems and fire trucks. A fire-safety activity area has hands-on exhibits for children. Guided 1-hour tours are available by reservation. **Time:** Allow 30 minutes minimum. **Hours:** Mon.-Fri. 8-4:30. Closed major holidays. **Cost:** Donations. **Phone:** (409) 880-3927.

## JOHN JAY FRENCH HISTORIC HOUSE MUSEUM
is off US 69/96/287 exit Lucas, then s. on access road to 3025 French Rd. This simple 1845 Greek Revival house is one of the area's first two-story, painted dwellings. The museum chronicles rural life in East Texas during the mid-19th century. The grounds include the Heritage Hall, a smokehouse, laundry shed, tannery, blacksmith shop and cemetery.

**Time:** Allow 30 minutes minimum. **Hours:** Tues.-Fri. 10-3, Sat. 10-2. Last tour begins 1 hour before closing. Closed major holidays. **Cost:** $3; $2 (ages 60+); $1 (students with ID). **Phone:** (409) 898-0348 or (409) 898-3267.

## McFADDIN-WARD HOUSE is at 1906 Calder Ave.
The W.P.H. McFaddin family acquired this 1906 Beaux Arts Colonial Revival-style mansion in 1907. The elegant furnishings include silver, porcelain and Oriental rugs. Tours start at the visitor center on Calder Avenue at Third Street, where a video presentation begins the 90-minute guided tour of the three-story house. After the tour visitors can explore the gardens and carriage house at their leisure. Guided tours of just the first floor also are offered.

**Time:** Allow 2 hours minimum. **Hours:** Full tours Tues.-Fri. at 10, 11, 1:30 and 2:30, Sat. at 10:30, 1:30 and 2:30. First-floor-only tours Sun. at 1. **Cost:** Full tour $3. First-floor-only tour free. Under 8 are not permitted. Reservations are recommended. **Phone:** (409) 832-2134.

## SPINDLETOP-GLADYS CITY BOOMTOWN MUSEUM is 5 mi. s. on US 69 to University Dr.
on the campus of Lamar University. An oil-field boomtown has been re-created at the museum, which features 16 buildings and equipment of the era that led to the liquid-fuel age. Gladys City history also is chronicled in a video. **Time:** Allow 1 hour minimum. **Hours:** Tues.-Sat. 10-5, Sun. 1-5. Closed major holidays. **Cost:** $5; $3 (ages 60+); $2 (ages 6-12). **Phone:** (409) 880-1750.

## TEXAS ENERGY MUSEUM is at 600 Main St.
Life-like robots describe the evolution of the petroleum industry and the history of the Spindletop Gusher. **Time:** Allow 1 hour, 30 minutes minimum. **Hours:** Tues.-Sat. 9-5, Sun. 1-5. Closed major holidays. **Cost:** $5; $3 (ages 6-12 and 65+). **Phone:** (409) 833-5100.

**BEST WESTERN JEFFERSON INN**          (409)842-0037

Hotel
$63-$80

**AAA Benefit:** Members save 10% or more with Best Western!

**Address:** 1610 I-10 S 77707 **Location:** I-10 exit 851 (College St); on westbound frontage road; 0.5 mi s of jct US 90. **Facility:** 119 units. 2 stories (no elevator), exterior corridors. **Pool(s):** outdoor. **Activities:** exercise room. **Guest Services:** coin laundry. **Featured Amenity: full hot breakfast.**

**COMFORT SUITES**          (409)840-6001

 **Hotel** $90-$140 **Address:** 5955 Walden Rd 77707 **Location:** I-10 exit 848 (Walden Rd), just n. **Facility:** 74 units. 4 stories, interior corridors. **Pool(s):** indoor. **Activities:** hot tub, exercise room. **Guest Services:** valet and coin laundry.

## DAYS INN (409)898-8150

Hotel
$59-$69

**Address:** 2155 N 11th St 77703 **Location:** I-10 exit 853B (11th St), just n. **Facility:** 152 units. 2 stories (no elevator), exterior corridors. **Pool(s):** outdoor. **Activities:** exercise room. **Guest Services:** coin laundry. **Featured Amenity:** full hot breakfast.

## HILTON GARDEN INN BEAUMONT (409)842-5646

Hotel $109-$139 **Address:** 3755 IH-10 S 77705 **Location:** I-10 exit 848 (Walden Rd); on eastbound frontage road. **Facility:** 100 units. 3 stories, interior corridors. **Terms:** 1-7 night minimum stay, cancellation fee imposed. **Pool(s):** heated outdoor. **Activities:** hot tub, exercise room. **Guest Services:** valet and coin laundry.

**AAA Benefit:** Members save up to 10%!

## HOLIDAY INN EXPRESS INN & SUITES 409/892-3600

Hotel. Rates not provided. **Address:** 7140 Eastex Frwy 77708 **Location:** US 69 exit 105; on northbound service road. **Facility:** 81 units. 3 stories, interior corridors. **Pool(s):** outdoor. **Activities:** hot tub, exercise room. **Guest Services:** valet and coin laundry.

## HOLIDAY INN HOTEL & SUITES BEAUMONT PLAZA (409)842-5995

Hotel
$109-$149

**Address:** 3950 I-10 S 77705 **Location:** I-10 exit 848 (Walden Rd), just n. **Facility:** 253 units, some two bedrooms. 8 stories, interior corridors. **Terms:** check-in 4 pm, cancellation fee imposed. **Pool(s):** heated indoor. **Activities:** hot tub, exercise room. **Guest Services:** valet and coin laundry. **Featured Amenity:** full hot breakfast.

## HOMEWOOD SUITES BY HILTON (409)842-9990

Extended Stay Hotel $109-$149 **Address:** 3745 IH-10 S 77705 **Location:** I-10 exit 848 (Walden Rd); on eastbound frontage road. **Facility:** 79 kitchen units, some two bedrooms. 3 stories, interior corridors. **Terms:** 1-7 night minimum stay, cancellation fee imposed. **Pool(s):** outdoor. **Activities:** exercise room. **Guest Services:** valet and coin laundry.

**AAA Benefit:** Members save up to 10%!

## MCM ELEGANTE HOTEL & CONFERENCE CENTER (409)842-3600

Hotel
$65-$129

**Address:** 2355 I-10 S 77705 **Location:** I-10 exit 850 (Washington Blvd); on eastbound frontage road. **Facility:** 276 units. 3-9 stories, interior corridors. **Amenities:** video games. **Pool(s):** outdoor. **Activities:** hot tub, exercise room, spa. **Guest Services:** valet and coin laundry, area transportation.

## RAMADA BEAUMONT (409)842-4420

Hotel
$59-$89

**Address:** 3985 College St 77707 **Location:** I-10 exit 851A (College St); on westbound frontage road. **Facility:** 77 units. 2 stories (no elevator), interior corridors. **Parking:** on-site (fee). **Amenities:** safes. **Pool(s):** outdoor. **Activities:** exercise room. **Guest Services:** valet and coin laundry.

## RED ROOF INN & SUITES - BEAUMONT (409)842-8200

Hotel $79-$150 **Location:** I-10 exit 850 (Washington Blvd) westbound; exit 851 (College St) eastbound. **Facility:** 94 units, some efficiencies. 4 stories, interior corridors. **Pool(s):** outdoor. **Activities:** exercise room. **Guest Services:** valet and coin laundry.

## SLEEP INN & SUITES (409)892-6700

Hotel $70-$100 **Address:** 2030 N 11th St 77703 **Location:** I-10 exit 853B (11th St), just n. **Facility:** 53 units. 3 stories, interior corridors. **Pool(s):** outdoor. **Activities:** exercise room. **Guest Services:** valet and coin laundry.

## WHERE TO EAT

## BRAZOS CATTLE COMPANY 409/895-0099

American. Casual Dining. $7-$23 **AAA Inspector Notes:** There is chicken-fried everything here, "moms fare" such as meat loaf and pot roast, as well as grilled steaks. The restaurant has a real Texas-country atmosphere with bison and longhorn heads on the walls. **Features:** full bar. **Reservations:** suggested. **Address:** 5055 Eastex Frwy 77706 **Location:** US 69/96 exit Dowlen Rd; on southbound frontage road.

## CAFE DEL RIO 409/347-0250

Tex-Mex. Casual Dining. $7-$16 **AAA Inspector Notes:** This place has a festive environment with a lively bar and a traditional Tex-Mex menu featuring tacos, fajitas and combo platters. **Features:** full bar, happy hour. **Address:** 2830 I-10 E 77703 **Location:** I-10 exit 853B (11th St); on westbound frontage road.

## THE GRILL BY ARFEEN, SMITH & PAYNE 409/866-0039

New American. Fine Dining. $20-$37 **AAA Inspector Notes:** This fine-dining option away from the crowded fast-food corridor is sophisticated and upscale with a menu to match. Dishes include the award-winning cognac-glazed field mushroom soup, Maytag-bleu bacon butter tournedos, blackened ahi tuna, Parmesan-crusted Chilean sea bass and their ever-popular chocolate tres leches dessert. Two upscale lounges and a patio with cabanas offer a special before- or after-dinner retreat. Check for entertainment times. **Features:** full bar, patio dining, Sunday brunch, happy hour. **Address:** 6680 Calder Ave 77706 **Location:** Corner of Dowlen St.

## PAPPADEAUX SEAFOOD KITCHEN 409/842-1339

Regional Seafood. Casual Dining. $9-$35 **AAA Inspector Notes:** A seafood lover's delight, the restaurant taps into a little bit of New Orleans with its Cajun dishes and elaborate menu selections. Patrons might start off with a creative choice of blackened oyster and shrimp fondeaux with crayfish and let the feast begin. While music plays in the background, patrons can dig into dirty rice or spicy gumbo loaded with seafood. Well-seasoned shrimp and fish are prepared in varied ways. **Features:** full bar. **Reservations:** suggested. **Address:** 4040 I-10 S 77707 **Location:** I-10 exit 848 (Walden Rd); on northwest corner.

**RAO'S BAKERY**                                          409/832-4342

Breads/Pastries Sandwiches. Casual Dining. $4-$8 **AAA Inspector Notes:** Since 1941, this bakery has been famous for its king cakes and pastries. Sandwiches, salads and soups also are available among the irresistible selection of iced cookies, individually decorated single-serving gourmet cake slices, trifle cup, panna cotta, cream puffs, brownies, petit fours and imported gelato. All temptations go better with one of their delicious fresh-made coffees. **Address:** 2596 Calder Ave 77702 **Location:** Corner of 10th St; in Olde Towne Plaza; downtown. [B] [L]

## BEDFORD (H-2) pop. 46,979, elev. 598'
• **Hotels & Restaurants map & index p. 257**

Bedford was named for a county in Tennessee, the original home of many of its early settlers. A general store and gristmill built by Weldon Bobo in the 1870s established the town as a gathering place for area farmers. The 62-acre Bedford Boys Ranch, a home for wayward boys, opened in 1949. The ranch is now a city park and aquatic center.

**OLD BEDFORD SCHOOL** is off SR 183 exit Bedford Rd., then .5 mi. n. to 2400 School Ln. Visitors to the restored 1915 school can view artifacts, photos, a movie and a period-furnished classroom. **Time:** Allow 30 minutes minimum. **Hours:** Guided tours are given Mon.-Fri. 8-5 by appointment. Closed major holidays. **Cost:** $5; $3 (ages 62+); $2 (ages 0-12). **Phone:** (817) 952-2290.

**COURTYARD BY MARRIOTT**               (817)545-2202  [46]

Hotel $79-$175 **Address:** 2201 W Airport Frwy 76021 **Location:** SR 121/183 exit Central Dr, just n to Plaza Dr. **Facility:** 145 units. 3 stories, interior corridors. **Activities:** exercise room. **Guest Services:** valet and coin laundry, area transportation.

> **AAA Benefit:** Members save 5% or more!

**HOMEWOOD SUITES BY HILTON**           (817)283-5006  [45]

Extended Stay Hotel $99-$129 **Address:** 2401 Airport Frwy 76021 **Location:** SR 183 exit Central Dr/Murphy Dr; on westbound frontage road. **Facility:** 83 efficiencies, some two bedrooms. 3 stories, interior corridors. **Terms:** 1-7 night minimum stay, cancellation fee imposed. **Amenities:** video games. **Pool(s):** outdoor. **Activities:** hot tub, limited exercise equipment. **Guest Services:** valet and coin laundry, area transportation.

> **AAA Benefit:** Members save up to 10%!

**LA QUINTA INN & SUITES DFW AIRPORT WEST-BEDFORD**
                                        (817)545-8105  [44]

Hotel $84-$124 **Address:** 1809 Hwy 121 S 76021 **Location:** SR 183 exit Murphy Dr; on westbound frontage road. **Facility:** 76 units. 4 stories, interior corridors. **Pool(s):** heated indoor. **Activities:** hot tub, exercise room. **Guest Services:** valet and coin laundry, area transportation.

**PAPPADEAUX SEAFOOD KITCHEN**            817/571-4696

Regional Seafood. Casual Dining. $11-$22 **AAA Inspector Notes:** A seafood lover's delight, the restaurant taps into a little bit of New Orleans with its Cajun dishes and elaborate menu selections. Patrons might start off with a creative choice of blackened oyster and shrimp fondeaux with crayfish and let the feast begin. While music plays in the background, patrons can dig into dirty rice or spicy gumbo loaded with seafood. Well-seasoned shrimp and fish are prepared in varied ways. **Features:** full bar, happy hour. **Address:** 2121 Airport Frwy 76021 **Location:** SR 121 exit Murphy Dr/Euless W Pkwy, 0.7 mi w. [L] [D]

**TEXAS LAND AND CATTLE STEAKHOUSE**      817/318-1811

Steak. Casual Dining. $7-$27 **AAA Inspector Notes:** A variety of large Prime steaks, delicious salads and scrumptious desserts await you at the friendly Texas ranch-style restaurant. Try the signature slow-smoked sirloin, which never fails to please, or the Caesar salad, another favorite. A Texas steakhouse means everything is bigger, from large cuts and oversize salads to potatoes and side dishes. Those not in the mood for beef can opt for chicken, quail or seafood. Dessert is an occasion. **Features:** full bar, Sunday brunch. **Address:** 1813 Hwy 121, Bldg B 76021 **Location:** SR 121 exit Murphy Dr/Euless W Pkwy, just w. [L] [D]

## BEEVILLE (G-8) pop. 12,863, elev. 215'

**BEEVILLE ART MUSEUM** is at 401 E. Fannin St. Various works by Texas artists are presented in changing exhibits. Works of art include sculptures and oil on canvas. This two-story house sits on park-like grounds and covers an entire block. **Time:** Allow 1 hour minimum. **Hours:** Mon.-Fri. 9-5, Sat. 10-2. Closed Memorial Day, July 4, Thanksgiving and Christmas. **Cost:** Free. **Phone:** (361) 358-8615.

**BEST WESTERN TEXAN INN**                (361)358-9999

Hotel $120-$170

> **AAA Benefit:** Members save 10% or more with Best Western!

**Address:** 2001 Hwy 59 78102 **Location:** US 181 at US 59, just e. Located in a quiet rural area. **Facility:** 61 units. 2 stories, interior/exterior corridors. **Pool(s):** outdoor. **Activities:** exercise room. **Guest Services:** coin laundry. **Featured Amenity:** full hot breakfast.

**HAMPTON INN**                           (361)362-2100

Hotel $109-$189 **Address:** 301 S Hall St 78102 **Location:** Just w of US 181. **Facility:** 70 units. 3 stories, interior corridors. **Terms:** 1-7 night minimum stay, cancellation fee imposed. **Pool(s):** outdoor. **Activities:** hot tub, exercise room. **Guest Services:** valet and coin laundry.

> **AAA Benefit:** Members save up to 10%!

## BELTON pop. 18,216

### BUDGET HOST INN

Hotel
$49-$75

(254)939-0744

**Address:** 1520 S I-35 76513 **Location:** I-35 exit 292 southbound; exit 293A northbound; on east frontage road. **Facility:** 50 units, some kitchens. 2 stories (no elevator), exterior corridors. **Terms:** 3 day cancellation notice-fee imposed. **Pool(s):** outdoor. **Featured Amenity:** continental breakfast.

### LA QUINTA INN & SUITES BELTON

(254)939-2772

Hotel $111-$146 **Address:** 229 W Loop 121 76513 **Location:** I-35 exit 292, just w. **Facility:** 72 units, some efficiencies. 3 stories, interior corridors. **Amenities:** video games. **Pool(s):** heated indoor. **Activities:** hot tub, exercise room. **Guest Services:** coin laundry.

### WHERE TO EAT

### LUIGI'S ITALIAN RESTAURANT

254/933-3214

Italian. Casual Dining. $7-$15 **AAA Inspector Notes:** All your favorite Italian dishes can be found here. I really enjoyed the pizza on my last visit, and the pasta dishes are served in generous portions. **Features:** beer & wine. **Address:** 2805 N Loop 121, Suite B 76513 **Location:** Jct US 190 and Loop 121, 2.7 mi n; across from Belton High School.   CALL

## BENBROOK pop. 21,234

• Hotels & Restaurants map & index p. 257

### BEST WESTERN WINSCOTT INN & SUITES

(817)249-0076  **62**

Hotel
$90-$149

**AAA Benefit:** Members save 10% or more with Best Western!

**Address:** 590 Winscott Rd 76126 **Location:** I-20 exit 429B, just n. **Facility:** 52 units, some efficiencies. 2 stories, interior corridors. **Amenities:** safes. **Pool(s):** outdoor. **Activities:** exercise room. **Guest Services:** valet and coin laundry.

### COMFORT SUITES

(817)249-8008  **63**

Hotel
$110-$190

**Address:** 8004 Winbrook Dr 76126 **Location:** I-20 exit 429B, just n. **Facility:** 55 units, some kitchens. 4 stories, interior corridors. **Amenities:** safes. **Pool(s):** indoor. **Activities:** hot tub, exercise room. **Guest Services:** valet and coin laundry. **Featured Amenity:** full hot breakfast.

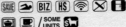

### MOTEL 6 - #4051

(817)249-8885  **64**

Hotel $67-$74 **Address:** 8601 Benbrook Blvd (Hwy 377 S) 76126 **Location:** I-20 exit 429A, 0.7 mi s. **Facility:** 63 units. 3 stories, interior corridors. **Terms:** 3 day cancellation notice. **Pool(s):** outdoor. **Guest Services:** coin laundry.

## BIG BEND NATIONAL PARK (F-3)

Elevations in the park range from 1,840 ft. along the Rio Grande as it leaves Big Bend to 7,825 ft. on Emory Peak. Refer to AAA maps for additional elevation information.

Big Bend National Park is southeast of Alpine on SR 118 and US 385. The park derives its name from a U-shaped bend of the Rio Grande bordering the park. This last great wilderness area of Texas offers mountain and desert scenery and a variety of unusual geological structures within its 801,163 acres.

The park encompasses the entire range of the Chisos Mountains. Three river canyons—Santa Elena, Mariscal and Boquillas—channel the Rio Grande as it forms the international border. Santa Elena Canyon's cliffs rise 1,513 feet above the river. The region is rugged, with volcanic rock formations, abrupt pinnacles, dry channels and deep-cut canyons. It was here that the fossilized bones of a pterosaur, a soaring reptile with a wingspan of 38 feet, were discovered in 1971.

When conditions are right, the lowlands bloom with desert flowers, shrubs and cacti. Piñon woodlands are found on the mountain slopes. High in the mountain canyons are forests of Arizona cypress, Douglas fir, juniper and oak.

Desert mule deer live in the area, and small white-tailed deer inhabit the Chisos Mountains. Coyotes, foxes and collared peccary or javelina also can be seen. More than 450 species of birds have been identified in the park.

## General Information and Activities

Big Bend National Park is open all year. Summer temperatures in the desert are usually high and afternoon thunderstorms are frequent July through September, but the mountains are pleasant in summer.

A trip from Marathon by way of park headquarters at Panther Junction and the Chisos Basin to Alpine provides a scenic 187-mile circle tour of the park. Hard-surfaced roads lead to Santa Elena and Boquillas canyons.

Many miles of trails are available for hiking. One of the more interesting hikes is along the self-guiding nature trail to Lost Mine Peak. The round-trip hike lasts about 3 hours. Other trips include the South Rim, the Window and a variety of desert or river's-edge hikes.

Guided walks and interpretive programs are given throughout the park; information is available at visitor centers. Illustrated talks by park interpreters are given year round.

Visitors can get assistance and information about planning back-country trips from the Panther Junction Visitor Center at the park headquarters. The visitor center, which also has exhibits, is open daily 8-6 (9-1 on Christmas).

Reservations for accommodations at Chisos Mountains Lodge should be made well in advance.

Write Big Bend Resorts, Basin Rural Station, Big Bend National Park, TX 79834; phone (432) 477-2291. *See Recreation Areas Chart.*

**ADMISSION** (valid for 7 days) is $20 per private vehicle or $10 per person age 16+ on bicycle or motorcycle. The park is open daily 24 hours. **Note:** Motorists should fill their gas tanks before leaving US 90; service stations in the park are open roughly 7 a.m.-8 p.m., November through mid-May, and 8-6 the rest of the year.

**PETS** must be on a leash or otherwise physically restricted and are not permitted in public buildings, the river or on trails.

**ADDRESS** inquiries to the Superintendent, Big Bend National Park, P.O. Box 129, TX 79834; phone (432) 477-2251.

## BIG SPRING (D-5) pop. 27,282, elev. 2,397'

The West Texas town of Big Spring was named for the spring that served as a watering place for buffaloes, antelopes, deer, mustangs and people. The spring is now part of 400-acre Comanche Trail Park *(see Recreation Areas Chart).* Since the discovery of oil in 1927, Big Spring has been a refining center and a distribution point for locally manufactured oil-well machinery.

**Big Spring Area Convention and Visitors Bureau:** 215 W. 3rd St., Big Spring, TX 79720. **Phone:** (432) 263-8235 or (866) 430-7100.

**BIG SPRING STATE PARK** is off I-20 exit 174 (eastbound) or 181A (westbound) on FM 700. Named for the only watering place for bison, antelopes and wild horses within a 60-mile radius, the park is atop a 200-foot mesa at the south city limits. Highlights of the 382-acre park include a prairie dog town, jogging and nature trails, a playground, picnic sites and a panorama from a 2.5-mile scenic drive around the mountain.

**Hours:** Daily 8 a.m.-dusk. **Cost:** Free. **Phone:** (432) 263-4931 or (800) 792-1112. 

**HANGAR 25 AIR MUSEUM,** 1911 Apron Dr., houses aircraft exhibits and displays describing the World War II-era bombardier school once located in this restored hangar on a former airbase. Visitors can see a training simulator, the nose of a B-52 bomber, a model airplane collection and such aircraft as a 1949 North American T-28A Trojan and a Cessna T-37B Tweety Bird as well as items from the Korean conflict and Vietnam War. **Time:** Allow 1 hour minimum. **Hours:** Tues.-Sat. 10-4. **Cost:** Donations. **Phone:** (432) 264-1999.

**HERITAGE MUSEUM** is at 510 Scurry St. Photographs and artifacts chronicle the development of this area from Native American life to the discovery of oil. Noteworthy are a collection of rare photographs from the late 1800s to the 1920s and a display of longhorn steer horns. **Time:** Allow 1 hour

minimum. **Hours:** Tues.-Fri. 8:30-4, Sat. 10-4. Closed major holidays. **Cost:** (Includes the Potton House) $3; $2 (ages 6-18, ages 60+ and college students with ID). **Phone:** (432) 267-8255.

**Potton House** is 1.5 mi. s. of I-20 on US 87 to 200 Gregg St. This 1901 red sandstone Victorian house reflects turn-of-the-20th-century living and features period furniture. Built for an Englishman who worked for the Texas and Pacific Railroad, the house contains many items original to the family. **Tours:** Guided tours are available. **Hours:** Tues.-Fri. by appointment. Closed Jan. 1, July 4, Thanksgiving and Christmas Eve-Dec. 31. **Cost:** (Includes the Heritage Museum) $3; $2 (ages 6-18, ages 60+ and college students with ID). **Phone:** (432) 267-8255.

**BEST WESTERN PALACE INN & SUITES**    (432)264-1500

Hotel
$99-$199

**AAA Benefit:** Members save 10% or more with Best Western!

**Address:** 915 Lamesa Hwy 79720 **Location:** I-20 exit 177, 2 blks s. **Facility:** 60 units. 3 stories, interior corridors. **Pool(s):** heated indoor. **Activities:** hot tub, exercise room. **Guest Services:** coin laundry. **Featured Amenity: full hot breakfast.**

**HAMPTON INN & SUITES**    432/264-9800

▼▼◇ Hotel. Rates not provided. **Address:** 805 W I-20 Hwy 79720 **Location:** I-20 exit 177; on south frontage road. **Facility:** 85 units. 3 stories, interior corridors. **Pool(s):** heated indoor. **Activities:** hot tub, exercise room. **Guest Services:** valet and coin laundry.

**HOLIDAY INN EXPRESS**    (432)263-5400

▼▼▼ Hotel $115-$171 **Address:** 1109 N Aylesford St 79720 **Location:** I-20 exit 177; on eastbound frontage road. **Facility:** 66 units. 3 stories, interior corridors. **Pool(s):** outdoor. **Activities:** hot tub, exercise room. **Guest Services:** valet and coin laundry.

**LA QUINTA INNS & SUITES BIG SPRING**    (432)264-0222

▼▼▼ Hotel $119-$214 **Address:** 1102 I-20 W 79720 **Location:** I-20 exit 177; on north frontage road. **Facility:** 73 units. 4 stories, interior corridors. **Pool(s):** outdoor. **Activities:** hot tub, exercise room. **Guest Services:** coin laundry.

## WHERE TO EAT

**K-C STEAK & SEAFOOD**    432/263-1651

▼▼▼ Steak Seafood. Casual Dining. $9-$22 **AAA Inspector Notes:** The restaurant has served simply good food throughout its 40 years in operation. Everything, from bread to salad dressing, is made from scratch. An elegant supper-club atmosphere remains the setting for a meal of delicious prime rib, steak, Alaskan crab or lobster. **Features:** beer & wine. **Address:** 2104 W I-20 79720 **Location:** N Service Rd to I-20 exit 176; 0.5 mi w of jct SR 176.

## BIG THICKET NATIONAL PRESERVE
(E-10)

Big Thicket National Preserve encompasses 15 units in southeast Texas. The 105,684-acre park protects one of the country's most biologically diverse wilderness areas. Until the 19th century, this region was a vast and almost impenetrable combination of woodlands and swamps.

The preserve's thicket of woods resulted from the unusual intermixing of elements from four major habitats—Southeastern swamps, Eastern forests, Central plains and the Appalachians. Within the remnants of this once-vast wilderness is an uncommon mix of plants and animals—Eastern bluebirds nest near road runners, and lush bogs border cactus- and yucca-dotted sandhills.

Big Thicket includes nine land units and six water corridors. Only the Turkey Creek, Beech Creek, Big Sandy and Hickory Creek Savannah units have hiking trails. The Big Sandy Creek Trail is a favorite for biking and horseback riding. Most other units include visitor day-use areas near unit boundaries. Walking is the best way to see the preserve, which offers trails varying in length from .5 to 18 miles. Naturalist programs are offered throughout the year. Another popular activity is canoeing on the Neches River, Pine Island Bayou and Village Creek.

Administered by the Nature Conservancy, the Roy E. Larsen Sandyland Sanctuary, in Hardin County off SR 327, offers numerous trails where nature lovers can view flora and fauna indicative of both desert and bog; phone (409) 385-0445.

The Big Thicket Visitor Center is about 7 miles north of Kountze at the junction of US 69 and FM 420. For more information contact the Superintendent, Big Thicket National Preserve, 6044 FM 420, Kountze, TX 77625. Picnicking is permitted. Allow 1 hour minimum. Visitor center open daily 9-5; closed Jan. 1,Thanksgiving and Christmas. Phone (409) 951-6700. *See Recreation Areas Chart.*

## BLANCO  pop. 1,739

**BEST WESTERN PLUS BLANCO LUXURY INN & SUITES**                    (830)833-5697

Hotel
$130-$230

**AAA Benefit:** Members save 10% or more with Best Western!

**Address:** 2218 Hwy 281 N 78606 **Location:** On US 281, 0.8 mi n. **Facility:** 51 units. 3 stories, interior corridors. **Terms:** 2 night minimum stay - seasonal and/or weekends, 5 day cancellation notice-fee imposed. **Pool(s):** outdoor. **Activities:** exercise room. **Guest Services:** coin laundry.

## BOERNE  (F-7) pop. 10,471, elev. 1,405'

Boerne's beginnings are evident in its old stone buildings with narrow windows, steep gables, outside stairways and gardens. Members of the idealist German colony of Bettina, students of the classics who founded several "Latin settlements" in Texas, first settled in the area in 1849. The immigrants designed their farm after Cicero's country home, Tusculum, and laid out the town to resemble the communities they had known in Europe.

Boerne (pronounced "bernie") was the home of George Wilkins Kendall, one of the founders of the *New Orleans Picayune*. At the outbreak of the Mexican War in 1846, Kendall organized a system of pony-express riders and ships to carry stories to his newspaper. So efficient was this method of reporting that the *Picayune* printed the text of the Treaty of Guadalupe before the U.S. government received a copy. Kendall's ranch, where he spent the last years of his life, encompassed most of what is modern Kendall County.

Situated along Cibolo Creek, the Cibolo Nature Center offers hiking trails, a boardwalk and a nature center; phone (830) 249-4616.

**Boerne Convention & Visitors Bureau:** 1407 S. Main St., Boerne, TX 78006. **Phone:** (830) 249-7277 or (888) 842-8080.

**CASCADE CAVERNS,** at 226 Cascade Caverns Rd. via I-10 exit 543, is part of a 105-acre park. Guided tours of the underground caves take visitors through spacious, 25- to 65-foot-high chambers and low, narrow passageways. You'll view unique rock formations like "chubby" stalactites and enormous solution domes; an underground lake; and such animals as Eastern Pipistrelle bats, cliff and leopard frogs, and the albino Cascade Cavern salamanders. The cavern walls, ceilings and floors are damp, and the temperature remains a constant 64 F.

The First Friday Flashlight Tour is a 1.5-hour night tour held the first Friday of the month. A tour of the lower cave also is offered.

**Note:** Sneakers are recommended, as the steps leading to the cavern are steep and the cavern floor can be slippery. **Time:** Allow 2 hours minimum. **Hours:** Park open Mon.-Fri. 9-5, Sat.-Sun. 9-6, Memorial Day-Labor Day; Tues.-Fri. 10-4, Mon. noon-4, Sat. 9-5, Sun. 10-5, rest of year. First tour begins 1 hour after opening; last tour begins 1 hour before closing. First Friday Flashlight Tour begins at dusk. Closed Jan. 1, Thanksgiving and Christmas.

**Cost:** $14.95; $9.50 (ages 4-11). First Friday Flashlight Tour $19.95. Reservations are required and age restrictions apply for First Friday Flashlight Tour. **Phone:** (830) 755-8080.

**ENCHANTED SPRINGS RANCH,** 242 SR 46W, is an 86-acre working ranch and entertainment park that serves as a movie set for Western films and TV shows. Visitors can walk through an Old West town complete with 40 rustic buildings; take a tractor wagon ride through an area where buffalo, deer, Texas longhorns and even zebras roam; and watch shooting and roping demonstrations, staged gunfights and a variety of other performances.

**Tours:** Guided tours are available. **Time:** Allow 2 hours minimum. **Hours:** Wed.-Sun. 10-5, mid-June to mid-Aug.; Sat.-Sun. 10-5, rest of year. Closed Jan. 1, Easter, Memorial Day, July 4, Labor Day, Thanksgiving, Christmas Eve, Christmas and Dec. 31. Phone ahead to confirm schedule. **Cost:** $14; $12 (ages 65+ and military with ID); $7 (ages 3-12). **Phone:** (830) 249-8222 or (800) 640-5917. ⬛⬛

## AMERICAS BEST VALUE INN
(830)249-9791

Motel
$79-$103

**Address:** 35150 IH-10 W 78006 **Location:** I-10 exit 540 (SR 46); westbound access road. **Facility:** 81 units, some kitchens. 2 stories, exterior corridors. **Pool(s):** outdoor. **Activities:** exercise room. **Guest Services:** coin laundry. **Featured Amenity: continental breakfast.**

⬛ ⬛ ⬛ ⬛ ⬛ ⬛ ⬛ ⬛ / SOME UNITS ⬛

## COMFORT INN & SUITES
(830)249-6800

⬛⬛⬛⬛ **Hotel** $79-$129 **Address:** 35000 I-10 W 78006 **Location:** I-10 exit 540 (SR 46), just e to Norris Ln, then just s. **Facility:** 62 units. 4 stories, interior corridors. **Pool(s):** outdoor. **Activities:** exercise room. **Guest Services:** coin laundry.

⬛ ⬛ ⬛ ⬛ ⬛ ⬛ ⬛ / SOME UNITS ⬛

## FAIRFIELD INN & SUITES BY MARRIOTT SAN ANTONIO BOERNE
(830)368-4167

⬛⬛⬛ **Hotel** $89-$209 **Address:** 6 Cascade Caverns Rd 78006 **Location:** I-10 exit 543 (Cascade Caverns Rd), just off westbound access road. Located in a quiet country side setting. **Facility:** 78 units. 4 stories, interior corridors. **Pool(s):** outdoor. **Activities:** hot tub, exercise room. **Guest Services:** valet and coin laundry.

**AAA Benefit:** Members save 5% or more!

⬛ ⬛ ⬛ ⬛ ⬛ ⬛ ⬛ / SOME UNITS ⬛ ⬛ ⬛

## HAMPTON INN & SUITES
(830)816-8800

⬛⬛⬛⬛
Hotel
$109-$169

 **AAA Benefit:** Members save up to 10%!

**Address:** 34935 IH-10 W 78006 **Location:** I-10 exit 540 (SR 46); on eastbound frontage road. Adjacent to interstate. **Facility:** 78 units. 4 stories, interior corridors. **Terms:** 1-7 night minimum stay, cancellation fee imposed. **Pool(s):** outdoor. **Activities:** hot tub, exercise room. **Guest Services:** coin laundry.

⬛ CALL ⬛ ⬛ ⬛ ⬛ ⬛ ⬛ ⬛ ⬛ ⬛

## LA QUINTA INN & SUITES BOERNE
(830)249-1212

⬛⬛⬛ **Hotel** $85-$134 **Address:** 36756 IH-10 W 78006 **Location:** I-10 exit 539 (Johns Rd) eastbound; exit 540 (Bandera Rd) eastbound, U-turn back; on westbound access road. Located in a quiet area. **Facility:** 67 units. 3 stories, interior corridors. **Pool(s):** outdoor. **Activities:** hot tub, exercise room. **Guest Services:** coin laundry.

CALL ⬛ ⬛ ⬛ ⬛ ⬛ ⬛ ⬛ ⬛ ⬛ / SOME UNITS ⬛

## THE RESORT AT TAPATIO SPRINGS
830/537-4611

⬛⬛⬛⬛ **Resort Hotel.** Rates not provided. **Address:** 1 Resort Way 78006 **Location:** I-10 exit 539 (Johns Rd), 3.5 mi w. **Facility:** This Hill Country hideaway, which caters to golfers, is large and spread out and offers dramatic views. Standard and large rooms are available. 111 units. 2 stories (no elevator), exterior corridors. **Terms:** check-in 4 pm. **Pool(s):** outdoor. **Activities:** sauna, hot tub, steamroom, regulation golf, tennis, exercise room. **Guest Services:** valet and coin laundry.

⬛ ⬛ ⬛ ⬛ ⬛ ⬛ ⬛ ⬛ ⬛

## YE KENDALL INN & LIMESTONE GRILLE
830/249-2138

⬛⬛⬛ **Historic Country Inn.** Rates not provided. **Address:** 128 W Blanco St 78006 **Location:** 2 blks w of Main St; facing town square. **Facility:** This is a large, restored 1859 property comprising a main house with several guest rooms and a series of themed buildings, including a large chapel circling a beautiful garden. 36 units, some cottages. 1-2 stories (no elevator), interior/exterior corridors. **Dining:** Limestone Grille, see separate listing. **Activities:** hot tub, exercise room.

⬛ ⬛ ⬛ ⬛ ⬛ ⬛ ⬛ / SOME UNITS ⬛ ⬛

## SPINELLI COUNTRY INN
830/249-9563

⬛ Not evaluated. **Address:** 911 S Main St 78006 **Location:** I-10 exit 542 (US 87/Main St), 1.5 mi n. Facilities, services, and décor characterize an economy property.

## WHERE TO EAT

## LIMESTONE GRILLE
830/249-9954

⬛⬛ Regional American. Casual Dining. $9-$28 **AAA Inspector Notes:** Located in a historic town inn overlooking the main city plaza, the casual, "down south" restaurant features popular selections with a Texas twang. **Features:** full bar. **Reservations:** suggested. **Address:** 128 W Blanco St 78006 **Location:** 2 blks w of Main St; facing town square; in Ye Kendall Inn & Limestone Grille.

⬛ ⬛ ⬛

## LITTLE GRETEL
830/331-1368

⬛⬛ Czechoslovakian. Casual Dining. $13-$29 **AAA Inspector Notes:** Overlooking a park and river, this Czech/German enclave features a variety of schnitzels, sausages, meatloaf, sandwiches, salads and flavorful pastries. **Features:** full bar, Sunday brunch. **Reservations:** suggested. **Address:** 518 River Rd 78006 **Location:** I-10 exit 540 (SR 46), 2.3 mi e. ⬛ ⬛ ⬛

## SPINELLI'S VISTRO RESTAURANT
830/816-2470

⬛ Not evaluated. Dramatic 35-foot-high walls with floor-to-ceiling book shelves and Texas memorabilia. House specialties include shrimp royale with onions, mushrooms and hot sauce. **Address:** 914 S Main St 78006

# BONHAM (C-9) pop. 10,127, elev. 568'

Named for James B. Bonham, a hero of the Alamo siege, Bonham is in the heart of the fertile Blacklands. Hamlets with names such as Telephone and Bug Tussle attest to the "down-homeness" of the area. During the Civil War the town was headquarters of the Texas Confederate forces.

In a park next to Sam Rayburn Library and Museum *(see attraction listing)* is Fort Inglish Museum and Village. Structures include three original, restored log cabins dating from the 1830s and a replica of the 1837 fort.

**Bonham Area Chamber of Commerce:** 119 E. Fifth St., Bonham, TX 75418. **Phone:** (903) 583-4811.

**FANNIN COUNTY MUSEUM OF HISTORY** is at 1 Main St. Twelve rooms of a restored 1900 train depot display Native American artifacts, fossils, antique farm tools, quilts and furniture, railroad memorabilia, vintage clothing, documents and photographs of area history. A World War II exhibit has a restored Fairchild PT19 airplane. A fire museum and memorabilia depicting the life and music of jazz guitarist Charlie Christian also are included.

**Time:** Allow 1 hour minimum. **Hours:** Tues.-Sat. 10-4, Apr. 1-Sept. 1; Tues.-Sat. noon-4, rest of year. Closed Jan. 1, July 4, Thanksgiving and Christmas. **Cost:** Donations. **Phone:** (903) 583-8042.

**SAM RAYBURN HOUSE MUSEUM** is 1.5 mi. w. on SR 56. The 12-room country house of the former Speaker of the House of Representatives contains family furnishings and belongings. Guided tours interpret the life and work of this powerful, long-term Congressional leader. **Time:** Allow 30 minutes minimum. **Hours:** Tues.-Sun. 9-4:30. Closed Jan. 1, Thanksgiving, Christmas Eve, Christmas and Dec. 31. **Cost:** $4; $3 (ages 6-18 and students with ID). **Phone:** (903) 583-5558.

**SAM RAYBURN LIBRARY AND MUSEUM** is 4 blks. w. on SR 56 at 800 W. Sam Rayburn Dr. The site preserves books and historical mementos collected by Speaker of the House Rayburn during a half-century of public service. A replica of the speaker's office at the United States Capitol contains the silver and crystal chandelier that hung in the White House from the terms of President Ulysses S. Grant to those of Theodore Roosevelt. **Time:** Allow 1 hour minimum. **Hours:** Mon.-Fri. 9-5, Sat. 10-2. Closed major holidays. Phone ahead to confirm schedule. **Cost:** Free. **Phone:** (903) 583-2455.

## BORGER (A-5) pop. 13,251

In 1926 the Panhandle Oil Field was discovered, and a boomtown of 45,000 people mushroomed on the site of Borger. The town remains a major petrochemical center. Before the oil boom, the area's most significant events were the Battles of Adobe Walls, which took place about 37 miles northeast of Borger in 1864 and 1874.

**Borger Chamber of Commerce:** 613 N. Main St., P.O. Box 490, Borger, TX 79008. **Phone:** (806) 274-2211.

**HUTCHINSON COUNTY MUSEUM** is at 618 N. Main St. Changing exhibits trace the history of the county and the town of Borger, depicting the Spanish exploration, the Plains Indians, the American frontier and the discovery of oil in 1859, when Borger's population grew from 15 to 35,000 in 3 months. An authentic cable tool drilling rig is displayed. **Time:** Allow 30 minutes minimum. **Hours:** Tues.-Fri. 9-5, Sat. 11-4:30. Closed major holidays. **Cost:** Donations. **Phone:** (806) 273-0130.

## BOWIE pop. 5,218

**PARK'S INN**                            940/872-1111

Motel
$60-$70

**Address:** 708 W Wise St 76230 **Location:** 0.5 mi n of jct SR 59; downtown. **Facility:** 40 units. 1 story, exterior corridors. **Terms:** cancellation fee imposed. **Pool(s):** outdoor. **Guest Services:** coin laundry.

## BOYS RANCH (A-5) pop. 282, elev. 3,202'

**CAL FARLEY'S BOYS RANCH** is off US 385 at 8 Julian Bivins Blvd. An Amarillo businessman founded the 120-acre ranch for wayward boys in 1939. Today, the 11,000-acre ranch is home to about 300 boys and girls. Facilities include a chapel, clinic, schools, visitor center, museum and 27 homes for children. A rodeo hosted by the residents is held Labor Day weekend. **Tours:** Guided tours are available. **Hours:** Ranch daily 8-5. Closed major holidays. **Cost:** Free. A fee is charged for special events. **Phone:** (806) 534-2211 or (866) 302-2789.

## BRACKETTVILLE (G-6) pop. 1,688

Established in 1852 as a supply center for Fort Clark, Brackettville became a trade center as the region filled with ranches and farms. This historic fort has been transformed into a resort with many of its original buildings serving as lodges and residences. During the 1950s the Brackettville area served as the setting for a handful of Hollywood films, including the John Wayne epic "The Alamo."

**Kinney County Chamber of Commerce:** P.O. Box 1738, Brackettville, TX 78832. **Phone:** (830) 563-2466.

## BRADY pop. 5,528

**BEST WESTERN BRADY INN**          (325)597-3997

Hotel
$85-$90

**AAA Benefit:** Members save 10% or more with Best Western!

**Address:** 2200 S Bridge St 76825 **Location:** 1.1 mi s on US 87/377. **Facility:** 40 units. 2 stories (no elevator), exterior corridors. **Pool(s):** outdoor. **Activities:** exercise room. **Guest Services:** coin laundry. **Featured Amenity:** continental breakfast.

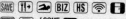

## BRECKENRIDGE (D-7) pop. 5,780, elev. 1,202'

**BOOMTOWN BRECKENRIDGE MURALS** are along Walker St. Murals adorn buildings lining the town's main street. Paintings inspired by 1920s black-and-white photographs depict city history. Maps for self-guiding tours are available at the Breckenridge Chamber of Commerce, 100 E. Elm St. **Time:** Allow 30 minutes minimum. **Hours:** Daily 24 hours. **Cost:** Free. **Phone:** (254) 559-2301 for the chamber of commerce.

**BRECKENRIDGE FINE ARTS CENTER** is at 207 N. Breckenridge Ave. The museum brings together an unusual variety of works ranging from such art museum mainstays as paintings and sculpture to the less typical—a large collection of dolls from around the world and lavish ball gowns from some of Texas' most renowned festivals. Changing exhibitions are presented throughout the year as well. **Time:** Allow 30 minutes minimum. **Hours:** Tues.-Fri. 10-5, Sat. 10-3, day after Labor Day-May 31; Tues.-Fri. 10-5, rest of year. Closed major holidays. **Cost:** Donations. **Phone:** (254) 559-6602.

**SWENSON MEMORIAL MUSEUM** is at 116 W. Walker St. Housed in the circa-1920 First National Bank building, the collection contains pioneer artifacts, photographs and traveling exhibits detailing the Breckenridge 1918-20 oil boom as well as the county's history. **Time:** Allow 30 minutes minimum. **Hours:** Tues.-Fri. 10-noon and 1-5. Closed major holidays. **Cost:** Donations. **Phone:** (254) 559-8471.

## BRENHAM (F-9) pop. 15,716, elev. 332'
• Hotels p. 126 • Restaurants p. 126

Brenham retains much of its mid-19th-century grandeur. The Main Street District contains restored 19th-century buildings that house restaurants and shops.

The city is the county seat for Washington County, which is home to some 120 historic sites and markers, many from the Texas Revolution. Brenham is home to Blinn College, the state's first county-owned junior college, which was founded in 1883.

Chappell Hill, 10 miles east, is the first town in Texas planned and laid out by a woman. Many of the original 19th-century structures remain, including the 1850s Stagecoach Inn, the 1869 Old Rock Store and the Browning Plantation of about 1857. The Masonic Cemetery contains the graves of Col. William Travis' family and Confederate soldiers. A museum and visitor center displays area artifacts.

Blue Bell Creameries, 1101 S. Blue Bell Rd., offers tours of the ice-cream plant and a film about the history of the creamery are offered on weekdays except holidays. Samples are served following the tour; phone (979) 836-7977 or (800) 327-8135.

**Washington County Convention and Visitors Bureau:** 115 W. Main St., Brenham, TX 77833. **Phone:** (979) 836-3696 or (888) 273-6426.

**Self-guiding tours:** Visitors to the area can view the bluebonnets and other wildflowers that bloom in profusion along country roads in the spring. The convention and visitors bureau provides a free map outlining the most scenic routes.

**ANTIQUE ROSE EMPORIUM** is 8.5 mi. n. of SR 105 on FM 50. More than 300 antique varieties of roses are represented on this early settler's 8-acre homestead. Herb, butterfly, perennial and water gardens also are on the grounds. **Time:** Allow 1 hour minimum. **Hours:** Mon.-Sat. 9-5:30, Sun. 11-5:30. Closed major holidays. **Cost:** Free. **Phone:** (979) 836-5548.

**TEXAS BAPTIST HISTORICAL MUSEUM** is at 10405 FM 50. The state's oldest continuously active Baptist church was established in the Republic of Texas in 1839. Museum exhibits relate to the church, the community, the founding of Baylor University and Baylor Female College and many of the area's notable residents, including Gen. Sam Houston. A nearby cemetery contains the graves of Mrs. Sam Houston and her mother, Nancy Lea. **Hours:** Tues.-Sat. 9-4, Apr.-Oct; Tues.-Sat. 10-4, rest of year. Closed major holidays. **Cost:** Donations. **Phone:** (979) 836-5117.

ANT STREET INN      979/836-7393

 **Classic Historic Country Inn** $145-$285 **Address:** 107 W Commerce St 77833 **Location:** US 290 exit Business Rt SR 36, 1.6 mi n to W Commerce St, then just e. Located in the historic district. **Facility:** All guest rooms are furnished with antiques at this property housed in a renovated historic mercantile building; common areas are spacious. 15 units. 2 stories (no elevator), interior corridors. **Terms:** age restrictions may apply, 10 day cancellation notice.

BEST WESTERN INN OF BRENHAM      (979)251-7791

Hotel $70-$190

**AAA Benefit:** Members save 10% or more with Best Western!

**Address:** 1503 Hwy 290 E 77833 **Location:** Jct SR 36 and US 290, 1.3 mi e. **Facility:** 59 units. 2 stories (no elevator), exterior corridors. **Pool(s):** outdoor. **Guest Services:** coin laundry. **Featured Amenity:** full hot breakfast.

COMFORT SUITES      (979)421-8100

Hotel $85-$180

**Address:** 2350 S Day St 77833 **Location:** US 290 exit SR 36 S, just n on Business Rt SR 36. **Facility:** 54 units. 3 stories, interior corridors. **Pool(s):** indoor. **Activities:** hot tub. **Guest Services:** coin laundry. **Featured Amenity:** full hot breakfast.

FAR VIEW BED & BREAKFAST      (979)836-1672

Classic Historic Bed & Breakfast $99-$210

**Address:** 1804 S Park St 77833 **Location:** US 290 exit Business Rt SR 36, 0.6 mi n to Lubbock St, then just e; between Park and Church sts. **Facility:** Extensive manicured grounds and 75-year-old live oaks contribute Gatsbylike elegance to this historic 1925 home. An outdoor kitchen is a new amenity. 9 units, some kitchens. 2 stories (no elevator), interior/exterior corridors. **Terms:** 7 day cancellation notice-fee imposed. **Pool(s):** outdoor. **Featured Amenity:** full hot breakfast.

HAMPTON INN & SUITES      (979)337-9898

 **Hotel** $99-$169 **Address:** 2605 Schulte Blvd 77833 **Location:** US 290 exit Business Rt SR 36; on south frontage road. **Facility:** 66 units. 3 stories, interior corridors. **Terms:** 1-7 night minimum stay, cancellation fee imposed. **Pool(s):** outdoor. **Activities:** hot tub, exercise room. **Guest Services:** valet and coin laundry.

**AAA Benefit:** Members save up to 10%!

## WHERE TO EAT

B T LONGHORN SALOON AND STEAKHOUSE      979/421-6700

Steak Seafood. Casual Dining. $9-$28 **AAA Inspector Notes:** Located in a historic downtown storefront, a massive wood bar serves as the centerpiece of this Western-style restaurant where steaks, seafood, chicken and ribs highlight the menu. Soups, salads, burgers and sandwiches also are available for lighter fare; lunch specials are available Monday through Friday. I really enjoyed the 14-ounce rib-eye steak, which was that lean, tender and very flavorful. **Features:** full bar. **Address:** 205 S Baylor St 77833 **Location:** Just off square; downtown. **Parking:** street only. L D

K-BOB'S STEAKHOUSE      979/836-7990

Steak. Casual Dining. $6-$22 **AAA Inspector Notes:** The steakhouse prepares a great variety of plump, juicy fillets. A fireplace opens up into both dining rooms, and antique clocks decorate the walls. Rustic wagon-wheel chandeliers illuminate the room. **Address:** 2120 Hwy 290 W 77833 **Location:** At Business Rt SR 36. L D

MANUEL'S MEXICAN RESTAURANT      979/277-9620

Mexican. Casual Dining. $6-$20 **AAA Inspector Notes:** A fiesta-like atmosphere punctuates the colorful dining room, where patrons nosh on tasty shrimp fajitas, Spanish rice and bean soup. Lovely murals depicting Mexican scenes adorn the walls, and bright ribbons and streamers add festive touches. I try to eat here on Wednesdays when they offer an incredible beef and vegetable soup that could easily be a meal unto itself. **Features:** full bar. **Address:** 409 W Main St 77833 **Location:** Just w of jct SR 36 and Main St. L D

VOLARE ITALIAN RESTAURANT      979/836-1514

Northern Italian. Casual Dining. $7-$23 **AAA Inspector Notes:** The historic downtown building provides the backdrop for dinners of pasta, chicken, seafood, steaks, lamb, veal and pork. **Features:** beer & wine. **Address:** 102 Ross St 77833 **Location:** At E Alamo and Ross sts; just e of downtown. **Parking:** street only. L D

## BROOKSHIRE pop. 4,702
• Part of Houston area — see map p. 301

LA QUINTA INN & SUITES BROOKSHIRE      (281)375-8888

**Hotel** $107-$142 **Address:** 721 FM 1489 77423 **Location:** I-10 exit 731; on south frontage road. **Facility:** 55 units. 3 stories, interior corridors. **Pool(s):** outdoor. **Activities:** hot tub, exercise room. **Guest Services:** coin laundry.

# BROWNFIELD   pop. 9,657

## BEST WESTERN CAPROCK INN

(806)637-9471

 Hotel
$99-$125

 **AAA Benefit:** Members save 10% or more with Best Western!

**Address:** 321 Lubbock Rd 79316 **Location:** Jct US 385 and 82, 2 blks n. **Facility:** 50 units. 1-2 stories, exterior corridors. **Pool(s):** outdoor.

  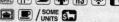

# BROWNSVILLE   (I-8) pop. 175,023, elev. 45'
• Hotels p. 128 • Restaurants p. 129

Brownsville is historically and economically intertwined with Matamoros, its sister city on the Mexican side of the border. As a major seaport and railhead, Brownsville exports the agricultural products of the Rio Grande Valley as well as a large percentage of Mexican commerce. Locally, both cities are often thought of as one. Brownsville is a bilingual city with strong Spanish cultural ties, and residents frequently cross the three international bridges to shop, visit and work.

During the 19th century, wars and banditry marked relations between the two communities. Brownsville was established in 1846 as Fort Brown to support the United States' claim to the Rio Grande as its southern border. The two battles at Palo Alto and Resaca de la Palma successfully defended that claim and started the Mexican War.

During the Civil War, Brownsville prospered as the Confederacy's chief cotton port, shipping materials out of Mexico to dodge the Union blockade. One of the last land battles of the Civil War was fought near Brownsville at Palmito Ranch; the Confederate troops had not heard of Gen. Robert E. Lee's surrender 1 month earlier. The dissent along the border did not end with the Civil War, however, as plots and counterplots by revolutionaries across the border kept Fort Brown busy during the rest of the 19th century and into the next.

Remnants of Fort Brown can still be seen east of the International Bridge on International Boulevard near Elizabeth Street. Several original fort buildings are part of the campus shared by Texas Southmost College and University of Texas at Brownsville, including the post hospital, guardhouse and post headquarters. Phone (956) 882-8200.

Other local sites and monuments remind visitors of the strife that occurred in Brownsville during the Mexican War. Battle sites include the Palo Alto Battlefield National Historical Park *(see attraction listing)*, at FM 1847 and FM 511; the Resaca de la Palma Battlefield Marker, on FM 1847 between Price and Coffee Port roads; and the Palmito Hill Battlefield Marker, 12 miles east on SR 4.

The ▼ Charro Days Fiesta in February celebrates the *charro* horsemen of Mexico with a grand ball, street dances, parades and a carnival; phone (956) 542-4245. Air Fiesta, held in March, is an air show featuring dozens of antique and modern military aircraft; phone (956) 541-8585. Latin Jazz Festival tunes fill the air in October; phone (956) 831-7818.

The city is known for its shrimp fleet and its dual-frontier *maquiladora* manufacturing program, which includes *Fortune* 500 companies in both Brownsville and Matamoros. Nearby are the wide sandy beaches of South Padre Island *(see place listing p. 538 and Padre Island National Seashore p. 430)*, which are reached via SRs 48 and 100 to Port Isabel, then over Laguna Madre Bay via the Queen Isabella Causeway.

Bird-watchers can find a variety of the winged species in the Brownsville area, including wild parrots and Brown Pelicans. More than 470 bird species call the area home.

**Brownsville Convention and Visitors Bureau:** 650 FM 802, Brownsville, TX 78520. **Phone:** (956) 546-3721 or (800) 626-2639.

**Self-guiding tours:** A map outlining the Brownsville Heritage Trail, which guides visitors around the historic downtown area, is available from the convention and visitors bureau.

**THE BROWNSVILLE HERITAGE COMPLEX,** jct. 13th and E. Washington sts., includes the 1850 Stillman House Museum, dedicated to Charles Stillman, the founder of Brownsville; the Brownsville Heritage Museum, which portrays the historical evolution of the city; the Aiken Education Center Gallery, which houses rotating cultural art and historical exhibitions; and Preservation Resource Center, home to a library and archives.

**Hours:** Tues.-Sat. 10-4. **Cost:** $5; $4 (ages 65+); $2 (ages 6-10 with adult and students with ID). **Phone:** (956) 541-5560.

**BROWNSVILLE MUSEUM OF FINE ART,** 660 E. Ringgold St., features a permanent collection of more than 350 works. The museum also offers a variety of changing exhibits and special events. **Time:** Allow 1 hour minimum. **Hours:** Mon.-Sat. 10-4 (also Wed. 4-8). Closed major holidays. **Cost:** $5; $3 (ages 6-12 and students with ID); free (Wed. after 5). **Phone:** (956) 542-0941.

▼GEM **GLADYS PORTER ZOO** is 2 mi. n. at 500 Ringgold St. Moats, streams, rocks and cave-like structures provide natural enclosures for more than 1,400 animals at the 26-acre zoo. More than 350 species are represented, including nearly 50 endangered.

Galapagos tortoises, spider monkeys and Cuban crocodiles inhabit Tropical America. Indo-Australia is home to orangutans, kangaroos, kookaburras and wallabies. The Asia environment features tigers, gibbons and dromedary camels. Popular residents of the Africa area include reticulated giraffes, zebras, lions, gorillas, chimpanzees and the rare Jentink's duiker antelope.

The zoo also offers a herpetarium, a free-flight aviary, bear grottoes and an exhibit of harbor seals. The children's zoo lets youngsters interact with Nigerian Dwarf Goats, miniature mules and other baby animals. **Hours:** Daily 9-5, with extended hours in summer. Train rides are available Sun. 1:30-3:30 (weather permitting). **Cost:** $9.50; $8 (ages 65+); $6.50 (ages 2-13). Train $2; $1 (ages 2-13). **Phone:** (956) 546-2177.

**Children's Museum of Brownsville** is at 501 E. Ringgold St. in the Gladys Porter Zoo complex. Interactive play-and-learn stations include a weather station, a construction zone, a farm and a health clinic. **Time:** Allow 2 hours minimum. **Hours:** Tues.-Sat. 10-5, Sun. noon-4. **Cost:** $6; free (ages 0-1). **Phone:** (956) 548-9300.

**HISTORIC BROWNSVILLE MUSEUM** is off SR 77/83 at the Boca Chica exit, then e. to 641 E. Madison St. Housed in a 1928 train depot, the museum offers interpretive exhibits from Brownsville's past, including the area's earliest military fort and the arrival of French teaching nuns. Agricultural and ranching tools, artifacts and pictures from the battles of the Mexican War and a restored Baldwin wood-burning, narrow-gauge railroad locomotive are included.

**Time:** Allow 30 minutes minimum. **Hours:** Tues.-Fri. 10-4, Sat. 10-2. Closed major holidays. **Cost:** $4; $2 (ages 0-15 and 65+). **Phone:** (956) 548-1313.

**PALO ALTO BATTLEFIELD NATIONAL HISTORICAL PARK,** 7200 Paredes Line Rd. is the setting of the first battle in 1846 of the 2-year Mexican War. An orientation video and exhibits may be seen in the visitor center. A .5-mile trail leads to a sweeping view of the battlefield; interpretive signs describe the battle scene. **Time:** Allow 1 hour minimum. **Hours:** Daily 8-5. Closed Jan. 1, Thanksgiving and Christmas. **Cost:** Free. **Phone:** (956) 541-2785.

**RESACA DE LA PALMA STATE PARK** is at 1000 New Carmen Rd. The summer tanager, yellow-breasted chat, black-bellied whistling duck and purple gallinule are just some of the bird species that call this 1,200-acre park home. On the grounds are more than 11 miles of biking, hiking and walking trails; a visitor center; and four observation decks. Visitors can take a tram tour, rent bikes and binoculars and participate in bird walks, nighttime hiking trips and other activities. *See Recreation Areas Chart.*

**Note:** During the summer months visitors are advised to visit in the early morning or late afternoon, wear a hat and bring mosquito repellent. **Tours:** Guided tours are available. **Time:** Allow 1 hour minimum. **Hours:** Grounds daily dawn-dusk. Visitor center daily 8-5, Dec.-Apr.; Thurs.-Sun. 8-5, rest of year. **Cost:** $4; $2 (ages 65+); free (ages 0-12 and those born before Sept. 1930). Bike rentals $5-$12 per day. Binocular rentals $3 per day. **Phone:** (956) 350-2920.

**RIO GRANDE VALLEY WING FLYING MUSEUM** is s. of the airport terminal at 955 S. Minnesota Ave. World War II military aircraft, antique vehicles, military uniforms and models are displayed. A 30-minute video features military aircraft operated and restored by the Commemorative Air Force. **Time:** Allow 30 minutes minimum. **Hours:** Wed.-Sat. 9:30-3:30, mid-Sept. to mid-June. Closed Jan. 1, Thanksgiving and Christmas. **Cost:** $6; $5 (ages 55+); $3 (ages 12-18); free (ages 0-11 with parent). **Phone:** (956) 541-8585.

---

BROWNSVILLE COMFORT SUITES     (956)541-3332
▼▼▼ Hotel $86-$169 **Address:** 651 Sunrise Blvd 78520 **Location:** US 77 and 83 exit Ruben Torres Sr Blvd (FM 802), just e off northbound frontage road. **Facility:** 75 units. 4 stories, interior corridors. **Pool(s):** outdoor. **Activities:** exercise room. **Guest Services:** valet and coin laundry.

---

COURTYARD BY MARRIOTT BROWNSVILLE    (956)350-4600
▼▼▼ Hotel $94-$139 **Address:** 3955 N Expwy 78520 **Location:** US 77 and 83 exit Ruben Torres Sr Blvd (FM 802). Located near Sunrise Mall. **Facility:** 90 units. 3 stories, interior corridors. **Pool(s):** heated outdoor. **Activities:** hot tub, exercise room. **Guest Services:** valet and coin laundry, area transportation.

**AAA Benefit:** Members save 5% or more!

---

HAMPTON INN & SUITES     (956)548-0005

▼▼▼ Hotel $99-$119

**AAA Benefit:** Members save up to 10%!

**Address:** 3000 N Expwy 78526 **Location:** US 77 and 83 exit Ruben Torres Sr Blvd (FM 802); on northbound frontage road. **Facility:** 98 units. 3 stories, interior corridors. **Terms:** 1-7 night minimum stay, cancellation fee imposed. **Amenities:** video games. **Pool(s):** outdoor. **Activities:** hot tub, exercise room. **Guest Services:** valet and coin laundry. **Featured Amenity:** continental breakfast.

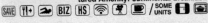

---

HOLIDAY INN     (956)547-1500

▼▼▼ Hotel $77-$85

**Address:** 3777 N Expwy 78520 **Location:** US 77 and 83 exit Ruben Torres Sr Blvd (FM 802); on southbound frontage road. **Facility:** 141 units. 2 stories (no elevator), interior corridors. **Amenities:** video games. **Pool(s):** heated outdoor. **Activities:** recreation programs, exercise room. **Guest Services:** valet and coin laundry.

## HOLIDAY INN EXPRESS HOTEL & SUITES

(956)550-0666

Hotel
$99-$129

**Address:** 1985 N Expwy 83 78520 **Location:** US 77 and 83 exit Ruben Torres Sr Blvd (FM 802); on southbound frontage road. **Facility:** 74 units. 3 stories, interior corridors. **Terms:** cancellation fee imposed, resort fee. **Pool(s):** outdoor. **Activities:** hot tub, exercise room. **Guest Services:** valet and coin laundry. **Featured Amenity: full hot breakfast.**

## HOMEWOOD SUITES BY HILTON

(956)574-6900

Extended Stay Hotel
$99-$139

**AAA Benefit:** Members save up to 10%!

**Address:** 3759 N Expwy 78520 **Location:** US 77 and 83 exit Ruben Torres Sr Blvd (FM 802); on southbound frontage road. Located in a light-commercial area. **Facility:** 86 units, some two bedrooms, efficiencies and kitchens. 3 stories, interior corridors. **Terms:** 1-7 night minimum stay, cancellation fee imposed. **Pool(s):** outdoor. **Activities:** hot tub, exercise room. **Guest Services:** valet and coin laundry, area transportation. **Featured Amenity: full hot breakfast.**

## LA QUINTA INN & SUITES BROWNSVILLE NORTH

(956)350-2118

Hotel $92-$127 **Address:** 5051 North Expwy (US 77) 78520 **Location:** US 77 exit Alton Gloor Rd southbound; exit Stillman Rd northbound U-turn; on southbound frontage road. **Facility:** 62 units. 3 stories, interior corridors. **Pool(s):** outdoor. **Activities:** hot tub, exercise room. **Guest Services:** coin laundry.

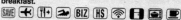

## RESIDENCE INN BY MARRIOTT BROWNSVILLE

(956)350-8100

Extended Stay Hotel
$89-$149 **Address:** 3975 N Expwy 83 78520 **Location:** US 77 and 83 exit Ruben Torres Sr Blvd (FM 802). Located near Sunrise Mall. **Facility:** 102 kitchen units, some two bedrooms. 3 stories, interior corridors. **Pool(s):** heated outdoor. **Activities:** hot tub, exercise room. **Guest Services:** valet and coin laundry, area transportation.

**AAA Benefit:** Members save 5% or more!

## STAYBRIDGE SUITES

(956)504-9500

Extended Stay Hotel $99-$129 **Address:** 2900 Pablo Kisel Blvd 78526 **Location:** US 77 and 83 exit Ruben Torres Sr Blvd (FM 802), 0.8 mi on frontage road to Pablo Kisel Blvd, then 0.5 mi e. **Facility:** 99 efficiencies, some two bedrooms. 4 stories, interior corridors. **Terms:** cancellation fee imposed. **Pool(s):** outdoor. **Activities:** hot tub, exercise room. **Guest Services:** complimentary and valet laundry, area transportation.

---

## WHERE TO EAT

### LUBY'S

956/546-1062

American. Cafeteria. $6-$12 **AAA Inspector Notes:** First opened in 1947 in south Texas, this cafeteria with over 100 outlets features a wide variety of salads, fresh fruits, seafood...including crunchy shrimp...pastas, meat, poultry and just baked cakes and pies. Ask about the kids specials and Lu Ann platters...an entrée with choice of 2 vegetables and a roll. Many locations offer drive-thru service. **Address:** 2124 Boca Chica Blvd 78521 **Location:** Jct US 83 and SR 48. [L] [D]

### TOSCAFINO

956/574-9888

Italian. Casual Dining. $20-$32 **AAA Inspector Notes:** Tucked into small strip mall, this restaurant was recommended by several locals. The interior features a theater kitchen and ultra-contemporary décor. Specials include osso buco and a very spicy frutti di mare. The crunch Toscachon dessert with ground oat flakes and meringue is outstanding. **Features:** full bar, happy hour. **Address:** 3001 Pablo Kisel Blvd, Suite N 78526 **Location:** US 77 and 83 exit Ruben Torres Sr Blvd (FM 802), 0.8 mi n on frontage road to Pablo Kisel Blvd, then 0.4 mi e. [L] [D] [LATE]

# Nearby Mexico

## MATAMOROS, TAMAULIPAS pop. 489,193

**Note:** For current information about safety/security issues in Matamoros, go to the U.S. State Department website (travel.state.gov). For general safety-related information *see Personal Safety, p. 243.*

Main port of entry to Mexico from the lower Rio Grande Valley, Matamoros (mah-tah-MOH-rohs) is connected with Brownsville, Tex. A destination for border-hopping tourists, it also is the most historically significant of the Rio Grande border towns. U.S. Gen. Zachary Taylor and his troops entered the city in 1846 and waged the first major battle of the Mexican-American War.

Three bridges span the Rio Grande. The two most helpful to visitors are the B & M Bridge, which enters Matamoros via Mexico Street in Brownsville, and the Gateway Bridge, also called the International Bridge, which enters via International Boulevard. Toll fees on the B & M Bridge are $2.25 (U.S.) for automobiles and pickups and 50c for pedestrians; the Gateway Bridge fees are $3 (U.S.) for automobiles and pickups and 75c for pedestrians. U.S. Customs and Border Protection offices as well as Mexican customs and immigration offices at both bridges are open daily 24 hours. Baggage must be inspected if you plan to travel into the interior.

The Casamata Museum, about 6 blocks east of Plaza Hidalgo (the main plaza) at avenidas Guatemala and Santos Degollado, is housed in the remains of a fort dating from 1845; never completed, it was supposed to help defend the city from U.S. attack. Exhibits include weapons, early city photographs and memorabilia associated with the 1910 Mexican Revolution. The museum is open Tues.-Fri. 8-4, Sat. 9-2, and admission is free; phone (868) 816-2071.

The Reforma Theater (Teatro Reforma) is a block north of Plaza Hidalgo at Calle 6 and Avenida Abasolo. It was built in 1861, demolished in 1956 and replaced with a movie theater, and then restored to its original architectural style in the early 1990s. It now serves as the venue for events associated with the International Autumn Festival in October.

**Shopping areas:** The Juárez Market (Mercado Juárez) occupies the block between Calles 9 and 10 and avenidas Abasolo and Matamoros, about 4 blocks northwest of Plaza Hidalgo. Here you can wander among more than 100 stalls and bargain for a variety of crafts and souvenirs. Sections of Calle 9 and Avenida Abasolo in the vicinity of the market are pedestrian only. Avenida Alvaro Obregón, which runs south from the Gateway Bridge toward Plaza Hidalgo, is lined with shops selling good-quality handicrafts, gifts and silver jewelry.

---

This ends the Brownsville section and resumes the alphabetical city listings for Texas.

---

# BROWNWOOD (E-7) pop. 19,288, elev. 1,342'

A cotton-buying center in its early days, Brownwood now relies on industry to sustain its economy. The city is rich in transportation history.

**Brownwood Area Chamber of Commerce:** 600 E. Depot St., Brownwood, TX 76801; P.O. Box 880, Brownwood, TX 76804. **Phone:** (325) 646-9535.

## HAMPTON INN                          (325)641-1122

▼▼▼ Hotel $99-$144 **Address:** 1103 Riverside Dr 76801 **Location:** Jct US 67/84/377 and Riverside Dr. **Facility:** 56 units. 3 stories, interior corridors. **Terms:** 1-7 night minimum stay, cancellation fee imposed. **Pool(s):** outdoor. **Activities:** exercise room. **Guest Services:** valet and coin laundry.

**AAA Benefit:** Members save up to 10%!

[icons]

## LA QUINTA INN & SUITES                 (325)641-1731

▼▼▼ Hotel $109-$144 **Address:** 103 Market Place Blvd 76801 **Location:** US 183, just e. **Facility:** 71 units. 4 stories, interior corridors. **Pool(s):** outdoor. **Activities:** hot tub, exercise room. **Guest Services:** coin laundry.

[icons] / SOME UNITS

---

# BRYAN (E-9) pop. 76,201, elev. 367'

Bryan is the county seat of Brazos County and a major educational and commercial center. Many of its first settlers were colonists who arrived with Stephen F. Austin, but not until the Houston & Texas Central Railroad arrived in 1860 did Bryan begin to take shape. The city has prospered with an economy based upon diversified agriculture and industry.

**Self-guiding tours:** A brochure about the historic district is available from the convention and visitors bureau.

## WINERIES

• **Messina Hof Winery & Resort** is 2 mi. e. off SR 6/Old Reliance Rd. exit, following signs to 4545

Old Reliance Rd. **Hours:** Tours are given Mon.-Fri. at 1, 2:30 and 5:30, Sat. at 11, 12:30, 2:30, 4 and 5:30, Sun. at 12:30, 2:30 and 4. Closed Jan. 1 and Christmas. **Phone:** (979) 778-9463 or (800) 736-9463.

## BEST WESTERN PREMIER OLD TOWN CENTER
(979)731-5300

▼▼▼▼
Hotel
$115-$500

**AAA Benefit:** Members save 10% or more with Best Western!

**Address:** 1920 Austins Colony Pkwy 77803 **Location:** SR 6 exit Briarcrest Dr; just n on east frontage road. **Facility:** 100 units. 5 stories, interior corridors. **Pool(s):** outdoor. **Activities:** hot tub, exercise room. **Guest Services:** valet and coin laundry. **Featured Amenity: full hot breakfast.**

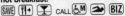

/ SOME UNITS

## FAIRFIELD INN BY MARRIOTT            (979)268-1552

▼▼▼ Hotel $109-$149 **Address:** 4613 S Texas Ave 77802 **Location:** Just n of jct SR 60 and 6 business route (Texas Ave). **Facility:** 62 units. 3 stories, interior corridors. **Pool(s):** heated indoor. **Activities:** hot tub, exercise room. **Guest Services:** valet and coin laundry. [icons]

**AAA Benefit:** Members save 5% or more!

## LASALLE HOTEL                          979/822-2000

▼▼▼▼
Historic Hotel
Rates not provided

**Address:** 120 S Main St 77803 **Location:** SR 6 exit Wm J Bryan Pkwy, 2.2 mi w to Main St, then 2 blks s. Located in a historic downtown area. **Facility:** This historical treasure's nostalgic touches belie its modern amenities; rooms are similar but the antique furniture and artwork distinguish each room. 55 units. 7 stories, interior corridors. **Guest Services:** valet laundry, area transportation. **Featured Amenity: continental breakfast.**

 / SOME UNITS

## THE VILLA AT MESSINA HOF             (979)778-9463

▼▼▼ ▼▼▼ Country Inn $165-$320 **Address:** 4545 Old Reliance Rd 77808 **Location:** Jct US 190 and SR 6 southbound, 1.7 mi e to Wallis Rd, 1.2 mi s to Old Reliance Rd, then 0.5 mi e; jct SR 6 and Old Reliance Rd northbound, 2 mi e. **Facility:** The property, located on a winery, offers upscale accommodations with a French flavor and an attached restaurant for fine dining. 11 units. 2 stories (no elevator), interior corridors. **Terms:** 2 night minimum stay - weekends, age restrictions may apply, 30 day cancellation notice. **Dining:** The Vintage House at Messina Hof, see separate listing. **Activities:** fishing, massage. [icons]

## WHERE TO EAT

## CAFFE CAPRI                           979/822-2675

▼▼ ▼▼ Italian. Casual Dining. $6-$13 **AAA Inspector Notes:** In a historic downtown building, the restaurant offers many favorite Italian dishes at attractive prices. **Features:** beer & wine. **Address:** 222 N Main St 77803 **Location:** Jct Main and 24th sts; downtown. **Parking:** street only. [L] [D]

### CHRISTOPHER'S WORLD GRILLE 979/776-2181

▼▼▼▼ American Fine Dining $13-$35

**AAA Inspector Notes:** *Classic.* From a converted 1911 home, Chef Christopher brings an interesting international flair to his seasonal menus, which offer patrons choices of inventive appetizers and entrees of steak, veal osso buco, lamb, seafood, duck and pasta, all served by an attentive and professional staff. **Features:** full bar. **Reservations:** suggested. **Address:** 5001 Boonville Rd 77802 **Location:** SR 6 Bypass exit University Dr, 2 mi e to Boonville Rd, then 0.5 mi n.

*Menu on AAA.com* L D CALL &M

**Prime Steaks, Fresh Seafood, Continental Cuisine**

### FRITTELLA ITALIAN CAFE 979/260-6666

▼ Italian. Casual Dining. $7-$9 **AAA Inspector Notes:** All homemade pasta dishes, frittellas (calzones) and wood-fired pizzas are served in the relaxed dining establishment. **Features:** beer & wine. **Address:** 3901 S Texas Ave 77802 **Location:** Jct Business SR 6 and 60, 0.6 mi n. L D

### LA RIVIERA RESTAURANT & BAKERY 979/846-5913

▼▼▼ Continental. Fine Dining. $9-$27 **AAA Inspector Notes:** Chef Alfonso brings some interesting flavors to the table at this bistrotype restaurant. Choose among beef, lamb, seafood, duck and chicken entrées, and you must save room for the superb desserts. **Features:** beer & wine. **Address:** 3700 S Texas Ave, Suite 300 77802 **Location:** Jct University Blvd, 0.5 mi n. L D

### THE VINTAGE HOUSE AT MESSINA HOF 979/778-9463

▼▼▼ American. Fine Dining. $9-$50 **AAA Inspector Notes:** Fine wines produced on site match with prime beef, seafood, duck or chicken selections. The French manor home exudes cozy ambience. **Features:** wine only. **Address:** 4545 Old Reliance Rd 77808 **Location:** Jct US 190 and SR 6, 1.7 mi w to Wallis Rd, 1.2 mi s to Old Reliance Rd, then 0.5 mi e; jct SR 6 and Old Reliance Rd northbound, 2 mi e; in The Villa at Messina Hof. L D

## BUDA pop. 7,295

### AMERICAS BEST VALUE INN (512)312-1550

▼▼▼▼ Hotel $59-$149

**Address:** 15101 IH-35 78610 **Location:** I-35 exit 220; on east frontage road. **Facility:** 41 units. 2 stories (no elevator), exterior corridors. **Terms:** cancellation fee imposed. **Pool(s):** outdoor. **Guest Services:** coin laundry. **Featured Amenity:** continental breakfast.

### BEST WESTERN SOUTHGATE INN & SUITES (512)295-4559

▼▼▼▼ Hotel $70-$150

*Best Western* **AAA Benefit:** Members save 10% or more with Best Western!

**Address:** 18658 S I-35 78610 **Location:** I-35 exit 217, just s on southbound frontage road. **Facility:** 50 units. 3 stories, interior corridors. **Terms:** 2-3 night minimum stay - seasonal. **Pool(s):** outdoor. **Activities:** exercise room. **Guest Services:** coin laundry. **Featured Amenity:** full hot breakfast.

### HAMPTON INN & SUITES (512)295-4900

▼▼▼▼ Hotel $99-$129

*Hampton* **AAA Benefit:** Members save up to 10%!

**Address:** 1201 Cabelas Dr 78610 **Location:** I-35 exit 220, just s on west frontage road to Cabelas Dr, then 1 mi w. **Facility:** 74 units. 4 stories, interior corridors. **Terms:** 1-7 night minimum stay, cancellation fee imposed. **Pool(s):** heated indoor. **Activities:** exercise room. **Guest Services:** coin laundry. **Featured Amenity:** full hot breakfast.

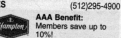  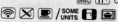 

### HOLIDAY INN EXPRESS BUDA (512)295-8040

▼▼▼ Hotel $110-$160 **Address:** 15295 IH-35 #600 78610 **Location:** I-45 exit 221; on east frontage road. **Facility:** 76 units. 3 stories, interior corridors. **Amenities:** safes. **Pool(s):** outdoor. **Activities:** hot tub, exercise room. **Guest Services:** coin laundry.

## BUFFALO pop. 1,856

### CRAIGS INN BUFFALO 903/322-5831

▼▼ Hotel. Rates not provided. **Address:** IH-45 & US 79 75831 **Location:** I-45 exit 178, just n on NW Frontage Rd. **Facility:** 59 units, some kitchens. 1-2 stories (no elevator), interior/exterior corridors. **Pool(s):** heated indoor. **Guest Services:** coin laundry.

### HAMPTON INN & SUITES (903)322-2223

▼▼▼ Hotel $119-$129 **Address:** 2624 W Commerce St 75831 **Location:** I-45 exit 178, just s. **Facility:** 77 units. 3 stories, interior corridors. **Terms:** 1-7 night minimum stay, cancellation fee imposed. **Pool(s):** heated indoor. **Activities:** hot tub, exercise room. **Guest Services:** coin laundry.

**AAA Benefit:** Members save up to 10%!

## BUFFALO GAP (D-6) pop. 464

• Restaurants p. 132

Buffalo Gap is at the site of a natural pass in the Callahan Divide through which buffalo traveled for many years. The town was a point on the Dodge Cattle Trail.

**BUFFALO GAP HISTORIC VILLAGE** is s. on FM 89, then 2 blks. w. on Elm St. This collection of 17 structures in three historic areas is centered on the 1879 Taylor County Courthouse and Jail. The 1875, 1905 and 1925 buildings include a pioneer log cabin, a medical display, barbershop, railroad depot with a working telegraph, blacksmith shop, two-room schoolhouse and more.

**Time:** Allow 1 hour minimum. **Hours:** Mon.-Sat. 10-6, Sun. noon-6, June 1-late Aug.; Mon.-Sat. 10-5, Sun. noon-5, rest of year. Closed Jan. 1, Thanksgiving and Christmas. **Cost:** $7; $6 (ages 55+); $4 (students with ID); free (ages 0-5 and active military with ID). **Phone:** (325) 572-3365.

**PERINI RANCH STEAKHOUSE**  325/572-3339

♦♦ Steak. Casual Dining. $13-$38 **AAA Inspector Notes:** History melds with old family recipes in the restaurant's rustic, Western setting. Guests can mosey in for some pork ribs, generous steaks, catfish and prime rib--menu highlights on Friday and Saturday. Quite honestly, you would be hard pressed to find better steaks anywhere in the United States. They're just outstanding. Lunch is served on weekends. **Features:** full bar, patio dining. **Reservations:** suggested. **Address:** 3002 FM 89 79508 **Location:** Jct US 83/84/277 and SR 89, 10.3 mi s. [D]

## BURKBURNETT pop. 10,811

**BURKBURNETT HAMPTON INN**  (940)569-8109

♦♦♦♦ Hotel $89-$139 **Address:** 1008 Sheppard Rd 76354 **Location:** I-44 exit 12, just e. **Facility:** 80 units. 4 stories, interior corridors. **Terms:** 1-7 night minimum stay, cancellation fee imposed. **Amenities:** video games. **Pool(s):** heated indoor. **Activities:** exercise room. **Guest Services:** coin laundry.

**AAA Benefit:** Members save up to 10%!

[icons]

## BURLESON pop. 36,690

### BEST WESTERN PLUS BURLESON INN & SUITES
(817)744-7747

♦♦♦♦ Hotel $80-$86

**AAA Benefit:** Members save 10% or more with Best Western!

**Address:** 516 Memorial Plaza 76028 **Location:** I-35W exit 36 northbound; exit 35 southbound; on northbound access road. **Facility:** 71 units. 3 stories, interior corridors. **Pool(s):** heated indoor. **Activities:** hot tub, exercise room. **Guest Services:** coin laundry.

[icons]

### COMFORT SUITES
(817)426-6666

♦♦♦ Hotel $75-$180

**Address:** 321 S Burleson Blvd 76028 **Location:** I-35W exit 35 southbound, 2 mi s to crossover, U-turn; exit 36 northbound; on northbound access road. **Facility:** 69 units, some kitchens. 3 stories, interior corridors. **Pool(s):** heated indoor. **Activities:** hot tub, exercise room. **Guest Services:** valet and coin laundry. **Featured Amenity:** full hot breakfast.

[icons]

### HAMPTON INN & SUITES
(817)295-2727

♦♦♦♦ Hotel $89-$115 **Address:** 13251 Jake Ct 76028 **Location:** I-35W exit 38 (Alsbury Blvd), just e, then just n. Adjacent to Fort Worth Spinks Airport. **Facility:** 88 units. 4 stories, interior corridors. **Terms:** 1-7 night minimum stay, cancellation fee imposed. **Pool(s):** heated indoor. **Activities:** hot tub, exercise room. **Guest Services:** valet and coin laundry.

**AAA Benefit:** Members save up to 10%!

[icons]

**HOLIDAY INN EXPRESS HOTEL & SUITES**  (817)426-0396

♦♦♦ Hotel $89-$119 **Address:** 13250 Jake Ct 76028 **Location:** I-35W exit 38 (Alsbury Blvd), just e to Jake Ct, then just n. **Facility:** 74 units. 3 stories, interior corridors. **Terms:** cancellation fee imposed. **Pool(s):** indoor. **Activities:** hot tub, exercise room. **Guest Services:** valet and coin laundry.

[icons]

**LA QUINTA INN & SUITES**  (817)447-6565

♦♦♦ Hotel $89-$124 **Address:** 225 E Alsbury Blvd 76028 **Location:** I-35E exit 38 (E Alsbury Blvd), just e. **Facility:** 77 units. 4 stories, interior corridors. **Pool(s):** heated indoor. **Activities:** hot tub, exercise room. **Guest Services:** valet and coin laundry.

[icons]

### WHERE TO EAT

**BABE'S CHICKEN DINNER HOUSE**  817/447-3400

♦ Chicken. Casual Dining. $6-$14 **AAA Inspector Notes:** Babe's offers an upbeat family atmosphere. Bowls filled with ample portions of green beans, corn, mashed potatoes and warm biscuits are served up for a home-style experience. BYOB allowed. Kids 5 and under eat free. **Address:** 120 S Main St 76028 **Location:** I-35W exit 36, just w on Renfro St. [L] [D]

**MEXICAN INN CAFE**  817/447-7661

♦♦ Tex-Mex. Casual Dining. $9-$19 **AAA Inspector Notes:** Established in the 1930s by notorious gambler Tiffin Hall, the small chain has grown to four restaurants in greater Fort Worth. Traditional Tex-Mex cuisine is served in a lively and colorful setting. This place prides itself on its homemade tostados and tortillas. **Features:** full bar. **Address:** 13155 S I-35 W 76028 **Location:** I-35W exit 38 (Alsbury Blvd), just n. [L] [D]

**SPRING CREEK BBQ**  817/426-6335

♦ Barbecue. Casual Dining. $8-$13 **AAA Inspector Notes:** Expect Texas-Style barbecue at its simple, homey best. Hickory smoked ribs, beef, pork and turkey lace the air with a spicy aroma that mingles with the scent of freshly baked rolls and cold ice cream slowly melting over a dish of homemade peach cobbler. Plates often are loaded with all the coleslaw, potato salad and corn on the cob they can support. Part of a small chain, this barbecue restaurant displays a rustic décor that gives patrons the impression they are "at the ranch." **Features:** beer only. **Address:** 13125 South Frwy W 76028 **Location:** I-35 exit 38 (Alsbury Blvd), just n. [L] [D]

## BURNET (E-8) pop. 5,987, elev. 1,304'

The town grew around Fort Croghan, established by ranchers in 1849 as part of a string of outposts on the Texas frontier. The region's many immense granite outcroppings proved a hindrance for early settlers. G.W. Lacy of nearby Marble Falls tried and failed to trade his granite mountain for a saddle horse. Later he deeded part of it to the state, which used the stone in the construction of the Texas Capitol. These outcroppings, some of the oldest in the world, are now prized by rock hounds and geologists.

Two other resources, water and wildflowers, have helped make Burnet a popular recreation center. Nine miles west via SR 29 is Inks Lake State Park (see Recreation Areas Chart), where 1,200 acres of woodlands and wildflowers border the lake. The visitor center at nearby Lake Buchanan (see Recreation Areas Chart) offers a panoramic view.

**Burnet Chamber of Commerce and Visitors Bureau:** 229 S. Pierce St., Burnet, TX 78611. **Phone:** (512) 756-4297.

**FORT CROGHAN MUSEUM** is at 703 Buchanan Dr. (SR 29W). On the 1849 Army fort grounds are seven restored 19th-century stone and log buildings, including a powder house and a one-room schoolhouse. **Hours:** Thurs.-Sat. 10-5, first Thurs. in Apr.-second Sat. in Oct. **Cost:** Donations. **Phone:** (512) 756-8281.

**LONGHORN CAVERN STATE PARK** is 6 mi. s. on US 281, then 6 mi. w. on Park Rd. 4S. Of interest are the Cathedral Room and two rooms of transparent crystal. The entire public part of the cave is lighted, and the temperature is a constant 68 F. Rubber-soled shoes are recommended. **Time:** Allow 1 hour, 30 minutes minimum. **Hours:** Tours daily 10-4, Memorial Day-Labor Day; Mon.-Fri. at 11, 1 and 3, Sat.-Sun. 10-4, rest of year. Closed Christmas Eve and Christmas. Phone ahead to confirm schedule. **Cost:** $12.99; $11.99 (ages 13-19, ages 60+ and military with ID); $8.99 (ages 2-12). **Phone:** (830) 598-2283 or (877) 441-2283.

**VANISHING TEXAS CRUISE** is 3 mi. w. on SR 29, then 14 mi. n. on FM 2341 to 443 Waterway Ln. The 2-hour Old Bluffton Cruise traverses Lake Buchanan and passes Garrett Island, home to migratory birds, including bald eagles, blue herons, egrets and ospreys.

**Hours:** Cruises depart Wed. and Sun. at 11, Sat. at 6. Phone ahead to confirm schedule. **Cost:** Morning cruise $20; $17.50 (ages 13-19, ages 60+ and military with ID); $12.75 (ages 2-12). Cruises with box lunch $27.50; $24.95 (ages 13-19, ages 60+ and military with ID); $19.50 (ages 2-12). Saturday evening cruise $25 (ride only); $36.99 (with dinner). Reservations are recommended. **Phone:** (512) 756-6986.

**BEST WESTERN POST OAK INN**          (512)756-4747

Motel
$67-$104

**AAA Benefit:** Members save 10% or more with Best Western!

**Address:** 908 Buchanan Dr 78611 **Location:** Jct US 281 and FM 29, 1 mi w. **Facility:** 46 units. 1 story, exterior corridors. **Terms:** 7 day cancellation notice-fee imposed. **Pool(s):** outdoor. **Featured Amenity:** full hot breakfast.

**COMFORT INN & SUITES**          (512)756-1789

Hotel $80-$210 **Address:** 810 S Water St (US 281) 78611 **Location:** Jct US 281 and FM 29, 0.5 mi s. **Facility:** 75 units, some kitchens. 3 stories, interior corridors. **Pool(s):** outdoor. **Activities:** exercise room. **Guest Services:** coin laundry.

**LOG COUNTRY COVE**          512/756-9132

Vacation Rental House $150-$3200 **Location:** Jct FM 1431 and 2342, 2 mi n; Park Rd 4 and FM 2342, 3 mi s. **Facility:** Upscale lodging in log homes up to 15,000 square feet is offered on the banks of Lake LBJ. The wooded sites have excellent views of the lake that can be enjoyed from relaxing decks and patios. 46 houses. 2 stories, exterior corridors. **Terms:** check-in 4 pm, 2 night minimum stay - seasonal and/or weekends, 60 day cancellation notice-fee imposed, resort fee. **Activities:** boat ramp, fishing, playground. **Guest Services:** complimentary and valet laundry.

**CANYON OF THE EAGLES: A CALIBRE RESORT**
512/334-2070

**fyi** Not evaluated. **Address:** 16942 Ranch Rd 2341 78611 **Location:** Jct US 281 and FM 29, 3 mi w to CR 2341, then 15 mi n. Facilities, services, and décor characterize an economy property.

## CALVERT   pop. 1,192

**PIN OAK BED & BREAKFAST**          (979)364-2935

**Classic Bed & Breakfast** $80-$95 **Address:** 503 Pin Oak 77837 **Location:** Jct SR 6 and Burnett St, 7 blks e. **Facility:** Built in 1900, this grand two-story home's property encompasses an entire city block and is dotted with century-old oaks. The spacious parlors and guest rooms have all been beautifully restored. 4 units. 2 stories (no elevator), interior corridors. *Bath:* some shared. **Parking:** street only. **Terms:** 14 day cancellation notice.

## CAMERON   pop. 5,552

**BUDGET HOST INN & SUITES**          (254)605-0610

Hotel
$89-$200

**Address:** 102 Lafferty Ave 76520 **Location:** US 77/190, 0.5 mi s. **Facility:** 40 units. 2 stories, interior corridors. **Terms:** cancellation fee imposed. **Pool(s):** outdoor. **Activities:** exercise room. **Guest Services:** coin laundry. **Featured Amenity:** breakfast buffet.

## CANADIAN   (A-6) pop. 2,649, elev. 2,425'
• Hotels p. 134

**THE CITADELLE ART FOUNDATION** is at 520 Nelson Ave. The 8,000-square-foot Citadelle mansion—embellished with elegant brickwork, columns and stained-glass windows—was built in 1910 as a church. It functioned as such until the 1970s, when it was sold and converted to a private residence. The owners later donated their home, along with their impressive art collection within, as a public art museum.

You'll start your visit with a video about the Citadelle's history and then set off on your own to explore the property. A handheld audio wand that describes 20-plus points of interest enhances the tour. More than 135 watercolors, pastels, oil paintings, pen-and-ink drawings and other works of American and European artists are on display. You'll also see a collection of some 250 antiques and a gallery devoted to changing exhibits.

If the weather's nice, you can unwind in four lovely gardens: The Four Seasons Garden, with ivy- and moss-covered brick walls and English sculptures; the Hathoot Garden, a tree-shaded, stone-adorned meadow; the Sculpture Garden, with a large bronze sculpture as its centerpiece; and the Pavilion Garden, featuring a classical-style pavilion and giant gates.

**Tours:** Guided tours are available. **Time:** Allow 1 hour, 30 minutes minimum. **Hours:** Thurs.-Sat. 11-4 (also Sun. 1-4, June-Sept.). Closed Jan. 1, Thanksgiving, Christmas Eve, Christmas and Dec. 31. **Cost:** $10; $8 (ages 65+); free (ages 0-18). **Phone:** (806) 323-8899.

**RIVER VALLEY PIONEER MUSEUM,** 118 N. 2nd St., chronicles the history and settlement of the Hemphill County area. Well-done exhibits focusing on regional geology, archeology, industry and other topics provide insight into what life was like here from the time giant mastodons roamed to the early 20th century. **Time:** Allow 45 minutes minimum. **Hours:** Mon.-Fri. 9-4. Closed major holidays. **Cost:** Donations. **Phone:** (806) 323-6548 or (806) 323-8993. 🏧

---

**BEST WESTERN OASIS INN**                    (806)323-9660

Hotel
$120-$170

**AAA Benefit:** Members save 10% or more with Best Western!

**Address:** 303 S 2nd St 79014 **Location:** 2 blks s on US 83; downtown. **Facility:** 55 units. 3 stories, interior corridors. **Pool(s):** heated indoor. **Activities:** exercise room. **Guest Services:** coin laundry.

---

## CANTON (D-9) pop. 3,581

Canton and its First Monday Trade Days are legendary in northern Texas. The tradition started in the 1850s when farmers began bringing horses, hunting hounds and other dogs to Canton to trade or sell. This event has continued uninterrupted over the years, growing into a huge flea market that runs for four days beginning on the Thursday before the first Monday of each month. About 7,000 exhibition stalls attract up to 200,000 people each month.

**Canton Chamber of Commerce:** 119 N. Buffalo St., Canton, TX 75103. **Phone:** (903) 567-2991.

---

**BEST WESTERN CANTON INN**                    (903)567-6591

Hotel
$80-$110

**AAA Benefit:** Members save 10% or more with Best Western!

**Address:** 2251 N Trade Days Blvd 75103 **Location:** Jct I-20 and SR 19 exit 527. Located in a semi-rural area. **Facility:** 82 units. 2 stories (no elevator), exterior corridors. **Terms:** 3 day cancellation notice-fee imposed. **Pool(s):** outdoor. **Guest Services:** coin laundry. **Featured Amenity:** breakfast buffet.

---

## CANYON (B-5) pop. 13,303, elev. 3,566'

Cattle ranches and the railroad sparked Canyon's commercial development at the turn of the 20th century. Agriculture and the campus of West Texas A&M University are the basis of the town's economy.

**Canyon Chamber of Commerce:** 1518 Fifth Ave., Canyon, TX 79015. **Phone:** (806) 655-7815.

**ELKINS RANCH** is e. off I-27 at SR 217, following signs to the entrance of Palo Duro Canyon State Park. Numerous jeep tours explore the rim, walls and floor of Palo Duro Canyon. The 1-hour Black Hawk tour travels to a waterfall and lookout points. The Hidden Spring Canyon tour lasts 2 hours, 15 minutes and explores a hidden finger of the canyon. The 3-hour Spirit of Palo Duro tour reaches the canyon floor.

**Hours:** Daily 8-6, Mar.-Nov.; by appointment rest of year (weather permitting). **Cost:** Black Hawk tour $25; $20 (ages 4-11). Hidden Spring Canyon tour $45; $30 (ages 4-11). Spirit of Palo Duro tour $65; $50 (ages 4-11). **Phone:** (806) 488-2100. ⓘ

**PALO DURO CANYON STATE PARK** is 12 mi. e. on SR 217. The canyon exposes geological formations more than 250 million years old, revealing colorful strata of red clay stone, white gypsum and yellow mudstone as well as layers of limestone and sandstone. Vegetation ranges from wildflowers to mesquite and juniper trees. Palo Duro is a Spanish reference to the canyon's hardwoods.

Deer, turkey, sheep, bobcats and rattlesnakes are among the wildlife visitors might encounter. There are 16 miles of scenic drives that descend to the canyon floor, some 1,000 feet below the rim. There also are 15 miles of bridle paths and more than 30 miles of bicycling and hiking trails. Camping facilities and cabins are available. *See Recreation Areas Chart.*

**Hours:** Daily 8 a.m.-10 p.m., June-Aug.; daily 8-8 (also Fri.-Sat. 8-10 p.m.), Apr.-May and in Sept.; Sun.-Thurs. 8-6, Fri.-Sat. 8-8, rest of year. **Cost:** $5; free (ages 0-12). **Phone:** (806) 488-2227.

**"Texas" Musical Drama** is held in the Pioneer Amphitheatre in Palo Duro Canyon State Park. The base of a 600-foot cliff serves as the backdrop for this outdoor musical drama about the Texas Panhandle, written by Paul Green. The production features more than 60 performers, live horses, light and sound effects and fireworks. Inquire about weather policies. Tickets are available at the theater and at the "Texas" Information Office at 1514 Fifth Ave.

**Time:** Allow 2 hours, 30 minutes minimum. **Hours:** Performances are given Tues.-Sun. at 8:30 p.m., early June to mid-Aug. Phone ahead to confirm schedule. **Cost:** Tickets $15.95-$29.95; $13.95-$27.95 (ages 60+ and military and students with ID); $11.95-$25.95 (ages 0-11). Park admission free to theater patrons after 5:30 p.m. Reservations are recommended. **Phone:** (806) 655-2181. ⓘ

**PANHANDLE-PLAINS HISTORICAL MUSEUM** is on the campus of West Texas A&M University at 2503 Fourth Ave., w. of I-27 on SR 217. The museum presents the cultural, geological and economic history of the region. Major exhibits are dedicated to western heritage, petroleum, paleontology and geology as well as decorative arts, textiles and fine art.

Highlights include a reconstructed pioneer town and the T-Anchor Ranch headquarters, one of the Panhandle's oldest buildings. The People of the Plains exhibit traces 14,000 years of human habitation; Native American artifacts include weavings, pottery, baskets and clothing. Windmills, oil rigs, antique vehicles, saddles, guns, textiles and dinosaur skeletons are among the many items on display. The museum's art collection includes works from the Taos and Santa Fe art colonies as well as a permanent gallery for Texan art.

**Time:** Allow 1 hour minimum. **Hours:** Mon.-Sat. 9-6, June-Aug.; Tues.-Sat. 9-5, rest of year. Closed Jan. 1, Thanksgiving, Christmas Eve and Christmas. **Cost:** $10; $9 (ages 65+); $5 (ages 4-12). **Phone:** (806) 651-2244.

### BEST WESTERN PALO DURO CANYON INN & SUITES
(806)655-1818

Hotel
$80-$111

**AAA Benefit:** Members save 10% or more with Best Western!

**Address:** 2801 4th Ave 79015 **Location:** I-27 exit 106, 1 mi w. **Facility:** 51 units. 3 stories, interior corridors. **Pool(s):** indoor. **Activities:** exercise room. **Guest Services:** coin laundry.

### BUFFALO INN
(806)655-2124

Motel
$45-$75

**Address:** 300 23rd St 79015 **Location:** I-27 exit 106, 2.7 mi w to US 87, then just n. **Facility:** 21 units. 1 story, exterior corridors. **Parking:** winter plug-ins. **Terms:** cancellation fee imposed.

### HOLIDAY INN EXPRESS HOTEL & SUITES
806/655-4445

Hotel
Rates not provided

**Address:** 2901 4th Ave 79015 **Location:** I-27 exit 106, 2 mi w. **Facility:** 66 units, some two bedrooms. 3 stories, interior corridors. **Parking:** winter plug-ins. **Pool(s):** heated indoor. **Activities:** hot tub, exercise room. **Guest Services:** coin laundry.

## CARROLLTON pop. 119,097
- **Hotels & Restaurants map & index p. 179, 184**
- **Part of Dallas area — see map p. 161**

RODEWAY INN    (972)245-9900   **47**

Hotel $50-$75 **Address:** 1832 N I-35 E 75006 **Location:** I-35E exit 443C (Frontage Rd) northbound; exit 443B (Belt Line Rd) southbound, U-turn, 1 mi n. **Facility:** 33 units. 3 stories, interior corridors. **Activities:** exercise room. **Guest Services:** coin laundry.

### WHERE TO EAT

BURGER ISLAND    972/245-4621   **39**

Burgers. Quick Serve. $4-$8 **AAA Inspector Notes:** Don't let the strip center scare you away, the burgers are big, juicy and loaded with flavor. They are made with 1/2-pound Angus beef and will require you to use multiple napkins; that's a good thing. For first timers, The Big Island is a customer favorite and is smothered with cheese, mushrooms and onions. **Address:** 1208 E Belt Line Rd 75006 **Location:** I-35 exit 443B (Belt Line Rd), just e. L D

GRANDY'S RESTAURANT

American. Quick Serve. $4-$8 **AAA Inspector Notes:** Fried chicken and country-fried steak are menu standbys at the restaurant, a regional franchise. They also offer a family-style dining menu. The décor is a step up from that of most quick-serve eateries and more resembles that of a conventional restaurant. Some elements of increased service include additional rolls, iced tea refills and tray removal. B L D

*For additional information, visit AAA.com*
**LOCATIONS:**
**Address:** 1753 I-35 S 75006 **Location:** I-35E exit 442; on northbound access road. **Phone:** 972/245-4302
**Address:** 3330 E Trinity Mills Rd 75006 **Location:** Just e of jct Midway. **Phone:** 972/250-1515

## CARTHAGE pop. 6,779

### BAYMONT INN & SUITES
(903)694-9075

Hotel
$89-$149

**Address:** 2313 SE Loop 75633 **Location:** Just n of jct E US 59 Loop and SR 699. **Facility:** 50 units. 2 stories (no elevator), interior corridors. **Terms:** 3 day cancellation notice-fee imposed. **Pool(s):** outdoor. **Activities:** limited exercise equipment. **Guest Services:** valet and coin laundry. **Featured Amenity:** full hot breakfast.

### BEST WESTERN INN OF CARTHAGE
(903)694-2809

Hotel
$68-$79

**AAA Benefit:** Members save 10% or more with Best Western!

**Address:** 2332 SE Loop 75633 **Location:** Jct E US 59 Loop and SR 699; southwest corner. **Facility:** 40 units. 2 stories (no elevator), exterior corridors. **Pool(s):** outdoor. **Guest Services:** coin laundry.

---

# Plan complete trip routings with the TripTik®
# Travel Planner on AAA.com/CAA.ca

## COMFORT INN & SUITES                (903)693-6700

Hotel
$64-$95

**Address:** 2235 SE Loop 75633 **Location:** Just n of jct E US 59 Loop and SR 699. **Facility:** 59 units. 3 stories, interior corridors. **Pool(s):** outdoor. **Activities:** hot tub, exercise room. **Guest Services:** valet and coin laundry. **Featured Amenity: full hot breakfast.**

SAVE CALL [&M] [≈] [BIZ] [HS] [≈]

[□] [□] [□] [□]

---

## CASTROVILLE (G-7) pop. 2,680

On Sept. 3, 1844, Henri Castro led Alsatian emigrants to this tranquil, tree-shaded area along the Medina River. Castro was consul general for the Republic of Texas in France and contracted with the French government to establish the settlement. With a guarantee of a town lot and 40 acres to farm, French settlers transformed the area into an independent farming center with its own gristmill and cotton gin.

**Castroville Area Chamber of Commerce:** 1115 Angelo St., P.O. Box 572, Castroville, TX 78009. **Phone:** (830) 538-3142 or (800) 778-6775.

**Self-guiding tours:** Information about a walking tour of historic homes and buildings is available from the chamber of commerce.

**LANDMARK INN STATE HISTORIC SITE** is .5 mi. e. on US 90 to jct. Florence and Fiorella sts. The state historic site comprises several buildings including an 1849 plastered limestone structure that has been restored as an 8-room bed and breakfast. A small museum adjacent to the inn's office contains memorabilia of the area. On the grounds are an 1850s two-story gristmill and dam and an old bathhouse. **Time:** Allow 30 minutes minimum. **Hours:** Daily 8-5. Phone ahead for holiday hours. **Cost:** $4; $3 (ages 6-17). **Phone:** (830) 931-2133.

SAMMY'S RESTAURANT                830/931-2204

[W] Comfort Food. Family Dining. $8-$15 **AAA Inspector Notes:** Home style dishes include juicy burgers, crab cakes, fried chicken and scalloped potatoes. All desserts are home made. Friendly south Texas style service. **Address:** 202 US Hwy 90 E 78009 **Location:** Downtown. [B] [L] [D]

---

## CAT SPRING

BLISSWOOD BED & BREAKFAST         713/301-3235

[fyi] Not evaluated. **Address:** 13300 Lehman Legacy Ln 78933 **Location:** Jct CR 949 and Newberg Rd, 1 mi w to "T", then 1 mi w. Facilities, services, and décor characterize a mid-scale property. Enjoy your stay on this rural, 600-acre working ranch complete with bison, camels and other exotic animals. Many secluded accommodations, including one with its own 27 acres of private space.

---

**WHERE TO EAT**

CAROL'S AT CAT SPRING             979/865-1100

[fyi] Not evaluated. Patrons experience upscale dining in the country, with entrees ranging from Texas favorites to palate-pleasing gourmet dinners. **Address:** 10745 CR 949 78933 **Location:** Downtown.

---

## CEDAR HILL pop. 45,028

• **Hotels & Restaurants map & index p. 197**
• **Part of Dallas area — see map p. 161**

## LA QUINTA INN & SUITES         (972)291-0008  [24]

Hotel
$89-$124

**Address:** 1419 N Hwy 67 75104 **Location:** US 67 exit Wintergreen Rd; on southbound frontage road. **Facility:** 60 units. 3 stories, interior corridors. **Pool(s):** outdoor. **Activities:** exercise room. **Guest Services:** coin laundry. **Featured Amenity:** breakfast buffet.

SAVE [Y↑+] CALL [&M] [≈] [BIZ] [HS]

[≈] [X] [□] [□] [□]

[/ SOME UNITS] [🐾]

---

**WHERE TO EAT**

SALTGRASS STEAKHOUSE             972/291-6348  [18]

[WW] Steak. Casual Dining. $9-$30 **AAA Inspector Notes:** Those looking for something different should try the comfortable steakhouse, which never says no to a special request. Born from the spirit of Texas cattle drives, the restaurant resembles a Texas lodge, with high ceilings and mounted animal heads. Baby back ribs are so tender the meat falls off the bone. Also on the menu are hearty steaks, prime rib, chicken, seafood and yummy desserts. **Features:** full bar. **Address:** 747 N Hwy 67 75104 **Location:** US 67 exit Pleasant Run Rd; on southbound frontage road.

SAVE [L] [D] [N]

VERACRUZ CAFE                    972/293-8926  [17]

[WW] Mexican. Casual Dining. $9-$17 **AAA Inspector Notes:** The cuisine is described as Mesoamerican and Aztec, and this illustrates the restaurant's commitment to a cuisine that goes beyond the usual Mexican fare. Enjoy handmade delicacies such as mole, cactus salad, Mexican bouillabaisse and almond-crusted oysters in a rustic cantina setting. **Features:** full bar, Sunday brunch, happy hour. **Address:** 1427 N Hwy 67 75104 **Location:** US 67 exit Wintergreen; on southbound frontage road. [L] [D] [N]

---

## CEDAR PARK (F-8) pop. 48,937, elev. 910'

• **Hotels & Restaurants map & index p. 86**

**AUSTIN STEAM TRAIN EXCURSIONS** departs from the Cedar Park Depot near the corner of US 183 & FM 1431. Sightseeing excursions include the Hill Country Flyer, a 6-hour round trip to the town of Burnet (see place listing p. 132), where shopping and dining are available; the 3-hour Bertram Flyer; and themed trips aboard the Twilight Flyer.

**Hours:** Hill Country Flyer departs Sat. at 10, Jan.-May and Sept.-Nov. Hours vary in Dec.; phone ahead. Bertram Flyer departs Sat. at 10, June-Aug.; Sun. at 2, Mar.-May and Oct.-Nov. Twilight Flyer and other specialty trains run year-round; phone for

---

(See map & index p. 86.)

schedule. Closed Christmas. Phone ahead to confirm schedule. **Cost:** Hill Country Flyer $30-$45; $27-$42 (ages 62+); $20-$35 (ages 3-13). Bertram Flyer $19-$34; $16-$31 (ages 62+); $14-$29 (ages 3-13). Phone for Twilight Flyer fares. Reservations are recommended. **Phone:** (512) 477-8468, ext. 2.

## BEST WESTERN CEDAR INN          (512)259-7300  94

Hotel
$85-$119

**AAA Benefit:** Members save 10% or more with Best Western!

**Address:** 425 E Whitestone Blvd 78613 **Location:** Jct US 183 and CR 1431, just e. **Facility:** 40 units. 2 stories (no elevator), exterior corridors. **Pool(s):** outdoor. **Activities:** exercise room.

## CANDLEWOOD SUITES          (512)986-4825  91

**Extended Stay Contemporary Hotel** $89-$159 **Address:** 1100 Cottonwood Creek Tr 78613 **Location:** Jct SR 183A and CR 1431, 1 mi e. **Facility:** 80 efficiencies. 3 stories, interior corridors. **Activities:** exercise room. **Guest Services:** complimentary and valet laundry.

## COMFORT INN          (512)259-1810  95

Hotel
$65-$200

**Address:** 300 E Whitestone Blvd 78613 **Location:** Jct US 183 and CR 1431, just e. **Facility:** 58 units. 2 stories, interior corridors. **Pool(s):** outdoor. **Guest Services:** coin laundry.

## HOLIDAY INN EXPRESS HOTEL & SUITES
(512)259-8200  92

**Hotel** $89-$169 **Address:** 1605 E Whitestone Blvd 78613 **Location:** Jct US 183 and CR 1431, 1.3 mi e. **Facility:** 62 units. 3 stories, interior corridors. **Pool(s):** outdoor. **Activities:** hot tub, exercise room. **Guest Services:** valet and coin laundry.

## LA QUINTA INN & SUITES AUSTIN - CEDAR PARK
(512)528-9300  93

**Hotel** $102-$164 **Address:** 1010 E Whitestone Blvd 78613 **Location:** Jct SR 183A and CR 1431; on southwest corner. **Facility:** 75 units. 4 stories, interior corridors. **Pool(s):** heated indoor. **Activities:** hot tub, exercise room. **Guest Services:** coin laundry.

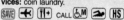

WHERE TO EAT

### 1431 CAFE          512/528-0018  72

Breakfast Comfort Food. Casual Dining. $5-$10 **AAA Inspector Notes:** Folks who love breakfast can get it all day long here, but the menu also features comfort food along the lines of fried chicken, chicken-fried steak, meatloaf and smoked pork loin. **Features:** full bar. **Address:** 501 E Whitestone Blvd 78613 **Location:** Jct US 183 and CR 1431, just e; in The Railyard Shopping Center.  B  L  D

### BELLINI'S TEXAS GRILL          512/528-8558  68

Comfort Food. Casual Dining. $6-$14 **AAA Inspector Notes:** Billed as Texas-Tuscan fusion with numerous selections of Texas comfort food as well as Italian favorites, including wood-fired pizzas, this place has rapidly become a very popular spot. Even the kids menu is inventive; is anyone up for spaghetti tacos? **Features:** full bar, Sunday brunch, happy hour. **Address:** 12800 W Parmer Ln 78613 **Location:** Jct CR 1431 and Parmer Ln, just s.  L  D  CALL

### C. R. SURF AND TURF          512/260-0600  71

Seafood Steak. Casual Dining. $7-$34 **AAA Inspector Notes:** From soups, salads and sandwiches to seafood, steak and combination dinners, this restaurant offers a relaxed and informal atmosphere. The filet mignon was cooked to perfection; prices are extremely fair. **Features:** beer & wine. **Address:** 601 E Whitestone Blvd 78613 **Location:** Jct US 183 and CR 1431, just e; in The Railyard Shopping Center.  L  D

### HEMINGWAY RESTAURANT AND BAR          512/219-6400  73

American. Casual Dining. $7-$17 **AAA Inspector Notes:** A nicely varied menu offering lighter fare of soups, salads and sandwiches to full entrées of steaks, seafood and some very nice comfort food selections. The meatloaf was a delightful surprise with its wild mushroom sauce. **Features:** full bar, Sunday brunch, happy hour. **Address:** 500 Cypress Creek Rd, Suite 170 78613 **Location:** Jct US 183 and Cypress Creek Rd, 0.5 mi w.  L  D

### MIGHTY FINE          512/528-5421  70

Burgers. Quick Serve. $4-$6 **AAA Inspector Notes:** All-American fare of juicy burgers, generous portions of french fries and handmade premium milk shakes are available at this simple and fun restaurant. **Address:** 1335 E Whitestone Blvd 78613 **Location:** Jct SR 183A and CR 1431; on northeast corner; in The Ranch Shopping Center.  L  D  CALL

### REUNION GRILLE          512/528-5644  69

Comfort Food. Casual Dining. $9-$19 **AAA Inspector Notes:** Comfort food with inventive sauces and spices highlight the menu where I really enjoyed both the meatloaf and barbecue ribs. The tempura okra fingers with a spicy ranch dipping sauce were very nice. Large dinner salads and steaks also tempt the patrons. **Features:** full bar, patio dining. **Address:** 1501 E New Hope Dr 78613 **Location:** Jct SR 183A and New Hope Dr; on northeast corner.  L  D  CALL

## CENTER  pop. 5,193

## BEST WESTERN CENTER INN          (936)598-3384

Hotel
$60-$70

**AAA Benefit:** Members save 10% or more with Best Western!

**Address:** 1005 Hurst St 75935 **Location:** On US 96; jct SR 87. **Facility:** 72 units. 2 stories (no elevator), exterior corridors. **Pool(s):** outdoor.

## BEST WESTERN PLUS CLASSIC INN & SUITES
(936)591-0002

Hotel
$75-$90

**AAA Benefit:** Members save 10% or more with Best Western!

**Address:** 210 Moffett Dr 75935 **Location:** Jct US 96 and SR 87, just n. **Facility:** 60 units. 4 stories, interior corridors. **Pool(s):** heated outdoor. **Activities:** hot tub, exercise room. **Guest Services:** valet and coin laundry. **Featured Amenity:** full hot breakfast.

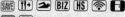

## HAMPTON INN & SUITES  (936)598-4447

Hotel $89-$139 **Address:** 141 Express Blvd 75935 **Location:** On US 96, just w of jct SR 87. **Facility:** 66 units. 3 stories, interior corridors. **Terms:** 1-7 night minimum stay, cancellation fee imposed. **Pool(s):** outdoor. **Activities:** hot tub, exercise room. **Guest Services:** coin laundry.

**AAA Benefit:** Members save up to 10%!

---

## CHANNELVIEW pop. 38,289

• **Hotels & Restaurants map & index p. 324**
• **Part of Houston area — see map p. 301**

---

## CLARION INN I-10 EAST  281/452-7304  109

Hotel. Rates not provided. **Address:** 15157 I-10 E 77530 **Location:** I-10 exit 783 (Sheldon Rd) eastbound; exit 781B westbound; on westbound frontage road. **Facility:** 120 units. 2-3 stories, exterior corridors. **Pool(s):** outdoor. **Activities:** exercise room. **Guest Services:** valet and coin laundry.

---

## DAYS INN & SUITES OF CHANNELVIEW
### (281)457-0140  107

Motel $70-$110

**Address:** 15765 I-10 E Frwy 77530 **Location:** I-10 exit 783 (Sheldon Rd); on westbound frontage road. **Facility:** 35 units. 2 stories (no elevator), exterior corridors. **Guest Services:** coin laundry. **Featured Amenity: continental breakfast.**

---

## FAIRFIELD INN & SUITES BY MARRIOTT CHANNELVIEW
### (281)457-0000  108

Hotel $104-$139 **Address:** 15822 East Frwy 77530 **Location:** I-10 exit 783 (Sheldon Rd); on south frontage road. **Facility:** 63 units. 3 stories, interior corridors. **Pool(s):** outdoor. **Activities:** exercise room. **Guest Services:** valet and coin laundry.

**AAA Benefit:** Members save 5% or more!

---

## CHILDRESS (B-6) pop. 6,105, elev. 1,877'

The economy of Childress is sustained by agriculture, particularly in the form of cotton, grains and livestock, as well as by small, diversified industry. Founded in 1876, the town is named for George Campbell Childress, author of the Texas Declaration of Independence.

**CHILDRESS COUNTY HERITAGE MUSEUM** is at 210 Third St. N.W. Housed in the old post office, the museum displays late 19th-century furniture, maps, photographs and other artifacts chronicling the history of Childress and the region. Transportation exhibits include automobiles, buggies and a train. **Hours:** Tues.-Sat. 10-5. Closed major holidays. **Cost:** Free. **Phone:** (940) 937-2261.

---

Learn about inspections
and Diamond Ratings at
AAA.com/Diamonds

---

## BEST WESTERN CHILDRESS  (940)937-6353

Hotel $85

**AAA Benefit:** Members save 10% or more with Best Western!

**Address:** 1801 Ave F NW (Hwy 287) 79201 **Location:** Jct US 62/83, just s. **Facility:** 65 units. 1-2 stories (no elevator), exterior corridors. **Parking:** winter plug-ins. **Amenities:** safes.

---

## HAMPTON INN & SUITES  (940)937-3500

Hotel $105-$129 **Address:** 400 Madison Ave 79201 **Location:** Jct US 298/83/62, just w. **Facility:** 64 units. 3 stories, interior corridors. **Terms:** 1-7 night minimum stay, cancellation fee imposed. **Pool(s):** heated indoor. **Activities:** hot tub, exercise room. **Guest Services:** coin laundry.

**AAA Benefit:** Members save up to 10%!

---

## QUALITY INN  (940)937-3434

Hotel $64-$89

**Address:** 2008 Ave F NW (Hwy 287) 79201 **Location:** On US 287, just n of jct US 62/83. **Facility:** 52 units. 2 stories (no elevator), interior corridors. **Pool(s):** heated indoor. **Activities:** hot tub, exercise room. **Guest Services:** coin laundry. **Featured Amenity: full hot breakfast.**

---

## SUPER 8 CHILDRESS  (940)937-8825

Motel $62-$122

**Address:** 411 Ave F NE (Hwy 287 S) 79201 **Location:** Jct US 83/287, 1.5 mi e. **Facility:** 44 units, some two bedrooms. 2 stories (no elevator), exterior corridors. **Amenities:** safes. **Pool(s):** indoor. **Activities:** hot tub, exercise room. **Guest Services:** coin laundry. **Featured Amenity: continental breakfast.**

---

### WHERE TO EAT

## K-BOB'S STEAKHOUSE  940/937-6184

American. Casual Dining. $6-$20 **AAA Inspector Notes:** The steakhouse prepares a great variety of plump, juicy fillets. A fireplace opens up into both dining rooms, and antique clocks decorate the walls. Rustic wagon-wheel chandeliers illuminate the room. **Address:** 1805 Ave F NW 79201 **Location:** Jct US 83/287, just e.

---

## CISCO pop. 3,899

## AMERICAS BEST VALUE INN  254/442-3735

Motel. Rates not provided. **Address:** 1898 Hwy 206 W 76437 **Location:** I-20 exit 330, just n. **Facility:** 31 units. 1 story, exterior corridors. **Pool(s):** outdoor. **Activities:** hot tub.

# CLARENDON pop. 2,026

## BEST WESTERN PLUS RED RIVER INN    (806)874-0160

**Hotel**
$95-$109

**AAA Benefit:** Members save 10% or more with Best Western!

**Address:** 902 W 2nd St 79226 **Location:** Jct US 287 and SR 70. **Facility:** 50 units. 3 stories, interior corridors. **Pool(s):** heated indoor. **Activities:** hot tub, exercise room. **Guest Services:** coin laundry.

### WHERE TO EAT

**BAR H BBQ N MORE**    806/874-0111

Barbecue. Casual Dining. $4-$8 **AAA Inspector Notes:** This place has a little something for everyone, with some steak offerings, barbecue and Mexican dishes. A nice selection of homemade pies is prepared daily. **Address:** 818 2nd St 79226 **Location:** Center.

# CLAUDE (B-5) pop. 1,196, elev. 3,407'

Armstrong City was established in 1887 as a stop on the Fort Worth and Denver City Railroad. The Panhandle settlement soon was renamed for Claude Ayers, the engineer who brought the first passenger train into town. Dr. W.A. Warner arrived in Claude in 1897 and is credited with founding one of the first Boy Scout troops west of the Mississippi.

**ARMSTRONG COUNTY MUSEUM** is 1 blk. n. of US 287 at 120 N. Trice St. Three historic downtown buildings are dedicated to the history of the Panhandle region. Exhibits chronicle the Red River Indian Wars, the founding of the 1.3-million-acre JA Ranch and the relocation of the Southern buffalo herd. A performance is presented once a month in the Gem Theater. An art gallery features local artists. **Time:** Allow 30 minutes minimum. **Hours:** Tues.-Sat. noon-4. Closed major holidays. **Cost:** Donations. **Phone:** (806) 226-2187.

# CLEAR LAKE CITY

• Hotels & Restaurants map & index p. 324

**CANDLEWOOD SUITES-HOUSTON-CLEAR LAKE**    281/461-3060    **123**

Extended Stay Hotel. Rates not provided. **Address:** 2737 Bay Area Blvd 77058 **Location:** I-45 exit 26 (Bay Area Blvd), 3.7 mi e. **Facility:** 122 efficiencies. 3 stories, interior corridors. **Activities:** exercise room. **Guest Services:** valet and coin laundry.

**HOMEWOOD SUITES BY HILTON HOUSTON/CLEAR LAKE**    281/486-7677    **125**

Extended Stay Hotel. Rates not provided. **Address:** 401 Bay Area Blvd 77598 **Location:** I-45 exit 26 (Bay Area Blvd), 1 mi e. **Facility:** 92 efficiencies, some two bedrooms. 3 stories, interior corridors. **Pool(s):** outdoor. **Activities:** exercise room. **Guest Services:** valet and coin laundry.

**AAA Benefit:** Members save up to 10%!

**RESIDENCE INN BY MARRIOTT HOUSTON CLEAR LAKE**    (281)486-2424    **124**

Extended Stay Hotel $143-$179 **Address:** 525 Bay Area Blvd 77058 **Location:** I-45 exit 26 (Bay Area Blvd), 1.2 mi e. **Facility:** 110 units, some two bedrooms, efficiencies and kitchens. 2 stories (no elevator), interior/exterior corridors. **Pool(s):** outdoor. **Activities:** hot tub, exercise room. **Guest Services:** valet and coin laundry.

**AAA Benefit:** Members save 5% or more!

### WHERE TO EAT

**PERRY'S ITALIAN GRILLE**    281/488-2626    **48**

Italian. Fine Dining. $12-$39 **AAA Inspector Notes:** This is an interesting variation of the Perry's Steakhouse restaurants and concentrates on steaks, chops and seafood prepared with an Italian flavor. Don't miss the wonderful pasta entrées. **Features:** full bar, happy hour. **Reservations:** required. **Address:** 1001 Pineloch Dr 77062 **Location:** I-45 exit 27, 0.9 mi e to Galveston Rd (SR 3), 0.8 mi n to Pineloch Dr, then 0.6 mi e to El Camino Real St; on northeast corner.

**PERRY'S STEAKHOUSE & GRILLE**    281/286-8800    **50**

Steak. Fine Dining. $15-$80 **AAA Inspector Notes:** In an upscale and professional atmosphere diners can feast on prime cuts of beef, rack of lamb, seafood, chicken or the signature pork chop carved tableside. Enjoy a relaxing evening with very good service. **Features:** full bar, Sunday brunch. **Address:** 487 Bay Area Blvd 77058 **Location:** I-45 exit 26 (Bay Area Blvd), 1.2 mi e. **Parking:** on-site and valet.

**TOMMY'S RESTAURANT & OYSTER BAR**    281/480-2221    **49**

Seafood Steak. Casual Dining. $6-$28 **AAA Inspector Notes:** The atmosphere here is relaxed but sophisticated with modern décor and professional and knowledgeable staff. The menu focuses on very fresh seafood from the nearby Gulf as well USDA Prime aged steaks. The happy hour is popular with oyster bar selections, appetizer specials and a nice wine list. The location is very convenient to many of the hotels and businesses of the Clear Lake-Webster-NASA area. **Features:** full bar, patio dining, happy hour. **Reservations:** suggested. **Address:** 2555 Bay Area Blvd 77598 **Location:** I-45 exit 26 (Bay Area Blvd), 3.1 mi e.

# CLEBURNE (D-8) pop. 29,337, elev. 764'

• Hotels p. 140 • Restaurants p. 140

Established in 1854 as Camp Henderson and renamed in 1867 after Confederate general Pat Cleburne, the town has large railroad construction and repair shops. Cleburne State Park, 12 miles south on US 67, contains a wildlife refuge and 116-acre Cedar Lake. *See Recreation Areas Chart.*

**Cleburne Chamber of Commerce:** 1511 W. Henderson St., P.O. Box 701, Cleburne, TX 76033. **Phone:** (817) 645-2455.

**LAYLAND MUSEUM** is at 201 N. Caddo St. in the 1905 Carnegie Building. The museum interprets home and family life in north-central Texas from the prehistoric period through 1970. Exhibits highlight Native Americans, early settlement and 20th-century home life. **Hours:** Tues.-Fri. 10-5, Sat. 10-4. Closed major holidays. **Cost:** Free. **Phone:** (817) 645-0940.

Get pet travel tips and enter the

photo contest at AAA.com/PetBook

## BEST WESTERN SMITHFIELD INN (817)556-3330

Motel
$50-$80

**AAA Benefit:** Members save 10% or more with Best Western!

**Address:** 1707 W Henderson St 76033 **Location:** 2.5 mi s of jct SR 4/171/174 and US 67 business route (Courthouse Square); on US 67 business route. **Facility:** 40 units. 1 story, exterior corridors. **Pool(s):** outdoor. **Activities:** exercise room. **Guest Services:** coin laundry.

SAVE 🏊 HS 📶 🍴 🖥 💻

## BUDGET HOST INN-SAGAMAR INN 817/556-3631

🔷🔷 **Motel.** Rates not provided. **Address:** 2107 N Main St 76033 **Location:** US 67 exit SR 174, just e. **Facility:** 28 units. 1 story, exterior corridors.

HS 📶 🍴 🖥 💻 / SOME UNITS 🐾

## COMFORT INN (817)641-4702

🔷🔷🔷 **Hotel** $80-$118 **Address:** 2117 N Main St 76033 **Location:** On SR 174, just s of jct US 67. **Facility:** 80 units, some two bedrooms. 3 stories, interior corridors. **Pool(s):** outdoor. **Activities:** exercise room. **Guest Services:** valet and coin laundry.

CALL 🖥M 🏊 HS 📶 🍴 🖥 💻 / SOME UNITS 🐾

## HAMPTON INN & SUITES (817)641-7770

🔷🔷🔷 **Hotel** $132-$145 **Address:** 1996 W Henderson St 76033 **Location:** Jct US 67 and 67 business route. Across from Texas Medical Center. **Facility:** 80 units. 4 stories, interior corridors. **Terms:** 1-7 night minimum stay, cancellation fee imposed. **Pool(s):** heated indoor. **Activities:** hot tub, exercise room. **Guest Services:** coin laundry.

**AAA Benefit:** Members save up to 10%!

CALL 🖥M 🏊 BIZ HS 📶 ✕ 💻 / SOME UNITS 🐾 🍴 🖥

## LA QUINTA INN & SUITES CLEBURNE (817)641-4455

🔷🔷🔷 **Hotel** $87-$122 **Address:** 107 E Kilpatrick Ave 76033 **Location:** Just n of jct SR 171/174 and FM 4. **Facility:** 62 units. 3 stories, interior corridors. **Pool(s):** outdoor. **Activities:** hot tub, exercise room. **Guest Services:** coin laundry.

🍴 CALL 🖥M 🏊 BIZ HS 📶 🍴 🖥 💻 / SOME UNITS 🐾

## WHERE TO EAT

### PASTAFINA 817/558-2220

🔷🔷 Italian. Casual Dining. $6-$19 **AAA Inspector Notes:** This clean and crisp restaurant offers both Northern and Southern Italian dishes as well as daily specials. The menu is nicely varied and has something for everyone. **Features:** full bar, happy hour. **Address:** 1670 W Henderson St 76033 **Location:** 1.7 mi w of downtown.

L D CALL 🖥M 🚭

### PURPLE TURNIP 817/558-6927

🔷🔷 American. Casual Dining. $8-$28 **AAA Inspector Notes:** Near the square downtown, the small restaurant presents a menu of American fare, including steaks, chicken and fish dishes. Salads, soups, pastas, quiche and sandwiches are featured for lunch. Hot-plate specials appeal to those who are a little more hungry. Home-made desserts are a perfect ending to the meal. **Address:** 104 N Pendell St 76033 **Location:** 1.8 mi sw of jct US 67 business route and SR 171/174 and FM 4 (Main St/Town Square/Court House) to Pendell St, then just e. L D

# CLEVELAND pop. 7,675
• Part of Houston area — see map p. 301

## BEST WESTERN CLEVELAND INN & SUITES (281)659-2700

🔷🔷🔷 Hotel $60-$160

**AAA Benefit:** Members save 10% or more with Best Western!

**Address:** 708 US Hwy 59 S 77328 **Location:** US 59 exit SR 105; northwest corner. **Facility:** 49 units. 3 stories, interior corridors. **Terms:** resort fee. **Pool(s):** outdoor. **Activities:** exercise room. **Guest Services:** coin laundry. **Featured Amenity: continental breakfast.**

SAVE 🍴 CALL 🖥M 🏊 BIZ HS 📶 ✕ 🍴 🖥 💻 / SOME UNITS 🐾

## HOLIDAY INN EXPRESS & SUITES (281)592-7500

🔷🔷🔷 Hotel $68 **Address:** 600 Hwy 59 S 77327 **Location:** US 59 exit Cleveland/Conroe northbound; exit Cleveland southbound; on northbound frontage road. **Facility:** 68 units. 3 stories, interior corridors. **Pool(s):** outdoor. **Activities:** hot tub, exercise room. **Guest Services:** coin laundry.

🍴 🏊 BIZ HS 📶 ✕ 🍴 🖥 💻 / SOME UNITS 🐾

## LA QUINTA INN & SUITES (281)806-3007

🔷🔷🔷 Hotel $94-$129 **Address:** 1004 Hwy 59 S 77327 **Location:** US 59 exit Washington Ave; on northbound frontage road. **Facility:** 56 units. 3 stories, interior corridors. **Pool(s):** outdoor. **Activities:** hot tub, exercise room. **Guest Services:** coin laundry.

🍴 CALL 🖥M 🏊 BIZ HS 📶 🍴 🖥 💻 / SOME UNITS 🐾

## SUPER 8 (281)432-8800

🔷🔷 Hotel $59-$109

**Address:** 427 W Southline St 77327 **Location:** US 59 exit SR 105, just e to W Southline St, then just s. **Facility:** 42 units. 2 stories (no elevator), interior corridors. **Terms:** 3 day cancellation notice-fee imposed. **Pool(s):** outdoor. **Activities:** hot tub. **Guest Services:** coin laundry. **Featured Amenity: continental breakfast.**

SAVE 🍴 🏊 📶 🍴 🖥 💻 / SOME UNITS 🐾

## WHERE TO EAT

### EL BURRITO MEXICAN RESTAURANT 281/592-1932

🔷🔷 Mexican. Casual Dining. $7-$12 **AAA Inspector Notes:** Since 1983, this brightly decorated restaurant has been serving great Mexican fare. New creations such as the brochette combo or mush-room chicken breast show up on the menu to keep locals coming back. Daily specials and dinners for two also are offered. **Features:** full bar. **Address:** 422 W Southline St 77327 **Location:** US 59 exit Cleveland, just e on SR 105. L D CALL 🖥M 🚭

# CLIFTON (E-8) pop. 3,442, elev. 671'

The late 1840s and early 1850s brought many im-migrants from Norway to the town now known as the Norwegian Capital of Texas. Cleng Peerson, said to be the Father of Norwegian Immigration to the

United States, led countless families to the area and helped turn it into a prosperous cultural and commercial center along the Bosque River.

**Clifton Chamber of Commerce:** 115 North Ave. D, Clifton, TX 76634. **Phone:** (254) 675-3720 or (800) 344-3720.

**BOSQUE MUSEUM** is at 301 S. Ave. Q. Cultural exhibits pertinent to the history of Bosque County include 11,000-year-old artifacts documenting the presence of early man in the region. An 1850s log cabin is furnished with frontier-style pieces. The collection of Norwegian immigrant artifacts is one of the largest in the South. **Time:** Allow 1 hour minimum. **Hours:** Tues.-Sat. 10-5. Closed Jan. 1, July 4, Thanksgiving and Christmas. **Cost:** $5; free (ages 0-10). **Phone:** (254) 675-3845.

### BEST WESTERN VELKOMMEN (254)675-8999

Hotel
$95-$105

**AAA Benefit:** Members save 10% or more with Best Western!

**Address:** 1215 N Ave G 76634 **Location:** SR 6, 1.5 mi n. **Facility:** 41 units. 2 stories, interior corridors. **Pool(s):** outdoor. **Activities:** exercise room. **Guest Services:** coin laundry. **Featured Amenity:** breakfast buffet.

## CLUTE pop. 11,211

### BAYMONT INN & SUITES CLUTE (979)388-0055

Hotel
$89-$139

**Address:** 900 Hwy 332 77531 **Location:** Just w of jct Business Rt SR 288. **Facility:** 45 units, some kitchens. 3 stories, interior corridors. **Pool(s):** outdoor. **Activities:** exercise room. **Guest Services:** coin laundry. **Featured Amenity:** full hot breakfast.

### HAMPTON INN & SUITES LAKE JACKSON-CLUTE (979)265-3200

**Hotel** $129-$189 **Address:** 1121 Hwy 332 W 77531 **Location:** On SR 288/332, just w of jct Business Rt SR 288. **Facility:** 67 units. 3 stories, interior corridors. **Terms:** 1-7 night minimum stay, cancellation fee imposed. **Amenities:** safes. **Pool(s):** outdoor. **Activities:** hot tub, exercise room. **Guest Services:** valet and coin laundry.

**AAA Benefit:** Members save up to 10%!

### LA QUINTA INN CLUTE LAKE JACKSON (979)265-7461

**Motel** $69-$100 **Address:** 1126 Hwy 332 W 77531 **Location:** On SR 288/332, just w of jct Business Rt SR 288. **Facility:** 135 units. 2 stories (no elevator), exterior corridors. **Pool(s):** outdoor. **Guest Services:** coin laundry.

### COLEMAN pop. 4,709

### BEST WESTERN COLEMAN INN (325)625-4176

Hotel
$72-S96

**AAA Benefit:** save 10% or more with Best Western!

**Address:** 1401 Hwy 84 Bypass 76834 **Location:** Jct US 84 and 283. **Facility:** 48 units. 1-2 stories (no elevator), exterior corridors. **Terms:** 2 night minimum stay - seasonal. **Pool(s):** outdoor.

## COLLEGE STATION (E-9) pop. 93,857, elev. 330'
**• Restaurants p. 143**

College Station is the home of Texas A&M University, the state's oldest public institution of higher education. The Agricultural and Mechanical College opened in 1876 with 106 students. The university is now the nation's sixth-largest, with an enrollment of more than 50,000.

**Bryan-College Station Convention and Visitors Bureau:** 715 University Dr. E., College Station, TX 77840. **Phone:** (979) 260-9898 or (800) 777-8292.

**GEORGE BUSH PRESIDENTIAL LIBRARY AND MUSEUM** is .8 mi. w. of Wellborn Rd. (FM 2154) at 1000 George Bush Dr. W. The 90-acre complex preserves an extensive collection of photographs, official and personal papers and video footage. Some 90,000 items include gifts of state and personal items. A film chronicles the 41st president's life.

Highlights of the museum are a World War II Avenger torpedo bomber, a 1947 Studebaker, a slab of the Berlin Wall and replicas of Bush's Oval Office, the White House Situation Room and the White House Press Room. Changing exhibits also are presented.

**Time:** Allow 1 hour, 30 minutes minimum. **Hours:** Mon.-Sat. 9:30-5, Sun. noon-5. Closed Jan. 1, Thanksgiving and Christmas. **Cost:** $7; $6 (ages 62+); $3 (ages 6-17); free (active-duty military and their families with ID). **Phone:** (979) 691-4000.

### COMFORT SUITES (979)268-5500

**Hotel** $89-$159 **Address:** 907 University Dr 77840 **Location:** Jct Texas Ave and University Dr, just e. **Facility:** 79 units, some kitchens. 3 stories, interior corridors. **Terms:** check-in 4 pm. **Pool(s):** outdoor. **Activities:** exercise room. **Guest Services:** valet and coin laundry.

### COMFORT SUITES AGGIELAND (979)680-9000

**Hotel** $90-$320 **Address:** 2313 Texas Ave S 77840 **Location:** Jct Business Rt SR 6 and University Dr, 1.5 mi s. **Facility:** 54 units, some efficiencies. 3 stories, interior corridors. **Pool(s):** outdoor. **Activities:** hot tub, exercise room. **Guest Services:** valet and coin laundry.

## COUNTRY INN & SUITES BY CARLSON   (979)693-7777

Hotel $99-$199 **Address:** 1010 Southwest Pkwy E 77840 **Location:** Jct SR 6 and Southwest Pkwy, just e. **Facility:** 64 units. 4 stories, interior corridors. **Terms:** 2 night minimum stay - seasonal and/or weekends. **Pool(s):** outdoor. **Activities:** hot tub, exercise room. **Guest Services:** coin laundry.

CALL [M] [symbols] BIZ HS [symbols]

## COURTYARD BY MARRIOTT   (979)695-8111

Hotel $109-$144 **Address:** 3939 SH 6 S 77845 **Location:** SR 6 S exit Rock Prairie Rd, just e. **Facility:** 125 units. 3 stories, interior corridors. **Pool(s):** outdoor. **Activities:** hot tub, exercise room. **Guest Services:** valet and coin laundry.

**AAA Benefit:** Members save 5% or more!

[symbols] CALL [M] [symbols] BIZ HS [symbols] / SOME UNITS [symbol]

## DAYS INN   (979)696-6988

Hotel $56-$143

**Address:** 2514 Texas Ave S 77840 **Location:** 2.4 mi s of jct SR 60 (University Dr). **Facility:** 98 units. 2 stories (no elevator), exterior corridors. **Pool(s):** outdoor. **Activities:** hot tub, playground. **Guest Services:** area transportation. **Featured Amenity:** continental breakfast.

SAVE [symbols]

## ECONO LODGE   (979)260-9150

Hotel $58-$250 **Address:** 901 University Dr E 77840 **Location:** Jct SR 6, 1 mi e. **Facility:** 98 units. 2 stories (no elevator), exterior corridors. **Pool(s):** outdoor. **Activities:** hot tub, exercise room. **Guest Services:** coin laundry.

[symbols] CALL [M] [symbols] / SOME UNITS [symbol]

## FOUR POINTS BY SHERATON COLLEGE STATION   (979)693-1741

Hotel $79-$289

FOUR POINTS BY SHERATON

**AAA Benefit:** Members get up to 20% off, plus Starwood Preferred Guest® bonuses!

**Address:** 1503 Texas Ave S 77840 **Location:** 1.3 mi s of jct SR 60. **Facility:** 126 units. 6 stories, interior corridors. *Bath:* shower only. **Terms:** cancellation fee imposed. **Pool(s):** outdoor. **Activities:** exercise room. **Guest Services:** valet laundry. **Featured Amenity:** breakfast buffet.

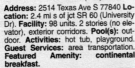

SAVE [symbols]

## HAMPTON INN & SUITES   979/694-2100

Hotel. Rates not provided. **Address:** 925 Earl Rudder Frwy S 77840 **Location:** Jct Bypass SR 6 and University Dr. **Facility:** 79 units. 3 stories, interior corridors. **Parking:** no self-parking. **Pool(s):** outdoor. **Activities:** hot tub, exercise room. **Guest Services:** valet and coin laundry.

**AAA Benefit:** Members save up to 10%!

[symbols] BIZ HS [symbols]

## HAMPTON INN-TEXAS A & M UNIVERSITY AREA   (979)846-0184

Hotel $119-$149 **Address:** 320 S Texas Ave 77840 **Location:** Just n of jct SR 60. **Facility:** 133 units. 4 stories, interior corridors. **Terms:** 1-7 night minimum stay, cancellation fee imposed. **Pool(s):** outdoor. **Activities:** exercise room. **Guest Services:** valet laundry, area transportation.

**AAA Benefit:** Members save up to 10%!

[symbols] / SOME UNITS [symbols]

## HAWTHORN SUITES BY WYNDHAM   (979)695-9500

Hotel $109-$269

**Address:** 1010 University Dr E 77840 **Location:** SR 6 exit University Dr, 0.5 mi w. **Facility:** 81 units. 3 stories, interior corridors. **Pool(s):** outdoor. **Activities:** exercise room. **Guest Services:** valet and coin laundry. **Featured Amenity:** full hot breakfast.

SAVE [symbols] CALL [M] [symbols] BIZ [symbols] / SOME UNITS [symbol]

## HILTON COLLEGE STATION & CONFERENCE CENTER   (979)693-7500

Hotel $119-$135 **Address:** 801 University Dr E 77840 **Location:** SR 6 exit University Dr, 1.1 mi w. **Facility:** 303 units. 11 stories, interior corridors. **Terms:** check-in 4 pm, 1-7 night minimum stay, cancellation fee imposed. **Dining:** Bell Ranch Steakhouse, see separate listing. **Pool(s):** outdoor. **Activities:** hot tub, exercise room. **Guest Services:** valet laundry, area transportation.

**AAA Benefit:** Members save 5% or more!

[symbols] BIZ [symbols] / SOME UNITS [symbols]

## HOLIDAY INN EXPRESS HOTEL & SUITES   (979)846-8700

Hotel $124-$134 **Address:** 1203 University Dr E 77840 **Location:** SR 6 exit University Dr, 1 mi w. **Facility:** 77 units. 3 stories, interior corridors. **Pool(s):** outdoor. **Activities:** exercise room. **Guest Services:** valet and coin laundry.

[symbols] CALL [M] [symbols] BIZ HS [symbols] / SOME UNITS [symbol]

## HOLIDAY INN HOTEL & SUITES — 979/485-8300

 Hotel. Rates not provided. **Address:** 2500 Earl Rudder Frwy 77840 **Location:** Jct SR 6 and Southwest Pkwy; on southwest corner. **Facility:** 116 units. 5 stories, interior corridors. **Pool(s):** heated indoor. **Activities:** hot tub, exercise room. **Guest Services:** valet and coin laundry.

---

## HOMEWOOD SUITES-COLLEGE STATION

(979)846-0400

Extended Stay Hotel
$129-$189

**AAA Benefit:** Members save up to 10%!

**Address:** 950 University Dr E 77840 **Location:** Jct SR 6 and 60, 1.5 mi e. **Facility:** 83 units, some two bedrooms and kitchens. 4 stories, interior corridors. **Terms:** 1-7 night minimum stay, cancellation fee imposed. **Pool(s):** outdoor. **Activities:** hot tub, exercise room. **Guest Services:** valet and coin laundry.

---

## HOWARD JOHNSON EXPRESS

(979)693-6810

Hotel
$59-$200

**Address:** 3702 Hwy 6 S 77845 **Location:** SR 6 exit Rock Prairie Rd southbound. **Facility:** 88 units. 1-2 stories (no elevator), exterior corridors. **Terms:** cancellation fee imposed. **Amenities:** safes. **Pool(s):** outdoor. **Guest Services:** coin laundry. **Featured Amenity:** continental breakfast.

---

## HYATT PLACE COLLEGE STATION

(979)846-9800

Hotel
$89-$379

**HYATT PLACE**
**AAA Benefit:** Members save 10%!

**Address:** 1100 University Dr E 77840 **Location:** Jct University Dr and Texas Ave, 1 mi e. **Facility:** 91 units. 4 stories, interior corridors. **Terms:** cancellation fee imposed. **Pool(s):** heated indoor. **Activities:** hot tub, exercise room. **Guest Services:** valet laundry, area transportation. **Featured Amenity:** breakfast buffet.

---

## LA QUINTA INN COLLEGE STATION

(979)696-7777

 Hotel $75-$144 **Address:** 607 Texas Ave 77840 **Location:** Just s on jct SR 60 and 6 business route to Live Oak St, just e. Across from Texas A & M University. **Facility:** 176 units. 2 stories (no elevator), exterior corridors. **Pool(s):** outdoor. **Guest Services:** valet laundry, area transportation.

---

## MANOR INN COLLEGE STATION

(979)764-9540

 Hotel $59-$179 **Address:** 2504 Texas Ave S 77840 **Location:** 2.4 mi s of jct SR 60 (University Dr). **Facility:** 116 units. 2 stories (no elevator), exterior corridors. **Terms:** 2 night minimum stay - seasonal and/or weekends, 14 day cancellation notice-fee imposed. **Pool(s):** outdoor. **Activities:** hot tub. **Guest Services:** coin laundry.

---

## QUALITY SUITES

(979)695-9400

 Hotel $90-$275 **Address:** 3610 Hwy 6 S 77845 **Location:** Jct SR 6 business route; just s on west access road. **Facility:** 81 units. 3 stories, interior corridors. **Pool(s):** outdoor. **Activities:** exercise room. **Guest Services:** valet and coin laundry.

---

## RAMADA COLLEGE STATION

(979)846-0300

Hotel
$85-$130

**Address:** 506 Earl Rudder Frwy S 77840 **Location:** Jct SR 6 and University Dr; on northwest corner. Located behind Home Depot and Olive Garden. **Facility:** 61 units. 3 stories, interior corridors. **Pool(s):** outdoor. **Activities:** exercise room. **Guest Services:** valet and coin laundry. **Featured Amenity:** full hot breakfast.

---

## RESIDENCE INN BY MARRIOTT COLLEGE STATION

(979)268-2200

Extended Stay Hotel
$119-$161

**Residence Inn Marriott**
**AAA Benefit:** Members save 5% or more!

**Address:** 720 University Dr E 77840 **Location:** Jct Texas Ave, 0.5 mi e. **Facility:** 84 units, some two bedrooms, efficiencies and kitchens. 4 stories, interior corridors. **Pool(s):** heated indoor. **Activities:** hot tub, exercise room. **Guest Services:** valet and coin laundry.

---

## SUPER 8-COLLEGE STATION

(979)846-8800

Motel
$79-$200

**Address:** 301 Texas Ave 77840 **Location:** Just n of jct SR 60. **Facility:** 89 units. 3 stories, interior corridors. **Amenities:** safes. **Guest Services:** coin laundry. **Featured Amenity:** continental breakfast.

---

## TOWNEPLACE SUITES BY MARRIOTT

(979)260-8500

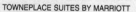 Extended Stay Contemporary Hotel $107-$144 **Address:** 1300 University Dr E 77840 **Location:** SR 6 exit University Dr, 1 mi w. **Facility:** 94 kitchen units. 3 stories, exterior corridors. **Terms:** check-in 4 pm. **Pool(s):** outdoor. **Activities:** exercise room. **Guest Services:** valet and coin laundry.

**AAA Benefit:** Members save 5% or more!

---

 **WHERE TO EAT**

## ABUELO'S THE FLAVOR OF MEXICO

979/260-3400

 Mexican. Casual Dining. $7-$19 **AAA Inspector Notes:** The kitchen staff prepares a nice selection of traditional Mexican dishes, which pair with inventive adult beverages. The spacious dining area has an upscale feel. **Features:** full bar. **Reservations:** suggested. **Address:** 840 University Dr E 77840 **Location:** Jct University Dr and Texas Ave, 1 mi e. L D

**BELL RANCH STEAKHOUSE**   979/693-7500

▼▼ ▼▼ American. Casual Dining. $9-$26 **AAA Inspector Notes:** Steak, chicken and seafood dishes share menu space with specialty salads and a nice selection of appetizers. Lunch is more relaxed and informal. **Features:** full bar, Sunday brunch. **Address:** 801 University Dr E 77840 **Location:** SR 6 exit University Dr, 1.1 mi w; in Hilton College Station & Conference Center. [B] [L] [D] CALL 🖳

**CAFE ECCELL**   979/846-7908

▼▼ ▼▼ American. Casual Dining. $9-$25 **AAA Inspector Notes:** Steaks, seafood and chicken entrées, as well as gourmet pizza made in a wood-fired oven, are at the heart of the university-area eatery's menu. Lighter lunch fare includes a nice variety of sandwiches. Homemade bread, sauces and soups are enjoyable. The penne with meatballs and sausage was very good, and I really enjoyed the tomato basil soup, which was very flavorful. **Features:** full bar. **Address:** 101 Church Ave 77840 **Location:** SR 6 exit University Dr, 0.8 mi sw to College Main, 1 blk n to Church Ave, then 4 blks sw. [L] [D] CALL 🖳

**CENARE**   979/696-7311

▼▼▼▼ Italian. Casual Dining. $9-$20 **AAA Inspector Notes:** Contributing to the inviting, romantic atmosphere are candlelight, white linens and Italian paintings. Among mouthwatering entrées are lasagna, salmon, shrimp rustica and veal marsala. **Features:** beer & wine, patio dining. **Address:** 404 University Dr E 77840 **Location:** SR 60 (University Blvd), 0.3 mi e of jct SR 6 business route (Texas Ave). [L] [D]

**FISH DADDY'S GRILL HOUSE**   979/260-1611

▼▼ ▼▼ American. Casual Dining. $7-$15 **AAA Inspector Notes:** Choices include fresh fish entrées, seafood platters, Cajun specialties and mixed grill selections. Among lighter-fare options are soups, salads, sandwiches and seafood baskets. The steak and shrimp dinner always is one of my favorites, and the shrimp pasta was super. **Features:** full bar. **Address:** 1611 University Dr 77840 **Location:** Jct SR 6 Bypass and University Dr, just w. [L] [D]

**LUIGI'S PATIO RISTORANTE**   979/693-2742

▼▼ ▼▼ Italian. Casual Dining. $6-$28 **AAA Inspector Notes:** Enjoy the formal dining room or the more casual indoor patio and choose from a large selection of Italian favorites, ranging from pasta and pizza to complete entrées of chicken, beef or seafood at this fun restaurant presenting an upscale dining experience. **Features:** full bar, Sunday brunch, happy hour. **Address:** 3975 SR 6 S 77845 **Location:** SR 6 exit Rock Prairie Rd southbound, just e. [L] [D] CALL 🖳

**OZONA GRILL AND BAR**   979/694-4618

▼▼ ▼▼ Regional American. Casual Dining. $8-$18 **AAA Inspector Notes:** Lining the nicely varied menu are soups, salads, sandwiches, platters, Mexican dishes, steaks and other specialties. Sunday brunch is worth a visit. **Features:** full bar, patio dining, Sunday brunch. **Address:** 520 Harvey Rd 77840 **Location:** Jct Business Rt SR 6 and 60, 2 mi s to SR 30, 0.5 mi e. [L] [D]

**THE REPUBLIC**   979/260-4120

▼▼▼▼▼

Steak
Fine Dining
$20-$44

**AAA Inspector Notes:** Procuring the freshest foods from local ranches, this restaurant specializes in prime cuts of beef with a professional staff attending to the needs of the patrons in an upscale and comfortable setting. My last visit to the restaurant saw a fabulous meal of a lump crab cake, lobster bisque, an outstanding rack of lamb and a very inventive single-malt brûlée for dessert, all with beautiful presentations. This is a true dining experience and never disappoints. **Features:** full bar. **Reservations:** suggested. **Address:** 701 University Dr, Suite 406 77840 **Location:** Jct Texas Ave, 0.5 mi e. [D] CALL 🖳

**VERITAS WINE & BISTRO**   979/268-3251

▼▼▼▼ American. Fine Dining. $7-$75 **AAA Inspector Notes:** The upscale restaurant features sashimi-grade seafood and Angus and Kobe beef selections served in a crisp and contemporary setting. **Features:** full bar. **Reservations:** suggested. **Address:** 830 University Dr E 77840 **Location:** Jct University Dr and Texas Ave, 0.5 mi e. [L] [D] CALL 🖳

**WINGS 'N MORE**   979/694-8966

▼▼ ▼▼ Wings Sandwiches. Casual Dining. $8-$36 **AAA Inspector Notes:** Buffalo-style chicken wings are the featured item, but guests also can nosh on baby back ribs, chicken, chicken-fried steak, seafood selections, soups and salads. **Address:** 3230 Texas Ave S 77845 **Location:** Jct SR 6 and 21. [L] [D]

**WINGS 'N MORE UNIVERSITY**   979/691-2100

▼▼ ▼▼ Wings. Casual Dining. $7-$17 **AAA Inspector Notes:** The many sauce choices for your meaty wings and the tasty sauce on those baby back ribs make this a popular sports-based gathering spot. **Features:** full bar, patio dining. **Address:** 1511 University Dr 77840 **Location:** Jct University Dr and Texas Ave, 1 mi e. [L] [D]

## COLLEYVILLE pop. 22,807
• Hotels & Restaurants map & index p. 257

**LA HACIENDA RANCH**   817/318-7500  (32)

▼▼ ▼▼ Tex-Mex. Family Dining. $11-$29 **AAA Inspector Notes:** The small chain prepares Tex-Mex and American cuisine. Contributing to the rustic ranch décor are stuffed, mounted animal heads, log rails and a wood ceiling. The specialty is steaks, both spicy Mexican and more subdued U.S. style. Many people like the large focal bar area, but families also appreciate the themed rooms and kids' lounge. **Features:** full bar, happy hour. **Address:** 5250 Hwy 121 76034 **Location:** SR 121 exit Hall-Johnson Rd; on southbound frontage road. [L] [D]

**MAC'S STEAKS & SEAFOOD**   817/318-6227  (33)

▼▼ ▼▼ Steak. Casual Dining. $10-$31 **AAA Inspector Notes:** Although the name aptly describes the fare, Mac's menu has broader appeal with regional items like crawfish étouffée, fish tacos and a Kobe steak burger. If you do opt for steak, spice it up a bit and go for the fillet pepperonata, a delicious sauce that will have you bathing your meat in it and licking your fork afterward. And while you are at it, just give in and try the seven-cheese mac 'n cheese, too. Even though it's called a steakhouse, the feeling is casual and very family-friendly. **Features:** full bar, Sunday brunch, happy hour. **Address:** 5120 Hwy 121 76034 **Location:** SR 121 exit Hall-Johnson Rd; on southbound frontage road. [L] [D]

## COLUMBUS (F-9) pop. 3,655, elev. 200'

Once at the site of a Native American village called Montezuma, Columbus was settled in 1823 by members of the Stephen F. Austin colony—groups of settlers led by pioneer Austin, who founded the first American settlements in Texas.

In 1836 Gen. Sam Houston deliberately burned the town to the ground in hopes of deterring Mexican general Antonio López de Santa Anna during the Texas Revolution. By the following year, Columbus citizens began to rebuild; many of those 19th-century structures can be seen in the downtown area. The restored 1886 Stafford Opera House, 425 Spring St., offers tours and family entertainment; phone (979) 732-5135.

The 1891 Colorado County Courthouse, on Milam Street, features a Tiffany-style stained-glass dome in the district courtroom and a four-face Seth Thomas clock. A 75-foot tree at 1218 Walnut St. is purported to be the second largest live oak in Texas.

Historically, Benjamin Beason Park marks the spot where Beason's ferry, operated by the Texas Army, once crossed the Colorado River. Today, the park offers camping, picnicking, fishing and ball fields.

**Columbus Chamber of Commerce:** 425 Spring St., Columbus, TX 78934. **Phone:** (979) 732-8385.

**Self-guiding tours:** Maps outlining a bicycle tour, a back-road bluebonnet tour, a talking house tour and a historical walking tour are available from the chamber of commerce.

### AMERICAS BEST VALUE INN    (979)732-6293

Hotel
$78-$150

**Address:** 2436 Hwy 71 S 78934 **Location:** I-10 exit 696 (SR 71). **Facility:** 40 units. 2 stories (no elevator), exterior corridors. **Terms:** cancellation fee imposed. **Pool(s):** outdoor. **Guest Services:** coin laundry. **Featured Amenity:** continental breakfast.

### COMFORT INN & SUITES    (979)732-3785

 Hotel $90-$134 **Address:** 2535 Hwy 71 S 78934 **Location:** I-10 exit 696 (SR 71), just s. **Facility:** 55 units, some efficiencies. 4 stories, interior corridors. **Pool(s):** outdoor. **Activities:** exercise room. **Guest Services:** coin laundry.

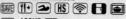

### HOLIDAY INN EXPRESS HOTEL & SUITES

(979)733-9300

Hotel
$99-$123

**Address:** 4321 I-10 78934 **Location:** I-10 exit 696 (SR 71), just w on westbound service road. **Facility:** 65 units. 3 stories, interior corridors. **Terms:** cancellation fee imposed. **Pool(s):** outdoor. **Activities:** exercise room. **Guest Services:** coin laundry. **Featured Amenity:** continental breakfast.

## WHERE TO EAT

### NANCY'S STEAKHOUSE    979/732-9700

Steak. Casual Dining. $8-$25 **AAA Inspector Notes:** The steakhouse's menu lists a wide variety of steaks, seafood, chicken and pasta entrées. Those looking for lighter fare will also find salads, burgers and sandwiches. **Features:** full bar, patio dining. **Address:** 2536 Hwy 71 S 78934 **Location:** I-10 exit 696 (SR 71), just s.

### SCHOBEL'S RESTAURANT    979/732-2385

American. Casual Dining. $7-$15 **AAA Inspector Notes:** In a convenient location near the interstate, the popular restaurant serves a widely varied noon buffet at a price that's easy on the budget. Simple dishes such as fried chicken offer a taste of home. **Features:** full bar. **Address:** 2020 Milam St 78934 **Location:** I-10 exit 696 (SR 71), just n.

Visit your AAA/CAA Travel

office to book a AAA Vacations®

Disney package

---

## COMANCHE pop. 4,335

### BEST WESTERN COMANCHE INN    (325)356-2300

Hotel
$78-$100

 **AAA Benefit:** Members save 10% or more with Best Western!

 **Address:** 1505 E Central Ave 76442 **Location:** 1 mi e on US 377. **Facility:** 50 units. 2 stories, interior corridors. **Pool(s):** outdoor. **Activities:** exercise room. **Guest Services:** coin laundry.

## COMSTOCK (F-5) elev. 1,550'

Settled in the 1880s along the Galveston, Harrisburg and San Antonio Railway, Comstock was named for a railroad dispatcher.

**SEMINOLE CANYON STATE PARK AND HISTORIC SITE** is 9 mi. w. on SR 90. The 2,172-acre archeological preserve contains hundreds of pictographs made by prehistoric inhabitants 2,000-8,000 years ago. Rock paintings on the walls of Fate Bell Shelter, a huge cliff overhang, may be viewed on a 90-minute guided hiking tour. A visitor center displays artifacts from the site's limestone shelters as well as dioramas of early man. *See Recreation Areas Chart.*

**Hours:** Daily 8-4:45. Guided tours are given Wed.-Sun. at 10 and 3, Sept.-May; Wed.-Sun. at 10, rest of year (weather permitting). **Cost:** $3; free (ages 0-12). Guided tour $5; free (ages 0-5). **Phone:** (432) 292-4464.

## CONROE (F-10) pop. 56,207, elev. 213'
• Hotels p. 146 • Restaurants p. 146
• Part of Houston area — see map p. 301

On the southern edge of Sam Houston National Forest, Conroe offers beautiful vistas of rolling hills, woodland lakes and tall pines. An oil field southeast of the city continues to produce.

Southern Empress Cruises, departing from 7039 Kingston Cove Ln. in Willis, offers cruises around Lake Conroe on a replica of an 1800s sternwheeler; phone (936) 588-3000.

**Conroe Area Convention and Visitors Bureau:** 505 W. Davis St., Conroe, TX 77301. **Phone:** (936) 522-3500 or (877) 426-6763.

**Shopping areas:** Outlets at Conroe, I-45 and League Line Rd., features such designer outlets as Guess, IZOD and Nike.

**HERITAGE MUSEUM OF MONTGOMERY COUNTY,** 1506 I-45N in Candy Cane Park, presents local-history exhibits focusing on influential people and events; the thriving oil, tobacco, cotton and timber industries; and the origins of the Texas flag. Kids will enjoy the Hands-On Children's Room. **Time:** Allow 1 hour minimum. **Hours:** Wed.-Sat. 9-4.

Closed major holidays, third week in July, week after Thanksgiving and week after Christmas. **Cost:** $1; 50c (ages 0-18). Cash only. **Phone:** (936) 539-6873.

## BAYMONT INN & SUITES-CONROE/WOODLANDS
(936)539-5100

Hotel
$69-$99

**Address:** 1506 Interstate 45 S 77304 **Location:** I-45 exit 85 (Gladstell St) northbound; exit 84 (Frazier St) southbound. **Facility:** 91 units. 4 stories, interior corridors. **Terms:** cancellation fee imposed. **Amenities:** safes. **Pool(s):** outdoor. **Activities:** exercise room. **Guest Services:** valet and coin laundry. **Featured Amenity: continental breakfast.**

## COMFORT INN-CONROE
(936)890-2811

Hotel
$90-$160

**Address:** 1115 League Line Rd 77303 **Location:** I-45 exit 91 (League Line Rd), just e. **Facility:** 57 units. 2 stories, interior corridors. **Pool(s):** outdoor. **Activities:** exercise room. **Guest Services:** valet and coin laundry. **Featured Amenity: continental breakfast.**

## FAIRFIELD INN & SUITES BY MARRIOTT HOUSTON CONROE
(936)756-3040

Hotel $89-$99 **Address:** 3010 I-45 N 77303 **Location:** I-45 exit 90 (Teas Nursery Rd) on northbound frontage road. **Facility:** 121 units. 5 stories, interior corridors. **Pool(s):** outdoor. **Activities:** exercise room. **Guest Services:** valet and coin laundry.

**AAA Benefit:**
Members save 5% or more!

## HAMPTON INN & SUITES CONROE I-45 NORTH
(936)539-1888

Hotel $140-$150 **Address:** 2242 Stoneside Rd 77303 **Location:** I-45 exit 88, just e on Milestone Rd, then just n; on northbound frontage road. **Facility:** 105 units. 4 stories, interior corridors. **Terms:** 1-7 night minimum stay, cancellation fee imposed. **Pool(s):** outdoor. **Activities:** exercise room. **Guest Services:** valet and coin laundry.

**AAA Benefit:**
Members save up to 10%!

## LA QUINTA INN & SUITES CONROE
(936)228-0790

Hotel $109-$167 **Address:** 4006 Sprayberry Ln 77303 **Location:** I-45 exit 91 (League Line Rd), just e. **Facility:** 50 units. 2 stories, interior corridors. **Pool(s):** heated indoor. **Activities:** hot tub, exercise room. **Guest Services:** valet and coin laundry.

### WHERE TO EAT

## 105 CAFE
936/539-3447

Breakfast. Casual Dining. $4-$10 **AAA Inspector Notes:** This is a humble breakfast haven that has all the usual suspects, but I think the best items here are the ones with some local flavor, including the huevos rancheros, pulled pork Benedict and the Southwest-style migas. A good range of salads and sandwiches can be ordered for lunch if you can get there before they close at 2. A senior discount is offered on Monday. **Features:** patio dining. **Address:** 3010 W Davis St 77301 **Location:** I-45 exit 87, 0.7 mi nw on SR 105. B L

## PAPPADEAUX SEAFOOD KITCHEN
936/321-4200

Regional Seafood. Casual Dining. $10-$36 **AAA Inspector Notes:** A seafood lover's delight, the restaurant taps into a little bit of New Orleans with its Cajun dishes and elaborate menu selections. Patrons might start off with a creative choice of blackened oyster and shrimp fondeaux with crayfish and let the feast begin. While music plays in the background, patrons can dig into dirty rice or spicy gumbo loaded with seafood. Well-seasoned shrimp and fish are prepared in varied ways. **Features:** full bar. **Address:** 18165 I-45 S 77385 **Location:** I-45 exit 77 (Tamina Rd); on east frontage road. L D CALL M

## SALTGRASS STEAKHOUSE
936/441-2121

Steak. Casual Dining. $10-$29 **AAA Inspector Notes:** Those looking for something different should try the comfortable steakhouse, which never says no to a special request. Born from the spirit of Texas cattle drives, the restaurant resembles a Texas lodge, with high ceilings and mounted animal heads. Baby back ribs are so tender the meat falls off the bone. Also on the menu are hearty steaks, prime rib, chicken, seafood and yummy desserts. **Features:** full bar. **Address:** 810 I-45 N 77301 **Location:** I-45 exit 87A northbound, 0.5 mi n on east frontage road; exit 87 southbound, U-turn, then just n. SAVE L D CALL M

# CONVERSE pop. 18,198
• Part of San Antonio area — see map p. 458

## BILL MILLER BAR-B-Q
210/659-1202

Barbecue. Quick Serve. $6-$11 **AAA Inspector Notes:** The relaxed, family-focused barbecue restaurant prepares ribs, chicken, brisket, turkey and sausage for sandwiches or plates. **Address:** 10676 Topperwein Rd 78109 **Location:** Just n of Kitty Hawk Rd. B L D

# COPPELL pop. 38,659
• Hotels & Restaurants map & index p. 191
• Part of Dallas area — see map p. 161

## 7 SALSAS
972/462-9006   1

Tex-Mex. Casual Dining. $7-$15 **AAA Inspector Notes:** The casual atmosphere provides a nice spot to catch up with friends over Mexican fare such as sizzling fajitas or the cha-cha chimichanga. Lunch specials present a good meal at the right price. **Features:** full bar. **Address:** 230 N Denton Tap Rd, Suite 106 75019 **Location:** I-635 exit 33 (Belt Line Rd), 3 mi n to Town Center; in Eleanor's Square. L D

## ANAMIA'S TEX-MEX
972/304-0321   2

Tex-Mex. Casual Dining. $6-$22 **AAA Inspector Notes:** Tex-Mex lovers will be pleased with the long list of traditional selections. No matter what their fancy-enchiladas, tacos, shrimp or chicken breast-it all can be found on the diverse menu. Located on a busy corner, the eatery fills quickly at lunch. **Features:** full bar, Sunday brunch. **Address:** 106 N Denton Tap Rd, Suite 240 75019 **Location:** I-635 exit 33 (Belt Line Rd), 3 mi n, then just e. L D

## PAN ACEAN
972/745-7788   3

Asian. Casual Dining. $6-$16 **AAA Inspector Notes:** Born from the family that has been feeding locals its Chinese food for more than 20 years, the restaurant presents a broad menu of Asian dishes that touch on multiple cuisines. Seafood is central to many of the stir-fries, noodle dishes and soups. The décor is casual upscale. **Features:** full bar. **Address:** 777 S MacArthur Blvd, Suite 401 75019 **Location:** I-635 exit 31 (MacArthur Blvd), 3.1 mi n; jct Belt Line Rd. L D

# COPPERAS COVE pop. 32,032

## BEST WESTERN INN & SUITES (254)518-3363

Hotel
$75-$90

**AAA Benefit:** Members save 10% or more with Best Western!

**Address:** 321 Constitution Dr 76522 **Location:** Just s of jct US 190. **Facility:** 60 units. 2 stories (no elevator), interior corridors. **Pool(s):** outdoor. **Activities:** exercise room. **Guest Services:** coin laundry. **Featured Amenity:** continental breakfast.

## COMFORT SUITES (254)518-8840

Hotel $90-$173 **Address:** 1816 Martin Luther King Jr Dr 76522 **Location:** Jct US 190 and Constitution Dr, just s. Located behind Walmart. **Facility:** 70 units. 4 stories, interior corridors. **Pool(s):** heated indoor. **Activities:** hot tub, exercise room. **Guest Services:** coin laundry.

### WHERE TO EAT

GIOVANNI'S ITALIAN RESTAURANT 254/518-2227

Italian. Casual Dining. $7-$24 AAA Inspector Notes: All your favorite pasta dishes and pizza choices, as well as seafood and steak selections, can be found here. I really enjoyed the lobster and shrimp ravioli. There's always a nice selection of luncheon specials at popular prices. **Features:** beer & wine. **Address:** 115 W Hwy 190 76522 **Location:** Just w; on south side of road.

# CORPUS CHRISTI (H-8) pop. 305,215, elev. 27'

- Hotels p. 151 • Restaurants p. 154
- Hotels & Restaurants map & index p. 149

Although first explored by Europeans in 1519, for more than 300 years Corpus Christi remained just the name of a landlocked bay. In 1839 Col. Henry Kinney established a trading post in the area, aggressively marketed his dusty settlement, and the town soon became a trade center for the nearby cattle ranches and the Mexican border towns.

Corpus Christi's transformation into an international port occurred when the Army Corps of Engineers dug a new ship channel in the mid-1920s. The completion of this project made the city the deepest port on the Texas coast and attracted many of the businesses that form its industrial base.

The city's importance was enhanced further with the addition of the Naval Air Station and its advanced flight-training school. This facility is one of the area's major employers and includes the Army Depot, the primary repair facility for Army helicopters.

Ironically, the city's metamorphosis into a booming cosmopolitan tourist mecca of hotels and palm-lined boulevards has fulfilled Henry Kinney's extravagant portrayal of this former patch of sand and sea at the end of nowhere as a resort area.

Despite its big-city stature, Corpus Christi has retained its earlier small-town flavor—a quality best expressed by the 2.5-mile-long seawall in the heart of the business district. Unlike other similar barricades, this seawall opens onto the bay, with stairs leading into the water. By adding this feature, Gutzon Borglum, its builder and the sculptor of Mount Rushmore, joined the vistas of blue water with the cityscape.

If the bay is Corpus Christi's front yard, then the more than 100 miles of beaches on nearby Padre and Mustang islands are its back yard. Hotels, condominiums and other resort facilities characterize North Padre Island, which mirrors the development at the south end of the island near Brownsville. Between these two extremes are almost 80 miles of beach in the Padre Island National Seashore (see place listing p. 430).

Nearby Mustang Island State Park (see Port Aransas p. 441) preserves many of the barrier beaches north of Padre Island. A freshwater alternative to these coastal areas is Lake Corpus Christi State Park, 35 miles northwest of the city. See Recreation Areas Chart.

In mid-October, head over to Heritage Park (see attraction listing) and soak up the sounds of the Texas Jazz Festival.

**Corpus Christi Convention and Visitors Bureau:** 1823 N. Chaparral St., Corpus Christi, TX 78401. **Phone:** (361) 561-2000 or (800) 766-2322.

**ART MUSEUM OF SOUTH TEXAS** is at 1902 N. Shoreline Blvd. The museum overlooks the bay and provides a unique view of the USS Lexington Museum on the Bay (see attraction listing). Within the permanent collection are hand-tooled and filigree saddles, Nicaraguan pottery, and Western oil paintings and bronze pieces. Traveling exhibitions feature artists ranging from traditional to contemporary. **Time:** Allow 1 hour minimum. **Hours:** Tues.-Sat. 10-5, Sun. 1-5. Closed major holidays. **Cost:** $8; $6 (ages 60+ and active military with ID); $4 (students with ID); free (ages 0-12). **Phone:** (361) 825-3500.

**CORPUS CHRISTI MUSEUM OF SCIENCE AND HISTORY** is in Bayfront Arts and Science Park at 1900 N. Chaparral St. Visitors can explore the 1554 Spanish shipwreck and the 1686 French LaBelle shipwreck. Replicas of Columbus' ships, the Pinta (available for tours) and Santa Maria, are moored outside the museum. Other areas of interest include the Children's Wharf and the history and natural history wings.

**Time:** Allow 1 hour, 30 minutes minimum. **Hours:** Tues.-Sat. 10-5, Sun. noon-5. Closed Thanksgiving and Christmas. **Cost:** $12.50; $9 (ages 65+, college students and active military with ID); $6 (ages 5-12 and non-college students with ID). **Phone:** (361) 826-4667.

(See map & index p. 149.)

**HERITAGE PARK** is on the 1600 block of N. Chaparral St. Twelve Victorian homes reside in this park. The Galván House is the park's headquarters and houses the Cultural Center, which contains changing exhibits focusing on the city's history; a carriage house, gazebo and rose garden are featured. **Time:** Allow 1 hour minimum. **Hours:** Mon.-Fri. 9-5. Closed Jan. 1, Thanksgiving and Christmas. **Cost:** Free. **Phone:** (361) 826-3417.

**SOUTH TEXAS BOTANICAL GARDENS & NATURE CENTER** is at 8545 S. Staples St. Comprising 182 acres, the grounds feature a 2,600-square-foot screened-in butterfly house, a bromeliad conservatory, an orchid house, and a rose garden with a pavilion. Other gardens include the Arid, Hummingbird and Sensory gardens plus the seasonal Plumeria Garden with a viewing platform. Nature tourists and bird lovers can explore the native habitat trail and birding platform on Gator Lake, learn about wetland plants and wildlife in the Palapa Grande and along the Wetlands Awareness Boardwalk, and soak up the cool in the Resident Reptiles exhibit.

**Time:** Allow 1 hour minimum. **Hours:** Daily 9-6. Closed Thanksgiving, Christmas Eve and Christmas. **Cost:** $7; $6 (ages 60+ and college students and military with ID); $3 (ages 3-12). **Phone:** (361) 852-2100.

**TEXAS STATE AQUARIUM**, 2710 N. Shoreline Blvd. on Corpus Christi Beach, displays thousands of animals representing over 330 species. Visitors to the aquarium enter under a waterfall representing a full submersion into the Gulf of Mexico. Dolphin Bay offers views of Atlantic bottlenose dolphins from above the water and in an underwater viewing room.

The Islands of Steel habitat, a replica of an offshore oil platform, features a 125,000-gallon tank with marine animals including sharks, sea turtles, tarpon and grouper. Exotic birds, poison-dart frogs, freshwater stingrays and boa constrictors live in the Amazon exhibit.

Guides answer questions about the animals and the aquarium's programs. Changing exhibits, dive shows, several touch pools, feeding demonstrations and hands-on experiences with sharks and stingrays also are available.

**Time:** Allow 1 hour, 30 minutes minimum. **Hours:** Daily 9-6, Mar. 1-Labor Day; 9-5, rest of year. Closed Thanksgiving and Christmas. **Cost:** $17.95; $16.95 (ages 65+ and military with ID); $12.95 (ages 3-12). **Parking:** $5. **Phone:** (361) 881-1200 or (800) 477-4853.

**TEXAS STATE MUSEUM OF ASIAN CULTURES AND EDUCATIONAL CENTER** is at 1809 N. Chaparral St. Life in Asia is portrayed through exhibits of pottery, kimonos, bronzeware, watercolors, Japanese dolls, masks, funerary and ancient Hindu art as well as objects from the Tang, Sung and Ming dynasties. A Buddhist art exhibit contains a large bronze Buddha made in 1766. **Hours:** Tues.-Sat. 10-4. **Cost:** $6; $4 (ages 65+ and students and military with ID); $3 (ages 4-12). **Phone:** (361) 881-8827.

**USS *LEXINGTON* MUSEUM ON THE BAY** is docked at 2914 N. Shoreline Blvd. Because this aircraft carrier was reported sunk no less than four times during World War II, it was nicknamed "The Blue Ghost" by the Japanese. Self-guiding tours of the 910-foot naval museum involve climbing steep stairways; comfortable walking shoes are recommended. Aboard the ship at the MEGA Theater, two movies are shown on a three-story screen.

**Time:** Allow 1 hour, 30 minutes minimum. **Hours:** Daily 9-6, Memorial Day-Labor Day; 9-5, rest of year. Closed Thanksgiving and Christmas. **Cost:** $13.95; $11.95 (ages 60+ and military with ID); $8.95 (ages 4-12). **Parking:** $3.50. **Phone:** (361) 888-4873 or (800) 523-9539.

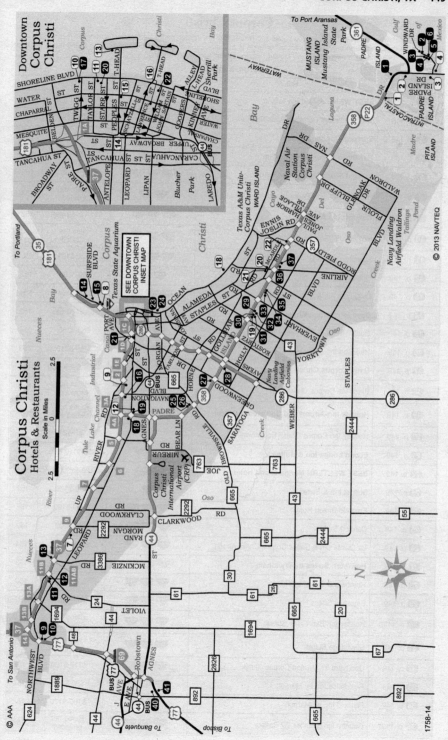

Downtown Corpus Christi

Corpus Christi
Hotels & Restaurants

# Corpus Christi

This index helps you to "spot" where approved hotels and restaurants are located on the corresponding detailed maps. Hotel daily rate range is for comparison only. Restaurant price range is a combination of lunch and/or dinner. Turn to the listing page for more detailed rate and price information and consult display ads for special promotions.

## CORPUS CHRISTI

| Map Page | Hotels | Diamond Rated | Rate Range | Page |
|---|---|---|---|---|
| **1** p. 149 | BEST WESTERN on the Island | ◆◆ | $90-$250 SAVE | 151 |
| **2** p. 149 | The Gulfstream Condominiums/North Padre Island | ◆◆ | $140-$300 | 153 |
| **3** p. 149 | Surfside Condominiums | ◆◆ | $140-$265 SAVE | 154 |
| **4** p. 149 | Hawthorn Suites by Wyndham | ◆◆ | $95-$170 SAVE | 153 |
| **5** p. 149 | Comfort Suites North Padre Island | ◆◆◆ | $80-$280 | 152 |
| **6** p. 149 | Holiday Inn North Padre Island | ◆◆ | Rates not provided | 153 |
| **9** p. 149 | Comfort Inn & Suites | ◆◆◆ | $119-$189 SAVE | 152 |
| **10** p. 149 | Holiday Inn Express & Suites | ◆◆◆ | Rates not provided | 153 |
| **11** p. 149 | Hampton Inn | ◆◆◆ | $129-$199 | 153 |
| **12** p. 149 | Garden Inn | ◆◆ | $99-$150 | 152 |
| **13** p. 149 | La Quinta Inn & Suites Northwest | ◆◆◆ | $105-$164 | 154 |
| **14** p. 149 | Days Inn-Corpus Christi Beach | ◆ | $65-$160 SAVE | 152 |
| **15** p. 149 | Quality Inn & Suites Sandy Shores | ◆◆ | $80-$290 | 154 |
| **16** p. 149 | Hampton Inn & Suites | ◆◆◆ | $119-$219 | 153 |
| **17** p. 149 | Omni Corpus Christi Hotel | ◆◆◆◆ | $129-$269 SAVE | 154 |
| **18** p. 149 | Plaza Inn Corpus Christi | ◆◆ | Rates not provided | 154 |
| **19** p. 149 | Holiday Inn-Airport and Conference Center | fyi | Rates not provided SAVE | 153 |
| **20** p. 149 | Holiday Inn Corpus Christi Downtown | fyi | $149-$249 | 153 |
| **21** p. 149 | Econo Lodge Inn & Suites | ◆◆ | $55-$110 SAVE | 152 |
| **22** p. 149 | BEST WESTERN Marina Grand Hotel | ◆◆ | $120-$180 SAVE | 151 |
| **23** p. 149 | Budget Inn & Suites | ◆ | $60-$170 | 152 |
| **24** p. 149 | Emerald Beach Hotel | ◆◆◆ | $139-$199 | 152 |
| **25** p. 149 | Comfort Suites | ◆◆◆ | $85-$200 | 152 |
| **26** p. 149 | La Quinta Inn & Suites Corpus Christi Airport | ◆◆◆ | $109-$180 | 154 |
| **27** p. 149 | Hawthorn Suites by Wyndham | ◆◆◆ | $89-$149 SAVE | 153 |
| **28** p. 149 | Homewood Suites by Hilton | ◆◆◆ | $99-$189 | 153 |
| **29** p. 149 | Embassy Suites Hotel | ◆◆◆ | $140-$250 | 152 |
| **30** p. 149 | Holiday Inn Express & Suites | ◆◆◆ | Rates not provided | 153 |
| **31** p. 149 | Staybridge Suites | ◆◆◆ | Rates not provided | 154 |
| **32** p. 149 | Courtyard by Marriott Corpus Christi | ◆◆◆ | $119-$199 | 152 |
| **33** p. 149 | Residence Inn by Marriott | ◆◆◆ | $90-$144 | 154 |
| **34** p. 149 | Fairfield Inn by Marriott | ◆◆ | $100-$170 | 152 |
| **35** p. 149 | Country Inn & Suites By Carlson | ◆◆◆ | Rates not provided | 152 |

## CORPUS CHRISTI (cont'd)

| Map Page | Hotels (cont'd) | Diamond Rated | Rate Range | Page |
|---|---|---|---|---|
| 36 p. 149 | La Quinta Inn Corpus Christi South | ▼▼ | $79-$160 | 154 |
| 37 p. 149 | **BEST WESTERN Paradise Inn** | ▼▼▼ | $84-$179 [SAVE] | 152 |

| Map Page | Restaurants | Diamond Rated | Cuisine | Price Range | Page |
|---|---|---|---|---|---|
| 1 p. 149 | Doc's Seafood & Steaks | ▼▼ | Seafood Steak | $10-$22 | 155 |
| 2 p. 149 | Padre Pizzeria | ▼ | Italian Pizza | $8-$20 | 155 |
| 3 p. 149 | Black Sheep Bistro | ▼▼ | Regional American | $14-$22 | 155 |
| 4 p. 149 | Island Italian Restaurant | ▼▼ | Italian | $8-$17 | 155 |
| 7 p. 149 | Peoples Restaurant and Lounge | ▼▼ | American | $10-$21 | 155 |
| 8 p. 149 | Blackbeards on the Beach | ▼▼ | Regional American | $9-$20 | 155 |
| 9 p. 149 | Bar B Q Man | ▼ | Regional Barbecue | $8-$15 | 154 |
| 10 p. 149 | **Republic of Texas Bar & Grill** | ▼▼▼ | Regional Steak Seafood | $19-$46 | 155 |
| 11 p. 149 | The Glass Pavilion | ▼▼▼ | American | $20-$35 | 155 |
| 12 p. 149 | Astor Restaurant | ▼▼ | Regional Steak Seafood | $10-$25 | 154 |
| 13 p. 149 | Landry's Seafood House | ▼▼ | Seafood | $12-$36 [SAVE] | 155 |
| 14 p. 149 | Portis Kountry Kitchen | ▼ | Regional Comfort Food | $7-$10 | 155 |
| 15 p. 149 | Thai Spice Cuisine | ▼▼ | Thai | $12-$28 | 155 |
| 16 p. 149 | Water Street Oyster Bar | ▼▼ | Regional Seafood | $8-$20 | 156 |
| 18 p. 149 | The Yardarm Restaurant | ▼▼ | Regional Seafood | $15-$32 | 156 |
| 19 p. 149 | China Garden & Kitchen | ▼ | Chinese | $7-$14 | 155 |
| 20 p. 149 | Bamboo Garden Restaurant | ▼▼ | Vietnamese | $10-$26 | 154 |
| 21 p. 149 | Catfish Charlie's | ▼ | Regional American | $9-$14 | 155 |
| 22 p. 149 | La Playa Mexican Cafe | ▼ | Regional Seafood | $8-$14 | 155 |

### ROBSTOWN

| Map Page | Hotels | Diamond Rated | Rate Range | Page |
|---|---|---|---|---|
| 40 p. 149 | **BEST WESTERN PLUS Tropic Inn** | ▼▼▼ | $99-$149 [SAVE] | 449 |
| 41 p. 149 | **Days Inn** | ▼▼▼ | $90-$143 [SAVE] | 449 |

**BEST WESTERN MARINA GRAND HOTEL**
(361)883-5111

 Hotel $120-$180

 **AAA Benefit:** Members save 10% or more with Best Western!

**Address:** 300 N Shoreline Blvd 78401 **Location:** Center of downtown. **Facility:** 173 units. 11 stories, interior corridors. **Terms:** check-in 4 pm, 2 night minimum stay - seasonal. **Amenities:** safes. **Pool(s):** outdoor. **Activities:** exercise room. **Guest Services:** valet and coin laundry.

**BEST WESTERN ON THE ISLAND**    (361)949-2300

 Motel $90-$250

 **AAA Benefit:** Members save 10% or more with Best Western!

**Address:** 14050 S Padre Island Dr 78418 **Location:** On Park Rd 22. **Facility:** 40 units. 2 stories (no elevator), exterior corridors. **Terms:** 2 night minimum stay - seasonal. **Pool(s):** outdoor. **Guest Services:** coin laundry.

(See map & index p. 149.)

## BEST WESTERN PARADISE INN (361)992-3100

**Motel**
**$84-$179**

**AAA Benefit:** Members save 10% or more with Best Western! .

**Address:** 6301 S Padre Island Dr 78412 **Location:** SR 358, just e of Airline Dr. Located at entrance to North Padre and Mustang Island. **Facility:** 50 units. 2 stories (no elevator), exterior corridors. **Terms:** 3 day cancellation notice-fee imposed. **Pool(s):** outdoor. **Activities:** hot tub. **Guest Services:** coin laundry.

SAVE YI+ CALL &M ~ BIZ HS
⌂ 🔽 /SOME UNITS 🔲 🔲

## BUDGET INN & SUITES (361)884-2485 23

🔽 **Motel** $60-$170 **Address:** 801 S Shoreline Blvd 78401 **Location:** I-37 exit Shoreline Blvd; between Park and Fuman aves. **Facility:** 30 units. 2 stories (no elevator), exterior corridors. **Terms:** 3 night minimum stay - seasonal and/or weekends, cancellation fee imposed. **Pool(s):** outdoor. **Guest Services:** coin laundry.

YI+ ~ HS ⌂ 🔲 🔲 🔲 /SOME UNITS 🔲

## COMFORT INN & SUITES (361)241-6363 9

**Hotel**
**$119-$189**

**Address:** 3838 Hwy 77 N 78410 **Location:** I-37 exit 14 northbound, 0.4 mi s over bridge, U-turn on northbound frontage road; exit 14A southbound. **Facility:** 61 units. 2 stories, interior corridors. **Pool(s):** outdoor. **Activities:** exercise room. **Guest Services:** coin laundry. **Featured Amenity:** full hot breakfast.

SAVE YI+ CALL &M ~ BIZ HS
⌂ 🔽 🔲 🔲 🔲

## COMFORT SUITES (361)299-2266 25

🔽🔽 **Hotel** $85-$200 **Address:** 538 S Padre Island Dr 78405 **Location:** SR 358 exit Old Brownsville Rd; on frontage road. **Facility:** 93 units. 4 stories, interior corridors. **Amenities:** *Some:* safes. **Pool(s):** outdoor. **Activities:** hot tub, exercise room. **Guest Services:** valet and coin laundry.

CALL &M ~ BIZ HS ⌂ 🔽 🔲 🔲 🔲

## COMFORT SUITES NORTH PADRE ISLAND (361)949-1112 5

🔽🔽 **Hotel** $80-$280 **Address:** 15209 Windward Dr 78418 **Location:** Park Rd 22 exit Whitecap Blvd; across from Gulf of Mexico. **Facility:** 79 units. some two bedrooms and kitchens. 4 stories, interior corridors. **Terms:** check-in 4 pm, 3 day cancellation notice. **Amenities:** safes. **Pool(s):** outdoor. **Activities:** hot tub, exercise room. **Guest Services:** valet and coin laundry.

CALL &M ~ BIZ HS ⌂ 🔽 🔲 🔲 🔲

## COUNTRY INN & SUITES BY CARLSON 361/985-8395 35

🔽🔽🔽 **Hotel.** Rates not provided. **Address:** 5209 Blanche Moore Dr 78411 **Location:** SR 358 E exit Everhart Rd, 0.3 mi e. Located in a modern commercial area. **Facility:** 64 units. 3 stories, interior corridors. **Pool(s):** heated indoor. **Activities:** hot tub, exercise room. **Guest Services:** valet and coin laundry.

YI+ ~ BIZ HS ⌂ 🔽 🔲 🔲 🔲

## COURTYARD BY MARRIOTT CORPUS CHRISTI (361)808-8400 32

🔽🔽🔽 **Hotel** $119-$199 **Address:** 5133 Flynn Pkwy 78411 **Location:** SR 358 exit Weber St. Located behind Embassy Suites Hotel. **Facility:** 105 units. 3 stories, interior corridors. **Pool(s):** outdoor. **Activities:** exercise room. **Guest Services:** valet and coin laundry.

**AAA Benefit:** Members save 5% or more!

YI+ ~ BIZ HS ⌂ 🔽 🔲 🔲 /SOME UNITS 🔲

## DAYS INN-CORPUS CHRISTI BEACH (361)882-3297 14

**Hotel**
**$65-$160**

**Address:** 4302 Surfside Blvd 78402 **Location:** 1 mi n off US 181 exit Beach St; at north end of Harbor Bridge. Located within walking distance of beach. **Facility:** 55 units. 3 stories, exterior corridors. **Terms:** cancellation fee imposed. **Amenities:** safes. **Pool(s):** outdoor. **Guest Services:** coin laundry. **Featured Amenity: continental breakfast.**

SAVE ~ HS ⌂ 🔲 🔲
/SOME UNITS 🔲

## ECONO LODGE INN & SUITES (361)883-7400 21

🔽🔽🔽 **Motel** **$55-$110**

**Address:** 722 N Port Ave 78408 **Location:** I-37 exit 1D (Port Ave); on southbound frontage road. **Facility:** 44 units. 2 stories (no elevator), exterior corridors. **Pool(s):** outdoor. **Activities:** hot tub, exercise room. **Guest Services:** coin laundry. **Featured Amenity: continental breakfast.**

SAVE ~ BIZ HS ⌂ 🔲 🔲 /SOME UNITS 🔲

## EMBASSY SUITES HOTEL (361)853-7899 29

🔽🔽🔽 **Hotel** $140-$250 **Address:** 4337 S Padre Island Dr 78411 **Location:** SR 358 exit Weber St. Located in a busy commercial area. **Facility:** 150 units, some two bedrooms. 3 stories, interior corridors. **Terms:** 1-7 night minimum stay, cancellation fee imposed. **Amenities:** video games. **Pool(s):** heated indoor. **Activities:** hot tub, exercise room. **Guest Services:** valet and coin laundry, area transportation.

**AAA Benefit:** Members save 5% or more!

🔀 YI 🔽 🍸 ~ BIZ SHS 🔇 🔲 🔲 🔲

## EMERALD BEACH HOTEL (361)883-5731 24

🔽🔽🔽 **Hotel** $139-$199 **Address:** 1102 S Shoreline Blvd 78401 **Location:** Oceanfront. 1.5 mi s on bay from downtown marina. **Facility:** 368 units. 2-7 stories, interior/exterior corridors. **Terms:** check-in 4 pm. **Pool(s):** heated indoor. **Activities:** hot tub, fishing, playground, game room, exercise room. **Guest Services:** valet laundry, area transportation.

🔀 YI 🔽 🍸 CALL &M ~ HS ⌂ 🔲
/SOME UNITS 🔲 🔲 🔲

## FAIRFIELD INN BY MARRIOTT (361)985-8393 34

🔽🔽 **Hotel** $100-$170 **Address:** 5217 Blanche Moore Dr 78411 **Location:** SR 358 E exit Everhart Rd, 0.3 mi e. Located in a modern commercial area. **Facility:** 68 units. 3 stories, interior corridors. **Pool(s):** outdoor. **Guest Services:** valet and coin laundry.

**AAA Benefit:** Members save 5% or more!

YI+ ~ BIZ HS ⌂ 🔽 🔲 /SOME UNITS 🔲 🔲

## GARDEN INN 361/241-6675 12

🔽🔽 **Motel** $99-$150 **Address:** 11217 I-37 78410 **Location:** I-37 exit 11B (Violet Rd); on southbound frontage road. **Facility:** 38 units. 2 stories (no elevator), exterior corridors. **Amenities:** safes. **Pool(s):** outdoor. **Activities:** hot tub, exercise room. **Guest Services:** coin laundry.

YI+ CALL &M ~ BIZ HS ⌂ 🔲 🔲 🔲
/SOME UNITS 🔲

(See map & index p. 149.)

### THE GULFSTREAM CONDOMINIUMS/NORTH PADRE ISLAND
361/949-8061  **2**

**Condominium** $140-$300 **Address:** 14810 Windward Dr 78418 **Location:** Oceanfront. Park Rd 22 on N Padre Island Dr, jct Whitecap Blvd, 1.2 mi ne. Located in a quiet area of condominiums and hotels on the beach. **Facility:** 79 condominiums. 6 stories, exterior corridors. **Terms:** check-in 4 pm, 2 night minimum stay - weekends, 3 day cancellation notice-fee imposed. **Amenities:** safes. **Pool(s):** heated outdoor. **Activities:** hot tub, fishing. **Guest Services:** coin laundry.

### HAMPTON INN
(361)241-9300  **11**

**Hotel** $129-$199 **Address:** 11233 I-37 78410 **Location:** I-37 exit 11B (Violet Rd); on southbound access road. **Facility:** 55 units. 3 stories, interior corridors. **Terms:** 1-7 night minimum stay, cancellation fee imposed. **Activities:** hot tub, exercise room. **Guest Services:** valet and coin laundry.

**AAA Benefit:** Members save up to 10%!

### HAMPTON INN & SUITES
(361)884-4444  **16**

**Hotel** $119-$219 **Address:** 917 N Navigation Blvd 78408 **Location:** I-37 exit 3A (Navigation Blvd); on southbound access road. **Facility:** 80 units. 4 stories, interior corridors. **Terms:** 1-7 night minimum stay, cancellation fee imposed. **Pool(s):** heated indoor. **Activities:** sauna, hot tub, exercise room. **Guest Services:** valet and coin laundry.

**AAA Benefit:** Members save up to 10%!

### HAWTHORN SUITES BY WYNDHAM
(361)854-3400  **27**

Extended Stay Hotel $89-$149

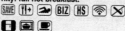

**Address:** 1442 S Padre Island Dr 78416 **Location:** SR 358; jct Greenwood Ave. **Facility:** 61 units, some two bedrooms and kitchens. 4 stories, interior corridors. **Terms:** cancellation fee imposed. **Pool(s):** outdoor. **Activities:** hot tub, exercise room. **Guest Services:** valet and coin laundry. **Featured Amenity:** full hot breakfast.

### HAWTHORN SUITES BY WYNDHAM
(361)949-2400  **4**

Extended Stay Hotel $95-$170

**Address:** 15201 Windward Dr 78418 **Location:** Park Rd 22 exit Whitecap Blvd; across from Gulf of Mexico. **Facility:** 54 units. 3 stories, interior corridors. **Terms:** check-in 4 pm, 3 day cancellation notice-fee imposed. **Activities:** exercise room. **Guest Services:** coin laundry. **Featured Amenity:** full hot breakfast.

### HOLIDAY INN-AIRPORT AND CONFERENCE CENTER
361/289-5100  **19**

fyi Hotel Rates not provided

Under major renovation, scheduled to be completed March 2013. **Last Rated:** **Address:** 5549 Leopard St 78408 **Location:** Jct SR 358 and Leopard St, 5.5 mi w. **Facility:** 237 units. 6 stories, interior corridors. **Pool(s):** heated indoor. **Activities:** hot tub, exercise room. **Guest Services:** valet and coin laundry. **Featured Amenity:** full hot breakfast.

### HOLIDAY INN CORPUS CHRISTI DOWNTOWN
(361)882-1700  **20**

**fyi Hotel** $149-$249 Under major renovation, scheduled to be completed September 2013. **Last Rated:** **Address:** 707 N Shoreline Blvd 78401 **Location:** Just n across from bay. **Facility:** 346 units. 20 stories, interior corridors. **Parking:** on-site (fee). **Terms:** cancellation fee imposed. **Amenities:** safes. **Pool(s):** heated outdoor, heated indoor. **Activities:** sauna, exercise room. **Guest Services:** valet and coin laundry.

### HOLIDAY INN EXPRESS & SUITES
361/857-7772  **30**

**Hotel.** Rates not provided. **Address:** 5213 Oakhurst Dr 78411 **Location:** SR 358 exit Weber St. Located behind Outback Steakhouse. **Facility:** 88 units. 3 stories, interior corridors. **Pool(s):** heated indoor. **Activities:** hot tub, exercise room. **Guest Services:** valet and coin laundry.

### HOLIDAY INN EXPRESS & SUITES
361/242-3330  **10**

**Hotel.** Rates not provided. **Address:** 13425 Brookhaven Dr 78410 **Location:** I-37 exit 11 (US 77 S); on northbound frontage road. **Facility:** 64 units. 4 stories, interior corridors. **Pool(s):** outdoor. **Activities:** exercise room. **Guest Services:** valet and coin laundry.

### HOLIDAY INN NORTH PADRE ISLAND
361/949-8041  **6**

**Hotel.** Rates not provided. **Address:** 15202 Windward Dr 78418 **Location:** Oceanfront. Park Rd 22, jct Whitecap Blvd, just e. **Facility:** 149 units. 6 stories, interior corridors. **Terms:** check-in 4 pm. **Amenities:** video games, safes. **Pool(s):** outdoor, heated outdoor. **Activities:** hot tub, limited beach access, fishing, recreation programs, game room, exercise room. **Guest Services:** valet and coin laundry.

### HOMEWOOD SUITES BY HILTON
(361)854-1331  **28**

**Extended Stay Hotel** $99-$189 **Address:** 5201 Crosstown Expwy (SR 286) 78417 **Location:** I-37 exit SR 358 E (Greenwood Dr), 0.6 mi e on eastbound access road. **Facility:** 86 efficiencies, some two bedrooms. 3 stories, interior corridors. **Terms:** check-in 4 pm, 1-7 night minimum stay, cancellation fee imposed. **Pool(s):** outdoor. **Activities:** hot tub, exercise room. **Guest Services:** valet and coin laundry.

**AAA Benefit:** Members save up to 10%!

(See map & index p. 149.)

### LA QUINTA INN & SUITES CORPUS CHRISTI AIRPORT
(361)299-2600  **26**

WWW Hotel $109-$180 **Address:** 546 S Padre Island Dr 78405 **Location:** SR 358 exit Old Brownsville Rd; on frontage road. Located in a light commercial area. **Facility:** 67 units. 3 stories, interior corridors. **Pool(s):** outdoor. **Activities:** hot tub, exercise room. **Guest Services:** valet and coin laundry.

### LA QUINTA INN & SUITES NORTHWEST
(361)241-4245  **13**

WWW Hotel $105-$164 **Address:** 10446 I-37 78410 **Location:** I-37 exit 11A (McKinzie Rd); on northbound frontage road. **Facility:** 66 units. 3 stories, interior corridors. **Pool(s):** outdoor. **Activities:** exercise room. **Guest Services:** coin laundry.

### LA QUINTA INN CORPUS CHRISTI SOUTH
(361)991-5730  **36**

WWW Hotel $79-$160 **Address:** 6225 S Padre Island Dr 78412 **Location:** SR 358 exit Airline Rd. **Facility:** 129 units. 3 stories, exterior corridors. **Pool(s):** outdoor. **Guest Services:** valet and coin laundry.

### OMNI CORPUS CHRISTI HOTEL
(361)887-1600  **17**

WWWW Hotel $129-$269 **Address:** 900 N Shoreline Blvd 78401 **Location:** Downtown; in marina district. **Facility:** This dramatic high-rise, located across the street from the bayfront marina, has elegant public areas, upscale guest rooms and decoratively striking bathrooms. Beautiful fine-dining facility on 20th floor. 475 units. 20 stories, interior corridors. **Parking:** valet and street only. **Terms:** cancellation fee imposed. **Amenities:** Some: safes. **Dining:** 2 restaurants, also, The Glass Pavilion, Republic of Texas Bar & Grill, see separate listings. **Pool(s):** heated outdoor. **Activities:** hot tub, spa. **Guest Services:** valet laundry, area transportation.

### PLAZA INN CORPUS CHRISTI
361/289-8200  **18**

WW Hotel. Rates not provided. **Address:** 2021 N Padre Island Dr 78408 **Location:** I-37 exit SR 358, just se at Leopard St. **Facility:** 105 units. 4 stories, interior corridors. **Pool(s):** outdoor. **Activities:** limited exercise equipment. **Guest Services:** valet and coin laundry.

### QUALITY INN & SUITES SANDY SHORES
(361)883-7456  **15**

WWW Hotel $80-$290 **Address:** 3202 Surfside Blvd 78402 **Location:** 1 mi n on US 181; at north end of Harbor Bridge exit Bridge St. Adjacent to north beach area and USS Lexington. **Facility:** 119 units, some efficiencies. 2 stories (no elevator), interior/exterior corridors. **Terms:** check-in 4 pm, 3 day cancellation notice. **Amenities:** safes. **Pool(s):** outdoor. **Activities:** hot tub. **Guest Services:** coin laundry.

### RESIDENCE INN BY MARRIOTT
(361)985-1113  **33**

WWW Extended Stay Hotel $90-$144 **Address:** 5229 Blanche Moore Dr 78411 **Location:** SR 358 E exit Everhart Rd, 0.3 mi e. Located in a modern commercial area. **Facility:** 66 kitchen units, some two bedrooms. 3 stories, interior corridors. **Pool(s):** heated indoor. **Activities:** hot tub, exercise room. **Guest Services:** valet and coin laundry.

**AAA Benefit:**
Members save 5% or more!

### STAYBRIDGE SUITES
361-857-7766  **31**

WWWW Extended Stay Hotel. Rates not provided. **Address:** 5201 Oakhurst Dr 78411 **Location:** SR 358 exit Weber St. Located behind Outback Steakhouse. **Facility:** 84 units, some two bedrooms, efficiencies and kitchens. 4 stories, interior corridors. **Pool(s):** outdoor. **Activities:** hot tub, exercise room. **Guest Services:** valet and coin laundry.

### SURFSIDE CONDOMINIUMS
361/949-8128  **3**

WWWW Condominium $140-$265 **Address:** 15005 Windward Dr 78418 **Location:** Park Rd 22 on N Padre Island Dr, jct Whitecap Blvd, 0.6 mi n to Windward Dr, then 0.8 mi w. **Facility:** 29 condominiums. 2 stories (no elevator), exterior corridors. **Terms:** check-in 4 pm, 2 night minimum stay, 3 day cancellation notice-fee imposed. **Pool(s):** heated outdoor. **Activities:** beach access. **Guest Services:** coin laundry.

### HOWARD JOHNSON
361/826-5100

**fyi** Not evaluated. **Address:** 6301 IH 37 78409 **Location:** I-37 exit 4 (Corn Products Rd); on northbound frontage road. Facilities, services, and décor characterize an economy property.

## WHERE TO EAT

### ASTOR RESTAURANT
361/289-0101  **12**

WW Regional Steak Seafood. Casual Dining. $10-$25 **AAA Inspector Notes:** Convenient to two major highways, this longtime city landmark features fine cuts of mesquite-grilled steaks and seafood. **Features:** full bar. **Address:** 5533 Leopard St 78408 **Location:** I-37 exit 4A (SR 358), just e. L D

### BAMBOO GARDEN RESTAURANT
361/993-7993  **20**

WW Vietnamese. Casual Dining. $10-$26 **AAA Inspector Notes:** Far East delicacies line two menus: one Chinese and one Vietnamese. The casual restaurant provides diners many choices. **Features:** full bar. **Address:** 1220 Airline Rd, Suite 115 78412 **Location:** Northeast corner of Airline and McArdle rds. L D

### BAR B Q MAN
361/888-4248  **9**

W Regional Barbecue. Quick Serve. $8-$15 **AAA Inspector Notes:** Just off the interstate, the casual south Texas 'cue shack has ample parking and a spacious dining area. On the menu are moist, tender cuts of chicken, pork and beef. **Features:** full bar. **Address:** 4931 I-37 S 78469 **Location:** I-37 exit 3A, just s; on southbound access road. L D

### BILL MILLER BAR-B-Q

W Barbecue. Quick Serve. $6-$11 **AAA Inspector Notes:** The relaxed, family-focused barbecue restaurant prepares ribs, chicken, brisket, turkey and sausage for sandwiches or plates. B L D

*For additional information, visit AAA.com*

**LOCATIONS:**
**Address:** 3942 US Hwy 77 78410 **Location:** I-37 exit 14, 1.8 mi s. **Phone:** 361/241-5880
**Address:** 7102 S Padre Island Dr 78412 **Location:** SR 358 and Ursa Blvd, just w. **Phone:** 361/993-7161
**Address:** 4940 Leopard St 78407 **Location:** I-37 exit 3A, on N Navigation Blvd, 0.4 mi to Leopard St, then just e. **Phone:** 361/881-8817
**Address:** 4946 Ayers St 78415 **Location:** SR 358 and Ayers St, 2 blks n. **Phone:** 361/852-0818

(See map & index p. 149.)

### BLACKBEARDS ON THE BEACH        361/884-1030  [8]
Regional American. Casual Dining. $9-$20 AAA Inspector Notes: Located in the north beach area near the USS Lexington, this casual restaurant focuses on classic American favorites, including made-to-order fresh seafood, burgers, soups and salads. An all-you-can-eat buffet is offered on Wednesdays. Saturdays feature all-you-can eat catfish and shrimp. Features: full bar. Address: 3117 N Surfside Blvd 78402 Location: US 181 exit Beach St, 0.4 mi e. [L] [D]

### BLACK SHEEP BISTRO        361/949-4819  [3]
Regional American. Casual Dining. $14-$22 AAA Inspector Notes: Tucked away on North Padre Island, this casual bistro offers interesting interpretations of bisques, quiches, sandwiches and desserts. I enjoyed my rich tomato basil soup, steak strips with roasted potatoes and a classic chilled crème brûlée with a warm crust. Features: beer & wine, patio dining, Sunday brunch. Address: 15201 S Padre Island Dr, Suite 120 78418 Location: Jct Park Rd 22. [D]

### CATFISH CHARLIE'S        361/993-0363  [21]
Regional American. Family Dining. $9-$14 AAA Inspector Notes: Family owned for 21 years, this casual eatery serves up scrumptious, made-from-scratch Southern comfort food. From the complimentary hush puppies to the crispy fried catfish fillets, every bite will make you feel right at home. Features: beer & wine. Address: 5830 McArdle Rd, Suite 12 78412 Location: SR 358 exit Airline Rd, 0.5 mi n; in Crossroads Shopping Village. [L] [D]

### CHINA GARDEN & KITCHEN        361/814-7888  [19]
Chinese. Quick Serve. $7-$14 AAA Inspector Notes: The buffet lines up ample selections, including sushi, seafood and shellfish, as well as such classic favorites as fried pork shish kebabs and cheese-filled dumplings. Address: 4101 S Padre Island Dr 78411 Location: SR 358 exit Weber Rd; on southbound access road. [L] [D]

### DOC'S SEAFOOD & STEAKS        361/949-6744  [1]
Seafood Steak. Casual Dining. $10-$22 AAA Inspector Notes: The large restaurant, elevated on stilts overlooking the intracoastal waterway, is tucked under the JFK Bridge and offers the freshest of coastal cuisine, including pan- or deep-fried crab cakes, seared tuna and herb-crusted flounder. Kids will love the chicken-fried steak, burgers and pasta. Be sure to ring the bell as you leave. Features: full bar. Address: 13309 S Padre Island Dr 78418 Location: Under the JFK Bridge; on Intracoastal Waterway. [L] [D]

### THE GLASS PAVILION        361/887-1600  [11]
American. Casual Dining. $20-$35 AAA Inspector Notes: This eatery offers a unique take on American dishes in upscale surroundings. Try the pavilion burger, which towers about 8 inches high. The devil's tower cake has four types of chocolate with house-made whipped cream and fresh strawberries. Features: full bar. Address: 707 N Shoreline Blvd 78401 Location: Downtown; in marina district; in Omni Corpus Christi Hotel. Parking: on-site and valet. [L] [D] CALL [&M]

### ISLAND ITALIAN RESTAURANT        361/949-7737  [4]
Italian. Casual Dining. $8-$17 AAA Inspector Notes: Tucked away on Padre Island, this longtime local favorite features thick lasagna, spiced meatballs and even snails. Island-style service is laid-back but caring and attentive. The menu is extensive. Guests are treated to live music Thursday through Sunday from 6:30 to 9 pm. Features: beer & wine. Address: 15370 S Padre Island Dr 78418 Location: 0.9 mi s of SR 361. [L] [D]

### LANDRY'S SEAFOOD HOUSE        361/882-6666  [13]
Seafood. Casual Dining. $12-$36 AAA Inspector Notes: An ideal spot for healthy seafood dinners and special occasions, the restaurant produces a wonderful clam chowder. Menu selections come from all the world's oceans. Features: full bar. Address: 600 N Shoreline Blvd 78401 Location: Center of harbor; on water. [SAVE] [L] [D]

### LA PLAYA MEXICAN CAFE        361/980-3909  [22]
Regional Seafood. Casual Dining. $8-$14 AAA Inspector Notes: Folks headed to the beach often stop at this small, informal spot on South Padre Island Drive for fresh seafood and friendly service. A recommendation is to request the snapper fillet prepared "al mojo," grilled and smothered in lightly toasted diced garlic and warm olive oil. Features: full bar, patio dining. Address: 7118 S Padre Island Dr 78412 Location: On SR 358, just se of Staples St. [L] [D] [⬟]

### LUBY'S        361/992-3262
American. Cafeteria. $6-$12 AAA Inspector Notes: First opened in 1947 in south Texas, this cafeteria with over 100 outlets features a wide variety of salads, fresh fruits, seafood...including crunchy entrees...pastas, meat, poultry and just baked cakes and pies. Ask about the kids specials and Lu Ann platters...an entrée with choice of 2 vegetables and a roll. Many locations offer drive-thru service. Address: 5730 Saratoga Blvd 78414 Location: Just e of FM 2444. [L] [D]

### PADRE PIZZERIA        361/949-0787  [2]
Italian Pizza. Casual Dining. $8-$20 AAA Inspector Notes: In a small strip mall on the island and with northern access to the John F Kennedy Causeway Bridge, the casual restaurant brings together quality ingredients in its pizzas, sandwiches, pastas and fresh salads. Features: beer & wine. Address: 14493 Park Rd 22 78418 Location: 0.3 mi n of CR 361. [L] [D]

### PEOPLES RESTAURANT AND LOUNGE        361/241-8087  [7]
American. Casual Dining. $10-$21 AAA Inspector Notes: The family restaurant serves local favorites such as fat burgers, hand-breaded shrimp platters, po' boys, big salads and chocolate cake with chocolate shavings on chocolate frosting. Features: full bar. Address: 9738 Up River Rd 78410 Location: I-37 exit 9 (Rand Morgan); on southbound frontage road. [L] [D]

### PORTIS KOUNTRY KITCHEN        361/885-7720  [14]
Regional Comfort Food. Quick Serve. $7-$10 AAA Inspector Notes: Take the elevator to the basement for authentic country cooking performed by a longtime city elder. The main dining room belies the flavorful dishes. Daily specials include two side dishes and sweet corn bread. Address: 615 N Upper Broadway 78477 Location: Downtown; on basement level of Well Fargo Bank Tower. Parking: on-site (fee) and street. [B] [L]

### REPUBLIC OF TEXAS BAR & GRILL
361/886-3515  [10]

Regional Steak Seafood Fine Dining $19-$46

AAA Inspector Notes: Sitting atop a high-rise hotel with impressive views of Corpus Christi Bay, this restaurant is well known for its steaks, seafood and large side dishes. Features: full bar. Reservations: suggested. Address: 900 N Shoreline Blvd 78401 Location: Downtown; in marina district; in Omni Corpus Christi Hotel. Parking: valet and street only. *Menu on AAA.com* [D]

### SIRLOIN STOCKADE        361/992-3878
Steak. Quick Serve. $9-$11 AAA Inspector Notes: The steakhouse lines up buffet items, including pizza, tacos, soups, salads and desserts, providing both excellent variety and a good value. Rotating theme nights allow for the sampling of sushi, barbecue and seafood. The buffet may also serve to complement a quality steak. Address: 5425 S Padre Island Dr, Suite 149 78411 Location: SR 358 exit Everhart Rd; on south side access road. [L] [D]

### THAI SPICE CUISINE        361/883-8884  [15]
Thai. Casual Dining. $12-$28 AAA Inspector Notes: At this authentic restaurant the Thai chef personally takes your order. Some dishes are served inside of coconuts and split pineapples. Features: beer & wine. Address: 523 N Water St 78401 Location: Just s of Peoples St; downtown. Parking: street only. [L] [D]

(See map & index p. 149.)

WATER STREET OYSTER BAR          361/881-9448   ⑯
♥♥ Regional Seafood. Casual Dining. $8-$20 **AAA Inspector Notes:** Close to where the replicas of the Pinta and Santa Maria are docked you will find meals hand prepared from only the highest quality ingredients. Several catch-of-the-day specials are offered, including mahi mahi, amberjack and red snapper. **Features:** full bar. **Address:** 309 N Water St 78401 **Location:** Just w of N Shoreline Dr. [L] [D] [LATE]

THE YARDARM RESTAURANT          361/855-8157   ⑱
♥♥ Regional Seafood. Casual Dining. $15-$32 **AAA Inspector Notes:** Inside this old wooden house overlooking picturesque Corpus Christi Bay is an intimate restaurant with an outdoor deck boasting the best view. The oysters Rockefeller and snapper papillote are fresh and delicious. **Features:** full bar, patio dining. **Address:** 4310 Ocean Dr 78412 **Location:** I-37 or US 181 exit Shoreline Dr, 5.3 mi s. [D]

## CORSICANA  (D-9) pop. 23,770, elev. 328'

Corsicana's officials were disappointed when oil was struck in 1894 during an attempt to locate a water supply for the town. Within a year not only water but also an abundance of oil had been discovered, and Corsicana became one of the first commercial oil-well and refinery sites west of the Mississippi. The rotary drill bit used in drilling operations for commercial wells was developed in Corsicana.

**Corsicana Area Chamber of Commerce:** 120 N. 12th St., Corsicana, TX 75110. **Phone:** (903) 874-4731 or (877) 376-7477.

**PEARCE MUSEUM AND THE COOK EDUCATION CENTER** is at 3100 W. Collin St. on the Navarro College campus. The Pearce Museum houses more than 15,000 original documents, photographs, diaries and artifacts from the Civil War as well as an extensive collection of contemporary Western art by both well-known and up-and-coming artists. The Cook Center Planetarium presents star shows and educational films.

**Time:** Allow 1 hour, 30 minutes minimum. **Hours:** Mon.-Fri. 10-4, Sat. noon-4. Phone ahead for planetarium show schedule. Closed major holidays. **Cost:** $8; $6 (ages 55+); $4 (ages 6-18 and students with ID). Phone ahead for planetarium show admission. **Phone:** (903) 875-7448 or (800) 988-5317.

**PIONEER VILLAGE** is 2 blks. n. of SR 22 at 912 W. Park Ave. This village of restored buildings and homes includes a Native American trading post, a smithy, eight log structures, a carriage house featuring Pancho Villa's surrey, a general store and slave quarters. Early Texas furniture, tools, toys and artifacts are displayed. The Sam Roberts Museum features western and Civil War items; the Lefty Frizzell Museum honors the Navarra County-born

country singer; and the Peace Officers Museum chronicles law enforcement legends and outlaws.

**Hours:** Mon.-Fri. 8-5, Sat. 9-4:30, Sun. 1-4:30. Closed major holidays. **Cost:** $5; $3 (ages 4-18). Prices may vary; phone ahead. **Phone:** (903) 654-4846.

**BEST WESTERN PLUS EXECUTIVE INN**   (903)872-0020

♥♥♥ Hotel $69-$199

**AAA Benefit:** Members save 10% or more with Best Western!

**Address:** 2100 E Hwy 31 75109 **Location:** I-45 exit 231, just e. **Facility:** 61 units. 3 stories, interior corridors. **Terms:** 3 day cancellation notice. **Pool(s):** outdoor. **Activities:** exercise room. **Guest Services:** valet and coin laundry. **Featured Amenity:** full hot breakfast.

[SAVE] CALL [&M] [🐾] [BIZ] [HS] [📶]
[🛗] [🖨] [💻] /[SOME UNITS] [🐕]

HOLIDAY INN EXPRESS & SUITES          903/874-7440
♥♥♥ Hotel. Rates not provided. **Address:** 620 Bryant's Way 75109 **Location:** I-45 exit 229 (US 287), just e then just n. **Facility:** 79 units. 4 stories, interior corridors. **Pool(s):** heated indoor. **Activities:** hot tub, exercise room. **Guest Services:** valet and coin laundry. [🍴] [🐾] [BIZ] [HS] [📶] [🛗] [🖨] [💻]

LA QUINTA INN & SUITES CORSICANA          (903)874-6292
♥♥♥ Hotel $85-$130 **Address:** 2020 Regal Dr 75110 **Location:** I-45 exit 231, just e. **Facility:** 56 units. 4 stories, interior corridors. **Pool(s):** indoor. **Activities:** exercise room. **Guest Services:** coin laundry. [🐾] [BIZ] [📶] [🛗] [🖨] [💻] /[SOME UNITS] [🐕]

### WHERE TO EAT

COLLIN STREET BAKERY          903/872-2157
♥ American. Quick Serve. $5-$7 **AAA Inspector Notes:** The original location is deep in Corsicana; this location is right on I-45, so it's an easy stop for travelers. The bakery has been in business for 110 years and their fruit cakes are legendary. So even though the savory items are limited to sandwiches and salads, the desserts are aplenty for those with a sweet tooth. This location offers free Wi-Fi. The building is hard to miss with white columns flanking the front facade, making it look very vintage. **Address:** 2035 S Hwy 45 75110 **Location:** I-45 exit 229 (US 287), just se to Corsicana Crossing, then just s. [L] [D] CALL [&M]

NAPOLI'S          903/874-9004
♥♥ Italian. Casual Dining. $6-$16 **AAA Inspector Notes:** Located in the center of this sleepy town, Napoli's has both pizza and pasta dishes, a welcoming staff and a separate bar that serves as a hangout for the locals. **Features:** full bar, happy hour. **Address:** 111 E Collin St 75110 **Location:** Center. **Parking:** street only. [L] [D]

SIRLOIN STOCKADE          903/874-0900
♥♥ Regional Steak. Casual Dining. $9-$11 **AAA Inspector Notes:** The steakhouse lines up buffet items, including pizza, tacos, soups, salads and desserts, providing both excellent variety and a good value. Rotating theme nights allow for the sampling of sushi, barbecue and seafood. The buffet may also serve to complement a quality steak. **Address:** 2508 W 7th St 75110 **Location:** Between N 34th and 35th sts. [L] [D] [◥]

Explore on-the-go travel tools at
AAA.com/mobile or CAA.ca/mobile

## COTULLA pop. 3,603

### BEST WESTERN COWBOY INN                    (830)879-3100

Hotel
$220-$240

**AAA Benefit:** Members save 10% or more with Best Western!

**Address:** 145 W FM 468 78014 **Location:** I-35 exit 57 (FM 468), just w. Located in a quiet area. **Facility:** 50 units. 2 stories (no elevator), interior/exterior corridors. **Pool(s):** outdoor. **Activities:** exercise room. **Guest Services:** coin laundry.

## CRAWFORD (E-8) pop. 717, elev. 734'

Crawford may be a small town, but as the Texas home of President George W. Bush it draws large crowds. Main Street is lined with shops, some specializing in presidential memorabilia. Tonkawa Park is just east of town where the Tonk River drops nearly 15 feet into a swimming hole during the rainy season.

**Crawford Chamber of Commerce:** P.O. Box 471, Crawford, TX 76638. **Phone:** (254) 744-6076.

## CRESSON pop. 741, elev. 1,054'

### BEST WESTERN CRESSON INN                    (817)396-4480

Hotel
$90-$159

**AAA Benefit:** Members save 10% or more with Best Western!

**Address:** 9120 E Hwy 377 76035 **Location:** 0.4 mi s of jct US 377 and SR 171. **Facility:** 62 units, some kitchens. 4 stories, interior corridors. **Amenities:** safes. **Pool(s):** outdoor. **Activities:** exercise room. **Guest Services:** coin laundry.

## CROCKETT pop. 6,950

HOLIDAY INN EXPRESS                    936/544-4488

Hotel. Rates not provided. **Address:** 1511 SE Loop 304 75835 **Location:** Just w of jct US 287 and S Loop 304. **Facility:** 53 units. 3 stories, interior corridors. **Pool(s):** outdoor. **Activities:** exercise room. **Guest Services:** valet and coin laundry.

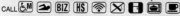

## CROSBYTON (C-5) pop. 1,741

Once the site of the Two Buckle Ranch, Crosbyton is an agricultural community. Associated Cotton Growers, reputedly the world's largest cotton-processing plant producing stripped cotton, serves 520 producers in a 50-mile radius.

**Crosbyton Chamber of Commerce:** 124 S. Berkshire St., Crosbyton, TX 79322. **Phone:** (806) 675-2261.

**CROSBY COUNTY PIONEER MUSEUM** is at 101 W. Main St. Pioneer life is depicted through replicas of houses and collections of household articles, crafts and equipment. Native American artifacts are displayed in the Wayne J. Parker Center for the Study of Native American Cultures. **Time:** Allow 1 hour, 30 minutes minimum. **Hours:** Tues.-Sat. 9-noon and 1-5. Closed major holidays. **Cost:** Donations. **Phone:** (806) 675-2331.

**MOUNT BLANCO FOSSIL MUSEUM** is at 124 W. Main St. Exhibits include dinosaur fossils and casts; a replica of a mastodon; amber from Madagascar; artifacts from tombs in Central Mexico and Peru; minerals; such fossil bones as a triceratops skull; and specimens of a metoposaurus (giant salamander). **Time:** Allow 30 minutes minimum. **Hours:** Mon.-Fri. 9-5. Closed major holidays. Phone ahead to confirm schedule. **Cost:** $4; $2 (ages 6-12). **Phone:** (806) 675-7777.

## CUERO pop. 6,841

### BEST WESTERN PARK HEIGHTS INN & SUITES
(361)524-5186

Hotel
$190

**AAA Benefit:** Members save 10% or more with Best Western!

**Address:** 308 Park Heights Dr 77954 **Location:** US 87, 0.5 mi s of downtown. **Facility:** 79 units. 3 stories, interior corridors. **Pool(s):** outdoor. **Activities:** exercise room. **Guest Services:** valet and coin laundry.

### WHERE TO EAT

FOSSATI'S DELICATESSEN                    361/576-3354

Deli. Quick Serve. $7-$12 **AAA Inspector Notes:** Located in a historic section of downtown, the deli serves authentic grinders, subs and gyros filled with quality meats and cheeses. **Features:** beer & wine. **Address:** 302 S Main St 77954 **Location:** In historic downtown. **Parking:** street only. [L]

## DALHART (A-4) pop. 7,930, elev. 3,984'
• Hotels p. 158 • Restaurants p. 158

First known as Twist, Dalhart grew from a junction of Denver City and Rock Island Railroad lines that crossed here in 1901. It was later named Denroc, a melding of the two railroad names, and finally its present Dalhart, a syllable combination of the two counties in which it resides, Dallam and Hartley. Dalhart now serves as a shipping point for cattle, grains and other agricultural products.

The Empty Saddle Monument north on US 87 was commissioned in 1940 to honor an XIT cowhand who died on his way to Dalhart for its annual reunion; the statue of a riderless horse has come to symbolize all pioneers who helped build the town.

**Dalhart Chamber of Commerce:** 102 E. Seventh St., P.O. Box 967, Dalhart, TX 79022. **Phone:** (806) 244-5646.

**XIT MUSEUM** is at 108 E. Fifth St. across from the courthouse. The XIT Ranch was once a working ranch of more than 3 million acres. Museum exhibits include a 1900 chapel, parlor, bedroom and kitchen; a chuck box; an antique switchboard; an antique gun collection; displays of wildlife common to the area; and works by Texas artists. **Tours:** Guided tours are available. **Time:** Allow 30 minutes minimum. **Hours:** Tues.-Sat. 9-5. Closed major holidays and Christmas-Dec. 31. **Cost:** Donations. **Phone:** (806) 244-5390.

## BEST WESTERN NURSANICKEL MOTEL  (806)244-5637

Hotel
$73-$110

**AAA Benefit:** Members save 10% or more with Best Western!

**Address:** 102 Scott Ave (Hwy 87 S) 79022 **Location:** Just s of jct US 54 and 87. **Facility:** 55 units. 2 stories (no elevator), exterior corridors. **Pool(s):** heated outdoor. **Activities:** hot tub. **Guest Services:** coin laundry. **Featured Amenity:** full hot breakfast.

### BUDGET INN                    806/244-4557

**Motel.** Rates not provided. **Address:** 415 Liberal St (Hwy 54) 79022 **Location:** On US 54, just e of US 87 and 385. **Facility:** 23 units. 1 story, exterior corridors. **Parking:** winter plug-ins.

### DAYS INN                      (806)244-5246

Hotel
$75

**Address:** 701 Liberal St (Hwy 54) 79022 **Location:** On US 54, 0.5 mi e. **Facility:** 42 units. 2 stories (no elevator), interior corridors. **Parking:** winter plug-ins. **Pool(s):** heated indoor. **Activities:** hot tub, limited exercise equipment. **Guest Services:** coin laundry. **Featured Amenity:** continental breakfast.

### RODEWAY INN                   (806)249-8585

Motel
$80-$150

**Address:** 918 Liberal St (Hwy 54 E) 79022 **Location:** 0.5 mi e of jct US 54 and 87. **Facility:** 36 units. 1 story, exterior corridors. **Pool(s):** outdoor. **Featured Amenity:** continental breakfast.

### SANDS MOTEL                   806/244-4568

**Motel.** Rates not provided. **Address:** 301 Liberal St (Hwy 54) 79022 **Location:** On US 54, just e of US 87 and 385. **Facility:** 23 units. 1 story, exterior corridors.

## SUPER 8                        (806)249-8526

Motel
$60-$85

**Address:** 403 Tanglewood Rd (Hwy 54 E) 79022 **Location:** Jct US 87 and 54, 0.5 mi e. **Facility:** 43 units. 2 stories (no elevator), interior corridors. **Parking:** winter plug-ins. **Featured Amenity:** continental breakfast.

Welcome to the Super 8 Dalhart, TX. Your stay here will be super, we promise!

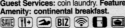
### WHERE TO EAT

### BAR-H STEAK HOUSE            806/244-3813

American. Casual Dining. $6-$22 **AAA Inspector Notes:** Thick steaks cut on the premises are the specialty at the rustic, Western-themed cafe. The salad bar is set up on an old-time frontier wagon, and wagon-wheel chandeliers hang from the ceiling of the softly lit dining room. **Features:** beer & wine. **Address:** 1010 US 54 E 79022 **Location:** On US 54, 0.5 mi e.

### EXTREME CUISINE             806/244-3287

Steak Chicken. Casual Dining. $7-$22 **AAA Inspector Notes:** New menus are offered daily at the upscale restaurant, where patrons enjoy food prepared from the freshest ingredients. **Features:** beer & wine. **Address:** 416 Denrock Ave 79022 **Location:** Downtown; across from courthouse. **Parking:** street only.

# Excite Your Travel Senses

Amp up your trip planning fun. Get the interactive **Top Destinations travel guides** in the iPad version AAA Mobile app with colorful photos, maps and "must do" recommendations from AAA travel experts.

Get the iPad version of the
**AAA Mobile app** on iTunes.

# Dallas

## Then & Now

With cars zipping by, squinting sightseers in Dealey Plaza imagine the sound of gunfire as they gaze at a chilling white X painted on Elm Street. Steps away, amateur photogs scrutinize the now-infamous grassy knoll before approaching the adjacent red-bricked building, the preserved site from which initial investigations ruled a lone sniper acted. This historic district—the location of President John F. Kennedy's assassination—is one of Dallas' most frenetic spots. Yet, in spite of all the activity, there's a palpable stillness in the air.

When, in 1963, America lost its 35th president here, ink and live images brought the world to Dallas, etching once everyday sites like a downtown plaza and a book depository building into the popular consciousness. With exposure like that, it's no wonder this modern metropolis is sometimes viewed as a hodgepodge of past events and larger-than-life people—many inspiring and some tragic.

Long before Lee Harvey Oswald became a household name, locals Bonnie Parker and Clyde Barrow fascinated the American public with a crime spree that ultimately led to their Dallas burials. On the other end of the spectrum, nearly 100 million viewers watched the Dallas Cowboys suit up for their record-breaking eighth Super Bowl appearance, making the 1996 championship game the most-watched U.S. television sporting event of its time. TV audiences also saw a hedonistic depiction of the petroleum hub and its boot-wearing oil barons in the prime-time soap "Dallas," which, in 1980, had *everyone* asking "Who shot J.R.?"

**Dealey Plaza**

It actually was the discovery of oil just east of town that catapulted the already burgeoning business center toward high-rolling status in the midst of the Great Depression. As a result, the community garnered such commercial plums as the 1936 Texas Centennial Exposition, which attracted millions of visitors to Dallas' Fair Park. A showcase for Art Deco architecture, the cultural complex continues to draw crowds with various events, including the State Fair of Texas.

During World War II, other industries like aviation and engineering furthered the city's wealth. More than 600 companies set up shop here over the next few decades; today the area boasts one of the country's highest concentrations of corporate headquarters. Among the most prominent is Texas Instruments, whose claims to fame include the integrated circuit, or microchip, devised in 1958, and the handheld calculator, invented in 1967 and snapped up by the mathematically challenged for $2,500 apiece.

(Continued on p. 162.)

# Destination Dallas

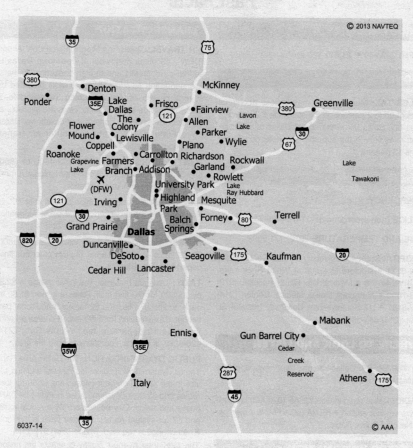

This map shows cities in the Dallas vicinity where you will find attractions, hotels and restaurants. Cities are listed alphabetically in this book on the following pages.

# Fast Facts

## ABOUT THE CITY

POP: 1,232,940 ▪ ELEV: 420 ft.

## MONEY

SALES TAX: Municipalities may impose additional rates of up to 2 percent on the statewide 6.25 percent sales tax. Sales tax in the city of Dallas is 8.25 percent; rates vary in the suburbs. The hotel occupancy tax is 13 percent.

## WHOM TO CALL

EMERGENCY: 911

POLICE (non-emergency): (214) 744-4444

TIME AND TEMPERATURE: (972) 771-0399

HOSPITALS: Baylor University Medical Center, (214) 820-0111 ▪ Doctors Hospital at White Rock Lake, (214) 324-6100 ▪ Medical City Dallas Hospital, (972) 566-7000 ▪ Methodist Dallas Medical Center, (214) 947-8181 ▪ UT Southwestern University Hospital–St. Paul, (214) 645-5555.

## WHERE TO LOOK AND LISTEN

NEWSPAPERS: Dallas has one daily newspaper, the Dallas Morning News.

RADIO: Dallas radio station WBAP (820 AM) is an all-news/weather station ▪ KERA (90.1 FM) is a member of National Public Radio.

## VISITOR INFORMATION

Dallas Convention and Visitors Bureau: 325 N. St. Paul St., Suite 700, Dallas, TX 75201. Phone: (214) 571-1000 or (800) 232-5527.

The visitor center is in the Old Red Courthouse and is open Mon.-Fri. 8-5; Sat.-Sun. 9-5. Phone (214) 571-1300.

## TRANSPORTATION

AIR TRAVEL: Dallas/Fort Worth International Airport (DFW), 18 miles northwest of downtown Dallas is served by domestic and foreign passenger carriers. Transportation to surrounding cities is provided by several shuttle services including SuperShuttle, a door-to-door ride-share system. Taxis are available at curbside. Seven miles northwest of downtown, Dallas Love Field (DAL) offers commuter air transit throughout the region.

RENTAL CARS: Hertz, (972) 453-4600 or (800) 654-3080, at Dallas/Fort Worth International Airport, offers discounts to AAA members.

RAIL SERVICE: Amtrak's Union Station is at 400 S. Houston St. for train schedule and ticket information phone (214) 653-1101 or (800) 872-7245.

BUSES: The Greyhound Lines Inc. bus station, (800) 231-2222, is at 205 S. Lamar St.; five other bus lines depart from this address.

TAXIS: Taxis are metered. The initial charge is $2.25 plus $1.80 for the first mile. Rates are then $1.80 for each additional mile, and $2 for each additional passenger. Taxis leaving from the airport charge an additional $4.10 departure fee. Yellow Cab, (214) 426-6262, is the main company serving the area.

PUBLIC TRANSPORTATION: The Dallas Area Rapid Transit System (DART) provides light-rail and bus service in the area. Two-hour passes are $2.50 for local routes and $3.50 for system routes including all DART buses and trains. Day passes are $5 for local routes and $7 for system routes. A 7-day pass is available. Exact change is required. Phone (214) 979-1111.

The McKinney Avenue Trolley connects the historic West End district downtown with Uptown Dallas. Beginning near the Dallas Museum of Art, the trolley runs up McKinney Avenue to Blackburn Street and the DART Cityplace Station, and then back downtown. The tree trolley runs every 15 to 20 minutes Mon.-Thurs. 7 a.m.-10 p.m., Fri. 7 a.m.-11 p.m. and every 25 minutes Sat. 10-midnight and Sun. and holidays 10-10. Phone (214) 855-0006.

(Continued from p. 160.)

But the steep cost of Texas Instruments' innovative calculating device was a pittance compared to AT&T Stadium's $1 billion-plus price tag. Opened in 2009, the largest domed arena on the planet—with a 72-by-160-foot high-def video board, another world record-holder—is a fitting home for "America's Team."

Minuscule in contrast to the behemoth stadium, a reconstruction of city founder John Neely Bryan's one-room abode sits in the cosmopolitan heart of Dallas. Eclipsing the tiny cabin are a towering skyscraper and, figuratively at least, a simple concrete edifice just opposite—the John Fitzgerald Kennedy Memorial, funded completely by Dallas citizens in 1970.

While the city will forever be linked to one of the saddest episodes in U.S. history, it also conjures notions of ingenuity, often meshed with characteristics associated with the state—individualism, affluence and sheer size. Moreover, Dallas' moments and people, along with the imprints both leave behind, offer a succinct glimpse at America's past, present and potential.

# Must Do: AAA Editor's Picks

- Listen as the somber voice of one of the first reporters to broadcast news of our 35th president's assassination directs you through 🎧 **The Sixth Floor Museum at Dealey Plaza.** Poignant exhibits documenting John F. Kennedy's life and legacy are housed in the former Texas School Book Depository, the building in which investigators found Lee Harvey Oswald's rifle and "sniper's perch" on Nov. 22, 1963.

- After visiting The Sixth Floor Museum (and *before* paying your respects at the nearby **John Fitzgerald Kennedy Memorial**), stroll around **Dealey Plaza.** Try to visualize the crowds cheering Kennedy's motorcade as it makes its ill-fated turn onto Elm Street. For the best view of the area, climb the infamous grassy knoll—at its crest, a concrete pergola honoring Dallas founder John Neely Bryan has become the unofficial headquarters for dedicated conspiracy theorists.

- Bring your wallet—and your appetite—to **Neiman Marcus' flagship store,** opened at Main and Ervay streets in downtown Dallas in 1914. While elegant displays peddle glittery baubles and satiny garments, the legendary strawberry butter-topped popovers of the **Zodiac Restaurant,** located on level six, pretty much sell themselves.

- Continue browsing throughout this stylish locale, which boasts more retail opportunities per capita than any other major U.S. city. For designer labels (Chanel and Diane von Furstenberg), exquisite jewels and timepieces (Harry Winston), and distinctive footwear (Jimmy Choo and Christian Louboutin), well-heeled Texans patronize **Highland Park Village,** a lovely, tree-shaded shopping center established in 1931.

- Snag tickets to see the NBA Mavericks or the NHL Stars play at the **American Airlines Center** in Victory Park, centered at the intersection of I-35, the Dallas North Tollway and SR 366 (Woodall Rodgers Freeway).

- Explore the 68-acre **Downtown Dallas Arts District,** southeast of SR 366 at Ross Avenue and St. Paul Street. In addition to sheltering such impressive cultural venues as the AT&T Performing Arts Center, the **Crow Collection of Asian Art,** the 🎧 **Dallas Museum of Art** and the **Nasher Sculpture Center,** the area boasts outdoor public artwork displays and architectural stunners like the Cathedral Shrine of the Virgin of Guadalupe, a High Victorian Gothic structure dedicated in 1902.

- Cheer on hard-knuckled athletes at the **Mesquite ProRodeo Series,** a rugged competition founded in Mesquite in 1958 by a group of cowboys—among them five-time world champion bull rider Harry Tomkins and Jim Shoulders, the "Babe Ruth of Rodeo." From June through August, participants showcase such essential Texan skills as lassoing and bronco riding in the slick Mesquite Arena.

- Ascend **Reunion Tower,** part of the **Hyatt Regency Dallas at Reunion** complex, and dine 560 feet off the ground at **Five Sixty by Wolfgang Puck,** which features fine Asian-style cuisine and floor-to-ceiling windows affording panoramic views of the city.

- Travel to nearby Arlington to see Dallas' five-time Super Bowl winners pull on their star-stamped helmets. If the Cowboys aren't playing, you can still tour the team's imposing (and costly) domed home, **AT&T Stadium.**

- Catch a concert, check out agricultural exhibits and indulge in deep-fried delicacies at the **State Fair of Texas.** Beginning in late September, the country's largest state fair attracts more than 3 million people annually to historic 🎧 **Fair Park.**

Browse the stylish Neiman Marcus flagship store

# Dallas 1-day Itinerary

AAA editors suggest these activities for a great short vacation experience.

## Morning

- Nab locally made garments, ceramics and jewelry in the Bishop Arts District, just southwest of downtown in Oak Cliff, the historic neighborhood where Bonnie Parker and Clyde Barrow met, Lee Harvey Oswald was captured and 7-Eleven originated. If you're an early riser, slurp eye-opening brews at hometown coffee joint Café Brazil, 611 N. Bishop Ave., or, if it's a Sunday, sleep in and do brunch at oh-so-chic **Hattie's.** A sound contender for any "Best of Dallas" list, this urbane eatery with a Southern accent doles out polished versions of your favorite stick-to-your-ribs comfort foods.

- After your morning cup of joe (and perhaps a few of Hattie's cornmeal griddlecakes), drive to one of the following AAA GEM attractions: the ▼**Dallas Zoo,** ▼**Fair Park** or the ▼**Dallas Arboretum.** Furry fun awaits at the state's largest and oldest zoo, and Fair Park's bounty of entertaining educational facilities keeps groups (especially those with little ones) busy for hours. Last but not least, the lush, 66-acre Dallas Arboretum, about 9 miles northeast of the Bishop Arts District, encompasses more than a dozen display gardens and overlooks scenic White Rock Lake, a haven for nature-loving recreationalists.

Enjoy a lavish dinner at The French Room in The Adolphus

## Afternoon

- Now that you've explored the Dallas outskirts a bit, make your way inward and investigate downtown. At the heart of the city is ▼**The Sixth Floor Museum at Dealey Plaza,** a thought-provoking exhibit space preserving a painful moment in U.S. history: the assassination of President John F. Kennedy. Preoccupied visitors mentally re-create the heart-wrenching day in 1963 when a sniper delivered a fatal blow to the country's youngest elected head of state. After investigating Dealey Plaza, most sightseers head east to pay their respects to the fallen leader at the **John Fitzgerald Kennedy Memorial,** a minimalist cenotaph designed by renowned American architect Philip Johnson.

- From the JFK memorial (on Market Street between Main and Commerce streets), walk a few blocks east to Main and Ervay streets and look for the red awnings outside the oldest Neiman Marcus in operation. As an alternative to window browsing at the high-end retailer's flagship store, peruse paintings and other inspirational works in the Downtown Dallas Arts District. The 19-block area at Ross Avenue and St. Paul Street encompasses several cultural gems, including the ▼**Dallas Museum of Art** and the **Nasher Sculpture Center.**

- If you chose colorful frocks over vibrant brushstrokes, enjoy an elegant lunch at Neiman Marcus' fashionable eatery, the **Zodiac**

**Restaurant.** Otherwise, seek out one of the Lone Star State staples north of downtown. Friendly crews rustle up tasty, slow-smoked vittles at the original **Sonny Bryan's BBQ** near Dallas Love Field, and at **Peggy Sue BBQ** you'll dine among Southern Methodist University undergrads well learned in Texas 'cue.

## Evening

- If you want to get gussied up, make reservations for **The French Room,** one of the finest gastronomic experiences this side of the Mississippi. Located in **The Adolphus** hotel, the lavish restaurant dazzles the eyes with ornate decor, while classic, expertly prepared recipes arouse cultivated taste buds. Or, for a dressed-down dinner, try cozy **Mia's Tex-Mex Restaurant,** a family-run eatery that tips its ten-gallon hat south of the border. A few bites of Butch's Original Brisket Tacos and you'll quickly understand why clued-in natives perpetually pack this low-key dining room.

- Attend an event at the American Airlines Center. Home to the NBA Mavericks and the NHL Stars, the well-appointed arena also welcomes an array of entertainers. For pre- or post-event cocktails, the surrounding Victory Park area (a developing playground for Dallas' "in crowd") has a handful of nightspots, though visiting VIPs like Jamie Foxx and Justin Timberlake favor the pulsing lounges of the **W Dallas Victory Hotel & Residences.** If you can't get tickets for an AAC event, barhop along Greenville or McKinney avenues or mingle with laid-back Dallasites in the Knox-Henderson area, where imaginative eateries cater to bohemian bellies.

# Top Picks for Kids

## Under 13

- At most **Dallas Children's Theater** productions, full-grown actors take center stage as princesses, villains and not-so-creepy bugs. But on occasion, rising talent from the youth conservatory steal the spotlight at these engaging shows held at the Rosewood Center for Family Arts.

- Armed with a little imagination, kids exploring the 19th- and 20th-century buildings at **Dallas Heritage Village at Old City Park** can discover what life was like for tough Texan pioneers.

- Themed dining areas and a zany waitstaff turn the tables on adults at the **Magic Time Machine.** While the longtime eatery isn't one of Dallas' trendy, high-end restaurants, it *is* extremely popular with VIGs—that is, Very Important Grade-schoolers. Dressed appropriately in superhero tights and fairy-tale frocks, servers crack jokes, sign autographs, and lead pint-size patrons to the "Salad Car," a salad bar whose vintage roadster design entices even finicky eaters to load up on veggies.

- Monets and Picassos in training get their scribble on at the **Dallas Museum of Art.** During regularly scheduled family-friendly events, fun activities—everything from paper leaf-making to story time with Arturo the Parrot, the museum's cartoon mascot—keep developing minds stimulated.

## Teens

- Think about it: Generation X and beyond have no firsthand knowledge of President John F.

Kennedy's assassination. But, through films, photos and eyewitness accounts, **The Sixth Floor Museum at Dealey Plaza** vividly re-creates one of the darkest days in American history. If the somber subject matter concerns you, ask for the toned-down youth version of the self-guiding audio tour.

- Cheering on the home team is guaranteed fun for young and old alike, as are behind-the-scenes tours of domed **AT&T Stadium** and jewel box–style **Rangers Ballpark in Arlington.** While gridiron action and the crack of the bat are only about 25 miles west of Dallas, an anxious "Are we there yet?" will be on teenage sports fans' lips before you even leave the hotel parking lot.

- **Six Flags Over Texas,** also in Arlington, is a no-brainer for groups with fearless youngsters in tow. When they're not launching 25 stories into the air on Superman: Tower of Power, kids will be texting their friends back home about the Texas Giant's "sick" (extremely awesome, in teen-speak) 79-degree drop. If you're visiting in summer, pack the swimsuits, too—just across the street is **Six Flags Hurricane Harbor,** which doles out enough splish-splashy action to keep the brood busy a second day.

## All Ages

- It doesn't matter if you're 4 or 14 going on 24—**Galleria Dallas** is a pretty cool place, and not just because it has an ice rink. At the American Girl store, beloved dolls can be treated to both brunch and a deluxe spa treatment. Your littlest wee ones will love running amok at Play Place; the cushiony jungle-themed playground on Level 3 is the site of the mall's free weekly kids event, Showtime Saturdays.

- A wild, unscripted reality show airs daily at the **Dallas Zoo.** Watch hulking African elephants flapping their ears to keep cool and young lions roughhousing to hone their hunting skills. On the other end of the spectrum are the koalas, which spend most of the day dozing. Why? Eucalyptus leaves, the cute-'n'-fuzzy marsupials' favorite treat, have a sedative effect.

- The stomping ground of many Dallas families, **Fair Park** hosts a fall fried foods bonanza (the **State Fair of Texas**) as well as sporting events, concerts and plays. It's also home to several year-round centers of learning. Drop by the **Children's Aquarium at Fair Park's** hair-raising stingray touch tank or check out the butterfly house and insectarium at **Texas Discovery Gardens at Fair Park.**

- Adventure awaits at **The Dallas World Aquarium.** Spirited kindergartners go bananas imitating very vocal red howler monkeys in the Orinoco South American rainforest experience. And brown, sawfish and bonnethead sharks in the Mundo Maya exhibit will capture the attention of older kids.

Take the family to Six Flags Over Texas

## Arriving
### By Car

Major highways provide quick access to the city. US 75 (North Central Expressway) and the Dallas North Tollway approach from the north, I-45 (South Central Expressway) from the southeast, I-20 and I-30 (R.L. Thornton Freeway) from the east, and I-30 (Tom Landry Freeway) from the west. I-35 runs northwest to southwest.

## Getting Around
### Street System

Because the streets of Dallas are not designed in the traditional grid pattern, it is wise to refer to a map when driving downtown. Major thoroughfares run from northwest to southeast and northeast to southwest. The principal street is Main Street, which runs southwest to northeast; other key streets include Elm Street, which is one way northeast.

The speed limit on most streets is 35 mph or as posted. Freeway limits range from 40 to 75 mph as posted. Rush hours are generally from 7:30 to 9 a.m. and from 4 to 6:30 p.m. Most signal lights are on the corners, but be alert for signals hanging in the center of intersections. Right turns are permitted on red; exceptions are marked.

### Parking

Numerous garages and parking lots compensate for the virtual absence of on-street parking downtown. Rates range from $3 to $5 each half-hour or $10 to $18 a day.

## Shopping

Even veteran shopaholics agree—Dallas's bevy of high-end retailers and local boutiques intensifies such fashionista pastimes as shoe hoarding and bargain bin diving. And, if choice must-haves ripped from the pages of *Elle* don't have you reaching for your wallet, the city's uptown art galleries and folksy antique spots surely will. For "Big D" exclusives, stray off the beaten path and follow the natives—department store divas and dapper dudes in designer denim—to Dallas's most splurge-worthy showrooms.

If you're *really* itching to shop 'til you drop, head north out of downtown Dallas. Mall walkers keep in tip-top shape at numerous suburban shopping centers, including the **Collin Creek Mall,** 18 miles north of Dallas in Plano. In town, at the intersection of the Dallas North Tollway and I-635, hundreds of stores encircle an indoor ice-skating art gallery in **Galleria Dallas,** anchored by Macy's, Nordstrom and Saks Fifth Avenue. Streamlined **NorthPark Center,** at the corner of SR 12 and US 75, keeps fashion-conscious Dallasites looking fab in everything from eclectic Betsey Johnson ensembles to luxurious textiles sold by Barneys New York and Burberry.

In **Uptown,** you'll rub elbows with decked-out mannequins and carefree natives pursuing the life of Riley. Drive along McKinney Avenue, this historic neighborhood's main thoroughfare, or hop on the McKinney Avenue Trolley to reach the trendy restaurants, hip art galleries and specialty boutiques that keep Uptown in vogue. Contemporary condos and lofts accommodate an abundance of young urbanites, as does **West Village,** a vibrant mix of national and local retailers and dining establishments at McKinney and Lemmon avenues.

The nearby **Park Cities** enclave, which comprises Dallas County municipalities Highland Park and University Park, boasts some of the highest per capita incomes in the state of Texas. As a result, this milieu is rife with posh salesrooms loaded with the same designer threads worshipped by East and West Coast elite. Among Park Cities' many shopping destinations, **Highland Park Village** at Preston Road and Mockingbird Lane is one of the most cherished, having served residents of picture-perfect vicinity mansions since 1931. The open-air, Mediterranean-style retail hub lures discerning buyers with tailor-made, hand-sewn garments; prestigious labels like Chanel, Escada and Hermès; and exquisite decorative baubles.

Named for two streets that meet at the North Central Expressway (US 75), the **Knox-Henderson** area near Southern Methodist University puts the spotlight on home décor. The west side (Knox Street) showcases big names like Pottery Barn and Restoration Hardware; the east side (Henderson Avenue) charms deal-hungry nostalgics with an array of whimsical antiques. **Froggie's 5 & 10,** a quirky Knox-Henderson toy shop, also attracts pranksters and pint-size shopaholics, while vintage clothes junkies pick through flashy boas and rhinestone-studded jewelry at resale shops like **Pandemonium! Ltd.**

Speed limit on most city streets is 35 mph

The flagship store of **Neiman Marcus,** founded in Dallas in the early 1900s, lies at the heart of downtown. Red awnings shade window-browsers at Main and Ervay streets, while elegant accouterments—from gold-trimmed escalators to ornate chandeliers—offer the red carpet treatment to those who venture inside. After perusing Neiman's extravagant trinkets, head to level six to nosh on decadent morsels (like strawberry butter-topped popovers) at the Zodiac Restaurant, a local institution for more than 50 years.

Though downtown doesn't have much of a central shopping district, recent revitalization projects have attracted some business owners to the Dallas core. Cruise through **Victory Park,** a developing shopping and entertainment hub at the intersection of I-35, the Dallas North Tollway and SR 366, and you'll find a handful of chic stores and eateries as well as this sleek area's crown jewel: the American Airlines Center. Home to the NBA Mavericks and the NHL Stars, the arena features a sports memorabilia shop (open Mon.-Sat. 10-5 with complimentary parking in Lot F) at Victory Avenue and All Star Way.

When they're not bicycling through the surrounding Oak Cliff neighborhood, active city dwellers stretch their imaginations in the compact **Bishop Arts District,** just southwest of downtown at Bishop Avenue and Davis Street.

## Nightlife

Having trouble deciding where to see and be seen in Dallas? Just cruise along **McKinney Avenue,** the main drag in the hip Uptown neighborhood, to find the city's most sizzling hot spots. For an upscale meal paired with a few late-night cocktails, several establishments fit the bill, including **Sambuca,** 2120 McKinney Ave., a small chain founded in Dallas in 1991. Playing everything from alternative country to jazz and blues, live bands keep hips swaying and toes tapping at the sultry dinner club; phone (214) 744-0820.

Two other tried-and-true Uptown mainstays—both cozy nighttime haunts loved by locals—are **The Quarter Bar,** 3301 McKinney Ave., and **The Ginger Man,** 2718 Boll St. Part of Bread Winners Cafe & Bakery, the former oozes New Orleans French Quarter charm and tempts voyeurs with a rooftop terrace overlooking McKinney. The latter welcomes any combination of sipping, slurping or chugging, especially when done al fresco in the bar's handsome beer garden. Phone (214) 754-4940 for The Quarter Bar or (214) 754-8771 for The Ginger Man.

Perfect your barhopping skills on **Greenville Avenue,** a commercial thoroughfare with casual eateries, stores and, most importantly, watering holes galore. Pockets of low-key taverns—many offering rooftop lounges—dot **Lower Greenville,** which runs between Ross Avenue and Mockingbird Lane. Fall in love with a fresh-faced indie band at **The Crown and Harp,** 1914 Greenville Ave., (214) 828-1914; snack, chat and swig at **The Libertine Bar,** 2101 Greenville Ave., (214) 824-7900; or groove in vintage style at **The Granada Theater,** 3524 Greenville

Groove in vintage style at The Granada Theater

Ave., (214) 824-9933, where alternative rock and funk sounds reverberate off Art Deco architectural elements.

In **Upper Greenville,** the bars are more spread out, though there's a small concentration of Southern Methodist University hangouts just north of Mockingbird Lane. Thirsty revelers settle in for cold pitchers and darts matchups at dives like the **Across the Street Bar, Milo Butterfingers** and **The Green Elephant,** all of which are near the intersection of Greenville and SMU Boulevard. Phone (214) 363-0660 for the Across the Street Bar, (214) 368-9212 for Milo Butterfingers or (214) 265-1338 for The Green Elephant.

SMU undergrads also party in the trendy **Knox-Henderson** area, named for two streets that meet at the North Central Expressway (from Ross Avenue in Lower Greenville, Henderson Avenue juts in a north-westerly direction toward Knox Street). Mingle with Ms. Pac-Man and Skee-Ball aficionados in retro-paradise **Barcadia,** 1917 N. Henderson Ave., or sip some sweet tea-infused vodka on the porch at **The Porch,** 2912 N. Henderson Ave. If ales, stouts and drafts are more your thing, drink with other foam-mustached patrons at **The Old Monk,** 2847 N. Henderson Ave. Chock-full of antiques, the seemingly age-old pub has been a local favorite since it opened in 1998. Phone (214) 821-7300 for Barcadia, (214) 828-2916 for The Porch or (214) 821-1880 for The Old Monk.

With the arrival of the American Airlines Center to downtown Dallas, high-end enterprises boasting high-tech amenities have sprung up in the surrounding **Victory Park** area like Texas wildflowers.

One of the most stunning additions to this still-developing district is the indulgent W Dallas Victory Hotel & Residences, 2440 Victory Park Ln. **The Living Room,** a chic but comfy lounge just off the W's lobby, has an outdoor patio, DJ music nightly and live jazz on Wednesday evenings; phone (214) 397-4100.

Near Continental Avenue and Houston Street in Victory Park, a handful of familiar bar/restaurants—[SAVE] Hard Rock Cafe, **Hooters** and **House of Blues**—stay open late Friday and Saturday evenings. Another fun pit stop when it's well past your bedtime is **Dick's Last Resort,** where bad behavior is rewarded. Smart-aleck servers take pride in ridiculing customers at the Dallas-based chain, which also brings new meaning to the word "obnoxious" in Boston, Chicago, San Diego and other major U.S. cities. Phone (469) 341-7625 for Hard Rock Cafe, (214) 979-9464 for Hooters, (214) 978-2583 for House of Blues or (214) 747-0001 for Dick's Last Resort.

**Deep Ellum**'s seen it all—from flapper do's and fedoras to Mohawks and metal piercings. Settled by freed slaves in the late 1800s, the neighborhood (east of downtown Dallas and centering on Main, Commerce and Elm streets) emerged as a hub for jazz and blues in the 1920s, with such entertainers as Bessie Smith and Robert Johnson packing 'em in nightly. Decades later, resourceful impresarios transformed the then-rundown district, turning empty warehouses into temples for worshiping punk rock gods like Black Flag and the Dead Kennedys.

Crowded with tattoo parlors, homespun eateries and nightclubs by the 1990s, Deep Ellum had found

Take a walk on the wild side in Deep Ellum

its calling—again. But then, the scene, as most do, died. These days, you'll largely find shuttered remnants from the entertainment district's most recent heyday; however, by many accounts, Deep Ellum stands poised for a comeback. In the meantime, lingering stalwarts like down-home **Adair's Saloon,** 2624 Commerce St.; the **Angry Dog** bar and grill, 2726 Commerce St., said to serve up the meanest, tastiest frankfurter in Dallas; and a newly renovated **Trees,** 2709 Elm St., known for "live, loud music" since Deep Ellum's glory days, remain popular with those who like to walk on the wild side. Phone (214) 939-9900 for Adair's Saloon, (214) 741-4406 for the Angry Dog or (214) 741-1122 for Trees.

## Big Events

Downtown on New Year's Day, floats and marching bands kick off Dallas' year with the **Comerica Bank New Year's Parade.** The AT&T Cotton Bowl Classic football game draws crowds to Arlington's **AT&T Stadium** in early January.

Spring is ushered in with **Dallas Blooms,** a festival of flowers held during March and early April at the **Dallas Arboretum.** Closing out spring is Dallas Symphony's free **Memorial Day Concert** at **Flagpole Hill.**

During the summer entertainers perform at **Fair Park**'s outdoor Gexa Energy Pavilion and the band shell. Another theatrical highlight is **Shakespeare in the Park,** which presents plays select days from mid-June through late September in **Samuell-Grand Park.**

Fair Park is home, mid-September to mid-October, to the **State Fair of Texas,** which many Texans consider the biggest and best state fair in the country.

In November, **Texas Stampede** offers championship rodeos and country music performances at the **Allen Events Center** in Allen.

## Sports & Rec

Athletes can enjoy many sports offered in and near Dallas. The list ranges from **golf** to **horseback riding** to **ice skating.** Many city parks have public golf courses, **tennis** courts and **swimming** pools. For **fishing, boating** and **water-skiing** enthusiasts, there are a number of lakes within an hour's drive.

A variety of professional sports is played in Dallas and nearby cities. Surely the best-known local team is the National **Football** League's **Dallas Cowboys,** who in 2009 inaugurated the 80,000-seat **AT&T Stadium** in Arlington (see attraction listing p. 66). The state-of-the-art sports complex hosts the annual AT&T Cotton Bowl Classic and was the venue for the 2011 Super Bowl XLV.

The National **Basketball** Association's **Dallas Mavericks,** who claimed their first NBA crown in 2011, and the National **Hockey** League's **Dallas Stars** play at American Airlines Center. The American League's **Texas Rangers** play **baseball** at **Rangers Ballpark in Arlington.** Rounding out

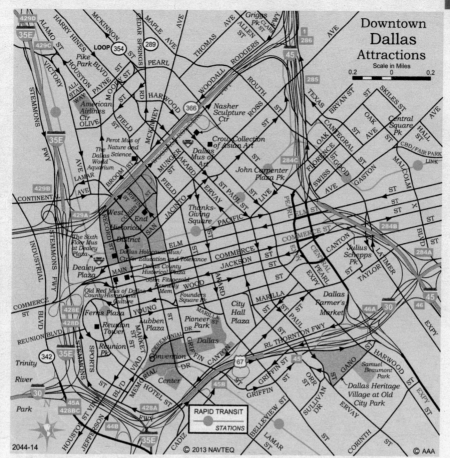

Downtown
**Dallas**
Attractions

Scale in Miles
0.2   0   0.2

RAPID TRANSIT

STATIONS

2044-14   © 2013 NAVTEQ   © AAA

the local professional-sports lineup, **FC Dallas** of Major League **Soccer** play at **FC Dallas Stadium.**

Also popular are amateur basketball and tennis tournaments. During fair weather, **sailing** buffs can enjoy the amateur races on Sunday at **White Rock Lake.** Professional **rodeos** are held weekends April through September in suburban Mesquite *(see place listing p. 416).*

## Performing Arts

September through May Dallas echoes with the sound of music. The celebrated **Dallas Symphony Orchestra** performs at **Morton H. Meyerson Symphony Center,** a short distance from the Dallas Museum of Art. Each spring the symphony heralds the arrival of the season with free park concerts; phone (214) 871-4000.

Summer brings the **Dallas Summer Musicals** to the **Music Hall at Fair Park** *(see attraction listing p. 172)* and varied performers to **Gexa Energy Pavilion.** The **Dallas Black Dance Theatre** troupe can be seen during the year at the **Dee and Charles Wyly Theatre** in the **AT&T Performing Arts Center,** 2403 Flora

Ave.; phone (214) 954-9925, or (214) 880-0202 for the box office. Stage plays are presented by **Dallas Theatre Center** at the Dee and Charles Wyly Theatre and the **Kalita Humphreys Theater,** 3636 Turtle Creek Blvd.; phone (214) 522-8499.

The **Dallas Children's Theater** presents family-friendly fare at the **Rosewood Center for Family Arts,** 5938 Skillman St. Performances typically take place Friday evenings at 7:30 and Saturdays and Sundays at 1:30 and 4:30; phone (214) 740-0051.

## ⚑ ATTRACTIONS

**CROW COLLECTION OF ASIAN ART** is at 2010 Flora St. Sculpture, jade artifacts, paintings, lacquer, ceramics, bronze works and silk screens from China, Japan, India and Southeast Asia are on display. Most art bears a religious significance, and the museum also houses items from the Qing dynasty. Gallery talks and tours are available. **Time:** Allow 30 minutes minimum. **Hours:** Tues.-Thurs. 10-9, Fri.-Sat.10-6, Sun. noon-6. Closed Christmas. **Cost:** Free. **Phone:** (214) 979-6430.

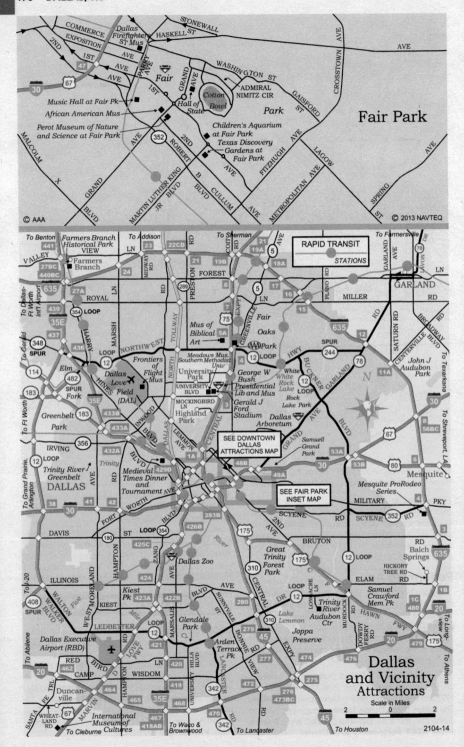

## Fair Park

- Music Hall at Fair Pk
- African American Mus
- Perot Museum of Nature and Science at Fair Park

Dallas Firefighters St Mus

COMMERCE
EXPOSITION
2ND
1ST
AVE
AVE
AVE
47
67
30

STONEWALL
HASKELL ST
WASHINGTON ST

Fair

Hall of State

Cotton Bowl

ADMIRAL NIMITZ CIR

Park

GRAND
AVE
1ST
352
2ND
ROBERT
B
CULLUM
AVE
FITZHUGH
AVE
METROPOLITAN AVE
LAGOW
SPRING
CROSSTOWN
GAISFORD

Children's Aquarium at Fair Park
Texas Discovery Gardens at Fair Park

MARTIN LUTHER KING JR BLVD
GRAND
BLVD
MALCOLM

© AAA                                        © 2013 NAVTEQ

## Dallas and Vicinity Attractions

RAPID TRANSIT
STATIONS

Scale in Miles
2   0   2

2104-14

**DALLAS ARBORETUM** is at 8525 Garland Rd. on White Rock Lake. The arboretum embraces 66 acres of trees, flowers and display gardens with ornamental, perennial and color themes. Visitors are encouraged to relax on the spacious lawn and take in a view of the picturesque gardens.

A Woman's Garden features an enclosed sanctuary, wind-activated harps and a reflective basin. The Texas Pioneer Adventure is a 2.5-acre exhibit with seven gardens, a sod house, two replica cabins, a Native American teepee, a covered wagon and interactive displays. Tours of the 1930s DeGolyer House and Gardens are available.

**Hours:** Daily 9-5. Closed Jan. 1, Thanksgiving and Christmas. **Cost:** $15; $12 (ages 65+); $10 (ages 3-12). **Parking:** $10. **Phone:** (214) 515-6500.

**DALLAS HERITAGE VILLAGE AT OLD CITY PARK** is downtown at 1515 S. Harwood St. The village is a collection of 38 relocated and restored 1840-1910 structures. On the 13-acre site are a working farm, several historic businesses, an antebellum mansion and a 1901 Conservative Jewish home. **Tours:** Guided tours are available. **Hours:** Tues.-Sat. 10-4, Sun. noon-4, Feb.-July and Sept.-Dec. Closed Jan. 1, Thanksgiving, Christmas Eve, Christmas and Dec. 31. **Cost:** $9; $6 (ages 65+); $5 (ages 4-12). **Phone:** (214) 421-5141.

**DALLAS HOLOCAUST MUSEUM/CENTER FOR EDUCATION AND TOLERANCE** is at 211 N. Record St., Suite 100. Dedicated to educating the public about the importance of tolerance and compassion, the museum features permanent and changing exhibits about the Nazi regime's systematic extermination of Jews and other groups during World War II. Audio guides, available in English and Spanish, provide narration during the self-guiding tour.

**Time:** Allow 1 hour, 30 minutes minimum. **Hours:** Mon.-Fri. 9:30-5, Sat.-Sun. 11-5. Closed Jan. 1, Easter, July 4, Rosh Hashanah, Yom Kippur, Thanksgiving, Christmas Eve and Christmas. **Cost:** (Includes audio guide) $8; $6 (ages 6-18, senior citizens and active military with ID). **Phone:** (214) 741-7500.

**DALLAS MUSEUM OF ART** is at 1717 N. Harwood St. Displays range from pre-Columbian and African artifacts to Impressionist and contemporary works. The permanent collection boasts Asian bronzeworks, masks from the Pacific, European paintings, African Congo sculpture, Colonial decorative arts and works by contemporary artists.

Exhibits include works by Henri Matisse, Claude Monet and John Singer Sargent, sculpture by Henry Moore and Auguste Rodin and paintings by Georgia O'Keeffe and Jackson Pollock. Traveling displays, smartphone tours and thematic guided tours are offered. Modern sculpture and fountains adorn the grounds.

**Time:** Allow 2 hours minimum. **Hours:** Tues.-Sun. 11-5 (also Thurs. 5-9 and third Fri. of the month 5-midnight). Closed July 4, Thanksgiving and Christmas. **Cost:** Free general admission (includes

Dallas Arboretum

entrance to the museum's galleries and most exhibitions). Some special exhibitions require a ticket of $16; $14 (ages 65+ and military with ID); $12 (students with Texas ID); free (ages 0-11). Phone ahead to verify when tickets are required. **Phone:** (214) 922-1200, or (214) 922-1818 for tickets.

**The Wendy and Emery Reves Collection** is on the third floor of the Dallas Museum of Art. The collection includes Impressionist and post-Impressionist works by such masters as Paul Cézanne, Paul Gauguin, Claude Monet, Pierre Auguste Renoir and Vincent van Gogh. Also displayed are antique furniture, Chinese porcelain and Winston Churchill memorabilia. The wing re-creates rooms of the Reves' Mediterranean villa. Guided tours are available by appointment. **Time:** Allow 1 hour minimum. **Cost:** Free with paid admission to Dallas Museum of Art. **Phone:** (214) 922-1200.

**THE DALLAS WORLD AQUARIUM** is 1 blk. n. of Ross Ave. at 1801 N. Griffin St. in the West End district. The aquarium is home to such marine life as stingrays, wrasses and rare leafy sea dragons. Monkeys, crocodiles, otters and manatees live in the Venezuelan rain forest habitat. A 40-foot tunnel allows visitors to surround themselves with sharks, rays and sawfish in the Mundo Maya exhibit. The Cape of Good Hope exhibit is home to a penguin colony.

**Time:** Allow 1 hour minimum. **Hours:** Daily 9-5, Mar.-Aug.; 10-5, rest of year. Closed Thanksgiving and Christmas. **Cost:** $20.95; $16.95 (ages 60+); $12.95 (ages 3-12). **Parking:** $5. **Phone:** (214) 720-2224 or (800) 732-7957.

**DALLAS ZOO** is 3 mi. s. on I-35E (Marsalis Ave. exit) at 650 S. R.L. Thornton Frwy. A 67.5-foot giraffe statue greets visitors at the entrance. The 106-acre zoo features rare and endangered species and includes a gorilla conservation center. Giants of the Savanna offers an urban safari experience, featuring African elephants, giraffes, lions, cheetahs and more. The 25-acre Wilds of Africa exhibit re-creates six habitats: bush, desert, forest, mountain, river and woodland. Visitors can take a monorail ride through the African exhibit or walk a 1,500-foot nature trail.

Sumatran tigers live in the ExxonMobil Endangered Tiger Habitat. The naturalistic, open-air environment of the Kimberly-Clark Chimpanzee Forest encourages the primates to climb, search for food and interact. African penguins frolic in another habitat, Otter Outpost features a family of Asian small-clawed otters, and Koala Walkabout is home to lorikeets, kookaburras and koalas. The Lacerte Family Children's Zoo features exhibits and activities related to wildlife conservation.

**Hours:** Daily 9-5. Monorail hours vary; phone ahead. Closed Christmas. **Cost:** Mar.-May $15; $12 (ages 3-11 and 65+). Rest of year $12; $9 (ages 3-11 and 65+). Monorail $3. Prices may vary; phone ahead. **Parking:** $8. **Phone:** (469) 554-7500.

**FAIR PARK** is 2 mi. e. of downtown off I-30. This 277-acre national historic landmark was the site of a world's fair and the 1936 Texas Centennial Exposition. The park is home to museums, performance facilities, the Texas Vietnam Veterans Memorial, the Cotton Bowl Stadium and a collection of 1930s Art Deco exposition-style architecture.

**Note:** When visiting the park at night, it is advisable to park in an attended lot and travel with a companion. **Hours:** Grounds daily 8-10. **Cost:** Free. Admission and hours for museums vary; phone ahead. **Phone:** (214) 670-8400, or (214) 421-9600 for event information.

**African American Museum** is at 3536 Grand Ave. Art, culture and history are preserved at this museum, which boasts high wooden ceilings. Historical collections such as the Texas Black Women's History Archives Collection and the Freedman's Cemetery Artifact Collection are included. Other artifacts, African American fine art, folk art and archives also are displayed. **Time:** Allow 30 minutes minimum. **Hours:** Tues.-Fri. and Martin Luther King Jr. Day 11-5, Sat. 10-5, Sun. 1-5. Closed major holidays. **Cost:** Free. **Phone:** (214) 565-9026.

**Children's Aquarium at Fair Park** is at 1462 First Ave. Bonnethead sharks, upside-down jellyfish and a 190-pound alligator snapping turtle are among the unusual creatures that call this kid-geared aquarium home. Visitors can feed stingrays, pet critters in a touch tank and watch feeding demonstrations.

**Time:** Allow 1 hour minimum. **Hours:** Daily 9-4:30. Closed Thanksgiving and Christmas. **Cost:** $8; $6 (ages 3-11 and 65+). **Phone:** (469) 554-7340.

**Dallas Firefighters Museum** is at 3801 Parry Ave. This museum commemorates the history and service of the Dallas Fire Department from 1872 to the present. Horse-drawn and motorized fire engines, fire-fighting equipment and memorabilia are displayed in the Old No. 5 Hook & Ladder Station, erected in 1907. **Hours:** Wed.-Sat. 9-4. Closed major holidays. **Cost:** $4; $2 (ages 3-18). **Phone:** (214) 821-1500.

**Hall of State** is at 3939 Grand Ave. The 1936 state building features the Museum of Texas History, statuary and two of the world's largest oil murals. A gold medallion symbolizing the six nations to which Texas has paid allegiance dominates the Great Hall. The Sharp Gallery features topical exhibits. **Hours:** Tues.-Sat. 9-5, Sun. 1-5. Closed Thanksgiving and Christmas. **Cost:** Free. **Phone:** (214) 421-4500.

**Music Hall at Fair Park** is at 909 First Ave. The hall presents the Dallas Summer Musicals and a variety of special performances. **Phone:** (214) 565-1116.

**Perot Museum of Nature and Science at Fair Park** is at 3535 Grand Ave. The museum features exhibits such as *Mineral Majesty*, *Light Play* and historical dioramas.

**Time:** Allow 1 hour minimum. **Hours:** Fri.-Sun. noon-5. Closed Thanksgiving and Christmas. **Cost:** $1; free (with admission ticket to Perot museum downtown). **Phone:** (214) 428-5555.

**Texas Discovery Gardens at Fair Park** is at 3601 Martin Luther King Jr. Blvd. The 7-acre site features

Fair Park

a two-story tropical butterfly habitat and 10 themed areas ranging from formal gardens to wildscapes. **Time:** Allow 1 hour minimum. **Hours:** Daily 10-5. Closed Jan. 1, Thanksgiving, Christmas Eve and Christmas. **Cost:** $8; $6 (ages 60+); $4 (ages 3-11). **Phone:** (214) 428-7476.

**FRONTIERS OF FLIGHT MUSEUM** is at the southeast corner of Dallas Love Field at 6911 Lemmon Ave. The *Apollo 7* spacecraft, a moon rock and a complete Southwest Airlines Boeing 737 are among items chronicling the history of aviation from early mythology through modern space travel. The museum also features exhibits about the Wright Brothers and World War II aircraft as well as displays of models, engines, missiles and a space suit.

  **Time:** Allow 1 hour minimum. **Hours:** Mon.-Sat. 10-5, Sun. 1-5. Closed Jan. 1, Thanksgiving and Christmas. **Cost:** $8; $6 (ages 65+); $5 (ages 3-17). **Phone:** (214) 350-3600 or (214) 350-1651.

**JOHN FITZGERALD KENNEDY MEMORIAL** is on Market St., between Main and Commerce sts. This monument to the 35th president, who was assassinated nearby in 1963, was designed by renowned American architect Philip Johnson as a cenotaph, or open tomb. Its stark design allows visitors to reflect and find their own spiritual meanings. **Cost:** Free. **Phone:** (214) 747-6660.

**MEDIEVAL TIMES DINNER AND TOURNAMENT** is off I-35 exit Market Center Blvd. (430B), then 1.5 mi. n.w. to 2021 N. Stemmons Frwy. Visitors are guests in a replica of an 11th-century castle, where, as in medieval days, a four-course dinner is served with no silverware. During dinner, knights on horseback compete in jousting matches and events of skill and accuracy. **Time:** Allow 3 hours minimum. **Hours:** Shows daily; phone for schedule. **Cost:** $58.95; $35.95 (ages 3-12). Reservations are recommended. **Phone:** (214) 761-1800 or (888) 935-6878. 🍴

**MUSEUM OF BIBLICAL ART,** 7500 Park Ln., displays biblically themed art from around the world, including paintings, sculptures and archeological pieces. Featured artists include John Singer Sargent, Andy Warhol, Marc Chagall, Emil Nolde and Francesco Guardi. A 12-foot-tall, 40-foot-wide mural entitled "The Resurrection," a research library and an outdoor sculpture garden are among the museum's highlights.

  **Tours:** Guided tours are available. **Time:** Allow 1 hour minimum. **Hours:** Tues.-Sat. 10-5 (also Thurs. 5-9), Sun. 1-5. Closed Thanksgiving and Christmas. **Cost:** $12; $10 (ages 65+ and students with ID); $8 (ages 6-12). **Phone:** (214) 368-4622.

**MUSEUM OF GEOMETRIC AND MADI ART** is at 3109 Carlisle St. Founded in the 1940s by South American artist Carmelo Arden Quin, the MADI art movement is characterized by abstract blends of geometric shapes and vivid colors. The museum showcases nearly 1,000 works of MADI and geometric art from around the world and features changing exhibits and special events. **Time:** Allow 1 hour minimum. **Hours:** Tues.-Sat. 11-5 (also Thurs. 5-7), Sun. 1-5. Closed major holidays. **Cost:** Free. **Phone:** (214) 855-7802.

**NASHER SCULPTURE CENTER** is adjacent to the Dallas Museum of Art between Harwood and Olive sts. at 2001 Flora St. The center highlights 20th-century sculpture within galleries that have barrel-vaulted glass ceilings and within a 1.4-acre walled garden. A lower level features a gallery for works that are sensitive to light. **Time:** Allow 1 hour minimum. **Hours:** Tues.-Sun. 11-5. Closed Jan. 1, July 4, Thanksgiving, Christmas Eve and Christmas. **Cost:** $10; $7 (ages 65+ and military with ID); $5 (students with ID); free (ages 0-12 and first Sat. of the month). **Phone:** (214) 242-5100.

**OLD RED MUSEUM OF DALLAS COUNTY HISTORY AND CULTURE** is at 100 S. Houston St. Featuring videos, interactive computers and more than 1,000 items, four exhibit areas trace the history of Dallas—from its founders and agricultural heritage to its big-name stars and strong support of corporate business. There's also a hands-on learning center for kids.

  **Tours:** Guided tours are available. **Time:** Allow 1 hour, 30 minutes minimum. **Hours:** Daily 9-5. Guided tours Mon.-Fri. at 2; phone ahead to confirm availability. Closed Thanksgiving and Christmas. **Cost:** $8; $6 (ages 65+ and students ages 17+ with ID); $5 (ages 3-16 and Sun. 9-noon). **Parking:** Garage voucher $4 with proof of visit to museum. **Phone:** (214) 745-1100. 🍴

**PEROT MUSEUM OF NATURE AND SCIENCE** is at 2201 Field St. Designed by Pritzker Prize-winning architect Thom Mayne, the 170-foot-tall, 180,000-square-foot building—a curiously textured precast concrete cube poised atop a base that's landscaped with native plants and rock shards—is an attraction in its own right. Protruding from the cube's exterior south wall is a glassed-in structure housing a 54-foot-long escalator; a "crack" in the cube's lower southeast corner reveals escalators and stairs behind a glass-and-steel atrium.

  Chock-full of simulators, computer and video animations, interactive games and the like, the state-of-the-art museum encourages a hands-on approach to learning. Eleven permanent exhibit halls explore such subjects as astronomy, human anatomy, energy, gems and minerals, ornithology, sports and engineering. The Moody Family Children's Museum, featuring entertaining and educational activities for the 5-and-under crowd, occupies one of the halls.

  Learning labs, a gallery devoted to changing exhibits and a 298-seat theater with cutting-edge projection and sound technology enhance the experience. **Note:** Tickets are timed at 30-minute intervals starting at 10 and are available on a first-come, first-served basis. Visitors are strongly advised to buy tickets in advance online to avoid sellouts and long lines.

**Hours:** Mon.-Sat. 10-6, Sun. noon-6 (also first Thurs. of the month 6-9 p.m.), late May-late Aug.; Mon.-Sat.10-5, Sun. noon-5, rest of year. Last admission 1.5 hours before closing. Closed for 4 days in late Aug. for maintenance. Phone ahead to confirm schedule. **Cost:** (Includes admission to Perot Museum of Nature and Science at Fair Park) $15; $12 (ages 12-17 and 65+); $10 (ages 2-11). Theater $5. A fee may be charged for traveling exhibits. Combination tickets are available. **Phone:** (214) 428-5555.

**REUNION TOWER** is at 300 Reunion Blvd. E. The 50-story tower is the focal point of the Reunion area, a settlement of French emigrants in the 19th century. Topped by a three-level geodesic sphere that houses a revolving restaurant and bar and an observation deck, the tower is illuminated at night.

Parking is available in the south lot at Reunion Boulevard and Sports Street. **Hours:** Observation deck Mon.-Thurs. 10-10, Fri. 10 a.m.-11:30 p.m., Sat. 9:30 a.m.-11:30 p.m., Sun. 9:30 a.m.-10 p.m. Last elevator departs 15 minutes before closing. Phone ahead to confirm schedule. **Cost:** Observation deck $16; $14 (ages 65+); $8 (ages 4-12). **Parking:** $6. **Phone:** (214) 571-5744.

**SIX FLAGS OVER TEXAS**—see Arlington p. 67.

**THE SIXTH FLOOR MUSEUM AT DEALEY PLAZA** is at 411 Elm St., in the building from which Lee Harvey Oswald shot President John F. Kennedy on Nov. 22, 1963. An audio tour, available in various languages, directs visitors through the sixth floor of the former Texas School Book Depository. Still shots taken from the well-known film captured by bystander Abraham Zapruder poignantly recreate Kennedy's final moments.

The "sniper's perch," where police found three spent cartridge shells shortly after the shooting, has been reconstructed and enclosed in glass. Near the end of the self-guiding tour, visitors also view the glass-protected corner staircase, where a rifle linked to Oswald was found.

In addition the museum showcases videos, artifacts and models that educate visitors about such topics as the social culture of the '60s and Kennedy's impact on America. Official forensic and ballistics tests, as well as other evidence used by the Warren Commission and other groups that investigated the assassination, are presented. A timeline depicts the events following the tragedy, from Oswald's capture to his own murder by local nightclub operator Jack Ruby.

Special exhibits are frequently presented in a seventh-floor gallery. **Time:** Allow 1 hour, 30 minutes minimum. **Hours:** Tues.-Sun. 10-6, Mon. noon-6. Closed Thanksgiving and Christmas. **Cost:** (Includes audio tour) $16; $14 (ages 65+); $13 (ages 6-18). Children's admission $4 (ages 0-5 with audio tour); free (ages 0-5 with no audio tour). **Phone:** (214) 747-6660 or (888) 485-4854.

**THANKS-GIVING SQUARE** is bounded by Pacific Ave. and Bryan and Ervay sts. Dedicated to promoting the spirit and unifying value of giving thanks in the community, nation and world, the square provides an oasis of calm in downtown Dallas with waterfalls, reflecting pools, a chapel, a bell tower and a meditation garden. The Hall of Thanksgiving presents detailed stories of American and other Thanksgiving traditions. **Tours:** Guided tours are available. **Hours:** Daily 10-4. **Cost:** Free. **Phone:** (214) 969-1977.

**TRINITY RIVER AUDUBON CENTER,** 6500 Great Trinity Forest Way, comprises 120 acres of hardwood forest and is home to 5 miles of nature trails, a children's garden and a variety of flora and fauna. The center's LEED-certified building was constructed with locally sourced materials and features energy-efficient heating, cooling, ventilation and electrical systems; a vegetated roof; and a rainwater collection system. Educational and recreational opportunities include guided hikes, birding classes, outdoor education, day camps, camping, kayak river adventures and owl prowls.

**Tours:** Guided tours are available. **Time:** Allow 2 hours minimum. **Hours:** Tues.-Sat. 9-4, Sun. 10-5. Closed major holidays. **Cost:** $6; $4 (ages 60+); $3 (ages 3-12); free (third Thurs. of the month). Guided tours $40. **Phone:** (214) 398-8722.

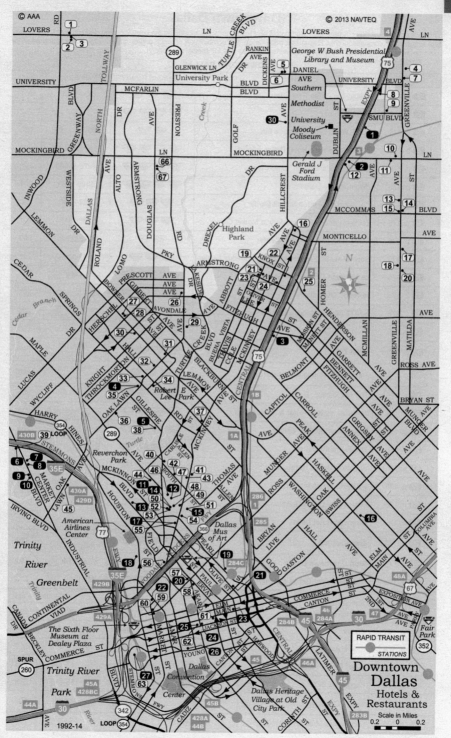

© AAA
© 2013 NAVTEQ

Downtown
Dallas
Hotels &
Restaurants

RAPID TRANSIT
STATIONS

Scale in Miles
0.2   0   0.2

George W Bush Presidential
Library and Museum

Southern
Methodist
University
Moody
Coliseum

Gerald J
Ford
Stadium

Highland
Park

Reverchon
Park

American
Airlines
Center

Trinity
River
Greenbelt

The Sixth Floor
Museum at
Dealey Plaza

Trinity River
Park

Dallas
Mus
of Art

Dallas
Convention
Center

Dallas Heritage
Village at Old
City Park

Fair
Park

1992-14

# Downtown Dallas

This index helps you "spot" where approved hotels and restaurants are located on the corresponding detailed maps. Hotel daily rate range is for comparison only. Restaurant price range is a combination of lunch and/or dinner. Turn to the listing page for more detailed rate and price information and consult display ads for special promotions.

## DOWNTOWN DALLAS

| Map Page | Hotels | Diamond Rated | Rate Range | Page |
|---|---|---|---|---|
| **1** p. 175 | Holiday Inn Dallas Park Cities | ◈◈◈ | $99-$109 | 201 |
| **2** p. 175 | **Hotel Palomar** | ◈◈◈◈ | $169-$397 SAVE | 202 |
| **3** p. 175 | **BEST WESTERN Cityplace Inn** | ◈◈ | $90-$130 SAVE | 200 |
| **4** p. 175 | **Warwick Melrose Hotel Dallas** | ◈◈◈◈ | $149-$599 SAVE | 204 |
| **5** p. 175 | Rosewood Mansion on Turtle Creek | ◈◈◈◈ | $270-$5000 | 203 |
| **6** p. 175 | Hilton Anatole Dallas | ◈◈◈◈ | $109-$359 | 201 |
| **7** p. 175 | Courtyard by Marriott-Market Center | ◈◈◈ | $84-$135 | 200 |
| **8** p. 175 | Fairfield Inn & Suites by Marriott Market Center | ◈◈◈ | $76-$110 | 201 |
| **9** p. 175 | **BEST WESTERN Market Center** | ◈◈ | $82-$200 SAVE | 200 |
| **10** p. 175 | DoubleTree by Hilton Hotel Dallas - Market Center | ◈◈◈ | $89-$309 | 201 |
| **11** p. 175 | **Le Méridien Dallas, The Stoneleigh** | ◈◈◈◈ | $119-$469 SAVE | 203 |
| **12** p. 175 | **Hotel St. Germain** | ◈◈◈◈ | $305-$700 SAVE | 202 |
| **13** p. 175 | **HYATT house Dallas/Uptown** (See ad p. 202.) | ◈◈◈ | $89-$299 SAVE | 203 |
| **14** p. 175 | Rosewood Crescent Hotel | ◈◈◈◈ | $300-$3000 | 203 |
| **15** p. 175 | **Hotel ZaZa** | ◈◈◈◈ | Rates not provided SAVE | 202 |
| **16** p. 175 | The Corinthian Bed & Breakfast | ◈◈◈ | Rates not provided | 200 |
| **17** p. 175 | The Ritz-Carlton, Dallas | ◈◈◈◈ | $399-$799 | 203 |
| **18** p. 175 | **W Dallas Victory Hotel & Residences** | ◈◈◈◈ | $279-$599 SAVE | 204 |
| **19** p. 175 | **Dallas Marriott City Center** | ◈◈◈◈ | $119-$289 SAVE | 201 |
| **20** p. 175 | **The Fairmont Dallas** | ◈◈◈◈ | $129-$699 SAVE | 201 |
| **21** p. 175 | **Sheraton Dallas Hotel** | ◈◈◈◈ | $299-$369 SAVE | 204 |
| **22** p. 175 | SpringHill Suites by Marriott | ◈◈◈ | $129-$189 | 204 |
| **23** p. 175 | Hotel Indigo Dallas Downtown | ◈◈◈ | $89-$149 | 202 |
| **24** p. 175 | **Magnolia Hotel Dallas** | ◈◈◈ | $129-$259 SAVE | 203 |
| **25** p. 175 | **The Adolphus** | ◈◈◈◈ | Rates not provided SAVE | 199 |
| **26** p. 175 | **Aloft Downtown Dallas** | ◈◈◈ | $109-$399 SAVE | 199 |
| **27** p. 175 | **Hyatt Regency Dallas at Reunion** | ◈◈◈◈ | $89-$499 SAVE | 203 |

| Map Page | Restaurants | Diamond Rated | Cuisine | Price Range | Page |
|---|---|---|---|---|---|
| 1 p. 175 | Dunston's Steak House | ◈◈ | Steak | $9-$25 | 206 |
| 2 p. 175 | **Bijoux** | ◈◈◈◈ | French | $12-$29 | 204 |
| 3 p. 175 | Cafe Instanbul | ◈◈ | Turkish | $11-$19 | 205 |
| 4 p. 175 | Prego Pasta House | ◈◈ | Italian | $7-$20 | 208 |
| 5 p. 175 | Peggy Sue BBQ | ◈◈ | Barbecue | $5-$15 | 208 |
| 6 p. 175 | Kuby's Sausage House | ◈ | Traditional German | $7-$25 | 207 |
| 7 p. 175 | Desperados Mexican Restaurant | ◈◈ | Tex-Mex | $8-$18 | 205 |

| Map Page | Restaurants (cont'd) | Diamond Rated | Cuisine | Price Range | Page |
|---|---|---|---|---|---|
| ⑧ p. 175 | Cafe Brazil University Park | ◊◊ | Breakfast | $7-$11 | 205 |
| ⑨ p. 175 | Twisted Root Burger Co | ◊ | Burgers | $6-$11 | 209 |
| ⑩ p. 175 | Burger Street | ◊ | Burgers | $3-$6 | 205 |
| ⑪ p. 175 | Campisi's Egyptian | ◊◊ | Italian | $9-$22 | 205 |
| ⑫ p. 175 | Central 214 | ◊◊◊ | New American | $8-$32 | 205 |
| ⑬ p. 175 | Aw Shucks | ◊ | Seafood | $6-$10 | 204 |
| ⑭ p. 175 | Snuffer's | ◊ | American | $7-$12 | 208 |
| ⑮ p. 175 | Woodfire Kirby's | ◊◊◊ | Steak | $13-$40 | 209 |
| ⑯ p. 175 | Javier's Gourmet Mexicano | ◊◊ | Mexican | $20-$29 | 207 |
| ⑰ p. 175 | St Martin's Wine Bistro | ◊◊◊ | French | $16-$29 | 208 |
| ⑱ p. 175 | Blue Goose Cantina | ◊◊ | Tex-Mex | $8-$20 | 205 |
| ⑲ p. 175 | Little Katana | ◊◊◊ | Japanese | $12-$32 | 207 |
| ⑳ p. 175 | The Grape | ◊◊ | French | $24-$35 | 207 |
| ㉑ p. 175 | Ziziki's Restaurant | ◊◊ | Mediterranean | $9-$26 | 209 |
| ㉒ p. 175 | Chuy's | ◊◊ | Tex-Mex | $7-$10 | 205 |
| ㉓ p. 175 | Cafe Madrid | ◊◊ | Spanish | $5-$15 | 205 |
| ㉔ p. 175 | **Abacus** | ◊◊◊◊ | Continental | $20-$60 | 204 |
| ㉕ p. 175 | The Porch | ◊◊ | American | $12-$25 | 208 |
| ㉖ p. 175 | Al Biernat's | ◊◊◊ | Steak | $20-$75 | 204 |
| ㉗ p. 175 | Mia's Tex-Mex Restaurant | ◊◊ | Tex-Mex | $7-$15 | 207 |
| ㉘ p. 175 | Bob's Steak & Chop House | ◊◊◊ | Steak | $25-$59 | 205 |
| ㉙ p. 175 | **Good Eats** | ◊◊ | American | $8-$17 | 206 |
| ㉚ p. 175 | Szechuan Chinese Restaurant | ◊ | Chinese | $7-$12 | 209 |
| ㉛ p. 175 | **Lucky's Cafe South** | ◊ | American | $7-$10 | 207 |
| ㉜ p. 175 | eatZi's | ◊ | Specialty | $5-$16 | 206 |
| ㉝ p. 175 | Green Papaya | ◊◊ | Vietnamese | $6-$13 | 207 |
| ㉞ p. 175 | Steel | ◊◊◊ | Asian | $10-$32 | 209 |
| ㉟ p. 175 | **The Landmark Restaurant** | ◊◊◊ | American | $12-$44 | 207 |
| ㊱ p. 175 | Zaguan Latin Cafe and Bakery | ◊◊ | Latin American | $7-$15 | 209 |
| ㊲ p. 175 | Bread Winners Cafe & Bakery | ◊◊ | American | $5-$30 | 205 |
| ㊳ p. 175 | The Mansion Restaurant at Rosewood Mansion on Turtle Creek | ◊◊◊◊ | Continental | $18-$64 | 207 |
| ㊴ p. 175 | SER Steak and Spirits | ◊◊◊ | Steak | $30-$50 | 208 |
| ㊵ p. 175 | Naan Sushi | ◊◊ | Sushi | $15-$25 | 208 |
| ㊶ p. 175 | Avanti Ristorante | ◊◊◊ | Italian | $14-$33 | 204 |
| ㊷ p. 175 | Dream Cafe | ◊◊ | American | $8-$20 | 206 |
| ㊸ p. 175 | S & D Oyster Company | ◊◊ | Southern Seafood | $10-$22 | 208 |
| ㊹ p. 175 | **T/X Restaurant** | ◊◊◊ | Regional American | $11-$37 | 209 |
| ㊺ p. 175 | The Meddlesome Moth | ◊◊◊ | American | $11-$28 | 207 |
| ㊻ p. 175 | The Old Warsaw | ◊◊◊ | Continental | $21-$45 | 208 |

| Map Page | Restaurants (cont'd) | Diamond Rated | Cuisine | Price Range | Page |
|---|---|---|---|---|---|
| 47 p. 175 | **Hotel St. Germain** | ▽▽▽▽ | French | $85 | 207 |
| 48 p. 175 | Arcodoro & Pomodoro | ▽▽▽ | Italian | $11-$36 | 204 |
| 49 p. 175 | Truluck's | ▽▽▽ | Seafood | $19-$45 | 209 |
| 50 p. 175 | Nobu | ▽▽▽ | Japanese | $18-$40 | 208 |
| 51 p. 175 | **Dragonfly** | ▽▽▽ | New American | $9-$35 | 206 |
| 52 p. 175 | The Capital Grille | ▽▽▽ | American | $13-$46 | 205 |
| 53 p. 175 | Palomino Restaurant | ▽▽▽ | Mediterranean | $7-$38 | 208 |
| 54 p. 175 | Morton's The Steakhouse | ▽▽▽ | Steak | $26-$70 | 207 |
| 55 p. 175 | Fearing's | ▽▽▽ | Southwestern | $18-$48 | 206 |
| 56 p. 175 | El Fenix | ▽▽ | Tex-Mex | $9-$16 | 206 |
| 57 p. 175 | **Pyramid Restaurant & Bar** | ▽▽▽▽ | American | $12-$35 | 208 |
| 58 p. 175 | Dakota's | ▽▽▽ | Steak | $12-$55 | 205 |
| 59 p. 175 | The Palm Restaurant | ▽▽▽ | Steak | $13-$52 | 208 |
| 60 p. 175 | Y.O. Ranch Steakhouse | ▽▽ | Steak | $9-$50 | 209 |
| 61 p. 175 | Zodiac Restaurant | ▽▽▽ | American | $13-$23 | 209 |
| 62 p. 175 | **The French Room** | ▽▽▽▽▽ | New French | $80 | 206 |
| 63 p. 175 | Five Sixty by Wolfgang Puck | ▽▽▽ | New Asian | $35-$70 | 206 |

**UNIVERSITY PARK**

| Map Page | Hotel | Diamond Rated | Rate Range | Page |
|---|---|---|---|---|
| 30 p. 175 | **The Lumen** | ▽▽▽ | Rates not provided [SAVE] | 558 |

**HIGHLAND PARK**

| Map Page | Restaurants | Diamond Rated | Cuisine | Price Range | Page |
|---|---|---|---|---|---|
| 66 p. 175 | Patrizio | ▽▽▽ | Northern Italian | $7-$24 | 298 |
| 67 p. 175 | Cafe Pacific | ▽▽▽ | Seafood | $12-$38 | 298 |

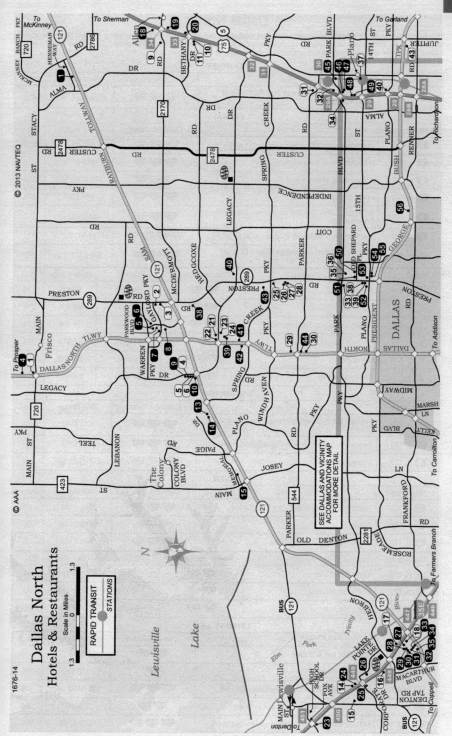

Dallas North
Hotels & Restaurants

# Dallas North

This index helps you "spot" where approved hotels and restaurants are located on the corresponding detailed maps. Hotel daily rate range is for comparison only. Restaurant price range is a combination of lunch and/or dinner. Turn to the listing page for more detailed rate and price information and consult display ads for special promotions.

## MCKINNEY

| Map Page | Hotel | Diamond Rated | Rate Range | Page |
|---|---|---|---|---|
| **1** p. 179 | **La Quinta Inn & Suites at The Ballfields at Craig Ranch** | ◆◆◆ | $95-$134 SAVE | 415 |

## FRISCO

| Map Page | Hotels | Diamond Rated | Rate Range | Page |
|---|---|---|---|---|
| **4** p. 179 | Comfort Suites - Frisco Square | ◆◆◆ | $89-$139 | 272 |
| **5** p. 179 | Hampton Inn & Suites-Frisco | ◆◆◆ | $89-$179 | 272 |
| **6** p. 179 | **Aloft Frisco** (See ad p. 210.) | ◆◆◆ | $71-$152 SAVE | 272 |
| **7** p. 179 | Hilton Garden Inn Frisco | ◆◆◆ | $99-$209 | 272 |
| **8** p. 179 | Embassy Suites Dallas-Frisco Hotel, Convention Center & Spa | ◆◆◆ | $120-$250 | 272 |
| **9** p. 179 | **The Westin Stonebriar** (See ad p. 273.) | ◆◆◆◆ | $109-$479 SAVE | 272 |
| **10** p. 179 | **Sheraton Stonebriar Dallas-Frisco** (See ad p. 273.) | ◆◆◆ | $99-$409 SAVE | 272 |

| Map Page | Restaurants | Diamond Rated | Cuisine | Price Range | Page |
|---|---|---|---|---|---|
| ① p. 179 | The Londoner | ◆◆ | English | $8-$15 | 274 |
| ② p. 179 | Platia Greek Kouzina | ◆◆ | Greek | $6-$24 | 274 |
| ③ p. 179 | Jinbeh Japanese Steakhouse | ◆◆ | Japanese | $8-$36 | 274 |
| ④ p. 179 | Kenny's Burger Joint | ◆ | Burgers | $7-$14 | 274 |
| ⑤ p. 179 | **Silver Fox** | ◆◆◆ | Steak | $15-$45 | 274 |
| ⑥ p. 179 | **Cantina Laredo** | ◆◆ | Mexican | $10-$26 | 274 |

## THE COLONY

| Map Page | Hotels | Diamond Rated | Rate Range | Page |
|---|---|---|---|---|
| **13** p. 179 | Fairfield Inn & Suites by Marriott-Plano/Frisco/The Colony | ◆◆◆ | $71-$143 | 551 |
| **14** p. 179 | Residence Inn by Marriott-Plano/Frisco/The Colony | ◆◆◆ | $89-$179 | 551 |
| **15** p. 179 | **Comfort Suites** | ◆◆◆ | $75-$200 SAVE | 551 |

## ALLEN

| Map Page | Hotels | Diamond Rated | Rate Range | Page |
|---|---|---|---|---|
| **18** p. 179 | Holiday Inn Express & Suites Allen/Dallas | ◆◆◆ | $95-$129 | 55 |
| **19** p. 179 | Pyramids Hotel | ◆◆ | $89-$149 | 55 |
| **20** p. 179 | Hilton Garden Inn Dallas/Allen | ◆◆◆ | $94-$189 | 55 |

| Map Page | Restaurants | Diamond Rated | Cuisine | Price Range | Page |
|---|---|---|---|---|---|
| ⑨ p. 179 | Silver Thai Cuisine | ◆◆ | Thai | $9-$28 | 56 |
| ⑩ p. 179 | Grimaldi's Pizzeria | ◆◆ | Pizza | $9-$18 | 55 |
| ⑪ p. 179 | The Londoner | ◆◆ | English | $8-$14 | 56 |

## LEWISVILLE

| Map Page | Hotels | Diamond Rated | Rate Range | Page |
|---|---|---|---|---|
| **23** p. 179 | **Baymont Inn & Suites** | ◆◆ | $69-$119 SAVE | 396 |
| **24** p. 179 | Motel 6 - #1288 | ◆ | $45-$65 | 396 |
| **25** p. 179 | **BEST WESTERN PLUS Lewisville/Coppell** | ◆◆◆ | $85-$130 SAVE | 396 |
| **26** p. 179 | Extended Stay America Dallas-Lewisville | ◆◆ | $70-$97 | 396 |
| **27** p. 179 | Holiday Inn Express & Suites, Dallas-Lewisville | ◆◆◆ | $79-$159 | 396 |

## LEWISVILLE (cont'd)

| Map Page | Hotels (cont'd) | Diamond Rated | Rate Range | Page |
|---|---|---|---|---|
| 28 p. 179 | Country Inn & Suites By Carlson | ♦♦ | $99-$119 | 396 |
| 29 p. 179 | Comfort Suites by Choice Hotels | ♦♦ | $62-$95 | 396 |
| 30 p. 179 | Residence Inn by Marriott Dallas/Lewisville | ♦♦♦ | $149-$164 | 396 |
| 31 p. 179 | TownePlace Suites by Marriott Dallas Lewisville | ♦♦♦ | $115-$140 | 396 |
| 32 p. 179 | Hampton Inn & Suites Dallas Lewisville/Vista Ridge Mall | ♦♦♦ | $89-$139 | 396 |
| 33 p. 179 | Fairfield Inn by Marriott-Lewisville | ♦♦ | $79-$119 | 396 |
| 34 p. 179 | Courtyard by Marriott | ♦♦♦ | $94-$169 | 396 |
| 35 p. 179 | Hilton Garden Inn Dallas/Lewisville | ♦♦♦ | $99-$189 | 396 |

| Map Page | Restaurants | Diamond Rated | Cuisine | Price Range | Page |
|---|---|---|---|---|---|
| 14 p. 179 | Aw Shucks Oyster Bar | ♦ | Seafood | $7-$12 | 397 |
| 15 p. 179 | Ojeda's Restaurant | ♦♦ | Tex-Mex | $6-$13 | 397 |
| 16 p. 179 | Cantina Laredo | ♦♦ | Mexican | $10-$26 | 397 |
| 17 p. 179 | Saltgrass Steakhouse | ♦♦ | Steak | $9-$30 SAVE | 397 |
| 18 p. 179 | Sweet Basil Thai Bistro | ♦♦ | Thai | $7-$14 | 397 |

## PLANO

| Map Page | Hotels | Diamond Rated | Rate Range | Page |
|---|---|---|---|---|
| 38 p. 179 | NYLO Plano at Legacy | ♦♦♦ | Rates not provided | 438 |
| 39 p. 179 | Marriott Dallas/Plano at Legacy Town Center | ♦♦♦ | $129-$299 | 438 |
| 40 p. 179 | Candlewood Suites-Plano | ♦♦ | Rates not provided | 437 |
| 41 p. 179 | Courtyard by Marriott | ♦♦♦ | $59-$189 SAVE | 438 |
| 42 p. 179 | Aloft Plano (See ad p. 210.) | ♦♦♦ | $79-$170 SAVE | 437 |
| 43 p. 179 | TownePlace Suites by Marriott | ♦♦ | $139-$179 | 439 |
| 44 p. 179 | Hyatt Place Dallas/Plano | ♦♦♦ | $79-$239 SAVE | 438 |
| 45 p. 179 | BEST WESTERN Park Suites Hotel | ♦♦ | $99-$104 SAVE | 437 |
| 46 p. 179 | Ramada Limited | ♦♦ | $50-$100 SAVE | 438 |
| 47 p. 179 | Holiday Inn Express Hotel & Suites Plano East | ♦♦♦ | $79-$109 | 438 |
| 48 p. 179 | Super 8-Plano | ♦♦ | $55-$90 SAVE | 439 |
| 49 p. 179 | Southfork Hotel | ♦♦♦ | $84-$119 SAVE | 439 |
| 50 p. 179 | Homewood Suites by Hilton | ♦♦♦ | $89-$159 | 438 |
| 51 p. 179 | Hampton Inn Plano | ♦♦♦ | $99-$139 | 438 |
| 52 p. 179 | Comfort Inn Near Plano Medical Center | ♦♦ | $55-$85 | 437 |
| 53 p. 179 | Courtyard by Marriott-Plano Parkway | ♦♦♦ | $59-$159 SAVE | 438 |
| 54 p. 179 | Fairfield Inn & Suites by Marriott Dallas Plano | ♦♦♦ | $67-$118 | 438 |
| 55 p. 179 | La Quinta Inn & Suites Dallas Plano West | ♦♦♦ | $79-$140 | 438 |
| 56 p. 179 | Staybridge Suites Plano/Richardson | ♦♦♦ | $109-$119 SAVE | 439 |

| Map Page | Restaurants | Diamond Rated | Cuisine | Price Range | Page |
|---|---|---|---|---|---|
| 21 p. 179 | Fireside Pies | ♦♦ | Pizza | $11-$16 | 439 |
| 22 p. 179 | Cafe Istanbul | ♦♦ | Turkish | $11-$19 | 439 |
| 23 p. 179 | Samui Thai | ♦♦ | Thai | $11-$20 | 440 |
| 24 p. 179 | Naan | ♦♦ | Japanese | $9-$36 | 440 |

| Map Page | Restaurants (cont'd) | Diamond Rated | Cuisine | Price Range | Page |
|----------|---------------------|---------------|---------|-------------|------|
| ㉕ p. 179 | Purple Cow Diner | ◆◆ | American | $6-$11 | 440 |
| ㉖ p. 179 | Japon Steakhouse & Sushi Bar | ◆◆ | Japanese | $10-$39 | 440 |
| ㉗ p. 179 | Bread Winner's Cafe | ◆◆ | American | $10-$25 | 439 |
| ㉘ p. 179 | Mignon | ◆◆◆ | French Steak | $14-$48 | 440 |
| ㉙ p. 179 | Chuy's | ◆◆ | Tex-Mex | $8-$12 | 439 |
| ㉚ p. 179 | Saltgrass Steakhouse | ◆◆ | Steak | $9-$30 SAVE | 440 |
| ㉛ p. 179 | Bavarian Grill | ◆◆ | German | $7-$20 | 439 |
| ㉜ p. 179 | Zenna Thai & Japanese Restaurant | ◆◆ | Thai | $7-$13 | 441 |
| ㉝ p. 179 | Osaka Sushi | ◆◆ | Japanese | $17-$30 | 440 |
| ㉞ p. 179 | Fishmongers Seafood Market & Cafe | ◆◆ | Regional Seafood | $7-$20 | 439 |
| ㊱ p. 179 | Patrizio | ◆◆ | Italian | $10-$17 | 440 |
| ㊲ p. 179 | Jorg's Cafe Vienna | ◆◆ | Austrian | $11-$23 | 440 |
| ㊳ p. 179 | Zorba's | ◆◆ | Greek | $6-$13 | 441 |
| ㊴ p. 179 | Luna De Noche | ◆◆ | Tex-Mex | $7-$22 | 440 |
| ㊵ p. 179 | Love & War in Texas | ◆◆ | Regional American | $8-$29 | 440 |

**RICHARDSON**

| Map Page | Restaurant | Diamond Rated | Cuisine | Price Range | Page |
|----------|------------|---------------|---------|-------------|------|
| ㊸ p. 179 | **Silver Fox** | ◆◆◆ | Steak | $17-$45 | 447 |

© AAA

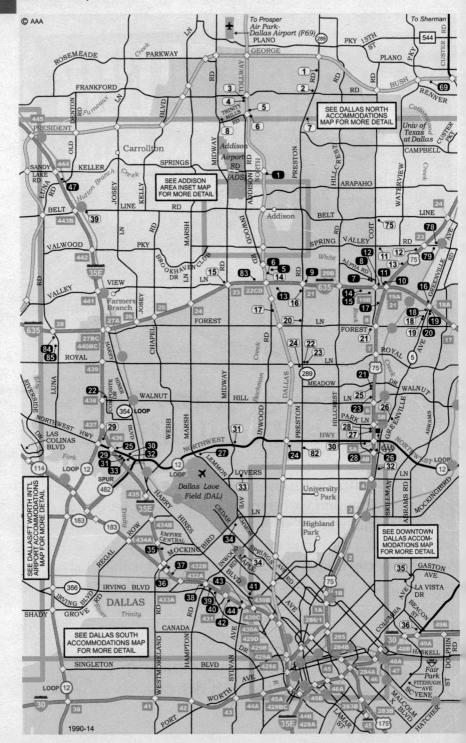

1990-14

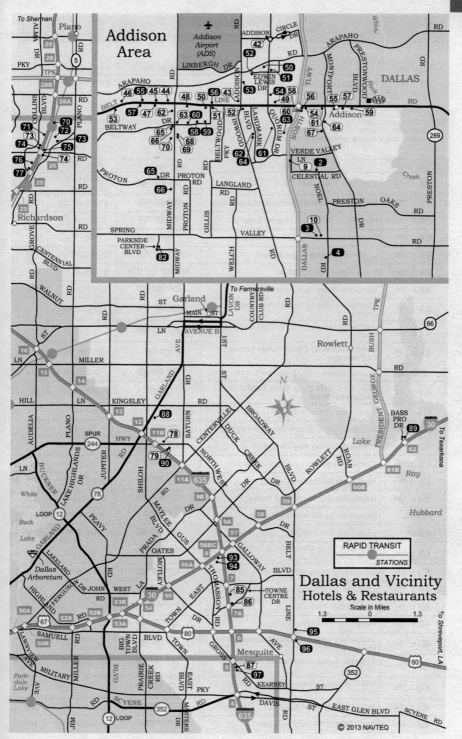

## ✈ Airport Hotels

| Map Page | DALLAS LOVE FIELD (Maximum driving distance from airport: 1.3 mi) | Diamond Rated | Rate Range | Page |
|---|---|---|---|---|
| 34 p. 184 | Wyndham Love Field, 1.3 mi | ◆◆◆ | $129-$260 SAVE | 218 |

# Dallas and Vicinity

This index helps you "spot" where approved hotels and restaurants are located on the corresponding detailed maps. Hotel daily rate range is for comparison only. Restaurant price range is a combination of lunch and/or dinner. Turn to the listing page for more detailed rate and price information and consult display ads for special promotions.

## DALLAS

| Map Page | Hotels | Diamond Rated | Rate Range | Page |
|---|---|---|---|---|
| 1 p. 184 | Staybridge Suites North Dallas | ◆◆◆ | Rates not provided | 217 |
| 2 p. 184 | Embassy Suites Hotel Dallas Near the Galleria | ◆◆◆ | $109-$199 SAVE | 212 |
| 3 p. 184 | Hyatt Place Dallas-North/by the Galleria | ◆◆◆ | $59-$189 SAVE | 216 |
| 4 p. 184 | Candlewood Suites-Dallas by the Galleria | ◆◆ | $80-$129 | 211 |
| 5 p. 184 | Le Meridien Dallas by the Galleria | ◆◆◆ | $109-$349 SAVE | 216 |
| 6 p. 184 | The Westin Galleria, Dallas | ◆◆◆◆ | $119-$449 SAVE | 217 |
| 7 p. 184 | Wyndham Dallas Park Central | ◆◆◆ | $79-$149 SAVE | 218 |
| 8 p. 184 | Hawthorn Suites by Wyndham Dallas Park Central | ◆◆◆ | $85-$120 SAVE | 214 |
| 9 p. 184 | Holiday Inn Express & Suites North Dallas at Preston | ◆◆◆ | $79-$209 | 215 |
| 10 p. 184 | Comfort Suites by Choice Hotels-Central Expressway | ◆◆ | $83-$99 SAVE | 211 |
| 11 p. 184 | Embassy Suites Hotel-Dallas/Park Central | ◆◆◆ | $129-$149 | 213 |
| 12 p. 184 | BEST WESTERN PLUS Dallas Hotel & Conference Center | ◆◆ | $96-$170 SAVE | 211 |
| 13 p. 184 | Hilton Dallas Lincoln Centre | ◆◆◆◆ | $129-$399 SAVE | 214 |
| 14 p. 184 | Residence Inn by Marriott-Dallas Park Central | ◆◆◆ | $80-$129 | 217 |
| 15 p. 184 | The Westin Dallas Park Central | ◆◆◆ | $99-$349 SAVE | 217 |
| 16 p. 184 | Candlewood Suites Dallas North/Richardson | ◆◆ | $65-$100 | 211 |
| 17 p. 184 | Hyatt Place Dallas/Park Central | ◆◆◆ | $69-$199 SAVE | 216 |
| 18 p. 184 | Holiday Inn Express Hotel & Suites | ◆◆◆ | $95-$115 SAVE | 216 |
| 19 p. 184 | Fairfield Inn by Marriott-Park Central | ◆◆ | $79-$129 | 214 |
| 20 p. 184 | Homewood Suites by Hilton - I-635 Greenville | ◆◆◆ | $89-$169 | 216 |
| 21 p. 184 | Residence Inn by Marriott Dallas Central Expressway | ◆◆◆ | $89-$189 | 217 |
| 22 p. 184 | Hampton Inn-Dallas North I-35 at Walnut Hill | ◆◆◆ | $79-$139 | 214 |
| 23 p. 184 | La Quinta Inn & Suites Dallas North Central | ◆◆ | $95-$144 | 216 |
| 24 p. 184 | Hilton Dallas Park Cities | ◆◆◆◆ | $129-$269 SAVE | 215 |
| 25 p. 184 | Holiday Inn Express Hotel & Suites | ◆◆◆ | $69-$139 | 215 |
| 26 p. 184 | DoubleTree by Hilton Dallas Campbell Centre (See ad p. 212.) | ◆◆◆ | Rates not provided SAVE | 212 |
| 27 p. 184 | Embassy Suites Hotel-Dallas/Love Field (See ad p. 213.) | ◆◆◆ | $99-$159 SAVE | 212 |
| 28 p. 184 | HYATT house Dallas/Lincoln Park (See ad p. 202.) | ◆◆◆ | $89-$299 SAVE | 216 |
| 29 p. 184 | MCM Elegante Hotel & Suites | ◆◆◆ | $89-$139 SAVE | 217 |
| 30 p. 184 | BEST WESTERN Northwest Inn | ◆◆ | $79-$149 SAVE | 210 |

**DALLAS (cont'd)**

| Map Page | Hotels (cont'd) | Diamond Rated | Rate Range | Page |
|---|---|---|---|---|
| **31** p. 184 | SpringHill Suites by Marriott-Stemmons | ◆◆◆ | $116-$128 | 217 |
| **32** p. 184 | **Baymont Inn & Suites Dallas Love Field** | ◆◆◆ | $79-$129 [SAVE] | 210 |
| **33** p. 184 | Country Inn & Suites Dallas Love Field / Medical Center | ◆◆◆ | Rates not provided | 211 |
| **34** p. 184 | **Wyndham Love Field** | ◆◆◆ | $129-$260 [SAVE] | 218 |
| **35** p. 184 | **Candlewood Suites Dallas Market Center** | ◆◆◆ | $89-$119 [SAVE] | 211 |
| **36** p. 184 | **Comfort Inn & Suites Market Center** | ◆◆ | $70-$140 [SAVE] | 211 |
| **37** p. 184 | Residence Inn by Marriott-Dallas Market Center | ◆◆◆ | $89-$209 | 217 |
| **38** p. 184 | Holiday Inn Express & Suites Dallas Central Market Center | ◆◆◆ | $119-$209 | 215 |
| **39** p. 184 | Homewood Suites Dallas Market Center | ◆◆◆ | $99-$179 | 216 |
| **40** p. 184 | **Embassy Suites Dallas-Market Center** *(See ad p. 213.)* | ◆◆◆ | $139-$199 [SAVE] | 212 |
| **41** p. 184 | Holiday Inn Dallas Market Center | ◆◆◆ | Rates not provided | 215 |
| **42** p. 184 | Dallas Marriott Suites Medical/Market Center | ◆◆◆ | $89-$209 | 211 |
| **43** p. 184 | Renaissance Dallas Hotel | ◆◆◆◆ | $115-$279 | 217 |
| **44** p. 184 | **Hilton Garden Inn Dallas/Market Center** *(See ad p. 215.)* | ◆◆◆ | $69-$309 [SAVE] | 215 |

| Map Page | Restaurants | Diamond Rated | Cuisine | Price Range | Page |
|---|---|---|---|---|---|
| **1** p. 184 | Lavendou Bistro Provencal | ◆◆◆ | French | $13-$31 | 220 |
| **2** p. 184 | Great China Restaurant | ◆◆ | Chinese | $10-$30 | 219 |
| **3** p. 184 | The Blue Fish | ◆◆ | Japanese | $11-$29 | 218 |
| **4** p. 184 | Thai Spice | ◆◆ | Thai | $10-$27 | 222 |
| **5** p. 184 | **Ill Forks** | ◆◆◆ | Steak | $29-$99 | 218 |
| **6** p. 184 | Maguire's Regional Cuisine | ◆◆◆ | Regional American | $15-$35 | 220 |
| **7** p. 184 | Afghan Grill | ◆◆ | Afghan | $14-$20 | 218 |
| **8** p. 184 | Sweet Basil Italian Grill | ◆◆ | Italian | $7-$20 | 221 |
| **9** p. 184 | Lawry's The Prime Rib | ◆◆◆ | Steak | $11-$48 | 220 |
| **10** p. 184 | Del Frisco's Double Eagle Steak House | ◆◆◆ | Steak | $30-$89 | 219 |
| **11** p. 184 | Cuquita's Restaurant | ◆◆ | Mexican | $7-$12 | 219 |
| **12** p. 184 | **El Chico** | ◆◆ | Tex-Mex | $7-$16 | 219 |
| **13** p. 184 | Saltgrass Steakhouse | ◆◆ | Steak | $9-$30 [SAVE] | 221 |
| **14** p. 184 | The Oceanaire Seafood Room | ◆◆◆ | Seafood | $14-$70 [SAVE] | 220 |
| **15** p. 184 | Saltgrass Steakhouse | ◆◆ | Steak | $9-$30 [SAVE] | 221 |
| **16** p. 184 | India Palace Restaurant & Bar | ◆◆ | Indian | $12-$25 | 219 |
| **17** p. 184 | Tupinamba | ◆◆ | Tex-Mex | $9-$17 | 222 |
| **18** p. 184 | **J.G.'s Old Fashioned Hamburgers** | ◆ | Burgers | $5-$8 | 219 |
| **19** p. 184 | Sushi Ichiban Japanese Restaurant | ◆◆ | Sushi | $6-$25 | 221 |
| **20** p. 184 | The Mercury | ◆◆◆ | New American | $14-$60 | 220 |
| **21** p. 184 | Asian Mint | ◆◆ | Thai | $9-$20 | 218 |
| **22** p. 184 | The Purple Cow | ◆ | American | $4-$10 | 221 |
| **23** p. 184 | **Cantina Laredo** | ◆◆ | Mexican | $10-$26 | 218 |

| Map Page | Restaurants (cont'd) | Diamond Rated | Cuisine | Price Range | Page |
|---|---|---|---|---|---|
| 24 p. 184 | Natalie's | ◆◆ | American | $12-$20 | 220 |
| 25 p. 184 | Bangkok Thai Cuisine | ◆◆ | Thai | $8-$17 | 218 |
| 26 p. 184 | Enchiladas Restaurant | ◆◆ | Tex-Mex | $7-$17 | 219 |
| 27 p. 184 | La Duni Latin Kitchen and Coffee Studio | ◆◆ | Latin American | $9-$27 | 219 |
| 28 p. 184 | P.F. Chang's China Bistro | ◆◆◆ | Chinese | $6-$25 | 221 |
| 29 p. 184 | Pappas Bros. Steakhouse | ◆◆◆ | Steak | $40-$95 | 220 |
| 30 p. 184 | Blue Mesa Grill | ◆◆ | Southwestern | $10-$17 | 218 |
| 31 p. 184 | Suze | ◆◆◆ | New American | $16-$36 | 221 |
| 32 p. 184 | Royal Thai Restaurant | ◆◆ | Thai | $8-$14 | 221 |
| 33 p. 184 | Celebration | ◆◆ | American | $12-$24 | 218 |
| 34 p. 184 | Herrera's Tex-Mex | ◆ | Tex-Mex | $7-$14 | 219 |
| 35 p. 184 | **Cantina Laredo** | ◆◆ | Mexican | $10-$26 | 218 |
| 36 p. 184 | Kalachandji's Garden Restaurant | ◆◆ | Vegetarian | $10-$13 | 219 |

## CARROLLTON

| Map Page | Hotel | Diamond Rated | Rate Range | Page |
|---|---|---|---|---|
| 47 p. 184 | Rodeway Inn | ◆◆ | $50-$75 | 135 |

| Map Page | Restaurant | Diamond Rated | Cuisine | Price Range | Page |
|---|---|---|---|---|---|
| 39 p. 184 | Burger Island | ◆ | Burgers | $4-$8 | 135 |

## ADDISON

| Map Page | Hotels | Diamond Rated | Rate Range | Page |
|---|---|---|---|---|
| 50 p. 184 | Holiday Inn-Addison/North Dallas | ◆◆ | $59-$299 | 51 |
| 51 p. 184 | **SpringHill Suites by Marriott Dallas/Addison** | ◆◆◆ | $61-$179 [SAVE] | 52 |
| 52 p. 184 | **HYATT house Dallas/Addison** | ◆◆◆ | $64-$169 [SAVE] | 51 |
| 53 p. 184 | **Hawthorn Suites by Wyndham** | ◆◆◆ | $76-$110 [SAVE] | 51 |
| 54 p. 184 | **Addison Quorum Courtyard By Marriott** | ◆◆◆ | $50-$179 [SAVE] | 50 |
| 55 p. 184 | Quality Inn & Suites | ◆◆ | $60-$150 | 51 |
| 56 p. 184 | **Comfort Suites by Choice Hotels** | ◆◆◆ | $69-$149 [SAVE] | 50 |
| 57 p. 184 | Hilton Garden Inn-Addison | ◆◆◆ | $99-$159 | 51 |
| 58 p. 184 | Homewood Suites by Hilton | ◆◆◆ | $99-$159 | 51 |
| 59 p. 184 | Hampton Inn | ◆◆◆ | $62-$129 | 51 |
| 60 p. 184 | Holiday Inn Express Hotel & Suites | ◆◆ | Rates not provided | 51 |
| 61 p. 184 | Residence Inn by Marriott-Addison | ◆◆◆ | $99-$169 | 51 |
| 62 p. 184 | **BEST WESTERN PLUS Addison Galleria Hotel** | ◆◆◆ | $59-$129 [SAVE] | 50 |
| 63 p. 184 | Dallas Addison Marriott Quorum by the Galleria | ◆◆◆ | $99-$259 | 51 |
| 64 p. 184 | La Quinta Inn & Suites Dallas Addison Galleria | ◆◆ | $75-$120 | 51 |
| 65 p. 184 | Courtyard by Marriott-Dallas Addison/Midway | ◆◆◆ | $54-$209 | 50 |
| 66 p. 184 | **Crowne Plaza North Dallas/Near the Galleria** (See ad p. 50.) | ◆◆◆ | $109-$219 [SAVE] | 50 |

| Map Page | Restaurants | Diamond Rated | Cuisine | Price Range | Page |
|---|---|---|---|---|---|
| 42 p. 184 | Antonio Ristorante | ◆◆ | Italian | $14-$29 | 52 |
| 43 p. 184 | Texas de Brazil | ◆◆◆ | Brazilian | $20-$45 | 54 |

| Map Page | Restaurants (cont'd) | Diamond Rated | Cuisine | Price Range | Page |
|---|---|---|---|---|---|
| 44 p. 184 | Andiamo Italian Restaurant | ◈◈◈ | Italian | $10-$30 | 52 |
| 45 p. 184 | Best Thai | ◈◈ | Thai | $9-$16 | 52 |
| 46 p. 184 | Lefty's Lobster & Chowder House | ◈◈ | Seafood | $6-$57 | 53 |
| 47 p. 184 | Fogo De Chao | ◈◈◈ | Brazilian | $32-$49 | 52 |
| 48 p. 184 | Tokyo One Japanese Restaurant | ◈◈ | Japanese | $17-$28 | 54 |
| 49 p. 184 | Magic Time Machine | ◈◈ | American | $12-$29 | 53 |
| 50 p. 184 | Cantina Laredo | ◈◈ | Tex-Mex | $10-$26 | 52 |
| 51 p. 184 | Remington's Seafood Grill | ◈◈ | Seafood | $12-$30 | 53 |
| 52 p. 184 | Benedict's Restaurant | ◈◈ | Breakfast | $5-$13 | 52 |
| 53 p. 184 | Jasmine Restaurant | ◈◈ | Chinese | $10-$25 | 53 |
| 54 p. 184 | Blue Mesa Grill | ◈◈ | Southwestern | $10-$17 | 52 |
| 55 p. 184 | India West by Ross Duggal | ◈◈◈ | Indian | $11-$32 | 53 |
| 56 p. 184 | Kenny's Italian Kitchen | ◈◈ | Italian | $10-$30 | 53 |
| 57 p. 184 | Houston's | ◈◈◈ | American | $15-$37 | 53 |
| 58 p. 184 | Canary by Gorji | ◈◈◈ | Mediterranean | $23-$36 | 52 |
| 59 p. 184 | Chamberlain's Steak & Chop House | ◈◈◈ | Steak | $23-$38 | 52 |
| 60 p. 184 | The Saffron House | ◈◈◈ | Indian | $9-$22 | 54 |
| 61 p. 184 | Addison Cafe | ◈◈◈ | Northern French | $10-$27 | 52 |
| 62 p. 184 | Nate's Seafood & Steakhouse | ◈◈ | Regional Seafood | $9-$30 | 53 |
| 63 p. 184 | The Londoner | ◈◈ | English | $7-$12 | 53 |
| 64 p. 184 | Mi Piaci | ◈◈◈ | Italian | $14-$38 | 53 |
| 65 p. 184 | Jaxx Steakhouse | ◈◈◈ | Steak | $13-$35 | 53 |
| 66 p. 184 | Loving Hut | ◈◈ | Vegan | $8-$17 | 53 |
| 67 p. 184 | Gloria's Latin Cuisine | ◈◈ | Latin American | $10-$17 | 53 |
| 68 p. 184 | The Blue Goose Cantina | ◈◈ | Tex-Mex | $10-$18 | 52 |
| 69 p. 184 | Snuffer's | ◈ | American | $8-$12 | 54 |
| 70 p. 184 | Ferrari's Italian Villa | ◈◈◈ | Italian | $11-$30 | 52 |

**RICHARDSON**

| Map Page | Hotels | Diamond Rated | Rate Range | Page |
|---|---|---|---|---|
| 69 p. 184 | Hilton Garden Inn Dallas/Richardson | ◈◈◈ | $109-$179 | 446 |
| 70 p. 184 | Renaissance Dallas-Richardson Hotel | ◈◈◈◈ | $72-$138 SAVE | 446 |
| 71 p. 184 | HYATT house Dallas/Richardson | ◈◈◈ | $69-$199 SAVE | 446 |
| 72 p. 184 | Residence Inn by Marriott Richardson | ◈◈◈ | $79-$189 SAVE | 446 |
| 73 p. 184 | Courtyard by Marriott Dallas Richardson at Campbell Rd | ◈◈◈ | $59-$169 SAVE | 445 |
| 74 p. 184 | DoubleTree by Hilton Hotel Dallas - Richardson | ◈◈◈ | Rates not provided | 446 |
| 75 p. 184 | Hyatt Regency North Dallas/Richardson | ◈◈◈ | $85-$249 SAVE | 446 |
| 76 p. 184 | Holiday Inn | ◈◈ | $105 | 446 |
| 77 p. 184 | Wingate by Wyndham Richardson | ◈◈◈ | $69-$125 SAVE | 447 |
| 78 p. 184 | Super 8 | ◈◈ | $55-$100 SAVE | 446 |
| 79 p. 184 | Courtyard by Marriott-Dallas Richardson at Spring Valley | ◈◈◈ | $53-$109 SAVE | 446 |

| Map Page | Restaurants | Diamond Rated | Cuisine | Price Range | Page |
|---|---|---|---|---|---|
| ⑦③ p. 184 | Cafe Brazil | ◈◈ | American | $7-$11 | 447 |
| ⑦④ p. 184 | Russo's Coal-Fired Pizzeria | ◈◈ | Pizza | $8-$16 | 447 |
| ⑦⑤ p. 184 | Thai Soon Restaurant | ◈◈ | Thai | $7-$14 | 447 |

### FARMERS BRANCH

| Map Page | Hotels | Diamond Rated | Rate Range | Page |
|---|---|---|---|---|
| ⑧② p. 184 | Fairfield Inn & Suites by Marriott Dallas North | ◈◈ | $89-$99 | 246 |
| ⑧③ p. 184 | **Sheraton Dallas Hotel by the Galleria** | ◈◈◈ | $85-$279 [SAVE] | 246 |
| ⑧④ p. 184 | Omni Dallas Hotel Park West | ◈◈◈◈ | $89-$209 | 246 |
| ⑧⑤ p. 184 | **DoubleTree by Hilton Hotel Dallas-Farmers Branch** | ◈◈◈ | $109-$139 [SAVE] | 246 |

### GARLAND

| Map Page | Hotels | Diamond Rated | Rate Range | Page |
|---|---|---|---|---|
| ⑧⑧ p. 184 | **Days Inn** | ◈◈ | $49-$109 [SAVE] | 283 |
| ⑧⑨ p. 184 | **BEST WESTERN Lakeview Inn** | ◈◈ | $65-$75 [SAVE] | 283 |
| ⑨⓪ p. 184 | **Microtel Inn & Suites by Wyndham Garland/Dallas** | ◈◈ | $55-$85 [SAVE] | 283 |

| Map Page | Restaurants | Diamond Rated | Cuisine | Price Range | Page |
|---|---|---|---|---|---|
| ⑦⑧ p. 184 | Cuquita's Restaurant | ◈◈ | Mexican | $6-$12 | 283 |
| ⑦⑨ p. 184 | **El Chico** | ◈◈ | Tex-Mex | $7-$16 | 283 |

### MESQUITE

| Map Page | Hotels | Diamond Rated | Rate Range | Page |
|---|---|---|---|---|
| ⑨③ p. 184 | Courtyard by Marriott Dallas/Mesquite | ◈◈◈ | $85-$130 | 416 |
| ⑨④ p. 184 | Fairfield Inn & Suites by Marriott Dallas Mesquite | ◈◈◈ | $89-$199 | 416 |
| ⑨⑤ p. 184 | **Comfort Suites** | ◈◈ | $65-$95 [SAVE] | 416 |
| ⑨⑥ p. 184 | **La Quinta Inn & Suites Dallas Mesquite** | ◈◈ | $89-$134 [SAVE] | 416 |
| ⑨⑦ p. 184 | Quality Inn Mesquite | ◈◈ | $60-$130 | 416 |

| Map Page | Restaurants | Diamond Rated | Cuisine | Price Range | Page |
|---|---|---|---|---|---|
| ⑧⑤ p. 184 | **El Chico** | ◈◈ | Tex-Mex | $7-$16 | 417 |
| ⑧⑥ p. 184 | Saltgrass Steakhouse | ◈◈ | Steak | $9-$30 [SAVE] | 417 |
| ⑧⑦ p. 184 | Soulman's Barbeque | ◈ | Barbecue | $9-$18 | 417 |

### UNIVERSITY PARK

| Map Page | Restaurant | Diamond Rated | Cuisine | Price Range | Page |
|---|---|---|---|---|---|
| ⑧② p. 184 | **R+D Kitchen** | ◈◈ | American | $12-$31 | 558 |

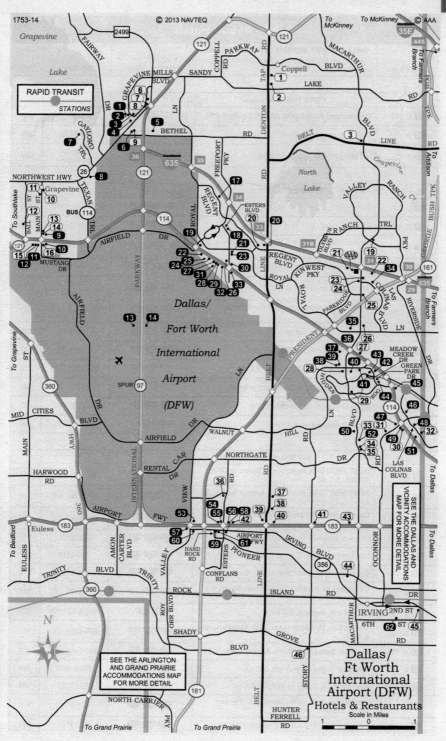

Dallas/
Fort Worth
International
Airport
(DFW)

Dallas/
Ft Worth
International
Airport (DFW)
Hotels & Restaurants

## ✈ Airport Hotels

| Map Page | DALLAS-FORT WORTH INTERNATIONAL (Maximum driving distance from airport: 8.8 mi) | Diamond Rated | Rate Range | Page |
|---|---|---|---|---|
| | **FORT WORTH-Hotels** | | | |
| 🔢 12 p. 257 | **Candlewood Suites DFW Airport South, 5.5 mi** | ◈◈◈ | $79-$139 SAVE | 263 |
| 🔢 14 p. 257 | DFW Airport Marriott South, 5.5 mi | ◈◈◈ | $79-$299 | 264 |
| 🔢 11 p. 257 | Holiday Inn DFW Airport South, 5.4 mi | ◈◈◈ | Rates not provided | 264 |
| | **GRAPEVINE-Hotels** | | | |
| 🔢 9 p. 191 | Comfort Inn, 6.6 mi | ◈◈◈ | $89-$159 | 289 |
| 🔢 5 p. 191 | Comfort Suites DFW North-Grapevine, 8.0 mi | ◈◈◈ | $79-$179 | 289 |
| 🔢 7 p. 191 | **Gaylord Texan Resort & Convention Center, 8.0 mi** | ◈◈◈◈ | $139-$449 SAVE | 289 |
| 🔢 13 p. 191 | **Grand Hyatt DFW, on airport property** | ◈◈◈◈ | $99-$449 SAVE | 289 |
| 🔢 8 p. 191 | Great Wolf Lodge-Grapevine, TX, 7.4 mi | ◈◈◈ | Rates not provided | 290 |
| 🔢 4 p. 191 | **Hilton DFW Lakes Executive Conference Center, 8.4 mi** | ◈◈◈ | $98-$242 SAVE | 290 |
| 🔢 11 p. 191 | Hilton Garden Inn, 6.8 mi | ◈◈◈ | $109-$299 | 290 |
| 🔢 2 p. 191 | Homewood Suites by Hilton, 8.7 mi | ◈◈◈ | $129-$159 | 290 |
| 🔢 3 p. 191 | **Hyatt Place Dallas/Grapevine, 8.6 mi** | ◈◈◈ | $69-$209 SAVE | 290 |
| 🔢 14 p. 191 | **Hyatt Regency DFW, on airport property** | ◈◈◈ | $89-$319 | 290 |
| 🔢 1 p. 191 | SpringHill Suites by Marriott, 8.8 mi | ◈◈◈ | $99-$199 | 290 |
| 🔢 10 p. 191 | **Super 8-Grapevine, 6.8 mi** | ◈◈ | $79-$109 SAVE | 290 |
| | **IRVING-Hotels** | | | |
| 🔢 58 p. 191 | **BEST WESTERN Irving Inn & Suites at DFW Airport, 5.7 mi** | ◈◈ | $69-$95 SAVE | 372 |
| 🔢 22 p. 191 | **BEST WESTERN PLUS DFW Airport Suites, 5.1 mi** | ◈◈ | $81-$139 SAVE | 372 |
| 🔢 57 p. 191 | **Comfort Inn & Suites DFW Airport South, 4.9 mi** | ◈◈◈ | $62-$119 SAVE | 372 |
| 🔢 29 p. 191 | Comfort Suites DFW Airport, 5.4 mi | ◈◈◈ | $99-$129 | 372 |
| 🔢 37 p. 191 | Comfort Suites Las Colinas Center, 8.8 mi | ◈◈◈ | $99-$119 | 372 |
| 🔢 17 p. 191 | Courtyard by Marriott-DFW Airport North, 6.4 mi | ◈◈◈ | $79-$189 | 372 |
| 🔢 53 p. 191 | **Courtyard by Marriott DFW Airport South, 5.1 mi** | ◈◈◈ | $89-$179 SAVE | 373 |
| 🔢 28 p. 191 | **DFW North Super 8, 5.4 mi** | ◈◈ | $55-$125 SAVE | 373 |
| 🔢 30 p. 191 | **DoubleTree by Hilton Hotel DFW Airport-North, 8.1 mi** | ◈◈◈ | $99-$289 SAVE | 373 |
| 🔢 20 p. 191 | **Element Dallas Fort Worth Airport North, 7.2 mi** | ◈◈◈ | $89-$162 SAVE | 374 |
| 🔢 60 p. 191 | Embassy Suites-DFW South, 5.0 mi | ◈◈◈ | $119-$229 | 374 |
| 🔢 27 p. 191 | Fairfield Inn & Suites by Marriott, 5.4 mi | ◈◈◈ | $67-$139 | 374 |
| 🔢 61 p. 191 | Fairfield Inn & Suites by Marriott DFW Airport South, 5.6 mi | ◈◈◈ | $75-$142 | 374 |
| 🔢 59 p. 191 | Hampton Inn-DFW Airport South, 5.5 mi | ◈◈◈ | $79-$159 | 374 |

| | IRVING-Hotels (cont'd) | | Diamond | Rate Range | Page |
|---|---|---|---|---|---|
| **32** p. 191 | Holiday Inn Express & Suites-DFW North, 5.6 mi | ▽▽▽ | | Rates not provided | 374 |
| **55** p. 191 | Holiday Inn Express DFW Airport South, 6.2 mi | ▽▽▽ | | $89-$189 | 374 |
| **25** p. 191 | Homewood Suites by Hilton Irving DFW Airport North, 5.3 mi | ▽▽▽ | | $109-$189 | 375 |
| **24** p. 191 | La Quinta Inn & Suites Dallas DFW Airport North, 5.2 mi | ▽▽ | | $85-$150 | 375 |
| **56** p. 191 | La Quinta Inn & Suites Dallas DFW Airport South/Irving, 7.9 mi | ▽▽▽ | | $85-$160 | 375 |
| **19** p. 191 | Marriott Hotel-DFW Airport North, 5.0 mi | ▽▽▽ | | $80-$227 [SAVE] | 376 |
| **31** p. 191 | Motel 6 - #4725 DFW North, 5.5 mi | ▽ | | Rates not provided | 376 |
| **23** p. 191 | Red Roof Inn/DFW Airport North, 6.2 mi | ▽▽ | | $49-$89 [SAVE] | 376 |
| **18** p. 191 | Residence Inn by Marriott-DFW North, 6.7 mi | ▽▽▽ | | $80-$160 | 376 |
| **33** p. 191 | Sheraton DFW Airport Hotel, 5.8 mi | ▽▽▽ | | $99-$359 [SAVE] | 376 |
| **54** p. 191 | Super 8 DFW South Irving, 5.9 mi | ▽▽ | | $55-$85 | 376 |
| **26** p. 191 | The Westin Dallas Fort Worth Airport, 6.2 mi | ▽▽▽ | | $89-$349 [SAVE] | 377 |
| **21** p. 191 | Wingate by Wyndham DFW Airport North, 6.2 mi | ▽▽▽ | | $79-$149 [SAVE] | 377 |

# Dallas/Ft. Worth International Airport

This index helps you "spot" where approved hotels and restaurants are located on the corresponding detailed maps. Hotel daily rate range is for comparison only. Restaurant price range is a combination of lunch and/or dinner. Turn to the listing page for more detailed rate and price information and consult display ads for special promotions.

## GRAPEVINE

| Map Page | Hotels | Diamond Rated | Rate Range | Page |
|---|---|---|---|---|
| **1** p. 191 | SpringHill Suites by Marriott | ▽▽▽ | $99-$199 | 290 |
| **2** p. 191 | Homewood Suites by Hilton | ▽▽▽ | $129-$159 | 290 |
| **3** p. 191 | Hyatt Place Dallas/Grapevine | ▽▽▽ | $69-$209 [SAVE] | 290 |
| **4** p. 191 | Hilton DFW Lakes Executive Conference Center | ▽▽▽ | $98-$242 [SAVE] | 290 |
| **5** p. 191 | Comfort Suites DFW North-Grapevine | ▽▽▽ | $79-$179 | 289 |
| **6** p. 191 | Embassy Suites Outdoor World | ▽▽▽ | $139-$289 | 289 |
| **7** p. 191 | Gaylord Texan Resort & Convention Center (See ad p. 200.) | ▽▽▽▽ | $139-$449 [SAVE] | 289 |
| **8** p. 191 | Great Wolf Lodge-Grapevine, TX | ▽▽▽ | Rates not provided | 290 |
| **9** p. 191 | Comfort Inn | ▽▽▽ | $89-$159 | 289 |
| **10** p. 191 | Super 8-Grapevine | ▽▽ | $79-$109 [SAVE] | 290 |
| **11** p. 191 | Hilton Garden Inn | ▽▽▽ | $109-$299 | 290 |
| **13** p. 191 | Grand Hyatt DFW | ▽▽▽▽ | $99-$449 [SAVE] | 289 |
| **14** p. 191 | Hyatt Regency DFW | ▽▽▽ | $89-$319 [SAVE] | 290 |

| Map Page | Restaurants | Diamond Rated | Cuisine | Price Range | Page |
|---|---|---|---|---|---|
| **6** p. 191 | Cozymel's Coastal Mex | ▽▽ | Tex-Mex | $8-$20 | 291 |
| **7** p. 191 | Love & War in Texas | ▽▽ | Steak | $10-$29 | 291 |
| **8** p. 191 | Saltwater Willy's Seafood & Steakhouse | ▽▽ | Seafood | $9-$20 | 291 |
| **9** p. 191 | Uncle Buck's Steakhouse & Brewery | ▽▽ | American | $9-$33 | 292 |
| **10** p. 191 | Napoli's Italian Cafe and Confectionary | ▽▽ | Italian | $9-$17 | 291 |
| **11** p. 191 | Big Fish Seafood Grill and Bar | ▽▽ | Seafood | $6-$20 | 290 |

| Map Page | Restaurants (cont'd) | Diamond Rated | Cuisine | Price Range | Page |
|---|---|---|---|---|---|
| ⑫ p. 191 | Silver Fox | ◆◆◆ | Steak | $20-$50 | 291 |
| ⑬ p. 191 | Fireside Pies | ◆◆ | Pizza | $11-$14 | 291 |
| ⑭ p. 191 | Mi Dia from Scratch | ◆◆◆ | Mexican | $9-$28 | 291 |
| ⑮ p. 191 | El Fenix | ◆◆ | Tex-Mex | $7-$12 | 291 |
| ⑯ p. 191 | Saltgrass Steakhouse | ◆◆ | Steak | $9-$30 [SAVE] | 291 |

## IRVING

| Map Page | Hotels | Diamond Rated | Rate Range | Page |
|---|---|---|---|---|
| ⑰ p. 191 | Courtyard by Marriott-DFW Airport North | ◆◆◆ | $79-$189 | 372 |
| ⑱ p. 191 | Residence Inn by Marriott-DFW North | ◆◆◆ | $80-$160 | 376 |
| ⑲ p. 191 | Marriott Hotel-DFW Airport North | ◆◆◆ | $80-$227 [SAVE] | 376 |
| ⑳ p. 191 | Element Dallas Fort Worth Airport North | ◆◆◆ | $89-$162 [SAVE] | 374 |
| ㉑ p. 191 | Wingate by Wyndham DFW Airport North | ◆◆◆ | $79-$149 [SAVE] | 377 |
| ㉒ p. 191 | BEST WESTERN PLUS DFW Airport Suites | ◆◆ | $81-$139 [SAVE] | 372 |
| ㉓ p. 191 | Red Roof Inn/DFW Airport North | ◆◆ | $49-$89 [SAVE] | 376 |
| ㉔ p. 191 | La Quinta Inn & Suites Dallas DFW Airport North | ◆◆ | $85-$150 | 375 |
| ㉕ p. 191 | Homewood Suites by Hilton Irving DFW Airport North | ◆◆◆ | $109-$189 | 375 |
| ㉖ p. 191 | The Westin Dallas Fort Worth Airport | ◆◆◆ | $89-$349 [SAVE] | 377 |
| ㉗ p. 191 | Fairfield Inn & Suites by Marriott | ◆◆◆ | $67-$139 | 374 |
| ㉘ p. 191 | DFW North Super 8 | ◆◆ | $55-$125 [SAVE] | 373 |
| ㉙ p. 191 | Comfort Suites DFW Airport (See ad p. 373.) | ◆◆◆ | $99-$129 | 372 |
| ㉚ p. 191 | DoubleTree by Hilton Hotel DFW Airport-North | ◆◆◆ | $99-$289 [SAVE] | 373 |
| ㉛ p. 191 | Motel 6 - #4725 DFW North | ◆ | Rates not provided | 376 |
| ㉜ p. 191 | Holiday Inn Express & Suites-DFW North | ◆◆◆ | Rates not provided | 374 |
| ㉝ p. 191 | Sheraton DFW Airport Hotel | ◆◆◆ | $99-$359 [SAVE] | 376 |
| ㉞ p. 191 | Hilton Garden Inn Las Colinas | ◆◆◆ | $135-$159 | 374 |
| ㉟ p. 191 | NYLO Dallas/Las Colinas | ◆◆◆ | $89-$499 [SAVE] | 376 |
| ㊱ p. 191 | HYATT house Dallas/Las Colinas | ◆◆◆ | $83-$189 [SAVE] | 375 |
| ㊲ p. 191 | Comfort Suites Las Colinas Center | ◆◆ | $99-$119 | 372 |
| ㊳ p. 191 | Staybridge Suites Dallas-Las Colinas | ◆◆◆ | $99-$229 | 376 |
| ㊴ p. 191 | Courtyard by Marriott-Dallas-Las Colinas | ◆◆◆ | $69-$209 [SAVE] | 372 |
| ㊵ p. 191 | Residence Inn by Marriott at Las Colinas | ◆◆◆ | $79-$219 | 376 |
| ㊶ p. 191 | Hampton Inn Las Colinas | ◆◆◆ | $119-$139 | 374 |
| ㊷ p. 191 | Fairfield Inn & Suites by Marriott-Las Colinas | ◆◆ | $89-$139 | 374 |
| ㊸ p. 191 | Hyatt Place Dallas/Las Colinas | ◆◆◆ | $69-$199 [SAVE] | 375 |
| ㊹ p. 191 | Candlewood Suites Dallas/Las Colinas | ◆◆◆ | $81-$109 | 372 |
| ㊺ p. 191 | Holiday Inn Express Hotel & Suites Irving Convention Center | ◆◆◆ | $79-$149 [SAVE] | 375 |
| ㊻ p. 191 | Dallas Marriott Las Colinas | ◆◆◆ | $104-$248 | 373 |
| ㊼ p. 191 | Wyndham-Las Colinas | ◆◆◆ | $79-$349 [SAVE] | 377 |
| ㊽ p. 191 | Omni Mandalay Dallas at Las Colinas | ◆◆◆◆ | $119-$329 | 376 |

**IRVING (cont'd)**

| Map Page | Hotels (cont'd) | Diamond Rated | Rate Range | Page |
|---|---|---|---|---|
| 49 p. 191 | Aloft Las Colinas *(See ad p. 210.)* | ◆◆◆ | $71-$161 [SAVE] | 372 |
| 50 p. 191 | La Quinta Inn & Suites Dallas - Las Colinas | ◆◆◆ | $82-$140 | 375 |
| 51 p. 191 | Homewood Suites by Hilton Las Colinas | ◆◆◆ | $99-$169 | 375 |
| 52 p. 191 | Four Seasons Resort and Club *(See ad p. 214.)* | ◆◆◆◆ | $280-$430 [SAVE] | 374 |
| 53 p. 191 | Courtyard by Marriott DFW Airport South | ◆◆◆ | $89-$179 [SAVE] | 373 |
| 54 p. 191 | Super 8 DFW South Irving | ◆◆ | $55-$85 [SAVE] | 376 |
| 55 p. 191 | Holiday Inn Express DFW Airport South | ◆◆◆ | $89-$189 | 374 |
| 56 p. 191 | La Quinta Inn & Suites Dallas DFW Airport South/Irving | ◆◆◆ | $85-$160 | 375 |
| 57 p. 191 | Comfort Inn & Suites DFW Airport South | ◆◆◆ | $62-$119 [SAVE] | 372 |
| 58 p. 191 | BEST WESTERN Irving Inn & Suites at DFW Airport | ◆◆ | $69-$95 [SAVE] | 372 |
| 59 p. 191 | Hampton Inn-DFW Airport South | ◆◆◆ | $79-$159 | 374 |
| 60 p. 191 | Embassy Suites-DFW South | ◆◆◆ | $119-$229 | 374 |
| 61 p. 191 | Fairfield Inn & Suites by Marriott DFW Airport South | ◆◆◆ | $75-$142 | 374 |
| 62 p. 191 | Jefferson Street Bed and Breakfast Inn | ◆◆ | $85-$280 [SAVE] | 375 |

| Map Page | Restaurants | Diamond Rated | Cuisine | Price Range | Page |
|---|---|---|---|---|---|
| 19 p. 191 | ZENse | ◆◆ | Thai | $9-$12 | 379 |
| 20 p. 191 | Cavalli Pizza Napoletana | ◆ | Pizza | $7-$12 | 377 |
| 21 p. 191 | Mayuri India Restaurant | ◆◆ | Indian | $10-$18 | 378 |
| 22 p. 191 | Saltgrass Steakhouse | ◆◆ | Steak | $9-$30 [SAVE] | 379 |
| 23 p. 191 | Mi Cocina | ◆◆ | Mexican | $9-$22 | 378 |
| 24 p. 191 | I Fratelli Italian Restaurant | ◆◆ | Italian | $9-$19 | 378 |
| 25 p. 191 | Paradise Indian Cuisine | ◆ | Indian | $10-$14 | 379 |
| 26 p. 191 | Blue Ginger | ◆◆ | Thai | $8-$16 | 377 |
| 27 p. 191 | The Blue Fish | ◆◆ | Japanese | $13-$27 | 377 |
| 28 p. 191 | Veranda Greek Cafe | ◆◆ | Greek | $7-$22 | 379 |
| 29 p. 191 | Cool River Cafe | ◆◆◆ | Steak | $13-$40 | 377 |
| 30 p. 191 | Chicago's Gourmet Pizza | ◆ | Pizza | $10-$25 | 377 |
| 31 p. 191 | Piman Asian Bistro | ◆◆ | Thai | $7-$14 | 379 |
| 32 p. 191 | Italian Cafe | ◆ | Italian | $4-$17 | 378 |
| 33 p. 191 | Café on the Green | ◆◆◆◆ | American | $18-$48 | 377 |
| 34 p. 191 | Midori Sushi | ◆◆ | Japanese | $7-$22 | 379 |
| 35 p. 191 | Via Real | ◆◆◆ | Southwestern | $8-$42 | 379 |
| 36 p. 191 | Kasbah Grill | ◆◆ | Moroccan | $5-$12 | 378 |
| 37 p. 191 | La Margarita | ◆◆ | Tex-Mex | $7-$15 | 378 |
| 38 p. 191 | Pasand Indian Cuisine | ◆◆ | Indian | $10-$18 | 379 |
| 39 p. 191 | Los Lupes VI | ◆◆ | Tex-Mex | $7-$16 | 378 |
| 40 p. 191 | Bangkok Orchid | ◆◆ | Thai | $9-$15 | 377 |
| 41 p. 191 | El Chico | ◆◆ | Tex-Mex | $6-$16 | 378 |
| 42 p. 191 | East Buffet | ◆ | Chinese | $8-$11 | 378 |

| Map Page | Restaurants (cont'd) | Diamond Rated | Cuisine | Price Range | Page |
|---|---|---|---|---|---|
| ④③ p. 191 | Taquera Arandas | ▼ | Mexican | $10-$15 | 379 |
| ④④ p. 191 | Angelo's Spaghetti & Pizza | ▼ | Italian | $6-$14 | 377 |
| ④⑤ p. 191 | Fred's Bar-B-Q | ▼ | Barbecue | $7-$16 | 378 |
| ④⑥ p. 191 | Mama's Daughters' Diner #5 | ▼ | Comfort Food | $5-$11 | 378 |

**COPPELL**

| Map Page | Restaurants | Diamond Rated | Cuisine | Price Range | Page |
|---|---|---|---|---|---|
| ① p. 191 | 7 Salsas | ▼▼ | Tex-Mex | $7-$15 | 146 |
| ② p. 191 | Anamia's Tex-Mex | ▼▼ | Tex-Mex | $6-$22 | 146 |
| ③ p. 191 | Pan Acean | ▼▼ | Asian | $6-$16 | 146 |

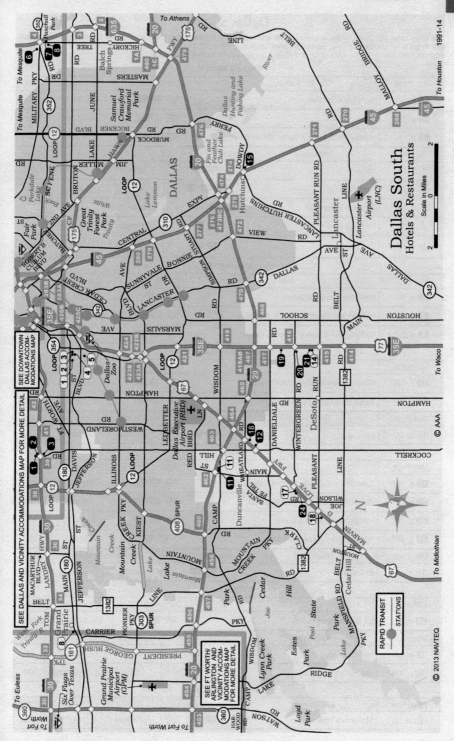

Dallas South
Hotels & Restaurants

# Dallas South

This index helps you "spot" where approved hotels and restaurants are located on the corresponding detailed maps. Hotel daily rate range is for comparison only. Restaurant price range is a combination of lunch and/or dinner. Turn to the listing page for more detailed rate and price information and consult display ads for special promotions.

## DALLAS SOUTH

| Map Page | Hotels | Diamond Rated | Rate Range | Page |
|---|---|---|---|---|
| **1** p. 197 | Hampton Inn & Suites | ◆◆◆ | $89-$119 | 222 |
| **2** p. 197 | Comfort Suites | ◆◆◆ | $94-$139 | 222 |
| **3** p. 197 | Holiday Inn Express & Suites Dallas West | ◆◆◆ | $119-$250 | 222 |

| Map Page | Restaurants | Diamond Rated | Cuisine | Price Range | Page |
|---|---|---|---|---|---|
| ① p. 197 | Bolsa | ◆◆ | American | $10-$27 | 222 |
| ② p. 197 | Hattie's | ◆◆◆ | American | $7-$32 | 222 |
| ③ p. 197 | Tillman's Roadhouse | ◆◆ | American | $9-$35 | 222 |
| ④ p. 197 | Veracruz Cafe | ◆◆ | Mexican | $9-$16 | 222 |
| ⑤ p. 197 | La Calle Doce | ◆◆ | Mexican Seafood | $7-$17 | 222 |

## MESQUITE

| Map Page | Hotels | Diamond Rated | Rate Range | Page |
|---|---|---|---|---|
| **6** p. 197 | **Days Inn Mesquite/Dallas** | ◆◆ | $55-$110 SAVE | 416 |
| **7** p. 197 | **Holiday Inn Express Hotel & Suites** | ◆◆◆ | $89-$139 SAVE | 416 |
| **8** p. 197 | Hampton Inn & Suites at Rodeo Center | ◆◆◆ | $80-$99 | 416 |

## DUNCANVILLE

| Map Page | Hotels | Diamond Rated | Rate Range | Page |
|---|---|---|---|---|
| **11** p. 197 | Hilton Garden Inn Dallas/Duncanville | ◆◆◆ | $99-$169 | 229 |
| **12** p. 197 | **BEST WESTERN PLUS Duncanville/Dallas** | ◆◆◆ | $90-$160 SAVE | 229 |

| Map Page | Restaurant | Diamond Rated | Cuisine | Price Range | Page |
|---|---|---|---|---|---|
| ⑪ p. 197 | Los Lupes | ◆◆ | Mexican | $6-$16 | 230 |

## DESOTO

| Map Page | Hotels | Diamond Rated | Rate Range | Page |
|---|---|---|---|---|
| **18** p. 197 | TownePlace Suites by Marriott Dallas DeSoto | ◆◆◆ | $89-$104 | 228 |
| **19** p. 197 | Hampton Inn & Suites Dallas/DeSoto | ◆◆◆ | $99-$149 | 228 |
| **20** p. 197 | Holiday Inn Express & Suites | ◆◆◆ | $89-$119 | 228 |
| **21** p. 197 | Americas Best Value Inn & Suites | ◆◆ | $59-$79 | 227 |

| Map Page | Restaurant | Diamond Rated | Cuisine | Price Range | Page |
|---|---|---|---|---|---|
| ⑭ p. 197 | **El Chico** | ◆◆ | Tex-Mex | $7-$16 | 228 |

## CEDAR HILL

| Map Page | Hotel | Diamond Rated | Rate Range | Page |
|---|---|---|---|---|
| **24** p. 197 | **La Quinta Inn & Suites** | ◆◆◆ | $89-$124 SAVE | 136 |

| Map Page | Restaurants | Diamond Rated | Cuisine | Price Range | Page |
|---|---|---|---|---|---|
| ⑰ p. 197 | Veracruz Cafe | ◆◆ | Mexican | $9-$17 | 136 |
| ⑱ p. 197 | Saltgrass Steakhouse | ◆◆ | Steak | $9-$30 SAVE | 136 |

## GRAND PRAIRIE

| Map Page | Restaurant | Diamond Rated | Cuisine | Price Range | Page |
|---|---|---|---|---|---|
| ⑧ p. 197 | Monterey's Little Mexico | ◆◆ | Tex-Mex | $6-$13 | 288 |

## DOWNTOWN DALLAS

### THE ADOLPHUS   214/742-8200  25

Classic Historic Hotel

Rates not provided

**Address:** 1321 Commerce St 75202 **Location:** Between Field and Akard sts. **Facility:** Built in 1912, this ornate hotel founded by the famous beer baron Adolphus Busch is a city landmark and features spacious rooms. Enjoy a meal at the renowned restaurant or take in afternoon tea. 422 units, some kitchens. 22 stories, interior corridors. **Parking:** valet only. **Amenities:** Some: safes. **Dining:** 3 restaurants, also, The French Room, see separate listing. **Activities:** exercise room, massage. **Guest Services:** valet laundry, area transportation.

SAVE | | | | CALL | M | BIZ
SHS | | X | | |
/SOME UNITS | | |

### ALOFT DOWNTOWN DALLAS   (214)761-0000  26

 Hotel

$109-$399

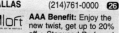

**AAA Benefit:** Enjoy the new twist, get up to 20% off + Starwood Preferred Guest® bonuses!

**Address:** 1033 Young St 75202 **Location:** Northeast corner of Griffin and Young sts. Across from convention center. **Facility:** 193 units. 9 stories, interior corridors. Bath: shower only. **Parking:** on-site (fee). **Terms:** cancellation fee imposed. **Amenities:** safes. **Pool(s):** heated outdoor. **Activities:** exercise room. **Guest Services:** coin laundry.

SAVE | | Y | CALL | M | | BIZ | HS | | X |
| /SOME UNITS |

(See map & index p. 175.)

## BEST WESTERN CITYPLACE INN  (214)827-6080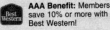

Hotel
$90-$130

**AAA Benefit:** Members save 10% or more with Best Western!

**Address:** 4150 N Central Expwy 75204 **Location:** US 75 exit 1B (Fitzhugh Ave) southbound; exit 2 (Fitzhugh Ave) northbound. **Facility:** 78 units, some two bedrooms. 2 stories (no elevator), exterior corridors. **Amenities:** safes. **Pool(s):** outdoor. **Activities:** exercise room. **Guest Services:** coin laundry.

## BEST WESTERN MARKET CENTER

(214)741-9000  **9**

Hotel
$82-$200

**AAA Benefit:** Members save 10% or more with Best Western!

**Address:** 2023 Market Center Blvd 75207 **Location:** I-35E exit 430B (Market Center Blvd), 0.3 mi se. **Facility:** 96 units. 3 stories, interior/exterior corridors. **Amenities:** safes. **Pool(s):** outdoor. **Activities:** exercise room. **Guest Services:** valet and coin laundry. **Featured Amenity:** continental breakfast.

## THE CORINTHIAN BED & BREAKFAST  214/818-0400  **16**

**Historic Bed & Breakfast.** Rates not provided. **Address:** 4125 Junius St 75246 **Location:** US 75 exit Lemmon Ave/Hall St, just se on Lemmon Ave to Haskell Dr, 1 mi s, then just e. **Facility:** This historic 1905 home has been carefully renovated to preserve an early-20th-century look. Baths are modern and rooms have elegant appointments. It's close to nightlife and many restaurants. 5 units, some kitchens. 2 stories (no elevator), interior/exterior corridors. **Terms:** age restrictions may apply.

## COURTYARD BY MARRIOTT-MARKET CENTER

(214)653-1166  **7**

Hotel $84-$135 **Address:** 2150 Market Center Blvd 75207 **Location:** I-35E exit 430B (Market Center Blvd), just se. **Facility:** 184 units. 5 stories, interior corridors. **Pool(s):** outdoor. **Activities:** hot tub, exercise room. **Guest Services:** valet and coin laundry, boarding pass kiosk, area transportation.

**AAA Benefit:** Members save 5% or more!

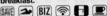

▼ See AAA listing p. 289 ▼

(See map & index p. 175.)

## DALLAS MARRIOTT CITY CENTER   (214)979-9000   🔟9️⃣

Hotel
$119-$289

**Marriott**
HOTELS & RESORTS

**AAA Benefit:**
Members save 5%
or more!

**Address:** 650 N Pearl St 75201 **Location:** Between San Jacinto and Bryan sts, 0.3 mi w of US 75 Central Expwy. **Facility:** The hotel features a stop on the light rail system, and its location at the Plaza of the America offers convenience to an indoor green area, food court and other shopping and services. 416 units. 14 stories, interior corridors. **Parking:** valet only. **Amenities:** safes. **Activities:** exercise room, massage. **Guest Services:** valet laundry, boarding pass kiosk.

SAVE 🍴 📶 ⅄ BIZ SHS 📶 ✕ 🎥 🖥

## DOUBLETREE BY HILTON HOTEL DALLAS - MARKET CENTER   (214)741-7481   🔟0️⃣

🌙🌙🌙 Hotel $89-$309 **Address:** 2015 Market Center Blvd 75207 **Location:** I-35E exit 430B (Market Center Blvd), just w. **Facility:** 227 units. 11 stories, interior corridors. **Terms:** 1-7 night minimum stay, cancellation fee imposed. **Pool(s):** outdoor. **Activities:** exercise room. **Guest Services:** valet and coin laundry, area transportation.

**AAA Benefit:**
Members save 5%
or more!

🍴 📶 ⅄ 🏊 BIZ HS 📶 ✕ 🎥 🖥 🖥

## FAIRFIELD INN & SUITES BY MARRIOTT MARKET CENTER
(214)760-8800   8️⃣

🌙🌙🌙 Hotel $76-$110 **Address:** 2110 Market Center Blvd 75207 **Location:** I-35E exit 430B (Market Center Blvd), just se. **Facility:** 116 units. 3 stories, interior corridors. **Pool(s):** heated indoor. **Guest Services:** valet and coin laundry, area transportation.

**AAA Benefit:**
Members save 5%
or more!

🏊 📶 ✕ 🖥 /SOME UNITS 🖥 🖥

## THE FAIRMONT DALLAS   (214)720-2020   2️⃣0️⃣

Hotel
$129-$699

**Address:** 1717 N Akard St 75201 **Location:** Corner of Ross Ave and N Akard St. **Facility:** Central to the arts, finance and entertainment districts, this hotel maintains the air of refinement and luxury expected with the name Fairmont. The guest units are all upscale and vary in size. 545 units. 19-25 stories, interior corridors. **Parking:** valet only. **Terms:** cancellation fee imposed. **Amenities:** safes. **Dining:** Pyramid Restaurant & Bar, see separate listing. **Pool(s):** outdoor. **Activities:** exercise room. **Guest Services:** valet laundry.

SAVE ECO 🍴 📶 ⅄ CALL 🅜

/SOME UNITS 🛏 🖥 🖥

## HILTON ANATOLE DALLAS   (214)748-1200   6️⃣

🌙🌙🌙 🌙🌙🌙 Hotel $109-$359 **Address:** 2201 N Stemmons Frwy 75207 **Location:** I-35E exit 430B (Market Center Blvd); on southbound frontage road. **Facility:** This hotel sits on nearly 50 acres of land, with a state-of-the-art recreational facility, a beautiful spa, lovely lawn and garden areas, and spacious meeting rooms and ballrooms. 1606 units. 12-27 stories, interior corridors. **Parking:** on-site (fee) and valet. **Terms:** 1-7 night minimum stay, cancellation fee imposed. **Amenities:** safes. **Dining:** 5 restaurants, also, SER Steak and Spirits, see separate listing, nightclub. **Pool(s):** outdoor, heated indoor. **Activities:** sauna, hot tub, steamroom, tennis, spa. **Guest Services:** valet laundry.

**AAA Benefit:**
Members save 5%
or more!

🍴 📶 ⅄ CALL 🅜 🏊 📶 BIZ SHS 📶 ✕

🎥 🖥 /SOME UNITS 🖥

## HOLIDAY INN DALLAS PARK CITIES   (214)750-6060   1️⃣

🌙🌙🌙 Hotel $99-$109 **Address:** 6070 N Central Expwy 75206 **Location:** US 75 exit 3 (Mockingbird Ln); on northbound frontage road. **Facility:** 292 units. 9 stories, interior corridors. **Terms:** cancellation fee imposed. **Pool(s):** heated indoor. **Activities:** exercise room. **Guest Services:** valet and coin laundry, area transportation.

🚭 🍴 📶 ⅄ 🏊 BIZ 📶 ✕ 🖥

/SOME UNITS 🛏 HS 🖥

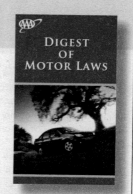

(See map & index p. 175.)

**HOTEL INDIGO DALLAS DOWNTOWN**  (214)741-7700  **23**

🚇🚇🚇 **Historic Hotel** $89-$149 **Address:** 1933 Main St 75201 **Location:** Jct Main and Harwood sts; on northwest corner. **Facility:** A Beaux Arts influence is evident in the terra-cotta, granite, cast iron and wrought iron ornamenting this landmark hotel founded in 1924. The inside, however, is done in a casual nautical theme. 170 units. 14 stories, interior corridors. *Bath:* shower only. **Parking:** on-site (fee) and valet. **Terms:** 3 day cancellation notice-fee imposed. **Activities:** exercise room. **Guest Services:** valet and coin laundry, area transportation.

🏨 🚗 🍴 BIZ HS 🛜 ✉ 🖥 / SOME UNITS 🛏 🧳 🖼

**HOTEL ST. GERMAIN**  (214)871-2516  **12**

Country Inn
$305-$700

**Address:** 2516 Maple Ave 75201 **Location:** I-35 exit 430A (Oak Lawn Ave), 0.5 mi e, then 1 mi s. **Facility:** This stately Victorian home features a variety of tastefully decorated guest rooms and inviting outdoor spaces. Feather beds, room service for breakfast and vintage baths with modern fixtures are offered. 7 units. 3 stories (no elevator), interior corridors. **Parking:** on-site and valet. **Terms:** closed 7/30-8/12, check-in 4 pm, 7 day cancellation notice-fee imposed. **Dining:** restaurant, see separate listing. **Activities:** massage. **Guest Services:** valet laundry. **Featured Amenity:** continental breakfast.

SAVE 🍴 🚗 🛜 ✉ / SOME UNITS 🛏

**HOTEL PALOMAR**  (214)520-7969  **2**

🚇🚇🚇 🚇🚇🚇
Hotel
$169-$397

**Address:** 5300 E Mockingbird Ln 75206 **Location:** US 75 exit 3 (Mockingbird Ln); on southeast corner. **Facility:** Upscale and modern accommodations with a friendly staff can be found at the conveniently located hotel near downtown and a short walk from the main SMU campus and several restaurants. 198 units. 9 stories, interior corridors. **Parking:** valet only. **Amenities:** video games, safes. **Dining:** Central 214, see separate listing. **Pool(s):** heated outdoor. **Activities:** hot tub, steamroom, exercise room, spa. **Guest Services:** valet laundry.

SAVE ECO 🚗 🍴 👤 🍸 CALL 📞M 🏊 BIZ HS
🛜 ✉ 🎥 / SOME UNITS 🐕

**HOTEL ZAZA**  214/468-8399  **15**

Hotel
Rates not provided

**Address:** 2332 Leonard St 75201 **Location:** Jct Maple Ave/Routh St and McKinney Ave; southeast corner. **Facility:** If ever a place had a vibe, this place is it. As the name insinuates, this hotel takes pride in differentiating itself from the pack and operating with a little whimsy. 155 units. 4 stories, interior corridors. **Parking:** valet only. **Terms:** check-in 4 pm. **Amenities:** safes. **Dining:** Dragonfly, see separate listing. **Pool(s):** outdoor. **Activities:** hot tub, steamroom, exercise room, spa. **Guest Services:** valet laundry, area transportation.

SAVE 🚗 🍴 👤 🍸 CALL 📞M
🏊 BIZ HS 🛜 ✉ 🎥 🧳 / SOME UNITS 🛏 🖼 🖥

(See map & index p. 175.)

## HYATT HOUSE DALLAS/UPTOWN (214)965-9990 🔟3️⃣

Extended Stay Hotel
$89-$299

**AAA Benefit:** Members save 10%!

**Address:** 2914 Harry Hines Blvd 75201 **Location:** I-35 exit 430A (Oak Lawn Ave), just n to Harry Hines Blvd, then 0.6 mi s. **Facility:** 141 efficiencies. 4 stories, interior corridors. **Parking:** on-site (fee). **Terms:** cancellation fee imposed. **Pool(s):** outdoor. **Activities:** hot tub, exercise room. **Guest Services:** valet and coin laundry, area transportation. **Featured Amenity:** breakfast buffet. (See ad p. 202.)

## HYATT REGENCY DALLAS AT REUNION
(214)651-1234 2️⃣7️⃣

Hotel
$89-$499

HYATT REGENCY
**AAA Benefit:** Members save 10%!

**Address:** 300 Reunion Blvd 75207 **Location:** I-35E and US 77 exit Reunion Blvd, just e; I-30 exit Commerce St eastbound, just n. **Facility:** Outfitted with electric blinds, modern design and neutral colors, the rooms at this hotel suit all travelers. Though the pool area is severely lacking, the bar scene is not. 1120 units. 15-28 stories, interior corridors. **Parking:** on-site (fee) and valet. **Terms:** cancellation fee imposed. **Amenities:** safes. **Dining:** 3 restaurants, also, Five Sixty by Wolfgang Puck, see separate listing. **Pool(s):** heated outdoor. **Activities:** exercise room. **Guest Services:** valet laundry, area transportation.

## LE MÉRIDIEN DALLAS, THE STONELEIGH
(214)871-7111 1️⃣1️⃣

Hotel
$119-$469

LE MÉRIDIEN **AAA Benefit:** Members get up to 20% off, plus Starwood Preferred Guest® bonuses!

**Address:** 2927 Maple Ave 75201 **Location:** I-35E exit 430A (Oak Lawn Ave), 0.5 mi e, then 1.2 mi s. **Facility:** Originally built in 1923 in this upscale neighborhood, the hotel is a Dallas landmark and has a colorful history. The renovated rooms retain their historical aspects. 170 units. 12 stories, interior corridors. **Parking:** valet only. **Terms:** cancellation fee imposed. **Amenities:** safes. **Dining:** T/X Restaurant, see separate listing. **Activities:** exercise room, spa. **Guest Services:** valet laundry, area transportation.

## MAGNOLIA HOTEL DALLAS (214)915-6500 2️⃣4️⃣

Historic Hotel
$129-$259

**Address:** 1401 Commerce St 75201 **Location:** Corner of Commerce and Akard sts. **Facility:** Large hotel in a renovated office building that used to be the headquarters of the old Magnolia Gas & Oil company. The interior has been redone with modern décor. 329 units, some kitchens. 28 stories, interior corridors. **Parking:** valet only. **Terms:** 3 day cancellation notice-fee imposed. **Activities:** exercise room. **Guest Services:** valet and coin laundry, area transportation.

## THE RITZ-CARLTON, DALLAS (214)922-0200 1️⃣7️⃣

Hotel $399-$799 **Address:** 2121 McKinney Ave 75201 **Location:** SR 366 (Woodall Rodgers Frwy) exit Pearl St, just sw to Olive St, then just nw. **Facility:** Located in uptown Dallas, with convenient access to shopping,

**AAA Benefit:** Unequaled service at special member savings!

dining, and local businesses, this hotel offers guests a variety of luxury rooms. The rooms are elegant but designed for both the leisure and business traveler. Museum quality artwork, an elegant roof-top pool and a nationally recognized restaurant are just a few of the reasons to spend the night here. 218 units. 8 stories, interior corridors. **Parking:** valet only. **Amenities:** video games, safes. **Dining:** Fearing's, see separate listing. **Pool(s):** heated outdoor. **Activities:** exercise room, spa. **Guest Services:** valet laundry, area transportation.

## ROSEWOOD CRESCENT HOTEL (214)871-3200 1️⃣4️⃣

Hotel $300-$3000 **Address:** 400 Crescent Ct 75201 **Location:** Corner of Crescent Ct and McKinney Ave; uptown. **Facility:** As part of a multi-use complex, one can do everything from banking to buying a wedding dress. Worth mentioning are the numerous fine restaurants, all within a short walk of this hotel. 220 units, some kitchens. 7 stories, interior corridors. **Parking:** on-site (fee) and valet. **Terms:** cancellation fee imposed. **Amenities:** safes. **Dining:** 4 restaurants, also, Nobu, see separate listing, entertainment. **Pool(s):** outdoor. **Activities:** sauna, hot tub, steamroom, spa. **Guest Services:** valet laundry, area transportation.

## ROSEWOOD MANSION ON TURTLE CREEK
(214)559-2100 5️⃣

Hotel $270-$5000 **Address:** 2821 Turtle Creek Blvd 75219 **Location:** 2 mi nw, entrance on Gillespie St, just e of jct Gillespie St and Oak Lawn Ave. Located in a residential area. **Facility:** Its location in a quiet upscale neighborhood makes this property an oasis in a large metropolitan city. Comfortable, intimate rooms are richly appointed and designed in chocolate and neutral hues. 143 units, some kitchens. 9 stories, interior corridors. **Parking:** valet only. **Terms:** cancellation fee imposed. **Amenities:** safes. **Dining:** The Mansion Restaurant at Rosewood Mansion on Turtle Creek, see separate listing. **Pool(s):** heated outdoor. **Activities:** sauna, hot tub, steamroom, exercise room, massage. **Guest Services:** valet laundry, area transportation.

(See map & index p. 175.)

## SHERATON DALLAS HOTEL (214)922-8000 [21]

▼▼▼▼ Hotel
$299-$369

**Sheraton** HOTELS & RESORTS

**AAA Benefit:** Members get up to 20% off, plus Starwood Preferred Guest® bonuses!

**Address:** 400 N Olive St 75201 **Location:** At Live Oak and Olive sts, just w off Central Expwy. **Facility:** With its large public spaces and three towers of rooms, this hotel is popular for large groups and convention-goers, but leisure travelers will be pleased to find it boasts a rooftop pool. 1840 units. 29-38 stories, interior corridors. **Parking:** on-site (fee) and valet. **Terms:** cancellation fee imposed. **Amenities:** video games, safes. **Dining:** 3 restaurants. **Pool(s):** heated outdoor. **Activities:** exercise room. **Guest Services:** valet and coin laundry.

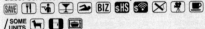

## SPRINGHILL SUITES BY MARRIOTT (214)999-0500 [22]

▼▼▼ Hotel $129-$189 **Address:** 1907 N Lamar St 75202 **Location:** Between Corbin Ave and Munger St; in Historic West End District. **Facility:** 148 units. 10 stories, interior corridors. **Parking:** valet and street only. **Pool(s):** outdoor. **Activities:** exercise room. **Guest Services:** valet and coin laundry, area transportation.

**AAA Benefit:** Members save 5% or more!

## WARWICK MELROSE HOTEL DALLAS (214)521-5151 [4]

▼▼▼ Historic Hotel
$149-$599

**Address:** 3015 Oak Lawn Ave 75219 **Location:** I-35E exit 430 (Oak Lawn Ave), 0.8 mi n; entrance off Cedar Springs, just n. Located in a quiet area. **Facility:** Built in 1924, this hotel offers varied-size rooms, all elegantly appointed. It is strategically located close to the Uptown, downtown and gay neighborhoods and close to numerous restaurants. 184 units. 8 stories, interior corridors. **Parking:** valet only. **Terms:** cancellation fee imposed, resort fee. **Amenities:** safes. **Dining:** The Landmark Restaurant, see separate listing. **Activities:** exercise room. **Guest Services:** valet laundry, area transportation.

## W DALLAS VICTORY HOTEL & RESIDENCES (214)397-4100 [18]

▼▼▼ Hotel
$279-$599

**W** HOTELS

**AAA Benefit:** Special member room rates, plus Starwood Preferred Guest® bonuses!

**Address:** 2440 Victory Park Ln 75219 **Location:** Southwest corner of Olive and N Houston sts; uptown Dallas; across from American Airlines Center. **Facility:** This über-trendy hotel has rooms with clean lines and amenities many techies will appreciate. The infinity pool on the roof is a big draw. 252 units. 33 stories, interior corridors. **Parking:** on-site (fee) and valet. **Terms:** cancellation fee imposed. **Amenities:** safes. Some: video games. **Pool(s):** heated outdoor. **Activities:** exercise room, spa. **Guest Services:** valet laundry, area transportation.

---

## ABACUS 214/559-3111 [24]

▼▼▼▼ Continental
Fine Dining
$20-$60

**AAA Inspector Notes:** Global contemporary cuisine is served in very modern and upscale rooms. Asian cuisine makes a lot of appearances, but Niman Ranch pork, short ribs and beef tenderloin also are sample items. This place is loved by the well-heeled and can get loud, but the view to the kitchen provides guests an opportunity to see the chefs at work. The lobster shooters are the signature item and should not be missed. **Features:** full bar. **Reservations:** suggested. **Address:** 4511 McKinney Ave 75205 **Location:** Corner of McKinney Ave and Armstrong St; between Knox St and Fitzhugh Ave. **Parking:** valet only. D

## AL BIERNAT'S 214/219-2201 [26]

▼▼▼ Steak. Fine Dining. $20-$75 **AAA Inspector Notes:** Located in the affluent Oak Lawn district, the restaurant offers seafood, but the menu is truly diverse and offers an enticing list of small plates and starters. Complete dessert and after-dinner ports also are available. **Features:** full bar, Sunday brunch. **Reservations:** suggested. **Address:** 4217 Oak Lawn Ave 75219 **Location:** Southwest corner of Oak Lawn and Herschel aves; between Wycliff Ave and Prescott St. **Parking:** valet only. L D

## ARCODORO & POMODORO 214/871-1924 [48]

▼▼▼ Italian. Fine Dining. $11-$36 **AAA Inspector Notes:** Known for signature recipes from the owner's home on the island of Sardinia, the eatery features award-winning pizzas baked in a wood-burning oven, excellent pasta with homemade sauces and a wide array of fresh fish and wild game entrées. **Features:** full bar, patio dining. **Reservations:** suggested. **Address:** 100 Crescent Ct, Suite 140 75201 **Location:** Woodall Rodgers Frwy exit Pearl St, n to McKinney Ave, just e to Maple Ave, then just n. **Parking:** valet and street only. L D

## AVANTI RISTORANTE 214/871-4955 [41]

▼▼▼ Italian. Fine Dining. $14-$33 **AAA Inspector Notes:** Traditional pasta dishes share menu space with veal, lamb and seafood entrées. This bistro is open for late-night dining on the weekends and is located in Uptown, which is crawling with young professionals. The cultural district also is nearby. **Features:** full bar. **Reservations:** suggested. **Address:** 2720 McKinney Ave 75204 **Location:** Jct Pearl St and McKinney Ave, 0.3 mi n. **Parking:** on-site and valet. L D

## AW SHUCKS 214/821-9449 [13]

▼ Seafood. Quick Serve. $6-$10 **AAA Inspector Notes:** This popular eatery with a modest nautical theme offers oysters, shrimp, gumbo and fried seafood baskets. Very popular are the fish tacos and signature seafood cocktail. Dining is no frills and they offer an unusual honor system for payment. Located on one of the city's main bar-hopping streets, it is regularly crowded. Expect parking to be a challenge. **Features:** beer & wine, patio dining. **Address:** 3601 Greenville Ave 75206 **Location:** US 75 exit 3 (Mockingbird Ln), 0.5 mi e to Greenville Ave, then 0.4 mi s. L D

## BIJOUX 214/350-6100 [2]

▼▼▼ French
Fine Dining
$12-$29

**AAA Inspector Notes:** This small gem features contemporary French cuisine served in an intimate dining room with soothing grays and greens. Seasonal menus may include items such as free-range rack of lamb, crisp pork belly, pan-seared prawns, Hudson Valley foie gras and desserts like coconut panna cotta. The staff provides service that makes any meal here memorable. The shopping center it is located in is pedestrian-friendly and has an eclectic collection of stores. **Features:** full bar. **Reservations:** suggested. **Address:** 5450 W Lovers Ln, Suite 225 75209 **Location:** Just w of Dallas North Tollway, jct Inwood Rd; in The Inwood Village Shopping Center. D

(See map & index p. 175.)

## BLUE GOOSE CANTINA  214/823-8339  [18]
▼▼ ▼▼ Tex-Mex. Casual Dining. $8-$20 **AAA Inspector Notes:** Guests can sample a best-selling margarita—grandma's favorite recipe—as they relax in a Mexican cantina setting. The sour cream enchiladas—a mixture of rice, beans and chicken in sour cream sauce rolled in a fresh tortilla—is a favorite selection. The restaurant is located in Dallas' lower Greenville area, a very popular spot for the locals. Parking during evenings and weekends can be challenging. **Features:** full bar, Sunday brunch. **Address:** 2905 Greenville Ave 75206 **Location:** N from US 75 exit 3 (Mockingbird Ln/University Blvd), 0.5 mi e to Greenville Ave, 0.9 mi s. [L] [D]

## BOB'S STEAK & CHOP HOUSE  214/528-9446  [28]
▼▼ ▼▼ Steak. Fine Dining. $25-$59 **AAA Inspector Notes:** Popular, award-winning steakhouse dining in a refined dining room setting is enhanced by mahogany booths and white tablecloths. Beef dominates the menu, with all entrées served with the signature colossal glazed carrot and choice of potato. The congenial service is crisp. **Features:** full bar. **Reservations:** suggested. **Address:** 4300 Lemmon Ave 75219 **Location:** Between US 75/Central Expwy and Dallas North Tollway. **Parking:** valet only. [D]

## BREAD WINNERS CAFE & BAKERY  214/754-4940  [37]
▼▼ ▼▼ American. Casual Dining. $5-$30 **AAA Inspector Notes:** A small plate stacked with delicious breads welcomes guests to the neighborhood eatery. Menus vary, but lunches normally consist of sandwiches, burgers and daily specials. More ambitious dinner entrées might include stuffed Chilean sea bass or honey-pecan-glazed pork tenderloin. Desserts and breads are sold in the storefront bakery. **Features:** full bar, patio dining, Sunday brunch. **Address:** 3301 McKinney Ave 75204 **Location:** Corner of Hall St; uptown.
[B] [L] [D] [M]

## BURGER STREET  214/823-3845  [10]
▼ Burgers. Quick Serve. $3-$6 **AAA Inspector Notes:** Tasty ingredients, including ground beef, crisp romaine lettuce, red onions, pickles and tomatoes, are the stars of this perpetually packed fastfood establishment. It's close to SMU and a popular bar-hopping area. A drive-thru is available. **Features:** patio dining. **Address:** 5657 E Mockingbird Ln 75206 **Location:** US 75 exit Mockingbird Ln, just e. [L] [D] CALL [M]

## CAFE BRAZIL UNIVERSITY PARK  214/691-7791  [8]
▼▼ ▼▼ Breakfast. Casual Dining. $7-$11 **AAA Inspector Notes:** There isn't much Brazilian about the food here. Popular with the university crowd, the restaurant focuses on breakfast specialties, sandwiches, heartier entrées such as chicken-fried chicken, and regional favorites like quesadillas and nachos. Specialty coffees are sold, and desserts are made in the bakery. The place won't win any design contests but reflects the laid-back, eclectic style of the employees and patrons. Parking can be an issue, especially at lunchtime and on weekends. **Address:** 6420 N Central Expwy 75206 **Location:** US 75 exit 3 (Mockingbird Ln); on northbound access road.
[B] [L] [D] [24]

## CAFE INSTANBUL  214/902-0919  [3]
▼▼ ▼▼ Turkish. Casual Dining. $11-$19 **AAA Inspector Notes:** The heat and smells radiating from the ovens at the entrance foretell a promising dining experience. The meze, or small plates, combine different flavors and textures. The tarama, for example, combines potato with red caviar. Rustic tile flooring, faux walls and rustic wood accents add to the authentic experience. The location makes it convenient for those with long layovers at Love Field airport and anyone who wants to take in a day of fun local shopping. **Features:** beer & wine. **Address:** 5450 W Lovers Ln, Unit 222 75209 **Location:** Just w of Dallas North Tollway; in The Inwood Village Shopping Center. [L] [D]

## CAFE MADRID  214/528-1731  [23]
▼▼ ▼▼ Spanish. Casual Dining. $5-$15 **AAA Inspector Notes:** Tapas in Spain are small, appetizer portions of food, usually a prelude to dinner. At Cafe Madrid, order several different tapas and share with your dinner companions. The shrimp in garlic sauce will leave you mopping your dish clean, and the goat cheese-stuffed piquillo peppers will leave you asking for more. Their signature sangria should not be missed. Sidewalk dining is available for smokers. Upscale retail outlets are nearby. **Features:** beer & wine, happy hour. **Address:** 4501 Travis St 75205 **Location:** US 75 exit 2 (Knox St/Henderson Ave), just w, then just s. [D] CALL [M] [☒]

## CAMPISI'S EGYPTIAN  214/827-0355  [11]
▼▼ ▼▼ Italian. Casual Dining. $9-$22 **AAA Inspector Notes:** "Egyptian" may be part of their name, but it relates nothing to what they are currently serving at this Dallas landmark. Traditional favorites like pan pizza, spaghetti, minestrone soup, salad and other pasta dishes take their place on the menu. This is a great place to bring kids, as simple dishes are the mainstays. A fun and energetic atmosphere is enhanced by an ever-smiling staff and upbeat jukebox music that can played straight from your table. **Features:** full bar. **Address:** 5610 E Mockingbird Ln 75206 **Location:** US 75 exit 3 (Mockingbird Ln), just e. [L] [D]

## THE CAPITAL GRILLE  214/303-0500  [52]
▼▼ ▼▼ American. Fine Dining. $13-$46 **AAA Inspector Notes:** Cherry wood and red leather assist in making this "clubby" dining room a beautiful spot to dine on excellent cuts of dry-aged beef. The staff is highly attentive and knowledgeable. **Features:** full bar, patio dining. **Reservations:** suggested. **Address:** 500 Crescent Ct, Suite 135 75201 **Location:** Corner of Crescent Ct and McKinney Ave; uptown. **Parking:** valet only. [L] [D]

## CENTRAL 214  214/443-9339  [12]
▼▼ ▼▼ New American. Fine Dining. $8-$32 **AAA Inspector Notes:** Seasonal menu offerings as well as Black Angus steaks and seafood are featured at this restaurant with a contemporary atmosphere. You might try the littleneck clams with melted leeks, bacon and mushrooms or striped bass paella with chorizo and roasted peppers before sinking in to some sweet potato donuts with mascarpone cream for dessert. Yum. **Features:** full bar, patio dining, Sunday brunch. **Reservations:** suggested. **Address:** 5860 N Central Expwy 75206 **Location:** US 75 exit 3 (Mockingbird Ln); on southeast corner; in Hotel Palomar. **Parking:** valet only. [B] [L] [D] CALL [M]

## CHUY'S  214/559-2489  [22]
▼▼ ▼▼ Tex-Mex. Family Dining. $7-$10 **AAA Inspector Notes:** This Texas original serves up Mexican kitsch like no else in its décor, but takes pride in its several house-made Chile sauces and hand-made tortillas. The menu is basic...fajitas, tacos and enchiladas. It's very family friendly but also located in an area frequented by young professionals. **Features:** full bar, patio dining, Sunday brunch, happy hour. **Address:** 4544 McKinney Ave 75205 **Location:** US 75 exit 2 (Knox St/Henderson Ave), just w. [L] [D]

## DAKOTA'S  214/740-4001  [58]
▼▼ ▼▼ Steak. Fine Dining. $12-$55 **AAA Inspector Notes:** The upscale American grill has the distinction of being located below street level with access from either a free-standing elevator or from the building across the street. They feature mostly grilled items such as beef, lamb, seafood and chicken. Don't overlook this place for lunch as they have a good variety of entrée salads and sandwiches. The entry is located on a small triangle of a block; look for the awning and the valet parking attendant. **Features:** full bar, patio dining. **Reservations:** suggested. **Address:** 600 N Akard St 75201 **Location:** Jct San Jacinto; lower level of Lincoln Plaza. **Parking:** valet only. [L] [D]

## DESPERADOS MEXICAN RESTAURANT  214/363-1850  [7]
▼▼ ▼▼ Tex-Mex. Casual Dining. $8-$18 **AAA Inspector Notes:** This small North Dallas restaurant located near Southern Methodist University, businesses and shopping has been in business for more than 35 years. Specializing in traditional Tex-Mex cuisine, the menu is full of your favorite dishes, including enchiladas, fajitas, flautas and tacos al carbon. Breakfast is available on Saturday and Sunday until 3 pm. **Features:** full bar, Sunday brunch, happy hour. **Address:** 4818 Greenville Ave 75206 **Location:** US 75 exit 4 (Lovers Ln), just e to Greenville Ave, then just s. [L] [D]

(See map & index p. 175.)

## DRAGONFLY  214/550-9500  51

**New American Casual Dining**
**$9-$35**

**AAA Inspector Notes:** A people-watcher's paradise, this modern restaurant features views of the hotel's perpetually hopping pool and lively bar. The décor is eclectic and the menu has been updated with items that are good for groups or those that prefer noshing to dining. Ahi tuna tacos, shrimp and chervil dumplings, Amish jerk chicken and fresh fish can be followed by creative desserts such as an ice cream sandwich made with two fresh chocolate chip cookies and paired with a delectable hot fudge dipping sauce. **Features:** full bar, patio dining, Sunday brunch. **Reservations:** suggested. **Address:** 2332 Leonard St 75201 **Location:** Jct Maple Ave/Routh St and McKinney Ave; southeast corner; in Hotel ZaZa. **Parking:** valet only. B L D CALL M

## DREAM CAFE  214/954-0486  42

American. Casual Dining. $8-$20 **AAA Inspector Notes:** Although you can savor items like almond shrimp, chicken potpie and chicken enchiladas at this eclectic Dallas eatery, the restaurant is legendary for its weekend brunches where you can nosh on items like granola-crusted French toast, Greek omelets and huevos rancheros. Families with young children like the inclusive feel, the young crowd enjoys its proximity to just about anything they need, and all diners enjoy the free Wi-Fi. **Features:** beer & wine, patio dining, Sunday brunch. **Address:** 2800 Routh St, Suite 170 75201 **Location:** Just w of jct McKinney Ave and Routh St to Laclede St, just n; in Quadrangle Center. B L D

## DUNSTON'S STEAK HOUSE  214/352-8320  1

Steak. Casual Dining. $9-$25 **AAA Inspector Notes:** Family-owned and -operated, this neighborhood restaurant is casual and friendly to all ages. Steaks are cooked over an open fire in the main dining room using mesquite wood. Desserts such as Key lime pie and bread pudding are made daily. Closed for lunch on Saturday and Sunday. **Features:** full bar. **Reservations:** suggested. **Address:** 5423 W Lovers Ln 75209 **Location:** Between Dallas North Tollway and Inwood Rd; on north side of road. L D

## EATZI'S  214/526-1515  32

Specialty. Quick Serve. $5-$16 **AAA Inspector Notes:** Epicureans rejoice! Diners' senses may be overwhelmed by the many choices of fresh bread, hot entrees, custom-made sandwiches and salads, and other delicacies. However, most locals appreciate this place for its selection of high-quality, made-from-scratch, prepackaged food for people on the go. Visitors also can pick up fresh flowers and wine to round out the makings for a great evening. **Features:** beer & wine. **Address:** 3403 Oak Lawn Ave 75219 **Location:** I-35E exit 430A (Oak Lawn Ave), 1.5 mi e. B L D

## EL FENIX  214/747-1121  56

Tex-Mex. Family Dining. $9-$16 **AAA Inspector Notes:** Since 1918 and now 21 restaurants strong, this iconic restaurant was an early originator of Tex-Mex cuisine. Started by Miguel Martinez, the restaurant still features many time-honored recipes. Many familiar items line the menu such as tacos, enchiladas, tamales and, of course, tortilla soup. Complimentary chips and salsa arrive quickly to the table as an early indication of the timely service. **Features:** full bar. **Address:** 1601 McKinney Ave 75202 **Location:** Corner of Caroline St and McKinney Ave. L D CALL M

## FEARING'S  214/922-4848  55

Southwestern. Fine Dining. $18-$48 **AAA Inspector Notes:** Not your common hotel restaurant experience, this eatery artfully combines global and regional ingredients to provide a menu of inspired cuisine that highlights the area's culinary treasures. Enjoy lobster coconut bisque, barbecue brisket sliders, crispy oysters, cactus pear-glazed antelope or pecan-crusted halibut. Everything is as you would expect in a world-class establishment, but you will find the staff to have a more casual approach. Consider taking dessert on the patio. **Features:** full bar, patio dining, Sunday brunch. **Reservations:** suggested. **Address:** 2121 McKinney Ave 75201 **Location:** SR 366 (Woodall Rodgers Frwy) exit Pearl St, just sw to Olive St, then just nw; in The Ritz-Carlton, Dallas. **Parking:** valet only. B L D CALL M

## FIVE SIXTY BY WOLFGANG PUCK  214/741-5560  63

New Asian. Fine Dining. $35-$70 **AAA Inspector Notes:** Five Sixty is located on the top of the Reunion Tower, offering bird's-eye views of the city while slowly revolving in full circle. Here you can enjoy the wonderful dining experience of Wolfgang Puck's famous cuisine. The Asian cuisine has been modernized with creative combinations and blending of flavors only such a chef could create. Chinese duckling, steamed king salmon, wok-fried whole sea bass and crispy quail are only a sample of menu offerings. **Features:** full bar, Sunday brunch. **Reservations:** suggested. **Address:** 300 Reunion Blvd E 75207 **Location:** I-35E and US 77 exit Reunion Blvd, just e; I-30 exit Commerce St eastbound, just n; in Hyatt Regency Dallas at Reunion. **Parking:** on-site (fee) and valet. D CALL M

## THE FRENCH ROOM  214/742-8200  62

**New French Fine Dining**
**$80**

**AAA Inspector Notes:** Entry into this restaurant takes diners a step back into the court of Louis XV in Versailles. Though the surroundings are formal, the food haute cuisine and the staff well trained, they succeed in making it a relaxed and enjoyable experience. Creative ingredient combinations such as jumbo lump crab cake with lemon grass lobster sauce and tomato jam or peanut butter chocolate cake with caramel corn ice cream assure a memorable meal. As promised, the crab cake may be the best you will ever have. **Features:** full bar. **Reservations:** suggested. Formal attire. **Address:** 1321 Commerce St 75202 **Location:** Between Field and Akard sts; in The Adolphus. **Parking:** valet only.  *Menu on AAA.com* D

### Easily among the top dining experiences in the world!

## GLORIA'S RESTAURANT  214/874-0088

Salvadoran. Casual Dining. $7-$15 **AAA Inspector Notes:** Authentic Salvadoran recipes with eye-catching presentation are served in a relaxing, colorful atmosphere and include regional specialty dishes such as plantain pupusa, tamales wrapped in banana leaves, fajitas, pollo asado and black beans with rice. The black bean dip for the chips is a welcome change from salsa. The location on Dallas' main bar-hopping drag means the bar here stays busy and patio fills up fast. **Features:** full bar, patio dining, happy hour. **Address:** 3715 Greenville Ave 75206 **Location:** US 75 exit Mockingbird Ln, 0.5 mi e to Greenville Ave, then 0.4 mi s. **Parking:** valet only. L D

## GOOD EATS  214/522-3287  29

**American Casual Dining**
**$8-$17**

**AAA Inspector Notes:** This Texas-style restaurant delivers home cooking with the likes of chicken potpie, meatloaf and Certified Angus steaks. Ask them what their best-seller is and they will probably say the chicken-fried steak. But sophistication is not lost here as they feature a variety of wines on a weekly basis. Located in a very busy and lively neighborhood. **Features:** full bar, patio dining. **Address:** 3888 Oak Lawn Ave, Suite 101 75219 **Location:** Just n of Lemmon and Oak Lawn aves; in Turtle Creek Village. L D

## GRANDY'S RESTAURANT  214/655-2677

American. Quick Serve. $4-$8 **AAA Inspector Notes:** Fried chicken and country-fried steak are menu standbys at the restaurant, a regional franchise. They also offer a family-style dining menu. The décor is a step up from that of most quick-serve eateries and more resembles that of a conventional restaurant. Some elements of increased service include additional rolls, iced tea refills and tray removal. **Address:** 901 Main St, Suite C-106A 75202 **Location:** Between Commerce and Elm sts. B L

---

### AAA/CAA travel information:

### Available online, on the go

### and in print!

(See map & index p. 175.)

**THE GRAPE**  214/828-1981  20

▼▼▼ French. Fine Dining. $24-$35 **AAA Inspector Notes:** The candlelight and soft music of this self-described urban bistro fill the dining room with cozy romance. An ever-changing menu features regional specialties from France, Italy and Asia, served in either the dining room with its grapevine motif or in the very European sidewalk café. Enjoy items such as chile-butter rainbow trout, Texas tomato and lump crab salad or a hot chorizo gratin. The restaurant is located in the artsy lower Greenville area. **Features:** full bar, patio dining, Sunday brunch, happy hour. **Reservations:** suggested. **Address:** 2808 Greenville Ave 75206 **Location:** US 75 exit 3 (Mockingbird Ln), 0.5 mi e to Greenville Ave, then 0.9 mi s. **Parking:** valet only. D

**GREEN PAPAYA**  214/521-4811  33

▼▼ Vietnamese. Casual Dining. $6-$13 **AAA Inspector Notes:** This neighborhood restaurant with a covered patio serves such dishes as fresh spring rolls, noodle plates and sauteed beef with lemongrass, vermicelli, lettuce and cucumbers. Parking is a challenge, so expect to valet. **Address:** 3211 Oak Lawn Ave, Suite B 75219 **Location:** I-35 exit 430A (Oak Lawn Ave), 0.9 mi e. **Parking:** valet only. L D 🐾

**HOTEL ST. GERMAIN**  214/871-2516  47

▼▼▼ French Fine Dining $85 **AAA Inspector Notes:** In the dining room of a country inn, the intimate restaurant presents diners a prix fixe dinner while overlooking a serene garden. Seven courses unfold as a gastronomical adventure. The atmosphere is formal but friendly. The staff here frequently offers themed dinners, so call ahead and see if anything special is going on during your visit. **Features:** full bar. **Reservations:** required. Semiformal attire. **Address:** 2516 Maple Ave 75201 **Location:** I-35 exit 430A (Oak Lawn Ave), 0.5 mi e, then 1 mi s. **Parking:** valet and street only. D

**JAVIER'S GOURMET MEXICANO**  214/521-4211  16

▼▼ Mexican. Casual Dining. $20-$29 **AAA Inspector Notes:** Round the curve too fast and you might miss it, but for 25 years locals have always known where to slow down for this neighborhood favorite. Appetizers like smoked chicken nachos and entrées like snapper with mushrooms and garlic are offered in a delightful Mexican colonial décor. The menu is traditional Mexico City cuisine. After dinner, relax in the trendy cigar bar. One room has an antique bar that offers a bustling feel to it. **Features:** full bar, patio dining. **Reservations:** suggested. **Address:** 4912 Cole Ave 75205 **Location:** US 75 exit Knox St/Henderson Ave, just w to McKinney Ave, then 0.4 mi n to Harvard Ave. **Parking:** valet only. D

**KUBY'S SAUSAGE HOUSE**  214/363-2231  6

▼ Traditional German. Casual Dining. $7-$25 **AAA Inspector Notes:** Decorated with family crests and a collection of steins, this eatery is located within a German food store. Homemade sausage is made from a family recipe more than two centuries old and brought over from Europe. Old World butcher-shop fare like knockwurst, bratwurst and schnitzel make up the menu. After 50 years in the neighborhood it's safe to call Kuby's an institution, and it's clear it's loved by the locals. Dinner is served Friday and Saturday only. **Features:** beer & wine, Sunday brunch. **Address:** 6601 Snider Plaza 75205 **Location:** Just w of jct Daniel and Hillcrest aves; in Snider Plaza; across from Southern Methodist University. **Parking:** street only. B L

**LA MADELEINE COUNTRY FRENCH CAFE**

▼ Traditional French. Casual Dining. $7-$12 **AAA Inspector Notes:** A fireplace creates the focal point at this cozy European style café where you can always get a quiche or savory stuffed puffed pastry on the go or stick around for a chicken crêpe or French dip sandwich. Heartier entrées like rotisserie chicken are offered and every season promises menu surprises. Whatever you decide on you probably will not get out the door without enjoying one of their tempting sweet pastries. B L D

*For additional information, visit AAA.com*

**LOCATIONS:**

**Address:** 3906 Lemmon Ave, Suite 110 75219 **Location:** Just w of Oak Lawn Ave. **Bar:** beer & wine. **Phone:** 214/521-0183

**Address:** 3072 Mockingbird Ln 75205 **Location:** Just w off US 75 (N Central Expwy) exit 3 (Mockingbird Ln); in Park City Plaza. **Bar:** wine only. **Phone:** 214/696-0800

**THE LANDMARK RESTAURANT**  214/224-3152  35

▼▼▼ American Fine Dining $12-$44 **AAA Inspector Notes:** In a dining room with abundant natural light and upscale decor, diners enjoy a menu of the steaks and chops noted for this area. The chef has included some worldly cuisine styles to balance out the menu. **Features:** full bar, Sunday brunch. **Reservations:** suggested. **Address:** 3015 Oak Lawn Ave 75219 **Location:** I-35E exit 430 (Oak Lawn Ave), 0.8 mi n; entrance off Cedar Springs, just n; in Warwick Melrose Hotel Dallas. **Parking:** valet only. L D

**LITTLE KATANA**  214/443-9600  19

▼▼▼ Japanese. Casual Dining. $12-$32 **AAA Inspector Notes:** Little Katana would be the quintessential restaurant for fine Asian fusion, sushi, delightfully prepared appetizers, soups, salads and various entrées, which are eye-catching and made to order. Its location, surrounded by numerous specialty stores, makes it a perfect end to a day of shopping. **Features:** full bar, patio dining. **Address:** 4527 Travis St 75205 **Location:** US 75 exit 2, just w on Knox St. L D

**LUCKY'S CAFE SOUTH**  214/522-3500  31

▼ American Casual Dining $7-$10 **AAA Inspector Notes:** This restaurant has the feel of a classic diner and offers comfort foods like meatloaf, chicken-fried steak, burgers and peach cobbler. Fair warning: Parking can be very tricky. **Features:** full bar, Sunday brunch. **Address:** 3531 Oak Lawn Ave 75219 **Location:** I-35 exit 430A (Oak Lawn Ave), 1.6 mi ne. B L D

**THE MANSION RESTAURANT AT ROSEWOOD MANSION ON TURTLE CREEK**  214/559-2100  38

▼▼▼ ▼▼▼ Continental. Fine Dining. $18-$64 **AAA Inspector Notes:** Guests pass through a courtyard entrance that leads to a richly appointed rotunda with marble floors and walls. From there, they are seated in one of several elegant dining rooms, where an attentive and intuitive staff serves such items as braised short ribs, lobster risotto and seared diver scallops. A lovely terrace is available and sets the perfect scene for a romantic evening or memorable afternoon meal. **Features:** full bar, Sunday brunch. **Reservations:** suggested. **Address:** 3411 Gillespie St 75219 **Location:** 2 mi nw, entrance on Gillespie St, just e of jct Gillespie St and Oak Lawn Ave; in Rosewood Mansion on Turtle Creek. **Parking:** valet only. B L D

**THE MEDDLESOME MOTH**  214/628-7900  45

▼▼▼ American. Gastropub. $11-$28 **AAA Inspector Notes:** In the up-and-coming design district, the Moth is for those who prefer ales in a stylish and lively atmosphere. It has 40 beers on tap and nearly 100 bottled varieties, including gluten-free options. Beer flights are a good way to acclimate, but you also can trust server recommendations. The menu pays homage to traditional English pubs with meat pies and fish and chips but also has roasted beet salad, shrimp and grits, steak frites and risotto. **Features:** full bar, Sunday brunch. **Address:** 1621 Oak Lawn Ave 75207 **Location:** I-35E exit 430A (Oak Lawn Ave), just w. **Parking:** valet only. L D ◥

**MIA'S TEX-MEX RESTAURANT**  214/526-1020  27

▼▼ Tex-Mex. Casual Dining. $7-$15 **AAA Inspector Notes:** You may think enchiladas are just normal fare. Try the chicken enchiladas with sour cream sauce and you'll see how special they can be. And if there is such a thing as Mexican cantina Art Deco this is the place to see it. It's very popular with folks around Dallas for good reasons. **Features:** full bar, patio dining, Sunday brunch. **Address:** 4322 Lemmon Ave 75219 **Location:** Between Wycliff Ave and Herschel St. L D

**MORTON'S THE STEAKHOUSE**  214/741-2277  54

▼▼▼ Steak. Fine Dining. $26-$70 **AAA Inspector Notes:** Patrons should make sure to reserve ahead for the popular, well-known steakhouse. Large portions, including huge cuts of fine beef and plentiful seafood, are the norm. Even the vegetables are oversized, with baked potatoes big enough for sharing. **Features:** full bar, happy hour. **Reservations:** suggested. **Address:** 2222 McKinney Ave 75201 **Location:** Woodall Rodgers Freeway exit Pearl St, just nw, then just e. **Parking:** valet only. D

(See map & index p. 175.)

**NAAN SUSHI**  214/772-6399  (40)

♦♦ Sushi. Casual Dining. $15-$25 **AAA Inspector Notes:** As part of a multi-use residential building, Naan is sure to fill up with residents, but diners are drawn from all parts for the enticing happy hour specials, late-night hours and creative fare like the Texas Tornado and Mt. Fuji rolls. A modern dining room with hard surfaces and tightly spaced tables ensure a loud and not-so-private meal. **Features:** full bar, happy hour. **Reservations:** suggested. **Address:** 2600 Cedar Springs Rd 75201 **Location:** I-35E exit 430 (Oak Lawn Ave), 0.4 mi ne to Maple Ave, 0.5 mi s to Carlisle St, then just e. **Parking:** valet and street only. [L] [D] [LATE]

**NOBU**  214/252-7000  (50)

♦♦♦ Japanese. Fine Dining. $18-$40 **AAA Inspector Notes:** Entry to this restaurant is through the hotel's marble-clad lobby. The international staff delivers Japanese cuisine with a crisp service style. An expanded wine list with a varied price range is available. **Features:** full bar. **Reservations:** suggested. **Address:** 400 Crescent Ct 75201 **Location:** Corner of Crescent Ct and McKinney Ave; uptown; in Rosewood Crescent Hotel. **Parking:** on-site (fee) and valet. [D]

**THE OLD WARSAW**  214/528-0032  (46)

♦♦♦ Continental. Fine Dining. $21-$45 **AAA Inspector Notes:** The well-established restaurant invites guests to unwind in the richly decorated dining room to sample preparations of seafood, meat and fowl as well as tempting appetizers. Everything at The Old Warsaw is done lavishly, so prepare for an evening with violin players and elaborately set tables. Jackets are preferred for men. **Features:** full bar. **Reservations:** required. **Address:** 2610 Maple Ave 75201 **Location:** Woodall Rodgers Frwy exit Pearl St, just n to McKinney Ave, just e to Maple Ave, then just n. **Parking:** valet only. [L] [D]

**THE PALM RESTAURANT**  214/698-0470  (59)

♦♦♦ Steak. Fine Dining. $13-$52 **AAA Inspector Notes:** This bustling restaurant is noted for Prime, dry-aged steaks and Nova Scotia lobsters. The huge portions are delivered by an attentive staff in an atmosphere that is fun and lively. At the end of the meal, servers present tempting pastries tableside. Caricature-lined walls lend to the feeling that patrons are dining in an art gallery. Even if you bring a big appetite you still may leave with a doggy bag. **Features:** full bar, happy hour. **Reservations:** suggested. **Address:** 701 Ross Ave 75202 **Location:** Corner of Market St and Ross Ave; in Historic West End District. **Parking:** valet only. [L] [D]

**PALOMINO RESTAURANT**  214/999-1222  (53)

♦♦♦ Mediterranean. Casual Dining. $7-$38 **AAA Inspector Notes:** This national chain restaurant offers patrons an impressive assortment of dishes including seafood, pasta and steak. Rounding out the menu are pizzas, salads and Tuscan-style rotisserie roasted chicken all served up in a trendy, casual upscale atmosphere. **Features:** full bar, patio dining, happy hour. **Reservations:** suggested. **Address:** 500 Crescent Ct, Suite 165 75201 **Location:** Woodall Rodgers Pkwy exit Pearl St, nw to McKinney Ave, n to Maple Ave, just nw, then just w. **Parking:** on-site and valet. [L] [D]

**PEGGY SUE BBQ**  214/987-9188  (5)

♦♦ Barbecue. Casual Dining. $5-$15 **AAA Inspector Notes:** Clad with old photographs of Western movie stars, this 1950s diner serves homemade barbecue and Mexican cuisine. Decorative hanging lamps give the two dining rooms a friendly glow. Start with the chicken quesadilla appetizer. **Features:** full bar, happy hour. **Address:** 6600 Snider Plaza 75205 **Location:** Just w of jct Daniel and Hillcrest aves; in Snider Plaza; across from Southern Methodist University Campus. **Parking:** street only. [L] [D]

**THE PORCH**  214/828-2916  (25)

♦♦ American. Casual Dining. $12-$25 **AAA Inspector Notes:** Located in a trendy area, the restaurant's casual décor is still suitable for a night on the town. The menu includes mac 'n cheese, a smoked brisket enchilada, grilled salmon, spinach-Parmesan dip and an array of sandwiches and salads. **Features:** full bar, patio dining, Sunday brunch. **Address:** 2912 N Henderson Ave 75206 **Location:** US 75 exit 2 (Knox St/Henderson Ave), just e. **Parking:** on-site and valet. [L] [D]

**PREGO PASTA HOUSE**  214/363-9204  (4)

♦♦ Italian. Casual Dining. $7-$20 **AAA Inspector Notes:** In business for 30 years, this family-owned and -operated restaurant prepares a good selection of traditional food, including veal, chicken, clam, calamari and shrimp dishes. Also on the menu are varied pasta preparations and some American-style sandwiches. Desserts, as well as sauces, are made in house. Pizza is a great choice. **Features:** full bar. **Address:** 4930 Greenville Ave 75206 **Location:** US 75 exit 4A (Lovers Ln/Southwestern Blvd) southbound, just s; exit 4 (University Blvd) northbound, just e, then just n. **Parking:** valet only. [L] [D]

**PYRAMID RESTAURANT & BAR**  214/720-5249  (57)

♦♦♦♦ American Fine Dining $12-$35 **AAA Inspector Notes:** Lots of travelers shy away from hotel restaurants, but Pyramid is not that kind of place. A vibrant bar scene greets guests on arrival, and sleek, contemporary dining rooms set the mood. The fare may sound standard—lamb, salmon and steaks—but it's the details that make it memorable, like port-infused cippolini onions, smoked mashed potatoes (can you say yuuumm?), house-made pickles, hand-cut fries and original libations of which the Fairmonts are known world round. **Features:** full bar, Sunday brunch. **Reservations:** suggested, for dinner. **Address:** 1717 N Akard St 75201 **Location:** Corner of Ross Ave and N Akard St; in The Fairmont Dallas. **Parking:** valet only. [B] [L] [D] CALL [M]

**ST MARTIN'S WINE BISTRO**  214/826-0940  (17)

♦♦♦ French. Fine Dining. $16-$29 **AAA Inspector Notes:** Intimate and attractive, this bistro's dining area has a gorgeous 14-foot ceiling, fabric wall coverings and dim lighting. Although the food is clearly the draw, the attentive staff helps make meals even more memorable. A talented pianist plays soothing music throughout the evening. **Features:** full bar, Sunday brunch. **Reservations:** suggested. **Address:** 3020 Greenville Ave 75206 **Location:** US 75 exit 3 (Mockingbird Ln/University Blvd), 0.5 mi e to Greenville Ave, then 1.2 mi s. **Parking:** valet only. [D]

**S & D OYSTER COMPANY**  214/880-0111  (43)

♦♦ Southern Seafood. Casual Dining. $10-$22 **AAA Inspector Notes:** Fresh Gulf Coast seafood is prepared New Orleans style in a 100-year-old building that once was a neighborhood grocery store. Oysters on the half-shell, royal red snapper and home-made icebox lemon meringue pie are the house specialties. **Features:** beer & wine. **Address:** 2701 McKinney Ave 75204 **Location:** Between Routh and Allen sts; n of downtown. [L] [D]

**SER STEAK AND SPIRITS**  214/761-7479  (39)

♦♦♦ Steak. Fine Dining. $30-$50 **AAA Inspector Notes:** The word "steakhouse" frequently conjures up images of white tablecloths and plainly presented meat. Forget those images and imagine a chic modern dining room, broad menu and unequaled views of the city skyline. Start with one of the raw dishes, the hamachi crudo or oysters, for example, move on to the richly flavored mushroom bisque, then pair your aged rib-eye or market-fish creation with the sweet onion rings. While the setting is attractive, it's not the place for quiet conversation. **Features:** full bar. **Reservations:** suggested. **Address:** 2201 N Stemmons Frwy 75207 **Location:** I-35E exit 430B (Market Center Blvd); on southbound frontage road; in Hilton Anatole Dallas. **Parking:** valet only. [D] CALL [M]

**SNUFFER'S**  214/826-6850  (14)

♦ American. Casual Dining. $7-$12 **AAA Inspector Notes:** For more than 20 years this restaurant has been a great spot for juicy hamburgers, margaritas and people-watching. Ask your server about the legend of the ghost. Period pictures and dark wooden booths distinguish the bustling dining room. **Features:** full bar, happy hour. **Address:** 3526 Greenville Ave 75206 **Location:** N on US 75 exit 3 (Mockingbird Ln), 0.5 mi e to Greenville Ave, then 0.5 mi s. [L] [D]

(See map & index p. 175.)

### THE SPAGHETTI WAREHOUSE   214/651-8475
WWWW Italian. Casual Dining. $7-$17 **AAA Inspector Notes:** The Italian-style restaurant chain sustains a festive family atmosphere. All entrees include bottomless tossed salad or soup. Patrons enjoy plentiful portions of such classic dishes as ravioli, lasagna, baked penne or the richly flavored cannelloni Florentine. Splurging on one of the many desserts, such as tiramisu, espresso mousse cake or carrot cake, is worthwhile. **Features:** full bar. **Address:** 1815 N Market St 75202 **Location:** In Historic West End District. L D

### STEEL   214/219-9908   34
WWWW Asian. Fine Dining. $10-$32 **AAA Inspector Notes:** This upscale Japanese-Indochine restaurant has both a creative flair in décor and meal selections that will intrigue your taste buds. Bursting with flavor but not too spicy, start off with sushi and enjoy the condiments that can pack some heat. You may be tempted to sample all the appetizers, but whatever you do, save room for the tantalizing entrées and desserts. Located in a lively neighborhood. **Features:** full bar, patio dining, happy hour. **Reservations:** suggested. **Address:** 3180 Welborn Ave 75219 **Location:** Corner of Cedar Springs Rd and Oak Lawn Ave; in Centrum Building. **Parking:** valet and street only.

L D CALL M

### SZECHUAN CHINESE RESTAURANT   214/521-2345   30
W Chinese. Casual Dining. $7-$12 **AAA Inspector Notes:** Szechuan food is at the heart of the menu at this small family-owned and –operated restaurant. A small buffet is set up for lunch and dinner, but guests can order from the menu at any time. Free delivery and takeout service are available. **Address:** 4117 Lemmon Ave 75219 **Location:** Between Dallas North Tollway and Oak Lawn Ave.

L D

### TRULUCK'S   214/220-2401   49
WWW Seafood. Fine Dining. $19-$45 **AAA Inspector Notes:** The chef's daily creations include jumbo fresh Florida stone crab claws, live Maine lobster, Australian cold water lobster tail, sesame-crusted ahi tuna, miso-glazed organic totem black cod, oysters Rockefeller, sautéed super-lump crab cake, juicy and flavorful Niman Ranch aged beef and a variety of delicious steamed sides including their signature Parmesan mashed potatoes. **Features:** full bar, patio dining, happy hour. **Reservations:** suggested. **Address:** 2401 McKinney Ave 75201 **Location:** Just n of Maple Ave. **Parking:** on-site and valet. L D

### TWISTED ROOT BURGER CO   214/361-2910   9
W Burgers. Quick Serve. $6-$11 **AAA Inspector Notes:** Order off of the inventive menu, then kick back in the comfy industrial-chic dining room and mingle with Dallas-area natives who support this homegrown business. Besides good ol' American beef you can find venison and ostrich on the burger menu as well as fried pickles and thick milk shakes. A full-service bar serves the predominantly SMU crowds. **Features:** full bar. **Address:** 5609 SMU Blvd, Suite 102 75206 **Location:** I-75 exit 3 (Mockingbird Ln) northbound, 0.6 mi n on frontage road, then just e; exit southbound, just e. **Parking:** street only. L D CALL M

### T/X RESTAURANT   214/871-7111   44
WWWW
**Regional American Fine Dining $11-$37**
**AAA Inspector Notes:** Although the seasonal menus are not extensive they pack a punch of local flavor with items such as tortilla-crusted snapper served with a tequila-orange butter, chicken quesadillas and cilantro salad with jicama and avocado. This trendy uptown spot features a well-appointed but light and airy dining room that can be enjoyed just as easily by the business traveler as the guest coming in to catch a basketball game or concert downtown. **Features:** full bar. **Reservations:** suggested. **Address:** 2927 Maple Ave 75201 **Location:** I-35E exit 430A (Oak Lawn Ave), 0.5 mi e, then 1.2 mi s; in Le Méridien Dallas, The Stoneleigh. **Parking:** valet only.

B L D CALL M

### UNCLE JULIO'S   214/520-6620
WW Tex-Mex. Casual Dining. $8-$20 **AAA Inspector Notes:** Open and airy dining rooms are filled with Mexican décor. You might start your meal with homemade tortilla soup and salsa with chips. The sizzle of the specialty fajitas can be heard throughout the dining rooms. The flan is praised for its sweet, caramel coating. **Features:** full bar, Sunday brunch, happy hour. **Address:** 4125 Lemmon Ave 75219 **Location:** Between Dallas North Tollway and Oak Lawn Ave.

L D

### WOODFIRE KIRBY'S   214/821-2122   15
WWW Steak. Fine Dining. $13-$40 **AAA Inspector Notes:** In a modern setting, patrons sit down to meals of chicken Florentine pizza, New York strip steak, classic cheeseburgers and Cobb salads. The bar is a draw and the kitchen is a focal point, so the dining rooms can get loud. Parking is hopeless; waste no time and just go straight to the valet. **Features:** full bar, patio dining. **Reservations:** suggested. **Address:** 3525 Greenville Ave 75206 **Location:** US 75 exit 3 (Mockingbird Ln/University Blvd), just e to Greenville Ave, then 0.4 mi s. **Parking:** valet only. D

### Y.O. RANCH STEAKHOUSE   214/744-3287   60
WW Steak. Casual Dining. $9-$50 **AAA Inspector Notes:** Opened in 1996, the restaurant has a license to use the Y.O. brand made famous by the Central Texas ranch of the same name. The menu centers on steaks and wild game from the Hill Country but also lists such exotic dishes as ostrich, quail, buffalo, venison, duck, alligator and wild boar, which are cooked to the diner's liking. Many foods are prepared with a Tex-Mex flair for those craving a more spicy touch. **Features:** full bar, patio dining. **Reservations:** suggested. **Address:** 702 Ross Ave 75202 **Location:** Southeast corner of Market St and Ross Ave. **Parking:** street only.

L D

### ZAGUAN LATIN CAFE AND BAKERY   214/219-8393   36
WW Latin American. Casual Dining. $7-$15 **AAA Inspector Notes:** This cafe is made even more casual by the several pastry boxes available for the numerous customers that drop by for the to-go items. On the savory side, the restaurant serves Venezuelan arepas and cachapas, fried plantains, Cuban ropa vieja and Argentinian empanadas. Outdoor seating is available. **Features:** beer & wine. **Address:** 2604 Oak Lawn Ave 75219 **Location:** I-35 exit 430 (Oak Lawn Ave), 0.4 mi ne.

B L D

### ZIZIKI'S RESTAURANT   214/521-2233   21
WW Mediterranean. Casual Dining. $9-$26 **AAA Inspector Notes:** This family-owned Art Deco Greek restaurant features plenty of family-inspired creations like Ziziki bread, Ziziki salad and Ziziki sauce. Fresh ingredients like cucumbers, tomatoes, yogurt and imported olives accompany signature dishes like the lamb lasagna. Enjoy upscale shopping after your meal. **Features:** full bar, patio dining, Sunday brunch. **Address:** 4514 Travis St, Suite 122 75205 **Location:** US 75 exit Knox St/Henderson Ave, just w to Travis St, then just s; in Travis Walk Shopping Complex. L D

### ZODIAC RESTAURANT   214/573-5800   61
WWWW American. Casual Dining. $13-$23 **AAA Inspector Notes:** The classic cafes talented chefs change the menu every six months for an ever-fresh selection of items such as lobster ravioli and braised pot roast as well as hearty salads and sandwiches. Their signature popovers with strawberry butter are a standard, however. The dining room is awash in silvery browns, bronze and white, providing a glamorous setting for a respite after a day at the original shopping mecca, Neiman Marcus. **Features:** full bar. **Reservations:** suggested. **Address:** 1618 Main St 75201 **Location:** Center; 6th floor of Neiman Marcus Department Store. **Parking:** on-site and valet. L

## DALLAS (D-9)

- Restaurants p. 218
- Hotels & Restaurants map & index p. 184

### BAYMONT INN & SUITES DALLAS LOVE FIELD
(214)350-5577

Hotel
$79-$129

**Address:** 2370 W Northwest Hwy 75220 **Location:** I-35E exit 436 Northwest Hwy (Loop 12), 0.8 mi e. **Facility:** 76 units. 3 stories, interior corridors. **Pool(s):** heated indoor. **Activities:** hot tub, exercise room. **Guest Services:** valet and coin laundry. **Featured Amenity: continental breakfast.**

### BEST WESTERN NORTHWEST INN    (214)353-8774

Hotel
$79-$149

**AAA Benefit:** Members save 10% or more with Best Western!

**Address:** 2361 W Northwest Hwy 75220 **Location:** I-35E exit 436, 0.4 mi e. **Facility:** 63 units. 3 stories, interior corridors. **Pool(s):** outdoor. **Activities:** hot tub, exercise room. **Guest Services:** coin laundry. **Featured Amenity: continental breakfast.**

(See map & index p. 184.)

## BEST WESTERN PLUS DALLAS HOTEL & CONFERENCE CENTER    (972)680-3000    12

Hotel
$96-$170

**AAA Benefit:** Members save 10% or more with Best Western!

**Address:** 8051 Lyndon B Johnson Frwy 75251 **Location:** I-635 exit 19B (Coit Rd), just n, then just e. **Facility:** 197 units. 6 stories, interior corridors. **Pool(s):** outdoor. **Activities:** exercise room. **Guest Services:** valet laundry.

## CANDLEWOOD SUITES-DALLAS BY THE GALLERIA    (972)233-6888    4

Extended Stay Hotel $80-$129 **Address:** 13939 Noel Rd 75240 **Location:** Jct Dallas Pkwy and Spring Valley, just e to Noel Rd, just s. **Facility:** 134 efficiencies. 3 stories, interior corridors. **Activities:** exercise room. **Guest Services:** complimentary and valet laundry, area transportation.

## CANDLEWOOD SUITES DALLAS MARKET CENTER    (214)631-3333    35

Extended Stay Hotel
$89-$119

**Address:** 7930 N Stemmons Frwy 75247 **Location:** I-35 exit 433B (Mockingbird Ln); on northbound frontage road. **Facility:** 150 efficiencies, some two bedrooms. 3 stories, interior corridors. **Pool(s):** outdoor. **Activities:** exercise room. **Guest Services:** complimentary and valet laundry, area transportation.

## CANDLEWOOD SUITES DALLAS NORTH/RICHARDSON    (972)669-9606    16

Extended Stay Hotel $65-$100 **Address:** 12525 Greenville Ave 75243 **Location:** I-635 exit 18A (Greenville Ave), just n, then just w on Amberton Pkwy. **Facility:** 122 efficiencies. 3 stories, interior corridors. **Terms:** cancellation fee imposed. **Activities:** exercise room. **Guest Services:** complimentary and valet laundry.

## COMFORT INN & SUITES MARKET CENTER    (214)461-2677    36

Hotel
$70-$140

**Address:** 7138 N Stemmons Frwy 75247 **Location:** I-35E exit 433B (Mockingbird Ln) northbound; exit 432B (Commonwealth Dr) southbound, turn under freeway, 0.7 mi on north access road. **Facility:** 62 units. 3 stories, interior corridors. **Activities:** exercise room. **Featured Amenity: full hot breakfast.**

## COMFORT SUITES BY CHOICE HOTELS-CENTRAL EXPRESSWAY    (972)699-7400    10

Hotel
$83-$99

**Address:** 13165 N Central Expwy 75243 **Location:** US 75 exit 22 (Midpark Rd); on southbound frontage road. Located in a commercial area. **Facility:** 78 units. 3 stories, interior corridors. **Pool(s):** heated indoor. **Activities:** hot tub, exercise room. **Guest Services:** valet and coin laundry. **Featured Amenity: full hot breakfast.**

## COUNTRY INN & SUITES DALLAS LOVE FIELD / MEDICAL CENTER    214/352-7676    33

Hotel. Rates not provided. **Address:** 2383 Stemmons Tr 75220 **Location:** I-35E exit 436, just e, then just s. **Facility:** 146 units. 3 stories, interior corridors. **Pool(s):** outdoor. **Activities:** hot tub, exercise room. **Guest Services:** valet and coin laundry, area transportation.

## DALLAS MARRIOTT SUITES MEDICAL/MARKET CENTER    (214)905-0050    42

Hotel $89-$209 **Address:** 2493 N Stemmons Frwy 75207 **Location:** I-35E exit 431 (Motor St); on southbound frontage road. **Facility:** 265 units. 12 stories, interior corridors. **Amenities:** video games. **Pool(s):** outdoor. **Activities:** hot tub, exercise room. **Guest Services:** complimentary and valet laundry, area transportation.

**AAA Benefit:** Members save 5% or more!

(See map & index p. 184.)

## DOUBLETREE BY HILTON DALLAS CAMPBELL CENTRE
214/691-8700

Hotel
Rates not provided

**AAA Benefit:** Members save 5% or more!

**Address:** 8250 N Central 75206 **Location:** US 75 exit 4B (Caruth-Haven Ln); on northbound access road. **Facility:** 300 units. 21 stories, interior corridors. **Activities:** exercise room. **Guest Services:** valet laundry, area transportation. *(See ad this page.)*

## EMBASSY SUITES DALLAS-MARKET CENTER
(214)630-5332

Hotel
$139-$199

**AAA Benefit:** Members save 5% or more!

**Address:** 2727 N Stemmons Frwy 75207 **Location:** I-35E exit 432A (Inwood Rd); on southbound frontage road. **Facility:** 244 units. 9 stories, interior corridors. **Terms:** 1-7 night minimum stay, cancellation fee imposed. **Activities:** hot tub, exercise room. **Guest Services:** valet and coin laundry. *(See ad p. 213.)*

## EMBASSY SUITES HOTEL-DALLAS/LOVE FIELD
(214)357-4500

Hotel
$99-$159

**AAA Benefit:** Members save 5% or more!

**Address:** 3880 W Northwest Hwy 75220 **Location:** Just se of jct Northwest Hwy (Loop 12) and Marsh Ln. **Facility:** 248 units. 8 stories, interior corridors. **Terms:** 1-7 night minimum stay, cancellation fee imposed. **Amenities:** video games. **Pool(s):** heated indoor. **Activities:** sauna, hot tub, steamroom, exercise room. **Guest Services:** valet and coin laundry, area transportation. *(See ad p. 213.)*

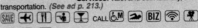

## EMBASSY SUITES HOTEL DALLAS NEAR THE GALLERIA
(972)364-3640

Hotel
$109-$199

**AAA Benefit:** Members save 5% or more!

**Address:** 14021 Noel Rd 75240 **Location:** Dallas North Tollway, 0.5 mi e on Spring Valley Rd, just s. **Facility:** 150 units. 6 stories, interior corridors. **Terms:** 1-7 night minimum stay, cancellation fee imposed. **Pool(s):** heated indoor. **Activities:** hot tub, exercise room. **Guest Services:** valet laundry, area transportation. **Featured Amenity:** full hot breakfast.

▼ *See AAA listing this page* ▼

Contact us about AAA/CAA Approved properties
at AAA.com/TourBookComments

(See map & index p. 184.)

**EMBASSY SUITES HOTEL-DALLAS/PARK CENTRAL**
(972)234-3300  **11**

Hotel $129-$149 **Address:** 13131 N Central Expwy 75243 **Location:** US 75 exit 22 (Midpark Rd) northbound; exit 21 southbound; on southbound frontage road. **Facility:** 279 units. 9 stories, interior corridors. *Bath:* shower only. **Terms:** 1-7 night minimum stay, cancellation fee imposed. **Amenities:** video games. **Pool(s):** heated indoor. **Activities:** hot tub, exercise room. **Guest Services:** valet and coin laundry, area transportation.

**AAA Benefit:** Members save 5% or more!

Visit your AAA/CAA Travel office to book a AAA Vacations® Disney package

(See map & index p. 184.)

### FAIRFIELD INN BY MARRIOTT-PARK CENTRAL
(972)437-9905 **19**

Hotel $79-$129 **Address:** 9230 LBJ Frwy 75243 **Location:** I-635 exit 18A (Greenville Ave S), just s, then just e. **Facility:** 94 units. 3 stories, interior corridors. **Pool(s):** heated indoor. **Activities:** hot tub, exercise room. **Guest Services:** valet laundry.

**AAA Benefit:** Members save 5% or more!

### HAMPTON INN-DALLAS NORTH I-35 AT WALNUT HILL
(972)484-6557 **22**

Hotel $79-$139 **Address:** 11069 Composite Dr 75229 **Location:** I-35E exit 438 (Walnut Hill Ln), just e, then n. **Facility:** 113 units. 4 stories, interior corridors. **Terms:** 1-7 night minimum stay, cancellation fee imposed. **Pool(s):** outdoor. **Activities:** exercise room. **Guest Services:** valet laundry.

**AAA Benefit:** Members save up to 10%!

### HAWTHORN SUITES BY WYNDHAM DALLAS PARK CENTRAL
(972)391-0000 **8**

Extended Stay Hotel
$85-$120

**Address:** 7880 Alpha Rd 75240 **Location:** I-635 exit 19B (Coit Rd), 0.3 mi n, then just w. **Facility:** 114 efficiencies, some two bedrooms. 3 stories, interior corridors. **Terms:** cancellation fee imposed. **Amenities:** video games. **Pool(s):** outdoor. **Activities:** hot tub, exercise room. **Guest Services:** complimentary and valet laundry, area transportation. **Featured Amenity:** full hot breakfast.

### HILTON DALLAS LINCOLN CENTRE
(972)934-8400 **13**

Hotel
$129-$399

Hilton
HOTELS & RESORTS

**AAA Benefit:** Members save 5% or more!

**Address:** 5410 LBJ Frwy 75240 **Location:** Jct I-635 and Dallas North Tollway/Dallas Pkwy; I-635 exit 22D (Dallas Pkwy) eastbound; exit 22B (Dallas Pkwy/Inwood Rd) westbound, just e on frontage road. Across from Galleria Mall. **Facility:** Though not in a pedestrian-friendly area, the restaurant and shopping options nearby are endless; the hotel van can even take you there. Rooms sparkle with contemporary flair. 500 units. 18 stories, interior corridors. **Parking:** on-site (fee) and valet. **Terms:** 1-7 night minimum stay, cancellation fee imposed. **Amenities:** video games, safes. **Dining:** 2 restaurants. **Pool(s):** outdoor. **Activities:** exercise room. **Guest Services:** valet laundry, area transportation.

▼ See AAA listing p. 374 ▼

(See map & index p. 184.)

## HILTON DALLAS PARK CITIES   (214)368-0400  **24**

Hotel
$129-$269

**AAA Benefit:** Members save 5% or more!

**Address:** 5954 Luther Ln 75225 **Location:** Dallas North Tollway exit Northwest Hwy (Loop 12), just e to Douglas Ave, then just s. **Facility:** Unlike many Hiltons, this hotel has a small footprint, offering a boutique experience with a very attentive staff. Located in an affluent neighborhood, within walking distance of shops and restaurants. 224 units. 11 stories, interior corridors. **Parking:** valet only. **Terms:** 1-7 night minimum stay, cancellation fee imposed. **Amenities:** safes. **Pool(s):** heated outdoor. **Activities:** exercise room. **Guest Services:** valet laundry.

## HILTON GARDEN INN DALLAS/MARKET CENTER   (214)634-8200  **44**

Hotel
$69-$309

**AAA Benefit:** Members save up to 10%!

**Address:** 2325 N Stemmons Frwy 75207 **Location:** I-35E exit 431; on eastbound service road. **Facility:** 240 units. 8 stories, interior corridors. **Terms:** 1-7 night minimum stay, cancellation fee imposed. **Amenities:** video games. **Pool(s):** outdoor. **Activities:** hot tub, exercise room. **Guest Services:** valet and coin laundry, area transportation. *(See ad this page.)*

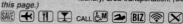

## HOLIDAY INN DALLAS MARKET CENTER   214/219-3333  **41**

**Hotel.** Rates not provided. **Address:** 4500 Harry Hines Blvd 75219 **Location:** I-35E exit 430B (Market Center Blvd), just e. **Facility:** 200 units. 9 stories, interior corridors. **Pool(s):** outdoor. **Activities:** exercise room. **Guest Services:** valet and coin laundry, area transportation.

## HOLIDAY INN EXPRESS & SUITES DALLAS CENTRAL MARKET CENTER   (214)905-1400  **38**

**Hotel** $119-$209 **Address:** 1521 Inwood Rd 75247 **Location:** I-35E exit 432A (Inwood Rd). **Facility:** 85 units. 4 stories, interior corridors. **Terms:** cancellation fee imposed. **Pool(s):** heated indoor. **Activities:** hot tub, exercise room. **Guest Services:** valet and coin laundry, area transportation.

## HOLIDAY INN EXPRESS & SUITES NORTH DALLAS AT PRESTON   (972)404-4500  **9**

**Hotel** $79-$209 **Address:** 6055 LBJ Frwy 75240 **Location:** I-635 exit 21 (Preston Rd); on westbound frontage road; eastbound, n on Preston Rd; turn at Walgreens. **Facility:** 103 units. 4 stories, interior corridors. **Amenities:** safes. **Pool(s):** heated indoor. **Activities:** hot tub, exercise room. **Guest Services:** valet and coin laundry, area transportation.

## HOLIDAY INN EXPRESS HOTEL & SUITES   (214)350-4011  **25**

**Hotel** $69-$139 **Address:** 2287 W Northwest Hwy 75220 **Location:** I-35E exit 436 (Northwest Hwy), just e. **Facility:** 103 units. 3 stories, interior corridors. **Terms:** 3 day cancellation notice-fee imposed. **Amenities:** safes. **Pool(s):** outdoor. **Activities:** exercise room. **Guest Services:** valet and coin laundry.

(See map & index p. 184.)

## HOLIDAY INN EXPRESS HOTEL & SUITES
(972)889-9972 **18**

Hotel
$95-$115

**Address:** 9089 Vantage Point Dr 75243 **Location:** I-635 exit 18A (Greenville Ave), just sw. **Facility:** 78 units. 4 stories, interior corridors. **Pool(s):** outdoor. **Activities:** hot tub, exercise room. **Guest Services:** valet and coin laundry, area transportation. **Featured Amenity: full hot breakfast.**

---

## HOMEWOOD SUITES BY HILTON - I-635 GREENVILLE
(972)437-6966 **20**

**Extended Stay Hotel**
$89-$169 **Address:** 9169 Markville Dr 75243 **Location:** I-635 exit 18A (Greenville Ave S), just s, then just e. **Facility:** 78 units, some two bedrooms, efficiencies and kitchens. 3 stories, interior corridors. **Terms:** 1-7 night minimum stay, cancellation fee imposed. **Pool(s):** heated indoor. **Activities:** hot tub, exercise room. **Guest Services:** valet and coin laundry.

**AAA Benefit:** Members save up to 10%!

---

## HOMEWOOD SUITES DALLAS MARKET CENTER
(214)819-9700 **39**

**Extended Stay Hotel**
$99-$179 **Address:** 2747 N Stemmons Frwy 75207 **Location:** I-35E exit 432A (Inwood Rd), just s. **Facility:** 137 efficiencies. 7 stories, interior corridors. **Terms:** 1-7 night minimum stay, cancellation fee imposed. **Amenities:** video games. **Pool(s):** outdoor. **Activities:** exercise room. **Guest Services:** valet and coin laundry, area transportation.

**AAA Benefit:** Members save up to 10%!

---

## HYATT HOUSE DALLAS/LINCOLN PARK
(214)696-1555 **28**

**Extended Stay Hotel**
$89-$299

**H HYATT house™**
**AAA Benefit:** Members save 10%!

**Address:** 8221 N Central Expwy 75225 **Location:** US 75 exit 5A southbound; exit 4B northbound, just w on Caruth Haven to Lincoln Pl, then just n. **Facility:** 155 units, some two bedrooms, efficiencies and kitchens. 4 stories, interior corridors. **Parking:** on-site (fee). **Terms:** cancellation fee imposed. **Pool(s):** outdoor. **Activities:** hot tub, exercise room. **Guest Services:** valet and coin laundry. **Featured Amenity:** breakfast buffet. *(See ad p. 202.)*

---

## HYATT PLACE DALLAS-NORTH/BY THE GALLERIA
(972)716-2001 **3**

Hotel
$59-$189

**Hyatt PLACE®**
**AAA Benefit:** Members save 10%!

**Address:** 5229 Spring Valley Rd 75254 **Location:** Jct Dallas North Tollway, just e. **Facility:** 123 units. 6 stories, interior corridors. **Terms:** cancellation fee imposed. **Pool(s):** heated outdoor. **Activities:** exercise room. **Guest Services:** valet laundry, area transportation. **Featured Amenity:** breakfast buffet.

---

## HYATT PLACE DALLAS/PARK CENTRAL
(972)458-1224 **17**

Hotel
$69-$199

**Hyatt PLACE®**
**AAA Benefit:** Members save 10%!

**Address:** 12411 N Central Expwy 75243 **Location:** US 75 exit 8B (Coit Rd) northbound; exit 8 (Coit Rd) southbound; on southbound access road. **Facility:** 126 units. 6 stories, interior corridors. **Terms:** cancellation fee imposed. **Pool(s):** outdoor. **Activities:** exercise room. **Guest Services:** valet laundry, area transportation. **Featured Amenity:** breakfast buffet.

---

## LA QUINTA INN & SUITES DALLAS NORTH CENTRAL
(214)361-8200 **23**

**Hotel** $95-$144 **Address:** 10001 N Central Expwy 75231 **Location:** US 75 exit 6 (Walnut Hill Ln/Meadow Rd) northbound, 0.5 mi n to Meadow Rd, then U-turn under highway; exit 7 (Royal St/Meadow Rd) southbound, 1 mi s on feeder. **Facility:** 127 units. 7 stories, interior corridors. **Pool(s):** heated outdoor. **Activities:** hot tub, exercise room. **Guest Services:** valet and coin laundry, area transportation.

---

## LE MERIDIEN DALLAS BY THE GALLERIA
(972)503-8700 **5**

Hotel
$109-$349

**Le MERIDIEN**
**AAA Benefit:** Members get up to 20% off, plus Starwood Preferred Guest® bonuses!

**Address:** 13402 Noel Rd 75240 **Location:** Dallas Pkwy exit Alpha Rd, just e to Noel Rd, then just s. **Facility:** 258 units. 11 stories, interior corridors. **Parking:** on-site (fee) and valet. **Terms:** cancellation fee imposed. **Amenities:** safes. **Pool(s):** heated indoor. **Activities:** exercise room. **Guest Services:** valet laundry, area transportation.

---

(See map & index p. 184.)

## MCM ELEGANTE HOTEL & SUITES (214)351-4477 [29]

Hotel
$89-$139

**Address:** 2330 W Northwest Hwy 75220 **Location:** I-35E exit 436, just e. **Facility:** 197 units. 8 stories, interior/exterior corridors. **Terms:** 7 day cancellation notice-fee imposed. **Amenities:** video games. **Pool(s):** outdoor. **Activities:** hot tub, exercise room. **Guest Services:** valet and coin laundry, area transportation. **Featured Amenity:** full hot breakfast.

---

## RENAISSANCE DALLAS HOTEL (214)631-2222 [43]

Hotel $115-$279 **Address:** 2222 N Stemmons Frwy 75207 **Location:** I-35E exit 430B (Market Center Blvd), 0.3 mi nw on access road. **Facility:** Shaped like an oval, with a polished granite exterior, this building is one that is quite easy to pick out of the Dallas skyline. Its location is convenient to downtown and the medical district. 514 units. 30 stories, interior corridors. **Parking:** valet only. **Amenities:** safes. **Pool(s):** heated outdoor. **Activities:** sauna, hot tub, exercise room. **Guest Services:** valet and coin laundry.

**AAA Benefit:** Members save 5% or more!

---

## RESIDENCE INN BY MARRIOTT DALLAS CENTRAL EXPRESSWAY (214)750-8220 [21]

Extended Stay Hotel $89-$189 **Address:** 10333 N Central Expwy 75231 **Location:** US 75 exit 6 (Walnut Hill Ln/Meadow Rd) northbound, 0.5 mi n to Meadow Rd, U-turn under highway; exit 7 (Royal St/Meadow Rd) southbound, 1 mi s on access road. **Facility:** 103 units, some two bedrooms, efficiencies and kitchens. 3 stories, interior/exterior corridors. **Pool(s):** outdoor. **Activities:** hot tub, exercise room. **Guest Services:** valet and coin laundry, area transportation.

**AAA Benefit:** Members save 5% or more!

---

## RESIDENCE INN BY MARRIOTT-DALLAS MARKET CENTER (214)631-2472 [37]

Extended Stay Hotel $89-$209 **Address:** 6950 N Stemmons Frwy 75247 **Location:** I-35E exit 432B (Commonwealth Ln), 0.6 mi n on northbound frontage road. **Facility:** 142 efficiencies, some two bedrooms. 3 stories, interior/exterior corridors. **Pool(s):** outdoor. **Activities:** hot tub, exercise room. **Guest Services:** valet and coin laundry, area transportation.

**AAA Benefit:** Members save 5% or more!

---

## RESIDENCE INN BY MARRIOTT-DALLAS PARK CENTRAL (972)503-1333 [14]

Extended Stay Hotel $80-$129 **Address:** 7642 LBJ Frwy 75251 **Location:** I-635 exit 20 (Hillcrest Ave); on eastbound access road. **Facility:** 139 units, some two bedrooms, efficiencies and kitchens. 3 stories, interior corridors. **Pool(s):** heated outdoor. **Activities:** hot tub, exercise room. **Guest Services:** valet and coin laundry.

**AAA Benefit:** Members save 5% or more!

---

## SPRINGHILL SUITES BY MARRIOTT-STEMMONS (214)350-2300 [31]

Hotel $116-$128 **Address:** 2363 Stemmons Tr 75220 **Location:** I-35E exit 436, just e, then just s. **Facility:** 96 units, some kitchens. 3 stories, interior corridors. **Pool(s):** outdoor. **Activities:** hot tub, exercise room. **Guest Services:** valet and coin laundry, area transportation.

**AAA Benefit:** Members save 5% or more!

---

## STAYBRIDGE SUITES NORTH DALLAS 972/726-9990 [1]

Extended Stay Hotel. Rates not provided. **Address:** 16060 N Dallas Pkwy 75248 **Location:** Dallas North Tollway exit Keller Springs, just e to Knoll Tr, then just s. **Facility:** 129 efficiencies. 3 stories, interior corridors. **Pool(s):** outdoor. **Activities:** hot tub. **Guest Services:** complimentary and valet laundry, area transportation.

---

## THE WESTIN DALLAS PARK CENTRAL (972)385-3000 [15]

Hotel
$99-$349

**WESTIN** HOTELS & RESORTS

**AAA Benefit:** Enjoy up to 20% off your next stay, plus Starwood Preferred Guest® bonuses!

**Address:** 12720 Merit Dr 75251 **Location:** I-635 exit 19C (Coit Rd) eastbound; exit 19B (US 75/Coit Rd) westbound; 0.3 mi w of jct US 75. **Facility:** 536 units. 19 stories, interior corridors. **Parking:** on-site (fee) and valet. **Amenities:** video games, safes. **Pool(s):** outdoor. **Activities:** exercise room. **Guest Services:** valet laundry, area transportation.

---

## THE WESTIN GALLERIA, DALLAS (972)934-9494 [6]

Hotel
$119-$449

**WESTIN** HOTELS & RESORTS

**AAA Benefit:** Enjoy up to 20% off your next stay, plus Starwood Preferred Guest® bonuses!

**Address:** 13340 Dallas Pkwy 75240 **Location:** Just n of jct I-635 and N Dallas Pkwy. **Facility:** As the only hotel located at the Galleria, this lodging has the advantage of having world-class shopping, an ice rink and numerous restaurants right at its doorstep. Rooms are contemporary. 448 units. 21 stories, interior corridors. **Parking:** on-site and valet. **Terms:** cancellation fee imposed. **Amenities:** safes. **Dining:** 2 restaurants, also, The Oceanaire Seafood Room, see separate listing. **Pool(s):** heated outdoor. **Activities:** exercise room, massage. **Guest Services:** valet laundry, boarding pass kiosk.

---

(See map & index p. 184.)

## WYNDHAM DALLAS PARK CENTRAL
(972)233-7600 **7**

Hotel
$79-$149

**Address:** 7800 Alpha Rd 75240 **Location:** I-635 exit 19C (Coit Rd) eastbound; exit 19B (Coit Rd) westbound, just n, then just w. **Facility:** 295 units. 10 stories, interior corridors. **Amenities:** video games. **Pool(s):** heated outdoor. **Activities:** hot tub, exercise room. **Guest Services:** valet and coin laundry, area transportation.

## WYNDHAM LOVE FIELD
(214)357-8500 **34**

Hotel
$129-$260

**Address:** 3300 W Mockingbird Ln 75235 **Location:** I-35 exit 433B (Mockingbird Ln), 2.3 mi e. **Facility:** 244 units. 8 stories, interior corridors. **Amenities:** video games, safes. **Pool(s):** outdoor. **Activities:** exercise room. **Guest Services:** valet and coin laundry, area transportation.

## WHERE TO EAT

### III FORKS
972/267-1776 **5**

Steak
Fine Dining
$29-$99

**AAA Inspector Notes:** All beef products served here are USDA Prime and include favorites such as filet mignon, bone-in-rib-eye, New York Strip, prime rib, burgers and pork chops. Seafood delicacies feature ahi tuna, shrimp, scallops and crab. The menu also offers Australian lobster, Chilean sea bass, lamb and Atlantic salmon. Staff members peruse the dining room serving fresh sliced and seasoned scallions and tomatoes. Finish off with homemade desserts which include a delectable bread pudding. **Features:** full bar. **Reservations:** suggested. **Address:** 17776 Dallas Pkwy 75287 **Location:** Dallas North Tollway exit Briargrove Ln. **Parking:** on-site and valet.

### USDA Prime beef, fresh fish, cold-water lobster tails

### AFGHAN GRILL
972/818-0300 **7**

Afghan. Casual Dining. $14-$20 **AAA Inspector Notes:** Located in the back corner of the Preston Plaza shopping center, the restaurant's mango- and crimson-colored walls provide a warm and inviting backdrop. For those who think Afghan cuisine may be too adventurous, at this restaurant the cuisine is remarkably similar to what one might find at a Lebanese or Greek eatery. Kebabs and lots of vegetarian items dominate the menu. **Features:** full bar. **Address:** 17370 Preston Rd, Suite 490 75252 **Location:** Dallas North Tollway exit Frankford Rd, 1.9 mi e, 0.7 mi s.

### ASIAN MINT
214/363-6655 **21**

Thai. Casual Dining. $9-$20 **AAA Inspector Notes:** Inside this small contemporary eatery designed completely in green and white, you will find Thai selections such as the classic pad thai and curry dishes as well as basil red snapper and garlic quail. Monday through Saturday evenings they add sushi to the menu, and there always is a refreshing and unexpected menu of pastries and specialty coffees. **Features:** full bar. **Address:** 11617 N Central Expwy, Suite 135 75243 **Location:** US 75 exit Forest Ln, just w.

### BANGKOK THAI CUISINE
214/739-3436 **25**

Thai. Casual Dining. $8-$17 **AAA Inspector Notes:** The small open dining room has simple décor, but the attention to detail and presentation given to dishes is a nice surprise. **Address:** 10207 N Central Expwy 75231 **Location:** US 75 exit 6 (Walnut Hill Ln/Meadow Rd) northbound, U-turn under highway; exit 7 (Royal/Meadow Rd) southbound; on south access road.

### THE BLUE FISH
972/250-3474 **3**

Japanese. Casual Dining. $11-$29 **AAA Inspector Notes:** The Japanese restaurant mixes contemporary décor and traditional food. Among dishes are sushi, sashimi and tempura preparations, as well as chicken, beef and seafood entrées. Guests also can sit at the sushi bar to watch the chef in action or enjoy the hibachi grill. **Features:** full bar, happy hour. **Address:** 18149 N Dallas Pkwy, Suite 100 75287 **Location:** Just w of jct N Dallas Pkwy and Frankford Rd.

### BLUE MESA GRILL
214/378-8686 **30**

Southwestern. Casual Dining. $10-$17 **AAA Inspector Notes:** Decorated in a rustic Southwestern motif, this café serves spicy entrées with a New Mexican flair. Guests can crunch on blue corn and sweet potato chips in the low-lit dining room before diving into a sampler plate such as one with an original tamale pie and mesquite-grilled skewers of meat. For dessert, try the dark chocolate empanadas served with a tart sangria sauce. Look out for their seasonal specials where they make ingredients like New Mexican Hatch chiles and peaches really shine. **Features:** full bar, Sunday brunch, happy hour. **Address:** 7700 W Northwest Hwy 75225 **Location:** US 75 exit Northwest Hwy (Loop 12), just w.

### CANTINA LAREDO
214/265-1610 **23**

Mexican
Casual Dining
$10-$26

**AAA Inspector Notes:** Modern yet relaxed, this restaurant features creative Mexican fare. A great starter of top-shelf guacamole, which is prepared tableside, primes the palate for an entree of enchiladas, tacos, fajitas and chiles rellenos. **Features:** full bar, Sunday brunch. **Address:** 6025 Royal Ln, Suite 250 75230 **Location:** In Preston Royal Shopping Center.

### Gourmet Mexican food, fresh-squeezed lime margaritas

### CANTINA LAREDO
214/821-5785 **35**

Mexican
Casual Dining
$10-$26

**AAA Inspector Notes:** Modern yet relaxed, this restaurant features creative Mexican fare. A great starter of top-shelf guacamole, which is prepared tableside, primes the palate for an entree of enchiladas, tacos, fajitas and chiles rellenos. **Features:** full bar, Sunday brunch. **Address:** 2031 Abrams Rd 75214 **Location:** In Lakewood Section; near Gaston Ave.

### Gourmet Mexican food, fresh-squeezed lime margaritas

### CELEBRATION
214/351-5681 **33**

American. Casual Dining. $12-$24 **AAA Inspector Notes:** Made-from-scratch cooking and family-style service make diners feel right at home. Dinner entrées are served with a choice of three side dishes such as glazed carrots, mashed potatoes and beans. Be sure to save room for a homemade dessert. The restaurant is located in a residential area near Dallas Love Field. **Features:** full bar, patio dining. **Address:** 4503 W Lovers Ln 75209 **Location:** Between Inwood Rd and Lemmon Ave.

(See map & index p. 184.)

**CUQUITA'S RESTAURANT**        214/575-3188  11

Mexican. Casual Dining. $7-$12 **AAA Inspector Notes:** This family-owned eatery is part of an iconic Mexican restaurant that eventually gave in to progress and was demolished. This location doesn't have the charm of the original house, but all the favorites are still on the menu. They offer authentic cuisine (think menudo, pozole, gorditas and handmade tortillas), not Tex Mex. They also open in the late morning for breakfast. **Features:** beer & wine. **Address:** 8076 Spring Valley Rd 75240 **Location:** Southeast corner of Coit and Spring Valley rds.  L  D

**DEL FRISCO'S DOUBLE EAGLE STEAK HOUSE**
972/490-9000  10

Steak. Fine Dining. $30-$89 **AAA Inspector Notes:** An iconic eatery in the area, the steaks are big, juicy and very tasty. If you aren't in the mood for beef, they also have a very good selection of seafood. All dishes are prepared à la carte, so you must order your vegetables separately; be careful ordering these side dishes as they are quite large. Desserts are made in house and are equally large. **Features:** full bar, happy hour. **Reservations:** suggested. **Address:** 5251 Spring Valley Rd 75254 **Location:** Jct Dallas Pkwy and Spring Valley Rd, just e. **Parking:** on-site and valet.  D

**EL CHICO**        972/238-0011  12

**Tex-Mex**
**Casual Dining**
**$7-$16**

**AAA Inspector Notes:** Inside and out, the decor of the popular Mexican restaurant is inviting. The menu features traditional favorites such as enchiladas, tacos, burritos and fajitas. The broad menu also lists a few American classics. **Features:** full bar. **Address:** 13937 N Central Expwy 75243 **Location:** US 75 exit 23, just sw.  L  D

**EL FENIX MEXICAN RESTAURANT**     214/363-5279

Tex-Mex. Casual Dining. $7-$16 **AAA Inspector Notes:** *Classic.* Since 1918, this Tex-Mex café has been serving traditional Tex-Mex in an inviting dining room that really transports you to another place. The expected dishes of nachos, fajitas, quesadillas and combination platters can be found alongside some classic egg dishes like huevos rancheros. **Features:** full bar, happy hour. **Address:** 6811 W Northwest Hwy 75225 **Location:** Just w of jct Hillcrest Ave.  L  D

**ENCHILADAS RESTAURANT**        214/363-8969  26

Tex-Mex. Casual Dining. $7-$17 **AAA Inspector Notes:** This small local chain serves up quesadillas, enchiladas, combo plates and other items such as carne asada and chipotle chicken. **Features:** full bar, patio dining, happy hour. **Address:** 7050 Greenville Ave 75231 **Location:** Between Walnut Hill and Park lns.  L  D

**GRANDY'S RESTAURANT**

American. Quick Serve. $4-$8 **AAA Inspector Notes:** Fried chicken and country-fried steak are menu standbys at the restaurant, a regional franchise. They also offer a family-style dining menu. The décor is a step up from that of most quick-serve eateries and more resembles that of a conventional restaurant. Some elements of increased service include additional rolls, iced tea refills and tray removal.  B  L  D

*For additional information, visit AAA.com*
**LOCATIONS:**
**Address:** 1607 Regal Row 75247 **Location:** I-35E exit 434B, just e. **Phone:** 214/689-9858

**Address:** 8228 E R L Thornton Frwy 75228 **Location:** I-30 exit 52A, just s. **Phone:** 214/324-1963

**Address:** 3738 Marvin D Love 75224 **Location:** Southeast corner of jct US 67 and S Polk St. **Phone:** 214/371-1613

**GREAT CHINA RESTAURANT**        972/732-8282  2

Chinese. Casual Dining. $10-$30 **AAA Inspector Notes:** In a small strip center near George Bush Tollway, the locally owned and operated restaurant prepares favorite Chinese dishes and Japanese sushi at its small sushi bar. Among choices worth trying is beef on a stick: slices of beef, onion, tomato and a cherry, complete with its own tiny hibachi grill. **Features:** full bar. **Address:** 18101 Preston Rd, Suite 106 75252 **Location:** Northwest corner of Frankford Blvd and Preston Rd.  L  D

**HERRERA'S TEX-MEX**        214/630-2599  34

Tex-Mex. Casual Dining. $7-$14 **AAA Inspector Notes:** The Dallas chain prepare Tex-Mex standards, including enchiladas, tamales and tacos. The menu, heavy on cheese and reliant on the traditional standards, is described by many as some of the best Tex-Mex the city has to offer. Menudo is available on the weekends, and although it is not open early you can catch breakfast here all day long. Finding it can be a challenge since its small sign is dwarfed by the large commercial building it is housed in. **Features:** full bar, happy hour. **Address:** 5427 Denton Dr 75235 **Location:** I-35E exit 432 (Inwood Rd), 1.4 mi n to Denton Dr, then just e.  B  L  D

**INDIA PALACE RESTAURANT & BAR**     972/392-0190  16

Indian. Casual Dining. $12-$25 **AAA Inspector Notes:** As one of the original Indian restaurants in this city, the Palace remains the one to imitate. Tandoori specialties are the focus, along with Indian-style barbecue with chicken, lamb and seafood. With its proximity to the Galleria, this conveniently located restaurant packs them in for their popular lunch buffet. Casual elegance describes the dining room, while service is relaxed but friendly. **Features:** full bar. **Reservations:** suggested, weekends. **Address:** 12817 Preston Rd, Suite 105 75230 **Location:** I-635 exit 21 (Preston Rd), just sw.  L  D

**J.G.'S OLD FASHIONED HAMBURGERS**
972/644-8628  18

**Burgers**
**Quick Serve**
**$5-$8**

**AAA Inspector Notes:** The place for burgers in the area, family-run JG's has been in business for more than 25 years. Burgers are served up simply; you dress them up any way you like at the dressings station. A small outdoor patio is available. **Features:** beer & wine. **Address:** 12101 N Greenville Ave, Suite 109 75243 **Location:** I-635 exit 18A (Greenville Ave), just s; in Highpoint Village Strip Center.  L  D

**KALACHANDJI'S GARDEN RESTAURANT**    214/821-1048  36

Vegetarian. Casual Dining. $10-$13 **AAA Inspector Notes:** This quaint restaurant is located in a garden courtyard with pleasant booth and table seating. Very reasonably priced and well-prepared vegetarian dishes are offered from the self-serve buffet tables. **Address:** 5430 Gurley Ave 75223 **Location:** I-30 exit 49A (E Grand Ave), just w to Phillip St, just ne to Fairview St, just n to Gurley Ave, then just e.  L  D

**LA DUNI LATIN KITCHEN AND COFFEE STUDIO**
214/987-2260  27

Latin American. Casual Dining. $9-$27 **AAA Inspector Notes:** There are many ways to enjoy this local favorite. Stop in to La Duni to recharge after some serious power shopping, enjoy a quick respite at the coffee studio or take in the tranquil courtyard with the afternoon tea service. This place has something for everyone. The menu features hearty sandwiches, empanadas, a multitude of delicious side items and entrées such as Argentine steak, roasted chicken, enchiladas and tacos. The desserts are the calling card, so be prepared to indulge. **Features:** full bar, patio dining, Sunday brunch. **Address:** 8687 N Central Expwy, Unit 1516 75225 **Location:** I-75 exit 75A Northwest Hwy (Loop 12), just w; in Northpark Center.  L  D

**(See map & index p. 184.)**

**LA MADELEINE COUNTRY FRENCH CAFE**

▼ Traditional French. Casual Dining. $7-$12 **AAA Inspector Notes:** A fireplace creates the focal point at this cozy European style café where you can always get a quiche or savory stuffed puffed pastry on the go or stick around for a chicken crêpe or French dip sandwich. Heartier entrées like rotisserie chicken are offered and every season promises menu surprises. Whatever you decide on you probably will not get out the door without enjoying one of their tempting sweet pastries. [B] [L] CALL [&M]

*For additional information, visit AAA.com*

**LOCATIONS:**
**Address:** 2121 San Jacinto St, Suite 120 75201 **Location:** Jct Ross Ave and N Pearl St, 1 blk se. **Bar:** beer & wine.
**Phone:** 214/220-3911
**Address:** 13350 Dallas Pkwy, Suite 400 75240 **Location:** Jct Dallas Pkwy and I-635; in Galleria Center. **Bar:** wine only.
**Phone:** 972/991-7788
**Address:** 4343 W Northwest Hwy, Suite 365 75220 **Location:** Jct Midway Rd and Northwest Hwy (Loop 12), just w. **Bar:** wine only.
**Phone:** 214/357-5621
**Address:** 11930 Preston Rd, Suite 100 75230 **Location:** Jct Preston Rd and Forest Ln, just n. **Bar:** wine only.
**Phone:** 972/233-6446
**Address:** 8319 Preston Rd 75225 **Location:** Jct Preston Rd and W Northwest Hwy (Loop 12). **Bar:** beer & wine. **Phone:** 214/346-9733
**Address:** 640 N Park Center 75225 **Location:** Jct N Central Expwy and W Northwest Hwy (Loop 12); in Park Center. **Bar:** beer & wine. **Phone:** 214/696-2398

**LAVENDOU BISTRO PROVENCAL**　972/248-1911　①

▼▼▼ French. Fine Dining. $13-$31 **AAA Inspector Notes:** The flavors are of the French countryside, the bistro ambience is full of energy, and the service is attentive. You'll enjoy molded pâtés, crusty breads and hearty dishes such as Provençal beef stew, coquilles St.-Jacques and rack of lamb with ratatouille. Also serving high tea weekday afternoons by reservation only. **Features:** full bar. **Address:** 19009 Preston Rd, Unit 200 75252 **Location:** Just s of jct George Bush Tpke. [L] [D]

**LAWRY'S THE PRIME RIB**　972/503-6688　⑨

▼▼▼▼ Steak. Fine Dining. $11-$48 **AAA Inspector Notes:** Frosted glass chandeliers hang from the ceiling of this upscale dining room. Tender prime rib is the specialty and is served tableside from stainless steel carts. Yorkshire pudding or creamed spinach can accompany most meals. Try the lofty banana cream pie for dessert. A sandwich bar serves as the lunch menu with several selections of meat, turkey and seafood cut by a chef when ordered. Prime rib lovers will be happy to know that it's available for lunch as well. **Features:** full bar, Sunday brunch. **Reservations:** suggested. **Address:** 14655 Dallas Pkwy 75254 **Location:** 0.5 mi s of jct Dallas Pkwy and Belt Line Rd; on west side service road. [L] [D]

**MAGUIRE'S REGIONAL CUISINE**　972/818-0068　⑥

▼▼▼▼ Regional American. Fine Dining. $15-$35 **AAA Inspector Notes:** Downtown restaurants certainly can provide a unique local experience, but head to the burbs and Maguire's will impress you with its sophisticated dining room, lively bar scene and superb staff, all the while providing an air of casualness. The Texas shrimp and grits are highlighted on the menu, and for good reason; the creamy grits blend well with the spiciness of the shrimp. Flatbreads, salads, steaks, grilled fish and a burger also can be enjoyed at this neighborhood favorite. **Features:** full bar, patio dining, Sunday brunch. **Reservations:** required. **Address:** 17552 N Dallas Pkwy 75287 **Location:** Jct Trinity Mills Rd and N Dallas Pkwy. **Parking:** on-site and valet. [L] [D] CALL [&M]

**MERCADO JUAREZ CAFE**　972/556-0796

▼▼ Tex-Mex. Casual Dining. $7-$15 **AAA Inspector Notes:** The look of a Mexican hacienda is created with brightly painted walls and window frames as well as a large focal-point tree. The menu includes fajitas, tacos al carbon and plenty of crunchy nachos. **Features:** full bar, happy hour. **Address:** 1901 W Northwest Hwy 75220 **Location:** 0.5 mi w of Northwest Hwy (Loop 12). [L] [D] CALL [&M]

**THE MERCURY**　972/960-7774　⑳

▼▼▼▼ New American. Fine Dining. $14-$60 **AAA Inspector Notes:** Menu offerings range from classic eggs Benedict at brunch to braised beef taquitos and wild mushroom risotto at lunch to crisped salmon and braised short ribs at dinner. In a small strip center, the restaurant is partially hidden away but well worth the search to find and convenient to lots of shopping. Those looking for a good bar scene will be pleased as well. **Features:** full bar. **Reservations:** suggested. **Address:** 11909 Preston Rd 75230 **Location:** Northwest corner of Preston Rd and Forest Ln. [L] [D]

**NATALIE'S**　214/739-0362　㉔

▼▼ American. Casual Dining. $12-$20 **AAA Inspector Notes:** Natalie's offers a broad menu with both Continental and American cuisine menu items. Chicken piccata, lasagna, osso buco, crab cakes and beef stroganoff are just a few of the selections. This neighborhood restaurant has a lovely dining room, reminiscent of a European bistro, and is popular with the area residents. **Features:** full bar, Sunday brunch. **Address:** 5940 Royal Ln 75230 **Location:** Jct Preston Rd and Royal Ln; southwest corner. [L] [D]

**THE OCEANAIRE SEAFOOD ROOM**　972/759-2277　⑭

▼▼▼ Seafood. Fine Dining. $14-$70 **AAA Inspector Notes:** Fresh fish and shellfish are flown in daily from around the globe. The sleek, handsomely designed dining room has a raw bar and is tastefully appointed in an Art Deco/nautical theme. The menu notes the seafood available daily and the varied preparation styles, such as broiled, grilled and blackened. **Features:** full bar. **Reservations:** suggested. **Address:** 13340 Dallas Pkwy 75240 **Location:** Just n of jct I-635 and N Dallas Pkwy; in The Westin Galleria, Dallas. **Parking:** on-site (fee). [SAVE] [L] [D] CALL [&M]

**PAPPADEAUX SEAFOOD KITCHEN**

▼▼ Regional Seafood. Casual Dining. $12-$47 **AAA Inspector Notes:** A seafood lover's delight, the restaurant taps into a little bit of New Orleans with its Cajun dishes and elaborate menu selections. Patrons might start off with a creative choice of blackened oyster and shrimp fondeaux with crayfish and let the feast begin. While music plays in the background, patrons can dig into dirty rice or spicy gumbo loaded with seafood. Well-seasoned shrimp and fish are prepared in varied ways. **Bar:** full bar. [L] [D]

*For additional information, visit AAA.com*

**LOCATIONS:**
**Address:** 18349 Dallas Pkwy 75287 **Location:** Just w of jct N Dallas Pkwy and Frankford Rd. **Phone:** 972/447-9616
**Address:** 10428 Lombardy Ln 75220 **Location:** I-35E exit 436 (Northwest Hwy/Loop 12), just w to Lombardy Ln.
**Phone:** 214/358-1912
**Address:** 3520 Oak Lawn Ave 75219 **Location:** I-35E exit 430A (Oak Lawn Ave), 1.5 mi ne. **Phone:** 214/521-4700

**PAPPAS BAR-B-QUE**　214/956-9038

▼▼ Barbecue. Casual Dining. $6-$20 **AAA Inspector Notes:** Hailing from the Houston Pappas family restaurant dynasty, the barbecue joint is all about casual, down-home dining. Barbecue sandwiches, brisket and dinner platters are served cafeteria style. Covered patio seating is an option. **Features:** beer only, patio dining. **Address:** 2231 W Northwest Hwy at Lombardy Ln 75220 **Location:** I-35E exit 436 Northwest Hwy (Loop 12) northbound, just w; exit southbound, just e. [B] [L] [D]

**PAPPAS BROS. STEAKHOUSE**　214/366-2000　㉙

▼▼▼ Steak. Fine Dining. $40-$95 **AAA Inspector Notes:** In-house-dried aged prime beef is the specialty of this upscale restaurant with signature steaks of filet mignon, New York strips, rib-eyes and porterhouses being featured. The wine list is extensive and includes rare cognac and single-malt scotch for the discerning diner. Although the dining here is sophisticated it is also surprisingly family-friendly. **Features:** full bar. **Reservations:** suggested. **Address:** 10477 Lombardy Ln 75220 **Location:** I-35 exit 436 westbound, 0.4 mi w on Northwest Hwy (Loop 12) to Lombardy Ln, then just n. **Parking:** on-site and valet. [D] CALL [&M]

Learn the local driving laws
at DrivingLaws.AAA.com

(See map & index p. 184.)

## PAPPASITO'S CANTINA   214/350-1970

◆ Mexican. Casual Dining. $7-$30 **AAA Inspector Notes:** Fine traditional offerings are served in an upscale cantina atmosphere. Often crowded during peak hours, the immensely popular stop dishes up generous portions of sizzling fajitas, enchiladas and other traditional Mexican favorites, including some shrimp specialties. The terrific margaritas are guaranteed to get attention. Tables in the large dining room are closely spaced. Ice cream with cinnamon on chocolate bread pudding shouldn't be missed. **Features:** full bar, patio dining, happy hour. **Address:** 10433 Lombardy Ln 75220 **Location:** Jct I-35E and SR 12, just s. L D

## P.F. CHANG'S CHINA BISTRO   972/818-3336 (28)

◆◆ Chinese. Casual Dining. $6-$25 **AAA Inspector Notes:** Trendy, upscale decor provides a pleasant backdrop for New Age Chinese dining. Appetizers, soups and salads are a meal by themselves. Vegetarian plates and sides, noodles, chow meins, chicken and meat dishes are created from exotic, fresh ingredients. **Features:** full bar. **Reservations:** suggested. **Address:** 18323 N Dallas Pkwy 75287 **Location:** Just w of jct N Dallas Pkwy and Frankford Rd. **Parking:** on-site and valet. L D

## THE PURPLE COW   214/373-0037 (22)

◆ American. Family Dining. $4-$10 **AAA Inspector Notes:** The eatery has been around for nearly 15 years and is a throwback to a '50s diner, with a fountain at the counter, metal chairs, black-and-white tile floors and background rock 'n' roll music. The main fare is burgers, fries and shakes, homemade soups and salads. Because kids abound in this family-friendly restaurant, one might forget adults can indeed enjoy a cocktail and frequently do during their Sunday happy hour. **Features:** full bar. **Address:** 6025 Royal Ln, Suite 110 75230 **Location:** Northeast corner of Preston Rd and Royal Ln; in Preston Royal Shopping Center. L D

## ROCKFISH SEAFOOD GRILL   214/823-8444

◆◆ Seafood. Casual Dining. $7-$20 **AAA Inspector Notes:** Patrons shuffle through peanut shells on the floor as they make their way to their seats and are easily distracted by the numerous pieces of hunting and fishing memorabilia adorning the walls and ceiling. Although guests kick back in a log cabin-style interior, the freshly caught fish gets more sophisticated preparation than campfire roasting. The chef uses an array of sauces and cooking styles, and soups are hearty and fresh. **Features:** full bar. **Address:** 5331 E Mockingbird Ln, Suite 160 75206 **Location:** I-75 exit 3 (Mockingbird Ln), just e; in Mockingbird Station Shopping Center. L D

## ROYAL THAI RESTAURANT   214/691-3555 (32)

◆◆ Thai. Casual Dining. $8-$14 **AAA Inspector Notes:** A subtle combination of spices, herbs and fresh ingredients, including ever-present chili peppers, flavors the restaurant's Thai cuisine. Good service by staff in traditional garb is a hallmark at the quaint spot, which is located in back of a busy shopping center. This place buzzes, which means waits should be expected. **Features:** beer & wine. **Address:** 5500 Greenville Ave, Suite 608 75206 **Location:** US 75 exit Lovers Ln, just e, then just n. L D

## SALTGRASS STEAKHOUSE

◆◆ Steak. Casual Dining. $9-$30 **AAA Inspector Notes:** Those looking for something different should try the comfortable steakhouse, which never says no to a special request. Born from the spirit of Texas cattle drives, the restaurant resembles a Texas lodge, with high ceilings and mounted animal heads. Baby back ribs are so tender the meat falls off the bone. Also on the menu are hearty steaks, prime rib, chicken, seafood and yummy desserts. **Bar:** full bar. SAVE L D

*For additional information, visit AAA.com*

**LOCATIONS:**
**Address:** 4101 LBJ Frwy 75244 **Location:** I-635 exit 23 (Midway Rd), just w on service road to Valley View. **Phone:** 972/243-9440 (15)
**Address:** 13561 N Central Expwy 75243 **Location:** I-75 exit 22 (Midpark Rd); on southbound frontage road.
**Phone:** 469/330-0152 (13)

## SONNY BRYAN'S BBQ   214/357-7120

◆ Barbecue. Quick Serve. $5-$15 **AAA Inspector Notes:** This 1958 Texas barbecue stand known for huge portions of hickory-smoked beef and ribs has served a wide variety of patrons from U.S. presidents to the cast of "Saving Private Ryan." When the barbecue's gone, it's gone, so come and get it before it goes! Much of the seating is outdoor picnic tables, but people from all walks of like pass through. **Features:** beer & wine. **Address:** 2202 Inwood Rd 75235 **Location:** I-35 exit 432A (Inwood Rd) eastbound, 0.5 mi ne. L D

## SUSHI ICHIBAN JAPANESE RESTAURANT   972/437-9514 (19)

◆ Sushi. Casual Dining. $6-$25 **AAA Inspector Notes:** Located in a strip mall, the paper globe lights, pictures of the Japanese countryside on the wall and bamboo wall coverings help bring the theme home. You can find an assortment of grilled, fried and other hot entrées as well as noodle dishes and sushi. **Features:** beer & wine. **Address:** 12101 Greenville Ave, Suite 112 75243 **Location:** I-635 exit 18A (Greenville Ave), just s. L D

## SUZE   214/350-6135 (31)

◆◆ New American. Fine Dining. $16-$36 **AAA Inspector Notes:** Tucked into the back of a shopping center, this small neighborhood restaurant offers a touch of Middle Eastern and Asian tastes to add zest to its menu. You might want to come early as they fill up fast and space is at a premium. Sample items such as crispy sesame lavosh pizza, fried green tomatoes, watermelon and French feta salad, baby rack of lamb and pan-roasted king salmon. **Features:** beer & wine. **Reservations:** suggested. **Address:** 4345 W Northwest Hwy, Suite 270 75220 **Location:** Dallas North Tollway exit W Northwest Hwy (Loop 12), 1.6 mi w; northeast corner of Northwest Hwy and Midway Rd; in Preston Hollow Shopping Center. D

## SWEET BASIL ITALIAN GRILL   972/733-1500 (8)

◆◆ Italian. Casual Dining. $7-$20 **AAA Inspector Notes:** This family-owned and -operated restaurant provides inviting rustic dining rooms that transport you to Italy. The menu is very well represented with beef, chicken, veal, pork, fresh seafood and several types of pasta. The lighting is low and the feeling intimate; it's the perfect place for a couple's night out or celebration. **Features:** full bar, Sunday brunch. **Address:** 17610 Midway Rd, Suite 150 75287 **Location:** Dallas North Tollway exit Trinity Mills Rd, 0.5 mi w; between Voss and Midway rds. L D

## TEXAS LAND AND CATTLE STEAKHOUSE   214/353-8000

◆◆ Steak. Casual Dining. $7-$27 **AAA Inspector Notes:** A variety of large Prime steaks, delicious salads and scrumptious desserts await you at the friendly Texas ranch-style restaurant. Try the signature slow-smoked sirloin, which never fails to please, or the Caesar salad, another favorite. A Texas steakhouse means everything is bigger, from large cuts and oversize salads to potatoes and side dishes. Those not in the mood for beef can opt for chicken, quail or seafood. Dessert is an occasion. **Features:** full bar. **Address:** 10250 Technology Blvd W 75220 **Location:** I-35E exit 436 Northwest Hwy (Loop 12), just e to Technology Blvd E, then just s. L D

(See map & index p. 184.)

**THAI SPICE**     469/533-8424   4

◆◆ ◆◆ Thai. Casual Dining. $10-$27 **AAA Inspector Notes:** The hip and funky atmosphere at this eatery is soothing and upbeat. A large water wall calms one's spirits upon entering. Customers are introduced to different levels of spiciness and are given a lot of choices for their meal. Wireless Internet access truly makes Thai Spice a hot spot. **Reservations:** suggested. **Address:** 18111 Dallas Pkwy, Unit 200 75287 **Location:** I-635 and Dallas North Tollway exit Frankford Rd, just sw. L D

**TUPINAMBA**     972/991-8148   17

◆◆ ◆◆ Tex-Mex. Casual Dining. $9-$17 **AAA Inspector Notes:** The loyalties are clear at this cavernous restaurant—this is Aggie town. No matter, all are welcome, and it's clear the locals love it and have for more than 60 years. Traditional Tex-Mex cuisine accompanies some tempting specialties like the sour cream chicken, grilled jalapeño catfish and the spicy camarones diablo (cascabel chile-spiced shrimp). **Features:** full bar. **Address:** 12270 Inwood Rd 75244 **Location:** I-635 exit 22D (Dallas Pkwy) eastbound; exit 22B (Dallas Pkwy/Inwood Rd) westbound, just s; in Summertree Shopping Center. L D

## DALLAS SOUTH
### • Hotels & Restaurants map & index p. 197

**COMFORT SUITES**     (214)267-0100   2

◆◆◆ ◆ Hotel $94-$139 **Address:** 4275 DFW Tpke 75211 **Location:** I-30 exit 39 (Cockrell Hill Rd), just n. **Facility:** 70 units. 3 stories, interior corridors. **Pool(s):** outdoor. **Activities:** hot tub, exercise room. **Guest Services:** coin laundry.

[icons]

**HAMPTON INN & SUITES**     (214)634-1800   1

◆◆◆ ◆ Hotel $89-$119 **Address:** 1718 N Cockrell Hill Rd 75211 **Location:** I-30 exit 39 (Cockrell Hill Rd), just s. **Facility:** 79 units. 4 stories, interior corridors. **Terms:** 1-7 night minimum stay, cancellation fee imposed. **Amenities:** safes. **Pool(s):** heated outdoor. **Activities:** hot tub, exercise room. **Guest Services:** valet and coin laundry.

**AAA Benefit:** Members save up to 10%!

[icons]

**HOLIDAY INN EXPRESS & SUITES DALLAS WEST**     (214)331-0505   3

◆◆◆ ◆ Hotel $119-$250 **Address:** 4321 Communications Dr 75211 **Location:** I-30 exit 39 (Cockrell Hill Rd), just s, then just e. **Facility:** 89 units. 4 stories, interior corridors. **Terms:** cancellation fee imposed. **Pool(s):** heated indoor. **Activities:** hot tub, exercise room. **Guest Services:** complimentary and valet laundry.

[icons]

### WHERE TO EAT

**BOLSA**     214/367-9367   1

◆◆ ◆◆ American. Casual Dining. $10-$27 **AAA Inspector Notes:** Housed in a restored service garage, this rustic eatery features an indoor/outdoor bar with a playful cocktail menu and an exposed kitchen. The ever-changing menu offers up locally grown and organic ingredients in items such as portobello flatbread, pickled beet salad, hanger steak and Berkshire pork loin. While the neighborhood is strictly blue collar the nearby Bishop Arts area boasts an eclectic mix of restaurants, boutiques and specialty stores. Avoid the waits, get there early. **Features:** full bar, patio dining, Sunday brunch. **Address:** 614 W Davis St 75208 **Location:** I-30 exit 43B (Sylvan Ave) westbound, 1.2 mi s to Davis St, then 0.5 mi e; exit 44A (Beckley Ave) eastbound, 0.7 mi s to Colorado Blvd, just w to N Bishop Ave, 0.8 mi s Davis St, then just w. L D

**GRANDY'S RESTAURANT**     972/296-1944

◆◆ American. Quick Serve. $4-$8 **AAA Inspector Notes:** Fried chicken and country-fried steak are menu standbys at the restaurant, a regional franchise. They also offer a family-style dining menu. The décor is a step up from that of most quick-serve eateries and more resembles that of a conventional restaurant. Some elements of increased service include additional rolls, iced tea refills and tray removal. **Address:** 3230 W Camp Wisdom Rd 75237 **Location:** US 67 exit W Camp Wisdom Rd, just w. B L D

**HATTIE'S**     214/942-7400   2

◆◆◆ ◆◆◆ American. Fine Dining. $7-$32 **AAA Inspector Notes:** Most people don't think of Oak Cliff for a night out, but Hattie's is perfectly situated in the Bishop Arts District, within walking distance of art galleries and boutique shopping. Guests enjoy updated Southern fare in a graceful white dining room touched with Southern accents. Menu items include Lowcountry shrimp on grilled grit cake, herb cheese-topped beef tenderloin, caramelized onion and cheese tart, fried green tomato sandwich and jalapeño-stuffed quail. **Features:** full bar, Sunday brunch. **Reservations:** suggested. **Address:** 418 N Bishop Ave 75208 **Location:** I-30 exit 43B (Sylvan Ave) westbound, 1.2 mi s to Davis St, 0.6 mi e to N Bishop Ave, then just s; exit 44A (Beckley Ave) eastbound, 0.7 mi s to Colorado Blvd, just w to N Bishop Ave, 0.8 mi s to Davis St, just w, then s. **Parking:** valet and street only. L D

**LA CALLE DOCE**     214/941-4304   5

◆◆ ◆◆ Mexican Seafood. Casual Dining. $7-$17 **AAA Inspector Notes:** For 30 years, the staff at this charming, rambling Craftsman with an enchanting courtyard and front-porch dining have been serving up delicious Mexican seafood dishes. You may want to start with sopa de pescado—cod stew with tomatoes, onions, potatoes and cilantro, Tampico Bay-style. Move on to a Spanish favorite like paella or try a Mexican dish like chile relleno de mariscos—poblano pepper stuffed with shrimp, scallops, octopus and fish. **Features:** full bar, patio dining, Sunday brunch. **Address:** 415 W 12th St 75208 **Location:** I-35 E exit 425A (Beckley Ave and Zang Blvd), 0.5 mi w. L D

**TILLMAN'S ROADHOUSE**     214/942-0988   3

◆◆ ◆◆ American. Casual Dining. $9-$35 **AAA Inspector Notes:** Although chuck wagon cuisine is what is served up in this kitschy eatery that has raw pine walls contrasting against sparkling chandeliers and velvet-backed banquettes, the menu items have common names and are done with a sophisticated spin. Options include venison Frito pie, chipotle-smoked barbecue ribs, orange-glazed crispy duck confit, hanger steak salad and tableside s'mores. Located in the trendy Bishop Arts neighborhood with art galleries, boutiques and a soda shop. **Features:** full bar, Sunday brunch. **Address:** 324 W 7th St 75208 **Location:** I-30 exit 43B (Sylvan Ave) westbound, 1.2 mi s to Davis St, 0.6 mi e to N Bishop Ave, just s, then just e; exit 44A (Beckley Ave) eastbound, 0.7 mi s to Colorado Blvd, just w to N Bishop Ave, 0.8 mi s to Davis St, just w, just s, then just e. **Parking:** street only. L D CALL

**VERACRUZ CAFE**     214/948-4746   4

◆◆ ◆◆ Mexican. Casual Dining. $9-$16 **AAA Inspector Notes:** The rich and colorful décor makes this restaurant the jewel in the heart of Oak Cliff. The menu serves up cuisine from the Mexican coastal state of Veracruz and takes pride in its made-from-scratch sauces and age-old recipes. The Mexican bouillabaisse is a customer favorite. The Bishop Arts area is thriving, so parking can be tricky on the weekends. **Features:** full bar, Sunday brunch. **Address:** 408 N Bishop Ave, Suite 107 75208 **Location:** I-30 exit 43B (Sylvan Ave) westbound, 1.2 mi s to Davis St, 0.6 mi e to N Bishop Ave, then just s; exit 44A (Beckley Ave) eastbound, 0.7 mi s to Colorado Blvd, just w to N Bishop Ave, 0.8 mi s to Davis St, just w, then s. **Parking:** street only. L D

# DAVY CROCKETT NATIONAL FOREST
(E-9)

Elevations in the forest range from 100 ft. at
Cochino Bayou to 460 ft. at Neches Bluff.
Refer to AAA maps for additional elevation
information.

Davy Crockett National Forest borders the
Neches River in East Texas. Since logging ended in
the 1920s, this pine and hardwood forest has made
a dramatic comeback. One of the best ways to see
the 161,500-acre area is via the 20-mile-long Four C
National Hiking Trail. The trail passes through a variety of terrains—sloughs, upland forests and pine
woods—as it follows an old tramway from Ratcliff
Lake Recreation Area to the Neches Overlook.

Near the forest is the Mission Tejas State Historic
Park *(see Recreation Areas Chart)*, which contains a
replica of the first Spanish mission in East Texas
and the Rice Stagecoach Inn.

For information contact the district ranger station
at 18551 SR 7E, Kennard, TX 75847, or write the
USDA Forest Supervisor, 2221 N. Raguet St.,
Lufkin, TX 75901-3801. Phone (936) 655-2299. *See
Recreation Areas Chart.*

# DAYTON pop. 7,242
• Part of Houston area — see map p. 301

### BEST WESTERN DAYTON INN & SUITES  (936)258-7600

Hotel
$79-$89

**AAA Benefit:** Members
save 10% or more with
Best Western!

**Address:** 1751 W Hwy 90 77535 **Location:** 0.4 mi w of SR 146. **Facility:** 56
units. 2 stories, interior/exterior corridors.
**Terms:** 4 day cancellation notice-fee imposed. **Pool(s):** outdoor. **Activities:** exercise room. **Guest Services:** coin
laundry. **Featured Amenity:** continental breakfast.

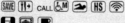

# DECATUR pop. 6,042

### BEST WESTERN DECATUR INN  (940)627-5982

Motel
$72-$86

**AAA Benefit:** Members
save 10% or more with
Best Western!

**Address:** 1801 S Hwy 287 76234 **Location:** 0.6 mi s of jct Business Rt US 380.
**Facility:** 45 units. 1 story, exterior corridors. **Pool(s):** outdoor. **Guest Services:**
coin laundry.

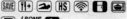

### ECONO LODGE DECATUR  (940)627-6919

Hotel $63-$93 **Address:** 1709 S US 287 76234 **Location:**
0.6 mi s of jct Business Rt US 380. **Facility:** 44 units. 2 stories (no
elevator), exterior corridors. **Pool(s):** outdoor. **Guest Services:** valet
and coin laundry.

### HAMPTON INN & SUITES DECATUR  (940)627-4900

Hotel
$79-$149

**AAA Benefit:**
Members save up to
10%!

**Address:** 110 S Hwy 81/287 76234 **Location:** Just s of jct US 380 and 287. **Facility:** 74 units. 4 stories, interior
corridors. **Terms:** 1-7 night minimum
stay, cancellation fee imposed. **Pool(s):**
heated indoor. **Activities:** hot tub, exercise room. **Guest Services:** valet and
coin laundry. **Featured Amenity: full
hot breakfast.**

### HOLIDAY INN EXPRESS HOTEL & SUITES
(940)627-0776

Hotel
$94-$144

**Address:** 1051 N Hwy 287 76234 **Location:** Just n of jct US 380 and 287.
**Facility:** 60 units. 3 stories, interior corridors. **Amenities:** safes. **Pool(s):** outdoor. **Activities:** hot tub, exercise room.
**Guest Services:** valet and coin laundry.
**Featured Amenity:** breakfast buffet.

## WHERE TO EAT

### YESTERDAY'S TEXAS  940/627-5866

 American. Casual Dining. $7-$14 **AAA Inspector Notes:**
This small diner located just off the main highway is decorated to resemble a typical 1950s eatery. It has a counter with bar stools along
one wall, just like the old diners. They even show TV footage of
"Howdy Doody" and "Bozo the Clown." The cuisine is typical of the
time—burgers, shakes, hot dogs, et cetera. One also can get
chicken-fried steak, chicken and some seafood. A nifty trip back in
time. **Address:** 100 S US 287 76234 **Location:** 0.3 mi s of jct US
287 and 380. L D

# DEER PARK pop. 32,010
• Restaurants p. 224
• Hotels & Restaurants map & index p. 324
• Part of Houston area — see map p. 301

### BEST WESTERN DEER PARK INN & SUITES
(281)476-1900  114

Hotel
$90-$150

**AAA Benefit:** Members
save 10% or more with
Best Western!

**Address:** 1401 Center St 77536 **Location:** SR 225 (La Porte Rd) exit Center
St, 0.9 mi s. Located in a busy commercial area. **Facility:** 54 units. 2 stories (no
elevator), exterior corridors. **Pool(s):** outdoor. **Activities:** hot tub, exercise room.
**Guest Services:** valet and coin laundry.
**Featured Amenity: full hot breakfast.**

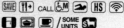

Explore on-the-go travel tools at
AAA.com/mobile or CAA.ca/mobile

(See map & index p. 324.)

### COMFORT SUITES DEER PARK/HOUSTON
(281)930-8888  **115**

WWW Hotel $93-$130 **Address:** 1501 Center St 77536 **Location:** SR 225 (La Porte Rd) exit Center St, 0.9 mi s. **Facility:** 56 units. 3 stories, interior corridors. **Amenities:** safes. **Pool(s):** outdoor. **Activities:** hot tub, exercise room. **Guest Services:** valet and coin laundry.

### HAMPTON INN
(281)930-9091  **116**

WWW Hotel $89-$159 **Address:** 1450 Center St 77536 **Location:** Jct SR 288 and Center St, 1 mi s. **Facility:** 63 units. 3 stories, interior corridors. **Terms:** 1-7 night minimum stay, cancellation fee imposed. **Pool(s):** outdoor. **Activities:** hot tub, exercise room. **Guest Services:** valet and coin laundry.

**AAA Benefit:** Members save up to 10%!

### LA QUINTA INN & SUITES DEER PARK
(281)476-5300  **113**

WWW Hotel $99-$150 **Address:** 1400 East Blvd 77536 **Location:** Jct SR 225 and East Blvd, 0.8 mi s. **Facility:** 74 units. 3 stories, interior corridors. **Pool(s):** heated indoor. **Activities:** hot tub, exercise room. **Guest Services:** coin laundry.

### SUPER 8
(281)930-4800  **112**

Hotel $70-$100

**Address:** 846 Center St 77536 **Location:** SR 225 exit Center St. **Facility:** 30 units. 2 stories (no elevator), exterior corridors. **Amenities:** safes. **Featured Amenity: continental breakfast.**

### WHERE TO EAT

### ANTONIO'S ITALIAN GRILL
281/479-0605  **45**

W Italian. Casual Dining. $7-$15 **AAA Inspector Notes:** A varied menu of soups, salads, sandwiches, pizza and full entrées ensures there is something for everyone at this very popular restaurant. **Features:** full bar. **Address:** 1105 Center St 77536 **Location:** Jct SR 225 and Center St, 1 mi s.

## DEL RIO (G-6) pop. 35,591, elev. 948'

San Felipe Springs, flowing at a rate of 90 million gallons daily, provides water for domestic use and for irrigation in the Del Rio area. The city is a major inland shipping point for wool and mohair and also is an international entry point. Directly across the Rio Grande is Ciudad Acuña, Mexico.

Amistad National Recreation Area, northwest of town, offers a variety of activities (see place listing p. 65 and Recreation Areas Chart).

**Del Rio Chamber of Commerce:** 1915 Veterans Blvd., Del Rio, TX 78840. **Phone:** (830) 775-3551.

**Self-guiding tours:** The chamber of commerce offers a brochure that outlines a walking tour past historic downtown structures.

**WHITEHEAD MEMORIAL MUSEUM** is at 1308 S. Main St. This 2.5-acre frontier village includes 14 buildings and 21 exhibit sites. Buildings include the 1871 Perry Mercantile, a chapel, a log cabin and a blacksmith shop. A barn houses early farming and transportation equipment. The Jersey Lily, a replica of Judge Roy Bean's saloon and court, contains his memorabilia. The graves of the judge and his son are on the grounds. **Hours:** Tues.-Sat. 9-4:30, Sun. 1-5. **Cost:** $5; $4 (ages 55+); $3 (ages 13-18); $2 (ages 6-12). **Phone:** (830) 774-7568.

### WINERIES
• **Val Verde Winery** is at 100 Qualia Dr. **Hours:** Mon.-Sat. 10-5. Closed major holidays. **Phone:** (830) 775-9714.

### BEST WESTERN INN OF DEL RIO
(830)775-7511

Motel $70-$80

**AAA Benefit:** Members save 10% or more with Best Western!

**Address:** 810 Veterans Blvd 78840 **Location:** Between E 6th and E 7th sts. **Facility:** 61 units. 2 stories (no elevator), exterior corridors. **Amenities:** safes. **Pool(s):** outdoor.

### HAMPTON INN & SUITES
830/775-9700

WWW Hotel. Rates not provided. **Address:** 2219 N Bedell Ave 78840 **Location:** Jct Veterans Blvd and Braddie Dr, just e. **Facility:** 65 units. 3 stories, interior corridors. **Pool(s):** outdoor. **Activities:** hot tub, exercise room. **Guest Services:** valet and coin laundry.

**AAA Benefit:** Members save up to 10%!

### LA QUINTA INN DEL RIO
(830)775-7591

WW Hotel $79-$114 **Address:** 2005 Veterans Blvd 78840 **Location:** 1.8 mi nw on US 90, 277 and 377. **Facility:** 101 units. 2 stories (no elevator), interior/exterior corridors. **Pool(s):** outdoor. **Guest Services:** valet and coin laundry.

### RAMADA
(830)775-1511

WWW Hotel $89-$169

**Address:** 2101 Veterans Blvd 78840 **Location:** 1.8 mi nw on US 90, 277 and 377. **Facility:** 183 units. 2 stories (no elevator), interior/exterior corridors. **Terms:** cancellation fee imposed. **Amenities:** Some: safes. **Pool(s):** outdoor, heated indoor. **Activities:** sauna, hot tub, exercise room. **Guest Services:** valet and coin laundry, area transportation. **Featured Amenity: full hot breakfast.**

Save on theme park tickets at
AAA.com/searchfordiscounts

## WHERE TO EAT

**RUDY'S COUNTRY STORE AND BAR-B-QUE**          830/774-0784

Barbecue. Quick Serve. $4-$8 **AAA Inspector Notes:** This small, informal barbecue chain has a twist: The tasty food is ordered by the pound. Guests can mix and match and order three-quarters of a pound of beef with a half-pound of turkey or pork, for example. Desserts and coleslaw are prepackaged, and precooked beans accompany the meat. A drive-through window is available at most locations. **Features:** beer & wine. **Address:** 330 Braddie Dr 78840 **Location:** Jct Veterans Blvd and Braddie Dr, just e.

B   L   D

**SIRLOIN STOCKADE**          830/774-0411

Steak. Quick Serve. $9-$11 **AAA Inspector Notes:** The steakhouse lines up buffet items, including pizza, tacos, soups, salads and desserts, providing both excellent variety and a good value. Rotating theme nights allow for the sampling of sushi, barbecue and seafood. The buffet may also serve to complement a quality steak. **Address:** 2015 Ave F (Veterans Blvd) 78840 **Location:** 1.8 mi nw on US 90, 277 and 377.   L   D

## DENISON  (C-9) pop. 22,682, elev. 742'

Before the Civil War, Denison was the home of buffalo hunters, traders and ranchers but not of lawmen. Following the war, former Confederate soldiers forced an end to the rowdiness that had earned the settlement a reputation as a tough town. The establishment of a railroad division point and permanent industry also helped tame the town.

The city is the birthplace of President Dwight D. Eisenhower and also serves as a base for recreational opportunities. Denison is within a five-minute drive of Eisenhower State Recreation Area *(see Recreation Areas Chart)* and Lake Texoma Recreation Area *(see attraction listing)*.

**Denison Area Chamber of Commerce:** 313 W. Woodard St., Denison, TX 75020. **Phone:** (903) 465-1551.

**Shopping areas:** Katy Depot, 101 E. Main St., houses shops and restaurants in a restored train station. There also are numerous galleries and antiques shops along Main Street.

**EISENHOWER BIRTHPLACE STATE HISTORIC SITE** is at 609 S. Lamar Ave. The two-story frame house in which Gen. Dwight D. Eisenhower was born has been restored to its 1890 appearance. Displays in the visitor center depict local history and Eisenhower's legacy. A 9-foot-tall bronze statue of the former president stands in the wooded 6-acre park, which includes gardens and picnic facilities. **Hours:** Tues.-Sat. 9-5, Sun. 1-5. Closed Jan. 1, July 4, Thanksgiving, Christmas Eve, Christmas and Dec. 31. **Cost:** $4; $3 (ages 6-18 and students with ID). **Phone:** (903) 465-8908.

**LAKE TEXOMA RECREATION AREA** lies along the Texas-Oklahoma border. The 89,000-acre Lake Texoma was created in 1944 with the construction of Denison Dam for flood control along the Red River. The 202,300-acre recreation area offers boating, camping, golf, hiking and swimming *(see Recreation Chart)*. For further information contact the Texoma Project Office, U.S. Army Corps of Engineers, 351 Corps Rd., Denison, TX 75020.

**Hours:** Daily 6 a.m.-dusk. **Cost:** Boat ramp $3. Beach $4 per private vehicle or $1 per person; free (ages 0-11). **Phone:** (903) 465-4990, (903) 465-1491 for lake level and temperature information, or (877) 444-6777 or campground reservations.

**BEST WESTERN PLUS TEXOMA HOTEL & SUITES**
(903)327-8883

Hotel
$81-$93

**AAA Benefit:** Members save 10% or more with Best Western!

**Address:** 810 N US Hwy 75 75020 **Location:** US 75 exit 69 (Morton Rd); on northbound frontage road. **Facility:** 77 units, some two bedrooms. 3 stories, interior corridors. **Pool(s):** heated indoor. **Activities:** hot tub, exercise room. **Guest Services:** coin laundry.

SAVE  CALL  M  BIZ  HS
/ SOME UNITS

**HAMPTON INN & SUITES-DENISON**          (903)464-9010

Hotel $79-$129 **Address:** 3415 Ansley Blvd 75020 **Location:** US 75 exit 69 (Morton Rd); on southbound frontage road. **Facility:** 79 units. 4 stories, interior corridors. **Terms:** 1-7 night minimum stay, cancellation fee imposed. **Pool(s):** outdoor. **Activities:** hot tub, exercise room. **Guest Services:** valet and coin laundry.  BIZ  HS

**AAA Benefit:** Members save up to 10%!

## DENTON  (G-2) pop. 113,383, elev. 662'
- Hotels p. 226 • Restaurants p. 227
- Part of Dallas area — see map p. 161

Named for John B. Denton, a lawyer and preacher, Denton was originally known as Mustang Branch and later renamed to Farmers Branch due its richness in farming and horse ranching. It has since developed with both industrial and commercial growth. The Bayless-Selby House Museum is a restored Eastlake Victorian house located near the county courthouse.

**Denton Chamber of Commerce:** 414 Parkway, Denton, TX 76201. **Phone:** (940) 382-9693.

**COURTHOUSE ON THE SQUARE MUSEUM** is at 110 W. Hickory St. Memorabilia pertinent to the history of early Denton and north Texas is displayed. Special collections include primitive to modern Native American pottery, weaponry and early American artifacts. **Time:** Allow 30 minutes minimum. **Hours:** Mon.-Fri. 10-4:30, Sat. 11-3. Closed major holidays. **Cost:** Donations. **Phone:** (940) 349-2850.

## BEST WESTERN PLUS DENTON INN & SUITES
(940)591-7726

Hotel
$92-$100

**AAA Benefit:** Members save 10% or more with Best Western!

**Address:** 2910 W University Dr 76201 **Location:** I-35E exit 469 (University Dr), just e. **Facility:** 65 units. 3 stories, interior corridors. **Terms:** 2 night minimum stay - seasonal and/or weekends. **Pool(s):** outdoor. **Activities:** hot tub, exercise room. **Guest Services:** coin laundry. **Featured Amenity: full hot breakfast.**

Free hot breakfast, Free WIFI, microfridge, coffee, pool w/spa, fitness center. Restaurant adjacent.

## BEST WESTERN PREMIER CROWN CHASE INN & SUITES
(940)387-1000

Motel
$99-$139

PREMIER

**AAA Benefit:** Members save 10% or more with Best Western!

**Address:** 2450 Brinker Rd 76208 **Location:** I-35E exit 462 (State School Rd), just n on frontage road, then just e. **Facility:** 74 units. 4 stories, interior corridors. **Terms:** 2 night minimum stay - seasonal. **Amenities:** safes. **Pool(s):** outdoor. **Activities:** hot tub, exercise room. **Guest Services:** valet and coin laundry. **Featured Amenity: full hot breakfast.**

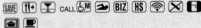

## COMFORT INN
(940)320-5150

Hotel
$75-$185

**Address:** 4050 Mesa Dr 76207 **Location:** I-35 exit 469 (University Dr), just w, then just n. **Facility:** 64 units. 4 stories, interior corridors. **Pool(s):** heated indoor. **Activities:** hot tub, exercise room. **Guest Services:** valet and coin laundry. **Featured Amenity: full hot breakfast.**

## COMFORT SUITES AT UNT
(940)898-8510

**Hotel** $80-$100 **Address:** 1100 N I-35 E 76205 **Location:** I-35 exit 465B southbound; exit 466A northbound; on northbound frontage road. **Facility:** 69 units. 3 stories, interior corridors. **Pool(s):** heated indoor. **Activities:** exercise room. **Guest Services:** valet and coin laundry.

## COURTYARD BY MARRIOTT DENTON
(940)382-4600

**Hotel** $94-$149 **Address:** 2800 Colorado Blvd 76210 **Location:** I-35E exit 463 (SR 288 Loop) southbound, just e, then 0.5 mi s; exit 462 (State School) northbound, 0.4 mi n on frontage road to Brinker Rd, just e, then just n. **Facility:** 92 units. 4 stories, interior corridors. **Pool(s):** heated indoor. **Activities:** hot tub, exercise room. **Guest Services:** valet and coin laundry, area transportation.

**AAA Benefit:** Members save 5% or more!

## DAYS INN DENTON
(940)383-1471

Hotel
$46-$70

**Address:** 4211 I-35 N 76207 **Location:** I-35 exit 469 (University Dr), just w, then just n. **Facility:** 110 units. 3 stories, interior corridors. **Pool(s):** outdoor. **Activities:** limited exercise equipment. **Guest Services:** coin laundry. **Featured Amenity: full hot breakfast.**

## FAIRFIELD INN & SUITES BY MARRIOTT-DENTON
(940)384-1700

**Hotel** $89-$112 **Address:** 2900 W University Dr 76201 **Location:** I-35 exit 469 (University Dr), just e. **Facility:** 75 units. 3 stories, interior corridors. **Pool(s):** heated indoor. **Activities:** hot tub, exercise room. **Guest Services:** complimentary and valet laundry.

**AAA Benefit:** Members save 5% or more!

## HAMPTON INN & SUITES-DENTON
(940)891-4900

**Hotel** $99-$114 **Address:** 1513 Centre Place Dr 76205 **Location:** I-35E exit 465A (Teasley Ln), just n on frontage road, then just e (turn right at Carino's). **Facility:** 85 units. 3 stories, interior corridors. **Terms:** 1-7 night minimum stay, cancellation fee imposed. **Pool(s):** outdoor. **Activities:** hot tub, exercise room. **Guest Services:** valet and coin laundry.

**AAA Benefit:** Members save up to 10%!

## THE HERITAGE INNS
940/565-6414

**Bed & Breakfast.** Rates not provided. **Address:** 815 N Locust St 76201 **Location:** Jct Ferguson St; 0.5 mi e of Court House Square. **Facility:** 5 units. 2 stories (no elevator), interior/exterior corridors.

## HOLIDAY INN HOTEL & SUITES
(940)383-4100

**Hotel** $79-$179 **Address:** 1434 Centre Place Dr 76205 **Location:** I-35E exit 465A (Teasley Ln); off northbound access road. **Facility:** 153 units, some efficiencies. 4 stories, interior corridors. **Pool(s):** heated indoor. **Activities:** hot tub, exercise room. **Guest Services:** valet and coin laundry, area transportation.

## HOMEWOOD SUITES BY HILTON-DENTON  (940)382-0420

▼▼▼ **Extended Stay Hotel** $139-$169 **Address:** 2907 Shoreline Dr 76210 **Location:** I-35E exit 462 (State School Rd), just w to Unicorn Lake, 0.4 mi n, then just w. **Facility:** 107 efficiencies, some two bedrooms. 4 stories, interior corridors. **Terms:** 1-7 night minimum stay, cancellation fee imposed. **Pool(s):** outdoor. **Activities:** exercise room. **Guest Services:** valet and coin laundry.

**AAA Benefit:** Members save up to 10%!

[icons] / SOME UNITS

## LA QUINTA INN & SUITES DENTON  (940)808-0444

▼▼▼ **Hotel** $89-$124 **Address:** 4465 N I-35 76207 **Location:** I-35 exit 469 (University Dr), just w, n on Mesa Dr, w on Barcelona St, then around to hotel; exit 471 southbound, on southbound frontage road. **Facility:** 88 units. 4 stories, interior corridors. **Pool(s):** heated indoor. **Activities:** hot tub, exercise room. **Guest Services:** valet and coin laundry.

[icons] / SOME UNITS

## SUPER 8-DENTON  (940)380-8888

▼▼ Hotel $63-$103

**Address:** 620 S I-35 E 76205 **Location:** I-35 exit 465A (Teasley Ln). **Facility:** 76 units. 3 stories, interior corridors. **Amenities:** safes. **Pool(s):** outdoor. **Featured Amenity:** continental breakfast.

[icons] / SOME UNITS

## WHERE TO EAT

## ANDAMAN THAI RESTAURANT  940/591-8790

▼▼ Thai. Casual Dining. $8-$15 **AAA Inspector Notes:** The small family-owned and -operated Thai restaurant specializes in traditional Thai cuisine, including several types of curries. The large menu also includes noodle, fish, duck and stir-fry dishes. Exposed ceilings, bright orange walls and concrete floors provide a modern theme. **Features:** beer & wine. **Address:** 221 E Hickory St 76201 **Location:** Just e of Court House Square; center. [L] [D]

## BETH MARIE'S OLD FASHIONED SODA FOUNTAIN
940/384-1818

▼ Specialty. Quick Serve. $3-$6 **AAA Inspector Notes:** Straight out of another era, this restaurant draws flocks of locals and tourists to the town square for filling lunches and scoops of tasty ice cream made on the premises. Lunch favorites include shaved turkey sandwiches and chicken salad. **Address:** 117 W Hickory St 76201 **Location:** Between Elm and Locust sts; on the square; downtown. **Parking:** street only. [L]

## EL MATADOR  940/387-1137

▼▼ Mexican. Casual Dining. $7-$11 **AAA Inspector Notes:** Owned and operated by a Denton native, the popular Mexican restaurant feeds guests delicious tacos, burritos and more in functional surroundings. **Features:** full bar. **Address:** 720 W University Dr 76201 **Location:** I-35 exit 469 (University Dr), 2.1 mi e, then just n; in Kroger Shopping Center. [L] [D] [◹]

## GERHARDS GERMAN RESTAURANT AND BAR  940/381-6723

▼▼ German. Casual Dining. $8-$17 **AAA Inspector Notes:** Located right in the historic town square, this beer garden infuses just the right amount of Bavaria to Texas. Enjoy schnitzel, brats, a Reuben sandwich and vegetarian casseroles at large communal tables while imbibing one of the several German beers on offer. If soccer is your thing, this restaurant is always hosting watching parties. Weekends frequently feature live music. **Features:** full bar, Sunday brunch, happy hour. **Address:** 222 W Hickory St 76201 **Location:** Center. **Parking:** street only. [L] [D]

## GIUSEPPE'S ITALIAN RESTAURANT  940/381-2712

▼▼ Italian. Casual Dining. $7-$16 **AAA Inspector Notes:** Near downtown and Texas Woman's University, the small, family-owned restaurant comprises a bottom-floor, turn-of-the-20th-century home and an upstairs B&B. On the menu are several pasta, veal and chicken dishes. The richly painted dining rooms are decorated with original art. **Features:** beer & wine, patio dining. **Address:** 821 N Locust St 76201 **Location:** Jct Ferguson and Locust sts, 0.5 mi e of Court House Square. [L] [D]

## GRANDY'S RESTAURANT

▼ American. Quick Serve. $4-$8 **AAA Inspector Notes:** Fried chicken and country-fried steak are menu standbys at the restaurant, a regional franchise. They also offer a family-style dining menu. The décor is a step up from that of most quick-serve eateries and more resembles that of a conventional restaurant. Some elements of increased service include additional rolls, iced tea refills and tray removal. [B] [L] [D]

*For additional information, visit AAA.com*

**LOCATIONS:**
**Address:** 808 W University Dr 76201 **Location:** Just w of jct University Dr and N Locust St. **Phone:** 940/387-7252
**Address:** 2217 S I-35 E 76201 **Location:** I-35E exit 463.
**Phone:** 940/565-8016

## HANNAH'S  940/566-1110

▼▼▼ Continental. Fine Dining. $10-$40 **AAA Inspector Notes:** Diners need not wait for a special occasion to visit this downtown eatery, where a fun and comfortable experience can be had either on the outside patio or in the dining room, which exudes rustic elegance. A long list of pleasing wine choices complements such mouthwatering delights as Thai curried mussels, rack of lamb and the signature steak, filet au poivre. The carrot cake warrants consideration as the menu boasts 2 pounds of carrots in every cake. Tapas are available at the bar. **Features:** full bar, patio dining, Sunday brunch, happy hour. **Reservations:** suggested, weekends. **Address:** 111 W Mulberry St 76201 **Location:** Just e of Cedar St; downtown. [L] [D]

## J&J'S PIZZA  940/382-7769

▼ Pizza. Quick Serve. $5-$14 **AAA Inspector Notes:** Students and locals alike love this pizzeria for its funky atmosphere—where else can a picture of the Virgin Mary and Richard Nixon be found in the same room?—and it's delicious pizza made on both New York and Chicago crusts. Live music is featured in their basement. **Features:** beer only. **Address:** 118 W Oak St 76201 **Location:** On town square; center. **Parking:** street only. [L] [D]

## THE LOOPHOLE COURTHOUSE PUB & GRILL  940/565-0770

▼▼ American. Casual Dining. $6-$16 **AAA Inspector Notes:** On the square across from the county courthouse, the neighborhood pub attracts the business crowd as well as local college students. Friendly servers treat everyone pleasantly. Choices range from burgers to tacos to fried mushrooms. The eatery converts to an adults-only bar at night, and as such will require ID. The nighttime smoke odor tends to persist into the day. **Features:** full bar, happy hour. **Address:** 119 W Hickory St 76201 **Location:** Between Elm and Locust sts; downtown. **Parking:** street only. [L] [D] [◹]

## SIAM OFF THE SQUARE  940/382-5118

▼▼ Thai. Casual Dining. $7-$14 **AAA Inspector Notes:** This small, cozy restaurant features a short menu of classic stir-fries and curries. Homemade coconut ice cream is worth the splurge. **Address:** 209 W Hickory St, Suite 104 76201 **Location:** Entrance on Cedar St; in historic downtown. [L] [D]

## DESOTO  pop. 49,047

- **Restaurants p. 228**
- **Hotels & Restaurants map & index p. 197**
- **Part of Dallas area — see map p. 161**

## AMERICAS BEST VALUE INN & SUITES  (972)224-8575  [21]

▼▼ Hotel $59-$79 **Address:** 1135 N I-35 E 75115 **Location:** I-35E exit 634 (Wintergreen Rd). **Facility:** 44 units. 2 stories (no elevator), exterior corridors. **Terms:** cancellation fee imposed. **Guest Services:** coin laundry. [icons]

(See map & index p. 197.)

HAMPTON INN & SUITES DALLAS/DESOTO
(972)228-0200 **19**

 Hotel $99-$149 **Address:** 1311 E Centre Park Blvd 75115 **Location: I**-35E exit 416 (Wintergreen Rd) southbound; exit 417 (Danieldale/Wheatland) northbound. **Facility:** 81 units. 4 stories, interior corridors. **Terms:** 1-7 night minimum stay, cancellation fee imposed. **Pool(s):** heated indoor. **Activities:** hot tub, exercise room. **Guest Services:** valet and coin laundry, area transportation.

**AAA Benefit:** Members save up to 10%!

CALL 🔲 ➰ BIZ HS 📶 🔲 🔲 🔲

HOLIDAY INN EXPRESS & SUITES
(972)224-3100 **20**

 Hotel $89-$119 **Address:** 1310 E Wintergreen Rd 75115 **Location:** I-35 exit 416 (Wintergreen Rd), just w. **Facility:** 88 units. 4 stories, interior corridors. **Terms:** cancellation fee imposed. **Amenities:** Some: safes. **Pool(s):** outdoor. **Activities:** hot tub, exercise room. **Guest Services:** valet and coin laundry, area transportation.

🍴➕ ➰ BIZ HS 📶 ✕ 🔲 🔲 🔲

TOWNEPLACE SUITES BY MARRIOTT DALLAS DESOTO
(972)780-9300 **18**

 Extended Stay Hotel $89-$104 **Address:** 2700 Travis St 75115 **Location:** US 67 exit Cockrell Hill; on northbound service road. **Facility:** 99 units, some two bedrooms, efficiencies and kitchens. 4 stories, interior corridors. **Pool(s):** heated indoor. **Activities:** exercise room. **Guest Services:** valet and coin laundry, area transportation.

**AAA Benefit:** Members save 5% or more!

🍴➕ CALL 🔲 ➰ HS 📶 ✕ 🔲 🔲 🔲
/ SOME UNITS 🐾

---

## WHERE TO EAT

EL CHICO
972/228-2133 **14**

Tex-Mex
Casual Dining
$7-$16

**AAA Inspector Notes:** Inside and out, the decor of the popular Mexican restaurant is inviting. The menu features traditional favorites such as enchiladas, tacos, burritos and fajitas. The broad menu also lists a few American classics. **Features:** full bar. **Address:** 1111 N I-35 E 75115 **Location:** I-35E exit 416 (Wintergreen Rd). L D

---

## D'HANIS pop. 847

J.M. KOCH'S HOTEL B&B
830/363-7500

🔲 Not evaluated. **Address:** Main St 78850 **Location:** Center of town. Facilities, services, and décor characterize a mid-scale property. A restored railroad hotel built in 1906, the property offers comfortable and relaxing accommodations of differing decor.

---

## DONNA pop. 15,798

SUPER 8
(956)461-2226

Motel
$52-$79

**Address:** 2005 E Expwy 83 78537 **Location:** US 83 exit CR 493. **Facility:** 40 units. 2 stories (no elevator), exterior corridors. **Amenities:** Some: safes. **Pool(s):** outdoor. **Guest Services:** coin laundry. **Featured Amenity:** continental breakfast.

SAVE 🍴➕ ➰ BIZ HS 📶 🔲
🔲 🔲 / SOME UNITS 🐾

---

VICTORIA PALMS INN & SUITES
(956)464-7801

 Hotel $55-$145 **Address:** 602 N Victoria Rd 78537 **Location:** US 83 exit Victoria Rd. Located in a quiet area. **Facility:** 120 units, some kitchens. 1 story, exterior corridors. **Terms:** check-in 4 pm. **Pool(s):** heated outdoor. **Activities:** hot tub, tennis, exercise room. **Guest Services:** coin laundry.

🔲 🍴 ➰ HS 📶 ✕ 🔲
/ SOME UNITS 🐾 🔲 🔲

---

## DRIFTWOOD pop. 144

SALT LICK BAR-B-Q
512/858-4959

🔲 Barbecue. Casual Dining. $7-$25 **AAA Inspector Notes:** Diners can take a short drive in the Hill Country to reach the restaurant, where they can get their hands on award-winning barbecue entrées of brisket, sausage, ribs and chicken made from recipes that date back to the Civil War. The Sunday menu also includes favorites such as prime rib and baby back ribs. It's BYOB and cash only. **Address:** 18300 FM 1826 78619 **Location:** 11 mi s on Loop 1 (Mo-Pac Expwy) merging with SR 45 W, 1.6 mi w to FM 1826, then 7.3 mi s. L D 🔲

---

## DRIPPING SPRINGS

SLEEP INN & SUITES
(512)858-2400

 Hotel $111-$350 **Address:** 2720 E US Hwy 290 78620 **Location:** On US 290, 2.5 mi e. **Facility:** 57 units. 3 stories, interior corridors. **Pool(s):** indoor. **Activities:** exercise room. **Guest Services:** valet and coin laundry.

CALL 🔲 ➰ HS 📶 ✕ 🔲 🔲 🔲 / SOME UNITS 🐾

---

## DUBLIN (D-7) pop. 3,654, elev. 1,463'

CENTRAL INN
(254)445-2138

Motel
$45-$55

**Address:** 723 N Patrick St 76446 **Location:** 1 mi n on US 67/377. **Facility:** 22 units. 1 story, exterior corridors. **Pool(s):** outdoor.

SAVE 🍴➕ ➰ 📶 🔲 🔲

---

## DUMAS (A-5) pop. 14,691, elev. 3,657'

**WINDOW ON THE PLAINS MUSEUM** is at 1820 S. Dumas Ave. Displays feature pioneer-era memorabilia donated by local families and include Native American artifacts, period clothing and antiques. A replica of a circa 1920s home as well as a blacksmith shop, general store and drug store are on-site. Farm equipment and a miniature-tractor display illustrate the importance of agriculture to the area. An art center with rotating exhibits is adjacent to the museum. **Time:** Allow 30 minutes minimum. **Hours:** Mon.-Sat. 10-5. Closed Jan. 1, Thanksgiving and Christmas. **Cost:** Donations. **Phone:** (806) 935-3113.

*Ratings Members Trust*

Learn more at **AAA.com/Diamonds**

## BEST WESTERN WINDSOR INN

(806)935-9644

Hotel
$62-$149

**AAA Benefit:** Members save 10% or more with Best Western!

**Address:** 1701 S Dumas Ave 79029 **Location:** US 287, 2 mi s of US 87 and SR 152. **Facility:** 57 units. 2 stories (no elevator), exterior corridors. **Pool(s):** heated indoor. **Activities:** sauna, hot tub, exercise room. **Guest Services:** coin laundry.

---

## COMFORT INN OF DUMAS

(806)935-6988

Hotel
$75-$125

**Address:** 1620 S Dumas Ave 79029 **Location:** US 287, 1 mi s of jct US 87 and SR 152. **Facility:** 51 units. 2 stories (no elevator), interior corridors. **Pool(s):** heated indoor. **Activities:** hot tub, exercise room. **Guest Services:** coin laundry. **Featured Amenity:** full hot breakfast.

---

## DAYS INN & SUITES

(806)935-2222

Hotel
$75-$108

**Address:** 1610 S Dumas Ave 79029 **Location:** Just s on US 287. **Facility:** 50 units. 2 stories, interior corridors. **Parking:** winter plug-ins. **Pool(s):** heated indoor. **Activities:** sauna, hot tub, exercise room. **Guest Services:** valet and coin laundry. **Featured Amenity:** continental breakfast.

---

## ECONO LODGE

(806)935-9098

Hotel
$65-$100

**Address:** 1719 S Dumas Ave 79029 **Location:** US 287, 2 mi s of US 87 and SR 152. **Facility:** 40 units. 2 stories (no elevator), exterior corridors. **Guest Services:** coin laundry.

---

## HAMPTON INN & SUITES

(806)935-6666

Hotel
$132-$170

**AAA Benefit:** Members save up to 10%!

**Address:** 2010 S Dumas Ave 79029 **Location:** US 287, 2.5 mi s of US 87 and SR 152. **Facility:** 78 units. 3 stories, interior corridors. **Terms:** 1-7 night minimum stay, cancellation fee imposed. **Pool(s):** heated indoor. **Activities:** sauna, hot tub, exercise room. **Guest Services:** valet and coin laundry. **Featured Amenity:** full hot breakfast.

---

## QUALITY INN

(806)935-4000

Hotel $69-$99 **Address:** 1525 S Dumas Ave 79029 **Location:** US 287, 1.1 mi s of US 87 and SR 152. **Facility:** 54 units. 2 stories (no elevator), interior corridors. **Pool(s):** outdoor. **Activities:** exercise room. **Guest Services:** coin laundry.

---

## SUPER 8

(806)935-6222

Motel
$79-$89

**Address:** 119 W 17th St 79029 **Location:** US 287, 2 mi s of US 87 and SR 152. **Facility:** 26 units. 2 stories (no elevator), exterior corridors. **Guest Services:** coin laundry. **Featured Amenity:** continental breakfast.

---

# DUNCANVILLE (I-3) pop. 38,524, elev. 725'

- Restaurants p. 230
- Hotels & Restaurants map & index p. 197
- Part of Dallas area — see map p. 161

**INTERNATIONAL MUSEUM OF CULTURES,** 411 US 67, represents the work of an organization that creates written language for peoples who have none. Lifestyles are reflected through pottery, interactive videos, habitat displays and depictions of the life of an indigenous people from birth to adulthood. Permanent exhibits highlight contemporary cultures of Amazonian Peru, Ecuador, Papua New Guinea, Ngbaka of the Congo, Southeast Asia, Mexico and others.

**Time:** Allow 1 hour minimum. **Hours:** Mon.-Fri. 10-4, Sat. noon-4. Closed major holidays. **Cost:** $5; $4 (ages 4-17, ages 50+ and students with ID). **Phone:** (972) 572-0462.

---

## BEST WESTERN PLUS DUNCANVILLE/DALLAS

(972)283-3000 **12**

Hotel
$90-$160

**AAA Benefit:** Members save 10% or more with Best Western!

**Address:** 922 E Hwy 67 75137 **Location:** US 67 exit Cockrell Hill Rd; on northbound frontage road. **Facility:** 70 units. 3 stories, interior corridors. **Terms:** 2-3 night minimum stay - seasonal. **Pool(s):** outdoor. **Activities:** hot tub, exercise room. **Guest Services:** valet and coin laundry.

---

## HILTON GARDEN INN DALLAS/DUNCANVILLE

(972)283-9777 **11**

Hotel $99-$169 **Address:** 800 N Main St 75116 **Location:** I-20 exit 462 (N Main St); southeast corner. **Facility:** 142 units. 5 stories, interior corridors. **Terms:** 1-7 night minimum stay, cancellation fee imposed. **Amenities:** video games. **Pool(s):** heated outdoor. **Activities:** hot tub, exercise room. **Guest Services:** valet and coin laundry.

**AAA Benefit:** Members save up to 10%!

(See map & index p. 197.)

## WHERE TO EAT

LOS LUPES                          972/780-2722  (11)

♦♦♦ Mexican. Casual Dining. $6-$16 **AAA Inspector Notes:**
Part of a small local chain, the restaurant serves up Mexican food for
both die-hard enchilada lovers and those that may be more adventurous. Beef tongue anyone? It tastes way better than you think, but
you'll never know if you don't try it. The homey dining room and staff
dressed in traditional garb illustrate why this place has been here for
more than 20 years. **Features:** full bar, patio dining. **Address:** 103 E
Camp Wisdom Rd 75116 **Location:** I-20 exit 462 (N Main St), just s,
then just e. [B] [L] [D]


PAPPADEAUX SEAFOOD KITCHEN          972/572-0580

♦♦ Regional Seafood. Casual Dining. $10-$36 **AAA Inspector Notes:** A seafood lover's delight, the restaurant taps into a
little bit of New Orleans with its Cajun dishes and elaborate menu selections. Patrons might start off with a creative choice of blackened
oyster and shrimp fondeaux with crayfish and let the feast begin.
While music plays in the background, patrons can dig into dirty rice
or spicy gumbo loaded with seafood. Well-seasoned shrimp and fish
are prepared in varied ways. **Features:** full bar, senior menu, happy
hour. **Address:** 800 E Hwy 67 75137 **Location:** US 67 at Cockrell
Hill Rd. [L] [D] CALL [&M] [✆]


## EAGLE PASS  (G-6) pop. 26,248, elev. 726'

The first known settlement at this river crossing
on the Mexican border was Camp Eagle Pass, a
temporary observation post during the Mexican War.
Fort Duncan was established by the First United
States Infantry in 1849. The village that grew up
around the fort earned the nickname "Camp California" when Forty-niners used it as a staging area
on their way through Mazatlán to the gold fields.
After the Civil War, an exiled Confederate force
crossed the Rio Grande into Mexico at Eagle Pass,
and the last flag to fly over Confederate troops was
buried in the river by General Joseph Orville Shelby.
The site came to be known as the "Grave of the
Confederacy."

A major port of entry into Mexico, Eagle Pass
serves as a tourism center and a retail/shipping hub
for the 40,000-acre irrigated winter-garden region.

**Eagle Pass Chamber of Commerce:** 400 Garrison
St., P.O. Box 1188, Eagle Pass, TX 78853. **Phone:**
(830) 773-3224 or (888) 355-3224.

## GAMBLING ESTABLISHMENTS

- **Kickapoo Lucky Eagle Casino** is off FM 1021 at
  794 Lucky Eagle Dr. **Hours:** Daily 24 hours.
  **Phone:** (888) 255-8259. *(See ad p. 498.)*


HAMPTON INN EAGLE PASS             (830)757-5565

♦♦♦♦ Hotel $89-$139 **Address:**
3301 E Main St 78852 **Location:** Just e      **AAA Benefit:**
of jct US 57 and Loop 431 (US 277). **Fa-**   Members save up to
**cility:** 65 units. 3 stories, interior corri-        10%!
dors. **Terms:** 1-7 night minimum stay,
cancellation fee imposed. **Amenities:** video games. **Pool(s):** outdoor. **Activities:** exercise room. **Guest Services:** valet and coin
laundry. [≥] [BIZ] [HS] [🛜] [🛁] [🖥] [🖵]


HOLIDAY INN EXPRESS HOTEL & SUITES

(830)757-3050

♦♦♦♦      **Address:** 2007 Veterans Blvd 78852
Hotel       **Location:** 1.5 mi n on Loop 431 (US
$99-$119   277). **Facility:** 100 units. 3 stories, inte-
           rior corridors. **Terms:** cancellation fee
           imposed. **Pool(s):** outdoor. **Activities:**
           hot tub, exercise room. **Guest Services:**
           valet and coin laundry. **Featured Ame-
           nity:** continental breakfast.

[SAVE] CALL [&M] [🖥] [BIZ] [🛜] [✕]
[🛁] [🖵] [🖵]


LA QUINTA INN EAGLE PASS           (830)773-7000

♦♦ Motel $99-$134 **Address:** 2525 E Main St **Loca-
tion:** Jct US 57 and Loop 431 (US 277). **Facility:** 130 units. 2 stories
(no elevator), exterior corridors. **Pool(s):** outdoor. **Guest Services:**
valet and coin laundry.

[🍴+] [≥] [HS] [🛜] [🖥] /[SOME UNITS] [🐾] [🛁] [🖵]


QUALITY INN & SUITES EAGLE PASS    830/758-1234

♦♦ Motel. Rates not provided. **Address:** 1923 N Veterans
Blvd 78852 **Location:** Jct US 57 and Loop 431 (US 277). **Facility:** 40
units. 2 stories (no elevator), exterior corridors. **Pool(s):** outdoor.
**Guest Services:** valet and coin laundry.

[🍴+] [≥] [BIZ] [HS] [🛜] [🛁] [🖵] [🖥]


TOWNEPLACE SUITES BY MARRIOTT EAGLE PASS

(830)757-0077

♦♦♦ Extended Stay Hotel
$89-$109 **Address:** 2033 N Veterans     **AAA Benefit:**
Blvd 78852 **Location:** 1.5 mi n on Loop   Members save 5%
431 (US 277). **Facility:** 80 units. 3 sto-      or more!
ries, interior corridors. **Pool(s):** heated
outdoor. **Activities:** exercise room. **Guest Services:** valet and coin
laundry.

[≥] [BIZ] [HS] [🛜] [✕] [🖥] [🖵] [🖵] /[SOME UNITS] [🅂]


KICKAPOO LUCKY EAGLE CASINO HOTEL   830/758-1936

[fyi] Not evaluated. **Address:** 794 Lucky Eagle Dr 78852 **Location:**
Off FM 1021. Facilities, services, and décor characterize a mid-scale
property. *(See ad p. 498.)*


MICROTEL INN & SUITES BY WYNDHAM EAGLE PASS

830/776-5661

[fyi] Not evaluated. **Address:** 2352 El Indio Hwy 78852. Facilities,
services, and décor characterize an economy property.


## WHERE TO EAT

SIRLOIN STOCKADE                   830/757-1400

♦♦ Steak. Quick Serve. $9-$11 **AAA Inspector Notes:** The
steakhouse lines up buffet items, including pizza, tacos, soups,
salads and desserts, providing both excellent variety and a good
value. Rotating theme nights allow for the sampling of sushi, barbecue and seafood. The buffet may also serve to complement a
quality steak. **Address:** 225 S Bibb Ave 78852 **Location:** US 57 and
Loop 431 (US 277), just s. [L] [D] [✆]

## EARLY pop. 2,762

### COMFORT INN                     (325)641-3400

Hotel
$95-$110

**Address:** 204 Early Blvd 76802 **Location:** Jct US 67/183/377, 2 blks w. **Facility:** 53 units. 3 stories, interior corridors. **Pool(s):** heated indoor. **Activities:** hot tub, exercise room. **Guest Services:** complimentary laundry. **Featured Amenity: continental breakfast.**

[SAVE] [📶] CALL [&M] [🏊] [BIZ] [HS]
[📶] [📱] [📷] [🖥]

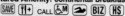
**WHERE TO EAT**

PRIMA PASTA                          325/641-8070

[📶] [📶] Italian. Casual Dining. $6-$20 **AAA Inspector Notes:** Italian favorites and pizza, as well as steaks and chicken entrées, make up the menu at this friendly restaurant. **Features:** full bar. **Address:** 210 Early Blvd 76802 **Location:** Jct US 67/183/377, 2 blks w. [L] [D] CALL [&M] [🖊]

## EASTLAND pop. 3,960

LA QUINTA INN & SUITES EASTLAND       (254)629-1414

[📶][📶][📶] **Hotel** $95-$134 **Address:** 10150 IH-20 76448 **Location:** I-20 exit 343; on north service road. **Facility:** 65 units. 3 stories, interior corridors. **Pool(s):** heated indoor. **Activities:** hot tub, exercise room. **Guest Services:** coin laundry.

[📶] CALL [&M] [🏊] [BIZ] [HS] [📶] [✖] [📱] [🖥] [🖥]
[/SOME UNITS] [🐕]

### SUPER 8 & RV PARK                 (254)629-3336

Motel
$50-$80

**Address:** 3900 I-20 E 76448 **Location:** I-20 exit 343; on north service road. **Facility:** 30 units. 1 story, exterior corridors. **Pool(s):** outdoor. **Featured Amenity: continental breakfast.**

[SAVE] [📶] [🏊] [HS] [📶] [📱] [📷]
[🖥] [/SOME UNITS] [🐕]

## EDINBURG (I-8) pop. 77,100, elev. 91'

Originally named Chapin for the townsite promoter, Edinburg was renamed in 1911. The city's soil is hospitable to vegetables and citrus. Among area industries are food processing, furniture and dairying.

**Edinburg Chamber of Commerce:** 602 W. University Dr., Edinburg, TX 78539. **Phone:** (956) 383-4974 or (800) 800-7214.

**EDINBURG SCENIC WETLANDS AND WORLD BIRDING CENTER,** 714 S. Raul Longoria Rd., offers various forms of wildlife viewing on its 40 acres. Winding trails and lagoon-side platforms enable visitors to view native birds, butterflies and other flora and fauna in their natural habitat. The Interpretive Center features telescopes, floor-to-ceiling windows and interactive exhibits about wildlife.

**Time:** Allow 1 hour minimum. **Hours:** Grounds open Mon.-Sat. 7-6. Interpretive Center open Mon.-Sat. 8-5. **Cost:** $3; $2 (ages 5-12, ages 55+ and students with ID). **Phone:** (956) 381-9922.

**MUSEUM OF SOUTH TEXAS HISTORY** is at 200 N. Closner Blvd. The museum has two facilities: a state-of-the-art museum and, across the courtyard, the 1910 Old County Jail Annex. The museum's premier permanent exhibition, Rio Grande Legacy—featuring unique artifacts, cutting-edge multimedia exhibits and bilingual text—takes visitors on a journey through the history of the region. The Old Jail features changing exhibits; a park adjoins the grounds.

**Time:** Allow 1 hour minimum. **Hours:** Tues.-Sat. 10-5, Sun. 1-5. Closed major holidays. **Cost:** $7; $5 (ages 62+ and students and active military with ID); $4 (ages 4-12). **Phone:** (956) 383-6911.

### BEST WESTERN PLUS EDINBURG INN & SUITES
(956)318-0442

[📶][📶][📶]
Hotel
$80-$180

**AAA Benefit:** Members save 10% or more with Best Western!

**Address:** 2708 S Bus Hwy 281 78539 **Location:** US 281 exit Canton Ave, 1 mi w to Business Rt US 281. **Facility:** 56 units. 2 stories, exterior corridors. **Pool(s):** outdoor. **Activities:** exercise room. **Guest Services:** valet and coin laundry.

[SAVE] [📶] CALL [&M] [🏊] [BIZ] [HS]
[📶] [📱] [📷] [🖥] [/SOME UNITS] [🐕]

## EDNA pop. 5,499

### BEST WESTERN LONE STAR INN          (361)781-0500

[📶][📶][📶]
Hotel
$145-$153

**AAA Benefit:** Members save 10% or more with Best Western!

**Address:** 310 E Houston Hwy 77957 **Location:** US 59 exit SR 111. **Facility:** 43 units. 2 stories, interior corridors. **Pool(s):** outdoor. **Activities:** hot tub. **Guest Services:** valet and coin laundry.

[SAVE] [🏊] [BIZ] [HS] [📶] [✖] [📱]
[📷] [🖥]

## EL CAMPO (G-9) pop. 11,602, elev. 110'
• Hotels p. 232

Painted on the sides of businesses, 24 giant murals detail the history of El Campo. Among scenes are a blacksmith, a pasture of longhorns, a rice and cotton harvest and a horse and buggy. A map is available from the chamber of commerce.

Be a better driver.

Keep your mind on the road.

**El Campo Chamber of Commerce:** 707 Fahrenthold St., El Campo, TX 77437. **Phone:** (979) 543-2713.

**EL CAMPO MUSEUM** is at 2350 N. Mechanic St. in the El Campo Civic Center. More than 300 big-game trophies from five continents are displayed. The Texas and Waterfowl exhibits feature animals indigenous to the area. A children's learning area contains hands-on exhibits and a holiday presentation incorporates the animals with Christmas displays. **Time:** Allow 30 minutes minimum. **Hours:** Tues.-Fri. 10-noon and 1-5, Sat. 10-3. Closed major holidays. **Cost:** Free. **Phone:** (979) 543-6885.

### BEST WESTERN EXECUTIVE INN EL CAMPO
(979)543-7033

Hotel
$90-$120

Best Western

**AAA Benefit:** Members save 10% or more with Best Western!

**Address:** 25880 US 59 77437 **Location:** US 59 exit SR 1163. **Facility:** 42 units. 2 stories (no elevator), exterior corridors. **Pool(s):** outdoor. **Activities:** exercise room. **Guest Services:** valet and coin laundry.

### ELGIN pop. 8,135

HOLIDAY INN EXPRESS          (512)285-3900
 **Hotel** $113-$133 **Address:** 258 Hwy 290 E 78621 **Location:** In town. **Facility:** 58 units. 3 stories, interior corridors. **Terms:** cancellation fee imposed, resort fee. **Pool(s):** outdoor. **Activities:** exercise room. **Guest Services:** valet and coin laundry.

MEYER'S ELGIN SMOKEHOUSE          512/281-3331
Barbecue. Quick Serve. $4-$12 **AAA Inspector Notes:** Meyer's Elgin Sausage is known throughout the Southwest for its retail smoked meats, and diners can enjoy all of them at the smokehouse at its headquarters. **Address:** 188 Hwy 290 78621 **Location:** In town. L D

SOUTHSIDE MARKET          512/285-3407
Barbecue. Casual Dining. $3-$14 **AAA Inspector Notes:** The family-friendly barbecue restaurant has been in operation since 1882. Sausage, beef and pork ribs, chicken and brisket dinners, as well as sandwiches, make up the menu. **Features:** beer only. **Address:** 1212 Hwy 290 W 78621 **Location:** Jct US 290 and SR 95, just e. B L D

## EL PASO (D-2) pop. 649,121, elev. 3,710'

- Hotels p. 239 • Restaurants p. 242
- Attractions map p. 234
- Hotels & Restaurants map & index p. 236

El Paso, on the Mexican border, is a popular winter tourist destination because of its international feel, warm dry climate and proximity to the Rio Grande. The name El Paso is a shortened version of El Paso del Rio del Norte (the pass through the river of the north), given to the river valley by conquistador Juan de Oñate. Through this juncture, Spanish explorers found their way into what is now America. "The Equestrian," a 36-foot-tall statue of Juan de Oñate, stands at the entrance to El Paso International Airport.

Agriculture adds to the city's financial well-being. The region is one of the few in the nation where long-staple Egyptian cotton is grown. Other contributors to the economy are manufacturers and the military.

Founded in 1682 with the establishment of the Mission Nuestra Señora del Carmen, the eastern suburb of Ysleta, is the oldest settlement in Texas.

(See map & index p. 236.)

Some of Ysleta's residents are among the last members of the Pueblo tribe in Texas. Ysleta Mission, built by Tigua Indians, Spanish refugees and Franciscan padres almost a century before the first California mission, adjoins the Tigua Indian Reservation.

Nearby is the *Camino Real,* the "Royal Highway." Once used by Spanish settlers and *conquistadores,* it is now a quiet farm road connecting Ysleta with two other Rio Grande Valley missions, La Purisima Socorro and San Elizario. These missions, which blend Spanish and Native American styles of architecture, still operate.

The Socorro Mission, 3 miles east of Ysleta, was built in 1681 by Piro Indians, members of the Pueblo Nation, who incorporated ancient Piro symbols in the construction. The mission was originally in Mexico, but the river shifted course, leaving the site on the Texas side. It contains a hand-carved statue of San Miguel and an ox-cart. It is said that when the ox-cart was used to bring the statue to the site, it mysteriously lodged itself into the mire in front of the church. All efforts to move the cart failed, convincing the parishioners that destiny dictated that the statue remain at Socorro.

San Elizario Presidio was established in 1789 to protect the river settlements of Ysleta and Socorro. The military garrison, which included barracks, corrals, storerooms and an adobe chapel, was abandoned during the Mexican War. The restored chapel stands on the site of the original that was washed away by the Rio Grande.

San Jacinto Plaza in downtown El Paso is bordered by Oregon, Main, Mesa and Mills streets. The plaza dates from the early 1800s, when El Paso's park and street commissioner built the tree-shaded square at his own expense and stocked it with alligators, which lived in the plaza until the 1960s.

North between US 80 and N. Piedras Street, a paved road leads to an overlook on the south side of the Franklin Mountains *(see Franklin Mountains State Park attraction listing).* The 15-minute scenic drive affords a spectacular view of El Paso and Ciudad Juárez, Mexico.

On New Year's Eve, college football fans gather at Sun Bowl Stadium for the annual ▽ Sun Bowl.

**El Paso Convention and Visitors Bureau:** 1 Civic Center Plaza, El Paso, TX 79901. **Phone:** (915) 534-0600, or (800) 351-6024 outside of Texas.

**Self-guiding tours:** A walking tour of downtown El Paso features 22 historic sites; a brochure is available from the convention and visitors bureau. The El Paso Public Library offers brochures and maps detailing walking tours of some of the buildings designed by Henry C. Trost, the prominent Southwestern architect who was greatly responsible for El Paso's present appearance.

**Shopping areas:** Cielo Vista Mall, I-10 and Hawkins Boulevard, offers Dillard's, JCPenney, Macy's and Sears. Sunland Park Mall, I-10 and Sunland Park Drive, includes Dillard's, Macy's and Sears. Bargain shoppers are drawn to The Outlet Shoppes at El Paso, at I-10 and Transmountain Road.

**CENTENNIAL MUSEUM AND CHIHUAHUAN DESERT GARDENS** is at University Ave. and Wiggins Rd. on the campus of the University of Texas at El Paso. This museum of natural and cultural history focuses on the Chihuahuan Desert region and features exhibits dealing with archeology, botany, ethnology, geology, mammalogy, ornithology and paleontology. The Chihuahuan Desert Gardens feature drought tolerant native plants of the Southwest. **Hours:** Museum Tues.-Sat. 10-4:30. Gardens daily dawn-dusk. Closed university holidays. **Cost:** Donations. **Phone:** (915) 747-5565.

**CHAMIZAL NATIONAL MEMORIAL** is at 800 S. San Marcial St. The 55-acre site commemorates the peaceful settlement in 1963 of a century-old dispute between Mexico and the United States over the international boundary. A museum and visitor center are on the grounds. **Time:** Allow 1 hour minimum. **Hours:** Memorial daily 5 a.m.-10 p.m. Visitor center Tues.-Sat. 10-5. Closed Jan. 1, Thanksgiving and Christmas. **Cost:** Free. **Phone:** (915) 532-7273.

**EL PASO HOLOCAUST MUSEUM,** 715 N. Oregon St., honors the memory of the more than 11 million people killed by the Nazis from 1933-45. Multimedia exhibits, survivor testimonies and artifacts tell the story of the Holocaust. **Tours:** Guided tours are available. **Time:** Allow 1 hour minimum. **Hours:** Tues.-Fri. 9-4, Sat.-Sun. 1-5. **Cost:** Free. **Phone:** (915) 351-0048.

**EL PASO MUSEUM OF ARCHAEOLOGY** is 8.5 mi. n. on US 54, then .5 mi. w. to 4301 Transmountain Rd. (Loop 375). The museum presents dioramas, exhibits and artifacts depicting Native Americans of the Southwest and northern Mexico. Permanent exhibits include basketry, ceramics, wood carvings, beaded leatherwork, textiles and stone tools. A 1-mile nature trail includes native plants and replicas of a Pueblo ruin, an Apache wikiup, tepee poles and a rock ring. The surrounding park offers more than 15 acres of nature trails amid scenic views of the Franklin Mountains.

**Time:** Allow 1 hour minimum. **Hours:** Tues.-Sat. 9-5, Sun. noon-5. Closed major holidays. **Cost:** Free. **Phone:** (915) 755-4332.

**EL PASO MUSEUM OF ART** is at One Arts Festival Plaza. The museum features 13th- to 18th-century European art, American art from the 18th- to 21st centuries and Mexican colonial pieces from both the Southwestern United States and Mexico. Films, lectures and workshops also are offered. **Time:** Allow 1 hour minimum. **Hours:** Tues.-Sat. 9-5 (also Thurs. 5-9), Sun. noon-5. Closed major holidays. **Cost:** Free. **Phone:** (915) 532-1707. ♿

(See map & index p. 236.)

**EL PASO MUSEUM OF HISTORY** is at 510 N. Santa Fe St. Five galleries provide visitors with a glimpse into the El Paso/Ciudad Juárez, Mexico, border region. Featured are historic documents, period clothing, photographs, machinery and weaponry. **Time:** Allow 1 hour minimum. **Hours:** Tues.-Sat. 9-5 (also Thurs. 5-9), Sun. noon-5. Closed major holidays. **Cost:** Free. **Phone:** (915) 351-3588.

**EL PASO ZOO** is at 4001 E. Paisano Dr. The 36-acre zoo features some 1,700 animals including birds, mammals, amphibians, reptiles and invertebrates in natural settings. Lions, giraffes and zebras are highlights of the African Savannah exhibit. The Asian Complex is home to elephants, tigers and orangutans. The Americas Aviary contains a walkway for visitors as well as a waterfall, flowers and plants. California sea lion shows and Asian elephant training demonstrations are presented daily.

**Time:** Allow 2 hours minimum. **Hours:** Daily 9:30-4 (also Sat.-Sun. 4-5, Memorial Day-Labor Day). Closed Jan. 1, Thanksgiving and Christmas. **Cost:** $10; $7.50 (ages 60+ and active military with ID); $6 (ages 3-12). **Phone:** (915) 521-1850. 🅰

**FORT BLISS MUSEUM AND STUDY CENTER—** see Fort Bliss p. 247.

**FRANKLIN MOUNTAINS STATE PARK** is off I-10 exit 6 (Canutillo), then 3.5 mi. e. on Transmountain Rd. (Loop 375). This park within El Paso city limits protects more than 26,000 acres of the Franklin Mountains range and is home to mule deer, cougars, golden eagles and Chihuahuan Desert plants. Multiuse trails are open to hikers and mountain bikers. *See Recreation Areas Chart.*

**Tours:** Guided tours are available. **Hours:** Mon.-Fri. 8-5, Sat.-Sun. 6:30 a.m.-8 p.m., Apr.-Sept.; daily 8-5, rest of year. Phone for guided tour schedule. **Cost:** $5; free (ages 0-12). **Phone:** (915) 566-6441 or (800) 792-1112. 🅰 🅰 🅰

**Wyler Aerial Tramway** is off I-10 exit US 54 (Patriot Frwy.), n. to Fred Wilson Blvd. exit, 1 mi. w. to Alabama St., then 1.5 mi. s. to 1700 McKinley Ave. Gondolas take passengers on a 4-minute narrated ride up the Franklin Mountains to the top of 5,632-foot Ranger Peak. The panoramic view from Wyler Observatory spans 7,000 square miles, encompassing three states and two countries. **Time:** Allow 30 minutes minimum. **Hours:** Fri.-Sat. noon-8, Sun. 10-6. Last tickets sold 1 hour before closing. Phone ahead to confirm schedule. **Cost:** $8; $4 (ages 0-12). Fares may vary; phone ahead. **Phone:** (915) 566-6622 or (915) 562-9899.

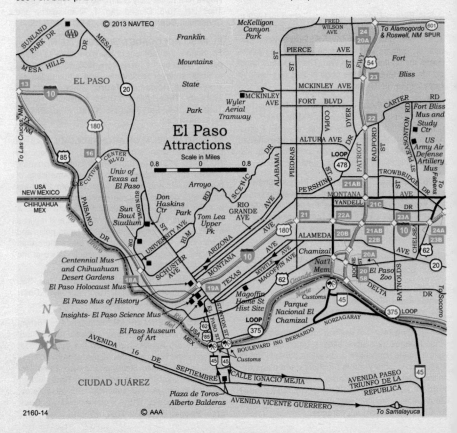

El Paso Attractions

Scale in Miles

(See map & index p. 236.)

**HUECO TANKS STATE PARK AND HISTORIC SITE** is 30 mi. e. on US 62/180, then 8 mi. n. on FM 2775 to 6900 Hueco Tanks Rd., #1. Used for almost 10,000 years, these rock basins, or *huecos,* collect rainwater. Some 2,000 pictographs and historic ruins serve as a legacy of the successive cultures that lived in the area. Bird-watching, hiking, rock climbing and camping opportunities are available *(see Recreation Areas Chart).*

Visitors are required to view an orientation video before entering. Picnicking is permitted; restrictions apply to use of fire. **Hours:** Mon.-Thurs. 8-6, Fri.-Sun. 7-7, May-Sept.; daily 8-6, rest of year. Only 70 people are permitted in self-guiding area at one time. Birding, bouldering, hiking and pictograph tours are available Wed.-Sun. by appointment. **Cost:** $7; free (ages 0-12). Reservations are recommended. **Phone:** (915) 857-1135, or (915) 849-6684 for tour reservations.

**INSIGHTS—EL PASO SCIENCE MUSEUM** is at 500 S. Hills St. Changing interactive exhibits about science and technology are offered. **Note:** At press time, the museum was closed during its move to a former school building at 500 S. Hills St.; reopening was scheduled for spring 2014. Phone for more information. **Phone:** (915) 534-0000.

**MAGOFFIN HOME STATE HISTORIC SITE** is at 1120 Magoffin Ave. Built around 1875, the adobe home is a prime example of Territorial-style architecture and its authentic art and furnishings reflect more than 100 years of continuous use by the Magoffins and their descendants. **Tours:** Guided tours are available. **Hours:** Tues.-Sun. 9-5. Guided tours are given on the hour 9-4. Closed Jan. 1, Thanksgiving, Christmas Eve, Christmas and Dec. 31.

**Cost:** $4; $3 (ages 6-18 and students with ID). **Phone:** (915) 533-5147.

**NATIONAL BORDER PATROL MUSEUM** is at 4315 Transmountain Rd. Covering more than 100 years of U.S. Border Patrol history throughout the United States, the museum exhibits books, uniforms, weapons, documents, photographs and other memorabilia. Displays describe mounted guards, canine units and traffic checkpoints. Visitors can sit inside the vehicles and aircraft on display. Guided tours are available by appointment. **Time:** Allow 30 minutes minimum. **Hours:** Tues.-Sun. Closed major holidays. **Cost:** Free. **Phone:** (915) 759-6060.

**TIGUA INDIAN RESERVATION AND PUEBLO** is 12 mi. w. via I-10 exit 32, then 3 mi. s.w. on Zaragosa Rd., then .7 mi. s.e. on Socorro Rd. to 305 Yaha Ln. The Tiguas (TEE-wahs) were relocated from New Mexico during the Pueblo Revolt of 1680. The tribe completed the Ysleta mission, one of the oldest in North America, under Spanish direction in 1682. The present structure incorporates the original foundations and some adobe walls. Adjacent is the Ysleta del Sur Pueblo Cultural Center, with a museum, bread ovens and a dance area. **Hours:** Wed.-Sun. 10-4. Closed major holidays. **Cost:** Free. **Phone:** (915) 859-7700.

**"VIVA EL PASO!"** is 2.5 mi. n. on Alabama St. in McKelligon Canyon Amphitheater in Franklin Mountains State Park *(see attraction listing).* The 2-hour musical gives the history of El Paso and its four cultures—Native American, Spanish, Mexican and American Pioneer. **Hours:** Shows are given Fri.-Sat. at 8:30, mid-June to mid-Aug. Two hours prior to the show, dinner is offered at an additional cost. **Cost:** Show tickets $18-$24; $16-$22 (senior citizens and military with ID); $14-$20 (ages 0-12 and students with ID). **Phone:** (915) 231-1165.

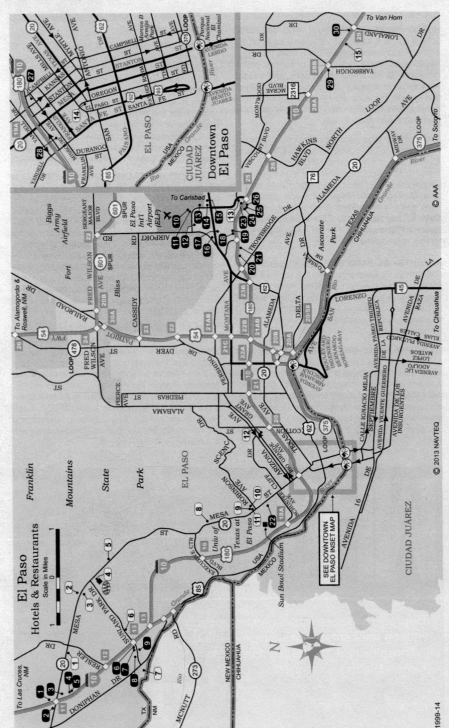

El Paso
Hotels & Restaurants
Scale in Miles

Downtown El Paso

SEE DOWNTOWN EL PASO INSET MAP

© AAA

© 2013 NAVTEQ

1999-14

## ✈ Airport Hotels

| Map Page | EL PASO INTERNATIONAL (Maximum driving distance from airport: 2.8 mi) | Diamond Rated | Rate Range | Page |
|---|---|---|---|---|
| 🄵 p. 236 | Chase Suites Hotel, 1.2 mi | ▽▽▽ | Rates not provided | 239 |
| 🄷 p. 236 | Coral Motel, 1.3 mi | ▽ | $49-$65 | 239 |
| 🄴 p. 236 | El Paso Marriott Hotel, 1.1 mi | ▽▽▽ | $90-$260 | 239 |
| ㉑ p. 236 | El Paso Suites Hotel, 2.8 mi | ▽▽▽ | $79-$99 | 239 |
| 🄫 p. 236 | GuestHouse International Suites, 0.9 mi | ▽▽▽ | $69-$135 | 239 |
| ㉓ p. 236 | **Hampton Inn & Suites, 2.0 mi** | ▽▽▽ | $89-$189 SAVE | 240 |
| ㉔ p. 236 | Hilton Garden Inn El Paso Airport, 2.0 mi | ▽▽▽ | $89-$289 | 240 |
| ㉖ p. 236 | Holiday Inn Express & Suites Airport Area, 2.0 mi | ▽▽▽ | $129-$149 | 240 |
| ⑳ p. 236 | **Hyatt Place El Paso Airport, 2.6 mi** | ▽▽▽ | $79-$209 SAVE | 240 |
| ⑪ p. 236 | **Microtel Inn & Suites by Wyndham El Paso Airport, 0.4 mi** | ▽▽ | $50-$89 SAVE | 241 |
| 🄶 p. 236 | Motel 6 El Paso-Airport-Fort Bliss - #4487, 1.7 mi | ▽▽ | Rates not provided | 241 |
| ⑬ p. 236 | **Radisson Hotel El Paso Airport, 1.0 mi** | ▽▽▽ | $99-$169 SAVE | 241 |
| ⑲ p. 236 | Residence Inn by Marriott El Paso, 2.6 mi | ▽▽▽ | $109-$189 | 241 |
| ㉕ p. 236 | Staybridge Suites Airport, 2.0 mi | ▽▽▽ | Rates not provided | 242 |
| ⑱ p. 236 | **Wingate by Wyndham, 2.7 mi** | ▽▽▽ | $88-$175 SAVE | 242 |
| ⑩ p. 236 | **Wyndham El Paso Airport, 0.3 mi** | ▽▽▽ | $89-$169 SAVE | 242 |

## El Paso

This index helps you "spot" where approved hotels and restaurants are located on the corresponding detailed maps. Hotel daily rate range is for comparison only. Restaurant price range is a combination of lunch and/or dinner. Turn to the listing page for more detailed rate and price information and consult display ads for special promotions.

### EL PASO

| Map Page | Hotels | Diamond Rated | Rate Range | Page |
|---|---|---|---|---|
| ① p. 236 | **Comfort Suites West** | ▽▽▽ | $101-$115 SAVE | 239 |
| ② p. 236 | Motel 6 El Paso West - #4583 | ▽▽ | Rates not provided | 241 |
| ③ p. 236 | La Quinta Inn El Paso West | ▽▽ | $72-$107 | 241 |
| ④ p. 236 | SpringHill Suites by Marriott El Paso West | ▽▽▽ | $103-$132 | 242 |
| ⑤ p. 236 | Fairfield Inn & Suites by Marriott El Paso | ▽▽▽ | $89-$138 | 239 |
| ⑥ p. 236 | Comfort Suites by Choice Hotels | ▽▽ | $74-$99 | 239 |
| ⑦ p. 236 | Sleep Inn by Choice Hotels | ▽▽ | $59-$99 | 242 |
| ⑧ p. 236 | **BEST WESTERN Sunland Park Inn** | ▽▽ | $79-$99 SAVE | 239 |
| ⑨ p. 236 | **Holiday Inn El Paso Sunland Park** | ▽▽▽ | $99-$149 SAVE | 240 |
| ⑩ p. 236 | Wyndham El Paso Airport | ▽▽▽ | $89-$169 SAVE | 242 |
| ⑪ p. 236 | **Microtel Inn & Suites by Wyndham El Paso Airport** | ▽▽ | $50-$89 SAVE | 241 |
| ⑫ p. 236 | GuestHouse International Suites | ▽▽▽ | $69-$135 | 239 |
| ⑬ p. 236 | **Radisson Hotel El Paso Airport** *(See ad p. 241.)* | ▽▽▽ | $99-$169 SAVE | 241 |
| ⑭ p. 236 | El Paso Marriott Hotel | ▽▽▽ | $90-$260 | 239 |
| ⑮ p. 236 | Chase Suites Hotel | ▽▽▽ | Rates not provided | 239 |

## EL PASO (cont'd)

| Map Page | Hotels (cont'd) | Diamond Rated | Rate Range | Page |
|---|---|---|---|---|
| **16** p. 236 | Motel 6 El Paso-Airport-Fort Bliss - #4487 | ◆◆ | Rates not provided | 241 |
| **17** p. 236 | Coral Motel | ◆ | $49-$65 | 239 |
| **18** p. 236 | **Wingate by Wyndham** | ◆◆◆ | $88-$175 [SAVE] | 242 |
| **19** p. 236 | Residence Inn by Marriott El Paso | ◆◆◆ | $109-$189 | 241 |
| **20** p. 236 | **Hyatt Place El Paso Airport** | ◆◆◆ | $79-$209 [SAVE] | 240 |
| **21** p. 236 | El Paso Suites Hotel | ◆◆◆ | $79-$99 | 239 |
| **22** p. 236 | Hilton Garden Inn El Paso-University of Texas | ◆◆◆ | $89-$229 | 240 |
| **23** p. 236 | **Hampton Inn & Suites** | ◆◆◆ | $89-$189 [SAVE] | 240 |
| **24** p. 236 | Hilton Garden Inn El Paso Airport | ◆◆◆ | $89-$289 | 240 |
| **25** p. 236 | Staybridge Suites Airport | ◆◆◆ | Rates not provided | 242 |
| **26** p. 236 | Holiday Inn Express & Suites Airport Area | ◆◆◆ | $129-$149 | 240 |
| **27** p. 236 | **Holiday Inn Express El Paso-Central** | ◆◆◆ | $79-$139 [SAVE] | 240 |
| **28** p. 236 | **DoubleTree by Hilton Hotel El Paso Downtown** | ◆◆◆ | $136-$159 [SAVE] | 239 |
| **29** p. 236 | La Quinta Inn & Suites El Paso East | ◆◆ | $72-$124 | 240 |
| **30** p. 236 | La Quinta Inn El Paso Lomaland | ◆◆ | $69-$100 | 241 |

| Map Page | Restaurants | Diamond Rated | Cuisine | Price Range | Page |
|---|---|---|---|---|---|
| **1** p. 236 | Paco Wong's Chinese Restaurant & Bar | ◆◆ | Chinese | $7-$21 | 243 |
| **2** p. 236 | Avila's Mexican Restaurant (West) | ◆◆ | Mexican | $7-$12 | 242 |
| **3** p. 236 | Koze Teppan Grill | ◆◆ | Sushi | $10-$34 | 243 |
| **4** p. 236 | Thyme Matters | ◆◆◆ | International | $9-$31 | 243 |
| **5** p. 236 | Villa Del Mar | ◆◆ | Seafood | $8-$32 | 243 |
| **6** p. 236 | The Greenery Restaurant & Market | ◆◆ | American | $8-$26 | 242 |
| **7** p. 236 | State Line Steaks & Barbecue | ◆◆ | Barbecue | $9-$29 | 243 |
| **8** p. 236 | Singapore Cafe | ◆◆ | Asian | $8-$15 | 243 |
| **9** p. 236 | GeoGeske | ◆◆ | American | $9-$32 | 242 |
| **10** p. 236 | Crave Kitchen & Bar | ◆◆ | New American | $10-$28 | 242 |
| **11** p. 236 | Ardovino's | ◆ | Pizza | $7-$18 | 242 |
| **12** p. 236 | La Tierra Cafe | ◆◆ | American | $9-$14 | 243 |
| **13** p. 236 | Dominguez Mexican Food | ◆ | Mexican | $6-$15 | 242 |
| **14** p. 236 | Cafe Central | ◆◆◆ | Continental | $11-$44 | 242 |
| **15** p. 236 | Julio's Cafe Corona Restaurant | ◆◆ | Mexican | $8-$25 | 243 |

(See map & index p. 236.)

CANDLEWOOD SUITES                  (915)755-9000

**Extended Stay Hotel** $99-$119 **Address:** 4631 Cohen Ave 79924 **Location:** US 54 exit 28 (Diana Dr) northbound, 1 mi n, then just e; exit southbound, 1 mi s, U-turn under freeway, 1 mi n, then just e. **Facility:** 95 efficiencies. 4 stories, interior corridors. **Activities:** exercise room. **Guest Services:** valet and coin laundry.

[icons] CALL [icons] BIZ HS [icons] / SOME UNITS

CHASE SUITES HOTEL                 915/772-8000   **15**

**Hotel.** Rates not provided. **Address:** 6791 Montana Ave 79925 **Location:** I-10 exit 25 (Airway Blvd), 1 mi n, then just e. **Facility:** 200 kitchen units, some two bedrooms. 2 stories (no elevator), exterior corridors. **Pool(s):** outdoor. **Activities:** hot tub. **Guest Services:** valet and coin laundry.

[icons] / SOME UNITS

COMFORT SUITES BY CHOICE HOTELS   (915)587-5300   **6**

**Hotel** $74-$99 **Address:** 949 Sunland Park Dr 79922 **Location:** I-10 exit 13 (Sunland Park Dr), just s. **Facility:** 61 units. 3 stories, interior corridors. **Amenities:** safes. **Pool(s):** heated indoor. **Activities:** hot tub, exercise room. **Guest Services:** valet and coin laundry.

[icons] BIZ HS [icons] / SOME UNITS

### COMFORT SUITES WEST            (915)585-2008   **1**

Hotel
$101-$115

**Address:** 5034 N Desert Blvd 79912 **Location:** I-10 exit 11 (Mesa St) northbound, just n; exit southbound, s to Mesa St, just e, then just n. **Facility:** 74 units. 4 stories, interior corridors. **Pool(s):** heated indoor. **Activities:** hot tub, exercise room. **Guest Services:** valet and coin laundry. **Featured Amenity:** full hot breakfast.

[SAVE] [icons] CALL [icons] BIZ HS [icons]

CORAL MOTEL                        915/772-3263   **17**

**Motel** $49-$65 **Address:** 6420 Montana Ave 79925 **Location:** I-10 exit 24 (Geronimo Dr) westbound; exit 24B eastbound, 0.5 mi n, then 0.5 mi e. **Facility:** 32 units. 1 story, exterior corridors.

[icons] HS [icons] / SOME UNITS

### DOUBLETREE BY HILTON HOTEL EL PASO DOWNTOWN
(915)532-8733   **28**

Hotel
$136-$159

DOUBLETREE

**AAA Benefit:**
Members save 5% or more!

**Address:** 600 N El Paso St 79901 **Location:** I-10 exit 19, just s. **Facility:** 200 units. 17 stories, interior corridors. **Terms:** 1-7 night minimum stay, cancellation fee imposed. **Dining:** 2 restaurants. **Pool(s):** heated outdoor. **Activities:** exercise room. **Guest Services:** valet laundry, area transportation.

[SAVE] [icons] CALL [icons]

[icons] BIZ HS [icons] / SOME UNITS

EL PASO MARRIOTT HOTEL            (915)779-3300   **14**

**Hotel** $90-$260 **Address:** 1600 Airway Blvd 79925 **Location:** I-10 exit 25 (Airway Blvd), 1 mi n. **Facility:** 293 units. 6 stories, interior corridors. **Terms:** check-in 4 pm. **Pool(s):** heated outdoor, heated indoor. **Activities:** sauna, hot tub, exercise room, spa. **Guest Services:** valet and coin laundry, area transportation.

**AAA Benefit:**
Members save 5% or more!

[icons] CALL [icons] BIZ SHS [icons] / SOME UNITS

EL PASO SUITES HOTEL              (915)779-6222   **21**

**Hotel** $79-$99 **Address:** 6100 Gateway Blvd E 79905 **Location:** I-10 exit 24B (Geronimo Dr) eastbound; exit 24 westbound, 0.6 mi to Trowbridge, U-turn under interstate, then 0.5 mi e. **Facility:** 184 units. 8 stories, interior corridors. **Terms:** 1-7 night minimum stay, cancellation fee imposed. **Amenities:** video games. **Pool(s):** heated indoor. **Activities:** hot tub, exercise room. **Guest Services:** valet and coin laundry.

[icons] BIZ [icons]

### FAIRFIELD INN & SUITES BY MARRIOTT EL PASO
(915)845-3100   **5**

**Hotel** $89-$138 **Address:** 7514 Remcon Cir 79912 **Location:** I-10 exit 11 (Mesa St). **Facility:** 95 units. 4 stories, interior corridors. **Pool(s):** indoor. **Activities:** hot tub, exercise room. **Guest Services:** valet and coin laundry.

**AAA Benefit:**
Members save 5% or more!

[icons] CALL [icons] BIZ HS [icons]

GUESTHOUSE INTERNATIONAL SUITES   (915)772-0395   **12**

**Hotel** $69-$135 **Address:** 1940 Airway Blvd 79925 **Location:** I-10 exit 25 (Airway Blvd), 1.2 mi n. **Facility:** 73 units. 4 stories, interior corridors. **Terms:** cancellation fee imposed. **Pool(s):** heated outdoor. **Activities:** exercise room. **Guest Services:** valet and coin laundry, area transportation.

[icons] CALL [icons] BIZ HS [icons] / SOME UNITS

(See map & index p. 236.)

## HAMPTON INN & SUITES
(915)771-6644

Hotel
$89-$189

**AAA Benefit:** Members save up to 10%!

**Address:** 6635 Gateway Blvd W 79925 **Location:** I-10 exit 25 (Airway Blvd); on westbound frontage road. **Facility:** 139 units, some efficiencies. 4 stories, interior corridors. **Terms:** 1-7 night minimum stay, cancellation fee imposed. **Pool(s):** heated outdoor. **Activities:** hot tub. **Guest Services:** valet and coin laundry, area transportation. **Featured Amenity: full hot breakfast.**

## HAMPTON INN & SUITES WEST
(915)833-7000

Hotel $109-$179 **Address:** 6411 S Desert Blvd 79932 **Location:** I-10 exit 8 (Artcraft Rd), just s. **Facility:** 93 units. 4 stories, interior corridors. **Terms:** 1-7 night minimum stay, cancellation fee imposed.

**AAA Benefit:** Members save up to 10%!

**Pool(s):** heated indoor. **Activities:** hot tub, exercise room. **Guest Services:** valet and coin laundry, area transportation.

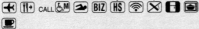

## HILTON GARDEN INN EL PASO AIRPORT
(915)772-4722

Hotel $89-$289 **Address:** 6650 Gateway Blvd E 79915 **Location:** I-10 exit 25 (Airway Blvd); just w to Robert E Lee Rd, s under freeway, then just e; exit 24 (Geronimo Dr) eastbound, just e. **Facility:** 145 units. 4 stories, interior corridors. **Terms:** 1-7 night minimum stay, cancellation fee imposed. **Pool(s):** heated outdoor. **Activities:** hot tub, exercise room. **Guest Services:** valet and coin laundry, area transportation.

**AAA Benefit:** Members save up to 10%!

## HILTON GARDEN INN EL PASO-UNIVERSITY OF TEXAS
(915)351-2121

Hotel $89-$229 **Address:** 111 W University Ave 79902 **Location:** I-10 exit 18A (Schuster Ave), jct Oregon St and University Ave; on UTEP Campus. **Facility:** 153 units. 5 stories, interior corridors. **Terms:** 1-7 night minimum stay, cancellation fee imposed. **Amenities:** video games. **Pool(s):** heated outdoor. **Activities:** hot tub, exercise room. **Guest Services:** valet and coin laundry, area transportation.

**AAA Benefit:** Members save up to 10%!

## HOLIDAY INN EL PASO SUNLAND PARK
(915)833-2900 **9**

Hotel
$99-$149

**Address:** 900 Sunland Park Dr 79922 **Location:** I-10 exit 13 (Sunland Park Dr), just s. **Facility:** 176 units. 2 stories, exterior corridors. **Terms:** cancellation fee imposed. **Pool(s):** heated outdoor. **Activities:** hot tub, exercise room. **Guest Services:** valet laundry, area transportation.

## HOLIDAY INN EXPRESS & SUITES AIRPORT AREA
(915)771-6200 **26**

Hotel $129-$149 **Address:** 6666 Gateway Blvd E 79915 **Location:** I-10 exit 25 (Airway Blvd) eastbound, just e; exit westbound, 0.5 mi w to Airway Blvd, then just sw. **Facility:** 102 units. 4 stories, interior corridors. **Terms:** cancellation fee imposed. **Pool(s):** heated outdoor. **Activities:** hot tub, exercise room. **Guest Services:** valet and coin laundry.

## HOLIDAY INN EXPRESS & SUITES WEST
915/587-5885

Hotel. Rates not provided. **Address:** 7935 Artcraft Rd 79932 **Location:** I-10 exit 8 (Artcraft Rd), just s; jct Berringer St. **Facility:** 96 units. 4 stories, interior corridors. **Pool(s):** indoor. **Activities:** hot tub, exercise room. **Guest Services:** valet and coin laundry, area transportation.

## HOLIDAY INN EXPRESS EL PASO-CENTRAL
(915)544-3333 **27**

Hotel $79-$139

**Address:** 409 E Missouri St 79901 **Location:** I-10 exit 19B westbound (downtown); exit 19 eastbound, just e. **Facility:** 112 units. 9 stories, interior corridors. **Pool(s):** heated outdoor. **Activities:** exercise room. **Guest Services:** valet and coin laundry, area transportation. **Featured Amenity: full hot breakfast.**

## HOLIDAY INN EXPRESS EL PASO EAST
915/590-3200

Hotel. Rates not provided. **Address:** 11825 Gateway Blvd W 79936 **Location:** I-10 exit 32; on westbound frontage road. **Facility:** 90 units. 4 stories, interior corridors. **Pool(s):** heated indoor. **Activities:** hot tub, exercise room. **Guest Services:** coin laundry.

## HYATT PLACE EL PASO AIRPORT
(915)771-0022 **20**

Hotel $79-$209

**AAA Benefit: Members save 10%!**

**Address:** 6030 Gateway Blvd E 79905 **Location:** I-10 exit 24B (Geronimo Dr) eastbound; exit 24 westbound, 0.6 mi to Trowbridge Dr, U-turn under interstate; on eastbound service road. **Facility:** 111 units. 6 stories, interior corridors. **Terms:** cancellation fee imposed. **Pool(s):** outdoor. **Activities:** exercise room. **Guest Services:** valet laundry, area transportation. **Featured Amenity: breakfast buffet.**

## LA QUINTA INN & SUITES EL PASO EAST
(915)591-3300 **29**

Hotel $72-$124 **Address:** 7944 Gateway Blvd E 79915 **Location:** I-10 exit 28B. **Facility:** 103 units. 4 stories, interior corridors. **Pool(s):** heated outdoor. **Activities:** exercise room. **Guest Services:** valet and coin laundry.

**(See map & index p. 236.)**

**LA QUINTA INN EL PASO LOMALAND**   (915)591-2244 **30**

▽▽ **Hotel** $69-$100 **Address:** 11033 Gateway Blvd W 79935 **Location:** I-10 exit 29 eastbound; exit 30 westbound, 1 mi w. **Facility:** 137 units. 2 stories (no elevator), exterior corridors. **Pool(s):** heated outdoor. **Guest Services:** valet laundry.

🍽️ CALL ⛰️M 🛄 🛜 💻 / SOME UNITS 🐕 [HS] 🚽 📷

**LA QUINTA INN EL PASO WEST**   (915)833-2522 **3**

▽▽ **Motel** $72-$107 **Address:** 7550 Remcon Cir 79912 **Location:** I-10 exit 11 (Mesa St). **Facility:** 130 units. 3 stories, exterior corridors. **Pool(s):** heated outdoor. **Guest Services:** valet and coin laundry. 🍽️ 🛄 🛜 🚽 💻 / SOME UNITS 🐕 📷

**MICROTEL INN & SUITES BY WYNDHAM EL PASO AIRPORT**   (915)772-3650 **11**

▽▽▽ Hotel $50-$89

**Address:** 2001 Airway Blvd 79925 **Location:** I-10 exit 25 (Airway Blvd), 1.3 mi n. **Facility:** 77 units. 3 stories, interior corridors. **Guest Services:** valet laundry, area transportation. **Featured Amenity: continental breakfast.**

[SAVE] ✈️ 🍽️ 🛄 CALL ⛰️M [BIZ] 🛜 🚽 💻 / SOME UNITS 🍴 📷

**MICROTEL INN & SUITES BY WYNDHAM EL PASO EAST**   (915)858-1600

▽▽ Hotel $55-$79

**Address:** 12211 Gateway Blvd W 79936 **Location:** I-10 exit 34 (Joe Battle Blvd); on westbound frontage road. **Facility:** 83 units. 3 stories, interior corridors. **Terms:** cancellation fee imposed. **Pool(s):** heated outdoor. **Activities:** limited exercise equipment. **Guest Services:** coin laundry, area transportation. **Featured Amenity: continental breakfast.**

[SAVE] ✈️ CALL ⛰️M 🛄 🛜 / SOME UNITS 🍴 🚽 📷 💻

**MOTEL 6 EL PASO-AIRPORT-FORT BLISS - #4487**
915/778-3311 **16**

▽▽ **Motel.** Rates not provided. **Address:** 6363 Montana Ave 79925 **Location:** I-10 exit 24 (Geronimo Dr) westbound; exit 24B eastbound, 0.5 mi n, then 0.5 mi e. **Facility:** 59 units. 2 stories (no elevator), exterior corridors. **Pool(s):** outdoor. **Guest Services:** coin laundry.

[ECO] ✈️ 🍽️ 🛄 [BIZ] 🛜 🚽 📷 / SOME UNITS 🐕

**MOTEL 6 EL PASO WEST - #4583**   915/584-4030 **2**

▽▽ **Hotel.** Rates not provided. **Address:** 7840 N Mesa St 79932 **Location:** I-10 exit 11 (N Mesa St), just s. **Facility:** 117 units. 2 stories (no elevator), exterior corridors. **Pool(s):** outdoor. **Guest Services:** coin laundry.

🍽️ 🛄 [BIZ] 🛜 🚽 📷 / SOME UNITS 🐕

**RADISSON HOTEL EL PASO AIRPORT**
(915)772-3333 **13**

▽▽▽ Hotel $99-$169

**Address:** 1770 Airway Blvd 79925 **Location:** I-10 exit 25 (Airway Blvd), 1.2 mi n. **Facility:** 239 units. 3-4 stories, interior/exterior corridors. **Terms:** 7 day cancellation notice-fee imposed. **Amenities:** *Some:* safes. **Pool(s):** heated outdoor, heated indoor. **Activities:** hot tub, exercise room. **Guest Services:** valet and coin laundry, area transportation. **Featured Amenity: full hot breakfast.** *(See ad this page.)*

[SAVE] ✈️ 🍽️ 🛜 ✖️ 🍷 🛄
[BIZ] [HS] 🛜 ✖️ 🚽 📷
💻

**RESIDENCE INN BY MARRIOTT EL PASO**
(915)771-0504 **19**

▽▽▽ **Extended Stay Hotel** $109-$189 **Address:** 6355 Gateway Blvd W 79925 **Location:** I-10 exit 24B (Geronimo Dr) eastbound, n to Edgemere, then just e; exit 25 (Airway Blvd) westbound; on westbound frontage road. **Facility:** 96 units, some two bedrooms, efficiencies and kitchens. 4 stories, interior corridors. **Pool(s):** heated indoor. **Activities:** hot tub, exercise room. **Guest Services:** valet and coin laundry.

**AAA Benefit:** Members save 5% or more!

🍽️ 🛄 [BIZ] 🛜 ✖️ 🚽 📷 💻 / SOME UNITS 🍴

▼ *See AAA listing this page* ▼

(See map & index p. 236.)

### SLEEP INN BY CHOICE HOTELS    (915)585-7577   **7**

◆◆ **Hotel** $59-$99 **Address:** 953 Sunland Park Dr 79922 **Location:** I-10 exit 13 (Sunland Park Dr), just w. **Facility:** 63 units. 3 stories, interior corridors. *Bath:* shower only. **Amenities:** safes. **Pool(s):** heated indoor. **Activities:** hot tub. **Guest Services:** valet laundry.

[icons]

### SPRINGHILL SUITES BY MARRIOTT EL PASO WEST
          (915)845-7400   **4**

◆◆◆ **Hotel** $103-$132 **Address:** 7518 Remcon Cir 79912 **Location:** I-10 exit 11 (Mesa St), just e, then just s. **Facility:** 103 units. 4 stories, interior corridors. **Pool(s):** heated outdoor. **Activities:** hot tub, exercise room. **Guest Services:** valet and coin laundry.

**AAA Benefit:**
Members save 5%
or more!

[icons]

### STAYBRIDGE SUITES AIRPORT    915/775-1212   **25**

◆◆◆ **Extended Stay Hotel.** Rates not provided. **Address:** 6680 Gateway Blvd E 79915 **Location:** I-10 exit 25 (Airway Blvd) eastbound, just e; exit westbound, 0.5 mi w to Airway Blvd, then just sw. **Facility:** 109 efficiencies, some two bedrooms. 4 stories, interior corridors. **Pool(s):** heated outdoor. **Activities:** hot tub, exercise room. **Guest Services:** valet and coin laundry, area transportation.

[icons]

### WINGATE BY WYNDHAM    (915)772-4088   **18**

◆◆◆
Hotel
$88-$175

**Address:** 6351 Gateway Blvd W 79925 **Location:** I-10 exit 24B (Geronimo Dr) westbound; exit 25 (Airway Blvd) eastbound, U-turn, 0.5 mi w. **Facility:** 102 units. 4 stories, interior corridors. **Terms:** cancellation fee imposed. **Amenities:** safes. **Pool(s):** heated outdoor. **Activities:** hot tub, exercise room. **Guest Services:** valet and coin laundry, area transportation. **Featured Amenity:** full hot breakfast.

[icons]

### WYNDHAM EL PASO AIRPORT    (915)778-4241   **10**

◆◆◆
Hotel
$89-$169

**Address:** 2027 Airway Blvd 79925 **Location:** I-10 exit 25 (Airway Blvd), 1.3 mi n. **Facility:** 272 units. 2-4 stories, interior corridors. **Terms:** 3 day cancellation notice-fee imposed. **Amenities:** video games, safes. **Pool(s):** heated outdoor. **Activities:** hot tub, exercise room, massage. **Guest Services:** valet and coin laundry, area transportation.

[icons]

## WHERE TO EAT

### ARDOVINO'S    915/532-9483   **11**

◆ Pizza. Casual Dining. $7-$18 **AAA Inspector Notes:** Opened in 1961 as a market specializing in Italian foods, the restaurant has evolved into a pizzeria and delicatessen. Diners can nibble on deliciously thin and crispy pizzas (arguably the best in El Paso), and buy wine, Italian specialties and gourmet chocolates. Across from the UTEP campus, the eatery attracts many students. **Features:** beer & wine. **Address:** 206 Cincinnati Ave 79902 **Location:** I-10 exit 18A (Schuster Ave), 0.7 mi ne to Mesa St, 0.6 mi n, then just e. **Parking:** street only. [L] [D]

### AVILA'S MEXICAN RESTAURANT (WEST)    915/584-3621   **2**

◆◆ Mexican. Casual Dining. $7-$12 **AAA Inspector Notes:** Hearty, modestly presented dishes draw patrons to the second Avila's location. Menu choices range from tacos and burritos to enchiladas and fajitas. **Features:** beer & wine. **Address:** 6232 N Mesa St 79912 **Location:** I-10 exit 13, 2 mi e to Mesa St, then just n. [L] [D]

### CAFE CENTRAL    915/545-2233   **14**

◆◆◆ Continental. Fine Dining. $11-$44 **AAA Inspector Notes:** This romantic restaurant features a changing seasonal menu and elegant surroundings. Creamy green chile soup is the house specialty. You can enjoy an entrée from the excellent variety of fish and shellfish selections and savor one of the spectacular house-made desserts. An award winning wine list is offered. **Features:** full bar, patio dining. **Reservations:** required. **Address:** 109 N Oregon St 79901 **Location:** I-10 exit 19B southbound; exit 19 northbound; jct Oregon and San Antonio sts. **Parking:** on-site and valet.
[L] [D]

### CRAVE KITCHEN & BAR    915/351-3677   **10**

◆◆ New American. Casual Dining. $10-$28 **AAA Inspector Notes:** This trendy neighborhood cafe puts a creative spin on modern American favorites. The fresh-squeezed ginger lemonade is thirst-quenching. The tomato basil soup is rich and creamy, and the vegetarian grilled portobello burger with paprika aioli can satisfy even die-hard meat eaters. An excellent selection of craft beers and wines is available. **Features:** beer & wine. **Address:** 300 Cincinnati Ave 79902 **Location:** Jct Stanton St; center; in Kern Place. **Parking:** on-site and street. [B] [L] [D] CALL [icon]

### DOMINGUEZ MEXICAN FOOD    915/772-2160   **13**

◆ Mexican. Casual Dining. $6-$15 **AAA Inspector Notes:** Home-style cooking is key at the laid-back establishment. Diners nosh on hearty portions of burritos, enchiladas, fajitas and more. **Features:** beer & wine. **Address:** 1201 Airway Blvd, Suite C-5 79925 **Location:** I-10 exit 25 (Airway Blvd), 0.3 mi n; in Junction Center. [L] [D]

### GEOGESKE    915/544-4242   **9**

◆◆ American. Casual Dining. $9-$32 **AAA Inspector Notes:** In eclectic Kern Place, the small eatery is known for its mod décor and well-heeled clientele. The open grill and bar provides a casual setting and relaxed service. The trendy and unusual menu changes often to offer diverse selections of seemingly contrasting foods that surprise and intrigue. **Features:** full bar. **Address:** 2701 N Stanton St 79902 **Location:** I-10 exit 19 eastbound; exit 19A (Mesa St) westbound, 1.2 mi n to Baltimore Dr, just e to Stanton St, then just s. [L] [D]

### GESKE'S FIRE GRILL    915/593-3473

◆◆ American. Casual Dining. $9-$29 **AAA Inspector Notes:** A great selection of burgers, steaks and seafood is fired-up in a relaxed contemporary setting. **Features:** full bar. **Address:** 1506 Lee Trevino Dr, Suite C 79936 **Location:** I-10 exit 30 (Lee Trevino Dr), 1 mi n; in Town Center. [L] [D]

### GRANDY'S RESTAURANT    915/598-8382

◆ American. Quick Serve. $4-$8 **AAA Inspector Notes:** Fried chicken and country-fried steak are menu standbys at the restaurant, a regional franchise. They also offer a family-style dining menu. The décor is a step up from that of most quick-serve eateries and more resembles that of a conventional restaurant. Some elements of increased service include additional rolls, iced tea refills and tray removal. **Address:** 10599 Vista Del Sol Dr 79924 **Location:** I-10 exit 28B, just ne on N Yarbrough Dr to Vista Del Sol Dr. [B] [L] [D]

### THE GREENERY RESTAURANT & MARKET
          915/584-6706   **6**

◆◆ American. Casual Dining. $8-$26 **AAA Inspector Notes:** This lively and locally popular restaurant features a creative menu that makes use of seasonal gourmet ingredients. An extensive wine list, whose selections also are available in the market, is offered. The on-site bakery has imported meats, cheeses and artisan breads. **Features:** beer & wine, Sunday brunch. **Address:** 750 Sunland Park Dr, Suite F5 79912 **Location:** I-10 exit 13 (Sunland Park Dr), just e; in Sunland Park Mall. [L] [D]

(See map & index p. 236.)

### JULIO'S CAFE CORONA RESTAURANT   915/591-7676  (15)
◆◆ Mexican. Casual Dining. $8-$25 **AAA Inspector Notes:** Popular with local residents, the eatery provides a casual, family-oriented atmosphere in which to taste a good variety of well-prepared dishes, including tacos, enchiladas, fajitas and fillet Tampiqueña. Some steak and seafood options add an even wider appeal. **Features:** full bar, Sunday brunch. **Reservations:** suggested. **Address:** 8050 Gateway Blvd E 79907 **Location:** I-10 exit 28B; on eastbound frontage road.  L  D

### KOZE TEPPAN GRILL   915/584-1128  (3)
◆◆ Sushi. Casual Dining. $10-$34 **AAA Inspector Notes:** This restaurant, located in a strip center with very modern décor, is popular with the locals for its creative sushi but even more so for its hibachi grills. Guests can gather around for a chef-directed culinary show. A line to see it is common, and people arrive as soon as the doors open. The bar scene also is thriving. Non-sushi options include entrées such as filet mignon with crabmeat and sea scallops with spicy sweet sauce. **Features:** full bar. **Address:** 6127 N Mesa St, Suite B 79912 **Location:** I-10 exit 13 (Sunland Park Dr), 1.3 mi ne to Mesa St, then just w.  L  D

### LA TIERRA CAFE   915/533-8890  (12)
◆◆ American. Casual Dining. $9-$14 **AAA Inspector Notes:** This lively and colorful little café serves a wide variety of creative items ranging from soups and salads to sandwiches and regional entrées. All are flavorful and made fresh. The green tuna tacos with pan-seared tuna and jalapeño cilantro sauce is a definite palate pleaser. The house-made desserts are luscious with several signature items plus a cake of the day. Black Russian Cake was my favorite, a multi layered Kahlua chocolate cake topped with a layer of creamy flan and whipped cream. **Address:** 1731 Montana Ave 79902 **Location:** I-10 exit Cotton St, just w; jct Williams St.  L  CALL M

### PACO WONG'S CHINESE RESTAURANT & BAR
915/581-7111  (1)
◆◆ Chinese. Casual Dining. $7-$21 **AAA Inspector Notes:** The restaurant provides flavorful Chinese favorites in an elegant setting with professional service. Live entertainment is presented nightly. **Features:** full bar. **Address:** 7111 N Mesa St 79912 **Location:** I-10 exit 11 (Mesa St), 1 mi e; jct Ressler Dr.  L  D

### RIPE EATERY   915/584-7473
◆◆ American. Casual Dining. $12-$26 **AAA Inspector Notes:** This casual neighborhood café serves up well-presented sandwiches, salads and entrées made with fresh, local and seasonal products. Vegetarians are easily accommodated. **Features:** beer & wine, patio dining, Sunday brunch, happy hour. **Address:** 910 E Redd Rd, Suite A 79912 **Location:** I-10 exit (Redd Rd), 2 mi e, jct Westwind.  L  D

### SINGAPORE CAFE   915/533-2889  (8)
◆◆ Asian. Casual Dining. $8-$15 **AAA Inspector Notes:** A favorite of locals, the eatery serves a variety of flavorful Asian dishes, including plenty of vegetarian selections. **Address:** 4120 N Mesa St 79902 **Location:** Between Eubank Ct and Greenwich Dr.  L  D

### STATE LINE STEAKS & BARBECUE   915/581-3371  (7)
◆◆ Barbecue. Casual Dining. $9-$29 **AAA Inspector Notes:** On the far west side of town near a casino, the popular, lodge-like restaurant is well worth the trip. Rolls of paper towels on the tables attest to the very informal yet friendly service you can expect. No-nonsense barbecue and steaks are served with traditional sides of beans, baked potatoes and sausage. Many diners eagerly await the homemade bread. Weekend waits are common, but on a nice summer night, sitting on the enormous outdoor patio lit up like a Christmas tree is a treat. **Features:** full bar. **Address:** 1222 Sunland Park Dr 79922 **Location:** I-10 exit 13 (Sunland Park Dr), 0.6 mi s.  L  D

### THYME MATTERS   915/585-0309  (4)
◆◆◆ International. Casual Dining. $9-$31 **AAA Inspector Notes:** This popular upscale cafe is a favorite of the local business community. The creative international menu features a variety of beef, chicken and fish entrées, plus soups, salads, sandwiches and pasta dishes. The delectable dessert offerings are made in house and include a luscious raspberry crème brûlée, which is a surprise with its sauce baked underneath. **Features:** full bar. **Reservations:** required. **Address:** 5857 N Mesa St, Suite 24 79912 **Location:** I-10 exit 13 (Sunland Park Dr), 1.5 mi e, then just s; jct Crestmont Dr.  L  D  CALL M

### VILLA DEL MAR   915/584-1888  (5)
◆◆ Seafood. Casual Dining. $8-$32 **AAA Inspector Notes:** This El Paso sister of the Juarez institution serves well-prepared Mexican-style seafood in generous portions. The shrimp al ajillo is flavorful with plenty of garlic and red chiles. **Features:** full bar, patio dining. **Address:** 5668 N Mesa St 79912 **Location:** Just s of Mesa Hills Dr.  L  D

## Visiting Mexico
### Personal Safety

Thousands of Americans routinely cross the border into Mexico on a daily basis for business and personal reasons without incident, and crimes directed at tourists are unlikely. The possibility does exist, however, particularly in cities that are centers of activity for Mexican drug cartels. This violence grabs news headlines and adversely affects the daily lives of many Mexicans.

But for the casual visitor, safety almost always boils down to good old common sense. Stash traveler's checks and cash in different places; for example, in money belts and extra pockets sewn inside clothing. Keep photocopies of passports, credit cards and other documents in a separate place from the originals. Use parking lots or garages whenever possible. Legal parking is designated by a sign showing a red circle with a capital "E" inside; no-parking zones have signs with a diagonal red line through the "E."

## Nearby Mexico
### CIUDAD JUÁREZ, CHIHUAHUA
pop. 1,332,131, elev. 5,000'
• Hotels p. 244 • Restaurants p. 244

**Note:** For current information about safety/security issues in Ciudad Juárez, go to the U.S. State Department website (travel.state.gov). For general safety-related information *see Personal Safety*, p. 243.

In 1581 Juan de Oñate crossed the Rio Grande in the vicinity of present-day Juárez (HWAH-res), the first Spanish explorer to do so. It wasn't until 1668, however, that Franciscan friar Father Garcia de San Francisco founded the Mission of Our Lady of Guadalupe (Misión de Nuestra Señora de Guadalupe), which still stands on the west side of Plaza de Armas in downtown Juárez. This sprawling border city is on the Rio Grande opposite El Paso, Tex.

### Border Tips

There are several border crossings between El Paso and downtown Juárez, including the Ysleta-Zaragoza Bridge, the Bridge of the Americas, the Stanton Street Bridge and the Santa Fe Street Bridge (also called the Paseo del Norte Bridge). The port of entry at Santa Teresa in nearby New Mexico is on the western edge of the El Paso/Juárez metropolitan area; take exit 8 (Artcraft Road) off I-10 and proceed west about 13 miles. Since it bypasses the city, this is the recommended crossing point for tourists and other travelers who are driving to Chihuahua and beyond or otherwise headed for interior Mexico. Banjercito offices at this border crossing and at the 30-kilometer (19-mile) mark on Mex. 45 (the Juárez-Chihuahua Highway) can process the paperwork necessary for vehicle travel into the interior.

Dollars or pesos are accepted when entering or departing Mexico or the United States. Baggage may be inspected at the customs offices. Both Mexican and U.S. Customs and Border Protection offices are open daily 24 hours at Ciudad Juárez. U.S. Customs and Border Protection offices at Santa Teresa are open daily 6 a.m.-midnight. AAA/CAA members can obtain Mexican automobile insurance at AAA Texas offices.

**El Paso Convention and Visitors Bureau:** 1 Civic Center Plaza, El Paso, TX 79901. **Phone:** (915) 534-0600, or (800) 351-6024 outside of Texas.

---

**BEST WESTERN PLUS PLAZA JUAREZ**    656/613-1310

Hotel
Rates not provided

**AAA Benefit:** Members save 10% or more with Best Western!

**Address:** Avenida Lincoln No. 722, Zona Pronaf 32315 **Location:** 2.1 mi (3.5 km) s of Bridge of the Americas. **Facility:** 162 units, some efficiencies. 2 stories (no elevator), exterior corridors. **Pool(s):** outdoor. **Activities:** exercise room. **Guest Services:** valet and coin laundry.

---

**HAMPTON INN-CIUDAD JUAREZ**    (656)227-1717

Hotel $72-$77 **Address:** Blvd Tomas Fernandez No. 7770 **Location:** Jct Tomas Fernandez and Vicente Guerrero, just e. **Facility:** 137 units. 5 stories, interior corridors. **Terms:** 1-7 night minimum stay, cancellation fee imposed. **Pool(s):** heated outdoor. **Activities:** exercise room. **Guest Services:** valet and coin laundry, area transportation.

**AAA Benefit:** Members save up to 10%!

---

**HOTEL LUCERNA**    656/629-9900

Hotel
Rates not provided

**Address:** Paseo Triunfo de la Republica 3976 **Location:** 2.3 mi (3.9 km) e on Chihuahua Hwy (Mex 45). **Facility:** 138 units. 8 stories, interior corridors. **Pool(s):** outdoor. **Activities:** hot tub, exercise room. **Guest Services:** valet laundry.

---

**HOLIDAY INN EXPRESS**    656/629-6000

[fyi] Not evaluated. **Address:** 3745 Paseo Triunfo de la Republica **Location:** 2.4 mi (4 km) e on Chihuahua Hwy (Mex 45). Facilities, services, and décor characterize a mid-scale property.

**HOTEL CASA GRANDE**    656/629-4000

[fyi] Not evaluated. **Address:** Ave Tecnologico 3620 **Location:** 6.2 mi (10 km) e on Chihuahua Hwy (Mex 45). Facilities, services, and décor characterize a mid-scale property.

**HOTEL KRYSTAL**    656/629-0994

[fyi] Not evaluated. **Address:** Ave Tecnologico 3750 **Location:** 6 mi (10 km) e on Chihuahua Hwy (Mex 45). Facilities, services, and décor characterize a mid-scale property.

## WHERE TO EAT

**SHANGRI-LA RESTAURANT**    656/613-0033

Chinese. Casual Dining. $10-$25 **AAA Inspector Notes:** This is a popular dining spot for tourists, local business people and El Paso, Texas residents who live just across the border. Skilled staff prepare and serve authentic Chinese dishes in a semiformal setting. **Features:** full bar. **Reservations:** suggested. **Address:** Ave de las Americas 133 **Location:** 2.7 mi (4.5 km) sw of Bridge of the Americas.

**FRIDA'S RESTAURANT & BAR**    656/639-0148

[fyi] Not evaluated. A tribute to Mexican artist Frida Kahlo, this popular restaurant is visually stimulating. The extensive menu features fresh seafood, beef and flavorful delicacies from all regions of Mexico. The house-made flan is luscious. **Address:** Paseo Triunfo de la Republica #2525 **Location:** 2.2 mi (3.7 km) e on Chihuahua Hwy (Mex 45), just w of Fiesta Inn Ciudad Juarez.

---

This ends the El Paso section and resumes the alphabetical city listings for Texas.

## EMORY

**BEST WESTERN PLUS EMORY AT LAKE FORK INN & SUITES**    903/473-2022

Hotel
$80-$100

**AAA Benefit:** Members save 10% or more with Best Western!

**Address:** 1026 E Lennon Dr 75440 **Location:** On US 69, just s of jct SR 515. **Facility:** 50 units. 3 stories, interior corridors. **Parking:** winter plug-ins. **Pool(s):** heated outdoor. **Activities:** hot tub, exercise room. **Guest Services:** valet and coin laundry. **Featured Amenity:** full hot breakfast.

---

**ENNIS** pop. 18,513
• Part of Dallas area — see map p. 161

**QUALITY INN ENNIS**    (972)875-9641

Hotel $79-$99 **Address:** 107 Chamber of Commerce Dr 75119 **Location:** I-45 exit 251B, just w. Located in a semi-rural area. **Facility:** 68 units. 2 stories (no elevator), exterior corridors. **Pool(s):** outdoor. **Activities:** hot tub. **Guest Services:** valet laundry.

---

AAA/CAA travel information: Available online, on the go and in print!

## EULESS pop. 51,277
• Hotels & Restaurants map & index p. 257

### LA QUINTA INN & SUITES DFW AIRPORT WEST - EULESS
(817)836-4000 **34**

Hotel
$95-$134

**Address:** 431 Airport Frwy 76040 **Location:** SR 183 exit Ector Dr; on eastbound frontage road. **Facility:** 71 units. 4 stories, interior corridors. **Pool(s):** heated indoor. **Activities:** hot tub, exercise room. **Guest Services:** valet and coin laundry, area transportation. **Featured Amenity:** full hot breakfast.

PLAZA SUITES DFW AIRPORT WEST (817)836-4040 **33**
Hotel $109-$129 **Address:** 421 Airport Frwy 76040 **Location:** SR 183 exit Ector Dr; on eastbound frontage road. **Facility:** 66 units. 4 stories, interior corridors. **Terms:** cancellation fee imposed. **Pool(s):** outdoor. **Activities:** hot tub, exercise room. **Guest Services:** valet and coin laundry, area transportation.

### WHERE TO EAT

NORTH MAIN BBQ 817/283-0884 **36**
Barbecue. Casual Dining. $8-$15 **AAA Inspector Notes:** Bring the family and your appetite to this all-you-can-eat buffet. Barbecue ribs, chicken, sausages and trimmings are offered in a simple setting with long tables that may require some social interaction. This local favorite is BYOB. **Address:** 406 N Main St 76039 **Location:** SR 183 exit Euless Blvd/Main St, just n. L D CALL

## FABENS pop. 8,257

CATTLEMAN'S STEAKHOUSE 915/544-3200
Western Steak. Casual Dining. $15-$40 **AAA Inspector Notes:** Some might say a visit to the city is incomplete without a meal at this classic steakhouse. A drive out into the Fabens Desert leads to the oasis, which is known for its outstanding steaks. Dining at the decidedly Western restaurant is like visiting a friend's ranch. Gracious hosts serve a short menu of steaks and sides family-style. **Address:** 3450 S Fabens Carlsbad Rd 79838 D

## FAIRVIEW
• Part of Dallas area — see map p. 161

PATRIZIO 972/363-2101
Italian. Casual Dining. $8-$24 **AAA Inspector Notes:** As a branch of the beloved original location in Dallas, this restaurant is also nuanced with richness and formality but welcomes all and is a favorite with couples and families alike. The menu focuses on pasta dishes, but a variety of entrée salads and pizza also is offered. Two private dining rooms can accommodate larger parties, and a signature patio also is available. There is a family play area and loads of good shopping in this dynamic shopping center. **Features:** full bar, patio dining. **Address:** 101 Fairview Station Pkwy 75069 **Location:** US 75 exit 36, just e, then just n; in Village at Fairview Shopping Center. L D CALL

## FALCON HEIGHTS (I-7) pop. 53

**FALCON STATE PARK** is 4 mi. s. on US 83, then about 5 mi. w. on FM 2098 to Park Rd. 46. Three miles of hiking and mountain biking trails make a complete loop around the park, and within the park is Falcon Lake, a popular fishing site *(see Recreation Areas Chart)*. Nearby Falcon Dam, a 5-mile-long earth- and rock-filled dam on the Rio Grande, is a combined effort of the United States and Mexico.

Simple metal shafts bearing the seals of both countries mark the international boundary. **Cost:** Park $3; free (ages 0-12). **Phone:** (956) 848-5327 or (800) 792-1112.

## FALFURRIAS (H-8) pop. 4,981, elev. 115'

**THE HERITAGE MUSEUM,** 515 N. St. Mary's St., features memorabilia from early frontier heritage and artifacts from pioneer days in Brooks County. Arrowheads, saddles, antique appliances and Victorian phonographs are just a few of the items exhibited. A room is dedicated to the Texas Rangers; weapons, uniforms and photos are on display. **Time:** Allow 30 minutes minimum. **Hours:** Tues.-Sat. 10-3. Closed Thanksgiving and Christmas. Phone ahead to confirm schedule. **Cost:** Donations. **Phone:** (361) 325-2907.

BEST WESTERN GARDEN INN (361)325-4848
Motel $80-$100

**AAA Benefit:** Members save 10% or more with Best Western!

**Address:** 2299 Hwy 281 S 78355 **Location:** 1.5 mi s of SR 285. **Facility:** 40 units. 1 story, exterior corridors. **Pool(s):** outdoor. **Activities:** exercise room. **Guest Services:** coin laundry.

DAYS INN (361)325-2515
Motel $60-$70
**Address:** 2116 Hwy 281 S 78355 **Location:** 1.5 mi s of SR 285. Located in a quiet area. **Facility:** 32 units. 1 story, exterior corridors. **Guest Services:** coin laundry. **Featured Amenity:** continental breakfast.

## FARMERS BRANCH (H-3) pop. 28,616, elev. 465'
• Hotels p. 246
• Attractions map p. 170
• Hotels & Restaurants map & index p. 184
• Part of Dallas area — see map p. 161

Originating as part of a land grant in 1841, Farmers Branch was originally known as Mustang Branch for its rich soil that produced wild grapes and other successful crops. Although it is no longer a farming community, it is part of the Dallas-Fort Worth greater-metropolitan area.

**Farmers Branch Convention & Visitors Bureau:** 13000 William Dodson Pkwy., Farmers Branch, TX 75234. **Phone:** (972) 247-3131.

Learn about inspections and Diamond Ratings at AAA.com/Diamonds

(See map & index p. 184.)

**FARMERS BRANCH HISTORICAL PARK** is off I-35E exit 441, then e. on Valley View Ln., then .7 mi. s. on Denton Dr., then e. to 2540 Farmers Branch Ln. Brick walkways link varied historic structures such as log houses, a depot, a church, a Queen Anne Victorian cottage, a 1920s general store and a school. The 1856 Gilbert House is the oldest house in Dallas County on its original foundation. **Time:** Allow 1 hour minimum. **Hours:** Mon.-Fri. 8-6, Sat.-Sun. noon-6. Closed Jan. 1, Easter, Thanksgiving and Christmas. **Cost:** Free. **Phone:** (972) 406-0184.

**DOUBLETREE BY HILTON HOTEL DALLAS-FARMERS BRANCH** (972)506-0055 **85**

Hotel
$109-$139

**AAA Benefit:** Members save 5% or more!

**Address:** 11611 Luna Rd 75234 **Location:** I-635 exit 28, just s. Located in a business park area. **Facility:** 160 units. 6 stories, interior corridors. **Terms:** 1-7 night minimum stay, cancellation fee imposed. **Pool(s):** heated outdoor. **Activities:** exercise room. **Guest Services:** valet laundry, area transportation.

**FAIRFIELD INN & SUITES BY MARRIOTT DALLAS NORTH** (972)661-9800 **82**

Hotel $89-$99 **Address:** 13900 Parkside Center Blvd 75244 **Location:** I-635 exit 23 (Midway Rd), 0.9 mi n to Spring Valley Rd, just w, then just s.

**AAA Benefit:** Members save 5% or more!

**Facility:** 107 units. 3 stories, interior corridors. **Pool(s):** indoor. **Activities:** hot tub, exercise room. **Guest Services:** valet and coin laundry, area transportation.

**OMNI DALLAS HOTEL PARK WEST** (972)869-4300 **84**

Hotel $89-$209 **Address:** 1590 LBJ Frwy 75234 **Location:** I-635 exit 29 (Luna Rd), just s. **Facility:** The hotel is close to DFW Airport, Las Colinas and the popular Galleria Mall. It features a wine bar, ever-so-rare complimentary covered parking and easy access to miles of running trails. 337 units. 12 stories, interior corridors. **Parking:** on-site and valet. **Terms:** cancellation fee imposed. **Amenities:** safes. **Pool(s):** heated outdoor. **Activities:** sauna, hot tub, exercise room. **Guest Services:** valet laundry, area transportation.

**SHERATON DALLAS HOTEL BY THE GALLERIA** (972)661-3600 **83**

Hotel
$85-$279

Sheraton

**AAA Benefit:** Members get up to 20% off, plus Starwood Preferred Guest® bonuses!

**Address:** 4801 LBJ Frwy 75244 **Location:** I-635 exit 22D (Dallas Pkwy) eastbound; exit 22B (Dallas Pkwy) westbound; on westbound frontage road. **Facility:** 309 units. 14 stories, interior corridors. **Parking:** on-site (fee). **Pool(s):** outdoor. **Activities:** exercise room. **Guest Services:** valet laundry, area transportation.

## FLORESVILLE pop. 6,448

• Part of San Antonio area — see map p. 458

**BEST WESTERN FLORESVILLE INN** (830)393-0443

Motel
$135-$145

Best Western

**AAA Benefit:** Members save 10% or more with Best Western!

**Address:** 1720 S 10th St 78114 **Location:** US 181, just s of downtown. Located in a quiet area. **Facility:** 42 units. 2 stories (no elevator), exterior corridors. **Pool(s):** outdoor. **Guest Services:** coin laundry. **Featured Amenity:** full hot breakfast.

### WHERE TO EAT

**ANGELICA'S MEXICAN RESTAURANT** 830/393-2182

Tex-Mex. Family Dining. $6-$12 **AAA Inspector Notes:** This is a great Tex-Mex pit stop. Try the chicken caldo. **Features:** beer & wine. **Address:** 604 Tenth St 78114 **Location:** Facing US 181, just s of Sutherland Springs Rd. B L D

**BILL MILLER BAR-B-Q** 830/393-8761

Barbecue. Quick Serve. $6-$11 **AAA Inspector Notes:** The relaxed, family-focused barbecue restaurant prepares ribs, chicken, brisket, turkey and sausage for sandwiches or plates. **Address:** 1615 Standish St 78114 **Location:** On CR 97, just s of US 181. B L D

## FLOWER MOUND pop. 64,669

• Part of Dallas area — see map p. 161

**EL CHICO** 972/539-6951

Tex-Mex
Casual Dining
$7-$16

**AAA Inspector Notes:** Inside and out, the decor of the popular Mexican restaurant is inviting. The menu features traditional favorites such as enchiladas, tacos, burritos and fajitas. The broad menu also lists a few American classics. **Features:** full bar. **Address:** 2111 Justin Rd, Suite 180 75028 **Location:** Just e of Morris Rd. L D

## FOREST HILL pop. 12,355

• Hotels & Restaurants map & index p. 257

**COMFORT INN** (817)551-5200 **55**

Hotel
$60-$70

**Address:** 3232 SE Loop 820 76140 **Location:** I-20/SE Loop 820 exit 440A (Wichita St); on eastbound access road. **Facility:** 59 units. 2 stories, interior corridors. **Amenities:** safes. **Pool(s):** outdoor. **Guest Services:** coin laundry.

**LA QUINTA INN & SUITES** (817)293-5800 **56**

Hotel $99-$143 **Address:** 3346 Forest Hill Cir 76140 **Location:** I-20 exit 440B (Forest Hill Cir), just s, then just w. **Facility:** 71 units. 3 stories, interior corridors. **Pool(s):** heated indoor. **Activities:** hot tub, exercise room. **Guest Services:** coin laundry.

# FORNEY pop. 14,661
• Part of Dallas area — see map p. 161

## BEST WESTERN PLUS CHRISTOPHER INN & SUITES
(972)552-1412

Hotel
$94-$114

**AAA Benefit:** Members save 10% or more with Best Western!

**Address:** 752 Pinson Rd 75126 **Location:** US 80 exit FM 740 (Pinson Rd), just ne. **Facility:** 70 units. 3 stories, interior corridors. **Pool(s):** outdoor. **Activities:** exercise room. **Guest Services:** valet and coin laundry. **Featured Amenity: full hot breakfast.**

## FORT BLISS (E-1)

**FORT BLISS MUSEUM AND STUDY CENTER** is off US 54, following signs to Bldg. 1735 on Marshall Rd. Museum exhibits chronicle the histories of the U.S. Army and the Air Defense Artillery branch in El Paso. An adjacent park contains anti-aircraft weapons and vehicles. Facing the main parade ground on Pleasonton Road is a replica of the 1854 Old Fort Bliss. Four adobe buildings contain exhibits depicting the lives and daily routines of 1850s soldiers and civilians. **Hours:** Mon.-Sat. 9-4:30. Closed major holidays. **Cost:** Donations. **Phone:** (915) 568-5412.

## FORT DAVIS (E-3) pop. 1,201, elev. 4,927'

In the heart of the Davis Mountains, Fort Davis grew as a strategic point on the San Antonio-El Paso Road. Established in 1854, the fort was named in honor of Jefferson Davis, then Secretary of War. Fort Davis was first manned by troops of the Eighth U.S. Infantry who, mounted on mules, fought the Comanches.

The canyon formed by Limpia Creek, which flows through the Davis Mountains, is a centuries-old oasis for travelers. Davis Mountains State Park embraces a part of the creek and 1,869 acres of the rolling grasslands and intermittent trees that cover these mountains. A 74-mile scenic highway, SR 166/118, makes a loop through the Davis Mountains and includes Madera Canyon and University of Texas McDonald Observatory.

**Fort Davis Chamber of Commerce:** 4 Memorial Sq., P.O. Box 378, Fort Davis, TX 79734. **Phone:** (432) 426-3015 or (800) 524-3015.

**CHIHUAHUAN DESERT NATURE CENTER & BOTANICAL GARDENS** is 3.5 mi. s. on SR 118. Included are a 20-acre botanical garden, a cactus greenhouse, indoor and outdoor interpretive exhibits, and hiking trails. The center is home to the Chihuahuan Desert Research Institute. **Time:** Allow 30 minutes minimum. **Hours:** Mon.-Sat. 9-5. Closed Jan. 1, Thanksgiving and Christmas. **Cost:** $6; free (ages 0-12). **Phone:** (432) 364-2499.

**FORT DAVIS NATIONAL HISTORIC SITE** is n. of town near Limpia Creek off SRs 17 and 118. Occupying 523 acres, this frontier military post was established to protect travelers, freighters and mail riders on the San Antonio-El Paso Road. In summer, interpreters in period dress staff the officers' quarters, barracks, kitchen and servants' quarters. Interpretive exhibits are displayed at the fort museum, which also features photographs, weapons, Native American artifacts and paintings. **Hours:** Daily 8-5. Closed Jan. 1, Martin Luther King Jr. Day, Thanksgiving and Christmas. **Cost:** $3; free (ages 0-15). **Phone:** (432) 426-3224.

**UNIVERSITY OF TEXAS McDONALD OBSERVATORY** is 16 mi. n.w. via SR 118 on Spur 78. A visitor center at the base of Mounts Locke and Fowlkes is the check-in point for all activities and offers exhibits about the observatory and research techniques. A giant Hobby-Eberly Telescope is connected to a gallery that offers interpretive programs. Evening Star Parties let guests view stars and planets through telescopes in the visitor center.

**Tours:** Guided tours are available. **Time:** Allow 2 hours, 30 minutes minimum. **Hours:** Daily 10-5:30. Evening Star Parties are offered year-round; phone for schedule. Closed Jan. 1, Thanksgiving and Christmas. **Cost:** Daytime Pass (includes video, exhibit hall, guided tour and sun viewing) $9; $8 (ages 6-12, ages 65+ and military with ID). Star Party Pass $14; $12 (ages 65+ and military with ID); $10 (ages 6-12). **Phone:** (432) 426-3640 or (877) 984-7827.

HISTORICAL PRUDE GUEST RANCH    432/426-3202

Ranch $61-$180 **Address:** 6 mi n Hwy 118 79734 **Location:** 4.5 mi n of jct SR 118 and 17. **Facility:** 41 units, some two bedrooms, kitchens and cabins. 1 story, exterior corridors. **Terms:** 2 night minimum stay - weekends, 3 day cancellation notice-fee imposed. **Pool(s):** heated indoor. **Activities:** tennis, picnic facilities, trails.

## FORT HOOD (E-7) pop. 29,589

This 217,000-acre installation is the only U.S. Army post large enough to station and train two heavy-armored divisions.

**1ST CAVALRY DIVISION MUSEUM** is at Fort Hood in Bldg. 2218 on 761st Tank Battalion and 56th St. The museum traces the history of the Cav trooper from the 1850s through activation of the Division in 1921 and onto the Division's involvement in World War II, the Korean War, Vietnam War, Bosnia, Operation Desert Storm and the conflicts in Iraq and Afghanistan.

Highlights include uniforms, weapons, aircraft and more than 125 vehicles. At Division Headquarters, visitors can view a memorial to the fallen soldiers of Operation Iraqi Freedom. **Note:** Visitors must enter at the main gate and through the Visitor Center and show photo ID, proof of insurance and vehicle registration. **Time:** Allow 1 hour minimum. **Hours:** Mon.-Fri. 9-4, Sat. 10-4, Sun. and federal holidays noon-4. Closed Jan. 1, Easter, Thanksgiving and Christmas. **Cost:** Free. **Phone:** (254) 287-3626.

## FORT McKAVETT (E-6) elev. 2,171'

**FORT McKAVETT STATE HISTORIC SITE** is 17 mi. w. on US 190, then 6 mi. s. on FM 864. The 80-acre site preserves the remains of Camp San Saba, established in 1852 to protect frontier settlers and travelers on the El Paso Road. Later named for an army captain, the fort was described by Gen. William T. Sherman as "the prettiest post in Texas." Two dozen limestone buildings have been restored; a museum features photographs, dioramas and artifacts.

**Time:** Allow 1 hour minimum. **Hours:** Daily 8-5. Closed Jan. 1, Thanksgiving, Christmas Eve, Christmas and Dec. 31. **Cost:** $4; $3 (ages 6-18 and students with ID). **Phone:** (325) 396-2358. ⛽

## FORT STOCKTON (E-4) pop. 8,283, elev. 3,000'

The town of Fort Stockton dates from 1858, when the U.S. Army established a cavalry post on the site. The first stores opened in 1870, and the community prospered as a trade center for a large ranching empire. The Yates oil field was discovered around 1925 in eastern Pecos County. Giant drilling rigs are part of the landscape, and the oil and gas industries are the mainstays of the local economy. Measuring 20 feet long by 11 feet tall and weighing 860 pounds, the giant roadrunner statue affectionately called Paisano Pete is a town landmark.

The Overland-Butterfield Stage Stop, 20 miles east on US 290 and I-10, is a reconstructed stage remount stand from the San Antonio-San Francisco route. Originally 1.5 miles southwest, the stand was dismantled and rebuilt on the present site using the original stones.

**Fort Stockton Chamber of Commerce Visitor Center:** 1000 Railroad Ave., Fort Stockton, TX 79735. **Phone:** (432) 336-2264 or (800) 336-2166.

**Self-guiding tours:** Brochures about historic downtown, including old Fort Stockton, are available from the chamber of commerce visitor center.

**ANNIE RIGGS MEMORIAL MUSEUM** is at 301 S. Main St. This 1900 adobe brick and wood hotel once catered to early travelers on the Overland-Butterfield route. The museum has some original furnishings, clothing, saddles, an archeology/geology exhibit and hosts free summer concerts. **Tours:** Guided tours are available. **Time:** Allow 30 minutes minimum. **Hours:** Mon.-Sat. 9-5, Sept.-May; Mon.-Sat. 9-6, rest of year. **Cost:** $3; $2.50 (ages 65+); $2 (ages 6-12). **Phone:** (432) 336-2167.

**HISTORIC FORT STOCKTON** is at 301 E. 3rd St. This frontier military post, active 1859-86, consisted of 35 adobe and limestone buildings. Three of the original eight officers' quarters, guard house and two reconstructed barracks with kitchens remain. Restored, they are now a small museum. A cemetery

also is near the grounds. Self-guiding tours are available. **Time:** Allow 30 minutes minimum. **Hours:** Mon.-Sat. 9-6, June-Aug.; Mon.-Sat. 9-5, rest of year. Closed Jan. 1, Thanksgiving and Christmas. **Cost:** $3; $2.50 (ages 65+); $2 (ages 6-12). **Phone:** (432) 336-2400.

**CANDLEWOOD SUITES**                          (432)336-7700

 **Extended Stay Hotel** $130-$140 **Address:** 2469 I-10 W 79735 **Location:** I-20 exit 257, just n; on north frontage road. **Facility:** 74 units, some efficiencies. 3 stories, interior corridors. **Terms:** cancellation fee imposed. **Pool(s):** outdoor. **Activities:** exercise room. **Guest Services:** valet and coin laundry.

**COMFORT SUITES**                              (432)336-3224

Hotel
$109-$169

**Address:** 3101 W Dickinson Blvd 79735 **Location:** I-10 exit 256, 0.5 mi e. **Facility:** 64 units. 3 stories, interior corridors. **Pool(s):** heated indoor. **Activities:** hot tub, exercise room. **Guest Services:** valet and coin laundry.

**DAYS INN**                                    (432)336-7500

Hotel
$69-$109

**Address:** 1408 N US Hwy 285 79735 **Location:** I-10 exit 257, just s. **Facility:** 50 units. 2 stories (no elevator), exterior corridors. **Pool(s):** outdoor. **Activities:** hot tub. **Featured Amenity: continental breakfast.** *(See ad p. 249.)*

**HAMPTON INN**                                 (432)336-9600

Hotel
$139-$169

**AAA Benefit:** Members save up to 10%!

**Address:** 2271 W I-10 79735 **Location:** I-10 exit 257, just s. **Facility:** 59 units. 3 stories, interior corridors. **Terms:** 1-7 night minimum stay, cancellation fee imposed. **Amenities:** video games. **Pool(s):** outdoor. **Activities:** hot tub, exercise room. **Guest Services:** valet and coin laundry.

**LA QUINTA INN FORT STOCKTON**                 (432)336-9781

Hotel $89-$130 **Address:** 1537 N US Hwy 285 79735 **Location:** I-10 exit 257. **Facility:** 97 units. 2 stories (no elevator), exterior corridors. **Pool(s):** outdoor. **Guest Services:** valet and coin laundry.

## QUALITY INN

Hotel
$74-S104

(432)336-5955
**Address:** 1308 N US Hwy 285 79735 **Location:** I-10 exit 257, just s. **Facility:** 44 units. 2 stories (no elevator), exterior corridors. **Pool(s):** outdoor. **Activities:** hot tub, exercise room. **Guest Services:** valet and coin laundry. **Featured Amenity: full hot breakfast.**

## SLEEP INN & SUITES
Hotel
$95-S140

(432)336-8338
**Address:** 3401 W Dickinson Blvd 79735 **Location:** I-10 exit 256, just e. **Facility:** 49 units. 3 stories, interior corridors. **Pool(s):** heated indoor. **Activities:** hot tub, exercise room. **Guest Services:** valet and coin laundry. **Featured Amenity: full hot breakfast.**

## SUPER 8

Hotel
$60-$116

(432)336-8531
**Address:** 3200 W Dickinson Blvd 79735 **Location:** I-10 exit 256, just s. **Facility:** 95 units. 2 stories (no elevator), interior corridors. **Terms:** cancellation fee imposed. **Amenities:** safes. **Pool(s):** outdoor. **Activities:** exercise room. **Guest Services:** valet and coin laundry. **Featured Amenity: continental breakfast.**

▼ See AAA listing p. 248 ▼

**WHERE TO EAT**

### K-BOB'S STEAKHOUSE
432/336-6233
American. Casual Dining. $7-$23 **AAA Inspector Notes:** The steakhouse prepares a great variety of plump, juicy fillets. A fireplace opens up into both dining rooms, and antique clocks decorate the walls. Rustic wagon-wheel chandeliers illuminate the room. **Address:** 2800 W Dickinson Blvd 79735 **Location:** Jct Dickinson Blvd and Pine St. L D

### TACOS O.J.
432/336-3066
Mexican. Family Dining. $6-$15 **AAA Inspector Notes:** The eatery sports a modest exterior with limited parking but a charming, warm, welcoming interior. The menu is a mix of traditional classic Mexican dishes as well as some specialties. There is a nice selection of seafood, and the grilled catfish tacos are a good choice. Desserts include the traditional tres leches cake. Breakfast is served on Saturday and Sunday. **Address:** 1303 N Main St 79735 **Location:** I-10 exit 259A, 1 mi s. L D

## FORT WORTH (I-2) pop. 741,206, elev. 610'
- Hotels p. 260 • Restaurants p. 262
- Attractions map p. 251
- Hotels & Restaurants map & index p. 255, 257

Fort Worth began in 1849 as a military post to protect a few struggling ranchers from Native American attacks. When the camp dissolved, the settlement became a trading post. After the Civil War the dusty trails were filled with longhorns as Texas cowboys came to town. On their heels were adventure-seekers, trailhands who lived it up for a night, dreamers who rode on, and the Native Americans, outlaws and settlers who stayed to make Fort Worth their home.

## Safety tip:
Keep a current AAA/CAA Road Atlas in every vehicle

(See maps & indexes p. 255, 257.)

The bubble of high hopes burst in 1873 when the first railroad, left stranded in nearby Dallas by a financial panic, failed to come to town. Unlike settlers in many Texas boomtowns, some Fort Worth citizens stayed and convinced the Texas and Pacific Railroad they could finish the 26 miles of roadbed before the land grant expired in 1876. Every person who could swing a pick or drive a mule helped lay the rails.

Once the railroad was finished, Fort Worth regained its prominence as the capital of the Southwestern cattle empire. By the end of the 19th century, stockyards had moved to the north side of the city, and the great meatpacking houses moved in.

More fuel was added to Fort Worth's boomtown frenzy when the north Texas oil fields began producing in 1912, sparking a tripling of the town's population in the next 2 decades. During the 1930s oil eclipsed the cattle industry and remained the city's leading industry for 30 years.

Fort Worth has blended frontier heritage with such industries as defense, high technology and aviation into a cosmopolitan mix of skyscrapers and historic buildings. Cattle drives are re-enacted twice daily as the Fort Worth longhorn herd makes its way down Exchange Avenue in the Stockyards.

Scattered throughout downtown are bronze plaques commemorating significant people and events of Fort Worth's past. Visitors also will find an innovative tribute to water at Water Garden, which features rushing and sprinkling water as well as water falling over stone slabs or lying quietly in pools. The garden now covers part of Hell's Half Acre, once a roaring, lawless area of saloons and brothels. Sundance Square, a 35-block entertainment district named for Butch Cassidy and the Sundance Kid, who once hid out there, is an active downtown area filled with restaurants, shops and galleries. Bass Performance Hall, adorned outside with herald angels, features outstanding acoustics and hosts the Fort Worth Opera, Fort Worth Symphony Orchestra, Texas Ballet Theater and major artists on tour.

The T operates a bus service to major entertainment districts, including the Cultural District, the Fort Worth Zoo, the Historic Stockyards and Sundance Square. The T offers a Free Zone located in downtown Fort Worth. For schedules and fares, phone the Fort Worth Transportation Authority at (817) 215-8600.

Forest Park, off Colonial Parkway, offers outdoor recreation and one of the longest miniature railroads in the United States. Two streamlined trains and an old-fashioned steam engine operate in the park. Log Cabin Village, within the park, has 10 restored frontier cabins furnished with pioneer articles that depict the life of early settlers. The village has a working gristmill. Spinning and candle-dipping demonstrations are given mornings and weekends; phone (817) 392-5881.

Leading educational institutions—Southwestern Baptist Theological Seminary, Texas Christian University, University of North Texas Health Science Center and Texas Wesleyan University—add further refinement to the city's cultural offerings. Among the institutional highlights is Southwestern Baptist Theological Seminary's Tandy Archeological Museum, which features Holy Land artifacts and biblical history, and the Monnig Meteorite Gallery at Texas Christian University, which contains more than 1,000 different meteorites.

Lakes now dot the once-empty prairie. Lake Worth, popular for its scenic vistas and water sports, lies within the city limits and was the first of several lakes built to meet the growing city's water needs. Other nearby lakes include Eagle Mountain to the northwest and Benbrook to the southwest.

The Fort Worth Stock Show and Rodeo, the popular name for the Southwestern Exposition & Livestock Show, has been held annually since 1896 and attracts more than 900,000 people to the Will Rogers Memorial Center from mid-January to early February. Texas Christian University's Amon G. Carter Stadium hosts the 🦇 Bell Helicopter Armed Forces Bowl in late December. Minor-league baseball is played at LaGrave Field, home of the Fort Worth Cats. For race fans, Texas Motor Speedway is north at I-35W exit 70; the AAA Texas 500, the eighth race in the NASCAR Sprint Cup series, is held there in November.

**Fort Worth Convention & Visitors Bureau:** 508 Main St., Fort Worth, TX 76102. **Phone:** (817) 336-8791 or (800) 433-5747.

**Self-guiding tours:** Maps and GPS Ranger devices for self-guiding walking tours of the historic stockyards at Stockyards National Historic District (see attraction listing p. 253) are available at 130 E. Exchange Ave.; phone (817) 625-9715 or (817) 624-4741.

**Shopping areas:** Stockyards Station, on East Exchange Avenue, has been restored and now accommodates restaurants, studios and crafts shops. Sundance Square is a 20-block area on Main Street where late 19th- and early 20th-century buildings have been restored. Additional shopping runs along historic Camp Bowie Boulevard and near the cultural district along University Drive, where the University Park Plaza is located.

**THE AMERICAN AIRLINES C.R. SMITH MUSEUM** is s. of Dallas/Fort Worth International Airport at 4601 US 360 and FAA Rd. American Airlines memorabilia from the 1930s to the present is housed at the museum. Displays illustrate the responsibilities of the cabin and cockpit crews, the effect of wind tunnels and how a plane is flown and maintained. Other exhibits include computer simulations, a jet engine and a restored DC3, American's flagship passenger plane.

**Time:** Allow 1 hour minimum. **Hours:** Tues.-Sat. 9-5. Closed Jan. 1, July 4, Thanksgiving, Christmas

(See maps & indexes p. 255, 257.)

Eve, Christmas and Dec. 31. Phone ahead to confirm schedule. **Cost:** $7; $4 (ages 2-8, ages 55+, and students and military with ID). **Phone:** (817) 967-1560.

**AMON CARTER MUSEUM OF AMERICAN ART** is 2.5 mi. w. at 3501 Camp Bowie Blvd. The museum's collection includes masterworks by such artists as Georgia O'Keeffe, Frederic Remington, Winslow Homer and Charles Russell. On display are paintings, sculpture, watercolors, prints and photographs. The interior walls of the museum are made of fossilized Texas shellstone. Visitors can view downtown Fort Worth through windows overlooking a landscaped plaza and lawn.

**Tours:** Guided tours are available. **Time:** Allow 1 hour, 30 minutes minimum. **Hours:** Tues.-Sat. 10-5 (also Thurs. 5-8), Sun. noon-5. Guided tours Thurs.-Sun. at 2. Closed major holidays. **Cost:** Free. **Phone:** (817) 738-1933.

**BALL-EDDLEMAN-McFARLAND HOUSE** is at 1110 Penn St. This 1899 Queen Anne-style house features Victorian-era architecture such as turrets, copper finials, a slate roof and marble exterior accents along with intricate interior woodwork. **Time:**

Allow 30 minutes minimum. **Hours:** Tours are given on the hour Wed.-Fri. 11-2, Sun. 1-3. Closed major holidays. Phone ahead to confirm schedule. **Cost:** (Includes Thistle Hill) $15; $7.50 (ages 7-12). **Phone:** (817) 332-5875.

**FORT WORTH BOTANIC GARDEN** is n. of I-30 off University Dr. at 3220 Botanic Garden Blvd., across from Trinity Park. This 110-acre complex features 23 specialty gardens, including a rose garden dating from 1933, a 10,000-square-foot conservatory with a tropical collection, a water conservation garden, a 7.5-acre Japanese garden, and one of the largest public perennial trial gardens in north-central Texas. An elevated boardwalk through a native forest features 13 interpretive stations. Special events are held throughout the year.

**Time:** Allow 4 hours minimum. **Hours:** Grounds daily 8-dusk. Conservatory Mon.-Sat. 10-6, Sun. 1-6, Mar.-Oct.; Mon.-Sat. 10-4, Sun. 1-4, rest of year. Phone for special-events schedule. **Cost:** Grounds free. Conservatory $2; $1 (ages 4-12 and 65+). Japanese garden $5; $4.50 (ages 65+); $3 (ages 4-12). **Phone:** (817) 871-7686.

**The Japanese Garden** is in the Fort Worth Botanic Garden. The garden combines water, plant material, stones, sculpture and structures to emphasize the

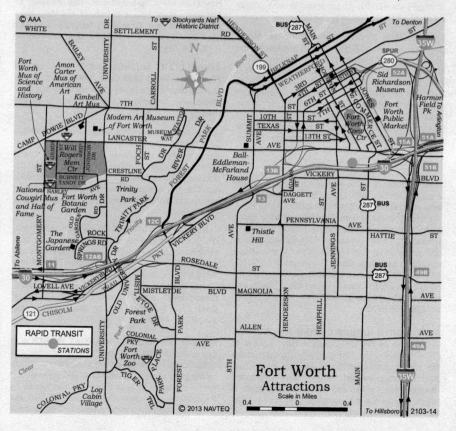
Fort Worth Attractions

(See maps & indexes p. 255, 257.)

beauty of seasonal changes and to foster tranquility. The 7.5-acre garden features a pagoda, teahouse, pavilion, five pools filled with koi fish and a moon-viewing deck. **Hours:** Daily 9-7, Apr.-Oct.; 9-5, rest of year. **Cost:** $5; $4.50 (ages 65+); $3 (ages 4-12). **Phone:** (817) 871-7686.

**FORT WORTH MUSEUM OF SCIENCE AND HISTORY** is at 1600 Gendy St. Hands-on displays focusing on science, history, art and technology stimulate the imagination of both kids and adults. The Energy Blast exhibit explores north Texas' energy resources and features a 4-D theater experience, a 50,000-pound vibrating truck and a 30-foot replica of a drilling rig. The Collections Gallery features changing exhibits.

The 10,000-square-foot Cattle Raisers Museum relates the development of the cattle industry. Visitors can participate in a simulated cattle drive, operate a computerized ranch and learn about the industry's role in the 21st century.

Designed for ages 8 and under, the Fort Worth Children's Museum has live amphibians and reptiles and an outdoor water play area. The Noble Planetarium's state-of-the-art projection system affords an amazing view of more than 7,000 stars.

**Time:** Allow 2 hours minimum. **Hours:** Mon.-Sat.10-5, Sun. noon-5. Planetarium show schedule varies; phone ahead. Closed Thanksgiving, Christmas Eve and Christmas. **Cost:** Museum $14; $10 (ages 2-12 and 65+). Planetarium $5; $4 (ages 2-12 and 65+). Combination museum, planetarium and Omni Theater documentary film $23; $17 (ages 2-12 and 65+). Combination museum and Omni Theater documentary film or planetarium $19; $14 (ages 2-12 and 65+). Parking lots and garages are available nearby for a fee. **Phone:** (817) 255-9300 or (888) 255-9300. 🍴

**Omni Theater** is at the Fort Worth Museum of Science and History, 1600 Gendy St. The theater presents educational and entertaining IMAX films on an eight-story dome screen. Programs change about every 4 months. **Time:** Allow 1 hour minimum. **Hours:** Shows are presented daily. Closed Thanksgiving, Christmas Eve and Christmas. Phone ahead to confirm schedule. **Cost:** Full-length film $10.50-$13; $8-$13 (ages 2-12 and 65+). Admission for 45-minute film $7; $6 (ages 2-12 and 65+). The theater often sells out; arrive early. **Phone:** (817) 255-9540 or (888) 255-9300.

**FORT WORTH NATURE CENTER AND REFUGE** is 9 mi. n.w. on SR 199/Jacksboro Hwy., 2 mi. w. of Lake Worth Bridge. Hiking and nature trails make the interior of this 3,620-acre preserve accessible. Animals frequently seen include bison, white-tailed deer, coyotes, turkeys and a wide variety of birds. A prairie dog town and bison range offer opportunities to see these animals in their natural habitat.

**Time:** Allow 2 hours, 30 minutes minimum. **Hours:** Refuge Mon.-Fri. 7-5, Sat.-Sun. 7-7, May-Sept.; daily 8-5, rest of year. Center daily 9-4:30. Closed Thanksgiving and Christmas. Phone ahead to confirm schedule. **Cost:** $5; $4 (military with ID); $3 (ages 65+); $2 (ages 3-12). **Phone:** (817) 392-7410.

**FORT WORTH ZOO** is off I-30 exit University Dr. S., then e. to 1989 Colonial Pkwy. Ranked as one of the nation's top zoos, the 64-acre complex is home to more than 7,000 animals from around the world. Visitors can stroll through the 30,000-square-foot Museum of Living Art (MOLA) herpetarium, which houses more than 100 species of amphibians and reptiles.

Other exhibits include World of Primates, Asian Falls, African Savannah, Raptor Canyon, Parrot Paradise, Australian Outback and Meerkat Mounds. More than 300 indigenous animals are featured at Texas Wild!, an 8-acre exhibit that re-creates an 1890s pioneer town and six geographic regions of the Lone Star State. Visitors also can hop aboard the Yellow Rose Express miniature train or take a ride on the Country Carousel.

**Time:** Allow 2 hours, 30 minutes minimum. **Hours:** Mon.-Fri. 10-5, Sat.-Sun. 10-6, mid-Mar. to mid-Sept.; daily 10-5, mid-Feb. to mid-Mar.; daily 10-4, rest of year. **Cost:** $12; $9 (ages 3-12 and ages 65+); half-price (Wed.). **Parking:** $5. **Phone:** (817) 759-7555.

**KIMBELL ART MUSEUM** is 2.5 mi. w. on Will Rogers Rd. W. to 3333 Camp Bowie Blvd., in the Cultural District. The vaulted building is the last completed work of architect Louis Kahn and is considered by many to be his masterpiece.

The museum's holdings range in period from antiquity to the 20th century, including works by Caravaggio, Matisse, Monet and Picasso. Other collections include Egyptian, Greek and Roman antiquities as well as Asian, African and pre-Columbian art. The museum provides an ongoing program of interpretive exhibitions, retrospectives and traveling exhibitions.

**Note:** At press time, a $135 million Renzo Piano-designed post-and-beam pavilion was under construction and was scheduled to open on the museum campus in late November 2013. **Time:** Allow 2 hours, 30 minutes minimum. **Hours:** Tues.-Thurs. and Sat. 10-5, Fri. noon-8, Sun. noon-5. Closed Jan. 1, July 4, Thanksgiving and Christmas. **Cost:** Free. Admission may be charged for special exhibitions. **Phone:** (817) 332-8451. 🏛

**MODERN ART MUSEUM OF FORT WORTH** is at Camp Bowie Blvd. and University Dr. Modern and contemporary works of art are featured and include paintings, sculpture, international photography and works on paper. The collection includes pieces by Pablo Picasso, Jackson Pollock, Mark Rothko and Andy Warhol. Educational programs include adult

(See maps & indexes p. 255, 257.)

and children's classes, guided tours, lectures and workshops.

**Time:** Allow 30 minutes minimum. **Hours:** Tues.-Sun. 10-5 (also Fri. 5-8). Closed major holidays. **Cost:** $10; $4 (ages 60+ and students with ID); free (ages 0-12). **Phone:** (817) 738-9215 or (866) 824-5566. [TI]

**NATIONAL COWGIRL MUSEUM AND HALL OF FAME,** 1720 Gendy St., celebrates the achievements of more than 200 western women who have played such roles as pathfinder, performer, rancher and artist. You'll be greeted by a Mehl Lawson sculpture of a cowgirl and her horse and a Richard Haas *trompe l'oeil* mural at the entrance. Within the museum's galleries, theaters and magnificent rotunda are more than 5,000 artifacts and 2,500 photographs related to cowgirls of the past and present.

Twelve optically illusory glass murals depicting cowgirls' lives add to the elegance of the rotunda, where you'll embark on your journey along the Spirit Trail. Lining the Rotunda Hall walls are shimmering glass stars bearing the names of influential females like Lewis and Clark's Shoshone interpreter Sacagawea, Nebraskan author Willa Cather and U.S. Supreme Court member and Arizonan Sandra Day O'Connor. Electronic "yearbooks" allow you to delve into the Hall of Famers' fascinating lives, and an 8-minute theater presentation highlights cowgirl diversity.

In the Into the Arena gallery you can see and hear authentic clips from famous rodeo rides, admire a revolving rack of polychromatic cowgirl attire and star in a recorded show of your own atop a mechanical bronc. Watch an interview on an interactive computer and let a pro tell you what it's like to be on the rodeo circuit.

In the Kinship with the Land gallery you'll be introduced to female ranchers whose love for the great outdoors is surpassed only by their untamable spirit. Special lighting effects are used in this room, which is illuminated with projected scenes of vast expanses of Western land and of cowgirls on the job. Youngsters will enjoy the kid-friendly activities in the Connie Reeves Discovery Corral.

Jukebox tunes of Patsy Cline, Reba McEntire and other country singers fill the air in the Claiming the Spotlight gallery. Must-sees include mementos and segments from the 1950s hit television shows "Annie Oakley" and "The Roy Rogers Show," a designer rhinestone-studded saddle and a dime novel collection. An old-fashioned theater presents a comical yet informative film about the cowgirl's place in Hollywood. Guided tours are available by reservation. **Time:** Allow 1 hour minimum. **Hours:** Tues.-Sat. 10-5 (also Mon. 10-5, June-Aug.), Sun. noon-5. **Cost:** $10; $8 (ages 3-12 and 60+). **Phone:** (817) 336-4475 or (800) 476-3263.

**SID RICHARDSON MUSEUM** is at 309 Main St. in Sundance Sq. Frederic Remington and Charles Russell are among the artists represented in the collection. **Time:** Allow 30 minutes minimum. **Hours:** Mon.-Sat. 9-5 (also Fri.-Sat. 5-8), Sun. noon-5. Closed major holidays. **Cost:** Free. **Phone:** (817) 332-6554 or (888) 332-6554.

**SIX FLAGS OVER TEXAS**—see Arlington p. 67.

**STOCKYARDS NATIONAL HISTORIC DISTRICT** is at N. Main St. and E. Exchange Ave. Galleries, restaurants and shops occupy many of the preserved stockyard structures covering 125 acres of what was once the largest livestock marketing center in the Southwest. Many of the stockyards' original structures such as Booger Red's Saloon, the Livestock Exchange Building and Stockyards Hotel remain, housing new businesses.

Visitors can watch a cattle drive demonstration as wranglers on horseback guide the Fort Worth Herd down East Exchange Avenue. Those wishing to take a self-guiding tour of the district can obtain free maps or rent GPS Rangers—handheld devices with narrated video, audio and photographs—at the visitor center. **Tours:** Guided tours are available. **Time:** Allow 2 hours minimum. **Hours:** Mon.-Fri. 8:30-6, Sat. 9-6, Sun. 11-5. Fort Worth Herd daily at 11:30 and 4. Closed Easter, Thanksgiving and Christmas. **Cost:** Free. **Phone:** (817) 625-9715. [TI] [A]

**Cowtown Cattlepen Maze** is at 145 E. Exchange Ave. Making it through this 5,400-square-foot maze constructed of wooden slats resembling livestock chutes is a challenge for all ages. A two-story observation deck is located within the maze. **Time:** Allow 1 hour minimum. **Hours:** Mon.-Thurs. 10-6, Fri.-Sat. 10-10, Sun. noon-6 (weather permitting). Closed Thanksgiving and Christmas. **Cost:** $6; free (ages 0-2). **Phone:** (817) 624-6666.

**Stockyards Museum** is n. of downtown in the Stockyards Livestock Exchange Building. Exhibits illustrate the livestock industry of Fort Worth and the history of the Stockyards. Western saddles, antiques from the 1800s and photographs portraying life in Fort Worth also are displayed. **Time:** Allow 30 minutes minimum. **Hours:** Mon.-Sat. 10-5 (also Sun. noon-5, Memorial Day-Labor Day). Closed Jan. 1, Thanksgiving, Christmas Eve and Christmas. **Cost:** Donations. **Phone:** (817) 625-5082.

**Stockyards Station Historical Walking Tours** depart from the visitor center at 130 E. Exchange Ave. Guided tours of the historic stockyard area include the Livestock Exchange Building, Cowtown Coliseum, Mule Alley, Cattlemen's Catwalk and old hog and sheep barns.

Visitors wishing to take a self-guiding tour can rent a GPS Ranger, a handheld device that automatically provides relevant audio and video narration based on locations within the district. Area history is chronicled in a video presentation, which also may be viewed without taking the tour for an additional fee.

(See maps & indexes p. 255, 257.)

**Time:** Allow 1 hour minimum. **Hours:** Guided tours depart Tues.-Sat. at 10, noon, 1:30 and 2:30, Sun. at noon, 2 and 4, Memorial Day-Labor Day; Tues-Fri. at 10, noon, 2 and 4, Sun. at noon, 2 and 4, rest of year. GPS Ranger tours Mon.-Sat. 9-5, Sun. 11-5. Closed Christmas. **Cost:** Guided tour (includes video presentation) $8; $7 (ages 65+); $6 (ages 6-12). GPS Ranger tour (includes video presentation) $12. Video presentation only $1. **Phone:** (817) 625-9715.

**Texas Cowboy Hall of Fame,** 128 E. Exchange Ave. inside Barn A, honors more than 100 world-champion cowboys and cowgirls. Individual booths contain personal memorabilia and a DVD depicting each hall-of-famer's life and career. Said to be the world's largest collection of lifestyle wagons, the Sterquell Wagon Collection features more than 60 wagons, carriages and sleighs. Other exhibits include the John Justin Trail of Fame, Chisholm Trail Exhibit, Zigrang Bit Collection and Adventures of the Cowboy Trail.

**Time:** Allow 1 hour minimum. **Hours:** Mon.-Sat. 10-6 (also Fri.-Sat. 6-7 p.m.), Sun. 11-5. Closed Easter, Thanksgiving and Christmas. **Cost:** $5; $4 (ages 13-17, ages 60+ and college students with ID); $3 (ages 5-12); free (military with ID). **Phone:** (817) 626-7131.

**TEXAS CIVIL WAR MUSEUM** is at 760 N. Jim Wright Frwy. Flags, textiles, clothing, weapons, tools and other artifacts from the Civil War period are displayed. Highlights include a collection of women's Victorian-era dresses and a 30-minute movie about Texas' role in the Civil War. **Time:** Allow 45 minutes minimum. **Hours:** Tues.-Sat. 9-5. Closed major holidays. **Cost:** $6; $3 (ages 7-12); free (ages 0-6 with adult). **Phone:** (817) 246-2323.

**THISTLE HILL** is at 1509 Pennsylvania Ave. This Georgian Revival mansion was built in 1904 for the daughter of a wealthy cattle baron. The restored house is furnished with period antiques. **Hours:** Tours are given on the hour Wed.-Fri. 11-2, Sun. 1-3. Closed major holidays. Phone ahead to confirm schedule. **Cost:** (Includes Ball-Eddleman-McFarland House) $15; $7.50 (ages 6-12). **Phone:** (817) 336-1212.

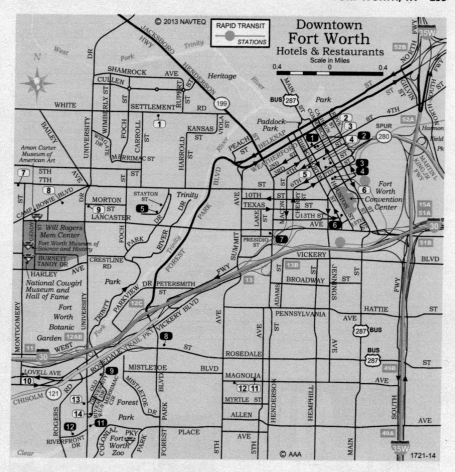

## Downtown Fort Worth

This index helps you "spot" where approved hotels and restaurants are located on the corresponding detailed maps. Hotel daily rate range is for comparison only. Restaurant price range is a combination of lunch and/or dinner. Turn to the listing page for more detailed rate and price information and consult display ads for special promotions.

### DOWNTOWN FORT WORTH

| Map Page | Hotels | Diamond Rated | Rate Range | Page |
|---|---|---|---|---|
| **1** this page | The Worthington Renaissance Fort Worth Hotel | ▽▽▽ | $129-$285 | 262 |
| **2** this page | Embassy Suites Fort Worth Downtown | ▽▽▽ | $169-$249 | 261 |
| **3** this page | The Ashton Hotel | ▽▽▽ | Rates not provided | 260 |
| **4** this page | Historic Hilton Fort Worth | ▽▽▽ | $149-$229 | 261 |
| **5** this page | Residence Inn by Marriott Fort Worth Cultural District | ▽▽▽ | $132-$229 | 262 |
| **6** this page | Omni Hotel | ▽▽▽▽ | $169-$349 | 261 |
| **7** this page | **Holiday Inn Express Hotel & Suites Fort Worth Downtown** (See ad p. 261.) | ▽▽▽ | $99-$229 [SAVE] | 261 |
| **8** this page | Hilton Garden Inn Fort Worth/Medical Center | ▽▽▽ | $129-$189 | 261 |
| **9** this page | Fairfield Inn & Suites by Marriott Fort Worth University Drive | ▽▽▽ | $120-$170 | 261 |

**DOWNTOWN FORT WORTH (cont'd)**

| Map Page | Hotels (cont'd) | Diamond Rated | Rate Range | Page |
|---|---|---|---|---|
| ⓫ p. 255 | Residence Inn by Marriott University | ▽▽ | $147-$169 | 262 |
| ⓬ p. 255 | Courtyard by Marriott Fort Worth University | ▽▽▽ | $137-$207 | 260 |

| Map Page | Restaurants | Diamond Rated | Cuisine | Price Range | Page |
|---|---|---|---|---|---|
| ① p. 255 | Angelo's Bar-B-Que | ▽ | Barbecue | $5-$13 | 262 |
| ② p. 255 | Cowtown Diner | ▽▽ | Comfort Food | $9-$29 | 262 |
| ③ p. 255 | Cabo Grande | ▽▽ | Tex-Mex | $8-$20 | 262 |
| ④ p. 255 | Mi Cocina Sundance Square | ▽▽ | Tex-Mex | $8-$22 | 263 |
| ⑤ p. 255 | **Cantina Laredo** | ▽▽ | Mexican | $10-$26 | 262 |
| ⑥ p. 255 | Del Frisco's Double Eagle Steak House | ▽▽▽ | Steak | $32-$89 | 262 |
| ⑦ p. 255 | Saint-Emilion | ▽▽▽ | French | $26-$39 | 263 |
| ⑧ p. 255 | The Buffet Restaurant at the Kimbell | ▽ | American | $10-$12 | 262 |
| ⑨ p. 255 | Dos Gringos Tex-Mex Cantina | ▽▽ | Tex-Mex | $9-$14 | 262 |
| ⑩ p. 255 | Flying Fish | ▽ | Seafood | $6-$16 | 263 |
| ⑪ p. 255 | Lili's bistro on Magnolia | ▽▽ | Comfort Food | $10-$32 | 263 |
| ⑫ p. 255 | Ellerbe Fine Foods | ▽▽▽ | Southern American | $10-$29 | 262 |
| ⑬ p. 255 | Blue Mesa Grill | ▽▽ | Southwestern | $10-$17 | 262 |
| ⑭ p. 255 | **Silver Fox** | ▽▽▽ | Steak | $14-$45 | 263 |

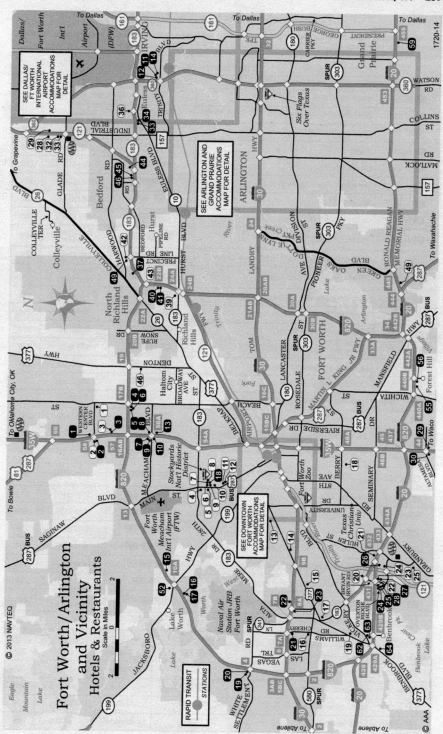

Fort Worth/Arlington and Vicinity
Hotels & Restaurants

# Fort Worth/Arlington and Vicinity

This index helps you "spot" where approved hotels and restaurants are located on the corresponding detailed maps. Hotel daily rate range is for comparison only. Restaurant price range is a combination of lunch and/or dinner. Turn to the listing page for more detailed rate and price information and consult display ads for special promotions.

## FORT WORTH

| Map Page | Hotels | Diamond Rated | Rate Range | Page |
|---|---|---|---|---|
| **1** p. 257 | **BEST WESTERN Inn** | ◈◈ | $90-$160 [SAVE] | 263 |
| **2** p. 257 | Comfort Inn-Western Center | ◈◈◈ | $90-$180 | 264 |
| **3** p. 257 | Residence Inn by Marriott-Fossil Creek | ◈◈◈ | $109-$189 | 265 |
| **4** p. 257 | **Super 8** | ◈◈ | $59-$129 [SAVE] | 266 |
| **5** p. 257 | Candlewood Suites | ◈◈ | $89-$99 | 263 |
| **6** p. 257 | Homewood Suites by Hilton | ◈◈◈ | $96-$189 | 265 |
| **7** p. 257 | **Super 8** | ◈◈ | $59-$139 [SAVE] | 266 |
| **8** p. 257 | La Quinta Inn & Suites Fort Worth North | ◈◈ | $99-$140 | 265 |
| **9** p. 257 | Holiday Inn North Fossil Creek | ◈◈◈ | Rates not provided | 264 |
| **10** p. 257 | Radisson Hotel Fort Worth North Fossil Creek | ◈◈◈ | $89-$169 | 265 |
| **11** p. 257 | Holiday Inn DFW Airport South | ◈◈◈ | Rates not provided | 264 |
| **12** p. 257 | **Candlewood Suites DFW Airport South** | ◈◈◈ | $79-$139 [SAVE] | 263 |
| **13** p. 257 | Hilton Garden Inn Fort Worth North | ◈◈◈ | $99-$189 | 264 |
| **14** p. 257 | DFW Airport Marriott South | ◈◈◈ | $79-$299 | 264 |
| **15** p. 257 | Holiday Inn Express Hotel & Suites | ◈◈◈ | $99-$125 | 264 |
| **16** p. 257 | La Quinta Inn & Suites Lake Worth | ◈◈◈ | $94-$129 | 265 |
| **17** p. 257 | Comfort Suites Lake Worth | ◈◈◈ | $85-$199 | 264 |
| **18** p. 257 | **Hyatt Place Fort Worth/Historic Stockyards** | ◈◈◈ | $99-$279 [SAVE] | 265 |
| **19** p. 257 | Staybridge Suites West Fort Worth | ◈◈◈ | $92-$179 | 265 |
| **20** p. 257 | **BEST WESTERN Fort Worth Inn & Suites** | ◈◈ | $80-$200 [SAVE] | 263 |
| **21** p. 257 | Holiday Inn Express Hotel & Suites-Fort Worth West | ◈◈◈ | Rates not provided | 264 |
| **22** p. 257 | Courtyard by Marriott Fort Worth I-30 West Near NAS JRB | ◈◈◈ | $125-$138 | 264 |
| **23** p. 257 | Fairfield Inn & Suites by Marriott - Fort Worth I-30 | ◈◈◈ | $109-$169 | 264 |
| **24** p. 257 | Courtyard by Marriott Fort Worth West at Cityview | ◈◈◈ | $99-$179 | 264 |
| **25** p. 257 | Homewood Suites Fort Worth Cityview | ◈◈◈ | $119-$179 | 265 |
| **26** p. 257 | Hampton Inn by Hilton-Southwest | ◈◈◈ | $89-$125 | 264 |
| **27** p. 257 | **Hyatt Place Ft. Worth/Cityview** | ◈◈◈ | $64-$219 [SAVE] | 265 |
| **28** p. 257 | La Quinta Inn & Suites Fort Worth Southwest | ◈◈ | $95-$150 | 265 |
| **29** p. 257 | **BEST WESTERN Fort Worth South Hotel** | ◈◈◈ | Rates not provided [SAVE] | 263 |
| **30** p. 257 | **Super 8 Fort Worth/Downtown Area** | ◈◈ | $65-$95 [SAVE] | 266 |

| Map Page | Restaurants | Diamond Rated | Cuisine | Price Range | Page |
|---|---|---|---|---|---|
| 1 p. 257 | Los Molcajetes | ◈◈ | Mexican | $8-$13 | 267 |
| 2 p. 257 | Rosa's Cafe Tortilla Factory | ◈ | Tex-Mex | $3-$10 | 268 |
| 3 p. 257 | Saltgrass Steakhouse | ◈◈ | Steak | $9-$30 [SAVE] | 268 |
| 4 p. 257 | Los Vaqueros | ◈◈ | Tex-Mex | $8-$15 | 267 |
| 5 p. 257 | The Star Cafe | ◈ | American | $7-$25 | 268 |

| Map Page | Restaurants (cont'd) | Diamond Rated | Cuisine | Price Range | Page |
|---|---|---|---|---|---|
| ⑥ p. 257 | Love Shack | ▼ | Burgers | $3-$8 | 267 |
| ⑦ p. 257 | Riscky's Barbeque | ▼ | Barbecue | $11-$16 | 268 |
| ⑧ p. 257 | Riscky's Steakhouse | ▼▼ | Steak | $9-$32 | 268 |
| ⑨ p. 257 | Lonesome Dove Western Bistro | ▼▼▼ | Western American | $9-$41 | 267 |
| ⑩ p. 257 | Joe T Garcia's | ▼▼ | Tex-Mex | $7-$14 | 267 |
| ⑪ p. 257 | Byblos Lebanese Restaurant | ▼▼ | Lebanese | $9-$25 | 266 |
| ⑫ p. 257 | El Rancho Grande | ▼▼ | Tex-Mex | $6-$13 | 266 |
| ⑬ p. 257 | Piola Italian Restaurant and Garden | ▼▼▼ | Italian | $7-$21 | 268 |
| ⑭ p. 257 | Kincaid's | ▼ | American | $4-$8 | 267 |
| ⑮ p. 257 | Hedary's Mediterranean Restaurant | ▼▼ | Mediterranean | $7-$32 | 267 |
| ⑯ p. 257 | West Side Cafe | ▼ | American | $6-$9 | 268 |
| ⑰ p. 257 | Edelweiss | ▼▼ | Traditional German | $9-$33 | 266 |
| ⑱ p. 257 | Fiesta Mexican Restaurant | ▼▼ | Tex-Mex | $5-$12 | 266 |
| ⑲ p. 257 | Pulido's Mexican Restaurant #2 | ▼▼ | Tex-Mex | $7-$16 | 268 |
| ⑳ p. 257 | Bonnell's Restaurant | ▼▼▼ | Wild Game | $11-$50 | 266 |
| ㉑ p. 257 | Chef Chen Restaurant Buffet & Bar | ▼▼ | Chinese | $7-$14 | 266 |
| ㉒ p. 257 | Rio Mambo | ▼▼ | Tex-Mex | $7-$18 | 268 |
| ㉓ p. 257 | Saltgrass Steakhouse | ▼▼ | Steak | $9-$30 [SAVE] | 268 |
| ㉔ p. 257 | Rosa's Cafe Tortilla Factory | ▼ | Tex-Mex | $6-$10 | 268 |
| ㉕ p. 257 | Maharaja Indian Restaurant & Bar | ▼▼ | Indian | $10-$15 | 267 |

**EULESS**

| Map Page | Hotels | Diamond Rated | Rate Range | Page |
|---|---|---|---|---|
| ㉝ p. 257 | Plaza Suites DFW Airport West | ▼▼▼ | $109-$129 | 245 |
| ㉞ p. 257 | La Quinta Inn & Suites DFW Airport West - Euless | ▼▼▼ | $95-$134 [SAVE] | 245 |

| Map Page | Restaurant | Diamond Rated | Cuisine | Price Range | Page |
|---|---|---|---|---|---|
| ㊱ p. 257 | North Main BBQ | ▼ | Barbecue | $8-$15 | 245 |

**NORTH RICHLAND HILLS**

| Map Page | Hotel | Diamond Rated | Rate Range | Page |
|---|---|---|---|---|
| ㊲ p. 257 | BEST WESTERN N.E. Mall Inn & Suites | ▼▼ | $80-$100 [SAVE] | 427 |

**RICHLAND HILLS**

| Map Page | Hotels | Diamond Rated | Rate Range | Page |
|---|---|---|---|---|
| ㊵ p. 257 | La Quinta Inn & Suites Fort Worth NE Mall | ▼▼▼ | $95-$130 | 448 |
| ㊶ p. 257 | Comfort Suites Near Northeast Mall | ▼▼▼ | $95-$125 | 448 |

| Map Page | Restaurant | Diamond Rated | Cuisine | Price Range | Page |
|---|---|---|---|---|---|
| ㊴ p. 257 | El Chico | ▼▼ | Tex-Mex | $7-$16 | 448 |

**BEDFORD**

| Map Page | Hotels | Diamond Rated | Rate Range | Page |
|---|---|---|---|---|
| ㊹ p. 257 | La Quinta Inn & Suites DFW Airport West-Bedford | ▼▼▼ | $84-$124 | 119 |
| ㊺ p. 257 | Homewood Suites by Hilton | ▼▼▼ | $99-$129 | 119 |
| ㊻ p. 257 | Courtyard by Marriott | ▼▼▼ | $79-$175 | 119 |

## HURST

| Map Page | Hotel | Diamond Rated | Rate Range | Page |
|---|---|---|---|---|
| 49 p. 257 | Hyatt Place Ft. Worth/Hurst | ◈◈◈ | $69-$209 SAVE | 371 |

| Map Page | Restaurants | Diamond Rated | Cuisine | Price Range | Page |
|---|---|---|---|---|---|
| 42 p. 257 | Italiannis | ◈◈ | Italian | $7-$26 | 371 |
| 43 p. 257 | Sweet Basil Thai Cuisine | ◈◈ | Thai | $7-$14 | 371 |

## LAKE WORTH

| Map Page | Hotel | Diamond Rated | Rate Range | Page |
|---|---|---|---|---|
| 52 p. 257 | BEST WESTERN PLUS Lake Worth Inn & Suites | ◈◈ | $79-$99 SAVE | 392 |

## FOREST HILL

| Map Page | Hotels | Diamond Rated | Rate Range | Page |
|---|---|---|---|---|
| 55 p. 257 | Comfort Inn | ◈◈ | $60-$70 SAVE | 246 |
| 56 p. 257 | La Quinta Inn & Suites | ◈◈◈ | $99-$143 | 246 |

## GRAND PRAIRIE

| Map Page | Hotel | Diamond Rated | Rate Range | Page |
|---|---|---|---|---|
| 59 p. 257 | La Quinta Inn & Suites South Grand Prairie | ◈◈◈ | $109-$154 | 288 |

## BENBROOK

| Map Page | Hotels | Diamond Rated | Rate Range | Page |
|---|---|---|---|---|
| 62 p. 257 | BEST WESTERN Winscott Inn & Suites | ◈◈ | $90-$149 SAVE | 120 |
| 63 p. 257 | Comfort Suites | ◈◈◈ | $110-$190 SAVE | 120 |
| 64 p. 257 | Motel 6 - #4051 | ◈ | $67-$74 | 120 |

## GRAPEVINE

| Map Page | Restaurants | Diamond Rated | Cuisine | Price Range | Page |
|---|---|---|---|---|---|
| 28 p. 257 | Cantina Laredo | ◈◈ | Mexican | $10-$26 | 291 |
| 29 p. 257 | Boi Na Braza | ◈◈ | Brazilian | $20-$48 | 290 |

## COLLEYVILLE

| Map Page | Restaurants | Diamond Rated | Cuisine | Price Range | Page |
|---|---|---|---|---|---|
| 32 p. 257 | La Hacienda Ranch | ◈◈ | Tex-Mex | $11-$29 | 144 |
| 33 p. 257 | Mac's Steaks & Seafood | ◈◈ | Steak | $10-$31 | 144 |

## HALTOM CITY

| Map Page | Restaurant | Diamond Rated | Cuisine | Price Range | Page |
|---|---|---|---|---|---|
| 46 p. 257 | Hoffbrau Steaks | ◈◈ | Steak | $8-$25 | 295 |

## ARLINGTON

| Map Page | Restaurant | Diamond Rated | Cuisine | Price Range | Page |
|---|---|---|---|---|---|
| 49 p. 257 | Corky's Brick Oven Pizzeria | ◈ | Pizza | $5-$12 | 73 |

# DOWNTOWN FORT WORTH

• Restaurants p. 262
• Hotels & Restaurants map & index p. 255

THE ASHTON HOTEL                817/332-0100  **3**
◈◈◈ **Boutique Hotel.** Rates not provided. **Address:** 610
Main St 76102 **Location:** Jct 6th and Main sts; center. **Facility:** As
part of the Small Luxury Hotels of the World, this boutique hotel presents intimate hospitality in a nurturing environment, featuring custom
mahogany furniture and large baths with pedestal sinks. 39 units. 6
stories, interior corridors. **Parking:** valet only. **Amenities:** safes. **Activities:** exercise room. **Guest Services:** valet laundry.

COURTYARD BY MARRIOTT FORT WORTH UNIVERSITY
                                (817)335-1300  **12**
◈◈◈ **Hotel** $137-$207 **Address:**          **AAA Benefit:**
3150 Riverfront Dr 76107 **Location:** I-30     Members save 5%
exit 12 (University Dr), 0.5 mi s. **Facility:**    or more!
130 units. 2 stories (no elevator), interior
corridors. **Pool(s):** outdoor. **Activities:**
hot tub, exercise room. **Guest Services:** valet and coin laundry.

(See map & index p. 255.)

EMBASSY SUITES FORT WORTH DOWNTOWN
(817)332-6900 **2**

▼▼▼▼ Hotel $169-$249 **Address:**
600 Commerce St 76102 **Location:**
Southwest corner of Commerce and 5th
sts. **Facility:** 156 units. 13 stories, interior corridors. **Parking:** valet only.
**Terms:** 1-7 night minimum stay, cancellation fee imposed. **Amenities:** video games. **Pool(s):** heated indoor. **Activities:** hot tub, exercise room. **Guest Services:** valet and coin laundry.

**AAA Benefit:**
Members save 5%
or more!

FAIRFIELD INN & SUITES BY MARRIOTT FORT WORTH
UNIVERSITY DRIVE
(817)335-2000 **9**

▼▼▼▼ Hotel $120-$170 **Address:**
1505 S University Dr 76107 **Location:**
I-30 exit 12 (University Dr), just s. **Facility:** 79 units. 4 stories, interior corridors. **Activities:**
hot tub, exercise room. **Guest Services:** valet and coin laundry.

**AAA Benefit:**
Members save 5%
or more!

HILTON GARDEN INN FORT WORTH/MEDICAL CENTER
(817)921-0788 **8**

▼▼▼▼ Hotel $129-$189 **Address:**
912 Northton St 76104 **Location:** I-30
exit 12B (Forest Park Blvd), just s. **Facility:** 157 units. 4 stories, interior corridors. **Terms:** 1-7 night minimum stay,
cancellation fee imposed. **Pool(s):** indoor. **Activities:** hot tub, exercise room. **Guest Services:** valet and coin laundry, area
transportation.

**AAA Benefit:**
Members save up to
10%!

Contact us about AAA/CAA
Approved properties at
AAA.com/TourBookComments

HISTORIC HILTON FORT WORTH
(817)870-2100 **4**

▼▼▼▼ Historic Hotel $149-$229
**Address:** 815 Main St 76102 **Location:**
Northeast corner of Main and 8th sts;
center. **Facility:** This hotel, a 1921 historic landmark, stands in the heart of the
city and opposite the convention center. Leisure guests will appreciate its proximity to Sundance Square and its nightlife activities. 294
units. 15 stories, interior corridors. **Parking:** valet only. **Terms:** 1-7
night minimum stay, cancellation fee imposed. **Dining:** 2 restaurants.
**Activities:** exercise room. **Guest Services:** valet laundry.

**AAA Benefit:**
Members save 5%
or more!

HOLIDAY INN EXPRESS HOTEL & SUITES FORT
WORTH DOWNTOWN
(817)698-9595 **7**

▼▼▼▼
Hotel
$99-$229

**Address:** 1111 W Lancaster Ave
76102 **Location:** I-30 exit 13B (Henderson St), just n. **Facility:** 132 units.
6 stories, interior corridors. **Pool(s):**
heated indoor. **Activities:** hot tub, exercise room. **Guest Services:** valet
and coin laundry, area transportation.
*(See ad this page.)*

OMNI HOTEL
(817)535-6664 **6**

▼▼▼▼ ▼▼▼ Hotel $169-$349 **Address:** 1300 Houston St 76102
**Location:** Between 12th and 14th sts. **Facility:** Behind the striking
glass facade of this hotel are rooms and public areas that celebrate
Fort Worth's history of being a cowtown, with purely sophisticated,
modern appointments. 614 units. 15 stories, interior corridors.
**Parking:** on-site (fee) and valet. **Terms:** cancellation fee imposed.
**Amenities:** safes. **Dining:** 4 restaurants. **Pool(s):** heated outdoor.
**Activities:** hot tub, exercise room, spa. **Guest Services:** valet
laundry, area transportation.

▼ See AAA listing this page ▼

(See map & index p. 255.)

## RESIDENCE INN BY MARRIOTT FORT WORTH CULTURAL DISTRICT
(817)885-8250 **5**

WWW **Extended Stay Hotel**
$132-$229 **Address:** 2500 Museum Way 76107 **Location:** I-30 exit 13B (Henderson St), 0.4 mi n to 7th St, 0.8 mi w to Stayton St, then just s. **Facility:** 149 efficiencies. 4 stories, interior corridors. **Pool(s):** heated outdoor. **Activities:** hot tub, exercise room. **Guest Services:** valet and coin laundry, area transportation.

**AAA Benefit:**
Members save 5% or more!

[icons]
/ SOME UNITS

## RESIDENCE INN BY MARRIOTT UNIVERSITY
(817)870-1011 **11**

WWW **Extended Stay Hotel**
$147-$169 **Address:** 1701 S University Dr 76107 **Location:** I-30 exit 12 (University Dr), 0.4 mi s. **Facility:** 120 kitchen units. 2 stories (no elevator), exterior corridors. **Pool(s):** outdoor. **Activities:** exercise room. **Guest Services:** valet and coin laundry.

**AAA Benefit:**
Members save 5% or more!

[icons] / SOME UNITS

## THE WORTHINGTON RENAISSANCE FORT WORTH HOTEL
(817)870-1000 **1**

WWWW **Hotel** $129-$285 **Address:** 200 Main St 76102 **Location:** Northwest corner of 2nd and Main sts. **Facility:** 504 units. 12 stories, interior corridors. **Parking:** on-site (fee) and valet. **Amenities:** safes. **Pool(s):** heated indoor. **Activities:** hot tub, tennis, exercise room, massage. **Guest Services:** valet laundry, boarding pass kiosk.

**AAA Benefit:**
Members save 5% or more!

[icons]
/ SOME UNITS

## WHERE TO EAT

## ANGELO'S BAR-B-QUE
817/332-0357 **1**

W Barbecue. Casual Dining. $5-$13 **AAA Inspector Notes:** In a commercial area, the restaurant attracts a diverse crowd, from bikers to businessmen. For lunch, have a fully loaded deli sandwich with salami, ham, turkey and homemade sauce. The barbecue beef and ribs are luscious. The simple dining room is decorated with wild game and hunting trophies. Although Angelo's has no ambience, it has a lot of history and is a regular hangout for a lot of locals. **Features:** beer & wine. **Address:** 2533 White Settlement Rd 76107 **Location:** 0.6 mi w of jct Henderson St and White Settlement Rd; just s of Trinity River Bridge. [L] [D]

## BLUE MESA GRILL
817/332-6372 **13**

WW Southwestern. Casual Dining. $10-$17 **AAA Inspector Notes:** Decorated in a rustic Southwestern motif, this café serves spicy entrées with a New Mexican flair. Guests can crunch on blue corn and sweet potato chips in the airy dining room before diving into a sampler plate such as one with an original tamale pie and mesquite-grilled skewers of meat. For dessert, try the dark chocolate empanadas served with a tart sangria sauce. Look out for their seasonal specials where they make ingredients like New Mexican Hatch chile and peaches really shine. **Features:** full bar, patio dining, Sunday brunch. **Address:** 1600 S University Dr 76107 **Location:** I-30 exit 12 (University Dr), just s; in University Park Strip Mall. [L] [D]

## THE BUFFET RESTAURANT AT THE KIMBELL
817/332-8451 **8**

W American. Casual Dining. $10-$12 **AAA Inspector Notes:** Don't let the word buffet scare you, the food here is as inviting as the art. Soup, salad, sandwiches and quiche are the highlights of this restaurant. You pick a plate, fill it as much as you can and pay one price. It also makes a great respite if you're taking in any of the surrounding museums, as admission to the Kimbell is not required. **Features:** beer & wine. **Address:** 3333 Camp Bowie Blvd 76107 **Location:** I-30 exit 11 (Montgomery St), 1 mi n to W Lancaster Ave, just e to Arch Adams St, then just n. [L]

## CABO GRANDE
817/348-8226 **3**

WW WW Tex-Mex. Casual Dining. $8-$20 **AAA Inspector Notes:** The cuisine focuses on seafood and Tex-Mex but also features such items as the caldo gallego soup from Spain and the Barcelona osso buco. Lighter fare includes a variety of salads such as the apple harvest salad with feta cheese and candied walnuts or the Dr. Wasserman steak salad with grilled vegetables and a ginger-lime dressing. The bar fills up with office dwellers and the dining rooms have TVs to watch a game. **Features:** full bar, patio dining, Sunday brunch. **Address:** 115 W 2nd St 76102 **Location:** Between Main and Houston sts; center. **Parking:** street only. [L] [D]

## COWTOWN DINER
817/332-9555 **2**

WW WW Comfort Food. Casual Dining. $9-$29 **AAA Inspector Notes:** Studded leather booths, lime-green upholstered chairs, rich woods and cowhide lampshades adorn what may be the fanciest diner you'll ever visit. Lucky for us they fancied up the menu, too, but didn't stray far from the comfort food one frequents a diner for. Frito pie, fried catfish and, get this, smoked chicken mac 'n cheese are served along with a full bar menu and wine list. Lest you think you can't eat healthy, they also feature a vegetarian dish, salads and grilled salmon. **Features:** full bar, patio dining. **Address:** 305 Main St 76102 **Location:** Between 2nd and 3rd sts. **Parking:** valet and street only. [B] [L] [D]

## DEL FRISCO'S DOUBLE EAGLE STEAK HOUSE
817/877-3999 **6**

WW WW Steak. Fine Dining. $32-$89 **AAA Inspector Notes:** The steaks are big, juicy and very tasty. If you aren't in the mood for beef, they also have a very good selection of seafood. This local favorite is strategically located near popular Sundance Square, which has a lot to offer in after-dinner entertainment. **Features:** full bar. **Reservations:** suggested. **Address:** 812 Main St 76102 **Location:** Northwest corner of 8th and Main sts; center. **Parking:** valet only. [D]

## DOS GRINGOS TEX-MEX CANTINA
817/338-9393 **9**

WW WW Tex-Mex. Casual Dining. $9-$14 **AAA Inspector Notes:** This family-owned and -operated Tex-Mex restaurant is in the Cultural District and has been in business for 35 years. They offer all the favorite dishes, including fajitas, enchiladas, tacos, quesadillas and chiles rellenos. Wednesday is fajita-frenzy time and features karaoke. **Features:** full bar, patio dining, happy hour. **Address:** 1015 University Dr 76107 **Location:** Just s of jct University Dr and 7th St/Camp Bowie. [L] [D]

## ELLERBE FINE FOODS
817/926-3663 **12**

WWW Southern American. Fine Dining. $10-$29 **AAA Inspector Notes:** A converted filling station turned genteel dining room, this eatery serves market-fresh food, which means the menu changes frequently. New Orleans barbecue shrimp, curried lamb chops, sautéed wild Alaskan halibut and wild boar are just a few of the examples of menu items you may find at this eatery, but because the chef takes great pride in her farm-to-table concept vegetarians will always find interesting items too, including a vegetable tartine. Mamas bread pudding is a standout. **Features:** beer & wine, patio dining. **Reservations:** suggested. **Address:** 1501 W Magnolia Ave 76104 **Location:** I-30 exit 13 (Summit Ave/8th Ave), 0.8 mi s, then just e. **Parking:** valet only. [L] [D]

(See map & index p. 255.)

### FLYING FISH
817/989-2277  (10)

Seafood. Quick Serve. $6-$16 AAA Inspector Notes: Locals come here for the fried seafood platters and Cajun-inspired selections. Grilled fish, po' boys and fish tacos are just a few of the other items that can be enjoyed. Vintage rock 'n' roll plays overhead, and the small parking lot fills up quickly. Quick tip: Everything comes out fairly quickly so if you don't want things to get cold, consider ordering them separately. **Features:** beer & wine, patio dining. **Address:** 2913 Montgomery St 76107 **Location:** I-30 exit 11 (Montgomery St), just s. L D

### HOFFBRAU STEAKHOUSE
817/870-1952

Steak. Casual Dining. $8-$24 AAA Inspector Notes: This restaurant's fare reflects the old chophouse tradition in which butchers set aside the best cuts of meat for local eateries. In addition to top cuts of steak and prime rib, the menu lists fish, shrimp and ribs. An area institution for 30 years, this place is known for its Hoffbrau chip appetizer and has a classic roadhouse feel. This location is convenient to Texas Christian University and the cultural district. **Features:** full bar, happy hour. **Address:** 1712 S University Dr 76107 **Location:** I-30 exit 12 (University Dr), 0.4 mi s. L D

### LILI'S BISTRO ON MAGNOLIA
817/877-0700  (11)

Comfort Food. Casual Dining. $10-$32 AAA Inspector Notes: This local favorite offers a relaxed setting in which to enjoy items such as Gorgonzola fries, chicken and étouffée, green chile enchiladas or a poblano burger. Portions are generous and vegetarian items also are an option. **Features:** beer & wine, patio dining. **Address:** 1310 W Magnolia Ave 76104 **Location:** I-30 exit 12B (Forest Park Blvd), just s to Rosedale St, just e to 8th Ave, just s, then just e. **Parking:** street only. L D

### MEXICAN INN CAFE
817/927-8541

Tex-Mex. Casual Dining. $9-$19 AAA Inspector Notes: Established in the 1930s by notorious gambler Tiffin Hall, the small chain now has four locations in greater Fort Worth. Traditional Tex-Mex cuisine is served in a lively and colorful setting. This place prides itself on its homemade tostados and tortillas. **Features:** beer & wine. **Address:** 1625 8th Ave 76104 **Location:** I-35W exit 49A, 1.5 mi w, then just n. L D

### MI COCINA SUNDANCE SQUARE
817/877-3600  (4)

Tex-Mex. Casual Dining. $8-$22 AAA Inspector Notes: Although it serves plenty of the traditional items found at most Tex-Mex restaurants, this eatery presents them in contemporary surroundings and with a bit of a modern spin. Enjoy brisket tacos, grilled chicken with mole and a selection of eight salsas with which to season your meal. With Sundance Square at its doorstep, this place is ideal for those wanting to take in the shopping and nightlife. **Features:** full bar, patio dining, Sunday brunch. **Address:** 509 Main St 76102 **Location:** Just s of Sundance Square; center. **Parking:** street only. L D

### SAINT-EMILION
817/737-2781  (7)

French. Fine Dining. $26-$39 AAA Inspector Notes: Country French cuisine is served in a delightful country inn atmosphere. Thoughtful touches like vases with fresh flowers at each table add to the graciousness of the experience. Bacon-wrapped shrimp makes a delicious, colorful and flavorful appetizer. **Features:** full bar. **Reservations:** suggested. **Address:** 3617 W 7th St 76107 **Location:** 0.5 mi w of University Dr. D

---

### SILVER FOX
817/332-9060  (14)

Steak
Fine Dining
$14-$45

AAA Inspector Notes: White tablecloth service, coffered ceilings, Americana art, rich woods and Texas-themed private dining rooms characterize this home-grown chain of steakhouses. Prime beef cuts dominate the menu, but there is also lots of seafood and a dinner-for-two special that allows couples to dine a bit more economically. **Features:** full bar, happy hour. **Reservations:** suggested. **Address:** 1651 S University Dr 76107 **Location:** I-30 exit 12 (University Dr), 0.5 mi s. D

**USDA Prime beef, fresh fish, lobster, local favorites**

---

## FORT WORTH (I-2)
- **Restaurants p. 266**
- **Hotels & Restaurants map & index p. 257**

### BEST WESTERN FORT WORTH INN & SUITES
(817)246-8777  (20)

Hotel
$80-$200

**AAA Benefit:** Members save 10% or more with Best Western!

**Address:** 201 W Loop 820 N 76108 **Location:** I-820 exit 4 (White Settlement Rd), just w. **Facility:** 50 units. 2 stories, interior corridors. **Pool(s):** outdoor. **Activities:** hot tub, exercise room. **Guest Services:** coin laundry. **Featured Amenity:** breakfast buffet.

SAVE 📶 🍴 🏊 HS 📶 ✕ 🔌 📠 📺

### BEST WESTERN FORT WORTH SOUTH HOTEL
817/293-3088  (29)

Hotel
Rates not provided

**AAA Benefit:** Members save 10% or more with Best Western!

**Address:** 100 Altamesa Blvd E 76134 **Location:** I-35W exit 44. **Facility:** 247 units. 6 stories, interior corridors. **Pool(s):** heated indoor. **Activities:** hot tub, exercise room. **Guest Services:** valet and coin laundry.

SAVE 🍴 🍴 🍽 🏊 BIZ 📶 ✕ 📺 / SOME UNITS 🐾 🔌 📠

### BEST WESTERN INN
(817)847-8484  (1)

Hotel
$90-$160

**AAA Benefit:** Members save 10% or more with Best Western!

**Address:** 6700 Fossil Bluff Dr 76137 **Location:** I-35W exit 58 (Western Center Blvd), just n on service road, then just e. **Facility:** 63 units. 3 stories, interior corridors. **Terms:** 7 day cancellation notice. **Amenities:** safes. **Pool(s):** outdoor. **Activities:** hot tub, exercise room. **Guest Services:** coin laundry.

SAVE 🍴 CALL 🛎 🏊 📶 🔌 📠 📺 / SOME UNITS HS

### CANDLEWOOD SUITES
(817)838-8229  (5)

Extended Stay Hotel $89-$99 **Address:** 5201 Endicott Ave 76137 **Location:** I-820 exit 17B (Beach St), just s, then w. **Facility:** 98 efficiencies. 3 stories, interior corridors. **Terms:** cancellation fee imposed. **Activities:** exercise room. **Guest Services:** complimentary and valet laundry.

🍴 HS 📶 🔌 📠 📺 / SOME UNITS 🐾

### CANDLEWOOD SUITES DFW AIRPORT SOUTH
(817)868-1900  (12)

Extended Stay Motel
$79-$139

**Address:** 4200 Reggis Ct 76155 **Location:** SR 360 exit Trinity Blvd, just e, then just n. **Facility:** 174 efficiencies. 4 stories, interior corridors. **Activities:** exercise room. **Guest Services:** complimentary and valet laundry, area transportation.

SAVE ✈ 🍴 HS 📶 🔌 📠 📺 / SOME UNITS 🐾

(See map & index p. 257.)

COMFORT INN-WESTERN CENTER (817)386-5666 **2**

▼▼▼ Hotel $90-$180 Address: 6455 Old Denton Rd 76131 Location: I-35 exit 58 (Western Center Blvd), just w. Facility: 70 units. 4 stories, interior corridors. Pool(s): heated indoor. Activities: hot tub, exercise room. Guest Services: valet and coin laundry.

COMFORT SUITES LAKE WORTH (817)237-2300 **17**

▼▼▼ Hotel $85-$199 Address: 5825 Quebec St 76135 Location: I-820 exit 9 (Quebec St), just sw. Facility: 68 units. 4 stories, interior corridors. Pool(s): heated outdoor. Activities: hot tub, exercise room. Guest Services: valet and coin laundry.

COURTYARD BY MARRIOTT FORT WORTH I-30 WEST NEAR NAS JRB (817)737-6923 **22**

▼▼▼ Hotel $125-$138 Address: 6530 West Frwy 76116 Location: I-30 exit 8A (Green Oaks Rd); on westbound access road. Facility: 92 units. 4 stories, interior corridors. Pool(s): outdoor. Activities: hot tub, exercise room. Guest Services: valet and coin laundry.

**AAA Benefit:** Members save 5% or more!

COURTYARD BY MARRIOTT FORT WORTH WEST AT CITYVIEW (817)294-7600 **24**

▼▼▼ Hotel $99-$179 Address: 6400 Overton Ridge Blvd 76132 Location: I-20 exit 431 (Bryant Irvin Rd), just s, then 0.5 mi w. Facility: 104 units. 4 stories, interior corridors. Pool(s): heated indoor. Activities: hot tub, exercise room. Guest Services: complimentary and valet laundry.

**AAA Benefit:** Members save 5% or more!

DALLAS FORT WORTH MARRIOTT HOTEL & GOLF CLUB AT CHAMPIONS CIRCLE (817)961-0800

▼▼▼ Hotel $71-$214 Address: 3300 Championship Pkwy 76177 Location: I-35W exit 70, 1.2 mi w on SR 114 to Championship Pkwy, then 0.4 mi s. Facility: 284 units. 10 stories, interior corridors. Amenities: video games, safes. Pool(s): outdoor. Activities: hot tub, regulation golf, exercise room. Guest Services: valet laundry, area transportation.

**AAA Benefit:** Members save 5% or more!

DFW AIRPORT MARRIOTT SOUTH (817)358-1700 **14**

▼▼▼ Hotel $79-$299 Address: 4151 Centreport Blvd 76155 Location: SR 360 exit Trinity Blvd, 0.3 mi e, then just n. Facility: 295 units. 8 stories, interior corridors. Pool(s): heated indoor. Activities: exercise room. Guest Services: valet and coin laundry, area transportation.

**AAA Benefit:** Members save 5% or more!

FAIRFIELD INN & SUITES BY MARRIOTT - FORT WORTH I-30 (817)731-9600 **23**

▼▼▼ Hotel $109-$169 Address: 6851 West Frwy 76116 Location: I-30 exit 7B, 0.8 mi e to Green Oaks Rd, then just s. Facility: 70 units. 3 stories, interior corridors. Pool(s): heated indoor. Activities: hot tub, exercise room. Guest Services: valet and coin laundry.

**AAA Benefit:** Members save 5% or more!

HAMPTON INN & SUITES-FORT WORTH ALLIANCE AIRPORT (817)439-0400

▼▼▼ Hotel $119-$139 Address: 13600 North Frwy 76177 Location: I-35W exit 66 (Westport Pkwy); on northbound access road. Facility: 102 units, some efficiencies. 5 stories, interior corridors. Terms: 1-7 night minimum stay, cancellation fee imposed. Pool(s): outdoor. Activities: exercise room. Guest Services: valet and coin laundry.

**AAA Benefit:** Members save up to 10%!

HAMPTON INN BY HILTON-SOUTHWEST (817)346-7845 **26**

▼▼▼ Hotel $89-$125 Address: 4799 SW Loop 820 76132 Location: I-20 exit 431 (Bryant Irvin Rd); on eastbound frontage road. Facility: 79 units. 4 stories, interior corridors. Terms: 1-7 night minimum stay, cancellation fee imposed. Pool(s): heated indoor. Activities: hot tub, exercise room. Guest Services: valet laundry.

**AAA Benefit:** Members save up to 10%!

HILTON GARDEN INN FORT WORTH NORTH (817)222-0222 **13**

▼▼▼ Hotel $99-$189 Address: 4400 North Frwy 76137 Location: I-35W exit 56A (Meacham Blvd), just e, then just s. Facility: 98 units. 3 stories, interior corridors. Terms: 1-7 night minimum stay, cancellation fee imposed. Amenities: video games. Pool(s): outdoor, heated indoor. Activities: hot tub, limited exercise equipment. Guest Services: valet and coin laundry.

**AAA Benefit:** Members save up to 10%!

HOLIDAY INN DFW AIRPORT SOUTH 817/399-1800 **11**

▼▼▼ Hotel. Rates not provided. Address: 14320 Centre Station Dr 76155 Location: SR 360 exit Trinity Blvd, just e to Centre Port, then just n. Facility: 143 units. 6 stories, interior corridors. Pool(s): outdoor. Activities: exercise room. Guest Services: valet and coin laundry, area transportation.

HOLIDAY INN EXPRESS HOTEL & SUITES (817)744-7755 **15**

▼▼▼ Hotel $99-$125 Address: 3541 NW Loop 820 76106 Location: I-820 exit 10A eastbound; exit 10B westbound. Facility: 69 units. 4 stories, interior corridors. Terms: cancellation fee imposed. Amenities: video games. Pool(s): outdoor. Activities: hot tub, exercise room. Guest Services: valet and coin laundry.

HOLIDAY INN EXPRESS HOTEL & SUITES-FORT WORTH WEST 817/560-4200 **21**

▼▼▼ Hotel. Rates not provided. Address: 2730 S Cherry Ln 76116 Location: I-30 exit 7A (Cherry Ln), just s. Facility: 60 units. 3 stories, interior corridors. Pool(s): outdoor. Activities: hot tub, exercise room. Guest Services: valet and coin laundry.

HOLIDAY INN NORTH FOSSIL CREEK 817/624-0002 **9**

▼▼▼ Hotel. Rates not provided. Address: 4635 Gemini Pl 76106 Location: I-35W exit 56A (Meacham Blvd), just w. Facility: 126 units. 5 stories, interior corridors. Amenities: safes. Pool(s): heated indoor. Activities: hot tub, exercise room. Guest Services: area transportation.

(See map & index p. 257.)

## HOMEWOOD SUITES BY HILTON

(817)834-7400 **6**

Extended Stay Hotel
$96-$189 **Address:** 3701 Tanacross Dr
76137 **Location:** I-820 exit 17B (Beach
St), just s, then just w. **Facility:** 137 efficiencies. 7 stories, interior corridors.
**Terms:** 1-7 night minimum stay, cancellation fee imposed. **Pool(s):**
outdoor. **Activities:** exercise room. **Guest Services:** complimentary
and valet laundry.

**AAA Benefit:** Members save up to 10%!

## HOMEWOOD SUITES FORT WORTH CITYVIEW

(817)585-1578 **25**

Hotel $119-$179 **Address:**
6350 Overton Ridge Blvd 76132 **Location:** I-20 exit 431 (Bryant Irvin Rd), just
s, then 0.5 mi w. **Facility:** 98 units. 4 stories, interior corridors. **Terms:** 1-7 night
minimum stay, cancellation fee imposed. **Pool(s):** heated indoor. **Activities:** hot tub. **Guest Services:** area transportation.

**AAA Benefit:** Members save up to 10%!

## HYATT PLACE FT. WORTH/CITYVIEW

(817)361-9797 **27**

Hotel $64-$219

**HYATT PLACE**
**AAA Benefit:** Members save 10%!

**Address:** 5900 Cityview Blvd 76132 **Location:** I-20 exit 431 (Bryant Irvin Rd),
just e on frontage road, then just s. **Facility:** 127 units. 6 stories, interior corridors. **Terms:** cancellation fee imposed.
**Amenities:** safes. **Pool(s):** heated outdoor. **Activities:** exercise room. **Guest
Services:** valet laundry. **Featured Amenity:** breakfast buffet.

## HYATT PLACE FORT WORTH/HISTORIC STOCKYARDS

(817)626-6000 **18**

Hotel $99-$279

**HYATT PLACE**
**AAA Benefit:** Members save 10%!

**Address:** 132 E Exchange Ave 76164
**Location:** In Historic Fort Worth Stockyards. **Facility:** 101 units. 5 stories, interior corridors. **Terms:** cancellation fee
imposed. **Amenities:** video games.
**Pool(s):** heated outdoor. **Activities:** exercise room. **Guest Services:** valet
laundry, area transportation. **Featured
Amenity:** breakfast buffet.

## LA QUINTA INN & SUITES FORT WORTH NORTH

(817)222-2888 **8**

Hotel $99-$140 **Address:** 4700 North Frwy 76137 **Location:** I-35W exit 56A (Meacham Blvd), just n. **Facility:** 133 units. 4
stories, interior corridors. **Pool(s):** outdoor. **Activities:** hot tub, exercise room. **Guest Services:** valet and coin laundry.

## LA QUINTA INN & SUITES FORT WORTH SOUTHWEST

(817)370-2700 **28**

Hotel $95-$150 **Address:** 4900 Bryant Irvin Rd 76132 **Location:** I-20 exit 431 (Bryant Irvin Rd), just s. **Facility:** 128 units. 4
stories, interior corridors. **Pool(s):** outdoor. **Activities:** hot tub, exercise room. **Guest Services:** valet and coin laundry.

## LA QUINTA INN & SUITES LAKE WORTH

(817)237-9300 **16**

Hotel $94-$129 **Address:** 5800 Quebec St 76135 **Loca-
tion:** I-820 exit 9 (Quebec St), just sw. **Facility:** 71 units. 4 stories, interior corridors. **Pool(s):** outdoor. **Activities:** hot tub, exercise room.
**Guest Services:** valet and coin laundry.

## MICROTEL INN & SUITES BY WYNDHAM FORT WORTH SOUTH

(817)551-7000

Hotel $50-$79

**Address:** 10675 South Frwy 76140 **Location:** I-35W exit 40; on northbound
frontage road. **Facility:** 63 units. 3 stories, interior corridors. **Guest Services:**
coin laundry. **Featured Amenity:** continental breakfast.

## RADISSON HOTEL FORT WORTH NORTH FOSSIL CREEK

(817)625-9911 **10**

Hotel $89-$169 **Address:** 2540 Meacham Blvd 76106
**Location:** I-35W exit 56A (Meacham Blvd), just w. **Facility:** 247 units.
6 stories, interior corridors. **Terms:** cancellation fee imposed.
**Pool(s):** heated indoor. **Activities:** hot tub, exercise room. **Guest
Services:** valet and coin laundry, area transportation.

## RESIDENCE INN BY MARRIOTT FORT WORTH ALLIANCE AIRPORT

(817)750-7000

Extended Stay Hotel
$79-$299 **Address:** 13400 North Frwy
76177 **Location:** I-35W exit 66. **Facility:**
111 units, some efficiencies and
kitchens. 5 stories, interior corridors.
**Pool(s):** outdoor. **Activities:** hot tub, exercise room. **Guest Services:** valet and coin laundry, area transportation.

**AAA Benefit:** Members save 5% or more!

## RESIDENCE INN BY MARRIOTT-FOSSIL CREEK

(817)439-1300 **3**

Extended Stay Hotel
$109-$189 **Address:** 5801 Sandshell Dr
76137 **Location:** I-35W exit 58 (Western
Center Blvd) northbound to Sandshell Dr,
0.7 mi s; exit southbound, first road to
right through strip center, just s to Sandshell Dr, then 0.7 mi s. **Facility:** 114 units, some efficiencies and kitchens. 3 stories, interior corridors. **Pool(s):** outdoor. **Activities:** hot tub, exercise room. **Guest
Services:** valet and coin laundry.

**AAA Benefit:** Members save 5% or more!

## STAYBRIDGE SUITES WEST FORT WORTH

(817)935-6500 **19**

Extended Stay Hotel $92-$179 **Address:** 229 Clifford
Center Dr 76108 **Location:** I-820 N exit 5A (Clifford Center Dr), just
w. **Facility:** 86 efficiencies, some two bedrooms. 3 stories, interior
corridors. **Terms:** cancellation fee imposed. **Pool(s):** heated outdoor.
**Activities:** exercise room. **Guest Services:** complimentary and valet
laundry.

(See map & index p. 257.)

**SUPER 8**       (817)222-0892 **4**

Hotel
$59-$129

**Address:** 5225 N Beach St 76137 **Location:** I-820 exit 17B (Beach St). **Facility:** 70 units. 3 stories, interior corridors. **Pool(s):** outdoor. **Activities:** exercise room. **Guest Services:** coin laundry. **Featured Amenity:** continental breakfast.

**SUPER 8**       (817)222-3220 **7**

Hotel
$59-$139

**Address:** 4665 Gemini Pl 76106 **Location:** I-35W exit 56A (Meacham Rd), just w. **Facility:** 55 units. 3 stories, interior corridors. **Pool(s):** outdoor. **Activities:** exercise room. **Guest Services:** coin laundry. **Featured Amenity:** continental breakfast.

**SUPER 8 FORT WORTH/DOWNTOWN AREA**
      (817)551-6700 **30**

Hotel
$65-$95

**Address:** 6500 South Frwy 76134 **Location:** I-35 exit 44; on southbound frontage road. **Facility:** 60 units. 2 stories (no elevator), interior corridors. **Pool(s):** outdoor. **Activities:** hot tub, exercise room. **Guest Services:** coin laundry. **Featured Amenity:** continental breakfast.

## WHERE TO EAT

**BONNELL'S RESTAURANT**     817/738-5489 **20**

Wild Game. Fine Dining. $11-$50 **AAA Inspector Notes:** Much-revered chef Bonnell offers up a delicious steak, but you also will find such delicacies as buffalo, quail, pork, chicken and some seafood. They strive to use organic, free-range and free-roaming game in all their dishes and their cheeses and other ingredients come from a local vendors. Desserts are all home made, and a very good wine selection is available. Check out the wall in the lounge—it's made from the corks from wine bottles that have been sold by the restaurant. **Features:** full bar. **Reservations:** suggested, weekends. **Address:** 4259 Bryant Irvin Rd 76109 **Location:** I-20 exit 431 (Bryant Irvin Rd), just n.
L D CALL M

**BYBLOS LEBANESE RESTAURANT**   817/625-9667 **11**

Lebanese. Casual Dining. $9-$25 **AAA Inspector Notes:** The authentic Lebanese artwork and musical instruments adorning the walls create a festive atmosphere. Taste buds will be pleasantly surprised by the slowly roasted lamb shank that literally falls off the bone. It's lightly spiced and served with seasonal vegetables. The palate-pleasing, skillet-fried sambouseck bel-lahm appetizer consists of a thinly rolled half moon of dough stuffed with ground sirloin, onions and pine nuts. **Features:** full bar. **Address:** 1406 N Main St 76106 **Location:** Corner of N Main St and Central Ave; 1.5 mi n of downtown. L D

**CHARLESTON'S RESTAURANT**     817/735-8900

American. Casual Dining. $9-$24 **AAA Inspector Notes:** This casual dining spot boasts a friendly, club-like atmosphere. Fine steak and seafood, as well as hardwood-grilled dishes, are at the heart of the menu. The noteworthy baked potato soup is rich with onions and bacon bits. **Features:** full bar. **Reservations:** suggested, weekends. **Address:** 3020 S Hulen St 76109 **Location:** I-20 exit 433, 1.9 mi n. L D

**CHEF CHEN RESTAURANT BUFFET & BAR**
      817/763-8886 **21**

Chinese. Casual Dining. $7-$14 **AAA Inspector Notes:** This south Fort Worth spot offers more than 100 items to choose from. **Features:** full bar. **Address:** 4840 SW Loop 820 76109 **Location:** I-20 exit 433, just w on access road. L D

**EDELWEISS**       817/738-5934 **17**

Traditional German. Casual Dining. $9-$33 **AAA Inspector Notes:** Eat, drink and dance to live music in a friendly, authentic German atmosphere. Traditional German fare includes cheese soup, marinated herring, sauerbraten with red cabbage and potato pancakes, and a luscious German cheesecake. Order carefully as portions are very generous. **Features:** full bar. **Address:** 3801-A Southwest Blvd 76116 **Location:** I-30 exit 7B, 1.3 mi s on SR 183 to Weatherford Traffic Circle. D

**EL RANCHO GRANDE**     817/624-9206 **12**

Tex-Mex. Casual Dining. $6-$13 **AAA Inspector Notes:** Mexican tile floors, ivory walls and ironwork decorate this family-run restaurant that serves up cuisine reminiscent of what mom made—if you grew up in a Mexican home that is. The homemade tortillas are a yummy accompaniment to the chile Colorado or chicken mole. Finish with a sliver of the tart margarita pie, then hop over to the Stockyards for some family entertainment. **Features:** full bar, patio dining, happy hour. **Address:** 1400 N Main St 76164 **Location:** Corner of N Main St and Central Ave; 1.5 mi n of downtown. L D

**FIESTA MEXICAN RESTAURANT**   817/923-6941 **18**

Tex-Mex. Casual Dining. $5-$12 **AAA Inspector Notes:** Terra cotta tile, brightly colored walls and a large mural of the Mexican countryside add to the festive atmosphere. Are the tortillas fresh? Patrons can stand by in the lobby and watch as they crank up the machine and make them. Typical Tex-Mex selections are offered alongside some more authentic Mexican fare. **Features:** full bar, happy hour. **Address:** 3233 Hemphill St 76110 **Location:** I-35W exit 48A, 0.7 mi w, then just s. B L D

**(See map & index p. 257.)**

**GRANDY'S RESTAURANT**

◆ American. Quick Serve. $4-$8 **AAA Inspector Notes:** Fried chicken and country-fried steak are menu standbys at the restaurant, a regional franchise. They also offer a family-style dining menu. The décor is a step up from that of most quick-serve eateries and more resembles that of a conventional restaurant. Some elements of increased service include additional rolls, iced tea refills and tray removal. B L D

*For additional information, visit AAA.com*

**LOCATIONS:**

**Address:** 4301 South Frwy 76115 **Location:** I-35W exit 46A southbound; exit 46B northbound. **Phone:** 817/927-7729

**Address:** 7201 Camp Bowie W 76116 **Location:** Just w of jct US 377 and SR 580. **Phone:** 817/244-5568

**Address:** 1050 N Beach St 76110 **Location:** Just n of jct SR 121. **Phone:** 817/834-3901

**HEDARY'S MEDITERRANEAN RESTAURANT**       817/731-6961  15

◆◆ Mediterranean. Casual Dining. $7-$32 **AAA Inspector Notes:** Serving Middle Eastern fare for nearly 35 years, this family-owned establishment offers a relaxing atmosphere with an open kitchen and Lebanese background music. Lamb, beef and chicken entrées, including the tasty shish kebab, are frequently featured with lemon and served with a warm pita. The restaurant is located on busy street with lots of shopping, dining and entertainment. **Features:** beer & wine, Sunday brunch. **Address:** 3308 Fairfield Ave 76116 **Location:** I-30 exit 9B (Camp Bowie Blvd), 0.3 mi sw, then just e. L D

**JOE T GARCIA'S**       817/429-5166  10

◆◆ Tex-Mex. Casual Dining. $7-$14 **AAA Inspector Notes:** Strolling cantors provide entertainment at this 60-year-old family-owned Mexican restaurant that is highly revered by the locals. The dining room is comfortable, but the patio area is endless, gorgeous and reminiscent of a courtyard in Mexico with fountains, foliage and statues. The dinner menu is limited to two choices—enchiladas or fajitas—so if it's chile rellenos or chimichangas you are looking for you better go for lunch. **Features:** full bar, patio dining, Sunday brunch. **Address:** 2201 N Commerce St 76164 **Location:** Corner of 22nd and Commerce sts. L D

**KINCAID'S**       817/732-2881  14

◆ American. Quick Serve. $4-$8 **AAA Inspector Notes:** This restaurant has been delighting locals for decades with its big, delicious hamburgers. **Features:** beer only. **Address:** 4901 Camp Bowie Blvd 76107 **Location:** I-30 exit 9B (Camp Bowie Blvd), 0.8 mi nw. L D

**LA MADELEINE COUNTRY FRENCH CAFE**       817/654-0471

◆ Traditional French. Casual Dining. $7-$12 **AAA Inspector Notes:** A fireplace creates the focal point at this cozy European style café where you can always get a quiche or savory stuffed puffed pastry on the go or stick around for a chicken crêpe or French dip sandwich. Heartier entrées like rotisserie chicken are offered and every season promises menu surprises. Whatever you decide on you probably will not get out the door without enjoying one of their tempting sweet pastries. **Features:** beer & wine. **Address:** 6140 Camp Bowie Blvd 76116 **Location:** Jct Bryant Irvin Rd and Camp Bowie Blvd. B L D

**LONESOME DOVE WESTERN BISTRO**       817/740-8810  9

◆◆◆ Western American. Fine Dining. $9-$41 **AAA Inspector Notes:** The acclaimed restaurant combines the influences of Texas, Mexico, California and China on its eclectic menu. Owner/Iron Chef Tim Love delves into state history to develop his creative style. Among choices are dishes utilizing chicken, beef, seafood, pheasant, lamb and even buffalo; although the cuisine is top notch, the servers are dressed to fit the theme and guests arrive in jeans and cowboy hats with regularity. **Features:** full bar. **Reservations:** suggested, for dinner. **Address:** 2406 N Main St 76164 **Location:** Just s of jct N Main St and E Exchange Ave; in Historic Fort Worth Stockyards area. **Parking:** valet and street only. L D

**LOS MOLCAJETES**       817/306-9000  1

◆◆ Mexican. Casual Dining. $8-$13 **AAA Inspector Notes:** In the far north reaches of the city, word of mouth has made this one hopping place. Happy hours fill the small eatery quickly; by the dinner hour the lines go out the door, so time your visit wisely. The menu features all the traditional plates but are well seasoned for those that appreciate a little spice in their life. **Features:** full bar, Sunday brunch. **Address:** 4320 Western Center Blvd 76137 **Location:** I-35W exit 58 (Western Center Blvd), 1 mi e. L D

**LOS VAQUEROS**       817/624-1511  4

◆◆ Tex-Mex. Casual Dining. $8-$15 **AAA Inspector Notes:** This longtime favorite serves traditional Tex-Mex in a sprawling converted warehouse. An extensive menu features popular dishes like quesadillas and nachos along with Mexican pepper steak. **Features:** full bar, happy hour. **Address:** 2629 N Main St 76164 **Location:** Just s of jct SR 183 and US 287; just n of Historic Fort Worth Stockyards. L D

**LOVE SHACK**       817/740-8812  6

◆ Burgers. Quick Serve. $3-$8 **AAA Inspector Notes:** Here the love is all about the burger. Named after chef Tim Love, this small outlet churns out burgers, hot dogs and milk shakes. From the upstairs deck of this Stockyards eatery, diners can enjoy great views of historic Exchange Avenue, where cattle and cowboys still roam. Live music can be found on the weekends, but beware inclement weather because outdoor dining is all that's offered. **Features:** beer & wine. **Address:** 110 E Exchange Ave 76164 **Location:** 0.5 mi s of jct US 287 and SR 183 to E Exchange Ave, just e; at Historic Fort Worth Stockyards. **Parking:** street only. L D ✕ ◥

**MAHARAJA INDIAN RESTAURANT & BAR**  817/263-7156  25

◆◆ Indian. Casual Dining. $10-$15 **AAA Inspector Notes:** This quiet northern Indian restaurant in a small shopping center near a mall and theaters is the perfect place for the novice Indian cuisine diner. The food is very mildly spiced, perfect for those who may have apprehensions about trying global cuisines. A lunch buffet and à la carte dinners feature tandoori items plus the always popular curry dishes. **Features:** full bar. **Address:** 6308 Hulen Bend Blvd 76132 **Location:** I-20 exit 433 (Hulen St), 1.4 mi s; in Starplex Cinema Shopping Center. L D

**MERCADO JUAREZ CAFE**       817/838-8285

◆◆ Tex-Mex. Casual Dining. $7-$15 **AAA Inspector Notes:** This eatery serves up its authentic cuisine in a large open area resembling a Mexican market. The brightly painted walls and interior help set the atmosphere. Specialties include sizzling shrimp and veggies, cabrito al pastor (young goat) and ribs al mesquite. Of course you also can get such basic entrées as enchiladas, fajitas, chile rellenos and combination plates with selections of several items. **Features:** full bar, Sunday brunch, happy hour. **Address:** 1651 E Northside Dr 76106 **Location:** I-35W exit 53, just w. L D

**PAPPADEAUX SEAFOOD KITCHEN**       817/877-8843

◆◆ Regional Seafood. Casual Dining. $12-$47 **AAA Inspector Notes:** A seafood lover's delight, the restaurant taps into a little bit of New Orleans with its Cajun dishes and elaborate menu selections. Patrons might start off with a creative choice of blackened oyster and shrimp fondeaux with crayfish and let the feast begin. While music plays in the background, patrons can dig into dirty rice or spicy gumbo loaded with seafood. Well-seasoned shrimp and fish are prepared in varied ways. **Features:** full bar. **Address:** 2708 West Frwy 76102 **Location:** I-30 exit 12B, just s. L D

**PAPPASITO'S CANTINA**       817/877-5546

◆◆ Mexican. Casual Dining. $10-$49 **AAA Inspector Notes:** Fine traditional offerings are served in an upscale cantina atmosphere. Often crowded during peak hours, the immensely popular stop dishes up generous portions of sizzling fajitas, enchiladas and other traditional Mexican favorites, including some shrimp specialties. The terrific margaritas are guaranteed to get attention. Tables in the large dining room are closely spaced. Ice cream with cinnamon on chocolate bread pudding shouldn't be missed. **Features:** full bar, happy hour. **Address:** 2704 West Frwy 76102 **Location:** I-30 exit 12 (Forest Park); on westbound frontage road. L D

(See map & index p. 257.)

### PIOLA ITALIAN RESTAURANT AND GARDEN    817/989-0007   13

▼▼/▼▼ Italian. Fine Dining. $7-$21 **AAA Inspector Notes:** Located in the cultural district, this small cottage holds promise for those seeking a romantic night out or celebrating a special occasion. The dining room is cozy and inviting, the menu replete with savory family recipes like buffalo meatballs, grandma's lasagna, smoked chicken fettuccine and lobster ravioli. **Features:** full bar, patio dining, happy hour. **Reservations:** suggested. **Address:** 3700 Mattison Ave 76107 **Location:** I-30 exit 11 (Montgomery St), 1.3 mi n, then just w.  L  D

### PULIDO'S MEXICAN RESTAURANT #2    817/732-7871   19

▼▼ ▼▼ Tex-Mex. Casual Dining. $7-$16 **AAA Inspector Notes:** This small chain specializes in traditional Tex-Mex favorites such as enchiladas, fajitas, tamales and tacos. The menu also lists a few American dishes. The stuffed jalapeño appetizer, which is served with bean-and-cheese nachos, is just the right degree of spicy. Overlooking a small creek, the tree-covered patio brings guests in touch with the great outdoors. **Features:** full bar, patio dining. **Address:** 5051 Hwy 377 S 76116 **Location:** 1.1 mi s of jct SR 183 and US 377.  L  D

### RIO MAMBO    817/423-3124   22

▼▼ ▼▼ Tex-Mex. Casual Dining. $7-$18 **AAA Inspector Notes:** Located in a shopping strip center, the restaurant prepares classic Tex-Mex favorites like quesadillas, fajitas and enchiladas. The menu also includes garlic shrimp, salmon and New York strip steak. **Features:** full bar, patio dining. **Address:** 6125 SW Loop 820, Suite 110 76132 **Location:** I-20 exit 431 (Bryant Irvin Rd), just sw; in CityView Strip Center.  L  D

### RISCKY'S BARBEQUE    817/626-7777   7

▼ Barbecue. Casual Dining. $11-$16 **AAA Inspector Notes:** This Texas barbecue house in the Stockyards has been in business since 1927. **Features:** full bar, patio dining, happy hour. **Address:** 140 E Exchange Ave, B100 76106 **Location:** 0.5 mi s of jct US 287 and SR 183 on N Main St to E Exchange Ave, then just e. **Parking:** street only.  L  D

### RISCKY'S STEAKHOUSE    817/624-4800   8

▼▼ ▼▼ Steak. Casual Dining. $9-$32 **AAA Inspector Notes:** In the heart of the Stockyards near downtown, the steak house draws hungry crowds. **Features:** full bar, happy hour. **Address:** 120 E Exchange Ave 76164 **Location:** 0.5 mi s of jct US 287 and SR 183 to E Exchange Ave, just e. **Parking:** street only.  L  D

### ROCKFISH SEAFOOD GRILL    817/738-3474

▼▼ ▼▼ Seafood. Casual Dining. $7-$20 **AAA Inspector Notes:** Patrons shuffle through peanut shells on the floor as they make their way to their seats and are easily distracted by the numerous pieces of hunting and fishing memorabilia adorning the walls and ceiling. Although guests kick back in a log cabin-style interior, the freshly caught fish gets more sophisticated preparation than campfire roasting. The chef uses an array of sauces and cooking styles, and soups are hearty and fresh. **Features:** full bar. **Address:** 3050 S Hulen St, Suite A 76109 **Location:** I-30 exit 10 (Hulen St), 1.8 mi s.  L  D

### ROSA'S CAFE TORTILLA FACTORY    817/361-5900   24

▼ Tex-Mex. Quick Serve. $6-$10 **AAA Inspector Notes:** Tex-Mex fare is served à la fast food, but the selection and taste are superior to other quick-serve restaurants. Tortillas are made fresh right in front of diners' eyes. The good food is a good value. The dining room is pleasantly decorated with talavera-topped tables, festive chairs and a salsa bar. Smoking allowed on patio. **Features:** beer only. **Address:** 5000 Overton Ridge Blvd 76132 **Location:** I-20 exit 431 (Bryant Irvine Rd), 0.4 mi s to Overton Ridge Blvd, then 0.7 mi e.  L  D  ◣

### ROSA'S CAFE TORTILLA FACTORY    817/306-8677   2

▼ Tex-Mex. Quick Serve. $3-$10 **AAA Inspector Notes:** This fast-casual restaurant offers traditional Mexican food like burritos and tacos but with more flavor and nutrition than the traditional fast-food place. A salsa bar allows for customization, and the bright décor provides a fun setting for dining in, while a drive-up window accommodates those on the go. **Features:** beer only. **Address:** 6551 Old Denton Rd 76137 **Location:** I-35W exit 58 (Western Center Blvd), just w.  L  D

### SALTGRASS STEAKHOUSE

▼▼ ▼▼ Steak. Casual Dining. $9-$30 **AAA Inspector Notes:** Those looking for something different should try the comfortable steakhouse, which never says no to a special request. Born from the spirit of Texas cattle drives, the restaurant resembles a Texas lodge, with high ceilings and mounted animal heads. Baby back ribs are so tender the meat falls off the bone. Also on the menu are hearty steaks, prime rib, chicken, seafood and yummy desserts. **Bar:** full bar.  SAVE  L  D  ◣

*For additional information, visit AAA.com*

**LOCATIONS:**
**Address:** 4601 City Lake Blvd W 76132 **Location:** I-20 exit 431 (Bryant Irvine Rd), just e. **Phone:** 817/263-5577   23
**Address:** 5845 Sandshell Dr 76137 **Location:** I-35W exit 58 (Western Center Blvd) northbound to Sandshell Dr, 0.4 mi s; exit southbound, take first road to right through strip center, just s to Sandshell Dr, then 0.4 mi s. **Phone:** 817/306-7900   3

### THE STAR CAFE    817/624-8701   5

▼ American. Casual Dining. $7-$25 **AAA Inspector Notes:** This restaurant in the heart of the historic Stockyards serves home cooking in a Western-style setting. The small cafe is packed with character and the food is packed with calories. Options include chicken-fried steak, juicy burgers and prime steak. The staff always recommends the famous pie. **Features:** full bar. **Address:** 111 W Exchange Ave 76106 **Location:** 0.5 mi s of jct US 287 and SR 183 to W Exchange Ave, just w. **Parking:** street only.  L  D

### WEST SIDE CAFE    817/560-1996   16

▼ American. Family Dining. $6-$9 **AAA Inspector Notes:** On the west side of the city near the interstate, the small cafe serves what it calls "good home-cooking." The basic menu lines up chicken, beef, fish, sandwiches and burgers. Many items are fried. This place is a local favorite, so expect a line on weekends. **Address:** 7950 Camp Bowie Blvd W 76116 **Location:** 0.7 mi w of jct SR 183 and Camp Bowie Blvd W.  B  L  D

### ZIO'S ITALIAN KITCHEN    817/232-3632

▼▼ ▼▼ Italian. Casual Dining. $8-$18 **AAA Inspector Notes:** The warm, comfortable atmosphere and Old World decor complement the menu. Meals are a good value, and so is the service. This small chain specializes in Italian cuisine, including oven-baked pizzas and pasta dishes. Guests are encouraged to get creative with their pizzas by mixing and matching from a list of 24 toppings. Particularly tempting dishes are Artichoke spinach pasta, chicken parmigiana, and Shrimp Limone. **Features:** full bar. **Address:** 6631 Fossil Bluff Dr 76137 **Location:** I-35W exit 58 (Western Center Blvd), just e to Sandshell Dr, then just n.  L  D

## FRANKLIN  pop. 1,564

### BEST WESTERN FRANKLIN INN & SUITES    (979)828-9090

▼▼/▼▼
Hotel
$100-$110

**AAA Benefit:** Members save 10% or more with Best Western!

**Address:** 790 W US 79 77856 **Location:** US 79, just w. **Facility:** 42 units. 2 stories, interior corridors. **Pool(s):** outdoor. **Activities:** hot tub. **Guest Services:** coin laundry.
SAVE  HS

## FREDERICKSBURG (F-7) pop. 10,530, elev. 1,742'
• Restaurants p. 271

Approximately 70 miles northwest of San Antonio, Fredericksburg was first settled by German farmers who began arriving in 1846. With one long, wide main street roughly paralleling the town creek, the town borrowed its layout from villages found along the Rhine, the longest river in Germany. Modern-day residents carry on many other old country traditions, much to the delight of day trippers seeking bier, bratwurst and everything in between.

Aside from its wealth of gastronomic indulgences, Fredericksburg is considered by many to be one of the most attractive small towns in Texas and boasts several restored stone houses. Also preserved are 19th-century Sunday Houses-one-room-and-loft structures used by ranchers and farmers when they traveled to town for shopping and church services. The eight-sided Vereins Kirche, a reproduction of the town's first church that shows off an ancient German building style, houses a local history collection at 100 W. Main St.; phone (830) 997-7832.

Agricultural pursuits also endure in Fredericksburg. From mid-May to early August, you can pick your own peaches in the area (you'll find a large cluster of peach farms along US 290 between Fredericksburg and Stonewall). Lavender, typically in bloom May through June, also is grown at a handful of local sites. In addition several vineyards are located in and around Fredericksburg, making the community a key stop on the Texas Hill Country Wine Trail. A wine connoisseur's dream, the tour covers a 15,000-square-mile appellation said to be the second-largest in the United States.

For more natural landscapes, visitors should venture to Lady Bird Johnson Municipal Park, which, in addition to such recreational facilities as an 18-hole golf course and six tennis courts, offers a 1-mile walking trail through riparian woodland, post oak savanna and shortgrass meadows. The park, 4.7 miles southwest off SR 16, is open daily 7 a.m.-10 p.m.; phone (830) 997-4202. Enchanted Rock State Natural Area, 18 miles north on RR 965, centers around a pink granite exfoliation dome that rises 425 feet and 640 acres *(see Recreation Areas Chart)*; phone (830) 685-3636.

Bird-watchers, along with black-capped vireos and golden-checked warblers, flock to both the municipal park and the state natural area. From May to October, millions of free-tailed bats can be spotted at the Old Tunnel Wildlife Management Area, 10619 Old San Antonio Rd. The nocturnal aviators emerge nightly from an abandoned railroad passageway; phone (866) 978-2287.

**Fredericksburg Convention and Visitors Bureau:** 302 E. Austin St., Fredericksburg, TX 78624. **Phone:** (830) 997-6523 or (888) 997-3600.

**Self-guiding tours:** A free brochure describing a walking tour of the historic district is available from the convention and visitors bureau.

**Shopping areas:** More than 150 shops and boutiques call Fredericksburg home, especially along Main Street between Elk and Milam streets. While away the day seeking out one-of-a-kind keepsakes, antiques and crafts—just be sure to hit up Opa's Smoked Meats on S. Washington Street (US 87) before the shop closes (Mon.-Fri. at 5:30, Sat. at 4).

Traditional German recipes make this Hill Country favorite's cured meats, blended sausages, and juicy hams and turkeys hard to resist.

**NATIONAL MUSEUM OF THE PACIFIC WAR** is at 340 E. Main St. The men and women who served in the Pacific, China, Burma, India and on the home front during World War II are honored here. The George H.W. Bush Gallery includes life-size exhibits such as the deck of the USS *Hornet,* an original two-man midget sub from the attack on Pearl Harbor and a replica of Henderson Field, Guadalcanal. The Admiral Nimitz Museum tells the story of Fleet Admiral Chester W. Nimitz through exhibits in his boyhood home, the historic Nimitz Hotel.

Veterans' memorials, a combat veteran P.T. boat, the Japanese Garden of Peace, the Plaza of the Presidents and an outdoor battlefield re-creation including a torpedo bomber displayed on the hangar deck of an aircraft carrier—in addition to numerous allied and Japanese emplacements—also are on the grounds.

**Time:** Allow 2 hours, 30 minutes minimum. **Hours:** Daily 9-5. Closed Thanksgiving, Christmas Eve and Christmas. **Cost:** $14; $12 (ages 65+); $10 (military with ID); $7 (ages 6-18 and college students with ID); free (ages 0-5 and World War II veterans). **Phone:** (830) 997-4379. 🎫

**PIONEER MUSEUM COMPLEX** is at 325 W. Main St. The 1849 stone house with eight furnished rooms and a wine cellar served as a house and store through the 1920s. Other buildings include the Fassel-Roeder house, Walton-Smith log cabin, a one-room schoolhouse, a barn and smokehouse and the Weber Sunday House. Self-guiding walking tour brochures are available. **Hours:** Mon.-Sat. 10-5, Memorial Day-Labor Day; Tues.-Sat. 10-5, rest of year. **Cost:** $5; $3 (ages 6-17). **Phone:** (830) 990-8441.

## WINERIES

- **Fredericksburg Winery** is at 247 W. Main St. **Hours:** Mon.-Sat. 10-5:15 (also Fri.-Sat. 5:30-7:15), Sun. noon-5:15. Closed Jan. 1, July 4, Thanksgiving and Christmas. **Phone:** (830) 990-8747.

**BEST WESTERN PLUS FREDERICKSBURG**

(830)992-2929

Hotel
$90-$180

**AAA Benefit:** Members save 10% or more with Best Western!

**Address:** 314 E Highway St 78624 **Location:** Jct US 87 (Washington St) and US 290, 0.7 mi s to E Highway St, then just e. **Facility:** 56 units, some kitchens. 2 stories, interior corridors. **Terms:** 2 night minimum stay - seasonal. **Pool(s):** outdoor. **Activities:** hot tub. **Guest Services:** valet laundry.

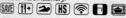

## COMFORT INN & SUITES (830)990-2552

▼▼▼▼ **Hotel** $69-$89 **Address:** 723 S Washington St 78624 **Location:** W on US 290 to US 87 (Washington St), then 0.7 mi s. **Facility:** 57 units, some efficiencies. 3 stories, interior corridors. **Pool(s):** outdoor. **Activities:** hot tub, exercise room. **Guest Services:** coin laundry.

[icons]

## DAS GARTEN HAUS 830/990-8408

▼▼▼▼ **Classic Bed & Breakfast** $135-$200 **Address:** 604 S Washington St 78624 **Location:** Jct US 290, Main and Washington sts, 0.6 mi s. **Facility:** Offering suites and a cottage, as well as a lovely garden, the B&B is just a short stroll from town. 3 units, some two bedrooms and cottages. 1-2 stories (no elevator), interior/exterior corridors. **Terms:** 2 night minimum stay - seasonal and/or weekends, age restrictions may apply, 7 day cancellation notice-fee imposed.

[icons]

## DAYS INN SUITES (830)997-1086

Hotel $60-$240

**Address:** 808 S Adams St 78624 **Location:** 0.6 mi sw of jct US 290 and SR 16. **Facility:** 30 units, some two bedrooms. 2 stories (no elevator), exterior corridors. **Terms:** cancellation fee imposed. **Pool(s):** outdoor. **Guest Services:** coin laundry. **Featured Amenity:** continental breakfast.

[icons] / SOME UNITS

## DIETZEL MOTEL 830/997-3330

Motel $54-$99

**Address:** 1141 W US 290 78624 **Location:** On US 290, 1 mi w; at US 87. **Facility:** 20 units. 1 story, exterior corridors. *Bath:* shower only. **Pool(s):** outdoor.

[icons] / SOME UNITS

## FREDERICKSBURG ECONO LODGE (830)997-3437

Motel $50-$120

**Address:** 810 S Adams St 78624 **Location:** Jct US 290 and SR 16 S, 1 mi s. **Facility:** 36 units. 1 story, exterior corridors. **Pool(s):** outdoor. **Activities:** hot tub. **Featured Amenity:** continental breakfast.

[icons] / SOME UNITS

## FREDERICKSBURG HILL COUNTRY HOTEL & RESORT
830/715-0088

▼▼▼▼ **Hotel.** Rates not provided. **Address:** 1220 N Hwy 87 78624 **Location:** 1 mi w on US 290. **Facility:** 52 units. 2 stories, interior corridors. **Terms:** check-in 4 pm. **Pool(s):** outdoor.

[icons] / SOME UNITS

## FREDERICKSBURG INN & SUITES (830)997-0202

Hotel $79-$229

**Address:** 201 S Washington St 78624 **Location:** US 290 and 87 (Washington St), 3 blks s. **Facility:** 103 units. 2 stories (no elevator), exterior corridors. **Terms:** 2 night minimum stay - seasonal and/or weekends, cancellation fee imposed. **Pool(s):** outdoor. **Activities:** hot tub. **Featured Amenity:** breakfast buffet.

[icons] / SOME

## INN ON BARONS CREEK (830)990-9202

Hotel $119-$239

**Address:** 308 S Washington St 78624 **Location:** Jct Main St and US 87 (Washington St), just s. **Facility:** 90 units, some two bedrooms, efficiencies and cottages. 3 stories, interior/exterior corridors. **Terms:** 2 night minimum stay - weekends, cancellation fee imposed. **Pool(s):** heated outdoor. **Activities:** hot tub, exercise room, spa. **Guest Services:** coin laundry.

[icons]

## LA QUINTA INN & SUITES FREDERICKSBURG (830)990-2899

▼▼▼▼ **Hotel** $119-$204 **Address:** 1465 E Main St 78624 **Location:** 1 mi e of downtown. **Facility:** 55 units. 3 stories, interior corridors. **Pool(s):** outdoor. **Activities:** hot tub, exercise room. **Guest Services:** coin laundry.

[icons] / SOME UNITS

## THE MAGNOLIA HOUSE (830)997-0306

Historic Bed & Breakfast $120-$190

**Address:** 101 E Hackberry St 78624 **Location:** SR 16, 0.6 mi n of jct US 290, just w. **Facility:** This restored 1923 home furnished with antiques includes a stone patio overlooking a tranquil fish pond. 5 units. 2 stories (no elevator), interior corridors. **Parking:** street only. **Terms:** 2 night minimum stay - weekends, 7 day cancellation notice-fee imposed. **Featured Amenity:** full hot breakfast.

[icons] / SOME UNITS

## MAIN STREET HAMPTON INN & SUITES 830/997-9696

▼▼▼▼ **Hotel.** Rates not provided. **Address:** 515 E Main St 78624 **Location:** 5 blks e on US 290. **Facility:** 55 units. 3 stories, interior corridors. **Terms:** check-in 4 pm. **Pool(s):** outdoor. **Activities:** hot tub, exercise room. **Guest Services:** coin laundry.

**AAA Benefit:** Members save up to 10%!

[icons] / SOME UNITS

## QUALITY INN (830)997-9811

▼▼ **Hotel** $68-$176 **Address:** 908 S Adams St 78624 **Location:** 0.8 mi sw on SR 16; 0.8 mi sw of jct US 87 and 290. **Facility:** 46 units. 2 stories (no elevator), exterior corridors. **Pool(s):** outdoor. **Activities:** tennis.

[icons] / SOME UNITS

**SUNDAY HOUSE INN & SUITES** (830)997-4484

▼▼▼ **Hotel** $99-$249 **Address:** 501 E Main St 78624 **Location:** 0.4 mi e on US 290. **Terms:** check-in 4 pm. **Pool(s):** outdoor.

**SUNSET INN MOTEL & SUITES** 830/997-9581

▼▼▼
Motel
$55-$95

**Address:** 900 S Adams St 78624 **Location:** 0.8 mi sw of jct US 290 and SR 16. **Facility:** 24 units, some efficiencies. 1 story, exterior corridors. **Guest Services:** coin laundry.

**COTTON GIN CABINS** 830/990-5734

[fyi] Not evaluated. **Address:** 2805 S Hwy 16 78624 **Location:** Jct US 290, 2.8 mi s. Facilities, services, and décor characterize a mid-scale property.

---

**WHERE TO EAT**

**ALTDORF RESTAURANT AND BIERGARTEN** 830/997-7865

▼▼▼ German. Casual Dining. $7-$18 **AAA Inspector Notes:** German and Tex-Mex fare, as well as sandwiches, are served in a relaxed atmosphere. Patrons can request indoor or outdoor seating. **Features:** beer only, patio dining. **Address:** 301 W Main St 78624 **Location:** On US 290; downtown. **Parking:** street only.

**AUGUST E'S** 830/997-1585

▼▼▼▼
Steak
Seafood
Fine Dining
$9-$59

**AAA Inspector Notes:** Upscale contemporary dining in the downtown district featuring sushi, seafood, steaks, chops and an interesting mixed grill of shrimp, filet mignon and quail. I had a superb meal of lobster tempura, cucumber soup, rack of lamb and crème brûlée during my last visit. **Features:** full bar. **Reservations:** suggested. **Address:** 203 E San Antonio St 78624 **Location:** 1 blk s of Main St; between Lincoln and Llano sts. *Menu on AAA.com*

**COTTON GIN CABERNET GRILL** 830/990-5734

▼▼▼ Cajun. Casual Dining. $20-$37 **AAA Inspector Notes:** A Hill Country flair punctuates the daily specials, which are among offerings that also include seafood and beef choices. The mixed grill of beef tenderloin, quail and pork tenderloin is very interesting. **Features:** full bar, patio dining. **Reservations:** suggested. **Address:** 2805 S Hwy 16 78624 **Location:** Jct US 290, 2.8 mi s; in Cotton Gin Cabins.

**DER LINDENBAUM** 830/997-9126

▼▼ German. Casual Dining. $8-$27 **AAA Inspector Notes:** Lunches and dinners consist of schnitzels, steak, sausages and chicken prepared in a traditional Bavarian manner. Guests also can savor excellent pastries, as well as German beer, wine and gourmet coffee. **Features:** beer & wine. **Address:** 312 E Main St 78624 **Location:** Downtown. **Parking:** street only.

**FRIEDHELM'S BAVARIAN INN** 830/997-6300

▼▼ German. Casual Dining. $8-$38 **AAA Inspector Notes:** A nicely varied menu of lighter-fare soups, salads and sandwiches in addition to full dinners of steak, chops, seafood and fine German fare are awaiting the patrons of this popular restaurant. **Features:** full bar. **Address:** 905 W Main St 78624 **Location:** On west side of town.

**K-BOB'S STEAKHOUSE** 830/307-3125

▼▼ Steak. Casual Dining. $6-$23 **AAA Inspector Notes:** The steakhouse prepares a great variety of plump, juicy fillets. A fireplace opens up into both dining rooms, and antique clocks decorate the walls. Rustic wagon-wheel chandeliers illuminate the room. **Features:** full bar. **Address:** 518 E Main St 78624 **Location:** Just e of downtown.

**MAMACITA'S MEXICAN RESTAURANT** 830/997-9546

▼▼ Mexican. Casual Dining. $5-$18 **AAA Inspector Notes:** The fun and colorful eatery serves such traditional foods as fajitas and rice. Large stained-glass windows cover the walls, and a central fountain fills the room with the relaxing sound of splashing water. **Features:** full bar. **Address:** 506 E Main St 78624 **Location:** US 290, just e of jct US 87.

**NAVAJO GRILL** 830/990-8289

▼▼▼ American. Fine Dining. $18-$33 **AAA Inspector Notes:** Salmon, trout, quail, chicken and steak selections are prepared in an upscale Southwestern style. The dining room sports the appropriate theme. **Features:** beer & wine. **Address:** 803 E Main St 78624 **Location:** 0.5 mi e on US 290.

**THE NEST RESTAURANT** 830/990-8383

▼▼▼ American. Fine Dining. $20-$37 **AAA Inspector Notes:** Upscale entrées of quail, shrimp, rack of lamb, filet mignon, chicken and daily specials are offered. The grilled shrimp appetizer with artichokes, hearts of palm and Asiago cheese was wonderful, as was the rack of lamb with the stone-ground demi-glace. Professional service accents the dining experience. **Features:** full bar. **Reservations:** required. **Address:** 607 S Washington St 78624 **Location:** Jct Main and Washington sts, 0.6 mi s.

**PASTA BELLA** 830/990-9778

▼▼ Italian. Casual Dining. $8-$14 **AAA Inspector Notes:** Make your selection among many different sauces for your favorite pastas at this downtown eatery. I truly enjoyed the seafood ravioli served with a very nice cream dill sauce. **Features:** beer & wine. **Address:** 103 S Llano St 78624 **Location:** Downtown. **Parking:** street only.

**FREER** pop. 2,818

**BEST WESTERN WINDWOOD INN & SUITES** (361)394-6200

▼▼▼
Motel
$130-$200

**AAA Benefit:** Members save 10% or more with Best Western!

**Address:** 1172 E Riley St 78357 **Location:** On US 59 and SR 44 E, just e of SR 16. **Facility:** 35 units. 1 story, exterior corridors. **Pool(s):** outdoor. **Activities:** exercise room. **Guest Services:** coin laundry. **Featured Amenity:** continental breakfast.

## FRIENDSWOOD  pop. 35,805
• **Hotels & Restaurants map & index p. 324**
• **Part of Houston area — see map p. 301**

PERRY & SONS MARKET & GRILLE        281/482-2842  (66)
Steak Seafood. Fine Dining. $9-$34 **AAA Inspector Notes:** Steaks and chops, chicken, seafood and pasta dishes, lighter-fare sandwiches and burgers and barbecue plates are served at this upscale establishment. The steak and shrimp dinner was very nice and was served with upbeat and professional service. **Features:** full bar. **Reservations:** required. **Address:** 614 S Friendswood Dr 77546 **Location:** I-45 exit 23 (SR 518), 6.7 mi w.  L D

## FRISCO  pop. 116,989
• **Restaurants p. 274**
• **Hotels & Restaurants map & index p. 179**
• **Part of Dallas area — see map p. 161**

ALOFT FRISCO        (972)668-6011  (6)

Hotel $71-$152
**AAA Benefit:** Enjoy the new twist, get up to 20% off + Starwood Preferred Guest® bonuses!

**Address:** 3202 Parkwood Blvd 75034 **Location:** Dallas North Tollway exit Warren Pkwy, 0.5 mi e to Parkwood Blvd, just s. **Facility:** 136 units. 5 stories, interior corridors. **Bath:** shower only. **Amenities:** safes. **Pool(s):** heated outdoor. **Activities:** exercise room. **Guest Services:** valet and coin laundry, area transportation. (See ad p. 210.)

COMFORT SUITES - FRISCO SQUARE        (972)668-9700  (4)
Hotel $89-$139 **Address:** 9700 Dallas Pkwy 75034 **Location:** Dallas North Tollway exit Main St, just n on frontage road. **Facility:** 109 units. 4 stories, interior corridors. **Pool(s):** heated indoor. **Activities:** hot tub, exercise room. **Guest Services:** valet and coin laundry.

EMBASSY SUITES DALLAS-FRISCO HOTEL, CONVENTION CENTER & SPA        (972)712-7200  (8)
Hotel $120-$250 **Address:** 7600 John Q Hammons Dr 75034 **Location:** SR 121 exit Parkwood, just n. Adjacent to Dr. Pepper/7-UP Ballpark. **Facility:** 330 units. 13 stories, interior corridors. **Parking:** on-site and valet. **Terms:** 1-7 night minimum stay, cancellation fee imposed. **Amenities:** video games, safes. **Dining:** 2 restaurants. **Pool(s):** heated indoor. **Activities:** sauna, hot tub, exercise room, spa. **Guest Services:** valet and coin laundry, area transportation.
**AAA Benefit:** Members save 5% or more!

HAMPTON INN & SUITES-FRISCO        (972)712-8400  (5)
Hotel $89-$179 **Address:** 3199 Parkwood Blvd 75034 **Location:** 1.1 mi n of jct SR 121 and Dallas Pkwy to Warren Pkwy, 0.5 mi e to Parkwood Blvd, then just s. **Facility:** 105 units. 6 stories, interior corridors. **Terms:** 1-7 night minimum stay, cancellation fee imposed. **Amenities:** video games. **Pool(s):** outdoor. **Activities:** exercise room. **Guest Services:** valet and coin laundry, area transportation.
**AAA Benefit:** Members save up to 10%!

HILTON GARDEN INN FRISCO        (469)362-8485  (7)
Hotel $99-$209 **Address:** 7550 Gaylord Pkwy 75034 **Location:** Dallas North Tollway exit Gaylord Pkwy, just e. **Facility:** 102 units. 5 stories, interior corridors. **Terms:** 1-7 night minimum stay, cancellation fee imposed. **Pool(s):** outdoor. **Activities:** exercise room. **Guest Services:** valet and coin laundry, area transportation.
**AAA Benefit:** Members save up to 10%!

SHERATON STONEBRIAR DALLAS-FRISCO        (972)668-8700  (10)

Hotel $99-$409

**AAA Benefit:** Members get up to 20% off, plus Starwood Preferred Guest® bonuses!
**Address:** 5444 State Hwy 121 75034 **Location:** SR 121 exit Legacy Dr; northwest corner. **Facility:** 119 units. 4 stories, interior corridors. **Activities:** exercise room. **Guest Services:** valet laundry, area transportation. (See ad p. 273.)

THE WESTIN STONEBRIAR        (972)668-8000  (9)
Hotel $109-$479
**WESTIN** HOTELS & RESORTS
**AAA Benefit:** Enjoy up to 20% off your next stay, plus Starwood Preferred Guest® bonuses!
**Address:** 1549 Legacy Dr 75034 **Location:** 0.3 mi n of jct SR 121. **Facility:** Located in one of the area's emerging entertainment centers and shopping destinations, this hotel exudes an upscale Western aesthetic. The large pool and sundeck are big draws for most guests. 301 units. 5 stories, interior corridors. **Parking:** on-site and valet. **Amenities:** safes. **Pool(s):** heated outdoor. **Activities:** sauna, hot tub, regulation golf, exercise room, massage. **Guest Services:** valet laundry, area transportation. (See ad p. 273.)

▼ See AAA listing p. 272 ▼

# Life is Better when Shared

## 10%-25% off
### Best Available Rate
(Single/Double 1-4 people)

## Sheraton
### Stonebriar
HOTEL

Sheraton.com/aaa

spg.
Starwood
Preferred
Guest

Approved

▼ See AAA listing p. 272 ▼

# FOR A BETTER YOU

Amazingly restful sleep. Energizing workout. Tempting, Super Foods. Everything that matters to you matters to us. Feel your very best on the road. AAA Members Save 10% – 25% off our Best Available Rates

## GO TO WESTIN.COM/AAA OR CALL 888.627.8441

spg.
Starwood
Preferred
Guest

www.WESTIN.COM/AAA

# Get There Better
## TripTik® Travel Planner

Plan your trips with better maps and better travel information. AAA.com and CAA.ca.

(See map & index p. 179.)

## WHERE TO EAT

**CANTINA LAREDO**          214/618-9860  [6]

*Mexican*
*Casual Dining*
*$10-$26*

**AAA Inspector Notes:** Modern yet relaxed, this restaurant features creative Mexican fare. A great starter of top-shelf guacamole, which is prepared tableside, primes the palate for an entree of enchiladas, tacos, fajitas and chiles rellenos. **Features:** full bar, Sunday brunch. **Address:** 1125 Legacy Dr, Suite 102 75034 **Location:** Just n of jct SR 121. [L] [D]

### Gourmet Mexican food, fresh-squeezed lime margaritas

**GLORIA'S RESTAURANT**          972/668-1555

Latin American. Casual Dining. $10-$18 **AAA Inspector Notes:** Salvadoran and Mexican dishes make up the menu here, and it makes for very popular fare. Among choices are plantains, seafood soup, grilled quail, flank steak enchiladas and quesadillas. Homemade tortillas and tamales add to the authenticity and accentuate many dishes. Sitting outside may be a preference on busy days as the dining room can get very loud. **Features:** full bar, patio dining, Sunday brunch, happy hour. **Address:** 8600 Gaylord Pkwy, Suite 5 75034 **Location:** 0.3 mi w of jct Preston Rd and Gaylord Pkwy. [L] [D]

**JINBEH JAPANESE STEAKHOUSE**          214/619-1200  [3]

Japanese. Casual Dining. $8-$36 **AAA Inspector Notes:** This Japanese steakhouse offers the usual hibachi selections of steak, chicken and shrimp in addition to items prepared in the large sushi and sashimi dining area and bar. It's located in a strip center near one of the area's larger shopping malls. **Features:** full bar. **Address:** 2693 Preston Rd, Suite 1040 75034 **Location:** Just n of jct SR 121 and Preston Rd. [L] [D]

**KENNY'S BURGER JOINT**          214/618-8001  [4]

Burgers. Casual Dining. $7-$14 **AAA Inspector Notes:** This eatery tops their sterling silver beef burgers with such options as Gruyère, wasabi mayo, Vermont cheddar, smoked bacon and Brie and serves them on ciabatta buns. Ribs and sandwiches round out the menu. A lively lunch scene amid the concrete floors makes it a little hard on the ears. **Features:** full bar, happy hour. **Address:** 1377 Legacy Dr 75034 **Location:** SR 121 exit Legacy Dr, just n; in Stonebriar Commons. [L] [D]

**THE LONDONER**          214/618-5025  [1]

English. Casual Dining. $8-$15 **AAA Inspector Notes:** For a real English pub feel visit the Londoner, which will take you across the pond with their menu of fish and chips, shepherd's pie and chicken tikka masala. Yup, an Indian dish is actually considered by many to be the national dish of England. Catch a soccer game or local sports on the TVs, lounge on their comfy sofas or play some darts—it may feel like a pub, but is very family-friendly. **Features:** full bar, patio dining, Sunday brunch. **Address:** 5454 Main St, Suite 123 75034 **Location:** George Bush Tpke exit Main St; on northeast corner. [L] [D] CALL [&M]

**PLATIA GREEK KOUZINA**          972/334-0031  [2]

Greek. Casual Dining. $6-$24 **AAA Inspector Notes:** Platia means "town center," and had I not been looking at the megamall across the way I may have believed I was at one in Greece. The dining room's rustic furniture, faux-finish walls and home-grown music nicely re-create a small Grecian eatery. Dolmas, gyros, moussakas, souvlaki and pita sandwiches can all be enjoyed. Desserts go way beyond baklava and can be picked up from the pastry case at the entry or enjoyed with a traditional Greek coffee. BYOB. **Features:** patio dining. **Address:** 2995 Preston Rd, Unit 1590 75034 **Location:** Dallas North Tollway exit Gaylord Pkwy, 1 mi e. [L] [D] CALL [&M]

**SILVER FOX**          214/618-5220  [5]

*Steak*
*Fine Dining*
*$15-$45*

**AAA Inspector Notes:** Prime beef cuts dominate the menu, but there is also lots of seafood and a dinner-for-two special that allows couples to dine a bit more economically. White tablecloth service in richly appointed dining rooms. **Features:** full bar. **Reservations:** suggested. **Address:** 1303 Legacy Dr 75034 **Location:** SR 121 exit Legacy Dr, just n. **Parking:** on-site and valet. [D]

### USDA Prime beef, fresh fish, lobster, local favorites

**TEXAS LAND AND CATTLE STEAKHOUSE**          972/668-2832

Steak. Casual Dining. $7-$27 **AAA Inspector Notes:** A variety of large Prime steaks, delicious salads and scrumptious desserts await you at the friendly Texas ranch-style restaurant. Try the signature slow-smoked sirloin, which never fails to please, or the Caesar salad, another favorite. A Texas steakhouse means everything is bigger, from large cuts and oversize salads to potatoes and side dishes. Those not in the mood for beef can opt for chicken, quail or seafood. Dessert is an occasion. **Features:** full bar. **Address:** 3191 Preston Rd 75034 **Location:** Jct SR 121, 0.5 mi n; in The Centre at Preston Ridge. [L] [D]

## FRITCH (A-5) pop. 2,117

Fritch was named for an agent of the Rock Island Railroad who plotted the region's first rail line in 1924. The town was incorporated in 1959 during construction of Sanford Dam, which created Lake Meredith *(see Lake Meredith National Recreation Area place listing p. 391).*

**ALIBATES FLINT QUARRIES NATIONAL MONUMENT**—see place listing p. 55.

**LAKE MEREDITH AQUATIC AND WILDLIFE MUSEUM** is at 101 N. Robey St. Dioramas show the habitats of animals and birds native to the Panhandle. Two aquariums display fish indigenous to the lake; artifacts representing the Plains Indians also are on display. **Hours:** Tues.-Sat. 10-5. Closed major holidays. **Cost:** Donations. **Phone:** (806) 857-2458.

## FULTON pop. 1,358

**HAMPTON INN & SUITES ROCKPORT-FULTON**
(361)727-2228

Hotel $99-$289 **Address:** 3677 SR 35 78358 **Location:** On SR 35, just n Mesquite St. **Facility:** 64 units. 3 stories, interior corridors. **Terms:** 1-7 night minimum stay, cancellation fee imposed. **Pool(s):** outdoor. **Activities:** sauna, hot tub, exercise room. **Guest Services:** valet and coin laundry.

**AAA Benefit:** Members save up to 10%!

[¶+] CALL [&M] [≈] [BIZ] [HS] [📶] [🔋] [🖥] [▭]

**THE INN AT FULTON HARBOR**          361/790-5888

Hotel. Rates not provided. **Address:** 215 N Fulton Beach Rd 78358 **Location:** Waterfront. Fulton Beach Rd at Cactus St. **Facility:** 45 units, some houses. 2 stories, exterior corridors. **Pool(s):** outdoor. **Activities:** hot tub, fishing. **Guest Services:** coin laundry.

[¶+] CALL [&M] [≈] [HS] [📶] [✕] [🔋] [🖥] [▭]

## WHERE TO EAT

### CHARLOTTE PLUMMER'S SEAFARE RESTAURANT
361/729-1185

▼▼ Regional American. Casual Dining. $9-$20 **AAA Inspector Notes:** Guests enjoy bayside views from the landmark restaurant's covered deck and rambling dining room, where tables are tucked into corners and niches. Fresh seafood options include oysters on ice. **Features:** full bar, patio dining, happy hour. **Address:** 202 N Fulton Beach Rd 78358 **Location:** Just e of SR 35.

[L] [D]

### HU-DAT RESTAURANT
361/790-7621

▼▼ Regional Asian. Casual Dining. $7-$18 **AAA Inspector Notes:** Dat Nguyen, a Dallas Cowboys football star, puts his name on this good spot for seafood, as well as Vietnamese and Chinese dishes, prepared by the Nguyen family. Eggs are plentiful in the egg drop soup, and Mongolian beef bursts with flavor. **Features:** beer & wine. **Address:** 61 Broadway St 78358 **Location:** Just s of SR 35.

[L] [D]

## GAINESVILLE pop. 16,002

### COMFORT SUITES
(940)665-5000

▼▼▼ Hotel $99-$150 **Address:** 1715 N I-35 76240 **Location:** I-35 exit 498B; jct Hwy 82; on northwest corner. **Facility:** 72 units. 4 stories, interior corridors. **Amenities:** safes. **Pool(s):** indoor. **Activities:** hot tub, exercise room. **Guest Services:** coin laundry.

### HAMPTON INN & SUITES
(940)612-4300

▼▼▼ Hotel $89-$299 **Address:** 4325 N I-35 76240 **Location:** I-35 exit 501, just w on FM 1202. **Facility:** 75 units. 4 stories, interior corridors. **Terms:** 1-7 night minimum stay, cancellation fee imposed. **Pool(s):** outdoor. **Activities:** hot tub, exercise room. **Guest Services:** valet and coin laundry.

**AAA Benefit:** Members save up to 10%!

### HOLIDAY INN EXPRESS HOTEL & SUITES
940/665-0505

▼▼▼ Hotel. Rates not provided. **Address:** 320 N I-35 76240 **Location:** I-35 exit 496B (California St); on northbound frontage road. **Facility:** 66 units. 3 stories, interior corridors. **Amenities:** safes. **Pool(s):** heated indoor. **Activities:** hot tub, exercise room. **Guest Services:** coin laundry.

### LA QUINTA INN & SUITES GAINESVILLE
(940)665-5700

▼▼▼ Hotel $95-$134 **Address:** 4201 N I-35 76240 **Location:** I-35 exit 501, just w on FM 1202, then just s on access road. **Facility:** 71 units. 4 stories, interior corridors. **Pool(s):** heated indoor. **Activities:** hot tub, exercise room. **Guest Services:** coin laundry.

## WHERE TO EAT

### EL TAPATIO
940/668-0740

▼▼ Mexican. Casual Dining. $5-$12 **AAA Inspector Notes:** This quaint restaurant serves up authentic Mexican food with handmade tortillas and homemade sauces. The menu is extensive and serves up traditional fare as well as specialty items like chile colorado and chilaquiles. The margaritas are a big draw. **Features:** beer & wine. **Address:** 1205 N Grand Ave 76240 **Location:** Just s of jct US 82. [L] [D]

## GALVESTON (G-10) pop. 47,743, elev. 17'
• Hotels p. 278 • Restaurants p. 282

To really know Galveston is to peel back the many layers of its colorful, multi-faceted personality and soak it up in all its glory and quirks. There are the lovely Victorian buildings, nostalgic gaslights and horse-drawn carriages in The Strand Historic District. There is the gentle lapping of waves from the Gulf against the sandy shore as seagulls circle overhead. And now, there are hulking cruise ships that make Galveston Bay their temporary home when they arrive to pick up passengers.

Something else that Galveston has is a background chock-full of drama and intrigue. Saying that Galveston has a storied history would be a classic understatement. Jean Lafitte and his pirates established a settlement in 1817 and the town was abandoned and burned when the United States forced Lafitte to leave a couple of years later. During the Texas Revolution the harbor served as the port for the Texas navy. By the Civil War, Galveston was Texas' principal seaport and leading commercial center. And by 1890, fully basking in its glory days, Galveston was Texas' largest and wealthiest city.

But Galveston lost everything to the hurricane of 1900, in which more than 6,000 people died. The barrier island was flooded by tides up to 15 feet high and lashed by winds in excess of 100 mph. Survivors found a devastated city in which entire sections along the Gulf Coast had been wiped away or were piled high with the debris of thousands of its buildings. Galveston would never be the same.

During Prohibition, Galveston began offering illegal drinks and gambling in its saloons. That, along with earlier acts of prostitution; earned Galveston the infamous nickname of "the sin city of the Gulf." Ultimately, Galveston lost its former status to its expanding neighbor, Houston. But in the 1970s and '80s and continuing today—even after Hurricane Ike ravaged several of its coastal communities in 2008—Galveston started initiatives that focused on renewal.

The centerpiece of Galveston's resurgence is the Victorian neighborhoods that have been restored to their original splendor. The most prominent among them is The Strand Historic District, once known as "The Wall Street of the Southwest." The 36-block area, which offers 100-plus shops, restaurants and galleries, is recognizable because of its iron-fronted buildings, one of the country's best-known collections of such architecture. It's these efforts and natural assets such as the 32 miles of sandy beaches that have made Galveston Island *(see Recreation Areas Chart)* a leading Gulf Coast resort.

But causing just as much interest is yet another development for Galveston—the arrival of the cruise industry. Previously, travelers had to go to Florida to set sail for the Caribbean. In 2000, however, Galveston joined a growing list of Southern cities that host major cruise lines and in no time at all has become one of the top cruise ports on the Gulf Coast. Carnival Cruise Lines and Royal Caribbean offer cruises from Galveston, with many vacationers enjoying excursions on Galveston Island before or after their voyage.

The cruise ships ply Galveston Bay's warm waters, silhouetted against the downtown skyline when they dock. From the decks of the ships, passengers can easily spot The Strand Historic District just one block from the cruise ship terminals on Harborside Drive.

One unforgettable tradition of this city is the annual 🐸 Mardi Gras! Galveston, a colorful celebration that includes parades, musical entertainment and costume balls on the two weekends preceding "Fat Tuesday."

But beaches have always been Galveston's primary recreational escape. One of the more popular areas is Stewart Beach Park, on the city's eastern edge at Seawall and Broadway boulevards. A scenic drive along the seawall and a ride on the harbor ferry are great diversions. Ferry services, which carry vehicles and passengers from the Bolivar Peninsula to Galveston Island and run 24 hours a day, have been publicly operated by the state since the 1930s; phone (409) 795-2230.

The restored Galveston Island Historic Pleasure Pier, on the waterfront at 2501 Seawall Blvd., is home to retail shops, restaurants and carnival-style rides and games; phone (855) 789-7437.

**Galveston Island Convention and Visitors Bureau:** 2328 Broadway, Galveston, TX 77550. **Phone:** (409) 797-5145 or (888) 425-4753.

**Self-guiding tours:** Scattered throughout the city are sculptures carved from some of the estimated 40,000 trees destroyed during Hurricane Ike. Brochures pinpointing these tree carvings are available at the convention and visitors bureau.

**BISHOP'S PALACE** is at 1402 Broadway. Designed for a local attorney in 1887, the three-story residence took 7 years to build. The exterior is sandstone, limestone and rough granite. The interior, furnished in period, features a hand-carved staircase, jeweled glass windows and a mantel that won first prize at the 1876 World Fair. The Catholic Diocese purchased the house to be the seat of the local bishop in 1923.

**Tours:** Guided tours are available. **Time:** Allow 1 hour minimum. **Hours:** Self-guiding audio tours available daily 11-5. Guided 1-hour tours depart daily at 12:30 and 3:30. Closed Thanksgiving and Christmas. **Cost:** $10; $7 (ages 6-18). **Phone:** (409) 762-2475.

**GALVESTON FERRY** departs from the end of Ferry Rd. on US. 87. A fleet of ferries crosses the Houston ship channel to Port Bolivar and back. An elevated deck offers views of the channel. Automobiles are permitted on board. **Time:** Allow 30 minutes minimum. **Hours:** Daily 24 hours. **Cost:** Free. **Phone:** (409) 795-2230.

**THE GRAND 1894 OPERA HOUSE** is at 2020 Postoffice St. Built in 1894, the theater survived the 1900 storm and has been restored to its Victorian-era grandeur. Al Jolson, John Philip Sousa and the Marx Brothers are among the celebrities who entertained on its stage. A year-round performing arts series continues to attract nationally and internationally known talent, including such performers as Bill Cosby, James Earl Jones, Bernadette Peters, Willie Nelson, Gladys Knight and Shirley MacLaine.

**Hours:** Mon.-Sat. 9-5. Phone ahead for performance schedule. Guided tours are offered by appointment. **Cost:** Guided tour $3. Self-guiding tour $2; free (ages 0-11). **Phone:** (409) 765-1894 or (800) 821-1894.

**LONE STAR FLIGHT MUSEUM** is .8 mi. n. of Seawall Blvd. on 83rd St. to the entrance of Galveston International Airport, following signs to 2002 Terminal Dr. Home of the Texas Aviation Hall of Fame, this museum details the history of aviation through exhibits of more than 40 restored aircraft as well as aviation artifacts and memorabilia. The impressive collection includes a P-47 Thunderbolt, an F4U Corsair, an F6F Hellcat and a Spitfire. Flight experiences are offered aboard several aircraft. **Time:** Allow 30 minutes minimum. **Hours:** Daily 9-5. Closed major holidays. **Cost:** $8; $5 (ages 5-17 and 65+). **Phone:** (409) 740-7722 or (888) 359-5736.

**MOODY GARDENS** is off I-45 exit 1A, 2 mi. s. to Seawall Blvd., 1.5 mi. w. to 81st St., then 10 mi. n. to 1 Hope Blvd. Three glass pyramids are the centerpiece of this 242-acre resort complex, which features beaches; paddle-wheel boat rides; the MG 3D, Ridefilm and 4D Special FX theaters; and a convention center.

The 12-story Aquarium at Moody Gardens is home to seals, penguins, sharks and other marine life from the oceans of the South Atlantic, North and South Pacific and Caribbean. The Rainforest Pyramid has streams, waterfalls, a Mayan colonnade, exotic plants, tropical fish and free-roaming monkeys and birds of the rain forests of Africa, Asia and South America. The Discovery Pyramid explores the world of science.

In the summer, Palm Beach offers a lazy river, a wave pool, waterslides, interactive splash areas and a white sand beach. **Time:** Allow 4 hours minimum. **Hours:** Daily 10-8, early June-early Aug.; 10-6, rest of year. Palm Beach daily 9-7, Memorial Day weekend-late Aug. Last admission 1 hour before closing. Phone ahead to confirm schedule.

**Cost:** Aquarium or Rainforest Pyramid $21.95; free (ages 0-3). Discovery Pyramid $9.95; free (ages 0-3). 4D Special FX Theater $10.95; free (ages 0-3). Ridefilm Theater $9.95; free (ages 0-3). Palm Beach $23.95; free (ages 0-3). One-day Value Pass (includes all Moody Gardens attractions) $49.95. Two-day Value Pass (includes all Moody Gardens attractions) $64.95. An additional fee may be charged for special events. **Phone:** (409) 744-4673 or (800) 582-4673. 🍴

**The *Colonel*** departs from the west parking lot in Moody Gardens. The three-deck paddle-wheel boat accommodates up to 750 passengers for narrated sightseeing cruises of Offatts Bayou. A dinner/dance cruise is available on Saturday evenings. **Hours:** Sightseeing cruises depart daily at 1, 3, 5 and 7, May-Aug.; Tues.-Fri. at 1, Sat.-Sun. at 1 and 3, rest of year (weather permitting). **Cost:** $10.95; free (ages 0-3). **Phone:** (409) 744-4673 or (800) 582-4673.

**MG 3D Theater** is off I-45 exit 1A, 2 mi. s. to Seawall Blvd., 1.5 mi. w. to 81st St., then 10 mi. n. to 1 Hope Blvd., at Moody Gardens. Three-dimensional images come to life on a six-story screen. Several films are offered. **Time:** Allow 1 hour minimum. **Hours:** Shows are presented daily 10-8; show times vary according to film. **Cost:** $10.95; free (ages 0-3). **Phone:** (409) 744-4673 or (800) 582-4673.

**THE MOODY MANSION** is at 2618 Broadway. Built about 1895 in the Richardsonian Romanesque style, the 32-room mansion was purchased by entrepreneur William L. Moody Jr. after the great hurricane of 1900. The interior features stained glass, carved wood, tile work, fancy plaster work and stenciling. Visitors can tour two floors where rooms are furnished in the opulence of a wealthy family in the early 1900s.

   **Tours:** Guided tours are available. **Hours:** Daily 10-3, Memorial Day-Labor Day; 11-3, rest of year. Closed Jan. 1, Easter, Thanksgiving, Christmas Eve and Christmas. **Cost:** $10; $8 (ages 65+); $5 (students with ID). **Phone:** (409) 762-7668.

**PIER 21 THEATER** is located at Pier 21 at Harborside Dr. and 21st St. "The Great Storm" is a 27-minute documentary about the hurricane of 1900 that killed an estimated 6,000 in Galveston, and the 18-minute "The Pirate Island of Jean Laffite" is the story of an early 19th-century pirate from Galveston. The hour-long "Galveston: Gateway to the Gulf" film evokes the stories of the more than 200,000 immigrants who entered the U.S. through Galveston 1835-1935.

   **Hours:** "The Great Storm" is shown daily on the hour 11-6. "The Pirate Island of Jean Lafitte" is shown daily on the half-hour 11:30-5:30. "Galveston: Gateway to the Gulf" is shown daily at 10 and 4. Seating is not permitted within 10 minutes of show time; arrive early. Closed Thanksgiving, Christmas Eve and Christmas. Phone ahead to confirm schedule. **Cost:** "The Great Storm" and "The Pirate Island of Jean Laffite" $6; $5 (ages 6-18). "Galveston: Gateway to the Gulf" $8; $7 (ages 6-18). **Phone:** (409) 763-8808.

**SCHLITTERBAHN GALVESTON ISLAND WATER-PARK** is at 2026 Lockheed St. More than 30 water attractions include two uphill water coasters, enclosed tube slides, speed slides, a lazy river system for floating, multiple areas for small children and an oversized hot tub. Wasserfest is a covered, climate-controlled area that maintains summertime air and water conditions during spring, fall and winter months, thus making the park accessible year-round.

   **Time:** Allow 3 hours minimum. **Hours:** Park opens daily at 10; closing times vary. **Cost:** Late Apr.-late Sept. $45.99; $35.50 (ages 3-11 and 55+). Rest of year $27.99; $22.99 (ages 3-11 and 55+). **Phone:** (409) 770-9283. 🍴 🏕

**TEXAS SEAPORT MUSEUM** is at Pier 22 and Harborside Dr. Home of tall ship The *Elissa*, this museum focuses on Texas' history of sea commerce and immigration. A database containing the names of more than 133,000 immigrants who entered the U.S. through Galveston, "The Ellis Island of the West," is open to visitors. **Time:** Allow 30 minutes minimum. **Hours:** Daily 10-5. Closed Jan. 1, Thanksgiving, Christmas Eve and Christmas. **Cost:** (Includes The *Elissa*) $8; $5 (ages 6-18). **Phone:** (409) 763-1877.

**The *Elissa*** is docked at Pier 22 at the foot of 22nd St. This 1877 iron barque was built in Scotland and once carried Texas cotton to the mills of Europe. The 400-ton square-rigger's masts tower 103 feet above the water. Visitors may walk the decks and view the sailors' living and working quarters. A theater presentation details the ship's rescue from the scrapyard and the 5-year restoration process. **Hours:** Daily 10-5. Closed Jan. 1, Thanksgiving, Christmas Eve and Christmas. **Cost:** Included in Texas Seaport Museum admission of $8; $5 (ages 6-18). **Phone:** (409) 763-1877.

## BAYMONT INN & SUITES          (409)744-3000

Hotel
$54-$299

**Address:** 2826 63rd St 77551 **Location:** 1 blk n of Seawall Blvd. **Facility:** 89 units. 3 stories, interior corridors. **Terms:** check-in 4 pm. **Amenities:** safes. **Pool(s):** outdoor. **Activities:** hot tub, exercise room. **Guest Services:** coin laundry. **Featured Amenity:** continental breakfast.

## BEACHFRONT PALMS HOTEL          (409)740-1261

Hotel
$60-$300

**Address:** 5914 Seawall Blvd 77551 **Location:** Oceanfront. Jct Seawall Blvd and 59th St. 3 stories, exterior corridors. **Amenities:** safes. **Pool(s):** outdoor. **Guest Services:** valet and coin laundry. **Featured Amenity:** continental breakfast. *(See ad this page.)*

## BEST WESTERN PLUS SEAWALL INN & SUITES BY THE BEACH          (409)766-7070

Hotel
$134-$254

Best Western
PLUS

**AAA Benefit:** Members save 10% or more with Best Western!

**Address:** 102 Seawall Blvd 77550 **Location:** Jct Seawall Blvd and 1st St. **Facility:** 62 units. 3 stories, interior corridors. **Terms:** check-in 4 pm. **Pool(s):** heated outdoor. **Activities:** exercise room. **Guest Services:** coin laundry. **Featured Amenity:** continental breakfast.

## CASA DEL MAR BEACHFRONT SUITES          (409)740-2431

Condominium
$89-$299

**Address:** 6102 Seawall Blvd 77551 **Location:** Oceanfront. Jct Seawall Blvd at 61st St. **Facility:** Each unit is a one-bedroom studio suite with kitchen, living room and Gulf-view balcony. 135 condominiums. 4 stories, interior/exterior corridors. **Terms:** check-in 4 pm, 2-3 night minimum stay - seasonal, cancellation fee imposed. **Pool(s):** outdoor, heated outdoor. **Guest Services:** coin laundry.

**Perfect for a family vacation or weekend for two! Beachfront Suites w/ kitchen amenities & 2 pools.**

COUNTRY INN & SUITES BY CARLSON          (409)763-5000

Hotel $139-$399 **Address:** 2818 Ave R 1/2 77550 **Location:** 1 blk from Seawall Blvd; corner of 29th St and Ave R 1/2. **Facility:** 60 units. 5 stories, interior corridors. **Terms:** cancellation fee imposed. **Pool(s):** indoor. **Activities:** hot tub, exercise room. **Guest Services:** valet and coin laundry, area transportation.

COURTYARD BY MARRIOTT GALVESTON ISLAND GULF FRONT          (409)497-2850

fyi Hotel $129-$229 Too new to rate. **Address:** 9550 Seawall Blvd 77554 **Location:** 5 mi w. **Amenities:** 80 units, restaurant, coffeemakers, microwaves, refrigerators, pool, exercise facility.

**AAA Benefit:** Members save 5% or more!

Explore on-the-go travel tools at
AAA.com/mobile or CAA.ca/mobile

▼ *See AAA listing this page* ▼

## FOUR POINTS BY SHERATON GALVESTON

(409)974-4796

Hotel
$89-$299

**FOUR POINTS** BY SHERATON

**AAA Benefit:** Members get up to 20% off, plus Starwood Preferred Guest® bonuses!

**Address:** 2300 Seawall Blvd 77550 **Location:** Jct Seawall Blvd and 23rd St. **Facility:** 125 units. 5 stories, interior corridors. **Terms:** 2 night minimum stay - seasonal and/or weekends. **Pool(s):** outdoor. **Activities:** exercise room. **Guest Services:** valet laundry.

---

## HAMPTON INN & SUITES-GALVESTON

(409)744-5600

Hotel
$109-$399

**AAA Benefit:** Members save up to 10%!

**Address:** 6431 Central City Blvd 77551 **Location:** 61st St, just w on Seawall Blvd, just n. **Facility:** 104 units. 5 stories, interior corridors. **Terms:** 1-7 night minimum stay, cancellation fee imposed. **Pool(s):** heated outdoor. **Activities:** hot tub, exercise room. **Guest Services:** valet laundry. **Featured Amenity: full hot breakfast.**

*Hampton Inn & Suites*

**Experience an island getaway, forty minutes south of Houston, seconds off the famous Galveston Seawall.**

---

## HARBOR HOUSE HOTEL & MARINA

(409)763-3321

**Boutique Hotel** $89-$249 **Address:** No 28 Pier 21 77550 **Location:** I-45 exit 1 (Harborside Dr), 2 mi w to Pier 21; in The Strand Historic District. **Facility:** This small hotel is surrounded by lively restaurants and is just steps from the charming downtown Strand area, but it's not near the beaches. 42 units. 3 stories, interior corridors. **Parking:** on-site (fee). **Terms:** check-in 4 pm, 2 night minimum stay - seasonal and/or weekends, 3 day cancellation notice-fee imposed, resort fee. **Guest Services:** valet laundry, area transportation.

---

## HILTON GALVESTON ISLAND RESORT

(409)744-5000

Hotel
$75-$509

**Hilton** HOTELS & RESORTS

**AAA Benefit:** Members save 5% or more!

**Address:** 5400 Seawall Blvd 77551 **Location:** Oceanfront. Jct Seawall Blvd at 54th St. Across from beach. **Facility:** This hotel has a great location and a friendly, professional staff. Guests have full access to the amenities of the San Luis Resort next door. 239 units. 6-10 stories, interior corridors. **Parking:** on-site and valet. **Terms:** check-in 4 pm, 1-7 night minimum stay, cancellation fee imposed. **Amenities:** video games, safes. **Pool(s):** heated outdoor. **Activities:** sauna, hot tub, limited beach access, cabanas, recreation programs, exercise room. **Guest Services:** valet and coin laundry, area transportation.

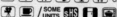

---

## HOLIDAY INN EXPRESS & SUITES GALVESTON

409/740-7900

**Hotel.** Rates not provided. **Address:** 8628 Seawall Blvd 77554 **Location:** Between 85th and 89th sts. Across from beach. **Facility:** 81 units. 4 stories, interior corridors. **Terms:** check-in 4 pm. **Pool(s):** outdoor. **Activities:** hot tub, exercise room. **Guest Services:** valet and coin laundry, area transportation.

## HOLIDAY INN RESORT ON THE BEACH    409/740-3581

Hotel
Rates not provided

**Address:** 5002 Seawall Blvd 77551 **Location:** Jct Seawall Blvd and 53rd St; just e. Across from beach. **Facility:** 178 units. 8 stories, interior/exterior corridors. **Terms:** check-in 4 pm. **Amenities:** safes. **Pool(s):** outdoor. **Activities:** beach access, playground, game room, exercise room. **Guest Services:** valet and coin laundry, area transportation.

## HOTEL GALVEZ AND SPA-A WYNDHAM GRAND HOTEL
(409)765-7721

Historic Hotel
$119-$350

**Address:** 2024 Seawall Blvd 77550 **Location:** Oceanfront. Jct 21st St. **Facility:** This historic Gulf-front hotel retains its classic look on the exterior and in lobby areas. The upscale resort pool and luxury spa that have been added in recent years fit in nicely. 224 units. 8 stories, interior corridors. **Parking:** on-site and valet. **Terms:** check-in 4 pm, 3 day cancellation notice-fee imposed. **Amenities:** safes. **Dining:** 2 restaurants. **Pool(s):** heated outdoor. **Activities:** hot tub, bicycles, exercise room, spa. **Guest Services:** valet laundry, area transportation.

## INN AT THE WATERPARK    (409)740-1155

Hotel
$89-$209

**Address:** 2525 Jones Dr 77551 **Location:** Jct Seawall Blvd and 81st St, 0.5 mi n. **Facility:** 151 units. 2-4 stories, interior/exterior corridors. **Terms:** 2 night minimum stay - seasonal and/or weekends, 3 day cancellation notice. **Pool(s):** outdoor. **Activities:** miniature golf. **Guest Services:** coin laundry, area transportation. **Featured Amenity:** continental breakfast.

## LA QUINTA INN & SUITES GALVESTON SEAWALL WEST
(409)740-9100

**Hotel** $79-$254 **Address:** 8710 Seawall Blvd 77554 **Location:** Between 85th and 89th sts. Across from beach. **Facility:** 120 units. 3 stories, interior corridors. **Terms:** check-in 4 pm. **Amenities:** safes. **Pool(s):** outdoor. **Activities:** hot tub, limited exercise equipment. **Guest Services:** coin laundry, area transportation.

## MOODY GARDENS HOTEL, SPA AND CONVENTION CENTER    (409)741-8484

Resort Hotel
$129-$409

**Address:** Seven Hope Blvd 77554 **Location:** I-45 exit 1A (61st St), 0.9 mi s to Stewart Rd, then 1 mi w on Stewart Rd/Jones Dr to entrance. **Facility:** Moody Gardens is a full-service resort offering spacious and comfortable rooms as well as a spa, health club and fine dining. 418 units, some two bedrooms. 7-9 stories, interior corridors. **Parking:** on-site and valet. **Terms:** check-in 4 pm, cancellation fee imposed. **Amenities:** safes. **Dining:** Sheam's Restaurant, Terrace Restaurant, see separate listings. **Pool(s):** heated outdoor, heated indoor. **Activities:** sauna, hot tub, boat dock, recreation programs in summer, spa. **Guest Services:** valet and coin laundry, area transportation. *(See ad this page.)*

▼ See AAA listing this page ▼

## QUALITY INN & SUITES   (409)740-1088

Hotel
$59-$309

**Address:** 5924 Seawall Blvd 77551 **Location:** I-45 exit 1A (61st St), 1.5 mi s, then just e. **Facility:** 91 units. 5 stories, interior corridors. **Terms:** check-in 4 pm. **Amenities:** safes. **Pool(s):** heated indoor. **Activities:** exercise room. **Guest Services:** valet and coin laundry. **Featured Amenity:** continental breakfast. *(See ad this page.)*

## THE SAN LUIS RESORT SPA & CONFERENCE CENTER
(409)744-1500

Resort Hotel
$119-$950

**Address:** 5222 Seawall Blvd 77551 **Location:** Oceanfront. Just e of jct Seawall Blvd and 53rd St. Across from beach. **Facility:** All of the rooms at this resort overlook the Gulf. They have a really nice resort-style pool with a swim-up bar, waterfall and luxury cabanas. The pool bar also becomes a popular nightspot. 243 units. 16 stories, interior corridors. **Parking:** on-site and valet. **Terms:** check-in 4 pm, 2 night minimum stay - seasonal and/or weekends, 3 day cancellation notice-fee imposed, resort fee. **Amenities:** safes. **Dining:** 3 restaurants, also, The Steakhouse, see separate listing. **Pool(s):** heated outdoor. **Activities:** sauna, hot tub, tennis, recreation programs in summer, playground, game room, exercise room, spa. **Guest Services:** valet laundry, area transportation.

## SPRINGHILL SUITES BY MARRIOTT GALVESTON
(409)740-9443

Hotel $119-$209 **Address:** 6303 Broadway St 77551 **Location:** I-45 N exit 1A (61st St); between 63rd and 64th sts. **Facility:** 74 units. 4 stories, interior corridors. **Pool(s):** heated indoor. **Activities:** hot tub, exercise room. **Guest Services:** valet and coin laundry.

**AAA Benefit:** Members save 5% or more!

## SUPER 8   (409)740-6640

Hotel
$58-$280

**Address:** 2825 1/2 B 61st St 77551 **Location:** Jct Seawall Blvd and 61st St, just n. Located in a commercial area. **Facility:** 57 units. 2 stories (no elevator), exterior corridors. **Terms:** check-in 4 pm. **Pool(s):** outdoor. **Guest Services:** coin laundry. **Featured Amenity:** continental breakfast.

## TOWNEPLACE SUITES BY MARRIOTT GALVESTON ISLAND
GULF FRONT   (409)497-2840

**fyi** **Extended Stay Contemporary Hotel** $129-$229 Too new to rate. **Address:** 9540 Seawall Blvd 77554 **Location:** Oceanfront. 5 mi w. **Amenities:** 80 units, pets, restaurant, coffeemakers, microwaves, refrigerators, pool, exercise facility. **Terms:** check-in 4 pm.

**AAA Benefit:** Members save 5% or more!

## THE TREMONT HOUSE-A WYNDHAM GRAND HOTEL
(409)763-0300

Historic Boutique Hotel
$115-$350

**Address:** 2300 Ship's Mechanic Row 77550 **Location:** Broadway Ave, 0.4 mi n on 23rd St; just w to entrance; downtown. Located in The Strand Historic District. **Facility:** This hotel has a unique style—part historic and part boutique. A highlight here is the rooftop bar and the downtown location right on The Strand. 119 units. 4 stories, interior corridors. **Parking:** valet and street only. **Terms:** check-in 4 pm, 2-3 night minimum stay - seasonal and/or weekends, 3 day cancellation notice-fee imposed. **Amenities:** safes. **Activities:** exercise room. **Guest Services:** valet laundry, area transportation.

Keep seasonal vehicles travel-ready with a AAA/CAA Battery Tender®

▼ *See AAA listing this page* ▼

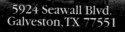

## THE VICTORIAN CONDO-HOTEL RESORT AND CONFERENCE CENTER     409/740-3555

Condominium
Rates not provided

**Address:** 6300 Seawall Blvd 77551 **Location:** Just w of 61st St. Across from beach. **Facility:** 152 condominiums, some two bedrooms. 3 stories, exterior corridors. **Terms:** check-in 4 pm. **Amenities:** safes. **Pool(s):** outdoor, heated outdoor. **Activities:** hot tub, tennis, exercise room. **Guest Services:** coin laundry, area transportation.

SAVE 🍴 🏊 📶 ✕ 📷 🔌
🍳 💻

### SAN LUIS CONDOMINIUMS     409/744-1500
[fyi] Not evaluated. **Address:** 5222 Seawall Blvd 77551. Facilities, services, and décor characterize an upscale property.

**WHERE TO EAT**

### FISHERMAN'S WHARF SEAFOOD GRILL     409/765-5708
♦♦ Seafood. Casual Dining. $9-$29 **AAA Inspector Notes:** Patrons can dine indoors or on the wharf patio at this harborside restaurant, which features a good choice of seafood favorites. **Features:** full bar, patio dining, happy hour. **Address:** 2200 Harborside Dr 77550 **Location:** At Pier 21. L D ✎

### FISH TALES     409/762-8545
♦♦ Seafood. Casual Dining. $10-$27 **AAA Inspector Notes:** Located directly on the Gulf of Mexico, the restaurant serves a large selection of seafood entrées. **Features:** full bar, happy hour. **Address:** 2502 Seawall Blvd 77550 **Location:** Jct Seawall Blvd and 25th St. L D

### GAIDO'S RESTAURANT     409/762-9625
♦♦♦ Seafood. Casual Dining. $17-$33 **AAA Inspector Notes:** This restaurant on the seawall has been a popular stop for more than 100 years. Gulf seafood is served in a classic atmosphere with very attentive service. A range of entrées is offered, including some steaks, but the best bet here is to keep it simple with one of the fresh seafood platters. **Features:** full bar. **Address:** 3800 Seawall Blvd 77550 **Location:** Between 38th and 39th sts.

L D CALL 🖐M ✎

### LANDRY'S SEAFOOD HOUSE     409/744-1010
♦♦ Seafood. Casual Dining. $10-$40 **AAA Inspector Notes:** An ideal spot for healthy seafood dinners and special occasions, the restaurant produces a wonderful clam chowder. Menu selections come from all the world's oceans. **Features:** full bar, happy hour. **Address:** 5310 Seawall Blvd 77551 **Location:** Next to convention center. SAVE L D

### MOSQUITO CAFE     409/763-1010
♦♦ Sandwiches. Casual Dining. $7-$15 **AAA Inspector Notes:** This place, just off the beaten path of tourist spots on the east end of town, is well worth a visit. Service is casual and friendly. The turkey divinity sandwich with house-roasted turkey, grilled apple, hickory-smoked bacon and melting brie on a baguette was excellent. Salads include some Thai flavors and one with goat cheese, pine nuts and figs. The kitchen also produces tasty pastries, cakes and cookies. Breakfast is served on weekends only and puts a creative twist on standard fare. **Features:** beer & wine, Sunday brunch, happy hour. **Address:** 628 14th St 77550 **Location:** Just n of Broadway St. **Parking:** street only. L D

### ORIGINAL MEXICAN CAFE     409/762-6001
♦♦ Tex-Mex. Casual Dining. $7-$16 **AAA Inspector Notes:** Historic. The name is fitting as this restaurant has been in operation since 1916. The décor is reminiscent of the Yucatan, but the menu of fresh, tasty Tex-Mex fare is closer to home. Expect the usual standards on the menu and basic but effective service. **Features:** full bar. **Address:** 1401 Market St 77550 **Location:** Jct W 14th St. **Parking:** on-site and street. L D

### SALTGRASS STEAKHOUSE     409/762-4261
♦♦ Steak. Casual Dining. $9-$30 **AAA Inspector Notes:** Those looking for something different should try the comfortable steakhouse, which never says no to a special request. Born from the spirit of Texas cattle drives, the restaurant resembles a Texas lodge, with high ceilings and mounted animal heads. Baby back ribs are so tender the meat falls off the bone. Also on the menu are hearty steaks, prime rib, chicken, seafood and yummy desserts. **Features:** full bar. **Address:** 1502 Seawall Blvd 77550 **Location:** At 15th St. SAVE L D ✎

### SALTWATER GRILL     409/762-3474
♦♦♦ Seafood. Casual Dining. $10-$30 **AAA Inspector Notes:** This popular downtown eatery offers a menu full of Gulf seafood and USDA prime steaks, and there are always some great daily specials and fresh gumbo. The upscale but casual atmosphere and friendly service are good matches for the cuisine. **Features:** full bar. **Address:** 2017 Post Office St 77550 **Location:** Across from Opera House; downtown. **Parking:** street only. L D CALL 🖐M

### SHEARN'S RESTAURANT     409/741-8484
♦♦♦ American Fine Dining $21-$42 **AAA Inspector Notes:** This is the finest and most elegant dining option in Galveston. The traditional menu does not break any new ground, but the quality is excellent. Crab and fresh seafood highlight the menu as expected, but other choices like USDA Prime beef and quality lamb are also offered. Service is very formal and refined. The dining room and lounge are on the top floor of the hotel and provide panoramic views of the island. **Features:** full bar. **Reservations:** suggested. **Address:** Seven Hope Blvd 77554 **Location:** I-45 exit 1A (61st St), 0.9 mi s to Stewart Rd, then 1 mi w on Stewart Rd/Jones Dr to entrance; in Moody Gardens Hotel, Spa and Convention Center. **Parking:** on-site and valet. D CALL 🖐M

### THE STEAKHOUSE     409/744-1500
♦♦♦♦ Steak Fine Dining $23-$46 **AAA Inspector Notes:** This is an intimate and luxurious restaurant with service that is attentive to the extreme. The menu has USDA Prime beef and all the items you'd expect at a fine steak house, but also selections such as live lobster, foie gras and market-fresh fish. Although it is designed as a fine dining experience, it retains a friendly and relaxed feel that fits the resort surroundings. The adjacent upscale lounge is a good stop before or after dinner and has live entertainment. **Features:** full bar. **Reservations:** suggested. **Address:** 5222 Seawall Blvd 77551 **Location:** Just e of jct Seawall Blvd and 53rd St; in The San Luis Resort Spa & Conference Center. **Parking:** on-site and valet. D CALL 🖐M

### TERRACE RESTAURANT     409/741-8484
♦♦ American. Casual Dining. $9-$31 **AAA Inspector Notes:** The casual restaurant's menu items range from salads, pasta and seafood to filet mignon, rib-eye steak and lighter fare. **Features:** full bar. **Reservations:** suggested. **Address:** Seven Hope Blvd 77554 **Location:** I-45 exit 1A (61st St), 0.9 mi s to Stewart Rd, then 1 mi w on Stewart Rd/Jones Dr to entrance; in Moody Gardens Hotel, Spa and Convention Center. **Parking:** on-site and valet. B L D CALL 🖐M

### WILLIE G'S     409/762-3030
♦♦ Seafood. Casual Dining. $10-$43 **AAA Inspector Notes:** Situated in The Strand Historic District on the waterfront, this restaurant with covered tables offers a wide selection of seafood, steaks and pasta dishes. **Features:** full bar. **Address:** 2100 Harborside Dr 77550 **Location:** At Pier 21. L D ✎

## GARLAND H-3 pop. 226,876, elev. 384'
• **Hotels & Restaurants map & index p. 184**
• **Part of Dallas area — see map p. 161**

**HAWAIIAN FALLS - GARLAND** is at 4550 N. Garland Ave. The Rush ride, featuring music and laser lights; Keiki Cove, an interactive water-play complex with slides, rope ladders and a dumping bucket;

(See map & index p. 184.)

Waikiki Wipeout, a 65-foot-tall body slide; and the racing mat slide Pineapple Express are among the highlights of this Hawaiian-themed water park.

Height restrictions apply on some rides. Lounge chairs are available on a first-come, first-served basis. Cabanas and lockers can be rented. Guests may bring their own food but must pay a $10 cooler fee. **Time:** Allow 4 hours minimum. **Hours:** Daily 10:30-6 (also Fri. 6-8 p.m.), Memorial Day-Labor Day. Schedule varies; phone ahead. **Cost:** $26.99; $19.99 (ages 55+ and under 48 inches tall); free (ages 0-2). Under 14 must be with an adult. **Phone:** (972) 675-8888 or (888) 544-7550.

## BEST WESTERN LAKEVIEW INN    (972)303-1601    89

Hotel
$65-$75

**AAA Benefit:** Members save 10% or more with Best Western!

**Address:** 1635 E I-30 at Bass Pro Rd 75043 **Location:** I-30 exit 62 (Bass Pro Rd) eastbound, s on Chaha Rd, over bridge to north frontage road. **Facility:** 49 units. 2 stories (no elevator), exterior corridors. **Pool(s):** outdoor. **Activities:** hot tub. **Guest Services:** coin laundry. **Featured Amenity:** full hot breakfast.

## DAYS INN    (972)840-0020    88

Hotel
$49-$109

**Address:** 3645 Leon Rd 75041 **Location:** I-635 exit 11B, just w on westbound frontage road, then 0.5 mi n. **Facility:** 44 units. 3 stories, interior corridors. **Terms:** cancellation fee imposed. **Amenities:** safes. **Pool(s):** outdoor. **Activities:** hot tub, limited exercise equipment. **Guest Services:** coin laundry. **Featured Amenity:** continental breakfast.

---

## HYATT PLACE DALLAS/GARLAND HOTEL AT FIREWHEEL CONVENTION CENTER    (972)414-3500

Hotel
$64-$219

**AAA Benefit:** Members save 10%!

**Address:** 5101 N President George Bush Hwy 75040 **Location:** Jct N Garland Ave, just e on frontage road. **Facility:** 153 units. 6 stories, interior corridors. **Terms:** cancellation fee imposed. **Pool(s):** heated outdoor. **Activities:** hot tub, exercise room. **Guest Services:** valet and coin laundry, area transportation. **Featured Amenity:** breakfast buffet.

**HYATT PLACE**
Vibrant Firewheel area.
Complimentary continental breakfast.
Shopping, golf, family fun, pool, shuttle.

---

## MICROTEL INN & SUITES BY WYNDHAM GARLAND/DALLAS    (972)270-7200    90

Hotel
$55-$85

**Address:** 1901 Pendleton Dr 75041 **Location:** I-635 exit 11B, just n to Pendleton Dr, then just e. **Facility:** 53 units. 3 stories, interior corridors. **Amenities:** safes. **Activities:** exercise room. **Guest Services:** coin laundry. **Featured Amenity:** continental breakfast.

---

## WHERE TO EAT

### CUQUITA'S RESTAURANT    214/227-5153    78

Mexican. Casual Dining. $6-$12 **AAA Inspector Notes:** Although it may not look like much from the outside, this restaurant was born from a longtime Dallas favorite. Inside you'll find inviting dining areas and staff dressed in traditional Mexican garb. They'll hook you up with complimentary freshly made corn tortillas and butter, then reel you in with classic Mexican cuisine like chicken mole, tacos and posole. **Features:** full bar. **Address:** 1957 Northwest Hwy 75041 **Location:** I-635 exit 11B, just n.

### EL CHICO    972/270-7580    79

Tex-Mex
Casual Dining
$7-$16

**AAA Inspector Notes:** Inside and out, the decor of the popular Mexican restaurant is inviting. The menu features traditional favorites such as enchiladas, tacos, burritos and fajitas. The broad menu also lists a few American classics. **Features:** full bar. **Address:** 1902 Eastgate Dr 75041 **Location:** I-635 exit 11B, just n to Pendleton Dr, then just e.

### GRANDY'S RESTAURANT

American. Quick Serve. $4-$8 **AAA Inspector Notes:** Fried chicken and country-fried steak are menu standbys at the restaurant, a regional franchise. They also offer a family-style dining menu. The décor is a step up from that of most quick-serve eateries and more resembles that of a conventional restaurant. Some elements of increased service include additional rolls, iced tea refills and tray removal. B L D

*For additional information, visit AAA.com*

**LOCATIONS:**

**Address:** 145 N Garland Ave 75046 **Location:** Just n of jct Garland Ave and Main St. **Phone:** 972/272-9922

**Address:** 2155 Northwest Hwy 75041 **Location:** I-635 exit 11B; on westbound access road. **Phone:** 972/278-0845

## GATESVILLE pop. 15,751
• Restaurants p. 284

### BEST WESTERN CHATEAU VILLE MOTOR INN    (254)865-2281

Hotel
$72-$89

**AAA Benefit:** Members save 10% or more with Best Western!

**Address:** 2501 E Main St 76528 **Location:** Jct US 84 and SR 36, 0.5 mi w. **Facility:** 56 units. 2 stories (no elevator), exterior corridors. **Pool(s):** outdoor.

---

AAA/CAA travel information: Available online, on the go and in print!

**PRIMA PASTA RISTORANTE ITALIANO & PIZZERIA**
254/865-8311

▼▼ ▼▼ Italian. Casual Dining. $6-$18 **AAA Inspector Notes:** Favorite Italian dishes and pizza, as well as steaks and chicken entrées, are available at this friendly restaurant. **Address:** 2503 E Main St 76528 **Location:** Jct US 84 and SR 36, 0.5 mi w. L D

**RANCHER'S STEAKHOUSE AND GRILL**
254/865-5863

▼▼ American. Casual Dining. $7-$24 **AAA Inspector Notes:** The eatery has a crowd-pleasing menu of comfort food favorites like burgers, steaks and pork chops, and even a salad bar to please healthier diets. But I'm still craving the chicken fried steak. Thick, juicy and with a crunchy breading, the dish will ensure you make your way back to this mom and pop eatery. It may not do much for your heart, but it will do lots for your faith in this Texas classic. **Address:** 107 Hwy 36 Bypass N 76528 **Location:** Jct US 84, just n.

B L D

## GEORGETOWN (E-8) pop. 47,400

Established in 1848 as a trade center for the agricultural region, Georgetown features black, fertile farmland and ranch lands. Downtown is noteworthy for its Victorian architecture.

**Georgetown Convention and Visitors Bureau:** 103 W. 7th St., P.O. Box 409, Georgetown, TX 78627. **Phone:** (512) 930-3545 or (800) 436-8696.

**INNER SPACE CAVERN** is 1 mi. s. off I-35 exit 259. The cave was discovered in 1963 during construction of I-35. Prehistoric relics also are displayed during the tours, which last at least an hour. **Hours:** Mon.-Sat. 9-6, Sun. 10-6, Memorial Day-Labor Day; Mon.-Fri. 9-4, Sat.-Sun. 10-5, rest of year. Closed Thanksgiving, Christmas Eve and Christmas. **Cost:** Adventure and Explorer tours $19.95-$21.95; $17.95-$19.95 (military with ID); $11.95-$13.95 (ages 4-12); $10.95-$12.95 (military children with ID). Wild Cave Tour $100. **Phone:** (512) 931-2283 or (877) 931-2283.

**BEST WESTERN PLUS GEORGETOWN INN & SUITES**
(512)868-8555

▼▼ ▼▼ Hotel $89-$109

**AAA Benefit:** Members save 10% or more with Best Western!

**Address:** 600 San Gabriel Village Blvd 78626 **Location:** I-35 exit 261A, 0.5 mi n on east frontage road, then just e. **Facility:** 76 units. 3 stories, interior corridors. **Pool(s):** outdoor. **Activities:** exercise room. **Guest Services:** coin laundry. **Featured Amenity: full hot breakfast.**

**COMFORT SUITES**
(512)863-7544

▼▼ ▼▼ Hotel $96-$179 **Address:** 11 Waters Edge Cir 78626 **Location:** I-35 exit 261, 0.6 mi n on east frontage road. **Facility:** 69 units, some efficiencies. 3 stories, interior corridors. **Pool(s):** indoor. **Activities:** hot tub, exercise room. **Guest Services:** valet and coin laundry.

**LA QUINTA INN GEORGETOWN**
(512)869-2541

▼▼ ▼▼ Hotel $75-$130 **Address:** 333 I-35 N 78628 **Location:** I-35 exit 264 northbound; exit 262 southbound; on west frontage road. **Facility:** 99 units, some two bedrooms and kitchens. 3 stories, exterior corridors. **Pool(s):** outdoor. **Activities:** hot tub. **Guest Services:** valet laundry.

**BURGER UNIVERSITY**
512/863-0100

▼ Burgers. Casual Dining. $5-$12 **AAA Inspector Notes:** Juicy burgers, fabulous onion rings and thick milk shakes are all found at this fun spot on the Square. **Address:** 119 W 7th St 78626 **Location:** On the square; downtown. **Parking:** street only. L D

**MILANO TRATTORIA PIZZA & PASTA**
512/869-0444

▼▼ Italian. Casual Dining. $6-$15 **AAA Inspector Notes:** Italian favorites with sharp, distinctive flavors are presented at this restaurant where I truly enjoyed the bruschetta, salad, chicken parmigiana and the tiramisu. **Features:** wine only. **Address:** 1015 W University Ave, Suite 420 78628 **Location:** I-35 exit 261, just w; in southeast section of Wolf Ranch Shopping Center. L D CALL

**WILDFIRE**
512/869-3473

▼▼▼ American. Casual Dining. $7-$34 **AAA Inspector Notes:** This fabulous menu features everything from soups and salads to sandwiches, half-pound burgers, seafood, steaks, chops, bison and elk. There are even some very nice comfort food selections. I had the shrimp chowder, scallops Alfredo and the bananas Wildfire and each course was terrific. **Features:** full bar, Sunday brunch, happy hour. **Address:** 812 S Austin Ave 78626 **Location:** Downtown; on south side of the square. **Parking:** street only. L D

**ZIO'S ITALIAN KITCHEN**
512/869-6600

▼▼ Italian. Casual Dining. $8-$18 **AAA Inspector Notes:** The warm, comfortable atmosphere and Old World decor complement the menu. Meals are a good value, and so is the service. This small chain specializes in Italian cuisine, including oven-baked pizzas and pasta dishes. Guests are encouraged to get creative with their pizzas by mixing and matching from a list of 24 toppings. Particularly tempting dishes are Artichoke spinach pasta, chicken parmigiana, and Shrimp Limone. **Features:** beer & wine. **Address:** 1007 W University Blvd 78628 **Location:** I-35 N exit 261, just w; in Wolf Ranch Shopping Center. L D CALL

## GEORGE WEST pop. 2,445

**BEST WESTERN GEORGE WEST EXECUTIVE INN**
(361)449-3300

▼▼▼ Motel $129-$139

**AAA Benefit:** Members save 10% or more with Best Western!

**Address:** 208 N Nueces St 78022 **Location:** Just n of US 59 on US 281. Located in a quiet area. **Facility:** 50 units. 2 stories (no elevator), exterior corridors. **Pool(s):** outdoor. **Activities:** exercise room. **Guest Services:** coin laundry. **Featured Amenity: full hot breakfast.**

## GIDDINGS pop. 4,881

### BEST WESTERN GIDDINGS INN & SUITES

(979)542-5000

Hotel
$115-$200

**AAA Benefit:** Members save 10% or more with Best Western!

**Address:** 2161 E Hempstead St 78942 **Location:** Jct US 290 and 77, 1.4 mi w. **Facility:** 51 units. 3 stories, interior corridors. **Pool(s):** outdoor. **Activities:** exercise room. **Guest Services:** coin laundry.

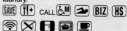

## GLEN ROSE (D-8) pop. 2,444, elev. 680'

Millions of years ago this region of central Texas was a coastal swampland where 60-foot dinosaurs dined on lush vegetation. The huge tracks of these prehistoric monsters can be seen in Dinosaur Valley State Park *(see Recreation Areas Chart)*.

Presented in the open-air Texas Amphitheatre at 5000 Texas Dr., "The Promise" is an epic musical drama portraying the life of Jesus. The 7-week performance runs in September and October. A variety of other performances are offered June through August; phone (254) 897-3926 or (800) 687-2661.

**Glen Rose Convention and Visitors Bureau:** 1505 NE Big Bend Tr., P.O. Box 2037, Glen Rose, TX 76043. **Phone:** (254) 897-3081 or (888) 346-6282.

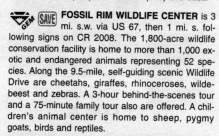 **FOSSIL RIM WILDLIFE CENTER** is 3 mi. s.w. via US 67, then 1 mi. s. following signs on CR 2008. The 1,800-acre wildlife conservation facility is home to more than 1,000 exotic and endangered animals representing 52 species. Along the 9.5-mile, self-guiding scenic Wildlife Drive are cheetahs, giraffes, rhinoceroses, wildebeest and zebras. A 3-hour behind-the-scenes tour and a 75-minute family tour also are offered. A children's animal center is home to sheep, pygmy goats, birds and reptiles.

**Tours:** Guided tours are available. **Time:** Allow 2 hours minimum. **Hours:** Daily 8:30-5:30, Mar.-Sept.; 8:30-4:30, in Oct.; 8:30-3:30, rest of year. Closed Thanksgiving, Christmas Eve and Christmas. **Cost:** $23.95; $20.95 (ages 62+); $17.95 (ages 3-11), Mar.-Oct.; $17.95; $14.95 (ages 62+); $11.95 (ages 3-11), rest of year. Behind-the-scenes tour Mar.-Oct. $52. Behind-the-scenes tour rest of year $47. Family tour Mar.-Oct. $38 per person. Family tour rest of year $32 per person. Under age 7 are not permitted on the behind-the-scenes tour. Tour reservations are required. Prices may vary; phone ahead. **Phone:** (254) 897-2960.

---

Be a better driver.
Keep your mind on the road.

---

### BEST WESTERN DINOSAUR VALLEY INN & SUITES

(254)897-4818

Hotel
$65-$126

**AAA Benefit:** Members save 10% or more with Best Western!

**Address:** 1311 NE Big Bend Tr 76043 **Location:** On US 67. **Facility:** 53 units, some two bedrooms. 3 stories, interior corridors. **Pool(s):** outdoor. **Activities:** hot tub, game room, exercise room. **Guest Services:** coin laundry.

COMFORT INN & SUITES (254)898-8900

Hotel $69-$189 **Address:** 1615 NE Big Bend Tr 76043 **Location:** On US 67. **Facility:** 70 units. 3 stories, interior corridors. **Pool(s):** outdoor. **Activities:** hot tub, exercise room. **Guest Services:** coin laundry.

### WHERE TO EAT

HAMMOND'S BBQ 254/897-3008

Barbecue. Casual Dining. $8-$11 **AAA Inspector Notes:** This no-frills restaurant features red picnic tables with rolls of paper towels (although finger licking is perfectly acceptable). Service is just as can be expected in a small Texas town, familiar and friendly. **Address:** 1106 NE Big Bend Tr 76043 **Location:** On US 67.

## GOLIAD (G-8) pop. 1,908, elev. 167'
• Hotels p. 286

One of the oldest towns in Texas, Goliad began in 1749 when the Presidio La Bahía and the Mission Espíritu Santo were established along the San Antonio River. From its inception and well into the early 19th century the military post was the site of many bitter contests between various contending armies. The most infamous was the massacre in 1836 of Col. James Fannin Jr. and 350 of his men by Mexican forces. The week prior they had surrendered to Gen. Antonio López de Santa Ana, led by Gen. José de Urrea following the battle of Coleto Creek near present-day Fannin.

News of the execution and the earlier defeat at the Alamo gave rise to the blood-curdling cry "Remember the Alamo! Remember Goliad!" that was shouted as Sam Houston's forces swept to victory at San Jacinto. Presidio La Bahía, said to be the most contested fort in Texas history and located 1.5 miles south on US 183, re-enacts the battle of Coleto Creek every March.

**Goliad County Chamber of Commerce:** 231 S. Market St., P.O. Box 606, Goliad, TX 77963. **Phone:** (361) 645-3563.

**Self-guiding tours:** A brochure detailing a walking tour of Courthouse Square is available from the chamber of commerce.

**FANNIN'S GRAVE** is 2 mi. s. on US 77A/183. The burial place of Col. James Fannin and his men is a few hundred yards from the Presidio La Bahía. **Hours:** Daily dawn-dusk. **Cost:** Free. **Phone:** (361) 645-3752.

**GOLIAD STATE PARK** is .2 mi. s. on US 77A/183. The Texans slain during the Battle of Goliad are commemorated at the site. The 188-acre park features nature trails, quarry ruins, old brick and tile kilns and displays of Native American and Spanish colonial items. *See Recreation Areas Chart.* **Time:** Allow 1 hour minimum. **Hours:** Daily 8-5. Closed Christmas. **Cost:** $3; free (ages 0-12). **Phone:** (361) 645-3405. 🎡

**Mission Espíritu Santo de Zuniga** is in Goliad State Park. The reconstructed 1749 church is furnished in period; the workshop displays period craft materials. A museum recounts mission history and daily life of missionaries and Native American converts. **Tours:** Guided tours are available. **Time:** Allow 30 minutes minimum. **Hours:** Mission and museum daily 8-5. Closed Christmas. **Phone:** (361) 645-3405.

**PRESIDIO LA BAHÍA** is 2 mi. s. on US 77A/183. The fortification was established in 1749 to protect Mission Espíritu Santo de Zuniga. Its chapel still is used for services. A museum shows articles found during restoration efforts indicating nine previous levels of civilization at this site. **Time:** Allow 30 minutes minimum. **Hours:** Daily 9-4:45. Closed Jan. 1, Easter, Thanksgiving and Christmas. **Cost:** $4; $3.50 (ages 60+); $1 (ages 6-11). **Phone:** (361) 645-3752.

**BEST WESTERN PLUS GOLIAD INN & SUITES**
361/645-3100

Hotel
Rates not provided

**AAA Benefit:** Members save 10% or more with Best Western!

**Address:** 754 E Pearl St 77963 **Location:** On US 59, just e of US 77 and 183. **Facility:** 42 units. 3 stories, interior corridors. **Pool(s):** exercise room. **Guest Services:** coin laundry. **Featured Amenity: full hot breakfast.**

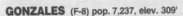

## GONZALES (F-8) pop. 7,237, elev. 309'

During the Texas Revolution, Gonzales citizens were the first to challenge the Mexicans. Rather than return a small brass cannon the Mexicans had left as protection against Native Americans, the community unfurled the first Lone Star battle flag— with the words "Come and Take It"—and used the cannon to fire the first shots of the revolution Oct. 2, 1835. The First Shot Monument is 7 miles southwest on SR 97.

The Gonzales Pioneer Village Living History Center, 2122 N. St. Joseph St., is a 12-acre site featuring restored 19th-century buildings on 7 acres, including log houses, a church, a smithy and a smokehouse. Phone (830) 672-2157 or (888) 672-1095.

**Gonzales Chamber of Commerce:** 414 St. Lawrence St., Gonzales, TX 78629. **Phone:** (830) 672-6532 or (888) 672-1095.

**Self-guiding tours:** Maps of historic points in Gonzales County can be obtained from the chamber of commerce.

**BEST WESTERN REGENCY INN & SUITES**
(830)672-5555

Motel
$160

**AAA Benefit:** Members save 10% or more with Best Western!

**Address:** 1811 E Sarah Dewitt Dr 78629 **Location:** 1.2 mi e of jct US 183 and Alternate Rt US 90. **Facility:** 27 units. 1 story, exterior corridors. **Pool(s):** outdoor. **Guest Services:** coin laundry.

**SLEEP INN & SUITES**
(830)672-1888

Hotel
$109-$189

**Address:** 2138 Water St 78629 **Location:** Jct US 183 N and Alternate Rt US 90, just n. **Facility:** 48 units. 2 stories, interior corridors. **Pool(s):** outdoor. **Guest Services:** coin laundry. **Featured Amenity:** full hot breakfast.

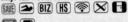

## GRAHAM pop. 8,903

**BEST WESTERN PLUS GRAHAM INN**
(940)521-0190

Hotel
$97-$117

**AAA Benefit:** Members save 10% or more with Best Western!

**Address:** 1707 Hwy 16 S 76450 **Location:** On SR 16, 2 mi s. **Facility:** 61 units. 3 stories, interior corridors. **Terms:** 2 night minimum stay - seasonal. **Pool(s):** outdoor. **Activities:** exercise room. **Guest Services:** complimentary laundry.

HOLIDAY INN EXPRESS & SUITES (940)521-9188
Hotel $99-$129 **Address:** 1581 Hwy 380 Bypass 76450 **Location:** Jct US 380 and SR 16, 1.3 mi e. **Facility:** 71 units. 3 stories, interior corridors. **Terms:** cancellation fee imposed. **Pool(s):** outdoor. **Activities:** hot tub, exercise room. **Guest Services:** coin laundry.

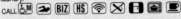

## GRANBURY (D-8) pop. 7,978, elev. 725'

Contemporary commerce takes on a 19th-century flavor in Granbury's historic town square. The 1891 courthouse, 1886 opera house, 1885 county jail, bank building and several other structures have been restored.

Visitors can view Jesse James' grave at Granbury Cemetery, N. Crockett and Moore streets.

**Shopping areas:** Antique lovers will find galleries and shops concentrated around the historic Granbury Square.

## BEST WESTERN GRANBURY INN & SUITES

(817)573-4239

Hotel
$70-$90

**AAA Benefit:** Members save 10% or more with Best Western!

**Address:** 1517 N Plaza Dr 76048 **Location:** On US 377 Bypass; 2.2 mi n of jct SR 144 and US 377 Bypass. **Facility:** 55 units, some efficiencies. 3 stories, interior corridors. **Activities:** hot tub, exercise room. **Guest Services:** valet and coin laundry. **Featured Amenity: full hot breakfast.**

---

## COMFORT SUITES

(817)579-5559

Hotel $70-$99 **Address:** 903 Harbor Lakes Dr 76048 **Location:** Jct SR 144 and US 377 Bypass, 1.9 mi n on US 377 Bypass. **Facility:** 70 units. 3 stories, interior corridors. **Pool(s):** heated indoor. **Activities:** hot tub, exercise room. **Guest Services:** coin laundry.

---

## HILTON GARDEN INN GRANBURY

(817)579-3800

Hotel $94-$169 **Address:** 635 E Pearl St 76048 **Location:** Waterfront. Jct US 377 and Business Rt US 377, 1 mi nw on Business Rt US 377; on Lake Granbury. **Facility:** 106 units. 3 stories, interior corridors. **Terms:** 1-7 night minimum stay, cancellation fee imposed. **Pool(s):** heated indoor. **Activities:** hot tub, limited beach access, exercise room. **Guest Services:** valet and coin laundry.

**AAA Benefit:**
Members save up to 10%!

---

## HOLIDAY INN EXPRESS & SUITES GRANBURY

(817)579-9977

Hotel $79-$99 **Address:** 1515 N Plaza Dr 76048 **Location:** On US 377 Bypass, 2.2 mi of jct SR 144 and US 377. **Facility:** 64 units. 4 stories, interior corridors. **Pool(s):** heated indoor. **Activities:** hot tub, exercise room. **Guest Services:** coin laundry.

---

## LA QUINTA INNS & SUITES-GRANBURY

(817)573-2007

Hotel $82-$117

**Address:** 880 Harbor Lakes Dr 76048 **Location:** Jct US 377 and SR 144. **Facility:** 57 units. 3 stories, interior corridors. **Pool(s):** heated outdoor. **Activities:** hot tub. **Guest Services:** valet and coin laundry. **Featured Amenity: full breakfast.**

---

## QUALITY INN & SUITES

(817)573-4411

Hotel $60-$200 **Address:** 800 Harbor Lakes Dr 76048 **Location:** Jct SR 144 and US 377 Bypass, 1.9 mi n on US 377 Bypass. **Facility:** 53 units. 2 stories (no elevator), interior corridors. **Amenities:** safes. **Pool(s):** outdoor. **Guest Services:** valet and coin laundry.

---

### BABE'S CHICKEN DINNER HOUSE

817/573-9777

American. Family Dining. $6-$14 **AAA Inspector Notes:** The home-style restaurant offers an upbeat family atmosphere. The portions are ample with serving bowls filled with green beans, corn, mashed potatoes and warm biscuits. BYOB is allowed. **Address:** 114 W Pearl St 76048 **Location:** On US 377 Bypass; between Lambert and Houston sts; center.

### BUFFALO GAP STEAKHOUSE & CANTINA

817/573-4471

Steak. Casual Dining. $8-$32 **AAA Inspector Notes:** Steaks and a varied selection of Tex-Mex favorites can be enjoyed while dining in the Western-lodge atmosphere of this popular restaurant. The stuffed quail-medallion appetizer is a big seller. **Features:** full bar, patio dining, happy hour. **Address:** 1470 Hwy 377 E 76048 **Location:** Jct US 67 N and Business Rt US 67; on north end of Kroger Shopping Center.

### EL CHICO

817/573-8833

Tex-Mex
Casual Dining
$7-$16

**AAA Inspector Notes:** Inside and out, the decor of the popular Mexican restaurant is inviting. The menu features traditional favorites such as enchiladas, tacos, burritos and fajitas. The broad menu also lists a few American classics. **Features:** full bar. **Reservations:** suggested. **Address:** 1151 Hwy 377, Suite 110 76048 **Location:** 2.5 mi e on US 377 Bypass.

### HOFFBRAU STEAKS

817/776-4982

Steak. Casual Dining. $7-$25 **AAA Inspector Notes:** Chicken-fried steak, center-cut fillets and fried catfish are all devoured in a rustic but delightfully bright country-themed dining room. Peach cobbler served in a hot skillet can be your indulgence, but I always pick the three-cheese mac as my guilty pleasure. **Features:** full bar, happy hour. **Address:** 315 E Hwy 377 76048 **Location:** Jct US 377 and SR 144, just n.

### PASTA FINA ITALIAN RESTAURANT

817/279-8669

Italian. Casual Dining. $6-$17 **AAA Inspector Notes:** Rustic decor incorporates a generous use of wood and rock throughout. Among specialties are veal and chicken piccata, Marsala, parmigiana and cacciatore. Other offerings include pasta dishes and pizzas. Strawberry shortcake lovers will enjoy the strawberry la bomba dessert. **Features:** full bar. **Address:** 1106 S Morgan St (SR 144) 76048 **Location:** Just e of jct US 377 and SR 144.

### PEARL STREET STATION

817/579-7233

American. Quick Serve. $7-$16 **AAA Inspector Notes:** Housed in an old Sinclair station, this little joint is easily identified by the green trim and old gas pump. It serves up generous portions of barbecue, gumbo, crawfish étouffée and a variety of sandwiches. Pinto beans may sound ordinary, but they're not when served with their amazing sourdough jalapeño cheese bread—yummy! **Features:** patio dining. **Address:** 120 W Pearl St 76048 **Location:** Center. **Parking:** street only.

### SPRING CREEK BBQ

817/579-7336

Barbecue. Casual Dining. $8-$13 **AAA Inspector Notes:** Expect Texas-Style barbecue at its simple, homey best. Hickory smoked ribs, beef, pork and turkey lace the air with a spicy aroma that mingles with the scent of freshly baked rolls and cold ice cream slowly melting over a dish of homemade peach cobbler. Plates often are loaded with all the coleslaw, potato salad and corn on the cob they can support. Part of a small chain, this barbecue restaurant displays a rustic décor that gives patrons the impression they are "at the ranch." **Features:** beer only. **Address:** 317 Hwy 377 E 76048 **Location:** 1.7 mi e on US 377 Bypass.

---

## GRAND PRAIRIE (I-2) pop. 175,396

• Hotels p. 288 • Restaurants p. 288
• Hotels & Restaurants map & index p. 68, 191, 197, 257
• Part of Dallas area — see map p. 161

Originally named Dechman at the close of the Civil War, Grand Prairie has long been a thoroughfare between Dallas and Fort Worth. A historical

# 288 GRAND PRAIRIE, TX

(See maps & indexes p. 68, 191, 197, 257.)

marker denotes the Cross Timbers region, a meeting place of commerce between settlers and Native Americans.

Lone Star Park, 1000 Lone Star Pkwy., holds Thoroughbred and quarter horse racing; phone (972) 263-7223 for schedule.

**Note:** Policies concerning admittance of children to pari-mutuel betting facilities vary. Phone for information.

**Grand Prairie Tourist Information Center:** 2170 N. Beltline Rd., Grand Prairie, TX 75050. **Phone:** (972) 263-9588 or (800) 288-8386.

**THE PALACE OF WAX AND RIPLEY'S BELIEVE IT OR NOT!** is 1.5 mi. n. of I-30 (Belt Line Rd. exit) at 601 E. Palace Pkwy. The Palace of Wax showcases realistic wax figures portraying personalities from history, religion, childhood stories, Hollywood and horror. Ripley's Believe It or Not! offers a collection of curiosities, oddities and illusions gathered by cartoonist and world traveler Robert Ripley. Simulations allow visitors to experience an earthquake, survive a Texas tornado and walk across a bed of hot coals.

The complex also features a mirror maze, a laser race and an animated shooting range. **Time:** Allow 1 hour minimum. **Hours:** Daily 10-9, Memorial Day weekend-Labor Day; Mon.-Fri. 10-5, Sat.-Sun. 10-6, rest of year. Last admission 1 hour before closing. **Cost:** Ripley's or The Palace of Wax $16.99; $8.99 (ages 4-12). Combination ticket $21.99-$29.99; $12.99-$19.99 (ages 4-12). Additional fees are charged for the mazes and shooting range. **Phone:** (972) 263-2391.

**BEST WESTERN PLUS ARLINGTON NORTH HOTEL & SUITES** (817)633-6311 27

Hotel $99-$399

AAA Benefit: Members save 10% or more with Best Western!

**Address:** 2075 N Hwy 360 75050 **Location:** I-30 exit 30, 1.7 mi n on SR 360 to Carrier Pkwy. **Facility:** 70 units. 4 stories, interior corridors. **Terms:** resort fee. **Amenities:** safes. **Pool(s):** outdoor. **Activities:** exercise room. **Guest Services:** valet and coin laundry. **Featured Amenity:** breakfast buffet.

**COMFORT SUITES** (214)412-1022 30

Hotel $79-$175 **Address:** 2504 I-20 W 75052 **Location:** I-20 exit 454 (Great Southwest Pkwy), just n, then just e. **Facility:** 68 units. 4 stories, interior corridors. **Amenities:** safes. **Pool(s):** heated indoor. **Activities:** hot tub, exercise room. **Guest Services:** valet and coin laundry.

**HAMPTON INN ARLINGTON/DFW AIRPORT AREA** (972)988-8989 26

Hotel $89-$169 **Address:** 2050 N Hwy 360 75050 **Location:** I-30 exit 30, 1.7 mi n on SR 360 (Watson Rd) exit Green Oaks Blvd/Carrier Pkwy.

AAA Benefit: Members save up to 10%!

**Facility:** 135 units. 4 stories, interior corridors. **Terms:** 1-7 night minimum stay, cancellation fee imposed. **Pool(s):** outdoor. **Activities:** exercise room. **Guest Services:** valet and coin laundry.

**HYATT PLACE DALLAS/NORTH ARLINGTON/GRAND PRAIRIE** (972)988-6800 28

Hotel $69-$279

HYATT PLACE
AAA Benefit: Members save 10%!

**Address:** 1542 N Hwy 360 75050 **Location:** SR 360 exit K/J aves southbound, U-turn at Ave J; exit Lamar Dr northbound, just n on frontage road. **Facility:** 134 units. 6 stories, interior corridors. **Terms:** cancellation fee imposed. **Pool(s):** heated outdoor. **Activities:** exercise room. **Guest Services:** valet and coin laundry, area transportation. **Featured Amenity:** breakfast buffet.

**LA QUINTA INN & SUITES SOUTH GRAND PRAIRIE** (214)412-3220 59

Hotel $109-$154 **Address:** 2131 W I-20 75052 **Location:** I-20 exit 454 (Great Southwest Pkwy); on eastbound frontage road. **Facility:** 73 units. 4 stories, interior corridors. **Pool(s):** outdoor. **Activities:** hot tub, exercise room. **Guest Services:** valet and coin laundry, area transportation.

**QUALITY INN & SUITES** (972)602-9400 29

Hotel $81-$100 **Address:** 3891 Great Southwest Pkwy 75052 **Location:** I-20 exit 454 (Great Southwest Pkwy), just ne. **Facility:** 51 units. 2 stories (no elevator), interior corridors. **Amenities:** safes. **Pool(s):** outdoor. **Guest Services:** coin laundry. **Featured Amenity:** continental breakfast.

**SUPER 8** (972)606-2800 31

Hotel $59-$99 **Address:** 4020 Great Southwest Pkwy 75052 **Location:** I-20 exit 454 (Great Southwest Pkwy), just s. **Facility:** 64 units. 2 stories (no elevator), exterior corridors. **Pool(s):** outdoor. **Guest Services:** coin laundry. **Featured Amenity:** continental breakfast.

**WHERE TO EAT**

**MONTEREY'S LITTLE MEXICO** 972/642-1237 8

Tex-Mex. Casual Dining. $6-$13 **AAA Inspector Notes:** This small regional chain sticks to the classics of Tex-Mex with enchiladas, tacos and fajitas. While they are not shy with the usage of cheese, that may be where the similarities with other Tex-Mex chains stop. The food is super savory and the staff eager to please. **Features:** full bar. **Address:** 602 Dalworth St 75050 **Location:** SR 360 exit Abrams, 2.2 mi e.

# GRAPEVINE (H-2) pop. 46,334

- **Restaurants p. 290**
- **Hotels & Restaurants map & index p. 191, 257**

The historic district of this small town offers antiques shops, art galleries, wineries and eateries. A Grapevine Opry musical showcase is held at the Palace Theater, 300 S. Main St.; phone (817) 481-8733. Wine tastings, car shows, carnival rides and a grape stomp are among the highlights of Grapefest, held downtown in September.

**Grapevine Convention & Visitors Bureau:** 636 S. Main St., Grapevine, TX 76051. **Phone:** (817) 410-3185 or (800) 457-6338.

**Shopping areas:** Grapevine Mills, SR 121N and International Pkwy., features more than 180 outlet stores, including Neiman Marcus Last Call and Saks Fifth Avenue OFF 5th.

**GRAPEVINE VINTAGE RAILROAD** departs from Cotton Belt Depot at 705 S. Main St. The locomotive engines are from the late 19th century and the coaches are from the mid-1920s. Cars travel approximately 21 miles to Fort Worth's Stockyards. A second route beginning at the Stockyards follows the Trinity River through the older areas of Fort Worth and back.

**Hours:** Trains depart Grapevine Fri.-Sun. at 1, June-Aug.; Sat.-Sun. at 1, mid-Feb. through May 31 and Sept.-Nov. Arrive 30 minutes prior to departure. **Phone** ahead to confirm schedule. **Cost:** Round-trip fare $10-$28; $18-$26 (ages 55+); $10-$18 (ages 3-12). **Phone:** (817) 410-8136.

**LEGOLAND DISCOVERY CENTER** is in the Grapevine Mills Mall, 3000 Grapevine Mills Pkwy. Visitors can build and race LEGO cars; design a LEGO tower and test its sturdiness on a shake table; watch a 4-D movie complete with sensory effects like wind and snow; sing karaoke in the Princess Palace; shoot laser guns on a chariot ride; drive an off-road LEGO vehicle; pedal their way to the ceiling on the Merlin's Apprentice ride; and be firefighters at LEGO City Play Zone & Fire Academy.

MINILAND is a LEGO re-creation of the Dallas/Fort Worth area. Designed with toddlers and preschoolers in mind, DUPLO Village is a playroom filled with bigger, softer plastic bricks. A factory tour details the LEGO-making process.

**Note:** Guaranteed-entry tickets, available online, are highly recommended during holidays and peak times. Visitors may have to wait in line. Socks are required for some play areas.

**Time:** Allow 2 hours minimum. **Hours:** Mon.-Fri. 10-8, Sat. 10-9, Sun. 11-6. Last admission 2 hours before closing. **Cost:** $19; $15 (ages 3-12). Children must be with an adult, and adults must be accompanied by at least one child. **Phone:** (469) 444-3050 or (877) 818-1677.

**COMFORT INN** (817)329-9300 **9**
Hotel $89-$159 **Address:** 301 Capitol St 76051 **Location:** SR 114 exit Main St, just n. **Facility:** 100 units. 4 stories, interior corridors. **Pool(s):** outdoor. **Activities:** limited exercise equipment. **Guest Services:** valet and coin laundry, area transportation.

**COMFORT SUITES DFW NORTH-GRAPEVINE**
(972)471-1900 **5**
Hotel $79-$179 **Address:** 1805 Enchanted Way 76051 **Location:** SR 121 exit Bass Pro Dr, just e. **Facility:** 96 units. 5 stories, interior corridors. **Pool(s):** outdoor. **Activities:** hot tub, exercise room. **Guest Services:** complimentary and valet laundry, area transportation.

**EMBASSY SUITES OUTDOOR WORLD** (972)724-2600 **6**
Hotel $139-$289 **Address:** 2401 Bass Pro Dr 76051 **Location:** SR 121 exit Bass Pro Dr, just w. **Facility:** 329 units. 12 stories, interior corridors. **Parking:** on-site and valet. **Terms:** 1-7 night minimum stay, cancellation fee imposed. **Pool(s):** heated indoor. **Activities:** sauna, hot tub, game room, exercise room, massage. **Guest Services:** valet and coin laundry, area transportation.

**AAA Benefit:** Members save 5% or more!

**GAYLORD TEXAN RESORT & CONVENTION CENTER**
(817)778-1000 **7**

Resort Hotel $139-$449

GAYLORD HOTELS

**AAA Benefit:** Members experience everything in one place with a special rate!

**Address:** 1501 Gaylord Tr 76051 **Location:** 1.3 mi sw of jct SR 121 and 26. **Facility:** This large resort offers convention facilities, seasonal activities and a water recreation area where guests can enjoy a lazy river complete with lagoons, water slides and a zip-line. 1511 units, some efficiencies. 9 stories, interior corridors. **Parking:** on-site (fee) and valet. **Terms:** resort fee. **Amenities:** safes. **Dining:** 5 restaurants, entertainment. **Pool(s):** heated outdoor, heated indoor. **Activities:** fishing, game room, exercise room, spa. **Guest Services:** valet and coin laundry. *(See ad p. 200.)*

**GRAND HYATT DFW** (972)973-1234 **13**

Hotel $99-$449

GRAND | HYATT

**AAA Benefit:** Members save 10%!

**Address:** 2337 S International Pkwy 75261 **Location:** In Dallas-Fort Worth International Airport; at Terminal D. **Facility:** Those with overnight layovers at DFW like the Hyatt because of the extensive workout facility, spa and lively lobby scene. Eastside rooms are quietest; for runway views choose fourth floor and above. 298 units. 9 stories, interior corridors. **Parking:** on-site (fee) and valet. **Terms:** cancellation fee imposed. **Amenities:** safes. **Pool(s):** heated outdoor. **Activities:** steamroom, exercise room, massage. **Guest Services:** valet and coin laundry.

(See maps & indexes p. 191, 257.)

## GREAT WOLF LODGE-GRAPEVINE, TX    817/488-6510    8

▼▼▼▼ **Hotel.** Rates not provided. **Address:** 100 Great Wolf Dr 76051 **Location:** 1.3 mi sw of jct SR 121 and 26, just e. **Facility:** 605 units, some two bedrooms. 8 stories, interior corridors. **Parking:** on-site and valet. **Terms:** check-in 4 pm. **Amenities:** video games, safes. **Dining:** 3 restaurants. **Pool(s):** heated outdoor, heated indoor. **Activities:** hot tub, recreation programs, game room, exercise room, spa. **Guest Services:** valet and coin laundry, area transportation.

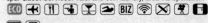

## HILTON DFW LAKES EXECUTIVE CONFERENCE CENTER    (817)481-8444    4

▼▼▼▼ **Hotel** $98-$242

**AAA Benefit:** Members save 5% or more!

**Address:** 1800 Hwy 26 E 76051 **Location:** SR 26A, 0.3 mi sw of jct SR 121; 0.5 mi nw of I-635 exit SR 121 N. **Facility:** 393 units. 10 stories, interior corridors. **Parking:** on-site and valet. **Terms:** 1-7 night minimum stay, cancellation fee imposed. **Amenities:** video games, safes. **Dining:** 2 restaurants. **Pool(s):** outdoor, heated indoor. **Activities:** sauna, hot tub, fishing, tennis, exercise room. **Guest Services:** valet laundry, area transportation.

## HILTON GARDEN INN    (817)421-1172    11

▼▼▼ **Hotel** $109-$299 **Address:** 205 W State Hwy 114 76051 **Location:** SR 114 exit Main St, just s. **Facility:** 110 units. 4 stories, interior corridors. **Terms:** 1-7 night minimum stay, cancellation fee imposed. **Pool(s):** heated indoor. **Activities:** exercise room. **Guest Services:** valet and coin laundry, area transportation.

**AAA Benefit:** Members save up to 10%!

## HOMEWOOD SUITES BY HILTON    (972)691-2427    2

▼▼▼ **Extended Stay Hotel** $129-$159 **Address:** 2214 Grapevine Mills Cir W 76051 **Location:** SR 121 N exit Bass Pro Dr. **Facility:** 105 units, some efficiencies and kitchens. 4 stories, interior corridors. **Terms:** 1-7 night minimum stay, cancellation fee imposed. **Pool(s):** indoor. **Activities:** hot tub, exercise room. **Guest Services:** valet and coin laundry, area transportation.

**AAA Benefit:** Members save up to 10%!

## HYATT PLACE DALLAS/GRAPEVINE    (972)691-1199    3

▼▼▼ **Hotel** $69-$209

**HYATT PLACE**

**AAA Benefit:** Members save 10%!

**Address:** 2220 Grapevine Mills Cir W 76051 **Location:** SR 121 N exit Bass Pro Dr, just w, then just e on SR 26. **Facility:** 125 units. 6 stories, interior corridors. **Terms:** cancellation fee imposed. **Pool(s):** outdoor. **Activities:** exercise room. **Guest Services:** valet laundry, area transportation. **Featured Amenity:** breakfast buffet.

## HYATT REGENCY DFW    (972)453-1234    14

▼▼▼ **Hotel** $89-$319

**HYATT REGENCY**

**AAA Benefit:** Members save 10%!

**Address:** 2334 N International Pkwy 75261 **Location:** In Dallas-Fort Worth International Airport Terminal C area. **Facility:** 811 units. 12 stories, interior corridors. **Parking:** on-site and valet. **Terms:** cancellation fee imposed. **Dining:** 2 restaurants. **Pool(s):** heated outdoor. **Activities:** exercise room. **Guest Services:** valet laundry, area transportation. **Featured Amenity:** full hot breakfast.

## SPRINGHILL SUITES BY MARRIOTT    (972)724-5500    1

▼▼▼ **Hotel** $99-$199 **Address:** 2240 W Grapevine Mills Cir 76051 **Location:** SR 121 W exit Bass Pro Dr northbound, just w, just ne on SR 26, then just w on Grapevine Mills Rd; exit southbound, 0.8 mi to Grapevine Mills Rd, then just w. **Facility:** 111 units. 4 stories, interior corridors. **Pool(s):** heated indoor. **Activities:** hot tub, exercise room. **Guest Services:** valet and coin laundry, area transportation.

**AAA Benefit:** Members save 5% or more!

## SUPER 8-GRAPEVINE    (817)329-7222    10

▼▼▼ **Hotel** $79-$109

**Address:** 250 E Hwy 114 76051 **Location:** SR 114 exit Main St. **Facility:** 100 units. 3 stories, interior corridors. **Amenities:** safes. **Pool(s):** outdoor. **Activities:** limited exercise equipment. **Guest Services:** valet and coin laundry, area transportation. **Featured Amenity:** continental breakfast.

---

## WHERE TO EAT

## BIG FISH SEAFOOD GRILL AND BAR    817/481-2010    11

▼▼ Seafood. Casual Dining. $6-$20 **AAA Inspector Notes:** Located along Grapevine's historic main street, Big Fish can provide a delicious respite from antique shopping or a day of window shopping. Fried pickles and oysters are great starters, and the fish tacos will fill you to the gills. Other choices include gumbo, oysters, po'boys, pasta, and red beans and rice. The menu definitely embraces Louisiana influences but also has a little Southwest flavor and daily fresh fish specials. There are no wrong choices here, so dig in. **Features:** full bar, happy hour. **Address:** 414 S Main St 76051 **Location:** SR 114 exit Main St, 0.8 mi s, then 0.9 mi e. **Parking:** street only.

## BOI NA BRAZA    817/329-5514    29

▼▼ Brazilian. Casual Dining. $20-$48 **AAA Inspector Notes:** Experience a gaucho-inspired type of cooking called churrasco. Large portions of prime meats are skewered and slowly roasted to perfection, then served to each table until diners say no more. Children 5 and under eat free. **Features:** full bar. **Reservations:** suggested. **Address:** 4025 William D Tate (Hwy 121) 76051 **Location:** SR 121 exit Hall-Johnson Rd northbound; exit Glade St southbound, 0.6 mi n on north access road.

(See maps & indexes p. 191, 257.)

---

**CANTINA LAREDO**     817/358-0505   28

◆◆◆

Mexican
Casual Dining
$10-$26

**AAA Inspector Notes:** Modern yet relaxed, this restaurant features creative Mexican fare. A great starter of top-shelf guacamole, which is prepared tableside, primes the palate for an entree of enchiladas, tacos, fajitas and chiles rellenos. **Features:** full bar, Sunday brunch. **Address:** 4020 William D Tate Ave, Suite 208 76051 **Location:** SR 121 exit Hall-Johnson Rd northbound. L D

## Gourmet Mexican food, fresh-squeezed lime margaritas

---

COZYMEL'S COASTAL MEX     972/724-0277   6

◆◆ Tex-Mex. Casual Dining. $8-$20 **AAA Inspector Notes:** People forget that Mexico has lots and lots of coastline, so seafood is just as much a part of its cuisine as tacos or burritos, and Cozymels shows that off. Grapevine locals and mall shoppers fill the place up because they know the menu has good selections from both land and sea. They can get anything from chimichangas and enchiladas to chipotle-glazed salmon and garlic shrimp. The separate bar is a good place to get started, and if the weather cooperates there is an outdoor dining area. **Features:** full bar, patio dining, Sunday brunch, happy hour. **Address:** 2655 Grapevine Mills Cir 76051 **Location:** SR 121 W exit Bass Pro Dr; in Grapevine Mills Mall Circle. L D 🐾

---

EL FENIX     817/421-1151   15

◆◆ Tex-Mex. Casual Dining. $7-$12 **AAA Inspector Notes:** This regional chain has been a Texas favorite since 1918. The menu is very traditional Tex-Mex, featuring the expected enchiladas, tacos and nachos. The Talavera tile accents, iron work and hacienda motif give one a feel of dining in old Mexico. **Features:** full bar, happy hour. **Address:** 401 State Hwy 114 76051 **Location:** SR 114 exit Main St, just s, then just w. L D

---

FIRESIDE PIES     817/416-1285   13

◆◆ Pizza. Casual Dining. $11-$14 **AAA Inspector Notes:** This pizza place draws the crowds as it has a hopping bar scene with an open kitchen; it can get loud. Pies are perfected in wood-fired ovens, and menu items are all served family style. On my visit, everything I sampled was absolutely delicious. **Features:** full bar, patio dining. **Address:** 1285 Main St 76051 **Location:** SR 114 exit Main St, just n. D

---

LA MADELEINE COUNTRY FRENCH CAFE     817/251-0255

◆ Traditional French. Casual Dining. $7-$12 **AAA Inspector Notes:** A fireplace creates the focal point at this cozy European style café where you can always get a quiche or savory stuffed puffed pastry on the go or stick around for a chicken crêpe or French dip sandwich. Heartier entrées are offered and every season promises menu surprises. Whatever you decide on you probably will not get out the door without enjoying one of their tempting sweet pastries. **Features:** wine only. **Address:** 900 Hwy 114 76051 **Location:** Jct SR 114 and William D Tate Ave. B L D

---

LOVE & WAR IN TEXAS     972/724-5557   7

◆◆ Steak. Casual Dining. $10-$29 **AAA Inspector Notes:** The Texas steak house prepares not only the usual steaks, pork chops, chicken and barbecue ribs but also wild game entrées centered on boar, buffalo, venison bratwurst, antelope, quail and catfish. Menu diversity means there's something for almost everyone. **Features:** full bar, patio dining, happy hour. **Address:** 2505 E Grapevine Mills Cir 76051 **Location:** SR 121 W exit Bass Pro Dr; in Grapevine Mills Mall Circle. L D

---

MI DIA FROM SCRATCH     817/421-4747   14

◆◆◆ Mexican. Casual Dining. $9-$28 **AAA Inspector Notes:** Yes, there will be a wait, but it will be worth it. Whether you opt for the guajillo-rubbed duck breast, banana-leaf-wrapped salmon or the blue corn tortilla enchiladas you are sure to find something on the menu that offers Mexican, Tex-Mex and New Mexican cuisine. An interesting drink menu and large and inviting patio draw the crowds. **Features:** full bar, patio dining. **Address:** 1295 S Main St 76051 **Location:** SR 114 exit Main St, just n. **Parking:** valet and street only. L D

---

NAPOLI'S ITALIAN CAFE AND CONFECTIONARY     817/310-0385   10

◆◆ Italian. Casual Dining. $9-$17 **AAA Inspector Notes:** Napoli's is a great place to start your stroll of this quaint historic area, have some pizza or pasta, then take in charming Main Street and work up your appetite for dessert on your return. Napoli's confectionery will treat you to a variety of gelatos, brownies, cookies and candies. **Features:** beer & wine. **Address:** 309 S Main St, Suite 100 76051 **Location:** Jct Main and Texas sts; southeast corner. L D

---

SALTGRASS STEAKHOUSE     817/329-1900   16

◆◆ Steak. Casual Dining. $9-$30 **AAA Inspector Notes:** Those looking for something different should try the comfortable steakhouse, which never says no to a special request. Born from the spirit of Texas cattle drives, the restaurant resembles a Texas lodge, with high ceilings and mounted animal heads. Baby back ribs are so tender the meat falls off the bone. Also on the menu are hearty steaks, prime rib, chicken, seafood and yummy desserts. **Features:** full bar. **Address:** 102 State Hwy 114 E 76051 **Location:** SR 114 exit Main St. SAVE L D 🔽

---

SALTWATER WILLY'S SEAFOOD & STEAKHOUSE     972/691-2659   8

◆◆ Seafood. Casual Dining. $9-$20 **AAA Inspector Notes:** After a day of shopping at the large adjacent outlet mall, this restaurant will satisfy the urges for seafood or steak and will do it with a Cajun flair. A crowd-pleasing menu of crawfish étouffée, fish tacos, coconut shrimp and chargrilled mahi mahi is offered in addition to perfectly made steaks. **Features:** full bar, patio dining, happy hour. **Address:** 2455 E Grapevine Mills Cir 76051 **Location:** SR 121 N exit Brass Pro Circle Dr; in E Grapevine Mills Circle Shopping Area. L D 🔽

---

**SILVER FOX**     817/329-6995   12

◆◆◆

Steak
Fine Dining
$20-$50

**AAA Inspector Notes:** This steakhouse features comfy booths, upholstered walls, a classy bar and private dining rooms. Prime beef cuts dominate the menu, but plenty of seafood and a dinner-for-two special that allows couples to dine a bit more economically are also on the menu. **Features:** full bar, happy hour. **Reservations:** suggested. **Address:** 1235 William D Tate Ave 76051 **Location:** SR 114 exit William D Tate Ave, just n. D 🔽

## USDA Prime beef, fresh fish, lobster, local favorites

---

THAI RIVERSIDE RESTAURANT     817/424-3765

◆◆ Thai. Casual Dining. $8-$15 **AAA Inspector Notes:** The cozy restaurant specializes in traditional Thai comfort food such as pad thai, Thai curry and peanut butter satay. A lunch buffet is offered on Friday. The staff is warm and friendly. **Address:** 2100 W Northwest Hwy, Suite 210 76051 **Location:** SR 114 exit E Southlake Blvd/Wall St, just nw on frontage road to SR 114, then just e; in Park Place Strip Mall (entrance on Park Blvd). L D

---

## Learn the local driving laws at DrivingLaws.AAA.com

(See maps & indexes p. 191, 257.)

UNCLE BUCK'S STEAKHOUSE & BREWERY
972/691-5100  [9]

♥♥♥ American. Casual Dining. $9-$33 **AAA Inspector Notes:** A state-of-the-art brewing facility encompasses one side of the restaurant. Hand-crafted beers and sodas are brewed using the finest ingredients. USDA Choice, grain-fed Midwestern beef is fresh, never frozen. The dining room, with mounted animal trophies, rock columns and log woodwork, transports diners to the great Northwest. **Features:** full bar. **Address:** 2501 Bass Pro Dr, Suite 100 76051 **Location:** SR 121 exit Bass Pro Dr, just nw. [L] [D]

## GREENVILLE (G-5) pop. 25,557, elev. 541'
• Part of Dallas area — see map p. 161

**THE AUDIE MURPHY/AMERICAN COTTON MUSEUM** is at 600 I-30E. This dual-theme museum follows the life of local farm boy Audie Murphy, one of the most decorated soldiers of World War II, while also illustrating the history of the cotton industry in the region. Exhibits include Murphy's medals, uniforms and memorabilia as well as information about other notable locals. Also on the grounds is the historic Ende-Gaillard House, which can be toured by appointment.

**Time:** Allow 45 minutes minimum. **Hours:** Tues.-Sat. 10-5. Closed Jan. 1, Thanksgiving, day after Thanksgiving, Christmas Eve and Christmas. **Cost:** $6; $4 (ages 60+, and college students and military veterans with ID); $2 (ages 6-18); free (active military with ID). **Phone:** (903) 450-4502.

**BEST WESTERN PLUS MONICA ROYALE INN & SUITES**
(903)454-3700

♥♥♥♥ Hotel $110-$205

**AAA Benefit:** Members save 10% or more with Best Western!

**Address:** 3001 Mustang Crossing 75402 **Location:** I-30 exit 93. **Facility:** 79 units. 3 stories, interior corridors. **Amenities:** safes. **Pool(s):** heated indoor. **Activities:** exercise room. **Guest Services:** valet and coin laundry.

SAVE [📶] CALL [⑤M] [🛁] [BIZ] [HS]
[📶] [✕] [🍽] [📺] [💻]
/ SOME UNITS [S🔒]

GREENVILLE COMFORT SUITES
(903)259-6343

♥♥♥ Hotel $74-$80 **Address:** 2005 Center Point Ln 75402 **Location:** I-30 exit 93, just e on service road; behind Home Depot. **Facility:** 77 units. 4 stories, interior corridors. **Pool(s):** heated indoor. **Activities:** hot tub, exercise room. **Guest Services:** coin laundry.

[🛁] [BIZ] [HS] [📶] [✕] [🍽] [📺] [💻]

HAMPTON INN & SUITES
(903)457-9200

♥♥♥♥ Hotel $89-$169 **Address:** 3001 Kari Ln 75402 **Location:** I-30 exit 93, just n. **Facility:** 75 units. 4 stories, interior corridors. **Terms:** 1-7 night minimum stay, cancellation fee imposed.

**AAA Benefit:** Members save up to 10%!

**Pool(s):** outdoor. **Activities:** hot tub. **Guest Services:** valet and coin laundry.

[📶] CALL [⑤M] [🛁] [♿] [BIZ] [HS] [📶] [✕] [🍽] [📺]
[💻]

HOLIDAY INN EXPRESS HOTEL & SUITES
(903)454-8680

♥♥♥♥ Hotel $99-$130 **Address:** 2901 Mustang Crossing 75402 **Location:** I-30 exit 93A. **Facility:** 80 units. 3 stories, interior corridors. **Amenities:** safes. **Pool(s):** outdoor. **Activities:** exercise room. **Guest Services:** valet and coin laundry.

[📶] CALL [⑤M] [🛁] [BIZ] [HS] [📶] [🍽] [📺] [💻]
/ SOME UNITS [S🔒]

### WHERE TO EAT

GRANDY'S RESTAURANT
903/450-1011

♥ American. Quick Serve. $4-$8 **AAA Inspector Notes:** Fried chicken and country-fried steak are menu standbys at the restaurant, a regional franchise. They also offer a family-style dining menu. The décor is a step up from that of most quick-serve eateries and more resembles that of a conventional restaurant. Some elements of increased service include additional rolls, iced tea refills and tray removal. **Address:** 6112 Wesley St 75401 **Location:** Between Terrell Rd and Eastland St. [B] [L] [D]

## GROESBECK pop. 4,328

QUALITY INN & SUITES
(254)729-0077

♥♥♥♥ Hotel $76-$120 **Address:** 1012 N Ellis St 76642 **Location:** Jct SR 14 and 164, 1 mi n. **Facility:** 42 units, some efficiencies. 2 stories, interior corridors. **Pool(s):** outdoor. **Activities:** exercise room. **Guest Services:** coin laundry.

CALL [⑤M] [🛁] [BIZ] [HS] [📶] [🍽] [📺] [💻] / SOME UNITS [S🔒]

## GROOM (B-5) pop. 574, elev. 3,214'

Groom was named for B.B. Groom, an English cattle breeder who worked as a land agent for the Francklyn Land and Cattle Company. Groom's ranch on White Deer Creek was noted for its Hereford cattle. Incorporated in 1911, Groom is located on historic Route 66.

**CROSS OF OUR LORD JESUS CHRIST** is at I-40 exit 112. The 190-foot-high, 2.5-million-pound cross is visible up to 20 miles away. Also on the grounds are a replica of the Shroud of Turin, a life-size Last Supper display, a 10 Commandments monument, and 14 life-size bronze stations of the cross, including an empty tomb display, Tomb of the Unborn and Calvary. **Hours:** Daily 24 hours. **Cost:** Donations. **Phone:** (806) 248-9006.

CHALET INN
806/248-7524

♥♥ Motel
Rates not provided

**Address:** I-40 FM 2300 79039 **Location:** I-40 exit 113, just s. **Facility:** 26 units. 1 story, exterior corridors.

SAVE [📶] CALL [⑤M] [HS] [📶] [♿]
[🍽] / SOME UNITS [S🔒]

## 🔷 GUADALUPE MOUNTAINS NATIONAL PARK (E-3)

Elevations in the park range from 3,689 ft. at Lewis Well to 8,749 ft. at Guadalupe Peak. Refer to AAA maps for additional elevation information.

Guadalupe Mountains National Park is 110 miles east of El Paso on US 62/180. The park's 86,416 acres occupy a rugged scenic section of the Guadalupe Mountains and include 8,749-foot Guadalupe Peak, the highest elevation in Texas.

The mountains are uplifted remains of the Capitan Reef Complex that originated some 250 million years ago during the Permian era when an inland sea covered part of what is now Texas and New Mexico. The 400-mile-long, horseshoe-shaped reef lies exposed in three places—the Apache, Glass and Guadalupe mountains. The Guadalupe Range forms a massive wedge towering above the West Texas desert; at the apex is the 2,000-foot sheer cliff, El Capitan.

Despite their barren appearance, the Guadalupes encompass stands of pine, fir and hardwoods that harbor elk and mule deer as well as javelinas, a variety of birds and an occasional cougar.

By the end of the 19th century the Mescalero Apaches, who had hunted and camped in the Guadalupes, had been expelled by the U.S. Army to make way for westward expansion and ranching activities. Relics of this period can be seen in the park, including buildings from the Williams and Frijole ranches as well as the remains of a Butterfield Stage Station. *See Recreation Areas Chart.*

## General Information and Activities

Guadalupe Mountains National Park and its facilities are open all year. Information about amphitheater programs and other park activities can be obtained at the Headquarters Visitor Center *(see attraction listing)* or the Dog Canyon Ranger Station.

There are no roads within the park. The only major route to the park is US 62/180. This road briefly crosses the southeast corner of the park and offers views of El Capitan, Guadalupe Peak and the eastern and western escarpment. Along the route are the ruins of The Pinery, a Butterfield Stage Station, just east of the Headquarters Visitor Center.

Three short spurs off US 62/180 lead to McKittrick Canyon, the Pine Springs/Headquarters Visitor Center campground complex and Frijole Ranch. Frijole Ranch House contains The Cultural Museum, which traces the human history of the area from more than 10,000 years ago to the present.

While the park lacks roads, it does offer 85 miles of trails for hikers, ranging from .5 to 18 miles. One of the more popular routes begins at McKittrick Canyon Visitor Center and progresses through the lush and twisting McKittrick Canyon. This trail, a relatively short round trip of 7 miles, is limited to day use.

An even shorter hike is the 2.3-mile loop from the Frijole historic site to Smith and Manzanita Springs and back. Longer hikes include travel to Guadalupe Peak, The Bowl and the base of El Capitan. Hikers should always carry water—at least one gallon per person per day.

Campgrounds at Pine Springs and Upper Dog Canyon are open all year on a first-come, first-served basis. Pine Springs is off US 62/180, and Upper Dog Canyon is at the end of New Mexico SR 137. Tent and RV camping are permitted at a cost of $8 per space per night; no hookups are available.

The closest gasoline stations are 35 miles northeast in White's City, 50 miles west in Dell City and 65 miles south in Van Horn.

The brilliant foliage of McKittrick Canyon makes fall the most popular season, but the spring also is beautiful and not as crowded. In general, the summers are warm and winters mild, with temperatures varying with the altitude. Be aware that sudden changes in the weather are common and often are accompanied by strong winds, electrical storms and occasional heavy downpours.

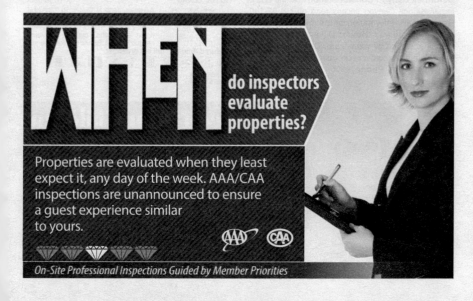

**ADMISSION** to the park, valid for 7 days, is $5; free (ages 0-15).

**PETS** must be on a leash or otherwise physically restricted; they are not permitted in public buildings or on trails.

**ADDRESS** inquiries to the Superintendent, Guadalupe Mountains National Park, 400 Pine Canyon Rd., Salt Flat, TX 79847; phone (915) 828-3251.

**McKITTRICK CANYON** is at the end of an access road off US 62/180. The canyon is a mixture of desert, canyon woodland and highland forest. Prickly pear and agaves grow at the entrance; farther along maples, ferns and wildflowers flourish. At the far end, the pine and Douglas fir of the mountain highlands appear. In late October the fall leaves resemble northern woods. Hiking is restricted to designated trails; maps are available at the visitor centers. **Hours:** Daily 8-6, Memorial Day weekend-Oct. 31; 8-4:30, rest of year. **Cost:** Included in park admission. **Phone:** (915) 828-3251.

**VISITOR CENTERS** are in two locations. They provide maps, brochures and information to enhance visits to the park. **Phone:** (915) 828-3251 for Headquarters Visitor Center, or (575) 981-2418 for Dog Canyon Ranger Station.

**Headquarters Visitor Center** is off US 62/180 at the top of Guadalupe Pass. Exhibits about natural and geologic histories are housed at the center, which also offers a 13-minute orientation film, schedules of interpretive activities and posted information. **Hours:** Daily 8-6 (Mountain time), Memorial Day-Labor Day; 8-4:30, rest of year. Closed Christmas. **Cost:** Included in park admission. **Phone:** (915) 828-3251.

**McKittrick Canyon Contact Station** is at the end of the McKittrick Canyon access road off US 62/180. General park information and exhibits about the canyon are offered. **Hours:** Days and hours vary (center is staffed by volunteers). Closed Christmas. Phone ahead to confirm schedule. **Cost:** Included in park admission. **Phone:** (505) 981-2418 or (915) 828-3251.

## GUN BARREL CITY  pop. 5,672
• Part of Dallas area — see map p. 161

### BEST WESTERN GUN BARREL CITY INN          (903)887-8886

Motel
$60-$100

**AAA Benefit:** Members save 10% or more with Best Western!

**Address:** 2111 W Main St 75156 **Location:** 4.1 mi e of jct SR 274 and 334. **Facility:** 35 units. 1 story, exterior corridors. Pool(s): outdoor. **Featured Amenity:** continental breakfast.

## HALLETTSVILLE  pop. 2,550

### BEST WESTERN EXECUTIVE INN          (361)798-9200

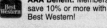
Hotel
$120-$160

**AAA Benefit:** Members save 10% or more with Best Western!

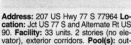

**Address:** 207 US Hwy 77 S 77964 **Location:** Jct US 77 S and Alternate Rt US 90. **Facility:** 33 units. 2 stories (no elevator), exterior corridors. **Pool(s):** outdoor. **Activities:** hot tub. **Guest Services:** coin laundry.

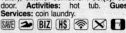

CHAPARRAL MOTEL          361/798-4385

**Motel.** Rates not provided. **Address:** 310 Hwy 77 S 77964 **Location:** Jct US 77 S and Alternate Rt US 90. **Facility:** 44 units. 2 stories (no elevator), exterior corridors. Pool(s): outdoor. **Guest Services:** coin laundry.

HOTEL TEXAS          (361)798-5900

Hotel
$80-$130

**Address:** 1632 N Texana St 77964 **Location:** Just s of CR 200. **Facility:** 40 units. 2 stories, interior corridors. **Terms:** resort fee. **Pool(s):** outdoor. **Activities:** hot tub. **Guest Services:** coin laundry.
**Featured Amenity:** full hot breakfast.

## HALTOM CITY   pop. 42,409
• Hotels & Restaurants map & index p. 257

HOFFBRAU STEAKS                                   817/498-1212   (46)

▼▼ Steak. Casual Dining. $8-$25 **AAA Inspector Notes:** Chicken-fried steak, center-cut fillets and fried catfish are all devoured in rustic, Western-themed dining rooms. Peach cobbler served in a hot skillet can be your indulgence, but I always pick the three-cheese mac as my guilty pleasure. **Features:** full bar, happy hour. **Address:** 4613 Denton Hwy 76117 **Location:** I-820 exit Denton Hwy, just s.

[L] [D] CALL [&M]

## HAMILTON   pop. 3,095

THE INN AT THE CIRCLE T                           (254)386-3209

Hotel
$89-$229

**Address:** 4021 W Hwy 36 76531 **Location:** 4.3 mi w. **Facility:** 57 units. 2 stories, interior corridors. **Terms:** cancellation fee imposed. **Pool(s):** outdoor. **Activities:** hot tub, exercise room. **Guest Services:** coin laundry. **Featured Amenity:** full hot breakfast.

SAVE [↑↓] CALL [&M] [≈] [HS] [♦]
[✕] [▯] [▭] [▱]

## HARKER HEIGHTS   pop. 26,700

AMERICAS BEST VALUE INN                           (254)690-3155

▼▼ Hotel $59-$79 **Address:** 511 Pan American Dr 76548 **Location:** US 190 exit Indian Trail Dr, just n. **Facility:** 48 units. 3 stories, interior corridors. **Terms:** cancellation fee imposed, resort fee. **Pool(s):** outdoor. **Activities:** exercise room.

[↑↓] [≈] [BIZ] [HS] [♦] [▯] [▭] [▱]

## HARLINGEN   (I-8) pop. 64,849, elev. 40'
• Restaurants p. 296

Named for a city in Holland, Harlingen earned a different moniker in its early days. Texas Rangers and U.S. Immigration and Customs officials patrolled the streets and railroad station in an attempt to maintain order in the border town, then known as "Six-shooter Junction."

Harlingen is the home of the Marine Military Academy. The academy, a private school, offers a training program designed to help its graduates gain admission to top colleges and universities. Another educational landmark is the 1928 Bowie Elementary School, a striking example of Aztec Revival architecture.

**Harlingen Area Chamber of Commerce:** 311 E. Tyler Ave., Harlingen, TX 78550. **Phone:** (956) 423-5565.

**HARLINGEN ARTS & HERITAGE MUSEUM** is 3 mi. n. in Harlingen Industrial Air Park at Boxwood and Raintree sts. The five-building complex features displays about the history of the lower Rio Grande Valley, especially its bicultural heritage. A 19th-century stagecoach inn is restored and furnished in period. The area's first hospital, which operated

1923-25, displays medical equipment of that era. The home of Lon C. Hill, founder of Harlingen, is on the grounds. A video presentation is offered.

**Time:** Allow 1 hour minimum. **Hours:** Tues.-Sat. 10-4, Sun. 1-4. Closed major holidays. **Cost:** Donations. **Phone:** (956) 216-4901.

◆ **IWO JIMA MEMORIAL** is on the south campus parade deck of the Marine Military Academy next to Harlingen International Airport. The original sculpture of World War II's Iwo Jima flag-raising was donated by its creator, Felix de Weldon, to the academy. This full-scale statue was the model used to cast the Marine Corps War Memorial for Arlington National Cemetery in Virginia. Buried next to the Iwo Jima Memorial is Harlon Block, one of the six flag-raisers.

Museum displays include items from the battle, brief biographies of the people portrayed in the sculpture, and the Hall of Fame of Iwo Jima Veterans, a series of books that contain information and "then and now" pictures of Iwo Jima veterans. A video documentary of the battle for Iwo Jima is shown daily. **Time:** Allow 1 hour minimum. **Hours:** Mon.-Sat. 10-4, Sun. 1-4. Closed major holidays. **Cost:** Donations. **Phone:** (956) 421-9234 or (800) 365-6006.

AMERICAS BEST VALUE INN                           956/425-1333

▼▼ Motel. Rates not provided. **Address:** 4401 S Expwy 83 78550 **Location:** US 83 and 77 exit Ed Carey Dr. **Facility:** 45 units. 1 story, exterior corridors. **Pool(s):** outdoor.

[≈] [BIZ] [HS] [♦] [▯] [▭]

BEST WESTERN CASA VILLA SUITES          (956)412-1500

▼▼ Hotel $77-$119

[Best Western logo] **AAA Benefit:** Members save 10% or more with Best Western!

**Address:** 4317 S Expwy 83 78550 **Location:** On US 83 and 77 exit Ed Carey Dr, just n; on northbound access road. **Facility:** 66 units. 3 stories, interior corridors. **Amenities:** safes. **Pool(s):** outdoor. **Activities:** hot tub, exercise room. **Guest Services:** valet and coin laundry. **Featured Amenity:** continental breakfast.

SAVE [↑↓] CALL [&M] [≈] [BIZ] [HS]
[♦] [✕] [▯] [▭] [▱]

COUNTRY INN & SUITES BY CARLSON           (956)428-0043

▼▼▼ Hotel $79-$99 **Address:** 3825 S Expwy 83 78550 **Location:** US 83 and 77 exit Ed Carey Dr. Located in a semi-rural area. **Facility:** 65 units. 3 stories, interior corridors. **Terms:** resort fee. **Pool(s):** outdoor. **Activities:** hot tub, exercise room. **Guest Services:** valet and coin laundry.

[✈] [≈] [BIZ] [HS] [♦] [▯] [▭] [▱]

COURTYARD BY MARRIOTT HARLINGEN          (956)412-7800

▼▼▼ Hotel $179-$199 **Address:** 1725 W Filmore Ave 78550 **Location:** US 83 and 77 exit M St, 0.5 mi n on Frontage Rd. Located in a commercial area. **Facility:** 114 units. 3 stories, interior corridors. **Pool(s):** outdoor. **Activities:** hot tub, exercise room. **Guest Services:** valet and coin laundry, area transportation.

**AAA Benefit:** Members save 5% or more!

[✈] [↑↓] [☰] CALL [&M] [≈] [BIZ] [HS] [♦] [✕] [▯]
[▱] / SOME UNITS [▭]

## HAMPTON INN & SUITES (956)428-9800

WWWW **Hotel** $109-$139 **Address:**
1202 Ed Carey Dr 78550 **Location:** US
83 and 77 exit Ed Carey Dr, n at light,
then 0.5 mi n. **Facility:** 70 units. 3 stories, interior corridors. **Terms:** 1-7 night
minimum stay, cancellation fee imposed. **Amenities:** video games.
**Pool(s):** outdoor. **Activities:** exercise room. **Guest Services:** valet
and coin laundry.

**AAA Benefit:**
Members save up to
10%!

## LA QUINTA INN HARLINGEN (956)428-6888

WW WW **Hotel** $69-$120 **Address:** 1002 S Expwy 83 78552 **Location:** US 83 and 77 exit M St. Across from a shopping mall. **Facility:** 128 units. 2 stories (no elevator), exterior corridors. **Pool(s):** outdoor. **Guest Services:** coin laundry, area transportation.

---

### WHERE TO EAT

## LA PLAYA MEXICAN CAFE 956/421-2000

WW WW Mexican. Casual Dining. $9-$18 **AAA Inspector Notes:**
The cafe serves authentic Mexican without the "Tex," so locals say.
Fresh local ingredients and produce combine in flavorful homemade
dishes prepared individually from the always-busy kitchen. Formally
attired waiters helpfully assist with tempting choices such as stuffed
avocado, eight kinds of enchiladas, fish de valle or the award-winning
carne guizada. **Features:** full bar. **Address:** 502 S 77 Sunshine Strip
78550 **Location:** US 83 and 77 exit Ed Carey Dr, 1 mi e, then 1.2 mi
n. L D

## LUBY'S

WW WW American. Cafeteria. $6-$12 **AAA Inspector Notes:** First
opened in 1947 in south Texas, this cafeteria with over 100 outlets
features a wide variety of salads, fresh fruits, seafood...including
crunchy shrimp...pastas, meat, poultry and just baked cakes and
pies. Ask about the kids specials and Lu Ann platters...an entrée with
choice of 2 vegetables and a roll. Many locations offer drive-thru
service. L D

*For additional information, visit AAA.com*

**LOCATIONS:**
**Address:** 2506 S 77 Sunshine Strip 78550 **Location:** Jct US 77 and
S Ed Carey Dr. **Phone:** 956/423-4812
**Address:** 822 Dixieland Rd 78552 **Location:** Just n of W Lincoln St.
**Phone:** 956/425-1525

---

## HEARNE pop. 4,459

## HOLIDAY INN EXPRESS & SUITES HEARNE 979/279-6600

WWWWW **Hotel.** Rates not provided. **Address:** 1645 N Market St
77859 **Location:** 1.7 mi n on SR 6. **Facility:** 64 units. 3 stories, interior corridors. **Pool(s):** outdoor. **Activities:** hot tub. **Guest Services:**
valet and coin laundry.

## OAK TREE INN (979)279-5599

WW WW **Hotel** $89-$120 **Address:** 1051 N Market St 77859 **Location:** 0.6 mi n of jct US 79 and SR 6. **Facility:** 116 units. 2 stories (no
elevator), interior/exterior corridors. **Activities:** exercise room. **Guest
Services:** coin laundry.

---

---

## HEBBRONVILLE pop. 4,558

### BEST WESTERN HEBBRONVILLE INN (361)527-3600

WWWW
**Hotel**
$99-$106

**AAA Benefit:** Members
save 10% or more with
Best Western!

**Address:** 37 E Hwy 359 78361 **Location:** On CR 359, just e of SR 16. Across
from US Border Patrol district office. **Facility:** 42 units. 1 story, interior corridors.
**Pool(s):** outdoor. **Activities:** exercise
room. **Guest Services:** coin laundry.

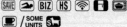

---

## HELOTES pop. 7,341

• Part of San Antonio area — see map p. 458

### BILL MILLER BAR-B-Q 210/372-0760

W Barbecue. Quick Serve. $6-$11 **AAA Inspector Notes:** The
relaxed, family-focused barbecue restaurant prepares ribs, chicken,
brisket, turkey and sausage for sandwiches or plates. **Address:**
12705 Bandera Rd 78023 **Location:** Just nw of Hausman Rd.
B L D

---

## HENDERSON (D-10) pop. 13,712

Henderson experienced two decades of rapid
growth before a devastating fire wiped out most of
its businesses in 1860. The discovery of oil in 1930
fueled a rebirth.

**Henderson Department of Tourism:** 1005 S. SR
64W, Henderson, TX 75652. **Phone:** (903)
392-8232 or (866) 650-5529.

**Self-guiding tours:** Information about walking tours
of the historic downtown district is available from
Henderson Department of Tourism.

**DEPOT MUSEUM AND CHILDREN'S DISCOVERY
CENTER** is at 514 N. High St. This living history museum features 12 historic buildings and a visitor
center. On the 5-acre grounds are an ornate Victorian outhouse, a syrup mill, an 1880 dogtrot house,
a caboose, a print shop, an oil derrick, a saw mill, a
cotton gin, a working carousel and an 1841 cabin. A
museum traces the history of Rusk County and features more than 100 hands-on activities for children.
**Time:** Allow 30 minutes minimum. **Hours:** Mon.-Fri.
9-5, Sat. 9-1. Closed state holidays. **Cost:** $3; $2
(ages 65+); $1 (ages 4-12). Carousel ride $1.
**Phone:** (903) 657-4303.

### BAYMONT INN & SUITES HENDERSON (903)657-7900

WWWW
**Hotel**
$79-$119

**Address:** 410 Hwy 79 75654 **Location:** Just n of jct US 259. **Facility:** 48
units, some two bedrooms. 3 stories (no
elevator), interior corridors. **Pool(s):** outdoor. **Activities:** exercise room. **Guest
Services:** valet and coin laundry. **Featured Amenity: continental breakfast.**

## BEST WESTERN INN OF HENDERSON (903)657-9561

Hotel
$81-$101

**AAA Benefit:** Members save 10% or more with Best Western!

**Address:** 1500 Hwy 259 S 75654 **Location:** 2 mi s, 0.7 mi s of jct US 79 and 259 S. **Facility:** 77 units. 2 stories (no elevator), interior/exterior corridors. **Pool(s):** outdoor. **Activities:** sauna, exercise room. **Guest Services:** coin laundry. **Featured Amenity:** full hot breakfast.

### HOLIDAY INN EXPRESS & SUITES - TRAFFIC STAR
903/657-5250

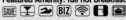 Hotel. Rates not provided. **Address:** 300 N Kilgore Dr 75652 **Location:** On US 259, just n of jct US 259/79 and SR 64/43. **Facility:** 64 units. 3 stories, interior corridors. **Pool(s):** heated outdoor. **Activities:** hot tub, exercise room. **Guest Services:** valet and coin laundry.

CALL

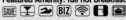
### WHERE TO EAT

### FRANCISCO'S MEXICAN RESTAURANT 903/392-8262

Mexican. Casual Dining. $6-$14 **AAA Inspector Notes:** Authentic fare made with fresh ingredients and prepared from slow-cooked family recipes are offered. You'll find all the favorites as well as such delicious specialties as Yaya's shrimp. **Features:** full bar, happy hour. **Address:** 505 Hwy 79 N 75652 **Location:** 0.5 mi n of jct US 259. L D

## HENRIETTA pop. 3,141

### BEST WESTERN HENRIETTA INN & SUITES
(940)538-6969

Hotel
$81-$140

**AAA Benefit:** Members save 10% or more with Best Western!

**Address:** 816 US Hwy 287 S 76365 **Location:** Jct US 287 and Spur 510 exit. **Facility:** 50 units. 3 stories, interior corridors. **Amenities:** safes. **Pool(s):** heated indoor. **Activities:** hot tub, exercise room. **Guest Services:** coin laundry.

## HEREFORD (B-4) pop. 15,370, elev. 3,806'

Known as the "town without a toothache," Hereford has a water supply high in natural fluoride, resulting in a low rate of dental decay. Dubbed "Beef Capital of the World" because of its abundance of cattle, the city is named for the white-faced cattle first bred in Hereford County, England. The area leads the state in cattle and agricultural production.

**Deaf Smith County Chamber of Commerce:** 701 N. Main St., P.O. Box 192, Hereford, TX 79045. **Phone:** (806) 364-3333.

**DEAF SMITH COUNTY HISTORICAL MUSEUM** is at 400 Sampson St. The museum preserves the county's history with re-creations of a general store

and a one-room school, an original jail and wagon barn, a hand-carved circus display and various tools, wagons and artifacts. The county was named for Erastus "Deaf" Smith, a Texas Revolution hero who lost his hearing in childhood. **Hours:** Mon.-Fri. 10-noon and 1-5, Sat. 10-noon and 1-3. Closed major holidays. **Cost:** Donations. **Phone:** (806) 363-7070.

## BEST WESTERN RED CARPET INN (806)364-0540

Hotel
$70-$90

**AAA Benefit:** Members save 10% or more with Best Western!

**Address:** 830 W 1st St 79045 **Location:** Jct US 385 and 60, just w. **Facility:** 90 units. 2 stories (no elevator), exterior corridors. **Parking:** winter plug-ins. **Pool(s):** outdoor. **Guest Services:** coin laundry. **Featured Amenity:** continental breakfast.

## HOLIDAY INN EXPRESS (806)364-3322

Hotel
$130-$169

**Address:** 1400 W 1st St 79045 **Location:** Jct US 385 and 60, just w. **Facility:** 59 units, some two bedrooms. 3 stories, interior corridors. **Pool(s):** heated indoor. **Activities:** hot tub, exercise room. **Guest Services:** coin laundry. **Featured Amenity:** full hot breakfast.

### WHERE TO EAT

### PARSON'S STEAKHOUSE 806/364-6413

Steak. Casual Dining. $7-$23 **AAA Inspector Notes:** The steakhouse prepares a great variety of plump, juicy fillets. A fireplace opens up into both dining rooms, and antique clocks decorate the walls. Rustic wagon-wheel chandeliers illuminate the room. **Address:** 215 S 25 Mile Ave 79045 **Location:** Jct US 385 and 60, just n.
L D

## HEWITT pop. 13,549

### SLEEP INN & SUITES (254)420-3200

Hotel $70-$200 **Address:** 209 Enterprise Blvd 76643 **Location:** I-35 exit 328; on northwest corner. **Facility:** 66 units. 3 stories, interior corridors. **Pool(s):** heated indoor. **Activities:** hot tub, exercise room. **Guest Services:** valet and coin laundry.

CALL

## HIDALGO (I-8) pop. 11,198, elev. 102'
• Hotels p. 298

**HIDALGO PUMPHOUSE** is at 902 S. 2nd St. A 45-minute guided tour takes visitors through the restored 1909 pump house. The original steam pumps and other machinery used to irrigate 40,000 acres of the Rio Grande Valley around Hidalgo are preserved here. Also on the grounds is a wing of the World Birding Center, where visitors can explore nature trails that are inhabited by birds and butterflies. **Tours:** Guided tours are available. **Time:** Allow 1 hour minimum. **Hours:** Pump house Mon.-Fri. 10-5. Birding center daily dawn-dusk. Closed major holidays. **Cost:** Pump house $3; $2 (ages 55+); $1 (ages 0-12 and students with ID). Birding center free. **Phone:** (956) 843-8686.

### SUPER 8 HIDALGO/MCALLEN AREA          (956)843-1234

Hotel
$60-$134

**Address:** 2520 N 10th St 78557 **Location:** US 83 exit 10th St, 6 mi s. Next to Dodge Arena. **Facility:** 66 units, some efficiencies. 3 stories, interior corridors. **Amenities:** safes. **Pool(s):** outdoor. **Activities:** hot tub, exercise room. **Guest Services:** valet and coin laundry. **Featured Amenity:** full hot breakfast.

## HIGHLAND PARK  pop. 8,564
• **Hotels & Restaurants map & index p. 175**
• **Part of Dallas area — see map p. 161**

### CAFE PACIFIC          214/526-1170  **67**

Seafood. Fine Dining. $12-$38 **AAA Inspector Notes:** For polished, professional service and appealing cuisine, this award-winning restaurant makes an impressive choice. Just a taste of dishes like short-smoked salmon and pepper steak with cognac sauce, and you are certain to agree. Serving as a neighborhood restaurant to its affluent guests, its windows look out onto the city's premier outdoor shopping center. Table spacing is tight, but Cafe Pacific still makes the perfect spot for a couple's night out or celebrations of any kind. **Features:** full bar, Sunday brunch. **Reservations:** suggested. **Address:** 24 Highland Park Shopping Village 75205 **Location:** Just sw of jct Mockingbird Ln and Preston Rd. **Parking:** on-site and valet.  L  D

### PATRIZIO          214/522-7878  **66**

Northern Italian. Casual Dining. $7-$24 **AAA Inspector Notes:** Pasta dishes and pizza are the main offerings at this favorite restaurant of the well-heeled set. No doubt that may be because it happens to be located in what is arguably the toniest shopping center in Dallas. The outdoor patio has been recognized as one of the most romantic the area has to offer, and I would definitely recommend it. That said, get there early as they are the first seats to go and on busy nights dining inside can get unpleasantly loud. **Features:** full bar. **Address:** 25 Highland Park Village 75205 **Location:** Between Mockingbird Ln and Preston Rd. **Parking:** on-site and valet.  L  D

## HILLSBORO  (D-8) pop. 8,456, elev. 617'

Hillsboro was established in the frontier tradition in the early 1800s. In fact, its first courthouse was a log cabin. Once a major cotton producer, the town is still rich in agriculture and is a gateway to Lake Whitney, a popular recreational spot. *See Recreation Areas Chart.*

**Hillsboro Convention and Visitors Bureau:** 115 N. Covington St., P.O. Box 358, Hillsboro, TX 76645. **Phone:** (254) 582-2481 or (800) 445-5726.

**Shopping areas:** Outlets at Hillsboro, off I-35, features some 45 factory outlet stores, including Polo Ralph Lauren and Nike. Known as the "antique capital of I-35," Hillsboro boasts multiple antique-shopping hot spots in the downtown area.

**TEXAS HERITAGE MUSEUM** is on the Hill College campus at 112 Lamar Dr. The museum explores the war experiences of Texans from 1836 to the present. Galleries feature wartime artifacts, uniforms and weapons, with a special section dedicated to Texan Audie Murphy, World War II's most decorated U.S. combat soldier. **Hours:** Mon.-Thurs. 8-4:30, Fri. 8-4 (also Sat. 9-4, June-Aug.). Phone ahead to confirm schedule. **Cost:** Free. **Phone:** (254) 659-7750.

### COMFORT SUITES          (254)582-8800

Hotel $80-$120 **Address:** 203 Outlet Dr 76645 **Location:** I-35 exit 368A northbound; exit 368 southbound, just e. **Facility:** 65 units. 4 stories, interior corridors. **Pool(s):** heated indoor. **Activities:** hot tub, exercise room. **Guest Services:** coin laundry.

### ECONO LODGE HILLSBORO          (254)582-3333

Hotel $50-$130 **Address:** 1515 Old Brandon Rd 76645 **Location:** I-35 exit 368A northbound; exit 368B southbound, just w. **Facility:** 50 units. 2 stories (no elevator), exterior corridors. **Parking:** winter plug-ins. **Pool(s):** outdoor.

### HAMPTON INN HILLSBORO          (254)582-9100

Hotel $89-$119 **Address:** 102 Dynasty Dr 76645 **Location:** I-35 exit 368B southbound; exit 368A northbound, just e. **Facility:** 70 units. 4 stories, interior corridors. **Terms:** 1-7 night minimum stay, cancellation fee imposed. **Pool(s):** outdoor. **Activities:** exercise room. **Guest Services:** valet and coin laundry.

**AAA Benefit:** Members save up to 10%!

### HOLIDAY INN EXPRESS          (254)582-0220

Hotel $89-$99 **Address:** 1505 Hillview Dr 76645 **Location:** I-35 exit 368 southbound; exit 368A northbound; on northbound access road. **Facility:** 53 units. 3 stories, interior corridors. **Terms:** cancellation fee imposed. **Pool(s):** outdoor. **Activities:** hot tub, exercise room. **Guest Services:** valet and coin laundry.

### LA QUINTA INN & SUITES HILLSBORO I-35
                              (254)580-1300

Hotel $82-$117

**Address:** 1513 Old Brandon Rd 76645 **Location:** I-35 exit 368A northbound; exit 368B southbound, just w. **Facility:** 65 units. 3 stories, interior corridors. **Pool(s):** outdoor. **Activities:** hot tub, exercise room. **Guest Services:** coin laundry. **Featured Amenity:** continental breakfast.

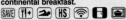

### SUPER 8          (254)580-0404

Hotel $70-$150

**Address:** 1512 Hillview Dr 76645 **Location:** I-35 exit 368A northbound; exit 368 southbound, just e. **Facility:** 49 units. 3 stories, interior corridors. **Pool(s):** heated indoor. **Activities:** hot tub, limited exercise equipment. **Guest Services:** coin laundry. **Featured Amenity:** continental breakfast.

**WHERE TO EAT**

EL CONQUISTADOR 254/582-9864

Tex-Mex. Casual Dining. $6-$14 **AAA Inspector Notes:** This local favorite features basic Tex-Mex cuisine with simple ingredients. **Features:** full bar. **Address:** 1516 Old Brandon Rd 76645 **Location:** I-35 exit 368A northbound; exit 368B southbound, just w.

L D

## HONDO pop. 8,803

**BEST WESTERN HONDO INN** (830)426-4466

Hotel
$85-$145

**AAA Benefit:** Members save 10% or more with Best Western!

**Address:** 301 Hwy 90 E 78861 **Location:** Just e of downtown. **Facility:** 57 units. 3 stories, interior corridors. **Amenities:** safes. **Pool(s):** outdoor. **Activities:** exercise room. **Guest Services:** coin laundry. **Featured Amenity: full hot breakfast.**

SAVE CALL BIZ HS

/ SOME UNITS

**WHERE TO EAT**

EL RODEO DE JALISCO 830/426-5050

Tex-Mex. Family Dining. $5-$10 **AAA Inspector Notes:** The restaurant serves homemade dishes and combinations such as carne guisada with enchiladas and a choice of fresh-made corn or flour tortillas. **Features:** beer & wine. **Address:** 409 19th St 78861 **Location:** On US 90. B L D

## HORSESHOE BAY pop. 3,418

**MARRIOTT HORSESHOE BAY RESORT** (830)598-8600

Resort Hotel
$127-$277

**AAA Benefit:** Members save 5% or more!

**Address:** 200 Hi Cir N 78657 **Location:** Jct US 281 and SR 2147, 6.6 mi w. **Facility:** A full-service resort with dramatic landscaping that includes a par-72 putting course, waterfalls and a flamingo pond, as well as a formal Japanese garden. 347 units, some two bedrooms, three bedrooms, efficiencies and kitchens. 2-7 stories, interior/exterior corridors. **Parking:** on-site and valet. **Terms:** check-in 4 pm, 3 day cancellation notice, resort fee. **Amenities:** video games, safes. **Dining:** Lantana Grille and Bar, see separate listing. **Pool(s):** outdoor. **Activities:** sauna, hot tub, steamroom, limited beach access, fishing, regulation golf, tennis, recreation programs, bicycles, game room, spa. **Guest Services:** complimentary laundry.

SAVE CALL BIZ HS

/ SOME UNITS

**WHERE TO EAT**

LANTANA GRILLE AND BAR 830/598-8600

American. Casual Dining. $11-$40 **AAA Inspector Notes:** Attentive service, a nice selection of entrées and a comfortable, relaxed and upscale setting combine for a pleasurable experience. **Features:** full bar, patio dining. **Address:** 200 Hi Cir N 78657 **Location:** Jct US 281 and SR 2147, 6.6 mi w; in Marriott Horseshoe Bay Resort. **Parking:** on-site and valet.

B L D CALL

# Houston

## Then & Now

Space City. H-Town. Bayou City. Capital of the Sunbelt. Clutch City. The Big Heart. Whatever you choose to call it, one thing's for certain: Houston is, well, a little bit of everything.

Space City is Houston's only official nickname. Because of the city's proximity to NASA's Johnson Space Center, the first word uttered by the first man on the moon in July 1969 was "Houston." In Tranquillity Park, which commemorates the Apollo 11 mission, you'll find mounds and depressions that resemble the lunar surface and towers that look like rockets. And don't pass up a trip to Space Center Houston, where you can learn all about space exploration.

Houston is also known for its vibrant arts and entertainment scene. The downtown Theater District boasts the nation's second-largest concentration of theater seats in one geographic

area. And top-notch museums, galleries and cultural establishments flourish in the Museum District. The nickname H-Town originated in the entertainment community, where everyone's heard of the H-Town Blues Festival, the Arena Theatre and the Houston-born hip-hop band H-Town, which made its debut in 1992.

Before there was a Houston there was a Harrisburg, a maritime trading post founded in 1824 by John Harris. In 1829 Harris died, leaving his brothers to resolve the inheritance of the town.

In 1836, the inheritance still unresolved, Augustus and John Allen attempted to purchase the town but felt the price was too high. They found a suitable plot of land near the junction of Buffalo and White Oak bayous and established Houston, named for Gen. Sam Houston, who had just defeated the Mexicans at nearby San Jacinto.

A 2,500-mile network of bayous flows through Houston, providing a vital habitat for diverse plant and animal species and a playground for outdoor enthusiasts. Not only have the numerous waterways helped sustain the Bayou City's environmental well-being, but they also have contributed to the town's economic success. The conversion of the winding, marshy Buffalo Bayou into the Houston Ship Channel precipitated rapid industrial growth. With cotton reigning as king in Houston at the turn of the 20th century, textile mills the world over received and processed this commodity. The timber-, cotton- and cattle-shipping town morphed into a major seaport (despite its location 50 miles inland from the Gulf of Mexico) and one of the energy capitals of the world.

The 20th century brought the discovery of oil, unleashing the potential of the refining and petrochemical industries. With petroleum, Houston became a boomtown,

Downtown's Tranquillity Park

(Continued on p. 302.)

# Destination Houston

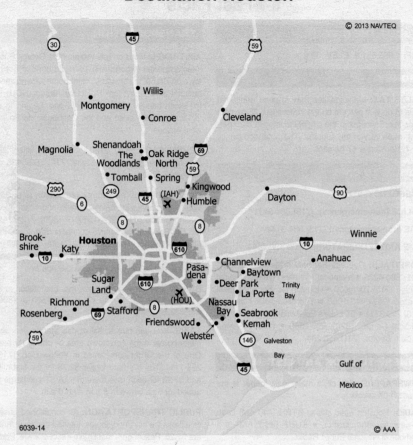

© 2013 NAVTEQ

6039-14

© AAA

This map shows cities in the Houston vicinity where you will find attractions, hotels and restaurants. Cities are listed alphabetically in this book on the following pages.

# Fast Facts

## ABOUT THE CITY

**POP:** 1,953,631 ▪ **ELEV:** 39 ft.

## MONEY

**SALES TAX:** Municipalities may impose additional rates of up to 2 percent on the statewide 6.25 percent sales tax. Sales tax in the city of Houston is 8.25 percent; rates vary in the suburbs. The hotel occupancy tax in Houston is 17 percent.

## WHOM TO CALL

**EMERGENCY:** 911

**POLICE (non-emergency):** (713) 884-3131

**FIRE (non-emergency):** (713) 884-3144

**TIME AND TEMPERATURE:** (713) 529-4444

**HOSPITALS:** Cypress Fairbanks Medical Center, (281) 890-4285 ▪ Memorial Hermann–Texas Medical Center, (713) 704-4000 ▪ Houston Northwest Medical Center, (281) 440-1000 ▪ The Methodist Hospital, (713) 790-3311 ▪ St. Luke's Episcopal Hospital–Texas Medical Center, (832) 355-1000 ▪ West Houston Medical Center, (281) 558-3444.

## WHERE TO LOOK AND LISTEN

**NEWSPAPERS:** The city's major daily paper is the *Houston Chronicle.*

**RADIO:** Houston radio station KTRH (740 AM) is an all-news/weather station ▪ KUHF (88.7 FM) is a member of National Public Radio.

## VISITOR INFORMATION

**Greater Houston Convention and Visitors Bureau:** 901 Bagby St., Suite 100, Houston, TX 77002-9396. **Phone:** (713) 437-5200 or (800) 446-8786.

## TRANSPORTATION

**AIR TRAVEL:** Houston has two airports. George Bush Intercontinental Airport (IAH), 23 miles north of downtown on US 59, is served by major domestic and international airlines. William P. Hobby Airport (HOU) to the south handles domestic flights and, beginning in 2015, flights to Mexico and the Caribbean via Southwest Airlines.

**RENTAL CARS:** Hertz, 2120 Louisiana St., offers discounts to AAA members; phone (713) 652-0436 or (800) 654-3080.

**RAIL SERVICE:** The Amtrak rail station is at 902 Washington Ave.; for train schedule and ticket information phone (713) 224-1577 or (800) 872-7245. METRORail light rail service connects downtown, the Museum District, Texas Medical Center and Reliant Stadium and costs $1.25 for one-way service and $2.50 for round-trip service; ages 0-5 ride free.

**BUSES:** The Greyhound Lines Inc. bus station is at 2121 S. Main St.; phone (713) 759-6565 or (800) 231-2222.

**TAXIS:** You can hire a taxi at cab stands near the major hotels in the downtown area or phone for one. One of the larger companies is Yellow Cab, (713) 236-1111. The standard fare is $2.75 for the first mile and $2.20 for each mile thereafter. A $1 surcharge is added for trips between 8 p.m. and 6 a.m.

**PUBLIC TRANSPORTATION:** Air-conditioned buses crisscross the city and suburbs. Limited and local fares are $1.25. Passengers must have exact change. Park-and-ride bus fares range from $2 to $4.50 and vary according to location. For details phone METRO Transit Authorities, (713) 635-4000.

**BOATS:** Houston is a leading world seaport, and the Port of Houston accommodates passenger ships.

---

(Continued from p. 300.)
ever growing, ever changing, ever maintaining its Capital of the Sunbelt status. In 1940 Houston was ranked as the country's 27th most populous city; by the late 1980s it had soared to 4th.

Because there are no zoning ordinances, Houston has experienced unrestricted development. This has resulted in the city having more than one skyline and being a proving ground for innovative architecture. The Astrodome, billed as the "eighth wonder of the world" when it opened in 1965, set a futuristic standard for stadium construction. Minute Maid Park and Reliant Stadium have ushered in a new generation of sports complexes.

Speaking of sports complexes, watching the Houston Rockets shoot three-pointers at Toyota Center is a fun diversion. Houston took its Clutch City nickname from the Rockets' furry mascot, Clutch the Bear, after the team captured two consecutive NBA championships in 1994-95.

Houston certainly has a lot to brag about, but its residents are bighearted—not bigheaded. It's the town's generosity, in fact, that yielded the moniker The Big Heart. After Hurricane Katrina wreaked havoc on neighboring Louisiana, Houstonians provided some 150,000 survivors with shelter, food and medical care.

# Must Do: AAA Editor's Picks

- Spend a few hours exploring history, science and art in the Houston Museum District, a cluster of museums within walking distance of one another. **The Menil Collection,** with its changing exhibits, single-artist installations and outdoor sculptures, is a must-see for art lovers. If you've got the kids in tow, let them burn off excess energy in the 14 fun-filled galleries comprising **The Children's Museum of Houston.**

- Also in the Museum District is 445-acre **Hermann Park,** where a number of Houston highlights are wrapped up in one pretty package. Meet some 6,000 animals at **Houston Zoo,** view all sorts of fascinating exhibits at **Houston Museum of Natural Science,** unwind in the Japanese Garden, rent a pedal boat on McGovern Lake, or enjoy some free entertainment at Miller Outdoor Theatre.

- Catch a show at **The Hobby Center for the Performing Arts,** the crown jewel of Houston's 17-block Theater District. The glass-walled contemporary building also houses the swanky **Artista** restaurant, where the service is speedy and the food is fab—it's a great pre- or post-performance dining spot.

- Practice self-discipline (or don't!) at the upscale **Houston Galleria** mall, which features 375-plus stores in addition to eateries, an ice-skating rink and two hotels. Whether or not you keep the credit card holstered, you'll enjoy wandering around this architectural stunner that's been touted as Houston's top shopping destination.

- Take a leisurely drive through **River Oaks,** an über-exclusive neighborhood whose stately mansions all come with impeccably groomed lawns and hefty price tags. The community was developed in the 1920s by brothers William and Michael Hogg; they lived with their sister, renowned philanthropist Ima Hogg, in the gorgeous Southern plantation home that's now **Bayou Bend Collection and Gardens,** a wing of **The Museum of Fine Arts, Houston.** If you have time, stop in and see the superb collection of furniture, glass, textiles and other American decorative arts dating from the Colonial era to the mid-19th century.

- Don a space helmet, hop aboard a simulator and defy gravity at **Space Center Houston.** Authentic spacecraft, spacesuits and other historic memorabilia; films; hands-on exhibits; plus tram and behind-the-scenes tours provide a mesmerizing lesson in space exploration.

- Munch on a picnic lunch in **Tranquillity Park,** then work off some calories on a "moon walk" across the park's grounds, which feature depressions and mounds that resemble the lunar surface. Snap a photo or two of the impressive 32-level fountain and the five rocket-like towers that rise from it.

- Take yourself out to the ballgame at **Minute Maid Park** and root, root, root for the home team, the MLB's **Houston Astros.** Even if you can't catch a game, a guided tour of this state-of-the-art, retractable-roofed stadium is a must.

- If basketball is your sport of choice, score tickets to watch the NBA's **Houston Rockets** sink jump shots at Toyota Center, a 750,000-square-foot, LEED-certified arena spanning six blocks in the heart of downtown.

- Let a seasoned guide sprinkle a savory blend of education and entertainment on your Houston experience during a walking, bus or van tour of the downtown area. **Houston Historical Tours** offers a variety of themed excursions highlighting the city's stadiums, parks, historic buildings, observation decks, underground tunnels and art displays.

Tour the Space Center Houston

# Houston 1-day Itinerary

AAA editors suggest these activities for a great short vacation experience.

## Morning

- Start your morning off with a picnic breakfast and a leisurely walk in **Tranquillity Park,** downtown next to City Hall. Named for the Apollo 11 astronauts' lunar landing site, this shady oasis features crater-like areas reminiscent of the moon's surface, a fountain with stainless-steel cylindrical towers that look just like rocket boosters, and a replica of the first human footprint left on the moon.

- A great way to familiarize yourself with the town is to take a guided bus or van tour (be sure to make reservations). Several tours of different themes and durations are offered through **Houston Historical Tours.** Opt for a tour that lasts between 1 and 4 hours, or choose a slightly longer one that includes a lunch break. Pickup and drop-off service is an added plus.

- As an alternative, join a guided walking tour of ◥ **Minute Maid Park,** at Crawford and Texas streets. (Though a 10 a.m. tour is almost always offered Monday through Saturday, it's a good idea to confirm the schedule before arriving). The renovated 1911 train terminal next door and the antique locomotive that chugs along the track on the left-field wall serve as reminders of the railroad industry's significant role in Houston's growth and development.

## Afternoon

- Hop the METRORail to the Houston Museum District. There are a whopping 19 museums to choose from, so you could spend days immersing yourself in art, science, culture and just about every other genre imaginable. Fortunately for those with limited time or transportation, the district's major points of interest lie within a walkable 1.5-mile radius of the Mecom Fountain, the glistening landmark at the center of the traffic circle at Main Street, Montrose Boulevard and Hermann Drive.

- Of course, you'll need to refuel before hoofing it the rest of the afternoon. If you're up for bangers and mash or shepherd's pie in an Old World atmosphere, stop at **The Black Labrador,** on Montrose Boulevard. Also on Montrose is **Brasserie Max & Julie,** a casual cafe serving up French fare like cassoulet and chateaubriand. From Tuesday through Friday you can (and should!) indulge in a prix fixe three-course lunch.

- A visit to ◥ **The Menil Collection** campus should be on every art aficionado's agenda. (Keep in mind that the buildings are closed on Mondays and Tuesdays.) Housed within the Renzo Piano-designed museum building on Sul Ross Street are changing exhibits ranging from medieval antiquities to contemporary European paintings. Be sure to check out the **Rothko Chapel,** at the junction of Sul Ross and Yupon streets; the Dan Flavin installation at Richmond

Downtown Aquarium brings you face-to-face with sea creatures

Hall, on Richmond Avenue; and the Cy Twombly Gallery, on Branard Street.

- If art just isn't your thing or if The Menil Collection is closed, spend the afternoon enjoying all that **Hermann Park** (on Fannin Street across from Rice University) has to offer. At **Houston Museum of Natural Science,** 5555 Hermann Park Dr., admire the dazzling emeralds and sapphires in the gem vault, explore the butterfly house, stargaze in the planetarium and watch a film in the Wortham Giant Screen Theatre. The 445-acre park also is home to **Houston Zoo** (6200 Hermann Park Dr.), a Japanese garden, an outdoor theater and a lake.

## Evening

- Set out for a night in the Theater District. Get tickets to a show at The Hobby Center for the Performing Arts (on Bagby Street); arrive early to enjoy the elaborate Grand Lobby and the contemporary art displays. Better yet, make pre-performance reservations at the center's posh **Artista** restaurant with its Latin American cuisine and spectacular views of the city, whether you're in the main dining room or on the balcony.

- Another evening entertainment option is **Downtown Aquarium,** also on Bagby Street. This Theater District highlight brings you face-to-face with more than 500 species of sea creatures and provides amusement-style fun with a Ferris wheel, a carousel and a train ride through a shark tank. At **Aquarium Restaurant** you can feast on fresh seafood while watching hundreds of kaleidoscopic fish in a 150,000-gallon saltwater tank.

## Arriving
### By Car

Entering Houston from the north, I-45 continues through town, exits southeast toward Space Center Houston at Clear Lake City and continues to Galveston. Hardy Toll Road parallels I-45 from north of Spring to I-610, which circles the city. I-10 enters the city from Louisiana, points east via Beaumont and picks up again as I-10 going to San Antonio.

From the northwest, US 290 connects Houston with Austin. From the northeast, US 59 runs from Texarkana through Houston to Victoria and the Mexican border.

## Getting Around
### Street System

Before tackling the freeway system, it is wise to study a city map. Freeways encircle and crisscross the city; names often change with the direction. The major city access routes spiral out from central downtown, not adhering to a north-south or east-west format.

The speed limit downtown is 35 mph or as posted. Rush hours generally occur Monday through Friday from 7 to 9 a.m. and from 4 to 6 p.m. Right turns on red are permitted unless otherwise posted.

### Parking

Metered parking is available and operational Monday through Saturday 7 a.m. to 6 p.m., with an average rate of $1.25 per hour. A Downtown Hopper Pass allowing visitors to park at spaces throughout the central business district is available for $7 and can be purchased at any pay station.

There are many commercial lots and garages downtown. The usual fee is $2 for the first 20 minutes, $5 per hour and $12 per day. Theater district parking garages charge $6 on weekends, beginning at 5 p.m. on Friday. Some places of business compensate for parking fees by stamping your parking ticket.

## Shopping

Whether you seek a 12-carat emerald or a $12 scarf, you are sure to find what you seek in one of the large department stores. Neiman Marcus, in **Houston Galleria** on the city's west side, is equipped to handle the wants of millionaires and eccentrics as well as those of browsers. The Galleria's 375 other stores include Macy's, Nordstrom and Saks Fifth Avenue, along with restaurants and an ice-skating rink.

Other malls offering restaurants, small shops, department stores and entertainment areas include **Baybrook Mall,** Bay Area Boulevard and I-45; **Greenspoint Mall,** North Belt and I-45; **Highland Village,** 4055 Westheimer Rd.; **Memorial City Mall,** Gessner Road and I-10; **The Shops at Houston Center,** on the east side of downtown; **PlazAmericas,** Bellaire Boulevard at US 59; **Town & Country Shopping Village,** I-10 at West Belt; **Uptown Park** on Post Oak Boulevard and I-610 W. Loop S.; and **Willowbrook Mall,** SR 249 and FM 1960.

Catch a rodeo while in town

There also are shops at **Rice Village** near Rice University. **Old Town Spring Shopping Village,** north on I-45 at exit 70A, has antique and specialty shops, galleries and restaurants in 180 restored Victorian cottages along tree-lined streets.

Urban cowboys and cowgirls will find boots, hats and other Western garb at various locations including **Cavender's Boot City.** Antique lovers are invited to forage for vintage treasures in **Lower Westheimer,** and those looking for rock 'n' roll souvenirs head to ⟨SAVE⟩ **Hard Rock Cafe,** 502 Texas Ave.

Most stores are open Mon.-Sat. 9-9. Most shopping centers are open Mon.-Sat. 10-9 and Sun. noon-6.

**Kemah Boardwalk,** 20 miles south of Houston off I-45 at exit 25, is a waterfront complex of shops, restaurants and amusements, including a Ferris wheel and roller coaster. **Katy Mills,** 25 miles west of Houston at 5000 Katy Mills Cir., offers 1.3 million square feet of designer outlet shopping; a Bass Pro Shops Outdoor World, with a 20,000-gallon aquarium, wildlife exhibits and sporting demonstrations; and more than 20 restaurants.

## Big Events

The rodeo opens the ⟨⟩ **Houston Livestock Show and Rodeo** at **Reliant Park** in late February or early March. The River Oaks Garden Club sponsors the **Azalea Trail** through **River Oaks** in March, when many houses and gardens are open to the public.

For golf lovers, the **Shell Houston Open** is played in late March at the **Redstone Golf Club** in northeast Houston. The city's cultural institutions, as well as those from other regions and countries, are presented during the **Houston International Festival (iFest).** This event, held in April or May, features music, dance and theater on 10 different stages.

During ❦ **Art Car Weekend** in May, a parade showcases cars and other wheeled objects turned polychromatic works of art.

A 16th-century English village is re-created 45 miles northwest of Houston, between Plantersville and Magnolia, for the **Texas Renaissance Festival.** Food, merchants, craft booths, entertainers, street characters, royalty, jousting, games and skills of the period are presented weekends from early October to late November. In early November the **George R. Brown Convention Center** hosts the 4-day ❦ **International Quilt Festival.**

The **Thanksgiving Day Parade,** a tradition since 1950, marches through downtown on Thanksgiving Day. During the second week in December the Heritage Society conducts ongoing **candlelight tours** through seven historic structures in **Sam Houston Park.**

## Sports & Rec

Sports thrive in Houston. Major League **Baseball's Houston Astros,** (713) 259-8000, play at **Minute Maid Park.** Houston's NFL **football** team, the **Houston Texans,** (832) 667-2000, hits the turf at **Reliant Stadium.** Major League **Soccer's Houston Dynamo,** (713) 276-7500, and Texas Southern University's **Tigers** football team, (713) 313-4263 or (713) 313-7011, call **BBVA Compass**

Root for the home team at Minute Maid Park

**Stadium** home. The University of Houston's **Cougars,** (713) 743-2255 or (877) 268-4275, will play the 2014-15 football season at the new **Houston Stadium.**

The NBA's **Houston Rockets,** (713) 627-3865, play **basketball** in **Toyota Center.** The AHL's **Houston Aeros,** (713) 974-7825, also play **hockey** here. The 19,000-seat arena hosts professional **boxing** and **wrestling** events; phone (713) 758-7200.

The various Rice University **Owls** teams, (713) 522-6957, draw large crowds to their 70,000-seat facility.

**Rodeos** always are sellouts, particularly those presented by The Houston Livestock Show and Rodeo.

Houston has many public **tennis** courts. **Golf** is available at many public courses in the city: **Bear Creek,** (281) 855-2447, at 16001 Clay Rd.; **Memorial Park,** (713) 862-4033, at 1001 Memorial Loop Dr. E.; and **Woodlands Resort and Conference Center,** (281) 882-3000, at 2301 N. Millbend Dr.

**Polo** is played near Memorial Park at the **Houston Polo Club,** 8552 Memorial Drive at I-610; phone (713) 681-8571.

**Challenger Seven Memorial Park,** 2301 W. NASA Pkwy. in Webster, (713) 440-1587, and **Mercer Arboretum and Botanic Gardens,** 22306 Aldine Westfield Rd. in Humble, (281) 443-8731, contain **hiking** trails as well as picnic areas. **Memorial Park,** 6501 Memorial Dr., features 6 miles of running trails as well as paths for **bicycling** and **skating.** Track cycling can be found at the Alkek Velodrome in **Cullen Park,** 19008 Saums Rd.; phone (281) 578-0858.

**Tom Bass Regional Park Section II** is at 3602 Fellows Rd. and contains jogging and nature trails as well as a 20-acre spring-fed **fishing** lake. Visitors can enjoy **canoeing** and a view of Houston's skyline from **Buffalo Bayou. Boating** is popular at **Clear Lake Park,** 5001 NASA Pkwy.

**Cypress Trails Equestrian Center** at 21415 Cypresswood Dr. in the town of Humble offers **horseback riding** trips along the trails threading through the undeveloped land around George Bush Intercontinental Airport. The equestrian center offers rides at other locations as well; phone (281) 446-7232.

**Horse racing,** both Thoroughbred and quarter horse, takes place at the **Sam Houston Race Park,** 7575 N. Sam Houston Pkwy. W. Simulcast racing is available daily. Phone (281) 807-8700.

**Note:** Policies concerning admittance of children to pari-mutuel betting facilities vary. Phone for information.

# Performing Arts

Houston has been musically inclined from its earliest days. As a result, a wide variety of musical entertainment, ranging from classical to modern, is currently available in the city.

The stage of **Jones Hall**, 615 Louisiana St., is used throughout the year for productions by the **Houston Symphony Orchestra,** phone (713) 224-7575, and the **Society for the Performing Arts;** phone (713) 227-4772. **Wortham Theater Center,** at Texas Avenue and Smith Street, is the home of the **Houston Grand Opera,** phone (713) 228-6737, and the **Houston Ballet;** phone (713) 227-2787.

The dramatic arts have flourished in the city. The centerpiece of the downtown theater district is **The Hobby Center for the Performing Arts,** 800 Bagby St.; phone (713) 315-2525. The center is the home of **Theatre Under the Stars,** phone (713) 558-2600; and **Broadway Across America Houston,** phone (713) 622-7469. Professional repertory can be found downtown at **Alley Theatre,** 615 Texas Ave.; phone (713) 228-9341. **Stages Repertory Theatre,** 3201 Allen Pkwy., is a performing arts company for original works and children's theater; phone (713) 527-0123. The **Bayou Music Center** at 520 Texas Ave. in Bayou Place attracts big-name performers and touring productions; phone (713) 230-1600. In addition to various performances, two art galleries can be found at **DiverseWorks Artspace,** 4102 Fannin St.

March through October the **Miller Outdoor Theatre** in Hermann Park presents free musicals and dramas as well as ballets and the Houston Symphony. Rock concerts are held at **Toyota Center.**

# INSIDER INFO:
## CityPASS

Houston CityPASS saves travelers 46 percent on combined admission costs to select Houston attractions. A Houston CityPASS ticket booklet includes prepaid admission to Space Center Houston, Downtown Aquarium and Houston Museum of Natural Science. Also included are two option tickets: one for either Houston Zoo or a Kemah Boardwalk All Day All Ride Pass and the other for either The Museum of Fine Arts, Houston or The Children's Museum of Houston.

The ticket booklet, valid for 9 days starting with the first date of use, is available online and from participating attractions.

# ◣ ATTRACTIONS

**BAYOU BEND COLLECTION AND GARDENS** is 4.5 mi. w. via Memorial Dr., then .5 mi. s. to 6003 Memorial Dr. The American decorative arts collection of The Museum of Fine Arts, Houston *(see attraction listing p. 311)* is housed in the former home of philanthropist Miss Ima Hogg. Displayed in more than 20 room settings, the collection traces the evolution in American style from the Colonial period to the mid-19th century. More than 5,000 works include ceramics, furniture, glass, paintings, paper, silver and textiles. The house is surrounded by 14 acres of woodlands and formal gardens with imported and native plants. The visitor and education center features exhibits, videos and a library.

**Hours:** Guided 1-hour or 90-minute house tours depart every 15 minutes Tues.-Thurs. 10-11:45 and 1-2:45, Fri.-Sat. 10-11:45, Sept.-July. Schedule varies rest of year; phone ahead. Self-guiding audio tours of the house Fri.-Sun. 1-5. Self-guiding garden tours Tues.-Sat. 10-5, Sun. 1-5. Closed Thanksgiving and Christmas. **Cost:** Guided 90-minute house tour (includes gardens) $15; $13.50 (ages 65+ and students with ID); $7.50 (ages 10-18). One-hour house tour (includes gardens) $12.50; $11 (ages 65+ and students with ID); $6.25 (ages 10-18). Gardens $5; free (ages 0-9). Ages 0-9 are not permitted on guided tours. Ages 10-16 must be with an adult. Reservations are required for guided tours. **Phone:** (713) 639-7750.

**BEER CAN HOUSE** is at 222 Malone St. The result of a project begun in 1968 by former homeowner John Milkovisch, the house and yard are said to showcase more than 50,000 beer cans. **Tours:** Guided tours are available. **Time:** Allow 15 minutes minimum. **Hours:** Sat.-Sun. noon-5. **Cost:** Guided tour $5. Self-guiding tour $2. Cash only. **Phone:** (713) 926-6368.

**BLAFFER ART MUSEUM AT THE UNIVERSITY OF HOUSTON** is off I-45 s. exit Cullen Blvd., then entrance 16 to the central campus. The museum features frequently changing exhibitions of contemporary art. **Hours:** Tues.-Sat. 10-5. Closed university holidays. **Cost:** Free. **Phone:** (713) 743-9530.

**THE CHILDREN'S MUSEUM OF HOUSTON** is at 1500 Binz St. Hands-on exhibits in 14 galleries represent such subjects as science, math, culture and the arts. Highlights include Kidtropolis, PowerPlay, FlowWorks, Invention Convention, Matter Factory and Cyberchase. **Time:** Allow 2 hours minimum. **Hours:** Tues.-Sat. 10-6 (also Thurs. 6-8 p.m.), Sun. noon-6. Schedule may vary Labor Day-Memorial Day; phone ahead. Closed Jan. 1, Easter, Thanksgiving and Christmas. **Cost:** $9; $8 (ages 65+ and military with ID); free (under 1 and Thurs. after 5 p.m.). **Parking:** $8 maximum. **Phone:** (713) 522-1138.

**CONTEMPORARY ARTS MUSEUM HOUSTON** is at 5216 Montrose Blvd. Changing exhibitions in the museum's two galleries focus on international, national and regional contemporary artists and themes. Various educational programs and lectures are offered. **Hours:** Tues.-Fri. 10-7 (also Thurs. 7-9 p.m.), Sat. 10-6, Sun. noon-6. Closed Jan. 1, Thanksgiving and Christmas. **Cost:** Free. **Phone:** (713) 284-8250.

**SAVE** **DOWNTOWN AQUARIUM,** 410 Bagby St., brings visitors up close to more than 500 species of marine life including stingrays, sawfish, sharks and eels. White Tigers of the Maharaha's Temple is among the aquarium's seven themed areas. The attraction also contains such amusement rides as a carousel, a Ferris wheel with views of the downtown Houston skyline, and Shark Voyage, a train ride through a shark tank.

**Time:** Allow 1 hour, 30 minutes minimum. **Hours:** Daily 10-10 (also Fri.-Sat. 10-11 p.m.). Closed Christmas. Phone ahead to confirm schedule. **Cost:** Aquarium exhibit $9.25; $8.25 (ages 65+); $6.25 (ages 2-12). Amusement ride fares vary. Combination ticket including all-day access to exhibits and rides $15.99. **Parking:** $7; valet parking $9. **Phone:** (713) 223-3474.

**THE HEALTH MUSEUM** is off SR 288 exit Calumet St., following service road to Binz St., then .5 mi. w. to La Branch St. at 1515 Hermann Dr. Throughout the museum, computer simulators, video touch screens and interactive exhibits provide hands-on learning about health and the workings of the human body.

Visitors can take a tour of the human body and learn about organs and bones inside the Amazing Body Pavilion or journey into the alien landscape of skin during the Planet You 3D film production. You: The Exhibit allows visitors to use body scanners, computer imaging and other multimedia and special-effects technology to explore their own bodies.

**Time:** Allow 30 minutes minimum. **Hours:** Mon.-Sat. 9-5, Sun. noon-5, June-Aug.; Tues.-Sat. 9-5, Sun. noon-5, rest of year. Closed Thanksgiving and Christmas. **Cost:** $8; $6 (ages 3-12 and 65+). **Parking:** $5. **Phone:** (713) 521-1515.

**THE HERITAGE SOCIETY** is at 1100 Bagby St. in Sam Houston Park. This outdoor museum features 10 historic houses, a general store and gallery exhibits. Buildings include the 1847 Kellum-Noble House, believed to be Houston's oldest brick house; the San Felipe Cottage, a German immigrant cottage of the 1860s; and the 1823 Old Place, a rough-hewn wooden frame said to be the oldest surviving building in Harris County.

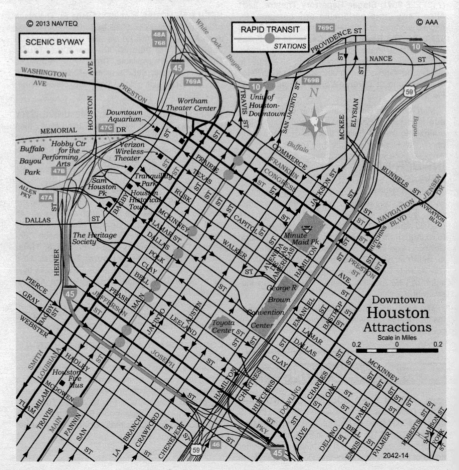

Downtown Houston Attractions

2042-14

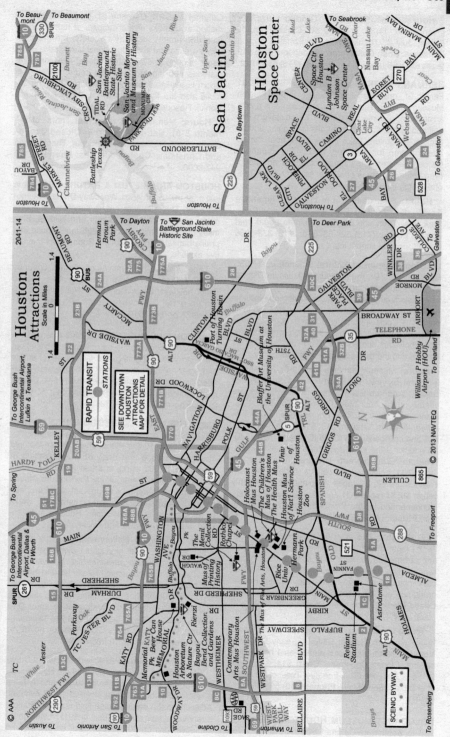

**Hours:** Tues.-Sat. 10-4. Guided tours are given at 10, 11:30, 1 and 2:30. Closed Jan. 1, Easter, July 4, Thanksgiving, Christmas Eve and Christmas. **Cost:** Gallery free. Guided tour $15; $12 (ages 65+); $6 (ages 6-18). **Phone:** (713) 655-1912.

**HERMANN PARK** is off Cambridge St. at 6001 Fannin St., opposite Rice University in the Houston Museum District. The 445-acre park contains a zoo, a museum, a miniature train, a water playground, golf and picnic facilities and trails for jogging and bicycling. McGovern Lake offers pedal boat rentals and a haven for migratory birds. The Japanese Garden features a tea house, waterfall and pond. Free entertainment is offered at Miller Outdoor Theatre March through November.

**Hours:** Park daily 6 a.m.-11 p.m. Japanese Garden daily 9-6, Mar.-Oct.; 9-5, rest of year. **Cost:** Park free. Train ride $3. Thirty-minute pedal boat ride $9. **Phone:** (713) 524-5876, or (713) 373-3386 for performance schedules.

**Houston Museum of Natural Science** is at 5555 Hermann Park Dr. in the Houston Museum District. Exhibits focus on astronomy, anthropology, geology, paleontology and natural history. Collections include Native American artifacts and a hall of gems and minerals. The Cockrell Butterfly Center is home to thousands of butterflies, insects and rain forest plants. Daily shows are offered at the Wortham Giant Screen Theatre and the Burke Baker Planetarium.

**Hours:** Museum exhibits daily 9-6, June-Aug.; 9-5, rest of year. Last admission 1 hour before closing. Wortham Giant Screen Theatre shows are offered on the hour Mon.-Fri. 10-5, Sat.-Sun. 11-5. Planetarium daily 11:30-5. Phone ahead to confirm schedule. **Cost:** Museum $15; $10 (ages 3-11, ages 62+ and college students with ID); free (Thurs. 2-5). An additional fee is charged for special exhibitions. Wortham Giant Screen Theatre shows $11; $9 (ages 3-11, ages 62+ and college students with ID). Planetarium $8; $7 (ages 3-11 and 62+). Butterfly center $8; $7 (ages 3-11 and 62+). Reservations are recommended for the Wortham Giant Screen Theater. **Phone:** (713) 639-4629.

**Houston Zoo** is at 6200 Hermann Park Dr. Lions, orangutans, chimpanzees and tigers are perennial favorites among some 6,000 animals representing more than 800 species. The 55-acre park includes the free-flight Tropical Bird House, orangutan and elephant habitats and an aquarium. Giraffe feedings and interactive keeper chats take place daily.

**Tours:** Guided tours are available. **Time:** Allow 2 hours minimum. **Hours:** Daily 9-7, early Mar.-early Nov.; 9-6, rest of year. Last admission 1 hour before closing. Closed Christmas. **Cost:** $14; $10 (ages 2-11); $7.50 (ages 65+); free (first Tues. of the month after 2 p.m., Sept.-May). **Phone:** (713) 533-6500.

**HOLOCAUST MUSEUM HOUSTON** is s. on SR 288 to Southmore/Calumet St., then .8 mi. w. on Calumet to 5401 Caroline St. Dedicated to promoting awareness of the dangers of hatred, prejudice and apathy in today's society, the museum offers a historical and educational view of the Holocaust through photographs, videos, survivors' oral histories and labeled historical items. A Memorial Room is available for contemplation. Changing exhibits also are featured in two galleries and in the Boniuk Resource Center.

**Hours:** Mon.-Fri. 9-5 (also first Thurs. of the month 5-8), Sat.-Sun. noon-5. Closed Jan. 1, Easter, Rosh Hashanah, Yom Kippur, Thanksgiving and Christmas. **Cost:** Donations. **Phone:** (713) 942-8000.

**HOUSTON ARBORETUM & NATURE CENTER** is just e. of I-610W at 4501 Woodway Dr. near Memorial Park. This 155-acre nature sanctuary supports many species of native plants and wildlife. Five miles of nature trails wind through forest, pond and prairie habitats. The Discovery Room offers interactive exhibits.

**Time:** Allow 1 hour minimum. **Hours:** Grounds daily 7-7. Discovery Room Tues.-Sun. 10-4. Closed major holidays. **Cost:** Donations. Reservations are required for Discovery Room. **Phone:** (713) 681-8433 or (866) 510-7219.

**HOUSTON FIRE MUSEUM** is at 2403 Milam St. An old firehouse contains fire equipment, exhibits about the history of firefighting and videos about safety and fires. An interactive junior firehouse area is offered for children. **Hours:** Tues.-Sat. 10-4. Closed major holidays. **Cost:** $5; $4 (ages 65+); $3 (ages 2-12). **Phone:** (713) 524-2526.

**THE MENIL COLLECTION,** 1533 Sul Ross St., is housed in a structure designed by Italian architect Renzo Piano. The museum features changing exhibits that draw from a collection of more than 17,000 works of art, including Byzantine and medieval art, antiquities, Pacific and African tribal arts, 16th-century to present-day European paintings, and surrealistic and contemporary works by such artists as Jasper Johns, Robert Rauschenberg, Mark Rothko and Andy Warhol.

The Cy Twombly Gallery contains work by the American artist. Other highlights include the nearby Rothko Chapel *(see attraction listing),* with huge canvases by the abstract expressionist, and the Barnett Newman sculpture "Broken Obelisk," dedicated to Martin Luther King Jr. Richmond Hall displays fluorescent work by the minimalist sculptor Dan Flavin. **Time:** Allow 1 hour, 30 minutes minimum. **Hours:** Wed.-Sun. 11-7. Closed major holidays. **Cost:** Free. **Phone:** (713) 525-9400.

**MINUTE MAID PARK** is downtown at Crawford and Texas sts. Home of the Houston Astros, the baseball stadium seats 40,950 and features a retractable roof that can close in 12-20 minutes. Adjacent to the natural-grass field is Union Station, a renovated train terminal built in 1911. A vintage locomotive runs on 800 feet of track on the left-field wall of the stadium. Guided 1-hour tours cover more than a mile of the facilities; Early Bird tours also are offered.

**Note:** Comfortable walking shoes are recommended. **Hours:** Tours depart Mon.-Sat. at 10, noon and 2. Early Bird tours depart Mon.-Sat. 1 hour prior to gate's opening for games during the Astros' regular season. Phone ahead to confirm schedule. **Cost:** Tour $11; $9 (ages 65+); $7 (ages 3-14). Early Bird tour $15; $13 (ages 65+); $11 (ages 3-14). **Phone:** (713) 259-8687.

**THE MUSEUM OF FINE ARTS, HOUSTON** is at 1001 Bissonnet between S. Main and Montrose Blvd. More than 63,000 art objects are contained in the museum's permanent collection. The Caroline Wiess Law Building houses an African gold collection, pre-Columbian and Asian art, and modern and contemporary works. The Audrey Jones Beck Building, 5601 Main St., features European art from antiquity to 1920 and American art through 1945. The museum's decorative arts collections are housed at Bayou Bend Collection and Gardens and Rienzi *(see attraction listings p. 307and p. 311, respectively).*

**Tours:** Guided tours are available. **Time:** Allow 2 hours minimum. **Hours:** Tues.-Wed. and Mon. holidays 10-5, Thurs. 10-9, Fri.-Sat. 10-7, Sun. 12:15-7. Sculpture garden daily 9 a.m.-10 p.m. Closed Thanksgiving and Christmas. **Cost:** $13; $8 (ages 65+); $6 (ages 6-18 and students with ID); free (Thurs.). Sculpture garden free. **Parking:** $6. **Phone:** (713) 639-7300 or TTY (713) 639-7390.

**MUSEUM OF PRINTING HISTORY** is at 1324 W. Clay between Montrose and Waugh. Antique printing equipment, fine art prints, rare books, prints and historic newspapers are displayed. Guided tours are available by reservation. **Time:** Allow 1 hour minimum. **Hours:** Tues.-Sat. 10-5. Closed major holidays. **Cost:** Guided tours $7; $5 (ages 60+); $3 (students with ID). Self-guiding tours free. **Phone:** (713) 522-4652.

**NATIONAL MUSEUM OF FUNERAL HISTORY** is off I-45 Richey Rd. exit w. under the interstate and w. to Ella Blvd., then s. to 415 Barren Springs Dr. The museum houses a collection of hearses, clothing, coffins, caskets, 19th-century mourning symbols and other exhibits tracing the history of funerals from the early Egyptians to the present. Replicas of King Tut's sarcophagus and Abraham Lincoln's coffin also are featured. **Time:** Allow 30 minutes minimum. **Hours:** Mon.-Fri. 10-4, Sat. 10-5, Sun. noon-5. Closed Jan. 1, Easter, Thanksgiving and Christmas. **Cost:** $10; $9 (ages 55+ and military with ID); $7 (ages 3-11). **Phone:** (281) 876-3063.

**PORT OF HOUSTON TURNING BASIN** is n.w. off the I-610 Clinton Dr. exit, in the 7300 block of Clinton Dr.; a security guard will direct visitors to

The Museum of Fine Arts, Houston

Gate 8. The basin is the navigational head of the 50-mile Houston Ship Channel. **Hours:** Narrated 90-minute boat tours of the Port of Houston aboard the MV *Sam Houston* are given Tues.-Wed. and Fri.-Sat. at 10 and 2:30, Thurs. and Sun. at 2:30, Jan.-Oct. and Dec. Closed major holidays. **Cost:** Free. Reservations are required and should be made at least 2 months in advance during the summer. **Phone:** (713) 670-2416.

**RIENZI** is off US 59 exit Kirby, then n. to 1406 Kirby Dr. The European decorative arts collection of The Museum of Fine Arts, Houston *(see attraction listing)* is displayed in the former home of philanthropists Carroll Sterling Masterson and Harris Masterson III. The villa, which is surrounded by formal gardens, is a showcase for 18th- and 19th-century European art and antiques, including more than 800 pieces of Worcester porcelain.

**Hours:** Guided 1-hour tours depart Wed.-Sat. at 10, 11, 1:30, 2:30 and 3:30, Sun. 1-5. Closed major holidays. **Cost:** $8; $5 (ages 65+, ages 12-18 with adult, and college students with ID). Under 12 must be with an adult. Reservations are recommended Wed.-Sat. **Phone:** (713) 639-7800.

**ROTHKO CHAPEL** is at 3900 Yupon St. at jct. Sul Ross St. American abstract expressionist Mark Rothko collaborated with architects Philip Johnson, Howard Barnstone and Eugene Aubrey to design this octagonal sanctuary, which contains 14 Rothko paintings that extend from the floor to the ceiling. The adjoining plaza features a Barnett Newman sculpture dedicated to the memory of Rev. Martin Luther King Jr. **Hours:** Daily 10-6. **Cost:** Free. **Phone:** (713) 524-9839.

**SPACE CENTER HOUSTON** is 25 mi. s.e. via I-45, then 3 mi. e. to 1601 NASA Pkwy. The official visitor center of NASA's Johnson Space Center tells the story of America's manned space flight program through historic artifacts, hands-on exhibits, live presentations and behind-the-scenes tours.

Visitors can try on space helmets, touch a moon rock and climb aboard computer simulators to retrieve a satellite, land the space shuttle and walk on the moon. Spacecraft on display include Mercury, Gemini and Apollo capsules, Skylab and Lunar Module Trainers and a full-size space shuttle replica. The Astronaut Gallery features spacesuits from every era of space exploration.

Guided 90-minute tram tours to Johnson Space Center stop at Mission Control, the Space Shuttle Training Facility and other NASA laboratories. Films are shown daily in the Destiny Theater and the five-story IMAX theater.

**Time:** Allow 5 hours minimum. **Hours:** Mon.-Fri. 10-5, Sat.-Sun. 10-6, with extended summer and holiday hours. Closed Christmas. Phone ahead to confirm schedule. **Cost:** $22.95; $21.95 (ages 65+); $18.95 (ages 4-11). **Parking:** $6. **Phone:** (281) 244-2100. 🍴

**TRANQUILLITY PARK** is downtown, bounded by Smith, Walker, Bagby and Rusk sts. The park commemorates the Apollo 11 mission and is named for the 1969 lunar landing on the Sea of Tranquillity. Five towers resembling rockets rise from a 32-level fountain and reflecting pool. Bronze plaques recount the Apollo story in 15 languages. **Hours:** Daily 6 a.m.-11 p.m. **Cost:** Free. **Phone:** (832) 395-7000.

## Sightseeing
### Bus and Van Tours
The easiest way to familiarize yourself with Houston is to take a bus or van tour of the city.

**HOUSTON HISTORICAL TOURS** usually departs from City Hall at 901 Bagby St.; transportation to and from local airports and hotels is offered. Visitors can explore Houston's parks, stadiums, historic buildings and more on one of eight narrated bus or van tours lasting between 2 and 9 hours. Other themed excursions include presidential tours, religious tours, ethnic tours, architectural walking tours and ghost tours.

**Time:** Allow 2 hours minimum. **Hours:** Tours are given daily. **Cost:** City tours $50-$225. Rates vary depending on tour selected. Fees apply for pickup and drop-off service outside the downtown area. Cash only. Reservations are required. **Parking:** Downtown parking maximum $12; free Sun. **Phone:** (713) 392-0867.

**HOUSTON TOURS** picks up passengers at all major hotels inside Loop 610. Lasting 3.5 hours, downtown tours begin at the Astrodome and continue through Rice University, Houston Museum District, the city center, River Oaks and the Houston Galleria area. Tours of Space Center Houston and Galveston Island also are offered.

**Hours:** Space Center Tour departs daily between 9 and 9:15. Phone to confirm dates and departure times for the downtown and Galveston Island tours. **Cost:** The 3.5-hour downtown tour $40; $20 (ages 4-11). Space Center Houston tour (includes admission to center) $60; $30 (ages 4-11). Reservations are required. **Phone:** (832) 630-9188.

### Driving Tours
Scenic drives wind through Memorial Park and residential River Oaks, with its large live oak trees and beautiful houses.

### Walking Tours
An area suited to walking tours is the original business district. Allen's Landing Park, at the corner of Main and Commerce, marks the site where Houston's founders, two brothers by the name of Allen, came ashore in 1836. Nearby Old Market Square is all that remains of Houston's original business section, bounded by Congress, Preston, Milam and Travis streets.

The 1847 Kennedy Trading Post, on the square at 813 Congress St., is Houston's oldest commercial building on its original site. The old Cotton Exchange Building is a four-story, Victorian-Italianate structure on the southwest corner of Travis and Franklin streets. Built in 1884, it served as a cotton exchange until 1923. The Old Sixth Ward is a residential-commercial area of Victorian gingerbread frame houses just northwest of downtown.

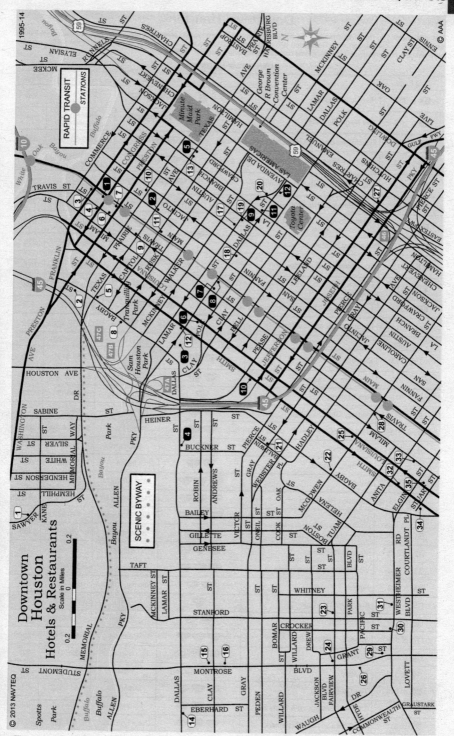

Downtown Houston
Hotels & Restaurants

RAPID TRANSIT STATIONS

SCENIC BYWAY

Scale in Miles
0      0.2

# Downtown Houston

This index helps you "spot" where approved hotels and restaurants are located on the corresponding detailed maps. Hotel daily rate range is for comparison only. Restaurant price range is a combination of lunch and/or dinner. Turn to the listing page for more detailed rate and price information and consult display ads for special promotions.

## DOWNTOWN HOUSTON

| Map Page | Hotels | Diamond Rated | Rate Range | Page |
|---|---|---|---|---|
| **1** p. 313 | Hotel Icon Houston | ◆◆◆ | Rates not provided | 334 |
| **2** p. 313 | **The Magnolia Hotel** | ◆◆◆ | Rates not provided (SAVE) | 334 |
| **3** p. 313 | DoubleTree by Hilton Hotel Houston Downtown | ◆◆◆ | $109-$299 | 332 |
| **4** p. 313 | **BEST WESTERN PLUS Downtown Inn & Suites** | ◆◆◆ | Rates not provided (SAVE) | 332 |
| **5** p. 313 | **The Westin Houston Downtown** | ◆◆◆ | Rates not provided (SAVE) | 335 |
| **6** p. 313 | **Hyatt Regency Houston** | ◆◆◆ | $89-$379 (SAVE) | 334 |
| **7** p. 313 | Residence Inn by Marriott Houston Downtown/ Convention Center | ◆◆◆ | $89-$399 | 335 |
| **8** p. 313 | Courtyard by Marriott Houston Downtown | ◆◆◆ | $89-$399 | 332 |
| **9** p. 313 | **Four Seasons Hotel Houston** | ◆◆◆◆ | Rates not provided (SAVE) | 333 |
| **10** p. 313 | Crowne Plaza Houston Downtown (See ad p. 333.) | ◆◆◆ | $90-$230 | 332 |
| **11** p. 313 | Embassy Suites Houston Downtown | ◆◆◆ | $142-$332 | 333 |
| **12** p. 313 | **Hilton Americas-Houston** (See ad p. 334.) | ◆◆◆◆ | $119-$549 (SAVE) | 334 |

| Map Page | Restaurants | Diamond Rated | Cuisine | Price Range | Page |
|---|---|---|---|---|---|
| **1** p. 313 | Beaver's | ◆◆ | Regional American | $8-$15 | 335 |
| **2** p. 313 | Aquarium Restaurant | ◆◆ | Seafood | $10-$33 (SAVE) | 335 |
| **3** p. 313 | Red Lantern | ◆ | Vietnamese | $6-$12 | 337 |
| **4** p. 313 | Hearsay Gastro Lounge | ◆◆ | New American | $6-$30 | 336 |
| **5** p. 313 | Hard Rock Cafe | ◆◆ | American | $10-$25 (SAVE) | 336 |
| **6** p. 313 | Treebeards | ◆ | Southern | $5-$15 | 337 |
| **7** p. 313 | Mia Bella Trattoria | ◆◆ | Italian | $7-$23 | 336 |
| **8** p. 313 | Artista | ◆◆◆ | Latin American | $26-$68 | 335 |
| **9** p. 313 | Sambuca Restaurant | ◆◆◆ | New American | $9-$28 | 337 |
| **10** p. 313 | 17 | ◆◆◆ | New American | $10-$42 | 335 |
| **11** p. 313 | Flying Saucer | ◆◆ | International | $8-$11 | 336 |
| **12** p. 313 | Massa's Restaurant | ◆◆◆ | Seafood | $16-$33 | 336 |
| **13** p. 313 | Vic & Anthony's Steakhouse | ◆◆◆ | Steak | $30-$56 | 337 |
| **14** p. 313 | Nino's | ◆◆ | Traditional Italian | $11-$35 | 337 |
| **15** p. 313 | Khun Kay Thai Cafe | ◆ | Thai | $7-$19 | 336 |
| **16** p. 313 | Pronto Cucinino | ◆◆ | Italian | $7-$13 | 337 |
| **17** p. 313 | Massa's Seafood Grill | ◆◆◆ | Seafood | $10-$30 | 336 |
| **18** p. 313 | **III Forks** | ◆◆◆ | Steak | $25-$60 | 335 |
| **19** p. 313 | **Quattro** | ◆◆◆◆ | Italian | $13-$52 | 337 |
| **20** p. 313 | The Grove | ◆◆◆ | American | $11-$32 | 336 |
| **21** p. 313 | The Fish Restaurant & Sushi Bar | ◆◆◆ | Asian Sushi | $9-$28 | 336 |
| **22** p. 313 | Charivari Specialty Restaurant | ◆◆◆ | New European | $11-$39 | 335 |

| Map Page | Restaurants (cont'd) | Diamond Rated | Cuisine | Price Range | Page |
|---|---|---|---|---|---|
| 23 p. 313 | Barnaby's Cafe | ▽▽ | American | $10-$17 | 335 |
| 24 p. 313 | La Mexicana Restaurant | ▽ | Mexican | $8-$23 | 336 |
| 25 p. 313 | Ibiza Food & Wine Bar | ▽▽▽ | New American | $9-$28 | 336 |
| 26 p. 313 | Niko Niko's | ▽ | Greek | $9-$23 | 336 |
| 27 p. 313 | Kim Son Restaurant | ▽▽ | Vietnamese | $7-$26 | 336 |
| 28 p. 313 | Reef | ▽▽▽ | New Seafood | $7-$29 | 337 |
| 29 p. 313 | Little Bigs | ▽ | Burgers | $2-$6 | 336 |
| 30 p. 313 | Katz's Deli & Bar | ▽▽ | Deli | $9-$15 | 336 |
| 31 p. 313 | Restaurant Indika | ▽▽▽ | New Indian | $12-$70 | 337 |
| 32 p. 313 | Damian's Cucina Italiana | ▽▽▽ | Italian | $15-$45 | 335 |
| 33 p. 313 | Van Loc Restaurant | ▽ | Vietnamese | $6-$15 | 337 |
| 34 p. 313 | Brennan's of Houston | ▽▽▽▽ | Creole | $16-$40 | 335 |
| 35 p. 313 | Piola | ▽▽ | Pizza | $9-$16 | 337 |

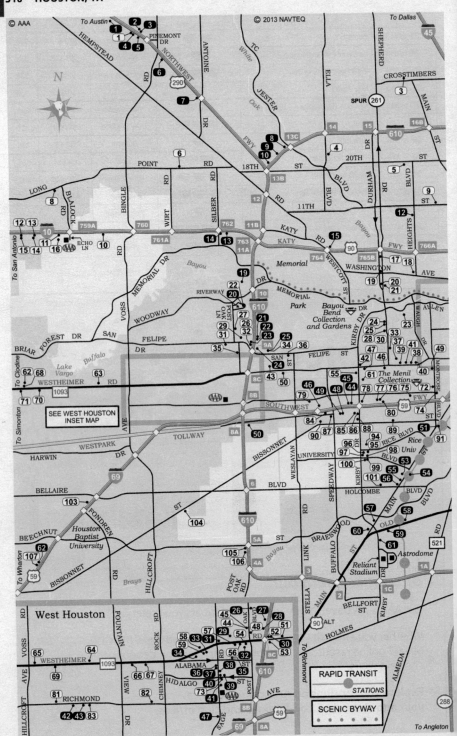

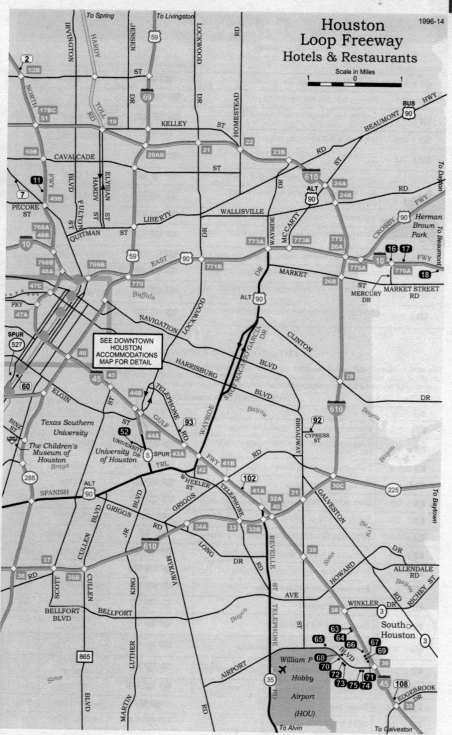

# Houston
# Loop Freeway
## Hotels & Restaurants

1996-14

Scale in Miles

## ✈ Airport Hotels

| Map Page | WILLIAM P HOBBY (Maximum driving distance from airport: 3.0 mi) | Diamond Rated | Rate Range | Page |
|---|---|---|---|---|
| 72 p. 316 | Best West Inn & Suites, 1.3 mi | ◆◆ | $109-$299 | 338 |
| 74 p. 316 | Comfort Suites Hobby Airport, 1.7 mi | ◆◆◆ | $79-$199 | 338 |
| 67 p. 316 | Courtyard by Marriott-Houston Hobby Airport, 2.0 mi | ◆◆◆ | $89-$159 | 339 |
| 75 p. 316 | Days Inn & Suites-Hobby Airport, 1.7 mi | ◆◆ | $85-$135 SAVE | 340 |
| 65 p. 316 | DoubleTree by Hilton Houston Hobby Airport, 0.9 mi | ◆◆◆ | $129-$349 | 340 |
| 69 p. 316 | Drury Inn & Suites-Houston Hobby, 2.0 mi | ◆◆◆ | $85-$219 | 341 |
| 63 p. 316 | Four Points by Sheraton Houston Hobby Airport, 2.4 mi | ◆◆◆ | $129-$179 SAVE | 341 |
| 70 p. 316 | Hampton Inn Houston-Hobby Airport, 1.1 mi | ◆◆◆ | $89-$209 | 342 |
| 64 p. 316 | Holiday Inn Express & Suites Hobby Airport, 2.5 mi | ◆◆◆ | Rates not provided | 343 |
| 68 p. 316 | Holiday Inn Houston Hobby Airport, 1.4 mi | ◆◆◆ | $89-$199 SAVE | 343 |
| 66 p. 316 | Houston Marriott South at Hobby Airport, 3.0 mi | ◆◆◆ | $99-$299 | 344 |
| 73 p. 316 | La Quinta Inn & Suites Houston Hobby Airport, 1.3 mi | ◆◆◆ | $95-$144 | 345 |
| 71 p. 316 | SpringHill Suites by Marriott (Houston/Hobby Airport), 2.0 mi | ◆◆◆ | $105-$129 | 347 |

## Houston Loop Freeway

This index helps you "spot" where approved hotels and restaurants are located on the corresponding detailed maps. Hotel daily rate range is for comparison only. Restaurant price range is a combination of lunch and/or dinner. Turn to the listing page for more detailed rate and price information and consult display ads for special promotions.

### HOUSTON (LOOP FREEWAY)

| Map Page | Hotels | Diamond Rated | Rate Range | Page |
|---|---|---|---|---|
| 1 p. 316 | Extended Stay America Houston-Northwest | ◆◆ | $89-$245 | 341 |
| 2 p. 316 | Sleep Inn & Suites Northwest Houston/Highway 290 | ◆◆◆ | $110-$150 | 346 |
| 3 p. 316 | TownePlace Suites by Marriott-Central | ◆◆◆ | $90-$270 | 347 |
| 4 p. 316 | Hampton Inn-Brookhollow | ◆◆◆ | $89-$174 | 342 |
| 5 p. 316 | Crowne Plaza Northwest Hotel (See ad p. 340.) | ◆◆◆ | $59-$179 SAVE | 340 |
| 6 p. 316 | Quality Inn & Suites | ◆◆ | $70-$150 | 345 |
| 7 p. 316 | BEST WESTERN PLUS Northwest Inn & Suites | ◆◆ | $100-$120 SAVE | 338 |
| 8 p. 316 | Courtyard by Marriott Houston Brookhollow | ◆◆◆ | $80-$260 | 339 |
| 9 p. 316 | SpringHill Suites by Marriott-Brookhollow | ◆◆◆ | $90-$310 | 347 |
| 10 p. 316 | Sheraton Houston Brookhollow | ◆◆◆ | $89-$299 SAVE | 346 |
| 11 p. 316 | Sleep Inn & Suites | ◆◆◆ | $90-$139 SAVE | 346 |
| 12 p. 316 | Sara's Inn on the Boulevard | ◆◆◆ | Rates not provided | 346 |
| 13 p. 316 | Crowne Plaza Houston Galleria Area | ◆◆◆ | Rates not provided SAVE | 339 |
| 14 p. 316 | Holiday Inn Express Hotel & Suites Memorial Area | ◆◆◆ | Rates not provided | 343 |
| 15 p. 316 | Hampton Inn & Suites Houston I-10 Central | ◆◆◆ | $99-$159 | 342 |
| 16 p. 316 | Quality Inn | ◆◆ | $65-$110 | 345 |
| 17 p. 316 | BEST WESTERN Heritage Inn | ◆◆◆ | $99-$109 SAVE | 338 |

## HOUSTON (LOOP FREEWAY) (cont'd)

| Map Page | Hotels (cont'd) | Diamond Rated | Rate Range | Page |
|---|---|---|---|---|
| 18 p. 316 | **Holiday Inn Express Hotel & Suites Houston East** | ◆◆◆ | $144-$154 SAVE | 343 |
| 19 p. 316 | **The Houstonian Hotel, Club & Spa** | ◆◆◆◆ | $199-$525 SAVE | 344 |
| 20 p. 316 | Omni Houston Hotel | ◆◆◆◆ | $199-$599 | 345 |
| 21 p. 316 | Drury Inn & Suites-Houston Near the Galleria | ◆◆◆ | $95-$239 | 341 |
| 22 p. 316 | La Quinta Inn & Suites Houston Galleria Area | ◆◆◆ | $85-$190 | 345 |
| 23 p. 316 | Houston Marriott West Loop By The Galleria | ◆◆◆ | $83-$339 | 344 |
| 24 p. 316 | **Hampton Inn Houston Near the Galleria** | ◆◆◆ | $85-$259 SAVE | 342 |
| 25 p. 316 | **The St. Regis Houston** | ◆◆◆◆◆ | $225-$780 | 346 |
| 26 p. 316 | **Hilton Houston Post Oak** | ◆◆◆◆ | $109-$289 SAVE | 342 |
| 27 p. 316 | **Royal Sonesta Hotel Houston** | ◆◆◆◆ | $109-$629 SAVE | 346 |
| 28 p. 316 | **Sheraton Suites Houston Near The Galleria** | ◆◆◆ | $139-$429 SAVE | 346 |
| 29 p. 316 | **Residence Inn by Marriott Houston by the Galleria** | ◆◆◆ | $102-$299 SAVE | 345 |
| 30 p. 316 | **Hotel Derek** | [fyl] | Rates not provided SAVE | 344 |
| 31 p. 316 | JW Marriott Houston | ◆◆◆◆ | $97-$369 | 345 |
| 32 p. 316 | **Westin Oaks Houston at the Galleria** | ◆◆◆◆ | $129-$449 SAVE | 347 |
| 33 p. 316 | **DoubleTree Suites by Hilton Hotel Houston by the Galleria** | ◆◆◆ | $109-$315 SAVE | 341 |
| 34 p. 316 | **Aloft Houston by the Galleria** | ◆◆◆ | $95-$499 SAVE | 338 |
| 35 p. 316 | **The Westin Galleria, Houston** | ◆◆◆◆ | $129-$449 SAVE | 347 |
| 36 p. 316 | Homewood Suites by Hilton Near the Galleria | ◆◆◆ | Rates not provided | 344 |
| 37 p. 316 | **Courtyard by Marriott Houston by the Galleria** | ◆◆◆ | $90-$330 SAVE | 339 |
| 38 p. 316 | Embassy Suites Houston Near the Galleria | ◆◆◆ | Rates not provided | 341 |
| 39 p. 316 | Hotel Indigo Houston at the Galleria | ◆◆◆ | $119-$259 | 344 |
| 40 p. 316 | **Sonesta ES Suites Houston** | ◆◆◆ | Rates not provided SAVE | 346 |
| 41 p. 316 | Hilton Garden Inn Houston Galleria Area | ◆◆◆ | $89-$329 | 342 |
| 42 p. 316 | **BEST WESTERN Fountainview Inn & Suites near Galleria** | ◆◆ | $85-$95 SAVE | 338 |
| 43 p. 316 | **Comfort Suites Galleria** | ◆◆◆ | $120-$189 SAVE | 338 |
| 44 p. 316 | **Crowne Plaza Houston River Oaks** | ◆◆◆ | $89-$229 SAVE | 339 |
| 45 p. 316 | **Four Points by Sheraton Houston Southwest** | ◆◆◆ | $79-$349 SAVE | 342 |
| 46 p. 316 | **DoubleTree by Hilton Hotel Houston - Greenway Plaza** (See ad p. 341.) | ◆◆◆ | $119-$429 SAVE | 340 |
| 47 p. 316 | **HYATT house Houston/Galleria** | ◆◆◆ | $89-$399 SAVE | 345 |
| 48 p. 316 | Courtyard by Marriott-West University | ◆◆◆ | $99-$209 | 339 |
| 49 p. 316 | Residence Inn by Marriott-West University | ◆◆◆ | $99-$209 | 345 |
| 50 p. 316 | Candlewood Suites Houston by the Galleria | ◆◆ | $79-$119 | 338 |
| 51 p. 316 | **Hotel ZaZa Houston Museum District** | ◆◆◆◆ | Rates not provided SAVE | 344 |
| 52 p. 316 | Hilton University of Houston | ◆◆◆ | $109-$269 | 343 |
| 53 p. 316 | Hilton Houston Plaza Medical Center | ◆◆◆ | $119-$359 | 342 |
| 54 p. 316 | Houston Marriott at the Texas Medical Center | ◆◆◆ | $125-$319 | 344 |

## HOUSTON (LOOP FREEWAY) (cont'd)

| Map Page | Hotels (cont'd) | Diamond Rated | Rate Range | Page |
|---|---|---|---|---|
| **55** p. 316 | BEST WESTERN Plaza Hotel & Suites at Medical Center | ▽▽▽ | $90-$115 [SAVE] | 338 |
| **56** p. 316 | Wyndham Houston Medical Center Hotel and Suites | ▽▽▽ | $99-$249 [SAVE] | 347 |
| **57** p. 316 | Residence Inn by Marriott-Medical Center/Reliant Park | ▽▽▽ | $109-$179 | 345 |
| **58** p. 316 | Hampton Inn & Suites Medical Center/Reliant Park | ▽▽▽ | $99-$189 | 342 |
| **59** p. 316 | SpringHill Suites by Marriott Houston-Medical Center Reliant Park | ▽▽▽ | $92-$399 | 347 |
| **60** p. 316 | Holiday Inn Express Hotel & Suites Houston Medical Center | ▽▽▽ | Rates not provided | 343 |
| **61** p. 316 | Holiday Inn Houston Reliant Park Area (See ad p. 343.) | ▽▽▽ | $99-$399 [SAVE] | 343 |
| **62** p. 316 | Crowne Plaza Suites Houston - Near Sugar Land | ▽▽▽ | $79-$159 | 340 |
| **63** p. 316 | Four Points by Sheraton Houston Hobby Airport | ▽▽▽ | $129-$179 [SAVE] | 341 |
| **64** p. 316 | Holiday Inn Express & Suites Hobby Airport | ▽▽▽ | Rates not provided | 343 |
| **65** p. 316 | DoubleTree by Hilton Houston Hobby Airport | ▽▽▽ | $129-$349 | 340 |
| **66** p. 316 | Houston Marriott South at Hobby Airport | ▽▽▽ | $99-$299 | 344 |
| **67** p. 316 | Courtyard by Marriott-Houston Hobby Airport | ▽▽▽ | $89-$159 | 339 |
| **68** p. 316 | Holiday Inn Houston Hobby Airport | ▽▽▽ | $89-$199 [SAVE] | 343 |
| **69** p. 316 | Drury Inn & Suites-Houston Hobby | ▽▽▽ | $85-$219 | 341 |
| **70** p. 316 | Hampton Inn Houston-Hobby Airport | ▽▽▽ | $89-$209 | 342 |
| **71** p. 316 | SpringHill Suites by Marriott (Houston/Hobby Airport) | ▽▽▽ | $105-$129 | 347 |
| **72** p. 316 | Best West Inn & Suites | ▽▽ | $109-$299 | 338 |
| **73** p. 316 | La Quinta Inn & Suites Houston Hobby Airport | ▽▽▽ | $95-$144 | 345 |
| **74** p. 316 | Comfort Suites Hobby Airport | ▽▽▽ | $79-$199 | 338 |
| **75** p. 316 | Days Inn & Suites-Hobby Airport | ▽▽ | $85-$135 [SAVE] | 340 |

| Map Page | Restaurants | Diamond Rated | Cuisine | Price Range | Page |
|---|---|---|---|---|---|
| **3** p. 316 | Barbecue Inn | ▽▽ | American | $6-$20 | 348 |
| **4** p. 316 | Tony's Mexican Restaurant & Cantina | ▽▽ | Tex-Mex | $7-$17 | 355 |
| **5** p. 316 | Shade | ▽▽▽ | New American | $8-$30 | 354 |
| **6** p. 316 | Otilia's | ▽▽ | Mexican | $9-$14 | 353 |
| **7** p. 316 | Spanish Flowers Mexican Restaurant | ▽▽ | Mexican | $6-$16 | 355 |
| **8** p. 316 | Korea Garden Restaurant | ▽▽ | Korean | $8-$20 | 352 |
| **9** p. 316 | Zelko Bistro | ▽▽▽ | American | $10-$22 | 356 |
| **10** p. 316 | Saltgrass Steakhouse | ▽▽ | Steak | $9-$30 [SAVE] | 354 |
| **11** p. 316 | Russo's New York Coal Fired Pizzeria | ▽▽ | Italian | $8-$20 | 354 |
| **12** p. 316 | Perry's Steakhouse & Grille | ▽▽▽ | Steak | $13-$48 | 353 |
| **13** p. 316 | Ciro's | ▽▽ | Italian | $12-$26 | 350 |
| **14** p. 316 | Denis' Seafood Restaurant | ▽▽▽ | Regional Seafood | $12-$25 | 350 |
| **15** p. 316 | Guadalajara Hacienda | ▽▽ | Mexican | $10-$24 | 351 |
| **16** p. 316 | Southwell's Hamburger Grill | ▽ | Burgers | $6-$10 | 355 |
| **17** p. 316 | Jax Grill | ▽ | American | $7-$19 | 351 |

| Map Page | Restaurants (cont'd) | Diamond Rated | Cuisine | Price Range | Page |
|---|---|---|---|---|---|
| 18 p. 316 | Hickory Hollow | ◆ | Regional Comfort Food | $8-$19 | 351 |
| 19 p. 316 | SOMA Sushi | ◆◆◆ | Japanese | $5-$25 | 354 |
| 20 p. 316 | BRC Gastropub | ◆◆ | American | $9-$24 | 349 |
| 21 p. 316 | Branch Water Tavern | ◆◆ | New American | $10-$32 | 348 |
| 22 p. 316 | **Noé Restaurant & Bar** | ◆◆◆◆ | New American | $21-$39 | 352 |
| 23 p. 316 | Daily Review Cafe | ◆◆ | New American | $11-$32 | 350 |
| 24 p. 316 | Tila's Restaurante & Bar | ◆◆ | Mexican | $11-$29 | 355 |
| 25 p. 316 | Backstreet Cafe | ◆◆ | American | $15-$39 | 348 |
| 26 p. 316 | Arturo's Uptown Italiano | ◆◆ | Italian | $13-$33 | 348 |
| 27 p. 316 | Post Oak Grill | ◆◆ | American | $10-$30 | 353 |
| 28 p. 316 | La Griglia | ◆◆ | Italian | $10-$36 | 352 |
| 29 p. 316 | Willie G's | ◆◆ | Seafood | $10-$43 | 356 |
| 30 p. 316 | Barnaby's Cafe | ◆◆ | American | $10-$17 | 348 |
| 31 p. 316 | Ciao Bello | ◆◆ | Italian | $11-$30 | 350 |
| 32 p. 316 | Yia Yia Mary's | ◆◆ | Greek | $9-$27 | 356 |
| 33 p. 316 | Mockingbird Bistro | ◆◆◆ | American | $22-$46 | 352 |
| 34 p. 316 | **The Remington Restaurant** | ◆◆◆◆ | American | $9-$42 | 354 |
| 35 p. 316 | RDG + Bar Annie | ◆◆◆ | Regional American | $16-$58 | 354 |
| 36 p. 316 | Ouisie's Table | ◆◆◆ | American | $8-$32 | 353 |
| 37 p. 316 | Te' House of Tea | ◆ | Coffee/Tea | $5-$9 | 355 |
| 38 p. 316 | Hugo's | ◆◆◆ | Regional Mexican | $15-$30 | 351 |
| 39 p. 316 | Empire Cafe | ◆ | Italian | $9-$11 | 350 |
| 40 p. 316 | DaMarco | ◆◆◆◆ | Italian | $14-$40 | 350 |
| 41 p. 316 | **Mark's American Cuisine** | ◆◆◆◆ | New American | $22-$57 | 352 |
| 42 p. 316 | Taco Milagro | ◆ | Mexican | $7-$14 | 355 |
| 43 p. 316 | Crapitto's Cucina Italiana | ◆◆ | Italian | $12-$39 | 350 |
| 44 p. 316 | Canyon Cafe | ◆◆ | Southwestern | $9-$18 | 349 |
| 45 p. 316 | Arcodoro | ◆◆◆ | Italian | $10-$35 | 348 |
| 46 p. 316 | Churrascos | ◆◆◆ | Latin American | $10-$56 | 349 |
| 47 p. 316 | Shanghai River | ◆◆ | Traditional Chinese | $7-$18 | 354 |
| 48 p. 316 | Kenny & Ziggy's Delicatessen Restaurant | ◆◆ | Deli Sandwiches | $11-$24 | 351 |
| 49 p. 316 | Cinq | ◆◆◆ | New European | $10-$48 | 350 |
| 50 p. 316 | Smith & Wollensky | ◆◆◆ | Steak | $15-$50 | 354 |
| 51 p. 316 | Sullivan's Steakhouse | ◆◆◆ | Steak | $20-$65 | 355 |
| 52 p. 316 | **Valentino** | ◆◆◆◆ | Italian | $16-$36 | 356 |
| 53 p. 316 | Grotto | ◆◆◆ | Italian | $10-$24 | 351 |
| 54 p. 316 | The Cheesecake Factory | ◆◆◆ | American | $9-$30 | 349 |
| 55 p. 316 | Pondicheri | ◆◆ | Indian | $8-$20 | 353 |
| 56 p. 316 | The Oceanaire Seafood Room | ◆◆◆ | Seafood | $11-$54 [SAVE] | 352 |

| Map Page | Restaurants (cont'd) | Diamond Rated | Cuisine | Price Range | Page |
|---|---|---|---|---|---|
| 57 p. 316 | Gigi's Asian Bistro & Dumpling Bar | ◇◇ | Asian | $12-$35 | 351 |
| 58 p. 316 | Truluck's | ◇◇◇ | Steak | $12-$45 | 356 |
| 59 p. 316 | The Capital Grille | ◇◇◇ | Steak Seafood | $23-$45 | 349 |
| 60 p. 316 | Sparrow Bar & Cookshop | ◇◇◇ | American | $15-$30 | 355 |
| 61 p. 316 | Fleming's Prime Steakhouse & Wine Bar | ◇◇◇ | Steak | $11-$49 | 350 |
| 62 p. 316 | Rudi Lechner's | ◇◇ | German | $12-$26 | 354 |
| 63 p. 316 | Fogo De Chao | ◇◇◇ | Brazilian | $35-$52 | 351 |
| 64 p. 316 | Cafe Mezza & Grille | ◇◇ | Mediterranean | $9-$30 | 349 |
| 65 p. 316 | Teppay Japanese Restaurant | ◇◇ | Japanese | $6-$26 | 355 |
| 66 p. 316 | Pappas Bros. Steakhouse | ◇◇◇◇ | Steak | $42-$80 | 353 |
| 67 p. 316 | Cafe Lili Lebanese Grill | ◇ | Lebanese | $5-$23 | 349 |
| 68 p. 316 | Ragin Cajun Seafood | ◇ | Cajun | $7-$21 | 353 |
| 69 p. 316 | Miyako Japanese Restaurant | ◇◇ | Japanese | $8-$25 | 352 |
| 70 p. 316 | Los Tios | ◇◇ | Tex-Mex | $3-$21 | 352 |
| 71 p. 316 | Churrascos-Westchase | ◇◇◇ | Latin American | $11-$29 | 349 |
| 72 p. 316 | The Black Labrador | ◇◇ | English | $7-$15 | 348 |
| 73 p. 316 | Alexander The Great | ◇◇ | Greek | $12-$28 | 347 |
| 74 p. 316 | Brasserie Max & Julie | ◇◇ | French | $12-$30 | 349 |
| 75 p. 316 | Maria Selma | ◇◇ | Mexican | $9-$22 | 352 |
| 76 p. 316 | Star Pizza | ◇ | Pizza | $7-$20 | 355 |
| 77 p. 316 | 59 Diner | ◇ | American | $7-$10 | 347 |
| 78 p. 316 | Haven | ◇◇◇ | Regional American | $11-$32 | 351 |
| 79 p. 316 | Tony's | ◇◇◇◇ | Continental | $19-$95 | 355 |
| 80 p. 316 | The Lexington Grille | ◇◇◇ | Continental | $12-$38 | 352 |
| 81 p. 316 | Thai Gourmet | ◇◇ | Thai | $9-$18 | 355 |
| 82 p. 316 | India's | ◇◇ | Indian | $14-$30 | 351 |
| 83 p. 316 | Ruth's Chris Steak House | ◇◇◇ | Steak | $40-$100 | 354 |
| 84 p. 316 | 100% Taquito | ◇ | Mexican | $4-$8 | 347 |
| 85 p. 316 | Goode Co. Seafood | ◇◇ | Regional Seafood | $12-$24 | 351 |
| 86 p. 316 | Goode Company Hamburgers & Taqueria | ◇ | American | $6-$23 | 351 |
| 87 p. 316 | Vietopia | ◇◇ | Vietnamese | $9-$19 | 356 |
| 88 p. 316 | Amazon Grill | ◇ | Latin American | $7-$27 | 348 |
| 89 p. 316 | Picnic | ◇ | Deli Breads/ Pastries | $7-$11 | 353 |
| 90 p. 316 | Cleburne Cafeteria | ◇ | American | $7-$14 | 350 |
| 91 p. 316 | Monarch | ◇◇◇ | Mediterranean | $10-$40 | 352 |
| 92 p. 316 | Brady's Landing | ◇◇ | American | $16-$34 | 348 |
| 93 p. 316 | Fiesta Loma Linda | ◇◇ | Tex-Mex | $6-$12 | 350 |
| 94 p. 316 | Benjy's | ◇◇ | American | $12-$29 | 348 |
| 95 p. 316 | Cafe Rabelais | ◇◇ | Traditional French | $8-$32 | 349 |

| Map Page | Restaurants (cont'd) | Diamond Rated | Cuisine | Price Range | Page |
|---|---|---|---|---|---|
| 96 p. 316 | Shiva Indian Restaurant | ▼▼ | Regional Indian | $11-$16 | 354 |
| 97 p. 316 | Prego Restaurant | ▼▼▼ | Italian | $12-$28 | 353 |
| 98 p. 316 | The Bombay Brasserie | ▼▼ | Indian | $11-$25 | 348 |
| 99 p. 316 | El Meson | ▼▼ | Latin American | $10-$32 | 350 |
| 100 p. 316 | Mi Luna Tapas Restaurant & Bar | ▼▼ | Small Plates | $4-$22 | 352 |
| 101 p. 316 | Southwell's Hamburger Grill | ▼ | Burgers | $4-$7 | 355 |
| 102 p. 316 | Bonnie's Beef & Seafood Co | ▼▼ | Steak Seafood | $9-$39 | 348 |
| 103 p. 316 | Fung's Kitchen | ▼▼ | Chinese | $8-$25 | 351 |
| 104 p. 316 | Cafe Piquet | ▼▼ | Cuban | $7-$17 | 349 |
| 105 p. 316 | Escalante's Mexican Grille | ▼▼ | Mexican | $8-$22 | 350 |
| 106 p. 316 | Saltgrass Steakhouse | ▼▼ | Steak | $9-$30 SAVE | 354 |
| 107 p. 316 | Saltgrass Steakhouse | ▼▼ | Steak | $9-$30 SAVE | 354 |
| 108 p. 316 | Taquerias Arandas | ▼ | Mexican | $8-$13 | 355 |

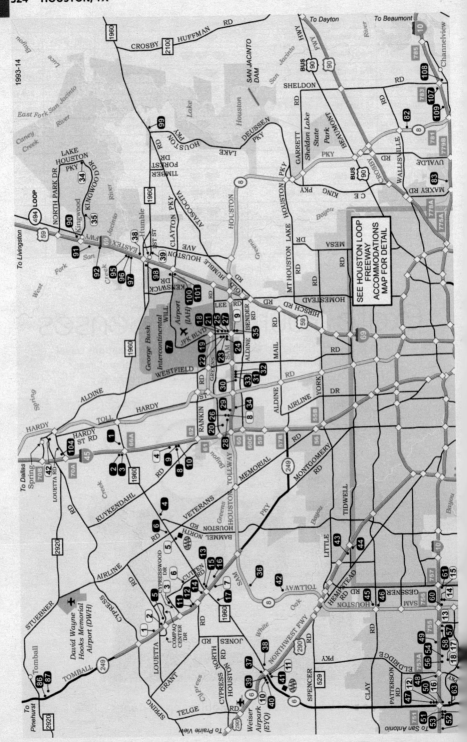

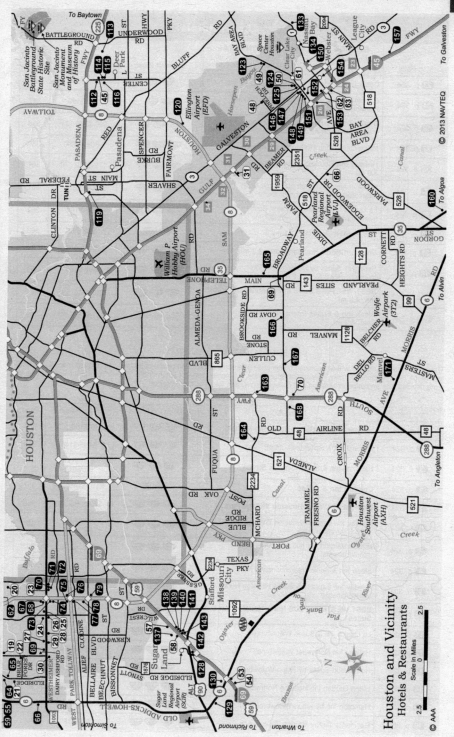

Houston and Vicinity
Hotels & Restaurants

## ✈ Airport Hotels

| Map Page | GEORGE BUSH INTERCONTINENTAL (Maximum driving distance from airport: 4.3 mi) | Diamond Rated | Rate Range | Page |
|---|---|---|---|---|
| 23 p. 324 | Comfort Suites Intercontinental Plaza, 3.2 mi | ◆◆ | $80-$130 | 357 |
| 24 p. 324 | Country Inn & Suites By Carlson, Houston Intercontinental AP-S, 3.2 mi | ◆◆ | $89-$199 | 357 |
| 19 p. 324 | DoubleTree by Hilton Hotel Houston Intercontinental Airport, 3.1 mi | ◆◆◆ | $99-$275 [SAVE] | 358 |
| 27 p. 324 | Hilton Garden Inn Houston/Bush Airport, 3.6 mi | ◆◆◆ | $99-$239 | 360 |
| 35 p. 324 | Holiday Inn Houston Intercontinental Airport, 3.9 mi | ◆◆◆ | $79-$219 [SAVE] | 361 |
| 7 p. 324 | Houston Airport Marriott at George Bush Intercontinental, on airport property | ◆◆◆ | $152-$279 | 362 |
| 25 p. 324 | La Quinta Inn & Suites Houston Bush Intercontinental Airport South, 3.7 mi | ◆◆◆ | $82-$164 | 362 |
| 22 p. 324 | Red Roof Houston IAH, 3.1 mi | ◆◆ | $59-$99 | 363 |
| 21 p. 324 | Sheraton North Houston Hotel, 3.2 mi | ◆◆◆ | $79-$279 [SAVE] | 364 |
| 18 p. 324 | SpringHill Suites by Marriott Houston Intercontinental Airport, 2.9 mi | ◆◆◆ | $89-$189 | 364 |
| 101 p. 324 | BEST WESTERN PLUS Intercontinental Airport Inn, 4.3 mi | ◆◆◆ | $90-$110 [SAVE] | 369 |
| 100 p. 324 | Sleep Inn & Suites Intercontinental Airport East, 4.3 mi | ◆◆◆ | $62-$150 [SAVE] | 369 |

# Houston and Vicinity

This index helps you "spot" where approved hotels and restaurants are located on the corresponding detailed maps. Hotel daily rate range is for comparison only. Restaurant price range is a combination of lunch and/or dinner. Turn to the listing page for more detailed rate and price information and consult display ads for special promotions.

## HOUSTON

| Map Page | Hotels | Diamond Rated | Rate Range | Page |
|---|---|---|---|---|
| 1 p. 324 | La Quinta Inn & Suites Houston I-45/1960 | ◆◆◆ | $99-$150 [SAVE] | 363 |
| 2 p. 324 | Fairfield Inn & Suites by Marriott - I-45 | ◆◆◆ | $135-$148 | 359 |
| 3 p. 324 | Hampton Inn & Suites Cypress Station | ◆◆◆ | Rates not provided | 359 |
| 4 p. 324 | Comfort Inn & Suites | ◆◆ | $110-$140 [SAVE] | 357 |
| 5 p. 324 | Element by Westin Houston Vintage Park | ◆◆◆ | $99-$299 [SAVE] | 358 |
| 6 p. 324 | Holiday Inn Express Houston Willowbrook FM 1960 Champions Area | ◆◆◆ | Rates not provided | 361 |
| 7 p. 324 | Houston Airport Marriott at George Bush Intercontinental | ◆◆◆ | $152-$279 | 362 |
| 8 p. 324 | Sleep Inn & Suites Intercontinental North | ◆◆◆ | $85-$130 | 364 |
| 9 p. 324 | Holiday Inn Express & Suites Houston North Intercontinental | ◆◆◆ | Rates not provided | 360 |
| 10 p. 324 | BEST WESTERN PLUS North Houston Inn & Suites | ◆◆◆ | $76-$210 [SAVE] | 356 |
| 11 p. 324 | La Quinta Inn & Suites Willowbrook | ◆◆◆ | $99-$159 | 363 |
| 12 p. 324 | Holiday Inn Northwest Willowbrook | ◆◆◆ | $99-$219 | 361 |
| 13 p. 324 | Homewood Suites by Hilton-Willowbrook | ◆◆◆ | $139-$219 | 361 |
| 14 p. 324 | Hilton Garden Inn Houston Northwest | ◆◆◆ | $89-$289 | 360 |
| 15 p. 324 | Hampton Inn by Hilton-Willowbrook | ◆◆◆ | $119-$199 | 360 |
| 16 p. 324 | Residence Inn by Marriott Willowbrook | ◆◆◆ | $99-$189 | 364 |

## HOUSTON (cont'd)

| Map Page | Hotels (cont'd) | Diamond Rated | Rate Range | Page |
|---|---|---|---|---|
| 17 p. 324 | Candlewood Suites Willowbrook | ◇◇◇ | Rates not provided | 357 |
| 18 p. 324 | SpringHill Suites by Marriott Houston Intercontinental Airport | ◇◇◇ | $89-$189 | 364 |
| 19 p. 324 | **DoubleTree by Hilton Hotel Houston Intercontinental Airport** *(See ad p. 358.)* | ◇◇◇ | $99-$275 (SAVE) | 358 |
| 20 p. 324 | Hilton Houston North | ◇◇◇ | $189-$209 | 360 |
| 21 p. 324 | **Sheraton North Houston Hotel** | ◇◇◇ | $79-$279 (SAVE) | 364 |
| 22 p. 324 | Red Roof Houston IAH | ◇◇ | $59-$99 | 363 |
| 23 p. 324 | Comfort Suites Intercontinental Plaza | ◇◇ | $80-$130 | 357 |
| 24 p. 324 | Country Inn & Suites By Carlson, Houston Intercontinental AP-S | ◇◇ | $89-$199 | 357 |
| 25 p. 324 | La Quinta Inn & Suites Houston Bush Intercontinental Airport South | ◇◇◇ | $82-$164 | 362 |
| 26 p. 324 | **Hyatt Place Bush Houston Intercontinental Airport** | ◇◇◇ | $69-$209 (SAVE) | 362 |
| 27 p. 324 | Hilton Garden Inn Houston/Bush Airport | ◇◇◇ | $99-$239 | 360 |
| 28 p. 324 | Houston Marriott North | ◇◇◇ | $159-$189 | 362 |
| 29 p. 324 | **Hyatt North Houston** | ◇◇◇ | $79-$249 (SAVE) | 362 |
| 30 p. 324 | **Super 8 IAH West/Greenspoint** | ◇◇ | $75-$140 (SAVE) | 364 |
| 31 p. 324 | Homewood Suites by Hilton Intercontinental Airport | ◇◇◇ | $129-$179 | 361 |
| 32 p. 324 | Comfort Suites-Greenspoint/IAH West | ◇◇◇ | $69-$149 | 357 |
| 33 p. 324 | **Wingate by Wyndham Houston Bush Intercontinental Airport IAH** | ◇◇◇ | $89-$180 (SAVE) | 365 |
| 34 p. 324 | Park Inn Houston North Hotel and Conference Center | ◇◇◇ | $69-$129 | 363 |
| 35 p. 324 | **Holiday Inn Houston Intercontinental Airport** | ◇◇◇ | $79-$219 (SAVE) | 361 |
| 36 p. 324 | **BEST WESTERN PLUS Sam Houston Inn & Suites** | ◇◇◇ | $90-$120 (SAVE) | 356 |
| 37 p. 324 | Homewood Suites by Hilton Houston Northwest Cy-Fair | ◇◇◇ | $129-$200 | 361 |
| 38 p. 324 | **Holiday Inn Express Northwest** | ◇◇◇ | $85-$169 (SAVE) | 361 |
| 39 p. 324 | Hampton Inn-Houston Northwest | ◇◇◇ | $114-$189 | 360 |
| 40 p. 324 | La Quinta Inn Houston Cy-Fair | ◇◇ | $79-$124 | 363 |
| 41 p. 324 | **BEST WESTERN Windsor Suites** | ◇◇ | $100-$130 (SAVE) | 357 |
| 42 p. 324 | Holiday Inn Express & Suites-West Road | ◇◇◇ | Rates not provided | 361 |
| 43 p. 324 | Crossland Economy Studios Houston-Northwest | ◇ | $52-$95 | 358 |
| 44 p. 324 | **Comfort Inn Hwy 290/NW** | ◇◇ | $80-$120 (SAVE) | 357 |
| 45 p. 324 | La Quinta Inn & Suites - Houston Clay Road | ◇◇◇ | $115-$184 | 363 |
| 46 p. 324 | **Sheraton Houston West Hotel** | ◇◇◇ | $89-$359 (SAVE) | 364 |
| 47 p. 324 | **Wyndham Houston West Energy Corridor** | ◇◇◇ | $99-$249 (SAVE) | 365 |
| 48 p. 324 | **Omni Houston Hotel Westside** | ◇◇◇◇ | $109-$379 (SAVE) | 363 |
| 49 p. 324 | **Embassy Suites Houston Energy Corridor** *(See ad p. 359.)* | ◇◇◇ | $239-$259 (SAVE) | 358 |
| 50 p. 324 | Drury Inn & Suites-Houston West | ◇◇◇ | $80-$229 | 358 |
| 51 p. 324 | TownePlace Suites by Marriott Houston I-10 West/Energy Corridor | ◇◇◇ | $81-$160 | 364 |

## HOUSTON (cont'd)

| Map Page | Hotels (cont'd) | Diamond Rated | Rate Range | Page |
|---|---|---|---|---|
| **52** p. 324 | La Quinta Inn & Suites Houston West Park 10 | ◆◆◆ | $72-$150 | 363 |
| **53** p. 324 | **HYATT house Houston-West/Energy Corridor** | ◆◆◆ | $59-$229 SAVE | 362 |
| **54** p. 324 | **Hilton Garden Inn Energy Corridor** | ◆◆◆ | $79-$359 SAVE | 360 |
| **55** p. 324 | Fairfield Inn & Suites by Marriott Houston I-10 West/Energy Corridor | ◆◆◆ | $81-$144 | 359 |
| **56** p. 324 | Courtyard by Marriott Houston West | ◆◆◆ | $99-$220 | 357 |
| **57** p. 324 | La Quinta Inn Houston Wilcrest | ◆◆ | $72-$107 | 363 |
| **58** p. 324 | Hampton Inn I-10 West/Energy Corridor Houston | ◆◆◆ | $89-$209 | 360 |
| **59** p. 324 | Houston Marriott Energy Corridor | ◆◆◆ | $95-$247 | 362 |
| **60** p. 324 | **Four Points by Sheraton Houston West** | ◆◆◆ | $149-$199 SAVE | 359 |
| **61** p. 324 | **Westin Houston Memorial City** | ◆◆◆◆ | $109-$369 SAVE | 364 |
| **62** p. 324 | Candlewood Suites at CITYCENTRE - Energy Corridor | ◆◆ | $99-$120 | 357 |
| **63** p. 324 | **Quality Inn & Suites Houston West/Energy Corridor** | ◆◆ | $70-$196 SAVE | 363 |
| **64** p. 324 | Holiday Inn Houston West Energy Corridor | ◆◆◆ | Rates not provided | 361 |
| **65** p. 324 | Staybridge Suites Houston West Energy Corridor | ◆◆◆ | $199-$219 | 364 |
| **66** p. 324 | Holiday Inn Express & Suites Houston Energy Corridor-West Oaks | ◆◆◆ | Rates not provided | 360 |
| **67** p. 324 | Fairfield Inn by Marriott-Westchase | ◆◆◆ | $90-$150 | 359 |
| **68** p. 324 | Homewood Suites by Hilton-Westchase | ◆◆◆ | $109-$229 | 361 |
| **69** p. 324 | La Quinta Inn & Suites Energy Corridor | ◆◆◆ | $95-$164 | 362 |
| **70** p. 324 | Hilton Houston Westchase | ◆◆◆ | $109-$299 | 360 |
| **71** p. 324 | Courtyard by Marriott Houston Westchase | ◆◆◆ | $242-$269 | 357 |
| **72** p. 324 | **Marriott Houston Westchase** | ◆◆◆ | $92-$269 SAVE | 363 |
| **73** p. 324 | **BEST WESTERN PLUS Westchase Mini-Suites** | ◆◆◆ | $89-$139 SAVE | 356 |
| **74** p. 324 | Red Roof Inns- Houston Westchase | ◆◆ | $49-$75 | 364 |
| **75** p. 324 | Holiday Inn Houston-Westchase | ◆◆◆ | $99-$229 | 361 |
| **76** p. 324 | Candlewood Suites-Westchase | ◆◆ | Rates not provided | 357 |
| **77** p. 324 | La Quinta Inn & Suites Houston - Westchase | ◆◆◆ | $99-$160 | 363 |
| **78** p. 324 | Hampton Inn & Suites at Westchase | ◆◆◆ | $139-$174 | 359 |
| **79** p. 324 | Hilton Garden Inn Houston Westbelt | ◆◆◆ | $89-$299 | 360 |
| **82** p. 324 | **La Quinta Inn & Suites Houston Channelview** | ◆◆◆ | $119-$154 SAVE | 362 |
| **83** p. 324 | La Quinta Inn & Suites Houston - Normandy | ◆◆◆ | $95-$144 | 363 |

| Map Page | Restaurants | Diamond Rated | Cuisine | Price Range | Page |
|---|---|---|---|---|---|
| ① p. 324 | Santa Fe Flats New Mex Grille | ◆◆ | Regional Southwestern | $9-$16 | 368 |
| ② p. 324 | Strata Restaurant & Bar | ◆◆◆ | New American | $8-$35 | 368 |
| ③ p. 324 | Perry's Steakhouse & Grille | ◆◆◆ | Steak | $24-$80 | 368 |
| ④ p. 324 | Saltgrass Steakhouse | ◆◆ | Steak | $9-$30 SAVE | 368 |
| ⑤ p. 324 | Matsu Japanese Restaurant | ◆◆ | Japanese | $9-$40 | 367 |

| Map Page | Restaurants (cont'd) | Diamond Rated | Cuisine | Price Range | Page |
|---|---|---|---|---|---|
| 6 p. 324 | The County Line Bar-B-Q | ◆ | Regional Barbecue | $9-$20 | 366 |
| 7 p. 324 | Saltgrass Steakhouse | ◆◆ | Steak | $9-$30 [SAVE] | 368 |
| 8 p. 324 | Jimmy G's Cajun Seafood Restaurant | ◆◆ | Cajun Seafood | $10-$29 | 366 |
| 9 p. 324 | **Good Eats** | ◆◆ | American | $8-$29 | 366 |
| 10 p. 324 | Harris County Smokehouse | ◆ | Barbecue | $4-$15 | 366 |
| 11 p. 324 | Chuy's | ◆◆ | Tex-Mex | $6-$12 | 366 |
| 12 p. 324 | Cattleguard Restaurant & Bar | ◆◆ | American | $9-$28 | 366 |
| 13 p. 324 | Brenner's Steakhouse | ◆◆◆ | Steak | $18-$65 | 365 |
| 14 p. 324 | Taste of Texas | ◆◆ | Steak | $10-$50 | 368 |
| 15 p. 324 | Il Mulino New York | ◆◆◆ | Italian | $10-$29 | 366 |
| 16 p. 324 | Lomonte's Italian Restaurant & Bar | ◆◆◆ | Italian | $12-$29 | 367 |
| 17 p. 324 | Lynn's Steakhouse and Seafood | ◆◆◆ | Steak | $13-$48 | 367 |
| 18 p. 324 | Carmelo's Ristorante | ◆◆◆ | Italian | $12-$34 | 366 |
| 19 p. 324 | Candelari's Pizzeria | ◆◆ | Italian Pizza | $9-$26 | 365 |
| 20 p. 324 | Empire Turkish Grill | ◆◆ | Turkish | $10-$22 | 366 |
| 21 p. 324 | Le Mistral | ◆◆◆ | French | $7-$34 | 367 |
| 22 p. 324 | Ashiana Fine Indian Cuisine | ◆◆ | Indian | $11-$26 | 365 |
| 23 p. 324 | Rio Ranch | ◆◆ | Steak Seafood | $12-$35 | 368 |
| 24 p. 324 | Bistro Le Cep | ◆◆ | Traditional French | $12-$29 | 365 |
| 25 p. 324 | Cafe Pita | ◆◆ | Mediterranean | $7-$20 | 365 |
| 26 p. 324 | **Cantina Laredo** | ◆◆ | Mexican | $10-$26 | 366 |
| 27 p. 324 | Cafe Caspian | ◆◆ | Persian | $10-$20 | 365 |
| 28 p. 324 | Nit Noi | ◆◆ | Thai | $10-$16 | 367 |
| 29 p. 324 | Burger Guys | ◆ | Burgers Hot Dogs | $8-$10 | 365 |
| 30 p. 324 | Sylvia's Enchilada Kitchen | ◆◆ | Mexican | $8-$18 | 368 |
| 31 p. 324 | Perry & Sons Market & Grille | ◆◆ | American | $5-$34 | 367 |

**TOMBALL**

| Map Page | Hotels | Diamond Rated | Rate Range | Page |
|---|---|---|---|---|
| 86 p. 324 | **Hampton Inn & Suites Tomball** | ◆◆◆ | $99-$149 [SAVE] | 554 |
| 87 p. 324 | Comfort Suites Tomball | ◆◆◆ | $99-$109 | 554 |

**KINGWOOD**

| Map Page | Hotels | Diamond Rated | Rate Range | Page |
|---|---|---|---|---|
| 90 p. 324 | Homewood Suites by Hilton at Kingwood Parc | ◆◆◆ | $99-$164 | 389 |
| 91 p. 324 | Holiday Inn Express Hotel & Suites-Kingwood | ◆◆◆ | $89-$189 | 389 |
| 92 p. 324 | Comfort Suites Kingwood-Humble | ◆◆◆ | $80-$140 | 389 |

| Map Page | Restaurants | Diamond Rated | Cuisine | Price Range | Page |
|---|---|---|---|---|---|
| 34 p. 324 | Hunan Garden Restaurant | ◆◆ | Chinese | $6-$13 | 389 |
| 35 p. 324 | Chelsea Deli & Cafe | ◆ | Deli | $3-$5 | 389 |

## HUMBLE

| Map Page | Hotels | Diamond Rated | Rate Range | Page |
|---|---|---|---|---|
| 95 p. 324 | Country Inn & Suites By Carlson Houston Airport East | ◈◈◈ | Rates not provided SAVE | 369 |
| 96 p. 324 | Fairfield Inn by Marriott | ◈◈ | $85-$133 | 369 |
| 97 p. 324 | Hampton Inn Humble | ◈◈◈ | $89-$299 | 369 |
| 98 p. 324 | Econo Lodge | ◈◈ | $65-$110 SAVE | 369 |
| 99 p. 324 | BEST WESTERN PLUS Atascocita Inn & Suites | ◈◈◈ | $90-$120 SAVE | 369 |
| 100 p. 324 | Sleep Inn & Suites Intercontinental Airport East | ◈◈◈ | $62-$150 SAVE | 369 |
| 101 p. 324 | BEST WESTERN PLUS Intercontinental Airport Inn | ◈◈◈ | $90-$110 SAVE | 369 |

| Map Page | Restaurants | Diamond Rated | Cuisine | Price Range | Page |
|---|---|---|---|---|---|
| 38 p. 324 | Saltgrass Steakhouse | ◈◈ | Steak | $9-$30 SAVE | 369 |
| 39 p. 324 | Jade Palace | ◈ | Chinese | $6-$12 | 369 |

## SPRING

| Map Page | Hotel | Diamond Rated | Rate Range | Page |
|---|---|---|---|---|
| 104 p. 324 | Comfort Suites Woodlands/Greenspoint | ◈◈◈ | $95-$149 | 541 |

| Map Page | Restaurant | Diamond Rated | Cuisine | Price Range | Page |
|---|---|---|---|---|---|
| 42 p. 324 | Wunsche Bros Cafe | ◈◈ | American | $6-$14 | 542 |

## CHANNELVIEW

| Map Page | Hotels | Diamond Rated | Rate Range | Page |
|---|---|---|---|---|
| 107 p. 324 | Days Inn & Suites of Channelview | ◈◈ | $70-$110 SAVE | 138 |
| 108 p. 324 | Fairfield Inn & Suites by Marriott Channelview | ◈◈◈ | $104-$139 | 138 |
| 109 p. 324 | Clarion Inn I-10 East | ◈◈ | Rates not provided | 138 |

## DEER PARK

| Map Page | Hotels | Diamond Rated | Rate Range | Page |
|---|---|---|---|---|
| 112 p. 324 | Super 8 | ◈◈ | $70-$100 SAVE | 224 |
| 113 p. 324 | La Quinta Inn & Suites Deer Park | ◈◈◈ | $99-$150 | 224 |
| 114 p. 324 | BEST WESTERN Deer Park Inn & Suites | ◈◈ | $90-$150 SAVE | 223 |
| 115 p. 324 | Comfort Suites Deer Park/Houston | ◈◈◈ | $93-$130 | 224 |
| 116 p. 324 | Hampton Inn | ◈◈◈ | $89-$159 | 224 |

| Map Page | Restaurant | Diamond Rated | Cuisine | Price Range | Page |
|---|---|---|---|---|---|
| 45 p. 324 | Antonio's Italian Grill | ◈◈ | Italian | $7-$15 | 224 |

## PASADENA

| Map Page | Hotels | Diamond Rated | Rate Range | Page |
|---|---|---|---|---|
| 119 p. 324 | Econo Lodge | ◈◈ | $60-$75 | 433 |
| 120 p. 324 | Hampton Inn & Suites-Houston/Pasadena | ◈◈◈ | $116-$152 | 433 |

## CLEAR LAKE CITY

| Map Page | Hotels | Diamond Rated | Rate Range | Page |
|---|---|---|---|---|
| 123 p. 324 | Candlewood Suites-Houston-Clear Lake | ◈◈ | Rates not provided | 139 |
| 124 p. 324 | Residence Inn by Marriott Houston Clear Lake | ◈◈◈ | $143-$179 | 139 |
| 125 p. 324 | Homewood Suites by Hilton Houston/Clear Lake | ◈◈◈ | Rates not provided | 139 |

| Map Page | Restaurants | Diamond Rated | Cuisine | Price Range | Page |
|---|---|---|---|---|---|
| 48 p. 324 | Perry's Italian Grille | ◈◈◈ | Italian | $12-$39 | 139 |

| Map Page | Restaurants (cont'd) | Diamond Rated | Cuisine | Price Range | Page |
|---|---|---|---|---|---|
| 49 p. 324 | Tommy's Restaurant & Oyster Bar | ♦♦♦ | Seafood Steak | $6-$28 | 139 |
| 50 p. 324 | Perry's Steakhouse & Grille | ♦♦♦ | Steak | $15-$80 | 139 |

### SUGAR LAND

| Map Page | Hotels | Diamond Rated | Rate Range | Page |
|---|---|---|---|---|
| 128 p. 324 | Drury Inn & Suites-Houston/Sugar Land | ♦♦♦ | $90-$229 | 544 |
| 129 p. 324 | **Hilton Garden Inn Houston Sugar Land** | ♦♦♦ | $99-$239 SAVE | 544 |
| 130 p. 324 | **Hyatt Place Houston/Sugar Land** | ♦♦♦ | $79-$269 SAVE | 544 |

| Map Page | Restaurants | Diamond Rated | Cuisine | Price Range | Page |
|---|---|---|---|---|---|
| 53 p. 324 | Perry's Steakhouse & Grille | ♦♦♦ | Steak | $24-$48 | 544 |
| 54 p. 324 | The Cheesecake Factory | ♦♦♦ | American | $9-$30 | 544 |

### NASSAU BAY

| Map Page | Hotels | Diamond Rated | Rate Range | Page |
|---|---|---|---|---|
| 133 p. 324 | Hilton Houston NASA Clear Lake | ♦♦♦ | $99-$209 | 424 |
| 134 p. 324 | Courtyard by Marriott NASA/Clear Lake | ♦♦♦ | $139-$153 | 424 |

### STAFFORD

| Map Page | Hotels | Diamond Rated | Rate Range | Page |
|---|---|---|---|---|
| 137 p. 324 | Staybridge Suites Stafford | ♦♦♦ | Rates not provided | 542 |
| 138 p. 324 | **Courtyard by Marriott Houston/Sugar Land** | ♦♦♦ | $79-$200 SAVE | 542 |
| 139 p. 324 | **Residence Inn by Marriott Houston/Sugar Land** | ♦♦♦ | $79-$200 SAVE | 542 |
| 140 p. 324 | La Quinta Inn & Suites Houston Stafford/Sugarland | ♦♦ | $82-$130 | 542 |
| 141 p. 324 | Stafford Hampton Inn by Hilton | ♦♦ | $80-$107 | 542 |
| 142 p. 324 | Comfort Suites | ♦♦ | $110-$160 | 542 |
| 143 p. 324 | Sleep Inn & Suites | ♦♦ | $79-$129 | 542 |

| Map Page | Restaurants | Diamond Rated | Cuisine | Price Range | Page |
|---|---|---|---|---|---|
| 57 p. 324 | Gringo's Mexican Kitchen | ♦♦ | Tex-Mex | $9-$21 | 542 |
| 58 p. 324 | Avalon Diner | ♦ | American | $6-$11 | 542 |

### WEBSTER

| Map Page | Hotels | Diamond Rated | Rate Range | Page |
|---|---|---|---|---|
| 146 p. 324 | Staybridge Suites Houston/ Clear Lake | ♦♦♦ | $99-$199 | 567 |
| 147 p. 324 | Holiday Inn NASA/ Webster | ♦♦♦ | Rates not provided | 566 |
| 148 p. 324 | Hampton Inn & Suites Houston Clear Lake/NASA | ♦♦♦ | $99-$209 | 566 |
| 149 p. 324 | La Quinta Inn & Suites Clearlake/Webster | ♦♦♦ | $109-$144 | 566 |
| 150 p. 324 | **Super 8-Houston-Webster-NASA** | ♦♦ | $79-$130 SAVE | 567 |
| 151 p. 324 | Extended Stay America Houston NASA-Bay Area Blvd | ♦♦ | $85-$100 | 566 |
| 152 p. 324 | Comfort Suites | ♦♦♦ | $90-$140 | 566 |
| 153 p. 324 | Holiday Inn Express Hotel & Suites | ♦♦♦ | $99-$139 | 566 |
| 154 p. 324 | SpringHill Suites by Marriott Houston Clear Lake/Webster | ♦♦♦ | $89-$299 | 566 |

| Map Page | Restaurants | Diamond Rated | Cuisine | Price Range | Page |
|---|---|---|---|---|---|
| 61 p. 324 | Tradicao | ♦♦♦ | Brazilian Steak | $40 | 567 |
| 62 p. 324 | Saltgrass Steakhouse | ♦♦ | Steak | $9-$30 SAVE | 567 |

| Map Page | Restaurants (cont'd) | Diamond Rated | Cuisine | Price Range | Page |
|---|---|---|---|---|---|
| ⟨63⟩ p. 324 | Pappas BBQ | ◆ | Barbecue | $6-$20 | 567 |

### LEAGUE CITY

| Map Page | Hotel | Diamond Rated | Rate Range | Page |
|---|---|---|---|---|
| 157 p. 324 | Hampton Inn & Suites Houston/League City | ◆◆◆ | $89-$209 | 395 |

### ALVIN

| Map Page | Hotel | Diamond Rated | Rate Range | Page |
|---|---|---|---|---|
| 160 p. 324 | Americas Best Value Inn & Suites | ◆◆ | $56-$66 | 57 |

### PEARLAND

| Map Page | Hotels | Diamond Rated | Rate Range | Page |
|---|---|---|---|---|
| 163 p. 324 | SpringHill Suites by Marriott Houston Pearland | ◆◆◆ | $99-$159 | 434 |
| 164 p. 324 | Hilton Garden Inn Houston/Pearland | ◆◆◆ | $95-$159 | 434 |
| 165 p. 324 | **BEST WESTERN Pearland Inn** | ◆◆ | $80-$180 SAVE | 433 |
| 166 p. 324 | Hampton Inn Pearland | ◆◆◆ | $99-$339 | 433 |
| 167 p. 324 | La Quinta Inn & Suites Pearland | ◆◆◆ | $99-$144 | 434 |
| 168 p. 324 | Courtyard by Marriott Houston Pearland | ◆◆◆ | $109-$209 | 433 |

| Map Page | Restaurants | Diamond Rated | Cuisine | Price Range | Page |
|---|---|---|---|---|---|
| ⟨69⟩ p. 324 | Central Texas Style BBQ | ◆ | Regional Barbecue | $5-$17 | 434 |
| ⟨70⟩ p. 324 | Saltgrass Steakhouse | ◆◆ | Steak | $9-$30 SAVE | 434 |

### MANVEL

| Map Page | Hotel | Diamond Rated | Rate Range | Page |
|---|---|---|---|---|
| 171 p. 324 | **BEST WESTERN PLUS Manvel Inn & Suites** | ◆◆◆ | $82-$179 SAVE | 409 |

### FRIENDSWOOD

| Map Page | Restaurant | Diamond Rated | Cuisine | Price Range | Page |
|---|---|---|---|---|---|
| ⟨65⟩ p. 324 | Perry & Sons Market & Grille | ◆◆◆ | Steak Seafood | $9-$34 | 272 |

## DOWNTOWN HOUSTON

- Restaurants p. 335
- Hotels & Restaurants map & index p. 313

### BEST WESTERN PLUS DOWNTOWN INN & SUITES
713/571-7733  **4**

Hotel
Rates not provided

**AAA Benefit:** Members save 10% or more with Best Western!

**Address:** 915 W Dallas St 77019 **Location:** Just w of I-45. **Facility:** 76 units. 4 stories, interior corridors. **Pool(s):** outdoor. **Activities:** hot tub, exercise room. **Guest Services:** valet and coin laundry, area transportation.

[SAVE] CALL [&M] [🚐] [BIZ] [HS] [📶]
[X] [🛗] [📷] [💻]

### COURTYARD BY MARRIOTT HOUSTON DOWNTOWN
(832)366-1600  **8**

◆◆◆ **Hotel** $89-$399 **Address:** 916 Dallas St 77002 **Location:** At Main St. **Facility:** 191 units. 9 stories, interior corridors. **Parking:** valet only. **Pool(s):** outdoor. **Activities:** hot tub, exercise room. **Guest Services:** valet and coin laundry, area transportation.

**AAA Benefit:** Members save 5% or more!

[🍴] [🛏] CALL [&M] [🚐] [BIZ] [HS] [📶] [X] [💻]
/ SOME UNITS [🛗] [📷]

### CROWNE PLAZA HOUSTON DOWNTOWN
(713)739-8800  **10**

◆◆◆◆ **Hotel** $90-$230 **Address:** 1700 Smith St 77002 **Location:** Corner of Pease St; west side. **Facility:** 259 units. 12 stories, interior corridors. **Parking:** valet only. **Terms:** cancellation fee imposed. **Amenities:** safes. **Pool(s):** outdoor. **Activities:** exercise room. **Guest Services:** valet laundry, area transportation. *(See ad p. 333.)*

[🍴] [🛏] [Y] CALL [&M] [🚐] [BIZ]
[HS] [📶] [X] [💻]

### DOUBLETREE BY HILTON HOTEL HOUSTON DOWNTOWN
(713)759-0202  **3**

◆◆◆ **Hotel** $109-$299 **Address:** 400 Dallas St 77002 **Location:** At Dallas and Bagby sts. Adjoins a pedestrian tunnel and sky bridge, across from Sam Houston Park. **Facility:** 350 units. 20 stories, interior corridors. **Parking:** valet only. **Terms:** 1-7 night minimum stay, cancellation fee imposed. **Activities:** exercise room. **Guest Services:** valet laundry, area transportation.

**AAA Benefit:** Members save 5% or more!

[🍴] [Y] [BIZ] [📶] [X] [💻] / SOME UNITS [🛏] [🛗] [📷]

Learn about inspections and Diamond

Ratings at AAA.com/Diamonds

(See map & index p. 313.)

**EMBASSY SUITES HOUSTON DOWNTOWN**
(713)739-9100

 **Hotel** $142-$332 **Address:** 1515 Dallas St 77010 **Location:** Between Crawford and La Branch sts. Across from Discovery Green Park. **Facility:** 262 units. 19 stories, interior corridors. **Parking:** valet only. **Terms:** 1-7 night minimum stay, cancellation fee imposed. **Amenities:** safes. **Pool(s):** heated outdoor. **Activities:** hot tub, exercise room. **Guest Services:** valet and coin laundry, area transportation.

> **AAA Benefit:**
> Members save 5% or more!

**FOUR SEASONS HOTEL HOUSTON** 713/650-1300

Hotel
Rates not provided

**Address:** 1300 Lamar St 77010 **Location:** Jct Lamar and Austin sts. Across from a shopping center. **Facility:** The style here is clean and refined, with luxurious décor. The outdoor pool is an oasis in this urban setting. The entire staff, as well as the on-site spa, are known for unmatched guest pampering. 404 units. 19 stories, interior corridors. **Parking:** valet only. **Amenities:** safes. **Dining:** Quattro, see separate listing, entertainment. **Pool(s):** heated outdoor. **Activities:** sauna, hot tub, exercise room, spa. **Guest Services:** valet laundry, area transportation.

▼ See AAA listing p. 332 ▼

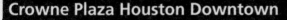

(See map & index p. 313.)

## HILTON AMERICAS-HOUSTON (713)739-8000

Hotel
$119-$549

**AAA Benefit:** Members save 5% or more!

Hilton
HOTELS & RESORTS

**Address:** 1600 Lamar St 77010 **Location:** Between Crawford St and Avenida De Las Americas; at George R Brown Convention Center. **Facility:** Conveniently located in downtown by Discovery Green Park, this hotel features a large, blown-glass chandelier in the lobby and includes the attached George R. Brown Convention Center to the side. Guests can enjoy stunning views on the 24th floor, which includes an indoor pool and outdoor patio, while the Toyota Center and Minute Maid Park are only a short walk away. 1200 units. 24 stories, interior corridors. **Parking:** on-site (fee) and valet. **Terms:** 1-7 night minimum stay, cancellation fee imposed. **Amenities:** video games, safes. **Pool(s):** heated indoor. **Activities:** sauna, hot tub, steamroom, spa. **Guest Services:** valet laundry, area transportation. *(See ad this page.)*

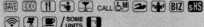

### HOTEL ICON HOUSTON 713/224-4266

**Historic Hotel.** Rates not provided. **Address:** 220 Main St 77002 **Location:** Between Travis and Main sts; entrance on Congress St. **Facility:** The luxurious hotel's rooms are done in shades of warm sage, rich cranberry and butter yellow and feature chandeliers and large baths with marble-topped vanities. 135 units. 12 stories, interior corridors. **Parking:** valet only. **Amenities:** safes. **Activities:** exercise room, spa. **Guest Services:** valet laundry, area transportation.

## HYATT REGENCY HOUSTON (713)654-1234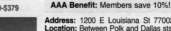

Hotel
$89-$379

HYATT REGENCY

**AAA Benefit:** Members save 10%!

**Address:** 1200 E Louisiana St 77002 **Location:** Between Polk and Dallas sts. **Facility:** This large luxury hotel with access to Houston's tunnel system has a soaring atrium lobby and a rooftop restaurant. The rooms are done in a modern but warm and comfortable style. 947 units. 30 stories, interior corridors. **Parking:** valet only. **Terms:** cancellation fee imposed. **Amenities:** safes. **Dining:** 3 restaurants. **Pool(s):** heated outdoor. **Activities:** exercise room. **Guest Services:** valet laundry, area transportation. **Featured Amenity:** full hot breakfast.

### THE MAGNOLIA HOTEL 713/221-0011

Hotel
Rates not provided

**Address:** 1100 Texas Ave 77002 **Location:** Between Fannin and San Jacinto sts. **Facility:** Housed in the historic building that was once the Post Dispatch newspaper, this modern hotel features large rooms done in an artistic and upscale style. 314 units, some efficiencies. 23 stories, interior corridors. **Parking:** valet only. **Amenities:** safes. **Pool(s):** outdoor. **Activities:** hot tub, exercise room, massage. **Guest Services:** valet and coin laundry, area transportation.

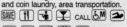

▼ See AAA listing this page ▼

Get pet travel tips and enter the photo contest at AAA.com/PetBook

(See map & index p. 313.)

**RESIDENCE INN BY MARRIOTT HOUSTON DOWNTOWN/ CONVENTION CENTER**   (832)366-1000   **7**

WVVV **Extended Stay Hotel** $89-$399 **Address:** 904 Dallas St 77002 **Location:** At Main St. **Facility:** 171 units, some two bedrooms, efficiencies and kitchens. 10 stories, interior corridors. **Parking:** valet only. **Pool(s):** outdoor. **Activities:** hot tub, exercise room. **Guest Services:** valet and coin laundry, area transportation.

**AAA Benefit:** Members save 5% or more!

CALL 🛎 🚐 BIZ HS 🛜 ✕ 🍴 🖥 🖵
/ SOME UNITS 🛏

---

## THE WESTIN HOUSTON DOWNTOWN

713/228-1520   **5**

WVVV WVVV   **WESTIN** HOTELS & RESORTS   **AAA Benefit:** Enjoy up to 20% off your next stay, plus Starwood Preferred Guest® bonuses!
Hotel
Rates not provided

**Address:** 1520 Texas Ave 77002 **Location:** Corner of Crawford St; center. **Facility:** This hotel is conveniently located right across the street from the Houston Astros' baseball stadium—so be prepared to see large groups of fans on some nights. 200 units. 12 stories, interior corridors. **Parking:** valet only. **Terms:** check-in 4 pm. **Amenities:** video games, safes. **Activities:** exercise room, massage. **Guest Services:** valet laundry, area transportation.

SAVE 🍴 🛁 🍸 CALL 🛎 HS 🛜 ✕ 🎥 🖵
/ SOME UNITS 🍴

---

### WHERE TO EAT

**17**   832/200-8888   **10**

WVVV New American. Fine Dining. $10-$42 **AAA Inspector Notes:** Tucked inside the Alden Houston downtown, the restaurant prepares American breakfast, lunch and dinner items with a creative and upscale touch. Patrons often visit for special occasions or group dinners. A mural illustrates the Battle of San Jacinto. Named for the 17 railroads that once all met in Houston, 17 oozes chic, contemporary style. Desserts are too sweet to pass up. **Features:** full bar. **Reservations:** suggested. **Address:** 1117 Prairie St 77002 **Location:** Jct San Jacinto; in Alden Houston. **Parking:** valet and street only.

B L D

---

**III FORKS**   713/658-9457   **18**

WVVV
Steak
Fine Dining
$25-$60

**AAA Inspector Notes:** All beef products served here are USDA Prime and include favorites such as filet mignon, bone-in-rib-eye, New York Strip, prime rib, burgers and pork chops. Seafood delicacies feature ahi tuna, shrimp, scallops and crab. The menu also offers Australian lobster, Chilean sea bass, lamb and Atlantic salmon. Staff members peruse the dining room serving fresh sliced and seasoned scallions and tomatoes. Finish off with homemade desserts which include a delectable bread pudding. **Features:** full bar. **Address:** 1201 San Jacinto St 77002 **Location:** Center of downtown. **Parking:** on-site (fee) and valet.   L D CALL 🛎

**USDA Prime beef, fresh fish, cold-water lobster tails**

---

Safety tip: Keep a current AAA/CAA
Road Atlas in every vehicle

---

**AQUARIUM RESTAURANT**   713/223-3474   **2**

WVV WVV Seafood. Casual Dining. $10-$33 **AAA Inspector Notes:** A truly impressive 150,000-gallon saltwater aquarium dominates the dining room. There is a lot to see with a myriad of fish large and small, including some sharks. Some may find it odd selecting from a menu of fresh seafood while watching the fish in the aquarium, but the food is excellent and the staff is friendly and attentive. **Features:** full bar, happy hour. **Address:** 410 Bagby St 77002 **Location:** Just n of Washington St. **Parking:** on-site (fee) and valet.

SAVE L D CALL 🛎

---

**ARTISTA**   713/278-4782   **8**

WVVV Latin American. Fine Dining. $26-$68 **AAA Inspector Notes:** Overlooking the Theater District, this contemporary restaurant offers great panoramic views of the city through full-size windows. The atmosphere is bustling as the staff competently and expediently serves guests to enable them to make the evening's performance. The seafood-rich menu (with three sauce choices) also includes chicken and vegetables. **Features:** full bar, patio dining. **Reservations:** suggested. **Address:** 800 Bagby St, Suite 400 77002 **Location:** In The Hobby Center for The Performing Arts. **Parking:** valet and street only.   L D CALL 🛎

---

**BARNABY'S CAFE**   713/522-0106   **23**

WVV WVV American. Casual Dining. $10-$17 **AAA Inspector Notes:** This place can be tough to find, as it's tucked away in a residential neighborhood. This is the original location of a small local chain that serves such classics as Cobb salad, hamburgers and meatloaf, but you will be pleasantly surprised with the diversity of the choices. The small dining room is accented with original artwork and has an eclectic and alternative atmosphere. **Features:** beer & wine. **Address:** 604 Fairview St 77006 **Location:** Just e of jct Montrose Blvd and Fairview St; between Stanford and Hopkins sts.

L D

---

**BEAVER'S**   713/864-2328   **1**

WVV WVV Regional American. Gastropub. $8-$15 **AAA Inspector Notes:** This is a gastropub Texas style. The menu is loaded with Texas comfort foods done with a creative twist and premium local ingredients. The barbecue is smoked on premises daily and includes brisket, pork and chicken. Menu items include pork belly BLT with avocado-orange mayo and marinated Texas tomatoes; house-made jalapeño sausage; and a huge seafood po'boy with shrimp, fish, crispy onions and spicy tartar sauce. Cocktails incorporate more Texas products and slightly obscure ingredients. **Features:** full bar, Sunday brunch. **Address:** 2310 Decatur St 77007 **Location:** Just s of jct Washington Ave and Sawyer St.   L D

---

**BRENNAN'S OF HOUSTON**   713/522-9711   **34**

WVV WVV WVV Creole. Fine Dining. $16-$40 **AAA Inspector Notes:** The restaurant has been totally rebuilt after a fire, and the setting is grander than ever. The menu still offers classic New Orleans flavors like turtle soup and entrées such as lamb mint julep, crawfish and maple leaf duck and the sublime signature Louisiana pecan-crusted fish. Finish with the superb Creole pudding soufflé or the signature bananas Foster flambé prepared at your table. The service is skilled and formal. **Features:** full bar, Sunday brunch. **Reservations:** suggested. **Address:** 3300 Smith St 77006 **Location:** Jct Smith and Stuart sts; southwest corner. **Parking:** valet only.   L D

---

**CHARIVARI SPECIALTY RESTAURANT**   713/521-7231   **22**

WVV WVV New European. Fine Dining. $11-$39 **AAA Inspector Notes:** Charivari means "a loud noise," and this restaurant near downtown is certainly making noise with the locals. European cuisine like no other reflects Transylvanian influences, and presentation could not be more beautiful. **Features:** full bar. **Address:** 2521 Bagby St 77006 **Location:** Corner of Bagby and McGowen sts.   L D

---

**DAMIAN'S CUCINA ITALIANA**   713/522-0439   **32**

WVV WVV WVV Italian. Fine Dining. $15-$45 **AAA Inspector Notes:** Near the Theater District, the attractive eatery features earth-colored walls and Italian countryside murals. Hanging copper pots and rich woods complete the look of a warm, rustic eatery. While the pasta menu is long, offerings also include many fish, veal, beef and chicken selections. Leave room for homemade tiramisu. **Features:** full bar. **Reservations:** suggested. **Address:** 3011 Smith St 77006 **Location:** 0.8 mi s, just n of Elgin St, just w of Main St. **Parking:** valet only.   L D

(See map & index p. 313.)

### THE FISH RESTAURANT & SUSHI BAR       713/526-5294   21
▼▼ Asian Sushi. Fine Dining. $9-$28 **AAA Inspector Notes:** Located within close proximity to the downtown area, this contemporary sushi bar offers a variety of cooked and uncooked Asian-influenced treats. You will find everything from macaroni gratin and gyoza to blue crab fried rice and fresh-water eel. **Features:** full bar, happy hour. **Address:** 309 Gray St, Suite 107 77002 **Location:** Jct Baldwin St. **Parking:** valet and street only. ☐ L ☐ D ☐ LATE

### FLYING SAUCER       713/228-7468   11
▼▼ International. Gastropub. $8-$11 **AAA Inspector Notes:** Part of a chain of beer emporiums located in six states, this is a fun place to chow on some American-, Mexican- and German-inspired dishes. Try the bratwurst plate or the nachos to satisfy the munchies. There's also an option to create your own pizza. The beer menu is encyclopedic. Learn how to earn your name on a flying dish saucer on their wall of fame. **Features:** full bar. **Address:** 705 Main St 77002 **Location:** Between Capitol and Rusk sts. **Parking:** on-site (fee) and street. ☐ L ☐ D ☐ LATE ⬓

### THE GROVE       713/337-7321   20
▼▼▼ American. Fine Dining. $11-$32 **AAA Inspector Notes:** This hot spot in Discovery Green Park offers "rustic American" cuisine in a dramatic setting. Chef Robert Del Grande uses local ingredients to prepare such items as Texas Quail skewers, pork belly sliders and charcoal-grilled skirt steak with tomatillo and fresh jalapeños. Besides appetizers and entrées, there are small plates, salads, sandwiches and an artisan cheese plate. The rooftop deck offers great views. Several hotels, the convention center, Toyota Center and Minute Maid Park are nearby. **Features:** full bar, patio dining, Sunday brunch, happy hour. **Reservations:** suggested. **Address:** 1611 Lamar St 77010 **Location:** In Discovery Green Park. **Parking:** valet and street only. ☐ L ☐ D CALL ⬓M 🐾

### HARD ROCK CAFE       713/227-1392   5
▼ American. Casual Dining. $10-$25 **AAA Inspector Notes:** Rock 'n' roll memorabilia decorates the walls of the popular theme restaurant. Live music on the weekends contributes to the bustling atmosphere. On the menu is a wide variety of American cuisine—from burgers and sandwiches to seafood, steaks and pasta. **Features:** full bar. **Address:** 502 Texas Ave 77002 **Location:** Between Bagby and Smith sts. **Parking:** street only. SAVE ☐ L ☐ D ☐ LATE

### HEARSAY GASTRO LOUNGE       713/225-8079   4
▼▼ New American. Gastropub. $6-$30 **AAA Inspector Notes:** *Historic.* Many will remember this gastropub for its setting in the W. L. Foley Building which is listed on the National Register of Historic Places. Local ingredients are used in its excellent and creative takes on comfort foods with items such as a Kobe beef hot dog, smoked brisket sandwich and entrées such as lamb chop pops and a chicken breast stuffed with goat cheese, spinach and sun-dried tomato. The crème brûlée is brought flaming to your table. Creative neo-classic cocktails are offered. **Features:** full bar, Sunday brunch. **Address:** 218 Travis St 77002 **Location:** At Congress St; in historic district. **Parking:** street only. ☐ L ☐ D ☐ LATE CALL ⬓M

### IBIZA FOOD & WINE BAR       713/524-0004   25
▼▼▼ New American. Casual Dining. $9-$28 **AAA Inspector Notes:** The trendy eatery pairs selections from its extremely large wine list with such succulent dishes as Colorado ruby trout, 6-hour-braised lamb shank and Belleville buffalo tenderloin. From creamy soups to decadent desserts, the attentive staff guides diners through a memorable meal. **Reservations:** suggested. **Address:** 2450 Louisiana St 77006 **Location:** Between McGowen and Hadley sts. **Parking:** on-site and valet. ☐ L ☐ D

### KATZ'S DELI & BAR       713/521-3838   30
▼▼ Deli. Quick Serve. $9-$15 **AAA Inspector Notes:** "Katz's never closes" is the motto at the New York-style delicatessen, an area institution since 1979. The extensive menu has something for everyone, including massive cold and hot sandwiches, hot dogs, soups, salads and entrées along the lines of roasted chicken and pot roast. Kosher ingredients are an additional draw. **Features:** full bar. **Address:** 616 Westheimer Rd 77006 **Location:** Just e of Montrose Blvd. ☐ B ☐ L ☐ D   24

### KHUN KAY THAI CAFE       713/524-9614   15
▼▼ Thai. Quick Serve. $7-$19 **AAA Inspector Notes:** Once a traditional Thai eatery, this restaurant has gone minimalist with IKEA-esque monochromatic furniture and nearly bare walls. Service is provided only at the counter. The menu features a variety of simple dishes. **Features:** beer & wine. **Address:** 1209 Montrose Blvd 77019 **Location:** Just s of jct W Dallas St and Montrose Blvd. ☐ L ☐ D

### KIM SON RESTAURANT       713/222-2461   27
▼▼ Vietnamese. Casual Dining. $7-$26 **AAA Inspector Notes:** The restaurant offers a large menu of various Asian preparations of beef, chicken and seafood entrées with vegetables, noodles and rice. The service is professional and efficient, and the décor is a step up from similar Vietnamese restaurants in the downtown area. The restaurant is large and gets very busy, but there is ample parking. **Features:** full bar, happy hour. **Address:** 2001 Jefferson St 77003 **Location:** US 59 exit Gray and Pierce sts; between Pease and Jefferson sts; on Chartres St. **Parking:** on-site and valet. ☐ L ☐ D

### LA MEXICANA RESTAURANT       713/521-0963   24
▼ Mexican. Casual Dining. $8-$23 **AAA Inspector Notes:** Those in the mood for home-style Mexican cooking should head to this spot near downtown. It's been around for generations and proves to be a favorite among the locals. **Features:** full bar, patio dining, happy hour. **Address:** 1018 Fairview St 77006 **Location:** Jct Fairview St and Montrose Blvd. ☐ B ☐ L ☐ D

### LITTLE BIGS       713/521-2447   29
▼ Burgers. Casual Dining. $2-$6 **AAA Inspector Notes:** This simple little burger joint serves only sliders, but they are made from premium ingredients such as freshly ground beef and freshly baked rolls. The fries are hand-cut fresh and fried to order. The limited menu also offers sliders of pulled pork, fried chicken and black bean. A selection of premium wines by the glass also is offered, as are beer, soft drinks and shakes. The staff is friendly, and there are many outdoor tables available. The place is open until 3 am on weekends. **Features:** beer & wine. **Address:** 2703 Montrose Blvd 77006 **Location:** Just n of Westheimer Rd. ☐ L ☐ D CALL ⬓M

### MASSA'S RESTAURANT       713/650-0837   12
▼▼▼ Seafood. Fine Dining. $16-$33 **AAA Inspector Notes:** A hot spot for business lunches or evening occasions, the restaurant presents a menu of seafood, meat and poultry dishes prepared with fresh sauces and vegetables with just a hint of Southern flavor. Chef Michael focuses on fine quality, and the trained staff watches over guests' leisurely meals. **Features:** full bar. **Address:** 1160 Smith St 77002 **Location:** Between Dallas and Lamar sts; center. **Parking:** street only. ☐ L ☐ D

### MASSA'S SEAFOOD GRILL       713/655-9100   17
▼▼▼ Seafood. Fine Dining. $10-$30 **AAA Inspector Notes:** The upscale, cosmopolitan restaurant has all the charm and elegance of the Old World. Staffers in white coats aim to please with expert service. Cajun influences are noticeable in dark roux gumbo and crayfish étouffée, while other tempting and sophisticated dishes also please the palate. **Features:** full bar, happy hour. **Address:** 1331 Lamar St 77010 **Location:** Corner of Austin and Lamar sts. **Parking:** street only. ☐ L ☐ D

### MIA BELLA TRATTORIA       713/237-0505   7
▼▼ Italian. Casual Dining. $7-$23 **AAA Inspector Notes:** With tall ceilings, dark woods and murals that recall Michelangelo, the eatery nurtures a distinct Old World atmosphere. Imaginative Italian dishes, including some design-your-own pasta choices, line the menu. **Features:** full bar, patio dining, Sunday brunch, happy hour. **Address:** 320 Main St 77002 **Location:** At Preston St. **Parking:** street only. ☐ L ☐ D

### NIKO NIKO'S       713/528-1308   26
▼ Greek. Quick Serve. $9-$23 **AAA Inspector Notes:** It's hard to find any Houstonian who hasn't visited or at least heard of this place. Established in 1977, it frequently earns accolades for its savory gyro sandwiches and yummy fries. The staff is always ready to help a newcomer make a selection from the lengthy menu. Although the little eatery is known for gyros, diners find a whole range of great food, including keftedes, moussaka and pastitsio. Sidewalk dining is available. **Features:** beer & wine, patio dining. **Address:** 2520 Montrose Blvd 77006 **Location:** Just n of Westheimer Rd. **Parking:** on-site and street. ☐ L ☐ D

(See map & index p. 313.)

NINO'S     713/522-5120   (14)

▼▼ ▼▼ Traditional Italian. Casual Dining. $11-$35 **AAA Inspector Notes:** In this casual setting, attentive servers present plates of traditional Italian cuisine such as pasta, chicken Marsala, veal and lamb chops and pizza. The restaurant shares a charming patio with other Italian restaurants in the complex. **Features:** full bar. **Reservations:** suggested. **Address:** 2817 W Dallas St 77019 **Location:** I-45 exit 47A (Allen Pkwy), 1.5 mi w to Montrose Blvd, s to W Dallas St, then just w. [L] [D]

PIOLA     713/524-8222   (35)

▼▼ ▼▼ Pizza. Casual Dining. $9-$16 **AAA Inspector Notes:** This trendy gourmet pizza restaurant has an international flair. The menu offers excellent thin-crust pies with interesting ingredients. Options include the Como with porcini mushrooms and prosciutto, and the Ortomisto with eggplant, spinach, sweet peppers and broccoli topped with fresh basil. There are a wide range of pizzas, as well as some great salads, carpaccio and a few pastas. The décor is modern and the atmosphere casual in this location near some of the popular midtown bars. **Features:** full bar. **Address:** 3201 Louisiana St, Suite 103 77006 **Location:** Just s of Elgin St. [L] [D]

PRONTO CUCININO     713/592-8646   (16)

▼▼ ▼▼ Italian. Quick Serve. $7-$13 **AAA Inspector Notes:** Enter into a warm, inviting interior marked by stone columns, arches and an open kitchen, decidedly unlike what you might expect to find in a quick-service spot. Step up to the counter to order food on par with that of full-service restaurants, including pizza, pasta, pork chops and lemon-garlic-roasted chicken. The experience focuses more on adult patrons, with wine and thoughtful entrée presentations. Sit on the sidewalk to watch the activity around the bookstore, grocery and other shops. **Features:** beer & wine. **Address:** 3191 W Holcombe Blvd 77025 **Location:** 3.1 mi s on US 59, 1.7 mi s on Buffalo Speedway. [L] [D]

QUATTRO     713/276-4700   (19)

▼▼ ▼▼ ▼▼
Italian
Fine Dining
$13-$52

**AAA Inspector Notes:** A subtle, refined ambience is achieved with a mix of classic and modern artwork and impeccable service. Diverse, artistically designed menu selections—ranging from foie gras to double-grilled lamb chops to crab cakes—combine with the chef's seasonal specials to create a distinct fusion of flavors. Located in the Four Seasons hotel, the restaurant delivers the refinement and luxury of its renowned location. **Features:** full bar, Sunday brunch. **Reservations:** suggested. **Address:** 1300 Lamar St 77010 **Location:** Jct Lamar and Austin sts; in Four Seasons Hotel Houston. **Parking:** valet only. [B] [L] [D] CALL [M]

RED LANTERN     713/237-0360   (3)

▼▼ Vietnamese. Casual Dining. $6-$12 **AAA Inspector Notes:** Simple eatery for a quick bite of Vietnamese-style cuisine. Limited menu but fairly quick service. The pho, a hearty beef soup, is one of the favorites. **Address:** 917 Franklin St, Suite 101 77002 **Location:** Between Main and Travis sts. [L] [D]

REEF     713/526-8282   (28)

▼▼ ▼▼ New Seafood. Fine Dining. $7-$29 **AAA Inspector Notes:** The menu from renowned Houston chef Bryan Caswell changes frequently, as you would expect from a restaurant that is focused on market fresh seafood. There is a wide variety here, including some fish that are not commonly seen in other restaurants. Some guests find the bustling dining room to be a bit loud and not really suited for relaxed, comfortable dining with one large main room with concrete floors and a simple pastel decor that vaguely recalls the ocean. Outdoor dining is available and the separate bar/lounge area is a lively and popular spot in the Midtown scene. **Features:** full bar, patio dining, happy hour. **Reservations:** suggested. **Address:** 2600 Travis St 77006 **Location:** At McGowen St; in Midtown District. **Parking:** valet and street only. [L] [D] CALL [M]

RESTAURANT INDIKA     713/524-2170   (31)

▼▼ ▼▼ ▼▼ New Indian. Fine Dining. $12-$70 **AAA Inspector Notes:** Even those who partake regularly of Indian food find this place a treat. The contemporary fare relies on an astute selection of spices and ingredients. Among dishes are coriander-encrusted tuna, slow-cooked spiced lamb shank, duck breast vindaloo and grilled chicken breast with mango chutney, as well as equally inspiring starters and desserts. This additional location is a departure from the charming cottage in west Houston but is just as chic and inviting. **Features:** full bar, Sunday brunch. **Reservations:** suggested, weekends. **Address:** 516 Westheimer Rd 77024 **Location:** Just w of jct Smith St. **Parking:** valet only. [L] [D]

SAMBUCA RESTAURANT     713/224-5299   (9)

▼▼ ▼▼ New American. Fine Dining. $9-$28 **AAA Inspector Notes:** This dinner club in the historic Rice building is the place to see live music, including rock, jazz, country and blues with different live bands each night. The menu offers a wide selection of entrées with fresh seafood, steaks and chops, as well as lighter items like salads, pizzas and small plates. The artistic décor and lively bar scene make for a very cosmopolitan atmosphere. **Features:** full bar, patio dining, happy hour. **Reservations:** suggested, weekends. **Address:** 909 Texas Ave 77002 **Location:** Between Travis and Main sts. **Parking:** valet and street only. [L] [D]

THE SPAGHETTI WAREHOUSE     713/229-9715

▼▼ ▼▼ Italian. Casual Dining. $7-$17 **AAA Inspector Notes:** The Italian-style restaurant chain sustains a festive family atmosphere. All entrees include bottomless tossed salad or soup. Patrons enjoy plentiful portions of such classic dishes as ravioli, lasagna, baked penne or the richly flavored cannelloni Florentine. Splurging on one of the many desserts, such as tiramisu, espresso mousse cake or carrot cake, is worthwhile. **Features:** full bar. **Address:** 901 Commerce St 77002 **Location:** At Travis St. [L] [D]

TREEBEARDS     713/228-2622   (6)

▼▼ Southern. Cafeteria. $5-$15 **AAA Inspector Notes:** This cafeteria-style eatery has been thriving for more than 30 years due to its simply delicious home-style food. Earthy gumbos, chunky red beans and rice with sausage, savory chili, jambalaya, and daily specials with fresh vegetables come together to give a great taste of Louisiana. The atmosphere is friendly and relaxed, with a diverse and loyal clientele dressed in everything from suits to ball caps. **Features:** beer only. **Address:** 315 Travis St 77002 **Location:** Corner of Travis and Preston sts; across from Market Square Park. **Parking:** street only. [L]

VAN LOC RESTAURANT     713/528-6441   (33)

▼▼ Vietnamese. Casual Dining. $6-$15 **AAA Inspector Notes:** The menu here is extensive and features all variations of Vietnamese cuisine. Spring rolls are very good and quite popular. A curry dish was found to be on the bland side, so feel free to request extra heat as desired. The downtown restaurant is very simple in décor. Service is quick and functional but not very informative. **Features:** beer & wine. **Address:** 3010 Milam St 77006 **Location:** 0.8 mi s on Milam St; just n of Elgin St. [L] [D]

VIC & ANTHONY'S STEAKHOUSE     713/228-1111   (13)

▼▼ ▼▼ ▼▼ Steak. Fine Dining. $30-$56 **AAA Inspector Notes:** The steakhouse décor can best be described as stunning. From luxurious marbles and rich woods to stained-glass lighting, the dining room gives off a royal air. Top-of-the-line USDA Prime grain-fed beef comes from Chicago. Surf-and-turf lovers can add in Maine or Australian rock lobster. Meals are done a la carte, and side dishes are huge enough for several people. An excellent selection of wines adds that extra touch to dinner. **Features:** full bar, happy hour. **Reservations:** suggested. **Address:** 1510 Texas Ave 77002 **Location:** Southeast corner of jct Texas Ave and La Branch St. **Parking:** valet only. [D]

# HOUSTON (LOOP FREEWAY)

- Restaurants p. 347
- Hotels & Restaurants map & index p. 316

## ALOFT HOUSTON BY THE GALLERIA
(713)622-7010 **34**

Hotel
$95-$499

**AAA Benefit:** Enjoy the new twist, get up to 20% off + Starwood Preferred Guest® bonuses!

**Address:** 5415 Westheimer Rd 77056 **Location:** I-610 exit 8C (Westheimer Rd) northbound; exit 9A (San Felipe Rd/Westheimer Rd) southbound, 0.8 mi w. **Facility:** 152 units. 10 stories, interior corridors. **Bath:** shower only. **Parking:** on-site (fee) and valet. **Terms:** cancellation fee imposed. **Amenities:** safes. **Pool(s):** heated indoor. **Activities:** exercise room. **Guest Services:** valet and coin laundry, area transportation.

## BEST WESTERN FOUNTAINVIEW INN & SUITES NEAR GALLERIA
(713)783-8388 **42**

Hotel
$85-$95

**AAA Benefit:** Members save 10% or more with Best Western!

**Address:** 6229 Richmond Ave 77057 **Location:** US 59 (Southwest Frwy) exit Fountain View Dr southbound; exit Hillcroft Ave northbound, 0.5 mi on service road to Fountain View Dr, just n to Richmond Ave, then just w. **Facility:** 67 units. 3 stories, interior corridors. **Terms:** check-in 4 pm. **Pool(s):** outdoor. **Activities:** exercise room. **Guest Services:** coin laundry. **Featured Amenity:** breakfast buffet.

## BEST WESTERN HERITAGE INN
(713)670-9100 **17**

Hotel
$99-$109

**AAA Benefit:** Members save 10% or more with Best Western!

**Address:** 10521 E Frwy 77029 **Location:** I-10 exit 776A (Mercury Dr) westbound; exit 776B (John Ralston Rd) eastbound; on westbound frontage road. **Facility:** 62 units. 3 stories, interior corridors. **Amenities:** safes. **Pool(s):** outdoor. **Activities:** exercise room. **Guest Services:** valet and coin laundry. **Featured Amenity:** full hot breakfast.

## BEST WESTERN PLAZA HOTEL & SUITES AT MEDICAL CENTER
(713)522-2811 **55**

Hotel
$90-$115

**AAA Benefit:** Members save 10% or more with Best Western!

**Address:** 6700 S Main St 77030 **Location:** I-610 exit 2 (Main St), 2.4 mi ne. **Facility:** 123 units. 6 stories, interior corridors. **Pool(s):** indoor. **Activities:** hot tub, exercise room. **Guest Services:** valet and coin laundry, area transportation. **Featured Amenity:** breakfast buffet.

 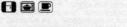

## BEST WESTERN PLUS NORTHWEST INN & SUITES
(713)290-1400 **7**

Hotel
$100-$120

**AAA Benefit:** Members save 10% or more with Best Western!

**Address:** 11611 NW Frwy 77092 **Location:** US 290 exit Antoine Dr, just s. **Facility:** 60 units. 3 stories, interior corridors. **Pool(s):** outdoor. **Activities:** hot tub, exercise room. **Guest Services:** valet and coin laundry.

## BEST WEST INN & SUITES
(713)943-2700 **72**

Hotel $109-$299 **Address:** 8778 Airport Blvd 77061 **Location:** I-45 exit 36 (Airport Blvd/College St), 1.2 mi w. **Facility:** 72 units. 3 stories, interior corridors. **Terms:** cancellation fee imposed. **Pool(s):** outdoor. **Activities:** exercise room. **Guest Services:** valet and coin laundry, area transportation.

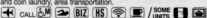

## CANDLEWOOD SUITES HOUSTON BY THE GALLERIA
(713)839-9411 **50**

Extended Stay Hotel $79-$119 **Address:** 4900 Loop Central Dr 77081 **Location:** I-610 exit 7 (Furnace Rd) southbound; exit 7 (Westpark Dr) northbound; on northbound frontage road. **Facility:** 122 efficiencies. 3 stories, interior corridors. **Terms:** cancellation fee imposed. **Activities:** exercise room. **Guest Services:** complimentary and valet laundry.

## COMFORT SUITES GALLERIA
(713)787-0004 **43**

Hotel
$120-$189

**Address:** 6221 Richmond Ave 77057 **Location:** US 59 (Southwest Blvd) exit Hillcroft St, 1 mi n to Richmond Ave, then 0.6 mi e. **Facility:** 61 units. 3 stories, interior corridors. **Pool(s):** outdoor. **Activities:** hot tub, exercise room. **Guest Services:** valet and coin laundry, area transportation. **Featured Amenity:** full hot breakfast.

## COMFORT SUITES HOBBY AIRPORT
(713)944-4400 **74**

Hotel $79-$199 **Address:** 9120 Airport Blvd 77061 **Location:** I-45 exit 36 (Airport Blvd/College St), just w. **Facility:** 59 units. 3 stories, interior corridors. **Pool(s):** outdoor. **Activities:** hot tub, exercise room. **Guest Services:** valet and coin laundry.

(See map & index p. 316.)

## COURTYARD BY MARRIOTT HOUSTON BROOKHOLLOW
(713)688-7711   **8**

 **Hotel $80-$260 Address:** 2504 N Loop W 77092 **Location:** I-610 exit 13C (TC Jester Blvd), just nw. **Facility:** 197 units. 3 stories, interior corridors. **Pool(s):** outdoor. **Activities:** exercise room. **Guest Services:** valet and coin laundry.

**AAA Benefit:** Members save 5% or more!

## COURTYARD BY MARRIOTT HOUSTON BY THE GALLERIA
(713)622-3611   **37**

 Hotel $90-$330

COURTYARD Marriott

**AAA Benefit:** Members save 5% or more!

**Address:** 2900 Sage Rd 77056 **Location:** I-610 exit 8C (Westheimer Rd) northbound, just w to Sage Rd, then just s; exit 8B (Hidalgo St/Richmond Ave) southbound, just w on Hidalgo St, then just s. **Facility:** 190 units. 15 stories, interior corridors. **Parking:** on-site (fee). **Pool(s):** heated indoor. **Activities:** hot tub, exercise room. **Guest Services:** valet and coin laundry.

## COURTYARD BY MARRIOTT-HOUSTON HOBBY AIRPORT
(713)910-1700   **67**

 **Hotel $89-$159 Address:** 9190 Gulf Frwy 77017 **Location:** I-45 exit 36 (Airport Blvd/College St) southbound; exit 38 (Monroe Rd/Bellfort St) northbound; on southbound service road. **Facility:** 153 units. 3 stories, interior corridors. **Pool(s):** outdoor. **Activities:** hot tub, exercise room. **Guest Services:** valet and coin laundry, area transportation.

**AAA Benefit:** Members save 5% or more!

## COURTYARD BY MARRIOTT-WEST UNIVERSITY
(713)661-5669   **48**

 **Hotel $99-$209 Address:** 2929 Westpark Dr 77005 **Location:** US 59 (Southwest Frwy) exit Kirby Dr, just s to Westpark Dr, then just w. **Facility:** 100 units. 3 stories, interior corridors. **Pool(s):** heated outdoor. **Activities:** hot tub, exercise room. **Guest Services:** valet and coin laundry, area transportation.

**AAA Benefit:** Members save 5% or more!

## CROWNE PLAZA HOUSTON GALLERIA AREA
713/680-2222   **13**

 Hotel Rates not provided

**Address:** 7611 Katy Frwy 77024 **Location:** I-10 exit 761 westbound, U-turn at Witt Ave; exit 762 eastbound; on south frontage road. **Facility:** 207 units. 6 stories, interior corridors. **Parking:** on-site and valet. **Pool(s):** heated outdoor. **Activities:** exercise room. **Guest Services:** valet laundry.

## CROWNE PLAZA HOUSTON RIVER OAKS
(713)523-8448   **44**

 Hotel $89-$229

**Address:** 2712 Southwest Frwy 77098 **Location:** US 59 (Southwest Frwy) exit Kirby Dr. **Facility:** 354 units. 18 stories, interior corridors. **Parking:** on-site (fee). **Terms:** cancellation fee imposed. **Pool(s):** outdoor. **Activities:** exercise room, massage. **Guest Services:** valet and coin laundry, area transportation.

(See map & index p. 316.)

## CROWNE PLAZA NORTHWEST HOTEL
(713)462-9977

Hotel
S59-S179

**Address:** 12801 Northwest Frwy 77040 **Location:** Nw on US 290 exit Hollister Rd, 0.7 mi e on south service road. **Facility:** 294 units. 3-10 stories, interior/exterior corridors. **Terms:** cancellation fee imposed. **Pool(s):** outdoor. **Activities:** hot tub, exercise room. **Guest Services:** valet and coin laundry, area transportation. *(See ad this page.)*

---

## CROWNE PLAZA SUITES HOUSTON - NEAR SUGAR LAND
(713)995-0123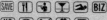

Hotel $79-$159 **Address:** 9090 Southwest Frwy 77074 **Location:** US 59 (Southwest Frwy) exit Beechnut St/Gessner Rd; on southbound frontage road. **Facility:** 243 units. 9 stories, interior corridors. **Terms:** cancellation fee imposed. **Amenities:** video games, safes. **Pool(s):** heated indoor. **Activities:** hot tub, exercise room. **Guest Services:** valet and coin laundry, area transportation.

---

## DAYS INN & SUITES-HOBBY AIRPORT
(713)944-3004

Motel
S85-S135

**Address:** 9114 Airport Blvd 77061 **Location:** I-45 exit 36 (Airport Blvd/College St), just w. **Facility:** 38 units, some kitchens. 2 stories (no elevator), exterior corridors. **Amenities:** safes. **Pool(s):** outdoor. **Activities:** hot tub, limited exercise equipment. **Guest Services:** valet and coin laundry. **Featured Amenity:** continental breakfast.

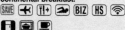

## DOUBLETREE BY HILTON HOTEL HOUSTON - GREENWAY PLAZA
(713)629-1200

Hotel
S119-S429

**AAA Benefit:** Members save 5% or more!

**Address:** 6 Greenway Plaza E 77046 **Location:** US 59 (Southwest Frwy) exit Buffalo Speedway. Located in Greenway Plaza Complex. **Facility:** The room layout at this upscale hotel is very comfortable, with spacious bathrooms and vanity areas. With a location next to a main freeway, the property is adjacent to many office complexes. 388 units. 20 stories, interior corridors. **Parking:** on-site (fee) and valet. **Terms:** check-in 4 pm, 1-7 night minimum stay, cancellation fee imposed. **Dining:** 3 restaurants. **Pool(s):** heated outdoor. **Activities:** exercise room. **Guest Services:** valet laundry, area transportation. *(See ad p. 341.)*

---

## DOUBLETREE BY HILTON HOUSTON HOBBY AIRPORT
(713)645-3000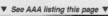

Hotel $129-$349 **Address:** 8181 Airport Blvd 77061 **Location:** I-45 exit 36 (Airport Blvd/College St), 1.5 mi w. **Facility:** 303 units. 9 stories, interior corridors. **Terms:** 1-7 night minimum stay, cancellation fee imposed. **Dining:** 3 restaurants. **Pool(s):** outdoor. **Activities:** exercise room. **Guest Services:** valet laundry, area transportation.

**AAA Benefit:** Members save 5% or more!

---

▼ See AAA listing this page ▼

(See map & index p. 316.)

### DOUBLETREE SUITES BY HILTON HOTEL HOUSTON BY THE GALLERIA
(713)961-9000  **33**

Hotel
$109-$315

**AAA Benefit:** Members save 5% or more!

**Address:** 5353 Westheimer Rd 77056 **Location:** I-610 8C (Westheimer Rd) northbound; exit 9A (San Felipe Rd/Westheimer Rd) southbound, 0.8 mi w. Next to Galleria Shopping Center. **Facility:** 380 units, some kitchens. 26 stories, interior corridors. **Parking:** on-site (fee) and valet. **Terms:** 1-7 night minimum stay, cancellation fee imposed. **Amenities:** video games, safes. **Pool(s):** outdoor. **Activities:** hot tub, exercise room. **Guest Services:** valet and coin laundry, area transportation.

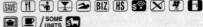

### DRURY INN & SUITES-HOUSTON HOBBY
(713)941-4300  **69**

Hotel $85-$219 **Address:** 7902 Mosley Rd 77061 **Location:** I-45 exit 36 (Airport Blvd/College St) northbound, just w on Airport Blvd, then just n; exit southbound, follow frontage road to Mosley Rd. **Facility:** 134 units. 5 stories, interior corridors. **Terms:** cancellation fee imposed. **Pool(s):** heated outdoor, heated indoor. **Activities:** hot tub, exercise room. **Guest Services:** valet and coin laundry.

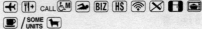

### DRURY INN & SUITES-HOUSTON NEAR THE GALLERIA
(713)963-0700  **21**

Hotel $95-$239 **Address:** 1615 W Loop S 77027 **Location:** I-610 exit 9 (San Felipe Rd) northbound; exit 9A (San Felipe Rd/Westheimer Rd) southbound; on east frontage road. **Facility:** 133 units. 5 stories, interior corridors. **Terms:** cancellation fee imposed. **Pool(s):** heated outdoor, heated indoor. **Activities:** hot tub, exercise room. **Guest Services:** valet and coin laundry.

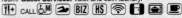

### EMBASSY SUITES HOUSTON NEAR THE GALLERIA
713/626-5444  **38**

Hotel. Rates not provided. **Address:** 2911 Sage Rd 77056 **Location:** I-610 exit 9A (San Felipe Rd/Westheimer Rd) southbound; exit 8C (Westheimer Rd) northbound, 0.4 mi w to Sage Rd, then just s. **Facility:** 150 units. 6 stories, interior corridors. **Parking:** on-site (fee). **Pool(s):** heated indoor. **Activities:** hot tub, exercise room. **Guest Services:** valet and coin laundry, area transportation.

**AAA Benefit:** Members save 5% or more!

### EXTENDED STAY AMERICA HOUSTON-NORTHWEST
(713)895-0965  **1**

Extended Stay Hotel $89-$245 **Address:** 5454 Hollister St 77040 **Location:** US 290 exit Tidwell Rd/Hollister St, just s. **Facility:** 85 kitchen units. 3 stories, interior corridors. **Terms:** cancellation fee imposed. **Pool(s):** outdoor. **Activities:** limited exercise equipment. **Guest Services:** coin laundry.

### FOUR POINTS BY SHERATON HOUSTON HOBBY AIRPORT
(713)948-0800  **63**

Hotel
$129-$179

**AAA Benefit:** Members get up to 20% off, plus Starwood Preferred Guest® bonuses!

**Address:** 8720 Gulf Frwy 77017 **Location:** I-45 exit 38 (Monroe Rd); on south frontage road. **Facility:** 79 units. 4 stories, interior corridors. **Pool(s):** outdoor. **Activities:** exercise room. **Guest Services:** valet and coin laundry, area transportation.

Enjoy exclusive member discounts and benefits from Hertz

▼ See AAA listing p. 340 ▼

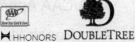

(See map & index p. 316.)

## FOUR POINTS BY SHERATON HOUSTON SOUTHWEST
(713)942-2111 **45**

Hotel
$79-$349

**AAA Benefit:** Members get up to 20% off, plus Starwood Preferred Guest® bonuses!

**Address:** 2828 Southwest Frwy 77098 **Location:** US 59 (Southwest Frwy) exit Kirby Dr; on southbound access road. **Facility:** 216 units. 9 stories, interior corridors. **Terms:** cancellation fee imposed. **Pool(s):** outdoor. **Activities:** exercise room. **Guest Services:** valet laundry, area transportation.

[SAVE] [icons] CALL [icons]
[BIZ] [HS] [icons]

## HAMPTON INN & SUITES HOUSTON I-10 CENTRAL
(713)869-9211 **15**

Hotel $99-$159 **Address:** 5820 Katy Frwy 77007 **Location:** I-10 exit 764 (Washington Ave); westbound frontage road. **Facility:** 90 units. 2 stories (no elevator), exterior corridors.
**AAA Benefit:** Members save up to 10%!
**Terms:** 1-7 night minimum stay, cancellation fee imposed. **Pool(s):** heated indoor. **Activities:** exercise room. **Guest Services:** valet and coin laundry.

[icons] [BIZ] [HS] [icons]

## HAMPTON INN & SUITES MEDICAL CENTER/RELIANT PARK
(713)797-0040 **58**

Hotel $99-$189 **Address:** 1715 Old Spanish Tr 77054 **Location:** I-635 exit 1B (Fannin St), 1.2 mi n, then just e. **Facility:** 120 units, some efficiencies. 5 stories, interior corridors. **Terms:**
**AAA Benefit:** Members save up to 10%!
1-7 night minimum stay, cancellation fee imposed. **Pool(s):** outdoor. **Activities:** exercise room. **Guest Services:** valet and coin laundry, area transportation.

[icons] CALL [icons]

## HAMPTON INN-BROOKHOLLOW
(713)939-7100 **4**

Hotel $89-$174 **Address:** 12909 Northwest Frwy 77040 **Location:** US 290 exit Hollister St; on eastbound access road. **Facility:** 81 units. 3 stories, interior corridors. **Terms:** 1-7 night minimum stay, cancellation fee imposed. **Pool(s):** outdoor. **Guest Services:** valet and coin laundry.
**AAA Benefit:** Members save up to 10%!

[icons] [BIZ] [icons] / SOME UNITS [icons]

## HAMPTON INN HOUSTON-HOBBY AIRPORT
(713)641-6400 **70**

Hotel $89-$209 **Address:** 8620 Airport Blvd 77061 **Location:** I-45 exit 36 (Airport Blvd/College St), 1.3 mi w. **Facility:** 119 units. 5 stories, interior corridors. **Terms:** 1-7 night minimum
**AAA Benefit:** Members save up to 10%!
stay, cancellation fee imposed. **Amenities:** video games. **Pool(s):** outdoor. **Activities:** hot tub, exercise room. **Guest Services:** valet laundry, area transportation.

[icons] CALL [icons] [BIZ] [icons] / SOME UNITS [icons]

Trust your vehicle to

AAA/CAA Approved

Auto Repair facilities

## HAMPTON INN HOUSTON NEAR THE GALLERIA
(713)871-9911 **24**

Hotel
$85-$259

**AAA Benefit:** Members save up to 10%!

**Address:** 4500 Post Oak Pkwy 77027 **Location:** I-610 exit 9 (San Felipe Rd) northbound; exit 9A (San Felipe Rd/Westheimer Rd) southbound; on northbound frontage road. **Facility:** 176 units. 6 stories, interior corridors. **Terms:** 1-7 night minimum stay, cancellation fee imposed. **Pool(s):** heated outdoor. **Activities:** exercise room. **Guest Services:** valet laundry. **Featured Amenity:** full hot breakfast.

[SAVE] [icons] CALL [icons] [BIZ] [icons]

## HILTON GARDEN INN HOUSTON GALLERIA AREA
(713)629-0101 **41**

Hotel $89-$329 **Address:** 3201 Sage Rd 77056 **Location:** I-610 exit 8C (Westheimer Rd) northbound, just w to Sage Rd, then just s; exit 8B (Hidalgo St/Richmond Ave) southbound,
**AAA Benefit:** Members save up to 10%!
just w, then just s. **Facility:** 182 units. 8 stories, interior corridors. **Parking:** on-site (fee). **Terms:** 1-7 night minimum stay, cancellation fee imposed. **Amenities:** video games, safes. **Pool(s):** outdoor. **Activities:** hot tub, exercise room. **Guest Services:** valet and coin laundry, area transportation.

[icons] CALL [icons] [BIZ] [HS] [icons]
[icons]

## HILTON HOUSTON PLAZA MEDICAL CENTER
(713)313-4000 **53**

Hotel $119-$359 **Address:** 6633 Travis St 77030 **Location:** I-610 exit 2 (Main St), 2.6 mi ne to Dryden St, just w to Travis St, then just n. **Facility:** 184 units. 19 stories, interior corridors.
**AAA Benefit:** Members save 5% or more!
**Parking:** on-site (fee) and valet. **Terms:** 1-7 night minimum stay, cancellation fee imposed. **Amenities:** safes. **Pool(s):** outdoor. **Activities:** exercise room. **Guest Services:** valet and coin laundry, area transportation.

[icons] CALL [icons] [BIZ] [icons]
[icons]

## HILTON HOUSTON POST OAK
(713)961-9300 **26**

Hotel
$109-$289

[Hilton logo]

**AAA Benefit:** Members save 5% or more!

**Address:** 2001 Post Oak Blvd 77056 **Location:** I-610 exit 8C (Westheimer Rd) northbound, just w; exit 9A (San Felipe Rd/Westheimer Rd) southbound; between San Felipe and Westheimer rds. Located in middle of Galleria business and shopping district. **Facility:** The property features good if somewhat ordinary rooms with work space geared toward the business traveler. The best reason to stay here is the convenient location to many offices, restaurants and shops at the Galleria. 448 units. 14 stories, interior/exterior corridors. **Parking:** on-site (fee) and valet. **Terms:** 1-7 night minimum stay, cancellation fee imposed. **Amenities:** video games, safes. **Pool(s):** outdoor. **Activities:** exercise room. **Guest Services:** valet laundry, area transportation.

[SAVE] [icons] [BIZ] [SHS] [icons]
 / SOME UNITS [icons]

**(See map & index p. 316.)**

HILTON UNIVERSITY OF HOUSTON (832)531-6300 **52**
▼▼▼▼ **Hotel** $109-$269 **Address:** 4800 Calhoun Rd 77204 **Location:** Between Wheeler Ave and University Dr; next to Conrad N Hilton College of Hotel & Restaurant Management; on campus of University of Houston. **Facility:** 86 units. 8 stories, interior corridors. **Parking:** on-site (fee). **Terms:** 1-7 night minimum stay, cancellation fee imposed. **Amenities:** safes. **Pool(s):** outdoor, heated indoor. **Activities:** sauna, hot tub, steamroom, tennis. **Guest Services:** valet laundry.

**AAA Benefit:**
Members save 5% or more!

HOLIDAY INN EXPRESS & SUITES HOBBY AIRPORT
713/941-6000 **64**
▼▼▼▼ **Hotel.** Rates not provided. **Address:** 8730 Gulf Frwy 77017 **Location:** I-45 exit 37 (Monroe Rd) southbound; exit 38 northbound; on south frontage road. **Facility:** 70 units. 4 stories, interior corridors. **Pool(s):** heated indoor. **Activities:** exercise room. **Guest Services:** valet and coin laundry.

**HOLIDAY INN EXPRESS HOTEL & SUITES HOUSTON EAST** (713)330-3800 **18**

▼▼▼▼
Hotel
$144-$154

**Address:** 11460 E Frwy I-10 77029 **Location:** I-10 exit 776B (John Ralston/Holland); on eastbound frontage road. **Facility:** 74 units. 3 stories, interior corridors. **Terms:** cancellation fee imposed. **Amenities:** safes. **Pool(s):** outdoor. **Activities:** hot tub, exercise room. **Guest Services:** valet and coin laundry. **Featured Amenity:** breakfast buffet.

HOLIDAY INN EXPRESS HOTEL & SUITES HOUSTON MEDICAL CENTER 713/665-4439 **60**
▼▼▼▼ **Hotel.** Rates not provided. **Address:** 8080 S Main St 77025 **Location:** I-610 exit 2 (Main St), 1.5 mi n. **Facility:** 79 units. 3 stories, interior corridors. **Activities:** exercise room. **Guest Services:** valet and coin laundry, area transportation.

HOLIDAY INN EXPRESS HOTEL & SUITES MEMORIAL AREA
713/688-2800 **14**
▼▼▼▼ **Hotel.** Rates not provided. **Address:** 7625 Katy Frwy 77024 **Location:** I-10 exit 762 (Silber Rd); on eastbound frontage road. **Facility:** 82 units. 7 stories, interior corridors. **Pool(s):** heated indoor. **Activities:** hot tub, exercise room. **Guest Services:** valet and coin laundry.

**HOLIDAY INN HOUSTON HOBBY AIRPORT**
(713)946-8900 **68**

▼▼▼▼
Hotel
$89-$199

**Address:** 8611 Airport Blvd 77061 **Location:** I-45 exit 36 (Airport Blvd/College St), 1.3 mi w. **Facility:** 194 units. 6 stories, interior corridors. **Terms:** cancellation fee imposed. **Pool(s):** outdoor. **Activities:** hot tub, exercise room. **Guest Services:** valet and coin laundry, area transportation.

**HOLIDAY INN HOUSTON RELIANT PARK AREA**
(713)790-1900 **61**

▼▼▼▼
Hotel
$99-$399

**Address:** 8111 Kirby Dr 77054 **Location:** I-610 exit 1C, 0.9 mi n. **Facility:** 238 units. 11 stories, interior corridors. **Terms:** check-in 4 pm, 3 day cancellation notice. **Pool(s):** outdoor. **Activities:** hot tub, exercise room. **Guest Services:** valet and coin laundry. *(See ad this page.)*

▼ See AAA listing this page ▼

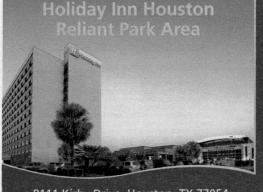

(See map & index p. 316.)

## HOMEWOOD SUITES BY HILTON NEAR THE GALLERIA
713/439-1305 **36**

▽▽▽ **Extended Stay Hotel.**
Rates not provided. **Address:** 2950
Sage Rd 77056 **Location:** I-610 exit 8C
(Westheimer Rd), just w to Sage Rd,
then just s. **Facility:** 162 efficiencies,
some two bedrooms. 14 stories, interior corridors. **Parking:** on-site
(fee). **Amenities:** video games. **Activities:**
hot tub, exercise room. **Guest Services:** valet and coin laundry.

**AAA Benefit:**
Members save up to
10%!

 CALL 🛌 🚗 BIZ HS 📶 📺 🔲 🎞 ☕
/SOME UNITS 🍳 🐾

## HOTEL DEREK
713/961-3000 **30**

**fyi**
Hotel
Rates not provided

Under major renovation, scheduled to
be completed September 2013. **Last
Rated:** ▽▽▽ **Address:** 2525 West
Loop S 77027 **Location:** I-610 exit 9A
(San Felipe Rd/Westheimer Rd) southbound; exit 8C (Westheimer Rd) northbound. **Facility:** 314 units. 14 stories,
interior corridors. **Parking:** valet and
street only. **Amenities:** safes. **Dining:**
Valentino, see separate listing. **Pool(s):**
outdoor. **Activities:** exercise room.
**Guest Services:** valet laundry, area
transportation.

SAVE 🍽 🍴 🍷 🚗 BIZ HS 📶 📺 🎞 ☕

/SOME UNITS 🍳 🐾 🔲

## HOTEL INDIGO HOUSTON AT THE GALLERIA
(713)621-8988 **39**

▽▽▽ **Hotel** $119-$259 **Address:** 5160 Hidalgo St 77056 **Location:** I-610 exit 9A (San Felipe Rd/Westheimer Rd) southbound;
exit 8C (Westheimer Rd) northbound, s to Post Oak, just e to Hidalgo
St, then just s. **Facility:** 131 units. 6 stories, interior corridors. *Bath:*
shower only. **Terms:** cancellation fee imposed. **Activities:** exercise
room. **Guest Services:** valet laundry.

🍽 🍴 🍷 CALL 🛌 BIZ HS 📶 📺 🎞 🔲
☕ /SOME UNITS 🍳 🐾

## HOTEL ZAZA HOUSTON MUSEUM DISTRICT
713/526-1991 **51**

▼▼ ▼▼
**Boutique Hotel**
Rates not provided

**Address:** 5701 Main St 77005 **Location:** US 59 (Southwest Frwy) exit Main
St northbound, 0.5 mi s; exit Fannin St
southbound, 0.5 mi s to Ewing St, then
just w. **Facility:** This stylish upscale hotel
is known for its cool and lively environment. The guest rooms are lush and
comfortable with a modern appeal. A
unique and eclectic mix of décor makes
this a true original. 315 units, some two
bedrooms. 12 stories, interior corridors.
**Parking:** valet only. **Terms:** check-in 4
pm. **Amenities:** safes. **Dining:** Monarch,
see separate listing. **Pool(s):** heated outdoor. **Activities:** steamroom, exercise
room, spa. **Guest Services:** valet laundry, area transportation.

SAVE 🍽 🍴 🍷 CALL 🛌 🚗 BIZ HS 📶 📺
🎞 /SOME UNITS 🍳 🐾 🔲

## THE HOUSTONIAN HOTEL, CLUB & SPA
(713)680-2626 **19**

▼▼ ▼▼
**Resort Hotel**
$199-$525

**Address:** 111 N Post Oak Ln 77024 **Location:** I-610 exit 10 (Woodway Dr), just
w to N Post Oak Ln, then 0.5 mi nw. **Facility:** The very upscale public spaces
and sleeping rooms here are impressive, but it is the other extras that really
set this hotel apart and make it a preferred spot for elite travelers. 289 units. 4
stories, interior corridors. **Parking:** onsite (fee) and valet. **Terms:** check-in 4
pm. **Amenities:** safes. **Dining:** 3 restaurants. **Pool(s):** heated outdoor. **Activities:** sauna, hot tub, tennis, recreation
programs, playground, spa. **Guest Services:** valet laundry, area transportation.
Affiliated with A Preferred Hotel.

SAVE 🍽 🍴 🍷 🚶 BIZ HS 📶 📺 🎞
☕

## HOUSTON MARRIOTT AT THE TEXAS MEDICAL CENTER
(713)796-0080 **54**

▽▽▽ **Hotel** $125-$319 **Address:**
6580 Fannin St 77030 **Location:** I-610
exit 2 (Main St), 2.5 mi ne to Holcombe
St, 0.3 mi e, then just n. Connected to
the medical center and shopping
venues. **Facility:** 394 units. 26 stories, interior corridors. **Parking:** onsite (fee) and valet. **Pool(s):** heated indoor. **Activities:** hot tub, exercise room. **Guest Services:** valet and coin laundry, area
transportation.

**AAA Benefit:**
Members save 5%
or more!

🍽 🍴 🍷 CALL 🛌 🚗 BIZ SHS 📶 📺 🎞
🔲 ☕ /SOME UNITS 🍳

## HOUSTON MARRIOTT SOUTH AT HOBBY AIRPORT
(713)943-7979 **66**

▽▽▽ **Hotel** $99-$299 **Address:**
9100 Gulf Frwy 77017 **Location:** I-45
exit 36 (Airport Blvd/College St) southbound; exit 38 (Monroe Rd) northbound,
on southbound frontage road. **Facility:**
287 units. 10 stories, interior corridors. **Dining:** 3 restaurants.
**Pool(s):** heated indoor. **Activities:** hot tub, exercise room. **Guest
Services:** valet laundry, area transportation.

**AAA Benefit:**
Members save 5%
or more!

🛫 🍽 🍴 🍷 🚗 BIZ 📶 📺 🎞 ☕
/SOME UNITS 🍳 🐾

## HOUSTON MARRIOTT WEST LOOP BY THE GALLERIA
(713)960-0111 **23**

▽▽▽ **Hotel** $83-$339 **Address:**
1750 W Loop S 77027 **Location:** I-610
exit 9 (San Felipe Rd) northbound, just
w; exit 9A (San Felipe Rd/Westheimer
Rd) southbound; entrance from San Felipe Rd or service road. **Facility:** 301 units. 14 stories, interior corridors. **Parking:** on-site (fee) and valet. **Amenities:** safes. **Dining:** 2
restaurants. **Pool(s):** heated indoor. **Activities:** sauna, exercise
room. **Guest Services:** valet and coin laundry, area transportation.

**AAA Benefit:**
Members save 5%
or more!

🍽 🍴 🍷 🚗 BIZ SHS 📶 📺 🔲 ☕

(See map & index p. 316.)

## HYATT HOUSE HOUSTON/GALLERIA
(713)629-9711 **47**

**Extended Stay Hotel**
**$89-$399**

**H**YATT **house**™
**AAA Benefit:** Members save 10%!

**Address:** 3440 Sage Rd 77056 **Location:** I-610 exit 9A (San Felipe Rd/Westheimer Rd) southbound; exit 8C (Westheimer Rd) northbound, just w to Sage Rd, then 0.8 mi s. **Facility:** 147 efficiencies, some two bedrooms. 4 stories, interior corridors. **Parking:** on-site (fee). **Terms:** cancellation fee imposed. **Amenities:** safes. **Pool(s):** outdoor. **Activities:** exercise room. **Guest Services:** valet and coin laundry, area transportation. **Featured Amenity: breakfast buffet.**

SAVE 🍴 BIZ 📶 🖥 🅿 🖨 🖳 / SOME UNITS 🅂🛏

---

JW MARRIOTT HOUSTON
(713)961-1500 **31**

🛆🛆🛆 🛆🛆🛆 Hotel $97-$369 **Address:** 5150 Westheimer Rd 77056 **Location:** I-610 exit 8C (Westheimer Rd) northbound; exit 9A (San Felipe Rd/Westheimer Rd) southbound, just w. Across from Galleria Mall. **Facility:** The

**AAA Benefit:** A deluxe level of comfort and a member rate!

moderately sized rooms here have a contemporary décor style. There are some extra recreational amenities, and the rooftop pool deck is the best of the hotels in this neighborhood. 515 units. 23 stories, interior corridors. **Parking:** on-site (fee) and valet. **Terms:** check-in 4 pm. **Amenities:** safes. **Dining:** 3 restaurants. **Pool(s):** heated outdoor. **Activities:** sauna, hot tub, steamroom. **Guest Services:** valet laundry, area transportation.

ECO 🍴 🖼 🍸 🏊 🏋 BIZ sHS 📶 🗡 🎥 🖳 / SOME UNITS 🅿

---

LA QUINTA INN & SUITES HOUSTON GALLERIA AREA
(713)355-3440 **22**

🛆🛆🛆 🛆🛆🛆 Hotel $85-$190 **Address:** 1625 W Loop S 77027 **Location:** I-610 exit 9 (San Felipe Rd) northbound; exit 9A (San Felipe Rd/Westheimer Rd) southbound; on northbound frontage road. **Facility:** 173 units. 6 stories, interior corridors. **Pool(s):** heated outdoor. **Activities:** hot tub, exercise room. **Guest Services:** valet and coin laundry.

🍴 CALL 🅂M 🏊 BIZ 📶 / SOME UNITS 🛏 HS 🅿 🖨

---

LA QUINTA INN & SUITES HOUSTON HOBBY AIRPORT
(713)490-1008 **73**

🛆🛆🛆 🛆🛆🛆 Hotel $95-$144 **Address:** 8776 Airport Blvd 77061 **Location:** I-45 exit 36 (Airport Blvd/College St), 1.3 mi w. **Facility:** 73 units. 3 stories, interior corridors. **Pool(s):** outdoor. **Activities:** exercise room. **Guest Services:** valet and coin laundry, area transportation.

♿ CALL 🅂M 🏊 BIZ HS 📶 🗡 🅿 🖨 🖳 / SOME UNITS 🛏

---

OMNI HOUSTON HOTEL
(713)871-8181 **20**

🛆🛆🛆 🛆🛆🛆 Hotel $199-$599 **Address:** Four Riverway 77056 **Location:** I-610 exit 10 (Woodway Dr), 0.3 mi w. **Facility:** Surrounded by relaxing green spaces and contemporary art sculptures, this hotel is like an enclave in the city. The lobby areas have a stylish sophistication, as do the salt and freshwater pool areas. 378 units. 11 stories, interior corridors. **Parking:** on-site (fee) and valet. **Terms:** cancellation fee imposed. **Amenities:** video games, safes. **Dining:** Noé Restaurant & Bar, see separate listing. **Pool(s):** outdoor, heated outdoor. **Activities:** sauna, hot tub, exercise room, spa. **Guest Services:** valet laundry, area transportation.

🍴 🖼 🍸 🏊 BIZ 📶 🗡 🎥 🖳 / SOME UNITS 🅂🛏

---

QUALITY INN
(713)673-4200 **16**

🛆🛆 🛆🛆 Motel $65-$110 **Address:** 828 Mercury Dr 77013 **Location:** I-10 exit 776A (Mercury Dr), just n. **Facility:** 88 units. 6 stories, interior corridors. **Pool(s):** outdoor. **Activities:** exercise room. **Guest Services:** valet and coin laundry.

🍴 🏊 📶 🖥 / SOME UNITS 🅿 🖨

---

QUALITY INN & SUITES
(713)957-8222 **6**

🛆🛆 🛆🛆 Hotel $70-$150 **Address:** 12439 Northwest Frwy 77092 **Location:** US 290 exit Bingle Rd; on eastbound feeder road. **Facility:** 62 units. 3 stories, interior corridors. **Pool(s):** outdoor. **Activities:** exercise room. **Guest Services:** valet and coin laundry.

CALL 🅂M 🏊 BIZ HS 📶 🗡 🅿 🖳 / SOME UNITS 🖨

---

## RESIDENCE INN BY MARRIOTT HOUSTON BY THE GALLERIA
(713)840-9757 **29**

🛆🛆🛆 🛆🛆🛆
**Extended Stay Hotel**
**$102-$299**

**Residence** Inn® Marriott.

**AAA Benefit:** Members save 5% or more!

**Address:** 2500 McCue Rd 77056 **Location:** I-610 exit 8C (Westheimer Rd) northbound; exit 9A (San Felipe Rd/Westheimer Rd) southbound, just w to McCue Rd, then just n. Located in a residential area. **Facility:** 146 units, some two bedrooms, efficiencies and kitchens. 2-3 stories, interior/exterior corridors. **Parking:** on-site (fee). **Pool(s):** outdoor. **Activities:** hot tub, exercise room. **Guest Services:** valet and coin laundry. **Featured Amenity: full hot breakfast.**

SAVE 🍴 🏊 BIZ HS 📶 🗡 🅿 🖨 🖳 / SOME UNITS 🅂🛏

---

RESIDENCE INN BY MARRIOTT-MEDICAL CENTER/RELIANT PARK
(713)660-7993 **57**

🛆🛆🛆 🛆🛆🛆 **Extended Stay Hotel** $109-$179 **Address:** 7710 S Main St 77030 **Location:** I-610 exit 2 (S Main St/Buffalo Speedway), 1.5 mi n. **Facility:**

**AAA Benefit:** Members save 5% or more!

143 kitchen units, some two bedrooms. 2 stories (no elevator), exterior corridors. **Pool(s):** outdoor. **Activities:** hot tub. **Guest Services:** valet and coin laundry, area transportation.

🍴 CALL 🅂M 🏊 BIZ HS 📶 🗡 🅿 🖨 🖳 / SOME UNITS 🅂🛏

---

RESIDENCE INN BY MARRIOTT-WEST UNIVERSITY
(713)661-4660 **49**

🛆🛆🛆 🛆🛆🛆 **Extended Stay Hotel** $99-$209 **Address:** 2939 Westpark Dr 77005 **Location:** US 59 (Southwest Frwy) exit Kirby Dr, just s, then just w. **Facility:** 120 units, some two bedrooms,

**AAA Benefit:** Members save 5% or more!

efficiencies and kitchens. 4 stories, interior corridors. **Pool(s):** heated outdoor. **Activities:** hot tub, exercise room. **Guest Services:** valet and coin laundry, area transportation.

CALL 🅂M 🏊 BIZ HS 📶 🗡 🅿 🖨 🖳 / SOME UNITS 🅂🛏

---

(See map & index p. 316.)

## ROYAL SONESTA HOTEL HOUSTON
(713)627-7600 **27**

Hotel
$109-$629

**Address:** 2222 W Loop S 77027 **Location:** I-610 exit 9 (San Felipe Rd) northbound; exit 9A (San Felipe Rd/Westheimer Rd) southbound. Located in Galleria business and shopping district. **Facility:** Located in the Galleria area, guest rooms at this property are well appointed and the public spaces have a very nice upscale decor. Try a room on an upper floor facing downtown the view. 485 units. 22 stories, interior corridors. **Parking:** on-site (fee) and valet. **Terms:** cancellation fee imposed. **Amenities:** video games, safes. **Pool(s):** heated outdoor. **Activities:** hot tub, exercise room. **Guest Services:** valet laundry, area transportation.

---

## THE ST. REGIS HOUSTON
(713)840-7600 **25**

Hotel
$225-$780

**AAA Benefit:** Legendary stays at a preferred rate!

**Address:** 1919 Briar Oaks Ln 77027 **Location:** I-610 exit 9A (San Felipe Rd/Westheimer Rd), 0.3 mi e. **Facility:** This hotel presents tasteful, refined luxury with sophisticated and polished service. The intimate lobby sets the tone for exclusivity and the rich appointments you will find throughout the hotel. 232 units, some two bedrooms and kitchens. 12 stories, interior corridors. **Parking:** valet only. **Terms:** cancellation fee imposed. **Amenities:** safes. **Dining:** The Remington Restaurant, see separate listing. **Pool(s):** heated outdoor. **Activities:** sauna, exercise room, spa. **Guest Services:** valet laundry.

**The St. Regis Houston is about the journey, each moment as it unfolds.**

ST REGIS
HOUSTON

---

## SARA'S INN ON THE BOULEVARD
713/868-1130 **12**

**Bed & Breakfast.** Rates not provided. **Address:** 941 Heights Blvd 77008 **Location:** I-10 exit 766 (Heights Blvd) westbound; exit 767A (Studemont St) eastbound, 0.5 mi n. Located in a quiet area of Historic Houston Heights District. **Facility:** Furnished with antiques and collectibles, this Queen Anne Victorian B&B is in the peaceful tree-lined Heights District. There are many good restaurants and eclectic shops nearby. 11 units. 2 stories (no elevator), interior corridors. **Terms:** age restrictions may apply.

---

Explore on-the-go travel

tools at AAA.com/mobile

or CAA.ca/mobile

---

## SHERATON HOUSTON BROOKHOLLOW
(713)688-0100 **10**

Hotel
$89-$299

Sheraton

**AAA Benefit:** Members get up to 20% off, plus Starwood Preferred Guest® bonuses!

**Address:** 3000 N Loop W 77092 **Location:** I-610 exit 13C (TC Jester Blvd); on southbound frontage road. **Facility:** 382 units. 10 stories, interior corridors. **Terms:** cancellation fee imposed. **Pool(s):** heated outdoor. **Activities:** hot tub, exercise room. **Guest Services:** valet laundry, boarding pass kiosk, area transportation.

---

## SHERATON SUITES HOUSTON NEAR THE GALLERIA
(713)586-2444 **28**

Hotel
$139-$429

Sheraton

**AAA Benefit:** Members get up to 20% off, plus Starwood Preferred Guest® bonuses!

**Address:** 2400 W Loop S 77027 **Location:** I-610 exit 9 (San Felipe Rd) northbound; exit 9A (San Felipe Rd/Westheimer Rd) southbound. **Facility:** 281 units. 12 stories, interior corridors. **Parking:** on-site (fee) and valet. **Terms:** cancellation fee imposed. **Amenities:** Some: safes. **Pool(s):** outdoor. **Activities:** hot tub, exercise room. **Guest Services:** valet laundry, area transportation.

---

## SLEEP INN & SUITES
(713)862-6300 **11**

Hotel
$90-$139

**Address:** 2475 North Frwy 77009 **Location:** I-45 exit 49B southbound; exit 50A northbound; entrance on southbound access road. **Facility:** 41 units. 3 stories, interior corridors. **Activities:** exercise room. **Guest Services:** coin laundry. **Featured Amenity:** continental breakfast.

---

## SLEEP INN & SUITES NORTHWEST HOUSTON/HIGHWAY 290
(713)996-0707 **2**

**Hotel** $110-$150 **Address:** 5451 NW Central Dr 77092 **Location:** US 290 exit Bingle Rd, westbound frontage road to NW Central Dr. **Facility:** 53 units. 3 stories, interior corridors. **Pool(s):** outdoor. **Activities:** exercise room. **Guest Services:** valet and coin laundry.

---

## SONESTA ES SUITES HOUSTON
713/355-8888 **40**

**Address:** 5190 Hidalgo St 77056 **Location:** I-610 exit 9A (San Felipe Rd/Westheimer Rd) southbound; exit 8C (Westheimer Rd) northbound, 0.4 mi w to Sage Rd, then just s. **Facility:** 93 efficiencies, some two bedrooms. 4 stories, interior corridors. **Amenities:** Some: safes. **Pool(s):** heated outdoor. **Activities:** exercise room. **Guest Services:** complimentary and valet laundry.

**Extended Stay Hotel**
Rates not provided

(See map & index p. 316.)

## SPRINGHILL SUITES BY MARRIOTT-BROOKHOLLOW

(713)290-9242   **9**

▼▼▼ **Hotel** $90-$310 **Address:**
2750 N Loop W 77092 **Location:** I-610
exit 13C (TC Jester Blvd), 0.4 mi on
westbound frontage road. **Facility:** 79
units.   3   stories,   interior   corridors.
**Pool(s):** heated indoor. **Activities:** hot tub, exercise room. **Guest Services:** valet laundry.

**AAA Benefit:**
Members save 5%
or more!

🍴⁺ CALL 🔥M 🏊 BIZ 📶 ✕ 🖥 📼 📺

## SPRINGHILL SUITES BY MARRIOTT (HOUSTON/HOBBY AIRPORT)

(713)943-1713   **71**

▼▼▼ **Hotel** $105-$129 **Address:**
7922 Mosley Rd 77061 **Location:** I-45
exit 36 (Airport Blvd/College St) southbound; off southbound service road; exit
36 northbound, just w on Airport Blvd,
then just n. **Facility:** 122 units. 5 stories, interior corridors. **Pool(s):**
outdoor. **Activities:** exercise room. **Guest Services:** valet and coin
laundry, area transportation.

**AAA Benefit:**
Members save 5%
or more!

✈ 🍴⁺ CALL 🔥M 🏊 BIZ 📶 ✕ 🎥 🖥 📼 📺

## SPRINGHILL SUITES BY MARRIOTT HOUSTON-MEDICAL CENTER RELIANT PARK

(713)796-1000   **59**

▼▼▼ **Hotel** $92-$399 **Address:**
1400 Old Spanish Tr 77054 **Location:**
I-610 exit 1C (Kirby Dr), 0.9 mi n, then
just e. **Facility:** 190 units. 7 stories, interior corridors. **Pool(s):** outdoor. **Activi-
ties:** hot tub, exercise room. **Guest Services:** valet and coin laundry,
area transportation.

**AAA Benefit:**
Members save 5%
or more!

CALL 🔥M 🏊 BIZ HS 📶 ✕ 🎥 🖥 📼 📺

## TOWNEPLACE SUITES BY MARRIOTT-CENTRAL

(713)690-4035   **3**

▼▼▼ **Extended Stay**
**Contemporary Hotel** $90-$270 **Ad-**
**dress:** 12820 Northwest Frwy (US 290)
77040 **Location:** US 290 exit Bingle
Rd/43rd St eastbound; exit Bingle
Rd/Pinemont Dr/43rd St westbound; on westbound feeder. Next to
movie theater complex. **Facility:** 85 units, some efficiencies. 3 stories, interior corridors. **Activities:** hot tub, exercise room. **Guest Ser-**
**vices:** valet and coin laundry.

**AAA Benefit:**
Members save 5%
or more!

🍴⁺ CALL 🔥M BIZ 📶 ✕ 🖥 📼 📺 / SOME UNITS 🆂

## THE WESTIN GALLERIA, HOUSTON

(713)960-8100   **35**

▼▼▼ ▼▼▼
**Hotel**
$129-$449

**WESTIN**
HOTELS & RESORTS
**AAA Benefit:** Enjoy
up to 20% off your
next stay, plus Starwood Preferred
Guest® bonuses!

**Address:** 5060 W Alabama St 77056
**Location:** I-610 exit 8C (Westheimer
Rd) northbound; exit 9A (San Felipe
Rd/Westheimer Rd) southbound, 0.5 mi
w on Westheimer Rd to Sage Rd, just s,
then just e. Located in Galleria Shopping
Mall. **Facility:** With doors opening right
into the famed Houston Galleria, you
cannot get any closer to the shopping
and restaurants. The rooms here are
large and well equipped but have a modern, minimalist décor.
487 units. 24 stories, interior corridors. **Parking:** on-site (fee)
and valet. **Terms:** cancellation fee imposed, resort fee. **Ameni-**
**ties:** safes. **Dining:** Daily Grill, see separate listing. **Pool(s):** outdoor. **Activities:** exercise room. **Guest Services:** valet laundry.

SAVE 🍴 🛎 🍸 CALL 🔥M 🏊 BIZ SHS 📶 ✕
🎥 📼 / SOME UNITS 🐾

## WESTIN OAKS HOUSTON AT THE GALLERIA

(713)960-8100   **32**

▼▼▼ ▼▼▼
Contemporary
Hotel
$129-$449

**WESTIN**
HOTELS & RESORTS
**AAA Benefit:** Enjoy
up to 20% off your
next stay, plus Starwood Preferred
Guest® bonuses!

**Address:** 5011 Westheimer Rd 77056
**Location:** I-610 exit 8C (Westheimer
Rd) northbound; exit 9A (San Felipe
Rd/Westheimer Rd) southbound. Located in Galleria Shopping Mall. **Fa-**
**cility:** Like its sister hotel, The Westin
Galleria, this hotel is right in the mall and
has sleek, contemporary rooms with a
minimalist but still elegant design style.
406 units. 21 stories, interior corridors.
**Parking:** on-site and valet. **Terms:** cancellation fee imposed, resort fee. **Amenities:** safes. **Pool(s):** outdoor. **Activities:** exercise room. **Guest Services:** valet laundry.

SAVE 🍴 🛎 🍸 CALL 🔥M 🏊 BIZ SHS 📶 ✕
🎥 📼 / SOME UNITS 🐾 🖥

## WYNDHAM HOUSTON MEDICAL CENTER HOTEL AND SUITES

(713)528-7744   **56**

▼▼▼
Hotel
$99-$249

**Address:** 6800 Main St 77030 **Loca-**
**tion:** I-610 exit 2 (Main St), 2.4 mi ne. **Fa-**
**cility:** 287 units, some two bedrooms
and efficiencies. 12 stories, interior corridors. **Parking:** on-site (fee). **Terms:** cancellation fee imposed. **Amenities:** video
games. **Pool(s):** outdoor. **Activities:** exercise room. **Guest Services:** valet and
coin laundry, area transportation.

SAVE 🍴 🛎 🍸 🏊 BIZ 📶
🎥 📼 / SOME UNITS 🖥 📺

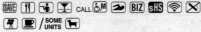
**WHERE TO EAT**

**100% TAQUITO**   713/665-2900   **84**

▼ Mexican. Quick Serve. $4-$8 **AAA Inspector Notes:** Those
who have been to Mexico might recognize that true Mexican food is
hard to find outside of the bordering neighbor. However, the search
ends here for the common "street" fare. The taqueria started as a
simple taco trailer and now allows more Houstonians to enjoy authentic tacos without lettuce, tomato and cheese but instead with cilantro, onions and salsa. Equally authentic are the drinks offered--try
cafe de olla, aguas frescas, Mexican hot chocolate and Mexican
bottled soft drinks. **Features:** beer only. **Address:** 3245 Southwest
Frwy 77027 **Location:** US 59 (Southwest Frwy) exit Edloe
St/Weslayan St westbound; exit Buffalo Speedway eastbound; on
eastbound frontage road. L D

**59 DINER**   713/523-2333   **77**

▼ American. Casual Dining. $7-$10 **AAA Inspector Notes:** Nos-
talgia abounds in the rock 'n' roll diner. Typifying the style of '50s and
'60s diners, the dining room features teal vinyl booths, a pink and
black tile floor, counter dining with low, red, padded stools and period
paraphernalia scattered throughout. True to its theme, the restaurant
specializes in burgers, hot dogs and such fountain drinks as root beer
floats and shakes. **Address:** 3801 Farnham St 77098 **Location:** US
59 (Southwest Frwy), just n on Shepherd Dr to Farnham St, just se.
B L D 24

**ALEXANDER THE GREAT**   713/622-2778   **73**

▼▼ Greek. Casual Dining. $12-$28 **AAA Inspector Notes:**
Located near The Gallery, this restaurant offers a wide variety of authentic dishes such as roasted eggplant, avgolemono soup and dol-
mathes (stuffed grape leaves). The patio is a great respite in spring.
**Features:** patio dining. **Address:** 3055 Sage Rd, Suite 170 77056
**Location:** I-610 exit 9A (San Felipe Rd/Westheimer Rd) southbound;
exit 8C (Westheimer Rd) northbound, 0.4 mi w to Sage Rd, then just
s; near The Galleria Shopping District. L D

(See map & index p. 316.)

## AMAZON GRILL
713/522-5888  (88)

Latin American. Quick Serve. $7-$27 **AAA Inspector Notes:** This is a great place for a quick meal with easy counter service and a menu of Latin comfort foods such as empanadas, flautas, fish tacos, chimichurri-grilled beef tenderloin, plantain-crusted chicken and a really good tres leche cake. The location makes it convenient and popular, especially at lunch. Some outdoor tables are available. **Features:** full bar, patio dining, happy hour. **Address:** 5114 Kirby Dr 77098 **Location:** US 59 (Southwest Frwy) exit Kirby Dr, just s.

L  D

## ARCODORO
713/621-6888  (45)

Italian. Fine Dining. $10-$35 **AAA Inspector Notes:** Offering Sardinian food, the upscale eatery boasts winning an international competition for the best ravioli in the world. Diners can partake of traditional dishes such as handmade gnocchi, risotto, pasta and a smart list of beef and fish dishes. Seating is available in formal and casual areas and on a patio. Homemade pastas, a wood-burning oven for pizza and the use of ingredients indigenous to Sardinia make for a very authentic experience. **Features:** full bar, Sunday brunch. **Reservations:** suggested. **Address:** 5000 Westheimer Rd, Suite 120 77056 **Location:** I-610 exit 9A (San Felipe Rd/Westheimer Rd) southbound; exit 8C (Westheimer Rd) northbound, just w; in Centre at Post Oak.  L  D

## ARTURO'S UPTOWN ITALIANO
713/621-1180  (26)

Italian. Casual Dining. $13-$33 **AAA Inspector Notes:** A mix of classic and contemporary Italian cuisine with rich interior décor and a more casual al fresco seating area. The antipasto starter is ideal for sharing and whetting the appetite before moving on to well-prepared entrée dishes such as the pork chop with a blackberry glaze and an array of pasta dishes. The selection of desserts, including panna cotta of the day, provides a sweet ending. **Features:** full bar, patio dining. **Reservations:** suggested. **Address:** 1180 Uptown Park Blvd, Suite 1 77056 **Location:** Just n of jct Uptown Park Blvd and S Post Oak Rd; in Uptown Park Shopping Complex. **Parking:** on-site (fee).  L  D

## BACKSTREET CAFE
713/521-2239  (25)

American. Fine Dining. $15-$39 **AAA Inspector Notes:** Most people enjoy the beautiful outdoor patio here, but the small relaxed dining rooms in the 1930s-era house also can be inviting. The seasonal menus are extensive, with frequent use of local items and a large separate vegetarian menu. Dinner entrées features creative but familiar items such as grilled bacon-wrapped quail, grilled paillards of lamb and shellfish risotto. Wine lovers will feel right at home with an interesting and carefully selected list and a knowledgeable service staff. **Features:** full bar, Sunday brunch. **Reservations:** suggested. **Address:** 1103 S Shepherd Dr 77019 **Location:** Between Dallas and Clay sts. **Parking:** valet only.  L  D

## BARBECUE INN
713/695-8112  (3)

American. Casual Dining. $6-$20 **AAA Inspector Notes:** This restaurant has been in business under the same family since 1947, and not much has changed in that time. The ribs are a very popular choice here, but barbecue is not really the main focus. The fork-tender chicken-fried steak is among the best in Texas, and many locals swear by the fried shrimp. Service here is quick and no nonsense with a classic Texas charm. The location is a little off the beaten path but worth the trip. **Features:** beer only. **Address:** 116 W Crosstimbers St 77018 **Location:** I-610 exit 16A, 1.4 mi n; northwest corner of Crosstimbers and Yale sts.  L  D

## BARNABY'S CAFE
713/520-5131  (30)

American. Casual Dining. $10-$17 **AAA Inspector Notes:** The cafe is a bigger and better version of the small eatery on Fairview Drive. Ceiling murals are whimsical, and the menu is the same. Huge portions of yummy meatloaf, pork chops, chicken tostadas and baby back ribs are served in a low-key, contemporary dining room; patio dining is available. **Features:** beer & wine. **Address:** 1701 S Shepherd Dr 77019 **Location:** US 59 (Southwest Frwy) exit Shepherd Dr, 1.5 mi n.  B  L  D

---

Learn the local driving laws

at DrivingLaws.AAA.com

## BENJY'S
713/522-7602  (94)

American. Casual Dining. $12-$29 **AAA Inspector Notes:** The hip cafe boasts such great items as gingered beef pot stickers, shrimp and pecan dumplings, penne pasta in chipotle sauce and pizza Margherita. The swanky lounge and village location makes this a popular meeting place. Tables in close proximity don't exactly allow for intimate conversations. **Features:** full bar, Sunday brunch, happy hour. **Reservations:** suggested. **Location:** 2424 Dunstan Rd 77005 **Location:** Jct US 59 (Southwest Frwy) and Kirby Dr, 0.8 mi s to Dunstan Rd, just e.  L  D

## BERRYHILL BAJA GRILL
713/526-8080

Mexican. Casual Dining. $6-$12 **AAA Inspector Notes:** This is the original location of a popular local chain. Most of the tables are on an outdoor patio. Tamales are the specialty, but exceptional fish tacos and many other Mexican favorites, including enchiladas and burritos, also are on the menu. Margaritas and cervezas are available. The service is quick and simple. **Features:** full bar. **Address:** 2639 Revere St 77098 **Location:** Corner of Westheimer Rd and Revere St; between Kirby and Shepherd drs.  L  D

## THE BLACK LABRADOR
713/529-1199  (72)

English. Casual Dining. $7-$15 **AAA Inspector Notes:** British and American cuisine are on the menu at this pub-like restaurant. Choices include kidney pie, fish and chips, bangers and mash, trifle, shepherd's pie and sausage with garlic-mashed potatoes, and for dessert, homemade bread pudding. Lending to the Old World feel are aged tables and chairs and the items on the walls. The one drawback is the steep beer prices. **Features:** full bar, patio dining, Sunday brunch. **Address:** 4100 Montrose Blvd 77006 **Location:** I-45 exit 47A (Allen Pkwy), 1.5 mi w to Montrose Blvd, then 3 mi s.  L  D

## THE BOMBAY BRASSERIE
713/355-2000  (98)

Indian. Casual Dining. $11-$25 **AAA Inspector Notes:** In the always bustling Rice Village, this slightly upscale restaurant puts forth a menu of traditional North Indian cuisine, including a vegetable samosa appetizer and tandoori, curry and vegetarian dishes. Patrons can unwind on the covered patio. **Features:** beer & wine. **Address:** 2414 University Blvd, Suite 210 77005 **Location:** US 59 (Southwest Frwy) exit Kirby Dr, 1 mi s, then just e; in Rice Village.  L  D

## BONNIE'S BEEF & SEAFOOD CO
713/641-2397  (102)

Steak Seafood. Casual Dining. $9-$39 **AAA Inspector Notes:** Sharp enough for business but comfortable enough for families, this steak house is well known for prime rib, strip steak, fried shrimp and baked potatoes with all the trimmings. The crowd-pleasing menu also lists seafood platters and a salad bar. Crates of produce over the salad bar give the impression of a farmers' market. Louisiana touches enhance the décor. **Features:** full bar, patio dining, happy hour. **Address:** 6867 Gulf Frwy 77087 **Location:** I-45 exit 41A; on northbound frontage road.  L  D

## BRADY'S LANDING
713/928-9921  (92)

American. Casual Dining. $16-$34 **AAA Inspector Notes:** The main attraction here is the waterfront location, although the view is of an industrial port area with large cargo ships. The restaurant is in a large, rustic wooden warehouse building and is a popular spot for weddings and events. The dinner menu has a focus on seafood with some steaks and salads available. Lunch is buffet only and includes a large selection of entrées, salads and desserts with items such as blackened catfish, lasagna, roast pork and a meat-carving station. **Features:** full bar, Sunday brunch. **Reservations:** suggested. **Address:** 8505 Cypress St 77012 **Location:** I-610 exit 30C (Lawndale Ave) southbound; exit 30D (Lawndale Ave) northbound, w to Broadway St, 0.6 mi n to Cypress St, then just e.  L  D

## BRANCH WATER TAVERN
713/863-7777  (21)

New American. Fine Dining. $10-$32 **AAA Inspector Notes:** This acclaimed restaurant pairs creative, refined food with relaxed service. The menu makes use of local and regional ingredients. Flavors are bold in the venison served with a sweet potato and brussels sprout hash, bacon confit and pomegranate jus. Other popular items include chicken-fried oysters, braised short rib "Flintstones style" and drum a la plancha with bok choy and red curry broth. The wine list is reasonably priced, and the bar has a deep roster of bourbons and other spirits. **Features:** full bar, Sunday brunch. **Reservations:** suggested. **Address:** 510 Shepherd Dr 77007 **Location:** 0.3 mi n of jct Memorial Dr. **Parking:** valet and street only.  L  D  CALL  M

**(See map & index p. 316.)**

### BRASSERIE MAX & JULIE    713/524-0070  74
WW WW  French. Casual Dining. $12-$30 **AAA Inspector Notes:** The dining here is simple with country-style décor and a casual cafe atmosphere. The menu covers many classic French dishes and includes items such as veal sweetbreads, beef Bourguignon, cassoulet and trout Provençal. Some guests will visit just for the selection of delicious desserts with soufflés, tarts and flan. The wine list has a deep selection from all regions of France. **Features:** beer & wine, Sunday brunch. **Address:** 4315 Montrose Blvd 77006 **Location:** At Richmond Ave. **Parking:** valet and street only. L D

### BRC GASTROPUB    713/861-2233  20
WW WW  American. Gastropub. $9-$24 **AAA Inspector Notes:** The hip and slightly dark dining room at this spot near Washington Street offers a menu of interesting comfort foods that incorporate premium local ingredients and sometimes fun childhood favorites. Options include Dr. Pepper-fried San Antonio quail, a "state fair" griddled cheese sandwich with pulled short rib and local cheeses, and a Rice Crispy ice cream sandwich. A good selection of entrées, salads and great burgers also are offered. There is a wide selection of craft beers and wines. **Features:** beer & wine, patio dining, Sunday brunch, happy hour. **Address:** 519 Shepherd Dr 77007 **Location:** 0.3 mi n of jct Memorial Dr. L D CALL M

### CADILLAC BAR    713/862-2020
WW WW  Tex-Mex. Casual Dining. $8-$36 **AAA Inspector Notes:** With a history going back more than 25 years, this classic eatery offers mesquite-roasted cabrito (baby goat), chorizo queso fundido and ceviche among its flavorful choices. Many familiar dishes also are offered, including fish tacos, tamales, chile rellenos, chalupas, flautas and chimichangas. Custom-made margaritas are very tempting. **Features:** full bar, Sunday brunch. **Address:** 1802 Shepherd Dr 77007 **Location:** I-10 exit 765B (N Durham Dr/N Shepherd Dr), just s. L D

### CAFE EXPRESS    713/522-3994
WW  American. Quick Serve. $7-$15 **AAA Inspector Notes:** Even if this place does serve burgers, its American/Mediterranean menu lists plenty of more healthful options, such as pasta dishes, roasted chicken and Caesar salad. Everything is made to order and served fast for people on the go. Those with a little more time to spare may want to enjoy some wine or the classic German chocolate cake. **Features:** beer & wine. **Address:** 3200 Kirby Dr, Suite 100 77098 **Location:** US 59 (Southwest Frwy) exit Kirby Dr, just n. B L D

### CAFE LILI LEBANESE GRILL    713/952-6969  67
WW  Lebanese. Casual Dining. $5-$23 **AAA Inspector Notes:** The Beijani family has a loyal following among the many Houstonians who drop by the inconspicuous strip mall that houses their restaurant. Diners can choose from small dishes and starters, including kebabs, shawarma, falafel and other items, including daily specials. Diners find lots of cold items and only a handful of hot ones. Several economical, small-portioned items are served individually to allow for experimenting. Although wine and beer are on the menu, diners can bring their own wine. **Features:** beer & wine. **Address:** 5757 Westheimer Rd, Suite 112 77057 **Location:** Between Chimney Rock Rd and Fountain View Dr; in Westheimer Plaza. L D

### CAFE MEZZA & GRILLE    713/334-2000  64
WW WW  Mediterranean. Casual Dining. $9-$30 **AAA Inspector Notes:** This comfortable restaurant with a casual feel is located in an upscale shopping plaza. The menu covers a wide range with everything from salads to pastas to kebabs and fresh fish, all done in an eclectic style that has influences of Mediterranean, Arabic, Southwestern and American cuisines. While it may sound a little complex, the food here is unpretentious and shows bright, interesting flavors. **Features:** full bar, patio dining, early bird specials. **Address:** 6100 Westheimer Rd, Suite 154 77057 **Location:** Between Fountainview and Voss rds. L D CALL M

### CAFE PIQUET    713/664-1031  104
WW  Cuban. Casual Dining. $7-$17 **AAA Inspector Notes:** The long menu outlines several house specialties such as top sirloin steak, roasted pork, Cuban shrimp Creole, ropa vieja and a selection of Cuban sandwiches. The portions are large, and meals are rounded out with sides such as fried plantains and black beans and rice. **Features:** beer & wine. **Reservations:** suggested. **Address:** 5757 Bissonnet St 77401 **Location:** US 59 (Southwest Frwy) exit Chimney Rock Rd, 1.6 mi s, then 0.4 mi w. L D

### CAFE RABELAIS    713/520-8841  95
WW WW  Traditional French. Casual Dining. $8-$32 **AAA Inspector Notes:** This small cafe near Rice University has a thoroughly French look and feel with tables surrounded by racks of wine bottles. It's a great lunch stop as well as an intimate dinner experience for couples. The hand-written chalkboard menus change regularly but focus on traditional French bistro fare. Salads and sandwiches dominate for lunch, but dinners include duck, beef, trout and salmon. The wine list reads like an encyclopedia of French wines but has a range of prices and bottle formats. **Features:** beer & wine. **Address:** 2442 Times Blvd 77005 **Location:** US 59 (Southwest Frwy) exit Kirby Dr, 1 mi s to Times Blvd, then just e. L D

### CANYON CAFE    713/629-5565  44
WW WW  Southwestern. Casual Dining. $9-$18 **AAA Inspector Notes:** With the look of a Santa Fe lodge, the trendy concept restaurant projects a perfect blend of wit and kitsch. This place presents a menu lined with enchiladas, quesadillas and tacos al carbon prepared with a Santa Fe flair. Also offered are King Ranch chicken casserole, chicken-fried steak, grilled tuna and several salads, as well as a plentiful choice of by-the-glass wines. Diners nibble blue tortilla chips with sweetened hot sauce inside and on the open-air terrace. **Features:** full bar. **Reservations:** suggested, weekends. **Address:** 5000 Westheimer Rd, Suite 250 77056 **Location:** I-610 exit 9A (San Felipe Rd/Westheimer Rd) southbound; exit 8C (Westheimer Rd) northbound, just w to Post Oak Blvd, then just n. L D

### THE CAPITAL GRILLE    713/623-4600  59
WW WW  Steak Seafood. Fine Dining. $23-$45 **AAA Inspector Notes:** Cherry wood and red leather assist in making this "clubby" dining room a beautiful spot to dine on excellent cuts of dry-aged beef. The staff is highly attentive and knowledgeable. **Features:** full bar. **Reservations:** suggested. **Address:** 5365 Westheimer Rd 77056 **Location:** I-610 exit 9A (San Felipe Rd/Westheimer Rd) southbound; exit 8C (Westheimer Rd) northbound, 0.5 mi w. **Parking:** on-site and valet. D

### THE CHEESECAKE FACTORY    713/840-0600  54
WW WW  American. Casual Dining. $9-$30 **AAA Inspector Notes:** A display case of mouthwatering cheesecakes is the first thing visitors see as they walk through the door. The extensive menu incorporates many types of cuisine, including Asian, Italian, Greek and Spanish. **Features:** full bar, Sunday brunch. **Address:** 5015 Westheimer Rd 77056 **Location:** I-610 exit 8C (Westheimer Rd) northbound; exit 9A (San Felipe Rd/Westheimer Rd) southbound, just w; in Galleria Mall. **Parking:** on-site and valet. L D LATE

### CHURRASCOS    713/527-8300  46
WW WW WW  Latin American. Fine Dining. $10-$56 **AAA Inspector Notes:** Authentic South American specialties include charcoal-grilled steak, seafood and the delicious grilled tenderloin that shares the restaurant's name. Plantain chips are just a sampling of the addictive appetizers, and tres leches, or three-milk cake, sweetly ends a meal. Clean lines, splashes of color, plush seating, whimsical art and a focal-point bar area provide this dining room with a comfortable yet upscale ambience that is decidedly adult. This place is popular with business diners. **Features:** full bar, patio dining, Sunday brunch, happy hour. **Reservations:** suggested. **Address:** 2055 Westheimer Rd 77098 **Location:** At Shepherd Dr; in Shepherd Square Shopping Center. **Parking:** valet and street only. L D

### CHURRASCOS-WESTCHASE    713/952-1988  71
WW WW  Latin American. Fine Dining. $11-$29 **AAA Inspector Notes:** This restaurant offers an upscale and delicious South American dining experience. The tender charcoal-grilled beef tenderloin with chimichurri was excellent and was served with grilled vegetables, plantains, fried yucca and rice. Plantain chips are an addictive appetizer, and tres leches, or three-milk cake, sweetly ends a meal. Other options include seafood and chicken done in the South American style. The décor follows the theme and is both rustic and sophisticated. **Features:** full bar, Sunday brunch, happy hour. **Reservations:** suggested. **Address:** 9705 Westheimer Rd 77042 **Location:** Just w of jct S Gessner Rd. L D

---

Keep seasonal vehicles

travel-ready with a AAA/CAA

Battery Tender®

**(See map & index p. 316.)**

### CIAO BELLO
713/960-0333 (31)

WWWW Italian. Casual Dining. $11-$30 AAA Inspector Notes: The atmosphere is sophisticated but relaxed. The theme carries through to the menu, which pairs family recipes with more contemporary and market-fresh items. Entrées such as stuffed quail and veal piccata Amalfi aren't really breaking new ground but are well done and make for a comfortable meal. The staff is friendly and seems to know many of the local residents who frequent the dining room and upscale bar. There also is a nice covered patio for pleasant afternoons and evenings. Features: full bar, patio dining, Sunday brunch, happy hour. Address: 5161 San Felipe Rd 77056 Location: I-610 exit San Felipe Rd, 0.6 mi w. [L] [D] CALL [&M]

### CINQ
713/524-7999 (49)

WWW New European. Fine Dining. $10-$48 AAA Inspector Notes: The dining room exudes charm in this restored mansion, which was built in 1923 by the founder of Exxon. The menu is split between modern, Texas-influenced European dishes and some long-time traditional favorites from the restaurant's past. Some local ingredients are incorporated. Items like braised beef short rib with corn veloute, red wine-stewed cabbage, mushrooms and veal demi-glace share spaces with snapper Cannes, which has lump crabmeat, tomato compote and lemon butter. Features: full bar, early bird specials. Reservations: suggested. Address: 3410 Montrose Blvd 77006 Location: Just s of jct Westheimer Rd; in La Colombe d'Or Hotel. Parking: valet and street only. [L] [D]

### CIRO'S
713/467-9336 (13)

WW Italian. Casual Dining. $12-$26 AAA Inspector Notes: Reminiscent of an Italian country inn, complete with outdoor boccie ball court. Specialties include flavorful artichoke brochette, tender osso buco and rich chocolate cake. The wine list is carefully crafted to pair well with menu selections. Features: full bar, patio dining. Address: 9755 Katy Frwy 77024 Location: I-10 exit 757 (Gessner Rd); eastbound frontage road. [L] [D]

### CLEBURNE CAFETERIA
713/667-2386 (90)

W American. Cafeteria. $7-$14 AAA Inspector Notes: Guests can count on cafeteria-line service at this cash-only restaurant. The original owner's artwork adorns the dining room walls. Traditional American fare, including broiled fish, roast beef and fried chicken, as well as an array of salads, breads, sides and desserts, is served in generous portions. Produce is purchased daily from the farmers market, and poultry and beef are delivered daily. Pastries are made daily in house, and even the mayonnaise and salad dressings are homemade. Address: 3606 Bissonnet St 77005 Location: Between Buffalo Speedway and Weslayan St. [L] [D] CALL [&M]

### CRAPITTO'S CUCINA ITALIANA
713/961-1161 (43)

WW Italian. Casual Dining. $12-$39 AAA Inspector Notes: This Italian bistro, set in a former house on a tree-lined side street, maintains a residential feel. Diners can enjoy their delicious meals in one of the quaint, intimate dining areas or on a spacious patio, shaded by century-old oaks. Features: full bar, patio dining, happy hour. Address: 2400 Mid Ln 77027 Location: I-610 exit 9A (San Felipe Rd/Westheimer Rd), just e on Westheimer Rd, then just n. Parking: valet only. [L] [D] CALL [&M]

### DAILY GRILL
713/960-5997

WW American. Casual Dining. $11-$34 AAA Inspector Notes: Steaks, rack of lamb, chicken and some seafood selections are among the offerings. The restaurant is reminiscent of upscale grills of the 1930s and 1940s. Features: full bar. Address: 5085 Westheimer Rd 77056 Location: I-610 exit 8C (Westheimer Rd) northbound; exit 9A (San Felipe Rd/Westheimer Rd) southbound, 0.5 mi w on Westheimer Rd to Sage Rd, just s, then just e; in The Westin Galleria, Houston. [B] [L] [D] CALL [&M]

### DAILY REVIEW CAFE
713/520-9217 (23)

WW New American. Casual Dining. $11-$32 AAA Inspector Notes: Diners can expect casual, casual dining in a simple bistro atmosphere. The well-rounded menu features items such as salmon tostada, achiote grilled shrimp, pizzas, pastas and salads. The Southern-fried chicken with all the traditional accompaniments is very popular. There is a covered patio for outdoor dining. Features: full bar, Sunday brunch. Reservations: suggested. Address: 3412 W Lamar St 77019 Location: Just s of Allen Pkwy; corner of W Lamar and Dunlavy sts. Parking: valet only. [L] [D]

### DAMARCO
713/807-8857 (40)

WWWW WWWW Italian. Fine Dining. $14-$40 AAA Inspector Notes: There is an understated sophistication about this eatery in a small cottage with intimate interiors. Although cozy and somewhat elegant, the dining room hums with activity and can get a little loud at times. Excellent food and service are the real reasons to come here. This is authentic, modern Italian cuisine with items like braised lamb ravioli, pappardelle with rabbit, grilled swordfish with cannellini and shrimp brodo and whole roasted fish. There is also a daily menu of specials. Features: full bar. Reservations: suggested. Address: 1520 Westheimer Rd 77006 Location: US 59 (Southwest Frwy) exit Shepherd Dr, 0.8 mi n, then 0.9 mi e. Parking: valet only. [L] [D]

### DENIS' SEAFOOD RESTAURANT
713/464-6900 (14)

WWWW Regional Seafood. Fine Dining. $12-$25 AAA Inspector Notes: A wide variety of fresh seafood with Cajun and 'Nawlins" influences. Specializing in whole fish preparations. The contemporary décor and high level of personalized service assure a satisfying experience. Features: full bar. Address: 9777 Katy Frwy 77024 Location: I-10 exit 757 (Gessner Rd); on eastbound frontage road. [L] [D]

### EL MESON
713/522-9306 (99)

WW Latin American. Casual Dining. $10-$32 AAA Inspector Notes: In an ever-popular university village area, the restaurant presents a menu that represents many Latin American and Spanish cuisines. Tapas are favorites at the laid-back spot, as is the extensive wine list. Parking is always challenging. Features: full bar. Address: 2425 University Blvd 77005 Location: US 59 (Southwest Frwy) exit Kirby Dr, 1 mi s to University Blvd, then just e. Parking: street only. [L] [D]

### EMPIRE CAFE
713/528-5282 (39)

W Italian. Casual Dining. $9-$11 AAA Inspector Notes: In the trendy Montrose area, the cafe offers a wholesome approach to quickly served food. Pasta, panini, pizza and homemade desserts make up much of the menu, but just as popular are the breakfast choices. The city's weather provides plenty of opportunity to take advantage of the sidewalk tables. Features: full bar. Address: 1732 Westheimer Rd 77098 Location: US 59 (Southwest Frwy) exit Shepherd Dr, 0.8 mi n, then 0.5 mi e. [B] [L] [D]

### ESCALANTE'S MEXICAN GRILLE
713/461-5400 (105)

WW Mexican. Casual Dining. $8-$22 AAA Inspector Notes: This family-friendly cantina is known for its made-at-the-table guacamole, which you get to scoop up with mega-thin chips. Enjoy traditional fajitas, enchiladas and tamales or, for a little twist, the shrimp and crabmeat enchilada or the grilled jumbo shrimp wrapped in bacon. Combination plates are available. The tortillas are made by hand, and you can watch the process in the showcase. The restaurant, including the very lively bar, is packed on the weekends. Outdoor seating is offered. Features: full bar, patio dining, Sunday brunch, happy hour. Address: 6582 Woodway Dr 77057 Location: Jct Woodway Dr and Voss Rd. [L] [D]

### FIESTA LOMA LINDA
713/924-6074 (93)

WW Tex-Mex. Casual Dining. $6-$12 AAA Inspector Notes: The owners have no lofty goals of keeping up with new trends in Mexican cuisine. The food, just like the decor, reflects the same traditional characteristics that have been satisfying customers for years. Features: full bar, happy hour. Address: 2111 Telephone Rd 77023 Location: I-45 exit 43B southbound; exit 43A northbound. [L] [D]

### FLEMING'S PRIME STEAKHOUSE & WINE BAR
713/520-5959 (61)

WWWW Steak. Fine Dining. $11-$49 AAA Inspector Notes: The warm, clubby atmosphere is the ideal setting for perfectly grilled steaks and seafood. Side dishes come in hearty portions, and salads are fresh and crisp. More than 100 wine selections are available. Features: full bar. Reservations: suggested. Address: 2405 W Alabama St 77098 Location: Just w of jct Shepherd Rd and W Alabama St. Parking: valet only. [D]

**(See map & index p. 316.)**

### FOGO DE CHAO   713/978-6500   63

▼▼▼▼ Brazilian. Casual Dining. $35-$52 **AAA Inspector Notes:** A meat lover's delight, the opulently decorated churrascaria offers excellent cuts of roasted beef, pork and chicken. Recipes are Brazilian, and the service is attentive. The salad bar is an experience in itself. Waiters in gaucho garb circulate through the spacious dining room. **Features:** full bar. **Address:** 8250 Westheimer Rd 77063 **Location:** Jct Westheimer and S Voss rds, just w. **Parking:** on-site and valet. L D CALL ⚐M

### FUNG'S KITCHEN   713/779-2288   103

▼ Chinese. Casual Dining. $8-$25 **AAA Inspector Notes:** The building's exterior resembles a Chinese pagoda, while the interior is peppered with exquisite Buddhist and Chinese statues. The extensive menu lists more than 400 dishes, which may seem overwhelming, but friendly servers are happy to help diners select a tasty meal. For something different, one of the traditional and attractively presented Chinese desserts is recommended. **Features:** beer & wine. **Address:** 7320 Southwest Frwy, Suite 115 77074 **Location:** US 59 (Southwest Frwy) exit Bellaire Blvd/Fondren Rd, just sw. L D

### GIGI'S ASIAN BISTRO & DUMPLING BAR   713/629-8889   57

▼ Asian. Casual Dining. $12-$35 **AAA Inspector Notes:** Cherry blossoms descending from the ceiling give the dining room an earthy and beautiful fairy tale feeling. The menu lists a variety of small plates, as well as more substantial fare such as pad thai, steak, Peking duck and crispy whole fish. As the name suggests, there is also a selection of dumplings. Smoking is allowed on the patio. **Features:** full bar, Sunday brunch. **Address:** 5085 Westheimer Rd, B2515 77056 **Location:** I-610 exit 8C (Westheimer Rd) northbound; exit 9A (San Felipe Rd/Westheimer Rd) southbound, just w; in Galleria Mall. L D

### GOODE COMPANY HAMBURGERS & TAQUERIA   713/520-9153   86

▼ American. Quick Serve. $6-$23 **AAA Inspector Notes:** This local favorite offers tasty mesquite-grilled burgers, crispy tacos, enchiladas and salads in a very laid-back setting with counter service only. A children's menu is offered. Adults can choose from a good selection of Mexican beers kept on ice. **Features:** beer & wine. **Address:** 4902 Kirby Dr 77098 **Location:** US 59 (Southwest Frwy) exit Kirby Dr, just s. B L D

### GOODE CO. SEAFOOD   713/523-7154   85

▼▼ Regional Seafood. Casual Dining. $12-$24 **AAA Inspector Notes:** Catering to a broad clientele (some in suits and ties and others in flip-flops), this spiffy railway diner is set in an old train car with nods to fishing aficionados. Southern and Mexican influences enhance lip-blistering gumbo, overstuffed, fried seafood po' boys, and boisterous fun. A special delight is the sweet seviche-like campeche with cubed avocado and chopped onion. **Features:** full bar. **Address:** 2621 Westpark Dr 77098 **Location:** 0.4 mi s of jct US 59 (Southwest Frwy) exit Kirby Dr. L D

### GROTTO   713/622-3663   53

▼▼▼ Italian. Casual Dining. $10-$24 **AAA Inspector Notes:** The chic and energetic Italian cafe is located just steps from the Galleria and serves homemade but unpredictable fare. A lavish assortment of antipasto can be seen in the display kitchen. Lively murals cover the walls. The focal points are the large wood-burning oven and the antipasto bar. **Features:** full bar, patio dining, Sunday brunch, happy hour. **Address:** 4715 Westheimer Rd 77027 **Location:** Southeast corner of Loop 610. **Parking:** on-site and valet. L D CALL ⚐M

### GUADALAJARA HACIENDA   713/461-5300   15

▼ Mexican. Casual Dining. $10-$24 **AAA Inspector Notes:** Reminiscent of a large hacienda with oversize wood beams, hand-painted Talavera tiles and a cantera stone fountain, guests will enjoy the authentic Mexican food. Chips are served with warm red salsa and a cool avocado cream sauce. First-time visitors are offered a complimentary dessert. **Features:** full bar. **Address:** 9799 Katy Frwy 77024 **Location:** I-10 exit 757 (Gessner Rd); eastbound frontage road. L D CALL ⚐M

### HAVEN   713/581-6101   78

▼▼▼▼ Regional American. Fine Dining. $11-$32 **AAA Inspector Notes:** This beautiful restaurant is in a quiet corner off Kirby Drive. An inviting outdoor patio makes this a great lunch stop. Chef Randy Evans prepares regional Texas cuisine with a modern flair. Local ingredients go into the ever-changing menu, which might include seared pork belly with shelling peas and mirepoix, shrimp corn dogs with lemonade and Tabasco mash remoulade, or Gulf fish in jumbo lump crab, okra, tomato and a cucumber-onion slaw. There also are some salads and vegetarian items. **Features:** full bar, patio dining, Sunday brunch, happy hour. **Reservations:** suggested. **Address:** 2502 Algerian Way 77098 **Location:** US 59 (Southwest Frwy) exit Kirby Dr, just n to Algerian Way, then just e. **Parking:** valet and street only. ECO ◄ L D CALL ⚐M

### HICKORY HOLLOW   713/869-6300   18

▼ Regional Comfort Food. Quick Serve. $8-$19 **AAA Inspector Notes:** Hickory Hollow has been featured on the Food Network's "Outrageous Food" program for its chicken-fried steaks, which are, to say the least, Texas-sized. A family of four could feast on the Large Rancher. I had the Small Plowman, and it was huge! This Texas café also offers steak platters, spare ribs and smoked sausage, as well as chicken, catfish and enormous loaded baked potatoes. **Features:** beer only. **Address:** 101 Heights Blvd 77007 **Location:** I-10 exit 767A, 0.5 mi s. L D

### HUGO'S   713/524-7744   38

▼▼▼▼ Regional Mexican. Casual Dining. $15-$30 **AAA Inspector Notes:** Mexican food lovers should know they won't find the cuisine that's most prevalent on this side of the border at this restaurant. Selections come from all over Mexico and include dishes most Americans likely have never even heard about. Among the good beverage pairings are choices from the impressive wine list and the signature hot chocolate. Live music can be heard during Sunday brunch. The dining room is casually elegant and appropriate for special occasions. **Features:** full bar, patio dining, Sunday brunch, happy hour. **Reservations:** suggested. **Address:** 1600 Westheimer Rd 77006 **Location:** Between Dunlavy St and Montrose Blvd. L D 🐾

### INDIA'S   713/266-0131   82

▼ Indian. Casual Dining. $14-$30 **AAA Inspector Notes:** Featuring seafood, lamb and chicken dishes, the cuisine emphasizes curried items as well as selections prepared in the tandoori, or clay oven, tradition. A well-stocked lunch buffet with items such as tandoori chicken and fried spinach is not only a good value but also a good way for novices to sample the variety in Indian cuisine. Dinner is a la carte. Chandelier lighting and an entire wall of mirrors enhance the atmosphere. Vegetarian options are plentiful. **Features:** full bar, Sunday brunch. **Reservations:** suggested. **Address:** 5704 Richmond Ave 77057 **Location:** Just n of US 59 (Southwest Frwy); between Chimney Rock and Fountainview rds. L D

### JAX GRILL   713/861-5529   17

▼ American. Quick Serve. $7-$19 **AAA Inspector Notes:** This popular and very casual restaurant features American and Mexican menu options with many daily specials. Outdoor seating is available when weather permits. **Features:** full bar. **Address:** 1613 Shepherd Dr 77007 **Location:** I-10 exit 765B westbound, just s on Durham Dr. L D ◣

### KENNY & ZIGGY'S DELICATESSEN RESTAURANT   713/871-8883   48

▼▼ Deli Sandwiches. Quick Serve. $11-$24 **AAA Inspector Notes:** The restaurant treats patrons to a New York delicatessen-style experience. The menu is an encyclopedia of sandwich choices, franks, bagels and lox, salads and such dinner plates as corned beef and cabbage. Although sandwich prices may seem high, the huge portions make them worthwhile. **Features:** beer & wine. **Address:** 2327 Post Oak Blvd 77056 **Location:** I-610 exit 8C (Westheimer Rd) northbound; exit 9A (San Felipe Rd/Westheimer Rd) southbound, just w on Westheimer Rd, then just n. B L D

Trust your vehicle to AAA/CAA

Approved Auto Repair facilities

(See map & index p. 316.)

**KOREA GARDEN RESTAURANT**    713/468-2800   (8)
▼▼ Korean. Casual Dining. $8-$20 **AAA Inspector Notes:** Most of the patrons who fill this restaurant for the authentic experience are regulars who enjoy eating barbecued meat prepared on gas grills set into the tables. You may cook the meat yourself or the staff will assist. The meat sizzles when it is laid on the hot grill and the table is laden with dipping sauce, sticky rice, lettuce leaves for wrapping the meat and a half-dozen condiments that are robust with flavor. **Features:** full bar. **Address:** 9501 Long Point Rd, Suite Z 77055 **Location:** I-10 exit 758 (Bunker Hill) eastbound; exit 759 (Bunker Hill) westbound, 0.6 mi n, then 0.4 mi e. [L] [D]

**LA GRIGLIA**    713/526-4700   (28)
▼▼▼ Italian. Casual Dining. $10-$36 **AAA Inspector Notes:** Noted as a place to see and be seen, the eatery should be appreciated more for its consistently well-made Italian fare. Diners shouldn't look for the standards here; instead, creative dishes like wild mushroom and roasted chicken lasagna leave them wanting more. Service is definitely attentive, and eating here can be fun, but it's also a decidedly adult experience. Whimsical best describes the colorful tile mosaics and murals, and a large pizza oven and antipasti bar are focal points. **Features:** full bar, patio dining, happy hour. **Address:** 2002 W Gray St 77019 **Location:** US 59 exit Shepherd Rd, 1.5 mi n, then just e. **Parking:** on-site (fee) and valet. [L] [D]

**THE LEXINGTON GRILLE**    713/524-9877   (80)
▼▼▼ Continental. Fine Dining. $12-$38 **AAA Inspector Notes:** The warm, intimate cottage provides a casual but elegant background for dining. Classic chicken, seafood and pasta dishes are presented with a modern flair. **Features:** full bar. **Reservations:** suggested, weekends. **Address:** 2005 Lexington St 77098 **Location:** US 59 (Southwest Frwy) exit Shepherd Dr/Greenbriar Rd, just n on Shepherd Dr to Lexington St, then just e. **Parking:** valet only. [L] [D]

**LOS TIOS**    713/784-0380   (70)
▼▼ Tex-Mex. Casual Dining. $3-$21 **AAA Inspector Notes:** Self-proclaimed as "The Food of the Border," Los Tios' specialty is puffy quesos, which are puffy, crispy shells smothered with fresh chile con queso. I enjoyed the Laredo Dinner, which consisted of a beef taco, cheese enchilada and a tamale topped with chili gravy. More Tex-Mex options include chalupas, mesquite-grilled fajitas, chalupas, nachos and quesadillas. Sopapillas or Mexican flan are a great way to conclude a meal. **Features:** full bar, happy hour. **Address:** 9527 Westheimer Rd 77063 **Location:** Sam Houston Pkwy (Beltway 8) exit Westheimer Rd, 0.3 mi e; in Tanglewilde Village. [L] [D] CALL [&M]

**MARIA SELMA**    713/528-4920   (75)
▼▼ Mexican. Casual Dining. $9-$22 **AAA Inspector Notes:** Amid mustard-colored walls and Talavera tile tables, the eatery serves Mexico City-style cuisine. Items such as shrimp in spicy chipotle adobo sauce and marinated beefsteak with grilled cactus share space with a selection of enchiladas, tortas and tacos. The palapa-covered patio and a long list of tequilas make this a neighborhood favorite. Breakfast is served on weekends. **Features:** full bar, Sunday brunch. **Reservations:** suggested. **Address:** 1617 Richmond Ave 77006 **Location:** US 59 (Southwest Frwy) exit Shepherd Dr, just n to Richmond Ave, then 0.7 mi e. [L] [D] [N]

**MARK'S AMERICAN CUISINE**    713/523-3800   (41)
▼▼▼ ▼▼
New American Fine Dining $22-$57

**AAA Inspector Notes:** Located within a restored 1920s church, Mark's draws a large congregation each night, and weekend reservations are a must. As beautiful and unique as the dining room is, the main draw here is the excellent food. The ever-changing menu includes premium items from around the world and also some local products. Appetizers include items like hearth-roasted Wianno oysters topped with a ragoût of jumbo crab meat, shrimp and roasted leeks in a truffle aioli vinaigrette. **Features:** full bar. **Reservations:** suggested. **Address:** 1658 Westheimer Rd 77006 **Location:** Northeast corner of Westheimer Rd and Dunlavy St.

**Parking:** on-site and valet. [L] [D]

**MI LUNA TAPAS RESTAURANT & BAR**    713/520-5025   (100)
▼▼ Small Plates. Casual Dining. $4-$22 **AAA Inspector Notes:** The focus is on tapas with a varied menu of boldly flavored foods served in small portions. The selections include such items as olives, marinated mushrooms, grilled scallops with a tomato-sherry wine sauce, empanadas, Moroccan sausage and grilled lamb with couscous. Several selections of paella also are on the menu. The myriad choices allow diners to try several items for a reasonable price. It can get pretty crowded with Rice University students on nights when live music is featured. **Features:** full bar, patio dining, happy hour. **Address:** 2441 University Blvd 77005 **Location:** US 59 exit Kirby Dr, 1.1 mi s. **Parking:** street only. [L] [D] [🐾]

**MIYAKO JAPANESE RESTAURANT**    713/781-6300   (69)
▼▼ Japanese. Casual Dining. $8-$25 **AAA Inspector Notes:** With a wide range of sushi and traditional dishes, the local favorite brings a touch of the Orient to mid-Texas. Combination plates with tempura, sushi and grilled meats are popular, as are tableside preparations of wok beef or chicken. Staff is attentive to diners' needs. Menu variety is bound to please even those that may not necessarily be too familiar with Asian cuisine. Parking is a nightmare, so going at odd hours may be best if you're not too interested in soaking up the scene. **Features:** full bar. **Address:** 6345 Westheimer Rd 77057 **Location:** US 59 S (Southwest Frwy) exit Fountain View Dr, 0.7 mi n, then 0.7 mi w. [L] [D] [LATE]

**MOCKINGBIRD BISTRO**    713/533-0200   (33)
▼▼▼ American. Fine Dining. $22-$46 **AAA Inspector Notes:** This neighborhood spot is popular and the atmosphere is relaxed and casual, but the noise level stays comfortable for dinner conversation, even on busy nights. The sophisticated seasonal menu reflects the chef's approach of using local market ingredients prepared with some French-country influences. Entrées might include seared sea scallops, grilled tuna, and organic chicken and lamb. **Features:** full bar, patio dining, Sunday brunch, happy hour. **Reservations:** suggested. **Address:** 1985 Welch St 77019 **Location:** US 59 (Southwest Frwy) exit Shepherd Dr, 0.8 mi n to Westheimer Rd, just e to McDuffie St, then 0.4 mi n. **Parking:** valet only. [L] [D] [🐾]

**MONARCH**    713/526-1991   (91)
▼▼▼ Mediterranean. Fine Dining. $10-$40 **AAA Inspector Notes:** Located in the swanky Hotel ZaZa, the sumptuous spot serves contemporary Mediterranean fare along the lines of crunchy crab cake with mango chipotle sauce, wild mushroom risotto and seared Chilean sea bass. Guests can relax in a trendy bar which offers plenty of seating or on the large outdoor patio. **Features:** full bar, Sunday brunch. **Reservations:** suggested. **Address:** 5701 Main St 77005 **Location:** US 59 (Southwest Frwy) exit Main St northbound, 0.5 mi s; exit Fannin St southbound, 0.5 mi s to Ewing St, then just w; in Hotel ZaZa Houston Museum District. **Parking:** valet only. [B] [L] [D]

**NOÉ RESTAURANT & BAR**    713/871-8181   (22)
▼▼▼ ▼▼
New American Fine Dining $21-$39

**AAA Inspector Notes:** Progressive American cuisine with an Asian influence is served at this stylish restaurant. The food reflects some Texas influences with use of some local ingredients. A recommended entrée is the seared diver scallops. There also is a selection of USDA Prime steaks and lamb. The separate lounge is a popular meeting place before or after dinner. **Features:** full bar. **Reservations:** suggested. **Address:** Four Riverway 77056 **Location:** I-610 exit 10 (Woodway Dr), 0.3 mi w; in Omni Houston Hotel. **Parking:** on-site and valet. [D] CALL [&M]

**THE OCEANAIRE SEAFOOD ROOM**    832/487-8862   (56)
▼▼▼ Seafood. Fine Dining. $11-$54 **AAA Inspector Notes:** Fresh fish and shellfish are flown in daily from around the globe. The sleek, handsomely designed dining room has a raw bar and is tastefully appointed in an Art Deco/nautical theme. The menu notes the seafood available daily and the varied preparation styles, such as broiled, grilled and blackened. **Features:** full bar. **Reservations:** suggested. **Address:** 5061 Westheimer Rd, Suite 8050 77056 **Location:** I-610 exit 8C (Westheimer Rd), just w; in Galleria Mall. **Parking:** on-site and valet. [SAVE] [L] [D]

**(See map & index p. 316.)**

### OTILIA'S
713/681-7203   [6]

◆◆ Mexican. Casual Dining. $9-$14 **AAA Inspector Notes:** The family-run eatery prepares food in the shell of an old burger drive-in, but the staff has deftly erased the fast-food history here. No one visits for the ambience, as it's all about the food: mole, gorditas, tacos and chiles rellenos. The refreshing menu offers dishes from the interior of Mexico, which is something offered in few Mexican restaurants north of the border. The east wall serves as a bragging station with the numerous local and national accolades this place has racked up. **Features:** full bar. **Address:** 7710 Long Point Rd 77055 **Location:** I-10 exit 761A (Wirt Rd), 1.3 mi n, then just e.   [L] [D]

### OUISIE'S TABLE
713/528-2264   [36]

◆◆◆ American. Fine Dining. $8-$32 **AAA Inspector Notes:** Request a seat in the understatedly elegant main dining hall or in the smaller, more intimate sunroom. Among the options are chicken-fried steak, grilled salmon, egg salad sandwiches, crispy crab cakes, brandied oysters, veal curry, and shrimp and cheese grits. Minutes from downtown, Ouisie's Table also entices you with daily changing blackboard menus that list gourmet surprises along the lines of salad with lime-poppy dressing and pumpkin seed-crusted salmon, as well as steaks and pasta dishes. **Features:** full bar, Sunday brunch. **Reservations:** suggested. **Address:** 3939 San Felipe Rd 77027 **Location:** Just w of Weslayan St, on south side of San Felipe Rd; between Weslayan St and Drexel Dr.   [B] [L] [D]

### PAPPADEAUX SEAFOOD KITCHEN

◆◆ Regional Seafood. Casual Dining. $12-$47 **AAA Inspector Notes:** A seafood lover's delight, the restaurant taps into a little bit of New Orleans with its Cajun dishes and elaborate menu selections. Patrons might start off with a creative choice of blackened oyster and shrimp fondeaux with crayfish and let the feast begin. While music plays in the background, patrons can dig into dirty rice or spicy gumbo loaded with seafood. Well-seasoned shrimp and fish are prepared in varied ways. **Bar:** full bar.   [L] [D]

*For additional information, visit AAA.com*

**LOCATIONS:**
**Address:** 6015 Westheimer Rd 77057 **Location:** US 59 (Southwest Frwy) exit Fountain View Dr, 0.8 mi n, then just w.
**Phone:** 713/782-6310

**Address:** 2410 Richmond Ave 77057 **Location:** Just e of Kirby Dr.
**Phone:** 713/527-9137

### PAPPAS BAR-B-QUE

◆◆ Barbecue. Casual Dining. $6-$17 **AAA Inspector Notes:** Step in for some delicious Texas barbecue. Cafeteria-style service allows guests to order from a selection of sandwiches, burgers, plate dinners and many side dishes, including cucumber salad and baked potatoes. Breakfast tacos are served weekday mornings at the drive-through only. **Bar:** beer only.   [L] [D]

*For additional information, visit AAA.com*

**LOCATIONS:**
**Address:** 4430 I-45 N 77076 **Location:** I-45 exit 52B (Crosstimbers St); on northbound frontage road. **Phone:** 713/697-9533
**Address:** 12917 Northwest Frwy 77040 **Location:** US Hwy 290 exit Bingle Rd, on W Frontage Rd. **Phone:** 713/462-2550

### PAPPAS BROS. STEAKHOUSE
713/780-7352   [66]

◆◆◆ ◆◆◆ Steak. Fine Dining. $42-$80 **AAA Inspector Notes:** The stars of Texas shine down in the classy restaurant with Western accents—think stone, wood and leather. Many consider this to be the best steakhouse in Houston. They have all the USDA Prime steaks you can imagine, as well as fresh seafood and lobster. Service is very refined and very attentive. The wine list includes more than 500 entries. A piano player entertains guests in the lounge before and after dinner. **Features:** full bar. **Reservations:** suggested. **Address:** 5839 Westheimer Rd 77057 **Location:** Between Chimney Rock St and Fountain View Dr. **Parking:** valet only.   [D]

### PAPPASITO'S CANTINA
713/784-5253

◆◆ ◆◆ Tex-Mex. Casual Dining. $10-$49 **AAA Inspector Notes:** Fine traditional offerings are served in an upscale cantina atmosphere. Often crowded during peak hours, the immensely popular shop dishes up generous portions of sizzling fajitas, enchiladas and other traditional Mexican favorites, including some shrimp specialties. The terrific margaritas are guaranteed to get attention. Tables in the large dining room are closely spaced. Ice cream with cinnamon on chocolate bread pudding shouldn't be missed. **Features:** full bar, Sunday brunch, happy hour. **Address:** 6445 Richmond Ave 77057 **Location:** US 59 (Southwest Frwy) exit Hillcroft St, 1 mi w, then just n.   [L] [D]

### PERRY'S STEAKHOUSE & GRILLE
832/358-9001   [12]

◆◆◆◆ Steak. Fine Dining. $13-$48 **AAA Inspector Notes:** An excellent selection of prime steaks, lamb and pork chops is served in this professional and upscale establishment. **Features:** full bar, happy hour. **Reservations:** required. **Address:** 9827 Katy Frwy 77024 **Location:** I-10 exit 763 (Gessner Rd), 1 mi e on S Frontage Rd.   [L] [D]  CALL ⑤M

### PICNIC
713/524-0201   [89]

◆ Deli Breads/Pastries. Quick Serve. $7-$11 **AAA Inspector Notes:** The great thing about this place is that it's just what it claims to be. Sandwiches are served in a box lunch that includes chips, fruit salad and a dessert. The chicken salad is excellent, and some soups and salads also are offered. Because it's also a working bakery, there are many breads, cookies and pastries to be sampled or purchased. The small space features two large picnic tables and a handful of bistro tables. This is a great stop for people doing the museum thing. **Address:** 1928 Bissonnet St 77005 **Location:** US 59 (Southwest Frwy) exit Kirby Dr, just s to Bissonnet St, then 0.7 mi e.   [L]

### PONDICHERI
713/522-2022   [55]

◆◆ Indian. Casual Dining. $8-$20 **AAA Inspector Notes:** This is a more casual cousin of Restaurant Indika, another popular Indian restaurant in the city. The menu has intense flavors and includes some classic dishes and traditional Indian street foods. The atmosphere is relaxed and very informal with counter service for breakfast and lunch and table service for dinner. The location on a busy corner of the trendy West Ave shopping/dining/residential complex makes it a popular spot that also affords easy parking, a rarity in this part of Houston. **Features:** beer & wine. **Address:** 2800 Kirby Dr, Suite B132 77098 **Location:** At Westheimer Ave; in West Ave Complex. **Parking:** on-site and valet.   [B] [L] [D]  CALL ⑤M

### POST OAK GRILL
713/993-9966   [27]

◆◆ American. Fine Dining. $10-$30 **AAA Inspector Notes:** Near the Galleria, the cozy dining room provides guests a straightforward menu of pasta dishes, grilled entrees and fresh salads, as well as sandwiches for lunch. Among the daily bistro classics are roasted lamb shanks and trout with lemon butter. **Features:** full bar. **Reservations:** suggested. **Address:** 1415 S Post Oak Ln 77056 **Location:** Between San Felipe Rd and Woodway Dr; just w of Post Oak Blvd.   [L] [D]

### PREGO RESTAURANT
713/529-2420   [97]

◆◆◆ Italian. Casual Dining. $12-$28 **AAA Inspector Notes:** Boisterous and bustling, this casual dining room features a mouthwatering variety of fresh, well-prepared dishes served in ample portions. The menu offers traditional Italian items and fresh seafood as well as some items with a Tex-Mex twist, including jalapeño fettuccine with grilled chicken, tomatoes, onions and black beans. Located near Rice University, this area is popular for its trendy shopping and eateries. **Features:** full bar, Sunday brunch. **Reservations:** suggested. **Address:** 2520 Amherst St 77005 **Location:** US 59 (Southwest Frwy) exit Kirby Dr, 1 mi s to Amherst St, then just e; in University Village.   [L] [D]

### RAGIN CAJUN SEAFOOD
832/251-7171   [68]

◆ Cajun. Casual Dining. $7-$21 **AAA Inspector Notes:** Quick service and fresh seafood prepared Cajun style are the name of the game at the modest, no-nonsense eatery. There's full bar service as well. The cocktail sauce for the boiled shrimp is terrific. The atmosphere is a bit noisy, and guests order at the counter before seating themselves at tables set with paper napkins and plastic utensils. The staff has a great sense of humor, and this is a great place to catch a Texans game. **Features:** full bar. **Address:** 9600 Westheimer Rd, Unit 80 77063 **Location:** Jct Westheimer and S Gessner rds; in Woodlake Square Center.   [L] [D]

### RA SUSHI BAR RESTAURANT
713/621-5800

◆◆ Sushi. Casual Dining. $7-$20 **AAA Inspector Notes:** The stylish restaurant serves a wide array of sushi and sashimi, as well as tempura and teriyaki dishes, so even those without a taste for raw fish can find something to like. The appetizers alone could be considered a meal for those with smaller appetites, and drink specialties abound in the lounge. **Features:** full bar, happy hour. **Address:** 3908 Westheimer Rd 77027 **Location:** US 59 (Southwest Frwy) exit Victoria, 0.5 mi via Southwest Frwy, then 0.8 mi on E Weslayan St. **Parking:** on-site and valet.   [L] [D] [LATE]

(See map & index p. 316.)

RDG + BAR ANNIE 713/840-1111 (35)

Regional American. Fine Dining. $16-$58 **AAA Inspector Notes:** In the trendy Galleria area, this place is a favorite for locals and tourists alike. Guests can dine in the more formal RDG Grill Room or the more casual Bar Annie. Both offer creative presentations of New American cuisine with heavy Southwestern and Texas influences. The refined service and sophisticated atmosphere further enhance the dining experience. **Features:** full bar, Sunday brunch. **Reservations:** suggested. **Address:** 1800 Post Oak Blvd 77056 **Location:** I-610 exit 9A (San Felipe Rd/Westheimer Rd), just w. **Parking:** on-site and valet. L D

**THE REMINGTON RESTAURANT** 713/403-2631 (34)

**American Fine Dining $9-$42**

**AAA Inspector Notes:** The Remington offers a menu of modern American dishes prepared with a Texas flair with choices like anise-scented chicken, grilled salmon with citrus mojo and five-spiced braised short ribs. There is a large, formal room accented with fine art pieces as well as an inviting conservatory with a glass ceiling. The energy and atmosphere can vary depending on the level of business at the hotel. The adjoining Remington bar is a lively and popular spot on weekends with live music and dancing on some nights. **Features:** full bar, Sunday brunch. **Reservations:** suggested. **Address:** 1919 Briar Oaks Ln 77027 **Location:** I-610 exit 9A (San Felipe Rd/Westheimer Rd), 0.3 mi e; in The St. Regis Houston. **Parking:** valet only. B L D

RUDI LECHNER'S 713/782-1180 (62)

German. Casual Dining. $12-$26 **AAA Inspector Notes:** The Old World restaurant serves some of the best German fare the city has to offer. Schnitzel, sauerbraten and Angus beef are but a few choices. Meals start with a serving of delicious warm zucchini bread, and a salad bar lets guests eat light. Live entertainment kicks up the atmosphere Friday and Saturday nights. **Features:** full bar. **Reservations:** suggested. **Address:** 2503 S Gessner Rd 77063 **Location:** Sam Houston Pkwy (Beltway 8) exit Westheimer Rd, 0.9 mi e, then just n. L D

RUSSO'S NEW YORK COAL FIRED PIZZERIA 713/647-9100 (11)

Italian. Casual Dining. $8-$20 **AAA Inspector Notes:** This place has the best New York-style pizza in Houston, but they also have a full menu with pasta, veal and chicken entrées. The restaurant itself has a comfortable family-friendly atmosphere with a wine bar and outdoor tables. The restaurant is convenient to area shopping and hotels. **Features:** beer & wine. **Address:** 9403 Katy Frwy, Suite B 77024 **Location:** I-10 exit 758B (Blalock Rd/Campbell Rd) eastbound; exit 758B (Echo Ln) westbound; on eastbound service road; in Hedwig Village Shopping Center. L D CALL &M

RUTH'S CHRIS STEAK HOUSE 713/789-2333 (83)

Steak. Fine Dining. $40-$100 **AAA Inspector Notes:** The main fare is steak, which is prepared from several cuts of Prime beef and cooked to perfection, but the menu also lists lamb, chicken and seafood dishes. Guests should come hungry because the side dishes, which are among the a la carte offerings, could make a meal in themselves. **Features:** full bar. **Address:** 6213 Richmond Ave 77057 **Location:** US 59 (Southwest Frwy) S exit Fountain View Dr, 0.3 mi n to Richmond Ave, then 0.8 mi w. **Parking:** valet only. D CALL &M

SALTGRASS STEAKHOUSE

Steak. Casual Dining. $9-$30 **AAA Inspector Notes:** Those looking for something different should try the comfortable steakhouse, which never says no to a special request. Born from the spirit of Texas cattle drives, the restaurant resembles a Texas lodge, with high ceilings and mounted animal heads. Baby back ribs are so tender the meat falls off the bone. Also on the menu are hearty steaks, prime rib, chicken, seafood and yummy desserts. **Bar:** full bar. SAVE L D

For additional information, visit AAA.com

**LOCATIONS:**

**Address:** 520 Meyerland Plaza 77096 **Location:** I-610 exit 5A (Beechnut St) southbound; exit 4A (Braeswood Blvd) northbound, just n to U-turn; just s on southbound frontage road to Meyerland Plaza Mall. **Phone:** 713/665-2226 (106)

**Address:** 8943 Katy Frwy 77024 **Location:** I-10 exit 759 (Campbell Rd) westbound; exit 760 (Bingle Rd/Voss Rd) eastbound; on eastbound frontage road. **Phone:** 713/461-6111 (10)

**Address:** 9110 Southwest Frwy 77074 **Location:** US 59 (Southwest Frwy) exit Bissonnet St; on northbound frontage road. **Phone:** 713/771-1777 (107)

SHADE 713/863-7500 (5)

New American. Casual Dining. $8-$30 **AAA Inspector Notes:** This restaurant exudes contemporary flair with its soft neutral colors. It also has a small outdoor patio. The seasonal menu is influenced by several cuisines and makes use of local market-fresh items. Dishes such as shrimp and crab campechana, sage- and garlic-grilled veal chop, and wasabi- and cucumber-crusted red snapper with Thai red curry coconut broth are expertly prepared. The house-made chocolate cherry croissant bread pudding shouldn't be missed. Brunch is offered on weekends. **Features:** full bar, Sunday brunch. **Reservations:** suggested. **Address:** 250 W 19th St 77008 **Location:** I-10 exit 766 (Heights Blvd) westbound; exit 767A (Studemont St) eastbound, 1.7 mi n on Heights Blvd, then just w. **Parking:** street only. L D CALL &M

SHANGHAI RIVER 713/528-5528 (47)

Traditional Chinese. Casual Dining. $7-$18 **AAA Inspector Notes:** Tended by friendly servers, this lovely restaurant prepares traditional offerings of chicken, beef, seafood and vegetarian fare. A delicious meal might include a large helping of cashew chicken and shrimp with fried rice, an egg roll and dark, crispy walnuts with a wonderful sugary taste. Shopping opportunities are nearby. **Features:** full bar. **Address:** 2407 Westheimer Rd 77098 **Location:** Between Kirby Dr and Shepherd Rd. L D

SHIVA INDIAN RESTAURANT 713/523-4753 (96)

Regional Indian. Casual Dining. $11-$16 **AAA Inspector Notes:** Catering to nearby Rice University, the small, quiet restaurant sets up afternoon buffets with ample selections of food. The twin metal cups on the tables are a traditional symbol of welcome and good fortune from the homeland. A favorite is the sharp yogurt dressing for the traditional cucumber salad. The dining room is washed in pink and a traditional tandoori oven is in view where fresh hot naan is made. Loads of vegetarian dishes are offered. **Features:** beer & wine. **Reservations:** suggested. **Address:** 2514 Times Blvd 77005 **Location:** Off Kirby Dr, just n of University Blvd. L D

SMITH & WOLLENSKY 713/621-7555 (50)

Steak. Fine Dining. $15-$50 **AAA Inspector Notes:** Patrons savor the flavors of New Orleans at the elegant, well-known steakhouse. A tempting menu awaits, as does the club-like atmosphere, which incorporates rich, dark woods and soft lighting. Service is professional and capable. **Features:** full bar, Sunday brunch. **Address:** 4007 Westheimer Rd 77027 **Location:** Just w of Weslayan St; at Highland Village. **Parking:** on-site and valet. L D LATE

SOMA SUSHI 713/861-2726 (19)

Japanese. Fine Dining. $5-$25 **AAA Inspector Notes:** If you love sushi and you are in Houston this is a must-stop for you. Creative and exotic combinations like the foie gras on yellowtail and the madai are exceptional, and the octopus is always a very good choice. But it is not just about sushi here, as the hot dishes such as the handmade pork buns are excellent. The servers at SOMA are quite knowledgeable, and the décor is contemporary and striking. **Features:** full bar. **Address:** 4820 Washington Ave 77007 **Location:** I-10 exit 765B, 0.3 mi s. L D CALL &M

**(See map & index p. 316.)**

### SOUTHWELL'S HAMBURGER GRILL    713/464-5268   16

Burgers. Quick Serve. $6-$10 **AAA Inspector Notes:** Locals of all ages love this no-frills burger joint, especially on weekends. The menu has a narrow focus on burgers and sandwiches, but the highlight is the freshly cut fries. This place will make burgers to order for those who can't find what they want on the menu. This Houston favorite occupies a somewhat-hidden location in the back of a large strip mall. **Address:** 9410 Gaylord St 77024 **Location:** I-10 exit 758B (Blalock Rd/Campbell Rd) eastbound; exit 758B (Echo Ln) westbound, just n, then just w.   L   D

### SOUTHWELL'S HAMBURGER GRILL    713/664-4959   101

Burgers. Quick Serve. $4-$7 **AAA Inspector Notes:** The menu at this small Houston chain in pretty limited, although there are a few surprises. In addition to the rather ordinary but delicious burgers, including one with jalapeños and another with avocado, there is a chicken sandwich and a very good BLT on Texas toast. The hand-cut french fries are definitely worth adding to any meal. The atmosphere here is simple and family friendly. **Address:** 2252 W Holcombe Blvd 77030 **Location:** I-610 exit 2 (S Main St), 2.4 mi n, then 0.5 mi w.   L   D

### SPANISH FLOWERS MEXICAN RESTAURANT
          713/869-1706   7

Mexican. Family Dining. $6-$16 **AAA Inspector Notes:** The casual family restaurant with an outdoor patio satisfies guests with choices such as traditional fajitas and carnitas tejanas with rice, beans and a small salad. Ice-cold Mexican aguas frescas, made from tamarind and rice-based horchata, go well with any menu item, and complimentary seasonal fruit is served after each meal. Flan and tres leches cake are delicious. On weekday evenings, a Latin trio enhances the atmosphere. **Features:** full bar, patio dining. **Address:** 4701 N Main St 77009 **Location:** Corner of Main St and Airline Dr.   B   L   D   24

### SPARROW BAR & COOKSHOP    713/524-6922   60

American. Casual Dining. $15-$30 **AAA Inspector Notes:** This is the restaurant of renowned chef Monica Pope, formerly of Boulevard Bistro. Organic Texas-grown ingredients flavor an ever-changing selection of Mediterranean-accented American dishes. The local themes continue to the interesting wine and cocktail list. Outdoor tables are offered. Guests also may dine in the casual and bustling dining room, which can be loud at times. A farmers market opens at the restaurant on Saturdays. **Features:** full bar. **Reservations:** suggested. **Address:** 3701 Travis St 77002 **Location:** Just n of Alabama St. **Parking:** valet only.   L   D

### STAR PIZZA    713/523-0800   76

Pizza. Casual Dining. $7-$20 **AAA Inspector Notes:** Near the arts district, this eatery offers outside dining on a spacious wraparound patio and a fun, whimsical interior. Service here is casual; the waitstaff can be quirky but always friendly. Pizza is sold by the pie or the slice and even buffet-style at lunch. Other menu selections include pasta dishes, sandwiches and salads. **Features:** beer & wine. **Address:** 2111 Norfolk St 77098 **Location:** US 59 (Southwest Frwy) S; between Shepherd and Greenbriar drs.   L   D

### SULLIVAN'S STEAKHOUSE    713/961-0333   51

Steak. Fine Dining. $20-$65 **AAA Inspector Notes:** Named for John L. Sullivan, heavyweight champion of the world in the 1880s, the upscale steakhouse prepares a wide selection of steaks, chops and seafood. Decorated with black-and-white photographs of Sullivan, Jack Dempsey and other boxing legends. **Features:** full bar. **Address:** 4608 Westheimer Rd 77027 **Location:** I-610 exit 8C (Westheimer Rd) northbound; exit 9A (San Felipe Rd/Westheimer Rd) southbound, just e. **Parking:** valet only.   L   D   LATE  

### TACO MILAGRO    713/522-1999   42

Mexican. Quick Serve. $7-$14 **AAA Inspector Notes:** Those without much time but who won't settle for drive-through food can satisfy a Mexican craving here. Delicious and sophisticated food is served fast in the restaurant, which includes a tequila bar, colorful dining room and large outdoor patio. Among menu items are tamales, enchiladas, chiles rellenos, burritos and tacos. Guests can serve themselves chips from the salsa and taco condiment bar. Musicians perform Thursday through Saturday nights. **Features:** full bar, happy hour. **Address:** 2555 Kirby Dr 77019 **Location:** US 59 (Southwest Frwy) exit Kirby Dr, 0.7 mi n.   L   D

### TAQUERIAS ARANDAS    713/910-2905   108

Mexican. Casual Dining. $8-$13 **AAA Inspector Notes:** One of several city locations, the taqueria prepares large portions of delicious food. Among standards are tacos, fajitas, burritos and tostadas, as well as many seafood choices. Guests also have the opportunity to try a real Mexican breakfast. The fare is not Tex-Mex but instead authentic Mexican, as evidenced by the number of Spanish speakers here. Spanish is helpful but not necessary. **Features:** beer only. **Address:** 10403-A S Gulf Frwy 77034 **Location:** I-45 exit 35 (Edgebrook Dr/Clearwood St); on northbound frontage road.
B   L   D   LATE  

### TE' HOUSE OF TEA    713/522-8868   37

Coffee/Tea. Casual Dining. $5-$9 **AAA Inspector Notes:** In a quiet residential area, the tea house has a peaceful interior with clean modern lines and earthy colors. Organic and fair-trade teas are among the many options that pair with pastries and some savory items, including panini sandwiches and crepes. Wi-Fi service is offered. There are regular theme nights each week, including open-mic night (Monday) foreign film night (Wednesday), swing dance (Saturday) and the very popular tango night (Friday). **Address:** 1927 Fairview St 77019 **Location:** US 59 (Southwest Frwy) exit Shepherd Dr, 1 mi n to Fairview St, then 0.3 mi e.   L   D

### TEPPAY JAPANESE RESTAURANT    713/789-4506   65

Japanese. Casual Dining. $6-$26 **AAA Inspector Notes:** This is not the place to find fancy and complex sushi rolls and trendy music. The small, traditional, family-run Japanese sushi bar specializes in presenting the freshest, highest quality fish to be found in Houston. They offer a moderate selection of simply presented sushi and usually a daily special. Some other Japanese items are offered, including noodles and teriyaki. A favorite among sushi-loving locals and visiting Japanese businessmen, the atmosphere is quaint and friendly but not well suited to children. **Features:** beer & wine. **Address:** 6516 Westheimer Rd, Suite A-2 77057 **Location:** At Voss Rd.   D

### THAI GOURMET    713/780-7955   81

Thai. Casual Dining. $9-$18 **AAA Inspector Notes:** In a strip center in west Houston, the small restaurant with a very friendly staff prepares a complete selection of dishes ranging from noodles and rice to beef, seafood, chicken and vegetables. Diners can order it spicy or a little milder, depending on their tastes. Dishes reflect influences from India, China and Java. Nearly 90 menu items are available. The wall features a large chalk mural that seems to be a work in progress. **Features:** beer & wine. **Address:** 6324 Richmond Ave 77057 **Location:** 0.7 mi w of Fountain View Dr; between Unity and Greenridge drs.   D

### TILA'S RESTAURANTE & BAR    713/522-7654   24

Mexican. Casual Dining. $11-$29 **AAA Inspector Notes:** The restaurant prides itself on serving authentic Mexico City cuisine, something that is not often seen in Tex-Mex country. Patio seating is available. **Features:** full bar. **Address:** 1111 S Shepherd Dr 77019 **Location:** I-10 exit 765B (Shepherd Dr), 1.5 mi s. **Parking:** on-site and valet.   L   D

### TONY'S    713/622-6778   79

Continental. Fine Dining. $19-$95 **AAA Inspector Notes:** This is regarded among the finest restaurants in the city, and for good reason. Although only mildly innovative, the food is expertly prepared and artfully presented. The refined menu reflects a blend of Italian classics, progressive American and traditional European flavors. The full dinner menu is served all day and includes items such as roasted sea bass amatriciana and stuffed truffled fillet of beef; a selection of lighter salads, pastas and a three-course business lunch also are offered. **Features:** full bar. **Reservations:** suggested. Semiformal attire. **Address:** 3755 Richmond Ave 77046 **Location:** I-610 exit US 59 (Southwest Frwy) southbound, just n to Richmond Ave, then 0.5 mi w; exit Weslayan St northbound, just n to Richmond Ave, then just e. **Parking:** valet only.   L   D   LATE   CALL   M

### TONY'S MEXICAN RESTAURANT & CANTINA
          713/862-6516   4

Tex-Mex. Casual Dining. $7-$17 **AAA Inspector Notes:** The simply made food targets any craving. From chiles rellenos to crispy tacos to enchilada plates, the selections are predictable but the choices seemingly endless. Patio dining is also available. This popular neighborhood restaurant is always packed, possibly because it is noted as having some of the best margaritas in Houston. **Features:** full bar. **Address:** 2222 Ella Blvd 77008 **Location:** I-610 exit 14 (Ella Blvd), 0.4 mi s. **Parking:** on-site and valet.
L   D

(See map & index p. 316.)

### TRULUCK'S
713/783-7270 58

Steak. Fine Dining. $12-$45 **AAA Inspector Notes:** The chef's daily creations include jumbo fresh Florida stone crab claws, live Maine lobster, Australian cold water lobster tail, sesame-crusted ahi tuna, miso-glazed organic totem black cod, oysters Rockefeller, sautéed super-lump crab cake, juicy and flavorful Niman Ranch aged beef and a variety of delicious steamed sides including their signature Parmesan mashed potatoes. **Features:** full bar. **Address:** 5350 Westheimer Rd 77057 **Location:** I-610 exit 9A (San Felipe Rd/Westheimer Rd) southbound; exit 8C (Westheimer Rd) northbound, 0.5 mi w. **Parking:** on-site and valet. [L] [D]

### VALENTINO
713/850-9200 52

Italian Fine Dining $16-$36

**AAA Inspector Notes:** This upscale and stylish dining room offers diners options of various tasting menus as well as à la carte choices. The modern Italian cuisine features selections of items such as hickory-smoked quails with warm asparagus salad and fig-grape-must dressing; three-color dumplings with rabbit sausage and mushroom cream; and black-truffle-crusted tuna medallions with fava beans and saffron sauce. The adjacent VinBar offers a lively scene and a lighter menu. **Features:** full bar. **Reservations:** suggested. **Address:** 2525A West Loop S 77027 **Location:** I-610 exit 9A (San Felipe Rd/Westheimer Rd) southbound; exit 8C (Westheimer Rd) northbound; in Hotel Derek. **Parking:** valet only. [B] [L] [D] [LATE] CALL [&][M]

### VIETOPIA
713/664-7303 87

Vietnamese. Casual Dining. $9-$19 **AAA Inspector Notes:** Many Asian cuisines are represented on the diverse menu, which includes some vegetarian dishes. The menu tries to cover a bit too much ground, so it's best to keep it simple when ordering. The lunch plates are a good value. Wood floors and high ceilings lend some style to this comfortable spot, which is conveniently located near shopping. **Features:** full bar. **Address:** 5176 Buffalo Speedway 77005 **Location:** US 59 (Southwest Frwy) exit Buffalo Speedway, just e. [L] [D]

### WILLIE G'S
713/840-7190 29

Seafood. Fine Dining. $10-$43 **AAA Inspector Notes:** Dark warm woods and cool art lend casual sophistication to this long-established Houston landmark, a great setting for impressing a business client or enjoying an intimate dinner. A touch of New Orleans infuses preparations of crab, shrimp, oysters and other fresh seafood, including gumbo, bisques, crawfish, Gulf red snapper prepared four ways. Grilled meats also pick up a bayou flavor. Smartly attired servers are knowledgeable, professional and speedy. **Features:** full bar, patio dining, Sunday brunch. **Address:** 1605 Post Oak Blvd 77056 **Location:** I-610 exit Post Oak Blvd, just w to San Felipe Rd. **Parking:** on-site and valet. [L] [D]

### YIA YIA MARY'S
713/840-8665 32

Greek. Casual Dining. $9-$27 **AAA Inspector Notes:** Known for its tremendously popular Mexican, barbecue and steak house restaurants, the Pappas family now gives the city a Greek restaurant to love. Popular and loud just like many of its other spots, this place presents a menu of traditional souvlaki, moussaka, dolmades and gyros. Large murals depicting Greek life and Greek music add to the festivity, and a location near the Galleria makes this a prime refueling spot for shoppers. Although the district is upscale, the restaurant is casual. **Features:** full bar. **Address:** 4747 San Felipe Rd 77056 **Location:** I-610 exit 9 northbound; exit 9A southbound; on southbound frontage road. [L] [D]

### ZELKO BISTRO
713/880-8691 9

American. Casual Dining. $10-$22 **AAA Inspector Notes:** The chef makes use of local ingredients and brings comfort food to the next level without over complicating it. The quality is outstanding. Entrées such as the captain's fried chicken and the fish tacos have garnered praise, but the best item tasted was the market-fresh fish of the day, which in this case was a pan-seared grouper simply presented with pineapple-tomato compote, white asparagus and an arugula salad. Desserts are high-quality renditions of classics like lemon icebox pie. **Features:** beer & wine, patio dining, Sunday brunch. **Address:** 705 E 11th St 77008 **Location:** 1 mi n of I-10 on Studewood St, just w; in Houston Heights. **Parking:** on-site and street. [L] [D] [🐾]

## HOUSTON (F-10)
- Restaurants p. 365
- Hotels & Restaurants map & index p. 324

### BEST WESTERN PLUS NORTH HOUSTON INN & SUITES
(281)873-7575 10

Hotel $76-$210

**AAA Benefit:** Members save 10% or more with Best Western!

**Address:** 14753 North Frwy 77090 **Location:** I-45 exit 63 (Airtex Dr); on southbound frontage road. **Facility:** 50 units. 3 stories, interior corridors. **Pool(s):** outdoor. **Activities:** exercise room. **Guest Services:** valet and coin laundry. **Featured Amenity:** full hot breakfast.

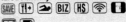

### BEST WESTERN PLUS SAM HOUSTON INN & SUITES
(281)970-7777 36

Hotel $90-$120

**AAA Benefit:** Members save 10% or more with Best Western!

**Address:** 8049 N Sam Houston Pkwy W 77064 **Location:** Sam Houston Pkwy (Beltway 8) exit Gessner Rd. **Facility:** 52 units. 3 stories, interior corridors. **Pool(s):** outdoor. **Activities:** exercise room. **Guest Services:** valet and coin laundry. **Featured Amenity:** full hot breakfast.

### BEST WESTERN PLUS WESTCHASE MINI-SUITES
(713)782-1515 73

Hotel $89-$139

**AAA Benefit:** Members save 10% or more with Best Western!

**Address:** 2950 W Sam Houston Pkwy S 77042 **Location:** Just w of Sam Houston Pkwy (Beltway 8) and Westheimer Rd; on southbound frontage road. **Facility:** 61 units. 2 stories (no elevator), interior corridors. **Pool(s):** outdoor. **Activities:** hot tub, exercise room. **Guest Services:** valet and coin laundry. **Featured Amenity:** full hot breakfast.

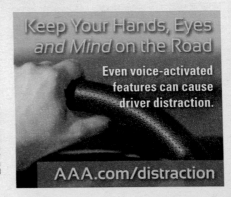

(See map & index p. 324.)

---

**BEST WESTERN WINDSOR SUITES**
(281)807-4007  **41**

Motel
$100-$130

**AAA Benefit:**
Members save 10% or more with
Best Western!

**Address:** 13371 FM 1960 W 77065
**Location:** Just s of US 290. **Facility:**
57 units. 2 stories (no elevator), exterior corridors. **Amenities:** safes.
**Pool(s):** outdoor. **Activities:** exercise
room. **Guest Services:** coin laundry.

Best Western

**Free full hot breakfast, WIFI,
pool, laundry. All rooms
w/microfridge, 42" LCD TV
w/HBO. Dining nearby**

---

**CANDLEWOOD SUITES AT CITYCENTRE - ENERGY
CORRIDOR**    (713)464-2677  **62**

▼▼ **Extended Stay Hotel** $99-$120 **Address:** 10503 Town &
Country Way 77024 **Location:** I-10 exit 755 eastbound, 1.2 mi on
frontage road to Attingham Dr, just s to Town and Country Way, then
just w; exit 756A westbound, U-turn under I-10, just e to Attingham Dr,
just s to Town and Country Way, then just w. **Facility:** 122 efficiencies. 3 stories, interior corridors. **Terms:** cancellation fee imposed.
**Activities:** exercise room. **Guest Services:** complimentary and valet
laundry.

---

**CANDLEWOOD SUITES-WESTCHASE**    713/780-7881  **76**

▼▼ **Extended Stay Hotel.** Rates not provided. **Address:**
4033 W Sam Houston Pkwy S 77042 **Location:** Sam Houston Pkwy
(Beltway 8) exit Westpark Dr; southeast corner of Westpark Dr and
Sam Houston Pkwy (Beltway 8); on northbound frontage road. **Facility:** 123 efficiencies. 3 stories, interior corridors. **Activities:** exercise room. **Guest Services:** complimentary and valet laundry.

---

**CANDLEWOOD SUITES WILLOWBROOK**    832/237-7300  **17**

▼▼ **Extended Stay Hotel.** Rates not provided. **Address:**
8719 FM 1960 W 77070 **Location:** Corner of Mills Rd and FM 1960
W; just w of Tomball Pkwy. **Facility:** 83 efficiencies. 3 stories, interior
corridors. **Pool(s):** outdoor. **Activities:** exercise room. **Guest Services:** valet and coin laundry.

---

**COMFORT INN & SUITES**    (281)444-5800  **4**

Hotel
$110-$140

**Address:** 3555 FM 1960 W 77068 **Location:** I-45 exit 66 (FM 1960), 3.5 mi w.
Across from Walmart. **Facility:** 56 units.
3 stories, interior corridors. **Pool(s):** outdoor. **Activities:** hot tub, exercise room.
**Guest Services:** valet and coin laundry.
**Featured Amenity:** full hot breakfast.

---

**COMFORT INN HWY 290/NW**    (713)690-1493  **44**

Hotel
S80-$120

**Address:** 7887 W Tidwell Rd 77040 **Location:** US 290 W exit W Tidwell Rd,
just w. **Facility:** 115 units. 5 stories, interior corridors. **Pool(s):** outdoor. **Activities:** exercise room. **Guest Services:**
valet and coin laundry. **Featured Amenity:** full hot breakfast.

---

**COMFORT SUITES-GREENSPOINT/IAH WEST**
(281)219-0400  **32**

▼▼ Hotel $69-$149 **Address:** 1350 N Sam Houston Pkwy E
77032 **Location:** Sam Houston Pkwy (Beltway 8) exit Aldine Westfield Rd eastbound, 0.8 mi e on service road; exit Hardy Toll Rd westbound, U-turn, then 1 mi e on service road. **Facility:** 72 units, some
efficiencies. 3 stories, interior corridors. **Pool(s):** outdoor. **Activities:**
hot tub, exercise room. **Guest Services:** valet and coin laundry, area
transportation.

---

**COMFORT SUITES INTERCONTINENTAL PLAZA**
(281)442-0600  **23**

▼▼ Hotel $80-$130 **Address:** 15555 John F Kennedy Blvd
77032 **Location:** Sam Houston Pkwy (Beltway 8) exit John F Kennedy Blvd, just n. **Facility:** 57 units, some kitchens. 3 stories, interior
corridors. **Pool(s):** outdoor. **Activities:** limited exercise equipment.
**Guest Services:** valet and coin laundry.

---

**COUNTRY INN & SUITES BY CARLSON, HOUSTON
INTERCONTINENTAL AP-S**    (281)987-2400  **24**

▼▼ Hotel $89-$199 **Address:** 15555B John F Kennedy Blvd
77032 **Location:** Sam Houston Pkwy (Beltway 8) exit John F Kennedy Blvd/Vickery Dr, just n. **Facility:** 57 units. 4 stories, interior corridors. **Pool(s):** outdoor. **Activities:** exercise room. **Guest Services:**
valet and coin laundry.

---

**COURTYARD BY MARRIOTT HOUSTON WEST**
(281)496-9090  **56**

▼▼▼ Hotel $99-$220 **Address:**
12401 Katy Frwy (I-10) 77079 **Location:**
I-10 exit 753B (Dairy Ashford), just s. **Facility:** 176 units. 2-3 stories, interior corridors. **Pool(s):** heated outdoor.

**AAA Benefit:**
Members save 5%
or more!

**Activities:** exercise room. **Guest Services:** valet and coin laundry,
area transportation.

---

**COURTYARD BY MARRIOTT HOUSTON WESTCHASE**
(713)784-3003  **71**

▼▼▼ Hotel $242-$269 **Address:**
9975 Westheimer Rd 77042 **Location:**
Sam Houston Pkwy (Beltway 8) exit
Westheimer Rd, then just e. **Facility:**
153 units. 3 stories, interior corridors.

**AAA Benefit:**
Members save 5%
or more!

**Pool(s):** outdoor. **Activities:** hot tub, exercise room. **Guest Services:** valet and coin laundry, area transportation.

---

# Plan complete trip routings with the TripTik®

## Travel Planner on AAA.com/CAA.ca

(See map & index p. 324.)

## CROSSLAND ECONOMY STUDIOS HOUSTON-NORTHWEST
(713)934-7600 **43**

Extended Stay Hotel $52-$95 **Address:** 5959 Guhn Rd 77040 **Location:** US 290 exit Fairbanks/N Houston Rd, 1 mi e on eastbound frontage road, then just s. **Facility:** 145 efficiencies. 3 stories, exterior corridors. **Terms:** cancellation fee imposed. **Guest Services:** coin laundry.

## DOUBLETREE BY HILTON HOTEL HOUSTON INTERCONTINENTAL AIRPORT
(281)848-4000 **19**

Hotel
$99-$275

**DOUBLETREE** BY HILTON

**AAA Benefit:** Members save 5% or more!

**Address:** 15747 John F Kennedy Blvd 77032 **Location:** Just n of Sam Houston Pkwy (Beltway 8). **Facility:** 313 units. 7 stories, interior corridors. **Terms:** 1-7 night minimum stay, cancellation fee imposed. **Amenities:** video games. **Dining:** 2 restaurants. **Pool(s):** outdoor. **Activities:** hot tub, exercise room. **Guest Services:** valet and coin laundry, area transportation.

*(See ad this page.)*

## DRURY INN & SUITES-HOUSTON WEST
(281)558-7007 **50**

Hotel $80-$229 **Address:** 1000 N Hwy 6 77079 **Location:** I-10 exit 751 (Addicks Rd/SR 6), just n. **Facility:** 119 units. 5 stories, interior corridors. **Terms:** cancellation fee imposed. **Pool(s):** heated indoor. **Activities:** hot tub, exercise room. **Guest Services:** valet and coin laundry.

## ELEMENT BY WESTIN HOUSTON VINTAGE PARK
(281)379-7300  **5**

Hotel
$99-$299

element by westin

**AAA Benefit:** Experience Element, get up to 20% off + Starwood Preferred Guest® bonuses!

**Address:** 14555 Vintage Preserve Pkwy 77070 **Location:** SR 249 exit Louetta Rd, just e to Chasewood Park, then just s. **Facility:** 123 units, some efficiencies. 4 stories, interior corridors. *Bath:* shower only. **Amenities:** safes. **Pool(s):** heated outdoor. **Activities:** bicycles, exercise room. **Guest Services:** valet and coin laundry, area transportation. **Featured Amenity:** full hot breakfast.

## EMBASSY SUITES HOUSTON ENERGY CORRIDOR
(281)531-7300 **49**

Hotel
$239-$259

**EMBASSY SUITES** HOTELS

**AAA Benefit:** Members save 5% or more!

**Address:** 11730 Katy Frwy 77079 **Location:** I-10 exit Kirkwood Dr, just w; on westbound access road. **Facility:** 216 units. 14 stories, interior corridors. **Parking:** on-site and valet. **Terms:** 1-7 night minimum stay, cancellation fee imposed. **Pool(s):** heated indoor. **Activities:** hot tub, exercise room. **Guest Services:** valet and coin laundry, area transportation.

*(See ad p. 359.)*

AAA/CAA travel information:
Available online, on the go and in print!

(See map & index p. 324.)

## FAIRFIELD INN & SUITES BY MARRIOTT HOUSTON I-10 WEST/ENERGY CORRIDOR
(281)646-0056 **55**

Hotel $81-$144 **Address:** 15111 Katy Frwy 77094 **Location:** I-10 exit 748 (Barker Cypress Rd) eastbound; exit 751 (US 6) westbound, just s to Grigsby Rd, then 0.3 mi w. **Facility:** 80 units. 3 stories, interior corridors. **Pool(s):** heated indoor. **Activities:** hot tub, exercise room. **Guest Services:** valet and coin laundry.

**AAA Benefit:** Members save 5% or more!

CALL ⑤M ⌷ BIZ 🛜 ✕ 💻 / SOME UNITS 🛏 🖼

## FAIRFIELD INN & SUITES BY MARRIOTT - I-45
(281)695-8989 **2**

Hotel $135-$148 **Address:** 17617 North Frwy (I-45) 77090 **Location:** I-45 exit 66 (FM 1960) southbound; exit 66A northbound, just w on FM 1960, just n on Westfield Pl, then just e on Wagon Point Dr. **Facility:** 62 units. 3 stories, interior corridors. **Pool(s):** heated indoor. **Activities:** hot tub, exercise room. **Guest Services:** valet and coin laundry.

**AAA Benefit:** Members save 5% or more!

🍴➕ CALL ⑤M ⌷ BIZ 🛜 ✕ 💻 / SOME UNITS 🛏 🖼

## FAIRFIELD INN BY MARRIOTT-WESTCHASE
(713)334-2400 **67**

Hotel $90-$150 **Address:** 2400 W Sam Houston Pkwy S 77042 **Location:** Sam Houston Pkwy (Beltway 8) exit Westheimer Rd; on southbound frontage road; nw of jct Westheimer Rd. **Facility:** 82 units. 3 stories, interior corridors. **Pool(s):** indoor. **Activities:** hot tub. **Guest Services:** valet laundry.

**AAA Benefit:** Members save 5% or more!

CALL ⑤M ⌷ BIZ 🛜 ✕ 💻 / SOME UNITS 🛏 🖼

---

## Learn about inspections and Diamond Ratings at AAA.com/Diamonds

---

## FOUR POINTS BY SHERATON HOUSTON WEST
(281)501-4600 **60**

Hotel $149-$199

FOUR POINTS BY SHERATON

**AAA Benefit:** Members get up to 20% off, plus Starwood Preferred Guest® bonuses!

**Address:** 10655 Katy Frwy 77024 **Location:** I-10 exit 756A westbound; exit 755 eastbound; southeast corner of I-10 and Sam Houston Pkwy (Beltway 8). **Facility:** 171 units. 2-15 stories, interior/exterior corridors. **Terms:** cancellation fee imposed. **Amenities:** safes. **Pool(s):** heated outdoor. **Activities:** exercise room. **Guest Services:** valet and coin laundry, area transportation. **Featured Amenity:** full hot breakfast.

SAVE 🍴 🛎 🍸 ⌷ BIZ HS 🛜 ✕ 💻 / SOME UNITS 🛏 🖼

## HAMPTON INN & SUITES AT WESTCHASE
(281)530-7776 **78**

Hotel $139-$174 **Address:** 6440 W Sam Houston Pkwy S 77072 **Location:** Sam Houston Pkwy (Beltway 8) exit Bellaire Blvd, just w to Rogerdale Rd, then just n. **Facility:** 82 units. 3 stories, interior corridors. **Terms:** 1-7 night minimum stay, cancellation fee imposed. **Amenities:** video games. Some: safes. **Pool(s):** outdoor. **Activities:** hot tub, exercise room. **Guest Services:** valet and coin laundry.

**AAA Benefit:** Members save up to 10%!

CALL ⑤M ⌷ BIZ HS 🛜 ✕ 🎦 🖼 💻

## HAMPTON INN & SUITES CYPRESS STATION
281/866-0404 **3**

Hotel. Rates not provided. **Address:** 150 Wagon Point Dr 77090 **Location:** I-45 exit 66 (FM 1960) southbound; on frontage road; exit 66A northbound, just w on FM 1960, just n on Westfield Pl, then just e. **Facility:** 74 units, some efficiencies. 3 stories, interior corridors. **Pool(s):** heated indoor. **Activities:** hot tub, exercise room. **Guest Services:** valet and coin laundry.

**AAA Benefit:** Members save up to 10%!

🍴➕ CALL ⑤M ⌷ BIZ HS 🛜 ✕ 🖼 💻

▼ See AAA listing p. 358 ▼

(See map & index p. 324.)

## HAMPTON INN BY HILTON-WILLOWBROOK
(281)955-2400 **15**

▼▼▼ **Hotel** $119-$199 **Address:** 7645 W FM 1960 77070 **Location:** Just e of jct SR 249 and FM 1960. Located at Willowbrook Mall. **Facility:** 74 units. 3 stories, interior corridors. **Terms:** 1-7 night minimum stay, cancellation fee imposed. **Pool(s):** heated indoor. **Activities:** hot tub, exercise room. **Guest Services:** valet laundry.

**AAA Benefit:** Members save up to 10%!

## HAMPTON INN-HOUSTON NORTHWEST    (281)890-2299 **39**

▼▼▼ **Hotel** $114-$189 **Address:** 20035 Northwest Frwy 77065 **Location:** W of jct US 290 and FM 1960. **Facility:** 62 units. 3 stories, interior corridors. **Terms:** 1-7 night minimum stay, cancellation fee imposed. **Amenities:** video games. **Pool(s):** outdoor. **Guest Services:** valet and coin laundry.

**AAA Benefit:** Members save up to 10%!

## HAMPTON INN I-10 WEST/ENERGY CORRIDOR HOUSTON
(713)935-0022 **58**

▼▼▼ **Hotel** $89-$209 **Address:** 11333 Katy Frwy 77079 **Location:** I-10 exit 754 (Kirkwood Rd), 0.5 mi e; on eastbound frontage road. **Facility:** 119 units. 4 stories, interior corridors. **Terms:** 1-7 night minimum stay, cancellation fee imposed. **Pool(s):** outdoor. **Activities:** exercise room. **Guest Services:** valet laundry.

**AAA Benefit:** Members save up to 10%!

## HILTON GARDEN INN ENERGY CORRIDOR
(281)531-0220 **54**

▼▼▼ Hotel $79-$359

**AAA Benefit:** Members save up to 10%!

**Address:** 12245 Katy Frwy 77079 **Location:** I-10 exit 753B (Dairy Ashford); on eastbound frontage road. **Facility:** 190 units. 7 stories, interior corridors. **Terms:** 1-7 night minimum stay, cancellation fee imposed. **Pool(s):** heated outdoor. **Activities:** hot tub, exercise room. **Guest Services:** valet and coin laundry, area transportation.

## HILTON GARDEN INN HOUSTON/BUSH AIRPORT
(281)449-4148 **27**

▼▼▼ **Hotel** $99-$239 **Address:** 15400 John F Kennedy Blvd 77032 **Location:** Just n of jct Sam Houston Pkwy (Beltway 8). **Facility:** 182 units. 6 stories, interior corridors. **Terms:** 1-7 night minimum stay, cancellation fee imposed. **Pool(s):** heated outdoor. **Activities:** hot tub, exercise room. **Guest Services:** valet and coin laundry.

**AAA Benefit:** Members save up to 10%!

## HILTON GARDEN INN HOUSTON NORTHWEST
(832)912-1000 **14**

▼▼▼ **Hotel** $89-$289 **Address:** 7979 Willow Chase Blvd 77070 **Location:** On SR 249 exit FM 1960; on northbound frontage road. **Facility:** 171 units. 6 stories, interior corridors. **Terms:** check-in 4 pm, 1-7 night minimum stay, cancellation fee imposed. **Pool(s):** outdoor. **Activities:** hot tub, exercise room. **Guest Services:** valet and coin laundry, area transportation.

**AAA Benefit:** Members save up to 10%!

## HILTON GARDEN INN HOUSTON WESTBELT
(713)270-6100 **79**

▼▼▼ **Hotel** $89-$299 **Address:** 6855 W Sam Houston Pkwy S 77072 **Location:** Sam Houston Pkwy (Beltway 8) exit Bellaire Blvd southbound, just e to entrance; exit Beechnut northbound; on northbound frontage road. **Facility:** 120 units. 6 stories, interior corridors. **Terms:** 1-7 night minimum stay, cancellation fee imposed. **Amenities:** *Some:* video games. **Pool(s):** heated outdoor. **Activities:** hot tub, exercise room. **Guest Services:** valet and coin laundry, area transportation.

**AAA Benefit:** Members save up to 10%!

## HILTON HOUSTON NORTH
(281)875-2222 **20**

▼▼▼ **Hotel** $189-$209 **Address:** 12400 Greenspoint Dr 77060 **Location:** I-45 exit 61 (Greens Rd), 0.5 mi e. **Facility:** 480 units. 15 stories, interior corridors. **Terms:** 1-7 night minimum stay, cancellation fee imposed. **Pool(s):** outdoor. **Activities:** exercise room. **Guest Services:** valet laundry.

**AAA Benefit:** Members save 5% or more!

## HILTON HOUSTON WESTCHASE
(713)974-1000 **70**

▼▼▼ **Hotel** $109-$299 **Address:** 9999 Westheimer Rd 77042 **Location:** Sam Houston Pkwy (Beltway 8) exit Westheimer Rd/Briar Forest Dr northbound; exit Westheimer Rd/Richmond Ave southbound, 0.5 mi e. **Facility:** 297 units. 13 stories, interior corridors. **Terms:** 1-7 night minimum stay, cancellation fee imposed. **Amenities:** safes. **Dining:** Rio Ranch, see separate listing. **Pool(s):** outdoor. **Activities:** sauna, hot tub, exercise room. **Guest Services:** valet laundry, area transportation.

**AAA Benefit:** Members save 5% or more!

## HOLIDAY INN EXPRESS & SUITES HOUSTON ENERGY CORRIDOR-WEST OAKS
281)497-9888 **66**

▼▼▼ **Hotel.** Rates not provided. **Address:** 2205 Barker Oaks Dr 77077 **Location:** I-10 exit 751 (Addicks Rd/SR 6), 2.9 mi s. **Facility:** 79 units. 3 stories, interior corridors. **Pool(s):** outdoor. **Activities:** exercise room. **Guest Services:** valet and coin laundry.

## HOLIDAY INN EXPRESS & SUITES HOUSTON NORTH INTERCONTINENTAL
281/876-7378 **9**

▼▼▼ **Hotel.** Rates not provided. **Address:** 125 Airtex Dr 77090 **Location:** I-45 exit 63 (Airtex Dr), just w. **Facility:** 109 units. 3-4 stories, interior corridors. **Amenities:** safes. **Pool(s):** outdoor. **Activities:** hot tub, exercise room. **Guest Services:** valet and coin laundry, area transportation.

(See map & index p. 324.)

### HOLIDAY INN EXPRESS & SUITES-WEST ROAD
713/896-4444  42

▼▼▼▼ **Hotel.** Rates not provided. **Address:** 9120 West Rd 77064 **Location:** Sam Houston Pkwy (Beltway 8) exit West Rd, just e. **Facility:** 87 units. 3 stories, interior corridors. **Pool(s):** outdoor. **Activities:** hot tub, exercise room. **Guest Services:** valet and coin laundry.

CALL 🛗M 🏊 BIZ HS 🛜 ✕ 🔌 📠 🖥

### HOLIDAY INN EXPRESS HOUSTON WILLOWBROOK FM 1960 CHAMPIONS AREA
281/866-0500  6

▼▼▼▼ **Hotel.** Rates not provided. **Address:** 4434 FM 1960 Rd W 77068 **Location:** Just e of jct Veterans Memorial Dr. **Facility:** 70 units. 3 stories, interior corridors. **Pool(s):** exercise room. **Guest Services:** valet and coin laundry, area transportation.

CALL 🛗M 🏊 BIZ HS 🛜 ✕ 🔌 📠 🖥

### HOLIDAY INN EXPRESS NORTHWEST
(832)237-4300  38

Hotel
$85-$169

**Address:** 12915 FM 1960 W 77065 **Location:** US 290 exit FM 1960, just e. **Facility:** 65 units. 3 stories, interior corridors. **Pool(s):** outdoor. **Activities:** hot tub, exercise room. **Guest Services:** valet and coin laundry. **Featured Amenity:** full hot breakfast.

SAVE 🍽 CALL 🛗M 🏊 BIZ HS
🛜 ✕ 🔌 📠 🖥
/ SOME UNITS 🛗

### HOLIDAY INN HOUSTON INTERCONTINENTAL AIRPORT
(281)449-2311  35

Hotel
$79-$219

**Address:** 15222 John F Kennedy Blvd 77032 **Location:** Jct N Sam Houston Pkwy (Beltway 8) E and John F Kennedy Blvd. **Facility:** 415 units. 5 stories, interior corridors. **Terms:** cancellation fee imposed. **Amenities:** video games. **Dining:** Good Eats, see separate listing. **Pool(s):** outdoor. **Activities:** tennis, exercise room. **Guest Services:** valet and coin laundry, area transportation.

SAVE ✈ 🍽 🛗 🏊 BIZ 🛜
✕ 🎦 🖥
/ SOME UNITS 🛗 📠

### HOLIDAY INN HOUSTON-WESTCHASE
(713)532-5400  75

▼▼▼▼ **Hotel** $99-$229 **Address:** 10609 Westpark Dr 77042 **Location:** Sam Houston Pkwy (Beltway 8) exit Westpark Dr, just w. **Facility:** 130 units. 5 stories, interior corridors. **Terms:** 2-3 night minimum stay - seasonal. **Amenities:** safes. **Pool(s):** indoor. **Activities:** exercise room. **Guest Services:** valet and coin laundry, area transportation.

🍽 🛗 🍸 CALL 🛗M 🏊 BIZ HS 🛜 ✕ 🔌
📠 🖥

### HOLIDAY INN HOUSTON WEST ENERGY CORRIDOR
281/679-6900  64

▼▼▼▼ **Hotel.** Rates not provided. **Address:** 1112 Eldridge Pkwy 77077 **Location:** I-10 exit 753A (Eldridge Pkwy), 1.1 mi s. **Facility:** 122 units. 5 stories, interior corridors. **Pool(s):** heated indoor. **Activities:** exercise room. **Guest Services:** valet and coin laundry.

🍽 🛗 🍸 CALL 🛗M 🏊 BIZ HS 🛜 ✕ 🔌
📠 🖥

### HOLIDAY INN NORTHWEST WILLOWBROOK
(281)970-4888  12

▼▼▼▼ **Hotel** $99-$219 **Address:** 18818 Tomball Pkwy 77070 **Location:** SR 249 (Tomball Pkwy) exit Grant Rd/Schroeder Rd, just n on Prestonwood Forrest Dr. **Facility:** 155 units. 3 stories, interior corridors. **Terms:** cancellation fee imposed. **Pool(s):** heated indoor. **Activities:** hot tub, exercise room. **Guest Services:** valet and coin laundry.

🍽 🛗 🍸 CALL 🛗M 🏊 BIZ HS 🛜 ✕ 🖥
/ SOME UNITS 🛗 🔌 📠

### HOMEWOOD SUITES BY HILTON HOUSTON NORTHWEST CY-FAIR
(832)237-2000  37

▼▼▼ **Extended Stay Contemporary Hotel** $129-$200 **Address:** 13110 Wortham Center Dr 77065 **Location:** US 290 exit FM 1960/SR 6, just w on westbound frontage road, then

**AAA Benefit:** Members save up to 10%!

just n. **Facility:** 123 efficiencies, some two bedrooms. 4 stories, interior corridors. **Terms:** 1-7 night minimum stay, cancellation fee imposed. **Amenities:** safes. **Pool(s):** outdoor. **Activities:** hot tub, exercise room. **Guest Services:** valet and coin laundry.

🍽 CALL 🛗M 🏊 BIZ HS 🛜 🔌 📠 🖥

### HOMEWOOD SUITES BY HILTON INTERCONTINENTAL AIRPORT
(281)219-9100  31

▼▼▼ **Extended Stay Hotel** $129-$179 **Address:** 1340 N Sam Houston Pkwy E 77032 **Location:** Sam Houston Pkwy (Beltway 8) exit Aldine Westfield Rd eastbound, 0.8 mi e on

**AAA Benefit:** Members save up to 10%!

frontage road; exit Hardy Toll Rd westbound, U-turn, 1 mi e on frontage road. **Facility:** 64 efficiencies, some two bedrooms. 3 stories, interior corridors. **Terms:** 1-7 night minimum stay, cancellation fee imposed. **Pool(s):** outdoor. **Activities:** hot tub, exercise room. **Guest Services:** valet and coin laundry, area transportation.

✈ CALL 🛗M 🏊 BIZ HS 🛜 🔌 📠 🖥
/ SOME UNITS 🛗

### HOMEWOOD SUITES BY HILTON-WESTCHASE
(713)334-2424  68

▼▼▼ **Extended Stay Hotel** $109-$229 **Address:** 2424 Rogerdale Rd 77042 **Location:** Sam Houston Pkwy (Beltway 8) exit Westheimer Rd, just w to Rogerdale Rd, then just n. **Facility:** 96

**AAA Benefit:** Members save up to 10%!

units, some two bedrooms, efficiencies and kitchens. 3 stories, interior corridors. **Terms:** 1-7 night minimum stay, cancellation fee imposed. **Pool(s):** heated indoor. **Activities:** hot tub, exercise room. **Guest Services:** valet and coin laundry.

CALL 🛗M 🏊 BIZ 🛜 🔌 📠 🖥 / SOME UNITS 🛗

### HOMEWOOD SUITES BY HILTON-WILLOWBROOK
(281)955-5200  13

▼▼▼ **Extended Stay Contemporary Hotel** $139-$219 **Address:** 7655 W FM 1960 77070 **Location:** Just e of jct SR 249 and FM 1960. Located at Willowbrook Mall. **Facility:** 72

**AAA Benefit:** Members save up to 10%!

efficiencies, some two bedrooms. 3 stories, interior corridors. **Terms:** 1-7 night minimum stay, cancellation fee imposed. **Pool(s):** heated indoor. **Activities:** hot tub, exercise room. **Guest Services:** valet and coin laundry.

🍽 CALL 🛗M 🏊 BIZ 🛜 🔌 📠 🖥 / SOME UNITS 🛗

(See map & index p. 324.)

### HOUSTON AIRPORT MARRIOTT AT GEORGE BUSH INTERCONTINENTAL
(281)443-2310 **7**

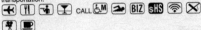

Hotel $152-$279 **Address:** 18700 John F Kennedy Blvd 77032 **Location:** At George Bush Intercontinental Airport. **Facility:** 565 units. 7 stories, interior corridors. **Parking:** on-site and valet. **Dining:** 3 restaurants. **Pool(s):** outdoor. **Activities:** hot tub, exercise room. **Guest Services:** valet and coin laundry, area transportation.

**AAA Benefit:** Members save 5% or more!

### HOUSTON MARRIOTT ENERGY CORRIDOR
(281)829-5525 **59**

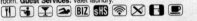

Hotel $95-$247 **Address:** 16011 Katy Frwy 77094 **Location:** I-10 exit 750 (Park Ten Pl); on south frontage road. **Facility:** 206 units. 10 stories, interior corridors. **Amenities:** safes. **Dining:** 2 restaurants. **Pool(s):** heated outdoor. **Activities:** hot tub, exercise room. **Guest Services:** valet laundry.

**AAA Benefit:** Members save 5% or more!

### HOUSTON MARRIOTT NORTH
(281)875-4000 **28**

Hotel $159-$189 **Address:** 255 N Sam Houston Pkwy E 77060 **Location:** Sam Houston Pkwy (Beltway 8) exit Imperial Valley Dr eastbound; exit Greenspoint Dr westbound; on westbound service road. **Facility:** 390 units. 12 stories, interior corridors. **Amenities:** video games. **Pool(s):** outdoor, heated indoor. **Activities:** hot tub, exercise room. **Guest Services:** valet and coin laundry, area transportation.

**AAA Benefit:** Members save 5% or more!

### HYATT HOUSE HOUSTON-WEST/ENERGY CORRIDOR
(281)646-9990 **53**

Extended Stay Hotel $59-$229

**HYATT house**

**AAA Benefit:** Members save 10%!

**Address:** 15405 Katy Frwy (I-10) 77094 **Location:** I-10 exit 751 (SR 6), just s to Grisby Rd, then just w. **Facility:** 116 efficiencies, some two bedrooms. 3 stories, interior corridors. **Terms:** cancellation fee imposed. **Pool(s):** outdoor. **Activities:** hot tub, exercise room. **Guest Services:** valet and coin laundry. **Featured Amenity:** breakfast buffet.

### HYATT NORTH HOUSTON
(281)445-9000 **29**

Hotel $79-$249

**HYATT**

**AAA Benefit:** Members save 10%!

**Address:** 425 N Sam Houston Pkwy E 77060 **Location:** Sam Houston Pkwy (Beltway 8) exit Imperial Valley Dr westbound; exit Hardy Toll Rd eastbound; on westbound frontage road. Located in Greenspoint Business District. **Facility:** 334 units. 8 stories, interior corridors. **Terms:** cancellation fee imposed. **Amenities:** safes. **Pool(s):** outdoor. **Activities:** hot tub, exercise room. **Guest Services:** valet and coin laundry, area transportation.

### HYATT PLACE BUSH HOUSTON INTERCONTINENTAL AIRPORT
(281)820-6060 **26**

Hotel $69-$209

**HYATT PLACE**

**AAA Benefit:** Members save 10%!

**Address:** 300 Ronan Park Pl 77060 **Location:** Sam Houston Pkwy (Beltway 8) exit Imperial Valley Dr westbound, 0.8 mi w on frontage road; exit Hardy Toll Rd eastbound, turn under parkway, 1.2 mi w on west frontage road. **Facility:** 126 units. 6 stories, interior corridors. **Terms:** cancellation fee imposed. **Pool(s):** heated outdoor. **Activities:** exercise room. **Guest Services:** valet laundry, area transportation. **Featured Amenity:** breakfast buffet.

### LA QUINTA INN & SUITES ENERGY CORRIDOR
(281)668-1068 **69**

Hotel $95-$164 **Address:** 2451 Shadow View Ln 77077 **Location:** 2.5 mi w of Sam Houston Pkwy (Beltway 8) on Westheimer Rd, just n. **Facility:** 77 units. 3 stories, interior corridors. **Pool(s):** outdoor. **Activities:** hot tub, exercise room. **Guest Services:** valet and coin laundry.

### LA QUINTA INN & SUITES HOUSTON BUSH INTERCONTINENTAL AIRPORT SOUTH
(281)219-2000 **25**

Hotel $82-$164 **Address:** 15510 John F Kennedy Blvd 77032 **Location:** Sam Houston Pkwy (Beltway 8) exit John F Kennedy Blvd/Vickery Dr, just n. **Facility:** 132 units. 5 stories, interior corridors. **Pool(s):** outdoor. **Activities:** hot tub, exercise room. **Guest Services:** valet and coin laundry, area transportation.

### LA QUINTA INN & SUITES HOUSTON CHANNELVIEW
(281)452-4402 **82**

Hotel $119-$154

**Address:** 5520 E Sam Houston Pkwy N 77015 **Location:** Sam Houston Pkwy exit Woodforest Blvd. **Facility:** 91 units. 4 stories, interior corridors. **Amenities:** safes. **Pool(s):** heated indoor. **Activities:** exercise room. **Guest Services:** valet and coin laundry. **Featured Amenity:** full hot breakfast.

(See map & index p. 324.)

### LA QUINTA INN & SUITES - HOUSTON CLAY ROAD
(713)939-1400   **45**

Hotel $115-$184 **Address:** 4424 Westway Park Blvd 77041 **Location:** Sam Houston Pkwy (Beltway 8) exit Clay Rd, just e. **Facility:** 58 units. 3 stories, interior corridors. **Pool(s):** indoor. **Activities:** hot tub, exercise room. **Guest Services:** valet and coin laundry.

### LA QUINTA INN & SUITES HOUSTON I-45/1960
(281)784-1112   **1**

Hotel $99-$150 **Address:** 415 FM 1960 Rd E 77073 **Location:** I-45 exit 66 (FM 1960), just e. **Facility:** 65 units. 3 stories, interior corridors. **Pool(s):** outdoor. **Activities:** hot tub, exercise room. **Guest Services:** valet and coin laundry.

### LA QUINTA INN & SUITES HOUSTON - NORMANDY
(713)451-0009   **83**

Hotel $95-$144 **Address:** 930 Normandy St 77015 **Location:** I-10 exit 778B, just n. **Facility:** 68 units. 3 stories, interior corridors. **Pool(s):** outdoor. **Activities:** hot tub, exercise room. **Guest Services:** valet and coin laundry.

### LA QUINTA INN & SUITES HOUSTON - WESTCHASE
(281)495-7700   **77**

Hotel $99-$160 **Address:** 10850 Harwin Dr 77072 **Location:** Sam Houston Pkwy (Beltway 8) exit Bellaire Blvd/Harwin Dr northbound; exit Westpark Dr/Harwin Dr southbound. **Facility:** 82 units. 3 stories, interior corridors. **Pool(s):** heated outdoor. **Activities:** hot tub, exercise room. **Guest Services:** valet and coin laundry.

### LA QUINTA INN & SUITES HOUSTON WEST PARK 10
(281)646-9200   **52**

Hotel $72-$150 **Address:** 15225 Katy Frwy 77094 **Location:** I-10 exit 748 (Barker Cypress Rd) eastbound, 2.6 mi on eastbound service road; exit 751 (SR 6) westbound, just s to Grisby Rd, then 0.5 mi w. **Facility:** 117 units. 4 stories, interior corridors. **Pool(s):** outdoor. **Activities:** hot tub, exercise room. **Guest Services:** valet and coin laundry, area transportation.

### LA QUINTA INN & SUITES WILLOWBROOK
(281)897-8868   **11**

Hotel $99-$159 **Address:** 18828 State Hwy 249 (Tomball Pkwy) 77070 **Location:** SR 249 exit Grant Rd/Schroeder Rd; on northbound frontage road. **Facility:** 76 efficiencies. 3 stories, interior corridors. **Pool(s):** outdoor. **Activities:** hot tub, exercise room. **Guest Services:** valet and coin laundry.

### LA QUINTA INN HOUSTON CY-FAIR
(281)469-4018   **40**

Motel $79-$124 **Address:** 13290 FM 1960 W 77065 **Location:** Just w of jct US 290 and FM 1960. **Facility:** 130 units. 3 stories, interior/exterior corridors. **Pool(s):** outdoor. **Guest Services:** valet and coin laundry.

### LA QUINTA INN HOUSTON WILCREST
(713)932-0808   **57**

Motel $72-$107 **Address:** 11113 Katy Frwy 77079 **Location:** I-10 exit 754 (Kirkwood Dr) westbound; exit 755 (Wilcrest Rd) eastbound; on eastbound service road. **Facility:** 172 units. 2 stories (no elevator), exterior corridors. **Pool(s):** outdoor. **Guest Services:** valet and coin laundry.

### MARRIOTT HOUSTON WESTCHASE
(713)978-7400   **72**

Hotel $92-$269

**Marriott** HOTELS & RESORTS

**AAA Benefit:** Members save 5% or more!

**Address:** 2900 Briarpark Dr 77042 **Location:** Just s of Westheimer Rd. **Facility:** 600 units. 10 stories, interior corridors. **Pool(s):** outdoor, heated indoor. **Activities:** hot tub, exercise room. **Guest Services:** valet and coin laundry, boarding pass kiosk, area transportation.

### OMNI HOUSTON HOTEL WESTSIDE
(281)558-8338   **48**

Hotel $109-$379 **Address:** 13210 Katy Frwy 77079 **Location:** I-10 exit 753A (Eldridge St), just n. **Facility:** This architecturally interesting hotel features tropical pools that give the illusion of running from outside and through the large lobby atrium. Koi fish and turtles are stocked in the pools. 400 units. 5 stories, interior corridors. **Parking:** on-site and valet. **Terms:** cancellation fee imposed. **Amenities:** safes. **Pool(s):** heated outdoor. **Activities:** hot tub, exercise room. **Guest Services:** valet laundry, area transportation.

### PARK INN HOUSTON NORTH HOTEL AND CONFERENCE CENTER
(281)931-0101   **34**

Hotel $69-$129 **Address:** 500 N Sam Houston Pkwy E 77060 **Location:** On eastbound service road of Sam Houston Parkway E (Beltway 8), just e of Imperial Valley Dr. **Facility:** 220 units. 2 stories, interior corridors. **Amenities:** Some: safes. **Pool(s):** outdoor. **Activities:** exercise room. **Guest Services:** valet laundry, area transportation.

### QUALITY INN & SUITES HOUSTON WEST/ENERGY CORRIDOR
(281)493-0444   **63**

Motel $70-$196 **Address:** 715 Hwy 6 S 77079 **Location:** I-10 exit 751 (Addicks Rd/Howell Rd), 0.4 mi s. **Facility:** 63 units. 2 stories (no elevator), exterior corridors. **Amenities:** safes. **Pool(s):** outdoor. **Guest Services:** valet and coin laundry.

### RED ROOF HOUSTON IAH
(832)243-7650   **22**

Hotel $59-$99 **Address:** 15675 John F Kennedy Blvd 77032 **Location:** Sam Houston Pkwy (Beltway 8) exit John F Kennedy Blvd, just n. **Facility:** 104 units. 3 stories, interior corridors. **Bath:** shower only. **Pool(s):** outdoor. **Activities:** exercise room. **Guest Services:** valet and coin laundry.

(See map & index p. 324.)

## RED ROOF INNS- HOUSTON WESTCHASE
(713)785-9909 **74**

Hotel $49-$75 **Address:** 2960 W Sam Houston Pkwy S 77042 **Location:** Sam Houston Pkwy (Beltway 8) exit Westheimer Rd; on southbound frontage road. **Facility:** 134 units. 3 stories, interior/exterior corridors. **Amenities:** safes. **Pool(s):** outdoor.

## RESIDENCE INN BY MARRIOTT WILLOWBROOK
(832)237-2002 **16**

Extended Stay Hotel $99-$189 **Address:** 7311 W Greens Rd 77064 **Location:** SR 249 exit Greens Rd, just e. Across from Willowbrook Mall. **Facility:** 96 units, some two bedrooms, efficiencies and kitchens. 3 stories, interior corridors. **Pool(s):** heated indoor. **Activities:** hot tub, exercise room. **Guest Services:** valet and coin laundry.

**AAA Benefit:** Members save 5% or more!

## SHERATON HOUSTON WEST HOTEL
(281)501-4200 **46**

Hotel $89-$359

Sheraton HOTELS & RESORTS

**AAA Benefit:** Members get up to 20% off, plus Starwood Preferred Guest® bonuses!

**Address:** 11191 Clay Rd 77041 **Location:** Sam Houston Pkwy (Beltway 8) exit Clay Rd, just e. **Facility:** 158 units. 5 stories, interior corridors. **Terms:** cancellation fee imposed. **Amenities:** safes. **Pool(s):** heated outdoor. **Activities:** hot tub, exercise room. **Guest Services:** valet and coin laundry, area transportation.

## SHERATON NORTH HOUSTON HOTEL
(281)442-5100 **21**

Hotel $79-$279

Sheraton HOTELS & RESORTS

**AAA Benefit:** Members get up to 20% off, plus Starwood Preferred Guest® bonuses!

**Address:** 15700 John F Kennedy Blvd 77032 **Location:** Sam Houston Pkwy (Beltway 8) exit John F Kennedy Blvd, just n. **Facility:** 420 units. 10 stories, interior corridors. **Amenities:** video games. **Pool(s):** outdoor, indoor. **Activities:** hot tub, exercise room. **Guest Services:** valet and coin laundry, area transportation.

## SLEEP INN & SUITES INTERCONTINENTAL NORTH
(281)872-6200 **8**

Hotel $85-$130 **Address:** 222 Airtex Dr 77090 **Location:** I-45 exit 63 (Airtex Dr), just w. **Facility:** 61 units. 3 stories, interior corridors. **Pool(s):** outdoor. **Activities:** hot tub, limited exercise equipment. **Guest Services:** valet and coin laundry.

Contact us about AAA/CAA

Approved properties at

AAA.com/TourBookComments

## SPRINGHILL SUITES BY MARRIOTT HOUSTON INTERCONTINENTAL AIRPORT
(281)442-2275 **18**

Hotel $89-$189 **Address:** 15840 John F Kennedy Blvd 77032 **Location:** 0.3 mi n of jct Sam Houston Pkwy (Beltway 8). **Facility:** 156 units. 6 stories, interior corridors. **Pool(s):** heated outdoor. **Activities:** exercise room. **Guest Services:** valet and coin laundry.

**AAA Benefit:** Members save 5% or more!

## STAYBRIDGE SUITES HOUSTON WEST ENERGY CORRIDOR
(281)759-7829 **65**

Extended Stay Contemporary Hotel $199-$219 **Address:** 1225 Eldridge Pkwy 77077 **Location:** I-10 exit 753A (Eldridge Pkwy), 1.8 mi s. **Facility:** 122 units, some two bedrooms, efficiencies and kitchens. 4 stories, interior corridors. **Terms:** cancellation fee imposed, resort fee. **Pool(s):** outdoor. **Activities:** exercise room. **Guest Services:** complimentary and valet laundry.

## SUPER 8 IAH WEST/GREENSPOINT
(281)987-7100 **30**

Hotel $75-$140

**Address:** 1230 N Sam Houston Pkwy E 77032 **Location:** Sam Houston Pkwy (Beltway 8) exit Aldine Westfield Rd eastbound; exit S Hardy Toll Rd westbound; on eastbound frontage road. **Facility:** 60 units, some efficiencies. 3 stories, interior corridors. **Pool(s):** outdoor. **Activities:** exercise room. **Guest Services:** coin laundry. **Featured Amenity:** continental breakfast.

## TOWNEPLACE SUITES BY MARRIOTT HOUSTON I-10 WEST/ENERGY CORRIDOR
(281)646-0058 **51**

Extended Stay Hotel $81-$160 **Address:** 15155 Katy Frwy 77094 **Location:** I-10 exit 751, just s on SR 6 to Grisby Rd, then w. **Facility:** 94 kitchen units, some two bedrooms. 3 stories, interior corridors. **Pool(s):** outdoor. **Activities:** exercise room. **Guest Services:** valet and coin laundry.

**AAA Benefit:** Members save 5% or more!

## WESTIN HOUSTON MEMORIAL CITY
(281)501-4300 **61**

Contemporary Hotel $109-$369

WESTIN HOTELS & RESORTS

**AAA Benefit:** Enjoy up to 20% off your next stay, plus Starwood Preferred Guest® bonuses!

**Address:** 945 Gessner Rd 77024 **Location:** I-10 exit 757 (Gessner Rd), just s. Next to hospital. **Facility:** This hotel has a sleek, modern look that includes a dramatic open air 18th floor pool deck. Guests will appreciate the convenient walkway that connects them to the upscale Memorial City shopping mall. 285 units, some condominiums. 21 stories, interior corridors. **Parking:** on-site and valet. **Terms:** cancellation fee imposed. **Amenities:** video games, safes. **Dining:** 3 restaurants, also, Il Mulino New York, see separate listing. **Pool(s):** heated outdoor. **Activities:** hot tub, exercise room, massage. **Guest Services:** valet laundry, area transportation.

(See map & index p. 324.)

### WINGATE BY WYNDHAM HOUSTON BUSH INTERCONTINENTAL AIRPORT IAH (281)372-1000 [33]

Hotel
$89-$180

**Address:** 1330 N Sam Houston Pkwy E 77032 **Location:** Off Sam Houston Pkwy (Beltway 8) exit Aldine Westfield Rd eastbound, 0.8 mi e on service road; exit Hardy Toll Rd westbound, U-turn, then 1 mi e on service road. **Facility:** 60 units. 3 stories, interior corridors. **Terms:** cancellation fee imposed. **Amenities:** safes. **Pool(s):** outdoor. **Activities:** hot tub, exercise room. **Guest Services:** valet and coin laundry. **Featured Amenity: full hot breakfast.**

### WYNDHAM HOUSTON WEST ENERGY CORRIDOR (281)558-5580 [47]

Hotel
$99-$249

**Address:** 14703 Park Row Blvd 77079 **Location:** I-10 exit 751 (Addicks Rd/SR 6), just n. **Facility:** 344 units. 20 stories, interior corridors. **Amenities:** video games. **Pool(s):** heated indoor. **Activities:** hot tub, exercise room. **Guest Services:** valet and coin laundry, area transportation.

---

## WHERE TO EAT

### ASHIANA FINE INDIAN CUISINE 281/679-5555 [22]

Indian. Casual Dining. $11-$26 **AAA Inspector Notes:** The Northern Indian menu includes lamb, prawns, fish and chicken selections, numerous naan choices and an extensive, award-winning wine list. Patrons receive white tablecloth service, but the family-friendly atmosphere at this local favorite is casual. **Features:** full bar. **Address:** 12610 Briar Forest Dr 77077 **Location:** I-10 exit 753B (Dairy Ashford Rd), 2.1 mi s.

### BABIN'S SEAFOOD HOUSE 281/477-9300

Seafood. Casual Dining. $9-$28 **AAA Inspector Notes:** Examples of the New Orleans-style seafood served here include crawfish étouffée, shrimp Creole, boiled seafood, grilled fish and fried seafood platters. Loud jazz plays over speakers as friendly and attentive servers stop to check on the families dining inside and on the patio. **Features:** full bar. **Address:** 17485 Tomball Pkwy (SH 249) 77064 **Location:** SR 249 exit Greens Rd, just s; in Willowbrook Plaza Shopping Center.

### BISTRO LE CEP 713/783-3985 [24]

Traditional French. Fine Dining. $12-$29 **AAA Inspector Notes:** Hardwood floors and lacy curtains are evocative of a small home in the French countryside. The traditional, simple bistro fare includes escargot and bouillabaisse, which match well with choices from a wine list that includes many by-the-glass options. Service is attentive. Crème brûlée is a satisfying way to end a meal. **Reservations:** suggested, Sat & Sun. **Address:** 11112 Westheimer Rd 77042 **Location:** Sam Houston Pkwy (Beltway 8) exit Westheimer Rd, 0.7 mi w.

### BOUDREAUX'S CAJUN KITCHEN

Cajun. Casual Dining. $6-$23 **AAA Inspector Notes:** Houstonians experience Cajun flavor via this restaurant's generous portions of fresh seafood, étouffée, boudin balls and dirty rice. Shrimp Creole also piques interest. The casual décor is evocative of a bayou shack. Kids eat free on Tuesdays. **Bar:** full bar.

*For additional information, visit AAA.com*

**LOCATIONS:**
**Address:** 17595 Tomball Pkwy 77064 **Location:** SR 249 exit FM 1960; on southbound frontage road. **Phone:** 281/469-8500
**Address:** 5475 W Loop S 77081 **Location:** I-610 exit 7 (Fournace Pl) southbound; exit 6 (Fournace Pl) northbound; on northbound frontage road. **Phone:** 713/838-2200

### BRENNER'S STEAKHOUSE 713/465-2901 [13]

Steak. Fine Dining. $18-$65 **AAA Inspector Notes:** Overlooking a beautiful garden with pools, waterfalls and a waterwheel, this dining room has been the setting for cozy meals since 1936. The menu features Prime steaks and seafood selections as well as some classic home-style recipes from the original owners such as beef stroganoff, German potatoes and the not-to-be-missed apple strudel. Service is refined and attentive. **Features:** full bar, patio dining. **Reservations:** suggested. **Address:** 10911 Katy Frwy 77079 **Location:** I-10 and US 90 exit 755 (Wilcrest Dr), just se on service road. **Parking:** valet only.

### BURGER GUYS 281/497-4897 [29]

Burgers Hot Dogs. Quick Serve. $8-$10 **AAA Inspector Notes:** This simple eatery takes the gourmet burger trend to the next level. The motto is "it's all about the meat," and they use premium Akaushi beef for the burgers. House-made toppings consist of local ingredients combined to create fresh flavors. Burger selections include the Houston Burger with onion bacon jam, ale mustard, pickled jalapeños and local cheese. Some items are even more complex, but simpler burgers also are offered, as well as an equally creative selection of hot dogs and classic sodas. **Address:** 12225 Westheimer Rd, Suite G 77077 **Location:** 2.2 mi w of Sam Houston Pkwy (Beltway 8).

### CAFE CASPIAN 281/493-4000 [27]

Persian. Casual Dining. $10-$20 **AAA Inspector Notes:** Tucked in a strip mall, the café prepares delicious cuisine. Diners relax in the casually sophisticated dining room and peruse a menu that lists such items as filling stews and lamb or beef kebabs. Whether noshing alone or sharing with friends, don't miss out on the satisfying appetizers, including the yogurt and cucumber dip. **Features:** beer & wine. **Address:** 12126 Westheimer Rd 77077 **Location:** Sam Houston Pkwy (Beltway 8) exit Westheimer Rd, 2 mi w.

### CAFE EXPRESS

American. Casual Dining. $7-$15 **AAA Inspector Notes:** Even if this place does serve burgers, its American/Mediterranean menu lists plenty of more healthful options, such as pasta dishes, roasted chicken and Caesar salad. Everything is made to order and served fast for people on the go. Those with a little more time to spare may want to enjoy some wine or the classic German chocolate cake. **Bar:** beer & wine.

*For additional information, visit AAA.com*

**LOCATIONS:**
**Address:** 780 W Sam Houston Pkwy N 77024 **Location:** Jct I-10 and Sam Houston Pkwy (Beltway 8); in Town & Country Village Shopping Center. **Phone:** 713/586-0800
**Address:** 5311 FM 1960 W 77069 **Location:** SR 249 exit FM 1960, 2.6 mi e. **Phone:** 832/484-9222

### CAFE PITA 713/953-7237 [25]

Mediterranean. Casual Dining. $7-$20 **AAA Inspector Notes:** Cafe Pita, featured on the Food Network program "Diners, Drive-Ins and Dives," features Bosnian cuisine with specialties such as Bosnian goulash and roasted lamb. Other favorites include a variety of kebabs, stuffed peppers, soups, salads, sandwiches and pizza. I had the fresh sardines, which were grilled and served with mixed veggies and basmati rice. Very good! **Features:** beer & wine. **Address:** 10890 Westheimer Rd 77042 **Location:** Sam Houston Pkwy (Beltway 8) exit Westheimer Rd, just w.

### CANDELARI'S PIZZERIA 281/497-0612 [19]

Italian Pizza. Casual Dining. $9-$26 **AAA Inspector Notes:** The bruschetta, Caesar salad and penne rustica were the courses I sampled at Candelari's, and they were all very fresh and delicious. The pasta course was one of the best I have had in some time. It consisted of coarsely ground Italian sausage, crimini mushrooms and spinach sautéed in rich tomato cream sauce. The pizzas looked tempting as well. **Features:** full bar, happy hour. **Address:** 14545 Memorial Dr 77079 **Location:** I-10 exit 753B (Dairy Ashford Rd), 1.1 mi s to Memorial Dr, then just e.

Visit your AAA/CAA Travel office
to book a AAA Vacations®
Disney package

(See map & index p. 324.)

## CANTINA LAREDO 713/952-3287 [26]
Mexican
Casual Dining
$10-$26

**AAA Inspector Notes:** Modern yet relaxed, this restaurant features creative Mexican fare. A great starter of top-shelf guacamole, which is prepared tableside, primes the palate for an entree of enchiladas, tacos, fajitas and chiles rellenos. **Features:** full bar, Sunday brunch. **Address:** 11129 Westheimer Rd 77042 **Location:** Sam Houston Pkwy (Beltway 8) exit Westheimer Rd, 0.7 mi w, then just s on Wilcrest. [L] [D] [LATE]

### Gourmet Mexican food, fresh-squeezed lime margaritas

## CARMELO'S RISTORANTE 281/531-0696 [18]
Italian. Fine Dining. $12-$34 **AAA Inspector Notes:** Owner-operated since 1981, this upscale dining spot serves a good variety of freshly prepared dishes that feature beef, chicken and seafood, in addition to table-side-prepared flambé dishes. Grilled chicken over pasta served with fresh steamed vegetables is a good lighter choice. Wall cutouts give the appearance of looking out to the Italian coastline. **Features:** full bar. **Reservations:** suggested. **Address:** 14795 Memorial Dr 77079 **Location:** I-10 exit 753B (Dairy Ashford Rd), 0.3 mi w. **Parking:** valet only. [L] [D]

## CATTLEGUARD RESTAURANT & BAR 281/493-5094 [12]
American. Casual Dining. $9-$28 **AAA Inspector Notes:** Patrons can unwind in a casually rustic atmosphere to savor premium gold Angus beef and award-winning chicken-fried steak. Burgers, Tex-Mex, wild game, pasta and ribs round out the menu. The restaurant is popular with guests of nearby hotels. **Features:** full bar. **Address:** 1010 N Hwy 6 77079 **Location:** I-10 exit 751 (Addicks-Howell Rd), just n. [L] [D]

## CHUY'S 281/970-0341 [11]
Tex-Mex. Casual Dining. $6-$12 **AAA Inspector Notes:** Family-friendly, loud and popular for its happy hour, this small Texas chain serves up enchiladas, tacos and combination plates. **Features:** full bar, patio dining, happy hour. **Address:** 19827 Northwest Frwy 77065 **Location:** Jct US 290 and FM 1960; off southbound frontage road. [L] [D] [🐾]

## CLAY'S RESTAURANT 281/859-3773
American. Casual Dining. $7-$15 **AAA Inspector Notes:** Although a bit off the beaten path, this place is popular with families because of its play area for kids, which includes a petting zoo and sandboxes, and its ability to enthusiastically accommodate large parties. Houstonians come for the burgers and monumental chicken-fried steak. Outdoor seating is a good nice-weather option, and smoking is permitted on the patio. **Features:** beer & wine, patio dining, happy hour. **Address:** 17717 Clay Rd 77084 **Location:** I-10 exit 748 (Barker Cypress Rd), 3.2 mi n, then 0.9 mi e. [L] [D] [🌙]

## THE COUNTY LINE BAR-B-Q 281/537-2454 [6]
Regional Barbecue. Casual Dining. $9-$20 **AAA Inspector Notes:** Nestled in a natural landscape that provides a haven from the bustle of the north Houston suburbs, this family restaurant dishes up helpings of excellent Texas barbecue and down-home side dishes. Baby back ribs and the sliced lean brisket are especially good with creamy potato salad. All-you-can-eat family-style meals and a lunch buffet are available. **Features:** full bar. **Address:** 13850 Cutten Rd 77069 **Location:** SR 249 exit FM 1960, just ne to Cutten Rd, then 0.7 mi n. [L] [D]

## EMPIRE TURKISH GRILL 713/827-7475 [20]
Turkish. Casual Dining. $10-$22 **AAA Inspector Notes:** Friendly staff, attractive décor and delicious food contribute to a truly enjoyable dining experience at this restaurant inside an eclectic shopping center. Even those unfamiliar with Turkish food are likely to enjoy filet mignon or chicken kebabs. Lamb and vegetarian options dominate the menu. The desserts are not to be missed. **Features:** beer & wine. **Address:** 12448 Memorial Dr 77024 **Location:** I-10 exit 757, 1.2 mi s on Gessner Dr, then just w; in Wick Lane Memorial Shopping Center. [L] [D]

## GOOD EATS 281/442-2815 [9]
American
Casual Dining
$8-$29

**AAA Inspector Notes:** Trying to find dining near the airport can be an exercise in futility, but this restaurant offers reliable Texas-style fare. Patrons can sample steak, meat loaf, pot roast, chicken-fried steak and other hearty items in a Lone Star State-inspired dining room. The bar is typically jumping with lots of business travelers. **Features:** full bar, Sunday brunch. **Address:** 15222 John F Kennedy Blvd 77032 **Location:** Jct N Sam Houston Pkwy (Beltway 8) E and John F Kennedy Blvd; in Holiday Inn Houston Intercontinental Airport. [B] [L] [D]

## HARRIS COUNTY SMOKEHOUSE 281/890-5735 [10]
Barbecue. Casual Dining. $4-$15 **AAA Inspector Notes:** The family-owned restaurant builds its menu on classic Texas food, meaning smoked meats, T-bone steak, sausage links, grilled chicken breast and tasty sides. When a table is available, a home-cooked breakfast is a must. **Features:** beer & wine. **Address:** 13280 FM 1960 W 77065 **Location:** Jct US 290 and FM 1960 W. [B] [L] [D]

## IL MULINO NEW YORK 832/358-0600 [15]
Italian. Casual Dining. $10-$29 **AAA Inspector Notes:** This is a more casual version of the renowned Il Mulino New York restaurants. The menu of traditional and rustic Italian dishes maintains the high quality standards of the original, although the service here is not as sharp or attentive. Platters of cured meats, imported cheeses and olives are popular for sharing. Other great items include beef carpaccio, veal saltimbocca and seared red snapper with broccoli rabe. The bar area is lively and often loud at happy hour. **Features:** full bar. **Address:** 945 Gessner Rd 77024 **Location:** I-10 exit 757 (Gessner Rd), just s; in Westin Houston Memorial City. **Parking:** on-site and valet. [B] [L] [D] CALL [🐾M]

## JIMMY G'S CAJUN SEAFOOD RESTAURANT 281/931-7654 [8]
Cajun Seafood. Casual Dining. $10-$29 **AAA Inspector Notes:** Locally owned and operated, the restaurant specializes in Cajun and Creole cuisine. At the center of the restaurant is an oyster bar where you can watch them boil crawfish. If you have a plane to catch, this place is convenient to Bush Airport. **Features:** full bar. **Address:** 307 N Sam Houston Pkwy E 77060 **Location:** Sam Houston Pkwy (Beltway 8) exit Imperial Valley Dr westbound, 0.8 mi on west frontage road; exit Hardy Toll Rd eastbound, turn under parkway, then 1.2 mi on west frontage road. [L] [D]

## LA MADELEINE COUNTRY FRENCH CAFE
Traditional French. Casual Dining. $7-$12 **AAA Inspector Notes:** A fireplace creates the focal point at this cozy European style café where you can always get a quiche or savory stuffed puffed pastry on the go or stick around for a chicken crêpe or French dip sandwich. Heartier entrées like rotisserie chicken are offered and every season promises menu surprises. Whatever you decide on you probably will not get out the door without enjoying one of their tempting sweet pastries. [B] [L] [D]

*For additional information, visit AAA.com*

**LOCATIONS:**

**Address:** 10001 Westheimer Rd, Suite 2123 77042 **Location:** Jct Westheimer Rd and Sam Houston Pkwy (Beltway 8), just e. **Bar:** wine only. **Phone:** 713/266-7686

**Address:** 6500 Woodway Dr 77057 **Location:** Jct Voss Rd and Woodway Dr, just ne. **Bar:** beer & wine. **Phone:** 713/722-8449

**Address:** 2047-A W Gray St 77019 **Location:** Jct W Gray St and Shepherd Dr, just e. **Bar:** beer & wine. **Phone:** 713/526-9666

**Address:** 6205 Kirby Dr 77005 **Location:** Jct Kirby Dr and Amherst St. **Bar:** beer & wine. **Phone:** 713/942-7081

**Address:** 4700 Beechnut St, Suite 620 77096 **Location:** I-610 exit 5A (Beechnut St) southbound; exit 4A (Braeswood Blvd) northbound, continue on frontage road to Beechnut St, then just w; in Meyerland Plaza Shopping Center. **Bar:** beer & wine. **Phone:** 713/218-8075

**Address:** 5015 Westheimer Rd, Suite 1420 77056 **Location:** In Galleria Shopping Center. **Bar:** beer & wine. **Phone:** 713/993-0287

**Address:** 5505-A FM 1960 77069 **Location:** Jct Champion Forest Dr and FM 1960, just e. **Bar:** beer & wine. **Phone:** 281/893-0723

**Address:** 19710 Northwest Frwy, Suite 100 77065 **Location:** Jct FM 1960 and US 290. **Bar:** beer & wine. **Phone:** 281/720-1000

**Address:** 770 W Sam Houston Pkwy N, Suite 100 77024 **Location:** In Town & Country Village Shopping Center. **Bar:** beer & wine. **Phone:** 713/465-7370

**(See map & index p. 324.)**

### LE MISTRAL
832/379-8322  **21**

WWWW French. Casual Dining. $7-$34 **AAA Inspector Notes:** Delicious traditional Provençal fare is served at this area favorite. The cuisine and sauces are lighter than what is typically found in other parts of France. The dining room is adorned with native art, suede and rich woods. A creamy white bovine adds to the feel that you're dining at a home in the French countryside. **Features:** full bar, Sunday brunch, happy hour. **Reservations:** suggested. **Address:** 1400 Eldridge Pkwy 77077 **Location:** I-10 exit 753A (Eldridge Pkwy), 1.8 mi s. L D

### LOMONTE'S ITALIAN RESTAURANT & BAR
281/496-0030  **16**

WWWW Italian. Fine Dining. $12-$29 **AAA Inspector Notes:** You can find some of the best pasta in Houston. I truly enjoyed the linguine with white clam sauce. Other options include ravioli dolce, shrimp diavolo and farfalle primavera. Many chicken and shrimp dishes are more of the delicious entrées to be found at Lomonte's. Tempting desserts include cannoli, tiramisu and gourmet cheesecake. An excellent selection of wines is available as well. **Features:** full bar, patio dining, happy hour. **Address:** 14510 Grisby Rd 77079 **Location:** I-10 exit 751, just s on SR 6 to Grisby Rd, then just e. L D CALL M

### LUPE TORTILLA MEXICAN RESTAURANT

WWW Mexican. Casual Dining. $8-$21 **AAA Inspector Notes:** Featuring an early Tex-Mex décor, the eatery pokes fun at itself with statements such as, "Es preetty good." However, the atypically good Mexican fare on the somewhat limited menu is nothing to laugh at. Unpretentious tacos, flautas, enchiladas, burritos, chile rellenos and chalupas are made from original recipes. This is the original location of what is now a Houston institution. The converted farmhouse includes a sandbox for kids, lively dining rooms and outdoor seating. **Bar:** full bar. L D

*For additional information, visit AAA.com*

**LOCATIONS:**

**Address:** 318 Stafford St 77079 **Location:** I-10 exit 751 (Addicks Rd/SR 6), just s to Grisby Rd; just e of jct Grisby Rd and SR 6. **Phone:** 281/496-7580

**Address:** 15315 North Frwy 77090 **Location:** I-45 exit 64 (Richey Rd); on southbound frontage road. **Phone:** 281/873-6220

### LYNN'S STEAKHOUSE AND SEAFOOD
281/870-0807  **17**

WWWW Steak. Fine Dining. $13-$48 **AAA Inspector Notes:** Guests can sip from a glass of award-winning wine selected from an extensive list as they relax in the intimate, rustic and dimly lit dining room. Thick steaks, rack of lamb and Australian rock lobster are favorites at the steakhouse. Its office building structure setting is deceptive, as the inside feels like a cozy cottage with small and romantic dining rooms. **Features:** full bar. **Reservations:** suggested. **Address:** 955 Dairy-Ashford Rd 77079 **Location:** I-10 exit 753, 0.5 mi s. L D

### MATSU JAPANESE RESTAURANT
281/893-8700  **5**

WW Japanese. Casual Dining. $9-$40 **AAA Inspector Notes:** This traditional restaurant serves sashimi, tempura and teriyaki dishes, and for lunch, the traditional bento meal. Lone diners will appreciate the many preparations displayed on the sushi bar; weekday happy hour sushi specials provide more bang for the buck. A meal in the tatami room is a relaxing treat. **Features:** beer & wine, happy hour. **Address:** 4855 FM 1960 W 77069 **Location:** I-45 exit 66, 5.2 mi w. L D

### MURPHY'S DELI
713/782-8818

W Deli. Quick Serve. $3-$9 **AAA Inspector Notes:** The delicatessen offers several selections such as the traditional tuna sandwich, hot ham and cheese, signature muffuletta and grilled chicken pita. There are no rules, and patrons can try plenty of side items, including macaroni, Greek and fruit salads, hummus, deviled eggs and tabbouleh. It's difficult to escape the register area without picking up a bag of delicious cookies. A full coffee bar is available for those who need their fix. **Features:** patio dining. **Address:** 10440 Richmond Ave 77042 **Location:** Sam Houston Pkwy (Beltway 8); 0.8 mi s of Westheimer Rd. B L

### NIT NOI
281/597-8200  **28**

WW Thai. Casual Dining. $10-$16 **AAA Inspector Notes:** Long a tradition in Houston, the restaurant presents a menu of Thai classics. Nearly 100 menu items means there is something for everyone, and this location allows west-side diners to partake more often. The small eatery has lovely murals of rural life in Thailand offset with modern lighting and rich woods. **Features:** beer & wine. **Address:** 11807 Westheimer Rd, Suite 580 77077 **Location:** Sam Houston Pkwy (Beltway 8) exit Westheimer Rd, 1.7 mi w. L D

### PAPPADEAUX SEAFOOD KITCHEN

WW Regional Seafood. Casual Dining. $12-$47 **AAA Inspector Notes:** A seafood lover's delight, the restaurant taps into a little bit of New Orleans with its Cajun dishes and elaborate menu selections. Patrons might start off with a creative choice of blackened oyster and shrimp fondeaux with crayfish and let the feast begin. While music plays in the background, patrons can dig into dirty rice or spicy gumbo loaded with seafood. Well-seasoned shrimp and fish are prepared in varied ways. **Bar:** full bar. L D

*For additional information, visit AAA.com*

**LOCATIONS:**

**Address:** 12109 Westheimer Rd 77077 **Location:** Sam Houston Pkwy (Beltway 8) exit Westheimer Rd, 2.2 mi w. **Phone:** 281/497-1110

**Address:** 7110 FM 1960 W 77069 **Location:** 0.9 mi e of jct SR 249 and FM 1960. **Phone:** 281/580-5245

**Address:** 10499 I-10 W 77024 **Location:** I-10 eastbound access road, just before Loop 8. **Phone:** 713/722-0221

**Address:** 13080 Northwest Frwy 77040 **Location:** US 290 exit Pinemont Rd/Bingle Rd; on north side. **Phone:** 713/460-1203

**Address:** 2525 South Loop W at S Main St 77054 **Location:** I-610 exit 2 westbound; exit 1C eastbound; on eastbound access road. **Phone:** 713/665-3155

### PAPPASITO'S CANTINA

WW Tex-Mex. Casual Dining. $10-$49 **AAA Inspector Notes:** Fine traditional offerings are served in an upscale cantina atmosphere. Often crowded during peak hours, the immensely popular stop dishes up generous portions of sizzling fajitas, enchiladas and other traditional Mexican favorites, including some shrimp specialties. The terrific margaritas are guaranteed to get attention. Tables in the large dining room are closely spaced. Ice cream with cinnamon on chocolate bread pudding shouldn't be missed. **Bar:** full bar. L D CALL M

*For additional information, visit AAA.com*

**LOCATIONS:**

**Address:** 7050 FM 1960 W 77069 **Location:** SR 249 exit FM 1960, 0.5 mi e. **Phone:** 281/893-5030

**Address:** 13070 Hwy 290 77040 **Location:** US 290 exit Bingle; on westbound frontage road. **Phone:** 713/462-0246

**Address:** 10409 I-10 W 77024 **Location:** I-10 exit 756A westbound; exit 755 eastbound; on eastbound frontage road. **Phone:** 713/468-1913

**Address:** 11831 I-10 E 77029 **Location:** I-10 exit 778A (Federal Rd) eastbound; exit 776B (John Ralston/Holland) westbound; on westbound frontage road. **Phone:** 713/455-8378

**Address:** 2515 South Loop W 77054 **Location:** I-610 exit 1C (Kirby) eastbound; exit 2 (Main St) westbound; on eastbound frontage road. **Phone:** 713/668-5756

**Address:** 15280 I-45 N at Airtex Dr 77090 **Location:** I-45 exit 63 (Airtex Dr); on northbound frontage road. **Phone:** 281/821-4500

### PAPPAS SEAFOOD HOUSE
281/999-9928

WW Seafood. Casual Dining. $12-$45 **AAA Inspector Notes:** This popular local seafood chain serves a great variety of extremely fresh seafood with Louisiana-inspired entrées, raw bar items, steaks, pasta and even sushi. The service is friendly and the atmosphere relaxed. **Features:** full bar, happy hour. **Address:** 11301 I-45 N 77037 **Location:** I-45 exit 60 (Aldine-Bender Rd); on west service road. L D

### PERRY & SONS MARKET & GRILLE
281/481-5214  **31**

WWW American. Casual Dining. $5-$34 **AAA Inspector Notes:** This place is an interesting combination of a meat market and a restaurant serving upscale cuts of beef and very tasty pasta entrées. **Features:** beer & wine. **Address:** 12830 Scarsdale Blvd 77089 **Location:** I-45 exit 31, just w. L D CALL M

(See map & index p. 324.)

**PERRY'S STEAKHOUSE & GRILLE**  281/970-5999  (3)

▼▼▼▼ Steak. Fine Dining. $24-$80 **AAA Inspector Notes:** Expect an excellent selection of prime steaks, lamb and pork chops all served in a professional and upscale establishment. **Features:** full bar, patio dining. **Reservations:** required. **Address:** 9730 Cypresswood Dr 77070 **Location:** SR 249 N exit Cypresswood Dr, 0.8 mi e to Schroder Rd; on northeast corner. **Parking:** on-site and valet.

[D] CALL [&M]

**RIO RANCH**  713/952-5000  (23)

▼▼ Steak Seafood. Casual Dining. $12-$35 **AAA Inspector Notes:** From the immense limestone walls to the mesquite-topped bar, this restaurant is all Texas with a delightful twist. While patrons can find chicken-fried steak here, they are equally as likely to find items such as wood-grilled boar chops, grilled Aussie rack of lamb, thick-cut sirloin and specials such as the mixed grill, which combines venison sausage, barbecue duck and chile-crusted quail. The fit-for-a-cowboy Sunday brunch buffet includes eggs, biscuits and gravy, and sausage and grits. **Features:** full bar, patio dining, Sunday brunch. **Address:** 9999 Westheimer Rd 77042 **Location:** Sam Houston Pkwy (Beltway 8) exit Westheimer Rd/Briar Forest Dr northbound; exit Westheimer Rd/Richmond Ave southbound, 0.5 mi e; in Hilton Houston Westchase. [L] [D]

**ROCKFISH SEAFOOD GRILL**

▼▼ Seafood. Casual Dining. $7-$20 **AAA Inspector Notes:** Patrons shuffle through peanut shells on the floor as they make their way to their seats and are easily distracted by the numerous pieces of hunting and fishing memorabilia adorning the walls and ceiling. Although guests kick back in a log cabin-style interior, the freshly caught fish gets more sophisticated preparation than campfire roasting. The chef uses an array of sauces and cooking styles, and soups are hearty and fresh. **Bar:** full bar. [L] [D]

*For additional information, visit AAA.com*

**LOCATIONS:**

**Address:** 11805 Westheimer Rd, Suite 370 77077 **Location:** Sam Houston Pkwy (Beltway 8) exit Westheimer Rd, 1.7 mi w. **Phone:** 281/558-7380

**Address:** 5500 FM 1960 Rd W 77069 **Location:** Between Champions Forest and Veterans Memorial drs; in Champions Forest Plaza. **Phone:** 281/587-2900

**SALTGRASS STEAKHOUSE**

▼▼ Steak. Casual Dining. $9-$30 **AAA Inspector Notes:** Those looking for something different should try the comfortable steakhouse, which never says no to a special request. Born from the spirit of Texas cattle drives, the restaurant resembles a Texas lodge, with high ceilings and mounted animal heads. Baby back ribs are so tender the meat falls off the bone. Also on the menu are hearty steaks, prime rib, chicken, seafood and yummy desserts. **Bar:** full bar. [SAVE] [L] [D] [◥]

*For additional information, visit AAA.com*

**LOCATIONS:**

**Address:** 17275 Tomball Pkwy 77064 **Location:** SR 249 exit Greens Rd; in Willowbrook Plaza; on southbound frontage road. **Phone:** 281/477-0952  (7)

**Address:** 14909 I-45 N 77090 **Location:** I-45 exit 64 (Richey Rd); on southbound frontage road. **Phone:** 281/872-4545  (4)

**SANTA FE FLATS NEW MEX GRILLE**  281/655-1400  (1)

▼▼ Regional Southwestern. Casual Dining. $9-$16 **AAA Inspector Notes:** This friendly and casual restaurant serves up cuisine from New Mexico in a comfortable space with a nice outdoor patio and even a small sandbox for the kiddies. The stacked green chile enchiladas are the house specialty, and there is a complimentary salsa bar with an assortment of zesty salsas and condiments. **Features:** full bar, Sunday brunch. **Address:** 21542 State Hwy 249, Suite 5 77070 **Location:** SR 249 exit Louetta Rd; on northbound frontage road. [L] [D] [◥]

**STRATA RESTAURANT & BAR**  281/379-2889  (2)

▼▼▼▼ New American. Fine Dining. $8-$35 **AAA Inspector Notes:** This upscale restaurant has an inviting patio for outdoor dining. The menu is creative and vast, although results are mixed. Start with appetizers like duck confit spring rolls and move to salads and steaks. This is a good place to sample wine and enjoy Texas striped bass with sautéed sweet potatoes, arugula and coconut curry; or braised lamb with pomodoro sauce and Israeli couscous. Vegetarian entrées, including a pasta made with a red wine mushroom demi-glacé, are offered. **Features:** full bar, Sunday brunch, happy hour. **Address:** 122 Vintage Park Blvd, Suite A 77070 **Location:** SR 249 exit Louetta Rd, just e to Vintage Park Shopping Complex.

[L] [D] CALL [&M]

**SYLVIA'S ENCHILADA KITCHEN**  281/679-8300  (30)

▼▼ Mexican. Casual Dining. $8-$18 **AAA Inspector Notes:** It is no surprise that the enchiladas are the menu's main attraction, and they are some of the best in the city. The selections reflect Mexico's diverse regions, while others are done up Tex-Mex style. Combination dishes also are offered with other Mexican favorites. The atmosphere is casual and friendly at this popular neighborhood restaurant. **Features:** full bar, happy hour. **Address:** 12637 Westheimer Rd 77077 **Location:** Sam Houston Pkwy (Beltway 8) exit Westheimer Rd, 2.8 mi w. [L] [D]

**TASTE OF TEXAS**  713/932-6901  (14)

▼▼ Steak. Casual Dining. $10-$50 **AAA Inspector Notes:** It is easy to see why the restaurant is a local favorite. Guests can pair their choice of certified Angus steak, or maybe chicken or seafood, with selections from the ample salad bar. For lighter eaters, freshly baked breads, sandwiches, salads and sides also make for a good meal. A casual, lodgelike atmosphere pervades the expansive eatery, in business since 1977. Friendly, trained servers help make dining here an experience. This place grinds its own coffee beans and bakes its own desserts. **Features:** full bar. **Address:** 10505 Katy Frwy 77024 **Location:** I-10 exit 756A (Frontage Rd) westbound; exit 755 Sam Houston Pkwy (Beltway 8) eastbound, 1.8 mi e on east service road. [L] [D]

**TEXAS LAND AND CATTLE STEAKHOUSE**

▼▼ Steak. Casual Dining. $7-$27 **AAA Inspector Notes:** A variety of large Prime steaks, delicious salads and scrumptious desserts await you at the friendly Texas ranch-style restaurant. Try the signature slow-smoked sirloin, which never fails to please, or the Caesar salad, another favorite. A Texas steakhouse means everything is bigger, from large cuts and oversize salads to potatoes and side dishes. Those not in the mood for beef can opt for chicken, quail or seafood. Dessert is an occasion. **Bar:** full bar. [L] [D]

*For additional information, visit AAA.com*

**LOCATIONS:**

**Address:** 8015 W FM 1960 77070 **Location:** Nw of jct FM 1960 and SR 249 (Tomball Pkwy). **Phone:** 281/469-3838

**Address:** 12313 Katy Frwy 77079 **Location:** I-10 exit 753; on southeast corner. **Phone:** 281/679-9900

**Address:** 11900 Dickinson Rd 77089 **Location:** I-45 exit 33, 1.3 mi s on Frontage Rd to Dickinson Rd, then 0.3 mi w. **Phone:** 281/922-6333

**ANTONE'S FAMOUS PO' BOYS**  713/623-4464

[fyi] Not evaluated. Try the Original or Super Original po'boy with ham, salami, provolone and chow chow. This place has been a city favorite for almost 50 years. Other options include oyster, shrimp and catfish po'boys, as well as cheesesteaks, deli sandwiches and flatbread. **Address:** 4520 San Felipe St 77027 **Location:** Near Reliant Stadium.

# HUMBLE pop. 15,133

- Hotels & Restaurants map & index p. 324
- Part of Houston area — see map p. 301

## BEST WESTERN PLUS ATASCOCITA INN & SUITES
(281)852-5665 **99**

Hotel $90-$120

**AAA Benefit:** Members save 10% or more with Best Western!

**Address:** 7730 FM 1960 Rd E 77346 **Location:** Jct US 59 and FM 1960, 6.8 mi e. **Facility:** 51 units. 3 stories, interior corridors. **Pool(s):** outdoor. **Activities:** hot tub, exercise room. **Guest Services:** valet and coin laundry. **Featured Amenity:** full hot breakfast.

## BEST WESTERN PLUS INTERCONTINENTAL AIRPORT INN
(281)548-1402 **101**

Hotel $90-$110

**AAA Benefit:** Members save 10% or more with Best Western!

**Address:** 7114 Will Clayton Pkwy 77338 **Location:** US 59 exit Will Clayton Pkwy, just w. **Facility:** 80 units. 3 stories, interior corridors. **Terms:** 2-3 night minimum stay - seasonal. **Pool(s):** outdoor. **Activities:** hot tub, exercise room. **Guest Services:** valet and coin laundry, area transportation. **Featured Amenity:** full hot breakfast.

## COUNTRY INN & SUITES BY CARLSON HOUSTON AIRPORT EAST
281/446-4977 **95**

Hotel
Rates not provided

**Address:** 20611 Hwy 59 N 77338 **Location:** US 59 exit Townsen Blvd; on southbound access road. **Facility:** 62 units. 4 stories, interior corridors. **Pool(s):** heated indoor. **Activities:** hot tub, exercise room. **Guest Services:** valet and coin laundry. **Featured Amenity:** full hot breakfast.

## ECONO LODGE
(281)548-2900 **98**

Hotel $65-$110

**Address:** 9821 W FM 1960 Business Route 77338 **Location:** US 59 exit FM 1960 business route, just w. **Facility:** 36 units. 2 stories (no elevator), exterior corridors. **Pool(s):** outdoor. **Guest Services:** coin laundry. **Featured Amenity:** continental breakfast.

Learn the local driving laws at DrivingLaws.AAA.com

## FAIRFIELD INN BY MARRIOTT
(281)540-3311 **96**

Hotel $85-$133 **Address:** 20525 Hwy 59 77338 **Location:** US 59 exit Townsen Rd; on southbound access road. **Facility:** 64 units. 3 stories, interior corridors. **Pool(s):** heated indoor. **Activities:** hot tub. **Guest Services:** valet laundry.

**AAA Benefit:** Members save 5% or more!

## HAMPTON INN HUMBLE
(281)446-4800 **97**

Hotel $89-$299 **Address:** 20515 Hwy 59 N 77338 **Location:** US 59 exit Townsen Rd; on southbound access road. **Facility:** 86 units. 4 stories, interior corridors. **Terms:** 1-7 night minimum stay, cancellation fee imposed. **Pool(s):** heated indoor. **Activities:** exercise room. **Guest Services:** valet and coin laundry, area transportation.

**AAA Benefit:** Members save up to 10%!

## SLEEP INN & SUITES INTERCONTINENTAL AIRPORT EAST
(281)446-4683 **100**

Hotel $62-$150

**Address:** 18150 McKay Dr 77338 **Location:** US 59 exit Will Clayton Pkwy, just w. **Facility:** 54 units. 3 stories, interior corridors. **Amenities:** safes. **Pool(s):** outdoor. **Activities:** hot tub, exercise room. **Guest Services:** valet and coin laundry. **Featured Amenity:** full hot breakfast.

 WHERE TO EAT

### JADE PALACE
281/446-1616 **39**

Chinese. Casual Dining. $6-$12 **AAA Inspector Notes:** This family-owned and –operated Chinese restaurant is a favorite of the local residents. It offers reasonable prices for a good selection of dishes. There is no buffet and no frills here; the food and service are just very straightforward and simple. Some American dishes such as a rib-eye steak and fried scallops are available as well. **Features:** beer & wine. **Address:** 330 First St 77338 **Location:** Jct US 59 and FM 1960A, 0.4 mi e.

### PAPPASITO'S CANTINA
281/540-8664

Tex-Mex. Casual Dining. $10-$49 **AAA Inspector Notes:** Fine traditional offerings are served in an upscale cantina atmosphere. Often crowded during peak hours, the immensely popular stop dishes up generous portions of sizzling fajitas, enchiladas and other traditional Mexican favorites, including some shrimp specialties. The terrific margaritas are guaranteed to get attention. Tables in the large dining room are closely spaced. Ice cream with cinnamon on chocolate bread pudding shouldn't be missed. **Features:** full bar, happy hour. **Address:** 10005 FM 1960 at Hwy 59 N 77338 **Location:** US 59 exit FM 1960, just w.

### PAPPAS SEAFOOD HOUSE
281/446-5053

Seafood. Casual Dining. $12-$42 **AAA Inspector Notes:** An extensive range of seafood selections can be found every day at this popular restaurant. **Features:** full bar, patio dining, happy hour. **Address:** 20410 Hwy 59 N 77338 **Location:** US 59 exit FM 1960, just n on northbound frontage road.

### SALTGRASS STEAKHOUSE
281/540-5116 **38**

Steak. Casual Dining. $9-$30 **AAA Inspector Notes:** Those looking for something different should try the comfortable steakhouse, which never says no to a special request. Born from the spirit of Texas cattle drives, the restaurant resembles a Texas lodge, with high ceilings and mounted animal heads. Baby back ribs are so tender the meat falls off the bone. Also on the menu are hearty steaks, prime rib, chicken, seafood and yummy desserts. **Features:** full bar. **Address:** 20090 Hwy 59 N 77338 **Location:** US 59 exit FM 1960; on northbound frontage road.

(See map & index p. 324.)

ZIO'S ITALIAN KITCHEN                                281/540-7787

Italian. Casual Dining. $9-$18 **AAA Inspector Notes:** The warm, comfortable atmosphere and Old World decor complement the menu. Meals are a good value, and so is the service. This small chain specializes in Italian cuisine, including oven-baked pizzas and pasta dishes. Guests are encouraged to get creative with their pizzas by mixing and matching from a list of 24 toppings. Particularly tempting dishes are Artichoke spinach pasta, chicken parmigiana, and Shrimp Limone. **Features:** full bar. **Address:** 20380 Hwy 59 77338 **Location:** US 59 exit FM 1960, just n on northbound frontage road.

L | D | CALL | M

# HUNTSVILLE (E-10) pop. 38,548, elev. 400'

Once known as a center of culture, the "Athens of Texas" was founded as a Native American trading post in 1836, the year of Texas independence. Sam Houston was among the prominent early Texans who resided in Huntsville.

Sam Houston's Grave is in Oakwood Cemetery at Sam Houston Memorial Drive. Also commemorating the Texas Revolutionary War hero is a 67-foot-tall Sam Houston statue titled "A Tribute to Courage" which stands on a 10-foot-tall granite base. The statue is off I-45 exit 109 at 7600 SR 75S. Phone (936) 291-9726.

The town also serves as the headquarters of the Texas prison system and is home to Sam Houston State University.

**Huntsville Convention and Visitors Bureau:** 7600 SR 75S, Huntsville, TX 77342-0538. **Phone:** (936) 291-9726 or (800) 289-0389.

**SAM HOUSTON MEMORIAL MUSEUM COMPLEX** is .5 mi. s. on the w. side of SR 75 Bus. Rte. at 1836 Sam Houston Ave. Two of Gen. Sam Houston's houses—Woodland, built in 1847, and the 1856 Steamboat House where he died—are preserved. On the grounds are his law office and the Sam Houston Memorial Museum containing his belongings and Texas Revolution artifacts. **Hours:** Tues.-Sat. 9-4:30, Sun. noon-4:30. Closed Jan. 1, Thanksgiving, Christmas Eve and Christmas. Phone ahead to confirm schedule. **Cost:** $4; $3 (ages 65+); $2 (ages 6-17). **Phone:** (936) 294-1832.

**TEXAS PRISON MUSEUM** is at 491 SR 75N. The museum chronicles the Texas prison system from its beginning in 1848 to the current system, which incarcerates 150,000 prisoners. **Time:** Allow 30 minutes minimum. **Hours:** Mon.-Sat. 10-5, Sun. noon-5. **Cost:** $4; $3 (ages 60+); $2 (ages 6-17). **Phone:** (936) 295-2155.

## BEST WESTERN PLUS HUNTSVILLE INN & SUITES
(936)295-9000

Hotel
$99-$149

**AAA Benefit:** Members save 10% or more with Best Western!

**Address:** 201 W Hill Park Cir 77320 **Location:** I-45 exit 116, just w on US 190. **Facility:** 56 units. 2 stories (no elevator), exterior corridors. **Pool(s):** outdoor. **Activities:** exercise room. **Guest Services:** valet and coin laundry. **Featured Amenity:** breakfast buffet.

## DAYS INN & SUITES
(936)438-8400

Hotel
$73-$87

**Address:** 160 I-45 S 77340 **Location:** I-45 exit 116, just off northbound access road. **Facility:** 48 units. 2 stories (no elevator), exterior corridors. **Terms:** 3 day cancellation notice. **Pool(s):** outdoor. **Guest Services:** coin laundry. **Featured Amenity:** continental breakfast.

## HOLIDAY INN EXPRESS HOTEL & SUITES HUNTSVILLE
(936)295-4300

Hotel
$129

**Address:** 148 S I-45 77340 **Location:** I-45 exit 116, just n. **Facility:** 87 units. 4 stories, interior corridors. **Terms:** cancellation fee imposed. **Pool(s):** heated indoor. **Activities:** hot tub, exercise room. **Guest Services:** valet and coin laundry. **Featured Amenity:** breakfast buffet.

## WHERE TO EAT

BOB LUBY'S SEAFOOD GRILL                          936/435-0944

Seafood. Casual Dining. $9-$20 **AAA Inspector Notes:** Many types of seafood and fish, including shrimp, salmon, red snapper and rainbow trout, are just a sampling of the daily fresh fish entrées found on this restaurant's chalkboard. Extras include fettuccine Alfredo, one chicken entrée and one steak entrée. Key lime pie is their dessert specialty. **Features:** full bar. **Address:** 139 IH-45 N 77320 **Location:** I-45 exit 116, just n. L | D

EL CHICO                                          936/295-9608

Tex-Mex
Casual Dining
$5-$15

**AAA Inspector Notes:** Inside and out, the decor of the popular Mexican restaurant is inviting. The menu features traditional favorites such as enchiladas, tacos, burritos and fajitas. The broad menu also lists a few American classics. **Features:** full bar, happy hour. **Address:** 170 S I-45 77340 **Location:** I-45 exit 116; on southbound frontage road. L | D

## HURST pop. 37,337
• Hotels & Restaurants map & index p. 257

### HYATT PLACE FT. WORTH/HURST   (817)577-3003   49

Hotel
$69-$209

HYATT PLACE
**AAA Benefit:** Members save 10%!

**Address:** 1601 Hurst Town Center Dr 76054 **Location:** SR 183 exit Precinct Line Rd, just n to Thousand Oaks Dr, then just w. **Facility:** 127 units. 6 stories, interior corridors. **Terms:** cancellation fee imposed. **Pool(s):** heated outdoor. **Activities:** exercise room. **Guest Services:** valet laundry, area transportation. **Featured Amenity:** breakfast buffet.

### WHERE TO EAT

ITALIANNIS   817/281-7272   42
Italian. Casual Dining. $7-$26 **AAA Inspector Notes:** The handsome dining room's generous booths, mosaic tile floors and brass accents provide the background for dining on your choice of pizza, pasta, grilled mahi mahi, stuffed pork chops or a refreshing strawberry salad. **Features:** full bar, Sunday brunch, happy hour. **Address:** 1601 Precinct Line Rd 76054 **Location:** SR 183 exit Precinct Line Rd, just n. L D

SWEET BASIL THAI CUISINE   817/268-2899   43
Thai. Casual Dining. $7-$14 **AAA Inspector Notes:** This small restaurant tucked behind North East Mall serves up a variety of noodle, curry and stir-fry dishes. The small but dedicated staff allows you to enjoy beautifully presented and consistently delicious food. **Address:** 977 Melbourne Rd 76053 **Location:** Loop 820 exit 23 (Pipeline Rd), just e to Melbourne Rd, then just n. L D CALL &M

## INGLESIDE pop. 9,387

### BEST WESTERN NAVAL STATION INN   (361)776-2767

Motel
$95-$140

Best Western
**AAA Benefit:** Members save 10% or more with Best Western!

**Address:** 2025 State Hwy 361 78362 **Location:** Jct SR 1069, 1 mi e. Located in a quiet semi-rural area. **Facility:** 37 units. 2 stories, exterior corridors. **Pool(s):** outdoor. **Guest Services:** valet and coin laundry.

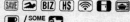

### COMFORT INN   (361)775-2700

Hotel
$80-$190

**Address:** 2800 State Hwy 361 78362 **Location:** On SR 361, 4 mi e of SR 35. Located in a quiet rural area. **Facility:** 40 units. 2 stories, interior corridors. **Amenities:** safes. **Pool(s):** outdoor. **Activities:** sauna, hot tub, exercise room. **Guest Services:** coin laundry. **Featured Amenity:** full hot breakfast.

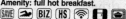

### MAINSTAY SUITES   (361)775-2000

Extended Stay Hotel
$99-$149

**Address:** 2787 State Hwy 361 78362 **Location:** Just w of city limits. **Facility:** 54 units, some efficiencies and kitchens. 4 stories, interior corridors. **Pool(s):** outdoor. **Activities:** hot tub, exercise room. **Guest Services:** coin laundry. **Featured Amenity:** full hot breakfast.

## IRVING (H-3) pop. 216,290
• Hotels p. 372 • Restaurants p. 377
• Hotels & Restaurants map & index p. 191
• Part of Dallas area — see map p. 161

Irving's proximity to the Dallas/Fort Worth International Airport fuels its prosperous service economy. Las Colinas Urban Center, the city's centerpiece, is a 12,000-acre development featuring high-rise office buildings housing hundreds of multinational companies. Shops, restaurants and outdoor cafes line the Mandalay Canal, which runs through the heart of the center.

Also of particular interest is the Irving Arts Center, which contains two performance theaters, four art galleries and a sculpture garden. Heritage Park, at Main and Second streets, features some historic structures including one of the city's original cabins, a windmill and a reconstructed railroad depot. Nearby stands Heritage House, 303 S. O'Connor Rd., which was built in 1912 and is one of Irving's oldest homes.

**Irving Convention and Visitors Bureau:** 500 W. Las Colinas Blvd., Irving, TX 75039. **Phone:** (972) 252-7476 or (800) 247-8464.

**THE MUSTANGS OF LAS COLINAS** are in Williams Square of Las Colinas Urban Center at 5205 N. O'Connor Blvd. In the pink granite plaza, nine larger-than-life bronze statues of wildly rushing mustangs appear to be splashing through a stream of water. This memorial to the heritage of Texas is believed to be the largest equestrian sculpture in the world.

**The Mustangs Sculpture Exhibit** is in the lobby of the West Tower at Williams Square. Photographs and a multimedia presentation explain the creation of the sculpture by renowned wildlife artist Robert Glen. Other works by Glen are displayed. **Time:** Allow 30 minutes minimum. **Hours:** Wed.-Sat. 11-5. Last film begins 30 minutes before closing. Closed major holidays. **Cost:** Donations. **Phone:** (972) 869-9047.

**THE NATIONAL SCOUTING MUSEUM OF THE BOY SCOUTS OF AMERICA** is at 1329 W. Walnut Hill Ln. Visitors can learn about the evolution of the Boy Scouts of America through hands-on and virtual reality exhibits, storytelling and other presentations. A Norman Rockwell art gallery also is included. Guided tours are available by reservation. **Time:** Allow 1 hour minimum. **Hours:** Mon.-Sat. 10-5 (also Mon. 5-7), Sun. 1-5. Closed major holidays. **Cost:**

(See map & index p. 191.)

$8; $6 (ages 4-12 and 60+); $5 (current and former Scouts); free (Sun.-Mon.). **Phone:** (972) 580-2100 or (800) 303-3047.

### ALOFT LAS COLINAS    (972)717-6100    49

Hotel
$71-$161

**AAA Benefit:** Enjoy the new twist, get up to 20% off + Starwood Preferred Guest® bonuses!

**Address:** 122 E John Carpenter Frwy 75062 **Location:** SR 114 exit O'Connor Rd, just s. **Facility:** 136 units. 5 stories, interior corridors. *Bath:* shower only. **Amenities:** safes. **Pool(s):** heated outdoor. **Activities:** exercise room. **Guest Services:** valet and coin laundry, area transportation. *(See ad p. 210.)*

### BEST WESTERN IRVING INN & SUITES AT DFW AIRPORT    (972)790-2262    58

Hotel
$69-$95

**AAA Benefit:** Members save 10% or more with Best Western!

**Address:** 4110 W Airport Frwy 75062 **Location:** SR 183 exit Esters Rd; on eastbound access road. **Facility:** 141 units. 2 stories (no elevator), exterior corridors. **Pool(s):** outdoor. **Activities:** hot tub, exercise room. **Guest Services:** valet and coin laundry, area transportation.

### BEST WESTERN PLUS DFW AIRPORT SUITES    (972)870-0530    22

Hotel
$81-$139

**AAA Benefit:** Members save 10% or more with Best Western!

**Address:** 5050 W John Carpenter Frwy 75063 **Location:** SR 114 exit Freeport Pkwy; on eastbound frontage road. **Facility:** 70 units. 3 stories, interior corridors. **Pool(s):** outdoor. **Activities:** hot tub, exercise room. **Guest Services:** valet and coin laundry.

### CANDLEWOOD SUITES DALLAS/LAS COLINAS    (972)714-9990    44

Extended Stay Hotel $81-$109 **Address:** 5300 Green Park Dr 75038 **Location:** SR 114 exit Walnut Hill Ln, just s. Located in a business center area. **Facility:** 117 efficiencies. 4 stories, interior corridors. **Terms:** 3 day cancellation notice-fee imposed. **Activities:** exercise room. **Guest Services:** complimentary and valet laundry, area transportation.

### COMFORT INN & SUITES DFW AIRPORT SOUTH    (972)790-7979    57

Hotel
$62-$119

**Address:** 4940 W Airport Frwy 75062 **Location:** SR 183 exit Valley View Ln. **Facility:** 93 units. 2 stories, interior corridors. **Amenities:** safes. **Pool(s):** outdoor. **Activities:** hot tub, exercise room. **Guest Services:** valet and coin laundry, area transportation.

### COMFORT SUITES DFW AIRPORT    (972)929-9097    29

Hotel $99-$129 **Address:** 4700 W John Carpenter Frwy 75063 **Location:** SR 114 exit Freeport Pkwy; on eastbound service road. **Facility:** 108 units. 3 stories, interior corridors. **Pool(s):** outdoor. **Activities:** hot tub, exercise room. **Guest Services:** valet and coin laundry. *(See ad p. 373.)*

### COMFORT SUITES LAS COLINAS CENTER    (972)518-0606    37

Hotel $99-$119 **Address:** 1223 Greenway Cir 75038 **Location:** Just sw of jct SR 114 and MacArthur Blvd, just s to Corporate Dr, then 0.3 mi w on Executive Dr. **Facility:** 54 units. 3 stories, interior corridors. **Amenities:** safes. **Activities:** exercise room. **Guest Services:** valet and coin laundry, area transportation.

### COURTYARD BY MARRIOTT-DALLAS-LAS COLINAS    (972)550-8100    39

Hotel
$69-$209

COURTYARD
*Marriott*

**AAA Benefit:** Members save 5% or more!

**Address:** 1151 W Walnut Hill Ln 75038 **Location:** SR 114 exit MacArthur Blvd, just s, then just w. **Facility:** 147 units. 3 stories, interior corridors. **Pool(s):** heated indoor. **Activities:** exercise room. **Guest Services:** valet and coin laundry, boarding pass kiosk, area transportation.

### COURTYARD BY MARRIOTT-DFW AIRPORT NORTH    (972)929-4004    17

Hotel $79-$189 **Address:** 4949 Regent Blvd 75063 **Location:** I-635 exit 34 (Freeport Pkwy), 0.5 mi s, then 0.5 mi w. **Facility:** 153 units. 3 stories, interior corridors. **Pool(s):** outdoor. **Activities:** exercise room. **Guest Services:** valet and coin laundry.

**AAA Benefit:** Members save 5% or more!

---

Be a better driver.
Keep your mind on the road.

(See map & index p. 191.)

## COURTYARD BY MARRIOTT DFW AIRPORT SOUTH
(972)790-8990 53

Hotel
$89-$179

**AAA Benefit:** Members save 5% or more!

**Address:** 2280 Valley View Ln 75062 **Location:** SR 183 exit Valley View Ln, just n. **Facility:** 154 units. 4 stories, interior corridors. **Amenities:** video games. **Pool(s):** outdoor. **Activities:** hot tub, exercise room. **Guest Services:** valet and coin laundry, area transportation.

/ SOME UNITS

### COURTYARD
Marriott
**Completely renovated with 154 rooms and 1700 s.f. of Meeting Space. Complimentary airport shuttle.**

## DALLAS MARRIOTT LAS COLINAS
(972)831-0000 46

Hotel $104-$248 **Address:** 223 W Las Colinas Blvd 75039 **Location:** SR 114 exit O'Connor Rd, just n to Las Colinas Blvd, then just w. Located in an office park. **Facility:** 364 units. 14 stories, interior corridors. **Parking:** on-site (fee) and valet. **Pool(s):** heated indoor. **Activities:** hot tub, exercise room. **Guest Services:** valet and coin laundry.

**AAA Benefit:** Members save 5% or more!

/ SOME UNITS

## DFW NORTH SUPER 8
(214)441-9000 28

Hotel
$55-$125

**Address:** 4770 W John Carpenter Frwy (SR 114) 75063 **Location:** SR 114 exit Freeport Pkwy; on east frontage road. **Facility:** 61 units. 3 stories, interior corridors. **Amenities:** safes. **Activities:** exercise room. **Guest Services:** valet and coin laundry. **Featured Amenity:** continental breakfast.

## DOUBLETREE BY HILTON HOTEL DFW AIRPORT-NORTH
(972)929-8181 30

Hotel
$99-$289

**AAA Benefit:** Members save 5% or more!

**Address:** 4441 W John Carpenter Frwy 75063 **Location:** N off SR 114 exit Esters Blvd. **Facility:** 282 units. 8 stories, interior corridors. **Terms:** 1-7 night minimum stay, cancellation fee imposed. **Amenities:** safes. **Pool(s):** outdoor. **Activities:** exercise room. **Guest Services:** valet and coin laundry, area transportation.

/ SOME UNITS

Enjoy exclusive member discounts and benefits from Hertz

▼ See AAA listing p. 372 ▼

(See map & index p. 191.)

## ELEMENT DALLAS FORT WORTH AIRPORT NORTH
(972)929-9800  **20**

Hotel
$89-$162

**AAA Benefit:** Experience Element, get up to 20% off + Starwood Preferred Guest® bonuses!

**Address:** 3550 IH 635 75063 **Location:** I-635 exit 33 (Belt Line Rd), just s. **Facility:** 123 units, some efficiencies. 4 stories, interior corridors. *Bath:* shower only. **Amenities:** safes. **Pool(s):** heated outdoor. **Activities:** exercise room. **Guest Services:** coin laundry, area transportation.

---

## EMBASSY SUITES-DFW SOUTH
(972)790-0093  **60**

Hotel $119-$229 **Address:** 4650 W Airport Frwy 75062 **Location:** SR 183 exit Valley View Ln, just s. **Facility:** 305 units. 10 stories, interior corridors. **Terms:** 1-7 night minimum stay, cancellation fee imposed. **Pool(s):** heated indoor. **Activities:** hot tub, exercise room. **Guest Services:** valet and coin laundry, area transportation.

**AAA Benefit:** Members save 5% or more!

---

## FAIRFIELD INN & SUITES BY MARRIOTT
(972)929-7257  **27**

Hotel $67-$139 **Address:** 4800 W John Carpenter Frwy 75063 **Location:** SR 114 exit Freeport Pkwy; on eastbound service road. **Facility:** 101 units. 3 stories, interior corridors. **Pool(s):** outdoor. **Activities:** exercise room. **Guest Services:** valet and coin laundry.

**AAA Benefit:** Members save 5% or more!

---

## FAIRFIELD INN & SUITES BY MARRIOTT DFW AIRPORT SOUTH
(214)441-9969  **61**

Hotel $75-$142 **Address:** 4210 W Airport Frwy 75062 **Location:** SR 183 exit Valley View Ln; on eastbound frontage road. **Facility:** 119 units. 4 stories, interior corridors. **Pool(s):** outdoor. **Activities:** exercise room. **Guest Services:** valet and coin laundry, area transportation.

**AAA Benefit:** Members save 5% or more!

---

## FAIRFIELD INN & SUITES BY MARRIOTT-LAS COLINAS
(972)550-8800  **42**

Hotel $89-$139 **Address:** 630 W John Carpenter Frwy 75039 **Location:** SR 114 exit Walnut Hill Ln. **Facility:** 117 units. 3 stories, interior corridors. **Pool(s):** heated indoor. **Activities:** hot tub, exercise room. **Guest Services:** valet and coin laundry, area transportation.

**AAA Benefit:** Members save 5% or more!

---

Explore on-the-go travel tools

at AAA.com/mobile or

CAA.ca/mobile

## FOUR SEASONS RESORT AND CLUB
(972)717-0700  **52**

Resort Hotel
$280-$430

**Address:** 4150 N MacArthur Blvd 75038 **Location:** SR 114 exit MacArthur Blvd, 1.5 mi s. **Facility:** A spa, golf course and high-end health club with tennis courts gives this luxury resort a retreat-like ambiance. The villas offer added seclusion. This resort setting is just outside of Dallas. 431 units. 2-9 stories, interior corridors. **Parking:** on-site and valet. **Terms:** cancellation fee imposed. **Amenities:** safes. **Dining:** 2 restaurants, also, Café on the Green, see separate listing. **Pool(s):** heated outdoor, heated indoor. **Activities:** sauna, hot tub, steamroom, regulation golf, tennis, recreation programs, playground, game room, spa. **Guest Services:** valet laundry, area transportation. *(See ad p. 214.)*

---

## HAMPTON INN-DFW AIRPORT SOUTH
(972)986-3606  **59**

Hotel $79-$159 **Address:** 4340 W Airport Frwy 75062 **Location:** SR 183 exit Valley View Ln; on southbound access road. **Facility:** 80 units. 4 stories, interior corridors. **Terms:** 1-7 night minimum stay, cancellation fee imposed. **Pool(s):** outdoor. **Activities:** exercise room. **Guest Services:** valet laundry, area transportation.

**AAA Benefit:** Members save up to 10%!

---

## HAMPTON INN LAS COLINAS
(972)753-1232  **41**

Hotel $119-$139 **Address:** 820 W Walnut Hill Ln 75038 **Location:** SR 114 exit MacArthur Blvd eastbound, just s, then just e; exit Walnut Hill Ln westbound, just sw. **Facility:** 135 units. 6 stories, interior corridors. **Terms:** 1-7 night minimum stay, cancellation fee imposed. **Pool(s):** outdoor. **Activities:** exercise room. **Guest Services:** valet laundry, area transportation.

**AAA Benefit:** Members save up to 10%!

---

## HILTON GARDEN INN LAS COLINAS
(972)444-8434  **34**

Hotel $135-$159 **Address:** 7516 Las Colinas Blvd 75063 **Location:** I-635 exit 31 (MacArthur Blvd), just s, then e. **Facility:** 173 units. 5 stories, interior corridors. **Terms:** 1-7 night minimum stay, cancellation fee imposed. **Pool(s):** heated outdoor. **Activities:** exercise room. **Guest Services:** valet and coin laundry, area transportation.

**AAA Benefit:** Members save up to 10%!

---

## HOLIDAY INN EXPRESS & SUITES-DFW NORTH
972/929-4499  **32**

Hotel. Rates not provided. **Address:** 4550 W John Carpenter Frwy 75063 **Location:** SR 114 exit Freeport Pkwy; on southbound service road. **Facility:** 163 units. 3 stories, interior corridors. **Pool(s):** outdoor. **Activities:** exercise room. **Guest Services:** valet and coin laundry.

---

## HOLIDAY INN EXPRESS DFW AIRPORT SOUTH
(972)659-1272  **55**

Hotel $89-$189 **Address:** 4235 W Airport Frwy 75062 **Location:** SR 183 exit Esters Rd; on westbound frontage road. **Facility:** 128 units. 6 stories, interior corridors. **Pool(s):** outdoor. **Activities:** exercise room. **Guest Services:** valet and coin laundry, area transportation.

(See map & index p. 191.)

## HOLIDAY INN EXPRESS HOTEL & SUITES IRVING CONVENTION CENTER  (972)910-0302 **45**

Hotel
$79-$149

**Address:** 333 W John Carpenter Frwy 75039 **Location:** SR 114 exit Hidden Ridge Rd. **Facility:** 128 units. 6 stories, interior corridors. **Terms:** cancellation fee imposed. **Pool(s):** heated outdoor. **Activities:** exercise room. **Guest Services:** valet and coin laundry, area transportation. **Featured Amenity:** full hot breakfast.

## HOMEWOOD SUITES BY HILTON IRVING DFW AIRPORT NORTH  (972)929-2202 **25**

**Extended Stay Hotel**
$109-$189 **Address:** 7800 Dulles Dr 75063 **Location:** SR 114 exit Freeport Pkwy, just se. **Facility:** 77 efficiencies. 4 stories, interior corridors. **Terms:** 1-7 night minimum stay, cancellation fee imposed. **Amenities:** video games. **Pool(s):** heated indoor. **Activities:** hot tub, exercise room. **Guest Services:** valet and coin laundry.

**AAA Benefit:** Members save up to 10%!

## HOMEWOOD SUITES BY HILTON LAS COLINAS  (972)556-0665 **51**

**Extended Stay Hotel**
$99-$169 **Address:** 4300 Wingren Dr 75039 **Location:** SR 114 exit O'Connor Rd/Wingren Dr eastbound, just e on frontage road, then just n; exit Rochelle Rd westbound, just w on frontage road, then just n. **Facility:** 136 efficiencies. 3 stories, interior/exterior corridors. **Terms:** 1-7 night minimum stay, cancellation fee imposed. **Amenities:** video games. **Pool(s):** outdoor. **Activities:** hot tub, exercise room. **Guest Services:** valet and coin laundry, area transportation.

**AAA Benefit:** Members save up to 10%!

## HYATT HOUSE DALLAS/LAS COLINAS  (972)831-0909 **36**

**Extended Stay Hotel**
$83-$189

**HYATT** house™

**AAA Benefit:** Members save 10%!

**Address:** 5901 N MacArthur Blvd 75039 **Location:** SR 114 exit MacArthur Blvd; northwest corner. **Facility:** 148 kitchen units, some two bedrooms. 2-3 stories (no elevator), interior/exterior corridors. **Terms:** cancellation fee imposed. **Pool(s):** outdoor. **Activities:** hot tub, exercise room. **Guest Services:** valet and coin laundry, area transportation. **Featured Amenity:** breakfast buffet.

## HYATT PLACE DALLAS/LAS COLINAS  (972)550-7400 **43**

Hotel
$69-$199

**HYATT PLACE**™

**AAA Benefit:** Members save 10%!

**Address:** 5455 Green Park Dr 75038 **Location:** SR 114 exit Walnut Hill Ln, just se. **Facility:** 122 units. 6 stories, interior corridors. **Terms:** cancellation fee imposed. **Pool(s):** heated outdoor. **Activities:** exercise room. **Guest Services:** valet laundry, area transportation. **Featured Amenity:** breakfast buffet.

## JEFFERSON STREET BED AND BREAKFAST INN  (972)253-2000 **62**

Bed & Breakfast
$85-$280

**Address:** 512 S Jefferson St 75060 **Location:** SR 183 exit O'Connor Rd, 2 mi s to 6th St, 0.3 mi e to Jefferson St, then just n. **Facility:** 9 units, some cottages. 1 story, exterior corridors. **Terms:** cancellation fee imposed. **Activities:** hot tub. **Guest Services:** complimentary and valet laundry. **Featured Amenity:** continental breakfast.

## LA QUINTA INN & SUITES DALLAS DFW AIRPORT NORTH  (972)915-4022 **24**

**Hotel** $85-$150 **Address:** 4850 W John Carpenter Frwy 75063 **Location:** SR 114 exit Freeport Pkwy; on eastbound frontage road. **Facility:** 140 units. 3 stories, interior corridors. **Pool(s):** outdoor. **Activities:** hot tub, exercise room. **Guest Services:** valet and coin laundry, area transportation.

## LA QUINTA INN & SUITES DALLAS DFW AIRPORT SOUTH/ IRVING  (972)252-6546 **56**

**Hotel** $85-$160 **Address:** 4105 W Airport Frwy 75062-5997 **Location:** SR 183 exit Esters Rd westbound; exit N Belt Line Rd eastbound; on westbound frontage road. **Facility:** 168 units. 5 stories, interior corridors. **Pool(s):** heated outdoor. **Activities:** hot tub, exercise room. **Guest Services:** valet and coin laundry, area transportation.

## LA QUINTA INN & SUITES DALLAS - LAS COLINAS  (972)261-4900 **50**

**Hotel** $82-$140 **Address:** 4225 N MacArthur Blvd 75038 **Location:** Se off SR 114 exit MacArthur Blvd, 1.4 mi s. **Facility:** 92 units. 2 stories, interior corridors. **Pool(s):** outdoor. **Activities:** exercise room. **Guest Services:** valet and coin laundry, area transportation.

(See map & index p. 191.)

## MARRIOTT HOTEL-DFW AIRPORT NORTH
(972)929-8800 **19**

Hotel
$80-$227

**Marriott**
HOTELS & RESORTS

**AAA Benefit:** Members save 5% or more!

**Address:** 8440 Freeport Pkwy 75063 **Location:** Nw off SR 114 exit Freeport Pkwy. **Facility:** 491 units. 20 stories, interior corridors. **Dining:** 2 restaurants. **Pool(s):** heated outdoor, heated indoor. **Activities:** hot tub, exercise room. **Guest Services:** complimentary and valet laundry.

SAVE 🚷 🍴 🐕 🍸 CALL 📶
🏊 BIZ 📶 ✕ 🎮 🖥
/ SOME UNITS 📦

## MOTEL 6 #4725 DFW NORTH
972/915-3993 **31**

◆ **Motel.** Rates not provided. **Address:** 7800 Heathrow Dr 75063 **Location:** SR 114 exit Freeport Pkwy, just se. **Facility:** 121 units. 3 stories, interior corridors. **Pool(s):** outdoor. **Guest Services:** coin laundry. 🚷 🏊 📶 / SOME UNITS 🐾

## NYLO DALLAS/LAS COLINAS
(972)373-8900 **35**

Hotel
$89-$499

**Address:** 1001 W Royal Ln 75039 **Location:** SR 114 exit MacArthur Blvd, just n, then just w. **Facility:** 200 units. 5 stories, interior corridors. *Bath:* shower only. **Terms:** cancellation fee imposed. **Amenities:** safes. **Pool(s):** heated outdoor. **Activities:** exercise room. **Guest Services:** valet laundry, area transportation.

SAVE 🍴 🍸 🏊 BIZ HS 📶
✕ 🖥 / SOME UNITS 🐾

## OMNI MANDALAY DALLAS AT LAS COLINAS
(972)556-0800 **48**

◆◆◆ ◆◆◆ **Hotel** $119-$329 **Address:** 221 E Las Colinas Blvd 75039 **Location:** SR 114 exit O'Connor Rd, just n, then just e. Located in a trendy office-park and residential area. **Facility:** For those searching for a scenic location and a slower pace, the Omni fronts a man-made lake and is centered in the perfectly manicured Las Colinas community. Close to restaurants and running trails. 421 units. 27 stories, interior corridors. **Parking:** on-site and valet. **Terms:** cancellation fee imposed. **Amenities:** safes. **Pool(s):** heated outdoor. **Activities:** sauna, hot tub, playground, exercise room, spa. **Guest Services:** valet laundry, area transportation.

🍴 🐕 🍸 🏊 BIZ 📶 ✕ 🎮 🖥
/ SOME UNITS 🐾 📦 🖥

## RED ROOF INN/DFW AIRPORT NORTH
(972)929-0020 **23**

Motel
$49-$89

**Address:** 8150 Esters Blvd 75063 **Location:** SR 114 exit Esters Blvd, just n. **Facility:** 156 units. 3 stories, exterior corridors. **Amenities:** video games, safes. **Guest Services:** coin laundry.

SAVE 🚷 🍴 📶
/ SOME UNITS 🐾 HS 📦 🖥 🖥

## RESIDENCE INN BY MARRIOTT AT LAS COLINAS
(972)580-7773 **40**

◆◆◆ **Extended Stay Hotel** $79-$219 **Address:** 950 W Walnut Hill Ln 75038 **Location:** SR 114 exit MacArthur Blvd, 0.5 mi s, then just e. **Facility:** 120 kitchen units. 2 stories (no elevator), exterior corridors. **Pool(s):** outdoor. **Activities:** exercise room. **Guest Services:** valet and coin laundry, area transportation.

**AAA Benefit:** Members save 5% or more!

ECO 🚷 CALL 📶 🏊 BIZ HS 📶 ✕ 📦 🖥
🖥 / SOME UNITS 🐾

## RESIDENCE INN BY MARRIOTT-DFW NORTH
(972)871-1331 **18**

◆◆◆ **Extended Stay Hotel** $80-$160 **Address:** 8600 Esters Blvd 75063 **Location:** SR 114 exit Esters Blvd, 0.9 mi n. **Facility:** 100 units, some efficiencies and kitchens. 3 stories, interior corridors. **Pool(s):** outdoor. **Activities:** hot tub, exercise room. **Guest Services:** valet and coin laundry, area transportation.

**AAA Benefit:** Members save 5% or more!

🚷 CALL 📶 🏊 BIZ HS 📶 ✕ 📦 🖥 🖥
/ SOME UNITS 🐾

## SHERATON DFW AIRPORT HOTEL
(972)929-8400 **33**

◆◆◆◆ Hotel $99-$359

**Sheraton** HOTELS & RESORTS

**AAA Benefit:** Members get up to 20% off, plus Starwood Preferred Guest® bonuses!

**Address:** 4440 W John Carpenter Frwy 75063 **Location:** SR 114 exit Esters Blvd, just s. **Facility:** 303 units. 12 stories, interior corridors. **Terms:** cancellation fee imposed, resort fee. **Pool(s):** heated outdoor. **Activities:** exercise room. **Guest Services:** valet laundry, area transportation.

SAVE 🚷 🍴 🐕 🍸 🏊 BIZ
sHS 📶 ✕ 🎮 🖥
/ SOME UNITS 🐾 📦

## STAYBRIDGE SUITES DALLAS-LAS COLINAS
(972)465-9400 **38**

◆◆◆ **Extended Stay Hotel** $99-$229 **Address:** 1201 Executive Cir 75038 **Location:** SR 114 exit MacArthur Blvd, just s to W Walnut Hill Ln, then just w. **Facility:** 117 efficiencies. 3 stories, interior corridors. **Terms:** cancellation fee imposed. **Pool(s):** heated outdoor. **Activities:** exercise room. **Guest Services:** complimentary and valet laundry, area transportation.

🏊 BIZ HS 📶 📦 🖥 🖥 / SOME UNITS 🐾

## SUPER 8 DFW SOUTH IRVING
(972)257-1810 **54**

◆◆ Hotel
$55-$85

**Address:** 4245 W Airport Frwy 75062 **Location:** SR 183 exit Esters Rd; on westbound frontage road. **Facility:** 101 units. 3 stories, interior corridors. **Guest Services:** valet and coin laundry. **Featured Amenity:** continental breakfast.

SAVE 🚷 🍴 📶
/ SOME UNITS 🐾 📦 🖥

(See map & index p. 191.)

## THE WESTIN DALLAS FORT WORTH AIRPORT
(972)929-4500  **26**

Hotel
$89-$349

**WESTIN** HOTELS & RESORTS **AAA Benefit:** Enjoy up to 20% off your next stay, plus Starwood Preferred Guest® bonuses!

**Address:** 4545 W John Carpenter Frwy 75063 **Location:** SR 114 exit Esters Blvd, just n. **Facility:** 506 units. 15 stories, interior corridors. **Parking:** on-site and valet. **Terms:** cancellation fee imposed. **Amenities:** safes. **Dining:** 2 restaurants. **Pool(s):** heated outdoor. **Activities:** hot tub, exercise room. **Guest Services:** valet laundry, area transportation.

## WINGATE BY WYNDHAM DFW AIRPORT NORTH
(972)929-4600  **21**

Hotel
$79-$149

**Address:** 8220 Esters Blvd 75063 **Location:** SR 114 exit Esters Blvd, just n. **Facility:** 113 units. 3 stories, interior corridors. **Terms:** 3 day cancellation notice-fee imposed. **Amenities:** video games, safes. **Pool(s):** heated outdoor. **Activities:** hot tub, exercise room. **Guest Services:** valet and coin laundry. **Featured Amenity:** full hot breakfast.

## WYNDHAM-LAS COLINAS
(972)650-1600  **47**

Hotel
$79-$349

**Address:** 110 W John Carpenter Frwy 75039 **Location:** Sw off SR 114 exit O'Connor Rd. **Facility:** 168 units. 3 stories, interior corridors. **Terms:** cancellation fee imposed. **Amenities:** video games. **Pool(s):** heated indoor. **Activities:** hot tub, exercise room. **Guest Services:** valet and coin laundry, area transportation.

## WHERE TO EAT

### ANGELO'S SPAGHETTI & PIZZA
972-254-7242  **44**

Italian. Casual Dining. $6-$14 **AAA Inspector Notes:** In business for more than 45 years, Angelo's is old-school Italian food served up by servers that have as much dedication to the restaurant as the community has had to it. You'll find that the place hasn't changed much since it opened in 1966. The numerous pizza boxes lined up at the entry expose one of their best-sellers. BYOB. **Address:** 1330 W Pioneer Dr 75061 **Location:** SR 183 exit Belt Line Rd, just s, then 1.9 mi w. L D

### BANGKOK ORCHID
972-252-7770  **40**

Thai. Casual Dining. $9-$15 **AAA Inspector Notes:** The shopping center may not be too appealing, but once through the doors of Bangkok Orchid guests experience a taste of Thailand without the travel. Dishes can be spicy, so a careful approach to the food is advised. Lime green and bright orange walls combine with contemporary furniture, Asian accents and an eclectic but groovy music selection for an enjoyable meal out. **Address:** 3311 W Airport Frwy 75062 **Location:** Jct SR 183 and N Belt Line Rd; northeast corner; in Irving Town Strip Mall. L D CALL M

### THE BLUE FISH
972-385-3474  **27**

Japanese. Casual Dining. $13-$27 **AAA Inspector Notes:** This contemporary restaurant features traditional and creative sushi preparations. Among dishes are sushi, sashimi and tempura preparations, as well as chicken, beef and seafood entrées. Guests can sit at the sushi bar to watch the chef in action or at the lively bar that routinely fills up with office dwellers. **Features:** full bar, happy hour. **Address:** 925 W John Carpenter Frwy, Unit 100 75039 **Location:** SR 114 exit MacArthur Blvd, just n. L D

### BLUE GINGER
972-373-9799  **26**

Thai. Casual Dining. $8-$16 **AAA Inspector Notes:** Popular with young local residents who come for the all-day weekend happy hours, this restaurant has modern décor and a nice assortment of dishes, including curries, stir-fries, noodle soups, duck and fish dishes. **Features:** full bar, patio dining, happy hour. **Address:** 6550 N MacArthur Blvd, Unit 150 75039 **Location:** SR 114 exit MacArthur Blvd, just n. L D

### CAFÉ ON THE GREEN
972-717-0700  **33**

American
Fine Dining
$18-$48

**AAA Inspector Notes:** A sophisticated a la carte menu with a creative American edge shows off the chef's artistic talents. Sample some chipotle barbecue prawns, chicken-fried quail, black bean quinoa cake or beef tenderloin. Breakfast and lunch feature both buffet dining or a la carte choices. **Features:** full bar, Sunday brunch. **Reservations:** suggested. **Address:** 4150 N MacArthur Blvd 75038 **Location:** SR 114 exit MacArthur Blvd, 1.5 mi s; in Four Seasons Resort and Club. **Parking:** valet only. B L D CALL M

### CAVALLI PIZZA NAPOLETANA
972-915-0001  **20**

Pizza. Casual Dining. $7-$12 **AAA Inspector Notes:** Certified by the Italian government as authentic Napolitana pizza, this independent pizzeria specializes in brick-oven pizza that blisters and chars around the edges. Whatever pizza you fancy, clams casino, pesto chicken or margherita perhaps, consider adding on the roasted cherry tomatoes. You'll be pleased when you experience the sweet explosion in your mouth. **Address:** 3601 Regent Blvd 75063 **Location:** I-635 exit 33 (Belt Line Rd), just s, then just w. L D

### CHICAGO'S GOURMET PIZZA
972-717-7770  **30**

Pizza. Casual Dining. $10-$25 **AAA Inspector Notes:** Small, cozy eatery featuring traditional Chicago deep-dish and hand-rolled pizza. While popular at lunch with area office workers, it's much slower in the evenings, but company is provided by whatever is playing on the TV. **Address:** 114 E John Carpenter Frwy 75062 **Location:** SR 114 exit O'Connor Rd, just s. L D

### COOL RIVER CAFE
972-871-8881  **29**

Steak
Fine Dining
$13-$40

**AAA Inspector Notes:** The café's dining room is rich with mahogany-style woods. Rock walls and large murals wrap the room. After trying the crab cake appetizer, diners might select one of the steak or chicken portions, which are served in ample portions. Guests can play pool while listening to live music from Thursday through Saturday. An extensive wine and liquor list comes from the full bar. This place is very popular with the local office workers. **Features:** full bar, happy hour. **Reservations:** suggested. **Address:** 1045 Hidden Ridge Rd 75038 **Location:** Se off SR 114 exit MacArthur Blvd, 1.5 mi s. **Parking:** on-site and valet. L D CALL M

**Steak, seafood, Southwestern fare, world-class bar**

Get more from your membership

with an upgrade to Plus or Premier

**(See map & index p. 191.)**

**EAST BUFFET** — 972/659-8999 **42**

Chinese. Casual Dining. $8-$11 **AAA Inspector Notes:** The complete buffet lines up a variety of appetizers, entrées and desserts. Diners can choose among everything from General Tso's chicken, kung pao chicken and Hunan pork to fried donuts and vegetable rolls. Also featured is a Mongolian grill, where beef, pork and chicken are cooked to order with varied vegetables, oils and toppings. Some American options also are offered. **Address:** 4023 W Airport Frwy 75062 **Location:** SR 183 exit Belt Line Rd; on westbound frontage road. L D CALL

**EL CHICO** — 972/659-1662 **41**

Tex-Mex
Casual Dining
$6-$16

**AAA Inspector Notes:** Inside and out, the decor of the popular Mexican restaurant is inviting. The menu features traditional favorites such as enchiladas, tacos, burritos and fajitas. The broad menu also lists a few American classics. **Features:** full bar, happy hour. **Address:** 2305 W Airport Frwy 75062 **Location:** SR 183 exit Mac-Arthur Blvd eastbound; exit Story Rd westbound; on westbound frontage road. L D

**FRED'S BAR-B-Q** — 972/579-7655 **45**

Barbecue. Quick Serve. $7-$16 **AAA Inspector Notes:** Located near the historic center of the city, the family-owned and -operated restaurant has been in business for 30 years and prepares nothing more than a variety of barbecue dished up in large portions. The atmosphere is rustic, and the owners are on-site for both good food and good cheer. **Address:** 808 E Irving Blvd 75060 **Location:** 0.9 mi w of jct S Loop 12 and SR 356 (Irving Blvd). L D

**GRANDY'S RESTAURANT** — 972/258-8584

American. Quick Serve. $4-$8 **AAA Inspector Notes:** Fried chicken and country-fried steak are menu standbys at the restaurant, a regional franchise. They also offer a family-style dining menu. The décor is a step up from that of most quick-serve eateries and more resembles that of a conventional restaurant. Some elements of increased service include additional rolls, iced tea refills and tray removal. **Address:** 2815 Beltline Rd 75062 **Location:** 1.5 mi n of jct SR 183 (Airport Frwy). B L D

**I FRATELLI ITALIAN RESTAURANT** — 972/501-9700 **24**

Italian. Casual Dining. $9-$19 **AAA Inspector Notes:** This Italian eatery, which is very family-friendly, features an array of Italian favorites, with pizza as the specialty. Surrounded by attractive wine racks, a variety of regional and international wines is available. You can dine inside where the atmosphere is warm and inviting or enjoy outside dining on their trendy patio. Be sure and try one of their homemade desserts to top off your meal. **Features:** full bar, happy hour. **Reservations:** suggested. **Address:** 7701 N MacArthur Blvd 75063 **Location:** I-635 exit 31 (MacArthur Blvd), just s. L D

**ITALIAN CAFE** — 972/401-0000 **32**

Italian. Casual Dining. $4-$17 **AAA Inspector Notes:** This family-owned and -operated restaurant prepares a good selection of traditional dishes, including chicken, veal, pasta and shrimp entrées, as well as pizzas. Pizza by the slice is available, and the slices are generous. Lunch is buffet only. **Features:** full bar, patio dining. **Address:** 387 E Las Colinas Blvd, Suite 120 75039 **Location:** SR 114 exit O'Connor Rd/Wingren Rd eastbound; exit Rochelle Rd westbound, just n to Las Colinas Blvd, 0.5 mi e; northeast corner of Wingren Rd and Las Colinas Blvd. L D

**JINBEH** — 972/869-4011

Japanese. Casual Dining. $10-$45 **AAA Inspector Notes:** The small restaurant offers a sushi bar, hibachi tables and tatami rooms, along with traditional cuisine, to give dining experiences a real Japanese flair. The lunch menu lists some good bargains for the business-lunch crowd. The selection of sushi and sashimi is excellent; during the week dinner is packed with business travelers and the eatery can become quite lively. **Features:** full bar. **Address:** 301 E Las Colinas Blvd 75039 **Location:** SR 114 exit O'Connor Rd/Wingren Dr, just n to Las Colinas Blvd, then just e. L D

**KASBAH GRILL** — 214/596-9206 **36**

Moroccan. Casual Dining. $5-$12 **AAA Inspector Notes:** This little restaurant grew its following out of a gas station but now greets its guests in a cozy dining room with offerings of tagines, couscous and kebabs. **Address:** 2851 Esters Rd 75062 **Location:** SR 183 exit Esters Rd, just n. L D

**LA MADELEINE COUNTRY FRENCH CAFE** — 469/385-1700

Traditional French. Quick Serve. $6-$12 **AAA Inspector Notes:** A fireplace creates the focal point at this cozy European style café where you can always get a quiche or savory stuffed puffed pastry on the go or stick around for a chicken crêpe or French dip sandwich. Heartier entrées like rotisserie chicken are offered and every season promises menu surprises. Whatever you decide on you probably will not get out the door without enjoying one of their tempting sweet pastries. **Features:** wine only, patio dining. **Address:** 6430 N MacArthur Blvd 75039 **Location:** Jct W Royal Ln and N MacArthur Blvd. B L D

**LA MARGARITA** — 972/570-1137 **37**

Tex-Mex. Casual Dining. $7-$15 **AAA Inspector Notes:** South-of-the-border cuisine is prepared with a focus on fresh ingredients and creative recipes. Colorful murals, festive lights and Spanish music make for an enjoyable dining experience. The tequila lounge is always full of people hanging out or watching a game. The restaurant mixes both traditional Tex-Mex and contemporary Mexican cuisine, which means it can accommodate both the enchilada lover and those looking for less commonplace dishes and flavors. **Features:** full bar, happy hour. **Address:** 2922 N Belt Line Rd 75062 **Location:** SR 183 exit Belt Line Rd, 0.5 mi n. L D

**LOS LUPES VI** — 972/870-1500 **39**

Tex-Mex. Casual Dining. $7-$16 **AAA Inspector Notes:** The small, regional, family-owned chain presents a menu of Tex-Mex fare. What differentiates this restaurant's food from most other Tex-Mex is that they venture in to more authentic preparations and offer items such as tongue, beef soup and labor-intensive tamales on the weekends. Tuesday night offers karaoke, and on Wednesday, Friday and Saturday the restaurant becomes a night club and stays open late. A buffet is offered for lunch on weekdays. **Features:** full bar, patio dining. **Address:** 3644 Irving Mall 75062 **Location:** SR 183 exit Belt Line Rd N; at Irving Mall. L D LATE

**MAMA'S DAUGHTERS' DINER #5** — 972/790-2778 **46**

Comfort Food. Casual Dining. $5-$11 **AAA Inspector Notes:** Note the "Mama-isms" written on the diner-style eatery's walls just to remind everyone who's boss. Good Southern-style cooking comes at a good price. On the menu are such classics as cornbread, turnip greens, and chicken and dumplings. **Address:** 2412 W Shady Grove Rd 75060 **Location:** SR 183 exit Story Rd, 2.3 mi s, then just w. B L D

**MAYURI INDIA RESTAURANT** — 972/910-8788 **21**

Indian. Casual Dining. $10-$18 **AAA Inspector Notes:** With a new location and a more extensive menu, Mayuri has refashioned itself for a second life. And it's a good thing because it now stands out from the numerous other Indian offerings in the area. Traditional preparations of southern and northern specialties can still be found alongside an added Indian-Chinese menu. Customers get good value with the lunch buffets, and for those with dietary restrictions there is an abundance of vegetarian options as well as halal meats. **Features:** beer & wine. **Address:** 1102 W I-635 75063 **Location:** I-635 exit 31 (MacArthur Park Dr), just s, then just w; in MacArthur Park Shopping Center; behind Target. L D

**MI COCINA** — 469/621-0451 **23**

Mexican. Casual Dining. $9-$22 **AAA Inspector Notes:** If you like Mexican cuisine but you prefer a more refined setting without the multicolored lights, village murals and bangity-bang music, then this is the place for you. While Mi Cocina still has the traditional queso, tacos and fajitas you can bring a date or celebrate something special and feel like you did it in style. **Features:** full bar, patio dining, happy hour. **Address:** 7750 N MacArthur Blvd 75063 **Location:** I-635 exit 31 (MacArthur Blvd), just s. L D

(See map & index p. 191.)

**MIDORI SUSHI** 972/887-1818 ③④
🔻🔻 Japanese. Casual Dining. $7-$22 **AAA Inspector Notes:** The small restaurant prepares traditional Japanese beef, chicken, seafood and vegetable dishes, as well as sushi and sashimi. Located in busy shopping center, it buzzes at lunchtime with people from the nearby business parks. **Features:** full bar. **Address:** 4020 N MacArthur Blvd, Suite 114 75038 **Location:** Se off SR 114 exit MacArthur Blvd, 1.6 mi s. [L] [D]

**PARADISE INDIAN CUISINE** 214/574-8500 ②⑤
🔻 Indian. Casual Dining. $10-$14 **AAA Inspector Notes:** Located in a busy retail area, this modern restaurant specializes in biryani (spice-laden rice dishes). Given the option, dinner is the better meal to have at this location. **Address:** 7300 N MacArthur Blvd, Suite 130 75063 **Location:** I-635 exit MacArthur Blvd, just s. [L] [D]

**PASAND INDIAN CUISINE** 972/594-0693 ③⑧
🔻🔻 Indian. Casual Dining. $10-$18 **AAA Inspector Notes:** Delicious traditional dishes include curries, tandoori entrées, dosas, stuffed pooris and more. The uninitiated may want to do the lunch buffets, as they provide an opportunity to try many things in small bites. The location just off the highway makes it a doable jaunt from DFW airport. **Features:** beer & wine. **Address:** 2600 N Belt Line Rd 75062 **Location:** SR 183 exit Belt Line Rd, just n; in strip mall. [L] [D]

**PIMAN ASIAN BISTRO** 972/650-0001 ③①
🔻🔻 Thai. Casual Dining. $7-$14 **AAA Inspector Notes:** Piman means heaven in Thai. This bistro, appropriate for any occasion, is justly named. The service is angelic, and the food is most pleasing. The extensive menu varies, with Japanese, Vietnamese and Chinese, but mainly Thai dishes, among the options. The intriguing sculpted heads that look over the dining room are characters from Thai literature. **Features:** beer & wine. **Address:** 4835 N O'Connor Rd, Unit 106 75062 **Location:** SR 114 exit O'Connor Rd, just s to O'Connor Ridge. [L] [D]

**ROCKFISH SEAFOOD GRILL** 214/574-4111
🔻🔻 Seafood. Casual Dining. $7-$20 **AAA Inspector Notes:** Patrons shuffle through peanut shells on the floor as they make their way to their seats and are easily distracted by the numerous pieces of hunting and fishing memorabilia adorning the walls and ceiling. Although guests kick back in a log cabin-style interior, the freshly caught fish gets more sophisticated preparation than campfire roasting. The chef uses an array of sauces and cooking styles, and soups are hearty and fresh. **Features:** full bar. **Address:** 7400 N MacArthur Blvd 75063 **Location:** SR 114 exit MacArthur Blvd, 1.3 mi n. [L] [D]

**SALTGRASS STEAKHOUSE** 972/373-9944 ②②
🔻🔻 Steak. Casual Dining. $9-$30 **AAA Inspector Notes:** Those looking for something different should try the comfortable steakhouse, which never says no to a special request. Born from the spirit of Texas cattle drives, the restaurant resembles a Texas lodge, with high ceilings and mounted animal heads. Baby back ribs are so tender the meat falls off the bone. Also on the menu are hearty steaks, prime rib, chicken, seafood and yummy desserts. **Features:** full bar. **Address:** 560 W LBJ Frwy 75063 **Location:** I-635 exit 31 (MacArthur Blvd). [SAVE] [L] [D] [🗙]

**SONNY BRYAN'S BBQ** 972/650-9564
🔻 Barbecue. Quick Serve. $8-$14 **AAA Inspector Notes:** In an upscale strip center in north Irving, the small restaurant, a barbecue legend for 100 years, serves a complete selection of beef, chicken, turkey and pork dishes to avid barbecue fans. Dine-in and takeout services are available. The food is simple but tasty. **Features:** beer only. **Address:** 4030 N MacArthur Blvd, Unit 222 75038 **Location:** SR 183 exit MacArthur Blvd, 1.5 mi n. [L] [D]

---

Discover free apps for mapping

and more at AAA.com/mobile

or CAA.ca/mobile

---

**SPRING CREEK BBQ** 972/313-0987
🔻 Barbecue. Casual Dining. $8-$13 **AAA Inspector Notes:** Expect Texas-Style barbecue at its simple, homey best. Hickory smoked ribs, beef, pork and turkey lace the air with a spicy aroma that mingles with the scent of freshly baked rolls and cold ice cream slowly melting over a dish of homemade peach cobbler. Plates often are loaded with all the coleslaw, potato salad and corn on the cob they can support. Part of a small chain, this barbecue restaurant displays a rustic décor that gives patrons the impression they are "at the ranch." **Features:** beer only. **Address:** 3514 W Airport Frwy 75061 **Location:** Jct SR 183 and Belt Line Rd; southwest corner. [L] [D]

**TAQUERA ARANDAS** 972/258-0789 ④③
🔻 Mexican. Casual Dining. $10-$15 **AAA Inspector Notes:** Restaurants in the small regional chain prepare Mexican standards, including enchiladas, quesadillas, fajitas, burritos and various combinations. Also offered are the classic torta and beef soup. What is sure is that the food here is not Tex-Mex, the salsa packs some heat and knowing Spanish is helpful. **Features:** full bar. **Address:** 1225 W Airport Frwy 75062 **Location:** SR 183 exit O'Connor Rd eastbound, U-turn under SR 183, then just w on access road; exit MacArthur Blvd westbound. [B] [L] [D]

**VERANDA GREEK CAFE** 972/518-0939 ②⑧
🔻🔻 Greek. Casual Dining. $7-$22 **AAA Inspector Notes:** The quiet restaurant presents a menu of traditional favorites, including spanakopita, souvlaki, moussaka and kebabs. Hummus is tasty with warm pita bread. The lunch buffet lines up interesting choices and offers a chance to sample with no commitment, but à la carte is available too. This place is popular for business lunches. **Features:** full bar. **Address:** 5433 N MacArthur Blvd 75038 **Location:** SR 114 exit MacArthur Blvd, just s. [L] [D]

**VIA REAL** 972/650-9001 ③⑤
🔻🔻🔻 Southwestern. Fine Dining. $8-$42 **AAA Inspector Notes:** This restaurant, designed with open beams, fireplaces and water fountains to evoke a New Mexican feel, features authentic recipes with an upscale flair. Enjoy flavorful selections like roasted pork loin, squash or spinach enchiladas, citrus-garlic shrimp and smoked mozzarella quesadillas. Its proximity to a luxury hotel makes it a popular place for business dinners—and keeps it very busy—which means sometimes it can get loud. **Features:** full bar, Sunday brunch. **Reservations:** suggested. **Address:** 4020 N MacArthur Blvd 75038 **Location:** SR 183 exit MacArthur Blvd, 1.5 mi n. **Parking:** on-site and valet. [L] [D]

**ZENSE** 972/401-0099 ①⑨
🔻🔻 Thai. Casual Dining. $9-$12 **AAA Inspector Notes:** The ping-pong balls hanging on the walls are a frequent topic of conversation, but the food is the real star at this small eatery. Curry, rice and noodle dishes are offered alongside items such as the tantalizing tom kha soup and crispy tilapia fillet. BYOB is allowed. **Address:** 8600 N MacArthur Blvd, Suite 142 75063 **Location:** I-635 exit 31 (MacArthur Blvd), just n. [L] [D]

## ITALY pop. 1,863
• Part of Dallas area — see map p. 161

**GRANDY'S RESTAURANT** 972/483-7601
🔻 American. Quick Serve. $4-$8 **AAA Inspector Notes:** Fried chicken and country-fried steak are menu standbys at the restaurant, a regional franchise. They also offer a family-style dining menu. The décor is a step up from that of most quick-serve eateries and more resembles that of a conventional restaurant. Some elements of increased service include additional rolls, iced tea refills and tray removal. **Address:** 101 L R Campbell Rd 76651 **Location:** I-35E exit 386. [B] [L] [D]

## JACKSBORO (C-8) pop. 4,511, elev. 1,084'

Jacksboro endured early existences as Lost Creek and Mesquiteville before it assumed its present identity. Some downtown buildings feature native limestone. Petroleum refining and related oil field services contribute to the economy.

**Jacksboro Chamber of Commerce:** 302 S. Main St., Jacksboro, TX 76458. **Phone:** (940) 567-2602.

**FORT RICHARDSON STATE HISTORIC SITE** is 1 mi. s. off US 281. Built in 1867, the fort was the northernmost in a chain of U.S. Cavalry posts used to halt Native American raids and to guard the Overland-Butterfield mail route. The fort was abandoned in 1878. Present-day Fort Richardson State Historic Site's 485 acres contain seven original and two replica buildings as well as picnic and camping facilities. *See Recreation Areas Chart.*

**Tours:** Guided tours are available. **Hours:** Grounds daily 8 a.m.-10 p.m. Guided tours daily at 10 and 2. Phone ahead to confirm schedule. **Cost:** $3; free (ages 0-12). Phone ahead for guided tour fees. **Phone:** (940) 567-3506.

## JACKSONVILLE (D-10) pop. 14,544, elev. 522'

**CHEROKEE TRACE DRIVE-THRU SAFARI** is at 1200 CR 4405. Exotic and endangered species roam freely in this 300-acre wildlife park. A self-guiding automobile drive allows visitors to view, feed and photograph fallow and sika deer, Indian antelope, a Watusi (African longhorn cow), bison and alligators.

**Time:** Allow 1 hour minimum. **Hours:** Mon.-Sat. 10-7, Sun. 1-7, June-Aug.; Mon.-Sat. 10-6, Sun. 1-6, Mar.-May; Mon.-Sat. 10-5, Sun. 1-5, rest of year. Last admission 90 minutes before closing. Closed Easter, Thanksgiving, Christmas Eve and Christmas. **Cost:** $15; $13 (ages 65+); $10 (ages 3-12). **Phone:** (903) 683-3322.

### BEST WESTERN EXECUTIVE INN     (903)586-0007

Hotel
$80-$90

**AAA Benefit:** Members save 10% or more with Best Western!

**Address:** 1659 S Jackson St 75766 **Location:** On US 69, 1.7 mi s of jct US 69 and 79. **Facility:** 53 units. 3 stories, interior corridors. **Pool(s):** heated indoor. **Activities:** hot tub, limited exercise equipment. **Guest Services:** coin laundry. **Featured Amenity:** full hot breakfast.

### COMFORT INN     (903)589-8500

Hotel $66-$119 **Address:** 1848 S Jackson St 75766 **Location:** On US 69, 2 mi s of jct US 69 and 79. **Facility:** 50 units. 2 stories (no elevator), interior corridors. **Pool(s):** outdoor. **Activities:** hot tub, exercise room. **Guest Services:** coin laundry.

### HOLIDAY INN EXPRESS & SUITES     903/589-8900

Hotel. Rates not provided. **Address:** 1923 S Jackson St 75766 **Location:** On US 69, 2.1 mi s of jct US 69 and 79. **Facility:** 68 units. 3 stories, interior corridors. **Pool(s):** heated indoor. **Activities:** hot tub, exercise room. **Guest Services:** valet and coin laundry.

### LA QUINTA INN & SUITES JACKSONVILLE     (903)586-6504

Hotel $99-$135 **Address:** 1902 S Jackson St 75766 **Location:** On US 69, 2.1 mi s of jct US 69 and 79. **Facility:** 62 units. 3 stories, interior corridors. **Pool(s):** heated indoor. **Activities:** exercise room. **Guest Services:** coin laundry.

## JASPER pop. 7,590

### BEST WESTERN INN OF JASPER     (409)384-7767

Hotel
$70-$90

**AAA Benefit:** Members save 10% or more with Best Western!

**Address:** 205 W Gibson St 75951 **Location:** US 190 and SR 63, 0.5 mi w of jct US 96. **Facility:** 59 units. 1-2 stories (no elevator), exterior corridors. **Amenities:** safes. **Pool(s):** outdoor. **Activities:** hot tub. **Guest Services:** coin laundry. **Featured Amenity:** breakfast buffet.

### HOLIDAY INN EXPRESS & SUITES     (409)384-8400

Hotel $100 **Address:** 501 W Gibson St 75951 **Location:** On US 190 and SR 63, 0.6 mi w of jct US 96. **Facility:** 65 units. 3 stories, interior corridors. **Pool(s):** outdoor. **Activities:** exercise room. **Guest Services:** valet and coin laundry.

### SUPER 8     (409)384-8600

Hotel
$65-$130

**Address:** 2100 N Wheeler St 75951 **Location:** US 96, 1.8 mi n of jct US 190. **Facility:** 57 units, some two bedrooms. 2 stories (no elevator), exterior corridors. **Pool(s):** outdoor. **Activities:** exercise room. **Guest Services:** coin laundry. **Featured Amenity:** continental breakfast.

## WHERE TO EAT

### ELIJAH'S CAFE     409/384-9000

Southern Comfort Food. Family Dining. $6-$13 **AAA Inspector Notes:** The family-oriented restaurant is known for such home-cooked staples as chicken-fried steak, pot roast, hamburgers and cobblers. **Address:** 201 W Gibson St 75951 **Location:** US 190 and SR 63, 0.5 mi w of jct US 96.

### LONE STAR BUFFET     409/381-8688

American. Quick Serve. $8-$12 **AAA Inspector Notes:** The family-owned and -operated buffet restaurant lines up a good selection of American fare, most of which is made in house. Families also can sample daily specials, including Cajun dishes on Friday night and chicken on Tuesday. Prices are reasonable. They're known for their signature mashed potato rolls, chicken and dumplings, barbecue ribs and smothered liver and onions. **Address:** 500 S Wheeler St 75951 **Location:** Jct US 190 and 96, 0.4 mi n.

## JEFFERSON (D-10) pop. 2,106, elev. 189'

Jefferson once was the state's largest city and a major inland port. Many families on their way west after the Civil War remained in the area, and sternwheelers traveling the Cypress River to St. Louis and New Orleans made stops in town. The city's rapid growth and development ended, however, with the decline of river transportation in the 1870s.

Jefferson's past is evident in a number of historical buildings reminiscent of the Old South. An example is House of the Seasons at 409 S. Alley St., built in 1872 in transitional style between Greek Revival and Victorian, with Italianate details. The house's name comes from its unusual cupola, which has stained-glass windows representing the seasons of the year. Guided tours are given by appointment for a fee; phone (903) 665-8000.

**Marion County Chamber of Commerce:** 101 N. Polk St., Jefferson, TX 75657. **Phone:** (903) 665-2672 or (888) 467-3529.

**Self-guiding tours:** Historic district maps are available from the chamber of commerce.

**"ATALANTA"** is at 211 W. Austin St. Named for a beautiful huntress of Greek mythology, the private railroad car of financier Jay Gould was built in 1890. The car has been restored to reflect the luxury of that era and contains four staterooms, a dining room, a lounge, a kitchen, a butler's pantry and a bathroom. **Time:** Allow 30 minutes minimum. **Hours:** Daily 10-3. Phone ahead to confirm schedule. **Cost:** $5. **Phone:** (903) 665-2513 or (800) 490-7270.

**EXCELSIOR HOUSE** is at 211 W. Austin St. Built by Capt. William Perry in 1850, the hotel welcomed such notable guests as Jay Gould, Ulysses S. Grant, Rutherford B. Hayes and Oscar Wilde. In addition to the guest registers on view in the lobby, displays feature original documents and furniture. **Hours:** Tours are given daily at 1 and 2. Closed major holidays. Phone ahead to confirm schedule. **Cost:** $8; $2 (ages 0-7). **Phone:** (903) 665-2513 or (800) 490-7270.

**JEFFERSON HISTORICAL MUSEUM** is at 223 W. Austin St. in the 1890 Federal Building. The museum depicts the life, industry and transportation of early East Texas. A collection of antique dolls from more than 20 countries is displayed. A replica 1900s train depot is located behind the museum and houses the R. D. Moses Texas and Pacific model railroad. **Hours:** Daily 9:30-4:30. Closed Jan. 1, Easter, Thanksgiving, Christmas Eve and Christmas. **Cost:** $7; $5 (ages 62+); $4 (ages 13-17); $3 (ages 6-12). **Phone:** (903) 665-2775.

THE CLAIBORNE HOUSE B & B                    (903)665-8800
**Classic Bed & Breakfast** $109-$199 **Address:** 312 S Alley St 75657 **Location:** Just e of jct US 59 and SR 49 to S Alley St, just s. Located in a quiet residential area. **Facility:** Original heart of pine floors are featured in this restored 1872 home decorated with antique furniture. All rooms feature different color schemes, including one with a dramatic black toile wallpaper. 6 units. 2 stories (no elevator), interior/exterior corridors. **Parking:** street only. **Terms:** 2 night minimum stay - weekends, 7 day cancellation notice-fee imposed. **Activities:** massage.

OLD MULBERRY INN AND COTTAGES            903/665-1945
**Bed & Breakfast.** Rates not provided. **Address:** 209 E Jefferson St 75657 **Location:** 0.3 mi s of jct US 59 and SR 49, just e. Located in a quiet residential area. **Facility:** This large, Greek Revival-style home mingles modern amenities with vintage touches such as antique claw-foot tubs. The home was built as a B&B in the '90s and has a large porch overlooking a garden. 10 units. 1 story, interior/exterior corridors.

WHERE TO EAT

AUSTIN STREET BISTRO                        903/665-9700
American. Casual Dining. $9-$21 **AAA Inspector Notes:** On first impression the rose-print tablecloths make this place look like a tea room, but on closer inspection you will hear Dave Matthews and Snow Patrol on the sound system and smoked Gouda grits on the menu. Bread lovers will appreciate their signature oatmeal molasses rolls and those with sweet tooths will be delighted by the numerous options, all made in house. **Address:** 117 E Austin St 75657 **Location:** Center. **Parking:** street only.

STILLWATER INN DINING ROOM                  903/665-8415
American. Casual Dining. $23-$51 **AAA Inspector Notes:** Historic. A restored turn-of-the-century home and inn, the Stillwater's loyal following is due to its talented and experienced chef. The menu features items like goat cheese salad, rack of lamb and their signature grilled breast of duck. **Features:** full bar. **Reservations:** suggested. **Address:** 203 E Broadway 75657 **Location:** Just e of jct US 59 and SR 49.

## AAA/CAA HELPS MAKE YOUR DISNEY DREAMS COME TRUE.

With *AAA Vacations*® packages, you can create the Disney dream vacation that fits your family, your taste and your budget while enjoying great savings and benefits along the way!

**Contact your AAA/CAA Travel professional to get started today.**
AAA.com

## JOHNSON CITY (F-7) pop. 1,656, elev. 1,193'

Named for the pioneer Johnson Family, ancestors of President Lyndon B. Johnson, the city is a retail center for a farm and ranch area. It also is the site of the Johnson City District of Lyndon B. Johnson National Historical Park *(see place listing p. 407)*, which includes the Lyndon B. Johnson Boyhood Home and the Johnson Settlement. Lyndon B. Johnson Ranch is 14 miles west.

A scenic overlook at Pedernales Falls State Park, 9 miles east on FM 2766, provides a view of the 3,000-foot-wide limestone canyon through which the Pedernales River has carved steps, cascades and pools. *See Recreation Areas Chart.*

**Johnson City Chamber of Commerce:** 100 E. Main St., P.O. Box 485, Johnson City, TX 78636. **Phone:** (830) 868-7684.

### BEST WESTERN JOHNSON CITY INN  (830)868-4044

Hotel $80-$130

**AAA Benefit:** Members save 10% or more with Best Western!

**Address:** 107 S Hwy 290/281 78636 **Location:** Jct US 281 and 290 N. **Facility:** 53 units. 2 stories (no elevator), exterior corridors. **Pool(s):** outdoor. **Guest Services:** coin laundry. **Featured Amenity:** full hot breakfast. *(See ad this page.)*
  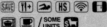

## WHERE TO EAT

### PECAN STREET BREWING  830/868-2500
American. Casual Dining. $8-$22 **AAA Inspector Notes:** Burgers, wood-fired pizzas and good-old comfort food are featured at this storefront location that's complete with a beer garden and dance hall. The meatloaf was super. **Features:** full bar, patio dining, Sunday brunch. **Address:** 106 E Pecan Dr 78636 **Location:** Downtown; on south side of town square. **Parking:** street only.

## JUNCTION pop. 2,574

### BEST WESTERN PLUS DOS RIOS  (325)446-3700

Hotel $110

**AAA Benefit:** Members save 10% or more with Best Western!

**Address:** 244 Dos Rios Dr 76849 **Location:** I-10 exit 456, just s. **Facility:** 52 units. 2 stories (no elevator), exterior corridors. **Pool(s):** outdoor. **Activities:** exercise room. **Guest Services:** coin laundry.

### MOTEL 6 JUNCTION - #4384  (325)446-3572
Hotel $65-$149 **Address:** 200 I-10 W 76849 **Location:** I-10 exit 456; on eastbound frontage road. **Facility:** 48 units. 2 stories (no elevator), exterior corridors. **Pool(s):** heated indoor. **Activities:** hot tub. **Guest Services:** coin laundry.

### RODEWAY INN  (325)446-4588
Hotel $60-$70 **Address:** 2343 N Main St 76849 **Location:** I-10 exit 456, just s on US 377. **Facility:** 29 units. 1 story, exterior corridors. **Pool(s):** outdoor. **Guest Services:** coin laundry.

▼ See AAA listing this page ▼

## WHERE TO EAT

### COOPER'S BAR-B-Q AND GRILL
325/446-8664

 Barbecue. Quick Serve. $6-$14 **AAA Inspector Notes:** Patrons can enjoy all their favorite barbecue dishes in this family-oriented restaurant. **Address:** 2423 N Main St 76849 **Location:** I-10 exit 456, just n. [L] [D]

---

## KATY (F-9) pop. 14,102, elev. 145'
### • Part of Houston area — see map p. 301

Katy is thought to have been named for the Missouri-Kansas-Texas (M-K-T) railroad, which laid track through town in 1893. Prosperity came with the 1934 discovery of the Katy gas field, which remains one of the largest natural gas sources in the state.

### BEST WESTERN PLUS KATY INN & SUITES
(281)395-6200

Hotel
$120-$150

**AAA Benefit:** Members save 10% or more with Best Western!

**Address:** 2006 Katy Mills Blvd 77494 **Location:** I-10 exit 741; on south frontage road. **Facility:** 78 units, some efficiencies. 3 stories, interior corridors. **Amenities:** safes. **Pool(s):** outdoor. **Activities:** hot tub, exercise room. **Guest Services:** valet and coin laundry. **Featured Amenity:** full hot breakfast.

### COMFORT INN & SUITES-WEST
(281)392-8700

 Hotel $109-$269 **Address:** 22025 I-10 W (Katy Frwy) 77450 **Location:** I-10 exit 745 (Mason Rd) eastbound, stay on frontage road; exit westbound, just s to Mason frontage road, then just w. **Facility:** 89 units, some kitchens. 2 stories, interior corridors. **Pool(s):** indoor. **Activities:** hot tub, exercise room. **Guest Services:** valet and coin laundry.

### COMFORT SUITES
(281)574-5900

Hotel $95-$200 **Address:** 25115 Katy Frwy 77494 **Location:** I-10 exit 741. **Facility:** 88 units. 3 stories (no elevator), interior corridors. **Pool(s):** outdoor. **Activities:** hot tub, exercise room. **Guest Services:** valet and coin laundry.

### HAMPTON INN & SUITES
(281)392-1000

Hotel $139-$169 **Address:** 22055 Katy Frwy 77450 **Location:** I-10 exit 743 (Grand Pkwy) westbound; exit 745 (Mason Rd) eastbound; on eastbound frontage road. **Facility:** 69 units. 3 stories, interior corridors. **Terms:** 1-7 night minimum stay, cancellation fee imposed. **Pool(s):** outdoor. **Activities:** hot tub, exercise room. **Guest Services:** valet and coin laundry.

**AAA Benefit:** Members save up to 10%!

### HILTON GARDEN INN KATY MILLS
(281)644-2400

Hotel $119-$259 **Address:** 2409 Taxmati Dr 77494 **Location:** I-10 exit 741; on south frontage road. **Facility:** 101 units. 4 stories, interior corridors. **Terms:** 1-7 night minimum stay, cancellation fee imposed. **Amenities:** safes. **Pool(s):** outdoor. **Activities:** hot tub, exercise room. **Guest Services:** valet and coin laundry, area transportation.

**AAA Benefit:** Members save up to 10%!

### LA QUINTA INN & SUITES KATY
(281)392-9800

Hotel
$129-$164

**Address:** 22455 Katy Frwy (I-10) 77450 **Location:** I-10 exit 745 (Mason Rd); on eastbound frontage road. **Facility:** 71 units, some efficiencies. 4 stories, interior corridors. **Pool(s):** outdoor. **Activities:** exercise room. **Guest Services:** valet and coin laundry.

### RESIDENCE INN BY MARRIOTT HOUSTON KATY MILLS
(281)391-7501

Extended Stay Contemporary Hotel $149-$229 **Address:** 25401 Katy Mills Pkwy 77494 **Location:** I-10 exit 740 (Pin Oak Rd) westbound; exit 741 (Pin Oak Rd) eastbound, just s; on south side of Kay Mills Mall. **Facility:** 126 units, some two bedrooms, efficiencies and kitchens. 4 stories, interior corridors. **Pool(s):** outdoor. **Activities:** hot tub, exercise room. **Guest Services:** valet and coin laundry.

**AAA Benefit:** Members save 5% or more!

### SPRINGHILL SUITES BY MARRIOTT HOUSTON-KATY MILLS
(281)644-4455

Hotel $93-$349 **Address:** 2501 Texmati Dr 77494 **Location:** I-10 exit 740 (Pin Oak Rd) westbound; exit 741 (Pin Oak Rd) eastbound; on eastbound frontage road. **Facility:** 69 units. 3 stories, interior corridors. **Pool(s):** outdoor. **Activities:** hot tub, exercise room. **Guest Services:** valet and coin laundry.

**AAA Benefit:** Members save 5% or more!

---

## WHERE TO EAT

### BABIN'S SEAFOOD HOUSE
281/829-9200

Cajun Seafood. Casual Dining. $9-$28 **AAA Inspector Notes:** This seafood house concentrates on doing things New Orleans style, so you will find plenty of Gulf fish and Louisiana favorites like shrimp Creole, gumbo, crawfish étouffée, fried seafood platters and a few steaks, too. Loud music plays over speakers. Colorful wood slats with lots of purple and gold reminds one of the New Orleans Saints or Mardi Gras. There's a bayou feeling overall. **Features:** full bar. **Address:** 21851 Katy Frwy 77450 **Location:** I-10 exit 745 (Mason Rd); on south frontage road. [L] [D]

### LANDRY'S SEAFOOD HOUSE
281/392-0452

Seafood. Casual Dining. $10-$40 **AAA Inspector Notes:** An ideal spot for healthy seafood dinners and special occasions, the restaurant produces a wonderful clam chowder. Menu selections come from all the world's oceans. **Features:** full bar, Sunday brunch. **Address:** 22215 Katy Frwy 77450 **Location:** I-10 exit 745 (Mason Rd), just e on south frontage road. [SAVE] [L] [D]

### PERRY'S STEAKHOUSE & GRILLE
281/347-3600

Steak. Fine Dining. $24-$80 **AAA Inspector Notes:** An excellent selection of prime steaks, lamb and pork chops is served at this professional and upscale establishment. **Features:** full bar, happy hour. **Reservations:** required. **Address:** 23501 Cinco Ranch Blvd 77494 **Location:** I-10 exit 743 (Grand Pkwy) westbound, 3.2 mi s to exit Cinco Ranch Blvd; southwest corner of La Centerra Shopping Center. [D] CALL

**SALTGRASS STEAKHOUSE**                      281/647-9400

 Steak. Casual Dining. $9-$30 **AAA Inspector Notes:** Those looking for something different should try the comfortable steakhouse, which never says no to a special request. Born from the spirit of Texas cattle drives, the restaurant resembles a Texas lodge, with high ceilings and mounted animal heads. Baby back ribs are so tender the meat falls off the bone. Also on the menu are hearty steaks, prime rib, chicken, seafood and yummy desserts. **Features:** full bar. **Address:** 21855 Katy Frwy 77450 **Location:** I-10 exit 745 (Mason Rd), 0.5 mi e; on south frontage road.

## KAUFMAN  pop. 6,703
• Part of Dallas area — see map p. 161

**BEST WESTERN LA HACIENDA INN**          (972)962-6272

Motel
$80-$100

**AAA Benefit:** Members save 10% or more with Best Western!

**Address:** 200 E Hwy 175 75142 **Location:** Just e of jct US 175 and SR 34. **Facility:** 40 units. 1 story, exterior corridors. **Pool(s):** outdoor. **Featured Amenity: full hot breakfast.**

## KEMAH  pop. 1,773
• Part of Houston area — see map p. 301

**BOARDWALK INN**                            (281)334-9880

Hotel
$129-$999

**Address:** 8 Kemah Waterfront 77565 **Location:** SR 146, 0.8 mi s; at Kemah Waterfront. **Facility:** 52 units. 2 stories, interior corridors. **Terms:** check-in 4 pm, cancellation fee imposed. **Pool(s):** heated outdoor. **Activities:** hot tub. **Guest Services:** valet laundry.

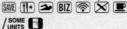

**AQUARIUM RESTAURANT**                       281/334-9010

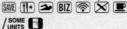 Seafood. Casual Dining. $10-$33 **AAA Inspector Notes:** Gigantic tropical fish in a cylindrical aquarium greet guests as they climb the stairs to the unusual restaurant. The decor transports diners to an underwater world, where they watch sharks and fish swim while they eat. Although the menu consists primarily of seafood dishes, beef and chicken choices are alternatives. Be sure to try one of the beautifully presented desserts. **Features:** full bar, happy hour. **Address:** 11 Kemah Boardwalk 77565 **Location:** I-45 exit 24 (NASA Rd 1), 7 mi e to SR 146, 0.8 mi s, then e to Kemah Waterfront.

**CADILLAC BAR**                             281/334-9049

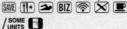 Tex-Mex. Casual Dining. $12-$24 **AAA Inspector Notes:** This restaurant and its welcoming patio offer a nice place to look out over the marina. Graffiti covers the walls, chairs, tables and ceilings, everywhere but the restroom. On the menu are large portions of Tex-Mex cuisine, including such classic favorites as tacos, enchiladas and fajitas, as well as fresh Gulf fish. I enjoyed the barbecue ribs and the sopapilla sundae. **Features:** full bar, patio dining, happy hour. **Address:** 7 Kemah Boardwalk 77565 **Location:** I-45 exit 24 (NASA Rd 1), 7 mi e to SR 146, 0.8 mi s, then e to Kemah Waterfront.

**THE FLYING DUTCHMAN**                       281/334-7575

 Seafood. Casual Dining. $9-$32 **AAA Inspector Notes:** This establishment is really two restaurants in one. Upstairs you'll find friendly, efficient and attentive servers who know their way around the extensive wine list and seafood-dominated menu. Downstairs is reserved for more casual dining. **Features:** full bar. **Address:** 9 Kemah Waterfront St 77565 **Location:** I-45 exit 24 (NASA Rd 1), 7 mi e to SR 146, 0.8 mi s, then e to Kemah Waterfront.

**LANDRY'S SEAFOOD HOUSE**                    281/334-2513

 Seafood. Casual Dining. $10-$40 **AAA Inspector Notes:** An ideal spot for healthy seafood dinners and special occasions, the restaurant produces a wonderful clam chowder. Menu selections come from all the world's oceans. **Features:** full bar. **Address:** 1 Kemah Boardwalk 77565 **Location:** On the Boardwalk.

**SALTGRASS STEAKHOUSE**                      281/538-5441

 Steak. Casual Dining. $9-$30 **AAA Inspector Notes:** Those looking for something different should try the comfortable steakhouse, which never says no to a special request. Born from the spirit of Texas cattle drives, the restaurant resembles a Texas lodge, with high ceilings and mounted animal heads. Baby back ribs are so tender the meat falls off the bone. Also on the menu are hearty steaks, prime rib, chicken, seafood and yummy desserts. **Features:** full bar. **Address:** 215 Kipp Ave 77565 **Location:** At the Boardwalk.

## KENEDY  pop. 3,296

**BEST WESTERN PLUS KENEDY INN**           (830)583-2121

Hotel
$160-$190

**AAA Benefit:** Members save 10% or more with Best Western!

**Address:** 205 Business Park Dr 78119 **Location:** Just e of US 181. **Facility:** 57 units. 3 stories, interior corridors. **Pool(s):** outdoor. **Activities:** hot tub, exercise room. **Guest Services:** coin laundry.

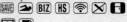

## KERMIT  pop. 5,708

**KERMIT INN**                                432/586-6693

[fyi] Not evaluated. **Address:** 304 E State Hwy 302 79745 **Location:** Jct Hwy 302 and 115, 4 blks e. Facilities, services, and décor characterize an economy property.

## KERRVILLE  (F-7) pop. 22,347, elev. 1,654'

Kerrville, in a rugged hill region along the Guadalupe River, is a popular summer and winter resort. Camp Verde, 11 miles south on FM 689, was the eastern terminus of a camel route to Fort Yuma, Calif., during the late 1850s.

**Kerrville Convention and Visitors Bureau:** 2108 Sidney Baker St., Kerrville, TX 78028. **Phone:** (830) 792-3535 or (800) 221-7958.

**THE MUSEUM OF WESTERN ART** is 1 mi. s.e. on FM 173 to 1550 Bandera Hwy. The center displays works by living Western American artists and Western Masters of the past. **Time:** Allow 2 hours minimum. **Hours:** Tues.-Sat. 10-4. Closed Jan. 1, Thanksgiving, Christmas Eve and Christmas. **Cost:** $7; $6 (ages 65+); $5 (ages 9-17 and students with ID); $4 (military with ID). **Phone:** (830) 896-2553.

---

### BEST WESTERN SUNDAY HOUSE INN   (830)896-1313

Hotel
$85-$90

**AAA Benefit:** Members save 10% or more with Best Western!

**Address:** 2124 Sidney Baker St 78028 **Location:** I-10 exit 508 (SR 16), just s. **Facility:** 97 units. 2 stories (no elevator), exterior corridors. **Pool(s):** outdoor. **Guest Services:** valet laundry.

---

### COMFORT INN   (830)792-7700

Hotel $74-$134 **Address:** 2001 Sidney Baker St 78028 **Location:** I-10 exit 508 (SR 16), 0.4 mi s. **Facility:** 55 units. 2 stories (no elevator), interior corridors. **Pool(s):** indoor. **Activities:** hot tub.

---

### DAYS INN OF KERRVILLE   (830)896-1000

Motel
$40-$99

**Address:** 2000 Sidney Baker St 78028 **Location:** I-10 exit 508 (SR 16), 0.5 mi s. Located in a light-commercial area. **Facility:** 42 units. 2 stories, interior/exterior corridors. **Terms:** cancellation fee imposed. **Pool(s):** outdoor. **Activities:** hot tub. **Featured Amenity:** continental breakfast.

---

### HAMPTON INN OF KERRVILLE   (830)257-0600

Hotel $99-$269 **Address:** 2038 Sidney Baker St 78028 **Location:** I-10 exit 508 (SR 16), 0.5 mi s. Located in a modern commercial area. **Facility:** 60 units. 3 stories, interior corridors.

**AAA Benefit:** Members save up to 10%!

**Terms:** 1-7 night minimum stay, cancellation fee imposed. **Pool(s):** outdoor. **Activities:** sauna, hot tub, exercise room. **Guest Services:** coin laundry.

---

### HOLIDAY INN EXPRESS HOTEL & SUITES   (830)895-9500

Hotel $99-$129 **Address:** 2114 Sidney Baker St 78028 **Location:** I-10 exit 508 (SR 16), just w. **Facility:** 64 units. 3 stories, interior corridors. **Pool(s):** outdoor. **Activities:** hot tub, exercise room. **Guest Services:** coin laundry.

---

### INN OF THE HILLS RESORT AND CONFERENCE CENTER   (830)895-5000

Hotel
$80-$134

**Address:** 1001 Junction Hwy 78028 **Location:** I-10 exit 505, 1.5 mi nw on SR 27. **Facility:** 166 units. 2 stories (no elevator), exterior corridors. **Terms:** check-in 4 pm, cancellation fee imposed. **Amenities:** video games, safes. **Pool(s):** outdoor. **Activities:** fishing, tennis, playground, massage. **Guest Services:** valet laundry, area transportation.

---

### LA QUINTA INN KERRVILLE   (830)896-9200

Hotel $89-$144 **Address:** 1940 Sidney Baker St 78028 **Location:** I-10 exit 508 (SR 16), 0.4 mi s. **Facility:** 65 units. 3 stories, interior corridors. **Pool(s):** heated indoor. **Activities:** hot tub, exercise room. **Guest Services:** coin laundry.

---

### Y. O. RANCH HOTEL & CONFERENCE CENTER   (830)257-4440

Hotel
$79-$129

**Address:** 2033 Sidney Baker St 78028 **Location:** I-10 exit 508 (SR 16), 0.3 mi s. Located in a light-commercial area at entrance to city. **Facility:** 190 units. 2 stories (no elevator), interior/exterior corridors. **Terms:** check-in 4 pm. **Amenities:** video games. **Dining:** The Branding Iron, see separate listing. **Pool(s):** outdoor. **Activities:** hot tub, tennis, exercise room. **Guest Services:** valet laundry. **Featured Amenity:** continental breakfast.

---

## WHERE TO EAT

### ACAPULCO RESTAURANT   830/257-6222

Tex-Mex. Casual Dining. $7-$14 **AAA Inspector Notes:** The casual Mexican restaurant features two dining rooms, a friendly staff and large portions of Tex-Mex and authentic Mexican seafood. **Features:** full bar. **Address:** 1718 Sidney Baker St 78028 **Location:** I-10 exit 508 (SR 16), 0.5 mi s. [B] [L] [D]

### THE BRANDING IRON   830/257-4440

American. Casual Dining. $10-$25 **AAA Inspector Notes:** The refined dining room is modern and inviting, trimmed in polished oak, iron chandeliers and large comfortable tables. Start the day with breakfast specials or enjoy an upscale dinner with more homemade desserts than ya'll can handle. A lunch buffet also is available. **Features:** full bar. **Address:** 2033 Sidney Baker St 78028 **Location:** I-10 exit 508 (SR 16), 0.3 mi s; in Y. O. Ranch Hotel & Conference Center. [B] [L] [D]

### COWBOY STEAK HOUSE   830/896-5688

Steak. Casual Dining. $10-$40 **AAA Inspector Notes:** The name says it all: large steaks à la south Texas. The eatery also features pork, chicken, quail and other homemade favorites. Nightly specials are featured like foie gras. **Features:** full bar. **Address:** 416 Main St 78028 **Location:** Corner of Sidney Baker and Main sts; downtown. [D] [X]

### THE LAKEHOUSE   830/895-3188

Regional Seafood Comfort Food. Casual Dining. $7-$15 **AAA Inspector Notes:** The eatery, overlooking the Guadalupe River, offers a wide variety of fresh seafood and country feel-good dishes uniquely prepared in Hill Country style. Service is attentive and friendly. The lodge-like space has a polished wood interior. **Features:** beer & wine. **Address:** 1655 Junction Hwy (SR 27) 78028 **Location:** On SR 27, just n of Goat Creek Rd. [L] [D]

---

## KILGORE (D-10) pop. 12,975, elev. 371'
• Hotels p. 386 • Restaurants p. 386

Kilgore is known for its collection of Art Deco buildings, many of which are being restored. Also prominent are the more than 70 star-topped reconstructed oil derricks around town. At one time, more than 1,200 such derricks operated within Kilgore.

**Kilgore Chamber of Commerce & Visitors Bureau:** 813 N. Kilgore St., P.O. Box 1582, Kilgore, TX 75663. **Phone:** (903) 984-5022.

**EAST TEXAS OIL MUSEUM** is off US 259 exit Ross St. on the Kilgore College campus. A tribute to the pioneers of the Texas oil industry, this museum traces the history and development of the vast East Texas Oil Field through exhibits, audio-visual presentations, photographs and a re-created 1930s boomtown. The Boomtown USA exhibit portrays a full-scale town with people, animals, stores and machinery common to a lively, booming oil town. Hand-painted murals and portraits of Texas oilmen cover the lobby walls. Geological tools and equipment also are displayed.

Educational videos focus on new technologies revolutionizing the energy industry, including horizontal drilling, salt water disposal, George Mitchell and Barnett Shale, fracturing and stimulation of wells in shale formations to capture hydrocarbons. An animatronic REA lineman on a utility pole describes his work of bringing electricity to rural East Texas.

**Time:** Allow 1 hour, 30 minutes minimum. **Hours:** Tues.-Sat. 9-5, Sun. 2-5, Apr.-Sept.; Tues.-Sat. 9-4, Sun. 2-5, rest of year. Closed Jan. 1, Easter, Thanksgiving and Christmas. **Cost:** $8; $5 (ages 3-11). **Phone:** (903) 983-8295.

**RANGERETTE SHOWCASE MUSEUM** is 1 blk. w. of US 259 at Broadway and Ross sts. Housed in the Physical Education Complex of Kilgore College, the museum traces the history and travels of the internationally known Kilgore College Rangerette Dance-Drill Team. A lounge features a tribute to Rangerette founder and originator of precision dance-drill, Gussie Nell Davis. Performances are showcased on two large television screens. **Time:** Allow 30 minutes minimum. **Hours:** Mon.-Fri. 9-4, Sat. 10-4. Closed Jan. 1, spring break, Thanksgiving and Christmas. **Cost:** Free. **Phone:** (903) 983-8265.

**BEST WESTERN INN OF KILGORE**　(903)986-1195

Hotel
$85-$120

**AAA Benefit:** Members save 10% or more with Best Western!

**Address:** 1411 N Hwy 259 75662 **Location:** I-20 exit 589, 3.9 mi s. **Facility:** 42 units. 2 stories (no elevator), exterior corridors. **Pool(s):** outdoor.

 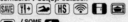

**HAMPTON INN KILGORE**　(903)983-3300

Hotel $79-$109 **Address:** 3109 N Hwy 259 75662 **Location:** I-20 exit 589, 2.1 mi s. **Facility:** 63 units. 3 stories, interior corridors. **Terms:** 1-7 night minimum stay, cancellation fee imposed. **Pool(s):** outdoor. **Activities:** exercise room. **Guest Services:** valet and coin laundry.

**AAA Benefit:** Members save up to 10%!

**HOLIDAY INN EXPRESS & SUITES KILGORE**　(903)986-3533

Hotel $72-$108 **Address:** 3308 US Hwy 259 N 75662 **Location:** I-20 exit 589A eastbound; exit 589B westbound, 2 mi s. **Facility:** 66 units. 3 stories, interior corridors. **Pool(s):** heated indoor. **Activities:** hot tub, exercise room. **Guest Services:** valet and coin laundry.

**KILGORE COMFORT SUITES**　(903)984-2385

Hotel $79-$150 **Address:** 1210 Hwy 259 N 75662 **Location:** I-20 exit 589, 4 mi s. **Facility:** 62 units. 4 stories, interior corridors. **Pool(s):** heated indoor. **Activities:** hot tub, exercise room. **Guest Services:** valet and coin laundry.

---

**WHERE TO EAT**

**COUNTRY TAVERN**　903/984-9954

Barbecue. Casual Dining. $7-$20 **AAA Inspector Notes:** It's thought to have some of the best barbecue in East Texas, but this place is not exactly convenient. But a drive west on the highway will take you to a large red edifice and neon sign. Once inside, the waitress will recite the short menu; order the ribs—that's what they are known for. If you find the sauce to be a little too sweet, the twice-baked potato casserole will provide some savory balance. In business since 1939. **Features:** full bar. **Address:** 1526 FM 2767 75662 **Location:** Jct SR 31 and FM 2767.

**KILLEEN** pop. 127,921

**BEST WESTERN KILLEEN**　(254)526-6651

Hotel
$69

**AAA Benefit:** Members save 10% or more with Best Western!

**Address:** 2709 E Veteran's Memorial Blvd 76543 **Location:** US 190 Bypass exit W S Young, 1.3 mi n to E Veteran's Memorial Blvd, then just e. **Facility:** 65 units. 2 stories (no elevator), exterior corridors. **Pool(s):** outdoor. **Guest Services:** valet laundry.

**CANDLEWOOD SUITES - FT. HOOD/KILLEEN**　254/501-3990

Extended Stay Hotel. Rates not provided. **Address:** 2300 Florence Rd 76542 **Location:** US 90 exit Jasper Rd, just s. **Facility:** 71 efficiencies. 3 stories, interior corridors. **Activities:** exercise room. **Guest Services:** valet and coin laundry.

---

**COURTYARD BY MARRIOTT KILLEEN**          (254)616-2000

▼▼▼▼ Hotel $99-$139 Address: 1721 E Central Texas Expwy 76541 Location: US 190 exit WS Young Dr, just n. Facility: 148 units. 6 stories, interior corridors. Pool(s): heated outdoor. Activities: exercise room. Guest Services: valet and coin laundry.

AAA Benefit: Members save 5% or more!

🍴 🍸 CALL 🅼 🏊 🅷🆂 🛜 ✖ 🗔 🖥 💻 / SOME UNITS 🖨

**DAYS INN KILLEEN MALL**          (254)554-2727

▼▼▼ Motel $69-$99

Address: 1602 E Central Texas Expwy 76541 Location: US 190 exit Trimmier Rd. Facility: 67 units. 2 stories (no elevator), exterior corridors. Activities: exercise room. Featured Amenity: continental breakfast.

SAVE 🅷🆂 🛜 🗔 🖥 💻 / SOME UNITS 🖨

**FAIRFIELD INN & SUITES BY MARRIOTT KILLEEN**          (254)526-3333

▼▼▼▼ Hotel $77-$119 Address: 200 E Central Texas 76541 Location: US 190 exit Fort Hood St; on eastbound frontage road. Facility: 86 units. 3 stories, interior corridors. Pool(s): outdoor. Activities: hot tub, exercise room. Guest Services: valet and coin laundry.

AAA Benefit: Members save 5% or more!

CALL 🅼 🏊 🅱🅸🆉 🅷🆂 🛜 ✖ 🗔 🖥 💻

**HAMPTON INN**          (254)554-7110

▼▼▼ Hotel $99-$159 Address: 2702 O W Curry Dr 76542 Location: US 190 exit W S Young Dr, just e on south frontage road. Facility: 62 units. 3 stories, interior corridors. Terms: 1-7 night minimum stay, cancellation fee imposed. Pool(s): outdoor. Activities: exercise room. Guest Services: valet laundry.

AAA Benefit: Members save up to 10%!

🍴 🏊 🅱🅸🆉 🛜 🗔 🖥 💻

**HAWTHORN SUITES BY WYNDHAM**          (254)634-7795

▼▼▼ Hotel $89-$125

Address: 1502 E Central Texas Expwy 76541 Location: US 190 exit Trimmier Rd; on south frontage road. Facility: 63 units, some efficiencies. 3 stories, interior corridors. Activities: exercise room. Guest Services: valet and coin laundry. Featured Amenity: full hot breakfast.

SAVE 🛜 🗔 🖥 💻 / SOME UNITS 🅷🆂

**HILTON GARDEN INN**          254/554-3900

▼▼▼ Hotel. Rates not provided. Address: 2704 O W Curry Dr 76542 Location: US 190 exit W S Young Dr, just e on south frontage road. Facility: 102 units. 4 stories, interior corridors. Pool(s): heated outdoor. Activities: hot tub, exercise room. Guest Services: valet and coin laundry.

AAA Benefit: Members save up to 10%!

🍴 CALL 🅼 🏊 🅱🅸🆉 🅷🆂 🛜 ✖ 🗔 🖥 💻

**HOLIDAY INN KILLEEN**          (254)690-5511

▼▼▼ Hotel $89-$149 Address: 300 E Central Texas Expwy 76541 Location: US 190 exit Fort Hood St/Jasper Rd (SR 195); on south frontage road. Facility: 99 units. 3 stories, interior corridors. Pool(s): outdoor. Activities: hot tub, exercise room. Guest Services: valet and coin laundry.

🍴 🍸 CALL 🅼 🏊 🅷🆂 🛜 ✖ 🗔 🖥 💻

**RESIDENCE INN BY MARRIOTT**          (254)634-1020

▼▼▼ Extended Stay Contemporary Hotel $103-$169 Address: 400 E Central Texas Expwy 76541 Location: US 190 exit Fort Hood St/Jasper Rd (SR 195); on south frontage road. Facility: 109 units, some two bedrooms, efficiencies and kitchens. 4 stories, interior corridors. Pool(s): heated outdoor. Activities: hot tub, exercise room. Guest Services: valet and coin laundry.

AAA Benefit: Members save 5% or more!

🍴 CALL 🅼 🏊 🅱🅸🆉 🅷🆂 🛜 ✖ 🗔 🖥 / SOME UNITS 🖨

**SHILO INN SUITES HOTEL - KILLEEN**          254/699-0999

▼▼▼▼ Hotel. Rates not provided. Address: 3701 S W S Young Dr 76542 Location: US 190 exit W S Young Dr, 1 mi s. Facility: 160 units, some kitchens. 4 stories, interior corridors. Amenities: safes. Dining: Shilo Restaurant-The Mark, see separate listing. Pool(s): heated indoor. Activities: sauna, hot tub, exercise room, massage. Guest Services: valet and coin laundry.

🏋 🍴 🍸 CALL 🅼 🏊 🅱🅸🆉 🅷🆂 🛜 🗔 🖥 💻 / SOME UNITS 🖨

**SLEEP INN & SUITES**          (254)616-2345

▼▼▼ Hotel $63-$129 Address: 700 E Central Texas Expwy 76541 Location: US 190 exit Trimmier Rd; on frontage road at Gateway Dr. Facility: 80 units. 3 stories, interior corridors. Amenities: safes. Activities: exercise room. Guest Services: valet and coin laundry.

🍴 🅷🆂 🛜 🗔 🖥 💻

**TOWNEPLACE SUITES BY MARRIOTT**          (254)554-8899

▼▼▼ Extended Stay Hotel $77-$87 Address: 2401 Florence Rd 76542 Location: US 190 exit Trimmier Rd to Jasper Rd, on south frontage road, 1 blk e to Florence Rd, then just s. Facility: 79 units, some efficiencies and kitchens. 3 stories, interior corridors. Pool(s): outdoor. Activities: exercise room. Guest Services: valet and coin laundry.

AAA Benefit: Members save 5% or more!

🍴 CALL 🅼 🏊 🅱🅸🆉 🛜 ✖ 🗔 🖥 💻 / SOME UNITS 🖨

## WHERE TO EAT

**EL CHICO**          254/634-0501

▼▼▼ Tex-Mex Casual Dining $7-$16

AAA Inspector Notes: Inside and out, the decor of the popular Mexican restaurant is inviting. The menu features traditional favorites such as enchiladas, tacos, burritos and fajitas. The broad menu also lists a few American classics. Features: full bar. Reservations: suggested. Address: 1701 E Central Texas Expwy 76541 Location: US 190 exit Trimmier Rd. 🅛 🅓

**LITTLE ITALY**          254/526-5163

▼▼ Italian. Casual Dining. $7-$17 AAA Inspector Notes: Near the military base and shopping, the small, family-owned restaurant presents a menu of Italian food, including pizza, spaghetti, veal and chicken Marsala. Features: beer & wine. Address: 1218 S Fort Hood St 76542 Location: Just s of jct US 190 and S Fort Hood St. 🅛 🅓 ◣

### RED ONION INDIAN BISTRO                    254/699-0006

▼ Indian. Casual Dining. $9-$18 **AAA Inspector Notes:** Daily lunch buffets are amplified in the evenings with choices of tandoori specialties and curries of chicken, lamb, seafood and vegetarian entrées, as well as Indo-Chinese selections. **Features:** full bar. **Address:** 1908 Central Texas Expwy 76541 **Location:** US 190 exit Trimmer Ave, just e on south frontage road. L D

### SHILO RESTAURANT-THE MARK                  254/247-3135

▼▼▼ American. Casual Dining. $13-$22 **AAA Inspector Notes:** The contemporary and upscale dining spot presents a menu of sandwiches, soups, salads, pasta dishes, pizza and full-course meals of beef and fish. **Features:** full bar, Sunday brunch. **Address:** 3701 S W S Young Dr 76542 **Location:** US 190 exit W S Young Dr, 1 mi s; in Shilo Inn Suites Hotel - Killeen. D CALL&M

### TAIWAN DRAGON                               254/526-2299

▼▼ Chinese. Casual Dining. $6-$13 **AAA Inspector Notes:** A wide selection of offerings with large portions served at popular prices await the patrons of this restaurant. The shrimp in lobster sauce was more than generous in portion size and was quite tasty. **Features:** beer & wine. **Address:** 308 E Ave G 76541 **Location:** Jct Business Rt US 190 and Gray St, just n to Ave G, just e; downtown. **Parking:** on-site and street. L D

### TEXAS LAND AND CATTLE STEAKHOUSE           254/699-5500

▼▼ Steak. Casual Dining. $9-$27 **AAA Inspector Notes:** A variety of large Prime steaks, delicious salads and scrumptious desserts await you at the friendly Texas ranch-style restaurant. Try the signature slow-smoked sirloin, which never fails to please, or the Caesar salad, another favorite. A Texas steakhouse means everything is bigger, from large cuts and oversize salads to potatoes and side dishes. Those not in the mood for beef can opt for chicken, quail or seafood. Dessert is an occasion. **Features:** full bar. **Reservations:** required. **Address:** 3404 E Central Texas Expwy 76543 **Location:** Jct US 190 and SR 3470, just nw. L D

---

## KINGSLAND pop. 6,030

### THE ANTLERS INN                            325/388-4411

▼▼▼
Classic Historic
Country Inn
$140-$550

**Address:** 1001 King Ct 78639 **Location:** On FM 1431; center. Located in historic railroad district. **Facility:** An early 1900s railroad hotel, the property today offers lodgings in the main building as well as in cabins, converted cabooses and coach cars. 19 units, some efficiencies, houses and cabins. 1-2 stories (no elevator), exterior corridors. **Terms:** cancellation fee imposed. **Activities:** boat dock, fishing, game room.

SAVE ⇥ 🛜
/SOME UNITS 🅿 🔲 📷 📠

### RIO VISTA RESORT                           325/388-6331

▼▼▼ Condominium $90-$950 **Address:** 234 Rio Vista Dr 78639 **Location:** Waterfront. Colorado River Bridge, 0.5 mi nw on FM 1431, 0.5 mi s on Reynolds St. **Facility:** Spacious accommodations are available at this lakeside property. 16 units, some houses, cottages and condominiums. 1-2 stories (no elevator), exterior corridors. **Terms:** 2 night minimum stay - seasonal and/or weekends, 30 day cancellation notice-fee imposed. **Pool(s):** outdoor. **Activities:** hot tub, boat dock, fishing. **Guest Services:** coin laundry.

🛥 🛜 ⊠ 🅿 📷 📠 /SOME UNITS 🐾

---

---

## KINGSVILLE (H-8) pop. 26,213

When Capt. Richard King, a Rio Grande riverboat pilot, camped along the Santa Gertrudis Creek in the south Texas region known as Wild Horse Desert, he saw its potential as a cattle range. The King Ranch, which covers 825,000 acres of protected habitat, is one of the largest privately owned ranches and is recorded on the National Register as the "Birthplace of American Ranching."

Kingsville, King Ranch Headquarters, was chartered on July 4, 1904, following development of a well-drilling system that could tap deeply buried water, and the construction of the railroad to enable King cattle to be shipped easily. The town prospered from its association with the ranch. It is known today for its agricultural and natural resources such as birding and wildlife. Texas A&M University-Kingsville and the Kingsville Naval Air Station also call the town home.

**Kingsville Visitor Center:** 1501 N. Hwy. 77, Kingsville, TX 78363. **Phone:** (361) 592-8516 or (800) 333-5032.

**JOHN E. CONNER MUSEUM** is on the Texas A&M University-Kingsville campus at 905 W. Santa Gertrudis St. The museum focuses on the heritage of south Texas. Displays range from prehistoric natural science to 19th-century ranch memorabilia, South Texas Native American and early Spanish artifacts and game trophies. **Time:** Allow 1 hour minimum. **Hours:** Mon.-Fri. 9-5, Sat. 10-4. Closed school holidays. **Cost:** Donations. **Phone:** (361) 593-2810.

**KING RANCH HEADQUARTERS** is w. off SR 141. In 1853 Capt. Richard King purchased the 15,500-acre Rincon de Santa Gertrudis Land Grant and stocked his ranch with longhorn cattle. Climate conditions and a demand for more flavorful and tender beef resulted in the creation of the Santa Gertrudis—the first beef cattle breed developed in the Western Hemisphere in more than 100 years. Today the ranch comprises 825,000 acres and offers a 90-minute narrated tour that focuses on its history and agricultural operations. A variety of nature tours also are offered.

**Hours:** History and agriculture tours depart Mon.-Sat. at 11 and 1, Sun. at 12:30 and 2:30. Departure times may vary; phone ahead. Closed major holidays. **Cost:** $10; $8 (ages 65+ and students and military with ID); $5 (ages 5-12). **Phone:** (361) 592-8055.

**King Ranch Museum** is at 405 N. Sixth St. On display are photographs of the ranch in the 1940s, saddle and branding iron collections, vintage carriages and automobiles. Videos about the ranch and residence are shown. **Time:** Allow 1 hour minimum. **Hours:** Mon.-Sat. 10-4, Sun. 1-5. Closed major holidays. **Cost:** $6; $5 (ages 65+ and students and military with ID); $3 (ages 5-12). **Phone:** (361) 595-1881.

## BEST WESTERN KINGSVILLE INN          (361)595-5656

 Motel
$90-$120

**AAA Benefit:** Members save 10% or more with Best Western!

**Address:** 2402 E King Ave 78363 **Location:** 1.5 mi e on US 77 Bypass; opposite jct SR 141. Located in a quiet rural area. **Facility:** 50 units. 2 stories, exterior corridors. **Pool(s):** outdoor. **Activities:** hot tub. **Guest Services:** coin laundry. **Featured Amenity: full hot breakfast.**

## COMFORT INN          (361)516-1120

 Hotel $100-$150 **Address:** 505 N Hwy 77 Bypass 78363 **Location:** Just off US 77. **Facility:** 47 units. 3 stories, interior corridors. **Pool(s):** outdoor. **Activities:** exercise room. **Guest Services:** coin laundry.

## HOLIDAY INN EXPRESS          (361)592-8333

Hotel $119-$149 **Address:** 2400 S Hwy 77 78363 **Location:** Just s of jct E General Cavazos Blvd; on northbound frontage road. **Terms:** cancellation fee imposed. **Pool(s):** outdoor. **Activities:** hot tub, exercise room. **Guest Services:** coin laundry.

## KINGSVILLE HAMPTON INN          361/592-9800

Hotel. Rates not provided.
**Address:** 2489 S US Hwy 77 78363 **Location:** Just s of jct E General Cavazos Blvd; on southbound frontage road. **Facility:** 51 units. 3 stories, interior corridors. **Amenities:** video games. **Activities:** exercise room. **Guest Services:** valet and coin laundry.

**AAA Benefit:** Members save up to 10%!

## QUALITY INN          (361)592-5251

 Hotel
$55-$70

**Address:** 221 S Hwy 77 Bypass 78363 **Location:** On US 77, just s of jct SR 141. **Facility:** 68 units. 2 stories, exterior corridors. **Pool(s):** outdoor. **Activities:** exercise room. **Guest Services:** coin laundry. **Featured Amenity: full hot breakfast.**

## SUPER 8          (361)592-6471

 Motel
$45-$69

**Address:** 105 S US Hwy 77 Bypass 78363 **Location:** 0.8 mi e on US 77. Located in a quiet rural area. **Facility:** 69 units. 2 stories, exterior corridors. **Terms:** cancellation fee imposed. **Pool(s):** outdoor. **Activities:** exercise room. **Guest Services:** coin laundry. **Featured Amenity: continental breakfast.**

Be a better driver.
Keep your mind on the road.

## SIRLOIN STOCKADE          361/595-1182

Steak. Quick Serve. $9-$11 **AAA Inspector Notes:** The steakhouse lines up buffet items, including pizza, tacos, soups, salads and desserts, providing both excellent variety and a good value. Rotating theme nights allow for the sampling of sushi, barbecue and seafood. The buffet may also serve to complement a quality steak. **Address:** 1500 S Brahma Blvd 78363 **Location:** US 77, 0.9 mi nw on Angle Rd, just s. L D

# KINGWOOD

- **Hotels & Restaurants map & index p. 324**
- **Part of Houston area — see map p. 301**

## COMFORT SUITES KINGWOOD-HUMBLE          (281)359-4448   92

Hotel $80-$140 **Address:** 22223 Hwy 59 N 77339 **Location:** US 59 exit Kingwood Dr northbound; exit McClellan southbound. **Facility:** 56 units. 3 stories, interior corridors. **Pool(s):** outdoor. **Activities:** hot tub, exercise room. **Guest Services:** valet and coin laundry.

CALL /SOME UNITS

## HOLIDAY INN EXPRESS HOTEL & SUITES-KINGWOOD          (281)359-2700   91

Hotel $89-$189 **Address:** 22675 US 59 N 77339 **Location:** US 59 exit Kingwood Dr; on southbound access road. **Facility:** 72 units. 3 stories, interior corridors. **Pool(s):** outdoor. **Activities:** exercise room. **Guest Services:** valet and coin laundry.

/SOME UNITS

## HOMEWOOD SUITES BY HILTON AT KINGWOOD PARC          (281)358-5566   90

Extended Stay Hotel $99-$164 **Address:** 23320 Hwy 59 N 77339 **Location:** US 59 exit Kingwood Dr, 1.4 mi n on northbound access road. **Facility:** 75 efficiencies, some two bedrooms. 3 stories, interior corridors. **Terms:** 1-7 night minimum stay, cancellation fee imposed. **Pool(s):** outdoor. **Activities:** hot tub, exercise room. **Guest Services:** valet and coin laundry, area transportation.

CALL

**AAA Benefit:** Members save up to 10%!

## CHELSEA DELI & CAFE          281/359-2972   35

Deli. Quick Serve. $3-$5 **AAA Inspector Notes:** A great spot for a quick lunch in the middle of the Kingwood community, this small deli restaurant is well known for its excellent chicken salad. The large deli sandwiches are a good choice with high quality meats and cheeses. Some breads and desserts also are made on the premises. **Address:** 1538 Kingwood Dr 77339 **Location:** US 59 exit Kingwood Dr, 1.3 mi e. B L D

## HUNAN GARDEN RESTAURANT          281/360-2668   34

Chinese. Casual Dining. $6-$13 **AAA Inspector Notes:** A nicely varied menu with generous portions is available here. The barbecue spare ribs and shrimp in lobster sauce were two very good options. **Address:** 4331 Kingwood Dr 77339 **Location:** US 59 exit Kingwood Dr, 4.3 mi e to W Lake Houston Pkwy; on northwest corner; in HEB Shopping Center. L D CALL

## LA MADELEINE COUNTRY FRENCH CAFE          281/360-1681

Traditional French. Casual Dining. $7-$12 **AAA Inspector Notes:** A fireplace creates the focal point at this cozy European style café where you can always get a quiche or savory stuffed puffed pastry on the go or stick around for a chicken crêpe or French dip sandwich. Heartier entrées like rotisserie chicken are offered and every season promises menu surprises. Whatever you decide on you probably will not get out the door without enjoying one of their tempting sweet pastries. **Features:** beer & wine. **Address:** 4570 Kingwood Dr 77345 **Location:** Jct Kingwood Dr and Lake Houston Pkwy, just w. B L D CALL

## KYLE pop. 28,016

**LA QUINTA INN & SUITES KYLE**                    (512)295-5599
▼▼▼ **Hotel** $90-$151 **Address:** 18869 IH-35 N 78640 **Location:** I-35 exit 217; on east frontage road. **Facility:** 66 units. 3 stories, interior corridors. **Pool(s):** outdoor. **Activities:** hot tub, exercise room. **Guest Services:** coin laundry.

## LA GRANGE (F-9) pop. 4,641, elev. 324'

Famed for its brave fighters during the revolt against Mexico, La Grange took its name from the country home of the Marquis de Lafayette. The town was founded in 1831 near the crossing of the Colorado River and an old Native American trail known as La Bahia Road.

**La Grange Area Chamber of Commerce:** 171 S. Main St., La Grange, TX 78945-2610. **Phone:** (979) 968-5756 or (800) 524-7264.

**MONUMENT HILL AND KREISCHE BREWERY STATE HISTORIC SITES** are 1.5 mi. s. on US 77, then .4 mi. w. on Spur 92. A memorial shaft marks a tomb containing the bodies of men murdered by Mexicans in the 1842 Dawson Massacre and members of the ill-fated Mier Expedition of 1843. The park also has the homestead and ruins of a brewery built in the 1860s by German immigrant Heinrich Kreische.

**Tours:** Guided tours are available. **Hours:** Park daily 8-5. Brewery tours are given Sat. at 2 and 3:30, Oct.-May; Sat. at 10, rest of year (weather permitting). Kreische House tours are given first and second Sun. of the month at 2 and 3. Phone ahead to confirm schedule. **Cost:** Free. **Phone:** (979) 968-5658. 🅰

**BEST WESTERN PLUS LA GRANGE INN & SUITES**
(979)968-6800

▼▼▼ Hotel $98-$150

**AAA Benefit:** Members save 10% or more with Best Western!

**Address:** 600 E State Hwy 71 Bypass 78945 **Location:** Jct US 77 and SR 71, just e on N Frontage Rd. **Facility:** 53 units, some kitchens. 4 stories, interior corridors. **Pool(s):** outdoor. **Activities:** exercise room. **Guest Services:** coin laundry.

**HAMPTON INN LA GRANGE**                    979/968-4900
▼▼▼ **Hotel.** Rates not provided. **Address:** 1624 W State Hwy 71 78945 **Location:** SR 71 W and W Business Rt 71, 1 mi e. **Facility:** 50 units. 3 stories, interior corridors. **Pool(s):** heated indoor. **Activities:** hot tub, exercise room. **Guest Services:** coin laundry.

**AAA Benefit:** Members save up to 10%!

---

**BISTRO 108**                    979/968-9108
▼▼ American. Casual Dining. $7-$35 **AAA Inspector Notes:** From wraps and burgers to full entrées of steaks, seafood, chicken and pasta dishes, this restaurant caters to all palates. **Features:** full bar, patio dining, early bird specials, Sunday brunch. **Reservations:** suggested. **Address:** 108 S Main St 78945 **Location:** Downtown. **Parking:** street only. L  D  🍴

## LAJITAS (G-3) elev. 2,342'

Lajitas (la-HEE-tas) is the Spanish word for "flagstones," which are noticeable in the area. The village was first established in 1915 when an Army post was stationed to protect the Big Bend area from the Mexican bandit Pancho Villa.

Known as the home of the late beer-drinking goat Clay Henry, Lajitas also serves as a base from which to explore Big Bend National Park *(see place listing p. 120)*, 20 miles east. Westbound travel on FM 170, also called The River Road, affords spectacular scenery as the paved highway climbs mountains and plunges into canyons along the Rio Grande.

**BARTON WARNOCK VISITOR CENTER** is 1 mi. e. on FM 170. Exhibits portray the natural history, geology and archeology of the Big Bend region. A courtyard showcases a yucca forest, and 2.5 acres of gardens are planted with local cacti, desert shrubs and trees. The center is the eastern entry point to Big Bend Ranch State Park *(see attraction listing p. 445)*. **Time:** Allow 1 hour minimum. **Hours:** Daily 8-4:30. Closed Christmas. **Cost:** $5; free (ages 0-12). **Phone:** (432) 424-3327. 🅰

**LAJITAS GOLF RESORT AND SPA**                    432/424-5000
▼▼▼ **Resort Hotel.** Rates not provided. **Address:** 1 Main St 79852 **Location:** Center. **Facility:** This property has the feel of a frontier fort and Old West town. Some fireplace units are offered. 103 units, some kitchens, houses and cottages. 1-2 stories (no elevator), interior/exterior corridors. **Amenities:** safes. **Dining:** Candelilla Cafe, see separate listing. **Pool(s):** outdoor. **Activities:** regulation golf, recreation programs, exercise room, spa. **Guest Services:** coin laundry.

---

**CANDELILLA CAFE**                    432/424-5000
▼▼ Regional American. Casual Dining. $8-$36 **AAA Inspector Notes:** Magnificent views of the Mexican mountains accentuate your dining experience in this relaxed environment featuring Southwestern cuisine. **Features:** full bar, patio dining, Sunday brunch. **Reservations:** suggested. **Address:** 1 Main St 79852 **Location:** Center; in Lajitas Golf Resort and Spa. B  L  D  CALL

---

**Trust your vehicle to AAA/CAA**

**Approved Auto Repair facilities**

## LAKE DALLAS pop. 7,105
• Part of Dallas area — see map p. 161

### BEST WESTERN PLUS LAKE DALLAS INN & SUITES
(940)497-1007

Hotel
$75-$160

**AAA Benefit:** Members save 10% or more with Best Western!

**Address:** 305 Swisher Rd 75065 **Location:** I-35E exit 458 (Swisher Rd), 0.6 mi on N Frontage Rd. **Facility:** 54 units. 3 stories, interior corridors. **Pool(s):** outdoor. **Activities:** hot tub, exercise room. **Guest Services:** valet and coin laundry.

## LAKE JACKSON (G-10) pop. 26,849, elev. 15'

Lake Jackson, named for the small oxbow lake on Maj. Abner Jackson's plantation, was founded as a model community by Dow Chemical Company. The town is known for curiously named streets such as Any Way, This Way and That Way.

**SEA CENTER TEXAS** is off SR 288 exit Plantation Dr., then .7 mi. s.w. to 300 Medical Dr. Aquariums feature marine life found in the Texas Gulf Coast region, such as redfish, groupers and sharks. The center also includes a touch tank containing blue and hermit crabs, anemones, urchins and clams; and a fish hatchery. **Hours:** Tues.-Sat. 9-4, Sun. 1-4. Closed Jan. 1, Easter, Thanksgiving, Christmas Eve and Christmas. **Cost:** Donations. **Phone:** (979) 292-0100.

### CANDLEWOOD SUITES-LAKE JACKSON-CLUTE
(979)297-0011
 **Extended Stay Contemporary Hotel** $110-$149 **Address:** 506 Hwy 332 77566 **Location:** Jct SR 288/332 and Plantation Dr, just n. **Facility:** 86 efficiencies. 2 stories, interior corridors. **Terms:** 2-6 night minimum stay - seasonal and/or weekends, cancellation fee imposed. **Pool(s):** outdoor. **Activities:** hot tub, exercise room. **Guest Services:** valet and coin laundry.

### CHEROTEL GRAND MARINER HOTEL
(979)297-1161
Hotel $74-$94 **Address:** 925 Hwy 332 77566 **Location:** On SR 288/332, just w of jct Business Rt SR 288. **Facility:** 131 units. 2 stories (no elevator), interior corridors. **Terms:** cancellation fee imposed, resort fee. **Pool(s):** outdoor. **Activities:** exercise room.

### WHERE TO EAT

### CAFE ANNICE
979/292-0060
American. Casual Dining. $7-$28 **AAA Inspector Notes:** Many of your favorites are offered at this restaurant that features pasta, sandwiches and full meals at lunchtime to steaks, seafood, pasta and chicken at the dinner hour. Lighter fare also is available in the evenings. **Features:** full bar. **Address:** 24 Circle Way St 77566 **Location:** Jct SR 332 and This Way, 1 blk s to Circle Way, then 2 blks e. **Parking:** street only. ⓛ ⓓ

### EL CHICO
979/297-4002

Tex-Mex
Casual Dining
$8-$16
**AAA Inspector Notes:** Inside and out, the decor of the popular Mexican restaurant is inviting. The menu features traditional favorites such as enchiladas, tacos, burritos and fajitas. The broad menu also lists a few American classics. **Features:** full bar. **Address:** 100 W Hwy 332 77566 **Location:** Jct SR 332 and This Way, 1 mi w. ⓛ ⓓ

### THE GRAPE TASTE WINE BISTRO
979/480-0424
American. Casual Dining. $7-$22 **AAA Inspector Notes:** Burgers, salads, sandwiches and pasta dishes for lunch are augmented with cheese selections, tapas, seafood and steaks for dinner at this cozy bistro. **Features:** full bar, patio dining, happy hour. **Address:** 145 Oyster Creek Dr, Suite 10 77566 **Location:** SR 288 exit Oyster Creek Dr, just e; in shopping center. ⓛ ⓓ CALL Ⓜ

### WURST HAUS
979/297-3003
German. Casual Dining. $6-$26 **AAA Inspector Notes:** Soups, salads, wurst plates, steaks and pasta dishes along with traditional German favorites like schnitzel and goulash are served in a relaxed environment. Brunch is offered daily. **Features:** full bar, patio dining, happy hour. **Address:** 102 This Way 77566 **Location:** Jct SR 288 and This Way, 2 blks e. Ⓑ ⓛ ⓓ 🐾

## LAKE MEREDITH NATIONAL RECREATION AREA (A-5)

Lake Meredith is about 45 miles northeast of Amarillo and 9 miles west of Borger via SR 136. Impounded by Sanford Dam on the Canadian River, the 10,000-acre lake offers recreational facilities at Blue West, Cedar Canyon, Fritch Fortress, Harbor Bay, Plum Creek and Sanford-Yake. Additional facilities are available at McBride and Bugbee Canyon. Fishing for walleye, crappie, bass, catfish and trout is a popular pastime. Hunters can pursue deer, dove, turkey, quail, pheasant and geese. Park open daily 24 hours. For more information about the recreation area, phone (806) 857-3151. *See Recreation Areas Chart.*

## LAKEWAY pop. 11,391
• Restaurants p. 392

### AUSTIN/LAKEWAY HAMPTON INN & SUITES
(512)263-7474
Hotel $134-$199 **Address:** 2013 RR 620 S 78734 **Location:** Jct SR 71 and FM 620, 1.5 mi e. **Facility:** 70 units. 3 stories, interior corridors. **Terms:** 1-7 night minimum stay, cancellation fee imposed. **Pool(s):** outdoor. **Activities:** hot tub, exercise room. **Guest Services:** coin laundry.

**AAA Benefit:** Members save up to 10%!

### LAKEWAY RESORT & SPA
(512)261-6600
Hotel
$119-$1300
**Address:** 101 Lakeway Dr 78734 **Location:** Jct FM 620 and Lakeway Blvd W, 1.5 mi to Lakeway Dr, 2.1 mi n. **Facility:** Upscale lodging and a range of recreational activities await the guests of this resort located on Lake Travis. 175 units, some condominiums. 6 stories, interior corridors. **Parking:** on-site and valet. **Terms:** check-in 4 pm, 2-4 night minimum stay - seasonal and/or weekends, 3 day cancellation notice-fee imposed, resort fee. **Pool(s):** outdoor. **Activities:** hot tub, marina, fishing, regulation golf, tennis, recreation programs, bicycles, playground, exercise room, spa. **Guest Services:** valet laundry.

## WHERE TO EAT

**THE GRILLE AT ROUGH HOLLOW**  103/261-3444

▼▼▼ Steak Seafood. Casual Dining. $12-$40 **AAA Inspector Notes:** With a beautiful location high atop Lake Travis, this restaurant presents steaks, chops, chicken and seafood. Sandwiches and salads are available for lighter appetites. **Features:** full bar, patio dining, Sunday brunch, happy hour. **Address:** 103 Yacht Club Cove 78738 **Location:** Jct SR 620 and Lakeway Blvd, 2.4 mi n to Highlands Blvd, 0.7 mi w to Rough Hollow Dr, 1.1 mi n to Rough Hollow Yacht Club, then 0.4 mi w. **Parking:** valet only. [L] [D]

**ROCCO'S GRILL**  512/263-8204

▼▼▼ Italian. Casual Dining. $9-$32 **AAA Inspector Notes:** Patrons can sample lamb, steak, chicken, seafood and pasta dishes in the trendy Art Deco establishment in the Lake Travis area. Upscale presentations can be enjoyed indoors or on the covered deck. **Features:** full bar, patio dining. **Address:** 900 RR 620 S 78734 **Location:** Jct FM 620 and Lakeway Blvd; in Lakeway Commons. [L] [D] CALL [&M]

# LAKE WORTH  pop. 4,584
• Hotels & Restaurants map & index p. 257

**BEST WESTERN PLUS LAKE WORTH INN & SUITES**
(817)238-1199  [52]

Hotel
$79-$99

**AAA Benefit:** Members save 10% or more with Best Western!

**Address:** 3920 Boat Club Rd 76135 **Location:** I-820 exit 10A (SR 199/Jacksboro Hwy), just w. **Facility:** 50 units. 2 stories, interior corridors. **Pool(s):** outdoor. **Activities:** hot tub, exercise room. **Guest Services:** valet and coin laundry. **Featured Amenity:** full hot breakfast.

# LAMESA  pop. 9,422

**BEST WESTERN LAMESA INN & SUITES**  (806)872-3888

Hotel
$130-$400

**AAA Benefit:** Members save 10% or more with Best Western!

**Address:** 506 N Dallas St 79331 **Location:** Jct US 180 and Business Rt 87; on northwest corner. **Facility:** 56 units, some efficiencies. 3 stories, interior corridors. **Pool(s):** heated indoor. **Activities:** hot tub, exercise room. **Guest Services:** coin laundry.

**SHILOH INN**  (806)872-6721

Motel
$69-$99

**Address:** 1707 Lubbock Hwy 79331 **Location:** Jct US 87 and 180, 1 mi n. **Facility:** 50 units. 1-2 stories (no elevator), exterior corridors. **Terms:** 3 day cancellation notice-fee imposed. **Pool(s):** outdoor.

# LAMPASAS  pop. 6,681

**INN AT LAMPASAS**  (512)556-9292

▼▼▼
Hotel
$89-$109

**Address:** 1200 Central Texas Expwy 76550 **Location:** 0.5 mi se of jct US 183 and 281. **Facility:** 59 units. 3 stories, interior corridors. **Terms:** cancellation fee imposed. **Pool(s):** heated outdoor. **Activities:** exercise room. **Guest Services:** coin laundry. **Featured Amenity:** full hot breakfast.

[SAVE] CALL [&M] [≈] [BIZ] [HS] [⊚] [▢]
/ SOME UNITS [🐕] [🔒] [▣]

# LANCASTER  pop. 36,361
• Part of Dallas area — see map p. 161

**GRANDY'S RESTAURANT**  972/224-5033

▼ American. Quick Serve. $4-$8 **AAA Inspector Notes:** Fried chicken and country-fried steak are menu standbys at the restaurant, a regional franchise. They also offer a family-style dining menu. The décor is a step up from that of most quick-serve eateries and more resembles that of a conventional restaurant. Some elements of increased service include additional rolls, iced tea refills and tray removal. **Address:** 3255 W Pleasant Run 75146 **Location:** I-35E exit 415 southbound; exit 416 northbound to Pleasant Run, just e. [B] [L] [D]

# LANGTRY  (F-5) elev. 1,315'

Langtry, on the Rio Grande, was the home of Judge Roy Bean. Though he never met actress Lillie Langtry, Judge Bean claimed he had named the town in her honor. Langtry actually was named for a railroad engineer.

**JUDGE ROY BEAN VISITOR CENTER** is on US 90 at Loop 25. The frontier judge dispensed beer and the "law west of the Pecos" from a saloon named the Jersey Lily, preserved at the center. Dioramas portray the judge's life. **Time:** Allow 30 minutes minimum. **Hours:** Daily 8-6, Memorial Day-Labor Day; 8-5, rest of year. Closed Jan. 1, Easter, Thanksgiving, Christmas Eve and Christmas. **Cost:** Free. **Phone:** (432) 291-3340.

# LA PORTE  (F-10) pop. 33,800
• Attractions map p. 309
• Part of Houston area — see map p. 301

When La Porte was founded in 1892, speculators advertised the area as a prime location for orange growers and farmers. Unfortunately, the land wasn't suited to many crops, but the town's location on Galveston Bay eventually made it a summer resort for Houston families.

**SAN JACINTO BATTLEGROUND STATE HISTORIC SITE** is 3 mi. n. of SR 225 on SR 134. The battle that resulted in Texas' independence from Mexico was fought on this 1,200-acre site April 21, 1836. **Hours:** Daily 9-6. Closed Thanksgiving, Christmas Eve and Christmas. **Cost:** Free. **Phone:** (281) 479-2431.

**Battleship *Texas*** is moored off San Jacinto Battleground. This vessel is the veteran of many campaigns of both World Wars. **Hours:** Daily 10-5. Closed Thanksgiving, Christmas Eve and Christmas. **Cost:** $12; $6 (ages 65+ and military with ID); free (ages 0-12). **Phone:** (281) 479-2431.

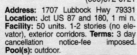

**San Jacinto Monument and Museum of History** is at One Monument Cir. Completed in 1939, the 570-foot limestone obelisk is said to be the world's tallest monument column. In the base of the monument, a museum depicts the region's history, from the Native American civilization found by Hernando Cortez through the Civil War period. A multi-image, digital show depicting the Battle of San Jacinto and the Texas revolution is offered. The observation deck, 489 feet above the battlefield, offers a spectacular view of the battlefield grounds, Houston skyline and ship channel.

**Hours:** Daily 9-6. Closed Thanksgiving, Christmas Eve and Christmas. **Cost:** (Includes show, elevator and special exhibits) $12; $10.50 (ages 65+); $8 (ages 0-11). **Phone:** (281) 479-2421.

COMFORT SUITES                                      (281)842-9200

Hotel $90-$180 **Address:** 902 S 8th 77571 **Location:** SR 146 exit Fairmont Pkwy, just e to S 8th, then just n. Located in a commercial area. **Facility:** 67 units, some two bedrooms. 3 stories, interior corridors. **Pool(s):** outdoor. **Activities:** hot tub, exercise room. **Guest Services:** coin laundry.

## LAREDO (H-7) pop. 236,091, elev. 438'
• Restaurants p. 394

A chief port of entry into Mexico, Laredo sits on the bank of the Rio Grande and is joined to Nuevo Laredo, Mexico, by four bridges. Laredo has been under seven flags since 1755, when it was founded by Don Tomás Sánchez, an officer of the Royal Army of Spain. At one time, Laredo was the capital of a separate republic known as "The Republic of the Rio Grande," which included south Texas and the area that is now the three northernmost states of Mexico.

The capitol of the republic stands in San Agustín Plaza, the site of the original town. An important commercial center, Laredo retains much of its colonial Spanish heritage and atmosphere.

**Laredo Convention and Visitors Bureau:** 501 San Agustín Ave., Laredo, TX 78040. **Phone:** (956) 795-2200 or (800) 361-3360.

**LAMAR BRUNI VERGARA ENVIRONMENTAL SCIENCE CENTER** is at W. End Washington St. on Laredo Community College campus. Highlights include four outdoor ponds with alligators, fish and turtles; a wetlands area; 50 species of native plants; a cactus garden; and a wildflower hill. **Time:** Allow 1 hour minimum. **Hours:** Mon.-Thurs. 8-6, Fri. 8-noon. **Cost:** $4; $2 (ages 4-18 and 60+). **Phone:** (956) 764-5701.

**REPUBLIC OF THE RIO GRANDE MUSEUM** is at 1005 Zaragoza St. During the Republic of the Rio Grande period (1839-41), this adobe building was used by neighboring communities in Texas and Mexico as the capitol of the proposed independent

nation. The house is furnished with frontier antiques. **Hours:** Tues.-Sat. 9-4. Closed major holidays. **Cost:** $2; free (Tues.). **Phone:** (956) 727-3480.

AMERICAS BEST VALUE INN                     (956)723-1510

Motel
$60-$90

**Address:** 5240 San Bernardo Ave 78041 **Location:** I-35 exit 3B (Mann Rd); on southbound frontage road. **Facility:** 133 units, some kitchens. 2 stories (no elevator), exterior corridors. **Terms:** resort fee. **Pool(s):** outdoor. **Activities:** hot tub. **Guest Services:** coin laundry, area transportation. **Featured Amenity: continental breakfast.**

BEST WESTERN SAN ISIDRO INN              (956)723-1600

Hotel
$115-$125

AAA Benefit: Members save 10% or more with Best Western!

**Address:** 1410 Hospitality Dr 78045 **Location:** Jct I-35 and Loop 20 (Bob Bullock Loop), 0.9 mi e. **Facility:** 81 units. 3 stories, interior/exterior corridors. **Amenities:** safes. **Pool(s):** outdoor. **Activities:** exercise room. **Guest Services:** valet and coin laundry. **Featured Amenity: full hot breakfast.**

COURTYARD BY MARRIOTT                          (956)725-5555

Hotel $85-$99 **Address:** 2410 Santa Ursula Ave 78040 **Location:** I-35 exit 2 (Jefferson St), just s; on southbound frontage road. **Facility:** 110 units. 5 stories, interior corridors. **Pool(s):** outdoor. **Activities:** hot tub, exercise room. **Guest Services:** valet and coin laundry, boarding pass kiosk, area transportation.

**AAA Benefit:** Members save 5% or more!

DAYS INN & SUITES                                      (956)724-8221

Hotel
$90-$170

**Address:** 7060 N San Bernardo Ave 78041 **Location:** I-35 exit 4 (San Bernardo Ave), just s; on southbound access road. **Facility:** 126 units. 2 stories, interior/exterior corridors. **Pool(s):** outdoor. **Activities:** game room, exercise room. **Guest Services:** coin laundry, area transportation. **Featured Amenity: full hot breakfast.**

FAIRFIELD INN & SUITES BY MARRIOTT        (956)722-4533

Hotel $94-$109 **Address:** 700 W Hillside Rd 78041 **Location:** I-35 exit 3A (Hillside Rd), just e. **Facility:** 115 units. 3 stories, interior corridors. **Pool(s):** heated outdoor. **Activities:** hot tub, exercise room. **Guest Services:** valet and coin laundry, area transportation.

**AAA Benefit:** Members save 5% or more!

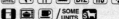

## HOLIDAY INN CIVIC CENTER          (956)727-5800

**Hotel** $99-$115 **Address:** 800 Garden St 78040 **Location:** I-35 exit 2 (Jefferson St), 2.3 mi n on US 81 and 83. **Facility:** 203 units. 14 stories, interior corridors. **Terms:** cancellation fee imposed. **Pool(s):** outdoor. **Activities:** hot tub, exercise room. **Guest Services:** valet and coin laundry, area transportation.

## HOLIDAY INN EXPRESS & SUITES          (956)218-8888

**Hotel** $130 **Address:** 7223 Bob Bullock Loop 78041 **Location:** I-35 exit 8 (Loop 20/Bob Bullock Loop), 5.8 mi e on Loop 20. **Facility:** 104 units. 4 stories, interior corridors. **Terms:** cancellation fee imposed. **Pool(s):** outdoor. **Activities:** hot tub, exercise room. **Guest Services:** valet and coin laundry, area transportation.

## LA POSADA HOTEL & SUITES          956/722-1701

**Hotel.** Rates not provided. **Address:** 1000 Zaragoza St 78040 **Location:** I-35 exit downtown; just e of International Bridge 1. Opposite San Agustin Plaza. **Facility:** 206 units. 3-4 stories, interior/exterior corridors. **Parking:** on-site (fee) and valet. **Terms:** check-in 4 pm. **Amenities:** safes. **Dining:** The Tack Room, Zaragoza Grill, see separate listings. **Pool(s):** outdoor. **Activities:** exercise room. **Guest Services:** valet and coin laundry, area transportation.

## LA QUINTA INN & SUITES LAREDO AIRPORT          (956)724-7222

**Hotel** $109-$170 **Address:** 7220 Bob Bullock Loop 78041 **Location:** I-35 exit 8 (Bob Bullock Loop E), 5.8 mi e. **Facility:** 101 units, some efficiencies. 3 stories, interior corridors. **Pool(s):** outdoor. **Activities:** hot tub, exercise room. **Guest Services:** valet and coin laundry.

## LA QUINTA INN LAREDO I-35          (956)722-0511

**Motel** $85-$124 **Address:** 3610 Santa Ursula Ave 78041 **Location:** I-35 exit 2 (Jefferson St); on southbound frontage road. **Facility:** 153 units, some two bedrooms. 2 stories (no elevator), exterior corridors. **Pool(s):** outdoor.

## MOTEL 6 SOUTH - #142          (956)725-8187

**Motel** $59-$71 **Address:** 5310 San Bernardo Ave 78041 **Location:** I-35 exit 3B (Mann Rd), just s; on southbound frontage road. **Facility:** 94 units. 2 stories (no elevator), exterior corridors. **Bath:** shower only. **Pool(s):** outdoor. **Guest Services:** coin laundry.

## RESIDENCE INN BY MARRIOTT LAREDO          (956)753-9700

**Extended Stay Hotel** $94-$123 **Address:** 310 Lost Oaks Blvd 78041 **Location:** I-35 exit 3B (Mann Rd), just n; on northbound frontage road. **Facility:** 109 units, some two bedrooms and kitchens. 4 stories, interior corridors. **Pool(s):** outdoor. **Activities:** hot tub, exercise room. **Guest Services:** valet and coin laundry, area transportation.

**AAA Benefit:** Members save 5% or more!

## SPRINGHILL SUITES BY MARRIOTT LAREDO          (956)717-0800

**Contemporary Hotel** $99-$109 **Address:** 5940 San Bernardo Ave 78041 **Location:** I-35 exit 4 (San Bernardo Ave), just s; on southbound frontage road. **Facility:** 108 units. 4 stories, interior corridors. **Amenities:** safes. **Pool(s):** outdoor. **Activities:** hot tub, exercise room. **Guest Services:** valet and coin laundry, area transportation.

**AAA Benefit:** Members save 5% or more!

## STAYBRIDGE SUITES-LAREDO          (956)722-0444

**Extended Stay Hotel** $109-$169 **Address:** 7010 Bob Bullock Loop 78041 **Location:** US 83 exit on Loop 20 (Bob Bullock Loop); on west side. **Facility:** 111 kitchen units. 3 stories, interior corridors. **Terms:** 2 night minimum stay - seasonal and/or weekends, 3 day cancellation notice. **Pool(s):** outdoor. **Activities:** hot tub, exercise room. **Guest Services:** complimentary laundry, area transportation.

## SUPER 8          (956)722-6321

**Motel** $90-$150

**Address:** 2620 Santa Ursula Ave 78040 **Location:** I-35 exit 2 (Jefferson St); on southbound frontage road. **Facility:** 71 units, some two bedrooms. 2 stories, exterior corridors. **Pool(s):** outdoor. **Guest Services:** coin laundry. **Featured Amenity: continental breakfast.**

## EMBASSY SUITES LAREDO          956/723-9100

[fyi] Not evaluated. **Address:** 110 Calle Del Norte 78041 **Location:** I-35 exit 3B (Mann Rd), just n. Facilities, services, and décor characterize a mid-scale property.

**AAA Benefit:** Members save 5% or more!

## WHERE TO EAT

## LUBY'S          956/717-8819

**American. Cafeteria.** $6-$12 **AAA Inspector Notes:** First opened in 1947 in south Texas, this cafeteria with over 100 outlets features a wide variety of salads, fresh fruits, seafood...including crunchy shrimp...pastas, meat, poultry and just baked cakes and pies. Ask about the kids specials and Lu Ann platters...an entrée with choice of 2 vegetables and a roll. Many locations offer drive-thru service. **Address:** 5300 N IH 35 78041 **Location:** I-35 exit 3B (Walton Rd); on northbound access road. [L] [D]

## MARIA BONITA          956/722-8123

**Mexican. Casual Dining.** $10-$18 **AAA Inspector Notes:** Like a small Mexican village with terrace windows looking down onto a plaza complete with cantera stone fountain. Unique Mexican dishes like machacado and ceviche. **Features:** full bar. **Address:** 4617 San Bernardo 78041 **Location:** I-35 exit 3A northbound, just w on Calton Rd, then just n; exit 3B southbound, 1.5 mi s. [L] [D]

## MCARTHUR GRILLE          956/723-7575

**Philippine. Casual Dining.** $8-$15 **AAA Inspector Notes:** "I shall return," stated the great general. So shall I, to this unique yet casual Filipino restaurant offering authentic dishes of pancit bihon and lumpia. **Address:** 1713 E Del Mar Blvd 78041 **Location:** Just ne of McPherson Rd. [L] [D]

## PALENQUE GRILL          956/728-1272

**Tex-Mex. Casual Dining.** $9-$15 **AAA Inspector Notes:** Creative Tex-Mex, including chorizo/bean dip, jicama-cucumber-carrot salad and chicken mole enchiladas, is served. The dining room resembles an upscale hacienda. **Features:** full bar, happy hour. **Address:** 7220 Bob Bullock Loop 78041 **Location:** I-35 exit 8 (Bob Bullock Loop E), 1.8 mi e on Loop 20. [L] [D] [LATE]

## POSH SUSHI          956/724-7674

**Sushi. Casual Dining.** $12-$18 **AAA Inspector Notes:** This contemporary restaurant offers upscale décor, knowledgeable and attentive staff, creative compositions of sushi and noodles, and desserts like caramel crêpes. **Features:** beer & wine, happy hour. **Address:** 2715 E Del Mar Blvd 78045 **Location:** 0.4 mi ne of McPherson Rd. [L] [D]

**SIRLOIN STOCKADE** 956/724-3800

▼▼ Steak. Quick Serve. $9-$11 **AAA Inspector Notes:** The steakhouse lines up buffet items, including pizza, tacos, soups, salads and desserts, providing both excellent variety and a good value. Rotating theme nights allow for the sampling of sushi, barbecue and seafood. The buffet may also serve to complement a quality steak. **Address:** 5301 San Dario Ave 78041 **Location:** I-35 exit 3A (Hillside Rd), just e on Calton Rd, then just n. L D

**THE TACK ROOM** 956/722-1701

▼▼▼ Steak. Fine Dining. $18-$32 **AAA Inspector Notes:** Situated on the banks of the Rio Grande, this is a longtime city favorite for perfectly cooked and tender steaks. **Reservations:** suggested. **Address:** 1000 Zaragoza St 78040 **Location:** I-35 exit downtown; just e of International Bridge 1; in La Posada Hotel & Suites. **Parking:** on-site and valet. D

**ZARAGOZA GRILL** 956/722-1701

▼▼▼ American. Casual Dining. $9-$21 **AAA Inspector Notes:** Located right on the border, this restaurant features upscale luxury, attentive service and a wide ranging menu. Try the pad thai, Reuben sandwich or fried tilapia. **Features:** full bar, Sunday brunch. **Address:** 1000 Zaragoza St 78040 **Location:** I-35 exit downtown; just e of International Bridge 1; in La Posada Hotel & Suites. **Parking:** on-site and valet. B L D

## LEAGUE CITY pop. 83,560
• Hotels & Restaurants map & index p. 324

**HAMPTON INN & SUITES HOUSTON/LEAGUE CITY**
(281)614-5437 [157]

▼▼▼ Hotel $89-$209 **Address:** 2320 Gulf Frwy S 77573 **Location:** I-45 exit 20, 1.5 mi n on east frontage road. **Facility:** 81 units. 4 stories, interior corridors. **Terms:** check-in 4 pm, 1-7 night minimum stay, cancellation fee imposed. **Pool(s):** outdoor. **Activities:** hot tub, exercise room. **Guest Services:** valet and coin laundry.

**AAA Benefit:** Members save up to 10%!

 CALL

**SOUTH SHORE HARBOUR RESORT & CONFERENCE CENTER** 281/334-1000

▼▼▼ Resort Hotel. Rates not provided. **Address:** 2500 S Shore Blvd 77573 **Location:** Waterfront. I-45 exit 23, 2.8 mi ne to SR 2094, then 1.5 mi e to resort entrance. Located on Clear Lake as part of a marina. **Facility:** This group-oriented property has many recreational amenities, some of which are located at the nearby health club. The rooms here are large, and many have balconies. 237 units. 11 stories, interior corridors. **Terms:** check-in 4 pm. **Pool(s):** outdoor. **Activities:** marina, regulation golf, massage. **Guest Services:** valet laundry.

## LEANDER pop. 26,521
• Hotels & Restaurants map & index p. 86

**LUIGI'S RISTORANTE ITALIANO** 512/260-8787 [65]

▼▼ Italian. Casual Dining. $7-$16 **AAA Inspector Notes:** Italian favorites, including seven different spaghetti entrées and pasta dinners featuring chicken and seafood, highlight the menu. Lighter fare of salads and sandwiches, as well as four sizes of pizzas, accommodate all hunger levels. The lobster ravioli was delicious and plentiful. **Features:** beer & wine. **Address:** 901 Crystal Falls Pkwy 78641 **Location:** Jct US 183 and Crystal Falls Pkwy, 0.5 mi w. L D

**TWO SAINTS BAKING CO. & CAFE** 512/260-5700

▼▼ Breads/Pastries. Quick Serve. $4-$8 **AAA Inspector Notes:** Wonderful pastries, cakes and pies complement the gourmet sandwich selection at this downtown bakery. **Features:** Sunday brunch. **Address:** 106 W Willis St 78641 **Location:** Downtown. B L

## LEON SPRINGS
• Part of San Antonio area — see map p. 458

**RUDY'S COUNTRY STORE AND BAR-B-QUE** 210/698-2141

▼ Barbecue. Quick Serve. $6-$18 **AAA Inspector Notes:** This small, informal barbecue chain has a twist: The tasty food is ordered by the pound. Guests can mix and match and order three-quarters of a pound of beef with a half-pound of turkey or pork, for example. Desserts and coleslaw are prepackaged, and precooked beans accompany the meat. A drive-through window is available at most locations. **Features:** beer & wine. **Address:** 24152 I-10 W 78257 **Location:** I-10 exit 551 (Boerne Stage Rd). L D

## LEON VALLEY pop. 10,151
• Hotels & Restaurants map & index p. 484
• Part of San Antonio area — see map p. 458

**SUPER 8 SEAWORLD AREA** (210)520-0888 [135]

▼▼ Hotel $60-$77

**Address:** 5336 Wurzbach Rd 78238 **Location:** I-410 exit Bandera Rd, just n to Wurzbach Rd, then just w. Located in a commercial area. **Facility:** 62 units. 3 stories, interior corridors. **Terms:** cancellation fee imposed. **Amenities:** safes. **Pool(s):** outdoor. **Guest Services:** coin laundry. **Featured Amenity:** continental breakfast.

**WHERE TO EAT**

**PICCOLO'S ITALIAN RESTAURANT** 210/647-5524 [90]

▼ Regional Italian. Quick Serve. $8-$22 **AAA Inspector Notes:** The local favorite is known for a casual relaxed atmosphere and freshly prepared dishes that are a good value. **Features:** beer & wine. **Address:** 5703 Evers Rd 78238 **Location:** I-410 exit Evers Rd, 0.3 mi n; between Loop 410 and Wurzbach Rd. L D

## LEVELLAND pop. 13,542

**BEST WESTERN SOUTH PLAINS INN & SUITES**
(806)894-9155

▼▼▼ Hotel $105-$130

**AAA Benefit:** Members save 10% or more with Best Western!

**Address:** 204 N College Ave 79336 **Location:** Jct US 385 N and SR 114, just n. **Facility:** 47 units. 3 stories, interior corridors. **Pool(s):** heated indoor. **Activities:** hot tub, exercise room. **Guest Services:** coin laundry. **Featured Amenity:** breakfast buffet.

**HOLIDAY INN EXPRESS HOTEL & SUITES** 806/894-8555

▼▼▼ Hotel. Rates not provided. **Address:** 703 E SR 114 79336 **Location:** Jct US 385 and SR 114, 0.5 mi e. **Facility:** 63 units. 3 stories, interior corridors. **Pool(s):** heated indoor. **Activities:** hot tub, exercise room. **Guest Services:** complimentary and valet laundry.

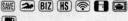

Learn the local driving laws

at DrivingLaws.AAA.com

# LEWISVILLE   pop. 95,290

- Hotels & Restaurants map & index p. 179
- Part of Dallas area — see map p. 161

## BAYMONT INN & SUITES          (972)420-1318  23

Hotel
$69-$119

**Address:** 885 S Stemmons Frwy 75067 **Location:** I-35E exit 451, just w. **Facility:** 54 units. 2 stories, interior corridors. **Terms:** 1-7 night minimum stay, cancellation fee imposed. **Pool(s):** outdoor. **Activities:** exercise room. **Guest Services:** valet and coin laundry. **Featured Amenity:** continental breakfast.

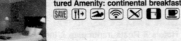

## BEST WESTERN PLUS LEWISVILLE/COPPELL
(972)459-5300  25

Hotel
$85-$130

**AAA Benefit:** Members save 10% or more with Best Western!

**Address:** 330 E Corporate Dr 75067 **Location:** I-35E exit 449 (Corporate Dr), just w. **Facility:** 64 units. 3 stories, interior corridors. **Pool(s):** outdoor. **Activities:** exercise room. **Guest Services:** valet and coin laundry.

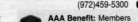

## COMFORT SUITES BY CHOICE HOTELS  (972)315-6464  29

**Hotel** $62-$95 **Address:** 755A Vista Ridge Mall Dr 75067 **Location:** I-35E exit 448A (Round Grove Rd) southbound; 0.5 mi s of jct I-35 and Round Grove Rd on southbound service road to Vista Ridge Mall Dr, then just w; exit 447B northbound, just w on SR 121 Bypass. **Facility:** 60 units. 3 stories, interior corridors. **Pool(s):** heated indoor. **Activities:** hot tub. **Guest Services:** valet and coin laundry.

## COUNTRY INN & SUITES BY CARLSON  (972)315-6565  28

**Hotel** $99-$119 **Address:** 755 E Vista Ridge Mall Dr 75067 **Location:** I-35E exit 448A (Round Grove Rd) southbound, 0.5 mi s on service road to Vista Ridge Mall Dr, then just w; exit 447B northbound, just w on SR 121 Bypass. **Facility:** 62 units. 3 stories, interior corridors. **Terms:** 3 day cancellation notice. **Pool(s):** heated indoor. **Activities:** hot tub. **Guest Services:** valet and coin laundry.

## COURTYARD BY MARRIOTT          (972)316-3100  34

**Hotel** $94-$169 **Address:** 2701 Lake Vista Dr 75067 **Location:** I-35E exit 447B northbound (SR 121); exit 448A southbound, just w on SR 121 Bypass. **Facility:** 122 units. 3 stories, interior corridors. **Pool(s):** heated outdoor. **Activities:** hot tub, exercise room. **Guest Services:** valet and coin laundry, area transportation.

**AAA Benefit:** Members save 5% or more!

## EXTENDED STAY AMERICA DALLAS-LEWISVILLE
(972)315-7455  26

**Extended Stay Hotel** $70-$97 **Address:** 1900 Lakepointe Dr 75057 **Location:** I-35E exit 449 (Corporate Dr), just e to Lakepointe Dr, then just s. **Facility:** 104 efficiencies. 3 stories, interior corridors. **Terms:** cancellation fee imposed. **Guest Services:** coin laundry.

## FAIRFIELD INN BY MARRIOTT-LEWISVILLE
(972)899-6900  33

**Hotel** $79-$119 **Address:** 2697 Lake Vista Dr 75067 **Location:** I-35E exit 448A (Round Grove Rd) southbound, just w on SR 121 Bypass; exit 447B northbound, just w on SR 121 Bypass. **Facility:** 71 units. 3 stories, interior corridors. **Pool(s):** heated indoor. **Activities:** hot tub, exercise room. **Guest Services:** valet laundry, area transportation.

**AAA Benefit:** Members save 5% or more!

## HAMPTON INN & SUITES DALLAS LEWISVILLE/VISTA RIDGE MALL                           (972)315-3200  32

**Hotel** $89-$139 **Address:** 2650 Lake Vista Dr 75067 **Location:** I-35E exit 447B northbound (SR 121); exit 448A southbound (SR 121), just w to Lake Vista Dr, then just n. **Facility:** 105 units. 6 stories, interior corridors. **Terms:** 1-7 night minimum stay, cancellation fee imposed. **Pool(s):** outdoor. **Activities:** hot tub, exercise room. **Guest Services:** valet and coin laundry.

**AAA Benefit:** Members save up to 10%!

## HILTON GARDEN INN DALLAS/LEWISVILLE
(972)459-4600  35

**Hotel** $99-$189 **Address:** 785 SH 121 Bypass 75067 **Location:** I-35E exit 448A (Round Grove Rd) southbound; exit 447B northbound, just w. **Facility:** 165 units. 6 stories, interior corridors. **Terms:** 1-7 night minimum stay, cancellation fee imposed. **Pool(s):** outdoor. **Activities:** hot tub, exercise room. **Guest Services:** valet and coin laundry, area transportation.

**AAA Benefit:** Members save up to 10%!

## HOLIDAY INN EXPRESS & SUITES, DALLAS-LEWISVILLE
(972)459-8000  27

**Hotel** $79-$159 **Address:** 780 E Vista Ridge Mall Dr 75067 **Location:** I-35E exit 448A (Round Grove Rd) to SR 121, just w; exit 447B northbound, just w on SR 121. **Facility:** 90 units. 4 stories, interior corridors. **Pool(s):** outdoor. **Activities:** exercise room. **Guest Services:** valet and coin laundry, area transportation.

## MOTEL 6 - #1288                 (972)436-5008  24

**Hotel** $45-$65 **Address:** 1705 Lakepointe Dr 75057 **Location:** I-35E exit 449 (Corporate Dr), just n on service road. **Facility:** 119 units. 3 stories, interior corridors. **Pool(s):** outdoor. **Guest Services:** coin laundry.

## RESIDENCE INN BY MARRIOTT DALLAS/LEWISVILLE
(972)315-3777  30

**Extended Stay Hotel** $149-$164 **Address:** 755 E Vista Ridge Mall Dr 75067 **Location:** I-35E exit 448A (Round Grove Rd) southbound, 0.5 mi s on frontage road, then just w; exit 447B northbound, just w to Lake Vista, just n. **Facility:** 72 units, some efficiencies and kitchens. 3 stories, interior corridors. **Pool(s):** heated indoor. **Activities:** hot tub, exercise room. **Guest Services:** valet and coin laundry.

**AAA Benefit:** Members save 5% or more!

## TOWNEPLACE SUITES BY MARRIOTT DALLAS LEWISVILLE
(972)459-1275  31

**Extended Stay Hotel** $115-$140 **Address:** 731 E Vista Ridge Mall Dr 75067 **Location:** I-35 exit 447B northbound (SR 121); exit 448A southbound (SR 121), just w to Lake Vista Dr, then just n. **Facility:** 118 units, some efficiencies and kitchens. 4 stories, interior corridors. **Pool(s):** heated outdoor. **Activities:** exercise room. **Guest Services:** valet and coin laundry, area transportation.

**AAA Benefit:** Members save 5% or more!

(See map & index p. 179.)

(See map & index p. 179.)

**WHERE TO EAT**

### AW SHUCKS OYSTER BAR   972/436-2520   14

Seafood. Quick Serve. $7-$12 **AAA Inspector Notes:** A long-time area favorite, this location offers delicious boiled and fried seafood, grilled fish and po'boys. Sit at the oyster bar or outside on the patio, or catch a game in the dining room. For a little local flavor enjoy the caldo (Mexican fish and shrimp soup) or the spicy shrimp cocktail with avocado and serrano peppers. **Features:** full bar, patio dining, happy hour. **Address:** 1630 S Stemmons Frwy 75067 **Location:** I-35E exit 449 (Corporate Dr); on northbound frontage road.

L   D

---

### CANTINA LAREDO   972/315-8100   16

Mexican
Casual Dining
$10-$26

**AAA Inspector Notes:** Modern yet relaxed, this restaurant features creative Mexican fare. A great starter of top-shelf guacamole, which is prepared tableside, primes the palate for an entree of enchiladas, tacos, fajitas and chiles rellenos. **Features:** full bar, Sunday brunch. **Address:** 2225 S Stemmons Frwy 75067 **Location:** I-35 exit 448A (Round Grove Rd) northbound; exit 449 (Corporate Dr); between Round Grove Rd and Corporate Dr; on southbound access road.

L   D

### Gourmet Mexican food, fresh-squeezed lime margaritas

---

### GRANDY'S RESTAURANT   972/436-3932

American. Quick Serve. $4-$8 **AAA Inspector Notes:** Fried chicken and country-fried steak are menu standbys at the restaurant, a regional franchise. They also offer a family-style dining menu. The décor is a step up from that of most quick-serve eateries and more resembles that of a conventional restaurant. Some elements of increased service include additional rolls, iced tea refills and tray removal. **Address:** 401 Stemmons Frwy 75067 **Location:** I-35E exit 453 southbound; exit 452 northbound; on southbound access road.

B   L   D

### JINBEH   214/488-2224

Japanese. Casual Dining. $9-$27 **AAA Inspector Notes:** This small restaurant offers a sushi bar and hibachi-grill cooking. The sushi list is extensive with good explanations of what you can expect. Although all the standards are there, try their signature rolls—they'll leave you wanting more. The lunch menu lists some good bargains for the business-lunch crowd. **Features:** full bar. **Address:** 2440-A S Stemmons Frwy 75067 **Location:** I-35E exit 448A (Round Grove Rd); on northbound frontage road; in strip center.

L   D

### LA MADELEINE COUNTRY FRENCH CAFE   972/459-5900

Traditional French. Casual Dining. $7-$12 **AAA Inspector Notes:** A fireplace creates the focal point at this cozy European style café where you can always get a quiche or savory stuffed puffed pastry on the go or stick around for a chicken crêpe or French dip sandwich. Heartier entrées like rotisserie chicken are offered and every season promises menu surprises. Whatever you decide on you probably will not get out the door without enjoying one of their tempting sweet pastries. **Features:** wine only. **Address:** 2417 S Stemmons Frwy, Suite 100 75067 **Location:** I-35E exit 448B (Hebron Pkwy); in Vista Ridge Mall; north corner.

B   L   D

### OJEDA'S RESTAURANT   972/434-2200   15

Tex-Mex. Casual Dining. $6-$13 **AAA Inspector Notes:** A Dallas fixture since 1969, they now have four locations. They are family-owned and -operated and serve simple Tex-Mex favorites. Customers love their cheese and onion enchiladas, puffed tacos and margaritas. **Features:** full bar, patio dining, happy hour. **Address:** 1680 S Hwy 121 Business 75067 **Location:** I-35E exit 450 (SR 121), 0.5 mi w.   L   D

---

### SALTGRASS STEAKHOUSE   972/316-0086   17

Steak. Casual Dining. $9-$30 **AAA Inspector Notes:** Those looking for something different should try the comfortable steakhouse, which never says no to a special request. Born from the spirit of Texas cattle drives, the restaurant resembles a Texas lodge, with high ceilings and mounted animal heads. Baby back ribs are so tender the meat falls off the bone. Also on the menu are hearty steaks, prime rib, chicken, seafood and yummy desserts. **Features:** full bar. **Address:** 2484 S Stemmons Frwy 75067 **Location:** I-35 exit 448B (SR 121) southbound, U-turn on SR 121, then just n; exit 448B (Round Grove Rd/Hebron Pkwy) northbound; on frontage road.

SAVE   L   D

### SWEET BASIL THAI BISTRO   214/488-1500   18

Thai. Casual Dining. $7-$14 **AAA Inspector Notes:** Among the many larger chains and fast-food joints sits this restaurant in a corner of a retail center. In addition to the traditional Thai offerings of noodle dishes, stir-fries and curries there are also duck and fish selections. The best value here may be at lunch, where one can dine on smaller portions but complete meals of appetizer, soup and entrée. **Address:** 2601 S Stemmons Frwy, Unit 450 75067 **Location:** I-35E exit 447B northbound; exit 448A southbound, just w.   L   D

---

## LINDALE   pop. 4,818

### BEST WESTERN LINDALE INN   (903)882-8884

Hotel
$66-$72

**AAA Benefit:** Members save 10% or more with Best Western!

**Address:** 3501 S Main St 75771 **Location:** I-20 exit 556, just n. **Facility:** 55 units. 2 stories (no elevator), exterior corridors. **Pool(s):** outdoor. **Activities:** exercise room. **Featured Amenity:** full hot breakfast.

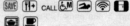

### COMFORT SUITES   (903)882-8613

Hotel $80-$140 **Address:** 200 W Centennial Blvd 75771 **Location:** I-20 exit 556, just n, then just w. **Facility:** 67 units. 3 stories, interior corridors. **Pool(s):** heated indoor. **Activities:** hot tub, exercise room. **Guest Services:** valet and coin laundry.

### HAMPTON INN   (903)882-1002

Hotel
$99-$139

Hampton

**AAA Benefit:** Members save up to 10%!

**Address:** 3505 S Main St 75771 **Location:** I-20 exit 556, just n. **Facility:** 62 units. 3 stories, interior corridors. **Terms:** 1-7 night minimum stay, cancellation fee imposed. **Amenities:** video games. **Pool(s):** outdoor. **Activities:** hot tub, limited exercise equipment. **Guest Services:** coin laundry. **Featured Amenity:** full hot breakfast.

**WHERE TO EAT**

### COLLIN STREET BAKERY   903/882-9205

American. Quick Serve. $5-$8 **AAA Inspector Notes:** The original has been in business for 110 years and its fruit cakes are legendary. So even though the savory items are limited to sandwiches and salads, the desserts are aplenty for those with a sweet tooth. This location also offers free Wi-Fi. The building is hard to miss with white columns flanking the front facade, making it look very vintage. **Address:** 17044 I-20 W 75771 **Location:** I-20 exit 552, just n.

L   D   CALL

# LITTLEFIELD pop. 6,372

### BEST WESTERN LITTLEFIELD INN & SUITES
(806)385-3400

Hotel
$102-$149

**AAA Benefit:** Members save 10% or more with Best Western!

**Address:** 2600 Hall Ave 79339 **Location:** Jct US 84 and 385, just s. **Facility:** 45 units. 2 stories, interior corridors. **Pool(s):** heated outdoor. **Activities:** hot tub, exercise room. **Guest Services:** coin laundry.

# LIVE OAK pop. 13,131
• Part of San Antonio area — see map p. 458

LA QUINTA INN SAN ANTONIO I-35 NORTH AT TOEPPERWEIN
(210)657-5500

 Hotel $69-$124 **Address:** 12822 I-35 N 78233 **Location:** I-35 exit 170B (Toepperwein Rd); on northbound access road. **Facility:** 136 units. 3-4 stories, interior/exterior corridors. **Pool(s):** outdoor. **Guest Services:** valet and coin laundry.

# LIVINGSTON (E-10) pop. 5,335, elev. 167'

**POLK COUNTY MEMORIAL MUSEUM** is at 514 W. Mill St. Exhibits describe local history and include an antique piano, organ, church bell and ranch bell. The Main Street Collection provides a glimpse of the town in the early 1900s. **Tours:** Guided tours are available. **Time:** Allow 30 minutes minimum. **Hours:** Mon.-Fri. 9-5. Closed major holidays. **Cost:** Donations. **Phone:** (936) 327-8192.

### BEST WESTERN PLUS LIVINGSTON INN & SUITES
(936)327-8500

Hotel
$85-$95

Best Western PLUS
**AAA Benefit:** Members save 10% or more with Best Western!

**Address:** 335 Hwy 59 Loop S 77351 **Location:** Just s of jct US 59 and 190; on southbound frontage road. **Facility:** 60 units. 3 stories, interior corridors. **Pool(s):** outdoor. **Activities:** hot tub, exercise room. **Guest Services:** coin laundry.

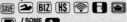

# LLANO pop. 3,232

### BEST WESTERN LLANO
(325)247-4101

Hotel
$70-$110

**AAA Benefit:** Members save 10% or more with Best Western!

**Address:** 901 W Young St 78643 **Location:** 1 mi w on SR 71 and 29. **Facility:** 40 units. 1-2 stories (no elevator), exterior corridors. **Pool(s):** outdoor.

### DAYS INN & SUITES
(325)247-1141

Hotel
$70-$139

**Address:** 609 Bessemer Ave 78643 **Location:** Jct SR 29 and 16/71, 2 blks s. **Facility:** 30 units. 2 stories (no elevator), exterior corridors. **Pool(s):** outdoor. **Activities:** hot tub. **Featured Amenity:** continental breakfast.

# LOCKHART pop. 12,698

### BEST WESTERN LOCKHART HOTEL & SUITES
(512)620-0300

Hotel
$100-$400

**AAA Benefit:** Members save 10% or more with Best Western!

**Address:** 1811 S Colorado St 78644 **Location:** On US 183, just s. **Facility:** 42 units, some efficiencies. 3 stories, interior corridors. **Pool(s):** outdoor. **Activities:** exercise room. **Guest Services:** coin laundry.

---

**WHERE TO EAT**

### BLACK'S BARBECUE
512/398-2712

Barbecue
Quick Serve
$4-$12
**AAA Inspector Notes:** Chicken, ribs, brisket, pork and turkey sold by the pound, as well as a selection of both hot and cold side dishes, tempt patrons of the classic barbecue restaurant. The atmosphere is rustic. **Address:** 215 N Main St 78644 **Location:** US 183 to Walnut St, 1 blk w. **Parking:** on-site and street.

### KREUZ MARKET
512/398-2361

 Barbecue. Quick Serve. $2-$18 **AAA Inspector Notes:** For more than 100 years, the restaurant has served smoked meats on butcher paper, and patrons eat without the benefit of forks. Only cash is accepted. **Features:** beer only. **Address:** 619 N Colorado St 78644 **Location:** US 183, 1 mi n of jct US 183 and SR 142.

### SIRLOIN STOCKADE
512/398-9931

 Comfort Food. Quick Serve. $7-$18 **AAA Inspector Notes:** The steakhouse lines up buffet items, including pizza, tacos, soups, salads and desserts, providing both excellent variety and a good value. Rotating theme nights allow for the sampling of sushi, barbecue and seafood. The buffet may also serve to complement a quality steak. **Reservations:** suggested. **Address:** 1420 S Colorado St 78644 **Location:** On US 183.

**SMITTY'S MARKET**       512/398-9344

Barbecue. Quick Serve. $2-$17 **AAA Inspector Notes:** Housed in a turn-of-the-century building that was home to Kreuz Market for more than 50 years before it moved, this restaurant was kept in the family and renamed. Informal family-style dining is the name of the game here, where barbecue is served in huge quantities every day. While waiting in line to place your order you literally come up close and personal with the fires smoking the meats. Cash only as credit cards are not accepted. **Features:** beer only. **Address:** 208 S Commerce St 78644 **Location:** Downtown; 2 blks s of courthouse.

L D

# LONGVIEW (D-10) pop. 80,455, elev. 339'
• Restaurants p. 400

Longview was founded in 1870 as a rail center for the region's timber mills and farms. In the 1930s, the discovery of oil tripled Longview's population of 6,000 and transformed the quiet East Texas agricultural community into an industrial center.

Within an hour's drive of Longview there are more than a dozen lakes, which range from 2,500 to 25,000 acres, including Caddo Lake, Lake O' the Pines and Martin Creek *(see Recreation Areas Chart)*. These lakes, as well as the surrounding pine and hardwood forests, make Longview a popular recreational center. Anglers and canoeists also enjoy the Sabine River, on the city's doorstep.

**Longview Convention and Visitors Bureau:** 410 N. Center St., Longview, TX 75601. **Phone:** (903) 753-3281.

**GREGG COUNTY HISTORICAL MUSEUM** is at 214 N. Fredonia St. The museum is housed in the 1910 Everett Building. Room reproductions include a bank president's office, a dentist's office, a print shop, a parlor, a log cabin and a general store. Audiovisual shows concern the histories of Texas, Gregg County and printing. There is a display and video about the 1894 Longview bank robbery by Bill Dalton and his gang. **Time:** Allow 1 hour minimum. **Hours:** Tues.-Fri. 10-4, Sat. noon-4. Closed major holidays. **Cost:** $2; $1 (ages 3-18 and 65+). **Phone:** (903) 753-5840.

**LONGVIEW MUSEUM OF FINE ARTS** is at 215 E. Tyler St. The works of Southwestern artists, particularly those from Texas, are displayed. Six separate permanent collections boast more than 300 pieces. Also among the museum's highlights is a 1956 drawing by artist Pablo Picasso. **Time:** Allow 30 minutes minimum. **Hours:** Tues.-Fri. 10-4, Sat. noon-4. Closed major holidays. **Cost:** $5. **Phone:** (903) 753-8103.

**BEST WESTERN LONGVIEW**      (903)757-8888

Hotel $89

**AAA Benefit:** Members save 10% or more with Best Western!

**Address:** 310 E Loop 28, Suite B 75605 **Location:** Loop 281, just w of jct US 259. **Facility:** 51 units. 3 stories, interior corridors. **Pool(s):** outdoor. **Activities:** exercise room. **Guest Services:** valet and coin laundry. **Featured Amenity:** full hot breakfast.

**BEST WESTERN REGENCY INN & SUITES**    (903)212-3333

Hotel $94-$154

**AAA Benefit:** Members save 10% or more with Best Western!

**Address:** 707 N Access Rd 75602 **Location:** I-20 exit 596 (Eastman Rd), just w. **Facility:** 59 units. 4 stories, interior corridors. **Pool(s):** outdoor. **Activities:** hot tub, exercise room. **Guest Services:** valet and coin laundry. **Featured Amenity:** full hot breakfast.

**COMFORT SUITES BY CHOICE HOTELS**    (903)663-4991

Hotel $80-$115 **Address:** 3307 N 4th St 75605 **Location:** Loop 281, just w of jct US 259. **Facility:** 60 units. 3 stories, interior corridors. **Pool(s):** heated indoor. **Activities:** hot tub, exercise room. **Guest Services:** valet laundry.

**FAIRFIELD INN BY MARRIOTT**    (903)663-1995

Hotel $95-$115 **Address:** 3305 N 4th St 75605 **Location:** Loop 281, just w of jct US 259. **Facility:** 64 units. 3 stories, interior corridors. **Pool(s):** heated indoor. **Activities:** hot tub. **Guest Services:** valet laundry.

**AAA Benefit:** Members save 5% or more!

## HAMPTON INN & SUITES LONGVIEW NORTH
(903)663-8670

Hotel
$79-$169

**AAA Benefit:** Members save up to 10%!

**Address:** 3044 N Eastman Rd 75605 **Location:** Just s of jct Loop 281 and US 259. **Facility:** 91 units. 4 stories, interior corridors. **Terms:** 1-7 night minimum stay, cancellation fee imposed. **Amenities:** video games. **Pool(s):** heated indoor. **Activities:** hot tub, exercise room. **Guest Services:** valet and coin laundry. **Featured Amenity: full hot breakfast.**

## HOLIDAY INN EXPRESS & SUITES-NORTH
903/663-6464

Hotel. Rates not provided. **Address:** 300 Tuttle Cir 75605 **Location:** Just e of jct Spur 63 (McMann Rd) and Loop 281 to Tuttle Blvd, just n. **Facility:** 70 units. 3 stories, interior corridors. **Pool(s):** heated indoor. **Activities:** sauna, hot tub, exercise room. **Guest Services:** valet and coin laundry.

## HOLIDAY INN EXPRESS HOTEL & SUITES LONGVIEW SOUTH
(903)247-3000

Hotel $84-$94 **Address:** 900 S Access Rd 75601 **Location:** I-20 exit 596. **Facility:** 90 units. 3 stories, interior corridors. **Terms:** cancellation fee imposed, resort fee. **Pool(s):** outdoor. **Activities:** exercise room. **Guest Services:** valet and coin laundry.

## LA QUINTA INN & SUITES LONGVIEW NORTH
(903)663-6611

Hotel $105-$140 **Address:** 908 E Hawkins Pkwy 75605 **Location:** Just w of jct US 259. **Facility:** 70 units. 3 stories, interior corridors. **Pool(s):** outdoor. **Activities:** hot tub, exercise room. **Guest Services:** valet and coin laundry.

## MICROTEL INN & SUITES BY WYNDHAM LONGVIEW
(903)234-2001

Hotel
$62-$82

**Address:** 803 N Access Rd 75602 **Location:** I-20 exit 596, just nw; on north service road. **Facility:** 50 units. 2 stories (no elevator), interior corridors. **Pool(s):** outdoor. **Activities:** exercise room. **Guest Services:** coin laundry. **Featured Amenity: continental breakfast.**

**Conveniently located near I-20, free Wi-Fi and free breakfast!**

## WINGATE BY WYNDHAM
(903)663-3196

Hotel
$95-$157

**Address:** 431 NE Loop 281 75605 **Location:** Loop 281, just w of jct US 259. **Facility:** 80 units. 4 stories, interior corridors. **Terms:** cancellation fee imposed. **Amenities:** safes. **Pool(s):** heated indoor. **Activities:** sauna, hot tub, exercise room. **Guest Services:** valet and coin laundry. **Featured Amenity: full hot breakfast.**

## STAYBRIDGE SUITES
903/212-3800

Not evaluated. **Address:** 3409 N Fourth St 75605 **Location:** Just n of jct SR 281/Loop 281. Facilities, services, and décor characterize a mid-scale property.

## WHERE TO EAT

### GRANDY'S RESTAURANT
903/758-9171

American. Quick Serve. $4-$8 **AAA Inspector Notes:** Fried chicken and country-fried steak are menu standbys at the restaurant, a regional franchise. They also offer a family-style dining menu. The décor is a step up from that of most quick-serve eateries and more resembles that of a conventional restaurant. Some elements of increased service include additional rolls, iced tea refills and tray removal. **Address:** 3305 S Eastman Rd 75607 **Location:** I-20 exit 596.
B  L  D

### THE JALAPENO TREE
903/757-4221

Tex-Mex. Casual Dining. $7-$17 **AAA Inspector Notes:** In small towns along I-30 in East Texas, the small chain of restaurants prepares standard Tex-Mex fare with a hint of New Mexico flair, courtesy of the red and green sauces found in that state. Outgoing servers do what they can to make meals a pleasure. The menu also lists American dishes and children's choices. A drive-through window offers convenience. Huge homemade sopapillas are shaped like jalapeños. **Features:** full bar. **Address:** 508 N Eastman Rd 75601 **Location:** Jct US 80 and 259; on southeast corner. L  D

### JOHNNY CACE'S SEAFOOD & STEAK HOUSE
903/753-7691

Regional Seafood Casual Dining
$8-$33

**AAA Inspector Notes:** Celebrating 63 years as a Longview tradition, this dining experience features New Orleans-style décor with chandeliers and a lovely courtyard. Broiled snapper, stuffed shrimp, flavorful fried catfish and delicious steaks, cut in-house, are just a few of the specialties. **Features:** full bar, Sunday brunch. **Address:** 1501 E Marshall Ave 75601 **Location:** US 80, 0.5 mi w of US 80 and 259 crossing. L  D

### PAPACITA'S MEXICAN RESTAURANT
903/663-1700

Tex-Mex. Casual Dining. $7-$18 **AAA Inspector Notes:** As the area's largest Mexican restaurant, this place does a brisk business in the evenings. Two colorful and distinctive stories surround a large, open central atrium. The specialty is Tex-Mex, and patrons can find all the standard fare, including enchiladas, chiles rellenos and tacos. One section of the menu is devoted to mesquite-grilled items like ribs and fajitas. **Features:** full bar, patio dining. **Address:** 305 W Loop 281 75605 **Location:** Just e of jct Loop 281 and Spur 63 (McCann Rd). L  D

## LOS FRESNOS (I-8) pop. 5,542, elev. 23'

**LAGUNA ATASCOSA NATIONAL WILDLIFE REFUGE** is at 22817 Ocelt Rd. Encompassing 88,000 acres of the former delta of the Rio Grande, Laguna Atascosa provides resting and feeding grounds for some 414 species of birds, including falcons, storks, sandhill cranes and waterfowl. Up to

80 percent of the continent's redheaded ducks winter here. The refuge also is home to coyotes, bobcats, ocelots, jaguarundis and white-tailed deer.

**Hours:** Refuge and tour road daily dawn-dusk. Visitor center daily 8-4. Closed major holidays. **Cost:** $3 (per private vehicle). **Phone:** (956) 748-3607. 🅰️

**LITTLE GRACELAND MUSEUM** is at 701 W. Ocean Blvd. The museum features Elvis Presley memorabilia collected by a former Army acquaintance of the singer. Displays include photographs, records, souvenir plates and an array of promotional collectibles. At the entrance is a replica of the Graceland gates in Memphis. **Time:** Allow 1 hour minimum. **Hours:** Thurs.-Sun. 10-noon and 2-5. Phone ahead to confirm schedule. **Cost:** Donations. **Phone:** (956) 233-5482.

# LUBBOCK (C-5) pop. 229,573, elev. 3,195'
**• Hotels p. 402 • Restaurants p. 405**

Lubbock was named for Col. Thomas S. Lubbock, a Confederate officer and brother of a Texas governor. The city's history as a commercial center dates back to the mid-1800s. One of the major agricultural centers of Texas, Lubbock ships livestock, grain and cotton and is one of America's largest cotton producers.

The Buddy Holly Walk of Fame, across from the Buddy Holly Center on Crickets Avenue, pays tribute to West Texas natives who have contributed to the fields of art, music and entertainment. Inductees include such celebrities as Dan Blocker, Mac Davis, Waylon Jennings, Roy Orbison and Tanya Tucker.

**Lubbock Convention and Visitors Bureau:** 1500 Broadway, Sixth Floor, Lubbock, TX 79401. **Phone:** (806) 747-5232 or (800) 692-4035.

**AMERICAN MUSEUM OF AGRICULTURE** is at 1121 Canyon Lake Dr. On display are 300 die-cast toy tractors, 71 pedal tractors, a threshing machine and other agricultural items from the early to mid-20th century. Other highlights include a 1920s blacksmith shop, a farm diorama and a cotton exhibit. **Time:** Allow 30 minutes minimum. **Hours:** Tues.-Sat. 10-5. **Cost:** $5; $10 (family of four). **Phone:** (806) 744-3786 or (877) 789-8335.

**AMERICAN WIND POWER CENTER** is at 1701 Canyon Lake Dr. A large indoor exhibit hall features more than 100 American-style windmills from 1868 to the present. The Linebery Windmill Park is 28 acres of rolling countryside that features more than 50 working windmills ranging in style from early wooden to modern metal; some stand more than 55 feet high. **Time:** Allow 1 hour minimum. **Hours:** Tues.-Sat. 10-5 (also Sun. 2-5, May-Sept.). Closed Jan. 1, July 4, Thanksgiving and Christmas. **Cost:** $5; $10 (family, up to four people); free (active military and their families with ID). **Phone:** (806) 747-8734. 🅰️

**BUDDY HOLLY CENTER** is at 1801 Crickets Ave. A guitar-shaped gallery chronicles the life and music of Lubbock native Buddy Holly. The depot also houses the Texas Musicians' Hall of Fame and Fine Arts Gallery, which offers changing exhibits by local, regional and national artists. **Time:** Allow 30 minutes minimum. **Hours:** Tues.-Sat. 10-5, Sun. 1-5. Closed major holidays. **Cost:** $5; $3 (ages 60+); $2 (ages 7-17 and college students with ID); free (ages 0-6 and active military in uniform). **Phone:** (806) 775-3560.

**LUBBOCK LAKE LANDMARK** is n. on University Ave. to Loop 289, then w. to Lubbock Lake exit. This archeological and natural history preserve is on more than 300 acres and contains evidence of

12,000 years of continuous human occupation. An interpretive center features artifacts, dioramas and interactive exhibits. Four miles of nature trails wind through a shortgrass prairie landscape.

**Time:** Allow 1 hour minimum. **Hours:** Tues.-Sat. 9-5, Sun. 1-5. Closed Jan. 1, Thanksgiving and Christmas Eve-Dec. 31. **Cost:** Donations. **Phone:** (806) 742-1116. 🏛

**MACKENZIE PARK** adjoins Lubbock on the northeast. Prairie Dog Town, a community of several hundred of the rodents, was established in the early 1940s. Park facilities include picnic areas, baseball fields, a golf course, disc golf course and an amusement park. **Phone:** (806) 775-2687 for the parks department. 🏛

**MUSEUM OF TEXAS TECH UNIVERSITY** is at Fourth St. and Indiana Ave. Exhibits emphasize the environment, history and cultures of Texas, the Southwest and arid and semiarid lands around the world. The museum's art collection includes sculpture, bronzes, ceramics, jades, ivories and Southwestern landscapes. There also are displays about Lubbock history, ethnohistory, natural history, dinosaurs and pre-Columbian and African art. The Moody Planetarium also is featured.

**Time:** Allow 1 hour minimum. **Hours:** Museum Tues.-Sat. 10-5, Sun. 1-5. Planetarium shows are given Tues.-Sat. at 11:30, 12:30, 2 and 3:30, Sun. at 2 and 3:30, June-Aug.; Wed.-Sun. at 2 and 3:30, rest of year. Laser shows are given Wed.-Sun. at 2. Closed major holidays. **Cost:** Museum free. Planetarium or laser show $5; $3 (ages 60+ and students with ID); free (ages 0-4). **Phone:** (806) 742-2490 or (806) 742-2456.

**NATIONAL RANCHING HERITAGE CENTER** is at 3121 4th St. This 19-acre historical park includes 48 relocated, restored structures from the early days of ranching. A self-guiding trail begins from the museum and goes through the historical park, which encompasses a ranch office, stone and log cabins, a Queen Anne-style rancher's home, a ranch cookhouse/dining hall, a horse barn, a bunkhouse, a one-room schoolhouse, windmills, a train and a depot. **Time:** Allow 1 hour minimum. **Hours:** Mon.-Sat. 10-5, Sun. 1-5. Closed major holidays. **Cost:** Donations. **Phone:** (806) 742-0498.

**SCIENCE SPECTRUM MUSEUM AND OMNI THEATER** is at 2579 S. Loop 289. This hands-on science and technology museum offers more than 250 interactive exhibits, an aquarium and rotating displays. Documentary and educational films are shown on a 58-foot dome screen in the OMNI Theater. **Time:** Allow 2 hours minimum. **Hours:** Mon.-Sat. 10-5 (also Sat. 5-6), Sun. 1-5. Phone for theater show schedule. **Cost:** Museum or theater $8; $6.50 (ages 3-12 and 60+). Combination ticket $13.50; $10.50 (ages 3-12 and 60+). **Phone:** (806) 745-2525, or (806) 745-6299 for the theater.

**SILENT WINGS MUSEUM** is at 6202 N. I-27 in the old Lubbock Airport terminal. Exhibits chronicle the history of the United States military glider program during World War II. A collection of more than 10,000 artifacts includes aircraft, vehicles, weapons and personal effects of soldiers and civilians. A fully restored glider sits inside the 30,000-square-foot gallery; a fully restored C-47 Skytrain is installed in front of the museum. **Time:** Allow 1 hour, 30 minutes minimum. **Hours:** Tues.-Sat. 10-5, Sun. 1-5. Closed Jan. 1, Thanksgiving and Christmas. **Cost:** $5; $3 (ages 60+); $2 (ages 7-17 and students with ID); free (ages 0-6 and active military in uniform). **Phone:** (806) 775-2047.

## WINERIES

- **Cap*Rock Winery** is 5.2 mi. s. of jct. I-27 and SR 289S on US 87, then .5 mi. e. on Woodrow Rd. to 408 E. Woodrow Rd. **Hours:** Mon.-Sat. 10-5, Sun. 12:30-5, May-Sept. Tours and tastings daily noon-5, May-Sept. Closed major holidays. **Phone:** (806) 686-4452.

- **Llano Estacado Winery** is 5 mi. s. of Loop 289 on US 87, then 3.2 mi. e. to 3426 E. FM 1585. **Hours:** Tours and tastings Mon.-Sat. 10-5, Sun. noon-5. Last tour departs 1 hour before closing. Closed Jan. 1, Thanksgiving and Christmas. **Phone:** (806) 745-2258.

- **Pheasant Ridge Winery** is 10 mi. n. on I-27 to exit 14, then 2 mi. e. on FM 1729, then 1 mi. s., following signs. **Hours:** Tours Fri.-Sat. noon-6, Sun. 1-5 and by appointment. Closed major holidays. **Phone:** (806) 746-6033.

**AMERICAS BEST VALUE INN - LUBBOCK**

(806)745-2515

Motel
$50-$199

**Address:** 150 Slaton Rd 79404 **Location:** I-27 exit 1, just e. on US 84. **Facility:** 71 units. 1 story, exterior corridors. **Terms:** 2-3 night minimum stay - seasonal and/or weekends, cancellation fee imposed, resort fee. **Pool(s):** outdoor. **Activities:** exercise room. **Guest Services:** coin laundry. **Featured Amenity:** full hot breakfast.

[SAVE] [➔] [BIZ] [HS] [🛜] [🛏] [▣] [▣] / SOME UNITS [🐾]

**ARBOR INN & SUITES**

(806)722-2726

Hotel
$89-$249

**Address:** 5310 Englewood Ave 79424 **Location:** Loop 289 exit 50th St, just w. **Facility:** 73 units, some efficiencies. 3 stories, interior corridors. **Amenities:** safes. **Pool(s):** heated outdoor. **Activities:** hot tub, exercise room. **Guest Services:** complimentary and valet laundry.

[SAVE] [📶] CALL [📞M] [➔] [BIZ] [HS] [🛜] [🛏] [▣] [▣] / SOME UNITS [🐾]

## ASHMORE INN & SUITES    (806)785-0060

Hotel $95-$199 **Address:** 4019 S Loop 289 79423 **Location:** Just s of jct Quaker Ave. **Facility:** 124 units, some efficiencies and kitchens. 2-3 stories (no elevator), interior corridors. **Terms:** cancellation fee imposed. **Pool(s):** heated outdoor. **Activities:** hot tub, exercise room. **Guest Services:** valet and coin laundry, area transportation.

   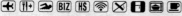 

## BAYMONT INN & SUITES LUBBOCK    (806)792-5181

Hotel
$69-$198

**Address:** 3901 19th St 79410 **Location:** Jct US 62/82 W and 19th St. **Facility:** 64 units. 3 stories, interior corridors. **Pool(s):** outdoor. **Activities:** exercise room. **Guest Services:** valet and coin laundry. **Featured Amenity:** continental breakfast.

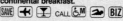

## BEST WESTERN PLUS LUBBOCK WINDSOR INN
(806)762-8400

Hotel
$80-$240

**AAA Benefit:** Members save 10% or more with Best Western!

**Address:** 5410 I-27 79404 **Location:** 3.5 mi s on I-27 exit 1B southbound; U-turn at exit 1A (50th St) northbound. **Facility:** 64 units. 2 stories, interior corridors. **Pool(s):** heated indoor. **Activities:** hot tub, exercise room. **Guest Services:** coin laundry.

## BEST WESTERN PLUS PALMS HOTEL & SUITES
(806)799-9999

Hotel
$85-$120

**AAA Benefit:** Members save 10% or more with Best Western!

**Address:** 6015 45th St 79407 **Location:** Jct US 62/82 and Loop 289, just w. **Facility:** 70 units, some efficiencies. 3 stories, interior corridors. **Terms:** 2 night minimum stay - seasonal. **Pool(s):** heated indoor. **Activities:** sauna, hot tub, exercise room. **Guest Services:** coin laundry.

## COMFORT INN & SUITES    (806)763-6500

Hotel $73-$210 **Address:** 5828 I-27 S 79404 **Location:** I-27 exit 1B, just s; on west frontage road. **Facility:** 66 units. 2 stories, interior corridors. **Pool(s):** heated indoor. **Activities:** hot tub, exercise room. **Guest Services:** valet and coin laundry.

## COMFORT SUITES    (806)798-0002

Hotel $89-$119 **Address:** 5113 S Loop 289 79424 **Location:** S on Loop 289 exit Slide Rd; on south frontage road. **Facility:** 65 units. 2 stories (no elevator), interior corridors. **Terms:** check-in 4 pm. **Pool(s):** outdoor. **Activities:** hot tub. **Guest Services:** valet and coin laundry.

## COUNTRY INN & SUITES BY CARLSON LUBBOCK
806/687-2500

Hotel. Rates not provided. **Address:** 5806 I-27 79404 **Location:** I-27 exit 1B; on southbound frontage road. **Facility:** 64 units. 3 stories, interior corridors. **Pool(s):** heated indoor. **Activities:** hot tub, exercise room. **Guest Services:** valet and coin laundry.

CALL

## COURTYARD BY MARRIOTT    (806)795-1633

Hotel $149-$164 **Address:** 4011 S Loop 289 79423 **Location:** Loop 289 exit Quarter Ave, 0.5 mi s. **Facility:** 78 units. 3 stories, interior corridors. **Pool(s):** heated indoor. **Activities:** hot tub, exercise room. **Guest Services:** valet and coin laundry.

**AAA Benefit:** Members save 5% or more!

## EMBASSY SUITES HOTEL LUBBOCK    (806)771-7000

Hotel $139-$179 **Address:** 5215 S Loop 289 79424 **Location:** Just sw of jct Slide Rd. **Facility:** 156 units. 3 stories, interior corridors. **Terms:** 1-7 night minimum stay, cancellation fee imposed. **Pool(s):** heated indoor. **Activities:** hot tub, exercise room. **Guest Services:** valet and coin laundry.

**AAA Benefit:** Members save 5% or more!

## FAIRFIELD INN BY MARRIOTT    (806)795-1288

Hotel $121-$133 **Address:** 4007 S Loop 289 79423 **Location:** Loop 289 exit Quaker Ave. **Facility:** 64 units. 3 stories, interior corridors. **Pool(s):** heated indoor. **Activities:** hot tub. **Guest Services:** valet laundry.

**AAA Benefit:** Members save 5% or more!

## HAMPTON INN & SUITES    (806)797-9600

Hotel
$139-$289

**AAA Benefit:** Members save up to 10%!

**Address:** 5614 Englewood Ave 79424 **Location:** Loop 289 exit 50th St, just w. **Facility:** 80 units. 4 stories, interior corridors. **Terms:** 1-7 night minimum stay, cancellation fee imposed. **Amenities:** Some: video games. **Pool(s):** heated indoor. **Activities:** hot tub, exercise room. **Guest Services:** valet and coin laundry, area transportation. **Featured Amenity:** breakfast buffet.

## HAMPTON INN BY HILTON    (806)795-1080

Hotel $152-$165 **Address:** 4003 S Loop 289 79423 **Location:** Loop 289 exit Quaker Ave. **Facility:** 80 units. 3 stories, interior corridors. **Terms:** 1-7 night minimum stay, cancellation fee imposed. **Pool(s):** heated indoor. **Activities:** hot tub, exercise room. **Guest Services:** valet laundry.

## HAWTHORN SUITES BY WYNDHAM (806)792-3600

Hotel
$85-$519

**Address:** 4435 Marsha Sharp Frwy 79407 **Location:** Just sw of jct US 62/82 and Quaker Ave. **Facility:** 132 units, some efficiencies. 4 stories, interior corridors. **Pool(s):** heated indoor. **Activities:** hot tub, exercise room. **Guest Services:** complimentary laundry. **Featured Amenity:** full hot breakfast.

SAVE ⬚ CALL &M ⬚ BIZ HS ⬚ ⬚ ⬚ ⬚ ⬚ ⬚ / SOME UNITS ⬚

## HOLIDAY INN EXPRESS HOTEL & SUITES 806/687-2600

**Hotel. Rates not provided. Address:** 6023 45th St 79407 **Location:** US 62/82 and Loop 289 W. **Facility:** 82 units. 4 stories, interior corridors. **Pool(s):** heated indoor. **Activities:** hot tub, exercise room. **Guest Services:** valet and coin laundry.

CALL &M ⬚ BIZ HS ⬚ ⬚ ⬚ ⬚ ⬚

## HOLIDAY INN PARK PLAZA (806)797-3241

**Hotel $79-$149 Address:** 3201 S Loop 289 79423 **Location:** Loop 289 S exit Indiana Ave; on south frontage road. **Facility:** 201 units. 2 stories (no elevator), interior/exterior corridors. **Terms:** check-in 4 pm. **Pool(s):** heated indoor. **Activities:** sauna, exercise room. **Guest Services:** valet and coin laundry.

⬚ ⬚ ⬚ BIZ ⬚ ⬚ / SOME UNITS ⬚ ⬚

## LA QUINTA INN & SUITES LUBBOCK NORTH
(806)749-1600

Hotel
$94-$139

**Address:** 5006 Auburn St 79416 **Location:** 1 mi sw of jct Loop 289 N and Quaker Ave; on N Service Rd. **Facility:** 109 units. 3 stories, interior corridors. **Pool(s):** heated indoor. **Activities:** hot tub, exercise room. **Guest Services:** valet and coin laundry, area transportation. **Featured Amenity:** continental breakfast.

SAVE ⬚ ⬚ BIZ ⬚ ⬚ ⬚ ⬚ ⬚ ⬚ / SOME UNITS ⬚

LA QUINTA INNS & SUITES

**Next door to the Lubbock Heart Hospital, minutes from TTU, hot breakfast, pet friendly!**

## LA QUINTA INN & SUITES LUBBOCK WEST MEDICAL CENTER (806)792-0065

**Hotel $89-$240 Address:** 4115 Marsha Sharp Frwy 79407 **Location:** Jct US 62/82 and Quaker Ave, just se. **Facility:** 132 units. 6 stories, interior/exterior corridors. **Pool(s):** outdoor. **Activities:** exercise room.

⬚ ⬚ BIZ ⬚ ⬚ / SOME UNITS ⬚ HS ⬚ ⬚

## LA QUINTA INN LUBBOCK CIVIC CENTER (806)763-9441

**Hotel $72-$220 Address:** 601 Ave Q 79401 **Location:** 0.8 mi nw on US 84. **Facility:** 137 units. 2 stories, exterior corridors. **Pool(s):** outdoor. **Guest Services:** valet laundry.

⬚ ⬚ ⬚ ⬚ / SOME UNITS ⬚ HS ⬚ ⬚

---

**Safety tip:**

**Keep a current AAA/CAA**

**Road Atlas in every vehicle**

## MCM ELEGANTE HOTEL AND SUITES 806/763-1200

Hotel
Rates not provided

**Address:** 801 Ave Q 79401 **Location:** Just s of jct 8th St. **Facility:** 295 units. 6 stories, interior corridors. **Terms:** check-in 4 pm. **Pool(s):** heated indoor. **Activities:** exercise room. **Guest Services:** valet and coin laundry, area transportation.

⬚ ⬚ ⬚ ⬚ ⬚ ⬚ BIZ ⬚ ⬚ / SOME UNITS ⬚ ⬚

## OVERTON HOTEL & CONFERENCE CENTER
(806)776-7000

Hotel
$150-$349

**Address:** 2322 Mac Davis Ln 79401 **Location:** US 82 (Marsha Sharpe Frwy), just s on University Ave. Across from Texas Tech University Football Stadium. **Facility:** The upscale, full-service property with a professional management team is conveniently located adjacent to Texas Tech University. 303 units. 15 stories, interior corridors. **Parking:** on-site and valet. **Terms:** check-in 4 pm, 7 day cancellation notice-fee imposed. **Dining:** Pecan Grill, see separate listing. **Pool(s):** outdoor. **Activities:** hot tub, exercise room. **Guest Services:** valet laundry.

SAVE ⬚ ⬚ ⬚ ⬚ CALL &M ⬚ BIZ HS ⬚ ⬚ ⬚ ⬚

## QUALITY INN & SUITES (806)780-4000

Hotel
$84-$119

**Address:** 3430 W Loop 289 79407 **Location:** W Loop 289 exit 34th St. **Facility:** 65 units. 3 stories, interior corridors. **Pool(s):** heated indoor. **Activities:** hot tub, exercise room. **Guest Services:** valet and coin laundry. **Featured Amenity:** full hot breakfast.

SAVE ⬚ BIZ HS ⬚ ⬚ ⬚ ⬚ ⬚

## RESIDENCE INN BY MARRIOTT (806)745-1963

**Extended Stay Hotel** $109-$199 **Address:** 2551 S Loop 289 79423 **Location:** Just w of jct University Ave; on south frontage road. **Facility:** 80 kitchen units, some two bedrooms. 2 stories (no elevator), exterior corridors. **Pool(s):** outdoor. **Activities:** hot tub, exercise room. **Guest Services:** valet and coin laundry.

**AAA Benefit:** Members save 5% or more!

⬚ ⬚ BIZ ⬚ ⬚ ⬚ ⬚ ⬚ / SOME UNITS ⬚ ⬚

## SLEEP INN & SUITES (806)368-6060

Hotel
$75-$210

**Address:** 5816 34th St 79407 **Location:** Loop 289 W exit 34th St, just e. **Facility:** 66 units. 4 stories, interior corridors. **Pool(s):** heated indoor. **Activities:** hot tub, exercise room. **Guest Services:** coin laundry. **Featured Amenity:** full hot breakfast.

SAVE CALL &M ⬚ BIZ HS ⬚ ⬚ ⬚ ⬚ ⬚ / SOME UNITS ⬚ ⬚

**New 2012. Free hot breakfast, WIFI, Bus. & fitness center. Indoor pool/hot tub. 1 min. to TTech & LCU.**

## STAYBRIDGE SUITES — 806/765-8900

▼▼▼ **Extended Stay Hotel.** Rates not provided. **Address:** 2515 19th St 79410 **Location:** Just sw of jct University Ave. **Facility:** 82 efficiencies. 3 stories, interior corridors. **Pool(s):** outdoor. **Activities:** hot tub, exercise room. **Guest Services:** complimentary and valet laundry.

## SUPER 8 — (806)771-8000

▼▼▼
Hotel
$65-$105

**Address:** 6510 I-27 79404 **Location:** I-27 exit 1B; on west frontage road. **Facility:** 75 units. 3 stories, interior corridors. **Pool(s):** heated indoor. **Activities:** sauna, hot tub, exercise room. **Guest Services:** valet and coin laundry. **Featured Amenity: continental breakfast.**

## TOWNEPLACE SUITES BY MARRIOTT — (806)799-6226

▼▼▼ **Extended Stay Hotel** $79-$159 **Address:** 5310 W Loop 289 79424 **Location:** 0.5 mi s of jct US 62/82. **Facility:** 88 units, some two bedrooms, efficiencies and kitchens. 3 stories, interior corridors. **Pool(s):** heated outdoor. **Activities:** hot tub, exercise room. **Guest Services:** valet and coin laundry.

**AAA Benefit:** Members save 5% or more!

## WHERE TO EAT

### 50TH STREET CABOOSE — 806/796-2240

▼▼ Mexican. Casual Dining. $6-$15 **AAA Inspector Notes:** One section of the restaurant is dedicated to a variety of video and arcade games. It can become quite lively with the combination of games and the large bar area. The menu is mainly Mexican cuisine, but some steak dishes and traditional bar/grill offerings also are available. **Features:** full bar. **Address:** 5027 50th St 79414 **Location:** Just e of jct Slide Rd.

### 50 YARD LINE RESTAURANT — 806/745-3991

▼▼ Steak Seafood. Casual Dining. $9-$36 **AAA Inspector Notes:** Among entrees are steak and seafood preparations, beef kebabs, pork chops and a selection of lighter fare. The setting is centered on football. **Features:** full bar. **Address:** 2549 S Loop 289 79423 **Location:** Loop 289 S exit Indiana Ave, just e; on southside frontage road.

### ABUELO'S THE FLAVOR OF MEXICO — 806/794-1762

▼▼ Mexican. Casual Dining. $7-$18 **AAA Inspector Notes:** Many traditional Mexican dishes are served in an upscale and spacious dining area. The adult beverages reflect an inventive spirit. **Features:** full bar. **Reservations:** suggested. **Address:** 4401 82nd St 79424 **Location:** Jct Quaker Ave and 82nd St; on southwest corner.

### CAFE J — 806/743-5400

▼▼ International. Casual Dining. $9-$42 **AAA Inspector Notes:** The varied menu showcases international flavors in preparations of pasta, crêpes, chicken, lamb, beef and salads. This restaurant has many pieces of original art that set the theme for the dining experience. **Features:** full bar. **Address:** 2605 19th St 79410 **Location:** 1 blk w of University Ave.

### CATTLE BARON STEAK & SEAFOOD — 806/798-7033

▼▼ American. Casual Dining. $8-$28 **AAA Inspector Notes:** A scrumptious array of menu selections includes steak, seafood, chicken and prime rib as well as desserts such as caramel apple pie. An upscale Western decor includes wood trim and distinctive chandeliers made from deer antlers. **Features:** full bar. **Address:** 8201 Quaker Ave 79423 **Location:** Jct Quaker Ave and 82nd St; on southeast corner.

### EL CHICO — 806/795-9445

▼▼▼
Tex-Mex
Casual Dining
$7-$17

**AAA Inspector Notes:** Inside and out, the decor of the popular Mexican restaurant is inviting. The menu features traditional favorites such as enchiladas, tacos, burritos and fajitas. The broad menu also lists a few American classics. **Features:** full bar. **Reservations:** suggested. **Address:** 4301 Marsha Sharp Frwy 79407 **Location:** W Loop 289 exit US 62/82, 2.7 mi w.

### MANNA BREAD & WINE — 806/791-5600

▼▼ Southwestern. Casual Dining. $8-$22 **AAA Inspector Notes:** Creative combinations of ingredients provide visually appealing and flavorful dishes. The intimate dining room has a nice view of the greenery in the courtyard. **Features:** full bar, patio dining. **Address:** 2610 Salem Ave, Suite 19 79410 **Location:** Just sw of jct US 62/82 and Quaker Ave.

### ORLANDO'S ITALIAN RESTAURANT — 806/797-8646

▼▼ Southern Italian. Casual Dining. $8-$18 **AAA Inspector Notes:** Large portions of your favorite Italian dishes at affordable prices are served at this very popular restaurant. **Features:** full bar. **Address:** 6951 Indiana Ave 79413 **Location:** Loop 289 exit Indiana Ave, just n.

### ORLANDO'S ITALIAN RESTAURANT — 806/747-3501

▼▼ Southern Italian. Casual Dining. $8-$18 **AAA Inspector Notes:** All your favorite traditional Italian dishes as well as pizzas and focaccia are found at this fun and popular location. **Features:** full bar. **Address:** 2402 Ave Q 79411 **Location:** Jct 24th St and Ave Q.

### PECAN GRILL — 806/776-7000

▼▼▼ American. Fine Dining. $8-$30 **AAA Inspector Notes:** A very nice selection of appetizers, soups, salads and entrées to please everyone are presented in a fine dining environment with a professional staff. I especially enjoyed the crab bisque and the rack of lamb. **Features:** full bar. **Address:** 2322 Mac Davis Ln 79401 **Location:** US 82 (Marsha Sharpe Frwy), just s on University Ave; in Overton Hotel & Conference Center.

### RIB CRIB BBQ AND GRILL — 806/798-3400

▼▼ Barbecue. Casual Dining. $6-$16 **AAA Inspector Notes:** Most guests need extra napkins to tackle the ribs, brisket, ham, pork and chicken selections. The menu also lists sandwiches and wraps, along with tempting sides and large desserts. The decor is decidedly Western. **Features:** beer & wine. **Address:** 8211 Slide Rd 79424 **Location:** Jct Slide Rd and 82nd St; on southeast corner.

### RIVER SMITH'S CHICKEN & CATFISH — 806/765-8165

▼ Seafood Chicken. Quick Serve. $5-$12 **AAA Inspector Notes:** Place your order at the counter, then wait for the servers to deliver your meal to the dining room. The menu offers a good variety of mainly fried items, though a few items are charbroiled. **Features:** beer only. **Address:** 406 Ave Q 79401 **Location:** Just s of jct US 82.

### ROCKFISH SEAFOOD GRILL — 806/780-7625

▼▼ Seafood. Casual Dining. $8-$34 **AAA Inspector Notes:** Patrons shuffle through peanut shells on the floor as they make their way to their seats and are easily distracted by the numerous pieces of hunting and fishing memorabilia adorning the walls and ceiling. Although guests kick back in a log cabin-style interior, the freshly caught fish gets more sophisticated preparation than campfire roasting. The chef uses an array of sauces and cooking styles, and soups are hearty and fresh. **Features:** full bar. **Address:** 6253 Slide Rd 79414 **Location:** Jct Loop 289 and Slide Rd; on northeast corner.

**TEXAS LAND AND CATTLE STEAKHOUSE**   806/791-0555

▼▼ ▼▼ Steak. Casual Dining. $9-$27 **AAA Inspector Notes:** A variety of large Prime steaks, delicious salads and scrumptious desserts await you at the friendly Texas ranch-style restaurant. Try the signature slow-smoked sirloin, which never fails to please, or the Caesar salad, another favorite. A Texas steakhouse means everything is bigger, from large cuts and oversize salads to potatoes and side dishes. Those not in the mood for beef can opt for chicken, quail or seafood. Dessert is an occasion. **Features:** full bar. **Address:** 7202 Indiana Ave 79423 **Location:** Jct Loop 289 S and Indiana Ave.

L  D  D  CALL 🔊M

**ZIO'S ITALIAN KITCHEN**   806/780-6003

▼▼ ▼▼ Italian. Casual Dining. $8-$18 **AAA Inspector Notes:** The warm, comfortable atmosphere and Old World decor complement the menu. Meals are a good value, and so is the service. This small chain specializes in Italian cuisine, including oven-baked pizzas and pasta dishes. Guests are encouraged to get creative with their pizzas by mixing and matching from a list of 24 toppings. Particularly tempting dishes are Artichoke spinach pasta, chicken parmigiana, and Shrimp Limone. **Features:** full bar. **Address:** 4414 82nd St 79424 **Location:** Jct 82nd St and Quaker Ave; on northwest corner. L  D

## LUFKIN (E-10) pop. 35,067, elev. 324'

Settled in 1882, Lufkin boasts the South's first paper mill. Currently the city's industries produce lumber, paper, metal castings, truck trailers, commercial gears and oil-drilling equipment.

**Lufkin Convention and Visitors Bureau:** 1615 S. Chestnut St., P.O. Box 1606, Lufkin, TX 75901. **Phone:** (936) 634-6305 or (800) 409-5659.

**Self-guiding tours:** A walking tour map of historic downtown is available at the chamber of commerce.

**ELLEN TROUT ZOO** is at 402 Zoo Cir. Home to nearly 700 mammals, birds and reptiles from around the world, the zoo features Masai giraffe and white rhinoceros exhibits, as well as a hippopotamus enclosure with an underwater viewing area. During the summer, a train takes visitors on a ride through the park. **Time:** Allow 1 hour minimum. **Hours:** Daily 9-5. **Cost:** $5; $2.50 (ages 4-11). Train $2. **Phone:** (936) 633-0399. 🍴

**MUSEUM OF EAST TEXAS** is at 503 N. Second St. This art collection represents the character, history and heritage of East Texas. Changing exhibits highlight the works of regionally, nationally and internationally known artists. **Time:** Allow 30 minutes minimum. **Hours:** Tues.-Fri. 9-5, Sat.-Sun. 1-5. Closed major holidays. **Cost:** Donations. **Phone:** (936) 639-4434.

**TEXAS FORESTRY MUSEUM** is w. of Loop 287 on SR 103E at 1905 Atkinson Dr. The museum explores the impact of lumbering and forest-products industries on East Texas. Outdoor exhibits, a hiking trail, a fire lookout tower and a logging train are on the grounds. **Time:** Allow 1 hour minimum. **Hours:** Mon.-Sat. 10-5. Closed Jan. 1, Easter, Thanksgiving, Christmas Eve, Christmas and Dec. 31. **Cost:** Donations. **Phone:** (936) 632-9535.

**BEST WESTERN PLUS CROWN COLONY INN & SUITES**   (936)634-3481

▼▼▼ Hotel $114-$149

**AAA Benefit:** Members save 10% or more with Best Western!

**Address:** 3211 S 1st St 75901 **Location:** 2 mi s of jct US 59 and Loop 287. **Facility:** 58 units, some two bedrooms. 3 stories, interior corridors. **Activities:** exercise room. **Guest Services:** coin laundry. **Featured Amenity:** full hot breakfast.

SAVE 🈂 BIZ HS 📶 ✕ 🔒
🖥 💻 / SOME UNITS 🐾

**COMFORT SUITES**   (936)632-4949

▼▼▼▼ Hotel $85-$149 **Address:** 4402 S 1st St 75901 **Location:** 2.2 mi s of jct US 59 and E Loop 287. **Facility:** 65 units, some kitchens. 3 stories, interior corridors. **Pool(s):** heated indoor. **Activities:** hot tub, exercise room. **Guest Services:** valet and coin laundry.

🍴 🈂 BIZ HS 📶 ✕ 🔒 🖥 💻

**COURTYARD BY MARRIOTT LUFKIN**   (936)632-0777

▼▼▼ Hotel $99-$149

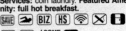

**AAA Benefit:** Members save 5% or more!

**Address:** 2130 S 1st St (Business Rt US 59) 75901 **Location:** Just s of jct Loop 287. **Facility:** 101 units. 4 stories, interior corridors. **Pool(s):** indoor. **Activities:** hot tub, exercise room. **Guest Services:** valet and coin laundry.

SAVE 🍴 🍽 🈂 BIZ HS 📶
✕ 🔒 🖥 💻

**HAMPTON INN & SUITES**   (936)699-2500

▼▼▼▼ Hotel $107-$143 **Address:** 4400 S 1st St 75901 **Location:** 2.2 mi s of jct US 59 and E Loop 287. **Facility:** 68 units. 4 stories, interior corridors. **Terms:** 1-7 night minimum stay, cancellation fee imposed. **Pool(s):** outdoor. **Activities:** exercise room. **Guest Services:** valet and coin laundry.

**AAA Benefit:** Members save up to 10%!

🍴 🈂 HS 📶 🔒 🖥 💻

**HOLIDAY INN EXPRESS & SUITES LUFKIN SOUTH**   936/699-3000

▼▼▼▼ Hotel. Rates not provided. **Address:** 4404 S 1st St 75901 **Location:** 2.2 mi s of jct US 59 and E Loop 287. **Facility:** 83 units. 4 stories, interior corridors. **Pool(s):** outdoor. **Activities:** exercise room. **Guest Services:** valet and coin laundry.

🍴 CALL 🔊M 🈂 BIZ HS 📶 ✕ 🔒 🖥 💻

**LA QUINTA INN LUFKIN**   (936)634-3351

▼▼ ▼▼ Hotel $85-$130 **Address:** 2119 S 1st St 75901 **Location:** US 59 exit Carriage Way northbound, 0.3 mi s of jct S Loop 287 and US 59 business route. **Facility:** 106 units. 2 stories (no elevator), exterior corridors. **Pool(s):** outdoor. **Guest Services:** valet laundry.

🍴 🈂 📶 💻 / SOME UNITS 🐾 HS 🔒 🖥

**EL CHICO**  936/632-5202

Tex-Mex
Casual Dining
$7–$15

**AAA Inspector Notes:** Inside and out, the decor of the popular Mexican restaurant is inviting. The menu features traditional favorites such as enchiladas, tacos, burritos and fajitas. The broad menu also lists a few American classics. **Features:** full bar. **Address:** 2104 S 1st St 75901 **Location:** US 59 exit Carriage Way northbound; jct S Loop 287 and US 59 business route.  L  D

**MANHATTAN FINE DINING**  936/639-8400

Continental. Casual Dining. $10–$30 **AAA Inspector Notes:** The grill serves traditional preparations of veal, chicken, spaghetti and an extensive selection of seafood. Entertainers usually perform on the weekend. The extensive wine list includes by-the-glass choices. **Features:** full bar. **Address:** 107 W Lufkin Ave 75901 **Location:** Between N 1st St and Cotton Square; in basement of Perry Building; downtown. **Parking:** street only.  L  D

**RALPH & KACOO'S**  936/634-8000

Seafood. Casual Dining. $8–$27 **AAA Inspector Notes:** The comfortable dining room has carpeted floors to muffle conversation from nearby tables. It has a lively bar for those wanting to catch up socially or discuss sports. The Louisiana fare includes crawfish étouffée, blackened fish, steaks and fried food platters. There's also a large dessert tray. Service is super friendly. Come on Wednesday for all-u-can-eat shrimp. **Features:** full bar. **Address:** 3107 S 1st St 75901 **Location:** 2 mi s of jct US 59 and Loop 287.

L  D  CALL ⒺⓂ

## LULING pop. 5,411

**BEST WESTERN PLUS LONGHORN INN & SUITES**
(830)875-5442

Hotel
$119–$149

**AAA Benefit:** Members save 10% or more with Best Western!

**Address:** 4120 E Pierce St 78648 **Location:** I-10 exit 632, on northwest corner. **Facility:** 54 units. 3 stories, interior corridors. **Terms:** cancellation fee imposed. **Pool(s):** outdoor. **Activities:** exercise room. **Guest Services:** coin laundry. **Featured Amenity: full hot breakfast.**

 / SOME UNITS

## LUMBERTON pop. 11,943

**ECONO LODGE**  (409)751-5557

Motel $74–$99 **Address:** 131 N LHS Dr 77657 **Location:** On US 69, 3 mi n of jct US 96. **Facility:** 50 units. 2 stories, interior corridors. **Pool(s):** outdoor. **Activities:** limited exercise equipment. **Guest Services:** coin laundry.

 / SOME UNITS

**LA QUINTA INN & SUITES**  (409)751-3999

Hotel
$104–$139

**Address:** 104 N LHS Dr 77657 **Location:** On US 69, 3 mi n of jct US 96. **Facility:** 56 units. 3 stories, interior corridors. **Pool(s):** outdoor. **Activities:** hot tub. **Guest Services:** coin laundry. **Featured Amenity: full hot breakfast.**

  / SOME UNITS

## LYNDON B. JOHNSON NATIONAL HISTORICAL PARK (E-7)

Lyndon B. Johnson National Historical Park is 2 blks. s. of US 290 in Johnson City *(see place listing p. 382)*. Covering 675 acres, some of which the Johnson family had owned since the late 1860s, the park consists of two districts, each once home to President Johnson. The home where he was born has been reconstructed on the site where the original once stood. His boyhood home remains in its original location. The visitor center chronicles LBJ's life and accomplishments and features a tribute to Lady Bird Johnson. The visitor center is open daily 8:45-5; closed Jan. 1, Thanksgiving and Christmas.

**JOHNSON CITY DISTRICT** is 2 blks. s. of US 290 on E. Lady Bird Ln. Lyndon Johnson's boyhood home is furnished in period, reflecting rural Texas life in the 1920s. **Hours:** Tours are given daily every half-hour 9-11:30 and 1-4:30. Johnson Settlement open daily dawn-dusk. Visitor Center daily 8:45-5. Closed Jan. 1, Thanksgiving and Christmas. **Cost:** Donations. **Phone:** (830) 868-7128, ext. 244.

**LBJ RANCH DISTRICT,** 14 mi. w. of Johnson City on US 290, is open to self-guiding automobile tours. Vehicle permits, as well as CDs providing a narrative of the tour route, are available at the visitor center at Lyndon B. Johnson State Park and Historic Site near Stonewall *(see attraction listing p. 543)*. Highlights of the tour include the farmhouse where LBJ was born, the one-room Junction School, the LBJ show barn, the "Texas White House" and the graves of former president Lyndon B. Johnson and Mrs. Johnson in the Johnson family cemetery.

**Time:** Allow 2 hours minimum. **Hours:** Daily 9-4:30. Texas White House tours daily 10-4:30. Closed Jan. 1, Thanksgiving and Christmas. **Cost:** Driving tour free. Texas White House tour $3; free (ages 0-17). **Phone:** (830) 868-7128, ext. 244.

## LYTLE pop. 2,492
• Restaurants p. 408

**BEST WESTERN PLUS LYTLE INN & SUITES**
(830)772-4949

Hotel
$126–$140

**AAA Benefit:** Members save 10% or more with Best Western!

**Address:** 19876 IH-35 S 78052 **Location:** I-35 exit 131, just s; on northbound access road. **Facility:** 64 units, some two bedrooms and efficiencies. 3 stories, interior corridors. **Pool(s):** heated indoor. **Activities:** hot tub, exercise room. **Guest Services:** valet and coin laundry. **Featured Amenity: full hot breakfast.**

## WHERE TO EAT

**BILL MILLER BAR-B-Q**                              830/772-4905

Barbecue. Quick Serve. $6-$11 **AAA Inspector Notes:** The relaxed, family-focused barbecue restaurant prepares ribs, chicken, brisket, turkey and sausage for sandwiches or plates. **Address:** 19715 I-35 S 78052 **Location:** I-35 exit 131 (CR 2790); on southbound frontage road. B L D

## MABANK pop. 3,035

• **Part of Dallas area — see map p. 161**

**COMFORT SUITES-MABANK**                           (903)887-0680

Hotel $82-$135 **Address:** 501 N FM 90 75147 **Location:** Jct US 175 and SR 198. **Facility:** 70 units. 3 stories, interior corridors. **Pool(s):** indoor. **Activities:** hot tub, exercise room. **Guest Services:** valet and coin laundry.

## MADISONVILLE pop. 4,396

**BEST WESTERN EXECUTIVE INN & SUITES**            (936)349-1700

Hotel
$100-$160

**AAA Benefit:** Members save 10% or more with Best Western!

**Address:** 3307 E Main St 77864 **Location:** I-45 exit 142, just e. **Facility:** 40 units. 2 stories, interior corridors. **Pool(s):** indoor. **Activities:** hot tub, exercise room. **Guest Services:** coin laundry.

**WOODBINE HOTEL AND RESTAURANT**                  (936)348-3333

**Historic Country Inn** $85-$165 **Address:** 209 N Madison St 77864 **Location:** I-45 exit 142, 2.2 mi w to town square, then 2 blks n. **Facility:** Spacious accommodations enhance this historic country inn offering eight rooms with differing amenities that include wet bars and whirlpool tubs. 8 units. 2 stories (no elevator), interior/exterior corridors. **Terms:** 7 day cancellation notice-fee imposed. **Dining:** restaurant, see separate listing.

## WHERE TO EAT

**WOODBINE HOTEL AND RESTAURANT**                  936/348-3333

American. Fine Dining. $7-$20 **AAA Inspector Notes:** *Classic Historic.* The nicely varied menu includes prime cuts of beef and interesting homemade soups. The two dining rooms are decorated in the early 20th-century tradition. **Features:** full bar, Sunday brunch. **Address:** 209 N Madison St 77864 **Location:** I-45 exit 142, 2.2 mi w to town square, then 2 blks n. L D

## MAGNOLIA pop. 1,393

• **Part of Houston area — see map p. 301**

**EXECUTIVE INN & SUITES**                          (281)259-8200

Motel $59-$250 **Address:** 17707 FM 1488 Rd 77354 **Location:** 1 mi e of jct FM 1774. **Facility:** 34 units, some kitchens. 2 stories (no elevator), exterior corridors. **Terms:** cancellation fee imposed. **Guest Services:** valet and coin laundry.

**MAGNOLIA INN & SUITES**                           (281)259-6119

Hotel $80-$125 **Address:** 18614 FM 1488 Rd 77354 **Location:** Jct FM 1488 and 1774. **Facility:** 24 units. 2 stories (no elevator), exterior corridors. **Terms:** resort fee. **Pool(s):** outdoor.

---

## MANSFIELD (I-2) pop. 56,368, elev. 604'

**HAWAIIAN FALLS - MANSFIELD** is at 490 Heritage Pkwy. S. Highlights of this Hawaiian-themed water park include the Hightide Whirlpool ride, the Pineapple Express racing mat slide, the Kona Kooler lazy river and the interactive water play structure Keiki Cove.

Height restrictions apply on some rides. Lounge chairs are available on a first-come, first-served basis. Cabanas and lockers can be rented. Guests may bring their own food but must pay a $10 cooler fee. **Time:** Allow 4 hours minimum. **Hours:** Daily 10:30-6, Memorial Day-Labor Day. Schedule varies; phone ahead. **Cost:** $26.99; $19.99 (ages 55+ and under 48 inches tall); free (ages 0-2). Under 14 must be with an adult. **Phone:** (817) 853-0050 or (888) 544-7550.

**BEST WESTERN PLUS MANSFIELD INN & SUITES**       (817)539-0707

Hotel
$79-$99

**AAA Benefit:** Members save 10% or more with Best Western!

**Address:** 775 N Hwy 287 76063 **Location:** US 287 exit Walnut Creek Rd; on southbound frontage road. **Facility:** 70 units. 3 stories, interior corridors. **Pool(s):** heated indoor. **Activities:** hot tub, exercise room. **Guest Services:** coin laundry. **Featured Amenity: full hot breakfast.**

**COMFORT INN**                                     (817)453-8848

Hotel $70-$130 **Address:** 175 N Hwy 287 76063 **Location:** US 287 S exit E Broad St. **Facility:** 59 units. 3 stories, interior corridors. **Pool(s):** outdoor. **Activities:** exercise room. **Guest Services:** valet and coin laundry.

**FAIRFIELD INN & SUITES BY MARRIOTT DALLAS/ MANSFIELD**                                        (817)473-2700

Hotel $99-$149 **Address:** 1480 US Hwy 287 N 76063 **Location:** US 287 exit Walnut Creek; on northbound frontage road. **Facility:** 82 units. 3 stories, interior corridors. **Pool(s):** heated indoor. **Activities:** hot tub, exercise room. **Guest Services:** valet and coin laundry.

**AAA Benefit:** Members save 5% or more!

**HAMPTON INN & SUITES MANSFIELD**                 (817)539-0060

Hotel
$105-$149

**AAA Benefit:** Members save up to 10%!

**Address:** 1640 US Hwy 287 N 76063 **Location:** US 287 exit Walnut Creek Rd; on northbound frontage road. **Facility:** 88 units. 3 stories, interior corridors. **Terms:** 1-7 night minimum stay, cancellation fee imposed. **Pool(s):** outdoor. **Activities:** hot tub, exercise room. **Guest Services:** valet and coin laundry. **Featured Amenity: breakfast buffet.**

HOLIDAY INN EXPRESS HOTEL & SUITES    (817)453-8722

WWWW Hotel $109-$199 **Address:** 201 Hwy 287 N 76063 **Location:** US 287 exit Walnut Creek Rd, just s on frontage road. **Facility:** 70 units, some two bedrooms. 3 stories, interior corridors. **Pool(s):** heated indoor. **Activities:** hot tub, exercise room. **Guest Services:** valet and coin laundry.

CALL 🔒M 🛏 BIZ HS 🛜 🔋 🖥 💻 / SOME UNITS 🐾

LA QUINTA INN & SUITES MANSFIELD    (817)453-5040

WWWW Hotel $89-$127 **Address:** 1503 Breckenridge Rd 76063 **Location:** US 287 exit Walnut Creek Rd/Debbie Ln, 1.2 mi n to Debbie Ln, then just e. **Facility:** 67 units. 4 stories, interior corridors. **Pool(s):** indoor. **Activities:** hot tub, exercise room. **Guest Services:** valet and coin laundry.

🍴 CALL 🔒M 🛏 BIZ HS 🛜 ✖ 🔋 🖥 💻 / SOME UNITS 🐾

SUZY Q'S SODA FOUNTAIN AND GRILL    817/539-8800

WW Comfort Food. Family Dining. $6-$10 **AAA Inspector Notes:** This restaurant features such classic American fare as hamburgers, fried chicken, pork chops and grilled cheese sandwiches. For a sense of place, some Tex-Mex is thrown in, too. An attached pharmacy with a novelty gift shop is an added amenity, but most people go for ice cream treats like floats and sundaes. **Address:** 1831 E Broad St 76063 **Location:** 0.5 mi e of jct US 287.

B L D CALL 🔒M

## MANVEL pop. 5,179

• Hotels & Restaurants map & index p. 324

BEST WESTERN PLUS MANVEL INN & SUITES
(281)489-2266    171

Hotel
$82-$179

**AAA Benefit:** Members save 10% or more with Best Western!

**Address:** 19301 Hwy 6 77578 **Location:** 1.3 mi e of jct SR 288. **Facility:** 50 units, some efficiencies and kitchens. 3 stories, interior corridors. **Pool(s):** indoor. **Activities:** hot tub, exercise room. **Guest Services:** coin laundry.

SAVE 🛏 BIZ HS 🛜 ✖ 🔋 🖥 💻 / SOME UNITS 🐾

## MARATHON pop. 430

THE GAGE HOTEL    432/386-4205

fyi Not evaluated. **Address:** Hwy 90 79842 **Location:** US 90; center. Facilities, services, and décor characterize a mid-scale property.

12 GAGE    432/386-4437

WWW Continental. Fine Dining. $18-$40 **AAA Inspector Notes:** In a restored historic ranch headquarters and hotel, the eatery serves eclectic Texas cuisine in four themed rooms: Native American, horns, skulls and the main 1800s Texas ranch. Outdoor seating is available. **Features:** full bar. **Reservations:** required. **Address:** 102 NW 1st St (US 90) 79842 **Location:** US 90; center; in The Gage Hotel. D

## MARBLE FALLS pop. 6,077

BEST WESTERN MARBLE FALLS INN    (830)693-5122

Hotel
$59-$159

**AAA Benefit:** Members save 10% or more with Best Western!

**Address:** 1403 US Hwy 281 78654 **Location:** 0.4 mi n of jct SR 281 and FM 1431. **Facility:** 62 units. 2 stories (no elevator), interior/exterior corridors. **Pool(s):** outdoor. **Activities:** hot tub, exercise room. **Guest Services:** coin laundry. **Featured Amenity:** full hot breakfast.

SAVE 🍴 CALL 🔒M 🛏 🛜 🔋 🖥 💻 / SOME UNITS 🐾 HS

HAMPTON INN ON THE LAKE-MARBLE FALLS    (830)798-1895

WWWW Hotel $109-$234 **Address:** 704 1st St 78654 **Location:** Waterfront. Jct US 281 and FM 1431, 0.5 mi s. Located on Lake Marble Falls at the river. **Facility:** 64 units. 3 stories, interior corridors. **Terms:** 1-7 night minimum stay, cancellation fee imposed. **Pool(s):** outdoor. **Activities:** hot tub, exercise room. **Guest Services:** coin laundry.

**AAA Benefit:** Members save up to 10%!

🍴 CALL 🔒M 🛏 HS 🛜 ✖ 🔋 🖥 💻

QUALITY INN-MARBLE FALLS    (830)693-7531

WW Hotel $75-$180 **Address:** 1206 Hwy 281 N 78654 **Location:** 0.3 mi n of jct US 281 and FM 1431. **Facility:** 49 units. 2 stories (no elevator), exterior corridors. **Amenities:** safes. **Pool(s):** outdoor. **Activities:** hot tub.

🍴 🛏 HS 🛜 🔋 🖥 💻 / SOME UNITS 🐾

DOCK'S FISH CAMP AND GRILL    830/693-2245

WW Seafood. Casual Dining. $11-$21 **AAA Inspector Notes:** Representative of the nautical-themed restaurant's quality, reasonably priced food are varied seafood and steak entrees. Thursday is prime rib night. **Features:** full bar. **Address:** 900 FM 1431 W 78654 **Location:** Jct US 281 and FM 1431; on southwest corner.

L D 🌙

RIVER CITY GRILLE    830/798-9909

WW American. Casual Dining. $7-$24 **AAA Inspector Notes:** A nautical theme provides the backdrop. Guests can select from steaks, seafood, chicken and pork chops, as well as lighter sandwiches and salads. **Features:** full bar, patio dining, happy hour. **Address:** 700 1st St 78654 **Location:** Jct US 281 and FM 1431, 0.5 mi s; at river. L D CALL 🔒M

RUSSO'S RESTAURANT    830/693-7091

WWW
Italian
Casual Dining
$8-$36

**AAA Inspector Notes:** Overlooking Lake Marble Falls, the modern establishment serves traditional fare. I always enjoy their Italian dishes, but hearty steaks and chops also are available. For lighter fare, soups, salads and sandwiches are offered. **Features:** full bar, Sunday brunch. **Address:** 602 Steve Hawkins Pkwy 78654 **Location:** Just s of Marble Falls Bridge; jct US 281 and FM 2147; on top of hill. *Menu on AAA.com* L D 🌙

## MARFA (F-3) pop. 1,981, elev. 4,685'
• Hotels p. 410 • Restaurants p. 410

THE CHINATI FOUNDATION, 1 Cavalry Row, behind the U.S. Customs and Border Protection office, is a contemporary art museum founded by artist Donald Judd. Situated on 340 acres at the site of former cavalry post Fort D.A. Russell, the museum explores the connection between the art, architecture and the natural landscape surrounding them. Eighteen buildings, including structures that once served as army barracks and artillery sheds, house works by Judd and 11 other artists. There are outdoor displays, too.

The site is accessible only by guided tour; visitors may choose from three different tours ranging from 30 minutes to 6 hours. Temporary exhibits and special programs are presented throughout the year.

**Note:** Photography is not permitted. **Time:** Allow 1 hour minimum. **Hours:** The 6-hour Full Collection tour (includes a 2-hour lunch break) departs Wed.-Sun. at 10. The 2-hour Selections tour departs Wed.-Sun. at 11. Closed Jan. 1, Thanksgiving and Christmas.

**Cost:** Full Collection tour $25; $10 (students with ID); free (ages 0-17). Selections tour $20; $10 (students with ID); free (ages 0-17). Reservations are recommended. **Phone:** (432) 729-4362.

---

HOTEL PAISANO                    432/729-3669

▼▼▼ **Classic Historic Hotel.** Rates not provided. **Address:** 207 N Highland Ave 79843 **Location:** Jct US 90 and SR 17, 3 blks n. **Facility:** With groundbreaking taking place in 1929, this hotel has been a focal point for the area for more than 80 years. Beautiful and relaxing public areas and comfortable guest rooms are offered. 41 units, some two bedrooms and kitchens. 2 stories (no elevator), interior corridors. **Parking:** street only. **Terms:** check-in 4 pm. **Dining:** Jett's Grill, see separate listing. **Pool(s):** indoor. **Activities:** exercise room.

🛏️ 🍽️ 🛋️ 📶 ❌ 🏋️
/SOME UNITS 🅂🅜 🚪 📺 💻

---

### WHERE TO EAT

JETT'S GRILL                    432/729-3838

▼▼▼ American. Casual Dining. $13-$29 **AAA Inspector Notes:** A courtyard atmosphere accents the Southwestern eatery. Beef, chicken and seafood selections are presented in an upscale manner. **Features:** full bar, patio dining. **Address:** 207 N Highland Ave 79843 **Location:** Jct US 90 and SR 17, 3 blks n; in Hotel Paisano. **Parking:** street only. [D]

MAIYA'S                    432/729-4410

▼▼▼ American. Fine Dining. $21-$33 **AAA Inspector Notes:** This urban, modern-hipster, art-world-style restaurant is housed in a renovated building in the heart of downtown, surrounded by Southwest Texas ranch country. The menu features local ingredients in favorites such as fungi lasagna with fresh-made pasta, portobello mushrooms, arrabbiata sauce, ricotta cheese, roasted red pepper, cream and Parmigiano-Reggiano. **Features:** full bar. **Reservations:** suggested. **Address:** 103 N Highland Ave 79843 **Location:** Jct US 90 and SR 17, 3 blks n. **Parking:** street only. [D] [🍷]

SQUEEZE MARFA                    432/729-4500

▼ American. Quick Serve. $4-$9 **AAA Inspector Notes:** A fun place to sit and relax and partake in a light breakfast, specialty protein drinks and smoothies as well as creamsicle sodas, Swiss chocolate drinks and a large selection of teas. Soups and sandwiches are available for lunch. **Address:** 215 N Highland Ave 79843 **Location:** On Courthouse Square. **Parking:** street only. [B] [L]

## MARLIN (E-8) pop. 5,967, elev. 383'

The thermomineral wells under Marlin, reputed to be the deepest in the world, expel more than 380,000 gallons of 147-degree-Fahrenheit water daily. The water is used in geothermal heating projects. The chamber of commerce and the Falls Community Memorial Hospital are heated by geothermal energy.

Agribusiness, primarily cattle and grain production, maintains Marlin's economy. When not at work, residents enjoy sports and recreation at Falls on the Brazos Park *(see Recreation Areas Chart)* on the Brazos River.

**Marlin Chamber of Commerce:** 245 Coleman St., Marlin, TX 76661. **Phone:** (254) 803-3301.

---

BEST WESTERN MARLIN INN & SUITES    (254)883-6000

Hotel
$85-$180

**AAA Benefit:** Members save 10% or more with Best Western!

**Address:** 100 FM 147 76661 **Location:** Jct SR 6 and 147 N. **Facility:** 56 units. 3 stories, interior corridors. **Pool(s):** outdoor. **Activities:** exercise room. **Guest Services:** coin laundry. **Featured Amenity: full hot breakfast.**

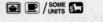

## MARSHALL (D-10) pop. 23,523, elev. 375'

During the Civil War Marshall was the capital of Missouri. It seemed strange that such a quiet town would be chosen by executives of Missouri and the Trans-Mississippi Department of the Confederacy as their administrative center. At that time Marshall was one of the biggest and wealthiest cities in the state, producing gun powder and ammunition for the Confederacy as well as saddles, harnesses and clothing.

On a major stagecoach route, Marshall became a stop on the Texas and Pacific Railroad in the 1870s. An original section of the old Stagecoach Road begins at the end of Poplar Street off US 59. The arrival of the railroad restored the town's fortunes—a prosperity expressed by the elegant Ginocchio Hotel built near the depot in 1896. This restored Victorian hostelry is the centerpiece of Marshall's three-block Ginocchio Historic District. At Christmas, millions of white lights decorate the downtown area in the Wonderland of Lights.

An abundance of red and white clay has made Marshall a center for pottery making. Stoneware is produced by more than a dozen companies in the area. Marshall Pottery, one of the country's largest manufacturers of terra-cotta flowerpots, was established in 1895.

**Marshall Convention and Visitors Bureau:** 301 N. Washington St., Marshall, TX 75670. **Phone:** (903) 702-7777.

**Self-guiding tours:** Maps outlining tours of historic Marshall and Harrison County are available from the convention and visitors bureau.

**HARRISON COUNTY HISTORICAL MUSEUM** is at 1 Peter Whetstone Sq. Exhibits highlight former well-known residents of Harrison County such as Lady Bird Johnson, Bill Moyers and George Foreman. Antiques and Civil War memorabilia are displayed. **Hours:** Tues.-Sat. 10-4. Closed major holidays. **Cost:** $6; $5 (ages 60+); $1 (students ages 16+ with ID); free (ages 0-15 with paying adult); half-price (Tues.). Prices may vary; phone ahead. **Phone:** (903) 935-8417.

**MICHELSON MUSEUM OF ART** is at 216 N. Bolivar St. The museum features more than 1,000 paintings, drawings and prints by Russian-born artist Leo Michelson, as well as African masks and works by American artists. The Dr. David Weisman Hirsch Discovery Room contains hands-on displays. **Time:** Allow 1 hour minimum. **Hours:** Guided tours Tues.-Fri. 10-4, Sat. 1-4. Closed major holidays. **Cost:** Donations. **Phone:** (903) 935-9480.

**STARR FAMILY STATE HISTORIC SITE** is at 407 W. Travis St. This two-story, wood-sided house was built in 1870 by James Franklin Starr, the son of former Republic of Texas treasurer, Dr. James Harper Starr. Expanded and altered during the 115 years the family occupied it, the house and its furnishings reflect the development of Texas. **Time:** Allow 1 hour minimum. **Hours:** Tours are given Tues.-Sat. 10-4, Sun. noon-4. Closed Jan. 1, Thanksgiving, Christmas Eve, Christmas and Dec. 31. **Cost:** $4; $3 (ages 6-18 and students with ID). **Phone:** (903) 935-3044 or (800) 792-1112.

**TEXAS AND PACIFIC RAILWAY MUSEUM** is at 800 N. Washington Ave. The history of the Texas and Pacific Railway is told through historical information and memorabilia. Located inside the restored 1912 Texas and Pacific Railway depot, the facility still functions as an Amtrak station. A steam locomotive and a caboose are displayed. **Time:** Allow 30 minutes minimum. **Hours:** Tues.-Sat. 10-4. Closed major holidays. **Cost:** $2; $1 (ages 5-12, ages 55+ and students with ID). **Phone:** (903) 938-9495.

**BEST WESTERN EXECUTIVE INN**          (903)935-0707

Hotel
$69-$90

**AAA Benefit:** Members save 10% or more with Best Western!

**Address:** 5201 E End Blvd S 75672 **Location:** I-20 exit 617, 0.4 mi n on US 59. **Facility:** 40 units. 2 stories (no elevator), exterior corridors. **Pool(s):** outdoor. **Guest Services:** coin laundry.

**COMFORT SUITES**          (903)927-1139

Hotel $84-$149 **Address:** 5204 E End Blvd S 75672 **Location:** I-20 exit 617, 0.3 mi n. **Facility:** 65 units. 3 stories, interior corridors. **Terms:** check-in 4 pm. **Pool(s):** outdoor. **Activities:** hot tub, exercise room. **Guest Services:** valet and coin laundry.

CALL 🅼 ⊠ HS ⊠ 🖥 🖨 💻

---

**FAIRFIELD INN & SUITES BY MARRIOTT**          (903)938-7666

Hotel $89-$129 **Address:** 105 W I-20 75672 **Location:** I-20 exit 617. **Facility:** 84 units. 3 stories, interior corridors. **Pool(s):** heated indoor. **Activities:** hot tub, exercise room. **Guest Services:** valet and coin laundry.

**AAA Benefit:** Members save 5% or more!

 CALL 🅼 ⊠ BIZ HS ⊠ ⊠ 🖥 🖨 💻

**HAMPTON INN MARSHALL**          (903)927-0079

Hotel $89-$116 **Address:** 5100 SE End Blvd 75672 **Location:** I-20 exit 617, 0.4 mi n on US 59. **Facility:** 68 units. 3 stories, interior corridors. **Terms:** 1-7 night minimum stay, cancellation fee imposed. **Pool(s):** outdoor. **Activities:** hot tub, exercise room. **Guest Services:** valet laundry.

**AAA Benefit:** Members save up to 10%!

CALL 🅼 ⊠ BIZ ⊠ 🖥 🖨 💻

**LA QUINTA INN & SUITES**          (903)934-3080

Hotel $105-$140 **Address:** 6015 E End Blvd S 75672 **Location:** I-20 exit 617, just s. **Facility:** 62 units. 3 stories, interior corridors. **Pool(s):** indoor. **Activities:** exercise room. **Guest Services:** coin laundry.

CALL 🅼 ⊠ BIZ HS ⊠ ⊠ ⊠ 🖥 🖨 💻 / SOME UNITS 🐾

**MOTEL 6 MARSHALL - #422**          (903)935-4393

Motel $43-$55 **Address:** 300 I-20 E 75670 **Location:** I-20 exit 617, just s, then just e. **Facility:** 121 units. 2 stories (no elevator), exterior corridors. *Bath:* shower only. **Pool(s):** outdoor. **Guest Services:** coin laundry. ⊠ ⊠ / SOME UNITS 🐾 🖥

**QUALITY INN**          (903)935-7923

Hotel $66-$101 **Address:** 4911 E End Blvd S 75672 **Location:** I-20 exit 617, 0.5 mi n on US 59. **Facility:** 58 units. 2 stories (no elevator), exterior corridors. **Pool(s):** outdoor. **Guest Services:** valet and coin laundry.

⊠ ⊠ HS ⊠ 🖥 🖨 💻

## WHERE TO EAT

**CENTRAL PERKS**          903/934-9902

American. Quick Serve. $8-$10 **AAA Inspector Notes:** Although known for its rich coffee drinks, this small café serves up a delicious lunch menu of wraps, quiche and sandwiches, all in very genteel dining rooms complete with lace tablecloths. Its location in the Weisman Center art gallery and gift boutique is perfect for some impromptu shopping. **Address:** 211-A N Washington Ave 75670 **Location:** Center. **Parking:** street only. L

**EL CHICO**          903/935-6861

Tex-Mex
Casual Dining
$7-$16

**AAA Inspector Notes:** Inside and out, the decor of the popular Mexican restaurant is inviting. The menu features traditional favorites such as enchiladas, tacos, burritos and fajitas. The broad menu also lists a few American classics. **Features:** full bar. **Address:** 205 E End Blvd 75670 **Location:** Jct US 59 and 80. L D

**THE JALAPENO TREE**          903/927-2777

Tex-Mex. Casual Dining. $7-$16 **AAA Inspector Notes:** A small chain operating in several towns along I-30 in east Texas, the restaurant prepares standard Tex-Mex fare with a hint of New Mexico flair, courtesy of the red and green sauces found in that state. Outgoing servers do what they can to make meals a pleasure. The menu also lists American dishes and children's choices. The huge homemade sopapillas are shaped like jalapeños. **Features:** full bar, patio dining. **Address:** 1000 E End Blvd S 75652 **Location:** 0.8 mi s of jct US 59 and 80. L D

**McALLEN** (I-8) pop. 129,877, elev. 122'
• Restaurants p. 414

McAllen was named in honor of its Scottish founder, John McAllen, who donated land for the establishment of a rail line in 1904. He also built the depot close to his hotel, thus increasing his occupancy rate. Construction of the McAllen-Hidalgo-Reynosa International Bridge in 1941 made the town a major port of entry into Mexico and a center for tourism. McAllen's culture reflects a strong Mexican influence.

Nicknamed the City of Palms for the 40 varieties of trees that line its streets, McAllen is a winter resort that lies on the same latitude as Fort Lauderdale and enjoys the same subtropical climate. The town bills itself as the "square dance capital of the world," attracting some 10,000 people each winter for daily promenades.

While you're exploring McAllen's 17th Street Entertainment District, look for the neon marquee (it's the original) of the Moderne-style Cine El Rey. Opened in 1947 as a Spanish-language theater, Cine El Rey catered to the town's Mexican community until the mid-1980s. Today it presents American independent films, concerts, theatrical performances and comedy shows; phone (956) 278-0626.

City parks offer year-round outdoor recreational opportunities. Park and Spray Ground, at the corner of 29th Street and Zinnia Avenue, has picnicking facilities, a skateboard park, a sand volleyball court and a "spray ground"—a playing surface containing hundreds of water jets. Camping, fishing, canoeing and kayaking can be enjoyed at Fireman's Park, 201 N. 1st St. At McAllen Nature Center, 4101 SR 83, hiking trails wind through a lush native forest that's home to a variety of flora and fauna.

McAllen Heritage Center, housed in the old post office building at 301 S. Main St., has artifacts, exhibits and special programs pertaining to the town's history; phone (956) 687-1904.

**McAllen Convention and Visitors Bureau:** 1200 Ash Ave., P.O. Box 790, McAllen, TX 78501. **Phone:** (956) 682-2871.

**Shopping areas:** Dillard's, JCPenney, Macy's and Sears are among the 150 stores in the 1.2 million-square-foot La Plaza Mall, 2100 S. 10th St.

McAllen's arts district, along Main Street in the heart of downtown, features a concentration of art galleries and studios exhibiting works by local artisans. The district's Art Walk, held the first Friday of each month from 6-10 p.m., is a popular event.

**INTERNATIONAL MUSEUM OF ART AND SCIENCE (IMAS)** is 3.2 mi. n.w. at jct. Nolana Ave. and Bicentennial Blvd. Galleries present changing exhibits of paintings, sculpture, photographs, graphics and crafts. RioScape Science Discovery Park is an interactive science playground with waterfalls, climbing walls and mazes. **Hours:** Tues.-Sat. 9-5 (also Thurs. 5-8), Sun. 1-5. Closed Jan. 1, Easter,

Memorial Day, July 4, Thanksgiving and Christmas. **Cost:** $7; $5 (ages 55+ and students with ID); $4 (ages 4-12); $1 (Thurs. 4-8). **Phone:** (956) 682-1564.

**NUEVO SANTANDER GALLERY**, 717 N. Main St., is housed in an architecturally striking reproduction of a Spanish mission. The exterior walls were built with locally quarried stone, and the entryway's Mexican-made doors and ironwork date back to the 1800s. The interior is adorned with stone columns, Talavera and Saltillo tile and native mesquite wood. Depicted on the building's stained-glass windows is the map used by conquistador José de Escandón when he founded Nuevo Santander, a province comprising portions of modern-day northern Mexico and southern Texas.

The gallery displays artifacts, artwork and changing exhibits representative of the Spanish Colonial period and the Old West. **Time:** Allow 1 hour minimum. **Hours:** Tues.-Fri. 10-5, Sat. 11-5. **Cost:** Free. **Phone:** (956) 618-4959.

**QUINTA MAZATLAN** is at 600 Sunset Dr. Affiliated with the World Birding Center organization, Quinta Mazatlan is a 10,000-square-foot historic 1930s Spanish Revival adobe hacienda set amid tropical gardens. Native plants and wild forest enhance the lush setting, where visitors may wander trails in search of various birds, including green jays, plain chachalacas, buff-bellied hummingbirds and olive sparrows. **Time:** Allow 30 minutes minimum. **Hours:** Tues.-Sat. 8-5 (also Thurs. 5-dusk). Closed major holidays. **Cost:** $2; $1 (ages 4-11 and 65+). **Phone:** (956) 681-3370.

**BEST WESTERN ROSE GARDEN INN & SUITES**
(956)630-3333

Hotel
$71-$96

**AAA Benefit:** Members save 10% or more with Best Western!

**Address:** 300 E Expwy 83 78503 **Location:** 0.5 mi e of jct US 83 exit 2nd St. Located in a commercial area. **Facility:** 92 units. 2 stories (no elevator), exterior corridors. **Pool(s):** outdoor. **Guest Services:** valet and coin laundry.

**COMFORT SUITES**
(956)213-0333

Hotel $70-$80 **Address:** 800 W Expwy 83 78501 **Location:** US 83 exit 10th St; on frontage road. **Facility:** 56 units, some two bedrooms. 3 stories, interior corridors. **Amenities:** safes. **Pool(s):** outdoor. **Activities:** hot tub, exercise room. **Guest Services:** valet and coin laundry.

**COURTYARD BY MARRIOTT**
(956)668-7800

Hotel $94-$109 **Address:** 2131 S 10th St 78503 **Location:** 0.3 mi s of US 83, just off S 10th St. Located in a commercial area. **Facility:** 110 units, some two bedrooms. 3 stories, interior corridors. **Pool(s):** heated outdoor. **Activities:** hot tub, exercise room. **Guest Services:** valet and coin laundry, area transportation.

**AAA Benefit:** Members save 5% or more!

## DRURY INN-MCALLEN
(956)687-5100

▼▼ Hotel $85-$149 Address: 612 W Expwy 83 78501 Location: US 83 exit 2nd St; on northwest frontage road. Located in a commercial area. Facility: 89 units. 3 stories, interior corridors. Terms: cancellation fee imposed. Pool(s): outdoor. Activities: exercise room. Guest Services: valet and coin laundry.

## DRURY SUITES-MCALLEN
(956)682-3222

▼▼▼ Extended Stay Hotel $105-$224 Address: 228 W Expwy 83 78501 Location: At US 83 and 6th St. Located in a modern commercial area. Facility: 90 units, some two bedrooms, efficiencies and kitchens. 6 stories, interior corridors. Terms: cancellation fee imposed. Pool(s): outdoor. Activities: hot tub, exercise room. Guest Services: valet and coin laundry.

## EMBASSY SUITES
(956)686-3000

▼▼▼ Hotel $109-$169 Address: 1800 S 2nd St 78501 Location: US 83 exit 2nd St, just s. Located close to mall, medical centers and restaurants. Facility: 262 units, some two bedrooms. 9 stories, interior corridors. Terms: 1-7 night minimum stay, cancellation fee imposed. Dining: entertainment. Pool(s): heated indoor. Activities: hot tub, exercise room. Guest Services: valet and coin laundry, area transportation.

**AAA Benefit:**
Members save 5% or more!

## FAIRFIELD INN & SUITES BY MARRIOTT
(956)971-9444

▼▼▼ Hotel $99-$109 Address: 2117 S 10th St 78503 Location: 0.4 mi s of US 83. Facility: 68 units. 3 stories, interior corridors. Pool(s): heated indoor. Activities: hot tub, exercise room. Guest Services: valet and coin laundry.

**AAA Benefit:**
Members save 5% or more!

## HAMPTON INN & SUITES
(956)661-1100

▼▼▼ Hotel $95-$129 Address: 10 W Expwy 83 78503 Location: US 83 exit 2nd and 10th sts; on northbound frontage road. Facility: 112 units. 5 stories, interior corridors. Terms: 1-7 night minimum stay, cancellation fee imposed. Pool(s): outdoor. Activities: hot tub, exercise room. Guest Services: valet and coin laundry, area transportation.

**AAA Benefit:**
Members save up to 10%!

## HOLIDAY INN EXPRESS HOTEL & SUITES
956/994-0505

▼▼▼ Hotel. Rates not provided. Address: 1921 S 10th St 78503 Location: 0.3 mi s of US 83. Across from La Plaza Mall. Facility: 191 units, some two bedrooms. 4-6 stories, interior/exterior corridors. Pool(s): heated indoor. Activities: hot tub, exercise room. Guest Services: valet and coin laundry, area transportation.

## HOMEWOOD SUITES BY HILTON
(956)630-0500

▼▼▼ Extended Stay Hotel $119-$139 Address: 3801 Expwy 83 78503 Location: US 83 exit Ware Rd, just s. Facility: 114 units, some two bedrooms and efficiencies. 4 stories, interior corridors. Terms: 1-7 night minimum stay, cancellation fee imposed. Pool(s): heated outdoor. Activities: exercise room. Guest Services: valet and coin laundry, area transportation.

**AAA Benefit:**
Members save up to 10%!

## MOTEL 6 MCALLEN - #212
(956)687-3700

▼ Motel $45-$59 Address: 700 W Expwy 83 78501 Location: US 83 exit 2nd St; on west frontage road. Facility: 93 units. 2 stories (no elevator), exterior corridors. Bath: shower only. Pool(s): outdoor. Guest Services: coin laundry.

## PEAR TREE INN BY DRURY
(956)682-4900

▼▼ Hotel $70-$124 Address: 300 W Expwy 83 78501 Location: US 83 exit 2nd St; on northwest frontage road. Located in a commercial area. Facility: 91 units. 4 stories, interior corridors. Terms: cancellation fee imposed. Pool(s): outdoor. Guest Services: valet laundry.

## POSADA ANA INN
(956)631-6700

▼▼ Hotel $77-$99 Address: 620 W Expwy 83 78501 Location: US 83 exit 2nd St; on northwest frontage road. Facility: 93 units. 3 stories, interior corridors. Terms: cancellation fee imposed. Guest Services: valet laundry.

## RENAISSANCE CASA DE PALMAS
(956)631-1101

▼▼▼ Historic Hotel $89-$169 Address: 101 N Main St 78501 Location: Just n of US 83 business route. Facility: Built in 1918, this hotel is characterized by Spanish architecture, refined guest rooms and historic ambience. 165 units. 3 stories, interior corridors. Pool(s): outdoor. Activities: exercise room. Guest Services: valet laundry, area transportation.

**AAA Benefit:**
Members save 5% or more!

## RESIDENCE INN BY MARRIOTT
(956)994-8626

▼▼▼ Extended Stay Hotel $89-$149 Address: 220 W Expwy 83 78501 Location: US 83 exit 2nd St, just w, then just n on 2nd St. Located in a quiet area. Facility: 78 units, some two bedrooms, efficiencies and kitchens. 3 stories, interior corridors. Amenities: Some: safes. Pool(s): outdoor. Activities: hot tub, tennis, exercise room. Guest Services: valet and coin laundry, area transportation.

**AAA Benefit:**
Members save 5% or more!

## SPRINGHILL SUITES BY MARRIOTT MCALLEN
(956)682-6336

▼▼▼ Contemporary Hotel $123-$139 Address: 1800 S Ware Rd 78503 Location: US 83 exit Ware Rd, just s. Facility: 102 units. 4 stories, interior corridors. Pool(s): heated indoor. Activities: hot tub, exercise room. Guest Services: valet and coin laundry, area transportation.

**AAA Benefit:**
Members save 5% or more!

## STAYBRIDGE SUITES MCALLEN-AIRPORT
956/213-7829

▼▼▼ Extended Stay Hotel. Rates not provided. Address: 620 Wichita Ave 78503 Location: 0.4 mi s of US 83, just e of S 10th St. Facility: 104 efficiencies, some two bedrooms. 4 stories, interior corridors. Pool(s): outdoor. Activities: hot tub, exercise room. Guest Services: complimentary and valet laundry, area transportation.

## HILTON GARDEN INN MCALLEN
956/664-2900

**fyi** Not evaluated. **Address:** 617 W Expwy 83 78503 **Location:** US 83 exit 10th St; on southeast frontage road. Facilities, services, and décor characterize a mid-scale property.

**AAA Benefit:** Members save up to 10%!

## WHERE TO EAT

### COSTA MESSA RESTAURANT
956/618-5449

Mexican. Casual Dining. $7-$20 **AAA Inspector Notes:** This small but popular restaurant offers spicy dishes that include fresh seafood. Try the combination fajita plate with shrimp, chicken and beef served on a sizzling platter with caramelized onions and fresh tortillas. **Features:** full bar. **Address:** 1621 N 11th St 78501 **Location:** From US 83, n on 10th St, just w on Pecan Blvd, then just n; between FM 495 and Redwood Ave. [L] [D]

### HOPTUNG CHINESE AND VIETNAMESE RESTAURANT
956/688-5888

Chinese. Casual Dining. $7-$15 **AAA Inspector Notes:** Inconspicuously tucked away in a small strip mall, this local favorite offers a large, diverse choice of menu items that are healthful and delicious. Hot pot, pho, dim sum, banh hoi (charcoal-broiled wraps) egg noodle nest and items from a full vegetarian menu are made from the freshest ingredients. Bubble teas and slushies are an added liquid treat. **Features:** beer & wine. **Address:** 4200 N 10th St, Suite 200 78504 **Location:** 2.7 mi n of Business Rt US 83.
[L] [D]

### LUBY'S
956/928-1853

American. Cafeteria. $6-$12 **AAA Inspector Notes:** First opened in 1947 in south Texas, this cafeteria with over 100 outlets features a wide variety of salads, fresh fruits, seafood...including crunchy shrimp...pastas, meat, poultry and just baked cakes and pies. Ask about the kids specials and Lu Ann platters...an entrée with choice of 2 vegetables and a roll. Many locations offer drive-thru service. **Features:** beer & wine. **Address:** 2200 S 10th St 78503 **Location:** US 83 exit S 10th St, just s. [L] [D]

### PALENQUE GRILL
956/994-8181

Mexican. Casual Dining. $10-$16 **AAA Inspector Notes:** Colorful décor, attentive staff and multiple choices of Mexican dishes define this popular restaurant. I really enjoyed my meal. The food is fresh, moist and flavorful. **Features:** full bar. **Address:** 606 E Expwy 83 78503 **Location:** US 83 eastbound; at McColl Rd.
[L] [D]

### P.F. CHANG'S CHINA BISTRO
956/664-1516

Chinese. Casual Dining. $5-$25 **AAA Inspector Notes:** Trendy, upscale decor provides a pleasant backdrop for New Age Chinese dining. Appetizers, soups and salads are a meal by themselves. Vegetarian plates and sides, noodles, chow meins, chicken and meat dishes are created from exotic, fresh ingredients. **Features:** full bar, patio dining. **Address:** 3100 W Expwy 83 78503 **Location:** W Expwy 83 exit Ware St; at Palms Crossing Shopping Center. [L] [D]

### PONCHO'S MEXICAN NUEVO RESTAURANT
956/630-2237

Tex-Mex. Casual Dining. $11-$20 **AAA Inspector Notes:** This large restaurant with decorative tiles, a Mexican bakery and very large portions is becoming a city landmark. **Features:** full bar. **Address:** 601 W Expwy 83 78503 **Location:** US 83 at 6th St; on eastbound frontage road. [L] [D]

### SAHADI CAFE
956/682-3419

Mediterranean. Casual Dining. $8-$25 **AAA Inspector Notes:** Established in 1989, this café gets its culinary inspiration from its gourmet grocery with exotic and sublime imports such as caviar, paté, bacalao and abalone. Menu items include escargot, ceviche, moussaka, souvlaki, stuffed grape leaves, lox and bagels. **Features:** beer & wine, patio dining. **Address:** 709 N 10th St 78501 **Location:** US 83 exit 10th St, just n of Business Rt US 83. [L] [D]

### THE SANTA FE STEAK HOUSE
956/630-2331

Steak. Fine Dining. $16-$35 **AAA Inspector Notes:** Subdued lighting veils an elegant dining room that's set for fine dining but is casually comfortable. Southwestern decor marks this place, which is known for its perfectly prepared high-quality steaks, laid-back service and lively separate bar. **Features:** full bar, patio dining. **Address:** 1918 S 10th St 78503 **Location:** US 83 exit 10th St, just s. [D] CALL [&M]

## McKINNEY (G-3) pop. 131,117, elev. 592'
- **Hotels & Restaurants map & index p. 179**
- **Part of Dallas area — see map p. 161**

McKinney, located 30 miles north of Dallas on US 75, is the county seat of Collin County and was named for Collin McKinney, a signer of the Texas Declaration of Independence. Diversified industry bolsters the city's economy.

**McKinney Chamber of Commerce:** 2150 S. Central Expy., Suite 150, McKinney, TX 75070. **Phone:** (972) 542-0163.

**HEARD NATURAL SCIENCE MUSEUM AND WILDLIFE SANCTUARY** is off US 75 exit 38A, then e. following signs to 1 Nature Pl. The 289-acre natural science and education center features 7 miles of hiking trails, a boardwalk over the wetlands, prairies, and a 2-acre native plant garden. Exhibits include the indoor Living Lab and Venomous Snakes of Texas. Fossils, minerals and seashells also are on display.

**Time:** Allow 1 hour, 30 minutes minimum. **Hours:** Tues.-Sat. 9-5, Sun. 1-5. Last admission to nature trails 1 hour before closing. Closed Jan. 1, Thanksgiving and Christmas. **Cost:** Admission Oct.-Jan. $11; $8 (ages 3-12 and 60+). Admission Feb.-May $10; $7 (ages 3-12 and 60+). Admission rest of year $9; $6 (ages 3-12 and 60+). **Phone:** (972) 562-5566. [A]

### BEST WESTERN PLUS MCKINNEY INN & SUITES
(972)548-3000

Hotel $81-$93

**AAA Benefit:** Members save 10% or more with Best Western!

**Address:** 480 Wilson Creek Blvd 75069 **Location:** US 75 exit 40A (Virginia St/Louisiana St). **Facility:** 68 units, some efficiencies. 3 stories, interior corridors. **Pool(s):** outdoor. **Activities:** hot tub, exercise room. **Guest Services:** valet and coin laundry.

[SAVE] [T+] CALL [&M] [pool] [BIZ] [wifi]

### COMFORT SUITES OF MCKINNEY
(972)548-9595

Hotel $89-$150 **Address:** 1590 N Central Expwy 75070 **Location:** US 75 exit 40B (Bob White Ave), 0.4 mi n on northbound frontage road. **Facility:** 63 units. 3 stories, interior corridors. **Pool(s):** outdoor. **Activities:** exercise room. **Guest Services:** valet and coin laundry.

[T+] CALL [&M] [pool] [BIZ] [HS] [wifi] [X] [fridge] [icon] [icon]

**(See map & index p. 179.)**

**HOLIDAY INN & SUITES MCKINNEY - FAIRVIEW**
(469)952-2044

▼▼▼ **Hotel** $99-$149 **Address:** 3220 Craig Dr 75070 **Location:** US 75 exit 39 (Eldorado Pkwy), just w, then just s. **Facility:** 99 units. 4 stories, interior corridors. **Terms:** cancellation fee imposed. **Amenities:** safes. **Pool(s):** heated indoor. **Activities:** hot tub, exercise room. **Guest Services:** valet and coin laundry, area transportation.

[Ⓣ] [Ⓨ] CALL[Ⓜ] [🔁] [BIZ] [HS] [📶] [✕] [🔒] [🖨]
[🅿]

**LA QUINTA INN & SUITES AT THE BALLFIELDS AT CRAIG RANCH**
(972)908-2370 🔟

▼▼▼
Hotel
$95-$134

**Address:** 6501 Henneman Way 75070 **Location:** SR 121 exit Stacy Rd, just n, then just w. **Facility:** 79 units. 4 stories, interior corridors. **Pool(s):** outdoor. **Activities:** hot tub, exercise room. **Guest Services:** coin laundry. **Featured Amenity:** breakfast buffet.

[SAVE] [Ⓣ] [🔁] [BIZ] [📶] [✕] [🔒]
[🖨] [🅿] [/SOME UNITS] [🐕]

**QUALITY INN**
(972)542-9471

▼▼ **Hotel** $70-$110 **Address:** 1300 N Central Expwy 75070 **Location:** US 75 exit 40B (Bob White Ave); on northbound frontage road. **Facility:** 93 units. 2 stories (no elevator), exterior corridors. **Pool(s):** outdoor. **Guest Services:** coin laundry.

[Ⓣ] [🔁] [📶] [🖨] [/SOME UNITS] [🛏] [🔒] [🖨]

**SUPER 8-MCKINNEY**
(972)548-8880

▼▼
Hotel
$59-$99

**Address:** 910 N Central Expwy 75070 **Location:** US 75 exit 40A (Virginia St/Louisiana St), 0.5 mi n on northbound frontage road. **Facility:** 75 units. 3 stories, interior corridors. **Amenities:** safes. **Pool(s):** outdoor. **Guest Services:** valet and coin laundry. **Featured Amenity:** continental breakfast.

[SAVE] [Ⓣ] [🔁] [📶] [🔒] [🖨] [🖨]
[/SOME UNITS] [🛏]

## WHERE TO EAT

**EL CHICO**
972/548-7526

▼▼▼
Tex-Mex
Casual Dining
$7-$16

**AAA Inspector Notes:** Inside and out, the decor of the popular Mexican restaurant is inviting. The menu features traditional favorites such as enchiladas, tacos, burritos and fajitas. The broad menu also lists a few American classics. **Features:** full bar. **Address:** 1222 N Central Expwy 75069 **Location:** US 75 exit 40B (White Ave). [L] [D]

**HANK'S TEXAS GRILL**
972/542-5144

▼▼ American. Casual Dining. $7-$15 **AAA Inspector Notes:** On the menu is just about every conceivable appetizer, as well as a variety of down-home, no-frills American, food but the specialty is barbecue. Texas artists frequently take the stage at this roadside eatery, so call ahead for cover charge and band information. **Features:** full bar. **Address:** 1310 N Central Expwy 75069 **Location:** US 75 exit 40B (White Ave). [L] [D] [LATE]

**LA MADELEINE COUNTRY FRENCH CAFE**
214/544-0765

▼▼ Traditional French. Casual Dining. $7-$12 **AAA Inspector Notes:** A fireplace creates the focal point at this cozy European style café where you can always get a quiche or savory stuffed puffed pastry on the go or stick around for a chicken crêpe or French dip sandwich. Heartier entrées like rotisserie chicken are offered and every season promises menu surprises. Whatever you decide on you probably will not get out the door without enjoying one of their tempting sweet pastries. **Features:** beer & wine. **Address:** 2730 S Central Expwy 75070 **Location:** In El Dorado Plaza Shopping Center. [B] [L] [D]

**THE PANTRY RESTAURANT**
972/542-2411

▼ American. Casual Dining. $6-$9 **AAA Inspector Notes:** This busy soup, salad and sandwich shop is open only for lunch on weekdays, with breakfast on the weekends, and patrons should be prepared to stand in line. The strictly self-serve and no-frills restaurant occupies an old restored building downtown. Blackboard specials are featured daily. **Address:** 214 E Louisiana St 75069 **Location:** Between Tennessee and Chestnut sts; just e of Town Square. [L]

**RICK'S CHOPHOUSE**
214/726-9251

▼▼▼ Steak. Fine Dining. $8-$45 **AAA Inspector Notes:** The restaurant, located in a historical hotel that dates back to 1885, is decorated with restored repousse (pressed tin) ceilings, leather and dark mahogany wood. Wrought-iron chandeliers, Western pictures, limestone walls and wood floors enhance the ambience, while the smoked chicken, broiled steaks, pan-barbecued shrimp and pecan-crusted salmon will please your palate. There also is seating on the front porch (street) and a large, cozy lounge in back. **Features:** full bar, Sunday brunch. **Address:** 107 N Kentucky St 75069 **Location:** On city square; west side; across from court house; in Grand Hotel. **Parking:** street only. [L] [D]

**ROCKFISH SEAFOOD GRILL**
972/542-2223

▼▼ Seafood. Casual Dining. $7-$20 **AAA Inspector Notes:** Patrons shuffle through peanut shells on the floor as they make their way to their seats and are easily distracted by the numerous pieces of hunting and fishing memorabilia adorning the walls and ceiling. Although guests kick back in a log cabin-style interior, the freshly caught fish gets more sophisticated preparation than campfire roasting. The chef uses an array of sauces and cooking styles, and soups are hearty and fresh. **Features:** full bar. **Address:** 2780 S Central Expwy (US 75) 75070 **Location:** US 75 exit 39 (Eldorado Pkwy), just w to Craig Rd, then just n. [L] [D]

**SALTGRASS STEAKHOUSE**
972/529-2200

▼▼ Steak. Casual Dining. $9-$30 **AAA Inspector Notes:** Those looking for something different should try the comfortable steakhouse, which never says no to a special request. Born from the spirit of Texas cattle drives, the restaurant resembles a Texas lodge, with high ceilings and mounted animal heads. Baby back ribs are so tender the meat falls off the bone. Also on the menu are hearty steaks, prime rib, chicken, seafood and yummy desserts. **Features:** full bar. **Address:** 2801 Craig Dr 75070 **Location:** US 75 exit 39 (Eldorado Pkwy), just w. [SAVE] [L] [D]

## McLEAN (B-6) pop. 778, elev. 2,812'

McLean began with a water well and a railroad switch built by the Choctaw, Oklahoma and Texas Railroad Company in 1901. This Texas Panhandle town became a shipping point for area farmers, who sent several hundred carloads of hogs and watermelons to market annually. McLean profited from the oil boom of the 1920s and the construction of Route 66. Efforts have been made to preserve buildings along the historic route, which was bypassed in the early 1980s. A vintage Phillips 66 gas station and an antique pumper can be seen at First and Gray streets.

**DEVIL'S ROPE MUSEUM** is at jct. Old Rte. 66 and Kingsley St. Housed in a former brassiere factory, the museum traces the history of barbed wire, the "devil's rope." Exhibits include tools for fence construction and entanglement wire used in warfare. Route 66 relics also are displayed. **Time:** Allow 1 hour minimum. **Hours:** Mon.-Fri. 9-5, Sat. 10-4, Mar.-Nov. Closed Thanksgiving. Phone ahead to confirm schedule. **Cost:** Donations. **Phone:** (806) 779-2225.

## MESQUITE (H-3) pop. 139,824, elev. 491'
- **Attractions map p. 170**
- **Hotels & Restaurants map & index p. 184, 197**
- **Part of Dallas area — see map p. 161**

Mesquite, an eastern suburb of Dallas, is the home of the Mesquite ProRodeo Series *(see attraction listing)*. Probably the best known of the nation's rodeos, the event has elevated to fame such riders and ropers as Don Gay, Larry Mahan, Charles Sampson and Jim Shoulders. Joe Kool, considered by many to have been the toughest bull to ride, often appeared in Mesquite.

**Mesquite Convention & Visitors Bureau:** 757 N. Galloway Ave., P.O. Box 850137, Mesquite, TX 75185-0137. **Phone:** (972) 204-4925 or (800) 541-2355.

**MESQUITE PRORODEO SERIES** is on I-635 at Military Pkwy. exit 4. Held in the 5,500-seat, air-conditioned Mesquite Arena, the rodeo competition includes professional bull and bronc riding, steer wrestling, tie-down and team roping, and barrel racing performed by cowgirls. Rodeo clowns, the Priefert Shark Cage, chuck wagon races and a calf scramble are part of the entertainment. Visitors can also ride a pony and have their photo taken while sitting on a bull.

**Time:** Allow 2 hours minimum. **Hours:** Fri.-Sat. at 7:30 p.m., June-Aug. and major holidays. Phone ahead to confirm holiday schedule. Gates open at 6:30 p.m. **Cost:** $24; $19 (active military with ID); $12 (ages 3-12). Reservations are recommended. **Parking:** $5. **Phone:** (972) 285-8777.

### COMFORT SUITES    (972)329-9400  95

Hotel
$65-$95

**Address:** 2100 N Belt Line Rd 75150 **Location:** US 80 exit Belt Line Rd, just n. **Facility:** 58 units. 2 stories, interior corridors. **Pool(s):** outdoor. **Activities:** hot tub, exercise room. **Guest Services:** coin laundry. **Featured Amenity:** full hot breakfast.

### COURTYARD BY MARRIOTT DALLAS/MESQUITE    (972)681-3300  93
Hotel $85-$130 **Address:** 2300 1-30 75150 **Location:** I-635 exit 7 (Town East Blvd), just w, then just n. **Facility:** 101 units. 4 stories, interior corridors. **Pool(s):** heated indoor. **Activities:** hot tub, exercise room. **Guest Services:** valet and coin laundry.

**AAA Benefit:** Members save 5% or more!

### DAYS INN MESQUITE/DALLAS    (972)285-1500  6

Hotel
$55-$110
**Address:** 140 Commerce Way 75149 **Location:** I-635 exit 4 (Military Pkwy), just w. **Facility:** 45 units. 2 stories (no elevator), interior corridors. **Amenities:** safes. **Pool(s):** indoor. **Activities:** hot tub. **Guest Services:** coin laundry. **Featured Amenity:** continental breakfast.

### FAIRFIELD INN & SUITES BY MARRIOTT DALLAS MESQUITE    (972)686-8286  94
Hotel $89-$199 **Address:** 4020 Towne Crossing Blvd 75150 **Location:** I-635 exit 7 (Military Pkwy), just w to Towne Crossing Blvd, then 0.5 mi n. **Facility:** 80 units. 3 stories, interior corridors. **Activities:** hot tub, exercise room. **Guest Services:** valet and coin laundry.

**AAA Benefit:** Members save 5% or more!

### HAMPTON INN & SUITES AT RODEO CENTER    (972)329-3100  8
Hotel $80-$99 **Address:** 1700 Rodeo Dr 75149 **Location:** I-635 exit 4 (Military Pkwy), 0.5 mi s on Hickory Tree Rd. **Facility:** 160 units, some efficiencies. 6 stories, interior corridors. **Terms:** check-in 4 pm, 1-7 night minimum stay, cancellation fee imposed. **Pool(s):** heated outdoor. **Activities:** exercise room. **Guest Services:** valet and coin laundry.

**AAA Benefit:** Members save up to 10%!

### HOLIDAY INN EXPRESS HOTEL & SUITES    (972)288-9900  7

Hotel
$89-$139

**Address:** 21850 I-635 (LBJ) 75149 **Location:** I-635 exit 4 (Military Pkwy), just s. **Facility:** 74 units. 5 stories, interior corridors. **Pool(s):** heated indoor. **Activities:** hot tub, exercise room. **Guest Services:** valet and coin laundry. **Featured Amenity:** full hot breakfast.

### LA QUINTA INN & SUITES DALLAS MESQUITE    (972)216-7460  96
Hotel
$89-$134
**Address:** 118 E Hwy 80 75149 **Location:** US 80E exit Belt Line Rd. **Facility:** 60 units. 3 stories, interior corridors. **Pool(s):** heated indoor. **Activities:** hot tub, exercise room. **Guest Services:** coin laundry. **Featured Amenity:** full hot breakfast.

### QUALITY INN MESQUITE    (972)285-6300  97
Hotel $60-$130 **Address:** 923 Windbell Cir 75149 **Location:** I-635 exit 5, just e, then just s. **Facility:** 62 units. 2 stories, interior corridors. **Pool(s):** heated indoor. **Activities:** hot tub, exercise room. **Guest Services:** valet and coin laundry.

(See maps & indexes p. 184, 197.)

## WHERE TO EAT

### EL CHICO
972/270-7727 [85]

Tex-Mex
Casual Dining
$7-$16

**AAA Inspector Notes:** Inside and out, the decor of the popular Mexican restaurant is inviting. The menu features traditional favorites such as enchiladas, tacos, burritos and fajitas. The broad menu also lists a few American classics. **Features:** full bar. **Address:** 2028 Town East Mall 75150 **Location:** I-635 exit 7 (Town East Blvd).
[L] [D]

### GRANDY'S RESTAURANT
972/681-8052

American. Quick Serve. $4-$8 **AAA Inspector Notes:** Fried chicken and country-fried steak are menu standbys at the restaurant, a regional franchise. They also offer a family-style dining menu. The décor is a step up from that of most quick-serve eateries and more resembles that of a conventional restaurant. Some elements of increased service include additional rolls, iced tea refills and tray removal. **Address:** 2009 N Town East Blvd 75150 **Location:** I-635 exit 7 (Town East Blvd) northbound; exit 7B (Town East Blvd) southbound, just w. [B] [L] [D]

### LUBY'S
972/279-6169

American. Cafeteria. $7-$12 **AAA Inspector Notes:** First opened in 1947 in south Texas, this cafeteria with over 100 outlets features a wide variety of salads, fresh fruits, seafood...including crunchy shrimp...pastas, meat, poultry and just baked cakes and pies. Ask about the kids specials and Lu Ann platters...an entrée with choice of 2 vegetables and a roll. Many locations offer drive-thru service. **Address:** 3301 Gus Thomasson Rd 75150 **Location:** Just s of jct Gus Thomasson Rd and N Town East Blvd. [L] [D]

### SALTGRASS STEAKHOUSE
972/270-5200 [86]

Steak. Casual Dining. $9-$30 **AAA Inspector Notes:** Those looking for something different should try the comfortable steakhouse, which never says no to a special request. Born from the spirit of Texas cattle drives, the restaurant resembles a Texas lodge, with high ceilings and mounted animal heads. Baby back ribs are so tender the meat falls off the bone. Also on the menu are hearty steaks, prime rib, chicken, seafood and yummy desserts. **Features:** full bar. **Address:** 18680 I-635 75150 **Location:** I-635E exit 7B (Town East Blvd) southbound; exit 7 (Town East Blvd) northbound; just s of Town East Mall. [SAVE] [L] [D]

### SOULMAN'S BARBEQUE
972/289-2300 [87]

Barbecue. Casual Dining. $9-$18 **AAA Inspector Notes:** At this local chain, guests can get their favorite barbecue dishes such as brisket, chicken, pork and sausage in generous portions. Prices won't pinch the pocketbook. **Address:** 1125 Gross Rd 75149 **Location:** I-635 exit 5, just e. [L] [D]

### THE SPAGHETTI WAREHOUSE
972/613-1478

Italian. Casual Dining. $7-$17 **AAA Inspector Notes:** The Italian-style restaurant chain sustains a festive family atmosphere. All entrees include bottomless tossed salad or soup. Patrons enjoy plentiful portions of such classic dishes as ravioli, lasagna, baked penne or the richly flavored cannelloni Florentine. Splurging on one of the many desserts, such as tiramisu, espresso mousse cake or carrot cake, is worthwhile. **Features:** full bar. **Address:** 3855 W Emporium Cir 75150 **Location:** I-635 exit 7B (Town East Blvd) southbound; exit 7 (Town East Blvd) northbound, just e, then just n.
[L] [D] [⬧]

### SPRING CREEK BBQ
972/682-3770

Barbecue. Casual Dining. $8-$13 **AAA Inspector Notes:** Expect Texas-Style barbecue at its simple, homey best. Hickory smoked ribs, beef, pork and turkey lace the air with a spicy aroma that mingles with the scent of freshly baked rolls and cold ice cream slowly melting over a dish of homemade peach cobbler. Plates often are loaded with all the coleslaw, potato salad and corn on the cob they can support. Part of a small chain, this barbecue restaurant displays a rustic décor that gives patrons the impression they are "at the ranch." **Features:** beer only. **Address:** 3939 W Emporium Cir 75150 **Location:** I-635 exit 7 (Town East Blvd), just e to Emporium Cir, just n to Pavillion Ct; southeast corner of Pavillion Ct and Emporium Cir.
[L] [D]

### MEXIA pop. 7,459

### BEST WESTERN LIMESTONE INN & SUITES
(254)562-0200

Hotel
$80-$100

**AAA Benefit:** Members save 10% or more with Best Western!

**Address:** 1314 E Milam St 76667 **Location:** Just e of CR 1365 on US 84; east side of town. **Facility:** 34 units. 2 stories, interior corridors. **Pool(s):** outdoor. **Activities:** exercise room. **Guest Services:** coin laundry.

### MIDLAND (D-5) pop. 111,147, elev. 2,769'
• Hotels p. 418 • Restaurants p. 419

Midland is a West Texas oil center that lies on the former Chihuahua Trail, the Emigrant Road to California and the Comanche War Trail. The settlement, named in 1880 for its location halfway between Fort Worth and El Paso, was a quiet farming town until its economy changed in 1923 with the tapping of the huge Permian Basin petroleum supply.

President George W. Bush spent his formative years in Midland; the Bush family lived in the area 1948-59. While working in Houston, George W. was introduced to Laura Welch, a young librarian from his home town. The couple married in 1977 and made their home in Midland.

**Midland Chamber of Commerce:** 109 N. Main St., Midland, TX 79701. **Phone:** (432) 683-3381 or (800) 624-6435.

**COMMEMORATIVE AIR FORCE AND AMERICAN AIRPOWER HERITAGE MUSEUM** is at Midland International Airport at 9600 Wright Dr. The facility features one of the world's foremost collections of World War II aircraft in flying condition. Also notable are the displays of Nose Art, a rare collection of American folk art cut from the fuselages of warbirds following World War II. Hands-on exhibits tell the story of World War II.

Hours: Tues.-Sat. 9-5. Closed Jan. 1, July 4, Thanksgiving, Christmas Eve, Christmas and Dec. 31. **Cost:** $10; $9 (ages 13-17 and 65+); $7 (ages 6-12). **Phone:** (432) 563-1000.

**GEORGE W. BUSH CHILDHOOD HOME** is at 1412 W. Ohio Ave. The fully restored childhood home of the 43rd president features furnishings authentic to the period of 1951-55, when the Bush family lived there. The 1,500-square-foot home also features photographic exhibits. **Hours:** Tues.-Sat. 10-5, Sun. 2-5. Closed Jan. 1, Easter, Thanksgiving and Christmas. **Cost:** $5; $3 (ages 65+ and military with ID); $2 (students with ID); free (ages 0-5). **Phone:** (432) 685-1112 or (866) 684-4380.

**HALEY LIBRARY & HISTORY CENTER**, 1805 W. Indiana Ave., preserves Western history and heritage with its extensive collection of printed materials about such topics as railroad history, the military, ranching and western exploration. Western art and historical items are on display and include paintings and sculptures by Veryl Goodnight, Joe Beeler and Charlie Dye. Cowboy photographs from the turn-of-the-20th-century by Erwin Smith also are in the collection.

**Time:** Allow 30 minutes minimum. **Hours:** Mon.-Fri. 9-5. Closed major holidays. **Cost:** Donations. **Phone:** (432) 682-5785.

**MUSEUM OF THE SOUTHWEST** is 1 blk. s. of US Bus. Rte. 80 at 1705 W. Missouri Ave. The museum houses art and archeological artifacts in a 1934 mansion designed by Anton F. Korn. The permanent collection includes works by founding members of the Taos Society of Artists, as well as graphics and sculpture. The museum also features traveling exhibitions and the Fredda Turner Durham Children's Museum, with hands-on exhibits.

**Time:** Allow 1 hour minimum. **Hours:** Tues.-Sat. 10-5, Sun. 2-5. Closed major holidays. **Cost:** Donations. Children's museum $3; free (ages 0-2). **Phone:** (432) 683-2882.

**Marian Blakemore Planetarium,** 1 blk. s. at Indiana and K sts., features interactive exhibits and a star projector. **Hours:** Tues.-Sat. 10-5. Phone ahead for astronomy show schedule. **Cost:** $3. Astronomy shows $6; $4 (ages 3-13). Prices may vary; phone ahead. **Phone:** (432) 683-2882.

**THE PETROLEUM MUSEUM** is at 1500 I-20W exit 136, .7 mi. w. of jct. SR 349 and I-20. Situated in the heart of the Permian Basin, this museum chronicles the origin and discovery of fossil fuels and their associated industries. Pioneers of the oil and gas industry are honored in the Petroleum Hall of Fame, where your tour begins.

In the Chaparral Gallery you'll learn about the history and innovations of the Midland-based auto racing team Chaparral Cars. You can view seven legendary Chaparral race cars, explore exhibits relating to aerodynamics and sit behind the wheel of a replica Chaparral 2E.

Other highlights include the Marine Diorama of the Ancient Permian Sea, the Boomtown Room, a well-fire display and antique drilling rigs. A permanent collection of Tom Lovell paintings is on display, and a research library is open to visitors.

**Tours:** Guided tours are available. **Time:** Allow 1 hour, 30 minutes minimum. **Hours:** Mon.-Sat. 10-5, Sun. 2-5. Research library by appointment. Closed Jan. 1, Thanksgiving, Christmas Eve and Christmas. **Cost:** $8; $6 (ages 12-17 and 65+); $5 (ages 6-11). **Phone:** (432) 683-4403.

---

Visit your AAA/CAA Travel office

for amazing AAA Vacations

tour and cruise packages

---

**COMFORT SUITES**                    (432)620-9191

Hotel
$90-$299

**Address:** 4706 N Garfield St 79705 **Location:** Loop 250 exit Garfield St, just n. **Facility:** 63 units. 2 stories, interior corridors. **Pool(s):** outdoor. **Activities:** hot tub, exercise room. **Guest Services:** valet and coin laundry. **Featured Amenity: full hot breakfast.**

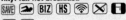

**COUNTRY INN & SUITES BY CARLSON**    (432)218-7980

Hotel
$100-$300

**Address:** 920 W Interstate 20 79701 **Location:** I-20 exit 136; on north frontage road. **Facility:** 66 units. 3 stories, interior corridors. **Terms:** cancellation fee imposed. **Pool(s):** outdoor. **Activities:** hot tub, exercise room. **Guest Services:** coin laundry. **Featured Amenity: continental breakfast.**

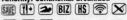

**COURTYARD BY MARRIOTT**              (432)689-9400

Hotel $123-$289 **Address:** 1505 Tradewind Blvd 79707 **Location:** Just w of jct Loop 250. **Facility:** 97 units. 5 stories, interior corridors. **Bath:** shower only. **Pool(s):** heated outdoor. **Activities:** exercise room. **Guest Services:** valet and coin laundry.

**DOUBLETREE BY HILTON**               (432)683-6131

Hotel $154-$284 **Address:** 117 W Wall St 79701 **Location:** Jct Loraine St; downtown. **Facility:** 255 units. 11 stories, interior corridors. **Parking:** onsite and valet. **Terms:** 1-7 night minimum stay, cancellation fee imposed. **Dining:** 2 restaurants. **Pool(s):** outdoor. **Activities:** hot tub, exercise room. **Guest Services:** valet laundry.

**FAIRFIELD INN & SUITES BY MARRIOTT**    (432)570-7155

Hotel $125-$229 **Address:** 2300 Faulkner Dr 79705 **Location:** Loop 250 exit Garfield St, just n. **Facility:** 69 units. 2 stories, interior corridors. **Pool(s):** heated indoor. **Activities:** hot tub, exercise room. **Guest Services:** valet and coin laundry.

**HAMPTON INN**                        (432)520-9600

Hotel $149-$310 **Address:** 5011 W Loop 250 N 79707 **Location:** Loop 250 exit Tremont Ave/Wadley Ave; on eastbound frontage road. **Facility:** 79 units. 3 stories, interior corridors. **Terms:** 1-7 night minimum stay, cancellation fee imposed. **Pool(s):** heated outdoor. **Activities:** exercise room. **Guest Services:** valet and coin laundry.

**HILTON GARDEN INN MIDLAND**          432/689-0022

**fyi** Hotel. Rates not provided. Too new to rate. **Address:** 1301 N Loop 250 79706 **Location:** Loop 250 W exit SR 158/191; on south frontage road. **Amenities:** 120 units, restaurant, coffeemakers, microwaves, refrigerators, pool, exercise facility.

## LA QUINTA INN & SUITES MIDLAND NORTH (432)694-1200

▼▼▼ Hotel $149-$279 **Address:** 2606 N Loop 250 W 79707 **Location:** 0.5 mi n of jct SR 158/191; on east frontage road. **Facility:** 74 units. 3 stories, interior corridors. **Pool(s):** outdoor. **Activities:** hot tub, exercise room. **Guest Services:** coin laundry.

CALL &M ≈ BIZ HS 📶 ✕ 🖥 📷 📖

## QUALITY INN MIDLAND (432)683-1111

▼▼▼ Hotel $119-$249 **Address:** 902 I-20 W 79701 **Location:** I-20 exit 136; on north service road. **Facility:** 68 units, some kitchens. 2 stories, interior corridors. **Pool(s):** indoor. **Activities:** hot tub, exercise room. **Guest Services:** valet and coin laundry.

🍴 ≈ BIZ HS 📶 🖥 📷 📖

## RESIDENCE INN BY MARRIOTT MIDLAND (432)689-3511

▼▼▼ Extended Stay Contemporary Hotel $135-$260 **Address:** 5509 Deauville Blvd 79706 **Location:** Just w of jct Loop 250; on south frontage road. **Facility:** 131 units, some two bedrooms, efficiencies and kitchens. 4 stories, interior corridors. **Pool(s):** heated outdoor. **Activities:** exercise room. **Guest Services:** valet and coin laundry.

**AAA Benefit:** Members save 5% or more!

🍴 CALL &M ≈ BIZ HS 📶 ✕ 🖥 📷 📖 / SOME UNITS 🍳🛒

## SLEEP INN & SUITES (432)694-4200

▼▼▼ Hotel $159-$229 **Address:** 5612 Deauville Blvd 79706 **Location:** Just w of jct Loop 250. **Facility:** 122 units. 4 stories, interior corridors. **Pool(s):** outdoor. **Activities:** hot tub, exercise room. **Guest Services:** coin laundry.

➕ 🍴 CALL &M ≈ BIZ HS 📶 ✕ 🖥 📷 📖

## WYNDHAM GARDEN MIDLAND (432)699-4144

▼▼▼ Hotel $99-$144

**Address:** 3100 W Wall St 79701 **Location:** Jct Powell St. **Facility:** 2 stories, interior corridors. **Pool(s):** heated indoor. **Activities:** hot tub, exercise room.

SAVE 🍷 ≈ BIZ 📶 ✕ 🖥 📷 📖

---

## WHERE TO EAT

## ABUELO'S THE FLAVOR OF MEXICO 432/685-3335

▼▼ Mexican. Casual Dining. $7-$19 **AAA Inspector Notes:** Guests sit down to a nice selection of traditional Mexican dishes in an upscale and spacious dining area. The adult beverages are inventive. **Features:** full bar. **Reservations:** suggested. **Address:** 4610 N Garfield Rd 79705 **Location:** Jct Loop 250 and Garfield Rd. L D CALL &M

## CATTLE BARON STEAK & SEAFOOD 432/683-2334

▼▼ American. Casual Dining. $8-$28 **AAA Inspector Notes:** A scrumptious array of menu selections includes steak, seafood, chicken and prime rib as well as desserts such as caramel apple pie. An upscale Western decor includes wood trim and distinctive chandeliers made from deer antlers. **Features:** full bar. **Address:** 418 W Wadley Ave 79705 **Location:** Loop 250 exit N Big Spring St, 1 mi s to Wadley Ave, then 1 blk w. L D

## CLEAR SPRINGS CAFE 432/522-1188

▼▼ American. Casual Dining. $8-$17 **AAA Inspector Notes:** Patrons relax in a fun Western atmosphere while enjoying offerings ranging from burgers to seafood to steaks. **Features:** full bar. **Address:** 5707 Andrews Hwy 79706 **Location:** Loop 250 W exit SR 158/191, just w on south frontage road. L D

## THE GARLIC PRESS 432/570-4020

▼▼▼ Italian. Casual Dining. $9-$33 **AAA Inspector Notes:** Eclectic offerings with upscale presentations are the restaurant's forte. The vibrant menu changes daily. Although many classic specialties center on seafood, others incorporate mouthwatering veal, chicken and beef. Quality ingredients and homemade preparations ensure freshness. **Features:** beer & wine. **Reservations:** suggested. **Address:** 2200 W Wadley Ave 79705 **Location:** Jct Wadley Ave and Garfield St. L D CALL &M 🚭

## THE HARVEST CAFFE 432/218-8331

▼▼ Coffee/Tea Breads/Pastries. Family Dining. $6-$12 **AAA Inspector Notes:** Located in a trendy area, you will often find a wait for a table. This coffeehouse with restaurant-style table service offers a menu made up of soups, salads and sandwiches. For a touch of comfort go for the grilled cheese panini and tomato basil soup. Numerous bakery items are available to satisfy your sweet tooth. **Features:** patio dining. **Address:** 2101 W Wadley Ave, Suite 8 79705 **Location:** Loop 250 exit Garfield St, 1.3 mi s. B L

## LUIGI'S ITALIAN RESTAURANT 432/683-6363

▼▼ Italian. Casual Dining. $5-$12 **AAA Inspector Notes:** Pizza and pasta dishes mingle with sandwiches and other wholesome foods on the tried-and-true menu. A casual, bistro-like ambience, decent portions and friendly servers distinguish the restaurant. **Features:** full bar. **Address:** 111 N Big Spring St 79701 **Location:** Just n of Wall St; downtown. L D

## STRAWBERRY FIELDS CAFE 432/684-5869

▼▼ Natural/Organic. Cafeteria. $6-$8 **AAA Inspector Notes:** Off of the Natural Foods Market, the menu is full of fresh organic produce. Choose among fresh salads, made-to-order sandwiches and wraps and the locally favorite burgers made from organic beef, turkey, wild-caught salmon or veggies. The sweets, made without refined sugars or hydrogenated oils, are guilt-free treats. **Features:** patio dining. **Address:** 2311 W Wadley Ave 79705 **Location:** Loop 250 exit Garfield St, 1 mi s, then just e. B L D

## VENEZIA RESTAURANT 432/687-0900

▼▼ Northern Italian. Casual Dining. $9-$20 **AAA Inspector Notes:** Generous portions and a good variety of well-prepared dishes make this a popular spot. Service is friendly, but during the busy lunchtime servers take care of the basics but appear rushed. **Features:** full bar, patio dining. **Address:** 2101 W Wadley #20 79705 **Location:** 0.9 mi s of jct Loop 250 and Garfield St. L D

## WALL STREET BAR & GRILL 432/684-8686

▼▼ American. Casual Dining. $10-$32 **AAA Inspector Notes:** The nostalgic bistro features late 19th-century decor, including a bar built in 1867. The menu comprises beef, chicken and seafood dishes, all homemade using fresh ingredients and meats cut on the premises. Savory crawfish etouffee is a house favorite. **Features:** full bar. **Address:** 115 E Wall St 79701 **Location:** Jct Wall St at Main St; downtown. L D

# MINEOLA pop. 4,515

## BEST WESTERN MINEOLA INN (903)569-5331

▼▼▼ Hotel $100-$115

**AAA Benefit:** Members save 10% or more with Best Western!

**Address:** 100 Debbie Ln 75773 **Location:** 1 mi s of jct US 80 and 69. **Facility:** 50 units. 2 stories, interior corridors. **Pool(s):** outdoor. **Activities:** hot tub, exercise room. **Guest Services:** coin laundry. **Featured Amenity:** full hot breakfast.

SAVE ≈ BIZ HS 📶 🖥 📷 📖

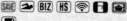

## MINERAL WELLS pop. 16,788

### BEST WESTERN CLUB HOUSE INN & SUITES
(940)325-2270

Hotel
$70-$110

**AAA Benefit:** Members save 10% or more with Best Western!

**Address:** 4410 Hwy 180 E 76067 **Location:** Jct US 180 and SR 1195; in East Mineral Wells. **Facility:** 50 units. 2 stories, interior corridors. **Pool(s):** outdoor. **Activities:** hot tub, exercise room. **Guest Services:** coin laundry. **Featured Amenity: full hot breakfast.**

SAVE CALL 🖢M 🛏 HS 📶 📶
📷 📺 / SOME UNITS 🐾

### COMFORT SUITES
(940)327-0077

🔻🔻🔻 **Hotel** $74-$119 **Address:** 105 Carl Kessler Blvd 76067 **Location:** Jct US 281 and 180, 2.5 mi w. **Facility:** 60 units. 3 stories, interior corridors. **Pool(s):** heated indoor. **Activities:** hot tub, exercise room. **Guest Services:** valet and coin laundry.

🍴 CALL 🖢M 🛏 HS 📶 ✕ 📷 📺
/ SOME UNITS 🐾

## MISSION (I-8) pop. 77,058, elev. 134'

Mission, in the Rio Grande Valley, was founded by Oblate Fathers in 1824. They are credited with being the first to plant citrus in this region, which is now known for Texas Ruby Red grapefruit. Situated on the migratory flyway between Central and South American and Canada, the Rio Grande Valley is a prime bird-watching destination; nearly 500 species have been sighted in the region.

Renowned football coach Tom Landry was born and grew up in Mission. A mural painted by local artist Manuel Hinojosa on a 95-foot wall facing Tom Landry Street depicts his life and football career, including playing in five Super Bowls with the Dallas Cowboys.

Los Ebanos Ferry, 17 miles southwest on FM 886, is thought to be the last remaining hand-drawn ferry in the country. It transports three cars and several passengers across the Rio Grande at a time.

**Mission Chamber of Commerce:** 202 W. Tom Landry St., Mission, TX 78572. **Phone:** (956) 585-2727 or (800) 580-2700.

**BENTSEN-RIO GRANDE VALLEY STATE PARK** is off US 83 exit FM 2062, following signs. The headquarters of the World Birding Center features a hawk tower, bird-feeding stations and observation blinds on 760 acres, allowing visitors ample birdwatching options as well as a glimpse of Mexico. Five miles of paved bicycle trails, 6 miles of nature trails, a tram ride, and birding and interpretive tours also are offered. *See Recreation Areas Chart.*

**Time:** Allow 1 hour minimum. **Hours:** Park daily 7 a.m.-10 p.m. Visitor center Mon.-Fri. 8-1, Sat.-Sun. 8-5. Tram rides depart hourly 7:30-4:30. Phone for birding and interpretive tour schedules. **Cost:** $5; free (ages 0-12). **Phone:** (956) 584-9156.

🔺 ✕ 🐾 🏕

**LA LOMITA CHAPEL** is 3 mi. s. on FM 1016. The "Little Hill" Chapel is one of the oldest Texas missions still in use. Measuring 12 feet by 25 feet, the sandstone structure was built by the Oblate Fathers in 1865 and relocated to its present site in 1899. Picnicking along nature trails in the surrounding 7-acre park is permitted. **Time:** Allow 30 minutes minimum. **Hours:** Daily dawn-dusk. **Cost:** Free. **Phone:** (956) 580-8760. 🏕

### BEST WESTERN LAS PALMAS INN
(956)583-9290

Hotel
$76-$126

**AAA Benefit:** Members save 10% or more with Best Western!

**Address:** 609 E Expwy 83 78572 **Location:** Off US 83 exit Conway Ave. Located in a quiet semi-rural area. **Facility:** 54 units. 2 stories (no elevator), exterior corridors. **Pool(s):** outdoor. **Activities:** hot tub, exercise room. **Guest Services:** coin laundry.

SAVE 🍴 🛏 BIZ HS 📶 📷
📷 📺

### EL ROCIO RETREAT
(956)584-7432

🔻🔻🔻 **Bed & Breakfast** $75-$315 **Address:** 2519 S Inspiration Rd 78572 **Location:** Jct US 83 at Inspiration Rd, 2 mi s. Located in a quiet area in natural surroundings. **Facility:** Surrounded by a wildlife refuge, the inn offers a peaceful getaway; guest rooms are uniquely decorated and offer a relaxed, inviting ambiance. 4 units, some houses. 1 story, interior/exterior corridors. *Bath:* some shared. **Terms:** 3 day cancellation notice-fee imposed. **Activities:** bicycles. **Guest Services:** complimentary laundry.

BIZ HS 📶 ✕ 📺 / SOME UNITS 🐾 📼

### HAMPTON INN & SUITES
(956)682-0333

🔻🔻🔻 **Hotel** $89-$189 **Address:** 2505 Victoria Dr 78572 **Location:** US 83 exit Shary Rd, just n. Across from large shopping complex. **Facility:** 107 units. 4 stories, interior corridors. **Terms:** 1-7 night minimum stay, cancellation fee imposed. **Pool(s):** outdoor. **Activities:** exercise room. **Guest Services:** valet and coin laundry.

**AAA Benefit:** Members save up to 10%!

🍴 CALL 🖢M 🛏 BIZ HS 📶 ✕ 📺
/ SOME UNITS 📷 📺

### HOLIDAY INN EXPRESS HOTEL & SUITES
(956)424-7788

🔻🔻🔻 **Hotel** $99-$169 **Address:** 901 S Shary Rd 78572 **Location:** Off US 83 exit Shary Rd. Located in a quiet semi-rural area. **Facility:** 85 units, some efficiencies. 2 stories, interior corridors. **Terms:** 3 day cancellation notice. **Pool(s):** outdoor. **Activities:** hot tub, exercise room. **Guest Services:** coin laundry.

🍴 CALL 🖢M 🛏 BIZ 📶 📺 / SOME UNITS HS 📷 📺

### LA QUINTA INN & SUITES
(956)581-7772

🔻🔻🔻 **Hotel** $94-$164 **Address:** 805 Travis St 78572 **Location:** US 83 exit Bryan Rd; on eastbound access road. **Facility:** 71 units. 4 stories, interior corridors. **Pool(s):** outdoor. **Activities:** hot tub, exercise room. **Guest Services:** coin laundry.

🍴 🛏 BIZ HS 📶 ✕ 📷 📷 📺
/ SOME UNITS 🐾

## WHERE TO EAT

**LONE STAR BAR-B-Q**                                956/585-2381

◆ Regional Barbecue. Quick Serve. $6-$12 **AAA Inspector Notes:** This is as south Texas as it gets, close to the border, se habla Español, moist smoked brisket, ribs, potato salad with iced tea. Casual, informal and Texas-friendly. **Address:** 2220 E Bus Hwy 83 78572 **Location:** US 83, 1 mi n on Shary Rd, just w.

L  D

**LUBY'S**                                            956/580-2555

◆◆ American. Cafeteria. $6-$12 **AAA Inspector Notes:** First opened in 1947 in south Texas, this cafeteria with over 100 outlets features a wide variety of salads, fresh fruits, seafood...including crunchy shrimp...pastas, meat, poultry and just baked cakes and pies. Ask about the kids specials and Lu Ann platters...an entrée with choice of 2 vegetables and a roll. Many locations offer drive-thru service. **Address:** 701 E Expwy 83 78572 **Location:** Between Conway Ave and Bryan Rd.  L  D

## MONAHANS (E-4) pop. 6,953, elev. 2,613'

Although the Spanish explored the area more than 400 years ago, it remained an undisturbed Native American habitat until the mid-1800s. Monahans was established about 1881 as a railroad city.

**Monahans Chamber of Commerce:** 401 S. Dwight Ave., Monahans, TX 79756. **Phone:** (432) 943-2187.

**MONAHANS SANDHILLS STATE PARK** is 5 mi. e. off I-20 to Park Rd. 41. The park includes 3,840 acres of sand dunes, part of a vast area that stretches into New Mexico. Many dunes are active, growing and changing shape, unlike most of the surrounding area, which has been stabilized by shin oak and other vegetation. Visitor center exhibits depict the history of the dunes as well as that of the area's former inhabitants. *See Recreation Areas Chart.*

**Hours:** Park daily 8 a.m.-10 p.m. Visitor center daily 8:30-4:30. **Cost:** $3; free (ages 0-12). **Phone:** (432) 943-2092.

**AMERICAS BEST VALUE COLONIAL INN**        432/943-4345

◆◆ Motel. Rates not provided. **Address:** 702 W I-20 79756 **Location:** I-20 exit 80, just s. **Facility:** 65 units. 1 story, interior/exterior corridors. **Guest Services:** coin laundry.

**BEST WESTERN PLUS MONAHANS INN & SUITES**
(432)943-3360

◆◆◆ Hotel $130-$500

Best Western PLUS

**AAA Benefit:** Members save 10% or more with Best Western!

**Address:** 2101 S Betty St 79756 **Location:** I-20 exit 80, just se. **Facility:** 51 units. 3 stories, interior corridors. **Terms:** 4 night minimum stay - seasonal. **Pool(s):** heated indoor. **Activities:** hot tub, exercise room. **Guest Services:** coin laundry. **Featured Amenity:** full hot breakfast.

**COMFORT INN & SUITES**                         (432)943-3000

◆◆◆◆ Hotel $150-$500 **Address:** 2200 S Stockton Ave 79756 **Location:** I-20 exit 80, just s. **Facility:** 61 units. 3 stories, interior corridors. **Terms:** 3 day cancellation notice. **Pool(s):** heated indoor. **Activities:** hot tub, exercise room. **Guest Services:** coin laundry.

## WHERE TO EAT

**PAPPY'S BAR B-Q**                                   432/943-9300

◆ Barbecue. Casual Dining. $4-$12 **AAA Inspector Notes:** A casual, laid-back atmosphere sets the stage for slow-roasted smoked meats sliced to order. Traditional sides accompany your meat order and it's all served up cafeteria style. The Texas beef brisket is a local favorite. **Address:** 1901 S Stockton Ave 79756 **Location:** I-20 exit 80, just nw.  L  D

## MONTGOMERY pop. 621
• Part of Houston area — see map p. 301

**BEST WESTERN LAKE CONROE INN**          (936)588-3030

◆◆◆ Hotel $72-$100

Best Western

**AAA Benefit:** Members save 10% or more with Best Western!

**Address:** 14643 Hwy 105 W 77356 **Location:** Just w of McCaleb Rd. **Facility:** 48 units. 2 stories (no elevator), exterior corridors. **Terms:** 2-4 night minimum stay - seasonal. **Pool(s):** outdoor.

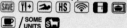

**LA TORRETTA LAKE RESORT & SPA**           936/448-4400

◆◆◆◆ Contemporary Resort Hotel Rates not provided

**Address:** 600 La Torretta Blvd 77356 **Location:** SR 105, 2.5 mi n on Walden Rd to La Torretta Blvd. **Facility:** I expect a resort to offer choices, and this place really does that with lots to do for kids, adults, business people and leisure travelers. 445 units, some cottages. 20 stories, interior/exterior corridors. **Parking:** on-site and valet. **Terms:** check-in 4 pm. **Amenities:** safes. **Dining:** 6 restaurants. **Pool(s):** outdoor, heated outdoor. **Activities:** hot tub, steamroom, limited beach access, boat ramp, fishing, regulation golf, miniature golf, tennis, recreation programs in summer, game room, spa. **Guest Services:** valet laundry.

## MOUNT PLEASANT pop. 15,564
• Restaurants p. 422

**BEST WESTERN MT. PLEASANT INN**          (903)572-5051

◆◆ Motel $55-$69

Best Western

**AAA Benefit:** Members save 10% or more with Best Western!

**Address:** 102 E Burton Rd 75455 **Location:** I-30 exit 162, just e. **Facility:** 57 units. 2 stories (no elevator), exterior corridors. **Pool(s):** outdoor. **Activities:** exercise room. **Guest Services:** coin laundry. **Featured Amenity:** continental breakfast.

## HAMPTON INN & SUITES · 903/572-7100

♦♦♦ **Hotel.** Rates not provided. **Address:** 2504 W Ferguson Rd 75455 **Location:** I-30 exit 160, just s. **Facility:** 76 units. 4 stories, interior corridors. **Pool(s):** heated indoor. **Activities:** exercise room. **Guest Services:** valet and coin laundry.

**AAA Benefit:**
Members save up to 10%!

[icons]

## HOLIDAY INN EXPRESS HOTEL & SUITES · (903)577-3800

♦♦♦ **Hotel** $85-$120 **Address:** 2306 Greenhill Rd 75455 **Location:** I-30 exit 162, just ne. **Facility:** 71 units. 3 stories, interior corridors. **Terms:** cancellation fee imposed. **Pool(s):** outdoor. **Activities:** exercise room. **Guest Services:** valet and coin laundry.

[icons]

## LA QUINTA INN & SUITES MT. PLEASANT · (903)572-5514

♦♦♦ **Hotel** $94-$129 **Address:** 1620 Rotan Ave 75455 **Location:** I-30 exit 160, just n. **Facility:** 89 units. 4 stories, interior corridors. **Pool(s):** heated indoor. **Activities:** hot tub, exercise room. **Guest Services:** coin laundry.

[icons]

## QUALITY INN · (903)577-7553

♦♦ Hotel $56-$95

**Address:** 2515 W Ferguson Rd 75455 **Location:** I-30 exit 160, just s. **Facility:** 59 units. 2 stories (no elevator), exterior corridors. **Pool(s):** outdoor. **Guest Services:** valet and coin laundry.

[icons]

## SUPER 8 · (903)572-9808

♦♦ Motel $50-$125

**Address:** 204 Lakewood Dr 75455 **Location:** I-30 exit 162 eastbound; exit 162A westbound, just n, then just w. **Facility:** 65 units. 2 stories (no elevator), exterior corridors. **Pool(s):** outdoor. **Guest Services:** coin laundry. **Featured Amenity:** continental breakfast.

[icons]

**WHERE TO EAT**

## EL CHICO · 903/572-1981

♦♦

Tex-Mex Casual Dining $7-$16

**AAA Inspector Notes:** Inside and out, the decor of the popular Mexican restaurant is inviting. The menu features traditional favorites such as enchiladas, tacos, burritos and fajitas. The broad menu also lists a few American classics. **Features:** full bar. **Address:** 2506 W Ferguson Rd 75455 **Location:** I-30 exit 160, just s. [L] [D]

## LUIGI'S · 903/577-9701

♦♦ Italian. Casual Dining. $7-$16 **AAA Inspector Notes:** This family-owned restaurant serves up classic Italian fare. On the menu are seafood, veal and chicken selections as well as several types of pasta. **Address:** 2213 W Ferguson Rd 75455 **Location:** I-30 exit 160, 0.5 mi s. [L] [D]

## TWO SENORITAS · 903/572-5057

♦♦ Tex-Mex. Casual Dining. $7-$16 **AAA Inspector Notes:** This restaurant is part of a small East Texas chain. The menu features such standards as enchiladas, chimichangas, fajitas and chile rellenos. A small selection of American cuisine also is available. **Features:** full bar, patio dining. **Address:** 2601 W Ferguson Rd 75455 **Location:** I-30 exit 160, just n. [L] [D] [icon]

# MOUNT VERNON · pop. 2,662

## SUPER 8 OF MOUNT VERNON · (903)588-2882

♦♦♦ Hotel $60-$90

**Address:** 401 W I-30 75457 **Location:** I-30 exit 147; on eastbound frontage road. **Facility:** 43 units. 2 stories (no elevator), exterior corridors. **Guest Services:** coin laundry. **Featured Amenity:** continental breakfast.

[icons]

# MUENSTER · pop. 1,544

## THE CENTER RESTAURANT & TAVERN · 940/759-2910

♦♦ German. Casual Dining. $8-$18 **AAA Inspector Notes:** You'll find authentic cuisine and décor here, but the restaurant also features American fare and homemade pizza. **Features:** full bar. **Address:** 603 E Hwy 82 76252 **Location:** E on US 82; between Mesquite and Sycamore sts. [B] [L] [D] [icon]

# MULESHOE · (C-4) pop. 5,158, elev. 3,769'

Muleshoe derived its name from a ranch of the same name. Ranches such as the Muleshoe, the Matador and the XIT represented large cattle syndicates that covered millions of acres on the High Plains in the late 19th century. The blizzard of 1888 spurred the demise of these ranches, which were eventually replaced by farms.

**Muleshoe Chamber of Commerce:** 115 E. American Blvd., P.O. Box 356, Muleshoe, TX 79347. **Phone:** (806) 272-4248.

**MULESHOE NATIONAL WILDLIFE REFUGE** is 20 mi. s. on SR 214 to CR 1248. The refuge encompasses 6,449 acres of rolling grasslands surrounding three lakes. From October to March the area has one of the country's largest concentrations of sandhill cranes. A favorite roosting area is Paul's Lake. During a wet year, waterfowl descend on the refuge, joining the cranes and resident prairie dogs. **Hours:** Daily 24 hours. **Cost:** Free. **Phone:** (806) 946-3341. [icons]

## IRISH INN AND SUITES · 806/272-4500

♦♦ Hotel. Rates not provided. **Address:** 104 E 6th St 79347 **Location:** Jct US 70/84, 0.5 mi e. **Facility:** 30 units, some efficiencies. 1 story, interior corridors. **Guest Services:** coin laundry.

[icons]

**NACOGDOCHES** (E-10) pop. 32,996,
elev. 283'
• **Restaurants p. 424**

Texas' oldest town, Nacogdoches (Nak-a-DOE-chez) was named for the region's earliest inhabitants, a Caddo Indian tribe. Hernando de Soto's lieutenant probably visited the area en route to Mexico 1541-42, after de Soto's death. The expedition of René-Robert Cavelier, Sieur de La Salle, documented the settlement in 1687.

A Spanish mission was built among the Nacogdoche Indians in 1716 by Father Margil, who founded the Mission of Our Lady of the Guadalupe of Nacogdoches. Finding the upkeep of the mission too costly, Spain recalled its subjects to San Antonio in 1772, removing many settlers by force. A group led by Antonio Gil Y'Barbo returned to the abandoned mission in 1779, and Nacogdoches was granted the official designation of *pueblo*, or town.

Serving as Spanish lieutenant governor, Y'Barbo built a stone house that served as the local seat of government and business until its demolition in 1902. A replica of the Stone Fort, as it came to be known, was built for the Texas Centennial celebration in 1936 *(see Stone Fort Museum attraction listing)*. During the early 1800s, the Stone Fort was the site of three failed attempts to establish a Republic of Texas, giving Nacogdoches the distinction of having nine national flags in its history, as opposed to the six that have flown over Texas.

**Nacogdoches Convention and Visitors Bureau:** 200 E. Main St., Nacogdoches, TX 75961. **Phone:** (936) 564-7351 or (888) 653-3788.

**DURST-TAYLOR HISTORIC HOUSE AND GARDENS** is at 304 North St. One of the oldest homes in the town, the restored house dates back to about 1835 and features porch columns, chimneys and paneled shutters. Guided tours take visitors through the period-furnished house and to the gardens, a blacksmith shop and a smokehouse. **Time:** Allow 30 minutes minimum. **Hours:** Tues.-Sat. 10-4. Closed major holidays. **Cost:** Donations. **Phone:** (936) 560-4443.

**MILLARD'S CROSSING HISTORIC VILLAGE** is at 6020 North St., .5 mi. n. off Loop 224 on US Bus. Rte. 59. The re-created East Texas village contains structures built 1830-1905, including log and framed houses, a school, a chapel and a country store. A 1.5-hour guided tour features a schoolhouse lesson and hands-on activities for children. **Time:** Allow 1 hour, 30 minutes minimum. **Hours:** Mon.-Sat. 9-4, Sun. 1-4. **Cost:** Guided tour $6; $5 (ages 5-11). Self-guiding tour $2; $1 (ages 5-11). **Phone:** (936) 564-6631.

**OAK GROVE CEMETERY** is at the e. end of Hospital St. at 200 Lanana St. Four signers of the Texas Declaration of Independence are buried here. **Hours:** Daily dawn-dusk. **Cost:** Free.

**OLD NACOGDOCHES UNIVERSITY BUILDING** is on Washington Sq. Completed in 1858, this is the only surviving structure of an institution of higher learning chartered by the Republic of Texas. The university building now is a house museum with antique furniture and silver. **Time:** Allow 30 minutes minimum. **Hours:** Tues.-Fri. 1-4, Sat. 10-4. **Cost:** Donations. **Phone:** (936) 569-7292, or (936) 564-7351 for tour information.

**STERNE-HOYA HOUSE MUSEUM/LIBRARY** is at 211 S. Lanana St. Restored sections of the 1830 house, which was built before the Texas Revolution, feature a collection of mid-1800s and 1900s antiques. **Time:** Allow 30 minutes minimum. **Hours:** Tues.-Sat. 10-4. Closed major holidays. **Cost:** Donations. **Phone:** (936) 560-5426.

**STONE FORT MUSEUM** is on the campus of Stephen F. Austin State University at 1808 Alumni Dr. N. Original stones were used in this reproduction of the 1788 Spanish Colonial stone house of Antonio Gil Y'Barbo, founder of Nacogdoches. Changing exhibits interpret the history of East Texas through 1900. Guided tours are offered by appointment. **Time:** Allow 1 hour minimum. **Hours:** Tues.-Sat. 9-5, Sun. 1-5. Closed major holidays. **Cost:** Donations. **Phone:** (936) 468-2408.

**BEST WESTERN INN OF NACOGDOCHES**

(936)560-4900

 Hotel $59-$65

 **AAA Benefit:** Members save 10% or more with Best Western!

 **Address:** 3428 South St 75964 **Location:** US 59, just s of jct Loop 224 and US 59 business route. **Facility:** 60 units. 2 stories (no elevator), exterior corridors. **Terms:** 2 night minimum stay - seasonal. **Pool(s):** outdoor. **Guest Services:** coin laundry. **Featured Amenity:** continental breakfast.

**BEST WESTERN NORTHPARK INN**  (936)560-1906

 Hotel $60-$125

**AAA Benefit:** Members save 10% or more with Best Western!

 **Address:** 4809 NW Stallings Dr 75964 **Location:** Jct US 59 N and Loop 224 exit Westward Dr. **Facility:** 79 units. 72 units. 2 stories (no elevator), exterior corridors. **Pool(s):** outdoor. **Guest Services:** coin laundry.

HAMPTON INN & SUITES  (936)560-9901

Hotel $99-$149 **Address:** 3625 South St 75964 **Location:** US 59, just s of jct Loop 224. **Facility:** 79 units. 3 stories, interior corridors. **Terms:** 1-7 night minimum stay, cancellation fee imposed. **Pool(s):** outdoor. **Activities:** hot tub, exercise room. **Guest Services:** valet and coin laundry.

**AAA Benefit:** Members save up to 10%!

## SUPER 8 NACOGDOCHES  (936)560-2888

Hotel
$59-$129

**Address:** 3909 South St 75964 **Location:** On US 59, just s of jct Loop 224. **Facility:** 60 units, some two bedrooms and kitchens. 3 stories, interior corridors. **Pool(s):** indoor. **Activities:** hot tub, exercise room. **Guest Services:** valet and coin laundry. **Featured Amenity:** continental breakfast.

### WHERE TO EAT

## CLEAR SPRINGS RESTAURANT  936/569-0489

American. Casual Dining. $10-$20 **AAA Inspector Notes:** Next to an old rail depot, the quintessential Texas café has hardwood floors, exposed brick walls, rustic ceilings and antique paraphernalia on the walls. The menu lists favorites such as hand-breaded onion rings, fried pickles and the best fried catfish around. Chicken-fried steak, fish tacos, catfish étouffée, po'boys, Cajun rice and fried oysters also top the list. Don't forget the banana pudding or slice of Key lime pie. Service is friendly and attentive. **Features:** full bar. **Address:** 211 Old Tyler Rd 75961 **Location:** Center. L D

## LA CARRETA MEXICAN RESTAURANT  936/569-2800

Tex-Mex. Casual Dining. $7-$15 **AAA Inspector Notes:** Near Stephen F. Austin University on the main road through town, the restaurant builds its menu on traditional Tex-Mex cuisine. American dishes also share menu space. Combination plates offer options to please just about everyone. Finish off the meal with a free ice cream cone, sopapilla or both. **Features:** full bar, happy hour. **Address:** 3000 North St (US 59 Business) 75961 **Location:** 1 mi n of main entrance to Stephen F. Austin University (Griffith Blvd).

L D

## SZECHUAN CHINESE RESTAURANT  936/569-2266

Chinese. Casual Dining. $7-$20 **AAA Inspector Notes:** Convenient to campus and downtown, the restaurant specializes in Szechuan cuisine. This place is one of the few Chinese restaurants that doesn't offer a buffet. The good selection of dishes is sure to please just about everyone. **Features:** full bar. **Address:** 3308 North St (US 59 Business) 75961 **Location:** 1.1 mi n of main entrance to Stephen F. Austin University (Griffith Blvd). L D

## NASSAU BAY pop. 4,002
• Hotels & Restaurants map & index p. 324
• Part of Houston area — see map p. 301

## COURTYARD BY MARRIOTT NASA/CLEAR LAKE
(281)333-0220  134

Hotel $139-$153 **Address:** 18100 Saturn Ln 77058 **Location:** I-45 exit 24, 3 mi e. Across from NASA Space Center. **Facility:** 124 units. 4 stories, interior corridors. **Pool(s):** outdoor. **Activities:** exercise room. **Guest Services:** valet and coin laundry.

**AAA Benefit:** Members save 5% or more!

## HILTON HOUSTON NASA CLEAR LAKE  (281)333-9300  133

Hotel $99-$209 **Address:** 3000 NASA Pkwy 77058 **Location:** Waterfront. 2 mi e of NASA Bypass road. **Facility:** 242 units. 13 stories, interior corridors. **Terms:** 1-7 night minimum stay, cancellation fee imposed. **Pool(s):** outdoor. **Activities:** exercise room. **Guest Services:** valet laundry, area transportation.

**AAA Benefit:** Members save 5% or more!

## NAVASOTA pop. 7,049

## BEST WESTERN INN OF NAVASOTA  (936)870-4100

Hotel
$80-$200

**AAA Benefit:** Members save 10% or more with Best Western!

**Address:** 8965 Hwy 6 N 77868 **Location:** Jct SR 6 and 90; on southeast corner. **Facility:** 44 units. 2 stories, exterior corridors. **Terms:** 2-3 night minimum stay - seasonal, 3 day cancellation notice-fee imposed. **Pool(s):** outdoor. **Guest Services:** coin laundry. **Featured Amenity:** continental breakfast.

## COMFORT INN & SUITES  (936)825-9464

Hotel $81-$249 **Address:** 9345 State Hwy 6 Loop S 77868 **Location:** SR 6 exit SR 105 and 90, 0.5 mi n on E Frontage Rd. **Facility:** 54 units. 3 stories, interior corridors. **Pool(s):** outdoor. **Activities:** hot tub, exercise room. **Guest Services:** coin laundry.

## NEW BOSTON pop. 4,550

## HOLIDAY INN EXPRESS HOTEL & SUITES  903/628-7805

Hotel. Rates not provided. **Address:** 1018 N Center St 75570 **Location:** I-30 exit 201, just s. **Facility:** 61 units. 3 stories, interior corridors. **Pool(s):** outdoor. **Activities:** hot tub, exercise room. **Guest Services:** coin laundry.

## NEW BRAUNFELS (F-8) pop. 57,740, elev. 637'
• Restaurants p. 427
• Part of San Antonio area — see map p. 458

New Braunfels was one of several towns north of San Antonio settled by Germans, one of the largest groups to immigrate to the new Republic of Texas. Settled in 1845, the town prospered from the region's plentiful water and rich soil, which soon produced a healthy agricultural economy. The city's German heritage and the region's natural beauty currently fuel a thriving tourism industry.

At the heart of the city is the spring-fed Comal River, a playground for inner tube riders and swimmers. The scenic Guadalupe River Road traverses the Hill Country through New Braunfels.

River Road, off SR 46, leads to Sattler and Canyon Dam before returning to the city via Sattler Road, Startzville and SR 46. The centerpiece of this scenic loop is the Guadalupe River Scenic Area, a popular river reserve for canoeing, inner tubing and fishing.

Another highlight is the restored late 19th-century community of Gruene and its historic district, which includes Texas' oldest dance hall as well as several general stores, antique stores, an art gallery and ethnic restaurants.

**New Braunfels Convention and Visitors Bureau:** 390 S. Seguin Ave., P.O. Box 311417, New Braunfels, TX 78131-1417. **Phone:** (830) 625-2385 or (800) 572-2626.

**HERITAGE VILLAGE/MUSEUM OF TEXAS HAND-MADE FURNITURE** is at 1370 Church Hill Dr. The 1858 Breustedt-Dillen house has a collection of furniture handmade by German cabinetmakers during the 1800s. An extensive collection of English ironstone complements the furniture. Other exhibits include a cabinetmaker's shop and tools, a summer kitchen and a restored dogtrot cabin built by one of New Braunfels' original settlers.

**Hours:** Tues.-Sat. 10-2, Sun. 1-4, June-July; Tues.-Sun. 1-4, Sept.-May; by appointment in Aug. and Dec. Last tour begins 30 minutes before closing. Closed major holidays. **Cost:** $5; $4 (ages 62+); $1 (ages 6-12). **Phone:** (830) 629-6504.

**LANDA PARK** is in the northwest section of town at 110 Golf Course Rd. Covering 196 acres, the recreation spot is unusual for Texas because of its tropical greenery. Tubing on the Comal River is a popular pastime, and paddleboats are available on 25-acre Landa Lake. There is a spring-fed swimming pool, an 18-hole golf course, a miniature golf course, a miniature train ride and facilities for fishing. **Hours:** Daily 6 a.m.-midnight. Park office Mon.-Fri. 8-5. **Phone:** (830) 608-2160.

**THE McKENNA CHILDREN'S MUSEUM** is at 801 W. San Antonio St. Interactive educational exhibits focus on science, history, geography, technology and art. Children learn about space exploration in Destination Space!, shop and work in a grocery store, do chores and learn about animals on Lend-A-Hand Ranch, treat patients in a hospital, and more. The Town Square exhibit features a bank, local newspaper, hardware store and construction site.

**Hours:** Mon.-Sat. 10-5. Closed Jan. 1, Easter, Memorial Day, July 4, Labor Day, Thanksgiving and Christmas. **Cost:** Memorial Day-Labor Day $7.50; free (under 1). Rest of year $5.50; free (under 1). **Phone:** (830) 606-9525. 🍴

**NEW BRAUNFELS CONSERVATION SOCIETY** is .5 mi. w. jct. I-35 and SR 46 at 1300 Church Hill Dr. Guided tours of the area's restored historic buildings are offered. Tours begin at Conservation Plaza and include a rose conservatory, a one-room school, a general store, a music studio, a saloon, a two-story pioneer house, a cabinetmaker's shop and house, and log cabins. **Hours:** Tues.-Fri. 10-2:30, Sat.-Sun. 2-4. **Cost:** $2.50; 50c (ages 6-18). **Phone:** (830) 629-2943.

**SCHLITTERBAHN WATERPARK RESORT** is at 305 W. Austin St. The 65-acre water park features 40 water attractions, including 17 waterslides, inner tube chutes, hot tubs, tubing rivers, a six-story uphill water coaster, black tunnel slides and children's water playgrounds. The park includes volleyball and picnic facilities.

Glass containers and alcohol are prohibited. **Hours:** Open daily at 10, mid-May to mid-Aug.; Sat.-Sun. at 10, late Apr. to mid-May and late Aug. to mid-Sept. Closing times vary between 6 and 8 p.m. **Cost:** $49.99; $39.99 (ages 3-11 and 55+). Admission after 3:30 p.m. for 8 p.m. closing or 2 p.m. for earlier closing $35.99; $28.99 (ages 3-11). Prices may vary; phone ahead. **Phone:** (830) 625-2351.
🍴 🏊

**SOPHIENBURG MUSEUM AND ARCHIVES** is at 401 W. Coll St. Prince Carl of Solms-Braunfels built a log fortress on this hilltop site. Displays include many of the nobleman's personal effects, Native American artifacts and household items of the pioneer era. Among the museum's highlights are the re-created bakery, pharmacy and barber shop. Archive documents highlight European immigration and settlement in Texas and the American southwest.

**Time:** Allow 30 minutes minimum. **Hours:** Tues.-Sat. 10-4. Closed major holidays. **Cost:** Archives $10; $1 (ages 0-18). Museum $5; $2 (ages 13-18); $1 (ages 6-12). **Phone:** (830) 629-1572.

**BAYMONT INN**                    (830)608-0334

Hotel
$69-$169

**Address:** 979 I-35 N 78130 **Location:** I-35 exit 189 (SR 46); on southbound access road. Located in a commercial area. **Facility:** 61 units. 2 stories, interior corridors. **Pool(s):** outdoor. **Activities:** hot tub, exercise room. **Guest Services:** coin laundry. **Featured Amenity:** continental breakfast.

**BEST WESTERN INN & SUITES**            (830)625-7337

Hotel
$70-$170

 **AAA Benefit:** Members save 10% or more with Best Western!

**Address:** 1493 I-35 N 78130 **Location:** I-35 exit 190; on southbound frontage road. Located in a quiet area. **Facility:** 61 units. 2 stories (no elevator), interior/exterior corridors. **Terms:** 2 night minimum stay - seasonal. **Pool(s):** outdoor. **Activities:** hot tub. **Guest Services:** coin laundry.

**COMFORT SUITES**                    (830)643-1100

💎💎 Hotel $75-$190 **Address:** 1489 I-35 N 78130 **Location:** I-35 exit 190; on southbound frontage road. Located in a quiet area. **Facility:** 62 units. 2 stories (no elevator), interior corridors. **Pool(s):** outdoor. **Activities:** hot tub, exercise room. **Guest Services:** valet and coin laundry.

## DAYS INN (830)608-0004

Motel
$60-$150

**Address:** 963 N IH-35 78130 **Location:** I-35 exit 189 (SR 46); on southbound frontage road. **Facility:** 60 units. 2 stories, exterior corridors. **Terms:** 2 night minimum stay - seasonal and/or weekends. **Amenities:** safes. **Pool(s):** outdoor. **Activities:** hot tub, exercise room. **Guest Services:** coin laundry. **Featured Amenity:** continental breakfast.

---

## ECONO LODGE INN & SUITES (830)625-2230

Hotel $70-$190 **Address:** 1254 FM 1101 78130 **Location:** I-35 exit 189, just s on SR 46. **Facility:** 50 units. 3 stories, interior corridors. **Pool(s):** outdoor. **Activities:** hot tub, exercise room. **Guest Services:** coin laundry.

---

## EXECUTIVE INN & SUITES (830)625-3932

Motel $44-$179 **Address:** 808 Hwy 46 S 78130 **Location:** I-35 exit 189, 0.4 mi e. **Facility:** 34 units. 2 stories (no elevator), exterior corridors. **Pool(s):** outdoor. **Activities:** hot tub. **Guest Services:** coin laundry.

---

## FAIRFIELD INN & SUITES BY MARRIOTT NEW BRAUNFELS (830)626-3133

Hotel
$89-$199

FAIRFIELD INN & SUITES Marriott

**AAA Benefit:** Members save 5% or more!

**Address:** 1465 IH-35 N 78130 **Location:** I-35 exit 190; on southbound frontage road. **Facility:** 89 units. 4 stories, interior corridors. **Parking:** no self-parking. **Pool(s):** heated indoor. **Activities:** hot tub, exercise room. **Guest Services:** valet and coin laundry. **Featured Amenity:** full hot breakfast.

---

## GRUENE APPLE BED & BREAKFAST 830/643-1234

Bed & Breakfast
Rates not provided

**Address:** 1235 Gruene Rd 78130 **Location:** I-35 exit 189 (SR 46), 1.6 mi w to Common St, just n to Gruene Rd, then 1.3 mi w; in Historic Gruene District. **Facility:** On a bluff overlooking the Guadalupe River, this B&B offers luxurious accommodations. The spacious manicured grounds feature a large fountain, and public areas are elegant and refined. 14 units. 2 stories, interior corridors. **Terms:** check-in 4 pm, age restrictions may apply. **Amenities:** safes. **Pool(s):** outdoor. **Activities:** hot tub, fishing.

## Savings for Your Inner Child

Show Your Card & Save

AAA.com/searchfordiscounts

---

## HAMPTON INN & SUITES NEW BRAUNFELS (830)608-0123

Hotel $119-$199 **Address:** 575 Hwy 46 S 78130 **Location:** I-35 exit 189 (SR 46), just e. **Facility:** 87 units. 4 stories, interior corridors. **Terms:** 1-7 night minimum stay, cancellation fee imposed. **Pool(s):** outdoor. **Activities:** hot tub, exercise room. **Guest Services:** valet and coin laundry.

**AAA Benefit:** Members save up to 10%!

---

## THE LAMB'S REST INN (830)609-3932

Bed & Breakfast $160-$260 **Address:** 1385 Edwards Blvd 78132 **Location:** Waterfront. I-35 exit 189 (SR 46), 3 mi w to River Rd, 0.4 mi n to Edwards Blvd, then 1.2 mi e. **Facility:** There is much to do at this property on the banks of the Guadalupe River, including sunning on the deck, sipping tea on the back porch or floating on an inner tube. 7 units, some two bedrooms, kitchens and cottages. 2 stories (no elevator), interior/exterior corridors. **Terms:** check-in 4 pm, 2 night minimum stay - weekends, age restrictions may apply, 7 day cancellation notice-fee imposed. **Pool(s):** outdoor. **Activities:** hot tub, fishing.

---

## LA QUINTA INN & SUITES NEW BRAUNFELS (830)627-3333

Hotel $99-$188 **Address:** 365 Hwy 46 S 78130 **Location:** I-35 exit 189 (SR 46), just e. **Facility:** 75 units. 3 stories, interior corridors. **Pool(s):** outdoor. **Activities:** hot tub, exercise room. **Guest Services:** valet and coin laundry.

---

## MICROTEL INN & SUITES BY WYNDHAM (830)557-4409

Hotel
$60-$170

**Address:** 1175 N Business IH 35 78130 **Location:** I-35 exit 189 (SR 46), just w. **Facility:** 65 units. 3 stories, interior corridors. **Pool(s):** outdoor. **Guest Services:** coin laundry. **Featured Amenity:** continental breakfast.

---

## QUALITY INN & SUITES (830)643-9300

Hotel $59-$360 **Address:** 1533 IH-35 N 78130 **Location:** I-35 exit 190; on southbound frontage road. Located in a quite area at northern edge of town. **Facility:** 71 units. 3 stories, interior corridors. **Amenities:** safes. **Pool(s):** indoor. **Activities:** hot tub, exercise room. **Guest Services:** coin laundry.

---

## RAMADA NEW BRAUNFELS (830)625-8017

Hotel
$80-$200

**Address:** 1051 I-35 E 78130 **Location:** I-35 exit 189 (SR 46); on southbound frontage road. **Facility:** 139 units. 2 stories (no elevator), exterior corridors. **Pool(s):** outdoor. **Activities:** exercise room. **Guest Services:** valet and coin laundry.

---

## SLEEP INN & SUITES (830)625-7700

Hotel $59-$266 **Address:** 1477 N IH-35 78130 **Location:** I-35 exit 190; on southbound frontage road. **Facility:** 57 units. 3 stories, interior corridors. **Pool(s):** outdoor. **Activities:** hot tub, exercise room. **Guest Services:** valet and coin laundry.

## SUPER 8-NEW BRAUNFELS (830)629-1155

Motel
$60-$220

**Address:** 510 Hwy 46 S 78130 **Location:** I-35 exit 189 (SR 46), just e. Located in a commercial area. **Facility:** 50 units. 2 stories (no elevator), exterior corridors. **Pool(s):** outdoor. **Activities:** hot tub. **Guest Services:** coin laundry. **Featured Amenity:** continental breakfast.

## WINGATE BY WYNDHAM (830)515-4701

Hotel
$84-$149

**Address:** 245 FM 306 N 78130 **Location:** I-35 exit 191 (FM 306), just w. Located in a quiet country setting just north of town. **Facility:** 72 units. 4 stories, interior corridors. **Amenities:** safes. **Pool(s):** heated indoor. **Activities:** hot tub, exercise room. **Guest Services:** coin laundry. **Featured Amenity:** full hot breakfast.

## HILTON GARDEN INN NEW BRAUNFELS 830/620-4200

[fyi] Not evaluated. **Address:** 1501 IH-35 N 78130 **Location:** I-35 exit 190; on southbound frontage road. Facilities, services, and décor characterize a mid-scale property.

**AAA Benefit:** Members save up to 10%!

**WHERE TO EAT**

## GRISTMILL RIVER RESTAURANT & BAR 830/625-0684

Regional American. Casual Dining. $9-$20 **AAA Inspector Notes:** *Historic.* Located inside a 19th-century grist mill, this eatery serves traditional foods like beef, chicken and fish. Chopped steak con queso and the slab-cut fries are the house specialty. The courtyard is perfect for sunset dining. **Features:** full bar. **Address:** 1287 Gruene Rd 78130 **Location:** I-35 exit 188, 2 mi w, follow signs; in Historic Gruene District. [L] [D]

## HUISACHE GRILL 830/620-9001

American. Casual Dining. $10-$25 **AAA Inspector Notes:** This eatery's influences can be seen in offerings such as seafood chowders, charbroiled chicken merida and grilled portobello mushroom sandwich. **Features:** beer & wine. **Address:** 303 W San Antonio St 78130 **Location:** I-35 exit 187 (Seguin Ave), just s of main plaza. [L] [D]

## MCADOO'S SEAFOOD COMPANY 830/629-3474

Seafood. Fine Dining. $10-$28 **AAA Inspector Notes:** Housed in a historic former post office, this popular spot features a wide variety of fresh seafood, chowders, fillets and multiple options of fresh and cooked oyster dishes. **Features:** full bar, happy hour. **Address:** 196 N Castell Ave 78130 **Location:** Just s of San Antonio St. **Parking:** street only. [L] [D]

## OMAS HAUS 830/625-3280

German. Casual Dining. $12-$22 **AAA Inspector Notes:** Potato pancakes, chicken or pork schnitzel with lumpy applesauce and tangy red cabbage and other Bavarian favorites are served in this German-style home from the early 1900s. Homemade sliced rye is served with a sausage sampler that includes knockwurst, bratwurst and kielbasa. The ultimate finish is a thick slice of German chocolate cake. **Features:** beer & wine. **Address:** 541 Hwy 46 S 78130 **Location:** I-35 exit 180, just e. [L] [D]

## SCHOBELS RESTAURANT 830/626-2200

American. Casual Dining. $9-$15 **AAA Inspector Notes:** The restaurant offers a daily changing buffet as well as à la carte selections, both with prices for kids under 12. Specialties in the large and modern dining room include Jägerschnitzel and roladen steak. A wide variety of vegetables is available. **Features:** full bar. **Address:** 1515 Kuehler Ave 78130 **Location:** I-35 exit 187 (Seguin Ave), just e. [L] [D]

**NEW CANEY**

## BEST WESTERN PLUS NEW CANEY INN & SUITES (281)354-7222

Hotel
$85-$139

**AAA Benefit:** Members save 10% or more with Best Western!

**Address:** 22033 N Hwy 59 77357 **Location:** US 59 northbound exit Community Dr, just e; southbound exit FM 1314, make U-turn. **Facility:** 49 units. 3 stories, interior corridors. **Pool(s):** outdoor. **Activities:** hot tub, exercise room. **Guest Services:** coin laundry. **Featured Amenity:** breakfast buffet.

## LA QUINTA INN & SUITES-NEW CANEY (281)354-1904

Hotel
$99-$134

**Address:** 22025 US Hwy 59 77357 **Location:** US 59 northbound exit Community Dr, just e; exit FM 1314 southbound, U-turn 1 mi n. **Facility:** 55 units. 3 stories, interior corridors. **Pool(s):** outdoor. **Activities:** hot tub, exercise room. **Guest Services:** valet and coin laundry. **Featured Amenity:** full hot breakfast.

## NEWCASTLE (C-7) pop. 585, elev. 1,126'

Petroleum production and agriculture have replaced coal mining in Newcastle, a town named after the English coal-mining city.

**FORT BELKNAP** is 3 mi. s. on FM 61. Once on the Overland-Butterfield Stage route, this 1851 outpost played an important part in defending the frontier. Seven original buildings are restored; two are small museums, and a third houses the county archives. **Hours:** Mon.-Tues. and Thurs.-Sat. 9-5, Sun. 1:30-5. **Cost:** Free. **Phone:** (940) 846-3222.

## NORTH RICHLAND HILLS pop. 63,343

- Restaurants p. 428
- Hotels & Restaurants map & index p. 257

## BEST WESTERN N.E. MALL INN & SUITES (817)656-8881 [37]

Hotel
$80-$100

**AAA Benefit:** Members save 10% or more with Best Western!

**Address:** 8709 Airport Frwy 76180 **Location:** SR 121/183 exit Precinct Line Rd eastbound; exit Bedford Euless Rd westbound; on westbound frontage road. **Facility:** 85 units, some efficiencies. 2 stories (no elevator), exterior corridors. **Pool(s):** outdoor. **Activities:** hot tub, exercise room. **Guest Services:** complimentary and valet laundry, area transportation. **Featured Amenity:** full hot breakfast.

(See map & index p. 257.)

(See map & index p. 257.)

## WHERE TO EAT

GRANDY'S RESTAURANT                    817/581-0667

◆ American. Quick Serve. $4-$8 **AAA Inspector Notes:** Fried chicken and country-fried steak are menu standbys at the restaurant, a regional franchise. They also offer a family-style dining menu. The décor is a step up from that of most quick-serve eateries and more resembles that of a conventional restaurant. Some elements of increased service include additional rolls, iced tea refills and tray removal. **Address:** 5205 Rufe Snow Dr 76118 **Location:** I-820 exit 20B, just n. B L D

## OAK RIDGE NORTH pop. 3,049
• Part of Houston area — see map p. 301

PALLOTTA'S ITALIAN GRILL                281/364-9555

◆◆ Italian. Casual Dining. $8-$24 **AAA Inspector Notes:** Casual, upscale and professional, this eatery surrounds its guests with an elegant, artsy décor that resounds with fine jazz music. Try the house specialty, chicken a la Pallotta in a rich cream and mushroom sauce. **Features:** full bar. **Address:** 27606 I-45 N 77385 **Location:** I-45 exit 76 (Robinson Rd/Woodlands Pkwy) southbound; exit 77 (Research Forest Dr/Tamina Rd) northbound; in Woodridge Plaza.

L D ◆

## ODESSA (D-4) pop. 99,940, elev. 2,891'

In 1881 Russian railroad laborers named Odessa after their homeland, which the wide, flat prairie resembled. By Texas standards, Odessa was a tame cow town, primarily because local Methodists outlawed saloons until 1898; the first bar was opened by the sheriff. The discovery of oil in 1926 brought prosperity and a population boom; by World War II, Odessa was one of the world's largest inland petroleum complexes.

After his graduation from Yale, George Herbert Walker Bush moved to Odessa in 1948 to work in the oil fields, bringing his wife and 2-year-old son George W. with him. The family lived in the Odessa-Midland area for 11 years.

The second largest known meteor crater in the United States is 8 miles west of the city, between I-20 and US 80. The world's largest known hare, the 8-foot Odessa Jackrabbit statue, is located at the corner of 8th and Sam Houston streets.

The Globe Theater, 2308 Shakespeare Rd. on the Odessa College campus, is a replica of Shakespeare's original playhouse. Community and professional productions are staged in the theater; tours are offered by appointment for a fee. Phone (432) 332-1586 or (432) 580-3177.

The Parker House Museum, 1118 Maple Ave., features photographs, documents and other memorabilia; phone (432) 335-9918.

**Odessa Convention and Visitors Bureau:** 700 N. Grant Ave., Suite 200, Odessa, TX 79761. **Phone:** (432) 333-7871 or (800) 780-4678.

**ELLEN NOËL ART MUSEUM** is off I-20 exit 121, then 1.3 mi. n. to 4909 E. University Blvd. near the U.T. Permian Basin campus. Three galleries feature 12-17 permanent and changing exhibits ranging from the Renaissance period to the present day and include such media as paintings, ceramics, prints, photography and sculpture. An outdoor sensory garden features bronze sculptures and fragrant herb beds for the visually impaired. The Art Haus is a special place for children to explore art.

**Time:** Allow 30 minutes minimum. **Hours:** Tues.-Sat. 10-5, Sun. 2-5. **Cost:** Donations. **Phone:** (432) 550-9696.

**THE ODESSA METEOR CRATER AND MUSEUM** is off I-20 exit 108, following signs. The meteor crater, formed by a meteor shower an estimated 63,000 years ago, measures 500 feet in diameter and 15 feet in depth. The museum contains exhibits about meteorites and historical videos. **Time:** Allow 30 minutes minimum. **Hours:** Tues.-Sat. 10-5, Sun. 1-5. Closed major holidays. **Cost:** Donations. **Phone:** (432) 381-0946.

**THE PRESIDENTIAL ARCHIVES AND LEADERSHIP LIBRARY** is off I-20 exit 121 (Loop 338), then 1.3 mi. n. to 4919 E. University Blvd. on the U.T. Permian Basin campus. Exhibits and educational programs are designed to provide a better understanding of the American presidency, campaigns and election procedures. Permanent displays include campaign memorabilia, documents and first ladies' inaugural gowns in miniature. Adjacent to the museum is the first Odessa home of George H.W. and George W. Bush. **Time:** Allow 1 hour minimum. **Hours:** Tues.-Sat. 10-5. Closed major holidays. **Cost:** $5; $3 (students with ID). **Phone:** (432) 363-7737. Ⓐ

BEST WESTERN GARDEN OASIS          (432)337-3006

Hotel
$225

**AAA Benefit:** Members save 10% or more with Best Western!

**Address:** 110 W I-20 79761 **Location:** Jct I-20 and US 385 exit 116, just w. **Facility:** 118 units. 2 stories (no elevator); interior/exterior corridors. **Pool(s):** heated indoor. **Activities:** sauna, hot tub, game room, exercise room. **Guest Services:** valet and coin laundry.

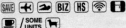

COMFORT INN & SUITES ODESSA        (432)332-0614

◆◆◆ Hotel $209-$229 **Address:** 801 S JBS Pkwy 79766 **Location:** I-20 exit 120, just ne. **Facility:** 79 units. 3 stories, interior corridors. **Pool(s):** outdoor. **Activities:** exercise room. **Guest Services:** valet and coin laundry.

CALL ⬛ ⬛ ⬛ ⬛ ⬛ ⬛ ⬛ ⬛ ⬛

COMFORT SUITES                     (432)362-1500

◆◆◆ Hotel $119-$400 **Address:** 4801 E 50th St 79762 **Location:** Jct JBS Pkwy and 42nd St, 0.5 mi n. **Facility:** 56 units. 3 stories, interior corridors. **Pool(s):** outdoor. **Activities:** exercise room. **Guest Services:** valet and coin laundry.

⬛ CALL ⬛ ⬛ ⬛ ⬛ ⬛ ⬛ ⬛ ⬛
/ SOME UNITS

## FAIRFIELD INN & SUITES BY MARRIOTT (432)363-1900

▼▼▼ **Hotel** $129-$350 **Address:** 3933 JBS Pkwy 79762 **Location:** I-20 exit 121, n to University Blvd, w to JBS Pkwy, then 0.5 mi n. **Facility:** 67 units. 3 stories, interior corridors. **Pool(s):** outdoor. **Activities:** exercise room. **Guest Services:** valet and coin laundry.

**AAA Benefit:** Members save 5% or more!

CALL 🛎️M 🛏️ BIZ HS 🛜 ❌ 🍴 🖥️ ☕

## HAMPTON INN (432)363-2900

▼▼▼ **Hotel** $144-$399 **Address:** 3923 JBS Pkwy 79762 **Location:** Jct University Blvd and JBS Pkwy, 0.5 mi n. **Facility:** 71 units. 3 stories, interior corridors. **Terms:** 1-7 night minimum stay, cancellation fee imposed. **Pool(s):** outdoor. **Activities:** exercise room. **Guest Services:** valet and coin laundry.

**AAA Benefit:** Members save up to 10%!

🍴➕ CALL 🛎️M 🛏️ BIZ HS 🛜 🍴 🖥️ ☕

## HILTON GARDEN INN ODESSA 432/366-5800

▼▼▼ **Hotel.** Rates not provided. **Address:** 5221 JBS Pkwy 79762 **Location:** Jct JBS Pkwy and N 52nd St, just n. **Facility:** 99 units. 3 stories, interior corridors. **Pool(s):** heated outdoor. **Activities:** hot tub, exercise room. **Guest Services:** valet and coin laundry.

**AAA Benefit:** Members save up to 10%!

✈️ 🍴 🍸 CALL 🛎️M 🛏️ BIZ HS 🛜 ❌ 🍴 🖥️ ☕

## HOLIDAY INN EXPRESS & SUITES ODESSA (432)362-6800

▼▼▼ **Hotel** $199-$329 **Address:** 5321 JBS Pkwy 79762 **Location:** Jct JBS Pkwy and N 52nd St, just n. **Facility:** 95 units. 3 stories, interior corridors. **Terms:** 3 day cancellation notice-fee imposed, resort fee. **Pool(s):** outdoor. **Activities:** hot tub, exercise room. **Guest Services:** valet and coin laundry.

🍴➕ CALL 🛎️M 🛏️ BIZ HS 🛜 ❌ 🍴 🖥️ ☕

## MICROTEL INN & SUITES BY WYNDHAM (432)614-4780

▼▼ ▼▼
Hotel
$170-$179

**Address:** 4300 E 50th St 79762 **Location:** Just sw of jct SR 191 and JBS Pkwy. **Facility:** 79 units. 3 stories, interior corridors. **Pool(s):** outdoor. **Activities:** exercise room. **Guest Services:** coin laundry. **Featured Amenity:** full hot breakfast.

SAVE 🍴➕ 🛏️ BIZ 🛜 ❌ 🍴 🖥️ ☕ /SOME UNITS 🐑

## TOWNEPLACE SUITES BY MARRIOTT (432)362-1077

▼▼▼ **Extended Stay Hotel** $118-$269 **Address:** 4412 Tanglewood Ln 79762 **Location:** Just n of jct JBS Pkwy and 42nd St. **Facility:** 108 efficiencies. 4 stories, interior corridors. **Pool(s):** heated outdoor. **Activities:** exercise room. **Guest Services:** valet and coin laundry.

**AAA Benefit:** Members save 5% or more!

🍴➕ CALL 🛎️M 🛏️ BIZ HS 🛜 ❌ 🍴 🖥️ ☕ /SOME UNITS 🐑

---

WHERE TO EAT

## THE BARN DOOR 432/337-4142

▼▼▼ Steak. Casual Dining. $8-$35 **AAA Inspector Notes:** Built in 1963, the newly remodeled building, which resembles a rustic barn, adjoins a historic train depot that serves as a bar. Complimentary homemade soup and bread are served with lunch in the saloon-style dining room. **Features:** full bar. **Address:** 2140 N Andrews Hwy 79761 **Location:** I-20 exit 116, 4 mi n; just s of University Blvd.

L D CALL 🛎️M

## HARRIGAN'S BAR & GRILL 432/617-8300

▼▼▼ Steak Seafood. Casual Dining. $9-$25 **AAA Inspector Notes:** The varied menu includes salads, burgers, steaks, seafood and Southern-style entrées. Prime rib is available after 5. The hot skillet apple pie a la mode is recommended for dessert. **Features:** full bar, Sunday brunch. **Address:** 2701 JBS Pkwy 79762 **Location:** Jct JBS Pkwy and University Blvd; on northwest corner.

L D CALL 🛎️M

## ZUCCHI'S RISTORANTE ITALIANO 432/550-7443

▼▼▼ Northern Italian. Fine Dining. $6-$30 **AAA Inspector Notes:** Diners can taste the treats from a nice selection of antipasto, gourmet pizzas, pasta dishes and entrées featuring chicken, salmon, fillet of beef and veal. Chops are also available. **Features:** full bar. **Address:** 1541 JBS Pkwy 79761 **Location:** I-20 exit 121, n to Business Rt I-20, 0.4 mi w to JBS Pkwy, then 0.8 mi n; in Old Town Shopping Center. L D CALL 🛎️M

# ORANGE (F-11) pop. 18,595, elev. 10'
• Hotels p. 430

Established in 1836, Orange's inland harbor, connected to the Gulf of Mexico by the Sabine-Neches waterway, was once frequented by Jean Lafitte's pirates. The port also was the berth of the Navy's Texas Group, Atlantic Reserve Fleet.

The First Presbyterian Church at 902 W. Green Ave. was completed in 1912. The copper-domed Greek Revival building features a beautiful collection of stained glass windows and an impressive 36-foot stained glass inner dome depicting 16 angels; phone (409) 883-2097.

**Orange Convention & Visitors Bureau:** 803 Green Ave., P.O. Box 520, Orange, TX 77631-0520. **Phone:** (409) 883-1011 or (800) 528-4906.

**STARK MUSEUM OF ART** is at 712 Green Ave. Five galleries chronicle the land, wildlife and people of the West. Among the exhibits are Audubon prints, works by members of the Taos Society of Artists, bronzes by Frederic Remington and Charles Russell and items crafted by tribes of the Great Plains and Southwest. Also displayed are Steuben crystal and Doughty porcelain. **Time:** Allow 1 hour, 30 minutes minimum. **Hours:** Tues.-Sat. 9-5. Closed major holidays. **Cost:** $6; $5 (ages 10-17, ages 65+ and students with ID); $2 (ages 4-9). **Phone:** (409) 886-2787.

**THE W.H. STARK HOUSE** is at 610 W. Main St. This restored three-story Victorian mansion was built in 1894. The 15 rooms, nine of which have fireplaces, are furnished with original Stark family pieces, including furniture, rugs, lamps, cut glass, statues and paintings. Manicured grounds surround the building. Tours involve climbing stairs. **Time:** Allow 1 hour minimum. **Hours:** Guided tours Tues.-Sat. 9-4. Last tour begins 30 minutes before closing.

Closed major holidays. **Cost:** $6; $5 (ages 10-17 and 65+). Under 10 are not permitted; ages 10-17 must be with an adult. Reservations are recommended. **Phone:** (409) 883-0871.

**COMFORT INN**                                              (409)745-0400

Hotel
$80-$90

**Address:** 2321 Hwy 62 S 77630 **Location:** I-10 exit 873, just s. **Facility:** 51 units. 4 stories, interior corridors. **Activities:** exercise room. **Guest Services:** valet and coin laundry. **Featured Amenity: full hot breakfast.**

**HOLIDAY INN EXPRESS & SUITES ORANGE**           (409)882-9222

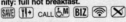

Hotel
$89-$129

**Address:** 2655 I-10 E 77630 **Location:** I-10 exit 877 eastbound; exit 876 westbound; on eastbound frontage road. **Facility:** 73 units. 3 stories, interior corridors. **Pool(s):** outdoor. **Activities:** exercise room. **Guest Services:** valet and coin laundry. **Featured Amenity:** breakfast buffet.

**LA QUINTA INN & SUITES ORANGE**              (409)883-0011

**Hotel** $99-$134 **Address:** 2220 Hwy 62 S 77630 **Location:** I-10 exit 873, just s. **Facility:** 58 units. 3 stories, interior corridors. **Pool(s):** heated indoor. **Activities:** hot tub, exercise room. **Guest Services:** valet and coin laundry.

**SLEEP INN & SUITES**                          (409)745-9393

**Hotel** $73-$90 **Address:** 2245 Hwy 62 S 77630 **Location:** I-10 exit 873, just s. **Facility:** 62 units. 3 stories, interior corridors. **Pool(s):** outdoor. **Activities:** exercise room. **Guest Services:** valet and coin laundry.

## OZONA pop. 3,225

**BEST WESTERN OZONA INN**                     (325)392-3791

Motel
$139-$169

**AAA Benefit:** Members save 10% or more with Best Western!

**Address:** 1307 Ave A 76943 **Location:** I-10 exit 365; on westbound frontage road. **Facility:** 50 units. 2 stories (no elevator), interior/exterior corridors. **Pool(s):** outdoor. **Activities:** exercise room. **Guest Services:** coin laundry.

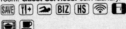

Trust your vehicle to AAA/CAA
Approved Auto Repair facilities

**HILLCREST INN & SUITES**                     (325)392-5515

Motel
$70-$90

**Address:** 1204 Sheffield Rd/Loop 466 W 76943 **Location:** I-10 exit 365, 2 blks n to Loop 466, then 1 mi w. **Facility:** 19 units. 1 story, exterior corridors. **Terms:** cancellation fee imposed. **Guest Services:** coin laundry. **Featured Amenity: continental breakfast.**

**HOLIDAY INN EXPRESS & SUITES OZONA**           325/392-9000

**Hotel.** Rates not provided. **Address:** 1308 Ave E 76943 **Location:** I-10 exit 365; on westbound frontage road. **Facility:** 70 units. 3 stories, interior corridors. **Pool(s):** outdoor. **Activities:** exercise room. **Guest Services:** coin laundry.

**TRAVELODGE OZONA**                           (325)392-2656

Motel
$99-$130

**Address:** 8 11th St 76943 **Location:** I-10 exit 368 westbound, 2 mi w; exit 365 eastbound to Loop 466, 1 mi e. Located in a quiet area. **Facility:** 40 units. 1 story, exterior corridors. **Terms:** cancellation fee imposed. **Amenities:** safes. **Pool(s):** outdoor. **Guest Services:** coin laundry. **Featured Amenity: full hot breakfast.**

# PADRE ISLAND NATIONAL SEASHORE
(H-8)

Padre Island National Seashore is parallel to the Gulf coast and reached via the JFK causeway at Corpus Christi. The national seashore covers 70 miles of 113-mile Padre Island, considered the longest undeveloped barrier island in the world. Some 600 species of plants and wildflowers can be found on the sand-duned strip of land, which is only .5 to 3 miles wide. To the east lies the Gulf and to the west the Laguna Madre, including a portion of the Intracoastal Waterway. On the Laguna Madre side lies the park's Bird Island Basin, a highly regarded and popular windsurfing spot.

In 1519, when the first Spanish fleet sailed along the shore, the island was peopled by the Karankawa Indians. Padre Island became infamous as a graveyard for ships blown onto the island during storms. Around 1804, Padre Nicholas Balli, for whom the island was named, used it for his ranching operation, the first permanent European settlement on the island.

Causeways at Corpus Christi and Port Isabel connect both ends of the island to the mainland, but there is no through road; a paved road extends for only 6 miles within the national seashore and a channel separates the two islands. There is no crossing for people or vehicles over the channel. Picnicking, sportfishing, camping and driving are allowed on the seashore, except for a 4.5-mile stretch at Malaquite Beach reserved for pedestrian traffic. The Malaquite Beach Visitor Center presents interpretive naturalist programs daily. Food is available.

Seashore open daily 24 hours. Visitor center open daily 9-5; closed Christmas. Admission, valid for 7 days, is $10 per private vehicle; $5 per person arriving by commercial vehicle, on foot or by bicycle. Phone (361) 949-8068. *See Recreation Areas Chart.*

## PAINT ROCK (E-6) pop. 273, elev. 1,631'

Paint Rock, founded in 1879, is named for the historic pictographs found on limestone cliffs bordering the nearby Concho River. These pictures are the remnants of once prosperous Native American settlements and nomads; archeologists surmise that some date from the prehistoric era.

**PAINT ROCK EXCURSIONS** departs .5 mi. n.w. on US 83. Guided 90-minute tours explore pictographs found along a nearby rock bluff. Most of the early paintings were made by nomadic tribes, while others may have been created by more permanent settlers such as Comanches and Apaches. **Hours:** Tours depart daily by appointment (weather permitting). Phone ahead to confirm schedule. **Cost:** $6; $3 (ages 5-18). There is a $15 minimum tour charge. Reservations are recommended. **Phone:** (325) 732-4376.

## PALESTINE (E-9) pop. 18,712, elev. 510'

In the 1840s it was discovered that the seat of Anderson County, Houston (not the major city of Harris County), was 2 miles off center. Literally obeying the legislature's guidelines that a county seat be at the center of the county, local residents constructed Palestine.

Pronounced "palas-teen," the town has old-fashioned charm, with Victorian and pioneer houses dating from 1849. The business area has preserved many of its original buildings.

**Palestine Convention and Visitors Bureau:** 825 W. Spring St., Palestine, TX 75801. **Phone:** (903) 723-3014 or (800) 659-3484.

### BEST WESTERN PALESTINE INN          (903)723-4655

Hotel
$84-$159

**AAA Benefit:** Members save 10% or more with Best Western!

**Address:** 1601 W Palestine Ave 75801 **Location:** Jct US 287/SR 19, 0.7 mi sw on US 79. **Facility:** 66 units. 1-2 stories (no elevator), exterior corridors. **Pool(s):** outdoor. **Guest Services:** coin laundry.

### COMFORT SUITES          (903)723-0284

Hotel $79-$109 **Address:** 301 Willow Creek Pkwy 75801 **Location:** 1.6 mi e of US 79 and Loop 256. **Facility:** 66 units. 3 stories, interior corridors. **Pool(s):** heated indoor. **Activities:** hot tub, exercise room. **Guest Services:** coin laundry.

### EXPRESS INN & SUITES          (903)729-3151

Motel $60 **Address:** 1100 E Palestine Ave 75801 **Location:** Jct US 79 and Loop 256, 0.4 mi s on US 79. **Facility:** 93 units. 2 stories (no elevator), exterior corridors. **Pool(s):** outdoor. **Activities:** exercise room. **Guest Services:** coin laundry.

### HOLIDAY INN EXPRESS          (903)723-4884

Hotel
$90-$145

**Address:** 1030 E Palestine Ave 75801 **Location:** Jct US 79 and Loop 256, 0.3 mi s on US 79. **Facility:** 62 units. 3 stories, interior corridors. **Terms:** 3 day cancellation notice. **Pool(s):** outdoor. **Activities:** sauna, hot tub, exercise room. **Guest Services:** coin laundry. **Featured Amenity: full hot breakfast.**

### LA QUINTA INN & SUITES PALESTINE          (903)723-1387

Hotel $94-$129 **Address:** 3000 S Loop 256 75801 **Location:** 1.8 mi e of jct US 79 and Loop 256. **Facility:** 60 units. 3 stories, interior corridors. **Pool(s):** outdoor. **Activities:** hot tub, exercise room. **Guest Services:** coin laundry.

## WHERE TO EAT

### BEIJING CHINA BUFFET          903/729-1188

Asian. Casual Dining. $6-$9 **AAA Inspector Notes:** You will find many familiar foods on the large buffet tables. Sushi and grill items also are available. Entrées like sweet and sour chicken, sesame chicken, beef and broccoli, kung pao chicken, lo mein and Mongolian beef, as well as soups and some salads are offered. The décor is bright and family friendly. **Address:** 2734 S Loop 256 75801 **Location:** 0.9 mi sw of jct US 287 and SR 19.

## PAMPA (A-6) pop. 17,994, elev. 3,234'

Founded in 1888 on the Santa Fe Railroad, Pampa was derived from the Spanish word *pampas*, meaning "plains." Recreational activities abound in the city's municipal parks.

**WHITE DEER LAND MUSEUM** is 3 blks. n. of US 60 at 112 S. Cuyler St. The 1916 headquarters of the White Deer Land Company contains 30 rooms and offices furnished in period, Native American artifacts, antiques and the Time-Line History Wall. Of interest is the David F. Barry photograph collection begun in the 1870s. **Time:** Allow 1 hour minimum. **Hours:** Guided tours are given Tues.-Sat. 1-4, Sun. by appointment. Closed major holidays. **Cost:** Donations. **Phone:** (806) 669-8041.

### AMERICINN LODGE & SUITES OF PAMPA          (806)665-4404

Hotel $110-$130 **Address:** 1101 N Hobart St 79065 **Location:** On SR 70; jct Hobart and Somerville sts. **Facility:** 52 units. 2 stories, interior corridors. **Amenities:** safes. **Pool(s):** heated indoor. **Activities:** hot tub, exercise room. **Guest Services:** valet and coin laundry.

## BEST WESTERN NORTHGATE INN (806)665-0926

Hotel
$89-$119

**AAA Benefit:** Members save 10% or more with Best Western!

**Address:** 2831 Perryton Pkwy 79065 **Location:** On SR 70, 3 mi n. **Facility:** 100 units. 2 stories (no elevator), exterior corridors. **Pool(s):** heated outdoor. **Guest Services:** valet and coin laundry.

SAVE ♀▎◈ 🛜 ▤ ▥ ▦
/SOME UNITS 🅂🄼 HS

## HAMPTON INN (806)669-1555

♥♥♥ Hotel $109-$159 **Address:** 2820 N Perryton Pkwy 79065 **Location:** Jct US 60 and SR 70, 3.0 mi n. **Facility:** 81 units. 3 stories, interior corridors. **Terms:** 1-7 night minimum stay, cancellation fee imposed. **Pool(s):** heated indoor. **Activities:** exercise room. **Guest Services:** coin laundry.

**AAA Benefit:**
Members save up to 10%!

♀▎ CALL 🄼 ◈ BIZ HS 🛜 ✕ ▤ ▥ ▦

## HOLIDAY INN EXPRESS & SUITES 806/665-9500

♥♥♥ Hotel. Rates not provided. **Address:** 3119 Perryton Pkwy 79065 **Location:** On SR 70, 3 mi n. **Facility:** 69 units. 3 stories, interior corridors. **Pool(s):** heated indoor. **Activities:** hot tub, exercise room. **Guest Services:** coin laundry.

CALL 🄼 ◈ BIZ HS 🛜 ✕ ▤ ▥ ▦

# PANHANDLE (B-5) pop. 2,452, elev. 3,451'

Aptly named for its location in the state, Panhandle counts wheat, cattle and petroleum products among its commodities.

**CARSON COUNTY SQUARE HOUSE MUSEUM** is 1 mi. n. of jct. US 60 and SR 207 at 501 Elsie St. Thirteen structures at the site include a 24-footsquare house built in the 1880s. Wildlife dioramas and more than 10,000 artifacts are displayed at the museum, which relates the story of 12,000 years of human adaptation to the north Texas plains. On the grounds are two art galleries, a windmill, a church, a barn, a dugout shelter and a railroad exhibit.

**Time:** Allow 1 hour minimum. **Hours:** Mon.-Sat. 9-5, Sun. 1-5. Closed Jan. 1, Easter, Thanksgiving and Christmas. **Cost:** Donations. **Phone:** (806) 537-3524. 🄰

# PANTEGO pop. 2,394

• **Hotels & Restaurants map & index p. 68, 257**

## EL CHICO 817/265-8335 🔢

Tex-Mex
Casual Dining
$7-$16

**AAA Inspector Notes:** Inside and out, the decor of the popular Mexican restaurant is inviting. The menu features traditional favorites such as enchiladas, tacos, burritos and fajitas. The broad menu also lists a few American classics. **Features:** full bar. **Address:** 1549 S Bowen Rd 76013 **Location:** Just s of W Park Row Dr.

L D

# PARIS (C-9) pop. 25,171, elev. 565'

Early settlement was rapid and constant in Lamar County, where Paris is situated. Between 1824,

when John Emberson built the first house along the banks of the Red River, and 1837, when Claiborne Chisum purchased land west of the present city, many families moved to the area from Kentucky, Tennessee, Alabama and Georgia.

The county straddles the ridge of the Red and Sulphur rivers, with their many creeks and tributaries. Furs as well as goods from New Orleans and Shreveport, La., were shipped up the Red River in flatboats and paddle wheelers and then transported overland by wagon and oxcart.

In 1844 the Central National Road of the Republic of Texas was cut through the county, intersecting the city. Markers on US 82 and CR 195 denote the historic route. With the coming of such railroads as the Texas and Pacific in 1876, the Gulf Colorado, the Santa Fe and the Paris and Great Northern in 1888, the Texas Midland in 1895 and the Paris and Mount Pleasant in 1910, the town emerged as a rail center.

John Chisum, a local cattle baron expanded into New Mexico, pioneering cattle trails from Fort Sumner to Las Animas and Tascosa. These routes are known as "Chisum Trails." A monument marks his gravesite at the railroad tracks southwest of town. Twelve miles north is the 8,000-acre Pat Mayse Lake recreation area *(see Recreation Areas Chart)*.

**Paris Visitors and Convention Council:** 8 W. Plaza, Paris, TX 75460. **Phone:** (903) 784-2501 or (800) 727-4789.

**Self-guiding tours:** Maps and brochures for driving tours of Paris and the surrounding countryside are available from the visitors and convention council.

**SAM BELL MAXEY HOUSE STATE HISTORIC SITE** is at 812 S. Church St. The 1868 High Italianate Victorian house was the residence of Sam Bell Maxey, Confederate general and U.S. senator. The home remained in the family for almost a century. Surrounded by landscaped grounds, it contains family heirlooms and Civil War items. **Hours:** Guided tours Tues.-Sun. on the hour 9-4. Last tour departs 1 hour before closing. Closed Jan. 1, Thanksgiving, Christmas Eve, Christmas and Dec. 31. **Cost:** $4; $3 (ages 6-17 and students with ID). **Phone:** (903) 785-5716.

## AMERICAS BEST VALUE INN PARIS (903)785-5566

Hotel
$59-$79

**Address:** 3755 NE Loop 286 75460 **Location:** Jct US 82 and E Loop 286, just n. Located in a commercial area. **Facility:** 77 units. 2 stories (no elevator), exterior corridors. **Pool(s):** outdoor. **Guest Services:** valet and coin laundry. **Featured Amenity:** continental breakfast.

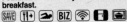

SAVE ♀▎ ◈ BIZ 🛜 ▤ ▥
▦ /SOME UNITS 🅂🄼 HS

## DAYS INN
(903)784-8164

Hotel
$55-$75

**Address:** 2650 N Main St 75460 **Location:** NE Loop 286 exit US 271, just n. **Facility:** 53 units. 2 stories (no elevator), exterior corridors. **Terms:** cancellation fee imposed. **Pool(s):** outdoor. **Featured Amenity: continental breakfast.**

[SAVE] 🚗 [BIZ] 📶 🛗 🍴 💻

## HAMPTON INN OF PARIS
903/784-6536

Hotel
Rates not provided

**AAA Benefit:** Members save up to 10%!

**Address:** 3563 NE Loop 286 75460 **Location:** Jct US 82 and E Loop 286, just n. **Facility:** 67 units. 3 stories, interior corridors. **Amenities:** video games. **Pool(s):** outdoor. **Activities:** hot tub, exercise room. **Guest Services:** valet and coin laundry. **Featured Amenity:** breakfast buffet.

[SAVE] [ii+] CALL [&M] 🚗 [BIZ] [HS] 📶 📹 🛗 🍴 💻

### WHERE TO EAT

## SIRLOIN STOCKADE
903/785-0319

Regional Steak. Casual Dining. $9-$11 **AAA Inspector Notes:** The steakhouse lines up buffet items, including pizza, tacos, soups, salads and desserts, providing both excellent variety and a good value. Rotating theme nights allow for the sampling of sushi, barbecue and seafood. The buffet may also serve to complement a quality steak. **Address:** 3525 NE Loop 286 75460 **Location:** Jct US 82 and E Loop 286, 0.5 mi n. [L] [D] [✂]

## PARKER (H-3) pop. 3,811
• Part of Dallas area — see map p. 161

**SOUTHFORK RANCH** is off US 75 exit 30, 5.5 mi. e. on Parker Rd., then .2 mi. s. on FM 2551 to 3700 Hogge Rd. This working ranch was the setting for the television series "Dallas." A guided tram tour of the renowned mansion is available. Memorabilia of the show's characters are displayed, and Texas longhorns and American paint horses can be seen along the tour. **Time:** Allow 1 hour minimum. **Hours:** Daily 9-5. Last tour begins 30 minutes before closing. Closed Thanksgiving and Christmas. **Cost:** $13.50; $11.50 (ages 60+); $8.50 (ages 5-12). **Phone:** (972) 442-7800.

## PASADENA (F-10) pop. 149,043, elev. 32'
• Hotels & Restaurants map & index p. 324
• Part of Houston area — see map p. 301

Pasadena's verdant landscape reminded early settlers of a similar city in California, from which the town took its name. The community became a major strawberry producer after Clara Barton donated 1.5 million plants to area farms damaged by the 1900 Galveston hurricane. Shipping and industry later replaced agriculture as mainstays in the local economy.

**ARMAND BAYOU NATURE CENTER** is 6.3 mi. e. of I-45 at 8500 Bay Area Blvd. A 2,500-acre preserve includes tall-grass prairie, estuarine bayou and coastal woods. On the preserve is an 1890s farm exhibit. Hiking trails are available; guided hikes and demonstrations are held Saturdays and Sundays. Adjacent is Bay Area Park, which has picnic facilities. **Time:** Allow 2 hours minimum. **Hours:** Wed.-Sat. 9-5, Sun. noon-5. Closed Jan. 1, Thanksgiving and Christmas. **Cost:** $4; $2 (ages 4-12 and 60+). **Phone:** (281) 474-2551. 🅰️

## ECONO LODGE
(713)477-4266  **119**

Motel $60-$75 **Address:** 823 W Pasadena Frwy 77506 **Location:** SR 225 (Pasadena Frwy) exit Richey St. **Facility:** 39 units. 2 stories (no elevator), exterior corridors.

[ii+] 📶 🛗 🍴

## HAMPTON INN & SUITES-HOUSTON/PASADENA
(281)998-3300  **120**

 Hotel $116-$152 **Address:** 4741 E Sam Houston Pkwy S 77505 **Location:** Beltway 8 exit Crenshaw Rd, just e. **Facility:** 90 units. 4 stories, interior corridors. **Terms:** 1-7 night minimum stay, cancellation fee imposed.

 **AAA Benefit:** Members save up to 10%!

**Pool(s):** outdoor. **Activities:** hot tub, exercise room. **Guest Services:** valet and coin laundry.

CALL [&M] 🚗 [BIZ] [HS] 📶 ✖️ 💻 / SOME UNITS 🛗 🍴

## PEARLAND pop. 91,252
• Restaurants p. 434
• Hotels & Restaurants map & index p. 324

## BEST WESTERN PEARLAND INN
(281)997-2000  **165**

Hotel
$80-$180

Best Western
**AAA Benefit:** Members save 10% or more with Best Western!

**Address:** 1855 N Main St 77581 **Location:** Jct Loop 8 S and SR 35, 1.5 mi s. **Facility:** 45 units. 2 stories (no elevator), exterior corridors. **Pool(s):** outdoor. **Activities:** hot tub, exercise room. **Guest Services:** coin laundry. **Featured Amenity: continental breakfast.**

[SAVE] [ii+] [BIZ] [HS] 📶 🛗 🍴 💻 / SOME UNITS 🔑

## COURTYARD BY MARRIOTT HOUSTON PEARLAND
(713)413-0500  **168**

Hotel $109-$209 **Address:** 11200 Broadway St 77584 **Location:** Jct SR 288 and 518; in Town Center Mall. **Facility:** 110 units. 5 stories, interior corridors. **Pool(s):** outdoor. **Activities:** hot tub, exercise room. **Guest Services:** valet and coin laundry.

**AAA Benefit:** Members save 5% or more!

[ii+] CALL [&M] 🚗 [BIZ] [HS] 📶 ✖️ 🛗 💻 / SOME UNITS 🍴

## HAMPTON INN PEARLAND
(832)736-9977  **166**

Hotel $99-$339 **Address:** 6515 W Broadway St (FM 518) 77581 **Location:** 4 mi e of SR 288. **Facility:** 61 units. 3 stories, interior corridors. **Terms:** 1-7 night minimum stay, cancellation fee imposed. **Pool(s):** outdoor. **Activities:** exercise room. **Guest Services:** valet and coin laundry.

**AAA Benefit:** Members save up to 10%!

[ii+] CALL [&M]  [BIZ]  [HS] 📶    💻

(See map & index p. 324.)

### HILTON GARDEN INN HOUSTON/PEARLAND
(713)340-0110 **164**

🔻🔻🔻 **Hotel $95-$159 Address:** 12101 Shadow Creek Pkwy 77584 **Location:** SR 288 exit Shadow Creek Pkwy, just w. **Facility:** 137 units. 5 stories, interior corridors. **Terms:** 1-7 night minimum stay, cancellation fee imposed. **Amenities:** safes. **Pool(s):** heated outdoor. **Activities:** hot tub, exercise room. **Guest Services:** coin laundry.

**AAA Benefit:** Members save up to 10%!

🍴 🍷 CALL 🔌M 🚭 BIZ HS 🛜 🔲 🖥 📺 📇

### LA QUINTA INN & SUITES PEARLAND
(281)412-5454 **167**

🔻🔻🔻 **Hotel $99-$144 Address:** 9002 Broadway St 77584 **Location:** Jct SR 288 and 518, 1.6 mi e. **Facility:** 56 units. 3 stories, interior corridors. **Pool(s):** outdoor. **Activities:** hot tub, exercise room. **Guest Services:** coin laundry.

CALL 🔌M 🚭 BIZ HS 🛜 ✖ 🔲 🖥 📇 / SOME UNITS 🐾

### SPRINGHILL SUITES BY MARRIOTT HOUSTON PEARLAND
(713)436-7377 **163**

🔻🔻🔻 **Hotel $99-$159 Address:** 1820 Country Place Pkwy 77584 **Location:** SR 288 exit Shadow Creek Pkwy, just e. **Facility:** 91 units. 3 stories, interior corridors. **Pool(s):** outdoor. **Activities:** exercise room. **Guest Services:** valet and coin laundry.

**AAA Benefit:** Members save 5% or more!

🍴 CALL 🔌M 🚭 BIZ HS 🛜 ✖ 📹 🔲 🖥 📇

---

## WHERE TO EAT

### CENTRAL TEXAS STYLE BBQ
281/485-9626 **69**

🔻 Regional Barbecue. Quick Serve. $5-$17 **AAA Inspector Notes:** The family-owned and -operated place has been feeding Pearland for more than 40 years. The name says it all—delicious down-home, hickory-smoked pit barbecue in the Texas tradition. The slow-smoked brisket and pork loin are excellent, as is the smoked turkey. The menu also includes ribs, chicken, smoked ham and jalapeño sausage. A good selection of fixins also is offered, including baked potatoes and home-made desserts. The décor is quaint and simple, like you're eating at home. **Address:** 4110 W Broadway St 77581 **Location:** Just w of Main St. L D

### SALTGRASS STEAKHOUSE
713/436-0799 **70**

🔻🔻 Steak. Casual Dining. $9-$30 **AAA Inspector Notes:** Those looking for something different should try the comfortable steakhouse, which never says no to a special request. Born from the spirit of Texas cattle drives, the restaurant resembles a Texas lodge, with high ceilings and mounted animal heads. Baby back ribs are so tender the meat falls off the bone. Also on the menu are hearty steaks, prime rib, chicken, seafood and yummy desserts. **Features:** full bar. **Address:** 3251 Silverlake Village Dr 77584 **Location:** SR 288 exit FM 518, just e, then just s. SAVE L D CALL 🔌M 🚭

---

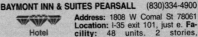
### LA QUINTA INN & SUITES
830/872-3277

fyi Not evaluated. **Address:** 170 Medical Dr 78061 **Location:** I-35 exit 101, just w; on southbound frontage road. Facilities, services, and décor characterize a mid-scale property.

---

## WHERE TO EAT

### COWPOKES TEXAS STYLE BAR-B-QUE
830/334-8000

🔻 Barbecue. Quick Serve. $6-$9 **AAA Inspector Notes:** Fall-apart tender and moist, flavorfully smoked barbecued meats and poultry are offered, as are homemade side dishes. The house-made pecan pie was the flakiest, crunchiest and lightest this inspector has tasted. **Address:** 1855 W Comal St 78061 **Location:** I-35 exit 101, just e. L D

---

## PECOS (E-4) pop. 8,780, elev. 2,580'

Tales of the Wild West are incomplete without a mention of Pecos. Prompted by a June 1883 dispute in front of Red Newell's saloon, cowhands from the Hashknife, W, Lazy Y and NA ranches competed the following Fourth of July to determine which spread had the best ropers and riders.

Saddle-bronc riding and steer-riding contests were held next to the courthouse, and nearly 1,000 spectators watched the cowboys compete for the $40 prize in this first rodeo—an event that did not earn its name until some 40 years later. The West of the Pecos Rodeo is held annually in late June.

**Pecos Area Convention and Visitors Bureau:** 100 E. 1st St., Pecos, TX 79772. **Phone:** (432) 445-2406.

**WEST OF THE PECOS MUSEUM** is at US 285 and Dot Stafford St. Occupying more than 50 rooms of the restored 1896 Orient Hotel and Saloon, the museum depicts the frontier history of Pecos. **Time:** Allow 1 hour minimum. **Hours:** Mon.-Sat. 9-5, Sun. 1-4, Memorial Day-Labor Day; Tues.-Sat. 9-5, rest of year. Closed Thanksgiving and Christmas Eve-Tues. after Christmas. **Cost:** $4; $3 (ages 65+); $1 (ages 6-18). **Phone:** (432) 445-5076.

## BEST WESTERN PLUS SWISS CHALET HOTEL & SUITES
(432)447-9477

Hotel
$160-$190

**AAA Benefit:** Members save 10% or more with Best Western!

**Address:** 141 S Frontage Rd 79772 **Location:** I-20 exit 40, just s. **Facility:** 81 units, some two bedrooms. 3 stories, interior corridors. **Amenities:** safes. **Pool(s):** heated indoor. **Activities:** hot tub, exercise room. **Guest Services:** complimentary and valet laundry. **Featured Amenity: full hot breakfast.**

## BEST WESTERN SWISS CLOCK INN
(432)447-2215

Motel
$120-$130

**AAA Benefit:** Members save 10% or more with Best Western!

**Address:** 133 S Frontage Rd, I-20 79772 **Location:** I-20 exit 40, just e. **Facility:** 104 units. 1 story, exterior corridors. **Dining:** Alpine Lodge Restaurant, see separate listing. **Pool(s):** outdoor. **Activities:** exercise room. **Guest Services:** complimentary and valet laundry.

## COMFORT SUITES
(432)445-1444

Hotel
$105-$199

**Address:** 110 Raul Florez Blvd 79772 **Location:** I-20 exit 39; on north frontage road. **Facility:** 58 units. 3 stories, interior corridors. **Pool(s):** heated indoor. **Activities:** hot tub, exercise room. **Guest Services:** coin laundry. **Featured Amenity: full hot breakfast.**

## HAMPTON INN
(432)447-0174

Hotel
$151-$161

**AAA Benefit:** Members save up to 10%!

**Address:** 215 S Frontage Rd 79772 **Location:** I-20 exit 39; on south frontage road. **Facility:** 64 units. 3 stories, interior corridors. **Terms:** 1-7 night minimum stay, cancellation fee imposed. **Amenities:** safes. **Pool(s):** heated indoor. **Activities:** hot tub, exercise room. **Guest Services:** coin laundry. **Featured Amenity: full hot breakfast.**

HOLIDAY INN EXPRESS & SUITES PECOS        432/445-9970

Hotel. Rates not provided. **Address:** 1900 S Cedar St 79772 **Location:** I-20 exit 42, just n. **Facility:** 71 units. 3 stories, interior corridors. **Pool(s):** heated outdoor. **Activities:** hot tub, exercise room. **Guest Services:** complimentary laundry.

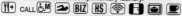

## KNIGHTS INN LAURA LODGE MOTEL & SUITES
(432)445-4924

Motel
$89-$130

**Address:** 1000 E Business I-20 79772 **Location:** I-20 exit 42, 1 mi nw to Business Rt I-20, then 0.5 mi e. **Facility:** 28 units. 2 stories (no elevator), exterior corridors. **Terms:** cancellation fee imposed. **Pool(s):** outdoor. **Activities:** hot tub. **Guest Services:** valet laundry. **Featured Amenity: continental breakfast.**

OAK TREE INN        (432)445-1628

Hotel $90-$115 **Address:** 22 N Frontage Rd 79772 **Location:** I-20 exit 42, just w on north frontage road. **Facility:** 61 units. 2 stories (no elevator), interior corridors. **Activities:** exercise room. **Guest Services:** valet and coin laundry.

### WHERE TO EAT

ALFREDO'S RESTAURANT        432/445-7776

Tex-Mex. Family Dining. $5-$15 **AAA Inspector Notes:** In an unassuming building near downtown, this restaurant serves up Tex-Mex, Mexican and American favorites. Locals keep coming back for the steak entrées. **Address:** 1002 N Cedar St 79772 **Location:** 1 mi s of downtown. L  D

ALPINE LODGE RESTAURANT        432/447-2215

American. Casual Dining. $8-$20 **AAA Inspector Notes:** The restaurant sustains the atmosphere of a European lodge. Offerings include all-day breakfast dishes, sandwiches, chicken, beef and local favorites. **Features:** full bar. **Address:** 133 S Frontage Rd, I-20 79772 **Location:** I-20 exit 40, just w; in BEST WESTERN Swiss Clock Inn. B  L  D

## PERRYTON (A-6) pop. 8,802, elev. 2,943'
• Hotels p. 436

In 1919, the Santa Fe Railway built a new line through the Texas Panhandle, bypassing the towns of Ochiltree, and Gray, Okla., eight miles to the north and south. Knowing their fortunes were tied to the railroad, residents of both towns loaded their belongings—and their buildings—onto wagons and relocated to Perryton. Called the "Wheatheart of the Nation" for its grain production, Perryton also is a major supplier of oil and natural gas, and is home to Lake Fryer and Wolf Creek Park.

**Perryton-Ochiltree Chamber of Commerce:** 2000 S. Main St., P.O. Box 789, Perryton, TX 79070. **Phone:** (806) 435-6575.

**MUSEUM OF THE PLAINS** is on US 83 at 1200 N. Main St. More than 10,000 items trace the regional history, paleontology and archeology of the High Plains. Exhibits include photographs, fossils, arrowheads, antique vehicles, an oil field display, Native American artifacts, a pioneer settlement and a Kiowa Indian village. Findings from the "Buried City," a settlement along Wolf Creek dating from A.D. 1100, also are displayed. **Time:** Allow 30 minutes minimum. **Hours:** Mon.-Fri. 9-5, Sat. 10-5, Sun. 1-5. Closed Jan. 1, Thanksgiving, Christmas Eve and Christmas. **Cost:** Donations. **Phone:** (806) 435-6400.

**BEST WESTERN PERRYTON INN** (806)434-2850

Hotel $150-$170

**AAA Benefit:** Members save 10% or more with Best Western!

**Address:** 3505 S Main St (US 83) 79070 **Location:** US 83, 2.2 mi s. **Facility:** 57 units. 2 stories, interior corridors. **Pool(s):** heated indoor. **Activities:** hot tub, exercise room. **Guest Services:** valet and coin laundry.

**Cook to order full hot breakfast, full service restaurant onsite, Internet, pool/spa & fitness center.**

## PFLUGERVILLE pop. 46,936
• Hotels & Restaurants map & index p. 86

**COMFORT SUITES AUSTIN (PFLUGERVILLE)** (512)251-9088

Hotel $100-$300

**Address:** 15112 FM 1825 78660 **Location:** I-35 exit 247, just n on E Frontage Rd. **Facility:** 64 units. 3 stories, interior corridors. **Pool(s):** heated indoor. **Activities:** hot tub, exercise room. **Guest Services:** valet and coin laundry.

### WHERE TO EAT

**FISH DADDY'S GRILL HOUSE** 512/989-3232
American. Casual Dining. $7-$15 **AAA Inspector Notes:** Choices include fresh fish entrées, seafood platters, Cajun specialties and mixed grill selections. Among lighter-fare options are soups, salads, sandwiches and seafood baskets. I always enjoy the steak and shrimp combination dinner. **Features:** full bar. **Address:** 15119-B I-35 N 78660 **Location:** I-35 exit 247, 1.2 mi n on E Frontage Rd.

## PHARR pop. 70,400

**HAMPTON INN & SUITES** (956)781-1116
Hotel $89-$159 **Address:** 300 W Nolana Loop 78577 **Location:** Just w of jct US 281 and Nolana Loop. **Facility:** 96 units. 4 stories, interior corridors. **Terms:** 1-7 night minimum stay, cancellation fee imposed. **Pool(s):** outdoor. **Activities:** hot tub, exercise room. **Guest Services:** coin laundry.

**AAA Benefit:** Members save up to 10%!

**HOLIDAY INN EXPRESS HOTEL & SUITES** 956/259-7829
Hotel. Rates not provided. **Address:** 205 W Nolana Loop 78577 **Location:** US 83 to US 281 N exit Nolana Loop, then w. **Facility:** 88 units. 4 stories, interior corridors. **Pool(s):** outdoor. **Activities:** hot tub, exercise room. **Guest Services:** valet and coin laundry.

**LA QUINTA INN & SUITES NORTH** (956)782-8832
Hotel $94-$134 **Address:** 4607 N Cage Blvd 78577 **Location:** US 281 exit Nolana Loop, just w. **Facility:** 67 units, some kitchens. 4 stories, interior corridors. **Pool(s):** outdoor. **Activities:** hot tub, exercise room. **Guest Services:** coin laundry.

**LA QUINTA INN & SUITES PHARR** (956)787-2900
Hotel $94-$134 **Address:** 4603 N Cage Blvd 78577 **Location:** US 281 northbound exit Nolana Loop, just w. **Facility:** 111 units, some two bedrooms and efficiencies. 3 stories, interior corridors. **Pool(s):** outdoor. **Activities:** hot tub, exercise room. **Guest Services:** coin laundry.

### WHERE TO EAT

**LUBY'S** 956/781-7717
American. Cafeteria. $6-$12 **AAA Inspector Notes:** First opened in 1947 in south Texas, this cafeteria with over 100 outlets features a wide variety of salads, fresh fruits, seafood...including crunchy shrimp...pastas, meat, poultry and just baked cakes and pies. Ask about the kids specials and Lu Ann platters...an entrée with choice of 2 vegetables and a roll. Many locations offer drive-thru service. **Address:** 500 N Jackson Rd 78577 **Location:** Just w.

## PLAINVIEW (C-5) pop. 22,194

Named for the magnificent view of the plains, Plainview has an abundant water supply as a result of a huge, shallow underground water belt. Milo, wheat, corn and cotton production as well as oil and gas contribute to the economy.

**Plainview Chamber of Commerce:** 1906 W. Fifth St., Plainview, TX 79072-6234. **Phone:** (806) 296-7431 or (800) 658-2685.

**MUSEUM OF THE LLANO ESTACADO** is at 1900 W. Eighth St. on the campus of Wayland Baptist University. Exhibits show the geological formation and historical development of the High Plains region known as Llano Estacado—the Staked Plain. Among the displays are Native American artifacts, replicas of pioneer rooms and cavalry and blacksmith equipment. **Hours:** Mon.-Thurs. 8-5; Fri. 8-4, Sat.-Sun. 1-5, Apr.-Nov. **Cost:** Donations. **Phone:** (806) 291-3660.

**BEST WESTERN CONESTOGA** (806)293-9454

Hotel $75

**AAA Benefit:** Members save 10% or more with Best Western!

**Address:** 600 N I-27 79072 **Location:** I-27 exit 49, just s of US 70; on eastbound access road. **Facility:** 79 units. 2 stories (no elevator), exterior corridors. **Pool(s):** outdoor. **Activities:** exercise room. **Guest Services:** coin laundry.

## COMFORT SUITES

(806)293-7700

Hotel
$89-$139

**Address:** 3615 Grandview Dr 79072 **Location:** I-27 exit 49; on southeast corner. **Facility:** 50 units. 2 stories, interior corridors. **Pool(s):** heated indoor. **Activities:** hot tub, exercise room. **Guest Services:** coin laundry. **Featured Amenity: full hot breakfast.**

HOLIDAY INN EXPRESS HOTEL & SUITES        806/296-9900

Hotel. Rates not provided. **Address:** 4213 W 13th St 79072 **Location:** I-27 exit 49 northbound, just w to Mesa, then just n; exit 50 southbound, just s to 13th St, then just w. **Facility:** 62 units. 3 stories, interior corridors. **Pool(s):** heated indoor. **Activities:** hot tub, exercise room. **Guest Services:** valet and coin laundry.

## PLANO (H-3) pop. 259,841, elev. 655'

- Restaurants p. 439
- Hotels & Restaurants map & index p. 179
- Part of Dallas area — see map p. 161

Originally known as Fillmore, Plano was renamed in 1851 when the post office was granted. Fires took a devastating toll on the city twice in the late 1800s. Proclaimed as the balloon capital of Texas, the city is host to the Plano Balloon Festival on the third weekend in September. It draws roughly 75,000 to Oak Point Park for the five balloon launches; concerts, skydiving and children's activities are also held.

**Plano Convention and Visitors Bureau:** 2000 E. Spring Creek Pkwy., Plano, TX 75074. **Phone:** (972) 941-5843 or (800) 817-5266.

**HERITAGE FARMSTEAD** is 1.2 mi. w. off US 75 exit 29 (FM 544) to 1900 W. 15th St. On the grounds of this 4-acre microcosm of early Texas farm life are a furnished late Victorian farmhouse and 12 outbuildings including a curing shed, a one-room schoolhouse and a windmill. The farmstead is furnished with period artifacts, including tools and vehicles.

Guided tours of the grounds and certain buildings are available. **Hours:** Self-guiding grounds tours Tues.-Sun. 10-4:30. Guided tours Tues.-Sat. at 10:30, Sun. at 1:30, June-Aug.; Tues.-Sun. at 1:30,

rest of year. Closed major holidays. **Cost:** Self-guiding grounds tours $2. Guided tours $5; $3.50 (ages 5-18 and 65+). **Phone:** (972) 881-0140.

## ALOFT PLANO

(214)474-2520   **42**

Hotel
$79-$170

**AAA Benefit:** Enjoy the new twist, get up to 20% off + Starwood Preferred Guest® bonuses!

**Address:** 6853 N Dallas Pkwy 75024 **Location:** Dallas North Tollway exit Spring Creek Pkwy/Tennyson Pkwy, just s of Tennyson Pkwy; on frontage road. **Facility:** 136 units. 5 stories, interior corridors. *Bath:* shower only. **Amenities:** safes. **Pool(s):** heated outdoor. **Activities:** exercise room. **Guest Services:** valet and coin laundry, area transportation. *(See ad p. 210.)*

## BEST WESTERN PARK SUITES HOTEL

(972)578-2243   **45**

Hotel
$99-$104

**AAA Benefit:** Members save 10% or more with Best Western!

**Address:** 640 Park Blvd E 75074 **Location:** US 75 exit 29A northbound, just e, then 0.5 mi s on frontage road; exit 29 southbound, just e on 15th St, then 0.5 mi n on frontage road. **Facility:** 84 units. 3 stories, interior corridors. **Pool(s):** outdoor. **Activities:** hot tub, exercise room. **Guest Services:** valet and coin laundry. **Featured Amenity: full hot breakfast.**

CANDLEWOOD SUITES-PLANO        972/618-5446   **40**

Extended Stay Hotel. Rates not provided. **Address:** 4701 Legacy Dr 75024 **Location:** Jct SR 289 (Preston Rd) and Legacy Dr, just e. **Facility:** 122 efficiencies. 3 stories, interior corridors. **Activities:** exercise room. **Guest Services:** complimentary and valet laundry, area transportation.

COMFORT INN NEAR PLANO MEDICAL CENTER

(972)733-4700   **52**

Hotel $55-$85 **Address:** 5021 W Plano Pkwy 75093 **Location:** Jct Plano Pkwy and (SR 289) Preston Rd; on northwest corner. **Facility:** 64 units. 2 stories, interior corridors. **Amenities:** safes. **Activities:** limited exercise equipment. **Guest Services:** valet and coin laundry.

(See map & index p. 179.)

## COURTYARD BY MARRIOTT (972)403-0802 **41**

Hotel
$59-$189

**AAA Benefit:** Members save 5% or more!

**Address:** 6840 N Dallas Pkwy 75024 **Location:** Dallas North Tollway exit Spring Creek Pkwy; on northbound frontage road. **Facility:** 153 units. 3 stories, interior corridors. **Pool(s):** outdoor. **Activities:** hot tub, exercise room. **Guest Services:** valet and coin laundry, boarding pass kiosk, area transportation.

SAVE ECO Y CALL M BIZ

🛜 ✕ 🖥 / SOME UNITS 🍴 🖼

## COURTYARD BY MARRIOTT-PLANO PARKWAY (972)867-8000 **53**

Hotel
$59-$159

**AAA Benefit:** Members save 5% or more!

**Address:** 4901 W Plano Pkwy 75093 **Location:** Jct Plano Pkwy and Preston Rd (SR 289). **Facility:** 149 units. 3 stories, interior corridors. **Pool(s):** outdoor. **Activities:** hot tub, exercise room. **Guest Services:** valet and coin laundry, area transportation.

SAVE ECO 🍴 CALL M 🏊

BIZ 🛜 ✕ 🖥 / SOME UNITS 🍴 🖼

## FAIRFIELD INN & SUITES BY MARRIOTT DALLAS PLANO (972)519-0303 **54**

Hotel $67-$118 **Address:** 4712 W Plano Pkwy 75093 **Location:** Just n of jct SR 289 (Preston Rd), then just e.

**AAA Benefit:** Members save 5% or more!

**Facility:** 99 units. 3 stories, interior corridors. **Pool(s):** heated indoor. **Activities:** hot tub, exercise room. **Guest Services:** valet and coin laundry. 🍴 🏊 BIZ 🛜 ✕ 🍴 🖼 🖥

## HAMPTON INN PLANO (972)519-1000 **51**

Hotel $99-$139 **Address:** 4901 Old Shepard Pl 75093 **Location:** 0.4 mi n of jct SR 289 (Preston Rd) and W Plano Pkwy, just e. **Facility:** 131 units.

**AAA Benefit:** Members save up to 10%!

5 stories, interior corridors. **Terms:** 1-7 night minimum stay, cancellation fee imposed. **Pool(s):** outdoor. **Activities:** exercise room. **Guest Services:** valet and coin laundry, area transportation.

🍴 🏊 BIZ 🛜 ✕ 🍴 🖼 🖥

## HOLIDAY INN EXPRESS HOTEL & SUITES PLANO EAST (972)881-1881 **47**

Hotel $79-$109 **Address:** 700 Central Pkwy E 75074 **Location:** Just e of US 75, 0.3 mi ne of jct FM 544; exit 29A northbound; exit 29 southbound, 0.5 mi s on frontage road, just e on 15th St, then 0.5 mi n on frontage road. **Facility:** 137 units. 6 stories, interior corridors. **Terms:** cancellation fee imposed. **Pool(s):** outdoor. **Activities:** hot tub, exercise room. **Guest Services:** valet and coin laundry.

🏊 BIZ HS 🛜 ✕ 🍴 🍴 🖼 🖥

## HOMEWOOD SUITES BY HILTON (972)758-8800 **50**

Extended Stay Hotel $89-$159 **Address:** 4705 Old Shepard Pl 75093 **Location:** Jct Plano Pkwy and SR 289 (Preston Rd), 0.4 mi n, then just e. **Facility:** 99 efficiencies. 4 stories, interior corridors. **Terms:** 1-7 night minimum stay, cancellation fee imposed. **Amenities:** video games. **Pool(s):** outdoor. **Activities:** exercise room. **Guest Services:** valet and coin laundry, area transportation.

CALL M 🏊 BIZ 🛜 📹 🍴 🖼 🖥 / SOME UNITS 🍴

## HYATT PLACE DALLAS/PLANO (972)378-3997 **44**

Hotel
$79-$239

🏨 HYATT PLACE

**AAA Benefit:** Members save 10%!

**Address:** 3100 Dallas Pkwy 75093 **Location:** Dallas Pkwy exit Park Blvd northbound; exit Parker Rd southbound; on northbound frontage road. **Facility:** 127 units. 6 stories, interior corridors. **Terms:** cancellation fee imposed. **Pool(s):** outdoor. **Activities:** exercise room. **Guest Services:** valet laundry, area transportation. **Featured Amenity:** breakfast buffet.

SAVE 🍴 CALL M 🏊 BIZ 🛜 ✕ 📹 🍴 🖼 🖥 / SOME UNITS 🍴 HS

## LA QUINTA INN & SUITES DALLAS PLANO WEST (972)599-0700 **55**

Hotel $79-$140 **Address:** 4800 W Plano Pkwy 75093 **Location:** Just e of jct SR 289 (Preston Rd). **Facility:** 129 units. 4 stories, interior corridors. **Pool(s):** outdoor. **Activities:** hot tub, exercise room. **Guest Services:** valet and coin laundry, area transportation.

🍴 CALL M 🏊 🛜 🖥 / SOME UNITS 🐾 HS 🍴 🖼

## MARRIOTT DALLAS/PLANO AT LEGACY TOWN CENTER (972)473-6444 **39**

Hotel $129-$299 **Address:** 7121 Bishop Rd 75024 **Location:** Dallas North Tollway exit Legacy Dr, just e to Bishop Rd, just s. **Facility:** 404 units. 6

**AAA Benefit:** Members save 5% or more!

stories, interior corridors. **Parking:** on-site (fee) and valet. **Amenities:** video games. **Pool(s):** heated outdoor. **Activities:** sauna, hot tub, steamroom, exercise room. **Guest Services:** valet laundry, area transportation.

🍴 🍴 Y CALL M 🏊 BIZ $HS 🛜 ✕ 📹 🖥 / SOME UNITS 🍴 🖼

## NYLO PLANO AT LEGACY 972/624-6990 **38**

Hotel. Rates not provided. **Address:** 8201 Preston Rd 75024 **Location:** Just s of jct SR 121. **Facility:** 176 units. 5 stories, interior corridors. **Bath:** shower only. **Amenities:** safes. **Pool(s):** heated outdoor. **Activities:** steamroom, exercise room. **Guest Services:** complimentary and valet laundry, area transportation.

🍴 🍴 Y 🏊 HS 🛜 ✕ 🍴 🖥 / SOME UNITS 🐾 🍴 🖼

## RAMADA LIMITED (972)424-5568 **46**

Hotel
$50-$100

**Address:** 621 Central Pkwy E 75074 **Location:** Just e of US 75 exit 29A northbound; exit 29 southbound, 0.5 mi s on frontage road, just e on 15th St, then 0.5 mi n on frontage road. **Facility:** 90 units. 3 stories, interior corridors. **Pool(s):** outdoor. **Guest Services:** valet and coin laundry.

SAVE 🍴 🏊 🛜 🖥 / SOME UNITS 🍴 🖼

(See map & index p. 179.)

### SOUTHFORK HOTEL
(972)578-8555 **49**

Hotel
$84-$119

**Address:** 1600 N Central Expwy 75074 **Location:** US 75 exit 29A northbound; exit 29 southbound; on northbound frontage road. **Facility:** 279 units. 3 stories, interior corridors. **Pool(s):** outdoor. **Activities:** hot tub, exercise room. **Guest Services:** valet and coin laundry, area transportation.

### STAYBRIDGE SUITES PLANO/RICHARDSON
(972)612-8180 **56**

Extended Stay Hotel
$109-$119

**Address:** 301 Silverglen Dr 75075 **Location:** George Bush Toll Rd exit Coit Rd, n to Mapleshade Ln, just e, then just s. **Facility:** 112 efficiencies. 4 stories, interior corridors. **Terms:** cancellation fee imposed. **Pool(s):** heated indoor. **Activities:** hot tub, exercise room. **Guest Services:** complimentary and valet laundry, area transportation. **Featured Amenity: full hot breakfast.**

### SUPER 8-PLANO
(972)423-8300 **48**

Hotel
$55-$90

**Address:** 1704 N Central Expwy 75074 **Location:** US 75 exit 29A (Park Blvd) northbound, just e; exit 29 southbound, 0.5 mi s on frontage road, just e on 15th St, then just n on frontage road. **Facility:** 98 units. 3 stories, interior corridors. **Amenities:** safes. **Guest Services:** coin laundry. **Featured Amenity: continental breakfast.**

### TOWNEPLACE SUITES BY MARRIOTT
(972)943-8200 **43**

**Extended Stay Hotel** $139-$179 **Address:** 5005 Whitestone Ln 75024 **Location:** Dallas North Tollway exit Spring Creek Pkwy, 1.9 mi e, just n on SR 289 (Preston Rd) to Whitestone Ln, then just w. **Facility:** 106 kitchen units, some two bedrooms. 3 stories, interior corridors. **Pool(s):** outdoor. **Activities:** exercise room. **Guest Services:** valet and coin laundry.

**AAA Benefit:** Members save 5% or more!

### WHERE TO EAT

#### ABUELO'S THE FLAVOR OF MEXICO
Mexican. Casual Dining. $9-$20 **AAA Inspector Notes:** Off the busy highway, this relaxed and inviting dining retreat employs welcoming, professional servers. Beautiful architectural enhancements make guests feel as though they're dining in the courtyard of a Mexican villa. Plants, archways, pillars and a fountain add interest to the inside dining area. Service is welcoming and professional. **Bar:** full bar.

*For additional information, visit AAA.com*

**LOCATIONS:**
**Address:** 3420 N Central Expwy 75075 **Location:** US 75 exit 30 (Parker Rd), just e, then just n; on frontage road. **Phone:** 972/423-9290

**Address:** 3701 N Dallas Pkwy 75093 **Location:** North Dallas Pkwy exit 29A (Parker Blvd) northbound; on south frontage road. **Phone:** 972/781-1613

#### BAVARIAN GRILL
972/881-0705 **31**
German. Casual Dining. $7-$20 **AAA Inspector Notes:** A traditional beer garden, with long wooden tables, steins along the wall, large pictures of a country home and Bavarian music, makes up one side of the restaurant. On the menu are such favorites as schnitzel, sauerkraut and strudel. A visit here feels like a trip to the Alps; a covered patio area accommodates smokers. **Features:** full bar, patio dining, happy hour. **Reservations:** suggested. **Address:** 221 W Parker Rd, Suite 527 75023 **Location:** US 75 exit 30 (Parker Rd), just w; in Ruisseau Village Strip Center.

#### BREAD WINNER'S CAFE
972/312-9300 **27**
American. Casual Dining. $10-$25 **AAA Inspector Notes:** A small plate stacked with delicious breads welcomes diners to this busy lunch spot. Menus vary, but lunches normally are comprised of sandwiches, burgers and daily specials. More ambitious dinner entrées might include such selections as stuffed Chilean sea bass or honey-pecan-glazed pork tenderloin. Desserts and breads are sold in the storefront bakery and are all made in-house. **Features:** full bar, patio dining, Sunday brunch. **Address:** 4021 Preston Rd 75093 **Location:** Between Lorimar Rd and Spring Creek Pkwy; in Lake Market Strip Center.

#### CAFE ISTANBUL
972/398-2020 **22**
Turkish. Casual Dining. $11-$19 **AAA Inspector Notes:** This eatery, located in an upscale outdoor shopping area, is designed for strolling and makes a great stop in between purchases. The menu features wraps, kebabs, pizzas and fish specialties. **Features:** full bar, patio dining. **Address:** 7300 Lone Star Dr 75024 **Location:** Dallas North Tollway exit Legacy Dr, just n on frontage road.

#### CHUY'S
469/467-2489 **29**
Tex-Mex. Casual Dining. $8-$12 **AAA Inspector Notes:** This Texas original serves up Mexican kitsch like no else in its décor but takes pride in its several house-made chile sauces and hand-made tortillas. Although the menu is familiar—fajitas, tacos and enchiladas—the freshness of the ingredients and chiles sets this place apart. The bar is always abuzz, but families are welcome. **Features:** full bar, patio dining. **Address:** 3908 Dallas Pkwy 75093 **Location:** Dallas North Tollway exit W Parker; on northbound frontage road.

#### FIRESIDE PIES
972/398-2700 **21**
Pizza. Casual Dining. $11-$16 **AAA Inspector Notes:** Expect rustic pizzas made with ingredients like goat cheese, sun-dried tomatoes, pine nuts and roasted red peppers. Menu items are made to be shared here, so come hungry or bring a mate. The bar draws a crowd, and the patio fills up fast. **Features:** full bar, patio dining. **Address:** 5717 Legacy Dr, Suite 110 75024 **Location:** Dallas North Tollway exit Legacy Dr, just e; in The Shops at Legacy.

#### FISHMONGERS SEAFOOD MARKET & CAFE
972/423-3699 **34**
Regional Seafood. Casual Dining. $7-$20 **AAA Inspector Notes:** Cajun, Tex-Mex and fried seafood dishes are the focus at this eatery. Shrimp tortilla soup, crawfish étouffée and what customers call the best homemade bread pudding in the world fill the menu with a variety of good tastes, but the baked scallops have a dedicated following. **Features:** full bar, happy hour. **Address:** 1901 N Central 75075 **Location:** US 75 exit 30 (Parker Rd), 0.8 mi s on west side access road; at Chisholm Rd; in Chisholm Plaza.

#### GRANDY'S RESTAURANT
American. Quick Serve. $4-$8 **AAA Inspector Notes:** Fried chicken and country-fried steak are menu standbys at the restaurant, a regional franchise. They also offer a family-style dining menu. The décor is a step up from that of most quick-serve eateries and more resembles that of a conventional restaurant. Some elements of increased service include additional rolls, iced tea refills and tray removal.

*For additional information, visit AAA.com*

**LOCATIONS:**
**Address:** 620 E 15th St 75074 **Location:** US 75 exit 29 northbound; exit 29 southbound to E 15th St, just e under US 75. **Phone:** 972/423-4744

**Address:** 8601 Ohio Dr 75024 **Location:** Just s of jct SR 121. **Phone:** 214/387-4933

**Address:** 2240 Coit Rd 75075 **Location:** Just n of jct Coit Rd and W Park Blvd. **Phone:** 972/867-3108

(See map & index p. 179.)

### JAPON STEAKHOUSE & SUSHI BAR          972/781-2818  26
▼▼ Japanese. Casual Dining. $10-$39 **AAA Inspector Notes:** In several major cities throughout Texas, this small chain specializes in steaks from hibachi grills and sushi and sashimi for those who really want a taste of Japan. The all-inclusive bento box lunch includes separate compartments with appetizers, rice, entrée and sushi/sashimi. Guests can order chicken, beef, shrimp or salmon teriyaki as the entrée. **Features:** full bar. **Reservations:** suggested. **Address:** 4021 Preston Rd, Suite 618 75093 **Location:** Between Lorimar Rd and Spring Creek Pkwy. L D

### JORG'S CAFE VIENNA          972/509-5966  37
▼▼▼ Austrian. Casual Dining. $11-$23 **AAA Inspector Notes:** This charming restaurant sits in the city's historic old town center, which seems worlds away from Dallas, yet is only minutes away. Schnitzel and sausage may be expected, but the delicious family-recipe sauces and specialties make this place singular. The owner hails from southern Austria, on the Italian border, and shows this geographical influence in such dishes as the wonderful tiramisu cake. A beer garden opens on warm summer nights. **Features:** full bar, patio dining. **Address:** 1037 E 15th St 75074 **Location:** Between K and I aves, just e of commuter railroad tracks; in Old Town Plano. **Parking:** street only. L D

### LA MADELEINE COUNTRY FRENCH CAFE
▼ Traditional French. Casual Dining. $7-$12 **AAA Inspector Notes:** A fireplace creates the focal point at this cozy European style café where you can always get a quiche or savory stuffed puffed pastry on the go or stick around for a chicken crêpe or French dip sandwich. Heartier entrées like rotisserie chicken are offered and every season promises menu surprises. Whatever you decide on you probably will not get out the door without enjoying one of their tempting sweet pastries. B L D

*For additional information, visit AAA.com*

**LOCATIONS:**
**Address:** 520 W 15th St 75075 **Location:** Jct E 15th St and N Central Expwy, just s. **Bar:** beer & wine. **Phone:** 972/398-3003
**Address:** 5000 W Park Blvd, Suite 100 75093 **Location:** Jct W Park Blvd and SR 289 (Preston Rd). **Bar:** wine only.
**Phone:** 972/407-1878

### LOVE & WAR IN TEXAS          972/422-6201  40
▼▼ Regional American. Casual Dining. $8-$29 **AAA Inspector Notes:** The Texas steakhouse prepares not only the usual steaks, pork chops, chicken and barbecue ribs but also wild game entrées centered on boar, buffalo, venison bratwurst, antelope, quail and catfish. The menu strives to represent the diversity of the Texas landscape and cuisine offerings, so it's a good place for large parties to do some sampling. **Features:** full bar, happy hour. **Address:** 601 E Plano Pkwy 75074 **Location:** US 75 exit 28A; northeast corner of Plano Pkwy and US 75. L D LATE

### LUNA DE NOCHE          972/818-2727  39
▼▼ Tex-Mex. Casual Dining. $7-$22 **AAA Inspector Notes:** Growing rapidly in the area, this small local chain offers such typical favorites as fajitas, enchiladas, chalupas, chile rellenos and flan. Portions are large, so it's a good idea to come with an appetite. Be sure to try the stuffed jalapeño platter as an appetizer. **Features:** full bar, patio dining, Sunday brunch. **Address:** 1401 Preston Rd 75093 **Location:** Just n of jct Preston Rd (SR 289) and N Plano Pkwy. L D

### MIGNON          972/943-3372  28
▼▼▼ French Steak. Fine Dining. $14-$48 **AAA Inspector Notes:** For anyone who shies away from French cuisine because of its reputation for being rich, sauce laden or pretentious, Mignon sets the record straight. With a clear adoration to all things Audrey Hepburn, this stylish restaurant has a menu that is sure to satisfy steak lovers, as that is what they have built their reputation on. But the menu also includes items like shrimp and sweet corn risotto, angus short ribs, grilled pear salad and barbecued shrimp and chorizo. **Features:** full bar, Sunday brunch, happy hour. **Reservations:** suggested. **Address:** 4005 Preston Rd, Suite 518 75093 **Location:** Between Lorimar Rd and Spring Creek Pkwy; in Lake Market Strip Center. L D CALL M

### NAAN          972/943-9288  24
▼▼▼ Japanese. Casual Dining. $9-$36 **AAA Inspector Notes:** Before or after shopping, stop in here for some delectable dishes featuring the spices and tastes of Asia. You might try freshly prepared sushi, spicy meat or vegetable mixtures prepared in a sizzling hot stone pot, or marinated beef, chicken or pork barbecue. In nice weather, the patio fills up fast, but the dining room provides a more upscale dining environment. **Features:** full bar, patio dining, Sunday brunch. **Address:** 7161 Bishop Rd, Unit G2 75024 **Location:** Dallas North Tollway exit Legacy Dr, just e, just s; 1.7 mi w on Preston Rd from jct Legacy Dr, just s. L D

### OSAKA SUSHI          972/931-8898  33
▼▼ Japanese. Casual Dining. $17-$30 **AAA Inspector Notes:** This restaurant specializes in an all-you-can-eat buffet featuring traditional Japanese favorites, including sushi, tempura, teriyaki steak and chicken. There also are some Korean and Chinese options. The choices are plentiful and the popularity of the place means items are always fresh. The restaurant is located in a strip center with excellent shopping nearby. **Features:** full bar. **Address:** 5012 W Park Blvd 75093 **Location:** Jct (SR 289) Preston Rd and W Park Blvd; southwest corner. L D

### PATRIZIO          972/964-2200  36
▼▼ Italian. Casual Dining. $10-$17 **AAA Inspector Notes:** As a branch of the beloved original location in Dallas, this restaurant also is nuanced with richness and formality but welcomes all and is a favorite with couples and families alike. The menu focuses on pasta dishes but a variety of entrée salads and pizza also is offered. It's located in an upscale shopping center. **Features:** full bar, patio dining, happy hour. **Address:** 1900 Preston Rd, Suite 343 75093 **Location:** Jct Preston Rd (SR 289) and W Park Blvd, just e. L D

### PURPLE COW DINER          972/473-6100  25
▼▼ American. Casual Dining. $6-$11 **AAA Inspector Notes:** The eatery is a throwback to a '50s diner, with a fountain at the counter, metal chairs, black-and-white tile floors and background rock 'n' roll music. The main fare is burgers, fries and shakes, but such daily specials as fried chicken, pork chops, catfish and lasagna have fans, too. **Features:** full bar. **Address:** 5809 Preston Rd, Suite 588 75093 **Location:** Just s of Spring Valley Rd; in Farmers Market Strip Center. L D

### ROCKFISH SEAFOOD GRILL          972/599-2190
▼▼ Seafood. Casual Dining. $7-$20 **AAA Inspector Notes:** Patrons shuffle through peanut shells on the floor as they make their way to their seats and are easily distracted by the numerous pieces of hunting and fishing memorabilia adorning the walls and ceiling. Although guests kick back in a log cabin-style interior, the freshly caught fish gets more sophisticated preparation than campfire roasting. The chef uses an array of sauces and cooking styles, and soups are hearty and fresh. **Features:** full bar. **Address:** 4701 W Park Blvd, Suite 105 75093 **Location:** Dallas North Tollway exit W Park Blvd, 2.5 mi e. L D

### SALTGRASS STEAKHOUSE          972/781-2202  30
▼▼ Steak. Casual Dining. $9-$30 **AAA Inspector Notes:** Those looking for something different should try the comfortable steakhouse, which never says no to a special request. Born from the spirit of Texas cattle drives, the restaurant resembles a Texas lodge, with high ceilings and mounted animal heads. Baby back ribs are so tender the meat falls off the bone. Also on the menu are hearty steaks, prime rib, chicken, seafood and yummy desserts. **Features:** full bar. **Address:** 3000 Dallas Pkwy 75093 **Location:** Dallas North Tollway exit Park Blvd; on northbound side. SAVE L D

### SAMUI THAI          972/398-2807  23
▼▼ Thai. Casual Dining. $11-$20 **AAA Inspector Notes:** Located in a popular retail area, the approach here is more upscale, with a subtle hint of Thailand in the modern décor. The degree of seasoning in traditional dishes can be customized to the diner's taste. The menu features stir-fries, noodle dishes and a variety of seafood specialties. Sticky rice, custard with seasonal mangoes and mint tea are a treat. **Features:** full bar. **Address:** 5700 Legacy Dr, Suite A-1 75024 **Location:** Jct Dallas Pkwy and Legacy Dr, just e. L D CALL M

(See map & index p. 179.)

THE SPAGHETTI WAREHOUSE                    972/516-8903

▼▼ Italian. Casual Dining. $7-$17 **AAA Inspector Notes:** The Italian-style restaurant chain sustains a festive family atmosphere. All entrees include bottomless tossed salad or soup. Patrons enjoy plentiful portions of such classic dishes as ravioli, lasagna, baked penne or the richly flavored cannelloni Florentine. Splurging on one of the many desserts, such as tiramisu, espresso mousse cake or carrot cake, is worthwhile. **Features:** full bar. **Address:** 1517 N Central Expwy 75075 **Location:** US 75 exit 29 northbound; exit 29A (Park Blvd/15th St) southbound; on southbound side of expressway. [L] [D]

TEXAS LAND AND CATTLE STEAKHOUSE           972/578-8707

▼▼ ▼▼ Steak. Casual Dining. $7-$27 **AAA Inspector Notes:** A variety of large Prime steaks, delicious salads and scrumptious desserts await you at the friendly Texas ranch-style restaurant. Try the signature slow-smoked sirloin, which never fails to please, or the Caesar salad, another favorite. A Texas steakhouse means everything is bigger, from large cuts and oversize salads to potatoes and side dishes. Those not in the mood for beef can opt for chicken, quail or seafood. Dessert is an occasion. **Features:** full bar. **Address:** 3945 N Central Expwy 75023 **Location:** US 75 exit 31 (Spring Creek Pkwy) northbound; exit 30 southbound; on southbound frontage road. [L] [D] [N]

ZENNA THAI & JAPANESE RESTAURANT    214/473-9797  (32)

▼▼ ▼▼ Thai. Casual Dining. $7-$13 **AAA Inspector Notes:** The small family-owned and -operated restaurant specializes in traditional Thai and Japanese cuisine. While the lunch menu features reasonably priced noodle, stir-fry, curry and sashimi bento boxes, a broader assortment of dishes is included on the dinner menu. Zenna is a rarity in Dallas as it is open until the wee hours of the night. This, combined with a great happy hour, sushi specials and very modern décor make it a big draw for the younger crowd. **Features:** full bar, patio dining, happy hour. **Address:** 2500 Central 75074 **Location:** US 75 exit 29A (Park Blvd/15th St) northbound; exit 29 southbound; on northbound frontage road. [L] [D] [LATE]

ZORBA'S                                    972/250-0002  (38)

▼▼ ▼▼ Greek. Casual Dining. $6-$13 **AAA Inspector Notes:** This family-owned and -operated restaurant is the type every neighborhood would be lucky to have. The décor and food take you to the Mediterranean, and its popularity makes it fun and lively. The small café specializes in preparations of chicken, lamb, pork and sausage, as well as pita sandwiches and such great desserts as baklava. **Address:** 1501 Preston Rd, Suite 150 75093 **Location:** Jct Plano Pkwy and SR 289 (Preston Rd), just n; in strip mall. [L] [D]

# PLEASANTON pop. 8,934

BILL MILLER BAR-B-Q                        830/569-3266

▼ Barbecue. Quick Serve. $6-$11 **AAA Inspector Notes:** The relaxed, family-focused barbecue restaurant prepares ribs, chicken, brisket, turkey and sausage for sandwiches or plates. **Address:** 301 S Main St 78064 **Location:** US 281, jct CR 97.

[B] [L] [D]

# PONDER pop. 1,395
• Part of Dallas area — see map p. 161

RANCHMAN'S CAFE "THE PONDER STEAKHOUSE"
                                           940/479-2221

▼ (diamond)
Steak
Casual Dining
$7-$32

**AAA Inspector Notes:** Featuring charming Western décor complete with longhorns and cowboy hats adorning the walls, this café serves steaks, burgers, homemade pies and cobblers. Call ahead for baked potatoes, as they are cooked slowly for one and a half hours. The restaurant is a landmark in the area, as it was a favorite for the cast and crew of "Bonnie and Clyde" and John Wayne always stopped in when in town. **Reservations:** suggested. **Address:** 110 W Bailey St 76259 **Location:** Center. *Menu on AAA.com*

 [L] [D] [N]

**PORT ARANSAS** (H-8) pop. 3,480, elev. 6'
• Restaurants p. 442

Port Aransas, known as Texas' forgotten island, is located on the northern tip of Mustang Island along the Central Texas Coast across from Corpus Christi and Aransas Bay. The barrier island, which took its name from the wild horses brought by Spanish explorers, was inhabited by the Karankawa Indians until the 19th century. First known as Sand Point, the town of Port Aransas was leveled by a hurricane in 1919.

Mustang Island State Park, 14 miles south, preserves nearly 4,000 acres of coastal dunes and 5 miles of gulf beach *(see Recreation Areas Chart)*. The island is connected to the mainland by the John F. Kennedy Causeway and a free car ferry.

**MARINE SCIENCE INSTITUTE VISITOR CENTER** is at 630 E. Cotter Ave. on the University of Texas Marine Science Institute campus. The center's seven aquariums re-create different Texas coastal habitats including a cordgrass salt marsh, black mangrove marsh, an oyster reef, an artificial reef, an open bay bottom and a rock jetty. Visitors can learn about the institute's research projects through exhibits, movies and educational programs housed in the main building. **Time:** Allow 1 hour minimum. **Hours:** Mon.-Fri. 8-5. Phone for movie schedule. **Cost:** Free. **Phone:** (361) 749-6729.

**PORT ARANSAS BIRDING CENTER** is s. on Cut-Off Rd. to the end of Ross Ave. Home to hundreds of resident and visiting birds, such as roseate spoonbills, least grebes, crested caracara and rails, this center includes four designated sites on the Great Texas Coastal Birding Trail. Boardwalks at two birding centers and an observation tower allow visitors to see more than 100 native Texas plant species, as well as wildlife including turtles, nutria and alligators. **Time:** Allow 1 hour minimum. **Hours:** Daily 24 hours. **Cost:** Free. **Phone:** (361) 749-4158.

BEACHGATE CONDOSUITES & MOTEL              (361)749-5900

▼ **Condominium** $40-$650 **Address:** 2000 On the Beach Dr 78373 **Location:** Oceanfront. Between beach markers 8 and 9; street access on Anchor Rd off 11th St. **Facility:** 84 condominiums. 1-4 stories, interior/exterior corridors. **Terms:** check-in 4 pm, 2-3 night minimum stay - seasonal and/or weekends, 30 day cancellation notice-fee imposed. **Pool(s):** outdoor, heated outdoor. **Activities:** hot tub, fishing. **Guest Services:** coin laundry.

 [HS]  [X] / SOME UNITS ▤ 🛏 ▦ ▣

BEST WESTERN OCEAN VILLA                   (361)749-3010

▼▼ ▼▼
Hotel
$69-$239

**AAA Benefit:** Members save 10% or more with Best Western!

**Address:** 400 E Ave G 78373 **Location:** Just se of S Alister St. Located in a quiet residential area. **Facility:** 48 units. 2 stories, exterior corridors. **Terms:** 2 night minimum stay - seasonal and/or weekends. **Pool(s):** heated outdoor. **Activities:** game room. **Guest Services:** coin laundry.

## THE COURTYARD CONDOMINIUMS
361/749-5243

◆◆ **Condominium** $79-$160 **Address:** 622 Beach Access Rd 1A 78373 **Location:** 2.5 mi s on SR 361. Located in a quiet residential area. **Facility:** 49 condominiums. 2 stories (no elevator), exterior corridors. **Terms:** check-in 4 pm, 2 night minimum stay, 7 day cancellation notice. **Pool(s):** outdoor. **Guest Services:** coin laundry.

🛟 🛜 ✕ 🖪 🖮 💻

## THE DUNES CONDOMINIUMS
361/749-5155

◆◆ **Condominium** $210-$480 **Address:** 1000 Lantana Dr 78373 **Location:** Oceanfront. SR 361, e on Beach St to Station St, 1 blk s. **Facility:** Located directly on the beach and adjacent to the city's fishing pier; all units have balconies and face the Gulf. 42 condominiums. 9 stories, exterior corridors. **Terms:** check-in 4 pm, 2 night minimum stay - seasonal and/or weekends, 7 day cancellation notice, resort fee. **Pool(s):** heated outdoor. **Activities:** hot tub, fishing, tennis, exercise room. **Guest Services:** coin laundry.

🍴 🛟 BIZ HS 🛜 ✕ 🖪 🖮 💻

## ISLAND HOTEL PORT ARANSAS
(361)749-8200

◆ **Motel** $59-$199 **Address:** 2607 Hwy 361 78373 **Location:** Just n of Paradise Dr. **Facility:** 57 units, some efficiencies. 2 stories, exterior corridors, *Bath:* shared. **Terms:** cancellation fee imposed. **Pool(s):** outdoor. **Guest Services:** coin laundry.

🛟 BIZ HS 🛜 ✕ 🖪 🖮 💻

## PLANTATION SUITES & CONFERENCE CENTER
(361)749-3866

◆◆◆ Motel $80-$200

**Address:** 1909 Hwy 361 78373 **Location:** On SR 361, 0.4 mi s; on Mustang Island. **Facility:** 52 units, some kitchens. 2 stories (no elevator), exterior corridors. **Terms:** check-in 4 pm, cancellation fee imposed. **Pool(s):** heated outdoor. **Activities:** hot tub. **Guest Services:** coin laundry. **Featured Amenity:** full hot breakfast.

SAVE 🍴 🛟 BIZ 🛜 ✕ 🖪 🖮 💻 / SOME UNITS 🛎

## MUSTANG ISLAND BEACH CLUB
361/749-5446

fyi Not evaluated. **Address:** 6275 SR 361 78373 **Location:** Just n on Island Estate Beach Rd; on Mustang Island. Facilities, services, and décor characterize a mid-scale property.

## PORT ROYAL OCEAN RESORT
361/749-5011

fyi Not evaluated. **Address:** 6317 State Hwy 361 78373 **Location:** On SR 361, just n of Mustang Island State Park. Facilities, services, and décor characterize a mid-scale property.

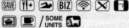

**WHERE TO EAT**

## BEACHES CAFE & BAKERY
361/749-2271

◆◆ American. Casual Dining. $10-$25 **AAA Inspector Notes:** Within walking distance of the beach, this recent addition to the local dining scene is a fun place with interesting dishes and a variety of homemade barbecue sauces. **Features:** beer & wine. **Address:** 118 Beach St 78373 **Location:** Jct N Alister St. [L] [D]

## THE CRAZY CAJUN
361/749-5069

◆ Regional Seafood. Quick Serve. $8-$16 **AAA Inspector Notes:** Just off Beach Street on the beach, the small and casual local favorite gets packed in season. A top choice is the Crazy Cajun, a family-sized pot of boiled shrimp, potatoes, crab, crawfish, corn on-the-cob and sausage, dumped out on your table to eat like true beachcombers. **Features:** beer & wine. **Address:** 303 Beach St 78373 **Location:** 3 blks se of jct Station St. [D]

## MOBY DICK'S
361/749-9447

◆◆ Regional American. Casual Dining. $8-$18 **AAA Inspector Notes:** Great for families, this restaurant has a fun nautical décor and offers fresh seafood dishes as well as some of the best burgers in town. Expect long lines for dinner in season. **Features:** full bar. **Address:** 515 S Alister St 78373 **Location:** Just off SR 361; between E and F aves. [B] [L] [D]

## SHRIMPS
361/749-6405

◆ Regional Seafood. Family Dining. $10-$25 **AAA Inspector Notes:** The large menu features a wide assortment of fresh seafood, pasta, steak and other favorites. Guests enjoy an evening of casual and fun dining on the island. The deck enhances the atmosphere. **Features:** full bar. **Address:** 337 Alister St 78373 **Location:** Just n of jct SR 361. [L] [D]

## TROUT STREET BAR & GRILL
361/749-7800

◆◆ Seafood. Casual Dining. $10-$30 **AAA Inspector Notes:** On the waterfront near the ferry landing, the landmark restaurant plies diners with delicious fresh local seafood. Guests are treated to great views of the harbor and channel. **Features:** full bar. **Address:** 104 W Cotter St 78373 **Location:** Just n of ferry landing; facing marina. [L] [D] [♦]

## VENETIAN HOT PLATE CUCINA ITALIANA
361/749-7617

◆◆ Italian. Family Dining. $12-$24 **AAA Inspector Notes:** The name says it all: hot plate casualness with Italian haute cuisine. Among the top dining spots on the island, the small spot focuses on fresh, distinctive pasta dishes served with seafood, veal, chicken and beef. **Features:** beer & wine. **Address:** 232 Beach St 78373 **Location:** 2 blks e of jct Beach Ave at SR 361. [D]

# PORT ARTHUR (F-11) pop. 53,818, elev. 8'

On Sabine Lake *(see Recreation Areas Chart)*, 11 miles from the Gulf of Mexico, Port Arthur is connected with the Gulf by a ship channel 36 feet deep and 400 feet wide at the bottom. SR 87, between Port Arthur and Sabine Pass, skirts the canal much of the way. Just northeast of the city, the 1.5-mile-long Rainbow Bridge spans the Neches River 176 feet above the water.

**Port Arthur Convention and Visitors Bureau:** 3401 Cultural Center Dr., Port Arthur, TX 77642. **Phone:** (409) 985-7822 or (800) 235-7822.

**MUSEUM OF THE GULF COAST** is at 700 Procter St. Artifacts, documents, photographs, fossils and memorabilia recount the area's history. The Gulf Coast Music Hall of Fame features mementos and recordings by such Port Arthur natives as Janis Joplin and The Big Bopper. The Sports Legends Gallery features audiovisual exhibits. Works by artist Robert Rauschenberg and a collection of decorative arts also are featured.

Time: Allow 30 minutes minimum. **Hours:** Mon.-Sat. 9-5, Sun. 1-5. Closed major holidays. **Cost:** $4; $3 (ages 62+ and college students with ID); $2 (ages 4-18). Children must be with an adult. **Phone:** (409) 982-7000.

**POMPEIIAN VILLA** is at 1953 Lakeshore Dr. Built in 1900 by barbed-wire tycoon Isaac Ellwood, the pink stucco house is patterned after an A.D. 79 Pompeiian villa. The residence is furnished with pieces dating from the 19th century to the present. **Time:** Allow 1 hour minimum. **Hours:** Guided tours are given Mon.-Fri. 10-2, Sat.-Sun. by appointment. Closed major holidays. **Cost:** $2. **Phone:** (409) 983-5977.

Be a better driver.

Keep your mind on the road.

## HAMPTON INN & SUITES PORT ARTHUR    (409)722 -6999

▼▼▼▼ **Hotel** $135-$145 **Address:** 7660 Memorial Blvd 77642 **Location:** US 69 exit Jimmy Johnson Blvd; on northbound access road. **Facility:** 72 units. 3 stories, interior corridors. **Terms:** 1-7 night minimum stay, cancellation fee imposed. **Pool(s):** outdoor. **Activities:** exercise room. **Guest Services:** valet and coin laundry.

**AAA Benefit:** Members save up to 10%!

[ⅱ→] CALL [🄻Ⓜ] [➛] [BIZ] [HS] [🛜] [✖] [🎥] [🅗] [🖵]
[▯]

## QUALITY INN & SUITES    409/722-1034

▼▼▼▼ **Hotel.** Rates not provided. **Address:** 7440 Memorial Blvd 77642 **Location:** US 69 to Jimmy Johnson Blvd, just e on Anchor Dr. **Facility:** 61 units. 3 stories, interior corridors. **Pool(s):** outdoor. **Activities:** exercise room. **Guest Services:** valet and coin laundry.

[ⅱ→] [➛] [BIZ] [HS] [🛜] [✖] [🅗] [🖵] [▯]

## THREE RIVERS INN & SUITES    409/983-8000

▼▼ **Hotel.** Rates not provided. **Address:** 2015 Henry O. Mills Hwy 77640 **Location:** SR 73, just w of jct SR 82. **Facility:** 80 units. 3 stories, interior corridors. **Guest Services:** coin laundry.

[HS] [🛜] [✖] [🅗] [🖵] [▯]

# PORT ISABEL (I-8) pop. 5,006, elev. 15'

The Queen Isabella Causeway crosses the Laguna Madre from Port Isabel to the town of South Padre Island *(see place listing p. 538)*, linking the mainland with the southern portion of Padre Island.

**Port Isabel Chamber of Commerce:** 421 E. Queen Isabella Blvd., Port Isabel, TX 78578. **Phone:** (956) 943-2262 or (800) 527-6102.

**DOLPHIN DOCKS** is at the base of the Queen Isabella Causeway at jct. Queen Isabella Blvd. and S. Garcia St. A 70-foot boat travels into the Laguna Madre Bay, where passengers will see bottlenose dolphins cavorting and feeding during a 90-minute cruise. Other sea life may be seen, including starfish and stingrays. **Time:** Allow 1 hour, 30 minutes minimum. **Hours:** Tours depart daily at 12:30, 5:30 and 7 p.m. **Cost:** Fare for 12:30 cruise $16; $13 (ages 3-12). Fare for 5:30 and 7 p.m. cruises $13; $10 (ages 3-12). **Phone:** (956) 943-3185.

**MUSEUMS OF PORT ISABEL** are on the corner of Railroad Ave. and Tarnava St. The complex is comprised of three sites within walking distance of one another, including the Port Isabel Historical Museum, the 1852 Port Isabel Lighthouse and the Treasures of the Gulf Museum. Each site depicts various aspects of the history of Port Isabel.

**Time:** Allow 1 hour minimum. **Hours:** Port Isabel Historical Museum Tues.-Sat. 10-4. Port Isabel Lighthouse Sun.-Thurs. 9-6, Fri.-Sat. 9-7, June 1-early Sept.; daily 9-5, rest of year. Treasures of the Gulf Museum Tues.-Sat. 10-5, June 1-early Sept.; Tues.-Sat. 10-4, rest of year. Port Isabel Historical Museum and Treasures of the Gulf Museum closed major holidays. **Cost:** Each site $3; $2 (ages 55+); $1 (students with ID); free (ages 0-4). Combination

ticket for all three sites $7; $5 (ages 55+); $2 (students with ID); free (ages 0-4). **Phone:** (956) 943-7602.

**Port Isabel Historical Museum** is opposite the lighthouse at 317 Railroad Ave. in the Champion Bldg. The museum, which includes a multilevel exhibit area and a theater, commemorates the history of the Port Isabel area. Displays depict Native American culture, Spanish exploration, the Mexican War, the Civil War, fishing and maritime history and border folklore. American, Mexican and Texas history also are highlighted.

**Time:** Allow 2 hours minimum. **Hours:** Tues.-Sat. 10-4. Last admission 30 minutes before closing. Closed major holidays. **Cost:** $3; $2 (ages 55+); $1 (students with ID); free (ages 0-4). Combination ticket with Port Isabel Lighthouse and Treasures of the Gulf Museum $7; $5 (ages 55+); $2 (students with ID); free (ages 0-4). **Phone:** (956) 943-7602.

**Port Isabel Lighthouse** is at Maxan and Tarnava sts. Visitors may climb to the top of the lighthouse, which guided ships through the barrier islands and Brazos Santiago 1852-1905. It is the only lighthouse along the coast of Texas open to the public. The lighthouse keeper's cottage, which houses the chamber of commerce, includes historic lighthouse-related items. **Note:** Rubber-soled shoes are recommended.

**Time:** Allow 30 minutes minimum. **Hours:** Sun.-Thurs. 9-6, Fri.-Sat. 9-7, June 1-early Sept.; daily 9-5, rest of year. Last admission 30 minutes before closing. **Cost:** $3; $2 (ages 55+); $1 (students with ID); free (ages 0-4). Combination ticket with Port Isabel Historical Museum and Treasures of the Gulf Museum $7; $5 (ages 55+); $2 (students with ID); free (ages 0-4). **Phone:** (956) 943-7602.

**Treasures of the Gulf Museum** is at 317 E. Railroad Ave. Exhibits explore three Spanish shipwrecks just 30 miles north of Port Isabel in 1554. Visitors can see artifacts and murals as well as participate in hands-on activities. The Ship Theatre and Children's Discovery Lab offer educational experiences.

**Time:** Allow 1 hour minimum. **Hours:** Tues.-Sat. 10-5, June 1-early Sept.; Tues.-Sat. 10-4, rest of year. Closed major holidays. **Cost:** $3; $2 (ages 55+); $1 (students with ID); free (ages 0-4). Combination ticket with Port Isabel Historical Museum and Port Isabel Lighthouse $7; $5 (ages 55+); $2 (students with ID); free (ages 0-4). **Phone:** (956) 943-7602.

## DIRTY AL'S PELICAN STATION    956/943-3344

▼▼▼ Regional Seafood. Casual Dining. $9-$28 **AAA Inspector Notes:** The friendly diner's American menu emphasizes seafood, salads and desserts. Specialties include crab cakes and distinctive slaws with jicama, carrots and mango. The steaks merit raves, as well. **Features:** full bar, patio dining. **Address:** 201 S Garcia St 78578 **Location:** Just s of Queen Isabella Cswy Bridge.

[B] [L] [D]

MARCELLO'S ITALIAN RESTAURANT                 956/943-7611

WWW Italian. Casual Dining. $8-$15 **AAA Inspector Notes:** Diners are greeted with a bowl of hot tomato sauce for dipping crusty homemade bread while their dinner is prepared. Casual and friendly, this is a great place for families or dining solo. **Features:** full bar. **Address:** 110 N Tarnava St 78578 **Location:** Just off Queen Isabella Blvd. L  D

# PORTLAND pop. 15,099

## BEST WESTERN PLUS NORTHSHORE INN
(361)777-3100

WWW
Hotel
$99-$189

Best Western
PLUS

**AAA Benefit:** Members save 10% or more with Best Western!

**Address:** 1707 State Hwy 181 78374 **Location:** US 181 exit Buddy Ganem Dr; south access road. **Facility:** 44 units, some efficiencies. 2 stories, interior corridors. **Pool(s):** outdoor. **Activities:** exercise room. **Guest Services:** valet and coin laundry. **Featured Amenity: full hot breakfast.**

## DAYS INN
(361)643-2222

WWW
Motel
$85-$109

**Address:** 1703 N Hwy 181 78374 **Location:** US 181 west access road exit FM 3239 northbound; exit Lang St southbound. **Facility:** 40 units. 2 stories, exterior corridors. **Terms:** cancellation fee imposed. **Pool(s):** outdoor. **Activities:** sauna, hot tub, exercise room. **Guest Services:** valet and coin laundry. **Featured Amenity: continental breakfast.**

**Visit our Days Inn Portland! Located near the Texas State Aquarium & the USS Lexington museum.**

## HAMPTON INN
(361)777-1500

WWW
Hotel
$129-$189

Hampton

**AAA Benefit:** Members save up to 10%!

**Address:** 1705 N Hwy 181 78374 **Location:** US 181 exit Buddy Ganem Dr; south access road. Across the highway from nearby Indian Point fishing pier. **Facility:** 54 units. 3 stories, interior corridors. **Terms:** 1-7 night minimum stay, cancellation fee imposed. **Pool(s):** outdoor. **Activities:** exercise room. **Guest Services:** valet and coin laundry. **Featured Amenity: full breakfast.**

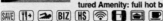

HOLIDAY INN EXPRESS HOTEL & SUITES CORPUS CHRISTI-PORTLAND                 361/777-1100

fyi Not evaluated. **Address:** 220 Reliant Dr 78374 **Location:** US 181 exit Buddy Ganem Dr; south access road. Facilities, services, and décor characterize a mid-scale property.

# PORT LAVACA (G-9) pop. 12,248

**CALHOUN COUNTY MUSEUM** is at 301 S. Ann St. The museum features local history exhibits including prehistoric Native American tools and items recovered from *La Belle,* one of French explorer René-Robert Cavelier, Sieur de La Salle's ships, which sank off the coast in 1686. Other displays describe the Karankawa Indians and German immigration into Texas by way of the nearby port city of Indianola. **Time:** Allow 30 minutes minimum. **Hours:** Tues.-Wed. 10:30-4:30, Thurs.-Fri. 10:30-5, Sat. 10-3. Closed major holidays. **Cost:** Free. **Phone:** (361) 553-4689.

## BEST WESTERN PORT LAVACA INN
(361)553-6800

WWW
Hotel
$99-$199

Best Western

**AAA Benefit:** Members save 10% or more with Best Western!

**Address:** 2202 N Hwy 35 77979 **Location:** Jct US 87 and SR 35, 2.5 mi e. **Facility:** 50 units, some two bedrooms. 2 stories, interior corridors. **Pool(s):** outdoor. **Activities:** exercise room. **Guest Services:** valet and coin laundry. **Featured Amenity: full hot breakfast.**

/ SOME UNITS

## LA QUINTA INN & SUITES PORT LAVACA
(361)552-8800

WWW
Hotel
$139-$174

**Address:** 910 Hwy 35 N 77979 **Location:** Jct US 87 and SR 35, 2 mi e. **Facility:** 57 units. 3 stories, interior corridors. **Pool(s):** outdoor. **Activities:** exercise room. **Guest Services:** valet and coin laundry. **Featured Amenity: full hot breakfast.**

/ SOME UNITS

# POST pop. 5,376

## BEST WESTERN POST INN
(806)495-9933

WWW
Hotel
$87-$160

Best Western

**AAA Benefit:** Members save 10% or more with Best Western!

**Address:** 1011 N Broadway 79356 **Location:** 1 mi n on US 84. **Facility:** 42 units. 2 stories, interior corridors. **Pool(s):** outdoor. **Activities:** exercise room. **Guest Services:** complimentary and valet laundry. **Featured Amenity: full hot breakfast.**

/ SOME UNITS

# PRESIDIO (F-3) pop. 4,426, elev. 2,594'

A sunbaked town of adobe houses along the Rio Grande, Presidio was settled in the 16th century by a handful of Spanish missionaries. By 1684 a series of missions had been constructed, and 2 centuries later the town became the Rio Grande crossing point of the Chihuahua Trail. Presidio is a popular departure point for those who wish to explore Mexico's Copper Canyon.

**Presidio Chamber of Commerce:** P.O. Box 2497, Presidio, TX 79845. **Phone:** (432) 229-3199.

**BIG BEND RANCH STATE PARK** is at 1900 Sauceda RR. The park protects 301,000 acres of Chihuahuan Desert wilderness. A 50-mile scenic drive follows the Rio Grande from the west entrance at Fort Leaton State Historic Site to the Barton Warnock Visitor Center in Lajitas *(see attraction listing p. 390)*. A 27-mile drive off FM 170 to Sauceda Headquarters and an additional 14 mile drive on a gravel road to Solitario leads to a an 8.5-mile-wide caldera. *See Recreation Areas Chart.*

Primitive camping is available. **Note:** Certain campsites along the river are closed indefinitely due to flood damage; phone for more information. **Hours:** Saucedo headquarters open daily 8-6. **Cost:** Admission Sept.-Apr. $5; free (ages 0-12). Admission rest of year $3; free (ages 0-12). Primitive camping $5-$8 per night. **Phone:** (432) 358-4444.

**FORT LEATON STATE HISTORIC SITE** is 3 mi. e. on FM 170. Former bounty hunter Benjamin Leaton established the border trading post in 1848. Twenty-five of the 47 rooms around the patio of the adobe fortress have been restored. Exhibits depict the area's Native American, Spanish, Mexican and American pioneer cultures. **Time:** Allow 30 minutes minimum. **Hours:** Daily 8-4:30. Closed Christmas. **Cost:** Admission Oct.-May $5; free (ages 0-12). Admission rest of year $3; free (ages 0-12). **Phone:** (432) 229-3613.

## QUANAH pop. 2,641

### BEST WESTERN QUANAH INN & SUITES
(940)663-5407

Hotel
$86-$100

**AAA Benefit:** Members save 10% or more with Best Western!

**Address:** 1100 W 11th St (Hwy 287) 79252 **Location:** 0.9 mi w. **Facility:** 50 units. 2 stories, interior corridors. **Amenities:** safes. **Pool(s):** heated indoor. **Activities:** hot tub, exercise room. **Guest Services:** coin laundry.

## RANCHO VIEJO pop. 2,437

RANCHO VIEJO RESORT & COUNTRY CLUB (956)350-4000

 **Resort Hotel** $149 **Address:** 1 Rancho Viejo Dr 78575 **Location:** US 77/83 exit Rancho Viejo. Located in a large quiet, residential complex. **Facility:** The resort is on beautifully manicured grounds, including a golf course, a landscaped 6,000-square-foot pool and villa-style guest units. 50 units. 1-2 stories, exterior corridors. **Terms:** check-in 4 pm, resort fee. **Dining:** 2 restaurants. **Pool(s):** outdoor. **Activities:** hot tub, boat dock, fishing, regulation golf, exercise room.

## RAYMONDVILLE pop. 11,284

LA QUINTA INN & SUITES RAYMONDVILLE (956)689-4000

 **Hotel** $94-$129 **Address:** 128 N Expwy 77 78580 **Location:** US 77, jct FM 186; on southbound access road. **Facility:** 60 units. 3 stories, interior corridors. **Pool(s):** outdoor. **Activities:** hot tub, exercise room. **Guest Services:** coin laundry.

## REFUGIO pop. 2,890

### BEST WESTERN REFUGIO INN
(361)526-4600

Hotel
$100-$180

**AAA Benefit:** Members save 10% or more with Best Western!

**Address:** 1007 N Victoria St 78377 **Location:** Just n of jct US 183 and 77. **Facility:** 42 units. 2 stories (no elevator), interior corridors. **Pool(s):** outdoor. **Activities:** exercise room. **Guest Services:** coin laundry.

## RICHARDSON pop. 99,223
- Restaurants p. 447
- Hotels & Restaurants map & index p. 179, 184
- Part of Dallas area — see map p. 161

### COURTYARD BY MARRIOTT DALLAS RICHARDSON AT CAMPBELL RD
(972)994-9933

Hotel
$59-$169

COURTYARD Marriott

**AAA Benefit:** Members save 5% or more!

**Address:** 2191 N Greenville Ave 75082 **Location:** US 75 exit 26 (Campbell Rd), just e to Greenville Ave, 0.4 mi n to Glenville Rd, then just w. **Facility:** 123 units, some two bedrooms. 4 stories, interior corridors. **Pool(s):** outdoor. **Activities:** hot tub, exercise room. **Guest Services:** valet and coin laundry, boarding pass kiosk, area transportation.

(See maps & indexes p. 179, 184.)

## COURTYARD BY MARRIOTT-DALLAS RICHARDSON AT SPRING VALLEY
(972)235-5000  **79**

Hotel
$53-$109

**COURTYARD Marriott**

**AAA Benefit:** Members save 5% or more!

**Address:** 1000 S Sherman St 75081 **Location:** US 75 exit 23 (Spring Valley Rd), just e. **Facility:** 149 units. 3 stories, interior corridors. **Pool(s):** outdoor. **Activities:** hot tub, exercise room. **Guest Services:** valet and coin laundry. **Featured Amenity:** breakfast buffet.

## DOUBLETREE BY HILTON HOTEL DALLAS - RICHARDSON
972/644-4000  **74**

**Hotel.** Rates not provided. **Address:** 1981 N Central Expwy 75080 **Location:** US 75 exit 26 (Campbell Rd), 1.8 mi n; Jct SR 5. **Facility:** 296 units. 13 stories, interior corridors. **Amenities:** video games, safes. **Pool(s):** outdoor. **Activities:** exercise room. **Guest Services:** valet and coin laundry, area transportation.

**AAA Benefit:** Members save 5% or more!

## HILTON GARDEN INN DALLAS/RICHARDSON
(972)792-9393  **69**

**Hotel** $109-$179 **Address:** 1001 W President George Bush Tpke 75080 **Location:** President George Bush Tpke (SR 190) exit Waterview Pkwy/Independence Pkwy, 0.4 mi e. **Facility:** 125 units. 4 stories, interior corridors. **Terms:** 1-7 night minimum stay, cancellation fee imposed. **Pool(s):** heated indoor. **Activities:** hot tub, exercise room. **Guest Services:** valet and coin laundry, area transportation.

**AAA Benefit:** Members save up to 10%!

## HOLIDAY INN
(972)238-1900  **76**

**Hotel** $105 **Address:** 1655 N Central Expwy 75080 **Location:** US 75 exit 26 (Campbell Rd); on southbound frontage road. **Facility:** 220 units. 6 stories, interior corridors. **Terms:** resort fee. **Pool(s):** outdoor, heated indoor. **Activities:** sauna, exercise room. **Guest Services:** valet and coin laundry, area transportation.

## HYATT HOUSE DALLAS/RICHARDSON
(972)671-8080  **71**

Extended Stay Hotel
$69-$199

**HYATT house**

**AAA Benefit:** Members save 10%!

**Address:** 2301 N Central Expwy 75080 **Location:** US 75 exit 26 (Campbell Rd), 0.5 mi w to Collins Blvd, then 0.6 mi n. **Facility:** 130 efficiencies. 2-3 stories, interior corridors. **Terms:** cancellation fee imposed. **Pool(s):** outdoor. **Activities:** hot tub, exercise room. **Guest Services:** valet and coin laundry, area transportation. **Featured Amenity:** breakfast buffet.

## HYATT REGENCY NORTH DALLAS/RICHARDSON
(972)619-1234  **75**

Hotel
$85-$249

**HYATT REGENCY**

**AAA Benefit:** Members save 10%!

**Address:** 701 E Campbell Rd 75081 **Location:** US 75 exit 26 (Campbell Rd) southbound; exit northbound; on frontage road. **Facility:** 342 units. 17 stories, interior corridors. **Terms:** cancellation fee imposed. **Amenities:** safes. **Pool(s):** heated outdoor. **Activities:** hot tub, exercise room. **Guest Services:** valet laundry, area transportation.

## RENAISSANCE DALLAS-RICHARDSON HOTEL
(972)367-2000  **70**

Hotel
$72-$138

**RENAISSANCE HOTELS**

**AAA Benefit:** Members save 5% or more!

**Address:** 900 E Lookout Dr 75082 **Location:** US 75 exit 27A (Gallatin Pkwy/Renner Rd) northbound; exit 26 (Gallatin Pkwy/Campbell Rd) southbound, just e. **Facility:** Ultra contemporary, with an atrium-style design featuring jewel-tone colors and sculpted furnishings, this hotel is on the Dallas light-rail line so one can easily enjoy the downtown sights. 336 units. 12 stories, interior corridors. **Parking:** on-site (fee) and valet. **Amenities:** safes. **Pool(s):** heated indoor. **Activities:** sauna, hot tub, exercise room. **Guest Services:** valet and coin laundry, area transportation.

## RESIDENCE INN BY MARRIOTT RICHARDSON
(972)669-5888  **72**

Extended Stay Hotel
$79-$189

**Residence Inn Marriott**

**AAA Benefit:** Members save 5% or more!

**Address:** 1040 Waterwood Dr 75082 **Location:** US 75 exit 26 (Campbell Rd), just e to Greenville Ave, 0.4 mi n to Glenville Rd, then just w. **Facility:** 120 units, some two bedrooms, efficiencies and kitchens. 3 stories, interior corridors. **Pool(s):** outdoor. **Activities:** hot tub, exercise room. **Guest Services:** valet and coin laundry, area transportation. **Featured Amenity:** full hot breakfast.

## SUPER 8
(972)680-8884  **78**

Hotel
$55-$100

**Address:** 220 W Spring Valley Rd 75081 **Location:** US 75 exit 23 (Spring Valley Rd), 0.3 mi e. **Facility:** 56 units. 2 stories (no elevator), exterior corridors. **Pool(s):** outdoor. **Activities:** hot tub, limited exercise equipment. **Guest Services:** coin laundry. **Featured Amenity:** continental breakfast.

(See maps & indexes p. 179, 184.)

## WINGATE BY WYNDHAM RICHARDSON

(972)234-5400    **77**

WVWVWV
Hotel
$69-$125

**Address:** 1577 Gateway Blvd 75080 **Location:** US 75 exit 26 (Campbell Rd); on southbound frontage road. **Facility:** 127 units. 4 stories, interior corridors. **Amenities:** safes. **Pool(s):** outdoor. **Activities:** exercise room. **Guest Services:** valet and coin laundry, area transportation. **Featured Amenity:** full hot breakfast.

SAVE  ⊞  ⫟⃗  CALL ⌖M  ⇲  BIZ
🛜  ✕  ⊟  ⌨  ⊡
/ SOME UNITS  HS

## WHERE TO EAT

### CAFE BRAZIL

972/783-9011    **73**

WVWV American. Casual Dining. $7-$11 **AAA Inspector Notes:** The cafe opens early for breakfast and serves it all day long. The food has a good variety of Tex-Mex-inspired cuisine, but sandwiches and salads also can be ordered. Specialty coffees are sold in bulk as well as in smaller-scale concoctions. Desserts made in the eatery's bakery are something special. **Address:** 2071 N Central Expwy 75080 **Location:** US 75 exit 26 (Campbell Rd) southbound; exit 27A (Galatyn Pkwy/Renner Rd) northbound; cross over to southbound frontage road. B  L  D  LATE

### GRANDY'S RESTAURANT

972/235-1373

WV American. Quick Serve. $4-$8 **AAA Inspector Notes:** Fried chicken and country-fried steak are menu standbys at the restaurant, a regional franchise. They also offer a family-style dining menu. The décor is a step up from that of most quick-serve eateries and more resembles that of a conventional restaurant. Some elements of increased service include additional rolls, iced tea refills and tray removal. **Address:** 106 W Campbell Rd 75080 **Location:** US 75 exit 26 (Campbell Rd). B  L  D

### LA MADELEINE COUNTRY FRENCH CAFE

972/671-4887

WV Traditional French. Casual Dining. $7-$12 **AAA Inspector Notes:** A fireplace creates the focal point at this cozy European style café where you can always get a quiche or savory stuffed puffed pastry on the go or stick around for a chicken crêpe or French dip sandwich. Heartier entrées like rotisserie chicken are offered and every season promises menu surprises. Whatever you decide on you probably will not get out the door without enjoying one of their tempting sweet pastries. **Features:** beer & wine. **Address:** 1320 W Campbell Rd 75080 **Location:** Jct Coit and Campbell rds, just n. B  L  D

### PAPPADEAUX SEAFOOD KITCHEN

972/235-1181

WV Regional Seafood. Casual Dining. $10-$36 **AAA Inspector Notes:** A seafood lover's delight, the restaurant taps into a little bit of New Orleans with its Cajun dishes and elaborate menu selections. Patrons might start off with a creative choice of blackened oyster and shrimp fondeaux with crayfish and let the feast begin. While music plays in the background, patrons can dig into dirty rice or spicy gumbo loaded with seafood. Well-seasoned shrimp and fish are prepared in varied ways. **Features:** full bar. **Address:** 725 S Central Expwy 75080 **Location:** US 75 exit 23 (Spring Valley Rd); on northbound frontage road. L  D

### PAPPASITO'S CANTINA

972/480-8595

WVWV Tex-Mex. Casual Dining. $11-$35 **AAA Inspector Notes:** Fine traditional offerings are served in an upscale cantina atmosphere. Often crowded during peak hours, the immensely popular stop dishes up generous portions of sizzling fajitas, enchiladas and other traditional Mexican favorites, including some shrimp specialties. The terrific margaritas are guaranteed to get attention. Tables in the large dining room are closely spaced. Ice cream with cinnamon on chocolate bread pudding shouldn't be missed. **Features:** full bar, patio dining, happy hour. **Address:** 723 S Central Expwy 75080 **Location:** US 75 exit 23 (Spring Valley Rd) southbound; exit 24 (Belt Line Rd/Main St) northbound; on northbound frontage road. L  D

### ROCKFISH SEAFOOD GRILL

972/267-8979

WVWVWV Seafood. Casual Dining. $7-$20 **AAA Inspector Notes:** Patrons shuffle through peanut shells on the floor as they make their way to their seats and are easily distracted by the numerous pieces of hunting and fishing memorabilia adorning the walls and ceiling. Although guests kick back in a log cabin-style interior, the freshly caught fish gets more sophisticated preparation than campfire roasting. The chef uses an array of sauces and cooking styles, and soups are hearty and fresh. **Features:** full bar. **Address:** 7639 Campbell Rd, Suite 800 75080 **Location:** I-635 exit 19C (Coit Rd) eastbound; exit 19B (Coit Rd) westbound, 3.8 mi n. L  D

### RUSSO'S COAL-FIRED PIZZERIA

972/235-7992    **74**

WVWV Pizza. Casual Dining. $8-$16 **AAA Inspector Notes:** Come to Russos for that neighborhood pizzeria feel; it's small, inviting and family friendly. The coal-fired pizza is the signature item here, but several pasta dishes, flatbread sandwiches and traditional Italian dishes like chicken Marsala and lobster ravioli also are served. **Features:** beer & wine, Sunday brunch. **Address:** 700 E Campbell Rd 75081 **Location:** US 75 exit 26 (Campbell Rd), just e. L  D  CALL ⌖M

---

### SILVER FOX

972/423-8121    **43**

WVWVWVWV
Steak
Fine Dining
$17-$45

**AAA Inspector Notes:** This quintessential steakhouse has comfy booths, mirrored walls, art on the walls and noise-reducing carpet that allows for good conversation. Prime beef cuts dominate the menu, but plenty of seafood and a dinner-for-two special that allows couples to dine a bit more economically also are offered. **Features:** full bar, happy hour. **Reservations:** suggested. **Address:** 3650 Shire Blvd 75082 **Location:** George Bush Tpke (SR 190) exit Jupiter, just s; in The Shire. D

## USDA Prime beef, fresh fish, lobster, local favorites

---

### SPRING CREEK BBQ

972/669-0505

WV Barbecue. Casual Dining. $8-$13 **AAA Inspector Notes:** Expect Texas-Style barbecue at its simple, homey best. Hickory smoked ribs, beef, pork and turkey lace the air with a spicy aroma that mingles with the scent of freshly baked rolls and cold ice cream slowly melting over a dish of homemade peach cobbler. Plates often are loaded with all the coleslaw, potato salad and corn on the cob they can support. Part of a small chain, this barbecue restaurant displays a rustic décor that gives patrons the impression they are "at the ranch." **Address:** 270 N Central Expwy 75080 **Location:** US 75 exit 24 southbound; exit 23 (Spring Valley Rd) northbound; between Belt Line and Arapaho rds; on northbound frontage road. L  D

### TEXAS LAND AND CATTLE STEAKHOUSE

972/705-9700

WVWV Steak. Casual Dining. $7-$27 **AAA Inspector Notes:** A variety of large Prime steaks, delicious salads and scrumptious desserts await you at the friendly Texas ranch-style restaurant. Try the signature slow-smoked sirloin, which never fails to please, or the Caesar salad, another favorite. A Texas steakhouse means everything is bigger, from large cuts and oversize salads to potatoes and side dishes. Those not in the mood for beef can opt for chicken, quail or seafood. Dessert is an occasion. **Features:** full bar. **Address:** 812 S Central Expwy 75080 **Location:** US 75 exit 22; jct Spring Valley Rd. L  D  CALL ⌖M

### THAI SOON RESTAURANT

972/234-6111    **75**

WVWV Thai. Casual Dining. $7-$14 **AAA Inspector Notes:** Located next to a ubiquitous coffee shop, this matchbox of a restaurant spices up traditional dishes to the diner's preference. The seasonal mango and sticky rice dessert is an especially nice treat after the meal. **Address:** 101 S Coit Rd, Suite 401 75080 **Location:** Jct Belt Line and Coit rds; southwest corner; in Dal-Rich Village Strip Center. L  D

## RICHLAND HILLS pop. 7,801
• Hotels & Restaurants map & index p. 257

COMFORT SUITES NEAR NORTHEAST MALL
(817)595-3332 **41**
♦♦♦ Hotel $95-$125 **Address:** 643 NE Loop 820 76118 **Location:** I-820 exit 23, just s of Glenview Dr. **Facility:** 72 units. 4 stories, interior corridors. **Pool(s):** heated indoor. **Activities:** hot tub, exercise room. **Guest Services:** valet and coin laundry.

LA QUINTA INN & SUITES FORT WORTH NE MALL
(817)595-4442 **40**
♦♦♦ Hotel $95-$130 **Address:** 653 NE Loop 820 76118 **Location:** I-820 exit 23, just s of Glenview Dr. **Facility:** 86 units. 4 stories, interior corridors. **Pool(s):** heated indoor. **Activities:** hot tub, exercise room. **Guest Services:** valet and coin laundry.

### WHERE TO EAT

EL CHICO
817/589-0737 **39**
♦♦ 
**Tex-Mex
Casual Dining
$7-$16**
**AAA Inspector Notes:** Inside and out, the decor of the popular Mexican restaurant is inviting. The menu features traditional favorites such as enchiladas, tacos, burritos and fajitas. The broad menu also lists a few American classics. **Features:** full bar. **Address:** 7621 Baker Blvd 76118 **Location:** I-820 exit 24A, just w. L D

## RICHMOND (F-9) pop. 11,679, elev. 104'
• Part of Houston area — see map p. 301

In 1822 Stephen Austin's colonists built a blockhouse at the foot of the great bend in the Brazos River, making Richmond one of Texas' oldest settlements. At that time the Brazos River was a major transportation corridor, and the crossing had strategic significance. Erastus "Deaf" Smith and Mirabeau Lamar, two important figures in Texas' fight for independence, are buried in local cemeteries. The 1908 Fort Bend County Courthouse is still in use.

Richmond, a southwest suburb of Houston, offers a variety of outdoor recreation. Ten miles southwest of town is Brazos Bend State Park (see Recreation Areas Chart), one of the state's largest parks. Almost 5,000 acres of aquatic wetlands, hardwood forests and coastal prairies make up the park, which attracts a diversity of birds and migratory waterfowl.

**Central Fort Bend Chamber Alliance:** 4120 Ave. H, Rosenberg, TX 77471. **Phone:** (281) 342-5464.

**FORT BEND MUSEUM** is at 500 S. Houston St. The museum traces the history of the county from its original 300 families. On the grounds, the John M. Moore house is an example of Greek Revival architecture. The Long-Smith cottage, also on the grounds, offers tours. **Hours:** Tues.-Fri. 9-5, Sat. 10-5. Closed major holidays. **Cost:** $5; $4 (ages 62+); $3 (ages 5-15). **Phone:** (281) 342-6478.

**GEORGE RANCH HISTORICAL PARK** is 8 mi. s. on US 59 to Crabb River Rd. exit, then 5 mi. e. to 10215 FM 762. This 500-acre living history site is located on a 23,000-acre working ranch. Trams take visitors to four areas representing a century of Texas history, including an 1830s stock farm; an 1860s prairie home; an 1890s Victorian mansion, cowboy camp, blacksmith shop and family cemetery; and a 1930s ranch house and cattle-working area. **Hours:** Tues.-Sat. 9-5. Closed Jan. 1, Thanksgiving, Christmas Eve and Christmas. **Cost:** $10; $9 (ages 62+); $5 (ages 5-15). **Phone:** (281) 343-0218.

## ROANOKE H-2 pop. 5,962, elev. 633'
• Part of Dallas area — see map p. 161

**HAWAIIAN FALLS - ROANOKE** is at 290 W. Byron Nelson Blvd. Highlights of this Hawaiian-themed water park include Mega WaterWorld, an interactive play structure with waterslides, a raft ride, dump buckets and more; the spiraling Hightide Whirlpool waterslide; the family-friendly Hawaiian Halfpipe raft ride; and the Kiki Cowabunga slide, designed for kids.

Height restrictions apply on some rides. Lounge chairs are available on a first-come, first-served basis. Cabanas and lockers can be rented. Guests may bring their own food but must pay a $10 cooler fee. **Time:** Allow 4 hours minimum. **Hours:** Park opens daily at 10:30, Memorial Day-Labor Day; closing times vary. Phone ahead to confirm schedule. **Cost:** $26.99; $19.99 (ages 55+ and under 48 inches tall); free (ages 0-2). Under 14 must be with an adult. **Phone:** (817) 853-0099 or (888) 544-7550.

### BEST WESTERN ROANOKE INN & SUITES
(817)490-9595
♦♦ 
**Hotel
$79**

**AAA Benefit:** Members save 10% or more with Best Western!

**Address:** 337 Dorman Rd 76262 **Location:** Just e of jct US 377 and SR 114. **Facility:** 58 units. 3 stories, interior corridors. **Pool(s):** outdoor. **Activities:** exercise room. **Guest Services:** coin laundry. **Featured Amenity:** full hot breakfast.

COMFORT SUITES NEAR ALLIANCE
(817)490-1455
♦♦ Hotel $85-$119 **Address:** 801 Byron Nelson Blvd 76262 **Location:** I-35 exit 70 (SR 114), 2 mi e. **Facility:** 88 units. 3 stories, interior corridors. **Pool(s):** outdoor. **Activities:** hot tub, exercise room. **Guest Services:** valet and coin laundry.

### WHERE TO EAT

BABE'S CHICKEN DINNER HOUSE
817/491-2900
♦♦ Chicken. Family Dining. $11 **AAA Inspector Notes:** This very popular country-themed restaurant located in the charming downtown area keeps things simple. You can choose fried chicken or chicken-fried steak served alongside corn, mashed potatoes and biscuits, and that's it. It's all served family style with endless servings of sides. It's a good choice for families or groups. **Address:** 104 N Oak St 76262 **Location:** Between Rusk and Main sts; downtown.

L D

**RENO RED'S**                                    817/491-4855

 American. Casual Dining. $6-$25 **AAA Inspector Notes:** Frontier cooking best describes such dishes as chicken-fried chicken, steaks, barbecued meats and grilled catfish. The rustic dining rooms have taxidermy lining the walls and country music playing in the background. On my visit I opted for the half rack of ribs, which proved to be only lightly moistened with barbecue sauce, allowing the smoky flavor of the meat to come through. I didn't even need the washcloth. If you're thinking of saving room for dessert, I wouldn't. **Features:** full bar, happy hour. **Address:** 304 S Hwy 377 76262 **Location:** Jct SR 114, 1 mi s.

## ROBSTOWN pop. 11,487
• Hotels & Restaurants map & index p. 149

**BEST WESTERN PLUS TROPIC INN**
                                      (361)767-3900   40

Hotel
$99-$149

**AAA Benefit:** Members save 10% or more with Best Western!

**Address:** 615 S Hwy 77 78380 **Location:** On US 77 southbound, just ne of CR 892 (Lincoln Ave). **Facility:** 40 units, some efficiencies. 2 stories, interior corridors. **Pool(s):** outdoor. **Activities:** exercise room. **Guest Services:** coin laundry.

**DAYS INN**                          (361)387-8600   41

Motel
$90-$143

**Address:** 650 Hwy 77 S 78380 **Location:** Just n of jct CR 892 (Lincoln Ave) and US 77. **Facility:** 35 units, some efficiencies. 1 story, exterior corridors. **Pool(s):** outdoor. **Guest Services:** coin laundry. **Featured Amenity:** continental breakfast.

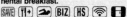  

## ROCKDALE pop. 5,595

**BEST WESTERN ROCKDALE INN**    (512)446-6163

Hotel
$85-$100

**AAA Benefit:** Members save 10% or more with Best Western!

**Address:** 381 N US Hwy 77 76567 **Location:** Jct US 77 and 79, just n. **Facility:** 43 units. 2 stories (no elevator), exterior corridors. **Terms:** 3 day cancellation notice-fee imposed. **Pool(s):** outdoor. **Guest Services:** valet and coin laundry.

## ROCKPORT (H-8) pop. 8,766, elev. 6'
• Restaurants p. 450

Rockport is a picturesque resort noted as an artists' colony and as one of the major birding areas in the country. Twice a year thousands of migratory waterfowl and other birds arrive to nest and breed on the nearby islands. A local wildlife refuge in Little Bay, Connie Hagar Wildlife Sanctuary was named for a legendary Rockport birder, whose efforts helped establish Rockport's birding reputation.

Birds are often the subject of Rockport's other major interest: art. By remodeling rundown buildings on Austin Street for use as galleries and studios, the Rockport Art Association sparked a restoration of neighboring buildings that now house shops and restaurants.

Twelve miles northeast is Goose Island State Park. *See Recreation Areas Chart.*

**Rockport-Fulton Area Chamber of Commerce:** 319 Broadway St., Rockport, TX 78382. **Phone:** (361) 729-6445 or (800) 242-0071.

**FULTON MANSION STATE HISTORIC SITE** is at 317 Fulton Beach Rd. at jct. Henderson St.; the Education and History Center is behind the mansion. This restored 1877 house was built in the French Second Empire style. The elaborate house incorporated such innovations as gas lighting, central heat and hot and cold running water. The Education and History Center offers interactive exhibits, history presentations and craft projects as well as a video and exhibits about the mansion's restoration work.

**Note:** The mansion is closed for renovations and is expected to reopen fall 2014. The Education and History Center remains open. Picnic tables are available on the mansion's south lawn. **Time:** Allow 1 hour minimum. **Hours:** Education and History Center open Tues.-Sat. 9:30-4:30, Sun. 12:30-4:30. Phone for mansion tour schedule when house reopens. Closed Jan. 1, Thanksgiving, Christmas Eve, Christmas and Dec. 31. Phone ahead to confirm schedule. **Cost:** $3; $1 (ages 6-18 and students with ID). Admission will return to $6 and $4 when the mansion reopens. **Phone:** (361) 729-0386.

**TEXAS MARITIME MUSEUM** is off SR 35 Bus. Rte. at the Rockport Harbor. This museum explores the maritime history of Texas, including Spanish and French exploration, seaport communities, maritime commerce and the search for offshore oil and gas. Nautical artifacts relate to shipbuilding, the oil industry and fishing. Highlights include a 1:12 scale model of *La Belle*, La Salle's flagship, and other artifacts related to the failed French colony.

**Time:** Allow 1 hour, 30 minutes minimum. **Hours:** Tues.-Sat. 10-4, Sun. 1-4. **Cost:** $8; $6 (ages 60+ and active military); $3 (ages 3-12). **Phone:** (361) 729-1271, (361) 729-6644 or (866) 729-2469.

**AMERICAS BEST VALUE INN**         (361)727-0283

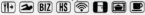 Hotel $59-$169 **Address:** 901 Hwy 35 N 78382 **Location:** On SR 35, just s of downtown historic area. **Facility:** 48 units. 2 stories, exterior corridors. **Terms:** 2 night minimum stay - seasonal and/or weekends. **Pool(s):** outdoor. **Guest Services:** coin laundry.

## DAYS INN (361)729-6379

Motel
$65-$105

**Address:** 1212 Laurel St 78382 **Location:** Jct Laurel St and Business Rt SR 35; center. **Facility:** 28 units. 3 stories (no elevator), exterior corridors. **Pool(s):** outdoor. **Activities:** hot tub. **Featured Amenity: continental breakfast.**

## HOLIDAY INN EXPRESS HOTEL & SUITES 361/729-4444

**Hotel.** Rates not provided. **Address:** 925 Lady Claire St 78382 **Location:** On SR 35. Across from city harbor, overlooking bay. **Facility:** 69 units. 3 stories, interior corridors. **Pool(s):** outdoor. **Activities:** exercise room. **Guest Services:** coin laundry.

## THE LIGHTHOUSE INN AT ARANSAS BAY (361)790-8439

Hotel
$109-$319

**Address:** 200 S Fulton Beach Rd 78382 **Location:** Oceanfront. SR 35, e on Broadway to Fulton Beach Rd, just s. **Facility:** 78 units, some kitchens. 3 stories, interior corridors. **Terms:** 2 night minimum stay - seasonal and/or weekends, 3 day cancellation notice-fee imposed. **Pool(s):** outdoor. **Activities:** hot tub, fishing, exercise room. **Guest Services:** coin laundry.

### WHERE TO EAT

#### THE BIG FISHERMAN 361/729-1997

Regional Seafood. Casual Dining. $6-$14 **AAA Inspector Notes:** Tucked away just off the main highway, this large and casual seafood restaurant is a local favorite known for large portions and excellent value. **Features:** full bar. **Address:** 510 SH 188 78336 **Location:** 0.3 mi w of SR 35.  L  D

#### THE DINER 361/729-4985

Regional American. Family Dining. $5-$10 **AAA Inspector Notes:** The basic diner features seafood, sandwiches and burgers. Specialty dishes include chicken-fried steak and fried chicken served with homemade mac 'n' cheese and mashed potatoes. This is also a local favorite for breakfast. **Address:** 205 Hwy 35 N 78382 **Location:** On SR 35 N; at N Church St.  B  L

#### HEMINGWAY'S BAR & GRILL 361/729-7555

American. Fine Dining. $18-$35 **AAA Inspector Notes:** This elegant and refined dining room includes rich woods and a floor-to-ceiling aquarium. The cuisine focuses on specialty farm-to-table ingredients and the freshest of seafood enhanced with a very complete wine list. It's among the better dining options in the area. **Features:** full bar, happy hour. **Address:** 1008 E North St 78382 **Location:** Just w of Loop 70.  L  D  CALL

#### JALISCO RESTAURANT 361/727-0555

Regional Mexican. Family Dining. $6-$10 **AAA Inspector Notes:** Mexican food in a fisherman's paradise? This is the place to eat delicious huevos rancheros, enchiladas and all sorts of tacos made with fresh tortillas. **Address:** 1701 Hwy 35 S 78382 **Location:** Jct W 3rd St.  B  L  D

#### J.J.'S BURGER WORKS AND CAFE 361/729-8787

American. Family Dining. $6-$12 **AAA Inspector Notes:** The restaurant's first-class home cooking includes moist and flavorful meatloaf, all types of seafood, and a complete soup and salad bar. Patrons also can order off the menu by telling the staff exactly what they want; chances are they can whip up a Vietnamese or Asian-style dish to match. It's an excellent value with some of the best prices in town. **Features:** patio dining. **Address:** 302 Hwy 35 N 78382 **Location:** Just s of E Laurel St.  B  L

#### LAT 28 02 COASTAL CUISINE 361/727-9009

Regional New World Seafood. Fine Dining. $12-$38 **AAA Inspector Notes:** Overlooking the Gulf of Mexico, the restaurant also offers sights inside in the fine art of the attached art gallery. The fine art of coastal cuisine comes alive in artistically presented preparations of fresh oysters, giant gulf shrimp and crab, as well as duck breast. **Features:** full bar. **Reservations:** suggested. **Address:** 105 N Austin St 78382 **Location:** Jct E Concho St.  D

## ROCKWALL pop. 37,490
### • Part of Dallas area — see map p. 161

## BEST WESTERN PLUS ROCKWALL INN & SUITES (972)722-3265

Hotel
$85-$150

**AAA Benefit:** Members save 10% or more with Best Western!

**Address:** 996 E I-30 75087 **Location:** I-30 exit 68; on westbound frontage road. **Facility:** 60 units. 3 stories, interior corridors. **Pool(s):** heated indoor. **Activities:** hot tub, exercise room. **Guest Services:** valet and coin laundry. **Featured Amenity: full hot breakfast.**

## HILTON DALLAS/ROCKWALL LAKEFRONT (214)771-3700

Hotel $119-$209 **Address:** 2055 Summer Lee Dr 75032 **Location:** I-30 E exit 67A (Horizon Rd) eastbound; exit 67B (Horizon Rd) westbound, just s to Summer Lee Dr, then 0.5

**AAA Benefit:** Members save 5% or more!

mi s. **Facility:** On the shores of Lake Ray Hubbard, this hotel has modern rooms, an inviting pool area and easy access to shopping and several restaurants. 231 units. 5 stories, interior corridors. **Parking:** on-site and valet. **Terms:** 1-7 night minimum stay, cancellation fee imposed. **Amenities:** video games, safes. **Pool(s):** outdoor. **Activities:** hot tub, boat dock, exercise room. **Guest Services:** valet laundry, area transportation.

## LA QUINTA INN & SUITES ROCKWALL (972)771-1685

Hotel $85-$124 **Address:** 689 E I-30 75087 **Location:** I-30 exit 67 (Ridge Rd) westbound; exit 67B (Horizon Rd) eastbound; on eastbound frontage road. **Facility:** 60 units. 3 stories, interior corridors. **Pool(s):** heated indoor. **Activities:** hot tub, exercise room. **Guest Services:** coin laundry.

### WHERE TO EAT

#### CULPEPPER STEAK HOUSE 972/771-1001

Steak. Fine Dining. $16-$45 **AAA Inspector Notes:** This popular restaurant features live jazz on the weekends. Steaks and other grilled specialties are served in a rustic mountain-lodge-like setting. **Features:** full bar, patio dining, Sunday brunch, happy hour. **Reservations:** suggested. **Address:** 309 I-30 75087 **Location:** I-30 exit 67 (Ridge Rd) westbound, 1 mi to Horizon Rd; on south access road; exit 67A (Horizon Rd) eastbound.  D

#### EL CHICO 972/771-8814

Tex-Mex
Casual Dining
$7-$16

**AAA Inspector Notes:** Inside and out, the decor of the popular Mexican restaurant is inviting. The menu features traditional favorites such as enchiladas, tacos, burritos and fajitas. The broad menu also lists a few American classics. **Features:** full bar. **Address:** 503 E I-30 75087 **Location:** I-30 E exit 67 (Ridge Rd) westbound, 0.5 mi to Horizon Rd; on south frontage road; exit 67A (Horizon Rd) eastbound.  L  D

### GLORIA'S RESTAURANT · 972/772-4088

Salvadoran. Casual Dining. $10-$20 **AAA Inspector Notes:** Salvadoran and Mexican dishes make up the menu at the popular restaurant. Among choices are plantains, seafood soup, grilled quail, flank-steak enchiladas and quesadillas. Homemade tortillas and tamales add to the authenticity and accentuate many dishes. Scenic views of Lake Ray Hubbard can be had from the patio or the large picture windows that cover the rear wall. **Features:** full bar, patio dining, Sunday brunch, happy hour. **Address:** 2079 Summer Lee Dr 75032 **Location:** I-30 E exit 67A (Horizon Rd), 0.5 mi s on Lake Ray Hubbard. L D

### GRANDY'S RESTAURANT · 972/772-3565

American. Quick Serve. $4-$8 **AAA Inspector Notes:** Fried chicken and country-fried steak are menu standbys at the restaurant, a regional franchise. They also offer a family-style dining menu. The décor is a step up from that of most quick-serve eateries and more resembles that of a conventional restaurant. Some elements of increased service include additional rolls, iced tea refills and tray removal. **Address:** 726 I-30 75087 **Location:** I-30 exit 68 eastbound; exit 67 (Ridge Rd) westbound; on westbound frontage road. B L D

### KYOTO JAPANESE STEAK HOUSE · 214/771-0688

Japanese. Casual Dining. $11-$21 **AAA Inspector Notes:** Families enjoy the theater at the hibachi grill while the sushi bar offers an array of offerings, including crawfish, sea urchin, octopus and a variety of tuna. **Features:** full bar, happy hour. **Address:** 1599 Laguna Dr 75087 **Location:** I-30 exit 67B (Horizon Rd) westbound; exit 67A (Horizon Rd) eastbound, just n. L D

### LUIGIS ITALIAN CAFE · 972/772-3522

Italian. Casual Dining. $8-$16 **AAA Inspector Notes:** The family-owned and -operated café has a menu featuring seafood, veal and chicken selections as well as several types of pasta. Those who like pizza can create their own by the pie or the slice. The homemade garlic rolls are popular. **Features:** beer & wine. **Address:** 2002 S Goliad St 75087 **Location:** I-30 exit 68, just n. L D

### THE OAR HOUSE · 972/771-9687

Italian Seafood. Casual Dining. $9-$28 **AAA Inspector Notes:** This family-owned restaurant concentrates on seafood. It has a rustic country-home atmosphere and a nautical theme. **Features:** full bar, Sunday brunch, happy hour. **Address:** 305 I-30 75087 **Location:** I-30 exit 67 (Ridge Rd) westbound, 1 mi to Horizon Rd; on south frontage road; exit 67A (Horizon Rd) eastbound. L D

### SALTGRASS STEAKHOUSE · 972/771-4999

Steak. Casual Dining. $9-$30 **AAA Inspector Notes:** Those looking for something different should try the comfortable steakhouse, which never says no to a special request. Born from the spirit of Texas cattle drives, the restaurant resembles a Texas lodge, with high ceilings and mounted animal heads. Baby back ribs are so tender the meat falls off the bone. Also on the menu are hearty steaks, prime rib, chicken, seafood and yummy desserts. **Features:** full bar. **Address:** 1649 Laguna Dr 75087 **Location:** I-30 exit 67A (Horizon Rd) eastbound; exit 67 (Ridge Rd) westbound; off westbound frontage road. SAVE L D

### SNUFFER'S ROCKWALL · 972/722-9811

Burgers. Casual Dining. $7-$12 **AAA Inspector Notes:** For more than 20 years, this small restaurant chain has been a great spot for juicy hamburgers, margaritas and people-watching. Period pictures and dark wooden booths distinguish the bustling dining room, which perches on a hill overlooking Lake Ray Hubbard to the west. **Features:** full bar. **Address:** 2901 Village Dr 75032 **Location:** I-30 exit 67 (Ridge Rd) westbound; exit 67A (Horizon Rd) eastbound. L D

### SOULMAN'S BAR-B-QUE · 972/771-0200

Barbecue. Quick Serve. $9-$19 **AAA Inspector Notes:** Barbecue is at the heart of the small chain of Dallas-Fort Worth area restaurants. The menu lists all the usual suspects: beef, chicken, turkey, sausage and ribs. Homemade banana pudding is a treat. Servings are ample to please hungry patrons. **Address:** 691 I-30 E 75087 **Location:** I-30 exit 67 (Ridge Rd) westbound; exit 67B (Horizon Rd) eastbound. L D CALL

### TREVINO'S TEX-MEX RESTAURANT · 972/771-1406

Tex-Mex. Casual Dining. $9-$17 **AAA Inspector Notes:** This family-owned and -operated restaurant serves all the traditional favorites such as fajitas, enchiladas and quesadillas. Breakfast is served on the weekends as well. **Features:** full bar. **Address:** 101 N Goliad Rd 75087 **Location:** Center; on town square. L D

## ROSENBERG pop. 30,618
• Part of Houston area — see map p. 301

### LA QUINTA INN & SUITES ROSENBERG · (832)595-6111

Hotel $100-$135 **Address:** 28332 Southwest Frwy 77471 **Location:** Jct US 59 and SR 36; on southbound frontage road. **Facility:** 56 units. 3 stories, interior corridors. **Pool(s):** outdoor. **Activities:** hot tub, exercise room. **Guest Services:** coin laundry.

### SPRINGHILL SUITES BY MARRIOTT ROSENBERG · (832)595-2220

Hotel $95-$119 **Address:** 6815 Reading Rd 77471 **Location:** US 59 S exit Reading Rd, just s; behind shopping mall. **Facility:** 118 units. 5 stories, interior corridors. **Pool(s):** heated outdoor. **Activities:** exercise room. **Guest Services:** coin laundry.

> **AAA Benefit:** Members save 5% or more!

## ROUND ROCK pop. 99,887
• Restaurants p. 453
• Hotels & Restaurants map & index p. 86

### AUSTIN MARRIOTT NORTH · (512)733-6767 · 113

Hotel $100-$300 **Address:** 2600 LaFrontera Blvd 78681 **Location:** I-35 exit 251, 0.6 mi w. **Facility:** 295 units. 8 stories, interior corridors. **Dining:** River City Grill, see separate listing. **Pool(s):** heated indoor. **Activities:** exercise room. **Guest Services:** valet and coin laundry.

> **AAA Benefit:** Members save 5% or more!

### BEST WESTERN EXECUTIVE INN · (512)255-3222 · 104

Hotel $87-$129

> **AAA Benefit:** Members save 10% or more with Best Western!

**Address:** 1851 N I-35 78664 **Location:** I-35 exit 253 northbound; exit 253A southbound, U-turn. **Facility:** 68 units. 2 stories (no elevator), exterior corridors. **Terms:** 2-3 night minimum stay - seasonal. **Pool(s):** outdoor. **Activities:** exercise room. **Guest Services:** coin laundry.

### CANDLEWOOD SUITES · 512/828-0899 · 107

Extended Stay Hotel. Rates not provided. **Address:** 521 S I-35 78664 **Location:** I-35 exit 252A, just n on northbound frontage road. **Facility:** 97 efficiencies. 3 stories, interior corridors. **Activities:** exercise room. **Guest Services:** complimentary and valet laundry.

---

Learn the local driving laws
at DrivingLaws.AAA.com

(See map & index p. 86.)

## COMFORT SUITES
(512)244-2700 **106**

▼▼▼ Hotel $89-$299 **Address:** 609 Chisholm Tr 78681 **Location:** I-35 exit 252B northbound; exit 252AB southbound, just w. **Facility:** 63 units, some two bedrooms and kitchens. 3 stories, interior corridors. **Pool(s):** outdoor. **Activities:** exercise room. **Guest Services:** valet and coin laundry.

## COUNTRY INN & SUITES BY CARLSON
(512)828-3800 **105**

▼▼▼ Hotel $89-$109

**Address:** 1560 N I-35 78681 **Location:** I-35 exit 254, 0.8 mi s on west frontage road. **Facility:** 63 units. 3 stories, interior corridors. **Terms:** cancellation fee imposed. **Pool(s):** outdoor. **Activities:** hot tub, exercise room. **Guest Services:** valet and coin laundry.

## COURTYARD BY MARRIOTT AUSTIN ROUND ROCK
(512)255-5551 **99**

▼▼▼ Hotel $89-$139 **Address:** 2700 Hoppe Tr 78681 **Location:** I-35 exit 254; on west frontage road. **Facility:** 113 units. 3 stories, interior corridors. **Pool(s):** outdoor. **Activities:** hot tub, exercise room. **Guest Services:** valet and coin laundry, boarding pass kiosk.

**AAA Benefit:** Members save 5% or more!

## EXTENDED STAY AMERICA AUSTIN-ROUND ROCK-N
(512)671-7872 **108**

▼▼ Extended Stay Hotel $49-$59 **Address:** 555 S I-35 City Centre Business Park 78664 **Location:** I-35 exit 252A; on northbound frontage road. **Facility:** 138 kitchen units. 3 stories, interior corridors. *Bath:* shower only. **Terms:** cancellation fee imposed. **Guest Services:** coin laundry.

## HAMPTON INN AUSTIN-ROUND ROCK
(512)248-9100 **111**

▼▼▼ Hotel $109-$199 **Address:** 110 Dell Way 78664 **Location:** I-35 exit 251; on east frontage road. **Facility:** 94 units. 6 stories, interior corridors. **Terms:** 1-7 night minimum stay, cancellation fee imposed. **Pool(s):** outdoor. **Activities:** hot tub, exercise room. **Guest Services:** valet laundry.

**AAA Benefit:** Members save up to 10%!

## HILTON GARDEN INN
(512)341-8200 **102**

▼▼▼ Hotel $99-$149 **Address:** 2310 N I-35 78681 **Location:** I-35 exit 254; on southbound frontage road. **Facility:** 122 units. 3 stories, interior corridors. **Terms:** 1-7 night minimum stay, cancellation fee imposed. **Pool(s):** outdoor. **Activities:** hot tub, exercise room. **Guest Services:** valet and coin laundry.

**AAA Benefit:** Members save up to 10%!

## HOLIDAY INN AUSTIN NORTH ROUND ROCK
512/246-7000 **100**

Hotel Rates not provided

**Address:** 2370 Chisholm Tr 78681 **Location:** I-35 exit 256 southbound; exit 254 northbound; just w. **Facility:** 116 units. 4 stories, interior corridors. **Amenities:** video games. **Pool(s):** heated indoor. **Activities:** hot tub, exercise room. **Guest Services:** valet and coin laundry.

## HOLIDAY INN EXPRESS & SUITES
(512)733-2630 **101**

▼▼▼▼ Hotel $105-$119 **Address:** 2340 N I-35 78681 **Location:** I-35 exit 254; on west frontage road. **Facility:** 91 units. 3 stories, interior corridors. **Pool(s):** outdoor. **Activities:** hot tub, exercise room. **Guest Services:** valet and coin laundry.

## HOMEWOOD SUITES BY HILTON
(512)394-9200 **110**

▼▼▼ Extended Stay Contemporary Hotel $129-$179 **Address:** 2201 S Mays St 78664 **Location:** I-35 exit 251, just n on east frontage road to Hesters Crossing, then just e. **Facility:** 115 efficiencies, some two bedrooms. 4 stories, interior corridors. **Terms:** 1-7 night minimum stay, cancellation fee imposed. **Pool(s):** outdoor. **Activities:** exercise room. **Guest Services:** valet and coin laundry, area transportation.

**AAA Benefit:** Members save up to 10%!

## LA QUINTA INN & SUITES AUSTIN ROUND ROCK NORTH
(512)255-6666 **103**

▼▼▼ Hotel $89-$144 **Address:** 2004 I-35 N 78681 **Location:** I-35 exit 254; on west frontage road. **Facility:** 116 units, some kitchens. 3 stories, interior corridors. **Amenities:** video games. **Pool(s):** outdoor. **Activities:** hot tub, exercise room. **Guest Services:** valet laundry.

## RESIDENCE INN BY MARRIOTT AUSTIN ROUND ROCK
(512)733-2400 **112**

▼▼▼ Extended Stay Hotel $89-$319

Residence Inn Marriott

**AAA Benefit:** Members save 5% or more!

**Address:** 2505 S I-35 78664 **Location:** I-35 exit 250 southbound; exit 251 northbound; on east frontage road. **Facility:** 96 units, some two bedrooms, efficiencies and kitchens. 3 stories, interior corridors. **Terms:** check-in 4 pm. **Pool(s):** heated outdoor. **Activities:** hot tub, exercise room. **Guest Services:** valet and coin laundry. **Featured Amenity: full hot breakfast.**

## SPRINGHILL SUITES BY MARRIOTT
(512)733-6700 **98**

▼▼▼ Hotel $83-$139 **Address:** 2960 Hoppe Tr 78681 **Location:** I-35 exit 256 southbound; exit 254 northbound; on west frontage road. **Facility:** 104 units. 4 stories, interior corridors. **Pool(s):** heated indoor. **Activities:** hot tub, exercise room. **Guest Services:** valet and coin laundry.

**AAA Benefit:** Members save 5% or more!

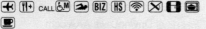

(See map & index p. 86.)

**STAYBRIDGE SUITES AUSTIN-ROUND ROCK**
(512)733-0942 **109**

WWW Extended Stay Contemporary Hotel $104-$189 Address: 520 I-35 S 78681 Location: I-35 exit 252B northbound; exit 252AB southbound; on west frontage road. Facility: 81 efficiencies, some two bedrooms. 4 stories, interior corridors. Terms: cancellation fee imposed. Pool(s): heated outdoor. Activities: exercise room. Guest Services: complimentary laundry.

## WHERE TO EAT

**FRENCH QUARTER** 512/433-6402 **79**

WWWW Southern American. Fine Dining. $10-$36 AAA Inspector Notes: *Historic.* In a stagecoach depot dating to 1848, the Louisiana-style café prepares chicken, seafood, beef tenderloin and pork dishes with a Cajun flair. Features: full bar, patio dining, happy hour. Reservations: required. Address: 901 Round Rock Ave 78681 Location: I-35 exit 252B northbound; exit 252A/B southbound, just w.

**GINO'S ITALIAN RESTAURANT** 512/218-9922 **83**

WW Italian. Casual Dining. $8-$22 AAA Inspector Notes: Since 1966, family-inspired dishes have been pleasing the guests of this popular restaurant. Features: beer & wine. Address: 1701 S Mays St 78664 Location: I-35 exit 251, just n on east frontage road to Hesters Crossing, just e to S Mays St, then just n; in South Towne Plaza.

**LA MADELEINE COUNTRY FRENCH CAFE** 512/863-0089

W Traditional French Breakfast Sandwiches. Casual Dining. $7-$12 AAA Inspector Notes: A fireplace creates the focal point at this cozy European style café where you can always get a quiche or savory puffed pastry on the go or stick around for a chicken crêpe or French dip sandwich. Heartier entrées like rotisserie chicken are offered and every season promises menu surprises. Whatever you decide on you probably will not get out the door without enjoying one of their tempting sweet pastries. Address: 4401 N I-35, Suite 2002 78664 Location: I-35 exit 256, just n; in Prime Outlet Mall.

**LA MARGARITA** 512/388-1103 **78**

WW Mexican. Casual Dining. $7-$16 AAA Inspector Notes: Traditional Mexican dishes are dished in generous portions at the cantina-style restaurant. Features: full bar. Address: 1530 N I-35 78681 Location: I-35 exit 254, 1.5 mi s on west frontage road.

**MAIN STREET GRILL** 512/244-7525 **81**

WWW American. Fine Dining. $9-$35 AAA Inspector Notes: Patrons appreciate not only the pleasant and relaxing atmosphere but also the nicely varied menu of steaks, chops, chicken, seafood and specialty items. Features: full bar. Address: 118 E Main St 78664 Location: At Main and S Lampasas sts; downtown. Parking: street only.

**MIGHTY FINE** 512/381-3310

W Burgers. Quick Serve. $5-$7 AAA Inspector Notes: All-American fare of large juicy burgers, generous portions of french fries and handmade premium milk shakes are available at this restaurant conveniently located near the Round Rock Outlet Mall. Features: beer only. Address: 201 University Oaks Blvd 78664 Location: I-35 exit 256, just e; behind IKEA.

**POK-E-JO'S SMOKEHOUSE** 512/388-7578

W Barbecue. Quick Serve. $4-$12 AAA Inspector Notes: This popular and relaxed spot slow-smokes delicious barbecue meats, which guests can order with a selection of tasty side dishes. Features: beer only. Address: 1202-C N I-35 78681 Location: I-35 exit 253; on northwest corner.

**RIVER CITY GRILL** 512/733-6767 **84**

WWW American. Casual Dining. $9-$32 AAA Inspector Notes: At lunch, the staff sets up a nice hot buffet, but guests also can choose from such menu items as sandwiches and salads. Patrons can unwind in a relaxed atmosphere over dinner entrees of beef, seafood, chicken and pasta. Barbecue ribs are a specialty. Features: full bar. Address: 2600 LaFrontera Blvd 78681 Location: I-35 exit 251, 0.6 mi w; in Austin Marriott North.

**RUDY'S COUNTRY STORE AND BAR-B-QUE** 512/244-2936

W Barbecue. Quick Serve. $4-$12 AAA Inspector Notes: This small, informal barbecue chain has a twist: The tasty beef is ordered by the pound. Guests can mix and match and order three-quarters of a pound of beef with a half-pound of turkey or pork, for example. Desserts and coleslaw are prepackaged, and precooked beans accompany the meat. A drive-through window is available at most locations. Features: beer & wine. Address: 2400 I-35 N 78681 Location: I-35 exit 254; on west frontage road.

**SALTGRASS STEAKHOUSE** 512/238-0091 **76**

WW Steak. Casual Dining. $9-$31 AAA Inspector Notes: Those looking for something different should try the comfortable steakhouse, which never says no to a special request. Born from the spirit of Texas cattle drives, the restaurant resembles a Texas lodge, with high ceilings and mounted animal heads. Baby back ribs are so tender the meat falls off the bone. Also on the menu are hearty steaks, prime rib, chicken, seafood and yummy desserts. Features: full bar. Address: 2300 N I-35 78681 Location: I-35 exit 254; on southwest frontage road.

**THE SALT LICK BAR-B-QUE** 512/386-1044 **77**

WW Barbecue. Casual Dining. $9-$23 AAA Inspector Notes: This renowned restaurant serves up heaping portions of your favorite smoked meats and side dishes. Don't pass up the pecan pie or cobblers for dessert. Features: full bar, patio dining. Address: 3350 Palm Valley Blvd 78665 Location: US 79, 2 mi e; at The Dell Diamond.

**SERRANO'S** 512/218-4888

WW Tex-Mex. Casual Dining. $6-$15 AAA Inspector Notes: The Tex-Mex cafe is known for its stuffed jalapenos, which tempt those with a taste for something spicy (and a nearby water glass). Among good choices are crunchy flautas and sizzling fajitas. Features: full bar. Reservations: suggested. Address: 2701 Parker Rd, Suite D200 78681 Location: I-35 exit 250, 0.4 mi w.

**SIRLOIN STOCKADE** 512/218-8600

WW American. Casual Dining. $7-$16 AAA Inspector Notes: The steakhouse lines up buffet items, including pizza, tacos, soups, salads and desserts, providing both excellent variety and a good value. Rotating theme nights allow for the sampling of sushi, barbecue and seafood. The buffet may also serve to complement a quality steak. Address: 1723 I-35 N 78664 Location: I-35 exit 253, 1 mi n on east frontage road.

**TARKA INDIAN KITCHEN ROUND ROCK** 512/246-1922

WW Indian. Casual Dining. $6-$9 AAA Inspector Notes: Many items are available to choose from at this modern restaurant, including naaminis, kebabs, biryanis, curried dishes and vegetarian choices. Features: beer & wine, patio dining. Address: 201 University Cir 78665 Location: I-35 exit 256, 1 blk e to University Oaks Blvd, then just s; behind IKEA.

**THAI SPOON RESTAURANT** 512/733-2233 **82**

WW Thai. Casual Dining. $6-$7 AAA Inspector Notes: A very nice selection of menu items is offered at popular prices. Features: beer & wine. Address: 3720 Gattis School Rd, Suite 400 78664 Location: I-354 exit 252A, just e to S Mays St, just n to Gattis School Rd, then 3.7 mi e; in HEB Shopping Center.

## ROUND TOP (F-9) pop. 90, elev. 390'
• Hotels p. 454 • Restaurants p. 454

In the late 1840s Alwin Soergel's octagonal building, or "the house with the round top," was a widely visible landmark in this open, rolling prairie and gave the town its name. Although some of Stephen Austin's colonists settled in the area, it was the German immigrants who gave the community its distinctive character and insularity.

This German heritage is preserved in such historic structures as the local Lutheran church, with its cedar pipe organ, and several of the buildings on the International Festival-Institute at Round Top campus (see attraction listing).

Another of the town's cultural institutions is the University of Texas' Winedale Historical Center on FM 2714. Devoted to the study of the ethnic cultures of central Texas, the 225-acre farmstead includes a visitor center, two historic structures, a nature trail and a picnic area.

**Round Top Area Chamber of Commerce:** 205 N. Line Oak, P.O. Box 216, Round Top, TX 78954. **Phone:** (979) 249-4042 or (888) 368-4783.

**INTERNATIONAL FESTIVAL-INSTITUTE AT ROUND TOP** is 8 mi. s. of jct. US 290 and SR 237 at Jaster Rd. Established in 1971, the 210-acre campus features historic buildings that were moved from other sites and restored, including the Edythe Bates Old Chapel, the 1885 Clayton House and the 1902 Menke House. Year-round concerts, from chamber music to major symphonic works, are held in the 1,100-seat Festival Concert Hall.

Guided tours are available by reservation. **Time:** Allow 1 hour minimum. **Hours:** Concert hall office Mon.-Fri. 8-noon and 1-5. Closed Jan. 1, Christmas Eve and Christmas. **Cost:** Free. Guided tour $10. **Phone:** (979) 249-3129.

THE PRAIRIE BY RACHEL ASHWELL                979/836-4975
▼▼▼▼ **Classic Bed & Breakfast** $200-$575 **Address:** 5808 Wagner Rd 78954 **Location:** Jct SR 237 and 1457, 5.8 mi e to Neumann Rd, just n. **Facility:** Many lodging types are offered at this reconstructed farm from the 1890s, including main-house rooms and cottages. 5 units, some kitchens and cottages. 1-2 stories (no elevator), interior/exterior corridors. **Terms:** 2 night minimum stay - seasonal and/or weekends, cancellation fee imposed, resort fee. **Activities:** fishing, bicycles, game room.
🏕 ✕ 🅦 🎿 🔋 🖵 / SOME UNITS 🖼

### WHERE TO EAT

ROYER'S CAFE                                 979/249-3611
▼▼ **American. Casual Dining.** $8-$43 **AAA Inspector Notes:** The family-owned cafe builds its menu on great regional American cuisine and wonderful pies. **Features:** beer & wine. **Address:** 105 Main St 78954 **Location:** Just e of jct SR 237 and 1457. **Parking:** street only. L D

## ROWLETT pop. 56,199
• **Part of Dallas area — see map p. 161**

COMFORT SUITES LAKE RAY HUBBARD             (972)463-9595
▼▼▼ **Hotel** $75-$109 **Address:** 8701 E I-30 75088 **Location:** I-30 exit 64 (Dalrock Rd). **Facility:** 62 units. 3 stories, interior corridors. **Amenities:** safes. **Pool(s):** outdoor. **Activities:** exercise room. **Guest Services:** valet and coin laundry.
CALL 🅗🅜 🏊 HS 🛜 ✕ 🔋 🖥 🖵 / SOME UNITS 🆂

**RUSK** (D-10) pop. 5,551, elev. 489'

In 1846 Rusk was selected as the seat of Cherokee County even though only one family lived in the town. The settlement was named after Thomas Jefferson Rusk, a signer of the Texas Declaration of Independence. The town was the birthplace of James S. Hogg and Thomas M. Campbell, the state's first two native-born governors. Rusk Park is 3 miles west on US 84 (see Recreation Areas Chart).

**Rusk Chamber of Commerce:** 184 S. Main St., P.O. Box 67, Rusk, TX 75785. **Phone:** (903) 683-4242 or (800) 933-2381.

**TEXAS STATE RAILROAD** is 2.7 mi. w. on US 84 at Park Rd. 76. The Texas state prison system began construction on the railroad in 1881. The line was built to transport iron ore to smelting furnaces at the East Texas State Penitentiary in Rusk. Today, passengers may travel through the "Pineywoods" region on 50-mile round-trip rides aboard late 19th- and early 20th-century trains. Along with regularly scheduled trips, several special-event train rides take place during the year.

**Time:** Allow 4 hours minimum. **Hours:** Pineywoods trips depart Sat.-Sun. at 11. Phone ahead for special-event trips schedule. **Cost:** $25-$75; $15-$40 (ages 0-12). Reservations are recommended. **Parking:** $5. **Phone:** (903) 683-2561 or (888) 987-2461.

**SABINE NATIONAL FOREST** (D-11)

Elevations in the forest range from 178 ft. in the Toledo Bend Reservoir to 550 ft. on a hilltop. Refer to AAA maps for additional elevation information.

Sabine National Forest stands in East Texas along the shores of the Toledo Bend Reservoir, which borders Louisiana. The forest encompasses 160,798 acres of Southern pine and hardwoods. Toledo Bend Reservoir, a 65-mile-long impoundment of the Sabine River, yields bass, bluegill, catfish and crappie; a number of recreation sites are along the shoreline.

Other areas of interest in the forest are Beech Ravines Scenic Area, Mill Cove Scenic Area, Red Hills Lake and Colorow Scenic Area. Recreation areas include Ragtown, Willow Oak, Lakeview, Indian Mounds and Indian Mounds Wilderness Area.

For information contact the district ranger station at 5050 SR 21E, Hemphill, TX 75948, or write the Forest Supervisor, 2221 N. Raguet St., Lufkin, TX 75904. Phone (409) 625-1940 in Hemphill. See Recreation Areas Chart.

# SALADO  pop. 2,126

## BEST WESTERN PLUS SALADO INN        (254)947-4001

Hotel
$85-$200

**AAA Benefit:** Members save 10% or more with Best Western!

**Address:** 10825 I-35 76571 **Location:** I-35 exit 286; on E Frontage Rd. **Facility:** 41 units. 4 stories, interior corridors. **Pool(s):** indoor. **Activities:** hot tub, exercise room. **Guest Services:** coin laundry.

SAVE CALL 🄼 🏊 BIZ HS 🛜 ✕ 🖥 🖨 📺

## HOLIDAY INN EXPRESS SALADO        254/947-4004

Hotel. Rates not provided. **Address:** 1991 N Stagecoach Rd 76571 **Location:** I-35 exit 286. **Facility:** 79 units. 3 stories, interior corridors. **Pool(s):** outdoor. **Activities:** exercise room. **Guest Services:** coin laundry.

CALL 🄼 🏊 BIZ HS 🛜 ✕ 🖥 🖨 📺 / SOME UNITS 🄂

## STAGECOACH INN        254/947-5111

Hotel. Rates not provided. **Address:** 401 S Stagecoach Rd 76571 **Location:** I-35 and US 81 exit 284 southbound; exit 283 northbound. **Facility:** 82 units. 2 stories (no elevator), exterior corridors. **Dining:** Stagecoach Inn Dining Room, see separate listing. **Pool(s):** outdoor. **Activities:** hot tub, tennis, playground, exercise room. 🍴 🏊 🛜 📺 / SOME UNITS 🐾 🖥 🖨

### WHERE TO EAT

## THE RANGE AT THE BARTON HOUSE        254/947-3828

American. Fine Dining. $25-$40 **AAA Inspector Notes:** Located in a historic stone and plaster home with abundant displays of original artwork, chef David Hermann uses the freshest ingredients to bring distinctive flavors to his steaks, chops, seafood and pasta offerings. Very nice and inventive sauces augment the delicious courses. **Features:** full bar, happy hour. **Reservations:** suggested. **Address:** 101 N Main St 76571 **Location:** I-35 exit 285; midtown.

D CALL 🄼

## STAGECOACH INN DINING ROOM        254/947-9400

American. Casual Dining. $9-$28 **AAA Inspector Notes:** *Historic.* Relax and dine where the early pioneers once stopped in their stagecoaches to rest and replenish for the next leg of their journeys. Roasted prime rib, hushpuppies and rich desserts are all offered from a verbal menu. **Features:** full bar. **Reservations:** suggested. **Address:** 401 S Stagecoach Rd 76571 **Location:** I-35 and US 81 exit 284 southbound; exit 283 northbound; in Stagecoach Inn. L D

# SAM HOUSTON NATIONAL FOREST
(E-10)

Elevations in the forest range from 100 ft. along the Neches River to 300 ft. within Montgomery, San Jacinto and Walher counties. Refer to AAA maps for additional elevation information.

Sam Houston National Forest is approximately 50 miles north of Houston on Lake Conroe. Offering hiking, camping, fishing, boating, hunting and other recreational activities, the 163,037-acre forest includes Double Lake and Cagle and Stubblefield recreation areas, Big Creek Scenic Area, Kellys Pond and Little Lake Creek Wilderness Area.

The 128-mile Lone Star Hiking Trail transects the forest, running from Richards in the west to near Cleveland in the east. A separate 85-mile system of multiuse trails is open for ATVs, mountain biking and horseback riding; the Cagle Recreation Area has a 2.2-mile loop around Lake Conroe.

For information contact the District Ranger, 394 FM 1375W, New Waverly, TX 77358. Phone (936) 344-6205 or (888) 361-6908. *See Recreation Areas Chart.*

# SAN ANGELO  (E-6) pop. 93,200, elev. 1,847'
• Restaurants p. 456

The establishment of an army post, Fort Concho, precipitated the settlement of San Angelo. Several trails used by drovers, stage lines and pioneers intersected at the townsite, providing a setting for such historical figures as Smoky Joe, Mystic Maud, Miss Goldie and the Fighting Parson. The latter used gaming halls as his church and the faro table as his pulpit. Only once did someone protest, and the Fighting Parson replied with a rap on the head from the butt of his six-shooter.

**San Angelo Convention and Visitors Bureau:** 418 W. Ave. B., San Angelo, TX 76903. **Phone:** (325) 655-4136 or (800) 375-1206.

**FORT CONCHO MUSEUM** is at 630 S. Oakes St. The fort's early days and the development of the San Angelo area are depicted. Among the remaining 20 original buildings are the headquarters building, officers' quarters, enlisted men's barracks and chapel. **Hours:** Mon.-Sat. 9-5, Sun. 1-5. Closed Jan. 1, Thanksgiving and Christmas. **Cost:** $3; $2 (ages 60+ and military with ID); $1.50 (ages 6-17). **Phone:** (325) 481-2646 or (325) 657-4444.

**SAN ANGELO MUSEUM OF FINE ARTS** is adjacent to the El Paseo de Santa Angela Heritage Trail at 1 Love St. This museum features permanent and changing exhibits of ceramics, sculpture and paintings, as well as an education wing with working studios and an outdoor kiln yard for university students. **Time:** Allow 30 minutes minimum. **Hours:** Tues.-Wed. and Sat. 10-4, Thurs. 10-6, Fri. 10-9, Sun. 1-4. Closed major holidays. **Cost:** $2; $1 (ages 60+); free (students and military with ID). **Phone:** (325) 653-3333.

## BEST WESTERN SAN ANGELO        (325)223-1273

Hotel
$125-$175

**AAA Benefit:** Members save 10% or more with Best Western!

**Address:** 3017 W Loop 306 76904 **Location:** Loop 306 exit College Hills Blvd, just s. **Facility:** 55 units. 2 stories (no elevator), exterior corridors. **Pool(s):** outdoor. **Featured Amenity: full hot breakfast.**

SAVE 🍴 🏊 BIZ HS 🛜 🖥
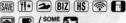
🖨 📺 / SOME UNITS 🄂

## CLARION HOTEL (325)658-2828

▼▼▼ Hotel $149-$229 **Address:** 441 Rio Concho Dr 76903 **Location:** US 87 to Concho Ave, 0.5 mi e; downtown. Adjacent to convention center. **Facility:** 148 units. 6 stories, interior corridors. **Pool(s):** heated outdoor. **Activities:** hot tub, exercise room. **Guest Services:** valet laundry. 🏊 🛜 ✕ 🛏 🖥 🖥

## COMFORT SUITES (325)944-8600

▼▼▼ Hotel $149-$229 **Address:** 4450 W Houston Harte 76901 **Location:** Loop 306 and Arden St; on west frontage road. **Facility:** 65 units. 3 stories, interior corridors. **Pool(s):** outdoor. **Activities:** hot tub, exercise room. **Guest Services:** valet and coin laundry.

🛗 CALL 🍽 🏊 BIZ HS 🛜 ✕ 🛏 🖥 🖥

## DAYS INN SAN ANGELO (325)658-6594

▼▼
Hotel
$160-$190

**Address:** 4613 S Jackson St 76903 **Location:** Jct US 87 and Jackson St. **Facility:** 113 units. 2 stories (no elevator), exterior corridors. **Pool(s):** outdoor. **Guest Services:** coin laundry. **Featured Amenity:** full hot breakfast.

SAVE 🍽 🏊 BIZ HS 🛜 🖥 / SOME UNITS 🐾 🛏 🖥

## FAIRFIELD INN & SUITES BY MARRIOTT (325)482-8400

▼▼▼ Hotel $219-$249 **Address:** 1459 Knickerbocker Rd 76904 **Location:** Jct US 87 S and Knickerbocker Rd, 1 mi w. **Facility:** 73 units. 3 stories, interior corridors. **Pool(s):** outdoor. **Activities:** hot tub, exercise room. **Guest Services:** valet and coin laundry.

**AAA Benefit:**
Members save 5% or more!

🍽 🏊 BIZ HS 🛜 ✕ 🛏 🖥 🖥

## HAMPTON INN BY HILTON (325)942-9622

▼▼▼ Hotel $249-$269 **Address:** 2959 W Loop 306 76901 **Location:** Loop 306 exit College Hills Blvd, just s. **Facility:** 63 units. 3 stories, interior corridors. **Terms:** 1-7 night minimum stay, cancellation fee imposed. **Pool(s):** heated indoor. **Activities:** hot tub, exercise room. **Guest Services:** valet laundry.

**AAA Benefit:**
Members save up to 10%!

🏊 BIZ 🛜 ✕ 🛏 🖥 🖥

## HOLIDAY INN EXPRESS HOTEL & SUITES 325/223-2200

▼▼▼ Hotel. Rates not provided. **Address:** 4613 Houston Harte Expwy 76901 **Location:** Loop 306 and Arden St; on east frontage road. **Facility:** 68 units. 3 stories, interior corridors. **Pool(s):** outdoor. **Activities:** hot tub, exercise room. **Guest Services:** valet and coin laundry.

🍽 CALL 🍽 🏊 BIZ HS 🛜 ✕ 🛏 🖥 🖥

## RODEWAY INN (325)944-2578

▼▼ Hotel $120-$185 **Address:** 2502 Loop 306 76904 **Location:** Loop 306 exit Knickerbocker Rd. **Facility:** 100 units. 2 stories (no elevator), exterior corridors. **Pool(s):** outdoor. **Activities:** hot tub, exercise room. **Guest Services:** coin laundry.

➕ 🍽 🏊 HS 🛜 🛏 🖥 / SOME UNITS 🐾

## SPRINGHILL SUITES BY MARRIOTT (325)949-6900

▼▼▼ Hotel $139-$299 **Address:** 2544 Southwest Blvd 76901 **Location:** Loop 306 and Arden St; on east frontage road. **Facility:** 96 units. 4 stories, interior corridors. **Pool(s):** outdoor. **Activities:** hot tub, exercise room. **Guest Services:** valet and coin laundry.

**AAA Benefit:**
Members save 5% or more!

🍸 CALL 🍽 🏊 BIZ HS 🛜 ✕ 🛏 🖥 🖥

## STAYBRIDGE SUITES (325)653-1500

▼▼▼ Extended Stay Contemporary Hotel $240-$270 **Address:** 1355 Knickerbocker Rd 76904 **Location:** US 87 S, 1 mi w. **Facility:** 80 units, some efficiencies. 3 stories, interior corridors. **Terms:** cancellation fee imposed. **Pool(s):** outdoor. **Activities:** hot tub, exercise room. **Guest Services:** complimentary and valet laundry.

🍽 🏊 HS 🛜 ✕ 🛏 🖥 🖥 / SOME UNITS 🐾

## WHERE TO EAT

## CHINA GARDEN RESTAURANT 325/949-2838

▼▼ Chinese. Casual Dining. $7-$15 **AAA Inspector Notes:** Lovely Chinese appointments come in soothing shades of green at the eatery, which features two dining areas separated by a large buffet room with four serving islands. Tasty dishes ranging from egg rolls to spicy chicken to desserts can be enjoyed in large portions. **Features:** full bar. **Address:** 4217 College Hills Blvd 76904 **Location:** Loop 306 exit College Hills Blvd. L D

## CORK & PIG TAVERN 325/227-6988

▼▼ American. Casual Dining. $12-$28 **AAA Inspector Notes:** This quaint restaurant offers a wide variety of American food. Specialties include handmade chicken-meatball spaghetti and various intriguing salads with almonds, bleu cheese and mandarin oranges. All desserts are homemade. **Features:** full bar, happy hour. **Address:** 2201 Knickerbocker Rd 76904 **Location:** Just n of Johnson St. L D

## GRANDY'S RESTAURANT 325/658-7424

▼ American. Quick Serve. $5-$7 **AAA Inspector Notes:** Fried chicken and country-fried steak are menu standbys at the restaurant, a regional franchise. They also offer a family-style dining menu. The décor is a step up from that of most quick-serve eateries and more resembles that of a conventional restaurant. Some elements of increased service include additional rolls, iced tea refills and tray removal. **Reservations:** suggested. **Address:** 109 N Koenigheim St 76903 **Location:** Just se of jct US 67/277/87. B L D

## THE WHARF 325/944-3414

▼▼ Seafood. Casual Dining. $15-$30 **AAA Inspector Notes:** Resembling a pier-front wooden structure, this cozy restaurant has a wide-ranging menu offering dishes with specialty sauces and housemade desserts. The servers are particularly well trained to ensure a memorable experience. **Features:** full bar. **Address:** 2302 W Loop 306 76904 **Location:** Loop 306 exit Knickerbocker Rd. D

## ZENTNER'S DAUGHTER STEAK HOUSE 325/949-2821

▼▼ Steak Comfort Food. Casual Dining. $5-$38 **AAA Inspector Notes:** The varied menu blends lighter fare, including salads and sandwiches, with steak and some seafood dinners. The restaurant is decorated in a tasteful German theme. **Features:** full bar. **Address:** 1901 Knickerbocker Rd 76904 **Location:** Jct US 87 and Knickerbocker Rd, 1.1 mi w. L D

# San Antonio

## Then & Now

Touted as Texas' top travel destination, San Antonio reels in more than 20 million visitors annually. Those who journey to this southwestern urban center come in search of everything from terrific Tex-Mex cuisine to exhilarating SeaWorld and Six Flags thrill rides. But San Antonio's appeal doesn't end at fajitas and roller coasters.

The Alamo, a source of pride for Texans, remains the city's shining star. The former Spanish mission, the first built along the San Antonio River, changed hands many times before misfortune elevated it to iconic status.

When the Texas Revolution barreled into the compound in 1836, the Alamo was a makeshift garrison manned by Texians, the local inhabitants fighting for independence from Mexico. Seeking control of San Antonio de Béxar (modern-day San Antonio), Mexico's dictator, Gen. Antonio López de Santa Anna, sent a large army to overtake the fort. The Alamo's defenders, a vastly outnumbered band of fewer than 200, fought valiantly to their deaths, staving off their attackers for nearly a fortnight.

With its soldiers proclaiming "Remember the Alamo!" the Texian Army eventually defeated Santa Anna's troops at the short-lived Battle of San Jacinto. Perhaps inspired by this rallying cry, the Daughters of the Republic of Texas began their own crusade to protect the Alamo around the turn of the 19th century, using personal funds and donations to save the historic site. In 1939, just outside walls so bravely protected, the Texas Centennial Commission erected the exquisitely carved, grey Georgia marble Alamo Cenotaph as a memorial to the outpost's slain guardians.

Arriving by the busload, reverent travelers now stroll the site hoping for a glimpse of heroes who gave their lives in pursuit of liberty. Displayed in the old chapel, where many of the last freedom fighters fell, are some of their belongings: co-commander William B. Travis' ring, a period hunting knife like the one wielded by Jim Bowie, and Davy Crockett's buckskin vest. Steps away, in a courtyard graced by flowering trees and cacti, docents attempt to separate fact from fiction while detailing events that occurred more than a century prior.

"Alamo City" also goes by the nickname "River City" thanks to its other prized possession, the River Walk. Like the Alamo, this picturesque stretch came into being after a period of heartache—in 1921, the San Antonio River overflowed during a violent storm, killing 50 people.

To prevent future tragedies, city officials wanted to create a giant storm drain by paving over the section of the untamed river cutting through downtown.

The Alamo remains the city's shining star

(Continued on p. 459.)

# Destination San Antonio

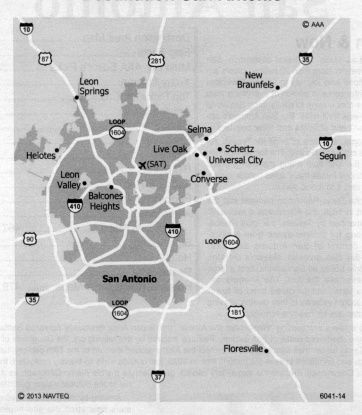

This map shows cities in the San Antonio vicinity where you will find attractions, hotels and restaurants. Cities are listed alphabetically in this book on the following pages.

# Fast Facts

## ABOUT THE CITY

**POP:** 1,296,682 ▪ **ELEV:** 650 ft.

## MONEY

**SALES TAX:** Municipalities may impose additional rates of up to 2 percent on the statewide 6.25 percent sales tax. Sales tax in the city of San Antonio is 8.25 percent; rates vary in the suburbs. The hotel occupancy tax is 19 percent.

## WHOM TO CALL

**EMERGENCY:** 911

**POLICE (non-emergency):** (210) 207-7273

**FIRE (non-emergency):** (210) 207-7744

**TIME:** (210) 226-3232

**TEMPERATURE:** (830) 609-2029

**HOSPITALS:** Baptist Medical Center, (210) 297-7000 ▪ Metropolitan Methodist Hospital, (210) 757-2200 ▪ Mission Trail Baptist Hospital, (210) 297-3000 ▪ Northeast Baptist Hospital, (210) 297-2000 ▪ University Hospital, (210) 358-4000.

## WHERE TO LOOK AND LISTEN

**NEWSPAPERS:** San Antonio prints one daily newspaper, the *San Antonio Express-News.*

**RADIO:** San Antonio radio station WOAI (1200 AM) is an all-news/weather station ▪ KSTX (89.1 FM) is a member of National Public Radio.

## VISITOR INFORMATION

**San Antonio Visitor Information Center:** 317 Alamo Plaza, San Antonio, TX 78205. **Phone:** (210) 207-6700 or (800) 447-3372.

## TRANSPORTATION

**AIR TRAVEL:** San Antonio International Airport (SAT), 7 miles north of downtown via Broadway Avenue, I-410 and SR 281, is served by U.S. and Mexican airlines. Taxis into the city charge $25-$29 depending on the departure point.

**RENTAL CARS:** Hertz, (210) 841-8800 or (800) 654-3080, offers discounts to AAA members.

**RAIL SERVICE:** The Amtrak station is at 350 Hoefgen Ave.; for train schedule and ticket information phone (210) 223-3226 or (800) 872-7245.

**BUSES:** The Greyhound Lines Inc. bus terminal is at 500 N. St. Mary's St.; phone (210) 270-5824 or (800) 231-2222.

**TAXIS:** San Antonio taxis are metered. The average fare is $2.50 when you enter the cab plus $2.60 for each mile. A $1 surcharge is added for trips between 9 p.m. and 5 a.m. Four passengers can ride for a single fare. The major company is Yellow Cab, (210) 222-2222. Boat taxis travel the river's downtown loop daily 9-9 (weather permitting). A one-way fare is $5, an all-day fare is $10, and a 3-day fare is $25. Phone (210) 244-5700 or (800) 417-4139.

**PUBLIC TRANSPORTATION:** VIA Metropolitan Transit provides public transportation consisting of buses and streetcars. Buses are routed through all sections of town; one bus even whisks shoppers from mall to mall on I-410. Express buses run daily from 6:30 to 9:30 a.m. Vintage streetcars travel three main city routes daily from 7 a.m. to 9 p.m. or later, swinging by attractions, shopping areas and other key locations about every 10 minutes.

The fare for basic bus and streetcar service is $1.20; 60c (ages 5-11 and 62+). The express bus fare is $2.50; $1.25 (ages 5-11 and 62+). Each transfer is 15c; 7c (ages 5-11 and 62+). Exact change is required. A one-day pass offering unlimited bus and streetcar service costs $4 and is available at the San Antonio Visitor Center or any VIA Information and Transit Center. For schedules, routing and other information phone (210) 362-2020 or TTY (210) 362-2019.

---

(Continued from p. 457.)

Thankfully, the women of the San Antonio Conservation Society fought this idea, turning the tide in favor of a flood-control program. Soon afterward, architect Robert H. H. Hugman began advocating his plan for a waterside urban park that included a system of dams and channels, footbridges and street-access stairways.

Hugman's vision became a reality in 1941, and today, sightseers looking for food and fun easily find both beside the sun-flecked San Antonio River. At the water's edge, majestic bald cypresses shade preening ducks, while the colorful umbrellas of Casa Rio, the River Walk's oldest restaurant, provide shelter to leisurely margarita-sipping patrons. Passing barge captains detail the history of the canal-like waterway, ferrying an estimated 1 million people through this downtown oasis each year.

The city's Catholic Hispanic traditions are the highlight of San Antonio Missions National Historical Park. At the park's four well-worn Spanish missions, contemporary worshipers carry out age-old rituals, along with newer customs.

After spirited Sunday services, locals crowd festive Market Square, the largest Mexican marketplace north of the border. Like other area attractions and locales, this colorful bazaar takes on new life during such special events as April's 11-day ◈ Fiesta San Antonio.

# Must Do: AAA Editor's Picks

- No visit to San Antonio is complete without a stroll along the ▽ **River Walk;** besides, this longtime attraction is pretty tough to avoid. Threading through downtown, the pedestrian stretch alongside the San Antonio River features cobblestone paths and garden-bedecked banks 20 feet below street level. **Rio San Antonio Cruises** offers visitors an overview of the canal-like waterway.

- Shop for handcrafted gifts at **La Villita,** Alamo City's first neighborhood. Today, scores of artisans, from glassblowers to weavers to leather workers, sell their wares in this historic area encompassing shaded patios, lively plazas, brick streets and adobe buildings.

- Zoom high into the clouds on the glass-walled elevator that climbs to the top of the **Tower of the Americas.** Built for the 1968 World's Fair, the 750-foot-tall **HemisFair Park** landmark attracts modern-day visitors with a sky-high revolving restaurant and an observation deck, both of which provide panoramic views of the city.

- "GO Spurs GO!" The fiery rallying cry for **San Antonio's professional basketball team,** consistently one of the top NBA franchises, thunders throughout the AT&T Center on game days. Order tickets in advance, and be sure to pack something black, white and silver.

Pick up a few souvenirs at Market Square

- Sidle up to the bar at the **Buckhorn Saloon & Museum** and see how many of the 520 wall-mounted species you can identify. The collection started in the 1880s, when dusty cowboys fresh off the trail traded deer antlers for whiskey shots. Of course, nowadays you'll have to plunk down hard cash for your libations, but if the stiff drinks don't have you seeing double, the eclectic museum, which features a two-headed calf and an eight-legged lamb, surely will.

- Follow your nose to **Mi Tierra Café Y Panadería,** a 24-hour restaurant and bakery known for its sweet bread, Mexican candies and strolling musicians. After your meal, pick up a few souvenirs at **Market Square,** the Mexican marketplace Mi Tierra calls home. Encircled by a kaleidoscope of colors created by piñatas, paper flowers and folklorico dancers in rainbow skirts, you'll find just the right memento to take home.

- The locals stay cool in the summer by **tubing** down the spring-fed Comal River, which meanders through New Braunfels, a German-settled hamlet on the outskirts of San Antonio. At times, everyone traipsing through town is wearing an inner tube.

- To describe something first-rate or excellent, Theodore Roosevelt favored the word "bully"; it's likely he used this adjective frequently in the cherry-paneled bar at **The Historic Menger Hotel,** where he recruited many of his Rough Riders. The elegant 1859 hotel, which has hosted presidents and celebrities, maintains many of its original architectural features; however, it's *also* said to be haunted by the ghosts of several past guests and employees.

- The **Spanish Governor's Palace,** though never home to a governor, was built in 1722 and is one of the last remnants of Spanish aristocratic life in 18th-century Texas. The one-story masonry house boasts private gardens and period-decorated interiors.

- Worship alongside San Antonians at the **Mariachi Mass** at ▽ **Mission San José y San Miguel de Aguayo,** when rich layers of guitars, trumpets and violins fill this wondrous centuries-old sanctuary. It starts at 12:30 p.m., but get there early, as this is a popular Sunday service with locals.

# San Antonio 1-day Itinerary

AAA editors suggest these activities for a great short vacation experience. Those staying in the area for a longer visit can access a 3-day itinerary at AAA.com/TravelGuide.

## Morning

- Begin your day at the 1749 **Spanish Governor's Palace** on Commerce Street. Notice the adobe-walled structure's elaborate wooden doors; it's said that the carved symbols relate the story of the Spanish conquest of the New World. Go inside and check out the period-furnished rooms, but be sure to spend some time outdoors, too—the formal landscaped gardens are lovely.

- Continue west on Commerce Street to the colorful **Market Square,** which is bounded by Dolorosa, Santa Rosa, W. Commerce Street and I-35. Here you can immerse yourself in Mexican culture by perusing stalls and carts overflowing with south-of-the-border arts, crafts and edibles.

## Afternoon

- Return to Market Square for lunch at **Mi Tierra Café Y Panadería,** a landmark Tex-Mex restaurant established in 1941. Sample the succulent fajitas and, for dessert, the delectable flan. For another take on Tex-Mex cuisine, try **La Margarita,** whose oysters on the half shell are a favorite with those in the know. Wash 'em down with an ice-cold Mexican soft drink or a fruity margarita (there are plenty of flavors to choose from).

- After you've grabbed a bite and a souvenir or two, walk a few blocks east to experience the ▽ **River Walk.** This is the town's main artery, and many would argue that it's the heart and soul of San Antone. It's impossible to visit the city without walking or riding along this picturesque stretch of the San Antonio River as it meanders through downtown. Find an access stairway and descend 20 feet below street level to the River Walk's breezy walkways. You'll saunter through serene parks and past trendy shops and eateries, fine hotels and locally made mosaic murals.

- While leisurely strolls along the lushly landscaped River Walk certainly are relaxing, you also can use this planned attraction to reach some of San Antonio's most treasured points of interest. For starters, take the Paseo del Alamo extension to get to ▽ **the Alamo;** from early to mid-afternoon the crowds aren't as heavy at the revered historical site. Pore over the artifacts exhibited in the Long Barrack Museum but don't overlook the amazing grounds planted with flora from four different ecological zones.

- Next, take Alamo Street south to the cobblestone streets of **La Villita,** the oldest neighborhood in the city. Once home to Coahuiltecan Indians, Spanish soldiers and 19th-century German and French immigrants, La Villita now shelters a vibrant arts and crafts

Stroll along the picturesque River Walk

community. The Spanish Colonial architecture is magnificent; plus, there are plenty of glassblowers, potters, weavers and leather workers to watch practicing their craft.

- Across Alamo Street, you'll spot a needle-shaped structure reaching toward the clouds. The 750-foot-tall **Tower of the Americas,** built for the 1968 World's HemisFair, features a 4-D theater as well as an observation deck from which to enjoy a panoramic view of the city. Take the elevator ride up at dusk, when the sun spreads a golden veil over San Antonio; as evening approaches, the hilly countryside beyond darkens to purple on the horizon.

## Evening

- Remain at the Tower of the Americas and linger over a scrumptious beef, chicken or seafood dinner at **Chart House,** which rotates 360 degrees to give diners spectacular views of the city. Another option is to head back to the twinkling, bustling River Walk, where there's no shortage of restaurants suitable for any palate or budget. At **Citrus,** imaginative cuisine is created with the freshest and finest local ingredients and presented in an elegant space in the **Hotel Valencia Riverwalk.** An extensive wine list complements the multi-course and a la carte menus, as is the case at **Las Canarias Restaurant,** where zesty aromas of Spanish specialties fill the air.

# Top Picks for Kids

### Under 13

- Hands-on learning—whether it involves operating a pint-size front-end loader, mining for gems, milking a cow or opening a bank account—is the name of the game at **San Antonio Children's Museum.** Kids can also create art, watch themselves on a video screen and climb to the tippy-top of a tree for an awesome view of the museum's three floors.

- One **Brackenridge Park** highlight is the 🔅 **San Antonio Zoo,** where an abandoned limestone quarry's cliffs provide natural habitats for more than 9,000 creatures. Kids will have a ball riding the miniature train, exploring the aquarium and reptile house, and meeting endangered animals like Komodo dragons and white rhinos. A special nature-themed area encourages toddlers and preschoolers to do everything *but* follow a "look, but don't touch" policy.

- At 🔅 **Natural Bridge Wildlife Ranch,** you can get up close and personal with even more animals without ever leaving your car. You'll pick up a free bag of feed at the entrance gate and use it to lure ostriches, emus, llamas, zebras and other curious critters to your open windows during a 4-mile, drive-through safari adventure.

### Teens

- The underground rooms and passages of 🔅 **Natural Bridge Caverns** showcase thousands of fascinating limestone formations, from the gigantic King's Throne and Watchtower to teeny-tiny soda straws. Special tours, some of which involve climbing and rappelling sans handrails, increase the wow factor big-time.

- In Alamo Plaza there are six Ripley's attractions that'll guarantee a good time: **Louis Tussaud's Wax Works, Ripley's Believe It or Not!, Ripley's 4D Moving Theater, Guinness World Records Museum, Ripley's Haunted Adventure,** and **Tomb Rider 3D Adventure Ride.** If you can only hit one, opt for the mind-bending Guinness World Records Museum with 16 exhibit galleries.

## All Ages

- You'll never run out of things to do at the city's "it" spot—the 🔅 **River Walk.** Go shopping, people watch, learn fun facts about the San Antonio River on a **Rio San Antonio Cruises** boat tour, or just meander along the breezy waterfront pathways. Refuel with a quesadilla or an enchilada under a crayon-colored umbrella outside **Casa Rio Mexican Restaurant,** the River Walk's oldest restaurant.

- Don't pass up a trip to 🔅 **SeaWorld San Antonio,** home to dolphins, sea lions, penguins and a whole bunch of other finned, furry and feathered friends (and perhaps *foes*, depending on your attitude toward sharks). What's more, the park offers adrenaline-pumping roller coasters and water rides as well as spectacular shows that will make anyone ooh and aah.

- Keeping the clan content all day long, 🔅 **Six Flags Fiesta Texas** celebrates Texas and the Southwest with live entertainment, thrill and family-style rides and a number of themed areas. The park's setting—the interior of a former rock quarry with 100-foot walls—is an attraction in and of itself. If you're visiting during the summer season, bring your swimsuit and prepare to splash and slide at White Water Bay.

- Check out Brackenridge Park's curiosity-piquing 🔅 **Witte Museum,** whose top-notch exhibits spotlight South Texas history, science and culture. You'll find mummies, dinosaur bones and creepy crawlers galore, and there's even a four-story tree house that lets you experiment with sound, weather and electricity.

- Opportunities for outdoor fun are endless at **Landa Park** in nearby **New Braunfels.** Float down the Comal River on an inner tube, take a dip in a spring-fed swimming hole, or rent a paddleboat on Landa Lake and give those legs a workout. If you'd rather play on dry land, other diversions include fishing, putt-putt, a nature hike and a miniature-train ride.

- You don't need an invitation to attend the city's biggest and best bash of the year—April's **Fiesta San Antonio.** What started out as a parade held in remembrance of fallen Texas heroes has mushroomed into an 11-day affair featuring carnivals, parades, fireworks, street dances, sports competitions and ethnic eats.

Kids will have a ball at the San Antonio Zoo

## Arriving
### By Car

Several of the country's more important transcontinental highways crisscross San Antonio.

The principal north-south route is I-35, heavy with traffic to and from the Mexican border and funneling an assortment of travelers from as far north as Lake Superior, near the Canadian border. US 281, similar in length and termini, carries a lighter flow of traffic. Sharing a frequently identical path with I-35 through much of Texas is US 81.

US 87 angles on a northwest-southeast course, bringing traffic from the ranches, the Great Plains and points along the Gulf of Mexico. US 181 also channels travelers from the Gulf area, but neither this nor US 87 is any match for I-37, a fast, wide link between San Antonio and Corpus Christi.

The major east-west route, I-10, connects San Antonio with the Atlantic and Pacific oceans. US 90 parallels and frequently merges with I-10 east of the city but maintains a separate course through much of West Texas.

These routes converge in San Antonio's center, enclosing the heart of downtown, part of the river and HemisFair Park, and providing easy access to major streets within the area. Farther out, I-410 is a completely circumferential highway that defines the outer limits of the city, interchanging not only with major highways but also with local streets.

**Note:** There are no service stations in downtown San Antonio.

## Getting Around
### Street System

The street system of downtown San Antonio was laid out more than 150 years ago, and in many instances follows old cattle trails. Because the system has been described as being roughly similar to a skillet of snakes, you should study a city map before starting out.

The speed limit on most streets is 30 mph or as posted. Freeway limits range from 40 to 75 mph. Rush hours generally are from 7 to 9 a.m. and 4 to 6:30 p.m. Right turns on red are permitted unless otherwise posted.

Use the circumferential loops to reach the different parts of the city. San Antonio is surrounded by two loops—Loop 1604 surrounds the outskirts, whereas I-410 encompasses the city's midsection. Interstates 10, 35 and 37 converge in the heart of San Antonio, forming another unofficial loop.

The proximity of most downtown attractions and accommodations to the San Antonio River prompts many visitors to use the River Walk or the boat taxis instead of driving. The outskirts of San Antonio tend to conform more closely to a grid pattern.

## Parking

Although some metered parking is available in certain downtown areas, public parking lots and garages are more plentiful throughout the city. Rates range from $1-$2 per half-hour to $6-$18 per day.

Grab your boots and hit the shops

## Shopping

For Macy's and other national chains, follow the mall rats to the **Rivercenter,** a complex on the **River Walk** *(see attraction listing p. 473)* with an IMAX theater and more than 70 restaurants and stores. Weary shopaholics find respite on the steps of the mall's lagoon, where the musical group Andean Fusion puts a New Age spin on Incan sounds Mondays through Saturdays. You'll also find a smorgasbord of memento-browsing opportunities elsewhere along the San Antonio River. Here lollygagging tourists flaunt newly purchased wares—from T-shirts touting Texas virtues to trucker hats promoting the Lone Star State's unofficial don't-mess-with-us policy, a popular slogan that evolved from a highway anti-littering campaign.

You may spot a few "Don't Mess with Texas" road signs on your way to San Antonio's favorite shopping destination: **I-410,** known locally as Loop 410. **Ingram Park Mall,** 6301 N.W. I-410, with Dillard's, JCPenney and Macy's, is along the northern arc of this route, as is **North Star Mall,** at San Pedro Avenue and I-410, which lays claim to the world's largest set of cowboy boots. Thanks to the 40-foot-tall sculpture, you'll have no trouble navigating to the stomping grounds of such upscale retailers as AIX Armani Exchange, Saks Fifth Avenue and Williams-Sonoma. Rustle up a few goodies then seek out the nearby smokestacks of **Alamo Quarry Market,** 255 E. Basse Rd., built on the site of a long-gone cement plant. At this open-air commercial plaza, you'll peruse everything from fine leather Lucchese boots to organic and recycled clothing from Whole Earth Provision Co.

**The Shops at La Cantera,** off SR 1604 (a.k.a. Loop 1604) next to Six Flags Fiesta Texas *(see attraction listing p. 476)*, presents an award-winning architectural blend of natural and man-made elements. Anchored by Dillard's, Macy's, Neiman Marcus and Nordstrom, the sophisticated center combines al fresco shopping with the traditional layout of an indoor mall. Along shaded walkways, Texan moms and daughters tote Abercrombie & Fitch and White House/Black Market purchases past waterfalls, lush greenery and a tiki-themed children's play area. Plus, everyone in the family will appreciate La Cantera's abundance of casual eateries, though the Yard House, where classic rock and draft beers rule, inevitably is the boys' first choice. To the east, on the opposite side of I-10/US 87, **The Rim** retail hub features Bass Pro Shops Outdoor World, JCPenney and an array of specialty stores.

Fashion mavens will largely be unimpressed by the downtown San Antonio shopping scene; however, the city's historic and artistic milieus will appeal to those seeking colorful tchotchkes, ethnic crafts and inexpensive keepsakes highlighting San Antonio's Tex-Mex culture. Bounded by Dolorosa, Santa Rosa, W. Commerce Street and I-35, lively **Market Square** *(see attraction listing p. 471)*, or El Mercado, delivers the flavors of Mexico to Alamo City—and we're not just talking tamales and tortillas! Indoor stalls beckon would-be customers with neat displays of imported leather goods, rich textiles and pottery; outside, it's more of the same vibrant eye candy, with strategically placed items like *lucha libre* (Mexican wrestling) masks, marionettes and sombreros attracting shoppers of all sizes.

San Antonio offers a variety of bars and late-night restaurants

Although Market Square has been central to the community since the 1900s, **La Villita** *(see attraction listing p. 471)* holds the title of oldest neighborhood in the city, having sheltered, at various times, Coahuiltecan Indians, Spanish soldiers and their families, and 19th-century European immigrants. With its cobblestone streets and quaint adobe and Victorian houses filled with handicrafts and artwork, the restored village serves as a leisurely detour for vacationers exploring the River Walk. The compact shopping venue at S. Alamo and E. Nueva streets also is accessible via the VIA streetcar system.

If the Texas heat has you longing for shade, head to **Paris Hatters**—you'll be following in the footsteps of Hollywood stars (Matt Damon and Tommy Lee Jones), rock gods (Eric Clapton and Paul McCartney) and world leaders (Pope John Paul II, Dwight Eisenhower and Harry Truman). Family owned and operated since 1917, this timeless operation just northwest of the Alamo at 119 Broadway keeps customers feeling and looking cool in stylish custom-fitted hats ranging from $20 to $7,000.

Vestiges of the past permeate San Antonio, so it's not surprising to see local history branded on assorted souvenirs sold in the area's many nondescript gift shops. At **Alamo Plaza**, a handful of stores fronting the Alamo *(see attraction listing p. 467)* hawk miniature versions of the mission-turned-fort as well as coffee mugs emblazoned with the poignant "Remember the Alamo!" battle cry.

## Nightlife

When it's time to let loose while vacationing in San Antone, there's little need to look much further than the **River Walk** *(see attraction listing p. 473)*. Offering access to a variety of clubs, casual watering holes and late-night restaurants, winding pathways along the banks of the San Antonio River are the liveliest means of traversing downtown after dark.

Most River Walk action is centered on the U-shaped channel (some call it "Horseshoe Bend" or the "River Loop") that shoots off the river's main north-south artery. With bass-thumping spots concentrated between **Presa and Commerce streets,** barkers poised by bar entrances try their best to entice passersby, though their shouts are muddled by the roar of raucous twentysomethings already partying inside. Drifting from **Howl at the Moon,** the dynamic sounds of dueling pianos lure those seeking high-energy nighttime entertainment; phone (210) 212-4770. Next door, [SAVE] **Hard Rock Cafe** draws a more laid-back clientele with its rock 'n' roll memorabilia and juicy burgers; phone (210) 224-7625.

The Paseo del Alamo, an extension of the River Walk built in 1981, flows through the atrium of the Hyatt Regency San Antonio and allows access to the Alamo *(see attraction listing p. 467)*. And, when the stars come out deep in the heart of Texas, thirsty revelers *also* use this shortcut to reach the **Menger Bar.** At the onset of the Spanish-American War, Theodore Roosevelt recruited many of his Rough Riders in this London-style pub, an 1887 addition to the Menger Hotel adorned with cherrywood paneling and beveled mirrors. Peruse the inn's well-kept collection of historical photographs and relics, then sip some cognac in the dimly lit bar. Of course, with the hotel rumored to be haunted, the fainthearted may want to settle their tabs before the witching hour strikes; phone (210) 223-4361.

Nearby, you'll find a 19th-century building that served as a USO center during World War II. The revamped edifice now houses **Bonham Exchange,** 411 Bonham St., where youthful club goers shake their booties through a maze of packed dance floors Wednesday through Saturday nights. Popular with gay San Antonians, the cavernous nightclub attracts a diverse crowd with cheap drinks, weekly dance contests and special celeb guests—from RuPaul to Charles Barkley.

For a few laughs, add the **Rivercenter Comedy Club,** on the third level of the Rivercenter (see Shopping), to your evening agenda; phone (210) 229-1420 for show times.

For effortless planning, simply seek out your beverage of choice. **Zinc Bistro & Bar** is just off the River Walk at 207 N. Presa St. This sophisticated but mellow haunt keeps choosy patrons happy with a menu that, in addition to wine, includes food, cigars and cocktails; phone (210) 224-2900. Meanwhile, at **Rio Rio Cantina's Naked Iguana Lounge,** you'll find a blender working overtime to dole out more than 20 variations of San Antonio's favorite tequila-infused concoction, the margarita. Located at 421 E. Commerce St. on the River Walk, the small contemporary hangout features several flat-screen TVs and balcony seating that's perfect for people watching; phone (210) 226-8462.

Those who adore craft beers and homemade sodas should hit up the **Blue Star Brewing Co.** in the Blue Star Arts Complex. (The arts complex is in the **Southtown** district on the south channel of the River Walk, but unless you're lodging nearby, it's easiest to drive or take a taxi there.) On select nights, jazz musicians jam at the funky brewery, but any day of the week newcomers can sample ales and lagers alongside the usual clientele of artisans and undergrads. Tickle your tongue with a preservative-free, sugar cane-sweetened orange cream soft drink, or choose from the plentitude of beers on tap, including the Texican, Blue Star's homage to Mexican-style lagers; phone (210) 212-5506.

Bohemian Southtown encompasses residential neighborhoods as well as the commercial corridors of S. Alamo, S. St. Mary's and S. Presa streets. While several area restaurants offer live entertainment and after-dinner dancing, the hip set practice their salsa and merengue moves at spicy establishments like **Azúca Nuevo Latina** and **Rosario's,** both on S. Alamo Street. Phone (210) 225-5550 for Azúca Nuevo Latina or (210) 223-1806 for Rosario's.

If you've officially added the River Walk to your been-there-done-that list, two music venues outside the city are worth the trip: **Gruene Hall,** about 40 minutes northeast of San Antonio in New Braunfels, and the **John T. Floore Country Store,** about 30

Celebrate Cinco de Mayo in Market Square

minutes northwest of town in Helotes. Cowboy boots still stomp weathered wood floors at the former, the state's oldest dance hall, while at the latter, a traditional Texas honky-tonk opened in 1942, audiences have swooned over the likes of Patsy Cline, Willie Nelson and the King of Rock 'n' Roll. Phone (830) 606-1281 for Gruene Hall or (210) 695-8827 for the John T. Floore Country Store.

# Big Events

Every other January (odd-numbered years) when the river is drained the **River Walk Mud Festival.** The festival features parades, entertainment and the crowning of the Mud King and Queen. In mid-February the **San Antonio Stock Show & Rodeo** takes place, complete with live music during all performances. In honor of St. Patrick, the San Antonio River is dyed green in March. The **Starving Artists Show** displays art at **La Villita** the first weekend in April.

The most widely celebrated event held in the city is the 11-day ⛨ **Fiesta San Antonio.** Honoring the heroes of Texas and fostering Pan-American friendship, the fiesta takes place the week of San Jacinto Day, April 21. More than 100 events are scheduled during the celebration. Highlights include concerts, an opening ceremony in front of the Alamo, fireworks, street dances and carnivals as well as vividly costumed participants and torchlit floats on the street and decorated barges parading down the San Antonio River.

Possibly the most distinctive features of the celebration are the cascarones, decorated confetti-filled eggshells sold for the express purpose of being crushed on any heads that happen to be within reach.

Market Square is the locale for a number of celebrations throughout the spring and summer, including Cinco de Mayo. Lasting 2 days in early May and featuring food and music from noon to midnight, this annual festival commemorates the Mexican militia's 1862 triumph over the invading French. Music fans from around the world gather in Rosedale Park for the 5-day Tejano Conjunto Festival en San Antonio, sponsored in mid-May by the Guadalupe Cultural Arts Center.

The Texas Folklife Festival in early June celebrates Texas' ethnic diversity and pioneer heritage. During this festival, hosted by The Institute of Texan Cultures in HemisFair Park, more than 40 ethnic groups share their traditions, crafts, music and foods. The Diez y Seis celebration in mid-September focuses on the city's Mexican heritage. In October, the Greek community celebrates its heritage during the Greek Funstival, held at St. Sophia Greek Orthodox Church.

The Christmas season is celebrated in colorful Mexican style during Fiestas Navideñas, complete with piñata parties, concerts and a blessing of children's pets by a priest. Ford Fiesta de las Luminarias features more than 2,500 candles in sand-filled bags lining the River Walk, symbolically showing the way for the holy family. Las Posadas is an ancient Spanish religious pageant. In late December or early January, college football fans head to the Alamodome for the ⛟ Valero Alamo Bowl.

## Sports & Rec

Mild winters and summers filled with sunshine provide outdoor recreational opportunities all year in

Majestic Theatre showcases touring Broadway shows

San Antonio. In addition to the 3,000 acres set aside for sports and recreation, three lakes within the city offer sailboating and fishing. Three 1-mile jogging and biking trails pass through the downtown area; information is available at the Marriott San Antonio Plaza, (210) 229-1000, 555 S. Alamo.

More than 80 municipal tennis courts can be found within the metropolitan area. Consult the telephone directories. Golf is available at six 18-hole courses in the city: Brackenridge Park, (210) 226-5612, at 2315 Ave. B; Cedar Creek, (210) 695-5050, at 8250 Vista Colina; Mission del Lago, (210) 627-2522, at 1250 Mission Grande; Olmos Basin, (210) 826-4041, at 7022 N. McCullough; Riverside, (210) 533-8371, at 203 McDonald; and Willow Springs, (210) 226-6721, at 202 AT&T Center Pkwy.

The surrounding Texas Hill Country has many lakes and dude ranches. Horseback riding is popular.

Spectator sports include the basketball games of the NBA San Antonio Spurs and WNBA San Antonio Silver Stars, who play at the AT&T Center, One AT&T Center Pkwy.; phone (800) 745-3000 for schedule and tickets. The San Antonio Missions of the Texas Baseball League play baseball April through September at Nelson W. Wolff Municipal Stadium at 5757 SR 90W; phone (210) 675-7275 for schedule and ticket information.

College teams add excitement to the sports seasons. The athletic program at Trinity University, One Trinity Pl., includes volleyball, soccer, tennis, football and basketball; phone (210) 999-8222. St. Mary's University offers soccer, volleyball, basketball and baseball; phone (210) 436-3528. The University of Texas at San Antonio also presents basketball games; phone (210) 458-8872.

Horse racing, both Thoroughbred and quarter horse, takes place at Retama Park; phone (210) 651-7000. Thoroughbred racing occurs Friday and Saturday from October through December; quarter horse racing occurs Friday and Saturday from June through August. Additionally, there are daily simulcasts.

Note: Policies concerning admittance of children to pari-mutuel betting facilities vary. Phone for information.

## Performing Arts

One of the few remaining movie and vaudeville theaters in the country, the Majestic, has been restored and revived as the Majestic Theatre, 224 E. Houston St. Touring Broadway productions and concerts are presented throughout the year; phone (210) 226-3333.

Lila Cockrell Theatre at the Henry B. Gonzalez Convention Center, Alamo and Market streets, is the scene of concerts, including pop, rock and jazz; phone (210) 207-8500 or (877) 504-8895 for schedule and tickets. The forum for instrumental soloists is Laurie Auditorium, on the campus of Trinity University, 1 Stadium Dr.; phone (210) 999-8119.

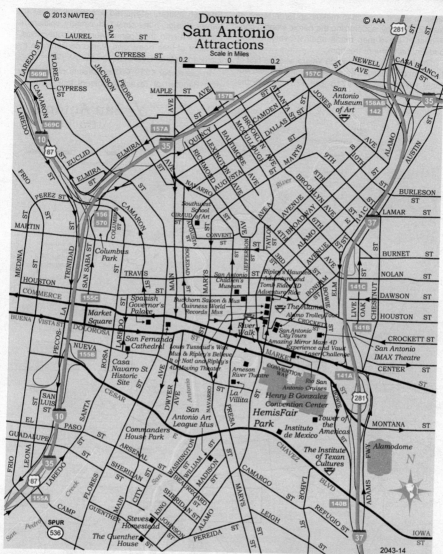

Strolling mariachi bands perform in the **Mexican Market** area along the River Walk.

**Beethoven Halle**, (210) 222-1521, and **Lila Cockrell Theatre**, (210) 207-8500, feature traveling dancers, including ballet troupes.

Trinity University's drama department presents several productions a year in its **Jane and Arthur Stieren Theater**. Ticket information can be obtained by phoning (210) 999-8515. Other colleges and the military bases occasionally produce theatrical shows.

Community theater also has a role in San Antonio's cultural environment. Presentations are held at **San Pedro Playhouse**, in San Pedro Park at Ashby Street and San Pedro Avenue; phone (210) 733-7258. **Harlequin Dinner Theater**, at Fort Sam Houston in Building 2652 on Harney Road, also offers performances; phone (210) 222-9694.

The most unusual of the city's theaters is **Arneson River Theatre** (see attraction listing p. 469), where performers are separated from the audience by the San Antonio River. The **San Antonio IMAX Theatre** (see attraction listing p. 474) in the Rivercenter presents "Alamo...The Price of Freedom."

## ATTRACTIONS

**THE ALAMO** is downtown at Alamo Plaza, bounded by Houston, Bonham, Alamo and Crockett sts. What this former Spanish mission lacks in size it more than makes up for in terms of historical legacy, epitomizing the heroic stand a contingent of brave men made against overwhelming odds in the name of freedom.

The Misión San Antonio de Valero was the first of five Spanish missions established along the San Antonio River between 1718 and 1731. When the Spanish military stationed a cavalry unit at the former mission in the early 19th century, soldiers renamed it Alamo, the Spanish word for "cottonwood," in honor of their hometown Alamo de Parras in the Mexican state of Coahuila.

In December 1835 Texian (citizens of the sovereign Republic of Texas) volunteers took control of

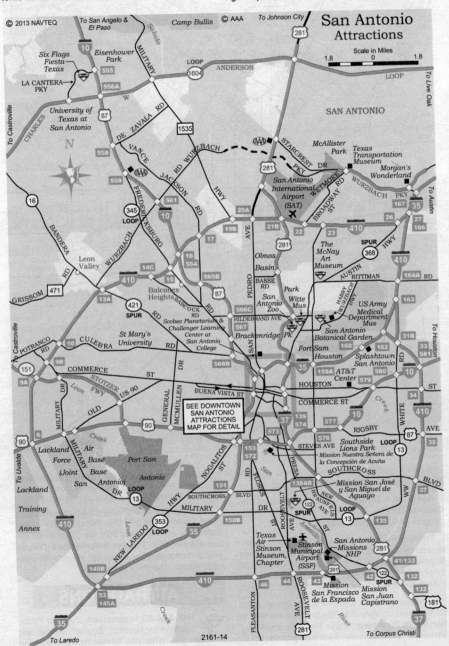

San Antonio Attractions

the Alamo, defeating Mexican forces quartered in the city. In response, Gen. Antonio López de Santa Anna launched an attack on the fortress that began on Feb. 23, 1836, and lasted 13 days. The badly outnumbered Alamo garrison (whose defenders included frontiersman Jim Bowie of hunting-knife fame and American folk hero David "Davy" Crockett) held their ground until Santa Anna's troops stormed the walls and breached the barricaded compound.

Gazing at this shrine to liberty today, it's hard to envision such fierce fighting. The Alamo's rough-hewn stone walls radiate a simple dignity. Wreaths and flowers inside the shrine are dedicated in memory of the men who lost their lives in battle. Exhibits here and in the Long Barrack Museum display Texas Revolution artifacts and personal items that belonged to the Alamo heroes. The Daughters of the Republic of Texas (DRT) Library contains books and documents pertaining to Texas history.

Regularly scheduled history talks in the Cavalry Courtyard tell the Alamo's story, as does the outdoor Wall of History. The lovely grounds and gardens are planted with flowering trees, cacti and ornamental plants. The waterway that runs behind the shrine and adjacent museum building is the remains of an irrigation system (acequia) that once served Spanish settlements along the river.

Snacks are available. **Time:** Allow 2 hours minimum. **Hours:** Daily 9-7, June-Aug.; 9-5:30, rest of year. Closed Thanksgiving, Christmas Eve and Christmas. **Cost:** Donations. **Phone:** (210) 225-1391.

**AMAZING MIRROR MAZE 4D EXPERIENCE AND VAULT LASER CHALLENGE** is at 217 Alamo Plaza, Suite 100, across from the Alamo. Visitors navigate through a network of passages surrounded by hundreds of mirrors, following the twists, turns, and moving mirrors forward and backward; the experience is enhanced with 3-D glasses. While racing through a vault, Vault Laser Challenge participants maneuver over, under and through laser beams in an effort to beat the clock without breaking any lasers and setting off alarms.

**Time:** Allow 1 hour minimum. **Hours:** Sun.-Thurs. 10 a.m.-11 p.m., Fri.-Sat. 10 a.m.-midnight, Memorial Day-Labor Day; Sun.-Thurs. 10-7, Fri.-Sat. 10 a.m.-11 p.m., rest of year. **Cost:** Each attraction $10.99; free (ages 0-3). Combination ticket for both attractions $13.99. **Phone:** (210) 224-2288. [TI]

**ARNESON RIVER THEATRE** is on the San Antonio River Walk adjacent to historic La Villita. Unequaled among the city's theaters, this outdoor amphitheater features tiers of grass seats on the south side of the river and a patio-type stage on the north side. Occasional passing river barges enhance audience enjoyment of the Mexican folk dances, opera, flamenco and other musical events. **Hours:** Events are presented most Fri.-Sat. nights, May-Aug. Phone ahead to confirm schedule. **Phone:** (210) 207-8614.

**BRACKENRIDGE PARK** is 2 mi. n. at 3700 N. St. Mary's St. The San Antonio River flows through this

343-acre park, which features Japanese tea gardens, walking and bicycling trails, a miniature railway and fishing and picnic facilities. **Hours:** Daily 5 a.m.-11 p.m. **Cost:** Free. **Phone:** (210) 207-7275. [A]

**Kiddie Park** is at 3015 Broadway St. Kids will have a ball and grown-ups will take a nostalgic walk down memory lane at this amusement park, which has been in operation since 1925. A 1918 carousel featuring colorful hand-carved wooden horses is a must-see. More thrills are provided by vintage airplane, boat, bus, car, helicopter and horse-drawn carriage rides. Even the ticket booth and snack bar are original. **Time:** Allow 1 hour minimum. **Hours:** Wed.-Sun. 10-7. **Cost:** Park free. Ride tickets $2.50 each; six tickets $11.25. Unlimited Ride Band $13. **Phone:** (210) 824-4351. [TI] [A]

**San Antonio Zoo** is at 3903 N. St. Mary's St. Quarried limestone cliffs provide natural habitats for approximately 9,000 animals representing 750 species. The 35-acre zoo is noteworthy for its endangered animals, including Sumatran tigers, white rhinos, whooping cranes and Komodo dragons.

An elephant, hippopotamuses, hyenas and lions inhabit African Hill, where a water hole brings ostriches, zebras, gazelles and antelopes together. Marmosets, sloths, giant anteaters, toucans, monkeys and jaguars are among the inhabitants of tropical Amazonia. Other highlights include Kronkosky's Tiny Tot Nature Spot, an interactive children's zoo for ages 5 and under. A miniature train offers daily trips through Brackenridge Park. **Hours:** Daily 9-5. **Cost:** $12; $10 (military with ID); $9.50 (ages 3-11 and 62+); $7.50 (physically impaired visitors ages 15+); $6 (physically impaired visitors ages 3-14). **Phone:** (210) 734-7184.

**Witte Museum,** 3801 Broadway St., focuses on science, natural history and South Texas heritage. Visitors can learn about the ecology of Texas; explore a four-story tree house that's filled with science-related exhibits; and see dinosaur bones, a 2,000-year-old mummy, live animals and historical homes. Featuring artifacts from the 1800s, the South Texas Heritage Center traces area history. Theater performances and interactive programs are other highlights.

**Time:** Allow 3 hours minimum. **Hours:** Mon.-Sat. 10-5 (also Tues. 5-8), Sun. noon-5. Closed third Mon. in Oct., Thanksgiving and Christmas. **Cost:** $10; $9 (ages 65+ and military with ID); $7 (ages 4-11); free (Tues. 3-8). **Phone:** (210) 357-1900.

**BUCKHORN SALOON & MUSEUM,** 318 E. Houston St., was built in 1881 and offers a step back to the Old West with artifacts from Texas history. Wildlife exhibits reflect African, Asian, Alaskan and North American themes. More than 520 mounted species are displayed, including fish from the seven seas. The Hall of Texas History presents life-size dioramas depicting milestones in the state's past.

**Time:** Allow 2 hours minimum. **Hours:** Daily 10-9, Memorial Day-Labor Day; 10-5, rest of year. Phone ahead to confirm schedule. **Cost:** (Includes Texas Ranger Museum) $18.99; $14.99 (ages 3-11). **Phone:** (210) 247-4000. ⏸

**Texas Ranger Museum** is at 318 E. Houston St. Exhibits of photographs, uniforms, insignia, weapons, memorabilia and confiscated items chronicle the history of the Texas Rangers. Also featured is a re-creation of old San Antonio with a saloon, jail, general store and other frontier storefronts. **Time:** Allow 1 hour minimum. **Hours:** Daily 10-9, Memorial Day-Labor Day; 10-5, rest of year. Phone ahead to confirm schedule. **Cost:** (Includes Buckhorn Saloon & Museum) $18.99; $14.99 (ages 3-11). **Phone:** (210) 247-4000. ⏸

**CASA NAVARRO STATE HISTORIC SITE** is at 228 S. Laredo St. This .7-acre complex in downtown San Antonio was the home of statesman José Antonio Navarro, a central figure in the formation of Texas. A signer of the Texas Declaration of Independence, Navarro served in the legislatures of both Mexico and Texas. The complex features multisensory exhibits; "Laredito," a mural by renowned artist Jesse Treviño; and an urban garden.

**Time:** Allow 1 hour minimum. **Hours:** Tues.-Sat. 10-4, Sun. noon-4. Closed major holidays. **Cost:** $4; $3 (ages 6-18 and students with ID). **Phone:** (210) 226-4801.

**FORT SAM HOUSTON** is off I-35 at the Walters St. exit. Founded in 1845, the complex is an active Army installation and home for several major Army groups. A museum chronicles the history of the fort from 1845 to the present. Maps are available. **Note:** Visitors may enter through the Walters Street gate or from a gate on Harry Wurzbach Road and must have a photo ID. **Time:** Allow 1 hour minimum. **Hours:** Wed.-Sun. 10-4. **Cost:** Free. **Phone:** (210) 221-1588.

**U.S. Army Medical Department Museum** is in Bldg. 1046 at the corner of Harry Wurzbach and Stanley rds. Beginning with the Revolutionary War, exhibits trace the history of the U.S. Army medical department through uniforms, U.S. Army and enemy medical equipment, POW memorabilia, photographs, scale models and emergency medical vehicles. **Note:** Visitors must enter on Harry Wurzbach Road and have a photo ID, proof of insurance and vehicle registration. **Time:** Allow 1 hour minimum. **Hours:** Tues.-Sat. 10-4. Closed major holidays. **Cost:** Free. **Phone:** (210) 221-6358.

**THE GUENTHER HOUSE** is at 205 E. Guenther St. This majestic 1860 home, which now operates as a museum and restaurant, was built along the San Antonio River by Pioneer Flour Mills founder Carl Hilmar Guenther. In the early 1900s the mansion was renovated by Guenther's youngest son, Erhard, who became the company's president.

Old-fashioned baking utensils and a collection of anniversary Dresden china plates are among the treasures displayed in the former library. The Victorian parlor is adorned with pine floors and exquisite window coverings, furniture and mirrors. Stop by the Art Nouveau-style restaurant for a peek at its stained-glass windows, copper light fixtures and ornate wood and plaster paneling. **Time:** Allow 30 minutes minimum. **Hours:** House Mon.-Sat. 8-4, Sun. 8-3. Restaurant daily 7-3. **Cost:** Free. **Phone:** (210) 227-1061 or (800) 235-8186. ⏸

**GUINNESS WORLD RECORDS MUSEUM** is w. off I-37 exit 141 (W. Commerce St.), then n. to 329 Alamo Plaza, directly across from the Alamo. Exhibits are based on the eccentric findings printed in the "Guinness Book of World Records." Amazing feats and human achievements are featured in exhibits, videos, touch screen computers, games, and interactive trivia spread out through the 16 galleries, including Human Achievement, Sports, Science and Technology, The Environment and Entertainment. The Gamers Zone provides a unique gaming experience with classic record-setting video games like Space Invaders and trendsetters like Guitar Hero.

**Time:** Allow 1 hour minimum. **Hours:** Sun.-Thurs. 10 a.m.-11 p.m., Fri.-Sat. 10 a.m.-midnight, Memorial Day-Labor Day; Sun.-Thurs. 10-7, Fri.-Sat. 10 a.m.-11 p.m., rest of year. **Cost:** $19.99; $11.99 (ages 3-11). Combination ticket with Ripley's Haunted Adventure or Tomb Rider 3D Adventure Ride $22.99; $14.99 (ages 3-11). Combination ticket for all three attractions $27.99; $17.99 (ages 3-11). **Phone:** (210) 226-2828.

**HEMISFAIR PARK** is bounded by I-37, César E. Chávez Blvd., and Market and Alamo sts. The 92-acre area was the site of San Antonio's World's Fair in 1968, which marked the city's 250th anniversary. It now is the center of downtown recreation and entertainment. **Hours:** Daily 24 hours. **Cost:** Donations. **Phone:** (210) 207-3677.

**Henry B. Gonzalez Convention Center** is on the northwestern quadrant of HemisFair Park. An extension of the San Antonio River flows through the heart of the complex, which houses an international conference center and a performing arts theater. Water taxis provide transportation to meetings from River Walk hotels. "The Confluence of Civilizations" mural is by Juan O'Gorman of Mexico; one of the exhibit halls features a mural by Carlos Merida. **Phone:** (210) 207-8500.

**The Institute of Texan Cultures** is on the University of Texas at San Antonio's Hemis-Fair Park Campus, 801 E. César E. Chávez Blvd. The museum presents the history and diverse cultures of Texas through art, artifacts, changing exhibits, events, festivals and programs. Exhibits are supplemented by demonstrations and a film in the dome show theater. **Time:** Allow 3 hours minimum. **Hours:** Mon.-Sat. 9-5, Sun. noon-5. Closed Jan. 1, Easter, Thanksgiving and Christmas. **Cost:** $8; $7 (ages 65+); $6 (ages 3-11 and military and college students with ID). **Phone:** (210) 458-2300.

**Instituto de Mexico** is at 600 HemisFair Park behind the Convention Center. The institute offers changing exhibits of works by contemporary Mexican and San Antonio artists as well as lectures, concerts, workshops and films. **Time:** Allow 1 hour, 30 minutes minimum. **Hours:** Tues.-Fri. 10-5, Sat.-Sun. 11-5. Closed holidays and Dec. 20-Jan. 5. **Cost:** Free. **Phone:** (210) 227-0123.

**Tower of the Americas** is adjacent to the Convention Center. The spire rises 750 feet, symbolizing the desire for achievement. A water park around the tower features calm water, fountains and waterfalls. Glass-fronted elevators speed passengers up the outside of the tower to an observation deck for views of the city and 100 miles of south Texas Hill Country. A 4-D theater ride takes passengers on a trip through Texas. The tower also has a revolving restaurant.

**Time:** Allow 1 hour minimum. **Hours:** Sun.-Thurs. 10-10, Fri.-Sat. 10 a.m.-11 p.m. **Cost:** (Includes observation deck and 4-D ride) $10.95; $9.95 (ages 65+ and military with ID); $8.95 (ages 0-12). **Parking:** $8. **Phone:** (210) 223-3101. 🍴

**LA VILLITA** is on the banks of the San Antonio River between E. Nueva and S. Alamo sts. La Villita (vee-YEE-tah) is a restoration of San Antonio's earliest residential settlement. Today La Villita is a thriving arts community that stands as a monument to San Antonio's past. A historic arts village since 1939, the galleries and shops occupying historical buildings offer unique art—oil paintings, sculptures, watercolors, metal art, rock art, textiles, copper wares, pottery, jewelry, stained glass and regional folk art—by local and regional artists.

Self-guiding tour maps documenting the historical structures are available throughout the village. **Time:** Allow 2 hours minimum. **Hours:** Daily 10-6. Closed major holidays. **Cost:** Free. **Phone:** (210) 207-8614.

**LOUIS TUSSAUD'S WAX WORKS,** across from the Alamo at 301 Alamo Plaza, features more than 200 wax figures from the annals of Hollywood, horror, history, religion and fairy tales. A 66-foot hand-painted mural depicts significant and strange events of the last 100 years.

**Time:** Allow 1 hour minimum. **Hours:** Opens daily at 10. Closing times vary. Phone ahead to confirm schedule. **Cost:** $19.99; $11.99 (ages 3-11). Combination ticket with Ripley's Believe It or Not! or Ripley's 4D Moving Theater $22.99; $14.99 (ages 3-11). Combination ticket for all three attractions $27.99; $17.99 (ages 3-11). **Phone:** (210) 224-9299. 🍴

**MARKET SQUARE** is bounded by Dolorosa, Santa Rosa, W. Commerce St. and I-35. Now renovated, the market has operated on this site for more than a century. The Farmers Market Plaza offers an assortment of Southwest- and Hispanic-themed shops and restaurants; El Mercado bills itself as the largest Mexican marketplace outside of Mexico. Visitors can watch artists at work in the outdoor plaza on weekends.

Morgan's Wonderland

Parking is available on the roof of the Farmers Market Plaza and under the freeway for a fee. **Time:** Allow 1 hour minimum. **Hours:** Daily 10-8, June-Aug.; 10-6, rest of year. Closed Jan. 1, Easter, Thanksgiving, Christmas Eve and Christmas. **Cost:** Free. **Phone:** (210) 207-8600. 🍴

◆GEM **THE McNAY ART MUSEUM** is at 6000 N. New Braunfels Ave. Housed in the 24-room Spanish Colonial Revival-style mansion of philanthropist Marion Koogler McNay, the museum showcases more than 16,000 19th- and 20th-century paintings, prints, drawings and sculpture. The collection features works by Paul Cézanne, Paul Gauguin, Edward Hopper, Pablo Picasso, Henri Matisse, Mary Cassatt and Georgia O'Keeffe. Traveling exhibitions can be viewed in the Jane and Arthur Stieren Center.

The 23 acres include fountains, broad lawns and a Japanese-inspired garden and fish pond. The Tobin Collection of Theatre Arts includes rare books, prints and stage-design drawings. **Time:** Allow 2 hours minimum. **Hours:** Tues.-Fri. 10-4 (also Thurs. 4-9), Sat. 10-5, Sun. noon-5. Closed Jan. 1, July 4, Thanksgiving and Christmas. **Cost:** $10; $5 (ages 65+ and students and military with ID); free (ages 0-12, Thurs. 4-9 and first Sun. of the month). Additional fees apply during special exhibitions. **Phone:** (210) 824-5368. 🏧

**MORGAN'S WONDERLAND** is off I-35 at 5223 David Edwards Dr. Inspired by the developer's daughter, this unique 25-acre park was designed with special-needs individuals in mind but is chock-full of activities, rides and themed areas for everyone to enjoy. Upon arrival all visitors are given a GPS Adventure Band that tracks their location, allowing parents and caregivers peace of mind from the get-go.

You can ride the Off-Road Adventure Ride and traverse a winding 1,800-foot-long track, take a trip on the Wonderland Express, or ride a horse or wheelchair-friendly chariot on the colorful carousel. Pirate- and butterfly-themed playgrounds, adaptive swings, a gigantic sandbox, a music garden and indoor gym add to the fun.

You can shoot water cannons or do some catch-and-release fishing at the wharf, then splash around in the Water Works play area. The interactive Sensory Village, designed to stimulate the imagination and senses, boasts a grocery, theater, car repair shop, TV station and stable.

Need a little break? "Escape" to a foreign country in one of several themed rest areas or unwind in the Sanctuary Garden. **Time:** Allow 2 hours minimum. **Hours:** Tues.-Fri. 9-4, Sat. 9-5, Sun. 11-4, June 1 to mid-Aug. Schedule varies Feb.-May and mid-Aug. through Dec. 31. **Cost:** $15; $10 (ages 3-10, ages 62+ and active military with ID); free (ages 0-2 and disabled individuals). Reservations are required. **Phone:** (210) 637-3434 or (210) 495-5888. 🍴 ⊠ 🪑

**NATURAL BRIDGE CAVERNS** is off I-35 exit 175, then 8 mi. w. on Natural Bridge Caverns Rd. (FM 3009). Determined to prove the existence of caverns beneath a 60-foot limestone bridge, four St. Mary's University students embarked on an unforgettable adventure in 1960. During their fourth trek they discovered 2 miles of underground corridors.

The guided 75-minute Discovery Tour takes visitors 180 feet below the surface through a half-mile of rooms and passages. Stunning formations range from the 40-foot King's Throne and Watchtower to tiny, delicate soda straws. Other highlights include Purgatory Creek, Sherwood Forest and the Natural Bridge.

Lasting 70 minutes, the Hidden Passages Tour explores two large underground areas adorned with soda straws, cave ribbon and other natural phenomena. A high-tech lighting network uses both light and darkness to intensify views—at one point total blackness envelops visitors. Adventure tours involving hiking, crawling and rappelling are offered.

Comfortable walking shoes are required. **Time:** Allow 1 hour, 30 minutes minimum. **Hours:** Caverns open daily at 9; closing times vary. Closed Jan. 1, Thanksgiving and Christmas. **Cost:** Discovery or Hidden Passages tour $19.99; $11.99 (ages 3-11). **Phone:** (210) 651-6101. 🍴 🪑

**NATURAL BRIDGE WILDLIFE RANCH** is off I-35 exit 175, then 7 mi. w. on Natural Bridge Caverns Rd. (FM 3009). This 400-acre, drive-through safari features more than 50 species of exotic animals that roam in open habitats, enticed to visitors' vehicles by a complimentary bag of food provided at the gate. The park also features enclosures for exotic birds and primates.

**Time:** Allow 1 hour, 30 minutes minimum. **Hours:** Opens daily at 9. Closing times vary. Closed Jan. 1, Thanksgiving and Christmas. Phone ahead to confirm schedule. **Cost:** $17.50; $16.50 (ages 65+); $9 (ages 3-11). **Phone:** (830) 438-7400. 🍴

**RIPLEY'S 4D MOVING THEATER,** 301 Alamo Plaza at jct. Crockett St., offers two different adventure rides created with giant movie screens, surround sound, special effects and seats that move in eight directions. Each ride lasts about 5 minutes; the complete experience lasts about 15 minutes.

**Note:** The rides are not recommended for people with neck, spine or joint injuries. **Time:** Allow 30 minutes minimum. **Hours:** Opens daily at 10. Closing times vary; phone ahead. **Cost:** $19.99; $11.99 (ages 3-11). Combination ticket with Ripley's Believe It or Not! or Louis Tussaud's Wax Works $22.99; $14.99 (ages 3-11). Combination ticket for all three attractions $27.99; $17.99 (ages 3-11). **Phone:** (210) 224-9299. 🍽

**RIPLEY'S BELIEVE IT OR NOT!,** 301 Alamo Plaza at jct. Crockett St., houses more than 500 exhibits from Robert Ripley's collection of oddities and curiosities from around the world. **Time:** Allow 1 hour minimum. **Hours:** Open daily at 10. Closing times vary; phone ahead. **Cost:** $19.99; $11.99 (ages 3-11). Combination ticket with Ripley's 4D Moving Theater or Louis Tussaud's Wax Works $22.99; $14.99 (ages 3-11). Combination ticket for all three attractions $27.99; $17.99 (ages 3-11). **Phone:** (210) 224-9299. 🍽

**RIPLEY'S HAUNTED ADVENTURE** is w. off I-37 exit 141 (W. Commerce St.), then n. to 329 Alamo Plaza, directly across from the Alamo. Beware of the crypt keeper, vampires and other figures of the undead lurking throughout the two-story haunted house. Live actors, bone-chilling special effects, animatronics, trap doors, disorienting light effects and optical illusions will keep visitors on their toes.

**Time:** Allow 1 hour minimum. **Hours:** Sun.-Thurs. 10 a.m.-11 p.m., Fri.-Sat. 10 a.m.-midnight, Memorial Day-Labor Day; Sun.-Thurs. 10-7, Fri.-Sat. 10 a.m.-11 p.m., rest of year. **Cost:** $19.99; $11.99 (ages 3-11). Combination ticket with Guinness World Records Museum or Tomb Rider 3D Adventure Ride $22.99; $14.99 (ages 3-11). Combination ticket for all three attractions $27.99; $17.99 (ages 3-11). Young children must be with an adult. **Phone:** (210) 226-2828.

**◆GEM RIVER WALK** runs 8 miles through downtown, extending as far north as Hildebrand Avenue and as far south as Mission Espada. It's hard to believe today, but downtown's standout attraction came into being as the result of efforts to tame the flood-prone San Antonio River. After a particularly devastating flood in 1921 that killed 50 people and caused millions of dollars in damage, Robert Hugman—an architect and native San Antonian—drafted an ambitious plan that would not only control the river's flow through damming and the construction of flood gates, but allow its banks to be developed for both commercial and beautification purposes.

The result is the prettiest place in the city. A long stretch of meandering waterways lined with big hotels, lots of restaurants and a sprinkling of specialty shops, River Walk is a tad reminiscent of the canals of Venice (that was Hugman's intention). Picturesque stone bridges arch across the water. The subtropical landscaping is lush. Pigeons coo, mallards quack and leaves rustle in the breeze. You can shop, have lunch, admire public art installations, learn about the river's history on a boat ride, stroll along paved walking paths shaded by pecan trees and tall cypresses, or simply sit on a bench, relax and watch people go by.

River Walk is just below street level, and that small difference is enough to give it a distinctly different feel. A series of entrance steps off downtown thoroughfares provide easy access. The scene becomes particularly festive in the evenings, on weekends and during major events like ◆ Fiesta San Antonio; lights twinkle, bars and clubs bustle and diners pack the waterside tables at restaurants like Casa Rio, which opened in 1946. But it's early morning, long after the crowds have dispersed, that a solitary ramble along the paved walkways offers an opportunity to really appreciate the loveliness of the setting.

The northern section of the River Walk is the Museum Reach, which links several downtown historic, commercial and cultural institutions, including the San Antonio Museum of Art, Witte Museum and the San Antonio Zoo; the southern portion is the Mission Reach. The winding river continues past the hotels and cafés where ongoing restoration projects are reclaiming the river and its environs. Dogs must be kept on a leash. **Hours:** Open daily. **Phone:** (210) 227-4262 for River Walk information. 🍽 🐾

**SAN ANTONIO ART LEAGUE MUSEUM** is at 130 King William St. Oil paintings, textiles, sculpture and ceramics are among the works by Texas artists and non-Texans that comprise a 400-piece permanent collection. Changing exhibitions also are offered. **Time:** Allow 2 hours minimum. **Hours:** Tues.-Sat. 10-3. Closed major holidays. **Cost:** Free. **Phone:** (210) 223-1140.

**◆GEM SAN ANTONIO BOTANICAL GARDEN** is 5 mi. n.e. at 555 Funston Pl. Covering 33 acres near Fort Sam Houston (see attraction listing p. 470), this botanical center balances formal gardens with 11 acres of indigenous plants. The Texas Native Trail includes three regions: East Texas Pineywoods, Hill Country, and South Texas Plains, which feature native flora and fauna, historical cabins and a limestone spring.

In the more formally cultivated areas are a rose garden, an old-fashioned garden, a Japanese garden, a sacred garden, and a touch and smell garden for the visually impaired. Occupying some of the highest ground in the city, the garden's glass Lucile Halsell Conservatory offers a glimpse of world climates inside its modern greenhouses.

**Hours:** Daily 9-5. Closed Jan. 1, Thanksgiving and Christmas. **Cost:** (Includes Lucile Halsell Conservatory) $8; $6 (ages 65+ and military and students with ID); $5 (ages 3-13). **Phone:** (210) 207-3250 or TTY (210) 207-3097.

**Lucile Halsell Conservatory** is at San Antonio Botanical Garden. Visitors enter this complex of exhibition greenhouses at ground level and take a tunnel 16 feet below the surface into a central courtyard with glass houses. These buildings include a tropical house, a desert house, a palm house and fern room. **Hours:** Daily 9-5. Closed Jan. 1, Thanksgiving and Christmas. **Phone:** (210) 207-3255.

**SAN ANTONIO CHILDREN'S MUSEUM** is at 305 E. Houston St. Interactive educational exhibits include a working elevator demonstrating leverage principles, a child-size operating front-end loader, a fictional airport and a grocery store. **Time:** Allow 2 hours minimum. **Hours:** Mon.-Fri. 9-5, Sat. 9-6, Sun. noon-5. **Cost:** $8; $7 (military with ID); free (ages 0-1). **Phone:** (210) 212-4453. *(See ad this page.)*

**SAN ANTONIO IMAX THEATRE** is in the Rivercenter, downtown at 849 E. Commerce St. The docudrama "Alamo: The Price of Freedom" is presented on a screen six stories tall. The film recounts the battle of the Alamo. Other digitally remastered and IMAX 3-D films also are shown. **Hours:** Daily 9 a.m.-10 p.m.; phone ahead for show times. **Cost:** $12.50-$15; $8.95-$15 (ages 3-11). Prices may vary; phone ahead. **Phone:** (210) 247-4629.

**SAN ANTONIO MISSIONS NATIONAL HISTORICAL PARK** includes four sites throughout the city; a visitor center is at 6701 San Jose Dr. next to the Mission San José y San Miguel de Aguayo. With the Alamo, these 18th-century missions were Spain's outposts along its northern frontier. A park map is available at the visitor center, which offers an orientation film and exhibits. **Tours:** Guided tours are available. **Hours:** Daily 9-5. Closed Jan. 1, Thanksgiving and Christmas. **Cost:** Donations. **Phone:** (210) 932-1001.

**Espada Dam and Aqueduct** is in Espada Park on Military Dr., just w. of the San Antonio River. Built by

Franciscans in 1745, the dam controlled the river and filled a network of *acequias,* or irrigation ditches, that furnished water to the Spanish Colonial missions. Remnants of sluice gate foundations are visible near Mission Espada; the aqueduct still carries water over Piedras creek to nearby farms. **Phone:** (210) 932-1001.

**Mission Nuestra Señora de la Concepción de Acuña** is at 807 Mission Rd. near Mitchell St. Relocated to its present location in 1731, the massive church with twin towers and dome was built by Franciscans and Native Americans. Reputedly the oldest unrestored stone church in the country, it is known for its great acoustics. The chapel and convent contain frescoes that date from the Colonial period. **Phone:** (210) 932-1001.

**Mission San Francisco de la Espada** is 10 mi. s. on US 281, w. on Espada Rd., then s. to 10040 Espada Rd. Founded in 1690 in East Texas, this mission was moved to its present site in 1731. The chapel doorway reflects Moorish influence. **Phone:** (210) 932-1001.

**Mission San José y San Miguel de Aguayo** is next to the visitor center at 6701 San Jose Dr. Founded in 1720, it is called the "Queen of Missions." Most of the compound—including outer walls containing Native American dwellings—has been restored. A 1794 Spanish Colonial gristmill, rebuilt outside the north wall, still is in operation. The domed church has a rich facade, and on its south side is one of the finest examples of stone carving in America, known as the Rose Window. **Time:** Allow 1 hour, 30 minutes minimum. **Phone:** (210) 932-1001.

**Mission San Juan Capistrano** is 6.5 mi. s. on Presa St., w. on Graf Rd., then .2 mi. s. to 9101 Graf Rd. The small chapel was relocated to the San Antonio River from East Texas in 1731 and restored in

1909; there are ruins of a larger church that was never completed. The southern loop of a nature trail on the grounds is open, but the northern loop is in need of maintenance and is closed; a reopening date is not available. **Phone:** (210) 932-1001.

**SAN ANTONIO MUSEUM OF ART** is at 200 W. Jones Ave. The complex occupies 10 buildings of the 1884 Lone Star Brewing Co. off Broadway. The historic brewhouse, with its modified Romanesque towers and turrets, is now the art museum. The West and East towers contain four levels of galleries. Glass elevators operate in each of the towers. The complex along the San Antonio River includes a 2.5-acre sculpture garden.

Permanent collections emphasize regional materials and art of the Americas. Exhibits include European and American paintings, decorative and contemporary arts, and Egyptian, Greek and Roman antiquities. The Nelson A. Rockefeller Center for Latin American Art features an extensive permanent collection of Spanish and Colonial art, modern and contemporary art, folk art and pre-Columbian art. An Asian wing houses Japanese, Korean, Indian and other Asian art.

**Time:** Allow 2 hours minimum. **Hours:** Tues. and Fri.-Sat. 10-9, Wed.-Thurs. 10-5, Sun. 10-6. Closed Jan. 1, Easter, Thanksgiving and Christmas. **Cost:** $10; $7 (ages 65+); $5 (students and military with ID); free (ages 0-12 and for all Tues. 4-9 and Sun. 10-noon). **Phone:** (210) 978-8100. ⓘ

**SAN FERNANDO CATHEDRAL** is at 115 W. Main Plaza. Colonists sent by King Philip of Spain arrived in San Antonio in 1731 and began work on the cathedral, the oldest parish in Texas. A French Gothic addition was completed in 1873; a modern restoration, which includes three gold-leaf *retablos* (altar pieces) in the colonial section, has been completed. Weekly services are held in the sanctuary, where a marble coffin is said to hold the remains of defenders of the Alamo. **Time:** Allow 1 hour minimum. **Hours:** Daily 8-5. Mariachi Mass is held Sat. at 5:30. **Cost:** Free. **Phone:** (210) 227-1297.

**SCOBEE PLANETARIUM & CHALLENGER LEARNING CENTER AT SAN ANTONIO COLLEGE** is 1 blk. e. of San Pedro Ave. on Park St. Shows are offered in addition to public viewings through the observatory telescope. **Note:** The planetarium is closed for extensive renovations; reopening is planned for early 2014. Phone ahead to confirm reopening date as well as schedule and admission information.

**Hours:** Shows are given Fri. at 6:30, 7:45 and 9 p.m., Sept. 1-late July. Telescope viewings Fri. at 9:45 (weather permitting). Closed major holidays. **Cost:** $5; $3 (ages 55+); $2 (ages 4-17). Age restrictions apply for some shows. Telescope viewings free. **Phone:** (210) 486-0100.

 **SEAWORLD SAN ANTONIO,** 10500 SeaWorld Dr., is a marine life adventure

Mission San Juan Capistrano

park offering shows, up-close animal encounters, attractions and rides. The high-energy show One Ocean blends killer-whale behaviors with music, choreography and colorful lights. The Azul show spotlights whales, dolphins, birds, high divers, synchronized swimmers, acrobats and water effects. Daredevil feats on water skis are the focus of the Cool Vibrations show, and The Cannery Row Caper show features the comical sea lion duo Clyde and Seamore.

The 3-acre Sesame Street Bay of Play offers family rides and the chance to meet and be photographed with Sesame Street characters. Sharks/Coral Reef brings you face-to-face with tropical fish, sharks and eels. There's also a feed-and-touch dolphin pool and a penguin habitat with more than 200 birds.

Journey to Atlantis combines the thrill of a coaster with the plunge of a water ride. Among the other rides are the Steel Eel coaster; Rio Loco, a river rapids ride; and The Great White, on which riders go heels-over-head five times.

Holiday-themed events include SeaWorld's Howl-O-Scream, held in October, and SeaWorld's Christmas Celebration, which runs from late November to early January.

**Note:** Swimsuits are recommended; rental lockers, changing facilities and showers are available. Pets are not permitted; kennels are available. **Tours:** Guided tours are available. **Hours:** Opens daily at 9 or 10, late May-late Aug.; days and hours vary rest of year. Phone ahead to confirm schedule. **Cost:** $62; $54 (ages 3-9). Combination ticket with Aquatica $87; $79 (ages 3-9). Admission and parking prices may vary; phone ahead. **Parking:** $15; $20 (preferred). **Phone:** (800) 700-7786. 🍴

**Aquatica** is at 10500 SeaWorld Dr.; access is via SeaWorld San Antonio's main gate. Visitors of this South Sea islands-inspired water park can get their adrenaline going on thrill rides; unwind on vast, sandy beaches with exotic flora and personal cabanas; and befriend stingrays, macaws and other creatures.

Stingray Falls, a park highlight, is a family-friendly raft ride through an underwater cavern inhabited by stingrays and colorful fish. A 1,200-foot-long lazy river, a three-story water play structure and multiple pool areas add to the fun.

**Note:** Swimsuits are recommended; rental lockers, changing facilities and showers are available. Pets are not permitted; kennels are available at SeaWorld San Antonio. **Tours:** Guided tours are available. **Time:** Allow 4 hours minimum. **Hours:** Opens daily at 9, 10 or 11, early June-late Aug.; opens Sat.-Sun. and some Mon. at 9, 10 or 11 in May and Sept.-Oct. Closing times vary. Phone ahead to confirm schedule. **Cost:** (Includes SeaWorld San Antonio) $87; $79 (ages 3-9). Admission and parking prices may vary; phone ahead. **Parking:** $15; $20 (preferred). **Phone:** (800) 700-7786. 🍴 ✖

🔺 💲SAVE **SIX FLAGS FIESTA TEXAS** is at 17000 I-10W. This 200-acre musical, theme and water park, in a former rock quarry with 100-foot cliff walls, celebrates Texas and the Southwest and offers live entertainment and both thrill and family-style rides.

Themed areas are Los Festivales, a Hispanic village with a continuous fiesta; the German village of Spassburg; Crackaxle Canyon, an old-time Texas town that celebrates the Fourth of July daily; Fiesta Bay Boardwalk; 1950s Rockville, where every day is homecoming; and White Water Bay, the free water park featuring more than 75 slides, a Texas-shaped wave pool, and a five-story interactive water tree house with mazes.

Iron Rattler, a snake-themed coaster made of wood and steel, has a 180-foot drop, four over-banked turns and an inverted barrel roll. The Sky-Screamer swing ride spins visitors around a 200-foot tower at speeds up to 40 mph, and the floorless Superman Krypton Coaster provides twists, turns, loops and corkscrews. Pandemonium is a spinning coaster, Scooby-Doo Ghostblasters is an interactive family ride, and Bugs' White Water Rapids is a log flume ride.

During summer more than a dozen live shows spotlight a variety of musical genres, including Latin and country; the evening Lone Star Nights Laser & Fireworks Celebration and the Broadway-style production Ovation are other summer options. The park also hosts Fright Fest in October and Holiday in the Park from late November to early January.

**Time:** Allow 4 hours minimum. **Hours:** Park open daily, late May-late Aug. (also in mid-Mar. for spring break); open Sat.-Sun. and some weekdays, late

Apr.-late May; open Sat.-Sun., Mar. 1 to mid-Mar. and late Mar.-late Apr.; open select days, Sept. 1-early Jan. Water park open daily, May 31-late Aug. Park and water park hours vary. Phone ahead to confirm schedule.

**Cost:** $63.99; $48.99 (under 48 inches tall); free (ages 0-2). Rates may vary; phone ahead. AAA members save on select services and merchandise. See guest relations for details. **Parking:** $18. **Phone:** (210) 697-5050. 🍴

**SOUTHWEST SCHOOL OF ART** is at jct. Navarro and Augusta sts. at 300 Augusta St. Adjacent campuses—Navarro and Ursuline—comprise the school. The former Ursuline Convent, established in 1851, has limestone architecture, gardens and courtyards. The Russell Hill Rogers Gallery on the Navarro campus exhibits works by emerging and prominent artists.

Guided tours of the Ursuline historic site are available. **Time:** Allow 2 hours minimum. **Hours:** History museum Mon.-Sat. 10-5, Sun. 11-4. Galleries Mon.-Sat. 9-5. Guided tours Mon.-Fri. 10-2 by reservation. **Cost:** Free. **Phone:** (210) 224-1848.

**SPANISH GOVERNOR'S PALACE** faces the back of City Hall at 105 Plaza de Armas. The adobe and stone structure dates back to the early 1700s and was the home and office of the captains of the Presidio San Antonio de Béjar. Now comprising 10 rooms, the building features hand-carved doors, tile and stone floors, period furnishings and a mosaic-tiled patio typical of Colonial Spain.

**Time:** Allow 1 hour minimum. **Hours:** Tues.-Sat. 9-5, Sun. 10-5. Closed Jan. 1, Easter, Battle of Flowers parade day, Thanksgiving, Christmas Eve and Christmas. **Cost:** $4; $3 (ages 60+ and military with ID); $2 (ages 7-13). **Phone:** (210) 224-0601.

**SPLASHTOWN SAN ANTONIO** is 3 mi. n. off I-35 exit 160 at 3600 N. Pan Am Expwy. A variety of aquatic amusements are offered, including water-slides and a wave pool. Lockers and showers are available. **Time:** Allow 3 hours minimum. **Hours:** Opens daily at 11, early June-late Aug. Closing times vary. Schedule varies rest of year; phone ahead. **Cost:** $29.99; $22.99 (under 48 inches tall); free (ages 0-2 and 65+). Admission after 4 p.m. Fri.-Sat. $18.99; free (ages 0-2 and 65+). Admission after 4 p.m. Sun.-Thurs. $16.99; free (ages 0-2 and 65+). **Phone:** (210) 227-1100.

**STEVES HOMESTEAD** is at 509 King William St. The site includes a lavish mansion built by German immigrant Edward Steves in 1876 and River House, what is said to be San Antonio's first swimming pool, as well as servants' buildings. The mansion and its furnishings reflect the lifestyle of this prominent family, who lived in the house for 53 years. **Hours:** Self-guiding tours daily 10-3:30. Guided tours depart daily at 1 and 11. Closed major holidays. Phone ahead to confirm schedule. **Cost:** Self-guiding tour $7.50; $5 (ages 65+, active military and students); free (ages 0-12). Guided tour $10; $7.50 (ages 65+, active military and students); free (ages 0-12). **Phone:** (210) 225-5924.

**TEXAS AIR MUSEUM, STINSON CHAPTER** is at the Stinson Airport at 1234 99th St. The museum explores the history of aviation. Some very rare aircraft are on display. **Time:** Allow 2 hours minimum. **Hours:** Tues.-Sat. 10-5. Closed Jan. 1, Thanksgiving, Christmas Eve, Christmas and Dec. 31. **Cost:** $4; $3 (ages 55+ and military with ID); $2 (ages 12-16); $1 (ages 0-11). Under 16 must be with an adult. **Phone:** (210) 977-9885.

**TEXAS TRANSPORTATION MUSEUM** is 3.5 mi. n. of jct. Loop 410 at 11731 Wetmore Rd. Vintage railcars, railroad exhibits, antique vehicles, antique fire equipment and horse-drawn carriages are housed at the museum. **Time:** Allow 1 hour minimum. **Hours:** Fri. 9:30-3, Sat.-Sun. 10-5. Train rides are available every 45 minutes Sat.-Sun. noon-4:30. Closed major holidays. **Cost:** (Includes train ride) $8; $7 (ages 65+ and retired military); $6 (ages 2-12); free (active military with ID). **Phone:** (210) 490-3554.

**TOMB RIDER 3D ADVENTURE RIDE** is w. off I-37 exit 141 (W. Commerce St.), then n. to 329 Alamo Plaza, directly across from the Alamo. The 3-D ride takes visitors on an adventure inside the tomb of an Egyptian god. Equipped with 3-D glasses and laser guns, riders battle the army of animatronic skeletons and mummies, competing with their partner for the highest score.

**Time:** Allow 30 minutes minimum. **Hours:** Daily 10 a.m.-11 p.m. (also Fri.-Sat. 11 p.m.-midnight), Memorial Day-Labor Day; 10-7 (also Fri.-Sat. 7-11 p.m.), rest of year. **Cost:** $19.99; $11.99 (ages 3-11). Combination ticket with Guinness World Records Museum or Ripley's Haunted Adventure $22.99; $14.99 (ages 3-11). Combination ticket for all three attractions $27.99; $17.99 (ages 3-11). **Phone:** (210) 226-2828.

# Sightseeing
## Boat Tours

**RIO SAN ANTONIO CRUISES** departs from three locations: the Rivercenter, under the Market Street Bridge at Alamo St. (across from the Hilton Palacio del Rio), and outside the Aztec Theatre at St. Mary's and Crockett sts. Board one of the motorized, open-air barges that follow the winding, canal-like waterway, gliding beneath cypress trees and arched stone pedestrian bridges and past lush growths of palms and flowering shrubs.

During the narrated 40-minute excursion tour guides point out various sites along the 2.5-mile stretch of the River Walk *(see attraction listing p. 473)* and offer historical tidbits pertaining to river and city history. If you prefer your River Walk views with a side of chips and salsa, dining boats are available through participating restaurants. **Time:** Allow 1

hour minimum. **Hours:** Daily 9-9. **Cost:** $8.25; $6 (ages 60+ and military with ID); $2 (ages 1-5). **Phone:** (210) 244-5700 or (800) 417-4139.

## Bus and Trolley Tours

The easiest way to familiarize yourself with San Antonio is to take a bus tour of the city. SAVE Gray Line offers sightseeing excursions along the city's historic Mission Trail as well as to the King William Historic District, La Villita and the River Walk; phone (800) 341-6000.

**ALAMO TROLLEY TOUR** departs from the Alamo Visitor Center. The 1-hour narrated tour passes the Alamo, HemisFair Park, La Villita, Mission Concepción, Mission San José, El Mercado Farmer's Market, the San Fernando Cathedral and the King William Historic District. With a Hop Pass, passengers may disembark and reboard the trolley.

**Hours:** Historic tours depart daily 9:30-4:15. Closed major holidays. **Cost:** 1-hour excursion $21.95; $10.95 (ages 4-12). Hop Pass $25.95; $12.95 (ages 4-12). **Phone:** (210) 247-0238.

**SAN ANTONIO CITY TOURS** departs from 321 Alamo Plaza. Guided bus tours of the city include the Alamo, River Walk, Mission Concepción, Japanese Sunken Garden, Farmers Market Plaza, El Mercado and Mission San José. Tours of the Hill Country also are available. **Hours:** Full-day city tour departs daily at 9. Half-day city tours depart daily at 9 and 1:30. Closed major holidays. **Cost:** Full-day city tour $54.50; $28.25 (ages 3-11). Half-day city tour $34.50; $17.25 (ages 3-11). **Phone:** (210) 228-9776.

Steves Homestead

## Walking Tours

The downtown loop of the San Antonio River provides unusual ways to see a portion of the city. The River Walk, which follows the riverbanks, affords walkers a leisurely view of downtown.

The San Antonio Conservation Society offers two self-guiding walking-tour brochures—Texas Star Trail and King William Historic District. Beginning at the Alamo, the 2.6-mile Texas Star Trail follows a signed route through the downtown area. The tour of the King William district spotlights many elegant Victorian houses built by prosperous German merchants during the mid-19th century.

For more information contact the Conservation Society at the Wulff House, 107 King William St., San Antonio, TX 78204; phone (210) 224-6163.

Beginning downtown, signs designate the Mission Trail, an 8-mile route linking the Alamo with the four sites of the San Antonio Missions National Historical Park *(see attraction listing p. 474).*

# Excite Your Travel Senses

Amp up your trip planning fun. Get the interactive **Top Destinations travel guides** in the iPad version AAA Mobile app with colorful photos, maps and "must do" recommendations from AAA travel experts.

read
share
see
plan
map

**The City**
Is Chicago the American city? You won't get an argument from us. Less intimidating than New York, more traditional than Los Angeles, it's always had a can-do attitude and a work ethic t...

**Fast Facts/Trivia**
Northwest Territory military outpost Fort Dearborn, the first glimmer of

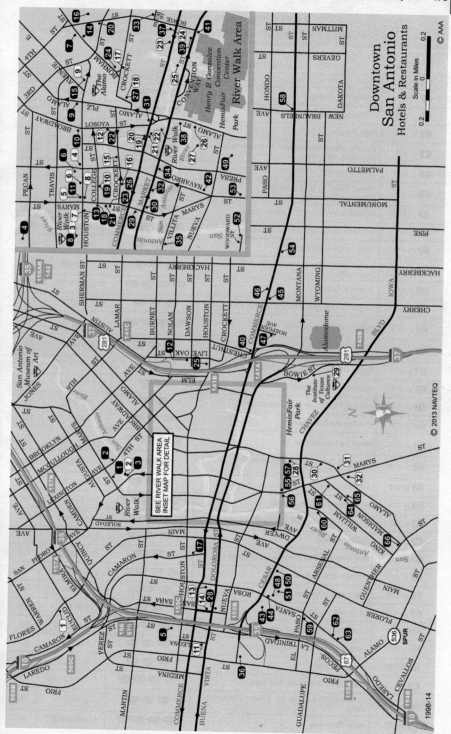

Downtown
San Antonio
Hotels & Restaurants

Scale in Miles

© AAA

© 2013 NAVTEQ

1998-14

# Downtown San Antonio

This index helps you "spot" where approved hotels and restaurants are located on the corresponding detailed maps. Hotel daily rate range is for comparison only. Restaurant price range is a combination of lunch and/or dinner. Turn to the listing page for more detailed rate and price information and consult display ads for special promotions.

## DOWNTOWN SAN ANTONIO

| Map Page | Hotels | Diamond Rated | Rate Range | Page |
|---|---|---|---|---|
| **1** p. 479 | Hotel Indigo Riverwalk | ◆◆◆ | $99-$179 | 497 |
| **2** p. 479 | El Tropicano Riverwalk | ◆◆◆ | $129-$169 | 495 |
| **3** p. 479 | Hotel Havana | ◆◆◆ | $100-$250 | 497 |
| **4** p. 479 | **The Wyndham San Antonio Riverwalk Hotel** *(See ad p. 502.)* | ◆◆◆ | $99-$235 SAVE | 503 |
| **5** p. 479 | Motel 6 - #1122 | ◆ | $55-$165 | 499 |
| **6** p. 479 | Home2 Suites by Hilton San Antonio Downtown-Riverwalk | ◆◆◆ | $109-$199 | 497 |
| **7** p. 479 | Residence Inn by Marriott Alamo Plaza | ◆◆◆ | $149-$229 | 500 |
| **8** p. 479 | Embassy Suites San Antonio Riverwalk-Downtown | ◆◆◆ | $179-$279 | 495 |
| **9** p. 479 | Hotel Indigo at the Alamo | ◆◆◆ | $130-$300 | 497 |
| **10** p. 479 | TownePlace Suites by Marriott San Antonio Downtown | ◆◆◆ | $109-$199 | 503 |
| **11** p. 479 | **Sheraton Gunter** | ◆◆◆◆ | $129-$269 SAVE | 502 |
| **12** p. 479 | Comfort Suites Alamo/Riverwalk *(See ad p. 494.)* | ◆◆◆ | $119-$239 | 494 |
| **13** p. 479 | **Hotel Valencia Riverwalk** | ◆◆◆◆ | Rates not provided SAVE | 497 |
| **14** p. 479 | Fairfield Inn & Suites by Marriott San Antonio Downtown/Alamo Plaza | ◆◆◆ | $99-$209 | 495 |
| **15** p. 479 | **Emily Morgan Hotel-DoubleTree by Hilton** | ◆◆◆ | $119-$179 SAVE | 495 |
| **16** p. 479 | Hampton Inn Downtown | ◆◆ | $119-$199 | 496 |
| **17** p. 479 | Holiday Inn Express Riverwalk Area | ◆◆ | $89-$189 | 497 |
| **18** p. 479 | **Holiday Inn Riverwalk** | ◆◆◆ | $129-$239 SAVE | 497 |
| **19** p. 479 | **Omni La Mansión del Rio** | ◆◆◆◆ | Rates not provided SAVE | 500 |
| **20** p. 479 | SpringHill Suites by Marriott San Antonio Downtown/Alamo Plaza | ◆◆◆ | $109-$209 | 502 |
| **21** p. 479 | Courtyard by Marriott San Antonio Riverwalk | ◆◆◆ | $169-$229 | 494 |
| **22** p. 479 | **Hyatt Regency San Antonio** | ◆◆◆◆ | $99-$359 SAVE | 498 |
| **23** p. 479 | Drury Inn & Suites-San Antonio Riverwalk | ◆◆◆ | $135-$229 | 495 |
| **24** p. 479 | **Crockett Hotel** | ◆◆◆ | $99-$295 SAVE | 494 |
| **25** p. 479 | **Red Roof Inn San Antonio (Downtown)** | ◆◆ | $69-$199 SAVE | 500 |
| **26** p. 479 | Mokara Hotel & Spa | ◆◆◆◆ | $269-$469 SAVE | 499 |
| **27** p. 479 | **The Historic Menger Hotel** | ◆◆◆ | $119-$299 SAVE | 496 |
| **28** p. 479 | La Quinta Inn San Antonio Market Square | ◆◆ | $89-$164 | 498 |
| **29** p. 479 | Drury Plaza Hotel-San Antonio Riverwalk | ◆◆◆ | $140-$284 | 495 |
| **30** p. 479 | Homewood Suites Riverwalk by Hilton | ◆◆◆ | $149-$249 | 497 |
| **31** p. 479 | Riverwalk Vista | ◆◆◆ | $127-$223 | 500 |
| **32** p. 479 | **The Westin Riverwalk, San Antonio** | ◆◆◆◆ | $119-$409 SAVE | 503 |
| **33** p. 479 | La Quinta Inn & Suites San Antonio Convention Center | ◆◆◆ | $145-$200 | 498 |
| **34** p. 479 | **Hotel Contessa** | ◆◆◆◆ | $159-$299 SAVE | 497 |

## DOWNTOWN SAN ANTONIO (cont'd)

| Map Page | Hotels (cont'd) | Diamond Rated | Rate Range | Page |
|---|---|---|---|---|
| 35 p. 479 | Riverwalk Plaza Hotel & Suites | ♦♦♦ | Rates not provided | 500 |
| 36 p. 479 | **DoubleTree by Hilton Hotel San Antonio Downtown** | ♦♦♦ | $99-$189 SAVE | 494 |
| 37 p. 479 | **San Antonio Marriott Rivercenter** | ♦♦♦ | $179-$299 SAVE | 500 |
| 38 p. 479 | Hilton Palacio del Rio | ♦♦♦ | $139-$389 | 496 |
| 39 p. 479 | **San Antonio Marriott Riverwalk** | ♦♦♦ | $179-$299 SAVE | 502 |
| 40 p. 479 | **BEST WESTERN PLUS Sunset Suites-Riverwalk** | ♦♦♦ | $90-$210 SAVE | 493 |
| 41 p. 479 | **Grand Hyatt San Antonio** | ♦♦♦ | $99-$359 SAVE | 496 |
| 42 p. 479 | **O'Brien Historic Hotel Riverwalk, an Ascend Hotel Collection Member** | ♦♦ | $99-$169 SAVE | 500 |
| 43 p. 479 | **Holiday Inn-Downtown-Market Square** | ♦♦♦ | $109-$189 SAVE | 496 |
| 44 p. 479 | Courtyard by Marriott San Antonio Downtown Market Square | ♦♦♦ | $119-$189 | 494 |
| 45 p. 479 | City View Inn & Suites | ♦ | Rates not provided | 494 |
| 46 p. 479 | Holiday Inn Express Hotel & Suites River Center Area | ♦♦♦ | $109-$199 | 496 |
| 47 p. 479 | **Staybridge Suites Downtown Convention Center** | ♦♦♦ | $109-$189 SAVE | 503 |
| 48 p. 479 | **Fairfield Inn & Suites by Marriott San Antonio Downtown/Market Square** | ♦♦♦ | $80-$140 SAVE | 495 |
| 49 p. 479 | The Fairmount Hotel | ♦♦♦ | Rates not provided | 496 |
| 50 p. 479 | La Quinta Inn & Suites San Antonio Downtown | ♦♦♦ | $119-$174 | 498 |
| 51 p. 479 | **Residence Inn by Marriott San Antonio Downtown/Market Square** | ♦♦♦ | $100-$170 SAVE | 500 |
| 52 p. 479 | Inn on the Riverwalk | ♦♦ | $99-$269 | 498 |
| 53 p. 479 | **Four Points by Sheraton San Antonio Downtown** | ♦♦♦ | $99-$279 SAVE | 496 |
| 54 p. 479 | **Knights Inn La Hacienda Inn** | ♦♦ | $64-$130 SAVE | 498 |
| 55 p. 479 | **Arbor House Suites Bed & Breakfast** | ♦♦♦ | $129-$207 SAVE | 493 |
| 56 p. 479 | **Hyatt Place San Antonio/Riverwalk** | ♦♦♦ | $99-$249 SAVE | 497 |
| 57 p. 479 | **Marriott Plaza San Antonio** (See ad p. 499.) | ♦♦♦♦ | $109-$169 SAVE | 499 |
| 58 p. 479 | **Alamo Inn** | ♦♦ | $45-$120 SAVE | 493 |
| 59 p. 479 | Holiday Inn Express Inn & Suites | ♦♦♦ | Rates not provided | 497 |
| 60 p. 479 | **Noble Inns-The Oge House Riverwalk** | ♦♦♦♦ | $199-$449 SAVE | 500 |
| 61 p. 479 | Noble Inns-The Jackson House | ♦♦♦ | $139-$299 | 500 |
| 62 p. 479 | **BEST WESTERN Alamo Suites** | ♦♦♦ | $109-$169 SAVE | 493 |
| 63 p. 479 | Candlewood Suites San Antonio Downtown | ♦♦♦ | $95-$139 | 493 |
| 64 p. 479 | A Yellow Rose Bed & Breakfast | ♦♦♦ | $110-$200 | 493 |
| 65 p. 479 | Brackenridge House B & B | ♦♦♦ | $109-$275 | 493 |
| 66 p. 479 | A Beckmann Inn & Carriage House Bed and Breakfast | ♦♦♦ | $119-$189 | 493 |

| Map Page | Restaurants | Diamond Rated | Cuisine | Price Range | Page |
|---|---|---|---|---|---|
| 2 p. 479 | Ocho Lounge | ♦♦ | Regional Cuban | $10-$22 | 504 |
| 3 p. 479 | Luke | ♦♦♦ | Cajun | $10-$18 | 504 |
| 4 p. 479 | Toscana Ristorante | ♦♦♦ | Italian | $12-$32 | 505 |

| Map Page | Restaurants (cont'd) | Diamond Rated | Cuisine | Price Range | Page |
|---|---|---|---|---|---|
| ⑤ p. 479 | Barron's | ◆◆◆ | American | $8-$15 | 503 |
| ⑥ p. 479 | **Bohanan's Prime Steaks & Seafood** | ◆◆◆◆ | Regional Steak Seafood | $18-$40 | 503 |
| ⑦ p. 479 | **Citrus** | ◆◆◆◆ | Regional International | $14-$40 | 504 |
| ⑧ p. 479 | Houston St. Bistro | ◆◆◆ | American | $8-$22 | 504 |
| ⑨ p. 479 | Oro Restaurant & Bar | ◆◆ | American | $10-$18 | 504 |
| ⑩ p. 479 | **Las Canarias Restaurant** | ◆◆◆ | American | $12-$30 | 504 |
| ⑪ p. 479 | Pico de Gallo | ◆◆ | Regional Mexican | $7-$16 | 505 |
| ⑫ p. 479 | Q on the Riverwalk | ◆◆◆ | Barbecue | $18-$29 | 505 |
| ⑬ p. 479 | La Margarita | ◆◆ | Regional Tex-Mex | $7-$12 | 504 |
| ⑭ p. 479 | Mi Tierra Café Y Panadería | ◆◆ | Regional Tex-Mex | $8-$18 | 504 |
| ⑮ p. 479 | Hard Rock Cafe | ◆◆ | American | $10-$28 SAVE | 504 |
| ⑯ p. 479 | **Ostra** | ◆◆◆◆ | Regional New World | $15-$65 | 505 |
| ⑰ p. 479 | Morton's The Steakhouse | ◆◆◆ | Steak | $27-$103 | 504 |
| ⑱ p. 479 | The Colonial Room | ◆◆ | Regional American | $8-$30 | 504 |
| ⑲ p. 479 | Boudro's on the Riverwalk | ◆◆◆ | Regional Tex-Mex | $10-$38 | 503 |
| ⑳ p. 479 | Rio Rio Cantina | ◆◆ | Regional Tex-Mex | $8-$25 | 505 |
| ㉑ p. 479 | Schilo's Delicatessen | ◆ | German Deli | $6-$12 | 505 |
| ㉒ p. 479 | Casa Rio Mexican Restaurant | ◆◆ | Regional Mexican | $7-$15 | 503 |
| ㉓ p. 479 | Luciano's On The River | ◆◆◆ | Italian | $10-$32 | 504 |
| ㉔ p. 479 | Sazo's Latin Grill | ◆◆◆ | Latin American | $12-$23 | 505 |
| ㉕ p. 479 | The Cactus Flower | ◆◆ | Regional American | $8-$20 | 503 |
| ㉖ p. 479 | Little Rhein Steak House | ◆◆◆ | Steak | $35-$45 | 504 |
| ㉗ p. 479 | Fig Tree Restaurant | ◆◆◆ | Traditional Continental | $24-$38 | 504 |
| ㉘ p. 479 | The Anaqua Room | ◆◆ | Regional American | $9-$25 | 503 |
| ㉙ p. 479 | Chart House | ◆◆◆ | Seafood | $8-$30 SAVE | 504 |
| ㉚ p. 479 | Azuca Nuevo Latino | ◆◆◆ | Regional Latin American | $12-$28 | 503 |
| ㉛ p. 479 | La Focaccia Italian Grill | ◆◆ | Italian | $12-$25 | 504 |
| ㉜ p. 479 | Rosario's | ◆◆ | Mexican | $15-$26 | 505 |

# Gear Up For Every Day

Make a statement at home or on vacation. Save from the bottom up on fashionable footwear and casual ensembles when you show your AAA/CAA membership card to save.

Use your mobile phone to find nearby discounts.

**AAA.com/searchfordiscounts**

Show Your Card & Save

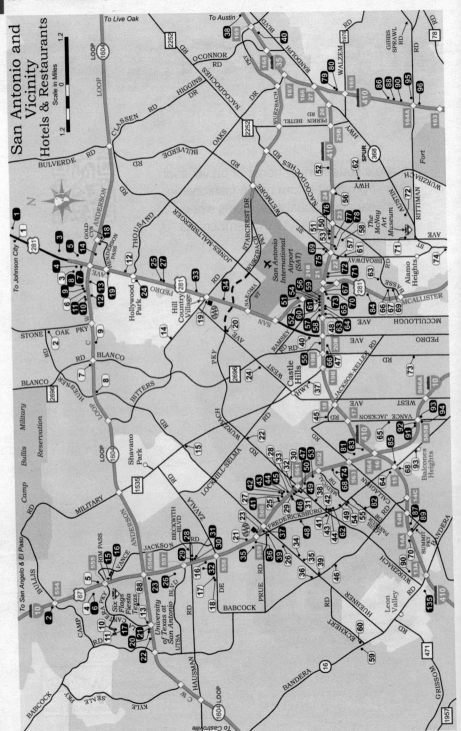

# San Antonio and Vicinity Hotels & Restaurants

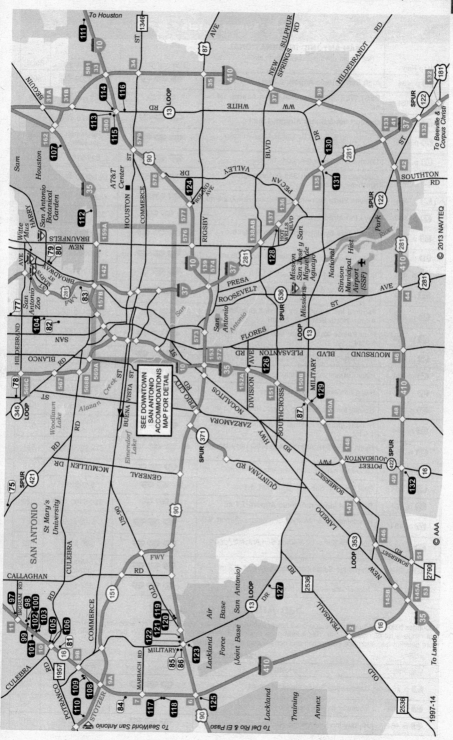

## ✈ Airport Hotels

| Map Page | SAN ANTONIO INTERNATIONAL (Maximum driving distance from airport: 4.2 mi) | Diamond Rated | Rate Range | Page |
|---|---|---|---|---|
| 66 p. 484 | Aloft San Antonio Airport, 2.7 mi | ▽▽▽ | $109-$399 SAVE | 506 |
| 73 p. 484 | BEST WESTERN Posada Ana Inn-Airport, 1.4 mi | ▽▽ | $90-$110 SAVE | 508 |
| 78 p. 484 | Comfort Inn & Suites Airport, 1.8 mi | ▽▽▽ | $80-$170 SAVE | 509 |
| 75 p. 484 | Country Inn & Suites By Carlson San Antonio Airport, 1.8 mi | ▽▽▽ | Rates not provided | 510 |
| 69 p. 484 | Courtyard by Marriott-Airport, 1.8 mi | ▽▽▽ | $99-$169 | 510 |
| 64 p. 484 | Courtyard by Marriott San Antonio Airport/Northstar, 1.9 mi | ▽▽▽ | $90-$150 SAVE | 510 |
| 76 p. 484 | Crowne Plaza San Antonio Airport Hotel, 2.6 mi | ▽▽▽ | $89-$199 SAVE | 511 |
| 72 p. 484 | Days Inn Airport, 1.1 mi | ▽▽ | $60-$70 SAVE | 511 |
| 58 p. 484 | DoubleTree by Hilton Hotel San Antonio Airport, 1.6 mi | ▽▽▽ | $99-$149 SAVE | 512 |
| 61 p. 484 | Drury Inn & Suites-San Antonio Airport, 1.3 mi | ▽▽▽ | $100-$199 | 512 |
| 51 p. 484 | Embassy Suites Hotel-Airport, 1.1 mi | ▽▽▽ | $119-$199 | 513 |
| 33 p. 484 | Extended Stay America-San Antonio-Airport, 4.2 mi | ▽▽ | $44-$59 | 513 |
| 65 p. 484 | Fairfield Inn & Suites by Marriott San Antonio Airport/North Star Mall, 2.0 mi | ▽▽ | $80-$140 SAVE | 513 |
| 56 p. 484 | Four Points by Sheraton San Antonio Airport, 1.3 mi | ▽▽ | Rates not provided SAVE | 514 |
| 54 p. 484 | Hampton Inn & Suites, 1.3 mi | ▽▽▽ | $119-$139 | 514 |
| 34 p. 484 | Hilton Garden Inn San Antonio Airport, 3.4 mi | ▽▽▽ | $99-$179 | 514 |
| 55 p. 484 | Hilton San Antonio Airport, 2.4 mi | ▽▽▽ | $109-$159 | 514 |
| 60 p. 484 | Holiday Inn Express-San Antonio Airport, 1.3 mi | ▽▽▽ | $99-$129 | 515 |
| 57 p. 484 | Holiday Inn San Antonio International Airport, 1.5 mi | ▽▽▽ | Rates not provided SAVE | 517 |
| 84 p. 484 | Hyatt Place San Antonio Airport/Quarry Market, 2.4 mi | ▽▽▽ | $79-$209 SAVE | 517 |
| 70 p. 484 | La Quinta Inn & Suites San Antonio Airport, 1.2 mi | ▽▽▽ | $89-$140 | 518 |
| 59 p. 484 | Pear Tree Inn San Antonio Airport, 1.1 mi | ▽▽ | $75-$139 | 520 |
| 52 p. 484 | Red Roof Inn-San Antonio Airport, 1.7 mi | ▽▽ | $50-$100 SAVE | 520 |
| 77 p. 484 | Residence Inn by Marriott San Antonio-Airport, 2.0 mi | ▽▽▽ | $109-$259 | 521 |
| 71 p. 484 | SpringHill Suites by Marriott San Antonio Airport, 1.0 mi | ▽▽▽ | $99-$199 | 522 |
| 63 p. 484 | Staybridge Suites San Antonio-Airport, 1.8 mi | ▽▽▽ | Rates not provided | 523 |
| 67 p. 484 | TownePlace Suites by Marriott, 1.2 mi | ▽▽▽ | $67-$149 | 523 |

## San Antonio and Vicinity

This index helps you "spot" where approved hotels and restaurants are located on the corresponding detailed maps. Hotel daily rate range is for comparison only. Restaurant price range is a combination of lunch and/or dinner. Turn to the listing page for more detailed rate and price information and consult display ads for special promotions.

### SAN ANTONIO

| Map Page | Hotels | Diamond Rated | Rate Range | Page |
|---|---|---|---|---|
| 1 p. 484 | Candlewood Suites Stone Oak Area | ▽▽▽ | Rates not provided | 509 |
| 2 p. 484 | Rodeway Inn-Six Flags Fiesta | ▽ | $50-$80 | 522 |
| 3 p. 484 | Holiday Inn San Antonio Hill Country | ▽▽▽ | $99-$139 | 516 |

## SAN ANTONIO (cont'd)

| Map Page | Hotels (cont'd) | Diamond Rated | Rate Range | Page |
|---|---|---|---|---|
| **4** p. 484 | **Hyatt Place San Antonio North Stone Oak** | ◆◆◆ | $79-$174 SAVE | 517 |
| **5** p. 484 | **Courtyard by Marriott San Antonio North/Stone Oak at Legacy** | ◆◆◆ | $79-$159 SAVE | 511 |
| **6** p. 484 | **Eilan Hotel Resort and Spa, Autograph Collection** (See ad p. 513.) | ◆◆◆◆ | $199-$500 SAVE | 512 |
| **7** p. 484 | **BEST WESTERN PLUS Hill Country Suites** | ◆◆◆ | $90-$180 SAVE | 507 |
| **8** p. 484 | **Residence Inn by Marriott North San Antonio** | ◆◆◆ | $79-$169 SAVE | 521 |
| **9** p. 484 | La Quinta Inn & Suites San Antonio North Stone Oak | ◆◆◆ | $137-$182 | 518 |
| **10** p. 484 | Drury Plaza San Antonio North | ◆◆◆ | $100-$204 | 512 |
| **11** p. 484 | Drury Inn & Suites-San Antonio North | ◆◆◆ | $80-$184 | 512 |
| **12** p. 484 | Staybridge Suites San Antonio-Stone Oak | ◆◆◆ | $99-$169 | 523 |
| **13** p. 484 | Fairfield Inn & Suites by Marriott North Stone Oak | ◆◆◆ | $69-$199 | 513 |
| **14** p. 484 | **Comfort Suites Stone Oak** | ◆◆◆ | $90-$130 SAVE | 510 |
| **15** p. 484 | Courtyard by Marriott San Antonio Northwest at the RIM | ◆◆◆ | $89-$189 | 511 |
| **16** p. 484 | Residence Inn by Marriott San Antonio Northwest at The RIM | ◆◆◆ | $99-$199 | 521 |
| **17** p. 484 | **The Westin La Cantera Hill Country Resort** | ◆◆◆◆ | $439-$2500 SAVE | 524 |
| **18** p. 484 | Hampton Inn San Antonio-Northwood | ◆◆◆ | $99-$150 | 514 |
| **19** p. 484 | **Days Inn & Suites San Antonio North/Stone Oak** | ◆◆ | $60-$100 SAVE | 511 |
| **20** p. 484 | **Four Points by Sheraton San Antonio Northwest** | ◆◆◆ | $100-$225 SAVE | 514 |
| **21** p. 484 | Comfort Inn-Fiesta | ◆◆ | $80-$110 | 509 |
| **22** p. 484 | Staybridge Suites NW Near Six Flags Fiesta | ◆◆◆ | Rates not provided | 523 |
| **23** p. 484 | Drury Inn & Suites San Antonio-La Cantera | ◆◆◆ | $95-$214 | 512 |
| **24** p. 484 | **Holiday Inn Express Airport North** (See ad p. 515.) | ◆◆◆ | Rates not provided SAVE | 514 |
| **25** p. 484 | Motel 6 - #4341 | ◆◆ | Rates not provided | 519 |
| **26** p. 484 | La Quinta Inn & Suites-Fiesta Texas | ◆◆◆ | $95-$154 | 518 |
| **27** p. 484 | **Microtel Inn & Suites by Wyndham** | ◆◆ | $69-$169 SAVE | 518 |
| **28** p. 484 | Sleep Inn & Suites at Six Flags | ◆◆◆ | $80-$180 | 522 |
| **29** p. 484 | Econo Lodge Inn & Suites Fiesta Park | ◆◆ | $40-$110 | 512 |
| **30** p. 484 | **BEST WESTERN PLUS Fiesta Inn** | ◆◆ | $90-$120 SAVE | 507 |
| **31** p. 484 | **Super 8-Six Flags Fiesta** | ◆◆ | $60-$100 SAVE | 523 |
| **32** p. 484 | Holiday Inn Northwest | ◆◆◆ | $89-$149 | 515 |
| **33** p. 484 | Extended Stay America-San Antonio-Airport | ◆◆ | $44-$59 | 513 |
| **34** p. 484 | Hilton Garden Inn San Antonio Airport | ◆◆◆ | $99-$179 | 514 |
| **35** p. 484 | Comfort Suites NW Near Six Flags | ◆◆◆ | $79-$149 | 510 |
| **36** p. 484 | SpringHill Suites by Marriott San Antonio Medical Center/Six Flags | ◆◆◆ | $89-$199 | 522 |
| **37** p. 484 | Quality Inn Six Flags Area | ◆◆ | $75-$100 | 520 |
| **38** p. 484 | **BEST WESTERN Garden Inn** | ◆◆ | $59-$109 SAVE | 506 |
| **39** p. 484 | TownePlace Suites by Marriott San Antonio Northwest | ◆◆◆ | $65-$139 | 524 |
| **40** p. 484 | **Comfort Suites** | ◆◆◆ | $79-$119 SAVE | 509 |

## SAN ANTONIO (cont'd)

| Map Page | Hotels (cont'd) | Diamond Rated | Rate Range | Page |
|---|---|---|---|---|
| **41** p. 484 | **Hyatt Place San Antonio-Northwest/Medical Center** | ▼▼▼ | $69-$179 SAVE | 517 |
| **42** p. 484 | Extended Stay America-San Antonio-Colonnade | ▼▼▼ | $59-$79 | 513 |
| **43** p. 484 | Homewood Suites by Hilton | ▼▼▼ | $89-$162 | 517 |
| **44** p. 484 | Staybridge Suites San Antonio NW-Colonnade | ▼▼▼ | $149-$249 | 523 |
| **45** p. 484 | Omni San Antonio Hotel at the Colonnade *(See ad p. 519.)* | ▼▼▼▼ | $119-$219 SAVE | 519 |
| **46** p. 484 | **Hawthorne Suites by Wyndham** | ▼▼▼ | $99-$199 SAVE | 514 |
| **47** p. 484 | Drury Inn & Suites-San Antonio Northwest Med Center | ▼▼▼ | $105-$289 | 512 |
| **48** p. 484 | **Regency Inn & Suites** | ▼▼ | $49-$159 SAVE | 521 |
| **49** p. 484 | **BEST WESTERN PLUS Posada Ana Inn - Medical Center** | ▼▼▼ | $60-$120 SAVE | 507 |
| **50** p. 484 | **Baymont Inns & Suites** | ▼▼ | $59-$109 SAVE | 506 |
| **51** p. 484 | Embassy Suites Hotel-Airport | ▼▼▼ | $119-$199 | 513 |
| **52** p. 484 | **Red Roof Inn-San Antonio Airport** | ▼▼ | $50-$100 SAVE | 520 |
| **53** p. 484 | Candlewood Suites Hotel | ▼▼▼ | $90-$110 | 508 |
| **54** p. 484 | Hampton Inn & Suites | ▼▼▼ | $119-$139 | 514 |
| **55** p. 484 | Hilton San Antonio Airport | ▼▼▼ | $109-$159 | 514 |
| **56** p. 484 | **Four Points by Sheraton San Antonio Airport** | ▼▼▼ | Rates not provided SAVE | 514 |
| **57** p. 484 | **Holiday Inn San Antonio International Airport** *(See ad p. 516.)* | ▼▼▼ | Rates not provided SAVE | 517 |
| **58** p. 484 | **DoubleTree by Hilton Hotel San Antonio Airport** | ▼▼▼ | $99-$149 SAVE | 512 |
| **59** p. 484 | Pear Tree Inn San Antonio Airport | ▼▼ | $75-$139 | 520 |
| **60** p. 484 | Holiday Inn Express-San Antonio Airport | ▼▼▼ | $99-$129 | 515 |
| **61** p. 484 | Drury Inn & Suites-San Antonio Airport | ▼▼▼ | $100-$199 | 512 |
| **62** p. 484 | Courtyard by Marriott-Medical Center | ▼▼▼ | $89-$169 | 510 |
| **63** p. 484 | Staybridge Suites San Antonio-Airport | ▼▼▼ | Rates not provided | 523 |
| **64** p. 484 | **Courtyard by Marriott San Antonio Airport/ Northstar** | ▼▼▼ | $90-$150 SAVE | 510 |
| **65** p. 484 | **Fairfield Inn & Suites by Marriott San Antonio Airport/North Star Mall** | ▼▼ | $80-$140 SAVE | 513 |
| **66** p. 484 | **Aloft San Antonio Airport** *(See ad p. 506.)* | ▼▼▼ | $109-$399 SAVE | 506 |
| **67** p. 484 | TownePlace Suites by Marriott | ▼▼▼ | $67-$149 | 523 |
| **68** p. 484 | Sleep Inn San Antonio | ▼▼ | $62-$119 | 522 |
| **69** p. 484 | Courtyard by Marriott-Airport | ▼▼▼ | $99-$169 | 510 |
| **70** p. 484 | La Quinta Inn & Suites San Antonio Airport | ▼▼▼ | $89-$140 | 518 |
| **71** p. 484 | SpringHill Suites by Marriott San Antonio Airport | ▼▼▼ | $99-$199 | 522 |
| **72** p. 484 | **Days Inn Airport** | ▼▼ | $60-$70 SAVE | 511 |
| **73** p. 484 | **BEST WESTERN Posada Ana Inn-Airport** | ▼▼ | $90-$110 SAVE | 508 |
| **74** p. 484 | La Quinta Inn & Suites Antonio Medical Center | ▼▼▼ | $109-$204 | 518 |
| **75** p. 484 | Country Inn & Suites By Carlson San Antonio Airport | ▼▼▼ | Rates not provided | 510 |
| **76** p. 484 | **Crowne Plaza San Antonio Airport Hotel** | ▼▼▼ | $89-$199 SAVE | 511 |
| **77** p. 484 | Residence Inn by Marriott San Antonio-Airport | ▼▼▼ | $109-$259 | 521 |

**SAN ANTONIO (cont'd)**

| Map Page | Hotels (cont'd) | Diamond Rated | Rate Range | Page |
|---|---|---|---|---|
| **78** p. 484 | **Comfort Inn & Suites Airport** | ◆◆◆ | $80-$170 SAVE | 509 |
| **79** p. 484 | Drury Inn & Suites Northeast | ◆◆◆ | $85-$164 | 512 |
| **80** p. 484 | Pear Tree Inn by Drury-San Antonio Northeast | ◆◆ | $70-$149 | 519 |
| **81** p. 484 | Embassy Suites Northwest | ◆◆◆ | $112-$199 | 513 |
| **82** p. 484 | Motel 6 - Medical Center South - #4429 | ◆◆ | Rates not provided | 519 |
| **83** p. 484 | **San Antonio Marriott Northwest** *(See ad p. 522.)* | ◆◆◆ | $99-$159 SAVE | 522 |
| **84** p. 484 | **Hyatt Place San Antonio Airport/Quarry Market** | ◆◆◆ | $79-$209 SAVE | 517 |
| **85** p. 484 | SpringHill Suites by Marriott San Antonio Medical Center/Northwest | ◆◆◆ | $89-$119 | 522 |
| **86** p. 484 | MainStay Suites | ◆◆ | $55-$139 | 518 |
| **87** p. 484 | **Baymont Inn** | ◆◆◆ | $89-$119 SAVE | 506 |
| **88** p. 484 | Hampton Inn & Suites San Antonio/Northeast I-35 | ◆◆◆ | Rates not provided | 514 |
| **89** p. 484 | **Quality Inn Medical** | ◆◆ | $69-$140 SAVE | 520 |
| **90** p. 484 | La Quinta Inn San Antonio I-35 North At Rittiman Rd | ◆◆ | $69-$124 | 518 |
| **91** p. 484 | Comfort Inn & Suites | ◆◆◆ | $69-$139 | 509 |
| **92** p. 484 | **Days Inn Northwest** | ◆◆ | $55-$75 SAVE | 511 |
| **93** p. 484 | La Quinta Inn San Antonio Vance Jackson | ◆◆ | $75-$130 | 518 |
| **94** p. 484 | Holiday Inn Express & Suites NW - Medical Center Area | ◆◆◆ | Rates not provided | 515 |
| **95** p. 484 | **BEST WESTERN Windsor Pointe Hotel & Suites-AT&T Center** | ◆◆ | $75-$260 SAVE | 508 |
| **96** p. 484 | Motel 6 Fort Sam Houston - #1350 | ◆ | $45-$65 | 519 |
| **97** p. 484 | M-Star SeaWorld | ◆◆ | $49-$119 | 519 |
| **98** p. 484 | Holiday Inn Express Hotel & Suites SeaWorld | ◆◆◆ | Rates not provided | 515 |
| **99** p. 484 | Courtyard by Marriott SeaWorld/Lackland A.F.B. | ◆◆◆ | $89-$199 | 511 |
| **100** p. 484 | Residence Inn by Marriott SeaWorld/Lackland AFB | ◆◆◆ | $109-$199 | 521 |
| **101** p. 484 | **BEST WESTERN Ingram Park Inn** | ◆◆ | $79-$139 SAVE | 507 |
| **102** p. 484 | **Red Roof Inn San Antonio (NW-SeaWorld)** | ◆◆ | $49-$89 SAVE | 520 |
| **103** p. 484 | Comfort Suites near SeaWorld | ◆◆◆ | $89-$129 | 509 |
| **104** p. 484 | Bonner Garden Bed & Breakfast | ◆◆◆ | $115-$180 | 508 |
| **105** p. 484 | La Quinta Inn San Antonio SeaWorld/Ingram Park | ◆◆ | $69-$154 | 518 |
| **106** p. 484 | **Ramada-SeaWorld Area** | ◆◆ | $49-$129 SAVE | 520 |
| **107** p. 484 | Quality Inn & Suites | ◆◆ | $70-$190 | 520 |
| **108** p. 484 | SpringHill Suites by Marriott San Antonio Seaworld/Lackland | ◆◆◆ | $89-$199 | 523 |
| **109** p. 484 | Sleep Inn & Suites-SeaWorld | ◆◆◆ | $65-$110 | 522 |
| **110** p. 484 | **Comfort Inn Near SeaWorld** *(See ad p. 515.)* | ◆◆◆ | $79-$149 SAVE | 509 |
| **111** p. 484 | La Quinta Inn San Antonio I-10 East | ◆◆ | $105-$140 | 518 |
| **112** p. 484 | **Econo Lodge Inn & Suites** | ◆◆ | $50-$200 SAVE | 512 |
| **113** p. 484 | **Rodeway Inn** | ◆ | $46-$85 SAVE | 521 |
| **114** p. 484 | Motel 6 East - #183 | ◆ | $45-$75 | 519 |
| **115** p. 484 | **Red Roof Inn- San Antonio Ft. Sam Houston** | ◆◆ | $50-$120 SAVE | 520 |

## SAN ANTONIO (cont'd)

| Map Page | Hotels (cont'd) | Diamond Rated | Rate Range | Page |
|---|---|---|---|---|
| 116 p. 484 | Americas Best Value Inn - San Antonio Downtown I-10 East | ◆◆ | $55-$75 SAVE | 506 |
| 117 p. 484 | Motel 6 - #651 | ◆ | $45-$85 | 519 |
| 118 p. 484 | Super 8 | ◆◆ | $59-$76 SAVE | 523 |
| 119 p. 484 | Rodeway Inn Lackland AFB/SeaWorld | ◆ | $49-$90 SAVE | 521 |
| 120 p. 484 | Holiday Inn Lackland | ◆◆◆ | Rates not provided | 515 |
| 121 p. 484 | Days Inn Lackland | ◆◆ | $80-$200 SAVE | 511 |
| 122 p. 484 | Red Roof Inn Lackland | ◆◆ | $60-$140 SAVE | 520 |
| 123 p. 484 | La Quinta Inn San Antonio Lackland | ◆◆ | $95-$140 | 518 |
| 124 p. 484 | Super 8 on Roland | ◆◆ | $79-$160 SAVE | 523 |
| 125 p. 484 | BEST WESTERN PLUS Atrea Hotel & Suites | ◆◆◆ | $130-$140 SAVE | 507 |
| 126 p. 484 | Econo Lodge Downtown South | ◆◆ | $49-$99 SAVE | 512 |
| 127 p. 484 | Travelodge Lackland | ◆◆ | $50-$250 SAVE | 524 |
| 128 p. 484 | Super 8 | ◆◆ | $69-$100 SAVE | 523 |
| 129 p. 484 | La Quinta Inn San Antonio South Park | ◆◆ | $79-$134 | 518 |
| 130 p. 484 | Quality Suites | ◆◆◆ | $105-$125 SAVE | 520 |
| 131 p. 484 | La Quinta Inn San Antonio AlamoDome South | ◆◆ | $121-$156 SAVE | 518 |
| 132 p. 484 | BEST WESTERN PLUS Palo Alto Inn & Suites | ◆◆◆ | $120-$180 SAVE | 507 |

| Map Page | Restaurants | Diamond Rated | Cuisine | Price Range | Page |
|---|---|---|---|---|---|
| 1 p. 484 | Luciano's Stone Ridge | ◆◆ | Italian | $8-$18 | 528 |
| 2 p. 484 | Cielito Lindo | ◆◆ | Regional Mexican | $8-$18 | 526 |
| 3 p. 484 | Perico's Mexican Cuisine | ◆◆ | Tex-Mex | $7-$12 | 528 |
| 4 p. 484 | Sustenio | ◆◆◆◆ | Regional Mexican | $14-$48 | 530 |
| 5 p. 484 | Maggiano's Little Italy | ◆◆◆ | Italian | $10-$25 | 528 |
| 6 p. 484 | Meson European Dining | ◆◆◆ | International | $9-$24 | 528 |
| 7 p. 484 | Aldino at the Vineyard | ◆◆◆ | Italian | $10-$30 | 524 |
| 8 p. 484 | Roaring Fork | ◆◆◆ | Regional American | $10-$18 | 529 |
| 9 p. 484 | Silo Elevated Cuisine and Bar-Loop 1604 | ◆◆◆ | New World | $18-$50 | 530 |
| 10 p. 484 | Brannon's Cafe | ◆◆◆ | Regional American | $19-$26 | 525 |
| 11 p. 484 | Francesca's at Sunset | ◆◆◆◆ | Regional American | $30-$60 | 526 |
| 12 p. 484 | Saltgrass Steakhouse | ◆◆ | Steak | $9-$31 SAVE | 529 |
| 13 p. 484 | Kona Grill | ◆◆◆ | Pacific Rim | $9-$30 | 527 |
| 14 p. 484 | Bin 555 Restaurant and Wine Bar | ◆◆◆ | New World | $14-$34 | 525 |
| 15 p. 484 | Frederick's Bistro | ◆◆◆ | New French Fusion | $15-$27 | 526 |
| 16 p. 484 | Matamoros Restaurant and Cantina | ◆◆ | Mexican | $7-$18 | 528 |
| 17 p. 484 | Rome's Pizza | ◆ | Italian Pizza | $7-$14 | 529 |
| 18 p. 484 | Thai Bistro & Sushi | ◆◆ | Thai | $8-$16 | 530 |
| 19 p. 484 | El Jarro de Arturo | ◆◆ | Regional Tex-Mex | $8-$16 | 526 |
| 20 p. 484 | Two Bros. BBQ Market | ◆◆ | Barbecue | $8-$15 | 531 |

| Map Page | Restaurants (cont'd) | Diamond Rated | Cuisine | Price Range | Page |
|---|---|---|---|---|---|
| ㉑ p. 484 | Saltgrass Steakhouse | ◆◆ | Steak | $9-$31 SAVE | 529 |
| ㉒ p. 484 | Milano on Wurzbach | ◆◆◆ | Italian | $8-$27 | 528 |
| ㉓ p. 484 | Fire Wok Asian Stir Fry | ◆ | Asian | $5-$12 | 526 |
| ㉔ p. 484 | India Oven | ◆◆ | Indian | $6-$18 | 526 |
| ㉕ p. 484 | Sea Island Shrimp House I-10 W | ◆ | Regional Seafood | $8-$22 | 529 |
| ㉖ p. 484 | M J China Bistro | ◆◆ | Chinese Sushi | $8-$15 | 528 |
| ㉗ p. 484 | The County Line Barbecue | ◆◆ | Barbecue | $11-$30 | 526 |
| ㉘ p. 484 | **Bolo's** | ◆◆◆ | Regional American | $8-$35 | 525 |
| ㉙ p. 484 | Alamo Cafe | ◆◆ | Tex-Mex | $8-$20 | 524 |
| ㉚ p. 484 | Sarovar Indian Cuisine | ◆ | Indian | $11-$16 | 529 |
| ㉛ p. 484 | Chester's Hamburgers | ◆ | Burgers | $7-$10 | 525 |
| ㉜ p. 484 | Broadway 50-50 | ◆◆ | American | $11-$22 | 525 |
| ㉝ p. 484 | Mama Margie's | ◆ | Tex-Mex | $5-$10 | 528 |
| ㉞ p. 484 | Sarika's Thai and Sushi | ◆◆ | Thai | $8-$14 | 529 |
| ㉟ p. 484 | Thai Topaz | ◆ | Thai | $7-$9 | 530 |
| ㊱ p. 484 | Regent Hunan Chinese Restaurant | ◆ | Regional Chinese | $6-$12 | 529 |
| ㊲ p. 484 | Sushihana Contemporary Japanese | ◆◆◆ | Sushi | $15-$30 | 530 |
| ㊳ p. 484 | Golden Wok Chinese Restaurant | ◆◆ | Dim Sum | $6-$17 | 526 |
| ㊴ p. 484 | Capparelli's Italian Restaurant | ◆ | Italian | $7-$12 | 525 |
| ㊵ p. 484 | Tokyo Steakhouse | ◆◆ | Japanese | $13-$47 | 530 |
| ㊶ p. 484 | Aldo's Ristorante Italiano | ◆◆◆ | Italian | $12-$40 | 524 |
| ㊷ p. 484 | Dry Dock Seafood Oyster Bar | ◆ | Seafood | $8-$22 | 526 |
| ㊸ p. 484 | Thai Corner | ◆◆ | Thai | $7-$12 | 530 |
| ㊹ p. 484 | **India Palace** | ◆◆ | Indian | $7-$15 | 527 |
| ㊺ p. 484 | Ernesto's Gourmet Restaurant | ◆◆◆ | Regional Mexican Seafood Steak | $8-$20 | 526 |
| ㊻ p. 484 | Shogun Steakhouse Restaurant | ◆ | Japanese | $8-$15 | 529 |
| ㊼ p. 484 | Lion and Rose British Restaurant and Pub | ◆◆ | British | $8-$14 | 527 |
| ㊽ p. 484 | Sea Island Shrimp House | ◆ | Seafood | $6-$14 | 529 |
| ㊾ p. 484 | Sompong's Thai & Chinese Cuisine | ◆ | Thai | $8-$15 | 530 |
| ㊿ p. 484 | Raffle's Restaurant and Bar | ◆◆ | American | $8-$14 | 529 |
| (51) p. 484 | Formosa Garden | ◆◆ | Chinese | $8-$18 | 526 |
| (52) p. 484 | Los Patios | ◆◆ | Regional American | $11-$21 | 527 |
| (53) p. 484 | Magic Time Machine | ◆◆ | American | $12-$40 | 528 |
| (54) p. 484 | Sarika's Thai Restaurant | ◆◆ | Thai | $8-$15 | 529 |
| (55) p. 484 | Mencius' Gourmet Hunan Chinese Restaurant | ◆◆ | Regional Chinese | $7-$20 | 528 |
| (56) p. 484 | Barbecue Station Restaurant | ◆ | Regional Barbecue | $6-$12 | 524 |
| (57) p. 484 | 410 Diner | ◆◆ | American | $8-$18 | 524 |
| (58) p. 484 | The Barn Door Restaurant | ◆◆ | Regional Steak | $13-$30 | 524 |

| Map Page | Restaurants (cont'd) | Diamond Rated | Cuisine | Price Range | Page |
|---|---|---|---|---|---|
| 59 p. 484 | Grady's Bar-B-Que #2 | ◆ | Barbecue | $6-$12 | 526 |
| 60 p. 484 | Cafe Milano | ◆◆ | Regional Italian | $7-$22 | 525 |
| 61 p. 484 | Beto's Comida Latina | ◆◆ | Regional Latin American | $7-$12 | 524 |
| 62 p. 484 | Crumpets Restaurant & Bakery | ◆◆ | Regional American | $9-$26 | 526 |
| 63 p. 484 | Paesano's Ristorante-Alamo Quarry | ◆◆◆ | Italian | $9-$30 | 528 |
| 64 p. 484 | La Fonda in Oakhills | ◆ | Tex-Mex | $8-$20 | 527 |
| 65 p. 484 | La Fogata Restaurant | ◆◆ | Mexican | $12-$28 | 527 |
| 66 p. 484 | Canyon Cafe | ◆◆ | Southwestern | $15-$30 | 525 |
| 67 p. 484 | J. Alexander's Restaurant | ◆◆ | American | $8-$27 | 527 |
| 68 p. 484 | Turquoise Grill | ◆◆ | Turkish Vegetarian | $9-$17 | 530 |
| 69 p. 484 | P.F. Chang's China Bistro | ◆◆◆ | Chinese | $5-$25 | 529 |
| 70 p. 484 | Mela Indian Bar & Grill | ◆◆ | Indian | $7-$13 | 528 |
| 71 p. 484 | Twin Sisters Bakery & Cafe | ◆◆ | Regional American | $8-$18 | 531 |
| 72 p. 484 | Silo Elevated Cuisine Alamo Heights | ◆◆◆ | New World | $10-$30 | 530 |
| 73 p. 484 | Los Barrios Mexican Restaurant | ◆◆ | Tex-Mex | $8-$18 | 527 |
| 74 p. 484 | Cappy's | ◆◆◆ | Regional American | $12-$32 | 525 |
| 75 p. 484 | Fatso's Sports Garden | ◆ | Regional Barbecue | $6-$18 | 526 |
| 77 p. 484 | Bistro Vatel | ◆◆◆ | Provincial French | $12-$30 | 525 |
| 78 p. 484 | Jacala Mexican Restaurant | ◆◆ | Regional Mexican | $5-$12 | 527 |
| 79 p. 484 | Van's Chinese Seafood Restaurant | ◆◆ | Chinese | $7-$19 | 531 |
| 80 p. 484 | Tomatillos Cafe y Cantina | ◆◆ | Regional Mexican | $8-$16 | 530 |
| 81 p. 484 | J. Anthony's Seafood Cafe | ◆ | Seafood | $8-$12 | 527 |
| 82 p. 484 | Cappy's LaFonda on Main | ◆◆◆ | Regional Mexican | $8-$21 | 525 |
| 83 p. 484 | Il Sogno Osteria | ◆◆◆ | Italian | $10-$28 | 526 |
| 84 p. 484 | Acadiana Cafe | ◆◆ | Regional Cajun | $7-$15 | 524 |
| 85 p. 484 | Mina & Dimi's Greek House Restaurant | ◆ | Greek | $6-$12 | 528 |
| 86 p. 484 | Sun Chinese Buffet | ◆ | Chinese | $7-$10 | 530 |
| 87 p. 484 | Sea Island Shrimp House | ◆ | Regional American | $6-$14 | 529 |
| 88 p. 484 | Perry's Steakhouse & Grille | ◆◆◆ | Steak | $31-$50 | 529 |

## LEON VALLEY

| Map Page | Hotel | Diamond Rated | | Rate Range | Page |
|---|---|---|---|---|---|
| 135 p. 484 | **Super 8 SeaWorld Area** | ◆◆ | | $60-$77 SAVE | 395 |

| Map Page | Restaurant | Diamond Rated | Cuisine | Price Range | Page |
|---|---|---|---|---|---|
| 90 p. 484 | Piccolo's Italian Restaurant | ◆ | Regional Italian | $8-$22 | 395 |

## BALCONES HEIGHTS

| Map Page | Restaurant | Diamond Rated | Cuisine | Price Range | Page |
|---|---|---|---|---|---|
| 93 p. 484 | Grady's Bar-B-Que | ◆ | Barbecue | $7-$10 | 114 |

# DOWNTOWN SAN ANTONIO

## A BECKMANN INN & CARRIAGE HOUSE BED AND BREAKFAST
(210)229-1449  **66**

 Historic Bed & Breakfast $119-$189 **Address:** 222 E Guenther St 78204 **Location:** 0.5 mi s, just w of S Alamo St; in King William Historic District. **Facility:** This restored, historic 1886 Victorian features burled-pine doors, 14-foot ceilings and a wraparound porch furnished with wicker. 5 units. 1-2 stories (no elevator), interior/exterior corridors. **Terms:** check-in 4 pm, 2 night minimum stay - seasonal and/or weekends, age restrictions may apply, 14 day cancellation notice-fee imposed. **Guest Services:** complimentary and valet laundry. 🍴 HS 🛜 ✕ 🛗

## ALAMO INN
(210)227-2203  **58**

Motel
$45-$120

**Address:** 2203 E Commerce St 78203 **Location:** I-37 exit 141A, 1.2 mi e at Commerce St and New Braunfels Ave. **Facility:** 15 units, some kitchens. 1 story, exterior corridors. **Terms:** cancellation fee imposed. **Amenities:** Some: safes. **Guest Services:** valet laundry, area transportation. **Featured Amenity: continental breakfast.**

SAVE HS 🛜 🛗 📶 / SOME UNITS 🛏

## ARBOR HOUSE SUITES BED & BREAKFAST
(210)472-2005  **55**

Historic Bed & Breakfast
$129-$207

**Address:** 109 Arciniega St 78205 **Location:** Just s of E Nueva St; between S Presa and S St. Mary's sts; near La Villita Historic District; in King William Historic District. **Facility:** Dating from 1903, this village of five houses features tranquil courtyards. The varied-size accommodations are individually decorated. A picnic-basket breakfast is delivered to each room daily. 7 units. 2 stories (no elevator), interior/exterior corridors. **Terms:** 14 day cancellation notice-fee imposed. **Activities:** hot tub. **Guest Services:** complimentary laundry. **Featured Amenity: continental breakfast.**

SAVE HS 🛜 ✕ 🛗 📶 / SOME UNITS 🛏

## A YELLOW ROSE BED & BREAKFAST
(210)229-9903  **64**

 Bed & Breakfast $110-$200 **Address:** 229 Madison St 78204 **Location:** Just s of S St. Mary's St; in King William Historic District. **Facility:** Porches with rocking chairs adjoin some accommodations at this restored, turn-of-the-century, Victorian B&B featuring spacious common areas. All rooms have private entrances. 5 units. 2 stories (no elevator), exterior corridors. **Terms:** 2 night minimum stay - seasonal and/or weekends, 14 day cancellation notice-fee imposed.

🍴 HS 🛜 ✕ 🛗 📶 / SOME UNITS 🛗

## BEST WESTERN ALAMO SUITES
(210)472-1002  **62**

Hotel
$109-$169

 **AAA Benefit:** Members save 10% or more with Best Western!

**Address:** 1002 S Laredo St 78204 **Location:** I-10/35 exit 155A (Alamo St), just s; on south side of interstate. **Facility:** 72 units. 3 stories, interior corridors. **Pool(s):** heated indoor. **Activities:** hot tub, exercise room. **Guest Services:** valet and coin laundry.

SAVE CALL 🛗♿ 🅼 🚲 BIZ HS 🛜 ✕ 🛗 📶 🛗 📶

## BEST WESTERN PLUS SUNSET SUITES-RIVERWALK
(210)223-4400  **40**

Historic Hotel
$90-$210

 **AAA Benefit:** Members save 10% or more with Best Western!

**Address:** 1103 E Commerce St 78205 **Location:** I-37 exit Commerce St, just e; in Historic Sunset Station. **Facility:** The beautifully restored historic building, conveniently facing the interstate, features polished wood plank lobbies, rich oak wood recliners and uniquely decorated guest rooms. 64 units. 4 stories, interior corridors. **Activities:** exercise room. **Guest Services:** valet and coin laundry.

SAVE 🍴 BIZ HS 🛜 ✕ 🛗 📶 🛗 📶

## BRACKENRIDGE HOUSE B & B
(210)271-3442  **65**

 Bed & Breakfast $109-$275 **Address:** 230 Madison St 78204 **Location:** Just s of S St. Mary's St at Cesar E Chavez Blvd; in King William Historic District. **Facility:** This B&B includes a suite in the carriage house in addition to guest rooms in the main house; all have TVs. A turn-of-the-century ambience is the hallmark of this comfortable B&B. 5 units, some cottages. 2 stories (no elevator), interior/exterior corridors. **Terms:** 2 night minimum stay - seasonal and/or weekends, age restrictions may apply, 14 day cancellation notice-fee imposed. HS 🛜 ✕ 🛗 📶 🛗

## CANDLEWOOD SUITES SAN ANTONIO DOWNTOWN
(210)226-7700  **63**

 Extended Stay Hotel $95-$139 **Address:** 1024 S Laredo St 78204 **Location:** I-10/35 exit Laredo St; on frontage road. **Facility:** 96 units, some efficiencies and kitchens. 3 stories, interior corridors. **Terms:** cancellation fee imposed. **Pool(s):** outdoor. **Activities:** hot tub, exercise room. **Guest Services:** complimentary and valet laundry.

🚲 BIZ HS 🛜 ✕ 🛗 📶 🛗 📶 / SOME UNITS 🛏

(See map & index p. 479.)

**CITY VIEW INN & SUITES**     210/222-2220   **45**

Motel. Rates not provided. **Address:** 1306 E Commerce St 78205 **Location:** Just e of downtown. **Facility:** 20 units. 3 stories, interior/exterior corridors. HS 🛜 ✕ 💻

**COMFORT SUITES ALAMO/RIVERWALK**   (210)227-5200   **12**

Hotel $119-$239 **Address:** 505 Live Oak St 78202 **Location:** I-37 exit 141B (Houston St), 2 blks n. **Facility:** 89 units. 5 stories, interior corridors. **Amenities:** safes. **Pool(s):** heated outdoor. **Activities:** exercise room. **Guest Services:** valet and coin laundry. *(See ad this page.)*

CALL 🛗 🏊 BIZ HS 🛜 ✕

📱 🍽 💻

**COURTYARD BY MARRIOTT SAN ANTONIO DOWNTOWN MARKET SQUARE**   (210)229-9449   **44**

Hotel $119-$189 **Address:** 600 S Santa Rosa Ave 78204 **Location:** I-10/35 exit 155B (Cesar E Chavez Blvd), 0.5 mi e. **Facility:** 149 units. 3 stories, interior corridors. **Pool(s):** outdoor.

**AAA Benefit:** Members save 5% or more!

**Activities:** hot tub, exercise room. **Guest Services:** valet and coin laundry, boarding pass kiosk.

🍽 🏊 BIZ HS 🛜 ✕ 📱 🍽 💻

**COURTYARD BY MARRIOTT SAN ANTONIO RIVERWALK**   (210)223-8888   **21**

Hotel $169-$229 **Address:** 207 N St. Mary's St 78205 **Location:** Between College and W Crockett sts. **Facility:** 217 units. 16 stories, interior corridors. **Parking:** valet only. **Pool(s):** heated outdoor. **Activities:** hot tub, exercise room. **Guest Services:** valet and coin laundry.

**AAA Benefit:** Members save 5% or more!

🍽 🍽 CALL 🛗 🏊 BIZ HS 🛜 ✕ 📱 💻

**CROCKETT HOTEL**     (210)225-6500   **24**

Hotel $99-$295

**Address:** 320 Bonham St 78205 **Location:** Center. Across from Alamo. **Facility:** 138 units. 3-7 stories, interior corridors. **Parking:** on-site and valet. **Terms:** cancellation fee imposed. **Pool(s):** outdoor. **Guest Services:** valet laundry. **Featured Amenity:** continental breakfast.

SAVE 🍽 🏊 BIZ HS 🛜 ✕

💻 / SOME UNITS 💻

---

**DOUBLETREE BY HILTON HOTEL SAN ANTONIO DOWNTOWN**   (210)224-7155   **36**

Hotel $99-$189

**AAA Benefit:** Members save 5% or more!

**Address:** 502 W Cesar E Chavez Blvd 78207 **Location:** I-35 exit 155B (Cesar E Chavez Blvd), 1 blk e; 8 blks from River Walk. Adjacent to University of Texas San Antonio downtown campus. **Facility:** 250 units. 6 stories, interior corridors. **Terms:** 1-7 night minimum stay, cancellation fee imposed. **Amenities:** video games. **Pool(s):** outdoor. **Activities:** exercise room. **Guest Services:** valet laundry, area transportation.

SAVE 🍽 📶 🍽 🏊 BIZ 🛜 ✕ 📱 💻

/ SOME UNITS HS 📱 💻

---

(See map & index p. 479.)

## DRURY INN & SUITES-SAN ANTONIO RIVERWALK

(210)212-5200 **23**

Historic Hotel $135-$229 **Address:** 201 N St. Mary's St 78205 **Location:** Just s of College St. **Facility:** This beautifully restored 1920s property features a grand player piano in the lobby. The public areas are elegant and guest units are large. 150 units. 7 stories, interior corridors. **Parking:** on-site (fee). **Terms:** cancellation fee imposed. **Pool(s):** outdoor. **Activities:** hot tub, exercise room. **Guest Services:** valet and coin laundry.

## DRURY PLAZA HOTEL-SAN ANTONIO RIVERWALK

(210)270-7799 **29**

Historic Hotel $140-$284 **Address:** 105 S St. Mary's St 78205 **Location:** Jct Commerce, St. Mary's and River sts. **Facility:** In the heart of the city in the landmark Alamo National Bank building, this high-rise has a green granite exterior and a 50-foot-high lobby ceiling brightened with stained-glass windows and detail. 366 units. 23 stories, interior corridors. **Parking:** valet only. **Terms:** cancellation fee imposed. **Pool(s):** heated outdoor, heated indoor. **Activities:** hot tub, exercise room. **Guest Services:** valet and coin laundry.

## EL TROPICANO RIVERWALK

(210)223-9461 **2**

Retro Hotel $129-$169 **Address:** 110 Lexington Ave 78205 **Location:** 0.3 mi s of jct Lexington Ave and I-35. **Facility:** This redecorated property overlooks the San Antonio River and has elegant Southwest décor mixed with contemporary retro accents. 308 units, some kitchens. 3-9 stories, interior corridors. **Parking:** on-site (fee) and valet. **Terms:** check-in 4 pm. **Pool(s):** outdoor. **Activities:** exercise room. **Guest Services:** valet and coin laundry.

## EMBASSY SUITES SAN ANTONIO RIVERWALK-DOWNTOWN

(210)226-9000 **8**

Hotel $179-$279 **Address:** 125 E Houston St 78205 **Location:** I-35 S/37 S exit 141A (Commerce St), just w. **Facility:** 285 units, some two bedrooms. 17 stories, interior corridors. **Parking:** on-site (fee) and valet. **Terms:** 1-7 night minimum stay, cancellation fee imposed. **Pool(s):** outdoor. **Activities:** hot tub, exercise room. **Guest Services:** valet and coin laundry.

**AAA Benefit:** Members save 5% or more!

## EMILY MORGAN HOTEL-DOUBLETREE BY HILTON

(210)225-8486 **15**

Historic Hotel $119-$179

**AAA Benefit:** Members save 5% or more!

**Address:** 705 E Houston St 78205 **Location:** Just n of Bonham St. Opposite the Alamo. **Facility:** The hotel offers spacious, high-ceilinged guest rooms, many overlooking the Alamo. 177 units. 12 stories, interior corridors. **Parking:** on-site (fee) and valet. **Terms:** 1-7 night minimum stay, cancellation fee imposed. **Amenities:** video games. **Dining:** Oro Restaurant & Bar, see separate listing. **Pool(s):** heated outdoor. **Activities:** hot tub, exercise room. **Guest Services:** valet laundry.

## FAIRFIELD INN & SUITES BY MARRIOTT SAN ANTONIO DOWNTOWN/ALAMO PLAZA

(210)212-6262 **14**

Hotel $99-$209 **Address:** 422 Bonham St 78205 **Location:** I-37 and US 281 exit Commerce St, just w to Bowie St, then 3 blks n. **Facility:** 89 units. 6 stories, interior corridors. **Parking:** on-site (fee) and valet. **Pool(s):** outdoor. **Activities:** hot tub, exercise room. **Guest Services:** valet and coin laundry.

**AAA Benefit:** Members save 5% or more!

## FAIRFIELD INN & SUITES BY MARRIOTT SAN ANTONIO DOWNTOWN/MARKET SQUARE

(210)299-1000 **48**

Hotel $80-$140

**AAA Benefit:** Members save 5% or more!

**Address:** 620 S Santa Rosa St 78204 **Location:** I-10/35 exit 155B (Cesar E Chavez Blvd), 0.5 mi e. **Facility:** 110 units. 4 stories, interior corridors. **Amenities:** video games. **Pool(s):** heated indoor. **Activities:** exercise room. **Guest Services:** valet and coin laundry. **Featured Amenity:** full hot breakfast.

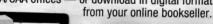

(See map & index p. 479.)

**THE FAIRMOUNT HOTEL**    210/224-8800 **49**

🔻🔻🔻 **Historic Hotel.** Rates not provided. **Address:** 401 S Alamo St 78205 **Location:** Opposite convention center and Hemisfair Plaza. Adjacent to La Villita Historic District. **Facility:** The historic hotel was physically moved from across town; it has a residential-style ambience. 37 units. 4 stories, interior/exterior corridors. **Parking:** on-site (fee) and valet. **Activities:** massage. **Guest Services:** valet laundry.

🍴 🛏 🚪 🛗 BIZ HS 🛜 ✕ 🖥
/ SOME UNITS 🐾 📠

---

**FOUR POINTS BY SHERATON SAN ANTONIO DOWNTOWN**    (210)354-1333 **53**

🔻🔻🔻 Contemporary Hotel $99-$279

FOUR POINTS BY SHERATON

**AAA Benefit:** Members get up to 20% off, plus Starwood Preferred Guest® bonuses!

**Address:** 524 S St. Mary's St 78205 **Location:** Just n of Cesar E Chavez Blvd. **Facility:** 116 units. 4 stories, interior corridors. **Parking:** no self-parking. **Pool(s):** outdoor. **Activities:** exercise room. **Guest Services:** valet laundry.

SAVE 🍴 🛗 CALL 👤M 🏊 BIZ
HS 🛜 ✕ 📠 🖥

---

**GRAND HYATT SAN ANTONIO**    (210)224-1234 **41**

🔻🔻🔻 Contemporary Hotel $99-$359

GRAND | HYATT

**AAA Benefit:** Members save 10%!

**Address:** 600 E Market St 78205 **Location:** I-37 exit 141A (Market St); between S Alamo St and I-37. Adjacent to San Antonio Convention Center. **Facility:** Overlooking the heart of the Riverwalk, this contemporary-style hotel opened in early 2008 and features striking lobbies, fanciful artwork and modern, state-of-the-art guest rooms. 1003 units. 24 stories, interior corridors. **Parking:** on-site (fee) and valet. **Terms:** check-in 4 pm, cancellation fee imposed. **Amenities:** video games, safes. **Dining:** 2 restaurants. **Pool(s):** heated outdoor. **Activities:** exercise room, massage. **Guest Services:** valet laundry.

SAVE ECO 🛗 🛗 CALL 👤M 🏊 BIZ SHS 🛜
🎥 🍴 🖥 / SOME UNITS 🐾 📠

---

**HAMPTON INN DOWNTOWN**    (210)225-8500 **16**

🔻🔻 Hotel $119-$199 **Address:** 414 Bowie St 78205 **Location:** Just nw of I-37 at Houston St. **Facility:** 169 units. 6 stories, interior corridors. **Parking:** on-site (fee). **Terms:** check-in 4 pm, 1-7 night minimum stay, cancellation fee imposed. **Pool(s):** outdoor. **Activities:** exercise room. **Guest Services:** valet and coin laundry.

**AAA Benefit:** Members save up to 10%!

🍴 CALL 👤M 🏊 BIZ HS 🛜 ✕ 🖥
/ SOME UNITS 📠 🖥

---

**HILTON PALACIO DEL RIO**    (210)222-1400 **38**

🔻🔻🔻 🔻🔻🔻 Hotel $139-$389 **Address:** 200 S Alamo St 78205 **Location:** Adjacent to convention center. Located on River Walk. **Facility:** Overlooking Hemisfair Plaza and the San Antonio River, this hotel displays a collection of Western riding saddles donated by celebrities. The room décor is very contemporary. 483 units. 22 stories, interior corridors. **Parking:** on-site (fee) and valet. **Terms:** 1-7 night minimum stay, cancellation fee imposed. **Amenities:** video games, safes. **Dining:** 2 restaurants, entertainment. **Pool(s):** outdoor. **Activities:** hot tub, exercise room. **Guest Services:** valet and coin laundry.

**AAA Benefit:** Members save 5% or more!

🍴 🛗 🛗 👤 CALL 👤M 🏊 BIZ SHS 🛜 ✕
🎥 📠 🖥

---

**THE HISTORIC MENGER HOTEL**    (210)223-4361 **27**

🔻🔻🔻 Historic Hotel $119-$299

**Address:** 204 Alamo Plaza 78205 **Location:** Just s of the Alamo. **Facility:** The elegant historic hotel dates to 1859. The public areas boast upscale sitting areas with period furnishings and beautiful central courtyards. 301 units. 4-5 stories, interior corridors. **Parking:** on-site (fee). **Terms:** cancellation fee imposed. **Amenities:** video games. **Dining:** The Colonial Room, see separate listing, entertainment. **Pool(s):** heated outdoor. **Activities:** hot tub, exercise room, massage. **Guest Services:** valet laundry. Affiliated with A Preferred Hotel.

SAVE 🚪 🍴 🛗 🏊 BIZ HS 🛜 ✕ 🎥
/ SOME UNITS 🐾 📠

---

**HOLIDAY INN-DOWNTOWN-MARKET SQUARE**    (210)225-3211 **43**

🔻🔻🔻 Hotel $109-$189

**Address:** 318 Cesar E Chavez Blvd 78204 **Location:** I-35 exit 155B (Cesar E Chavez Blvd), 1 blk e. Adjacent to Market Square. **Facility:** 313 units. 4 stories, interior corridors. **Terms:** cancellation fee imposed. **Amenities:** video games. **Pool(s):** outdoor. **Activities:** hot tub, exercise room. **Guest Services:** valet and coin laundry, area transportation.

SAVE 🍴 🛗 🛗 CALL 👤M 🏊
BIZ HS 🛜 ✕ 🎥 🖥

---

**HOLIDAY INN EXPRESS HOTEL & SUITES RIVER CENTER AREA**    (210)220-1010 **46**

🔻🔻🔻 Hotel $109-$199 **Address:** 1309 E Commerce St 78205 **Location:** I-37 exit 141 (Commerce St), just e. **Facility:** 81 units. 4 stories, interior corridors. **Terms:** check-in 4 pm, cancellation fee imposed. **Amenities:** video games. **Pool(s):** outdoor. **Activities:** hot tub, exercise room. **Guest Services:** valet and coin laundry, area transportation.

🍴 🏊 BIZ HS 🛜 ✕ 📠 🖥 🖥

---

**(See map & index p. 479.)**

**HOLIDAY INN EXPRESS INN & SUITES** 210/277-1000 **59**

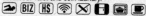 **Hotel.** Rates not provided. **Address:** 102 El Paso St 78204 **Location:** I-35 exit 155B (Cesar E Chavez Blvd); jct Frio St. Located in a quiet area. **Facility:** 79 units. 4 stories, interior corridors. **Pool(s):** heated outdoor. **Activities:** hot tub, exercise room. **Guest Services:** valet and coin laundry.

**HOLIDAY INN EXPRESS RIVERWALK AREA**

(210)281-1400 **17**

 **Hotel** $89-$189 **Address:** 120 Camaron St 78205 **Location:** I-37 exit 141 (Commerce St) southbound to one-way street; between Houston and Camaron sts. **Facility:** 82 units. 5 stories, interior corridors. **Parking:** on-site (fee). **Terms:** 2 night minimum stay - seasonal and/or weekends, 3 day cancellation notice. **Pool(s):** outdoor. **Activities:** hot tub, exercise room. **Guest Services:** valet and coin laundry.

**HOLIDAY INN RIVERWALK** (210)224-2500 **18**

Hotel
$129-$239

**Address:** 217 N St. Mary's St 78205 **Location:** Jct Houston St, just s. Located on San Antonio River. **Facility:** 313 units. 23 stories, interior corridors. **Parking:** on-site (fee) and valet. **Terms:** check-in 4 pm, cancellation fee imposed. **Amenities:** Some: safes. **Pool(s):** heated outdoor. **Activities:** hot tub, exercise room. **Guest Services:** valet laundry.

**HOME2 SUITES BY HILTON SAN ANTONIO DOWNTOWN-RIVERWALK** (210)354-4366 **6**

**Extended Stay Contemporary Hotel** $109-$199 **Address:** 603 Navarro St 78205 **Location:** Jct E Houston St. **Facility:** 128 units. 14 stories, interior corridors. **Parking:** valet only. **Terms:** 1-7 night minimum stay, cancellation fee imposed. **Pool(s):** heated indoor. **Activities:** exercise room. **Guest Services:** valet and coin laundry.

**AAA Benefit:** Members save up to 10%!

**HOMEWOOD SUITES RIVERWALK BY HILTON**

(210)222-1515 **30**

**Extended Stay Hotel** $149-$249 **Address:** 432 W Market St 78205 **Location:** Corner of St. Mary's and W Market sts; center. **Facility:** 146 kitchen units, some two bedrooms. 10 stories, interior corridors. **Parking:** valet only. **Terms:** 1-7 night minimum stay, cancellation fee imposed. **Pool(s):** heated outdoor. **Activities:** hot tub, exercise room. **Guest Services:** valet and coin laundry.

**AAA Benefit:** Members save up to 10%!

**HOTEL CONTESSA** (210)229-9222 **34**

Hotel
$159-$299

**Address:** 306 W Market St 78205 **Location:** At St. Mary's St. **Facility:** This large modern, all-suite hotel is constructed in an upscale Texas theme with columns of limestone, wrought iron and related oversize artwork. Guest units include honor bars, safes and large bathrooms. 265 units. 13 stories, interior corridors. **Parking:** on-site (fee) and valet. **Terms:** check-in 4 pm, cancellation fee imposed, resort fee. **Amenities:** video games, safes. **Pool(s):** outdoor. **Activities:** hot tub, exercise room, spa. **Guest Services:** valet laundry.

**HOTEL HAVANA** (210)222-2008 **3**

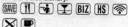 **Historic Country Inn** $100-$250 **Address:** 1015 Navarro St 78205 **Location:** Just s of N St. Mary's St. Located in a quiet area. **Facility:** Overlooking a quiet section of the River Walk, the hotel has a laid-back atmosphere and a Latin flavor. 27 units. 3 stories, interior corridors. **Parking:** on-site (fee). **Terms:** 3 day cancellation notice-fee imposed. **Dining:** Ocho Lounge, see separate listing. **Guest Services:** valet laundry.

**HOTEL INDIGO AT THE ALAMO** (210)933-2000 **9**

 **Historic Boutique Hotel** $130-$300 **Address:** 105 N Alamo Plaza 78205 **Location:** I-37 exit 141 (Commerce St), just s. Across from the Alamo. **Facility:** Unique public areas contrast with guest rooms beautifully decorated with wood floors, pillowtop beds, bright accents and upscale bathrooms. 91 units. 8 stories, interior corridors. *Bath:* shower only. **Parking:** valet only. **Terms:** cancellation fee imposed. **Activities:** exercise room. **Guest Services:** valet laundry.

**HOTEL INDIGO RIVERWALK** (210)527-1900 **1**

 **Contemporary Hotel** $99-$179 **Address:** 830 N St. Mary's St 78205 **Location:** Just n of Navarro St. Located on River Walk at tour boat landing. **Facility:** 149 units. 3 stories, interior corridors. *Bath:* shower only. **Terms:** cancellation fee imposed. **Pool(s):** outdoor. **Activities:** exercise room. **Guest Services:** valet laundry.

**HOTEL VALENCIA RIVERWALK** 210/227-9700 **13**

Boutique Contemporary Hotel
Rates not provided

**Address:** 150 E Houston St 78205 **Location:** Just e of N St. Mary's St. **Facility:** Overlooking the River Walk, the hotel offers a unique, upscale, Art Deco experience with a very high level of service. 213 units. 12 stories, interior corridors. **Parking:** valet only. **Terms:** check-in 4 pm. **Dining:** 2 restaurants, also, Citrus, see separate listing. **Activities:** exercise room, spa. **Guest Services:** valet laundry.

**HYATT PLACE SAN ANTONIO/RIVERWALK**

(210)227-6854 **56**

Contemporary Hotel
$99-$249

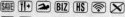 **HYATT PLACE**

**AAA Benefit:** Members save 10%!

**Address:** 601 S St. Mary's St 78205 **Location:** I-35 exit 155B (Cesar E Chavez Blvd), 0.9 mi e. **Facility:** 131 units. 7 stories, interior corridors. **Terms:** cancellation fee imposed. **Pool(s):** heated outdoor. **Activities:** exercise room. **Guest Services:** valet laundry. **Featured Amenity:** breakfast buffet.

**Download eTourBook® Guides**

AAA.com/ebooks

(See map & index p. 479.)

## HYATT REGENCY SAN ANTONIO   (210)222-1234  22

Hotel
$99-$359

HYATT REGENCY'

**AAA Benefit:** Members save 10%!

**Address:** 123 Losoya St 78205 **Location:** Between College and Crockett sts. Located on River Walk at Paseo del Alamo. **Facility:** Southwestern styling creates a casual ambiance at this hotel. The River Walk and river take the spotlight in the lower lobby. 632 units. 14 stories, interior corridors. **Parking:** on-site (fee) and valet. **Terms:** cancellation fee imposed. **Amenities:** safes. **Dining:** Q on the Riverwalk, see separate listing. **Pool(s):** heated outdoor. **Activities:** hot tub, exercise room. **Guest Services:** valet laundry.

## INN ON THE RIVERWALK   (210)225-6333  52

Bed & Breakfast $99-$269 **Address:** 129 Woodward Pl 78204 **Location:** Just n of W Cesar E Chavez Blvd. Located in a quiet area. **Facility:** 13 units. 3 stories (no elevator), interior/exterior corridors. **Terms:** 7 day cancellation notice-fee imposed.

## KNIGHTS INN LA HACIENDA INN   (210)272-0391  54

Motel
$64-$130

**Address:** 1524 E Commerce St 78205 **Location:** I-37 exit 141 (Commerce St), 0.4 mi e. **Facility:** 19 units. 2 stories (no elevator), interior corridors. **Featured Amenity: continental breakfast.**

## LA QUINTA INN & SUITES SAN ANTONIO CONVENTION CENTER   (210)222-9181  33

Hotel $145-$200 **Address:** 303 Blum St 78202 **Location:** 0.5 mi ne. Opposite convention center and Hemisfair Plaza. **Facility:** 348 units. 15 stories, interior/exterior corridors. **Parking:** on-site (fee). **Pool(s):** outdoor. **Activities:** hot tub, exercise room. **Guest Services:** valet and coin laundry.

## LA QUINTA INN & SUITES SAN ANTONIO DOWNTOWN   (210)212-5400  50

Hotel $119-$174 **Address:** 100 Cesar E Chavez Blvd 78204 **Location:** I-35 exit 155B (Cesar E Chavez Blvd), 3 blks e of jct E Flores St. **Facility:** 151 units. 6 stories, interior corridors. **Pool(s):** outdoor. **Activities:** hot tub, exercise room. **Guest Services:** valet and coin laundry.

## LA QUINTA INN SAN ANTONIO MARKET SQUARE   (210)271-0001  28

Hotel $89-$164 **Address:** 900 Dolorosa St 78207 **Location:** I-10/35 exit Cesar E Chavez Blvd, just n on Santa Rosa St, then just w on Nueva St. Adjacent to Market Square. **Facility:** 125 units. 2 stories, exterior corridors. **Pool(s):** outdoor. **Guest Services:** valet laundry.

(See map & index p. 479.)

## MARRIOTT PLAZA SAN ANTONIO

(210)229-1000   57

**Marriott** HOTELS & RESORTS

Hotel
$109-$169

**AAA Benefit:** Members save 5% or more!

**Address:** 555 S Alamo St 78205 **Location:** Opposite convention center and Hemisfair Plaza. Adjacent to La Villita Historic District. **Facility:** This property includes a large garden courtyard/pool/spa area. The spacious and comfortable dining room has large high-back chairs, creative dishes and breakfast buffets. 252 units. 5-7 stories, interior corridors. **Parking:** on-site (fee) and valet. **Dining:** The Anaqua Room, see separate listing. **Pool(s):** heated outdoor. **Activities:** sauna, hot tub, tennis, bicycles, exercise room, massage. **Guest Services:** valet and coin laundry. *(See ad this page.)*

SAVE ⬥ 🍴 🛏 🍸 CALL 📞M 🏊 BIZ sHS 🛜 ✖ ⬥ 📺 /SOME UNITS 🍷

## MOKARA HOTEL & SPA

(210)396-5800   26

Hotel
$269-$469

**Address:** 212 W Crockett St 78205 **Location:** Between St. Mary's and Navarro sts; on River Walk. **Facility:** Among San Antonio's newest downtown spas, this hotel overlooks the River Walk. An upscale yet sublime elegance exudes throughout the hotel. The large, sumptuous guest rooms have whirlpool baths. 99 units. 8 stories, interior corridors. **Parking:** valet only. **Terms:** cancellation fee imposed. **Amenities:** safes. **Dining:** Ostra, see separate listing. **Pool(s):** heated outdoor. **Activities:** hot tub, exercise room, spa. **Guest Services:** valet laundry.

SAVE ⬥ 🍴 🛏 🍸 📶 CALL 📞M 🏊 BIZ HS
🛜 ✖ 🎦 📺 /SOME UNITS 🍷

### MOTEL 6 - #1122

(210)225-1111   5

Motel $55-$165 **Address:** 211 N Pecos St 78207 **Location:** I-10/35 exit 155B (Pecos St); on southbound frontage road. Located in a busy commercial area. **Facility:** 119 units. 2 stories (no elevator), exterior corridors. **Pool(s):** outdoor. **Guest Services:** coin laundry.

🍴 🏊 sHS 🛜 /SOME UNITS 🐕 🍷

---

▼ *See AAA listing this page* ▼

**(See map & index p. 479.)**

## NOBLE INNS-THE JACKSON HOUSE (210)223-2353 61

▼▼▼▼ **Historic Bed & Breakfast** $139-$299 **Address:** 107 Madison St 78204 **Location:** Just s of jct Cesar E Chavez Blvd and St. Mary's sts; in King William Historic District. **Facility:** Gas fireplaces and period antiques are featured in all guest rooms at this 1894 home built in the King William Historical District and a short distance from the attractions of downtown. 6 units. 2 stories (no elevator), interior corridors. **Terms:** 2 night minimum stay - weekends, 14 day cancellation notice-fee imposed. **Pool(s):** heated indoor. **Activities:** hot tub. **Guest Services:** valet laundry.

[icons]

## NOBLE INNS-THE OGE HOUSE RIVERWALK (210)223-2353 60

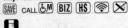

Historic Bed & Breakfast $199-$449

**Address:** 209 Washington St 78204 **Location:** At Turner Ave; in King William Historic District. **Facility:** On the National Register of Historic Places, this dramatic two-story 1857 inn provides guests an experience similar to pre-Civil War San Antonio. 10 units. 3 stories (no elevator), interior corridors. **Terms:** 2 night minimum stay - weekends, 14 day cancellation notice-fee imposed. **Guest Services:** valet laundry. **Featured Amenity:** full hot breakfast.

SAVE CALL &M BIZ HS 🛜 ✕ 🚻

## O'BRIEN HISTORIC HOTEL RIVERWALK, AN ASCEND HOTEL COLLECTION MEMBER (210)527-1111 42

▼▼▼ Hotel $99-$169

**Address:** 116 Navarro St 78205 **Location:** Corner of Navarro and S St. Mary's sts. **Facility:** 39 units. 3 stories, interior corridors. **Parking:** on-site (fee). **Guest Services:** valet laundry. **Featured Amenity:** continental breakfast.

SAVE 🍴 BIZ HS 🛜 ✕ 🖥

## OMNI LA MANSIÓN DEL RIO 210/518-1000 19

▼▼▼▼ Hotel Rates not provided

**Address:** 112 College St 78205 **Location:** Just s on the River Walk. **Facility:** Spanish-style décor enhances this property offering many accommodations with balconies overlooking the San Antonio River Walk. 338 units, some kitchens. 3 stories, interior/exterior corridors. **Parking:** on-site (fee) and valet. **Amenities:** video games. **Dining:** Las Canarias Restaurant, see separate listing, entertainment. **Pool(s):** heated outdoor. **Activities:** exercise room. **Guest Services:** valet laundry.

SAVE 🛬 🍴 👤 🍸 🛝 BIZ
🔥HS 🛜 ✕ 🖥

/ SOME UNITS 🖼 🚻 🖼

## RED ROOF INN SAN ANTONIO (DOWNTOWN) (210)229-9973 25

▼▼ Hotel $69-$199

**Address:** 1011 E Houston St 78205 **Location:** I-37 exit 141 (Commerce St) northbound; exit 141B southbound. **Facility:** 215 units. 6 stories, interior corridors. **Amenities:** video games, safes. **Pool(s):** outdoor. **Guest Services:** valet laundry.

SAVE 🛝 HS 🛜 ✕ 🐾 🖥
/ SOME UNITS 🐾 🚻 🖼

## RESIDENCE INN BY MARRIOTT ALAMO PLAZA (210)212-5555 7

▼▼▼ **Extended Stay Hotel** $149-$229

**AAA Benefit:** Members save 5% or more!

**Address:** 425 Bonham St 78205 **Location:** I-37 and US 281 exit Commerce St, just w to Bowie St, then 4 blks n. **Facility:** 220 units, some two bedrooms, efficiencies and kitchens. 13 stories, interior corridors. **Parking:** on-site (fee). **Pool(s):** heated outdoor. **Activities:** hot tub, exercise room. **Guest Services:** valet and coin laundry.

🍴 🛬 BIZ HS 🛜 ✕ 🚻 🖼 🖼 🖥
/ SOME UNITS S🔩

## RESIDENCE INN BY MARRIOTT SAN ANTONIO DOWNTOWN/MARKET SQUARE (210)231-6000 51

▼▼▼ Extended Stay Hotel $100-$170

Residence Inn Marriott.

**AAA Benefit:** Members save 5% or more!

**Address:** 628 S Santa Rosa Blvd 78204 **Location:** I-10/35 exit 155B (Cesar E Chavez Blvd), 0.5 mi e. Located in a quiet area. **Facility:** 95 units, some two bedrooms, efficiencies and kitchens. 3 stories, interior corridors. **Amenities:** video games. **Pool(s):** outdoor. **Activities:** hot tub, exercise room. **Guest Services:** valet and coin laundry. **Featured Amenity:** full hot breakfast.

SAVE 🍴 🛬 BIZ HS 🛜 ✕ 🚻 🖼 🖥
/ SOME UNITS S🔩

## RIVERWALK PLAZA HOTEL & SUITES 210/225-1234 35

▼▼▼▼ Hotel. Rates not provided. **Address:** 100 Villita St 78205 **Location:** Just e of I-35; center. Next to Bexar County Courthouse & Main Plaza. **Facility:** 129 units. 6 stories, interior/exterior corridors. **Parking:** on-site (fee). **Amenities:** safes. **Pool(s):** heated outdoor. **Activities:** exercise room. **Guest Services:** valet laundry.

🍴 👤 🛬 BIZ HS 🛜 🚻 🖥 / SOME UNITS 🖼

## RIVERWALK VISTA (210)223-3200 31

▼▼▼ Hotel $127-$223 **Address:** 262 Losoya St 78205 **Location:** Jct Losoya and Commerce sts. Located in a converted historic building. **Facility:** 17 units. 3 stories, interior corridors. *Bath:* shower only. **Parking:** no self-parking. **Terms:** 2 night minimum stay - weekends, 10 day cancellation notice-fee imposed. **Amenities:** safes. **Guest Services:** valet laundry.

🍴 BIZ HS 🛜 ✕ 🚻 🖥

## SAN ANTONIO MARRIOTT RIVERCENTER (210)223-1000 37

▼▼▼▼ Hotel $179-$299

**Marriott** HOTELS & RESORTS

**AAA Benefit:** Members save 5% or more!

**Address:** 101 Bowie St 78205 **Location:** Corner of Bowie and Commerce sts. Adjacent to Rivercenter Mall on River Walk. **Facility:** Towering over San Antonio, this landmark high-rise full-service hotel with upscale guest rooms overlooks the River Walk and is connected to Rivercenter Mall. 1001 units. 38 stories, interior corridors. **Parking:** on-site (fee) and valet. **Terms:** check-in 4 pm. **Amenities:** safes. **Dining:** Sazo's Latin Grill, see separate listing. **Activities:** sauna, hot tub, exercise room. **Guest Services:** complimentary and valet laundry.

SAVE 🍴 📺 🖥 CALL &M BIZ 🔥HS 🛜 ✕ 🖥
/ SOME UNITS 🚻

(See map & index p. 479.)

## SAN ANTONIO MARRIOTT RIVERWALK
(210)224-4555 **39**

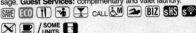

Hotel
$179-$299

**Marriott** HOTELS & RESORTS

**AAA Benefit:** Members save 5% or more!

**Address:** 889 E Market St 78205 **Location:** Opposite convention center and Hemisfair Plaza; across from San Antonio Marriott Rivercenter. **Facility:** 512 units. 30 stories, interior corridors. **Parking:** on-site (fee) and valet. **Terms:** check-in 4 pm. **Amenities:** safes. **Dining:** The Cactus Flower, see separate listing. **Pool(s):** heated outdoor, heated indoor. **Activities:** exercise room, massage. **Guest Services:** complimentary and valet laundry.

---

## SHERATON GUNTER
(210)227-3241 **11**

Historic Hotel
$129-$269

**AAA Benefit:** Members get up to 20% off, plus Starwood Preferred Guest® bonuses!

**Address:** 205 E Houston St 78205 **Location:** Center. **Facility:** This hotel's refined, formal lobby, trimmed in rich wood tones, evokes an appealing aura of days gone by. 322 units. 12 stories, interior corridors. **Parking:** on-site (fee) and valet. **Terms:** cancellation fee imposed. **Amenities:** video games. **Dining:** Barron's, see separate listing. **Pool(s):** heated outdoor. **Activities:** hot tub, exercise room. **Guest Services:** valet laundry.

**Sheraton** HOTELS & RESORTS

Lobby, Rooms and Restaurant renovated in 2013. Features Pool, Fitness, Restaurant, Pub and Bakery.

---

Visit your AAA/CAA Travel office for amazing AAA Vacations tour and cruise packages

SPRINGHILL SUITES BY MARRIOTT SAN ANTONIO DOWNTOWN/ALAMO PLAZA
(210)222-2121 **20**

Contemporary Hotel
$109-$209 **Address:** 411 Bowie St 78205 **Location:** I-37 and US 281 exit Commerce St, just w to Bowie St, then 3 blks n. **Facility:** 118 units. 6 stories, interior corridors. **Parking:** valet only. **Pool(s):** heated outdoor. **Activities:** hot tub, exercise room. **Guest Services:** valet and coin laundry.

**AAA Benefit:** Members save 5% or more!

▼ See AAA listing p. 503 ▼

(See map & index p. 479.)

## STAYBRIDGE SUITES DOWNTOWN CONVENTION CENTER
(210)444-2700  47

Extended Stay Hotel
$109-$189

**Address:** 123 Hoefgen Blvd 78205 **Location:** In Historic Sunset Station. Adjacent to Sunset Station complex. **Facility:** 138 kitchen units, some two bedrooms. 11 stories, interior corridors. **Pool(s):** outdoor. **Activities:** exercise room. **Guest Services:** complimentary laundry.

## TOWNEPLACE SUITES BY MARRIOTT SAN ANTONIO DOWNTOWN
(210)271-3444  10

**Extended Stay Hotel** $109-$199 **Address:** 409 E Houston St 78205 **Location:** 1 blk w of Broadway St. **Facility:** 117 units, some two bedrooms, efficiencies and kitchens. 4 stories, interior corridors. **Parking:** on-site (fee). **Pool(s):** heated outdoor. **Activities:** exercise room. **Guest Services:** valet and coin laundry.

**AAA Benefit:** Members save 5% or more!

## THE WESTIN RIVERWALK, SAN ANTONIO
(210)224-6500  32

Hotel $119-$409

**WESTIN** HOTELS & RESORTS **AAA Benefit:** Enjoy up to 20% off your next stay, plus Starwood Preferred Guest® bonuses!

**Address:** 420 W Market St 78205 **Location:** 2 blks w of Navarro St. Located on River Walk. **Facility:** Overlooking the River Walk, the hotel features luxurious public areas, haute cuisine, elegant guest rooms and attentive service. 473 units. 15 stories, interior corridors. **Parking:** on-site (fee) and valet. **Terms:** cancellation fee imposed. **Amenities:** video games, safes. **Pool(s):** outdoor. **Activities:** steamroom, exercise room, spa. **Guest Services:** valet laundry.

## THE WYNDHAM SAN ANTONIO RIVERWALK HOTEL
(210)354-2800  4

Hotel $99-$235

**Address:** 111 Pecan St E 78205 **Location:** Corner of Pecan and Soledad sts. **Facility:** 410 units. 21 stories, interior corridors. **Parking:** valet only. **Amenities:** video games. **Pool(s):** heated outdoor. **Activities:** sauna, hot tub, exercise room. **Guest Services:** valet and coin laundry. (See ad p. 502.)

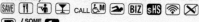

Save on theme park tickets at
AAA.com/searchfordiscounts

## WHERE TO EAT

### THE ANAQUA ROOM
210/229-1000  28
Regional American. Casual Dining. $9-$25 **AAA Inspector Notes:** Overlooking a hotel garden, the dining room has fountains and Mediterranean-style decor. The Southwestern cuisine includes tender filet covered in crawfish ragu. Make sure you have plenty to drink when you try the spicy twisted pasta with mushrooms. **Features:** full bar. **Reservations:** suggested. **Address:** 555 S Alamo St 78205 **Location:** Opposite convention center and Hemisfair Plaza; in Marriott San Antonio Plaza. **Parking:** on-site (fee) and valet.
B L D

### AZUCA NUEVO LATINO
210/225-5550  30
Regional Latin American. Casual Dining. $12-$28 **AAA Inspector Notes:** Distinctive ingredients from across the continents are combined in exciting specialties presented in artistic concepts. The outdoor terrace provides a seating alternative. **Features:** full bar, patio dining, happy hour. **Address:** 713 S Alamo St 78205 **Location:** 2 blks n of S St. Mary's St.
L D

### BARRON'S
210/227-3241  5
American. Family Dining. $8-$15 **AAA Inspector Notes:** A resplendent dining room features lovely paintings and hotel memorabilia, and showcases an impressive display of wines. Shrimp cocktail, crab cakes and decadent offerings like German chocolate cake and eclairs are house specialties not to be missed. **Features:** full bar. **Address:** 205 E Houston St 78205 **Location:** Center; in Sheraton Gunter. **Parking:** valet only.
B L D

### BOHANAN'S PRIME STEAKS & SEAFOOD
210/472-2600  6
Regional Steak Seafood Fine Dining $18-$40
**AAA Inspector Notes:** Aged beef, fresh seafood and other quality ingredients from around the world are combined in artistic creations. The dining room is elegant and the service refined. The restaurant is said to be among San Antonio's best. **Features:** full bar. **Reservations:** suggested. **Address:** 219 E Houston St, Suite 275 78205 **Location:** Between S St. Mary's and Navarro sts. **Parking:** valet only.
Menu on AAA.com   L D

### BOUDRO'S ON THE RIVERWALK
210/224-8484  19
Regional Tex-Mex. Casual Dining. $10-$38 **AAA Inspector Notes:** Fresh floral arrangements, steel pictographs and framed mirrors hang from the limestone walls at this Riverwalk restaurant. The blackened prime rib is seared in Cajun spices and the seafood has a Southern flair. Try the delicious homemade chicken and tortilla soup with avocado, queso fresco, cilantro and calabacitas. Finish with the slightly tart lemon chess pie that is well balanced with homemade whipped cream. **Features:** full bar, patio dining. **Reservations:** suggested. **Address:** 421 E Commerce St 78205 **Location:** Just w of jct Commerce and Alamo sts. **Parking:** no self-parking.
L D

### THE CACTUS FLOWER
210/224-4555  25
Regional American. Casual Dining. $8-$20 **AAA Inspector Notes:** Located near the Alamo, this Southwestern café has a splendid view overlooking the river. Mexican cuisine like tortilla soup is loaded with seasonings and Monterey Jack cheese. They are closed from 2:30 to 5:30 pm every afternoon. Hours are subject to change depending on business. **Features:** full bar. **Address:** 711 E River Walk 78205 **Location:** Opposite convention center and Hemisfair Plaza; across from San Antonio Marriott Rivercenter; in San Antonio Marriott Riverwalk. **Parking:** on-site (fee) and valet.
B L D

### CASA RIO MEXICAN RESTAURANT
210/225-6718  22
Regional Mexican. Family Dining. $7-$15 **AAA Inspector Notes:** Tables with colorful umbrellas are lined along the River Walk. This is a popular place for couples to dine. The green-chicken enchiladas are made with fresh, homemade tortillas. Be sure to sip on a margarita with fresh lime juice. **Features:** full bar. **Address:** 430 E Commerce St 78205 **Location:** 1 blk from Hemisfair Plaza; just e of Alamo St. **Parking:** on-site (fee) and street.
L D

(See map & index p. 479.)

**CHART HOUSE**  210/223-3101  (29)

▼▼▼ Seafood. Casual Dining. $8-$30 **AAA Inspector Notes:** Examples of the fabulous food include prime rib, filet mignon, tomato-basil chicken and varied fresh fish and seafood dishes. **Features:** full bar. **Reservations:** suggested. **Address:** 701 S Bowie St 78205 **Location:** Just s of Market St; in Hemisfair Plaza atop the Tower of Americas. **Parking:** on-site (fee). [SAVE] [L] [D]

**CITRUS**  210/227-9700  (7)

◈◈◈◈ **AAA Inspector Notes:** Elegantly sub-dued, the fine-dining restaurant uses special ingredients to make traditional classics. Try the tropical fresh-water agua frescas. The restaurant closes from 2 to 5 pm daily. **Features:** full bar. **Reservations:** suggested. **Address:** 150 E Houston St 78205 **Location:** Just e of N St. Mary's St; in Hotel Valencia Riverwalk. **Parking:** on-site (fee) and valet. [B] [L] [D]

Regional International Fine Dining $14-$40

**THE COLONIAL ROOM**  210/223-4361  (18)

▼▼ Regional American. Casual Dining. $8-$30 **AAA Inspector Notes:** This restaurant's famous mango ice cream was served at President Clinton's inauguration. Designed in 1909, the light-colored dining room has attractive archways and a fireplace and has the feel of Colonial Williamsburg. Fill your plate at the breakfast and lunch buffets. **Features:** full bar. **Address:** 204 Alamo Plaza 78205 **Location:** Just s of the Alamo; in The Historic Menger Hotel. **Parking:** on-site and valet. [B] [L] [D]

**FIG TREE RESTAURANT**  210/224-1976  (27)

▼▼▼ Traditional Continental. Fine Dining. $24-$38 **AAA Inspector Notes:** Historic. Savor beef Wellington with a full-bodied Cabernet in this cozy New England-style cottage overlooking the River Walk. Elegant tables, classic Continental dishes and an attentive dining room staff make for a memorable dining experience. **Features:** full bar, patio dining. **Reservations:** suggested. **Address:** 515 Villita St 78205 **Location:** Just e of S Presa St; in La Villita Historic District. **Parking:** street only. [D]

**HARD ROCK CAFE**  210/224-7625  (15)

▼▼ American. Casual Dining. $10-$28 **AAA Inspector Notes:** Rock 'n' roll memorabilia decorates the walls of the popular theme restaurant. Live music on the weekends contributes to the bustling atmosphere. On the menu is a wide variety of American cuisine—from burgers and sandwiches to seafood, steaks and pasta. **Features:** full bar. **Address:** 111 W Crockett St 78205 **Location:** Between Presa and Navarro sts. **Parking:** on-site (fee). [SAVE] [L] [D] [LATE]

**HOUSTON ST. BISTRO**  210/476-8600  (8)

▼▼▼ American. Casual Dining. $8-$22 **AAA Inspector Notes:** Deep in the heart of Texas, the restaurant is a favorite of the downtown crowd. Among hallmarks are good food like the grilled chicken breast with an artichoke lemon-butter-basil sauce. The atmosphere is business casual with fast, friendly service. **Features:** full bar, patio dining. **Address:** 204 E Houston St 78205 **Location:** Just e of N St. Mary's St. **Parking:** no self-parking. [L] [D]

**LA FOCACCIA ITALIAN GRILL**  210/223-5353  (31)

▼▼ Italian. Casual Dining. $12-$25 **AAA Inspector Notes:** The restaurant features Old World décor and classic Italian dishes such as chicken marsala, mussels and stuffed pastas. **Features:** beer & wine. **Address:** 800 S Alamo St 78205 **Location:** Jct S Presa and S Alamo sts; near King William Historic District. [L] [D]

**LA MARGARITA**  210/227-7140  (13)

▼▼ Regional Tex-Mex. Casual Dining. $7-$12 **AAA Inspector Notes:** Munch on a never-ending bowl of chips and salsa as you admire the Mexican paintings hanging on this restaurant's brick walls. Begin with the fajita and shrimp cocktail or oysters on ice. Spicy mole is served over chicken with a side of rice and beans. **Features:** full bar, patio dining, happy hour. **Address:** 120 Produce Row 78207 **Location:** I-35 exit 155B (Cesar E Chavez Blvd), just s of El Mercado; between Commerce and Dolores sts; in Market Square. **Parking:** on-site (fee). [L] [D]

**LAS CANARIAS RESTAURANT**  210/518-1000  (10)

◈◈◈◈ **AAA Inspector Notes:** This eatery is within walking distance of the famous Alamo. Sit on the outdoor River Walk terrace and dine on exceptional cuisine with an international flair. Sunday brunch 10 am-2 pm. **Features:** full bar, patio dining, Sunday brunch. **Reservations:** suggested. **Address:** 112 College St 78205 **Location:** Just s on the River Walk; in Omni La Mansión del Rio. **Parking:** on-site (fee) and valet. [B] [L] [D]

American Fine Dining $12-$30

**LITTLE RHEIN STEAK HOUSE**  210/225-2111  (26)

▼▼▼ Steak. Family Dining. $35-$45 **AAA Inspector Notes:** Historic. Tender prime rib and lobster are house specialties. The Little Rhein dessert is an ice cream ball rolled in crushed Oreo cookies, topped with hot fudge, strawberries and whipped cream. The historic dining room is filled with antiques. **Features:** full bar. **Reservations:** suggested. **Address:** 231 S Alamo St 78205 **Location:** Jct Alamo and La Villita sts; next to Fig Tree Restaurant; opposite convention center and Hemisfair Plaza. **Parking:** valet only. [D] [⬟]

**LUCIANO'S ON THE RIVER**  210/223-0500  (23)

▼▼▼ Italian. Casual Dining. $10-$32 **AAA Inspector Notes:** This large, attractively decorated restaurant features house-made pastas and sauces. I recommend the flounder al limone and the cheese raviolis. **Features:** full bar, patio dining. **Reservations:** suggested. **Address:** 849 Commerce St 78205 **Location:** On River Walk level of Rivercenter Mall. **Parking:** on-site (fee). [L] [D]

**LUKE**  210/227-5853  (3)

▼▼ Cajun. Casual Dining. $10-$18 **AAA Inspector Notes:** Overlooking the River Walk, this casual New Orleans-style restaurant features classic dishes like crabmeat bisque and a variety of fresh oysters. **Features:** full bar, patio dining, Sunday brunch. **Address:** 125 Houston St 78205 **Location:** Between N St. Marys and N Main sts. **Parking:** valet and street only. [L] [D]

**MI TIERRA CAFÉ Y PANADERÍA**  210/225-1262  (14)

▼▼ Regional Tex-Mex. Casual Dining. $8-$18 **AAA Inspector Notes:** This San Antonio landmark looks like Christmas year-round. Photographs of longtime customers hang in the lobby of this Tex-Mex café, which opened in 1941. A three-dimensional clay mural covers one wall. Juicy fajitas are seasoned to perfection, and the flan is coated with caramel. **Features:** full bar. **Address:** 218 Produce Row 78207 **Location:** Just off Dolorosa St; in Market Square. **Parking:** on-site and street. [B] [L] [D] [24]

**MORTON'S THE STEAKHOUSE**  210/228-0700  (17)

▼▼▼ Steak. Fine Dining. $27-$103 **AAA Inspector Notes:** Patrons should make sure to reserve ahead for the popular, well-known steakhouse. Large portions, including huge cuts of fine beef and plentiful seafood, are the norm. Even the vegetables are oversized, with baked potatoes big enough for sharing. **Features:** full bar. **Reservations:** suggested. **Address:** 300 E Crockett St 78205 **Location:** Adjacent to Rivercenter Mall. **Parking:** valet only. [D]

**OCHO LOUNGE**  210/222-2008  (2)

▼▼ Regional Cuban. Casual Dining. $10-$22 **AAA Inspector Notes:** Overlooking a quiet area of the River Walk, the eatery offers indoor and terrace dining; specialties include tapas-style Spanish food. **Features:** full bar, patio dining, happy hour. **Address:** 1015 Navarro St 78205 **Location:** Just s of N St. Mary's St; in Hotel Havana. [B] [L] [D]

**ORO RESTAURANT & BAR**  210/225-8486  (9)

▼▼ American. Casual Dining. $10-$18 **AAA Inspector Notes:** The casual yet refined setting is within sight of the Alamo. The focus of this popular restaurant is on local farm-to-table cuisine. **Features:** full bar. **Address:** 705 E Houston St 78205 **Location:** Just n of Bonham St; in Emily Morgan Hotel-DoubleTree by Hilton. **Parking:** valet and street only. [B] [L] [D]

(See map & index p. 479.)

## OSTRA
210/396-5817 (16)

Regional
New World
Fine Dining
$15-$65

**AAA Inspector Notes:** Specializing in seafood prepared in exciting and sometimes exotic methods, you also will be intrigued by the ambient lighting schemes and fresh seafood bar with claws, tails and shells. You can taste the roasted Sonoran flavor of their seafood cocktail. And the organic quinoa-grain salad is loaded with protein. On the famed River Walk. **Features:** full bar. **Reservations:** suggested. **Address:** 212 W Crockett St 78205 **Location:** Between St. Mary's and Navarro sts; on River Walk; in Mokara Hotel & Spa. **Parking:** valet only.

[B] [L] [D] CALL [&][M]

## PICO DE GALLO
210/225-6060 (11)

Regional Mexican. Casual Dining. $7-$16 **AAA Inspector Notes:** Family-owned for three generations, this Mexican restaurant offers unique decorations, full wall murals and a fiesta atmosphere. Savor the original-recipe pepper steak entrée. For dessert, try the bola bola with ice cream covered with coconut and chocolate. **Features:** full bar. **Address:** 111 S Leona St 78207 **Location:** Just w of I-10/35; between W Commerce and Buena Vista sts.

[B] [L] [D]

## Q ON THE RIVERWALK
210/222-1234 (12)

Barbecue. Casual Dining. $18-$29 **AAA Inspector Notes:** World-class barbecue means high-quality ingredients, while the décor and service are trendy, professional and focused. **Features:** full bar. **Address:** 123 Losoya St 78205 **Location:** Between College and Crockett sts; in Hyatt Regency San Antonio. **Parking:** valet only. [B] [L] [D]

## RIO RIO CANTINA
210/226-8462 (20)

Regional Tex-Mex. Family Dining. $8-$25 **AAA Inspector Notes:** Overlooking the Riverwalk, this informal eatery offers outdoor seating. The rellenos, made with shredded beef, raisins and nuts, are an excellent choice. You definitely won't leave hungry after chowing down on the restaurant's large botana platter filled with beef and chicken fajitas and queso flamedo alongside rice and beans. Fun specialty cocktails and martinis in flavors such as cucumber and jalapeño are sure to keep you lingering. **Features:** full bar. **Address:** 421 E Commerce St 78205 **Location:** Between S Presa and Losoya sts. **Parking:** on-site (fee). [L] [D]

## ROSARIO'S
210/223-1806 (32)

Mexican. Family Dining. $15-$26 **AAA Inspector Notes:** A descendent of the famous Rosario's once located a few blocks away, this King William hot spot straddles the Tex-Mex line with dishes such as pozole, mole, green enchiladas and flan. **Features:** full bar. **Address:** 910 S Alamo St 78205 **Location:** In King William Historic District. **Parking:** on-site and street.

[L] [D]

## SAZO'S LATIN GRILL
210/223-1000 (24)

Latin American. Casual Dining. $12-$23 **AAA Inspector Notes:** Contemporary décor with Latin American- and Spanish-influenced dishes. Be sure to get a seat by the large windows in order to enjoy the view of the River Walk while you dine. **Features:** full bar. **Address:** 101 Bowie St 78205 **Location:** Corner of Bowie and Commerce sts; in San Antonio Marriott Rivercenter. **Parking:** on-site (fee) and valet. [L] [D]

## SCHILO'S DELICATESSEN
210/223-6692 (21)

German Deli. Family Dining. $6-$12 **AAA Inspector Notes:** *Historic.* In the heart of downtown, the delicatessen has been serving city residents and visitors since 1900. Stacked sandwiches taste great with sides of warm and chilled potato salad and choices from the large pastry bar. **Features:** beer & wine. **Address:** 424 E Commerce St 78205 **Location:** Between N Presa and Losoya sts. **Parking:** on-site (fee). [B] [L] [D]

## TOSCANA RISTORANTE
210/222-2865 (4)

Italian. Casual Dining. $12-$32 **AAA Inspector Notes:** This upscale Italian restaurant features tender pasta purses stuffed with ricotta cheese and pan-fried savory lump crab cakes. The refined staff can expertly match your favorite dishes to their ample wine list. Located in the heart of downtown. **Features:** full bar. **Address:** 301 E Houston St 78205 **Location:** Jct E Houston and Navarro sts. **Parking:** no self-parking. [L] [D]

## CHARLIE WANTS A BURGER
210/227-0864

[fyi] Not evaluated. Located in the heart of the Riverwalk, this restaurant features a dog-friendly outdoor patio, gourmet burgers and a well-stocked bar. All burgers are made with 80/20 ground chuck and certified Angus beef brisket. Pick your own toppings from the long list of specialty condiments and sauces, including salsa verde, wasabi ketchup and creamy horseradish mayo. Wash it down with a classic milk shake. **Address:** 223 Losoya St 78205 **Location:** Between Commerce and Crockett sts; on River Walk.

# SAN ANTONIO (F-8)

- Restaurants p. 524
- Hotels & Restaurants map & index p. 484

## ALOFT SAN ANTONIO AIRPORT  (210)541-8881  66

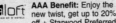

Contemporary Hotel
$109-$399

**AAA Benefit:** Enjoy the new twist, get up to 20% off + Starwood Preferred Guest® bonuses!

**Address:** 838 NW Loop 410 78216 **Location:** I-410 exit Blanco Rd, just s. **Facility:** 141 units. 5 stories, interior corridors. *Bath:* shower only. **Amenities:** safes. **Pool(s):** heated outdoor. **Activities:** exercise room. **Guest Services:** valet and coin laundry, area transportation. *(See ad this page.)*

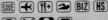   

## AMERICAS BEST VALUE INN - SAN ANTONIO DOWNTOWN I-10 EAST  (210)359-8080  116

Hotel
$55-$75

**Address:** 170 S WW White Rd 78219 **Location:** I-10 exit 580 (WW White Rd), just s. Located in a light-commercial area. **Facility:** 42 units, some efficiencies. 2 stories (no elevator), exterior corridors. **Terms:** cancellation fee imposed. **Amenities:** safes. **Pool(s):** outdoor. **Guest Services:** coin laundry. **Featured Amenity: continental breakfast.**

Visit AAA.com/Travel or CAA.ca/Travel for vacation planning and reservations

## BAYMONT INN  (210)684-9966  87

Hotel
$89-$119

**Address:** 4803 Manitou Dr 78228 **Location:** I-410 exit Callaghan Rd eastbound; exit Evers Rd westbound, take turn around; on eastbound access road. Located in a commercial area. **Facility:** 122 units. 5 stories, interior corridors. **Terms:** 1-7 night minimum stay, cancellation fee imposed. **Amenities:** video games. **Pool(s):** outdoor. **Activities:** exercise room. **Guest Services:** valet laundry. **Featured Amenity: continental breakfast.**

## BAYMONT INNS & SUITES  (210)593-0338  50

Hotel
$59-$109

**Address:** 9542 I-10 W 78230 **Location:** I-10 exit 561 (Wurzbach Rd), just e on eastbound access road. Located in a commercial area. **Facility:** 106 units. 2 stories (no elevator), exterior corridors. **Pool(s):** outdoor. **Featured Amenity: continental breakfast.**

## BEST WESTERN GARDEN INN  (210)599-0999  38

Hotel
$59-$109

**AAA Benefit:** Members save 10% or more with Best Western!

**Address:** 11939 N I-35 78233 **Location:** I-35 exit 170 (Judson Rd); on southbound frontage road. **Facility:** 70 units. 2 stories (no elevator), exterior corridors. **Pool(s):** outdoor. **Activities:** hot tub, exercise room. **Guest Services:** coin laundry.

▼ See AAA listing this page ▼

(See map & index p. 484.)

## BEST WESTERN INGRAM PARK INN
(210)520-8080  **101**

Motel
$79-$139

**AAA Benefit:** Members save 10% or more with Best Western!

**Address:** 6855 NW Loop 410 78238 **Location:** I-410 exit 11 (Ingram Rd); on westbound frontage road. **Facility:** 78 units, some two bedrooms. 2 stories (no elevator), exterior corridors. **Pool(s):** outdoor. **Activities:** exercise room. **Guest Services:** coin laundry.

## BEST WESTERN PLUS ATREA HOTEL & SUITES
(210)298-8880  **125**

Contemporary Hotel
$130-$140

**AAA Benefit:** Members save 10% or more with Best Western!

**Address:** 3635 Crooked Tr 78227 **Location:** I-410 exit 6 (US 90); on Loop 410 southbound frontage road. Near Lackland AFB Training Annex. **Facility:** 77 units, some kitchens. 4 stories, interior corridors. **Pool(s):** heated indoor. **Activities:** hot tub, exercise room. **Guest Services:** valet and coin laundry.

## BEST WESTERN PLUS FIESTA INN
(210)696-2400  **30**

Hotel
$90-$120

**AAA Benefit:** Members save 10% or more with Best Western!

**Address:** 13535 I-10 W 78249 **Location:** I-10 exit 557 westbound; exit 558 eastbound; on westbound access road. **Facility:** 60 units, some two bedrooms. 2 stories, exterior corridors. **Pool(s):** outdoor. **Activities:** exercise room. **Guest Services:** coin laundry. **Featured Amenity:** full hot breakfast.

## BEST WESTERN PLUS HILL COUNTRY SUITES
(210)490-9191  **7**

Hotel
$90-$180

**AAA Benefit:** Members save 10% or more with Best Western!

**Address:** 18555 US Hwy 281 N 78258 **Location:** US 281 exit Sonterra Blvd, just w. Located in a modern commercial area. **Facility:** 77 units, some efficiencies. 3 stories, interior corridors. **Pool(s):** outdoor. **Activities:** hot tub, exercise room. **Guest Services:** valet and coin laundry. **Featured Amenity:** full hot breakfast.

## BEST WESTERN PLUS PALO ALTO INN & SUITES
(210)298 9990  **132**

Hotel
$120-$180

**AAA Benefit:** Members save 10% or more with Best Western!

**Address:** 12507 SW Loop 410 78224 **Location:** I-410 exit 49 (Palo Alto Rd); on eastbound access road. **Facility:** 75 units, some efficiencies. 4 stories, interior corridors. **Terms:** 2 night minimum stay - seasonal. **Pool(s):** heated indoor. **Activities:** hot tub, exercise room. **Guest Services:** valet and coin laundry.

## BEST WESTERN PLUS POSADA ANA INN - MEDICAL CENTER
(210)691-9550  **49**

Hotel
$60-$120

**AAA Benefit:** Members save 10% or more with Best Western!

**Address:** 9411 Wurzbach Rd 78240 **Location:** I-10 exit 561 (Wurzbach Rd); on eastbound access road. Located in a commercial area. **Facility:** 79 units. 4 stories, interior corridors. **Pool(s):** outdoor. **Activities:** exercise room. **Guest Services:** valet and coin laundry.

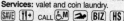

(See map & index p. 484.)

## BEST WESTERN PLUS SAN ANTONIO EAST INN & SUITES
(210)661-8669

Hotel
$85-$180

PLUS

**AAA Benefit:** Members save 10% or more with Best Western!

**Address:** 8669 I-10 E 78109 **Location:** I-10 exit 585 (Martinez Converse Rd); on westbound frontage road. **Facility:** 67 units, some kitchens. 3 stories, interior corridors. **Pool(s):** outdoor. **Activities:** hot tub, exercise room. **Guest Services:** coin laundry. (See ad this page.)

## BEST WESTERN POSADA ANA INN-AIRPORT
(210)342-1400  73

Hotel
$90-$110

**AAA Benefit:** Members save 10% or more with Best Western!

**Address:** 8600 Jones Maltsberger Rd 78216 **Location:** Loop 410 exit 21A (Jones Maltsberger Rd), just s. Located in a quiet area. **Facility:** 60 units. 2 stories, interior corridors. **Pool(s):** outdoor. **Activities:** exercise room. **Guest Services:** valet and coin laundry, area transportation.

## BEST WESTERN WINDSOR POINTE HOTEL & SUITES-AT&T CENTER
(210)655-6800  95

Hotel
$75-$260

**AAA Benefit:** Members save 10% or more with Best Western!

**Address:** 4639 Rittiman Rd 78218 **Location:** I-35 exit 164A (Rittiman Rd), just e. **Facility:** 54 units, some three bedrooms. 4 stories, interior corridors. **Pool(s):** outdoor. **Activities:** exercise room. **Guest Services:** coin laundry. **Featured Amenity:** continental breakfast.

## BONNER GARDEN BED & BREAKFAST  (210)733-4222  104
Historic Bed & Breakfast $115-$180 **Address:** 145 E Agarita Ave 78212 **Location:** Corner of McCullough and E Agarita aves; in Monte Vista Historic District. **Facility:** This restored, Italian-style 1910 villa features a pool/lawn area, a rooftop terrace offering expansive views of downtown and an extensive art collection featuring Mary Bonner. Three rooms with fireplaces. 6 units. 2 stories (no elevator), interior/exterior corridors. **Terms:** 2 night minimum stay - weekends, 3 day cancellation notice-fee imposed. **Pool(s):** outdoor.

## CANDLEWOOD SUITES HOTEL  (210)615-0550  53
Extended Stay Hotel $90-$110 **Address:** 9350 I-10 W 78230 **Location:** I-10 W exit 561 (Wurzbach Rd), between Wurzbach Rd and Medical Dr; eastbound access road. Located in a quiet area. **Facility:** 112 units, some efficiencies. 4 stories, interior corridors. **Terms:** cancellation fee imposed. **Pool(s):** outdoor. **Activities:** exercise room. **Guest Services:** complimentary and valet laundry.

Explore on-the-go travel tools at
AAA.com/mobile or CAA.ca/mobile

**(See map & index p. 484.)**

CANDLEWOOD SUITES SAN ANTONIO WEST SEAWORLD AREA                                    (210)523-7666

◆◆◆ **Extended Stay Hotel** $89-$129 **Address:** 9502 Amelia Pass 78254 **Location:** Loop 1604 at Braun Rd; on northbound frontage road. **Facility:** 81 units, some efficiencies and kitchens. 4 stories, interior corridors. **Terms:** cancellation fee imposed, resort fee. **Pool(s):** outdoor. **Activities:** exercise room. **Guest Services:** complimentary and valet laundry.

CANDLEWOOD SUITES STONE OAK AREA                  210/545-2477 **1**

◆◆◆ **Extended Stay Hotel.** Rates not provided. **Address:** 21103 Encino Commons Blvd 78259 **Location:** US 281 exit Evans Rd; on northbound frontage road. 4 stories, interior corridors. Pool(s): heated indoor. **Activities:** hot tub, exercise room. **Guest Services:** valet and coin laundry.

COMFORT INN & SUITES                                      (210)733-8080 **91**

◆◆◆ **Hotel** $69-$139 **Address:** 6039 IH-10 W 78201 **Location:** I-10 exit Vance Jackson Rd; on westbound access road. **Facility:** 82 units. 4 stories, interior corridors. **Pool(s):** heated indoor. **Activities:** hot tub, exercise room. **Guest Services:** valet and coin laundry.

COMFORT INN & SUITES AIRPORT   (210)249-2000 **78**

Hotel
$80-$170

**Address:** 8640 Crownhill Blvd 78209 **Location:** I-410 exit Airport Blvd, just off eastbound frontage road; just e of Broadway Ave. **Facility:** 100 units. 4 stories, interior corridors. **Pool(s):** outdoor. **Activities:** exercise room. **Guest Services:** coin laundry. **Featured Amenity: full hot breakfast.**

COMFORT INN-FIESTA                          (210)696-4766 **21**

◆◆ **Motel** $80-$110 **Address:** 6755 N Loop 1604 W 78249 **Location:** I-10 exit CR 1604 W, 0.5 mi w of La Cantera Pkwy. Opposite University of Texas at San Antonio. **Facility:** 124 units. 4 stories, interior corridors. **Terms:** check-in 4 pm. **Pool(s):** outdoor.

COMFORT INN NEAR SEAWORLD   (210)522-0700 **110**

Hotel
$79-$149

**Address:** 8731 State Hwy 151 78245 **Location:** I-410 exit SR 151 (SeaWorld); on northbound access road. **Facility:** 78 units. 4 stories, interior corridors. **Pool(s):** heated indoor. **Activities:** hot tub, exercise room. **Guest Services:** coin laundry. **Featured Amenity: continental breakfast.** (See ad p. 515.)

COMFORT SUITES                                 (210)656-4600 **40**

Hotel
$79-$119

**Address:** 11526 I-35 N 78233 **Location:** I-35 exit 168 (Weidner Rd), 0.4 mi n. **Facility:** 57 units. 3 stories, interior corridors. **Pool(s):** indoor. **Activities:** hot tub, exercise room. **Guest Services:** valet and coin laundry. **Featured Amenity: full hot breakfast.**

COMFORT SUITES NEAR SEAWORLD   (210)681-6000 **103**

◆◆◆ **Hotel** $89-$129 **Address:** 8021 Alamo Downs Pkwy 78238 **Location:** I-410 exit 10 (Culebra Rd); on eastbound access road. **Facility:** 75 units, some efficiencies. 3 stories, interior corridors. **Pool(s):** heated indoor. **Activities:** hot tub, exercise room. **Guest Services:** valet and coin laundry.

(See map & index p. 484.)

**COMFORT SUITES NW NEAR SIX FLAGS**    (210)448-5400

 Hotel $79-$149 **Address:** 5130 Vantage Way 78249 **Location:** I-10 exit 558 (De Zavala Rd), just off eastbound frontage road. **Facility:** 82 units. 4 stories, interior corridors. **Pool(s):** outdoor. **Activities:** hot tub, exercise room. **Guest Services:** valet and coin laundry.

 / SOME UNITS

**COMFORT SUITES STONE OAK**    (210)495-5557   14

Hotel
$90-$130

**Address:** 1754 N Loop 1604 E 78232 **Location:** Off Loop 1604, just e of US 218; on eastbound access road in Northwood shopping complex; behind HEB Supermarket. **Facility:** 95 units. 4 stories, interior corridors. **Pool(s):** outdoor. **Activities:** exercise room. **Guest Services:** valet and coin laundry. **Featured Amenity:** full hot breakfast.

SAVE

**COUNTRY INN & SUITES BY CARLSON SAN ANTONIO AIRPORT**    210/822-1554   75

 Contemporary Hotel. Rates not provided. **Address:** 8505 Broadway St 78217 **Location:** I-410 E exit 22 (Broadway St), just n. **Facility:** 126 units. 4 stories, interior corridors. **Amenities:** safes. **Pool(s):** outdoor. **Activities:** hot tub, exercise room. **Guest Services:** valet and coin laundry, area transportation.

*Ratings*
*Members*
*Trust*

Learn more at AAA.com/Diamonds

**COURTYARD BY MARRIOTT-AIRPORT**    (210)828-7200   69

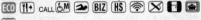 Hotel $99-$169 **Address:** 8615 Broadway St 78217 **Location:** I-410 exit 22 (Broadway St), just n. Located in a quiet area. **Facility:** 145 units. 4 stories, interior corridors. **Pool(s):** outdoor. **Activities:** hot tub, exercise room. **Guest Services:** valet and coin laundry, boarding pass kiosk, area transportation.

> **AAA Benefit:**
> Members save 5% or more!

ECO

**COURTYARD BY MARRIOTT-MEDICAL CENTER**    (210)614-7100   62

Hotel $89-$169 **Address:** 8585 Marriott Dr 78229 **Location:** Jct I-410, 1.8 mi n off Fredericksburg Rd. Located in a quiet area. **Facility:** 146 units. 3 stories, interior corridors. **Terms:** check-in 4 pm. **Pool(s):** outdoor. **Activities:** hot tub, exercise room. **Guest Services:** valet and coin laundry.

> **AAA Benefit:**
> Members save 5% or more!

ECO

**COURTYARD BY MARRIOTT SAN ANTONIO AIRPORT/ NORTHSTAR**    (210)530-9881   64

Hotel
$90-$150

COURTYARD Marriott

> **AAA Benefit:**
> Members save 5% or more!

**Address:** 80 Loop 410 NE 78216 **Location:** I-410 exit 21A (Jones Maltsberger Rd); on eastbound frontage road. Located in a commercial area. **Facility:** 78 units. 4 stories, interior corridors. **Pool(s):** heated indoor. **Activities:** hot tub, exercise room. **Guest Services:** valet and coin laundry, boarding pass kiosk, area transportation.

SAVE  / SOME UNITS

▼ See AAA listing p. 557 ▼

(See map & index p. 484.)

## COURTYARD BY MARRIOTT SAN ANTONIO NORTH/ STONE OAK AT LEGACY
(210)545-3100  **5**

Contemporary Hotel
$79-$159

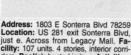

**AAA Benefit:** Members save 5% or more!

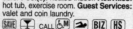

**Address:** 1803 E Sonterra Blvd 78259 **Location:** US 281 exit Sonterra Blvd, just e. Across from Legacy Mall. **Facility:** 107 units. 4 stories, interior corridors. **Pool(s):** heated indoor. **Activities:** hot tub, exercise room. **Guest Services:** valet and coin laundry.

## COURTYARD BY MARRIOTT SAN ANTONIO NORTHWEST AT THE RIM
(210)558-7774  **15**

Hotel $89-$189 **Address:** 5731 Rim Pass Dr 78257 **Location:** I-10 exit 555 (La Cantera Pkwy); in Rim Shopping Complex; off westbound access road. **Facility:** 124 units. 4 stories, interior corridors. **Pool(s):** heated outdoor. **Activities:** exercise room. **Guest Services:** valet and coin laundry.

**AAA Benefit:** Members save 5% or more!

## COURTYARD BY MARRIOTT SAN ANTONIO SEAWORLD WESTOVER HILLS
(210)509-3700

Contemporary Hotel $129-$199 **Address:** 11605 State Hwy 151 78251 **Location:** I-410 exit SR 151 (Westover Hills); on northbound access road. **Facility:** 179 units. 4 stories, interior corridors. **Activities:** hot tub, exercise room. **Guest Services:** valet and coin laundry, area transportation.

**AAA Benefit:** Members save 5% or more!

## COURTYARD BY MARRIOTT SEAWORLD/LACKLAND A.F.B.
(210)647-4100  **99**

Hotel $89-$199 **Address:** 6738 NW Loop 78238 **Location:** I-410 exit 10 (Culebra Rd); on eastbound frontage road. **Facility:** 96 units. 4 stories, interior corridors. **Pool(s):** heated indoor. **Activities:** hot tub, exercise room. **Guest Services:** valet and coin laundry.

**AAA Benefit:** Members save 5% or more!

## CROWNE PLAZA SAN ANTONIO AIRPORT HOTEL
(210)828-9031  **76**

Hotel $89-$199

**Address:** 1111 NE Loop 410 78209 **Location:** I-410 exit Nacogdoches Rd; on westbound frontage road. Located in a commercial area. **Facility:** 224 units, some efficiencies. 10 stories, interior corridors. **Terms:** cancellation fee imposed. **Amenities:** video games. **Pool(s):** outdoor. **Activities:** hot tub, exercise room. **Guest Services:** valet and coin laundry, area transportation.

## DAYS INN AIRPORT
(210)930-3300  **72**

Motel $60-$70

**Address:** 542 NE Loop 410 78216 **Location:** I-410 exit 21 (Airport Blvd), Loop 410 eastbound access road; between Airport Blvd and Wetmore Rd. **Facility:** 49 units. 2 stories, interior corridors. **Terms:** check-in 4 pm. **Amenities:** safes. **Pool(s):** outdoor. **Activities:** hot tub. **Featured Amenity:** continental breakfast.

## DAYS INN & SUITES SAN ANTONIO NORTH/STONE OAK
(210)545-5400  **19**

Hotel $60-$100

**Address:** 1505 Bexar Crossing 78232 **Location:** Jct US 281 and Loop 1604 (Anderson Loop), 0.5 mi s on southbound access road. **Facility:** 60 units, some efficiencies. 3 stories, interior corridors. **Pool(s):** outdoor. **Activities:** exercise room. **Guest Services:** valet and coin laundry. **Featured Amenity:** full hot breakfast.

**The Perfect hotel for business or pleasure at a great value, Located in the Northside Stone Oak area.**

## DAYS INN LACKLAND
(210)675-9690  **121**

Hotel $80-$200

**Address:** 6815 Hwy 90 W 78227 **Location:** I-410 exit US 90 eastbound, 0.8 mi e to Military Dr; on westbound frontage road. **Facility:** 98 units. 2 stories (no elevator), exterior corridors. **Amenities:** video games, safes. **Pool(s):** outdoor. **Featured Amenity:** continental breakfast.

## DAYS INN NORTHWEST
(210)736-1900  **92**

Hotel $55-$75

**Address:** 6023 NW I-10 W 78201 **Location:** I-10 exit 565B eastbound; exit 565C (Vance Jackson Rd) westbound, just n. **Facility:** 75 units. 2 stories, exterior corridors. **Pool(s):** outdoor. **Activities:** hot tub. **Featured Amenity:** continental breakfast.

Save on theme park tickets at
AAA.com/searchfordiscounts

(See map & index p. 484.)

## DOUBLETREE BY HILTON HOTEL SAN ANTONIO AIRPORT   (210)366-2424  58

Hotel
$99-S149

**AAA Benefit:** Members save 5% or more!

**Address:** 37 NE Loop 410 78216 **Location:** I-410 exit 20B (McCullough Ave); on westbound access road. Across from North Star Mall. **Facility:** 290 units. 5 stories, interior/exterior corridors. **Terms:** 1-7 night minimum stay, cancellation fee imposed. **Amenities:** safes. **Pool(s):** outdoor. **Activities:** hot tub, exercise room. **Guest Services:** valet and coin laundry, area transportation.

/ SOME UNITS

## DRURY INN & SUITES NORTHEAST   (210)657-1107  79

Hotel $85-$164 **Address:** 4900 Crestwind Dr 78239 **Location:** I-35 exit 165 (Walzem Rd); on northbound access road. Located in a quiet area. **Facility:** 79 units. 4 stories, interior corridors. **Terms:** cancellation fee imposed. **Pool(s):** outdoor. **Activities:** exercise room. **Guest Services:** valet and coin laundry.

/ SOME UNITS

## DRURY INN & SUITES-SAN ANTONIO AIRPORT   (210)308-8100  61

Hotel $100-$199 **Address:** 95 NE Loop 410 78216 **Location:** I-410 exit 21A (Jones Maltsberger Rd), 1.8 mi w of airport. **Facility:** 284 units, some efficiencies. 6 stories, interior corridors. **Terms:** cancellation fee imposed. **Pool(s):** outdoor. **Activities:** hot tub, exercise room. **Guest Services:** valet and coin laundry, area transportation.

/ SOME UNITS

## DRURY INN & SUITES SAN ANTONIO-LA CANTERA   (210)696-0800  23

Hotel $95-$214 **Address:** 15806 IH-10 W 78249 **Location:** I-10 exit Loop 1604; on eastbound access road. Adjacent to nature area. **Facility:** 223 units. 11 stories, interior corridors. **Terms:** cancellation fee imposed. **Pool(s):** heated indoor. **Activities:** hot tub, exercise room. **Guest Services:** coin laundry.

/ SOME UNITS

## DRURY INN & SUITES-SAN ANTONIO NORTH   (210)404-1600  11

Hotel $80-$184 **Address:** 801 N Loop 1604 E 78232 **Location:** Jct Loop 1604 and US 281, just w. Located in a wooded area facing Loop. **Facility:** 120 units. 6 stories, interior corridors. **Terms:** cancellation fee imposed. **Pool(s):** outdoor. **Activities:** hot tub, exercise room. **Guest Services:** valet and coin laundry.

/ SOME UNITS

## DRURY INN & SUITES-SAN ANTONIO NORTHWEST MED CENTER   (210)561-2510  47

Hotel $105-$289 **Address:** 9806 I-10 W 78230 **Location:** I-10 exit 561 (Wurzbach Rd); on southeast corner. Located in a commercial area. **Facility:** 213 units. 5 stories, interior corridors. **Terms:** cancellation fee imposed. **Pool(s):** indoor. **Activities:** hot tub, exercise room. **Guest Services:** valet and coin laundry.

/ SOME UNITS

## DRURY PLAZA SAN ANTONIO NORTH   (210)494-2420  10

Contemporary Hotel $100-$204 **Address:** 823 N Loop 1604 E 78232 **Location:** Jct Loop 1604 and US 281, just w. **Facility:** 194 units. 6 stories, interior corridors. **Terms:** cancellation fee imposed. **Pool(s):** valet and coin laundry. outdoor. **Activities:** hot tub, exercise room. **Guest Services:** valet and coin laundry.

/ SOME UNITS

## ECONO LODGE INN & SUITES   (210)229-9220  112

Motel
$50-$200

**Address:** 2755 N Panam Expwy 78208 **Location:** I-35 exit 160 (Splashtown Ave); on southbound access road. **Facility:** 47 units. 2 stories (no elevator), exterior corridors. **Amenities:** safes. **Pool(s):** outdoor. **Featured Amenity:** continental breakfast.

/ SOME UNITS

## ECONO LODGE INN & SUITES FIESTA PARK   (210)690-5500  29

Motel $40-$110 **Address:** 13575 I-10 W 78249 **Location:** I-10 exit 557 westbound; exit 558 eastbound; on westbound access road. **Facility:** 62 units. 2 stories, exterior corridors. **Pool(s):** outdoor. **Guest Services:** coin laundry.

/ SOME UNITS

## EILAN HOTEL RESORT AND SPA, AUTOGRAPH COLLECTION   (210)598-2900  6

Boutique Hotel
S199-S500

AUTOGRAPH COLLECTION

**AAA Benefit:** Fresh, inventive and positively unique with special member savings!

**Address:** 17103 La Cantera Pkwy 78256 **Location:** I-10 exit 554 (La Cantera Pkwy), just w; in Eilan office/shopping complex. **Facility:** This elegant and upscale boutique hotel opened in the spring of 2012 and features dramatic public areas, refined guest rooms and one-of-a-kind suites. 165 units. 5 stories, interior corridors. **Parking:** valet only. **Terms:** resort fee. **Amenities:** safes. **Dining:** Sustenio, see separate listing. **Activities:** exercise room, spa. **Guest Services:** valet laundry. (See ad p. 513.)

/ SOME UNITS

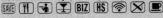

(See map & index p. 484.)

## EMBASSY SUITES HOTEL-AIRPORT
(210)525-9999 **51**

 Hotel $119-$199 **Address:** 10110 Hwy 281 N 78216 **Location:** US 281 exit Jones Maltsberger Rd; on northbound frontage road. Located close to San Antonio International Airport. **Facility:** 261 units. 9 stories, interior corridors. **Terms:** check-in 4 pm, 1-7 night minimum stay, cancellation fee imposed. **Pool(s):** heated indoor. **Activities:** sauna, hot tub, playground, exercise room. **Guest Services:** valet and coin laundry, area transportation.

**AAA Benefit:** Members save 5% or more!

## EMBASSY SUITES NORTHWEST
(210)340-5421 **81**

 Hotel $112-$199 **Address:** 7750 Briaridge Dr 78230 **Location:** I-10 just n of Loop 410 via Callaghan Rd exit, just n to Pinebrooke Dr, then 0.3 mi e. Located in a quiet area. **Facility:** 216 units. 8 stories, interior corridors. **Terms:** check-in 4 pm, 1-7 night minimum stay, cancellation fee imposed. **Pool(s):** heated indoor. **Activities:** hot tub, exercise room. **Guest Services:** valet and coin laundry, area transportation.

**AAA Benefit:** Members save 5% or more!

## EXTENDED STAY AMERICA-SAN ANTONIO-AIRPORT
(210)491-9009 **33**

Extended Stay Motel $44-$59 **Address:** 1015 Central Pkwy S 78232 **Location:** I-410 exit US 281 (San Pedro Ave), just n of Bitters Rd; on northbound frontage road. **Facility:** 153 kitchen units. 2 stories, exterior corridors. **Terms:** cancellation fee imposed. **Guest Services:** coin laundry.

## EXTENDED STAY AMERICA-SAN ANTONIO-COLONNADE
(210)694-1229 **42**

Extended Stay Hotel $59-$79 **Address:** 4331 Spectrum One 78230 **Location:** I-10 exit 561 (Wurzbach Rd), just nw. **Facility:** 84 units, some efficiencies and kitchens. 4 stories, interior corridors. **Terms:** cancellation fee imposed. **Pool(s):** outdoor. **Activities:** exercise room. **Guest Services:** coin laundry.

## FAIRFIELD INN & SUITES BY MARRIOTT NORTH STONE OAK
(210)491-9595 **13**

Hotel $69-$199 **Address:** 80 Trail Crest 78232 **Location:** On Loop 1604 eastbound access road, just w of US 281. **Facility:** 84 units. 3 stories, interior corridors. **Pool(s):** heated indoor. **Activities:** hot tub, exercise room. **Guest Services:** valet and coin laundry.

**AAA Benefit:** Members save 5% or more!

## FAIRFIELD INN & SUITES BY MARRIOTT SAN ANTONIO AIRPORT/NORTH STAR MALL
(210)530-9899 **65**

 Hotel $80-$140

**AAA Benefit:** Members save 5% or more!

**Address:** 88 Loop 410 NE 78216 **Location:** I-410 exit 21A (Jones Maltsberger Rd); between San Pedro Ave and Jones Maltsberger Rd; on eastbound frontage road. Located in a busy commercial area. **Facility:** 120 units. 5 stories, interior corridors. **Amenities:** video games. **Pool(s):** heated indoor. **Activities:** hot tub, exercise room. **Guest Services:** valet and coin laundry, area transportation. **Featured Amenity:** full hot breakfast.

## FAIRFIELD INN & SUITES BY MARRIOTT - SAN ANTONIO/SEAWORLD
(210)682-6800

Hotel $89-$149 **Address:** 4026 Wiseman Blvd 78251 **Location:** SR 151 W exit Wiseman Blvd, 0.6 mi ne. **Facility:** 98 units. 3 stories, interior corridors. **Pool(s):** outdoor. **Activities:** hot tub, exercise room. **Guest Services:** valet and coin laundry, area transportation.

**AAA Benefit:** Members save 5% or more!

▼ See AAA listing p. 512 ▼

(See map & index p. 484.)

## FOUR POINTS BY SHERATON SAN ANTONIO AIRPORT
210/348-9960 **56**

Contemporary Hotel

Rates not provided

**AAA Benefit:** Members get up to 20% off, plus Starwood Preferred Guest® bonuses!

**Address:** 8818 Jones Maltsberger Rd 78216 **Location:** I-410 exit 21A (Jones Maltsberger Rd); on westbound frontage road. **Facility:** 121 units. 4 stories, interior corridors. **Pool(s):** outdoor. **Activities:** hot tub, exercise room. **Guest Services:** valet and coin laundry, boarding pass kiosk, area transportation.

## FOUR POINTS BY SHERATON SAN ANTONIO NORTHWEST
(210)690-0300 **20**

Hotel
$100-$225

**AAA Benefit:** Members get up to 20% off, plus Starwood Preferred Guest® bonuses!

**Address:** 6809 N Loop 1604 W 78260 **Location:** On Loop 1604, just w of La Cantera Pkwy. **Facility:** 130 units. 6 stories, interior corridors. **Bath:** shower only. **Terms:** cancellation fee imposed. **Pool(s):** outdoor. **Activities:** hot tub, exercise room. **Guest Services:** valet laundry, area transportation.

## HAMPTON INN & SUITES
(210)558-3999 **54**

Hotel $119-$139 **Address:** 8902 Jones Maltsberger Rd 78216 **Location:** I-410 exit 21A (Jones Maltsberger Rd); on westbound frontage road. **Facility:** 106 units. 3 stories, interior corridors. **Terms:** 1-7 night minimum stay, cancellation fee imposed. **Amenities:** video games. **Pool(s):** outdoor. **Activities:** hot tub, exercise room. **Guest Services:** valet and coin laundry, area transportation.

**AAA Benefit:** Members save up to 10%!

## HAMPTON INN & SUITES SAN ANTONIO/NORTHEAST I-35
210/599-4800 **88**

Hotel. Rates not provided. **Address:** 6718 IH-35 N 78218 **Location:** I-35/410 exit 164A (Rittiman Rd); on northbound frontage road. **Facility:** 76 units. 4 stories, interior corridors. **Pool(s):** heated indoor. **Activities:** hot tub, exercise room. **Guest Services:** valet and coin laundry.

**AAA Benefit:** Members save up to 10%!

## HAMPTON INN SAN ANTONIO-NORTHWOOD
(210)404-1144 **18**

Hotel $99-$150 **Address:** 2127 Gold Canyon Dr 78232 **Location:** Loop 1604 exit Gold Canyon; on eastbound frontage road. **Facility:** 97 units. 4 stories, interior corridors. **Terms:** 1-7 night minimum stay, cancellation fee imposed. **Amenities:** video games. **Pool(s):** outdoor. **Activities:** exercise room. **Guest Services:** valet and coin laundry.

**AAA Benefit:** Members save up to 10%!

## HAWTHORNE SUITES BY WYNDHAM
(210)561-9660 **46**

Extended Stay Hotel
$99-$199

**Address:** 4041 Bluemel Rd 78240 **Location:** I-10 exit 561 (Wurzbach Rd), 0.3 mi w on eastbound access road; set back from interstate. **Facility:** 128 units, some efficiencies and kitchens. 2 stories (no elevator), exterior corridors. **Terms:** 2 night minimum stay - weekends. **Amenities:** video games. **Pool(s):** outdoor. **Activities:** hot tub, exercise room. **Guest Services:** valet and coin laundry. **Featured Amenity:** full hot breakfast.

## HILTON GARDEN INN SAN ANTONIO AIRPORT
(210)494-7600 **34**

Hotel $99-$179 **Address:** 12828 San Pedro Ave 78216 **Location:** US 281 exit Nakoma Rd southbound; exit Bitters Rd northbound; on northbound access road. Set back from highway in quiet area. **Facility:** 117 units. 4 stories, interior corridors. **Terms:** 1-7 night minimum stay, cancellation fee imposed. **Amenities:** video games. **Pool(s):** heated indoor. **Activities:** exercise room. **Guest Services:** valet and coin laundry, area transportation.

**AAA Benefit:** Members save up to 10%!

## HILTON HILL COUNTRY HOTEL & SPA
(210)509-9800

Resort Hotel $129-$199 **Address:** 9800 Westover Hills Blvd 78251 **Location:** Between Loop 410 and 1604, just off CR 151. Located in a wooded area, across from SeaWorld. **Facility:** This up-to-date ranch-style resort nestled on 27 rolling acres features guest rooms with designer touches; suites offer scenic views. 227 units. 5 stories, interior corridors. **Terms:** check-in 4 pm, 1-7 night minimum stay, cancellation fee imposed. **Amenities:** video games. **Dining:** 2 restaurants. **Pool(s):** heated outdoor. **Activities:** hot tub, recreation programs in season, playground, spa. **Guest Services:** valet and coin laundry, area transportation.

**AAA Benefit:** Members save 5% or more!

## HILTON SAN ANTONIO AIRPORT
(210)340-6060 **55**

Hotel $109-$159 **Address:** 611 NW Loop 410 78216 **Location:** Loop 410 exit San Pedro Ave; on westbound access road. Located in a busy commercial area. **Facility:** 386 units. 13 stories, interior corridors. **Terms:** 1-7 night minimum stay, cancellation fee imposed. **Amenities:** video games. **Pool(s):** heated outdoor. **Activities:** sauna, hot tub, exercise room. **Guest Services:** valet and coin laundry, area transportation.

**AAA Benefit:** Members save 5% or more!

## HOLIDAY INN EXPRESS AIRPORT NORTH
210/402-3300 **24**

Hotel
Rates not provided

**Address:** 16315 US Hwy 281 N 78232 **Location:** US 281 exit Thousand Oaks; on southbound frontage road. **Facility:** 67 units. 3 stories, interior corridors. **Pool(s):** outdoor. **Activities:** hot tub, exercise room. **Guest Services:** valet and coin laundry, area transportation. *(See ad p. 515.)*

**(See map & index p. 484.)**

HOLIDAY INN EXPRESS & SUITES NW - MEDICAL CENTER AREA      210/738-2200 **94**
WWWW **Hotel.** Rates not provided. **Address:** 102 Spencer Ln 78201 **Location:** I-10 exit 565B eastbound; exit 565C (Vance Jackson Rd) westbound, just s. **Facility:** 80 units. 3 stories, interior corridors. **Pool(s):** outdoor. **Activities:** hot tub, limited exercise equipment. **Guest Services:** valet and coin laundry.

HOLIDAY INN EXPRESS HOTEL & SUITES SEAWORLD      210/520-4200 **98**
WWWW **Hotel.** Rates not provided. **Address:** 2861 Cinema Ridge 78238 **Location:** I-410 exit 10 (Culebra Rd), just w of Ingram Rd; on eastbound frontage road. **Facility:** 84 units, some two bedrooms. 4 stories, interior corridors. **Terms:** check-in 4 pm. **Pool(s):** heated indoor. **Activities:** hot tub, exercise room. **Guest Services:** valet and coin laundry.

HOLIDAY INN EXPRESS-SAN ANTONIO AIRPORT      (210)308-6700 **60**
WWWW **Hotel** $99-$129 **Address:** 91 NE Loop 410 78216 **Location:** Loop 410 exit 21A (Jones Maltsberger Rd) eastbound; exit 20B westbound; between San Pedro Ave and Jones Maltsberger Rd; on westbound access road. Located in a commercial area. **Facility:** 154 units. 10 stories, interior corridors. **Pool(s):** outdoor. **Activities:** exercise room. **Guest Services:** valet and coin laundry, area transportation.

HOLIDAY INN EXPRESS SAN ANTONIO WEST - SEAWORLD AREA      210/684-7666
WWWW **Hotel.** Rates not provided. **Address:** 9536 Amelia Pass 78254 **Location:** Loop 1604 at Braun Rd; on northbound frontage road. **Facility:** 80 units. 4 stories, interior corridors. **Pool(s):** outdoor. **Activities:** hot tub, exercise room. **Guest Services:** valet and coin laundry.

HOLIDAY INN LACKLAND      210/678-0444 **120**
WWWW **Hotel.** Rates not provided. **Address:** 6502 Old Hwy 90 W 78227 **Location:** US 90 exit Old US 90, 0.3 mi ne. Located in a quiet area across from Lackland AFB. **Facility:** 74 units, some efficiencies. 2 stories (no elevator), interior corridors. **Pool(s):** outdoor. **Activities:** hot tub, exercise room. **Guest Services:** valet and coin laundry.

HOLIDAY INN NORTHWEST      (210)549-2434 **32**
WWWW **Hotel** $89-$149 **Address:** 5535 University Heights 78249 **Location:** I-10 exit 557 (De Zavala Rd), just off eastbound access road. Next to Sams Club. **Facility:** 122 units. 4 stories, interior corridors. **Terms:** cancellation fee imposed, resort fee. **Pool(s):** outdoor. **Activities:** hot tub, exercise room. **Guest Services:** valet and coin laundry, area transportation.

(See map & index p. 484.)

## HOLIDAY INN NORTHWEST-SEAWORLD
210/520-2508

Hotel
Rates not provided

**Address:** 10135 State Hwy 151 78251 **Location:** I-410 exit SR 151, 3 mi n on northbound access road. **Facility:** 194 units. 5 stories, interior corridors. **Pool(s):** outdoor, heated indoor. **Activities:** hot tub, exercise room. **Guest Services:** valet and coin laundry. *(See ad this page.)*

## HOLIDAY INN SAN ANTONIO HILL COUNTRY
(210)298-8820  **3**

Hotel **$99-$139 Address:** 19280 Redland Rd 78259 **Location:** US 281 exit Redland Rd; on northbound frontage road. **Facility:** 111 units. 4 stories, interior corridors. **Terms:** cancellation fee imposed. **Amenities:** safes. **Pool(s):** heated outdoor. **Activities:** hot tub, exercise room. **Guest Services:** valet and coin laundry.

Trust your vehicle to AAA/CAA
Approved Auto Repair facilities

▼ See AAA listing this page ▼

## Near SeaWorld/Aquatica

- Great family-friendly hotel with indoor & outdoor pools/ hot tub
- State of the art fitness center
- Sporting News Grill
- Complimentary WIFI
- Shuttle Service (5 miles)
- Weekday Newspaper
- Rooms feature Micro/frig, Coffee Maker, HD TVs

**Holiday Inn Northwest-SeaWorld**
10135 State Highway 151
San Antonio, Texas 78251
## 210-520-2508
www.holidayinn.com/sanantonionw

*Kids Eat Free is available for kids age 12 and under. Call hotel or visit www.holidayinn.com for details.*

▼ See AAA listing p. 517 ▼

# Holiday Inn San Antonio International Airport

- Full Service Hotel with Bravo Bar & Grill and Java Express
- 397 Guest Rooms with Mini-fridges & Microwaves
- Complimentary High Speed Wireless Internet
- Fitness Center, Outdoor Pool & Spa
- Room Service & Breakfast Buffet
- Convenient ATM & Business Center
- Meeting Facilities & Services Available
- Across from North Star Mall
- Complimentary Parking
- Pet Friendly Hotel

**Newly Renovated for 2014**

**Holiday Inn**
**Great Hotels Guests Love**

1-888-615-0518
## 1-800-HOLIDAY
holidayinn.com/sat-intlapt

**77 N.E. Loop 410 • San Antonio, TX 78216**

(See map & index p. 484.)

## HOLIDAY INN SAN ANTONIO INTERNATIONAL AIRPORT
210/349-9900 **57**

Hotel
Rates not provided

**Address:** 77 NE Loop 410 78216 **Location:** I-410 exit 20B (McCullough St); on westbound access road. Located in a commercial area. **Facility:** 397 units. 11 stories, interior corridors. **Terms:** check-in 4 pm. **Amenities:** video games. **Pool(s):** outdoor. **Activities:** hot tub, exercise room. **Guest Services:** coin laundry, area transportation. *(See ad p. 516.)*

## HOMEWOOD SUITES BY HILTON
(210)696-5400 **43**

**Extended Stay Hotel**
$89-$162 **Address:** 4323 Spectrum One 78230 **Location:** I-10 exit 561 (Wurzbach Rd), 0.3 mi w; off westbound access road. Located in a quiet area adjacent to upscale mall. **Facility:** 123 kitchen units, some two bedrooms. 4 stories, interior corridors. **Terms:** 1-7 night minimum stay, cancellation fee imposed. **Amenities:** video games. **Pool(s):** outdoor. **Activities:** exercise room. **Guest Services:** valet and coin laundry.

**AAA Benefit:** Members save up to 10%!

## HYATT PLACE SAN ANTONIO AIRPORT/QUARRY MARKET
(210)930-2333 **84**

Contemporary Hotel
$79-$209

**HYATT PLACE**

**AAA Benefit:** Members save 10%!

**Address:** 7615 Jones Maltsberger Rd 78216 **Location:** US 281 exit Jones Maltsberger Rd; on Loop 410. **Facility:** 126 units. 6 stories, interior corridors. **Terms:** cancellation fee imposed. **Pool(s):** heated outdoor. **Activities:** exercise room. **Guest Services:** valet and coin laundry, area transportation. **Featured Amenity:** breakfast buffet.

## HYATT PLACE SAN ANTONIO NORTH STONE OAK
(210)545-2810 **4**

Contemporary Hotel
$79-$174

**HYATT PLACE**

**AAA Benefit:** Members save 10%!

**Address:** 1610 E Sonterra Blvd 78258 **Location:** US 281 exit Sonterra Blvd, just w. **Facility:** 126 units. 6 stories, interior corridors. **Terms:** cancellation fee imposed. **Pool(s):** heated indoor. **Activities:** exercise room. **Guest Services:** valet and coin laundry, boarding pass kiosk.

## HYATT PLACE SAN ANTONIO-NORTHWEST/MEDICAL CENTER
(210)561-0099 **41**

Contemporary Hotel
$69-$179

**HYATT PLACE**

**AAA Benefit:** Members save 10%!

**Address:** 4303 Hyatt Place Dr 78230 **Location:** I-10 exit 561 (Wurzbach Rd), 0.5 mi on westbound access road. Located in a quiet commercial area. **Facility:** 126 units. 6 stories, interior corridors. **Terms:** cancellation fee imposed. **Pool(s):** heated outdoor. **Activities:** exercise room. **Guest Services:** valet laundry, area transportation. **Featured Amenity:** breakfast buffet.

## HYATT REGENCY HILL COUNTRY RESORT AND SPA
(210)647-1234

Resort Hotel
$149-$439

**HYATT REGENCY**

**AAA Benefit:** Members save 10%!

**Address:** 9800 Hyatt Resort Dr 78251 **Location:** Between Loop 410 and 1604, just off CR 151 exit Hyatt Resort Dr. Across from SeaWorld. **Facility:** Wood-trimmed porches and walls of regionally quarried limestone distinguish this sprawling resort, which is known for its lazy river ride. 500 units. 5 stories, interior corridors. **Parking:** on-site and valet. **Terms:** check-in 4 pm, 3 day cancellation notice-fee imposed, resort fee. **Amenities:** safes. **Dining:** 3 restaurants, also, Antlers Lodge, see separate listing. **Pool(s):** heated outdoor. **Activities:** sauna, hot tub, regulation golf, tennis, recreation programs, bicycles, playground, spa. **Guest Services:** valet and coin laundry, area transportation. **Featured Amenity:** full hot breakfast.

## JW MARRIOTT SAN ANTONIO HILL COUNTRY RESORT & SPA
(210)276-2500

Contemporary Resort Hotel
$189-$399

 JW MARRIOTT.

**AAA Benefit:** A deluxe level of comfort and a member rate!

**Address:** 23808 Resort Pkwy 78261 **Location:** Loop 1604 exit US 281, 1.3 mi n to TPC Pkwy, then 1.5 mi e. **Facility:** This elegant large resort in South Texas Hill Country has expansive public areas and features a state-of-the-art floating river, kid's water park and quiet adult-swim area. 1002 units. 9 stories, interior corridors. **Parking:** on-site and valet. **Terms:** check-in 4 pm, 3 day cancellation notice, resort fee. **Amenities:** safes. **Dining:** 4 restaurants, also, Cibolo Moon, see separate listing. **Pool(s):** heated outdoor. **Activities:** regulation golf, tennis, recreation programs, bicycles, playground, spa. **Guest Services:** valet and coin laundry.

---

Be a better driver.
Keep your mind on the road.

(See map & index p. 484.)

### LA QUINTA INN & SUITES
(210)447-8000

Hotel $73-$135 **Address:** 11155 W Loop 1604 N 78023 **Location:** Just w of Bandera Rd. **Facility:** 76 units. 4 stories, interior corridors. **Pool(s):** outdoor. **Activities:** hot tub, exercise room. **Guest Services:** valet and coin laundry.

### LA QUINTA INN & SUITES ANTONIO MEDICAL CENTER
(210)525-8090  **74**

Hotel $109-$204 **Address:** 4431 Horizon Hill Blvd 78229 **Location:** I-10 exit 562; between Callaghan and Wurzbach rds; on eastbound frontage road. **Facility:** 168 units. 8 stories, interior corridors. **Amenities:** safes. **Pool(s):** outdoor. **Activities:** hot tub, exercise room. **Guest Services:** valet and coin laundry.

### LA QUINTA INN & SUITES DOMINION
(210)564-6700

Hotel $84-$129 **Address:** 25042 I-I-10 W 78257 **Location:** I-10 exit 550 (Johns Rd), just e; on westbound access road. **Facility:** 75 units. 3 stories, interior corridors. **Amenities:** safes. **Pool(s):** outdoor. **Activities:** exercise room. **Guest Services:** coin laundry.

### LA QUINTA INN & SUITES-FIESTA TEXAS
(210)696-0100  **26**

Hotel $95-$154 **Address:** 5622 Utex Blvd 78249 **Location:** I-10 exit Loop 1604, 0.7 mi e; on eastbound access road. **Facility:** 93 units. 4 stories, interior corridors. **Pool(s):** outdoor. **Activities:** hot tub, exercise room. **Guest Services:** valet and coin laundry.

### LA QUINTA INN & SUITES SAN ANTONIO AIRPORT
(210)342-3738  **70**

Hotel $89-$140 **Address:** 850 Halm Blvd 78216 **Location:** I-410 exit 21A (Jones Maltsberger Rd); on eastbound frontage road. **Facility:** 276 units. 8 stories, interior corridors. **Amenities:** video games. **Pool(s):** heated outdoor. **Activities:** hot tub, exercise room. **Guest Services:** valet and coin laundry, area transportation.

### LA QUINTA INN & SUITES SAN ANTONIO NORTH STONE OAK
(210)497-0506  **9**

Hotel $137-$182 **Address:** 18502 Hardy Oak Blvd 78258 **Location:** Jct Loop 1604 and US 281, just w. **Facility:** 85 units. 4 stories, interior corridors. **Pool(s):** heated indoor. **Activities:** hot tub, exercise room. **Guest Services:** valet and coin laundry.

### LA QUINTA INN SAN ANTONIO ALAMODOME SOUTH
(210)337-7171  **131**

Hotel
$121-$156

**Address:** 3180 Goliad Rd 78223 **Location:** I-37 exit 135 (Brooks City Base/SE Military Dr), just w of interstate. **Facility:** 115 units. 2 stories, interior corridors. **Amenities:** video games. **Pool(s):** outdoor. **Activities:** exercise room. **Guest Services:** coin laundry.

### LA QUINTA INN SAN ANTONIO I-10 EAST
(210)661-4545  **111**

Hotel $105-$140 **Address:** 6075 IH-10 E Foster Rd 78219 **Location:** I-10 exit 583 (Foster Rd); on westbound frontage road. Located in a quiet rural area. **Facility:** 52 units. 3 stories, interior corridors. **Pool(s):** heated indoor. **Activities:** hot tub, exercise room. **Guest Services:** coin laundry.

### LA QUINTA INN SAN ANTONIO I-35 NORTH AT RITTIMAN RD
(210)653-6619  **90**

Hotel $69-$124 **Address:** 6410 I-35 78218 **Location:** I-35 exit 164A (Rittiman Rd); on northbound frontage road. Located in a quiet area. **Facility:** 130 units. 2 stories (no elevator), exterior corridors. **Amenities:** video games. **Pool(s):** outdoor. **Guest Services:** valet and coin laundry.

### LA QUINTA INN SAN ANTONIO LACKLAND
(210)674-3200  **123**

Hotel $95-$140 **Address:** 6511 Military Dr W 78227 **Location:** Sw of jct US 90 and Military Dr W. Located at entrance to Lackland AFB. **Facility:** 175 units. 2 stories (no elevator), exterior corridors. **Pool(s):** outdoor. **Activities:** exercise room. **Guest Services:** coin laundry.

### LA QUINTA INN SAN ANTONIO SEAWORLD/INGRAM PARK
(210)680-8883  **105**

Hotel $69-$154 **Address:** 7134 NW Loop 410 78238 **Location:** I-410 exit 10 (Culebra Rd); on eastbound access road. **Facility:** 195 units, some two bedrooms. 3 stories, exterior corridors. **Amenities:** video games. **Pool(s):** outdoor. **Guest Services:** valet and coin laundry.

### LA QUINTA INN SAN ANTONIO SOUTH PARK
(210)922-2111  **129**

Hotel $79-$134 **Address:** 7202 S Pan Am 78224 **Location:** I-35 exit 150A (Military Dr) northbound; exit 150B southbound; s of jct I-35 and Military Dr SW. **Facility:** 122 units. 2 stories (no elevator), exterior corridors. **Guest Services:** coin laundry.

### LA QUINTA INN SAN ANTONIO VANCE JACKSON
(210)734-7931  **93**

Motel $75-$130 **Address:** 5922 I-10 W 78201 **Location:** I-10 exit 565B eastbound; exit 565C (Vance Jackson Rd) westbound; on eastbound access road. Located in a light-commercial area. **Facility:** 111 units. 2 stories (no elevator), exterior corridors. **Pool(s):** outdoor.

### MAINSTAY SUITES
(210)798-3900  **86**

Extended Stay Hotel $55-$139 **Address:** 6900 IH-35 N 78218 **Location:** I-35/410 exit 164A (Rittiman Rd); on northbound access road. **Facility:** 66 kitchen units. 3 stories, interior corridors. **Amenities:** safes. **Pool(s):** outdoor. **Activities:** exercise room. **Guest Services:** valet and coin laundry.

### MICROTEL INN & SUITES BY WYNDHAM
(210)404-1900  **27**

Hotel
$69-$169

**Address:** 15314 Hwy 281 N 78232 **Location:** US 281 N exit Brook Hollow; on northbound frontage road. **Facility:** 79 units. 3 stories, interior corridors. **Pool(s):** outdoor. **Guest Services:** valet and coin laundry. **Featured Amenity:** continental breakfast.

(See map & index p. 484.)

### MICROTEL INN & SUITES BY WYNDHAM SAN ANTONIO/NEAR SEAWORLD/LACKLAND AFB
(210)255-8608

Hotel
$79-$189

**Address:** 1605 W Loop 1604 S 78245 **Location:** Loop 1604 exit Military Dr; on eastbound frontage road. **Facility:** 83 units. 3 stories, interior corridors. **Terms:** check-in 4 pm. **Pool(s):** outdoor. **Activities:** hot tub. **Guest Services:** area transportation. **Featured Amenity: continental breakfast.**

---

### MOTEL 6 - #4341
210/447-9000 **25**

**Hotel.** Rates not provided. **Address:** 126 Kenley Pl 78232 **Location:** US 281 exit Brook Hollow Blvd, just n on northbound frontage road. **Facility:** 79 units. 3 stories, interior corridors. **Pool(s):** outdoor. **Activities:** hot tub, exercise room. **Guest Services:** coin laundry.

---

### MOTEL 6 - #651
(210)673-9020 **117**

**Motel** $45-$85 **Address:** 2185 SW Loop 410 78227 **Location:** I-410 exit 7 (Marbach Rd), 0.7 mi w; on westbound access road. **Facility:** 122 units. 3 stories, exterior corridors. **Pool(s):** outdoor. **Guest Services:** coin laundry.

---

### MOTEL 6 EAST - #183
(210)333-1850 **114**

**Motel** $45-$75 **Address:** 138 N WW White Rd 78219 **Location:** I-10 exit 580 (WW White Rd); just off eastbound frontage road. **Facility:** 101 units. 2 stories (no elevator), exterior corridors. **Bath:** shower only. **Pool(s):** outdoor. **Guest Services:** coin laundry.

---

### MOTEL 6 FORT SAM HOUSTON - #1350
210/661-8791 **96**

**Motel** $45-$65 **Address:** 5522 N Pan Am Expwy 78218 **Location:** I-35/410 exit 164 (Rittiman Rd), just s on northbound access road; just off Goldfield St. **Facility:** 154 units, some kitchens. 2 stories, exterior corridors. **Pool(s):** outdoor. **Guest Services:** coin laundry.

---

### MOTEL 6 - MEDICAL CENTER SOUTH - #4429
210/616-0030 **82**

**Hotel.** Rates not provided. **Address:** 7500 Louis Pasteur Dr 78229 **Location:** I-410 exit 14C (Babcock Rd), 1 mi nw, then 0.5 mi n. **Facility:** 48 units. 3 stories, interior corridors. **Guest Services:** coin laundry, area transportation.

---

### M-STAR SEAWORLD
(210)647-8000 **97**

**Motel** $49-$119 **Address:** 6360 NW Loop 410 78238 **Location:** I-410 exit 11 (Ingram Rd); on eastbound access road. Located in a commercial area. **Facility:** 43 units. 2 stories (no elevator), exterior corridors. **Terms:** cancellation fee imposed. **Amenities:** safes. **Pool(s):** outdoor. **Guest Services:** coin laundry.

---

### OMNI SAN ANTONIO HOTEL AT THE COLONNADE
(210)691-8888 **45**

Hotel
$119-$219

**Address:** 9821 Colonnade Blvd 78230 **Location:** I-10 exit 561 (Wurzbach Rd); on westbound frontage road. Located in Colonnade Mall. **Facility:** This luxury property overlooks the rolling Hill Country and offers refined public areas and guest rooms. Indoor and outdoor pools and a complete exercise room are offered. 326 units. 20 stories, interior corridors. **Terms:** cancellation fee imposed. **Dining:** Bolo's, see separate listing, entertainment. **Pool(s):** outdoor, heated indoor. **Activities:** sauna, hot tub, exercise room, massage. **Guest Services:** valet laundry, area transportation. *(See ad this page.)*

---

### PEAR TREE INN BY DRURY-SAN ANTONIO NORTHEAST
(210)654-1144 **80**

**Hotel** $70-$149 **Address:** 8300 I-35 N 78239 **Location:** I-35 exit 165 (Walzem Rd); northbound access road. **Facility:** 105 units. 4 stories, interior/exterior corridors. **Terms:** cancellation fee imposed. **Pool(s):** outdoor. **Activities:** exercise room. **Guest Services:** valet and coin laundry.

▼ See AAA listing this page ▼

(See map & index p. 484.)

### PEAR TREE INN SAN ANTONIO AIRPORT
(210)366-9300 **59**

Hotel $75-$139 **Address:** 143 NE Loop 410 78216 **Location:** I-410 exit 21 (Jones Maltsberger Rd ); on westbound frontage road. **Facility:** 125 units. 4 stories, interior corridors. **Terms:** cancellation fee imposed. **Pool(s):** outdoor. **Activities:** exercise room. **Guest Services:** valet and coin laundry, area transportation.

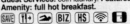

### QUALITY INN & SUITES
(210)226-4361 **107**

Hotel $70-$190 **Address:** 3855 I-35 N 78219 **Location:** I-35 exit 162 (Binz-Engleman Rd) southbound; exit 161 northbound, on southbound access road. **Facility:** 180 units, some kitchens. 2 stories (no elevator), exterior corridors. **Pool(s):** outdoor. **Activities:** exercise room. **Guest Services:** valet and coin laundry.

### QUALITY INN & SUITES BANDERA POINTE
(210)372-9900

Hotel $59-$190 **Address:** 9522 Brimhall Rd (Loop 1604) 78254 **Location:** Loop 1604 exit Bandera Rd; on westbound access road. **Facility:** 64 units. 3 stories, interior corridors. **Pool(s):** heated outdoor. **Activities:** hot tub, exercise room. **Guest Services:** coin laundry.

### QUALITY INN MEDICAL
(210)684-8606 **89**

Hotel $69-$140 **Address:** 4 Piano Pl 78228 **Location:** I-410 exit Evers Rd westbound; exit 14 (Callahan Rd/Babcock Rd) eastbound. **Facility:** 55 units. 2 stories (no elevator), exterior corridors. **Amenities:** safes. **Pool(s):** outdoor. **Activities:** hot tub. **Guest Services:** coin laundry. **Featured Amenity:** full hot breakfast.

### QUALITY INN SIX FLAGS AREA
(210)561-9058 **37**

Hotel $75-$100 **Address:** 11010 I-10 W 78230 **Location:** I-10 exit 560 (Huebner Rd) westbound; exit 559 eastbound. Located in a busy commercial area. **Facility:** 120 units. 6 stories, interior corridors. **Amenities:** video games. **Pool(s):** outdoor. **Activities:** exercise room. **Guest Services:** valet and coin laundry.

### QUALITY SUITES
(210)798-5000 **130**

Hotel $105-$125 **Address:** 3602 Military Hwy SE 78223 **Location:** I-37 exit 135 (Military Hwy), just off westbound frontage road. **Facility:** 65 units. 3 stories, exterior corridors. **Pool(s):** outdoor. **Activities:** hot tub. **Guest Services:** coin laundry. **Featured Amenity:** breakfast buffet.

Texas size rooms and nearby restaurants.

### RAMADA-SEAWORLD AREA
(210)521-1485 **106**

Hotel $49-$129 **Address:** 7043 Culebra Rd 78238 **Location:** I-410 exit 10 (Culebra Rd); on eastbound access road. **Facility:** 72 units. 2 stories (no elevator), exterior corridors. **Terms:** cancellation fee imposed. **Amenities:** safes. **Pool(s):** outdoor. **Guest Services:** coin laundry. **Featured Amenity:** full hot breakfast.

### RED ROOF INN LACKLAND
(210)675-4120 **122**

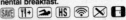

Hotel $60-$140 **Address:** 6861 Hwy 90 W 78227 **Location:** Ne of jct US 90 and Military Dr W; access via Renwick St, off Military Dr, just n of jct US 90. **Facility:** 156 units. 2 stories (no elevator), exterior corridors. **Pool(s):** heated outdoor. **Activities:** exercise room. **Guest Services:** coin laundry. **Featured Amenity:** continental breakfast.

### RED ROOF INN-SAN ANTONIO AIRPORT
(210)340-4055 **52**

Hotel $50-$100 **Address:** 333 Wolfe Rd 78216 **Location:** Just s of US 281 at Isom Rd; on southbound frontage rd. Located in a quiet area. **Facility:** 135 units. 3 stories, interior/exterior corridors. **Amenities:** video games, safes.

### RED ROOF INN- SAN ANTONIO FT. SAM HOUSTON
(210)333-9430 **115**

Hotel $50-$120 **Address:** 4403 I-10 E 78219 **Location:** I-10 exit 580 (WW White Rd); on westbound access road. **Facility:** 120 units. 2-3 stories (no elevator), exterior corridors. **Amenities:** safes. **Pool(s):** outdoor. **Guest Services:** coin laundry, area transportation. **Featured Amenity:** continental breakfast.

### RED ROOF INN SAN ANTONIO (NW-SEAWORLD)
(210)509-3434 **102**

Hotel $49-$89 **Address:** 6880 NW Loop 410 78238 **Location:** I-410 exit 11 (Alamo Downs Pkwy); on eastbound frontage road. **Facility:** 123 units. 3 stories, interior/exterior corridors. **Amenities:** safes. **Pool(s):** outdoor.

(See map & index p. 484.)

## REGENCY INN & SUITES (210)690-2255 **48**

Motel
$49-$159

**Address:** 9727 Fredericksburg Rd 78240 **Location:** I-10 exit 560 (Huebner Rd), just w to Fredericksburg Rd, then 0.9 mi s; across from USAA. Located in a quiet area. **Facility:** 33 units. 2 stories (no elevator), exterior corridors. **Terms:** cancellation fee imposed. **Guest Services:** coin laundry. **Featured Amenity:** continental breakfast.

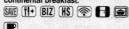

## RESIDENCE INN BY MARRIOTT NORTH SAN ANTONIO
(210)490-1333 **8**

Extended Stay Hotel
$79-$169

**AAA Benefit:** Members save 5% or more!

**Address:** 1115 N SR 1604 E 78232 **Location:** Loop 1604, just w of US 281; on westbound frontage road. **Facility:** 88 units, some two bedrooms, efficiencies and kitchens. 4 stories, interior corridors. **Pool(s):** heated outdoor. **Activities:** exercise room. **Guest Services:** valet and coin laundry, area transportation.

## RESIDENCE INN BY MARRIOTT SAN ANTONIO-AIRPORT
(210)805-8118 **77**

Extended Stay Hotel $109-$259 **Address:** 1014 NE Loop 410 78209 **Location:** Loop 410 exit Broadway St, 0.4 mi e on eastbound access road. **Facility:** 120 units, some two bedrooms and kitchens. 2-3 stories, exterior corridors. **Terms:** check-in 4 pm. **Pool(s):** outdoor. **Activities:** hot tub, tennis, exercise room. **Guest Services:** valet and coin laundry.

**AAA Benefit:** Members save 5% or more!

## RESIDENCE INN BY MARRIOTT SAN ANTONIO NORTHWEST AT THE RIM
(210)561-0200 **16**

Extended Stay Hotel $99-$199 **Address:** 5707 Rim Pass Dr 78257 **Location:** I-10 exit 555 (La Cantera Pkwy); on westbound access road; in The Rim Shopping Complex. **Facility:** 131 kitchen units, some two bedrooms. 6 stories, interior corridors. **Pool(s):** heated outdoor. **Activities:** exercise room. **Guest Services:** valet and coin laundry.

**AAA Benefit:** Members save 5% or more!

## RESIDENCE INN BY MARRIOTT SEAWORLD/LACKLAND AFB
(210)509-3100 **100**

Extended Stay Contemporary Hotel $109-$199 **Address:** 2838 Cinema Ridge 78238 **Location:** I-410 exit 10 (Ingram Rd); on eastbound frontage road. **Facility:** 109 units, some two bedrooms and kitchens. 4 stories, interior corridors. **Amenities:** safes. **Pool(s):** heated indoor. **Activities:** hot tub, exercise room. **Guest Services:** valet and coin laundry.

**AAA Benefit:** Members save 5% or more!

## RODEWAY INN (210)359-7268 **113**

Motel
$46-$85

**Address:** 211 N WW White Rd 78219 **Location:** I-10 exit 580 (WW White Rd), just n. Located in a busy commercial area near city Loop 410 and I-10. **Facility:** 92 units. 2 stories, exterior corridors. **Pool(s):** outdoor. **Guest Services:** coin laundry. **Featured Amenity:** continental breakfast.

## RODEWAY INN LACKLAND AFB/SEAWORLD
(210)674-1511 **119**

Motel
$49-$90

**Address:** 6500 Old Hwy 90 W 78227 **Location:** US 90 exit Old US 90, 0.3 mi ne. Located in a quiet area across from Lackland AFB. **Facility:** 40 units. 1 story, exterior corridors. **Pool(s):** outdoor. **Guest Services:** coin laundry. **Featured Amenity:** continental breakfast.

(See map & index p. 484.)

RODEWAY INN-SIX FLAGS FIESTA          (210)698-3991  **2**

♦ **Motel** $50-$80 **Address:** 19793 I-10 W 78257 **Location:** I-10 exit 554 (Camp Bullis Rd), westbound; exit 552 (Dominion) and U-turn onto eastbound access road. **Facility:** 72 units. 2 stories (no elevator), exterior corridors. **Pool(s):** outdoor. **Guest Services:** coin laundry.

---

## SAN ANTONIO MARRIOTT NORTHWEST
(210)377-3900  **83**

**Marriott**
HOTELS & RESORTS

Hotel
$99-$159

**AAA Benefit:** Members save 5% or more!

**Address:** 3233 NW Loop 410 78213 **Location:** I-410 exit 17 (Vance Jackson Rd/Cherry Ridge Dr), 1 mi on westbound access road. **Facility:** 296 units. 11 stories, interior corridors. **Terms:** check-in 4 pm. **Amenities:** video games. **Pool(s):** outdoor. **Activities:** exercise room. **Guest Services:** valet and coin laundry. *(See ad this page.)*

---

SLEEP INN & SUITES AT SIX FLAGS          (210)561-6100  **28**

♦♦♦ **Hotel** $80-$180 **Address:** 5042 Beckwith Blvd 78249 **Location:** I-10 exit 557 (UTSA Blvd) westbound; exit 558 eastbound; on westbound access road; 1 mi n of De Zavala Rd. **Facility:** 60 units. 4 stories, interior corridors. **Amenities:** safes. **Pool(s):** indoor. **Activities:** hot tub, exercise room. **Guest Services:** coin laundry.

---

SLEEP INN & SUITES-SEAWORLD          (210)670-2500  **109**

♦♦♦ **Hotel** $65-$110 **Address:** 143 Richland Hills Dr 78245 **Location:** I-410 exit 9A, jct I-410 and SR 151. **Facility:** 72 units, some two bedrooms. 4 stories, interior corridors. **Pool(s):** heated indoor. **Activities:** hot tub, exercise room. **Guest Services:** coin laundry.

---

SLEEP INN SAN ANTONIO          (210)344-5400  **68**

♦♦ **Hotel** $62-$119 **Address:** 8318 I-10 W 78230 **Location:** I-10 exit 561 (Callaghan Rd); on eastbound frontage road. Located in a quiet area. **Facility:** 104 units. 3 stories, interior corridors. *Bath:* shower only. **Terms:** check-in 4 pm. **Amenities:** video games. **Pool(s):** outdoor. **Guest Services:** coin laundry, area transportation.

---

SPRINGHILL SUITES BY MARRIOTT SAN ANTONIO AIRPORT
(210)804-2266  **71**

♦♦♦ **Contemporary Hotel** $99-$199 **Address:** 514 NE Loop 410 78216 **Location:** Loop 410 exit 21 (Airport Blvd), just e on eastbound frontage road; between Airport Blvd and Wetmore Rd. **Facility:** 116 units. 4 stories, interior corridors. **Pool(s):** heated outdoor. **Activities:** exercise room. **Guest Services:** valet and coin laundry, area transportation.

**AAA Benefit:** Members save 5% or more!

---

SPRINGHILL SUITES BY MARRIOTT SAN ANTONIO MEDICAL CENTER/NORTHWEST          (210)737-6086  **85**

♦♦♦ **Contemporary Hotel** $89-$119 **Address:** 3636 NW Loop 410 78201 **Location:** I-410 E exit Fredericksburg Rd. **Facility:** 112 units. 4 stories, interior corridors. **Pool(s):** outdoor. **Activities:** exercise room. **Guest Services:** valet and coin laundry, area transportation.

**AAA Benefit:** Members save 5% or more!

---

SPRINGHILL SUITES BY MARRIOTT SAN ANTONIO MEDICAL CENTER/SIX FLAGS          (210)697-8900  **36**

♦♦♦ **Contemporary Hotel** $89-$199 **Address:** 11426 IH-10 W 78230 **Location:** I-10 exit 558 (De Zavala Rd), 0.7 mi e on access road. **Facility:** 109 units. 4 stories, interior corridors. **Pool(s):** indoor. **Activities:** hot tub, exercise room. **Guest Services:** valet and coin laundry.

**AAA Benefit:** Members save 5% or more!

---

(See map & index p. 484.)

SPRINGHILL SUITES BY MARRIOTT SAN ANTONIO
SEAWORLD/LACKLAND               (210)520-6655  **108**

▽▽▽ **Contemporary  Hotel**
$89-$199 **Address:** 138 Richland Hills
Dr 78245 **Location:** I-410 exit 9A (Sea-
World), just w on westbound access
road. **Facility:** 116 units. 4 stories, inte-
rior corridors. **Pool(s):** heated indoor. **Activities:** exercise room.
**Guest Services:** valet and coin laundry.

[❚↑] [☎] [BIZ] [HS] [☞] [✕] [🔒] [🖨] [💻]

| **AAA Benefit:** |
| Members save 5% |
| or more! |

STAYBRIDGE SUITES NW NEAR SIX FLAGS FIESTA
                                210/691-3443  **22**

▽▽▽ **Extended Stay Hotel.** Rates not provided. **Address:**
6919 N Loop 1604 W 78249 **Location:** Loop 1604 exit La Cantera
Pkwy; on westbound frontage road. **Facility:** 120 kitchen units, some
two bedrooms. 4 stories, interior corridors. **Pool(s):** outdoor. **Activities:** hot tub, exercise room. **Guest Services:** valet and coin laundry,
area transportation.

[☎] [BIZ] [HS] [☞] [✕] [🔒] [🖨] [💻] / SOME UNITS [🐾]

STAYBRIDGE SUITES SAN ANTONIO-AIRPORT
                                210/341-3220  **63**

▽▽▽ **Extended Stay Hotel.** Rates not provided. **Address:** 66
NE Loop 410 78216 **Location:** I-410 exit 20B (McCullough St); on
eastbound access road. Next to Texas Land & Cattle Restaurant. **Facility:** 136 efficiencies, some two bedrooms. 9 stories, interior corridors. **Terms:** check-in 4 pm. **Pool(s):** heated outdoor. **Activities:** hot
tub, exercise room. **Guest Services:** complimentary and valet
laundry, area transportation.

[✈] [❚↑] [☎] [BIZ] [HS] [☞] [🔒] [🖨] [💻]
/ SOME UNITS [🐾]

STAYBRIDGE SUITES SAN ANTONIO NW-COLONNADE
                                (210)558-9009  **44**

▽▽▽ **Extended Stay Hotel** $149-$249 **Address:** 4320 Spectrum One 78230 **Location:** I-10 exit 561 (Wurzbach Rd), 0.3 mi w; off
westbound access road. **Facility:** 118 units, some two bedrooms, efficiencies and kitchens. 3 stories, interior corridors. **Terms:** cancellation fee imposed. **Pool(s):** heated outdoor. **Activities:** exercise room.
**Guest Services:** complimentary laundry, area transportation.

[❚↑] [☎] [BIZ] [HS] [☞] [🔒] [🖨] [💻] / SOME UNITS [🐾]

STAYBRIDGE SUITES SAN ANTONIO-STONE OAK
                                (210)497-0100  **12**

▽▽▽ **Extended Stay Hotel** $99-$169 **Address:** 808 N Loop
1604 E 78232 **Location:** On Loop 1604, 0.4 mi w of US 281. **Facility:** 135 kitchen units, some two bedrooms. 5 stories, interior corridors. **Terms:** cancellation fee imposed. **Amenities:** safes. **Pool(s):**
outdoor. **Activities:** hot tub, exercise room. **Guest Services:** valet
and coin laundry, area transportation.

[❚↑] CALL [📞M] [☎] [BIZ] [HS] [☞] [✕] [🔒] [🖨] [💻]
/ SOME UNITS [🐾]

STAYBRIDGE SUITES-SEAWORLD SAN ANTONIO
                                210/767-1100

▽▽▽ **Extended Stay Hotel.** Rates not provided. **Address:**
10919 Town Center Dr 78251 **Location:** SR 151 exit Westover Hills,
just off northbound access road. Across from SeaWorld. **Facility:** 98
units, some two bedrooms, efficiencies and kitchens. 4 stories, interior corridors. **Pool(s):** heated outdoor. **Activities:** exercise room.
**Guest Services:** valet and coin laundry, area transportation.

[❚↑] [☎] [BIZ] [HS] [☞] [🔒] [🖨] [💻]

SUPER 8                         (210)678-0888  **118**

▽▽ ▽▽
Motel
$59-$76

**Address:** 2211 SW Loop 410 78227
**Location:** I-410 exit 7 (Marbach Rd), 0.7
mi w; on westbound access road. **Facility:** 60 units. 2 stories, exterior corridors. **Amenities:** safes. **Pool(s):**
outdoor. **Guest Services:** coin laundry.
**Featured  Amenity:  continental
breakfast.**

[SAVE] [☎] [HS] [☞] [🔒] [🖨] [💻]

SUPER 8                         (210)265-8888  **128**

▽▽ ▽▽
Hotel
$69-$100

**Address:** 723 Hot Wells Blvd 78223 **Location:** I-410 exit 137 (Hot Wells Blvd);
on southbound access road. **Facility:** 49
units. 3 stories, interior corridors.
**Pool(s):** indoor. **Activities:** sauna, exercise room. **Guest Services:** coin
laundry. **Featured Amenity:** continental breakfast.

[SAVE] [❚↑] [☎] [HS] [☞] [🔒] [🖨]
[💻] / SOME UNITS [🐾]

SUPER 8 ON ROLAND              (210)798-5500  **124**

▽▽ ▽▽
Hotel
$79-$160

**Address:** 302 Roland Ave 78210 **Location:** I-10 exit 577 (Roland Ave); on
eastbound access road. **Facility:** 55
units. 2 stories, exterior corridors.
**Pool(s):** outdoor. **Guest Services:** coin
laundry. **Featured Amenity:** continental breakfast.

[SAVE] [❚↑] [☎] [BIZ] [HS] [☞] [🔒]
[🖨] [💻] / SOME UNITS [🐾]

SUPER 8-SIX FLAGS FIESTA       (210)696-6916  **31**

▽▽ ▽▽
Hotel
$60-$100

**Address:** 5319 Casa Bella 78249 **Location:** I-10 exit 557 westbound; exit 558
eastbound; on westbound frontage road.
**Facility:** 71 units. 3 stories, interior corridors. **Pool(s):** outdoor. **Guest Services:** coin laundry. **Featured Amenity:**
continental breakfast.

[SAVE] [☎] [BIZ] [HS] [☞] [🔒] [🖨]
[💻] / SOME UNITS [🐾]

TOWNEPLACE SUITES BY MARRIOTT  (210)308-5510  **67**

▽▽▽ **Extended  Stay  Hotel**
$67-$149 **Address:** 214 NE Loop 410
78216 **Location:** I-410 exit 21A (Jones
Maltsberger Rd); on eastbound frontage

| **AAA Benefit:** |
| Members save 5% |
| or more! |

road. **Facility:** 106 units, some two bed-
rooms, efficiencies and kitchens. 4 stories, interior corridors. **Pool(s):**
outdoor. **Activities:** exercise room. **Guest Services:** valet and coin
laundry, boarding pass kiosk, area transportation.

[✈] [☎] [BIZ] [HS] [☞] [✕] [🔒] [🖨] [💻]
/ SOME UNITS [🐾]

# Learn the local driving laws

## at DrivingLaws.AAA.com

(See map & index p. 484.)

## TOWNEPLACE SUITES BY MARRIOTT SAN ANTONIO NORTHWEST (210)694-5100 **39**

Extended Stay Hotel $65-$139 **Address:** 5014 Prue Rd 78240 **Location:** I-10 exit 560 (Huebner Rd) westbound; exit 559 eastbound, 1 blk sw to Fredericksburg Rd, then just n. **Facility:** 123 kitchen units. 3 stories, interior corridors. **Pool(s):** outdoor. **Activities:** exercise room. **Guest Services:** valet and coin laundry, area transportation.

**AAA Benefit:** Members save 5% or more!

## TRAVELODGE LACKLAND (210)645-1561 **127**

Hotel $50-$250

**Address:** 120 Rustleaf Dr 78242 **Location:** I-410 exit 3B (Medina Base Rd), 1.9 mi se to Whitewood Dr, n to Military Hwy, then 0.3 mi nw. Adjacent to Lackland AFB West Gate. **Facility:** 32 units. 2 stories (no elevator), exterior corridors. **Terms:** 3 day cancellation notice-fee imposed. **Amenities:** safes. **Pool(s):** outdoor. **Activities:** hot tub. **Guest Services:** coin laundry. **Featured Amenity:** continental breakfast.

## THE WESTIN LA CANTERA HILL COUNTRY RESORT (210)558-6500 **17**

Resort Hotel $439-$2500

WESTIN HOTELS & RESORTS **AAA Benefit:** Enjoy up to 20% off your next stay, plus Starwood Preferred Guest® bonuses!

**Address:** 16641 La Cantera Pkwy 78256 **Location:** I-10 exit La Cantera Pkwy, access via Loop 1604 at La Cantera Pkwy. **Facility:** Overlooking San Antonio, this elegant, expansive resort features design details that embody the Texas Hill Country style. 508 units. 7 stories, interior corridors. **Parking:** on-site and valet. **Terms:** check-in 4 pm, 3 day cancellation notice, resort fee. **Amenities:** video games, safes. **Dining:** 2 restaurants, also, Brannon's Cafe, Francesca's at Sunset, see separate listings. **Pool(s):** outdoor, heated outdoor. **Activities:** regulation golf, tennis, playground, spa. **Guest Services:** valet laundry, area transportation.

## WHERE TO EAT

### 410 DINER 210/822-6246 **57**

American. Quick Serve. $8-$18 **AAA Inspector Notes:** The retro diner with a friendly staff offers unique creations. I sampled an excellent cream of tomato soup, a club sandwich with spinach and a light chocolate cake. **Features:** full bar. **Address:** 8315 Broadway St 78209 **Location:** I-410 exit Broadway St, just s. L D

### ACADIANA CAFE 210/674-0019 **84**

Regional Cajun. Family Dining. $7-$15 **AAA Inspector Notes:** Cajun-style cuisine served in a modest, down home atmosphere is what this restaurant is all about. Delicious food served hot and well-seasoned includes crisp salad, spicy gumbo, fried oysters with French fries, and warm, homemade peach cobbler. **Features:** full bar. **Address:** 1289 SW Loop 410 78227 **Location:** I-410 exit 8 (Marbach Rd), on westbound access road; next to Westlakes Mall. L D

### ALAMO CAFE 210/691-8827 **29**

Tex-Mex. Family Dining. $8-$20 **AAA Inspector Notes:** Southwestern cuisine, including enchiladas, chicken-fried steak and fajitas, are served here by a cordial waitstaff. The hamburgers are loaded with the works. This large and busy dining establishment is a good family eating spot, and the margarita pie has a kick to it. **Features:** full bar. **Address:** 10060 W I-10 78216 **Location:** I-10 exit 561 (Wurzbach Rd) eastbound; exit 560 (Huebner Rd) westbound, U-turn. L D

### ALDINO AT THE VINEYARD 210/340-0000 **7**

Italian. Casual Dining. $10-$30 **AAA Inspector Notes:** A sister property to well-known Aldo's, this new establishment prepares mostly Italian dishes but includes some Continental selections such as smoked salmon and cream soups. Among the specialties are minestrone and lasagna. **Features:** full bar. **Address:** 1203 N Loop 1604 78258 **Location:** Loop 1604 at Blanco St; on westbound access road. L D

### ALDO'S RISTORANTE ITALIANO 210/696-2536 **41**

Italian. Fine Dining. $12-$40 **AAA Inspector Notes:** Set inside a 100-year-old Italian-style villa, this romantic bistro boasts a relaxing garden surrounded by tall oak trees. Try the snapper di Aldo—sautéed fillet with crabmeat, artichoke hearts and white wine basil sauce. **Features:** full bar. **Address:** 8539 Fredericksburg Rd 78229 **Location:** I-10 exit 561 (Wurzbach Rd); in South Texas Medical Center. L D

### ANTLERS LODGE 210/647-1234

American Fine Dining $38-$67

**AAA Inspector Notes:** Dominated by an enormous antler chandelier, this upscale resort restaurant offers the freshest seafood, aged steaks and select game, as well as pasta, scallops and crab chowder. The service is phenomenal, with custom recommendations and follow-up attention. Guests can expect the manager to visit to ensure satisfaction. **Features:** full bar. **Reservations:** suggested. **Address:** 9800 Hyatt Resort Dr 78251 **Location:** Between Loop 410 and 1604, just off CR 151 exit Hyatt Resort Dr; in Hyatt Regency Hill Country Resort and Spa. **Parking:** on-site and valet. D CALL

### BARBECUE STATION RESTAURANT 210/824-9191 **56**

Regional Barbecue. Quick Serve. $6-$12 **AAA Inspector Notes:** From a converted gas station, the restaurant prepares tender smoked brisket, sausages and chicken with homemade sauces and serves them with homemade sides, such as pintos, creamed corn and chunky potato salad. Shelves are stocked with products and canned goods from the 1960s. **Features:** beer only. **Address:** 1610 NE Loop 410 78209 **Location:** I-410 exit (Nacogdoches Rd), on eastbound frontage road. L D

### THE BARN DOOR RESTAURANT 210/824-0116 **58**

Regional Steak. Casual Dining. $13-$30 **AAA Inspector Notes:** This barn-like structure is noted for its red, rustic, Western décor. Various photographs and store memorabilia decorate the walls. Charcoal-broiled steaks are a specialty. **Features:** full bar. **Reservations:** suggested. **Address:** 8400 N New Braunfels Ave 78209 **Location:** I-410 exit 22 (Broadway St), 0.4 mi e on eastbound access road to N New Braunfels, then just s. L D

### BETO'S COMIDA LATINA 210/930-9393 **61**

Regional Latin American. Casual Dining. $7-$12 **AAA Inspector Notes:** What's an empanada? The root word is "pan," which means bread. The rest you can find out for yourself, but it's warm, flaky and delicious. Try the specialty mojitos and margaritas. **Features:** beer & wine, patio dining. **Address:** 8142 Broadway St 78209 **Location:** I-410 exit 22 (Broadway St), 0.3 mi s of Loop 410. L D

**(See map & index p. 484.)**

## BILL MILLER BAR-B-Q

Barbecue. Quick Serve. $6-$11 **AAA Inspector Notes:** The relaxed, family-focused barbecue restaurant prepares ribs, chicken, brisket, turkey and sausage for sandwiches or plates.

(B) (L) (D)

*For additional information, visit AAA.com*

**LOCATIONS:**

**Address:** 2750 Bill Miller Ln 78223 **Location:** Just s of E Southcross Blvd. **Phone:** 210/533-5143

**Address:** 6950 W Military Dr 78227 **Location:** Just n of US 90. **Phone:** 210/673-1122

**Address:** 5250 De Zavala Rd 78249 **Location:** I-10 exit De Zavala Rd, just e. **Phone:** 210/690-0054

**Address:** 3200 Fredericksburg Rd 78201 **Location:** Just s of Vance Jackson Rd; jct Babcock Rd. **Phone:** 210/736-4211

**Address:** 430 S Santa Rosa Ave 78207 **Location:** Just n of Cesar E Chavez Blvd. **Phone:** 210/302-1510

**Address:** 2110 Jackson Keller Rd 78213 **Location:** I-410 exit 17 (Jackson Keller Rd); on eastbound access road. **Phone:** 210/341-6119

**Address:** 2911 Thousand Oaks Dr 78247 **Location:** Just se of Jones Maltsberger Rd. **Phone:** 210/496-2958

**Address:** 5113 Walzem Rd 78218 **Location:** I-35 exit 165 (Walzem Rd), just e. **Phone:** 210/656-6262

**Address:** 11842 Perrin Beitel Rd 78217 **Location:** Just s of Thousand Oaks Dr. **Phone:** 210/657-3074

**Address:** 4500 Broadway St 78209 **Location:** Just n of E Hildebrand Ave. **Phone:** 210/829-7688

**Address:** 3511 Roosevelt Ave 78214 **Location:** Just s of SE Military Dr. **Phone:** 210/924-1666

**Address:** 135 S WW White Rd 78219 **Location:** I-10 exit 580 (WW White Rd), just s. **Phone:** 210/333-4830

**Address:** 12345 US Hwy 87 S 78101 **Location:** Just s of Loop 1604. **Phone:** 210/649-4567

## BIN 555 RESTAURANT AND WINE BAR   210/496-0555 (14)

New World. Casual Dining. $14-$34 **AAA Inspector Notes:** Unusual combinations like pan-fried salmon with spicy Indian potato salad are matched with wine and cheese from around the world. The staff is exceptionally well versed in all the exotic ingredients, and the ambience is relaxing and inviting. The over-size booths contribute to the sharing concept of this facility. **Features:** full bar. **Address:** 555 W Bitters Rd 78216 **Location:** Jct US 281, 2 mi w.

(L) (D) (⬟)

## BISTRO VATEL   210/828-3141 (77)

Provincial French. Fine Dining. $12-$30 **AAA Inspector Notes:** This place, with its crowded dining room, maroon painted ceiling, framed art pieces, wine bottles on shelves and ledges, stylish lighting and viewable kitchen, is like a scene from the Left Bank. Just off Olmos Circle, the tight bistro immediately transports guests, if only figuratively, to France. Daily specials scrawled on the large blackboard include the most authentic of French onion soup and flavorful and tender duck in casserole. **Features:** beer & wine. **Address:** 218 E Olmos Dr 78212 **Location:** McCullough Ave at Olmos Circle.

(L) (D)

## BOLO'S   210/691-8888 (28)

Regional American Casual Dining $8-$35

**AAA Inspector Notes:** Perceptive staff fulfills your every wish as you sample culinary delights from deep in the heart of Texas. Evidence of the chef's artistic talents include a sausage trio—beef, venison and chicken—and excellent lump crab cakes. **Features:** full bar. **Reservations:** suggested. **Address:** 9821 Colonnade Blvd 78230 **Location:** I-10 exit 561 (Wurzbach Rd); on westbound frontage road; in Omni San Antonio Hotel at the Colonnade. *Menu on AAA.com* (B) (L) (D)

## BRANNON'S CAFE   210/558-6500 (10)

Regional American. Casual Dining. $19-$26 **AAA Inspector Notes:** This spot is locally known for unique Southwest dishes like seafood Campechana and flautas. The dining room is refined with plate glass walls showcasing the striking Hill Country of south Texas. **Features:** full bar. **Address:** 16641 La Cantera Pkwy 78256 **Location:** I-10 exit La Cantera Pkwy, access via Loop 1604 at La Cantera Pkwy; in The Westin La Cantera Hill Country Resort. **Parking:** on-site and valet. (B) (L) (D)

## BROADWAY 50-50   210/691-5050 (32)

American. Casual Dining. $11-$22 **AAA Inspector Notes:** The classic diner cuisine offered includes a wide variety of choices like fried chicken, pulled pork, deli sandwiches, sweet potato fries, shakes, floats and spicy Elvis deviled eggs. **Features:** full bar, Sunday brunch, happy hour. **Address:** 9837 IH-10 W 78230 **Location:** I-10 exit 11 (Alamo Downs Pkwy); on westbound access road; in Colonnade Shopping Complex. (L) (D)

## CAFE MILANO   210/680-8111 (60)

Regional Italian. Casual Dining. $7-$22 **AAA Inspector Notes:** An attentive staff, a unique Old World decor and authentic Milano dishes make this cheerful eatery a very pleasant place to visit. Servers work in teams to present baskets of fresh, hot rolls, a delicious antipasto, fresh seafood and flavorful vegetables. **Features:** beer & wine. **Address:** 7530 Bandera Rd 78238 **Location:** I-410 exit 13A (Bandera Rd); northeast jct Bandera Rd (SR 16); at Eckert Rd. (L) (D)

## CANYON CAFE   210/821-3738 (66)

Southwestern. Casual Dining. $15-$30 **AAA Inspector Notes:** The trendy, casual restaurant offers a west coast menu and Texas-friendly service. **Features:** full bar, patio dining. **Address:** 255 E Basse Rd, Unit 600 78209 **Location:** 0.4 mi e of US 281 (McAllister Frwy); in Alamo Quarry Market. (L) (D)

## CAPPARELLI'S ITALIAN RESTAURANT   210/690-6036 (39)

Italian. Casual Dining. $7-$12 **AAA Inspector Notes:** The small, quaint setting belies the rich and flavorful Italian specialties. This place serves the Medical Center area. **Features:** beer & wine. **Address:** 8822 Huebner Rd 78240 **Location:** Jct Babcock Rd; on southeast corner. (L) (D)

## CAPPY'S   210/828-9669 (74)

Regional American. Fine Dining. $12-$32 **AAA Inspector Notes:** All dishes are pleasant surprises with unexpected ingredients and preparations. One of the city's favorite restaurants, it provides friendly, interesting décor and a wide range of menu options. The trendy place is located in upscale Alamo Heights. **Features:** full bar. **Address:** 5011 Broadway Ave 78209 **Location:** Just n of Hildebrand St; in Alamo Heights. (L) (D)

## CAPPY'S LAFONDA ON MAIN   210/733-0621 (82)

Regional Mexican. Casual Dining. $8-$21 **AAA Inspector Notes:** Recently joining the Cappy family of city restaurants, this favorite from 1939 is now infused with new flavors and combinations like the poblano avocado soup. Kick back, relax and enjoy your meal on the outdoor patio next to a huge 300-year-old oak tree. **Features:** full bar, patio dining. **Address:** 2415 N Main Ave 78212 **Location:** Just s of Woodlawn Ave. (L) (D)

## CHESTER'S HAMBURGERS   210/699-1222 (31)

Burgers. Quick Serve. $7-$10 **AAA Inspector Notes:** Made-to-order hamburgers with toppings of bacon, chili, green chili or just the basics of tomato, mustard or mayonnaise. Fresh-cut french fries, onion rings, stuffed jalapeños, hand-dipped shakes and more than 200 kinds of beer and wine also are available at this local favorite. **Features:** beer & wine, patio dining. **Address:** 9980 I-10 W 78230 **Location:** I-10 exit 561 (Wurzbach Rd); on southeast corner. (L) (D)

## CIBOLO MOON   210/276-2500

American. Casual Dining. $22-$40 **AAA Inspector Notes:** Self-described as Texas cuisine, the farm-to-table menu includes dishes like enchilada stack, Gulf crab salad, bison meatloaf and apple pie with vanilla bean ice cream. Sweeping views of the South Texas Hill Country enhance the experience. **Features:** full bar. **Address:** 23808 Resort Pkwy 78261 **Location:** Loop 1604 exit US 281, 1.3 mi n to TPC Pkwy, then 1.5 mi e; in JW Marriott San Antonio Hill Country Resort & Spa. **Parking:** on-site and valet. (B) (L) (D)

**(See map & index p. 484.)**

## CIELITO LINDO    210/545-6965   (2)

◇◇ ◇◇ Regional Mexican. Casual Dining. $8-$18 **AAA Inspector Notes:** On the far north side of the city, this popular spot focuses its menu on authentic Mexican dishes, such as albondigas (spicy meatballs), cochinita pibil (marinated pork) and mole. Flavorful Aztec sauce is made with peanuts, chocolate and 20-some ingredients. **Features:** full bar. **Address:** 19941 Stone Oak Pkwy 78258 **Location:** Just s; jct Huebner Rd. (B) (L) (D) CALL (&M)

## THE COUNTY LINE BARBECUE    210/641-1998   (27)

◇◇ ◇◇ Barbecue. Casual Dining. $11-$30 **AAA Inspector Notes:** The Texas roadhouse-style barbecue restaurant serves great brisket, a gigantic full rack of baby back ribs and an enjoyable array of accompanying sides. **Features:** full bar. **Address:** 10101 I-10 W 78230 **Location:** I-10 exit 561 (Wurzbach Rd); on west access road, n of Wurzbach Rd. (L) (D) CALL (&M)

## CRUMPETS RESTAURANT & BAKERY    210/821-5454   (62)

◇◇ ◇◇ Regional American. Casual Dining. $9-$26 **AAA Inspector Notes:** Floor-to-ceiling windows let guests enjoy the surroundings, which include woods. The aroma of luscious cakes and pastries wafts from the in-house bakery, and homemade whipped cream over strawberries is a favorite. Enjoy the live music of a jazz pianist on Saturday and harpist or classical guitar on Sunday. **Features:** full bar, Sunday brunch. **Address:** 3920 Harry Wurzbach Rd 78209 **Location:** 0.8 mi s of I-410; jct Wurzbach Rd and Oakwell Dr. (L) (D)

## DRY DOCK SEAFOOD OYSTER BAR    210/692-3959   (42)

◇◇ Seafood. Casual Dining. $8-$22 **AAA Inspector Notes:** Fresh seafood is served in simple, nautical surroundings in a landmark, boat-shaped building. Enjoy seasonal crawfish specialties and fresh, cold oysters served on the half shell. **Features:** beer & wine, patio dining. **Address:** 8522 Fredericksburg Rd 78240 **Location:** I-10 exit 561 (Wurzbach Rd), 0.5 mi s; corner of Wurzbach and Fredericksburg rds. (L) (D)

## EL JARRO DE ARTURO    210/494-5084   (19)

◇◇ ◇◇ Regional Tex-Mex. Casual Dining. $8-$16 **AAA Inspector Notes:** The large Tex-Mex restaurant serves a wide variety of specialties, including enchiladas verdes and carne asada. The friendly, attentive staff greets guests with chips and fresh-made salsa. Lunch features a wide-ranging buffet. **Features:** full bar, patio dining. **Address:** 13421 San Pedro Ave 78216 **Location:** Jct US 281 and Bitters Rd; on southwest corner; next to AAA office. (L) (D)

## ERNESTO'S GOURMET RESTAURANT    210/344-1248   (45)

◇◇ ◇◇ ◇◇ Regional Mexican Seafood Steak. Casual Dining. $8-$20 **AAA Inspector Notes:** Cozy like a neighborhood tea room, this café has candlelit dining. Feast on imaginative blends of French and Mexican cuisine. Grilled seafood dishes are brushed with one of nine specialty butter sauces. Shrimp nachos and seafood crêpes are tasty. **Features:** full bar. **Address:** 2559 Jackson-Keller Rd 78230 **Location:** I-410 exit Vance Jackson Rd, 0.3 mi n to Jackson-Keller Rd; in Corner's at Jackson Shopping Complex. (L) (D)

## FATSO'S SPORTS GARDEN    210/432-0121   (75)

◇◇ Regional Barbecue. Quick Serve. $6-$18 **AAA Inspector Notes:** I've been eating their 'que since 1968. The brisket, served with pintos and 'tato salad or slaw, is excellent. Texas-style hot wings are smothered in original wing sauce. The baby back ribs are baked in beer and then placed on a mesquite grill. Watch a volleyball tournament from the huge outdoor deck. **Features:** full bar. **Address:** 1704 Bandera Rd 78228 **Location:** I-410 exit Bandera Rd, 1.5 mi s. (L) (D) (�)

## FIRE WOK ASIAN STIR FRY    210/691-0880   (23)

◇◇ Asian. Casual Dining. $5-$12 **AAA Inspector Notes:** The great concept includes having the patrons fill an oversize bowl with a wide array of fresh ingredients, rice and sauces and letting the chef prepare the food to order. Tableside a la carte service also is available. **Address:** 11075 I-10 W, Suite 311 78230 **Location:** 0.4 mi w of Huebner Rd, off I-10 westbound access road; in Huebner Oaks Shopping Mall. (L) (D)

## FORMOSA GARDEN    210/828-9988   (51)

◇◇ ◇◇ Chinese. Casual Dining. $8-$18 **AAA Inspector Notes:** Classic. The elegant and upscale dining room offers unique presentations of Far Eastern favorites as well as attentive and friendly service. Visit the new hibachi room or the decorative sushi bar. Early bird specials are offered. **Features:** full bar. **Address:** 1011 NE Loop 410 78209 **Location:** Loop 410 westbound frontage road; between Nacogdoches Rd and Broadway St. (L) (D)

## FRANCESCA'S AT SUNSET    210/558-6500   (11)

◇◇◇ ◇◇◇

**Regional American Fine Dining $30-$60**

**AAA Inspector Notes:** The kitchen blends fresh ingredients from local specialty farms into such dramatic and distinctive dishes as seared foie gras, Wagyu rib-eye and watermelon bisque. Service is equally flawless and attentive. Enjoy striking Hill Country sunsets while you dine. **Features:** full bar. **Reservations:** suggested. **Address:** 16641 La Cantera Pkwy 78256 **Location:** I-10 exit La Cantera Pkwy, access via Loop 1604 at La Cantera Pkwy; in The Westin La Cantera Hill Country Resort. **Parking:** on-site and valet. (D)

## FREDERICK'S BISTRO    210/888-1500   (15)

◇◇◇◇ New French Fusion. Fine Dining. $15-$27 **AAA Inspector Notes:** Quiet and refined, this far-north eatery features a strong wine list and such interesting offerings as duck confit and veal piccata. **Features:** full bar, happy hour. **Address:** 14439 NW Military Hwy 78231 **Location:** Jct Huebner Rd. (L) (D)

## GOLDEN WOK CHINESE RESTAURANT    210/615-8282   (38)

◇◇ Dim Sum. Casual Dining. $6-$17 **AAA Inspector Notes:** The dramatic décor includes huge mirrors bordered with ornate dragons like those in Hong Kong. Known for the large portions, the restaurant features a chicken supreme dish, which is filled with yellow corn and colored mushrooms in a wine sauce. The egg foo yung is very good. **Features:** full bar. **Address:** 8822 Wurzbach Rd 78240 **Location:** 0.4 mi e of Fredericksburg Rd. (L) (D)

## GRADY'S BAR-B-QUE #2    210/684-2899   (59)

◇◇ Barbecue. Quick Serve. $6-$12 **AAA Inspector Notes:** The menu features South Texas smoked meats such as brisket, sausage and ribs. Dishes are served up with sides of homemade beans and potato salad. **Features:** beer & wine. **Address:** 7400 Bandera Rd 78238 **Location:** I-410 exit Bandera Rd, just n of Huebner Rd. (L) (D)

## GREY MOSS INN    210/695-8301

◇◇◇ ◇◇◇

**Steak Fine Dining $20-$49**

**AAA Inspector Notes:** Leave the city behind and relish the country inn ambience at this oak-studded Hill Country restaurant. Most entrées are mesquite grilled, including lamb chop T-bones with a rosemary wine sauce. A selection from the lengthy wine list enhances the relaxed mood. **Features:** full bar, patio dining. **Reservations:** suggested. **Address:** 19010 Scenic Loop Rd 78023 **Location:** 12 mi n of Loop 1604 on Babcock Rd to Scenic Loop Rd, then 2 mi w. *Menu on AAA.com* (D) (◁)

## IL SOGNO OSTERIA    210/223-3900   (83)

◇◇◇ Italian. Fine Dining. $10-$28 **AAA Inspector Notes:** Retro décor, a viewable kitchen and interesting, well-crafted dishes are highlights of this downtown-close osteria. **Features:** full bar, patio dining. **Reservations:** suggested. **Address:** 200 E Grayson St, Suite 100 78215 **Location:** Just w of Broadway Ave; in Historic Pearl Brewery Shopping Complex. (B) (L) (D)

## INDIA OVEN    210/366-1030   (24)

◇◇ Indian. Quick Serve. $6-$18 **AAA Inspector Notes:** This hideaway offers buffet style dining featuring a wide variety of spicy dishes loaded with flavor. Samosas, pakoras, and tandoori selections are enhanced with Mulligatawny soup, mango pudding or their refreshing garbanzo salad. This is a long time local favorite. **Features:** beer & wine. **Address:** 1031 Patricia Dr, Suite 106 78213 **Location:** Just w of jct West Ave; in Churchill West Plaza. (L) (D)

(See map & index p. 484.)

## INDIA PALACE  210/692-5262  44

◆◆◆
Indian
Quick Serve
$7-$15

**AAA Inspector Notes:** Serving the Medical Center area, this casual but dignified restaurant features authentic dishes rich with color, flavor and variety. **Features:** beer & wine. **Address:** 8474 Fredericksburg Rd 78229 **Location:** I-10 exit 561 (Wurzbach Rd), 1 mi w to Fredericksburg Rd; on southeast corner. *Menu on AAA.com*

L  D

## JACALA MEXICAN RESTAURANT  210/732-5222  78

◆◆◆ Regional Mexican. Casual Dining. $5-$12 **AAA Inspector Notes:** Dating from 1946, this is one of the oldest, originally owned Mexican restaurants in the city. A mural of the San Antonio River decorates the dining room. Spicy salsa is perfect for dipping crunchy tortilla chips. The chicken tacos with mole are authentic. **Features:** full bar. **Address:** 606 West Ave 78201 **Location:** I-10 exit West Ave, 0.3 mi s, then just n of Fredericksburg Rd.

L  D

## J. ALEXANDER'S RESTAURANT  210/824-0275  67

◆◆◆ American. Casual Dining. $8-$27 **AAA Inspector Notes:** The busy and casual restaurant prepares classic fare--including steak, grilled fish and prime rib--in the open kitchen. The dessert menu is excellent. **Features:** full bar. **Address:** 255 E Basse Rd, Suite 1300 78209 **Location:** US 281 exit Basse Rd, 0.4 mi ne; in Alamo Quarry Market.  L  D  LATE

## J. ANTHONY'S SEAFOOD CAFE  210/647-8681  81

◆ Seafood. Quick Serve. $8-$12 **AAA Inspector Notes:** Simple and attractive, this seafood café offers fresh seafood prepared in a variety of ways. The ceviche is fresh, and my grilled tilapia fillet was large. A great family value. **Address:** 7210 NW Loop 410 78238 **Location:** I-410 exit 10 northbound; exit 9B westbound; on eastbound frontage road.  L  D

## KONA GRILL  210/877-5355  13

◆◆◆ Pacific Rim. Casual Dining. $9-$30 **AAA Inspector Notes:** The eclectic menu reflects Pacific influences. In addition to noodle dishes and sushi, it lists specialties of macadamia nut chicken and lemon grass-encrusted swordfish. The dining room has a large aquarium, a private area and a sushi bar. The patio opens during warm weather. **Features:** full bar. **Address:** 15900 La Cantera Pkwy, Bldg 7 78256 **Location:** 0.5 mi n of Loop 1604; in The Shops at La Cantera.  L  D  LATE

## LA FOGATA RESTAURANT  210/340-1337  65

◆ Mexican. Casual Dining. $12-$28 **AAA Inspector Notes:** The outdoor patio has a dramatic stone fountain. Indoors you will find an attractive, brightly colored dining room set with metal chairs. Try the hearty stuffed peppers or soft enchiladas filled with gooey cheese. **Features:** full bar, patio dining, happy hour. **Address:** 2427 Vance Jackson Rd 78213 **Location:** Loop 410 exit Vance Jackson Rd, 0.8 mi s; between Loop 410 and I-10.

L  D  ⬦

## LA FONDA IN OAKHILLS  210/342-8981  64

◆ Tex-Mex. Casual Dining. $8-$20 **AAA Inspector Notes:** This longtime city landmark serves authentic Mexican dishes in a quiet and refined setting. **Features:** full bar. **Address:** 350 Northaven Dr 78210 **Location:** I-410 exit Fredericksburg Rd, just n of Loop 410.

L  D

---

Trust your vehicle to

AAA/CAA Approved

Auto Repair facilities

## LA MADELEINE COUNTRY FRENCH CAFE

◆ Traditional French. Casual Dining. $6-$12 **AAA Inspector Notes:** A fireplace creates the focal point at this cozy European style café where you can always get a quiche or savory stuffed puffed pastry on the go or stick around for a chicken crêpe or French dip sandwich. Heartier entrées like rotisserie chicken are offered and every season promises menu surprises. Whatever you decide on you probably will not get out the door without enjoying one of their tempting sweet pastries. **Bar:** wine only.

B  L  D

*For additional information, visit AAA.com*

**LOCATIONS:**

**Address:** 11745 I-10 W, Suite 101 78230 **Location:** Jct Woodstone Dr and I-10; in Huebner Oaks Shopping Center. **Phone:** 210/691-1227

**Address:** 4820 Broadway Ave 78209 **Location:** Jct Broadway and Harrigan Ct. **Phone:** 210/829-7291

**Address:** 18030 US Hwy 281 N, Suite 201 78232 **Location:** On US 281, s of Loop 1604; in Northwoods Shopping Center. **Phone:** 210/499-0208

## LION AND ROSE BRITISH RESTAURANT AND PUB  210/798-4154  47

◆◆ British. Gastropub. $8-$14 **AAA Inspector Notes:** A fun place for meals and libations, including 36 types of bottled beer. Irish, English, German and Czech draft labels are offered. Ales, lagers and guest taps can be paired with classic British food like angles on horseback, Scotch eggs, cock-a-leekie and Picadilly pastries. I tried the roasted vegetable soup and corned beef sandwich with marinated cabbage on marble rye with a Smithwick's Irish red ale. **Features:** full bar, happy hour. **Location:** I-410 exit Blanco Rd, just s; in Park North Shopping Center. **Parking:** on-site and valet.  L  D  LATE

## LOS BARRIOS MEXICAN RESTAURANT  210/732-6017  73

◆ Tex-Mex. Casual Dining. $8-$18 **AAA Inspector Notes:** One of San Antonio's premier family-owned restaurants serving a wide selection of tacos, enchiladas, fajitas, freshly made tortillas and hearty Mexican soups. **Features:** full bar. **Address:** 4223 Blanco Rd 78212 **Location:** Just s of Basse Rd.

B  L  D

## LOS PATIOS  210/655-6171  52

◆◆ Regional American. Casual Dining. $11-$21 **AAA Inspector Notes:** Set amid a canopy of oak trees, the Spanish architecture includes a gazebo with airy dining rooms. Buttery, homemade biscuits accompany such delicious entrees as Los Patios shrimp and crepes. Huge, homemade desserts are to die for. **Features:** full bar, patio dining. **Address:** 2015 NE Loop 410 78217 **Location:** I-410 exit Starcrest Dr; on westbound frontage road.

L  D

## LUBY'S

◆◆ American. Cafeteria. $6-$12 **AAA Inspector Notes:** First opened in 1947 in south Texas, this cafeteria with over 100 outlets features a wide variety of salads, fresh fruits, seafood...including crunchy shrimp...pastas, meat, poultry and just baked cakes and pies. Ask about the kids specials and Lu Ann platters...an entrée with choice of 2 vegetables and a roll. Many locations offer drive-thru service.  L  D

*For additional information, visit AAA.com*

**LOCATIONS:**

**Address:** 911 N Main Ave 78212 **Location:** I-35 exit Main St, just n. **Phone:** 210/223-1911

**Address:** 13400 San Pedro Ave 78216 **Location:** Just n of Heimer Rd. **Phone:** 210/496-2559

**Address:** 11811 W Loop 1604 N 78250 **Location:** Just w of Bandera Rd. **Phone:** 210/695-4494

**Address:** 9251 Floyd Curl Dr 78240 **Location:** Just s of Huebner Rd. **Phone:** 210/699-6652

**Address:** 4541 Fredericksburg Rd 78201 **Location:** Just s of Hillcrest Dr. **Phone:** 210/733-0372

**Address:** 2310 SW Military Dr 78224 **Location:** On southbound access road. **Phone:** 210/924-7162

**Address:** 8511 Tesoro Dr 78217 **Location:** I-410 exit Nacogdoches Rd, just off westbound access road. **Phone:** 210/930-3227

(See map & index p. 484.)

**LUCIANO'S STONE RIDGE**   210/495-0188  (1)

ᵂ ᵂ Italian. Quick Serve. $8-$18 **AAA Inspector Notes:** Little brother to Luciano's on the Riverwalk, guests are greeted by a loaded display case showing off fresh salads, pizzas, a wide variety of pasta dishes and house-made desserts. This location boasts the same extensive wine list as its Riverwalk counterpart. **Features:** full bar. **Address:** 20811 Hwy 281 N, Suite 426 78258 **Location:** US 281 exit Evans Rd; on southbound frontage road. L  D

**MAGGIANO'S LITTLE ITALY**   210/451-6000  (5)

ᵂ ᵂ ᵂ Italian. Casual Dining. $10-$25 **AAA Inspector Notes:** Diners savor scrumptious, traditional favorites served in a bustling atmosphere reminiscent of Little Italy. The dining area projects an early-20th-century feel; loud conversations bouncing off high ceilings evoke a sense of the Roaring '20s. **Features:** full bar. **Address:** 17603 I-10 W 78257 **Location:** I-10 exit The Rim; in The Rim Shopping Complex. L  D

**MAGIC TIME MACHINE**   210/828-1478  (53)

ᵂ ᵂ American. Casual Dining. $12-$40 **AAA Inspector Notes:** A costumed staff creates a boisterous party atmosphere more suited to special-occasion dinners. Super heroes prance around the dining room while you enjoy prime rib and other specialties. This is a great place for the young at heart. **Features:** full bar. **Address:** 902 NE Loop 410 78209 **Location:** I-410 exit Broadway St; on eastbound access road. D

**MAMA MARGIE'S**   210/561-0400  (33)

ᵂ Tex-Mex. Quick Serve. $5-$10 **AAA Inspector Notes:** The large, decorative restaurant features fast service, typical Tex-Mex cuisine and plenty of salsas and self-serve condiments. Margaritas are available. **Features:** beer only. **Address:** 9950 I-10 W 78230 **Location:** I-10 exit 561 (Marbach Rd), just w; on eastbound frontage road; at Colonial Square Dr. B  L  D  24

**MATAMOROS RESTAURANT AND CANTINA**   210/558-3200  (16)

ᵂ ᵂ Mexican. Casual Dining. $7-$18 **AAA Inspector Notes:** The large, pleasant dining room has a wide variety of selections and a friendly staff. **Address:** 12844 IH 10 W 78249 **Location:** I-10 exit De Zavala Rd, just w; on westbound access road. L  D

**MELA INDIAN BAR & GRILL**   210/682-1234  (70)

ᵂ ᵂ Indian. Casual Dining. $7-$13 **AAA Inspector Notes:** Sanskrit for "festival," Mela offers a new approach to Indian cuisine. The professionally designed dining room is contemporary, elegant and even suave. The menu features traditional lamb kababs and chicken tandoori enhanced with coconut, ginger, mango and secret tangy spices. There is a full bar. The staff excels at making you feel welcome and cared for. The restaurant is conveniently located just off the main city loop. An evening buffet is the only option Monday through Wednesday. **Features:** full bar. **Address:** 4987 NW Loop 410 78229 **Location:** I-410 exit 14A (Summit Pkwy); on westbound frontage road. L  D

**MENCIUS' GOURMET HUNAN CHINESE RESTAURANT**   210/615-1288  (55)

ᵂ ᵂ Regional Chinese. Casual Dining. $7-$20 **AAA Inspector Notes:** Oriental sauces are served in attractive ceramic dishes, and the dining room features black lacquer tables. The specialty is the Hunan triple delight, which consists of shrimp, chicken and beef with stir-fry vegetables. Finish your meal with an exotic Asian dessert. **Features:** full bar. **Address:** 7959 Fredericksburg Rd, Suite 147 78229 **Location:** Jct Fredericksburg Rd and Medical Dr; southwest corner; in Oakhills Center Mall. L  D

**MESON EUROPEAN DINING**   210/690-5811  (6)

ᵂ ᵂ ᵂ International. Casual Dining. $9-$24 **AAA Inspector Notes:** New creations in international cuisine are the hallmarks of this cozy restaurant in the Stone Oak area. **Features:** full bar, patio dining. **Address:** 927 N Loop 1604 E, Suite 115 78258 **Location:** Loop 1604, just w of Stone Oak Dr. L  D

**MILANO ON WURZBACH**   210/493-3611  (22)

ᵂ ᵂ ᵂ Italian. Casual Dining. $8-$27 **AAA Inspector Notes:** A bit more dressed up than its Bandera Road counterpart, the restaurant feeds diners a variety of pasta dishes, meaty-rich or buttery-light, as well as soups, salads and freshly made desserts. **Features:** full bar, Sunday brunch. **Address:** 11802 Wurzbach Rd 78230 **Location:** Just s of Lockhill-Selma Rd. L  D

**MINA & DIMI'S GREEK HOUSE RESTAURANT**   210/674-3464  (85)

ᵂ Greek. Quick Serve. $6-$12 **AAA Inspector Notes:** Zesty Greek cuisine is served by a cordial staff. A charming dining room has homemade decorations hanging on the wall. Crisp salads are covered with oils and feta. The gyro has a soft, fresh pita with tangy sauce and tender cuts of beef. Come for the buffet on Friday and the belly dancers on Saturday night. **Features:** beer & wine. **Address:** 7159 W Hwy 90 78227 **Location:** Across from Lackland AFB; at Military Dr W and US 90; entrance on SW Military Dr; in Gateway Plaza. L  D

**M J CHINA BISTRO**   210/265-5800  (26)

ᵂ ᵂ Chinese Sushi. Casual Dining. $8-$15 **AAA Inspector Notes:** Serving the Medical Center area, the restaurant offers an upscale dining experience with interesting combinations and lunch specials. The specialty is custom-made sushi dishes. **Features:** beer & wine. **Address:** 10103 Huebner Rd 78240 **Location:** Just ne of Floyd Curl Dr; in Medical Center. L  D  CALL 🄼

**PAESANO'S RISTORANTE-ALAMO QUARRY**   210/828-5191  (63)

ᵂ ᵂ ᵂ Italian. Casual Dining. $9-$30 **AAA Inspector Notes:** This is a cool place with low lighting, contemporary décor and very good food. Fresh-made pasta options include my mini cheese ravioli in a delicate cream tomato sauce, which were served with moist and satisfying veal meatballs and topped with a bright red, zesty tomato sauce. You'll find some of the best fresh-baked loaves in the city, including a crusty dark rye with nuts and fruit. **Features:** full bar. **Address:** 555 E Basse Rd, Suite 100 78209 **Location:** US 281 exit Basse Rd, 0.6 mi ne; in Alamo Quarry Market. L  D

**PAPPADEAUX SEAFOOD KITCHEN**   210/340-7143

ᵂ ᵂ Regional Seafood. Family Dining. $10-$36 **AAA Inspector Notes:** A seafood lover's delight, the restaurant taps into a little bit of New Orleans with its Cajun dishes and elaborate menu selections. Patrons might start off with a creative choice of blackened oyster and shrimp fondeaux with crayfish and let the feast begin. While music plays in the background, patrons can dig into dirty rice or spicy gumbo loaded with seafood. Well-seasoned shrimp and fish are prepared in varied ways. **Features:** full bar, patio dining, happy hour. **Address:** 76 NE Loop 410 78216 **Location:** I-410 exit McCullough Ave; on eastbound access road. L  D

**PAPPASITO'S CANTINA**   210/691-8974

ᵂ ᵂ Tex-Mex. Casual Dining. $11-$44 **AAA Inspector Notes:** Fine traditional offerings are served in an upscale cantina atmosphere. Often crowded during peak hours, the immensely popular stop dishes up generous portions of sizzling fajitas, enchiladas and other traditional Mexican favorites, including some shrimp specialties. The terrific margaritas are guaranteed to get attention. Tables in the large dining room are closely spaced. Ice cream with cinnamon on chocolate bread pudding shouldn't be missed. **Features:** full bar, happy hour. **Address:** 10501 I-10 W 78230 **Location:** I-10 exit 561 (Wurzbach Rd); between Wurzbach and Huebner rds; on westbound access road. L  D

**PERICO'S MEXICAN CUISINE**   210/402-6006  (3)

ᵂ ᵂ Tex-Mex. Casual Dining. $7-$12 **AAA Inspector Notes:** The large, hacienda-style dining room is set back on a wooded lot and decorated with hand-painted Mexican tiles and rustic artwork. The wide-ranging menu offers cheesy enchiladas, spicy chile rellenos and flavorful mole. Patio dining is available. **Features:** full bar. **Address:** 1439 E Sonterra Blvd 78258 **Location:** Just w of US 281. B  L  D

(See map & index p. 484.)

**PERRY'S STEAKHOUSE & GRILLE**   210/558-6161   88
Steak. Fine Dining. $31-$50 **AAA Inspector Notes:** Elegant décor with mahogany walls and an open kitchen design create an inviting atmosphere, but the menu, with a variety of seafood and steak entrées, is more than reason enough to stop by. Sink into the chocolate-brown leather chairs and enjoy the Chateaubriand carved tableside for two or the popular pork chops that are slow smoked and caramelized before being served with homemade apple sauce. For dessert, try the reconstructed lemon meringue pie or the Rocky Road bread pudding. **Features:** full bar, patio dining, happy hour. **Address:** 15900 LaCantera Pkwy, Suite 22200 78256 **Location:** I-10 exit 555 (La Cantera Pkwy), access via Loop 1604; at La Cantera Pkwy; in Shops at La Cantera. **Parking:** on-site and valet.  D  CALL M

**P.F. CHANG'S CHINA BISTRO**   210/507-1000   69
Chinese. Casual Dining. $5-$25 **AAA Inspector Notes:** Trendy, upscale decor provides a pleasant backdrop for New Age Chinese dining. Appetizers, soups and salads are a meal by themselves. Vegetarian plates and sides, noodles, chow meins, chicken and meat dishes are created from exotic, fresh ingredients. **Features:** full bar. **Address:** 225 E Basse Rd 78209 **Location:** US 281 exit Basse Rd, just e; in Alamo Quarry Market.  L  D

**RAFFLE'S RESTAURANT AND BAR**   210/826-7118   50
American. Casual Dining. $8-$14 **AAA Inspector Notes:** Opened in 2012, a large wooden bar dominates this restaurant, which features classic American and Tex-Mex dishes. Tortilla soup, crisp salads and spicy enchiladas are among the favorites. It's open for dinner on Tuesday, Friday and Saturday. **Features:** full bar. **Address:** 1039 NE Loop 410 78209 **Location:** I-410 exit Nacogdoches Rd; on westbound frontage road.  L

**REGENT HUNAN CHINESE RESTAURANT**
210/690-8499   36
Regional Chinese. Family Dining. $6-$12 **AAA Inspector Notes:** Casual decor, low prices and a varied menu make the neighborhood favorite worth the visit. **Address:** 5865 Babcock Rd 78240 **Location:** Just n of Huebner Rd; in Carillion Hills Shopping Center.  L  D

**ROARING FORK**   210/479-9700   8
Regional American. Fine Dining. $10-$18 **AAA Inspector Notes:** In the artistic and dramatic dining rooms patrons eat pork green chili and flavorful fish tacos along with steaks. A complete wine list is available. **Features:** full bar, patio dining, Sunday brunch. **Address:** 1806 N Loop 1604 W 78248 **Location:** Just w of Huebner Rd; on eastbound access road; in Plaza Las Campanas.  L  D  CALL M

**ROME'S PIZZA**   210/691-2070   17

Italian
Pizza
Quick Serve
$7-$14

*Menu on AAA.com*

**AAA Inspector Notes:** A San Antonio family favorite, the casual restaurant uses quality ingredients in its strombolis, calzones, salads, subs and pizzas. **Features:** beer & wine. **Address:** 5999 De Zavala Rd 78249 **Location:** I-10 exit 558 (De Zavala Rd), 0.4 mi s to Cogburn Dr; in Post Office Central Plaza.  L  D

Get There Better
*TripTik® Travel Planner*
AAA.com and CAA.ca

**SALTGRASS STEAKHOUSE**
Steak. Casual Dining. $9-$31 **AAA Inspector Notes:** Those looking for something different should try the comfortable steakhouse, which never says no to a special request. Born from the spirit of Texas cattle drives, the restaurant resembles a Texas lodge, with high ceilings and mounted animal heads. Baby back ribs are so tender the meat falls off the bone. Also on the menu are hearty steaks, prime rib, chicken, seafood and yummy desserts. **Bar:** full bar. SAVE  L  D

*For additional information, visit AAA.com*
**LOCATIONS:**
**Address:** 11745 I-10 W 78230 **Location:** I-10 exit 560 (Huebner Rd) westbound; exit 559 eastbound; in Huebner Oaks Shopping Center. **Phone:** 210/641-6447   21
**Address:** 16910 US 281 N 78232 **Location:** US 281 exit Thousand Oaks/Mecca; on northbound access road. **Phone:** 210/402-6621   12

**SARIKA'S THAI AND SUSHI**   210/877-0888   34
Thai. Quick Serve. $8-$14 **AAA Inspector Notes:** The sister property to longtime city landmark Sarika's, this casual restaurant offers traditional Thai cuisine. The fresh sushi is decorated with a whimsical use of garnish. Don't be surprised to be served by Sarika herself. **Address:** 9620 Huebner Rd, Suite 109 78240 **Location:** Just nw of jct Babcock Rd.  L  D

**SARIKA'S THAI RESTAURANT**   210/692-3200   54
Thai. Casual Dining. $8-$15 **AAA Inspector Notes:** Tucked into a small corner of an office complex, the casual dining room offers a surprisingly varied array of Thai dishes. **Features:** beer & wine. **Address:** 4319 Medical Dr 78229 **Location:** Just w of Fredericksburg Rd; in Medical Park Plaza Mall.  L  D

**SAROVAR INDIAN CUISINE**   210/558-8289   30
Indian. Quick Serve. $11-$16 **AAA Inspector Notes:** Authentic Indian cuisine is featured at the complete lunchtime buffet. Beware, some dishes are very spicy, but the wide variety and exotic ingredients promise a realistic Indian feast. The dinner menu is à la carte. **Features:** beer & wine. **Address:** 10227 Ironside Dr 78230 **Location:** I-10 exit 561 (Wurzbach Rd), just n on Wurzbach Rd to Ironside Dr, then just e.  L  D

**SCENIC LOOP CAFE & BAR**   210/687-1818
Regional American. Casual Dining. $10-$30 **AAA Inspector Notes:** Located northwest in the beautiful Texas Hill country, by day the eatery is a casual family place offering burgers to scallops; by night it's a hot-spot with dancing on the outdoor terrace. **Features:** full bar, patio dining, Sunday brunch. **Address:** 25615 Boerne Stage Rd 78255 **Location:** Just nw of Boerne Stage Rd; jct Scenic Loop Rd.  L  D  CALL M

**SEA ISLAND SHRIMP HOUSE**   210/342-7771   48
Seafood. Family Dining. $6-$14 **AAA Inspector Notes:** This cavernous dining room is a casual place to enjoy excellent seafood. Some whole-fish selections are available. **Features:** beer & wine. **Address:** 322 W Rector St 78216 **Location:** I-410 exit San Pedro Ave, 0.4 mi s, then just e.  L  D

**SEA ISLAND SHRIMP HOUSE**   210/921-9700   87
Regional American. Casual Dining. $6-$14 **AAA Inspector Notes:** A wide variety of fresh seafood, including whole fish, is offered. **Features:** beer & wine. **Address:** 2119 SW Military Dr 78224 **Location:** I-35 exit Military Dr, just w.  L  D

**SEA ISLAND SHRIMP HOUSE I-10 W**   210/558-8989   25
Regional Seafood. Family Dining. $8-$22 **AAA Inspector Notes:** Although shrimp gets the mention in the restaurant's name, the menu also includes fresh fish fillets, oysters, soups and salads. The specialty is actually whole fish. **Features:** beer & wine. **Address:** 4323 Amerisuites Dr 78230 **Location:** I-10 exit 562 (Wurzbach Rd), on westbound frontage road.  L  D

**SHOGUN STEAKHOUSE RESTAURANT**   210/696-8638   46
Japanese. Casual Dining. $8-$15 **AAA Inspector Notes:** Featuring teppan-style and traditional seating, this longtime favorite is known for freshly prepared dishes and lively chef interactions. Brunch on Saturday and Sunday. **Features:** full bar, Sunday brunch. **Address:** 5500 Babcock Rd 78240 **Location:** Just w on Eckert Rd; in Northgate Village Mall.  D

(See map & index p. 484.)

### SILO ELEVATED CUISINE ALAMO HEIGHTS
210/824-8686   72

New World. Fine Dining. $10-$30 **AAA Inspector Notes:** Refined New World dishes include bisques, sirloin Asian salads, seared tuna, double chops and small tasting plates, all flavored with fresh herbs and seasonings. Among other good choices are spring rolls and top-quality ahi tuna. **Features:** full bar. **Reservations:** suggested. **Address:** 1133 Austin Hwy 78209 **Location:** I-410 exit 561 (Wurzbach Rd), 1.4 mi s to Austin Hwy, then 1.8 mi s.   L  D

### SILO ELEVATED CUISINE AND BAR-LOOP 1604
210/483-8989   9

New World. Fine Dining. $18-$50 **AAA Inspector Notes:** The name hints at the second-floor location as well as a higher style of dining. Duck, oysters, 32-day-aged prime rib-eyes and foie gras all are prepared in original methods that layer gentle flavors, aromas and textures. **Features:** full bar, Sunday brunch. **Address:** 434 N Loop 1604 W 78232 **Location:** Loop 1604 exit Blanco St; on eastbound access road; in Ventura Plaza Mall.   L  D

### SOMPONG'S THAI & CHINESE CUISINE   210/614-0845   49

Thai. Quick Serve. $8-$15 **AAA Inspector Notes:** Just off Fredericksburg Road in the Medical Center area, the restaurant pleases patrons with exciting Thai and Chinese dishes in a quiet, relaxed atmosphere. **Features:** beer & wine. **Address:** 8110 Fredericksburg Rd 78229 **Location:** Just n of jct Medical Center Dr.   L  D

### THE SPAGHETTI WAREHOUSE   210/299-1114

Italian. Casual Dining. $6-$16 **AAA Inspector Notes:** The Italian-style restaurant chain sustains a festive family atmosphere. All entrees include bottomless tossed salad or soup. Patrons enjoy plentiful portions of such classic dishes as ravioli, lasagna, baked penne or the richly flavored cannelloni Florentine. Splurging on one of the many desserts, such as tiramisu, espresso mousse cake or carrot cake, is worthwhile. **Features:** full bar. **Address:** 1226 E Houston St 78205 **Location:** US 281/I-37 exit 141 (Commerce St/downtown) northbound, just n on Chestnut, then just e; exit 141B (Houston St) southbound, just e.   L  D

### SUN CHINESE BUFFET   210/678-0863   86

Chinese. Quick Serve. $7-$10 **AAA Inspector Notes:** Convenient to Lackland and Kelly Air Force Base, this Chinese buffet has a chef's station where fresh cuts of beef, chicken and seafood are prepared. Accompanying these are the varied soups, rice dishes and desserts on the buffet tables. **Features:** beer & wine. **Address:** 7121 W US 90 78227 **Location:** Across from Lackland AFB at Military Dr W and US 90; in Gateway Plaza; entrance off Military Dr.   L  D

### SUSHIHANA CONTEMPORARY JAPANESE
210/340-7808   37

Sushi. Casual Dining. $15-$30 **AAA Inspector Notes:** The modern, California-style sushi house offers a wide assortment of fresh seafood, chicken, beef and vegetarian rolls with side dishes of rice, vegetables and tofu in dazzling presentations. **Features:** beer & wine, happy hour. **Address:** 1810 NW Military Hwy, Suite B 78213 **Location:** I-410 E exit NW Military Hwy, 0.7 mi n.   L  D

### SUSTENIO   210/598-2950   4

Regional Mexican Fine Dining $14-$48

**AAA Inspector Notes:** Inspired by celebrity chef Stephen Pyles, this is imaginative and artistic haute cuisine in a modern elegant setting served by a knowledgeable and well-trained staff. My gazpacho was aromatic, refreshing and flavorful. The salmon confit featured crisp skin and clean flavor throughout. **Features:** full bar. **Reservations:** suggested. **Address:** 17103 La Cantera Pkwy 78256 **Location:** I-10 exit 554 (La Cantera Pkwy), just w; in Eilan office/shopping complex; in Eilan Hotel Resort & Spa. **Parking:** valet only.   B  L  D

### TEXAS LAND AND CATTLE STEAKHOUSE

Regional Steak. Family Dining. $7-$27 **AAA Inspector Notes:** A variety of large Prime steaks, delicious salads and scrumptious desserts await you at the friendly Texas ranch-style restaurant. Try the signature slow-smoked sirloin, which never fails to please, or the Caesar salad, another favorite. A Texas steakhouse means everything is bigger, from large cuts and oversize salads to potatoes and side dishes. Those not in the mood for beef can opt for chicken, quail or seafood. Dessert is an occasion. **Bar:** full bar.   L  D

*For additional information. visit AAA.com*

**LOCATIONS:**
**Address:** 60 NE Loop 410 78216 **Location:** I-410 exit McCullough Ave; on eastbound access lane. **Phone:** 210/342-4477
**Address:** 9911 W IH-10 78230 **Location:** I-10 exit 561 (Wurzbach Rd); on westbound access road. **Phone:** 210/699-8744

### TEXAS PRIDE BARBEQUE   210/649-3730

Regional Barbecue. Quick Serve. $7-$16 **AAA Inspector Notes:** Take it from this 23-year veteran AAA inspector: This place serves some of the very best 'que in the county. It's worth driving out to this converted 1950s gas station—now a casual barbecue shack—for the most tender, moist and meaty ribs, brisket and sausages. **Features:** full bar, patio dining. **Address:** 2980 E Loop 1604 78101 **Location:** On Loop 1604; between I-10 and US 87.   L  D

### THAI BISTRO & SUSHI   210/558-6707   18

Thai. Casual Dining. $8-$16 **AAA Inspector Notes:** Guests of this restaurant are greeted at the door by the owner. Most dishes come with a choice of tofu, chicken, beef or pork. The Thai teas are refreshing. **Features:** beer & wine. **Address:** 5999 De Zavala Rd 78249 **Location:** I-10 exit 558 (De Zavala Rd), 0.6 mi w.   L  D

### THAI CORNER   210/615-8424   43

Thai. Casual Dining. $7-$12 **AAA Inspector Notes:** Casual yet authentic dishes, including restorative consommé, spicy pad thai and crispy spring rolls, are popular selections. **Features:** beer & wine, patio dining. **Address:** 8498 Fredericksburg Rd 78229 **Location:** Jct Wurzbach Rd.   L  D

### THAI TOPAZ   210/690-6000   35

Thai. Quick Serve. $7-$9 **AAA Inspector Notes:** Near the Medical Center area, this small and casual family-operated restaurant features healthful selections prepared without monosodium glutamate. Light lunch options include soup. **Address:** 9386 Huebner Rd 78240 **Location:** Jct Floyd Curl Dr.   L  D

### TOKYO STEAKHOUSE   210/341-4461   40

Japanese. Family Dining. $13-$47 **AAA Inspector Notes:** You will get your share of food and entertainment at this restaurant. A quirky, talented chef cooks large portions of fried rice, shrimp, chicken and beef at your table. The full sushi bar offers colorful entrées of fresh seafood and shrimp stir-fry. **Features:** full bar. **Reservations:** suggested. **Address:** 9405 San Pedro Ave 78216 **Location:** Loop 410 exit San Pedro Ave N, 0.3 mi n.   L  D

### TOMATILLOS CAFE Y CANTINA   210/824-3005   80

Regional Mexican. Casual Dining. $8-$16 **AAA Inspector Notes:** This cantina makes all of its Tex-Mex cuisine from scratch. The interior is brightly colored like a Mexican fiesta. While you wait for your meal, munch on chips and spicy salsa. The specialty quesadillas are filled with fresh meat, chicken and cheese. **Features:** full bar, patio dining, happy hour. **Address:** 3210 Broadway St 78209 **Location:** US 281 exit Hildebrand Ave, 0.5 mi e to Broadway St, then 0.7 mi s.   L  D

### TURQUOISE GRILL   210/736-2887   68

Turkish Vegetarian. Casual Dining. $9-$17 **AAA Inspector Notes:** A friendly, knowledgeable staff serves a wide selection of fresh-made house specialties, including many vegetarian selections. The dining room features Turkish décor. **Address:** 3720 NW Loop 410 78229 **Location:** Loop 410 exit Fredericksburg Rd; on eastbound frontage road.   L  D

(See map & index p. 484.)

TWIN SISTERS BAKERY & CAFE               210/822-0761  (71)
♦♦ ♦♦ Regional American. Casual Dining. $8-$18 **AAA Inspector Notes:** Light, healthy selections with an emphasis on some vegetarian dishes, including vegetable lasagna, are on the menu. Check out the daily specials. This place is also well known for fresh delightful pastries. **Features:** beer & wine. **Address:** 6322 N New Braunfels Ave 78209 **Location:** In Alamo Heights; just n of Broadway St. [B] [L] [D]

TWO BROS. BBQ MARKET                     210/496-0222  (20)
♦♦ ♦♦ Barbecue. Quick Serve. $8-$15 **AAA Inspector Notes:** One of local celebrity chef Jason Dady's restaurants, this authentic south Texas barbecue shack serves wide variety of smoked meats and classic side dishes. Beverages include grape Kool-Aid. **Features:** beer & wine. **Address:** 12656 West Ave 78216 **Location:** Just n of w Nakoma Dr. [L] [D]

VAN'S CHINESE SEAFOOD RESTAURANT
                                         210/828-8449  (79)
♦♦ ♦♦ Chinese. Casual Dining. $7-$19 **AAA Inspector Notes:** Homemade Chinese and Vietnamese cuisine is served at this friendly restaurant. The garlic chicken is very sweet and served with white rice, and the egg drop soup is very spicy. The wine list is extensive. **Features:** beer & wine. **Address:** 3214 Broadway St 78209 **Location:** Just n of E Mulberry Ave; opposite Brackenridge City Park. [L] [D]

ZIO'S ITALIAN KITCHEN                    210/697-7222
♦♦ ♦♦ Italian. Casual Dining. $6-$18 **AAA Inspector Notes:** The warm, comfortable atmosphere and Old World decor complement the menu. Meals are a good value, and so is the service. This small chain specializes in Italian cuisine, including oven-baked pizzas and pasta dishes. Guests are encouraged to get creative with their pizzas by mixing and matching from a list of 24 toppings. Particularly tempting dishes are Artichoke spinach pasta, chicken parmigiana, and Shrimp Limone. **Features:** full bar. **Address:** 12858 W I-10 78249 **Location:** I-10 exit 558 (De Zavala Rd); just n; on eastbound access road. [L] [D]

## SAN BENITO (I-8) pop. 24,250, elev. 36'

**FREDDY FENDER MUSEUM** is at 210 E. Heywood St. On display are awards, guitars, amplifiers and a Harley-Davidson belonging to the legendary musician and San Benito native. Visitors also can view several photographs from Fender's early years. **Time:** Allow 30 minutes minimum. **Hours:** Thurs.-Sat. 10-4. **Cost:** $3; free (ages 0-9). Cash only. **Phone:** (956) 361-3800.

**BEST WESTERN GARDEN INN & SUITES**
                                         (956)361-2222

♦♦ ♦♦
Motel
$63-$160

**AAA Benefit:** Members save 10% or more with Best Western!

**Address:** 175 W Expwy 83 78586 **Location:** US 77 and 83 exit Sam Houston Blvd; on southbound access road. **Facility:** 43 units. 2 stories (no elevator), exterior corridors. **Pool(s):** outdoor. **Activities:** limited exercise equipment. **Guest Services:** coin laundry.

[SAVE] CALL [&M] [➔] [BIZ] [HS] [📶]
[🛏] [🖨] [🖵]

---

Explore on-the-go travel tools at
AAA.com/mobile or CAA.ca/mobile

---

WHERE TO EAT

LONGHORN CATTLE COMPANY BARBEQUE & STEAK RESTAURANT                               956/399-4400
♦♦ Steak Barbecue. Quick Serve. $6-$22 **AAA Inspector Notes:** Visit the enormous screened porch decorated with mounted longhorns. Western relics cover the walls, and ceiling fans twirl above. Guests are greeted with a spicy cup of pintos at their table. Texas barbecue is the specialty at this bustling eatery. **Features:** beer & wine, patio dining. **Address:** 3055 W Expwy 83 78586 **Location:** US 83 exit Paseo Real Hwy, 0.5 mi e; on eastbound access road. [L] [D]

## SAN MARCOS (F-8) pop. 44,894, elev. 581'
• Hotels p. 532 • Restaurants p. 532

One mile northwest of San Marcos are the headwaters of the San Marcos River at Aquarena Springs. Created by the Balcones Fault, the San Marcos Springs, from which the river flows, produce 150 million gallons of ice-cold water daily. San Marcos is the input point for the Texas Water Safari, a 260-mile, nonstop canoe race to the Gulf town of Seadrift. The record for this grueling race is 29 hours, 46 minutes.

**San Marcos Convention and Visitors Bureau:** 617 I-35 N., San Marcos, TX 78666. **Phone:** (512) 393-5930 or (888) 200-5620.

**Shopping areas:** Bargain shopping is popular at Prime Outlets and [SAVE] Tanger Outlet Center, both at I-35 exit 200.

**AQUARENA CENTER** is off I-35 exit 206, then w. to 929 Aquarena Springs Dr. Glass-bottom boats take visitors over the San Marcos Springs, which produce 150 million gallons of artesian water a day. The Natural Aquarium displays endangered species, and a wetlands walkway, nature trails and historic sites are on the grounds. Spring Lake Hall, next to Spring Lake at the headwaters of the San Marcos River, features interactive exhibits about Texas' waterways.

**Time:** Allow 3 hours minimum. **Hours:** Grounds daily dawn-dusk. Boat tours depart 10-6, late May-Labor Day; 10-5, rest of year. Spring Lake Hall daily 10-5. **Cost:** Aquarium, grounds and exhibit center free. Boat tour $9; $7.50 (ages 60+); $6 (ages 4-15). **Phone:** (512) 245-7570. [📅]

**WONDER WORLD PARK** is at 1000 Prospect St. One of the largest earthquake-formed caves in the United States, this underground labyrinth was discovered in 1893. A 90-minute guided tour includes the Balcones Fault Line Cave, the Tejas Observation Tower, the Anti-Gravity House and a train ride through the Wildlife Park, where visitors can feed native and exotic deer and other animals.

**Hours:** Daily 8-8, June-Aug.; Mon.-Fri. 9-5, Sat.-Sun. 9-6, rest of year. Tours depart every 15 minutes. Last admission 1 hour, 30 minutes before closing. **Cost:** All-inclusive admission $19.95; $14.95 (ages 6-11 and 65+); $12.95 (active military with ID); $8.50 (ages 3-5). **Phone:** (512) 392-3760.

## BEST WESTERN SAN MARCOS          (512)754-7557

Hotel
$92-$142

**AAA Benefit:** Members save 10% or more with Best Western!

**Address:** 917 I-35 N 78666 **Location:** I-35 exit 204B; on west side frontage road. **Facility:** 50 units. 2 stories (no elevator), interior corridors. **Pool(s):** outdoor. **Guest Services:** coin laundry.

## COMFORT SUITES NEAR TEXAS STATE UNIVERSITY
(512)392-1006

Hotel
$100-$220

**Address:** 104 I-35 N 78666 **Location:** I-35 exit 204B; on east frontage road. **Facility:** 53 units. 3 stories, interior corridors. **Pool(s):** outdoor. **Activities:** hot tub, exercise room. **Guest Services:** valet and coin laundry. **Featured Amenity: full hot breakfast.**

## COUNTRY INN & SUITES BY CARLSON          (512)392-8111

 Hotel $94-$159 **Address:** 1560 IH-35 S 78666 **Location:** I-35 exit 202; on west frontage road. **Facility:** 84 units. 4 stories, interior corridors. **Terms:** cancellation fee imposed. **Pool(s):** heated indoor. **Activities:** hot tub, exercise room. **Guest Services:** coin laundry.

## DAYS INN          (512)353-5050

Hotel
$55-$100

**Address:** 1005 I-35 N 78666 **Location:** I-35 exit 205 northbound; exit 204B southbound, jct SR 80; on southbound frontage road. **Facility:** 61 units. 2 stories (no elevator), exterior corridors. **Terms:** cancellation fee imposed. **Pool(s):** outdoor. **Featured Amenity: continental breakfast.**

## ECONO LODGE          (512)353-5300

Hotel
$45-$130

**Address:** 811 S Guadalupe St 78666 **Location:** I-35 exit 204 northbound; exit 204A southbound; on west frontage road. **Facility:** 54 units, some kitchens. 2 stories (no elevator), exterior corridors. **Pool(s):** outdoor. **Featured Amenity: continental breakfast.**

## EMBASSY SUITES-SAN MARCOS HOTEL, SPA AND CONFERENCE CENTER          512/392-6450

 Hotel. Rates not provided. **Address:** 1001 E McCarty Ln 78666 **Location:** I-35 exit 201; on east frontage road. **Facility:** 283 units. 10 stories, interior corridors. **Amenities:** safes. **Dining:** Rocky River Grill, see separate listing. **Pool(s):** heated outdoor. **Activities:** hot tub, exercise room, spa. **Guest Services:** valet and coin laundry, area transportation.

**AAA Benefit:** Members save 5% or more!

## HAMPTON INN & SUITES SAN MARCOS          (512)754-7707

 Hotel $139-$299 **Address:** 106 I-35 N 78666 **Location:** I-35 exit 204; on northbound frontage road. **Facility:** 90 units. 4 stories, interior corridors. **Terms:** 1-7 night minimum stay, cancellation fee imposed. **Pool(s):** heated outdoor. **Activities:** exercise room. **Guest Services:** valet and coin laundry.

**AAA Benefit:** Members save up to 10%!

## LA QUINTA INN SAN MARCOS          (512)392-8800

 Hotel $79-$150 **Address:** 1619 I-35 N 78666 **Location:** I-35 exit 206 southbound, 0.5 mi s; on west frontage road; exit northbound, 1 mi n to turnaround to west frontage road, then 1.5 mi s. **Facility:** 117 units. 2 stories, interior/exterior corridors. **Amenities:** video games. **Pool(s):** outdoor.

## RAMADA LIMITED          (512)395-8000

Hotel
$60-$160

**Address:** 1701 I-35 N 78666 **Location:** I-35 exit 206 southbound, 0.4 mi s on west frontage road; exit northbound, 1 mi n to turnaround for west frontage road, then 1.4 mi s. **Facility:** 38 units. 2 stories (no elevator), exterior corridors. **Terms:** cancellation fee imposed. **Pool(s):** outdoor. **Guest Services:** valet and coin laundry. **Featured Amenity: continental breakfast.**

## RODEWAY INN          (512)353-8011

Hotel $40-$150 **Address:** 1635 Aquarena Springs Dr 78666 **Location:** I-35 exit 206, 0.5 mi s. **Facility:** 95 units. 2 stories (no elevator), exterior corridors. **Pool(s):** outdoor.

## SAN MARCOS HOTEL & SUITES          (512)754-6621

Hotel $109-$159 **Address:** 108 I-35 N 78666 **Location:** I-35 exit 204A southbound; exit 204 northbound; on east frontage road. **Facility:** 105 units. 3 stories, interior corridors. **Pool(s):** outdoor. **Activities:** exercise room. **Guest Services:** valet and coin laundry.

## TRAVELODGE SAN MARCOS          (512)396-5665

Hotel
$59-$89

**Address:** 1611 I-35 N 78666 **Location:** I-35 exit 206; on southbound frontage road. **Facility:** 54 units. 2 stories (no elevator), exterior corridors. **Pool(s):** outdoor. **Featured Amenity: continental breakfast.**

## WHERE TO EAT

## PALMER'S RESTAURANT BAR & COURTYARD          512/353-3500

Seafood Steak. Casual Dining. $10-$29 **AAA Inspector Notes:** The dining room nurtures a rustic, homey atmosphere, while the courtyard has a comfortable, breezy feel. On the varied menu are pasta, Tex-Mex, seafood and premium Angus beef dishes. **Features:** full bar, Sunday brunch. **Address:** 218 W Moore St 78666 **Location:** I-35 exit 205, 1.6 mi w on CR 12 to Hutchinson St.

ROCKY RIVER GRILL   512/392-6450

WWWW American. Casual Dining. $8-$32 **AAA Inspector Notes:** The nicely varied menu lists upscale presentations, including both steaks and lighter fare for lunch and dinner. **Features:** full bar. **Address:** 1001 E McCarty Ln 78666 **Location:** I-35 exit 201; on east frontage road; in Embassy Suites-San Marcos Hotel, Spa and Conference Center. [L] [D] CALL [&M]

SALTGRASS STEAKHOUSE   512/396-5255

WW Steak. Casual Dining. $8-$30 **AAA Inspector Notes:** Those looking for something different should try the comfortable steakhouse, which never says no to a special request. Born from the spirit of Texas cattle drives, the restaurant resembles a Texas lodge, with high ceilings and mounted animal heads. Baby back ribs are so tender the meat falls off the bone. Also on the menu are hearty steaks, prime rib, chicken, seafood and yummy desserts. **Features:** full bar, happy hour. **Address:** 100 Sessoms Dr 78666 **Location:** I-35 exit 206, 1.1 mi w to Sessoms Dr, then just n.

[SAVE] [L] [D]

SAN MARCOS RIVER PUB & GRILL   512/353-3747

WW American. Casual Dining. $8-$15 **AAA Inspector Notes:** The rustic riverfront restaurant offers indoor and outdoor seating. On the menu is a good selection of appetizers, salads, steaks, seafood, chicken and pasta, as well as such lighter fare as burgers, chicken and club sandwiches and tacos. Portions are generous. **Features:** full bar. **Address:** 701 Cheatham St 78666 **Location:** I-35 exit 204, 0.3 mi n on FM 82/12 to Cheatham St, then 0.6 mi e.

[L] [D] [LATE] CALL [&M] [↘]

## SCHERTZ pop. 31,465
• **Part of San Antonio area — see map p. 458**

FAIRFIELD INN & SUITES BY MARRIOTT   (210)658-1466

WWWW Hotel $113-$179 **Address:** 5008 Corridor Loop Rd 78154 **Location:** I-35 exit 175 (Natural Bridge Cavern Rd); just off northbound frontage road. **Facility:** 118 units. 5 stories, interior corridors. **Pool(s):** heated outdoor. **Activities:** hot tub, exercise room. **Guest Services:** valet and coin laundry.

**AAA Benefit:** Members save 5% or more!

[icons] /SOME UNITS

HAMPTON INN & SUITES   (210)566-6110

WWWW Hotel $89-$129 **Address:** 17702 IH-35 N 78154 **Location:** I-35 exit 175 (Natural Bridge Cavern Rd); just off northbound frontage road. **Facility:** 98 units. 4 stories, interior corridors. **Terms:** 1-7 night minimum stay, cancellation fee imposed. **Amenities:** video games. **Pool(s):** outdoor. **Activities:** exercise room. **Guest Services:** valet and coin laundry.

**AAA Benefit:** Members save up to 10%!

[icons] /SOME UNITS

LA QUINTA INN & SUITES   (210)655-2700

WWWW Hotel $94-$159 **Address:** 17650 4 Oaks Ln 78154 **Location:** I-35 exit 175 (Natural Bridge Cavern Rd), just w. Located behind Walmart. **Facility:** 81 units. 4 stories, interior corridors. **Pool(s):** outdoor. **Activities:** hot tub, exercise room. **Guest Services:** valet and coin laundry.

[icons] /SOME UNITS

### WHERE TO EAT

BILL MILLER BAR-B-Q   210/659-5514

W Barbecue. Quick Serve. $6-$11 **AAA Inspector Notes:** The relaxed, family-focused barbecue restaurant prepares ribs, chicken, brisket, turkey and sausage for sandwiches or plates. **Address:** 17600 IH-35 N 78154 **Location:** I-35 exit 174B (CR 3009), just n.

[B] [L] [D]

## SCHULENBURG (F-9) pop. 2,852

Schulenburg was founded in the mid-19th century by German, Austrian and Czech settlers. The town was named for Louis Schulenburg, who donated land for construction of the Southern Pacific Railroad in 1873. The Schulenburg Oil Mill, said to be the longest continuously operating cottonseed mill, ran from 1883 until the 1950s.

**STANZEL MODEL AIRCRAFT MUSEUM** is off I-10 exit 674, then 2 mi. s. on US 77 to 311 Baumgarten St. Schulenburg natives Victor and Joe Stanzel began building airplane models after Charles Lindbergh's flight across the Atlantic in 1927. The brothers designed the Tiger Shark, the first controlline model airplane kit, and eventually opened a toy company.

The museum houses interactive exhibits and displays; the family farmhouse is open to the public. The Stanzel Brothers Factory Museum displays machinery. **Time:** Allow 30 minutes minimum. **Hours:** Mon., Wed. and Fri.-Sat. 10:30-4:30. Closed major holidays. **Cost:** $4; $2 (ages 65+); free (ages 0-12). **Phone:** (979) 743-6559.

BEST WESTERN PLUS SCHULENBURG INN & SUITES   (979)743-2030

WWWW Hotel $119-$159

**AAA Benefit:** Members save 10% or more with Best Western!

**Address:** 101 Huser Blvd 78956 **Location:** I-10 exit 674, just s. **Facility:** 52 units. 3 stories, interior corridors. **Pool(s):** heated outdoor. **Activities:** hot tub, exercise room. **Guest Services:** coin laundry. **Featured Amenity:** full hot breakfast.

[icons] /SOME UNITS

## SEABROOK pop. 11,952
• **Restaurants p. 534**
• **Part of Houston area — see map p. 301**

COMFORT INN & SUITES-NASA CLEARLAKE   (281)326-3301

WWWW Hotel $89-$159 **Address:** 2901 NASA Pkwy 77586 **Location:** 1 mi w of jct W SR 146. **Facility:** 49 units. 3 stories, interior corridors. **Amenities:** safes. **Pool(s):** heated indoor. **Activities:** exercise room. **Guest Services:** valet and coin laundry.

[icons] /SOME UNITS

COMFORT SUITES SEABROOK   (281)291-9090

WWW Hotel $89-$150

**Address:** 5755 Bayport Blvd 77586 **Location:** 1.5 mi n on SR 146. **Facility:** 86 units. 3 stories, interior corridors. **Pool(s):** outdoor. **Activities:** exercise room. **Guest Services:** valet and coin laundry, area transportation. **Featured Amenity:** full hot breakfast.

[icons] /SOME UNITS

HAMPTON INN NASA/JOHNSON SPACE CENTER HOUSTON
(281)532-9200

WWWW Hotel $109-$179 **Address:** | **AAA Benefit:**
3000 NASA Pkwy 77586 **Location:** 1 mi | Members save up to
w of jct SR 146. **Facility:** 70 units. 3 sto- | 10%!
ries, interior corridors. **Terms:** 1-7 night
minimum stay, cancellation fee imposed.
**Pool(s):** outdoor. **Activities:** exercise room. **Guest Services:** valet
laundry.

LA QUINTA INN & SUITES HOUSTON NASA SEABROOK
(281)326-7300

WWWW Hotel $105-$154 **Address:** 3636 NASA Pkwy 77586 **Location:** I-45 exit 25 (NASA Rd 1), 6 mi e; SR 146, 2 mi w. **Facility:**
54 units. 3 stories, interior corridors. **Pool(s):** outdoor. **Activities:** hot
tub, exercise room. **Guest Services:** valet and coin laundry.

QUALITY INN & SUITES
(281)326-7200

WWWW Hotel $90-$299 **Address:** 2720 NASA Rd 1 77586 **Location:** Jct SR 146 and NASA Rd 1, 0.6 mi w. **Facility:** 60 units. 2
stories, interior corridors. **Amenities:** safes. **Pool(s):** outdoor. **Activities:** exercise room. **Guest Services:** coin laundry.

SPRINGHILL SUITES BY MARRIOTT HOUSTON/NASA/
SEABROOK
(281)474-3456

WWWW Hotel $109-$249 **Address:** | **AAA Benefit:**
2120 NASA Pkwy 77586 **Location:** Jct | Members save 5%
SR 146 and NASA Rd 1, just w. **Facility:** | or more!
88 units. 3 stories, interior corridors.
**Pool(s):** outdoor. **Activities:** exercise
room. **Guest Services:** valet and coin laundry.

### WHERE TO EAT

VILLA CAPRI
281/326-2373

WW Italian. Casual Dining. $7-$30 **AAA Inspector Notes:** This
renovated home is set amid a boat dock and a Roman-style garden.
Seafood entrées include stuffed ravioli in a savory crabmeat sauce
and scampi piccata soaked in a buttery garlic-herb sauce. A salad
bar, specialty sauces and outdoor seating are among the other highlights. **Features:** full bar, patio dining, Sunday brunch. **Address:**
3713 NASA Pkwy 77586 **Location:** 1.5 mi w of SR 146.
L D

## SEAGOVILLE pop. 14,835
• Part of Dallas area — see map p. 161

BEST WESTERN EXECUTIVE INN
(972)287-9100

WWW | **AAA Benefit:** Members
Hotel | save 10% or more with
$66-$90 | Best Western!

**Address:** 1910 N US Hwy 175 75159
**Location:** US 175 exit Seagoville
Rd/Kaufman St; on westbound frontage
road. **Facility:** 49 units. 2 stories (no elevator), interior corridors. **Amenities:**
safes. **Pool(s):** outdoor. **Guest Services:** coin laundry.

## SEALY pop. 6,019

AMERICAS BEST VALUE INN OF SEALY (979)885-3707

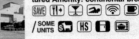

WWW
Hotel
$70-$95

**Address:** 2107 Hwy 36 S 77474 **Location:** I-10 exit 720. **Facility:** 66 units. 2
stories (no elevator), exterior corridors.
**Terms:** 3 day cancellation notice-fee imposed. **Pool(s):** outdoor. **Activities:** hot
tub. **Guest Services:** coin laundry. **Featured Amenity: continental breakfast.**

SUPER 8
(979)885-2121

WWW
Hotel
$80-$160

**Address:** 267 Gebhardt Rd 77474 **Lo-
cation:** I-10 exit 720. **Facility:** 50 units.
2 stories (no elevator), exterior corridors.
**Pool(s):** outdoor. **Activities:** hot tub.
**Guest Services:** coin laundry. **Featured
Amenity: continental breakfast.**

### WHERE TO EAT

HINZE'S BAR-B-QUE
979/885-7808

W Barbecue. Quick Serve. $4-$13 **AAA Inspector Notes:** The
homey eatery is a great place to stop for a fast but mouthwatering
meal of pork ribs, bacon cheeseburger or fried catfish. Lighter eaters
will appreciate the numerous vegetable sides. Homemade pies melt
in the mouth. **Features:** beer only. **Address:** 2101 Hwy 36 S 77474
**Location:** I-10 exit 720. L D

MARIBELLI ITALIAN RISTORANTE
979/627-7665

WW Italian. Casual Dining. $6-$21 **AAA Inspector Notes:** In
addition to the expected pizza and pasta dishes, the restaurant prepares chicken, veal, seafood and steak entrees in its pleasing setting.
**Features:** full bar. **Address:** 2352 S Hwy 36 77474 **Location:** I-10
exit 720, just s. L D CALL

## SEGUIN (F-8) pop. 25,175
• Part of San Antonio area — see map p. 458

Home of the world's largest pecan, Seguin (pronounced "sa-geen") was founded as Walnut Springs
in 1838. The name was changed to honor Col. Juan
N. Seguin, a distinguished Tejano patriot who
served under Sam Houston in the fight for Texas
independence. A statue of Col. Seguin stands in
Central Park at South River and Nolte streets.

The giant pecan—a sculpture on the courthouse
lawn—marks Seguin as a major cultivator of the nut.
Guided tours of the area include sites from Janice
Woods Windle's historical novel "True Women." The
town's first church, built for a Methodist conference
in 1849, is among the oldest surviving protestant
churches in the state. Seguin also is the home of
Texas Lutheran University.

**Seguin Convention and Visitors Bureau:** 116 N.
Camp St., Seguin, TX 78156. **Phone:** (830)
379-6382 or (800) 580-7322.

**Self-guiding tours:** Brochures for a walking tour of historic downtown Seguin and a driving tour of sites from "True Women" are available from the convention and visitors bureau.

**SEGUIN WAVE POOL** is 3 mi. s. off I-10 exit 609, following SR 123 to Max Starcke Park. Aquatic amusements include a 15,000-square-foot wave pool and a splash pool. Dressing rooms and grass volleyball courts are available. **Hours:** Tues.-Sun. 1-7, early June-late Aug. **Cost:** $5; $4 (ages 4-11 and 60+). **Phone:** (830) 401-2480.

COMFORT INN & SUITES (830)372-3990

▼▼▼ **Hotel** $89-$199 **Address:** 3013 N SR 123 Bypass 78155 **Location:** I-10 exit 610 (SR 123), just n. Located in a rural area. **Facility:** 72 units. 3 stories, interior corridors. **Pool(s):** outdoor. **Activities:** hot tub, exercise room. **Guest Services:** coin laundry.

HAMPTON INN 830/379-4400

▼▼▼ **Hotel.** Rates not provided. **Address:** 1130 Larkin Ave 78155 **Location:** I-10 exit 610 (SR 123), just n. **Facility:** 68 units. 3 stories, interior corridors. **Pool(s):** outdoor. **Activities:** exercise room. **Guest Services:** valet and coin laundry.

> **AAA Benefit:** Members save up to 10%!

HOLIDAY INN EXPRESS & SUITES SEGUIN 830/379-4440

▼▼▼ **Hotel.** Rates not provided. **Address:** 2801 Jay Rd 78155 **Location:** I-10 exit 610 (SR 123), just n. **Facility:** 89 units. 4 stories, interior corridors. **Pool(s):** outdoor. **Activities:** exercise room. **Guest Services:** coin laundry.

LA QUINTA INN & SUITES SEGUIN (830)372-0567

▼▼▼ **Hotel** $139-$174 **Address:** 1501 Hwy 46 N 78155 **Location:** I-10 exit 607 (SR 46), just off westbound frontage road. **Facility:** 66 units. 3 stories, interior corridors. **Pool(s):** outdoor. **Activities:** hot tub, exercise room. **Guest Services:** coin laundry.

SUPER 8 OF SEGUIN (830)379-6888

▼▼▼ Hotel
$69-$190

**Address:** 1525 N Hwy 46 78155 **Location:** I-10 exit 607 (SR 46); on eastbound frontage road. Located in a quiet rural area. **Facility:** 49 units. 2 stories (no elevator), interior corridors. **Featured Amenity:** continental breakfast.

## WHERE TO EAT

BILL MILLER BAR-B-Q 830/372-2668

▼ Barbecue. Quick Serve. $6-$11 **AAA Inspector Notes:** The relaxed, family-focused barbecue restaurant prepares ribs, chicken, brisket, turkey and sausage for sandwiches or plates. **Address:** 1823 W IH-10 78155 **Location:** I-35 exit 607 (SR 46); on northbound frontage road. [B] [L] [D]

EL RANCHITO 830/303-7802

▼▼ Mexican. Family Dining. $7-$12 **AAA Inspector Notes:** Since 1940 and now in its newest location on the outskirts of town, the specialties here include enchiladas and chiles relleno stuffed with cheese and smothered in meat gravy. Combo plates are also popular, including the version with a chicken enchilada, pork tamal and crispy taco served with rice and beans. **Features:** beer & wine. **Address:** 983 N Hwy 123 Bypass 78155 **Location:** I-10 exit 610 (SR 123), 0.8 mi s. [L] [D]

## SELMA pop. 5,540
• Part of San Antonio area — see map p. 458

COMFORT INN & SUITES (210)447-2305

▼▼▼ **Hotel** $79-$109 **Address:** 15771 IH 35 N 78154 **Location:** I-35 exit 174A (Selma Shertz CR 1518); on southbound frontage road. Located in a quiet area. **Facility:** 88 units. 3 stories, interior corridors. **Pool(s):** outdoor. **Activities:** hot tub, exercise room. **Guest Services:** valet and coin laundry.

HAMPTON INN & SUITES (210)590-3388

▼▼▼ **Hotel** $119-$139 **Address:** 14655 IH-35 N Access Rd 78154 **Location:** I-35 exit 173 (The Forum Pkwy); on southbound access road. **Facility:** 85 units. 4 stories, interior corridors. **Terms:** 1-7 night minimum stay, cancellation fee imposed. **Pool(s):** heated indoor. **Activities:** exercise room. **Guest Services:** coin laundry.

> **AAA Benefit:** Members save up to 10%!

HOLIDAY INN EXPRESS & SUITES SELMA (210)651-3885

▼▼▼ **Hotel** $109-$125 **Address:** 15408 I-35 N, Suite 2 78154 **Location:** I-35 exit 173 (Olympia Pkwy); on northbound frontage road. **Facility:** 84 units. 4 stories, interior corridors. **Terms:** cancellation fee imposed. **Pool(s):** outdoor. **Activities:** hot tub, exercise room. **Guest Services:** coin laundry.

## SEMINOLE pop. 6,430

SEMINOLE INN 432/758-9881

▼▼ Motel
Rates not provided

**Address:** 2200 Hobbs Hwy 79360 **Location:** 1.5 mi w on US 62 and 180. **Facility:** 40 units. 1 story, exterior corridors.

## SHAFTER

CIBOLO CREEK RANCH 432/229-3737

[fyi] Not evaluated. **Address:** US Hwy 67 N 79843 **Location:** On US 67, 6 mi n; 33 mi s from Marfa. Facilities, services, and décor characterize an upscale property. Distinguishing this 30,000-acre resort ranch are upscale accommodations in refitted private forts dating to 1857; many activities are offered.

## SHAMROCK (B-6) pop. 1,910, elev. 2,342'
• Hotels p. 536

Incorporated in 1911, Shamrock originally was established as a post office 21 years prior at the home of an Irish sheep rancher. Cattle and farming sustain the economy of the Texas Panhandle town. The 1936 Tower Station and U-Drop Inn are Art Deco landmarks at the crossroads of historic Route 66 and US 83.

**Shamrock Chamber of Commerce:** 105 E. 12th St., Shamrock, TX 79309. **Phone:** (806) 256-2501.

**PIONEER WEST MUSEUM** is at 204 N. Madden St. More than 20 rooms contain artifacts, Native American arrowheads, articles on loan from Houston Space Center, doctors' and dentists' office equipment and military items. A barn and a renovated doctor's office are on the grounds. **Hours:** Mon.-Fri. 10-3. **Cost:** Donations. **Phone:** (806) 256-3941.

### BEST WESTERN PLUS SHAMROCK INN & SUITES
(806)256-1001

 Hotel $88-$110

 **AAA Benefit:** Members save 10% or more with Best Western!

 **Address:** 1802 N Main St 79079 **Location:** I-40 exit 163, just n. **Facility:** 46 units, some kitchens. 3 stories, interior corridors. **Terms:** 14 day cancellation notice. **Pool(s):** heated indoor. **Activities:** hot tub, exercise room. **Guest Services:** coin laundry.

HOLIDAY INN EXPRESS & SUITES        806/256-5022

 Hotel. Rates not provided. **Address:** 101 E 13th St 79079 **Location:** I-40 exit 163, just s. **Facility:** 65 units. 3 stories, interior corridors. **Pool(s):** heated indoor. **Activities:** hot tub, exercise room. **Guest Services:** coin laundry.

### SLEEP INN & SUITES
(806)256-2227

 Hotel $119-$199

 **Address:** 111 E 15th St 79079 **Location:** I-40 exit 163, 1 blk s. **Facility:** 53 units, some kitchens. 3 stories, interior corridors. **Amenities:** safes. **Pool(s):** heated indoor. **Activities:** hot tub, exercise room. **Guest Services:** coin laundry.

### WESTERN MOTEL
(806)256-3244

 Motel $59-$169

 **Address:** 104 E 12th St 79079 **Location:** Business Rt I-40 and US 83. **Facility:** 24 units. 2 stories, exterior corridors.

## SHEFFIELD (E-5) elev. 2,168'

The San Antonio-El Paso Road was forged in 1851 to carry U.S. mail and passengers west. Despite Native American attacks, the stage line transported thousands of travelers as far as San Diego.

By 1900, a small community had formed at a ford in the Pecos River where the stage line crossed, and the town eventually took the name of a local rancher, Will Sheffield. Oil was discovered in 1920, and natural gas became the town's second major commodity in the 1970s.

**FORT LANCASTER STATE HISTORIC SITE** is off I-10 exit 343, then 8 mi. w. on US 290. Established in 1855, the fort was a defense post against Native American attacks along the San Antonio-El Paso Road. The installation grew to 25 buildings before it was abandoned at the onset of the Civil War. An interpretive center features artifacts, maps and exhibits about the site's history, natural history and archeology. The 82-acre park includes a nature trail and picnic facilities.

**Time:** Allow 1 hour minimum. **Hours:** Daily 9-5. Closed Jan. 1, Thanksgiving, Christmas Eve, Christmas and Dec. 31. Phone ahead to confirm schedule. **Cost:** $4; $3 (ages 6-18 and students with ID). **Phone:** (432) 836-4391. ⛺

## SHENANDOAH pop. 2,134
• **Part of Houston area — see map p. 301**

TOWNEPLACE SUITES BY MARRIOTT THE WOODLANDS
(936)273-7772

Extended Stay Hotel $161-$189 **Address:** 107 Vision Park Blvd 77384 **Location:** I-45 exit 79 (College Park/Needham Rd), 1 mi s; on southbound frontage road. **Facility:** 124 efficiencies. 3 stories, interior corridors. **Pool(s):** heated outdoor. **Activities:** exercise room. **Guest Services:** valet and coin laundry.

**AAA Benefit:** Members save 5% or more!

### WHERE TO EAT

BABIN'S SEAFOOD HOUSE        281/419-6333

Regional Seafood. Casual Dining. $9-$28 **AAA Inspector Notes:** This small chain specializes in seafood with a Cajun flair. At least 10 fresh fish choices are offered daily. Check out the list or menu board to learn about the "catches" of the day. Many varieties of seafood and preparations, as per your request, are available. Specialty cocktails are fresh and delicious. **Features:** full bar. **Address:** 19529 I-45 S 77385 **Location:** I-45 exit 76 southbound; exit 77 northbound; on northbound frontage road. L D

SALTGRASS STEAKHOUSE        281/298-7527

Steak. Casual Dining. $9-$30 **AAA Inspector Notes:** Those looking for something different should try the comfortable steakhouse, which never says no to a special request. Born from the spirit of Texas cattle drives, the restaurant resembles a Texas lodge, with high ceilings and mounted animal heads. Baby back ribs are so tender the meat falls off the bone. Also on the menu are hearty steaks, prime rib, chicken, seafood and yummy desserts. **Features:** full bar. **Address:** 19533 I-45 N 77385 **Location:** I-45 exit 76 (Woodlands Pkwy/Robinson Rd) southbound; exit 77 (Lake Woodlands Dr/Research Forest Dr/Tamina Rd) northbound, on northbound frontage road.

## SHERMAN (C-9) pop. 38,521, elev. 728'

Laid out in 1846 as the seat of Grayson County, Sherman gained early prominence when the Butterfield Stage was routed through town. The town is named for Sidney Sherman, who coined the phrase "Remember the Alamo!" during the Battle of San Jacinto. It is nicknamed "Helldorado on the Cross" and "The Athens of Texas."

**Sherman Department of Tourism:** 405 N. Rusk St., P.O. Box 1106, Sherman, TX 75091. **Phone:** (903) 957-0310.

**Self-guiding tours:** A brochure that outlines a driving tour of historic Sherman is available from the department of tourism.

**HAGERMAN NATIONAL WILDLIFE REFUGE** is 13 mi. n. on FM 1417, then 6 mi. w. to 6465 Refuge Rd. This 11,320-acre area on the southern end of the Big Mineral Arm of Lake Texoma is a resting and feeding place for migratory birds and a winter home for geese and ducks. Shore bird migrations peak in the summer. The visitor center provides interpretive displays and bird lists. Fishing, hiking and picnicking are permitted all year; boating is permitted mid-March through September. **Hours:** Refuge daily dawn-dusk. Visitor center Mon.-Fri. 7:30-4, Sat. 9-4, Sun. 1-5. **Cost:** Free. **Phone:** (903) 786-2826.

**THE SHERMAN MUSEUM** is at 301 S. Walnut St. Displays pertain to life in northern Texas from the mid-19th century to the present. Permanent exhibits include a farm and ranch room, general store and map corner. Temporary exhibits rotate every 6 months. **Time:** Allow 1 hour minimum. **Hours:** Tues.-Sat. 10-4. Closed major holidays. **Cost:** $5; $3 (ages 60+); $2 (students). **Phone:** (903) 893-7623.

COMFORT SUITES OF SHERMAN            (903)893-0499
▼▼▼ Hotel $84-$119 **Address:** 2900 US Hwy 75 N 75090 **Location:** US 75 exit 63, 0.3 mi s of jct US 82. **Facility:** 67 units. 2 stories (no elevator), interior corridors. **Pool(s):** outdoor. **Activities:** hot tub, exercise room. **Guest Services:** valet and coin laundry.

HAMPTON INN            (903)893-9333
▼▼▼ Hotel $99-$129 **Address:** 2904 Michelle Dr 75090 **Location:** US 75 exit 63, just s of jct US 82. **Facility:** 69 units. 3 stories, interior corridors. **Terms:** 1-7 night minimum stay, cancellation fee imposed. **Pool(s):** heated indoor. **Activities:** hot tub, exercise room. **Guest Services:** valet and coin laundry.

**AAA Benefit:** Members save up to 10%!

LA QUINTA INN & SUITES SHERMAN DENISON            (903)870-1122
▼▼▼ Hotel $82-$127 **Address:** 2912 US 75 N 75090 **Location:** US 75 exit 63; on southbound frontage road. **Facility:** 115 units. 4 stories, interior corridors. **Pool(s):** outdoor. **Activities:** hot tub, exercise room. **Guest Services:** valet and coin laundry.

AAA/CAA travel information:
Available online, on the go and in print!

**WHERE TO EAT**

EL CHICO            903/893-2663
▼▼▼
Tex-Mex
Casual Dining
$6-$16
**AAA Inspector Notes:** Inside and out, the decor of the popular Mexican restaurant is inviting. The menu features traditional favorites such as enchiladas, tacos, burritos and fajitas. The broad menu also lists a few American classics. **Features:** full bar. **Address:** 2815 N Sam Rayburn Frwy 75090 **Location:** US 75 exit 63, just sw of jct US 82.

LA MESA MEXICAN RESTAURANTE & CANTINA
            903/892-1644
▼ Tex-Mex. Casual Dining. $7-$20 **AAA Inspector Notes:** This cozy restaurant presents a good variety of offerings with a few American dishes included. **Features:** full bar. **Address:** 2124 Texoma Pkwy 75090 **Location:** Jct US 82 and Texoma Pkwy, 0.4 mi s.

TOKYO HIBACHI & SUSHI            903/892-2001
▼▼ Japanese. Casual Dining. $14-$40 **AAA Inspector Notes:** A good variety of fresh seafood is served. The at-table preparation is entertaining. **Features:** full bar. **Address:** 2916 Hwy 75, Suite 300 75092 **Location:** US 75 exit 63, just sw of jct US 82.

## SINTON pop. 5,665

BEST WESTERN SINTON            (361)364-2882
▼▼▼
Motel
$95-$100

**AAA Benefit:** Members save 10% or more with Best Western!

**Address:** 8108 US Hwy 77 78387 **Location:** 0.5 mi s of SR 188. Located in a rural area. **Facility:** 32 units. 1 story, exterior corridors. **Pool(s):** outdoor. **Activities:** exercise room. **Guest Services:** coin laundry.

## SMITHVILLE pop. 3,817

AMERICAS BEST VALUE INN & SUITES            512/237-2040
▼▼ Motel. Rates not provided. **Address:** 1503 Dorothy Nichol Ln 78957 **Location:** Jct SR 71 and Dorothy Nichol Ln. **Facility:** 34 units. 2 stories (no elevator), exterior corridors. **Pool(s):** outdoor. **Activities:** hot tub. **Guest Services:** coin laundry.

## SNYDER pop. 11,202

BEST WESTERN SNYDER INN            (325)574-2200
▼▼▼
Hotel
$85-$199

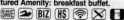
**AAA Benefit:** Members save 10% or more with Best Western!

**Address:** 810 E Coliseum Dr 79549 **Location:** 1 mi w of US 84. **Facility:** 39 units. 1 story, exterior corridors. **Pool(s):** outdoor. **Activities:** exercise room. **Featured Amenity:** breakfast buffet.

### PURPLE SAGE MOTEL
(325)573-5491

Motel
$59-$79

**Address:** 1501 E Coliseum Dr 79549
**Location:** 1 mi w on US 180 from jct US
84. **Facility:** 63 units, some efficiencies.
1 story, exterior corridors. **Terms:** cancellation fee imposed. **Pool(s):** outdoor.
**Guest Services:** coin laundry. **Featured
Amenity:** breakfast buffet.

SAVE 🛏 HS 📶 🛁 🖼 💻
/ SOME UNITS 🐾

### SONORA (F-6) pop. 3,027, elev. 2,120'

The town was settled on the western slope of the
Edwards Plateau in 1889 after a water well was
drilled on what is now the Sutton County Courthouse lawn. Sonora produces wool, mohair, meat
goats and natural gas.

**Sonora Chamber of Commerce:** 205 SR 277N,
Suite B, P.O. Box 1172, Sonora, TX 76950. **Phone:**
(325) 387-2880 or (888) 387-2880.

**Self-guiding tours:** The Sonora Walking Tour features 15 points of interest and historical information
including the place where outlaw Will Carver was
shot. Self-guiding walking tour brochures are available from the chamber of commerce or from Friends
of Historic Sonora at 105 N. Concho St., phone
(325) 387-2248 or (888) 387-2880.

**CAVERNS OF SONORA** is 8 mi. n.w. off
I-10 exit 392 and 7 mi. s. on Cavern Rd.
(Ranch Rd. 1989). A 1.75-mile trail winds through
the cave, where the temperature is a constant 70
degrees F. Stalagmites, stalactites and helictites
cover the walls, ceiling and floor of the cave. These
translucent formations exhibit a wide range of
natural colors.

The guided Crystal Palace Tour lasts 1 hour, 45
minutes and takes visitors through the original entrance, covering the 1.75-mile interior and all of the
cave's major features, including Horseshoe Lake,
the Corinthian Room and the Crystal Palace Room.

Tours involve climbing stairs. Comfortable walking
shoes are recommended. **Hours:** Daily 8-6, Mar.
1-Labor Day; 9-5, rest of year. Closed Christmas.
**Cost:** Crystal Palace tour $20; $16 (ages 4-11).
Prices may vary. **Phone:** (325) 387-3105. 🍴 🎡

### BEST WESTERN SONORA INN
(325)387-9111

Hotel
$108-$119

**AAA Benefit:** Members
save 10% or more with
Best Western!

**Address:** 270 Hwy 277 N 76950 **Location:** I-10 exit 400, just s. **Facility:** 54
units. 2 stories (no elevator), exterior
corridors. **Pool(s):** outdoor. **Activities:**
exercise room. **Guest Services:** coin
laundry. **Featured Amenity: full hot
breakfast.**

SAVE 🍴 🛏 📶 🛁 🖼 💻
/ SOME UNITS 🍳 HS

### COMFORT INN OF SONORA
(325)387-5800

Hotel $110-$130 **Address:** 311 N Hwy 277 76950 **Location:** I-10 exit 400, just s. **Facility:** 52 units. 2 stories (no elevator),
exterior corridors. **Pool(s):** outdoor. **Activities:** exercise room. **Guest
Services:** coin laundry.

🍴 🛏 HS 📶 ✕ 🛁 🖼 💻

### HOLIDAY HOST MOTEL
325/387-2532

Motel
$45-$55

**Address:** 127 Loop 467 (Hwy 290) E
76950 **Location:** Loop 467 exit 404
westbound, 3 mi w; exit 399 eastbound,
3 mi e. **Facility:** 20 units. 1 story, exterior corridors. **Pool(s):** outdoor. **Featured Amenity: continental breakfast.**

SAVE 🛏 📶 🛁 🖼 💻
/ SOME UNITS 🐾

### SOUTHLAKE pop. 26,575

#### COAL VINES
817/310-0850

Pizza. Casual Dining. $10-$15 **AAA Inspector Notes:**
This pizzeria pays homage to New York and prefers you to customize
the pizzas to your liking, including offering a gluten-free dough. The
coal ovens make the pizza deliciously crispy and tasty. They also
offer some non-pizza options, including baked eggplant, fennel-crusted salmon and rigatoni. **Features:** full bar, patio dining, Sunday
brunch, happy hour. **Address:** 1251 E Southlake Blvd 76092 **Location:** SR 114 exit Carroll Ave, just s; in Shops of Southlake Shopping
Center. D

#### ROCKFISH SEAFOOD GRILL
817/442-0131

Seafood. Casual Dining. $7-$20 **AAA Inspector Notes:**
Patrons shuffle through peanut shells on the floor as they make their
way to their seats and are easily distracted by the numerous pieces
of hunting and fishing memorabilia adorning the walls and ceiling. Although guests kick back in a log cabin-style interior, the freshly
caught fish gets more sophisticated preparation than campfire
roasting. The chef uses an array of sauces and cooking styles, and
soups are hearty and fresh. **Features:** full bar. **Address:** 228 State
St 76092 **Location:** SR 114 exit Southlake Blvd, 2 mi w to Southlake
Town Square. L D

### SOUTH PADRE ISLAND (I-8) pop. 2,816
• Restaurants p. 541

The southernmost 5 miles of Padre Island, the resort town of South Padre Island, are connected by a
causeway to Port Isabel on the mainland. The area
is a haven for artists, photographers and ecologists.
Gulls, herons and rare brown pelicans are found
among the island's tropical foliage, waterways,
dunes and long white beaches.

There is a seemingly limitless supply of seashells,
and rumors allude to buried treasure beneath the
sand—pirate plunder and debris from 5 centuries of
shipwrecks.

Laguna Madre, the bay that separates the island
from the mainland, has excellent fishing all year.
Charter boats leave daily in search of red snapper,
king mackerel, marlin, tarpon and sailfish in the Gulf.
There also is fishing from the lighted 5,000-foot Sea
Ranch Fishing Pier.

South Padre Island offers swimming, diving, windsurfing, sailing, parasailing and horseback riding.
Boat ramps, slips and marinas accommodate all
sizes of craft.

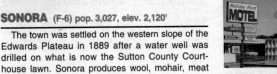

**South Padre Island Convention and Visitors Bureau:** 610 Padre Blvd., South Padre Island, TX 78597. **Phone:** (956) 761-6433 or (800) 767-2373.

**SCHLITTERBAHN BEACH WATERPARK** is .5 mi. s. of Queen Isabella Cswy. at 33261 State Park Rd. 100. This indoor and outdoor water park features a Brazilian beach and tree-house theme. A half-mile river system carries visitors to rides throughout the park, including four uphill water coasters, a 245-foot tube chute, two five-story tube slides, twin tidal wave rivers, multiple kids' areas and one of the world's largest bodyboarding rides. The five-story Sandcastle features water slides and computerized water features.

Glass containers and alcohol are prohibited. **Time:** Allow 3 hours minimum. **Hours:** Park opens daily at 10, mid-May to late Aug.; Sat.-Sun. at 10, late Apr. to mid-May and late Aug.-late Sept. Closing times vary from 6 to 8 p.m. **Cost:** $45.99; $35.99 (ages 3-11). After 3 p.m. $32.99; $28.99 (ages 3-11). Prices may vary; phone ahead. **Phone:** (956) 772-7873. 🍴 🏕

**SEA TURTLE, INC.,** 6617 Padre Blvd., rehabilitates injured sea turtles and promotes sea turtle conservation. Educational talks featuring live sea turtles describe how different species are identified, how they have become injured and what you can do to help protect them. **Time:** Allow 1 hour minimum. **Hours:** Tues.-Sun. 10-4. Educational talks are given every 45 minutes. Closed Christmas. **Cost:** $3; $2 (ages 5-18). **Phone:** (956) 761-4511.

**SOUTH PADRE ISLAND BIRDING AND NATURE CENTER** is at 6801 Padre Blvd. Boardwalks and nature trails winding through intertidal flats, salt marshes, dune meadows and wooded areas; a five-story observation tower; and seven blinds afford views of waterfowl and such migratory birds as peregrine falcons, thrushes and warblers. Visitors also can participate in bird walks and educational programs and enjoy the center's movies and hands-on exhibits.

**Tours:** Guided tours are available. **Hours:** Boardwalks and nature trails daily dawn-dusk. Center daily 9-5. Guided tours are given daily during birding season; every other Sat. at 9:30 and 2:30, rest of year. Phone for tour schedule. **Cost:** $5; $4 (ages 55+ and students ages 13-18 with ID); $2 (ages 4-12). **Phone:** (956) 243-8179.

**THE UNIVERSITY OF TEXAS-PAN AMERICAN COASTAL STUDIES LABORATORY** is at the southern tip of the island in Isla Blanca Park. This marine-biology research and education center offers self-guiding afternoon tours. Displays identify local flora and fauna; an aquarium holds colorful vertebrate and invertebrate species. **Hours:** Mon.-Fri. 1:30-4:30. Closed major holidays. **Cost:** Donations. Park entrance $5 per private vehicle. **Phone:** (956) 761-2644.

## RECREATIONAL ACTIVITIES
### Horseback Riding

- **Island Equestrian Center** is 1 mi. n. of the South Padre Island Convention Center at 8805 Padre Blvd. The center offers guided horseback rides on the beach. Other activities are offered. **Hours:** Daily 9-6. Phone ahead to confirm schedule. **Phone:** (956) 761-4677.

COMFORT SUITES                                   (956)772-9020

▼▼▼ **Hotel** $60-$350 **Address:** 912 Padre Blvd 78597 **Location:** Opposite Queen Isabella Cswy. Located behind McDonalds. **Facility:** 74 units. 4 stories, interior corridors. **Terms:** 3 day cancellation notice. **Pool(s):** heated outdoor. **Activities:** hot tub, beach access. **Guest Services:** coin laundry.
🍴 🏊 BIZ HS 📶 ❌ 🛗 📺 💻

HILTON GARDEN INN SOUTH PADRE ISLAND    956/761-8700

◆◆◆ **Hotel.** Rates not provided. **Address:** 7010 Padre Blvd 78597 **Location:** Oceanfront. 3 mi n of Queen Isabella Cswy. **Facility:** 156 units. 4 stories, interior corridors. **Amenities:** safes. **Pool(s):** heated outdoor. **Activities:** hot tub, exercise room. **Guest Services:** valet and coin laundry.

**AAA Benefit:**
Members save up to 10%!

[icons]

HOLIDAY INN EXPRESS HOTEL & SUITES    956/761-8844

◆◆◆ **Hotel.** Rates not provided. **Address:** 6502 Padre Blvd 78597 **Location:** Oceanfront. 3 mi n of Queen Isabella Cswy. **Facility:** 104 units. 4 stories, interior corridors. **Amenities:** video games. **Pool(s):** outdoor. **Activities:** hot tub, exercise room. **Guest Services:** valet and coin laundry.

[icons]

THE INN AT SOUTH PADRE    956/761-5658

◆◆ **Hotel.** Rates not provided. **Address:** 1709 Padre Blvd 78597 **Location:** 0.9 mi n of Queen Isabella Cswy; corner of W Palm St. **Facility:** some two bedrooms, three bedrooms, efficiencies and kitchens. 3 stories, interior corridors. **Amenities:** safes. **Pool(s):** outdoor. **Activities:** hot tub. **Guest Services:** valet and coin laundry.

[icons]

### ISLA GRAND BEACH RESORT    (956)761-6511

◆◆◆
Resort Hotel
$89-$625

**Address:** 500 Padre Blvd 78597 **Location:** Oceanfront. 0.3 mi n of Queen Isabella Cswy. **Facility:** Featuring an eye-catching lobby, this property is located on a notable beach. Rooms are in a main tower building and alongside the pool area. 91 units, some condominiums. 2-12 stories, interior/exterior corridors. **Terms:** 3 day cancellation notice-fee imposed. **Amenities:** safes. **Dining:** entertainment. **Pool(s):** outdoor, heated outdoor. **Activities:** hot tub, tennis, recreation programs in summer, exercise room. **Guest Services:** valet and coin laundry.

[icons]

LA COPA INN BEACH HOTEL    (956)761-6000

◆◆◆ **Hotel** $50-$400 **Address:** 350 Padre Blvd 78597 **Location:** Oceanfront. Just s of Queen Isabella Cswy. **Facility:** 146 units, some two bedrooms and kitchens. 4 stories, interior corridors. **Terms:** 3 day cancellation notice-fee imposed, resort fee. **Amenities:** safes. **Pool(s):** heated outdoor. **Activities:** hot tub, exercise room. **Guest Services:** valet and coin laundry.

[icons]

LA QUINTA INN & SUITES SOUTH PADRE BEACH
    (956)772-7000

◆◆◆ **Hotel** $120-$275 **Address:** 7000 Padre Blvd 78597 **Location:** Oceanfront. 3 mi n of Queen Isabella Cswy. **Facility:** 147 units. 4 stories, interior corridors. **Amenities:** safes. **Pool(s):** heated outdoor. **Activities:** hot tub, fishing, exercise room. **Guest Services:** coin laundry.

[icons]

MOTEL 6 SOUTH PADRE ISLAND - #1237    (956)761-7911

◆ **Motel** $35-$125 **Address:** 4013 Padre Blvd 78597 **Location:** 2 mi n of Queen Isabella Cswy. **Facility:** 52 units. 2 stories (no elevator), exterior corridors. *Bath:* shower only. **Pool(s):** outdoor. **Guest Services:** coin laundry.

[icons]

PENINSULA ISLAND RESORT & SPA    956/761-2514

◆◆◆ **Condominium.** Rates not provided. **Address:** 340 Padre Blvd 78597 **Location:** Oceanfront. Just s of Queen Isabella Cswy, jct Padre Rd and Padre Blvd. **Facility:** Elegant, spacious accommodations. Upscale pool area. 39 units, some two bedrooms, efficiencies, kitchens and condominiums. 6 stories, interior corridors. **Terms:** check-in 4 pm. **Amenities:** safes. **Pool(s):** heated outdoor. **Activities:** hot tub, limited beach access, exercise room, spa. **Guest Services:** coin laundry.

[icons]

### ROYALE BEACH & TENNIS CLUB    (956)761-1166

◆◆
Condominium
$138-$450

**Address:** 400 Padre Blvd 78597 **Location:** Oceanfront. Just s of Queen Isabella Cswy. **Facility:** 134 units, some condominiums. 14 stories, interior/exterior corridors. **Terms:** check-in 4 pm, 3 day cancellation notice-fee imposed. **Pool(s):** outdoor, heated outdoor. **Activities:** hot tub, tennis. **Guest Services:** complimentary and valet laundry.

[icons]

SUITES AT SUNCHASE, AN ASCEND HOTEL COLLECTION MEMBER    (956)761-7711

◆◆◆ **Hotel** $100-$250 **Address:** 1004 Padre Blvd 78597 **Location:** 0.3 mi n of Queen Isabella Cswy; in Sunchase Mall Complex. **Facility:** 90 units. 4 stories, interior corridors. **Pool(s):** outdoor. **Activities:** hot tub, beach access, exercise room. **Guest Services:** coin laundry.

[icons]

### SUPER 8

(956)761-6300

Hotel
$69-$299

**Address:** 4205 Padre Blvd 78597 **Location:** 2.7 mi n of Queen Isabella Cswy. **Facility:** 65 units, some efficiencies. 2 stories (no elevator), exterior corridors. **Terms:** cancellation fee imposed. **Amenities:** safes. **Pool(s):** outdoor. **Activities:** hot tub. **Guest Services:** coin laundry. **Featured Amenity: continental breakfast.**

### TRAVELODGE

(956)761-4744

Hotel
$60-$310

**Address:** 6200 Padre Blvd 78597 **Location:** 3 mi n of Queen Isabella Cswy. **Facility:** 144 units, some two bedrooms and kitchens. 2 stories (no elevator), exterior corridors. **Amenities:** safes. **Pool(s):** heated outdoor. **Activities:** hot tub, exercise room. **Guest Services:** coin laundry. **Featured Amenity: continental breakfast.**

### GALLEON BAY CLUB

956/761-7808

[fyi] Not evaluated. **Address:** 4901 Laguna Blvd 78597 **Location:** 1 blk w of Padre Blvd; jct Capricorn Dr. Facilities, services, and décor characterize an economy property.

### INVERNESS AT SOUTH PADRE

956/761-7919

[fyi] Not evaluated. **Address:** 5600 Gulf Blvd 78597 **Location:** Oceanfront. 2.7 mi n on SR 100 from Queen Isabella Cswy. Facilities, services, and décor characterize an economy property.

### SUNCHASE IV CONDOMINIUMS BY SOUTH PADRE RESORT

956/761-6818

[fyi] Not evaluated. **Address:** 1000 Padre Blvd 78597 **Location:** Queen Isabella Cswy. 0.6 mi n, turn left; just before Sunchase Mall. Facilities, services, and décor characterize an upscale property.

---

## WHERE TO EAT

### BLACKBEARD'S RESTAURANT

956/761-2962

Regional Seafood. Casual Dining. $10-$21 **AAA Inspector Notes:** Elevated beach home structure offers choice seafood, steaks burgers and sandwiches in a fun, island like atmosphere. Try the seviche, followed by a flaky flounder and finish with a rich carrot cake. **Features:** full bar, patio dining. **Address:** 103 E Saturn St 78597 **Location:** 2.7 mi n of Queen Isabella Cswy.

### DADDY'S SEAFOOD & CAJUN KITCHEN

956/761-1975

Regional Seafood. Casual Dining. $8-$19 **AAA Inspector Notes:** The menu is bursting with plentiful portions of local fish and shrimp, flavorful Cajun selections, burgers and po' boys. The luscious homemade carrot cake is a must. **Features:** full bar, patio dining. **Address:** 1808 Padre Blvd 78597 **Location:** 1 mi n of Queen Isabella Cswy.

### LOUIE'S BACKYARD

956/761-6406

Seafood. Casual Dining. $15-$22 **AAA Inspector Notes:** The waterfront dining area is the perfect place to watch a splendid sunset and to catch a tropical breeze. Seafood and hand-cut steaks are served by a friendly waitstaff. The upstairs sports bar has 14 TVs to satisfy even the biggest sports fan. **Features:** full bar, patio dining. **Address:** 2305 Laguna Blvd 78597 **Location:** 1.5 mi n of Queen Isabella Cswy; corner of Ling St and Laguna Blvd.

### SEA RANCH RESTAURANT & BAR

956/761-1314

Seafood. Casual Dining. $9-$33 **AAA Inspector Notes:** The adjacent marina and restaurant namesake provide an ideal waterside setting for enjoying the freshest available red snapper and other seasonal fresh seafood. Signature items include king crab legs, live Maine lobster, Gulf Coast shrimp and shrimp scampi. The more casual Dirty Dave's Deck also allows a relaxing view of fishing and sailing boats' arrivals and departures. **Features:** full bar. **Address:** 33330 State Park Rd 100 78597 **Location:** Just s of Queen Isabella Cswy.

## SPICEWOOD (F-8) elev. 768'

### RECREATIONAL ACTIVITIES

#### Ziplines

- **Cypress Valley Canopy Tours** is at 1223 Paleface RR. **Hours:** Tues.-Sat. 9-dusk, Sun. noon-dusk, in summer; Fri.-Sat. 9-dusk, Sun. noon-dusk, Tues.-Thurs. by appointment, rest of year. **Cost:** Reservations are required. **Phone:** (512) 264-8880.

## SPRING (F-10) pop. 54,298

- Restaurants p. 542
- Hotels & Restaurants map & index p. 324
- Part of Houston area — see map p. 301

Orcoquiza Indians were the first inhabitants of the region along Spring Creek, which was settled by a number of Stephen F. Austin's colonists in the 1820s. German farmers arrived in the mid-19th century, followed by immigrants from Louisiana and other southern states. Spring experienced a decline after the International-Great Northern Railroad moved its switchyard to Houston in 1923, but with the metropolitan area's northward expansion, Spring has become a thriving suburb.

Old Town Spring is a collection of Victorian cottages that now house antique stores, art galleries, specialty shops and restaurants.

**SPLASHTOWN** is off I-45 Louetta Rd. exit. This wooded 40-acre park features slides, chutes, pools and lagoons. Highlights include Tornado, a giant funnel sending riders over 5,000 gallons of water at 30 mph; Thunder Run, a five-story aqua speedway; and Crocodile Isle, a children's play area.

**Time:** Allow 4 hours minimum. **Hours:** Park opens daily at 10, late May-late Aug.; closing times vary. Park opens Sat.-Sun. and some Fri. between 10 and noon, late Apr.-late May and late Aug.-late Sept.; closing times vary. Phone ahead to confirm schedule. **Cost:** $36.99; $28.99 (under 48 inches tall and ages 65+); free (ages 0-2). Prices may vary; phone ahead. **Parking:** $10. **Phone:** (281) 355-3300.

### COMFORT SUITES WOODLANDS/GREENSPOINT

(281)288-5515  [104]

Hotel $95-$149 **Address:** 323 E Louetta Rd 77373 **Location:** I-45 exit 68 (Louetta Rd) southbound; exit 70A (Tomball/FM 2920) northbound, just e. **Facility:** 62 units. 3 stories, interior corridors. **Pool(s):** outdoor. **Activities:** hot tub, exercise room. **Guest Services:** valet and coin laundry.

(See map & index p. 324.)

## WHERE TO EAT

**WUNSCHE BROS CAFE**    281/350-1902    42

American. Casual Dining. $6-$14 **AAA Inspector Notes:** *Historic.* In a wood-frame house built in 1902 is an old Texas saloon offering excellent comfort food. Try its famous fried chicken, luscious bread pudding, sausage crumb salad and homemade beer bread. It's not just the house that has been here since 1902, the business has, too, originally opening as a hotel and saloon as a stop on the original rail route between Galveston and Palestine. It's in quaint Old Town Spring, a cluster of shops and restaurants preserved in historic homes and edifices. **Features:** full bar. **Address:** 103 Midway St 77373 **Location:** I-45 exit 70A (Spring-Cypress Rd), 0.9 mi e to jct Gentry/Midway sts and Spring-Cypress Rd, then just e. **Parking:** street only. L D

## STAFFORD pop. 17,693

- Hotels & Restaurants map & index p. 324
- Part of Houston area — see map p. 301

**COMFORT SUITES**    (281)565-5566    142

Hotel $110-$160 **Address:** 4820 Techniplex Dr 77477 **Location:** US 59 exit Corporate Dr southbound; exit Airport Blvd/Kirkwood Rd northbound; on service road. **Facility:** 67 units. 3 stories, interior corridors. **Pool(s):** outdoor. **Activities:** hot tub, exercise room. **Guest Services:** valet and coin laundry.

**COURTYARD BY MARRIOTT HOUSTON/SUGAR LAND**    (281)491-7700    138

Hotel
$79-$200

COURTYARD Marriott

**AAA Benefit:** Members save 5% or more!

**Address:** 12655 Southwest Frwy 77477 **Location:** US 59 exit Corporate Dr southbound; exit Airport Blvd/Kirkwood Rd northbound; on northbound service road. **Facility:** 112 units. 4 stories, interior corridors. **Pool(s):** outdoor. **Activities:** hot tub, exercise room. **Guest Services:** valet and coin laundry.

SAVE CALL SOME UNITS HS

**LA QUINTA INN & SUITES HOUSTON STAFFORD/SUGARLAND**    (281)240-2300    140

Hotel $82-$130 **Address:** 12727 Southwest Frwy 77477 **Location:** US 59 exit Corporate Dr southbound; exit Airport Blvd/Kirkwood Rd northbound; eastbound service road. **Facility:** 125 units. 4 stories, interior corridors. **Pool(s):** outdoor. **Activities:** exercise room. **Guest Services:** valet and coin laundry.

SOME UNITS

**RESIDENCE INN BY MARRIOTT HOUSTON/SUGAR LAND**    (281)277-0770    139

Extended Stay
Contemporary
Hotel
$79-$200

Residence Inn Marriott

**AAA Benefit:** Members save 5% or more!

**Address:** 12703 Southwest Frwy 77477 **Location:** US 59 exit Corporate Dr southbound; exit Airport Blvd/Kirkwood Rd northbound; on northbound service road. Located in the business district. **Facility:** 78 efficiencies, some two bedrooms. 3 stories, interior corridors. **Amenities:** video games. **Pool(s):** outdoor. **Activities:** hot tub, exercise room. **Guest Services:** valet and coin laundry.

**Featured Amenity: full hot breakfast.**

SAVE / SOME UNITS

**SLEEP INN & SUITES**    (281)494-2900    143

Motel $79-$129 **Address:** 4810 Alpine Dr 77477 **Location:** US 59 exit Corporate Dr southbound; exit Alternate Rt 90/Stafford northbound, just n on northbound frontage road, then just e. **Facility:** 63 units. 2 stories, interior corridors. **Amenities:** safes. **Pool(s):** indoor. **Activities:** limited exercise equipment. **Guest Services:** valet and coin laundry.

CALL

**STAFFORD HAMPTON INN BY HILTON**    (281)565-0559    141

Hotel $80-$107 **Address:** 4714 Techniplex Dr 77477 **Location:** US 59 exit Corporate Dr southbound; exit Airport Blvd/Kirkwood Rd northbound; eastbound service road. **Facility:** 85 units. 3 stories, interior corridors. **Terms:** 1-7 night minimum stay, cancellation fee imposed. **Pool(s):** heated indoor. **Activities:** hot tub, exercise room. **Guest Services:** valet laundry.

**AAA Benefit:** Members save up to 10%!

CALL / SOME UNITS

**STAYBRIDGE SUITES STAFFORD**    281/302-6535    137

Extended Stay Hotel. Rates not provided. **Address:** 11101 Fountain Lake Dr 77477 **Location:** US 59 exit Kirkwood Rd, just nw. **Facility:** 90 efficiencies, some two bedrooms. 4 stories, interior corridors. **Pool(s):** outdoor. **Activities:** exercise room. **Guest Services:** valet and coin laundry, area transportation.

CALL / SOME UNITS

## WHERE TO EAT

**AVALON DINER**    281/240-0213    58

American. Casual Dining. $6-$11 **AAA Inspector Notes:** A good place to begin a day of attacking the nearby shops and movie theater is this retro diner, which features teal booths, checkered floors and servers dressed in old-style bow ties and paper hats. Hamburgers, hot dogs and blue-plate specials share menu space with old-fashioned floats and desserts. For late risers, breakfast is served all day. **Address:** 12810 Southwest Frwy 77477 **Location:** US 59 exit Corporate Dr southbound; exit Kirkwood Rd/Airport Blvd northbound; on southbound service road; in Fountains Shopping Center. B L D

**GRINGO'S MEXICAN KITCHEN**    281/980-7482    57

Tex-Mex. Casual Dining. $9-$21 **AAA Inspector Notes:** This small Houston chain has what most people are looking for in a Mexican restaurant: great food and a fun, festive, family-friendly atmosphere. The traditional Mexican and Tex-Mex offerings include chalupas, tamales, flautas and enchiladas. The "Rita Cantina" bar is popular with its good selection of margaritas. The rustic but slightly upscale décor feels more like a Mexican resort than a small village cantina. Guests are treated to complimentary soft-serve ice cream. **Features:** full bar, happy hour. **Address:** 12330 Southwest Frwy 77477 **Location:** US 59 exit Airport Blvd; on southbound frontage road. L D CALL

(See map & index p. 324.)

PAPPADEAUX SEAFOOD KITCHEN                281/240-5533

◆◆ Regional Seafood. Casual Dining. $11-$40 AAA Inspector Notes: A seafood lover's delight, the restaurant taps into a little bit of New Orleans with its Cajun dishes and elaborate menu selections. Patrons might start off with a creative choice of blackened oyster and shrimp fondeaux with crayfish and let the feast begin. While music plays in the background, patrons can dig into dirty rice or spicy gumbo loaded with seafood. Well-seasoned shrimp and fish are prepared in varied ways. Features: full bar. Address: 12711 Hwy 59 S 77477 Location: US 59 exit Corporate Dr southbound; exit Airport Blvd/Kirkwood Rd northbound; eastbound service road.

L  D

TEXAS LAND AND CATTLE STEAKHOUSE        281/494-8844

◆◆ Steak. Casual Dining. $7-$27 AAA Inspector Notes: A variety of large Prime steaks, delicious salads and scrumptious desserts await you at the friendly Texas ranch-style restaurant. Try the signature slow-smoked sirloin, which never fails to please, or the Caesar salad, another favorite. A Texas steakhouse means everything is bigger, from large cuts and oversize salads to potatoes and side dishes. Those not in the mood for beef can opt for chicken, quail or seafood. Dessert is an occasion. Features: full bar. Address: 12710 Southwest Frwy S 77477 Location: US 59 exit Corporate Dr southbound; exit Airport/Kirkwood northbound; on southbound access road; in Fountains Shopping Center.   L  D  CALL 🔊M

## STANTON pop. 2,492

COMFORT INN                              (432)756-1100

◆◆◆ Hotel $90-$239 Address: 3414 W I-20 79782 Location: I-20 exit 156 (SR 137); on south frontage road. Facility: 70 units, some efficiencies. 2 stories, interior corridors. Pool(s): heated indoor. Activities: hot tub, exercise room. Guest Services: valet and coin laundry.

 BIZ HS 📶 ✕ 🛅 🖥 💻 / SOME UNITS 🐾

## STEPHENVILLE pop. 17,123

### AMERICAS BEST VALUE INN - CROSS TIMBERS          (254)968-2114

◆◆ Hotel $60-$65 Address: 1625 W South Loop (US 377) 76401 Location: 1.8 mi sw on US 377 Bypass and 67. Facility: 49 units. 2 stories (no elevator), exterior corridors. Terms: cancellation fee imposed. Pool(s): outdoor. Guest Services: coin laundry. Featured Amenity: full hot breakfast.

SAVE 🍴 ➡ HS 📶 🛅 🖥 💻 / SOME UNITS 🐾

LA QUINTA INN & SUITES STEPHENVILLE      (254)918-2444

◆◆◆ Hotel $94-$129 Address: 105 Christy Plaza 76401 Location: US 67/377 S, 5 mi s of jct US 281. Facility: 68 units. 3 stories, interior corridors. Pool(s): outdoor. Activities: hot tub, exercise room. Guest Services: coin laundry.

🍴 CALL 🔊M ➡ BIZ HS 📶 ✕ 🛅 🖥 💻 / SOME UNITS 🐾

STEPHENVILLE HAMPTON INN & SUITES        (254)918-5400

◆◆◆ Hotel $119-$161 Address: 910 S Harbin Dr 76401 Location: US 67/377 S, 3 mi s of jct US 281. Facility: 64 units. 3 stories, interior corridors. Terms: 1-7 night minimum stay, cancellation fee imposed. Pool(s): heated indoor. Activities: hot tub, exercise room. Guest Services: valet and coin laundry.

CALL 🔊M ➡ BIZ HS 📶 💻 / SOME UNITS 🐾 🛅 🖥

PASTAFINA ITALIAN RISTORANTE             254/918-5553

◆◆ Italian. Casual Dining. $7-$17 AAA Inspector Notes: The varied menu offers selections from both Northern and Southern Italy. Features: beer & wine. Address: 2897 W Washington St 76401 Location: 5 mi sw on US 377.   L  D  CALL 🔊M

## STONEWALL (F-7) pop. 505, elev. 1,449'

Established in 1860, Stonewall was named for Gen. Stonewall Jackson and is known for its Gillespie County peaches. Lyndon B. Johnson, 36th president, was born near here Aug. 27, 1908.

LYNDON B. JOHNSON STATE PARK AND HISTORIC SITE is 2 mi. e. on US 290 on Park Rd. 52. At the state park visitor center complex, memorabilia chronicle Johnson's life and Texas Hill Country history. The 732-acre site includes the Sauer-Beckmann Living History Farm, restored dog-run cabins, nature trails and picnic facilities. See Recreation Areas Chart. Hours: Park daily 8-5. Farm daily 8-4:30. Closed Jan. 1, Thanksgiving and Christmas. Cost: Park and farm free. Phone: (830) 644-2252.

❌ 🎣 🏕

ROSE HILL MANOR                          830/644-2247

◆◆◆ ◆◆◆
Country Inn
Rates not provided

Address: 2614 Upper Albert Rd 78671 Location: Jct US 290, 2 mi s on Ranch Rd 1623 to Upper Albert Rd, then just w. Located on a peaceful 40-acre ranch. Facility: In a quiet rural setting, the country inn features upscale accommodations. Large rooms fill both the main house and detached lodgings. 12 units, some cottages. 1-2 stories, interior/exterior corridors. Terms: age restrictions may apply. Dining: Austin's, The Restaurant at Rose Hill Manor, see separate listing. Activities: bicycles. Featured Amenity: full hot breakfast.

SAVE 🍴 🍸 📶 ✕ 💻 / SOME UNITS 🛅 🖥

AUSTIN'S, THE RESTAURANT AT ROSE HILL MANOR
                                         830/644-2247

◆◆◆ American. Fine Dining. $9-$45 AAA Inspector Notes: Surrounded by distant views and gently rolling country hills, this excellent restaurant near Fredericksburg offers a surprisingly high level of artistic and flavorful cuisine at a leisurely European pace. A tasting menu is available, or guests can select from a la carte favorites like risotto, truffles and jumbo lump crab cakes. Features: full bar. Reservations: suggested. Address: 2614 Upper Albert Rd 78671 Location: Jct US 290, 2 mi s on Ranch Rd 1623 to Upper Albert Rd, then just w; in Rose Hill Manor.   D

AAA.com/
TourBook
Comments

Let Your
Voice
Be Heard

## SUGAR LAND pop. 78,817
- Hotels & Restaurants map & index p. 324
- Part of Houston area — see map p. 301

### BEST WESTERN SUGARLAND INN   (281)232-0680

Hotel
$105-$125

**AAA Benefit:** Members save 10% or more with Best Western!

**Address:** 6330 E Riverpark Dr 77479 **Location:** US 59 exit SR 99 (Grand Pkwy), just w to Riverpark Dr, then just n. **Facility:** 61 units, some kitchens. 3 stories, interior corridors. **Pool(s):** outdoor. **Activities:** hot tub, exercise room. **Guest Services:** valet and coin laundry. **Featured Amenity: full hot breakfast.**

### DRURY INN & SUITES-HOUSTON/SUGAR LAND
(281)277-9700   128

Hotel $90-$229 **Address:** 13770 Southwest Frwy 77478 **Location:** US 59 exit Dairy Ashford Rd/Sugar Creek Blvd; on north frontage road. **Facility:** 133 units. 5 stories, interior corridors. **Terms:** cancellation fee imposed. **Pool(s):** heated outdoor, heated indoor. **Activities:** hot tub, exercise room. **Guest Services:** valet and coin laundry.

### HILTON GARDEN INN HOUSTON SUGAR LAND
(281)491-7777   129

Hotel
$99-$239

**AAA Benefit:** Members save up to 10%!

**Address:** 722 Bonaventure Way 77478 **Location:** US 59 and SR 6, 1.2 mi n on SR 6 to University Blvd, just w, then just n. **Facility:** 202 units. 6 stories, interior corridors. **Terms:** 1-7 night minimum stay, cancellation fee imposed. **Pool(s):** heated outdoor. **Activities:** hot tub, exercise room. **Guest Services:** valet and coin laundry. **Featured Amenity: breakfast buffet.**

### HYATT PLACE HOUSTON/SUGAR LAND
(281)491-0300   130

Hotel
$79-$269

**HYATT PLACE**
**AAA Benefit:** Members save 10%!

**Address:** 16730 Creek Bend Dr 77478 **Location:** Jct US 59 and SR 6, just n on SR 6 to Fluor Daniel Dr, just e. **Facility:** 214 units. 9 stories, interior corridors. **Terms:** cancellation fee imposed. **Pool(s):** heated outdoor. **Activities:** exercise room. **Guest Services:** valet laundry. **Featured Amenity: breakfast buffet.**

Safety tip: Keep a current AAA/CAA

Road Atlas in every vehicle

## WHERE TO EAT

### BAKER ST. PUB & GRILL   713/986-8635
British. Casual Dining. $8-$19 **AAA Inspector Notes:** A lively and fun spot to meet and eat. Indoor or sidewalk dining is available for those looking for some British delights. **Features:** full bar, happy hour. **Address:** 15970 City Walk 77479 **Location:** Jct US 59 and SR 6; on southeast corner; in Town Square District.

### BERRYHILL BAJA GRILL   281/313-8226
Mexican. Casual Dining. $4-$12 **AAA Inspector Notes:** The large portrait of Elvis holding a fish taco says it all. This place is known for them, but the tamales and burritos deserve a second look. The grill is a city institution, and that history benefits anyone who stops in for the varied Mexican treats. The chunky tomato salsa is reason enough to dine here. Both locals and guest of nearby hotels unwind in the lively bar. **Features:** full bar. **Address:** 13703 Southwest Frwy 77478 **Location:** US 59 exit Alternate Rt US 90/Spur 41 southbound; exit Dairy Ashford Rd/Sugar Creek Blvd northbound; on northbound frontage road.

### CAFE EXPRESS   281/980-9222
American. Casual Dining. $7-$15 **AAA Inspector Notes:** Even if this place does serve burgers, its American/Mediterranean menu lists plenty of more healthful options, such as pasta dishes, roasted chicken and Caesar salad. Everything is made to order and served fast for people on the go. Those with a little more time to spare may want to enjoy some wine or the classic German chocolate cake. **Features:** beer & wine. **Address:** 15930 City Walk 77479 **Location:** US 59 exit SR 6, just e.

### THE CHEESECAKE FACTORY   281/313-9500   54
American. Casual Dining. $9-$30 **AAA Inspector Notes:** A display case of mouthwatering cheesecakes is the first thing visitors see as they walk through the door. The extensive menu incorporates many types of cuisine, including Asian, Italian, Greek and Spanish. **Features:** full bar, Sunday brunch. **Address:** 16535 Southwest Frwy 77479 **Location:** US 59 and SR 6; in First Colony Mall; on southeast corner. **Parking:** on-site and valet.

### LA MADELEINE COUNTRY FRENCH CAFE   281/494-4400
Traditional French. Casual Dining. $7-$12 **AAA Inspector Notes:** A fireplace creates the focal point at this cozy European style café where you can always get a quiche or savory stuffed puffed pastry on the go or stick around for a chicken crêpe or French dip sandwich. Heartier entrées like rotisserie chicken are offered and every season promises menu surprises. Whatever you decide on you probably will not get out the door without enjoying one of their tempting sweet pastries. **Features:** beer & wine. **Address:** 2675 Town Center Blvd 77479 **Location:** US 59 and SR 6; on southeast corner; in First Colony Mall.

### PAPPASITO'S CANTINA   281/565-9797
Mexican. Casual Dining. $10-$49 **AAA Inspector Notes:** Fine traditional offerings are served in an upscale cantina atmosphere. Often crowded during peak hours, the immensely popular stop dishes up generous portions of sizzling fajitas, enchiladas and other traditional Mexican favorites, including some shrimp specialties. The terrific margaritas are guaranteed to get attention. Tables in the large dining room are closely spaced. Ice cream with cinnamon on chocolate bread pudding shouldn't be missed. **Features:** full bar, Sunday brunch, happy hour. **Reservations:** suggested. **Address:** 13750 Hwy 59 S 77478 **Location:** US 59 exit Dairy Ashford Rd/Sugar Creek Blvd; on west frontage road.

### PERRY'S STEAKHOUSE & GRILLE   281/565-2727   53
Steak. Fine Dining. $24-$48 **AAA Inspector Notes:** An excellent selection of prime steaks, lamb and pork chops are served in an professional and upscale establishment. **Features:** full bar. **Reservations:** suggested. **Address:** 2115 Town Square Place 77479 **Location:** US 59 exit SR 6, just s; in Town Square Shopping Center. **Parking:** on-site and valet.

(See map & index p. 324.)

SALTGRASS STEAKHOUSE                281/232-3502

▼▼ Steak. Casual Dining. $9-$30 AAA Inspector Notes: Those looking for something different should try the comfortable steakhouse, which never says no to a special request. Born from the spirit of Texas cattle drives, the restaurant resembles a Texas lodge, with high ceilings and mounted animal heads. Baby back ribs are so tender the meat falls off the bone. Also on the menu are hearty steaks, prime rib, chicken, seafood and yummy desserts. Features: full bar. Address: 19720 Southwest Frwy 77479 Location: US 59 exit SR 99 (Grand Pkwy); on west frontage road.

[SAVE] [L] [D] CALL [&M]

## SULPHUR SPRINGS (C-9) pop. 15,449, elev. 494'

With nearly 500 dairies, the Sulphur Springs/Hopkins County area is one of the leading dairy producers in Texas. The town is named for its abundant underground springs; a source under the town square once heated a swimming pool.

Hopkins County Chamber of Commerce: 300 Connally St., P.O. Box 347, Sulphur Springs, TX 75483. Phone: (903) 885-6515.

MUSIC BOX EXHIBIT is in the city library at 611 N. Davis St. More than 150 unusual and antique music boxes collected during a 50-year period are displayed. Time: Allow 30 minutes minimum. Hours: Mon.-Wed. and Fri. 9-6, Thurs. 11-8, Sat. 9-1. Closed major holidays. Cost: Donations. Phone: (903) 885-4926.

SOUTHWEST DAIRY MUSEUM is at 1210 Houston St. The center traces the history of the dairy industry from rural farm life before electricity to modern milking methods, bottling and transportation. Exhibits include a re-created 1930s kitchen and dairy barn. Tours: Guided tours are available. Time: Allow 30 minutes minimum. Hours: Mon.-Fri. 9-4. Closed major holidays. Cost: Donations. Phone: (903) 439-6455. [↑↓]

BEST WESTERN TRAIL DUST INN & SUITES
                                    (903)885-7515

Hotel
$64-$74

AAA Benefit: Members save 10% or more with Best Western!

Address: 1521 Shannon Rd 75482 Location: I-30 exit 127; on eastbound frontage road. Facility: 99 units. 2 stories (no elevator), interior/exterior corridors. Pool(s): outdoor. Activities: exercise room. Guest Services: valet and coin laundry.

[SAVE] [+K] [↑↓] [Y] [🛏] [BIZ] [📶]

HAMPTON INN                          (903)439-4646

▼▼▼ Hotel $75-$94 Address: 1202 Mockingbird Ln 75482 Location: I-30 exit 124, just n, then just e. Facility: 70 units. 4 stories, interior corridors. Terms: 1-7 night minimum stay, cancellation fee imposed. Pool(s): outdoor. Activities: hot tub, exercise room. Guest Services: valet laundry.

AAA Benefit: Members save up to 10%!

CALL [&M] [🛏] [BIZ] [HS] [📶] [X] [💻] / SOME UNITS [🔋] [🖨]

---

HOLIDAY INN EXPRESS HOTEL & SUITES     903/885-6851

▼▼▼ Hotel. Rates not provided. Address: 411 E Industrial Dr 75482 Location: I-30 exit 125; on westbound frontage road. Facility: 72 units. 3 stories, interior corridors. Pool(s): outdoor. Activities: exercise room. Guest Services: valet and coin laundry.

[↑↓] CALL [&M] [🛏] [BIZ] [HS] [📶] [X] [🔋] [🖨] [💻]

LA QUINTA INN & SUITES SULPHUR SPRINGS
                                    (903)885-8181

▼▼▼ Hotel $90-$125 Address: 1344 Eaton Dr 75482 Location: I-30 exit 125; on westbound frontage road. Facility: 65 units. 3 stories, interior corridors. Pool(s): heated indoor. Activities: hot tub, exercise room. Guest Services: valet and coin laundry.

CALL [&M] [🛏] [BIZ] [HS] [📶] [🔋] [🖨] [💻] / SOME UNITS [🐾]

## WHERE TO EAT

BURTON'S FAMILY RESTAURANT            903/885-5976

▼ American. Casual Dining. $9-$19 AAA Inspector Notes: Just off the interstate, the family-owned and -operated restaurant serves simple home cooking for the whole family. Patrons can pair beef, chicken, seafood and pork dishes with a selection of home-style vegetables. Don't neglect a slice of freshly baked pie. Wednesday through Saturday it stays open 24 hours. Address: 1505 Shannon Rd E 75482 Location: I-30 exit 127; on south side road.

[B] [L] [D] [🔧]

## SWEETWATER (D-6) pop. 10,906, elev. 2,164'
• Hotels p. 546 • Restaurants p. 546

Many streams around Sweetwater are tainted by gypsum deposits, which are good for the local wallboard industry but not for drinking. Sweetwater Creek offered early settlers the only potable water in the area.

During World War II an experiment in military aviation took place outside Sweetwater at Avenger Field. More than 1,000 women were trained 1943-44 as military pilots in a program almost identical to that given their male counterparts. As part of the Women Airforce Service Pilots (WASP), they flew every aircraft the Army Air Force had (see National WASP World War II Museum attraction listing). Now Avenger Field is the municipal airport.

Sweetwater Chamber of Commerce: 810 E. Broadway, P.O. Box 1148, Sweetwater, TX 79556. Phone: (325) 235-5488 or (800) 658-6757.

NATIONAL WASP WORLD WAR II MUSEUM is at 210 Loop 170 on Avenger Field, the original WASP (Women Airforce Service Pilots) training base. Highlights include photographs, a duty-station map, a re-created sleeping bay and a model of the gate that guarded Avenger Field. Also on display is a statue of Walt Disney's female gremlin Fifinella, who became the WASP mascot. Tours: Guided tours are available. Time: Allow 1 hour minimum. Hours: Wed.-Sat. 10-5, Sun.1-5. Cost: Free. Phone: (325) 235-0099.

PIONEER CITY COUNTY MUSEUM is at 610 E. Third St. This 1906 house, partly decorated in period, displays Native American artifacts, pioneer farming and ranching equipment, photographs and paintings of pioneer families, late 19th-century fashions, toys and dolls. One room is dedicated to the Women Air Force Service Pilots (WASP) who trained at Avenger Field to ferry aircraft during World

War II. **Time:** Allow 30 minutes minimum. **Hours:** Tues.-Fri. 1-4. Closed major holidays. **Cost:** Donations. **Phone:** (325) 235-8547.

## BEST WESTERN PLUS SWEETWATER INN & SUITES
(325)236-6512

Hotel
$101-$119

**AAA Benefit:** Members save 10% or more with Best Western!

**Address:** 300 NW Georgia Ave 79556 **Location:** I-20 exit 244; jct US 70. **Facility:** 58 units. 3 stories, interior corridors. **Terms:** check-in 4 pm. **Pool(s):** heated outdoor. **Activities:** hot tub, exercise room. **Guest Services:** valet and coin laundry.

## HAMPTON INN SWEETWATER
(325)235-3337

Hotel
$79-$169

**AAA Benefit:** Members save up to 10%!

**Address:** 302 SE Georgia Ave 79556 **Location:** I-20 exit 244; on south frontage road. **Facility:** 72 units. 4 stories, interior corridors. **Terms:** 1-7 night minimum stay, cancellation fee imposed. **Pool(s):** heated indoor. **Activities:** hot tub, exercise room. **Guest Services:** coin laundry. **Featured Amenity:** breakfast buffet.

## RANCH HOUSE MOTEL & RESTAURANT
325/236-6341

Hotel
$65-$75

**Address:** 301 SW Georgia Ave 79556 **Location:** I-20 exit 244, just w of jct SR 70; on south frontage road. **Facility:** 49 units. 2 stories (no elevator), interior/exterior corridors. **Terms:** cancellation fee imposed. **Pool(s):** outdoor. **Featured Amenity:** full hot breakfast.

### WHERE TO EAT

BUCK'S STEAKS & BBQ
325/235-4049

Steak Barbecue. Casual Dining. $5-$29 **AAA Inspector Notes:** The rustic family restaurant serves steaks, pork chops, chicken, quail and a barbecue buffet that includes brisket, ham, sausage and ribs. Burgers and a children's menu are also available. **Address:** 103 SW Georgia Ave 79556 **Location:** I-20 exit 244.

## TAYLOR pop. 15,191

### BEST WESTERN TAYLOR INN
(512)352-5292

Hotel
$99-$129

**AAA Benefit:** Members save 10% or more with Best Western!

**Address:** 2600 W 2nd St 76574 **Location:** US 79, 1 mi w. **Facility:** 40 units. 2 stories (no elevator), exterior corridors. **Pool(s):** outdoor. **Featured Amenity:** full hot breakfast.

### WHERE TO EAT

LOUIE MUELLER BARBECUE
512/352-6206

Barbecue. Quick Serve. $4-$19 **AAA Inspector Notes:** Now owned by the third generation of Mueller's, this landmark barbecue dates back to 1949 and has won numerous awards and been featured in several movies. The brisket is very special—don't pass it up! **Features:** beer only. **Address:** 206 W 2nd St 76574 **Location:** On Business Rt US 79; downtown.

## TEMPLE (E-8) pop. 66,102, elev. 736'

Temple began as a rail and retail center serving the cattle trade. Currently, the city is best known for its concentration of hospitals and the proximity of one of the country's largest military bases, Fort Hood.

**Temple Visitor Center:** 120 W. Central Ave., Temple, TX 76501. **Phone:** (254) 298-5900 or (800) 479-0338.

**RAILROAD AND HERITAGE MUSEUM** is off I-35 exit 301, .9 mi. on Central Ave. to 7th St., then s. to 315 W. Ave. B. Housed in a restored 1911 Santa Fe depot and working Amtrak station, the museum depicts railroad history and local heritage. Exhibits include railroad equipment, model trains, a telegraph room and listening stations for train communications. Locomotives, cabooses and passenger cars are displayed outside. **Time:** Allow 1 hour minimum. **Hours:** Tues.-Sat. 10-4. **Cost:** $4; $3 (ages 60+); $2 (ages 5-12). **Phone:** (254) 298-5172.

### BAYMONT INN & SUITES TEMPLE
(254)770-0300

Hotel
$64-$84

**Address:** 1415 N General Bruce Dr 76504 **Location:** I-35 exit 302. **Facility:** 58 units. 2 stories (no elevator), interior corridors. **Terms:** 3 day cancellation notice. **Pool(s):** outdoor. **Guest Services:** valet and coin laundry. **Featured Amenity:** full hot breakfast.

## BEST WESTERN TEMPLE INN & SUITES  (254)742-1122

Hotel
$89-$149

AAA Benefit: Members save 10% or more with Best Western!

**Address:** 602 N General Bruce Dr 76504 **Location:** I-35 exit 302; on east frontage road. **Facility:** 60 units. 2 stories (no elevator), interior corridors. **Pool(s):** outdoor. **Activities:** exercise room. **Guest Services:** coin laundry. **Featured Amenity: full hot breakfast.**

## COUNTRY INN & SUITES BY CARLSON   254/778-6700

◆◆◆ **Hotel.** Rates not provided. **Address:** 1414 SW H K Dodgen Loop 76504 **Location:** I-35 exit 299, 1.5 mi e on Loop 363 (US 190) at SR 36; on north frontage road. **Facility:** 60 units. 3 stories, interior corridors. **Pool(s):** heated indoor. **Activities:** hot tub, exercise room. **Guest Services:** valet and coin laundry.

## FAIRFIELD INN BY MARRIOTT   (254)771-3030

◆◆ **Hotel** $90-$127 **Address:** 1402 SW H K Dodgen Loop 76504 **Location:** 0.5 mi s on Loop 363 (US 190) at SR 36. **Facility:** 62 units. 3 stories, interior corridors. **Pool(s):** heated indoor. **Activities:** hot tub. **Guest Services:** valet laundry.

**AAA Benefit:** Members save 5% or more!

## HILTON GARDEN INN-TEMPLE   (254)773-0200

◆◆◆ **Hotel** $99-$199 **Address:** 1749 Scott Blvd 76504 **Location:** I-35 exit 299, 1.5 mi e, then 0.3 mi nw of jct Loop 363 (US 190) and SR 36. Across from hospital. **Facility:** 133 units. 4 stories, interior corridors. **Terms:** check-in 4 pm, 1-7 night minimum stay, cancellation fee imposed. **Pool(s):** heated indoor. **Activities:** hot tub, exercise room. **Guest Services:** valet and coin laundry.

**AAA Benefit:** Members save up to 10%!

## LA QUINTA INN & SUITES TEMPLE   (254)771-2980

◆◆ **Hotel** $75-$114 **Address:** 1604 W Barton Ave 76504 **Location:** SR 53, just e; jct I-35 and US 81 exit 301. **Facility:** 106 units. 3 stories, interior/exterior corridors. **Pool(s):** outdoor.

## QUALITY INN   254/770-1100

◆◆◆ **Hotel.** Rates not provided. **Address:** 1610 W Nugent Ave 76504 **Location:** I-35 exit 302. **Facility:** 85 units. 3 stories, interior corridors. **Pool(s):** outdoor. **Activities:** exercise room. **Guest Services:** valet and coin laundry.

## RESIDENCE INN BY MARRIOTT   (254)773-8400

◆◆◆ **Extended Stay Contemporary Hotel** $94-$142 **Address:** 4301 S General Bruce Dr 76502 **Location:** I-35 exit 298; on east frontage road. **Facility:** 103 units, some efficiencies and kitchens. 3 stories, interior corridors. **Pool(s):** heated outdoor. **Activities:** hot tub, exercise room. **Guest Services:** valet and coin laundry.

## SUPER 8   (254)778-0962

Hotel
$60-$90

**Address:** 5505 S General Bruce Dr 76502 **Location:** I-35 exit 297. **Facility:** 94 units. 2 stories (no elevator), exterior corridors. **Pool(s):** outdoor. **Activities:** exercise room. **Guest Services:** coin laundry. **Featured Amenity: continental breakfast.**

### WHERE TO EAT

## CHEEVES BROS. STEAK HOUSE   254/742-2300

◆◆◆ Steak. Fine Dining. $10-$67 **AAA Inspector Notes:** The fine-dining steakhouse's specialty is prime beef, and the menu touts that this place has been voted to have the best steaks in central Texas. Also offered is a good selection of seafood, chicken and pasta. The restaurant boasts one of the area's best wine cellars. **Features:** full bar, happy hour. **Address:** 14 E Ave A 76501 **Location:** Between S Main and S 2nd sts; downtown. **Parking:** valet and street only.
L D

## EL CHICO   254/771-3080

◆◆◆
Tex-Mex
Casual Dining
$5-$15

**AAA Inspector Notes:** Inside and out, the decor of the popular Mexican restaurant is inviting. The menu features traditional favorites such as enchiladas, tacos, burritos and fajitas. The broad menu also lists a few American classics. **Features:** full bar. **Reservations:** suggested. **Address:** 3303 S 31st St 76502 **Location:** 0.5 mi w on Loop 363 (US 190). L D

## MONTEREY'S LITTLE MEXICO   254/778-9212

◆◆ Tex-Mex. Casual Dining. $7-$23 **AAA Inspector Notes:** Serving traditional Tex-Mex cuisine since 1955, the family-friendly restaurant serves up a festive mercado atmosphere and tasty fajitas. The restaurant is conveniently located near the Temple Mall on the south side of town and is easily accessible from the interstate. **Features:** full bar. **Address:** 1712 SW H K Dodgen Loop 76504 **Location:** US 190, jct SR 36, 0.7 mi s on Loop 363 (US 190). L D

## PIGNETTI'S RESTAURANT   254/778-1269

◆◆◆ Italian. Casual Dining. $7-$30 **AAA Inspector Notes:** On this downtown eatery's menu are steak, veal, chicken, seafood, pasta and pizza choices. Portions are ample. This place is popular, so reservations are suggested. **Features:** beer & wine. **Reservations:** suggested. **Address:** 14 S 2nd St 76501 **Location:** Between E Ave A and E Centra St, just e of Main St; downtown. **Parking:** valet and street only. L D

## TERLINGUA (G-3) pop. 58, elev. 2,891'

Once a prime source of quicksilver, Terlingua became a ghost town after the collapse of the Chisos Mining Company in 1942. In recent years, tourism and an annual chili cook-off have put the village back on the map. Located in the Big Bend region, Terlingua is a departure point for river-rafting expeditions on the Rio Grande.

**BIG BEND RIVER TOURS** departs from jct. SR 118 and FM 170. River tours ranging from a half-day to 21 days take visitors through the Rio Grande canyons of Big Bend National Park and Big Bend Ranch State Park. Also available are canoe, hiking, backroad, interpretive and combination float and horseback trips.

Pets are not permitted. **Hours:** Trips depart daily; phone for schedule. **Cost:** Half-day trips $60-69.

Full-day trips $130-$155. Overnight trips start at $290. Prices exclude river-use fees. Minimum age varies from 2 to 6, depending on trip. Reservations are recommended. **Phone:** (432) 371-3033 or (800) 545-4240.

**FAR FLUNG OUTDOOR CENTER** is just outside the west entrance to Big Bend National Park. A va-

riety of float trips range from a half-day to 10 days through the Rio Grande canyons of Big Bend National Park. Jeep rentals and tours, guided ATV tours, and guided walking tours also are available.

**Hours:** Trips are available year-round. **Cost:** Half-day river trips $69-$74; $130 (full-day); $325 (overnight per person). Prices include park admission and river-use fees. Rates may vary; phone ahead. Reservations are required. **Phone:** (432) 371-2633 or (800) 839-7238.

## TERRELL pop. 15,816
• Part of Dallas area — see map p. 161

**BEST WESTERN COUNTRY INN** (972)563-1521

Hotel
$90-$100

**AAA Benefit:** Members save 10% or more with Best Western!

**Address:** 1604 Hwy 34 S 75160 **Location:** I-20 exit 501 (SR 34), just n. **Facility:** 44 units. 2 stories (no elevator), exterior corridors. **Terms:** 2-4 night minimum stay - seasonal, 3 day cancellation notice. **Pool(s):** outdoor. **Guest Services:** coin laundry.

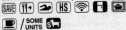

**HOLIDAY INN EXPRESS HOTEL & SUITES TERRELL** (972)563-7888

Hotel
$124-$134

**Address:** 300 Tanger Dr 75160 **Location:** I-20 exit 501 (SR 34), just s, then just w. **Facility:** 68 units. 4 stories, interior corridors. **Terms:** cancellation fee imposed. **Pool(s):** heated indoor. **Activities:** hot tub, exercise room. **Guest Services:** coin laundry. **Featured Amenity:** breakfast buffet.

## WHERE TO EAT

**NAPOLI'S** 972/524-8170

Italian. Casual Dining. $9-$17 **AAA Inspector Notes:** For most travelers, Terrell may be just a small stop on the interstate with little hope for good dining. But venture off the interstate for a few short minutes and you can enjoy a nice selection of Northern Italian cuisine at this family run-restaurant. The very broad menu includes chicken, veal, pasta and pizza. **Features:** beer & wine. **Address:** 101 Hwy 205 75160 **Location:** Just n of jct US 80 and SR 205.

## TEXARKANA (C-10) pop. 36,411, elev. 290'

The Arkansas-Texas state line runs approximately through the center of the dual municipality of Texarkana, which has a combined population of about 61,000.

For hundreds of years before European settlement in the area, the Great Southwest Trail, the major route between the Native American villages of the Mississippi Valley and the West and Southwest, crossed the area around what is now Texarkana. The Grand Caddoes, hospitable to explorers and settlers, farmed in the vicinity and maintained six villages along the banks of the Red River.

Shortly after 1840 a permanent settlement was established at Lost Prairie, 15 miles east of Texarkana. A number of mounds and other traces of former Native American civilizations remain within a 30-mile radius of the town.

During the 1850s the Cairo and Fulton Railroad served portions of Arkansas and by 1874 had crossed the Red River into Texas, establishing direct rail service to St. Louis. The Texas and Pacific Railroad had laid track to the Arkansas boundary, and the place where the two lines met became a town—Texarkana.

The state line runs through the middle of the Texarkana Post Office and Courthouse, said to be the only federal building situated in two states. Built in 1932 of pink granite from Texas and limestone from Arkansas, the post office has two separate zip codes. Residents on both sides of the border enjoy the Perot Theatre, 221 Main St., a restored 1924 facility that presents a variety of Broadway shows.

**Texarkana Chamber of Commerce:** 819 N. State Line Ave., Texarkana, TX 75501. **Phone:** (903) 792-7191 or (877) 275-5289.

**ACE OF CLUBS HOUSE MUSEUM** is at 420 Pine St. This 22-sided house was built in 1885 reputedly from the winnings of a poker game. The Italianate Victorian-style building has three octagonal wings and one rectangular wing and features original furniture. A 15-minute video presentation is followed by a 1-hour guided tour. High heels and photography are not permitted. **Time:** Allow 1 hour, 30 minutes minimum. **Hours:** Tues.-Fri. by appointment, Sat. 10-4. Last tour begins 1 hour before closing. Closed major holidays. **Cost:** $6; $5 (ages 60+); $4 (students with ID). **Phone:** (903) 793-4831.

**DISCOVERY PLACE CHILDREN'S MUSEUM** is at the corner of Pine St. and State Line Ave. at 215 Pine St. Educational and entertaining hands-on exhibits focus on science and history. A theater, a science lab and a 12-foot sound wall sculpture enhance the learning environment. **Time:** Allow 1 hour minimum. **Hours:** Tues.-Sat. 10-4. Closed major holidays. **Cost:** $4.50; free (ages 0-4). **Phone:** (903) 793-4831.

**MUSEUM OF REGIONAL HISTORY** is 4 blks. s. of US 59/67/71/82 at 219 N. State Line Ave. Housed in an 1879 brick building, this museum traces the region's history from the early Caddo Indians through

20th-century citizens, including early industry, post World War II and the civil rights movement. In addition to the Native American Gallery, the Scott Joplin Gallery is dedicated to the composer's early life and career in Texarkana. **Hours:** Tues.-Sat. 10-4. Closed major holidays. **Cost:** $5; $4 (ages 60+ and students ages 12-18 with ID); $3.50 (ages 5-11). **Phone:** (903) 793-4831.

## CANDLEWOOD SUITES TEXARKANA      (903)334-7418

Extended Stay Hotel
$79-$89

**Address:** 2901 S Cowhorn Creek Loop 75503 **Location:** I-30 exit 220 (Richmond Rd) westbound, just s on Cowhorn Creek Rd, then just w; exit 220B (Richmond Rd) eastbound, 1.5 mi on frontage road, then just s. **Facility:** 80 efficiencies. 4 stories, interior corridors. **Activities:** exercise room. **Guest Services:** complimentary and valet laundry.

## COMFORT SUITES      (903)223-0951

Hotel $79-$99 **Address:** 215 Richill Dr 75503 **Location:** I-30 exit 220B (Richmond Rd); on westbound frontage road. **Facility:** 70 units. 3 stories, interior corridors. **Amenities:** safes. **Pool(s):** heated indoor. **Activities:** exercise room. **Guest Services:** valet and coin laundry.

## COUNTRY INN & SUITES BY CARLSON TEXARKANA
903/838-6955

Hotel. Rates not provided. **Address:** 1918 University Ave 75503 **Location:** I-30 exit 219, just s. **Facility:** 81 units. 4 stories, interior corridors. **Pool(s):** heated indoor. **Activities:** hot tub. **Guest Services:** valet and coin laundry.

## COURTYARD BY MARRIOTT      (903)334-7400

Hotel
$119-$139

COURTYARD Marriott

**AAA Benefit:** Members save 5% or more!

**Address:** 5001 N Cowhorn Creek Loop 75503 **Location:** I-30 exit 222 (Summerhill Rd), just w on frontage road, then just n. **Facility:** 90 units. 3 stories, interior corridors. **Pool(s):** heated indoor. **Activities:** hot tub, exercise room. **Guest Services:** valet and coin laundry.

## FAIRFIELD INN & SUITES BY MARRIOTT      (903)306-0473

Hotel $109-$129 **Address:** 4209 Mall Dr 75501 **Location:** I-30 exit 219; on eastbound frontage road. **Facility:** 83 units. 4 stories, interior corridors. **Pool(s):** heated indoor. **Activities:** exercise room. **Guest Services:** valet and coin laundry.

**AAA Benefit:** Members save 5% or more!

## HAMPTON INN & SUITES      (903)832-3499

Hotel
$129-$169

Hampton

**AAA Benefit:** Members save up to 10%!

**Address:** 4601 Cowhorn Creek Rd 75503 **Location:** I-30 exit 220B (Richmond Rd), 0.5 mi e on eastbound frontage road to Cowhorn Creek Loop, then just sw. **Facility:** 81 units. 4 stories, interior corridors. **Terms:** 1-7 night minimum stay, cancellation fee imposed. **Pool(s):** heated indoor. **Activities:** exercise room. **Guest Services:** valet and coin laundry.

## HILTON GARDEN INN      (903)792-1065

Hotel $99-$169 **Address:** 2910 S Cowhorn Creek Loop 75503 **Location:** I-30 exit 220 (Richmond Rd) westbound, just s on Cowhorn Creek Rd; exit 220B eastbound, 1.5 mi on frontage road, then just s. **Facility:** 154 units. 6 stories, interior corridors. **Terms:** 1-7 night minimum stay, cancellation fee imposed. **Pool(s):** indoor. **Activities:** hot tub, exercise room. **Guest Services:** valet and coin laundry.

**AAA Benefit:** Members save up to 10%!

## TOWNEPLACE SUITES BY MARRIOTT      (903)334-8800

Extended Stay Hotel
$99-$129

TownePlace SUITES Marriott

**AAA Benefit:** Members save 5% or more!

**Address:** 5020 N Cowhorn Creek Loop 75503 **Location:** I-30 exit 222 (Summerhill Rd), w on frontage road, then just n. **Facility:** 85 units, some two bedrooms, efficiencies and kitchens. 4 stories, interior corridors. **Pool(s):** heated outdoor. **Activities:** exercise room. **Guest Services:** valet and coin laundry.

## WHERE TO EAT

### BRYCE'S CAFETERIA      903/792-1611

American. Cafeteria. $4-$7 **AAA Inspector Notes:** This cafeteria has moved around a bit, but it's hard to argue with longevity. It's been a local tradition for more than 80 years. No matter what you think of cafeteria food, they serve several standouts among such classic favorites as meatloaf, spaghetti and pecan pie. The service here is a vestige of when this cafeteria got its start perhaps, genteel and friendly. **Address:** 2021 Mall Dr 75503 **Location:** I-30 exit 222 (Summerhill Rd), just s to Mall Dr, then just w. L D

### DIXIE DINER #2      903/223-0841

American. Casual Dining. $8-$13 **AAA Inspector Notes:** Area residents rely on this small restaurant chain for down-home family favorites. Beef, chicken, pork, fish and vegetable dishes all are made in house. A slice of homemade pie is the perfect finish to a meal. **Address:** 4115 N Kings Hwy, Suite 120 75503 **Location:** I-30 exit 218, just n. L D

## GRANDY'S RESTAURANT
903/832-5206

 American. Quick Serve. $4-$8 **AAA Inspector Notes:** Fried chicken and country-fried steak are menu standbys at the restaurant, a regional franchise. They also offer a family-style dining menu. The décor is a step up from that of most quick-serve eateries and more resembles that of a conventional restaurant. Some elements of increased service include additional rolls, iced tea refills and tray removal. **Address:** 1720 Richmond Rd 75503 **Location:** I-30 exit 220B (Richmond Rd), 0.7 mi s. [B] [L] [D]

## IRONWOOD GRILL
903/223-4644

American. Casual Dining. $6-$20 **AAA Inspector Notes:** Like a beam of light shining from the sea of chain restaurants, this place seems more like it's in Boulder or Austin. This laid-back eatery exudes a rustic purity with sagey green walls, natural wood beams, corrugated metal and indie music playing over the speakers. Here they pay attention to the details and elevate what would otherwise be a common menu of pizza, steaks, burgers, salads and sandwiches. The children's sandbox makes this a family favorite. **Features:** full bar, patio dining. **Address:** 4312 Morris Ln 75503 **Location:** I-30 E exit 220B (Richmond Rd), 1.1 mi n, then just w. [L] [D]

## JULIE'S DELI & MARKET
903/792-3354

American. Quick Serve. $7-$10 **AAA Inspector Notes:** Just a quick hop off the interstate, this deli has a great selection of cold and hot sandwiches, quiches, salads and desserts. Road trippers and RV travelers should consider this place to load up on wholesome food for the road since the market area sells frozen casseroles for parties large and small. Items by the pound, including chicken salad, meatloaf, black bean salsa and rosemary potatoes, also are sold from their cold cases. The friendly staff is just a bonus. **Address:** 4055 Summerhill Square 75503 **Location:** I-30 exit 222 (Summerhill Rd), just s. [L] CALL [M]

# Nearby Arkansas

## TEXARKANA pop. 29,919

### BEST WESTERN PLUS TEXARKANA INN & SUITES
(870)774-1534

Hotel
$89-$109

**AAA Benefit:** Members save 10% or more with Best Western!

**Address:** 5219 Crossroads Pkwy 71854 **Location:** I-30 exit 1 (Jefferson Ave); on westbound frontage road. **Facility:** 76 units. 3 stories, interior corridors. **Pool(s):** outdoor. **Activities:** exercise room. **Guest Services:** valet and coin laundry. **Featured Amenity:** full hot breakfast.

SAVE CALL [M] [pool] [BIZ] [HS] [wifi]
[X] [fridge] [micro] [coffee]

### HOLIDAY INN EXPRESS HOTEL & SUITES TEXARKANA EAST
(870)216-0083

Hotel
$76-$95

**Address:** 5210 Crossroads Pkwy 71854 **Location:** I-30 exit 1 (Jefferson Ave); on westbound frontage road. **Facility:** 88 units. 4 stories, interior corridors. **Terms:** cancellation fee imposed. **Pool(s):** heated indoor. **Activities:** hot tub, exercise room. **Guest Services:** valet and coin laundry. **Featured Amenity:** breakfast buffet.

SAVE CALL [M] [pool] [BIZ] [HS] [wifi]
[coffee] / SOME UNITS [fridge] [micro]

## CATTLEMANS STEAKHOUSE
870/774-4481

Steak. Casual Dining. $10-$25 **AAA Inspector Notes:** This restaurant features the traditional steak dishes with basic presentations and preparation methods, but they also serve a nice variety of chicken and fried, broiled or blackened seafood. The dark lighting, paneled walls and vintage furniture resonate with the locals and visitors that have kept this place in business for 45 years. Prime rib is their big seller, but all entrées include salad, soup and vegetables. **Features:** full bar. **Address:** 4018 State Line Ave 71854 **Location:** I-30 exit 223A, 0.5 mi s. [D]

## EL CHICO
870/779-0300

Tex-Mex
Casual Dining
$8-$18

**AAA Inspector Notes:** Inside and out, the decor of the popular Mexican restaurant is inviting. The menu features traditional favorites such as enchiladas, tacos, burritos and fajitas. The broad menu also lists a few American classics. **Features:** full bar, happy hour. **Address:** 420 Realtor Rd 71854 **Location:** I-30 exit 1 (Jefferson Ave), just s then just w. [L] [D]

## OLD TYME BURGER SHOPPE
870/772-5775

[fyi] Not evaluated. This little burger joint has been in business for over twenty years. You can also enjoy breakfast here. **Address:** 1205 Arkansas Blvd 71854 **Location:** I-30 exit 1 (Jefferson Ave), just s.

---

This ends the Texarkana section and resumes the alphabetical city listings for Texas.

---

## TEXAS CITY pop. 45,099

### BEST WESTERN MAINLAND INN & SUITES
(409)986-6600

Hotel
$80-$100

**AAA Benefit:** Members save 10% or more with Best Western!

**Address:** 10620 Emmett F Lowry Expwy 77591 **Location:** I-45 exit 16, 1 mi s to Century Blvd exit, 0.5 mi w. Next to shopping mall. **Facility:** 52 units. 3 stories, interior corridors. **Terms:** 2 night minimum stay - seasonal. **Pool(s):** outdoor. **Activities:** exercise room. **Guest Services:** valet and coin laundry. **Featured Amenity:** full hot breakfast.

SAVE [pool] [BIZ] [HS] [wifi] [fridge] [micro]
[coffee]

### FAIRFIELD INN BY MARRIOTT
(409)986-3866

Hotel $99-$149 **Address:** 10700 Emmett F Lowry Expwy 77591 **Location:** I-45 exit 16, 1 mi s to Century Blvd exit, 0.5 mi w. Next to shopping mall. **Facility:** 64 units. 3 stories, interior corridors. **Pool(s):** heated indoor. **Activities:** hot tub. **Guest Services:** valet laundry.

**AAA Benefit:** Members save 5% or more!

[accessible] CALL [M] [pool] [wifi] [X] [coffee] / SOME UNITS [fridge] [micro]

#### HOLIDAY INN EXPRESS & SUITES TEXAS CITY
(409)986-6700

▼▼/▼▼ **Hotel** $99-$169 **Address:** 2440 Gulf Frwy 77591 **Location:** I-45 exit 15, just n. **Facility:** 70 units. 4 stories, interior corridors. *Bath:* shower only. **Terms:** 2 night minimum stay - seasonal and/or weekends. **Amenities:** safes. **Pool(s):** outdoor. **Activities:** exercise room. **Guest Services:** valet and coin laundry.

CALL 🆓Ⓜ 🛥 BIZ HS 🛜 ✕ 🛏 🖨 🖥

#### TEXAS CITY HAMPTON INN
(409)986-6686

▼▼/▼▼ **Hotel** $109-$159 **Address:** 2320 FM 2004 77591 **Location:** I-45 exit 15, just n. Next to shopping mall. **Facility:** 63 units. 3 stories, interior corridors. **Terms:** 1-7 night minimum stay, cancellation fee imposed. **Pool(s):** heated indoor. **Activities:** hot tub, exercise room. **Guest Services:** valet laundry.

> **AAA Benefit:** Members save up to 10%!

🍴 CALL 🆓Ⓜ 🛥 🛜 🖥 / SOME UNITS 🛏 🖨

---

### WHERE TO EAT

#### GRINGO'S MEXICAN KITCHEN
409/986-6864

▼/▼ Tex-Mex. Casual Dining. $7-$16 **AAA Inspector Notes:** This local chain offers great Tex-Mex in a fun atmosphere. All the usual favorites are available, including fajitas, enchiladas and burritos. They have a great margarita selection, too. This location is close to many hotels. **Features:** full bar, happy hour. **Address:** 10200 Emmett F Lowry Expwy 77591 **Location:** I-45 exit 16, 1 mi s to Century Blvd exit, then just w. L D CALL 🆓Ⓜ

#### THE REEF SEAFOOD HOUSE
409/945-6151

▼ Seafood. Casual Dining. $8-$27 **AAA Inspector Notes:** The menu focuses on fried seafood, and guests can build their own platter from selections including shrimp, clams, catfish, frog legs and crawfish. Burgers and some grilled fish and steak also are offered. The family-friendly atmosphere is very casual. The place can be a bit hard to find as it's tucked just behind the buildings on Palmer Highway (FM 1764). **Features:** full bar. **Address:** 1301 31st 1/2 St 77590 **Location:** I-45 exit 15, 5.2 mi e on FM 1764 to 31st 1/2 St.

L D CALL 🆓Ⓜ 🚫

---

### THE COLONY H-3 pop. 36,328, elev. 591'
• **Hotels & Restaurants map & index p. 179**
• **Part of Dallas area — see map p. 161**

**HAWAIIAN FALLS - THE COLONY** is at 4400 Paige Rd. Highlights of this Hawaiian-themed water park include the kid-friendly Breaker Bay wave pool, the Kona Kooler lazy river, speed and tube slides and Whirlwind 360, featuring two launching capsules.

Height restrictions apply on some rides. Lounge chairs are available on a first-come, first-served basis. Cabanas and lockers can be rented. Guests may bring their own food but must pay a $10 cooler fee. **Time:** Allow 4 hours minimum. **Hours:** Daily 10:30-6, Memorial Day-Labor Day. Days and hours vary; phone ahead. **Cost:** $26.99; $19.99 (ages 55+ and under 48 inches tall); free (ages 0-2). Under 14 must be with an adult. **Phone:** (972) 370-4327 or (888) 544-7550. 🍴 🎡

---

#### COMFORT SUITES
(972)668-5555 **15**

▼▼/▼▼ **Hotel** $75-$200

**Address:** 4796 Memorial Dr 75056 **Location:** SR 121 exit Blair Oaks southbound; exit Main St northbound, just n to Memorial Dr, then just e. **Facility:** 71 units. 3 stories, interior corridors. **Pool(s):** heated indoor. **Activities:** hot tub, exercise room. **Guest Services:** valet and coin laundry. **Featured Amenity: full hot breakfast.**

SAVE 🍴 CALL 🆓Ⓜ 🛥 BIZ 🛜 ✕ 🛏 🖥 / SOME UNITS 🐾

#### FAIRFIELD INN & SUITES BY MARRIOTT-PLANO/FRISCO/THE COLONY
(972)370-7732 **13**

▼▼/▼▼ **Hotel** $71-$143 **Address:** 5909 Stone Creek Dr 75056 **Location:** SR 121 exit Spring Creek Pkwy; on southbound frontage road. **Facility:** 104 units. 4 stories, interior corridors.

> **AAA Benefit:** Members save 5% or more!

**Pool(s):** outdoor. **Activities:** hot tub, exercise room. **Guest Services:** valet and coin laundry, area transportation.

🛥 BIZ HS 🛜 ✕ 🖥 / SOME UNITS 🛏 🖨

#### RESIDENCE INN BY MARRIOTT-PLANO/FRISCO/THE COLONY
(214)469-1155 **14**

▼▼/▼▼ **Extended Stay Hotel** $89-$179 **Address:** 6600 Cascades Ct 75056 **Location:** SR 121 exit Spring Creek Pkwy; on southwest frontage road. **Facility:** 102 units, some efficiencies and kitchens. 4 stories, interior corridors. **Pool(s):** outdoor.

> **AAA Benefit:** Members save 5% or more!

**Activities:** hot tub, exercise room. **Guest Services:** valet and coin laundry, area transportation.

💳 🍴 🛥 BIZ HS 🛜 ✕ 🛏 🖨 🖥 / SOME UNITS 🐾

---

### THE WOODLANDS pop. 93,847
• **Restaurants p. 553**
• **Part of Houston area — see map p. 301**

#### BEST WESTERN PLUS THE WOODLANDS
(936)271-2378

▼▼/▼▼ **Hotel** $109-$149

> **AAA Benefit:** Members save 10% or more with Best Western!

**Address:** 17081 I-45 S 77385 **Location:** I-45 exit 79 (College Park Dr/Needham Rd) northbound; northeast corner of SR 242; on northbound frontage road. **Facility:** 62 units. 4 stories, interior corridors. **Pool(s):** outdoor. **Activities:** exercise room. **Guest Services:** valet and coin laundry. **Featured Amenity: full hot breakfast.**

SAVE 🍴 🛥 HS 🛜 🛏 🖥

🖥 / SOME UNITS 🐾

#### COMFORT SUITES
(936)273-1500

▼▼ **Hotel** $109-$249 **Address:** 18456 I-45 S 77384 **Location:** I-45 exit 79 (College Park Dr/Needham Rd) southbound; exit 79A (College Park Dr/Needham Rd) northbound; on southbound frontage road. **Facility:** 64 units. 3 stories, interior corridors. **Terms:** check-in 4 pm. **Amenities:** safes. **Pool(s):** outdoor. **Activities:** hot tub, limited exercise equipment. **Guest Services:** valet and coin laundry.

🍴 CALL 🆓Ⓜ 🛥 HS 🛜 ✕ 🛏 🖨 🖥

---

### COURTYARD BY MARRIOTT-HOUSTON THE WOODLANDS
(281)292-3262

Hotel $109-$299 Address: 1020 Lake Front Cir 77380 Location: I-45 exit 79 (College Park Dr/Needham Rd) northbound; exit 77 (Research Forest Dr/Tamina Rd) southbound; just off southbound frontage road. Facility: 90 units. 3 stories, interior corridors. Pool(s): heated indoor. Activities: hot tub, exercise room. Guest Services: valet and coin laundry.

**AAA Benefit:** Members save 5% or more!

### DRURY INN & SUITES-HOUSTON/THE WOODLANDS
(281)362-7222

Hotel $105-$209 Address: 28099 I-45 N 77380 Location: I-45 exit 77 (Research Forest Dr/Tamina Rd) southbound; on southbound frontage road. Facility: 150 units. 7 stories, interior corridors. Terms: cancellation fee imposed. Activities: hot tub, exercise room. Guest Services: valet and coin laundry.

### FAIRFIELD INN & SUITES BY MARRIOTT THE WOODLANDS
(936)271-0110

Hotel $79-$129 Address: 16850 I-45 S 77384 Location: I-45 exit 79 (College Park Dr/Needham Rd); on northwest corner. Located behind Chevron. Facility: 83 units. 3 stories, interior corridors. Pool(s): heated indoor. Activities: exercise room. Guest Services: valet and coin laundry.

**AAA Benefit:** Members save 5% or more!

### HAMPTON INN-THE WOODLANDS I-45 N
(936)273-3400

Hotel $125-$179 Address: 18484 I-45 S 77384 Location: I-45 exit 79 (College Park Dr/Needham Rd) southbound; exit 79A (College Park Dr/Needham Rd) northbound; on southbound frontage road. Facility: 78 units. 2 stories (no elevator), exterior corridors. Terms: 1-7 night minimum stay, cancellation fee imposed. Pool(s): outdoor. Activities: hot tub, exercise room. Guest Services: valet and coin laundry.

**AAA Benefit:** Members save up to 10%!

### HILTON GARDEN INN-HOUSTON/THE WOODLANDS
(281)364-9300

Hotel $229-$249 Address: 9301 Six Pines Dr 77380 Location: I-45 exit 77 (Lake Woodlands Dr/Research Forest Dr/Tamina Rd), 0.4 mi w on Lake Woodlands Dr, then just n. Facility: 117 units. 4 stories, interior corridors. Terms: 1-7 night minimum stay, cancellation fee imposed. Pool(s): outdoor. Activities: hot tub, exercise room. Guest Services: valet and coin laundry.

**AAA Benefit:** Members save up to 10%!

### HOLIDAY INN EXPRESS HOTEL & SUITES
(281)681-8088

Hotel $99-$159

Address: 24888 I-45 N 77386 Location: I-45 exit 73 (Rayford Rd/Sawdust Rd); on northbound access road. Facility: 120 units. 3 stories, interior corridors. Pool(s): outdoor. Activities: sauna, hot tub, steamroom, exercise room. Guest Services: valet and coin laundry. Featured Amenity: full hot breakfast.

### HYATT MARKET STREET THE WOODLANDS
(281)203-5005

Boutique Contemporary Hotel $169-$349

 HYATT

**AAA Benefit:** Members save 10%!

Address: 9595 Six Pines Dr, Suite 1100 77380 Location: I-45 exit 76B (Woodlands Pkwy) northbound; center; in Market Street complex. Facility: The boutique hotel offers stylish but comfortable rooms and lively public spaces. The second-floor patio offers a sleek pool area by day and an inviting lounge with outdoor fire pits and entertainment at night. 70 units, some two bedrooms. 5 stories, interior corridors. Parking: valet and street only. Terms: check-in 4 pm, cancellation fee imposed. Amenities: safes. Some: video games. Dining: 2 restaurants, entertainment. Pool(s): heated outdoor. Activities: hot tub, exercise room. Guest Services: valet laundry, area transportation.

### LA QUINTA INN & SUITES - THE WOODLANDS SOUTH
(281)681-9188

Hotel $104-$139 Address: 24868 I-45 N 77386 Location: I-45 exit 73 (Rayford Rd/Sawdust Rd); on northbound access road. Facility: 92 units, some efficiencies and kitchens. 3 stories, interior corridors. Pool(s): outdoor. Activities: hot tub, exercise room. Guest Services: valet and coin laundry.

### RESIDENCE INN BY MARRIOTT LAKE FRONT
(281)292-3252

Extended Stay Hotel $109-$309 Address: 1040 Lake Front Cir 77380 Location: I-45 exit 79 (College Park Dr/Needham Rd) northbound; exit 77 (Research Forest Dr/Tamina Rd) southbound; just off southbound frontage road. Facility: 90 units, some two bedrooms, efficiencies and kitchens. 3 stories, interior corridors. Pool(s): heated indoor. Activities: hot tub, exercise room. Guest Services: valet and coin laundry.

**AAA Benefit:** Members save 5% or more!

### SPRINGHILL SUITES BY MARRIOTT THE WOODLANDS
(936)271-0051

Hotel $99-$189 Address: 16520 I-45 S 77384 Location: I-45 exit 79 (College Park Dr/Needham Rd); just w; in College Park Shopping Plaza. Facility: 138 units. 4 stories, interior corridors. Pool(s): outdoor. Activities: hot tub, exercise room. Guest Services: valet and coin laundry.

**AAA Benefit:** Members save 5% or more!

## THE WOODLANDS WATERWAY MARRIOTT HOTEL & CONVENTION CENTER    (281)367-9797

Contemporary Hotel
$170-$309

**Marriott** HOTELS & RESORTS

**AAA Benefit:** Members save 5% or more!

**Address:** 1601 Lake Robbins Dr 77380 **Location:** I-45 exit 76B (Woodlands Pkwy) northbound, 1.6 mi w to Six Pines, then just n; exit 77 (Research Forest Dr/Tamina Rd) southbound, 0.5 mi w. **Facility:** Situated directly on the scenic Woodlands Waterway in a pleasant walking neighborhood of shops and restaurants, this contemporary property has updated rooms and expansive meeting space. 343 units. 13 stories, interior corridors. **Parking:** on-site (fee) and valet. **Terms:** check-in 4 pm. **Amenities:** *Some:* safes. **Pool(s):** heated outdoor. **Activities:** hot tub, exercise room, spa. **Guest Services:** valet and coin laundry.

SAVE ECO ⏹ ⏹ ⏹ CALL &M ⏹ BIZ SHS ⏹
⏹ ⏹ ⏹ / SOME UNITS ⏹

## WHERE TO EAT

### AMERIGO'S GRILL    281/362-0808
Italian. Fine Dining. $14-$43 **AAA Inspector Notes:** Patrons sit on the patio or in the upscale dining room adorned with original art and enjoy original Italian specialties, perhaps starting with the lobster cake appetizer, then savoring a hearty Caesar salad, veal Marsala with penne pasta and a glass of wine. Other options include braised short ribs, filet mignon and several fish dishes. The sauces and pastas are made in house. For dessert, the moist tiramisu is a must. **Features:** full bar. **Address:** 25250 Grogan's Park Dr 77380 **Location:** I-45 exit 73 (Rayford Rd/Sawdust Rd), 0.8 mi w on Sawdust and Grogans Mill rds; in Grogan's Mill Mall. ⏹L ⏹D

### CRABBY DADDY SEAFOOD & STEAKHOUSE    281/296-2722
Seafood. Casual Dining. $10-$35 **AAA Inspector Notes:** This casual family-run restaurant and oyster bar is attached to the seafood market next door and serves a good range of grilled, fried and steamed seafood. Clams, shrimp, crawfish, crabs and various seasonal fish share the menu with a selection of steaks. There is a large covered patio and a large open bar area where smoking is permitted, so nonsmokers should choose their table carefully. **Features:** full bar, happy hour. **Address:** 25186 I-45 N, Suite 4G 77386 **Location:** I-45 exit 73 (Rayford Rd/Sawdust Rd), just e. ⏹L ⏹D CALL &M ⏹

### FLEMING'S PRIME STEAKHOUSE & WINE BAR    281/362-0103
Steak. Casual Dining. $12-$49 **AAA Inspector Notes:** The warm, clubby atmosphere is the ideal setting for perfectly grilled steaks and seafood. Side dishes come in hearty portions, and salads are fresh and crisp. More than 100 wine selections are available. **Features:** full bar. **Address:** 1201 Lake Woodlands Dr 77380 **Location:** I-45 exit 77 (Lake Woodlands Dr/Research Forest Dr/Tamina Rd), just w on Lake Woodlands Dr; at The Woodlands Mall. **Parking:** on-site and valet. ⏹D

### GROTTO    281/419-4252
Italian. Casual Dining. $12-$29 **AAA Inspector Notes:** Very good preparations of Italian standards with a few more creative items to make it interesting are offered. The penne with shrimp, shaved garlic and asparagus in a citrus sauce and the pear salad carpaccio are good choices. The large dessert cart has some great cakes. The attractive restaurant has a wood-burning oven and antipasto bar in the middle of the dining room. The atmosphere can be loud and lively on busy nights, so try one of the outdoor tables for a more intimate experience. **Features:** full bar, patio dining, Sunday brunch, happy hour. **Reservations:** suggested. **Address:** 9595 Six Pines, Suite 100 77380 **Location:** I-45 exit 77 (Lake Woodlands Dr/Research Forest Dr/Tamina Rd) 0.9 mi w on Lake Woodlands Dr; in Market Street complex. **Parking:** on-site and valet. ⏹L ⏹D CALL &M

### GUADALAJARA HACIENDA    281/362-0774
Mexican. Casual Dining. $9-$22 **AAA Inspector Notes:** Across from the mall and next to a big-box shopping center, the restaurant serves Tex-Mex favorites in a Mexican market interior. Murals, plants and Spanish writing blanket the plastered walls. Those interested in something different should consider stuffed camarones—shrimp wrapped in crispy bacon. **Features:** full bar, patio dining, Sunday brunch, happy hour. **Address:** 27885 I-45 N 77381 **Location:** I-45 exit 79 (College Park Dr/Needham Rd) southbound; exit 79A (College Park Dr/Needham Rd) northbound. ⏹L ⏹D ⏹

### JASPER'S    281/298-6600
Regional American. Casual Dining. $10-$40 **AAA Inspector Notes:** Chef Kent Rathbun serves up "gourmet backyard cuisine" in this beautiful and stylish restaurant located in the heart of the Market Street complex. The menu features creative takes on items such as Texas peach barbecued pork tenderloin, pistachio-wasabi pea-crusted rainbow trout and candied pecan crusted shrimp as well as prime steaks and chops. Save room for desserts such as butterfinger creme brulee and banana parfait with homemade "Nilla" wafers. The restaurant decor is hip but comfortable, and there are outdoor tables available. **Features:** full bar, Sunday brunch, happy hour. **Address:** 9595 Six Pines Dr 77380 **Location:** I-45 exit 77 (Lake Woodlands Dr/Research Forest Dr/Tamina Rd) 0.9 mi w on Lake Woodlands Dr; in Market Street complex. **Parking:** street only. ⏹L ⏹D CALL &M

### KOBE JAPANESE STEAK HOUSE & SUSHI    281/298-2000
Japanese. Casual Dining. $16-$41 **AAA Inspector Notes:** This Japanese steak house does it all with its sushi bar, hibachi grill and more traditional dining room. There is a wide selection of specialty sushi rolls and good quality sashimi, and the chefs put on an entertaining show at the hibachi tables. **Features:** full bar. **Reservations:** suggested. **Address:** 433 Sawdust Rd 77380 **Location:** I-45 exit 73 (Rayford Rd/Sawdust Rd), just w; in The Woodwinds Shopping Plaza. ⏹L ⏹D ⏹

### LA MADELEINE COUNTRY FRENCH CAFE    281/419-5826
Traditional French. Casual Dining. $7-$12 **AAA Inspector Notes:** A fireplace creates the focal point at this cozy European style café where you can always get a quiche or savory stuffed puffed pastry on the go or stick around for a chicken crêpe or French dip sandwich. Heartier entrées like rotisserie chicken are offered and every season promises menu surprises. Whatever you decide on you probably will not get out the door without enjoying one of their tempting sweet pastries. **Features:** beer & wine. **Address:** 9595 Six Pines Dr, Suite 100 77380 **Location:** I-45 exit 77 (Lake Woodlands Dr/Research Forest Dr/Tamina Rd) 0.9 mi w on Lake Woodlands Dr; in Market Street complex. ⏹B ⏹L ⏹D CALL &M

### PERRY'S STEAKHOUSE & GRILLE    281/362-0569
Steak. Fine Dining. $24-$48 **AAA Inspector Notes:** An excellent selection of prime steaks, lamb and pork chops is served in a professional and upscale establishment. **Features:** full bar. **Reservations:** required. **Address:** 6700 Woodlands Pkwy 77382 **Location:** I-45 exit 76 (Woodlands Pkwy), 6 mi w to Kuykendahl Rd; on northwest corner; in Sterling Ridge Shopping Center. ⏹D CALL &M

### PIT-MASTER BBQ CAFE    281/419-3644
Barbecue. Casual Dining. $7-$19 **AAA Inspector Notes:** The small barbecue cafe in a strip mall just off I-45 is appointed in interesting Western décor and offers patio seating and drive-up service. **Features:** beer & wine. **Address:** 343 Sawdust Rd 77380 **Location:** I-45 exit 73 (Rayford Rd/Sawdust Rd), just w; in The Woodwinds Shopping Plaza. ⏹L ⏹D

### TAIPEI CHINA BISTRO    281/363-9188
Chinese. Casual Dining. $5-$15 **AAA Inspector Notes:** This small chain restaurant offers everything from noodles to chow mein. A small bar is available for those waiting to dine. It is conveniently located and is one of the few Chinese restaurants in the area that doesn't offer a buffet. **Features:** full bar, early bird specials. **Address:** 25807 I-45 77380 **Location:** I-45 exit 73 (Rayford Rd/Sawdust Rd); on southbound access road. ⏹L ⏹D

**THEP THAI RESTAURANT**　　　　281/419-7619

◆◆ Thai. Casual Dining. $8-$16 **AAA Inspector Notes:** This family-owned and –operated restaurant is somewhat hidden in a strip shopping center, but it's worth a visit. A tropical atmosphere lends to the authentic Thai feel. Brave souls who appreciate a spicy treat should try some of the blazing curries on the menu. The restaurant does not serve alcohol, but guests can bring their own and pay a small corkage fee. **Address:** 421 Sawdust Rd 77380 **Location:** I-45 exit 73 (Rayford Rd/Sawdust Rd), just w; in The Woodwinds Shopping Plaza. L D

**UNI SUSHI**　　　　281/298-7177

◆◆ Sushi. Casual Dining. $10-$25 **AAA Inspector Notes:** The upscale décor of this restaurant in the heart of the Market Street shopping district features onyx and marble. Outdoor sidewalk dining also is available. The Japanese/European-fusion menu offers very high-quality, creative sushi selections but also a range of entrées such as champagne apple pork tenderloin and split bone-in rib-eye steak. A range of lunch bentos are available. **Features:** full bar. **Address:** 9595 Six Pines Dr, Suite 860 77380 **Location:** I-45 exit 77 (Lake Woodlands Dr/Research Forest Dr/Tamina Rd), 0.9 mi w on Lake Woodlands Dr; in Market Street Complex. **Parking:** street only. L D CALL ♿M

**WILLIE GRILL & ICE HOUSE**　　　　936/321-0065

◆ Regional American. Casual Dining. $6-$15 **AAA Inspector Notes:** The small south Texas chain caters to families. On the menu are hamburgers, steaks, chicken and salads. A playroom and outdoor sandbox occupy children while their parents relax with a cold drink and a meal. Outdoor seating is available on the covered patio. Country music can be heard, the TVs broadcast sports and neon beer signs are everywhere. **Features:** beer & wine, patio dining. **Address:** 16846 I-45 S 77384 **Location:** I-45 exit 79 (SR 242); on southbound frontage road; in Walmart strip center. L D

# THREE RIVERS pop. 1,848

**BEST WESTERN INN-THREE RIVERS**　　　(361)786-2000

Motel
$139-$199

**AAA Benefit:** Members save 10% or more with Best Western!

**Address:** 900 N Harborth Ave 78071 **Location:** I-37 exit 72 (US 281), 1.8 mi s; jct US 281 and SR 72. **Facility:** 38 units. 2 stories (no elevator), exterior corridors. **Pool(s):** outdoor. **Featured Amenity:** continental breakfast.

SAVE ⫯⫯+ ⊇ BIZ HS 🛜 🕮 🍽 🖥 / SOME UNITS 🐕

**BASS INN**　　　　361/786-3521

fyi Not evaluated. **Address:** 3149 Hwy 72 W 78071 **Location:** SR 72, 7.5 mi w of jct US 281. Facilities, services, and décor characterize an economy property.

# TOMBALL pop. 10,753
• Hotels & Restaurants map & index p. 324
• Part of Houston area — see map p. 301

**COMFORT SUITES TOMBALL**　　　(281)290-7070　87

◆◆◆ Hotel $99-$109 **Address:** 13636 Michel Rd 77375 **Location:** Business Rt SR 249, just s of FM 2920, then e. **Facility:** 55 units. 3 stories, interior corridors. **Pool(s):** heated indoor. **Activities:** hot tub, exercise room. **Guest Services:** valet and coin laundry.

⫯⫯+ ⊇ BIZ HS 🛜 ✕ 🖥 🍽 🖥

**HAMPTON INN & SUITES TOMBALL**
　　　　(281)357-1500　86

Hotel
$99-$149

**AAA Benefit:** Members save up to 10%!

**Address:** 14100 Medical Complex Dr 77377 **Location:** Jct FM 2920 and Business Rt SR 249, just s to Medical Complex Dr, then just w. **Facility:** 81 units. 4 stories, interior corridors. **Terms:** 1-7 night minimum stay, cancellation fee imposed. **Pool(s):** outdoor. **Activities:** exercise room. **Guest Services:** valet and coin laundry, area transportation. **Featured Amenity:** full hot breakfast.

SAVE ⫯⫯+ CALL ♿M ⊇ BIZ HS 🛜 ✕ 🖥 🍽 🖥

# TULIA pop. 4,967

**EXECUTIVE INN**　　　　806/995-3248

◆◆ Motel. Rates not provided. **Address:** 1591 I-27 79088 **Location:** I-27 exit 74; on west frontage road. **Facility:** 36 units. 1 story, exterior corridors. **Guest Services:** coin laundry.

⫯⫯+ CALL ♿M 🛜 🖥 🍽 / SOME UNITS 🐕

# TYLER (D-10) pop. 96,900, elev. 558'
• Restaurants p. 556

Incorporated in 1846, Tyler was named for President John Tyler, who was instrumental in bringing Texas into the Union. The area is well known for its field-grown rosebushes, which are sold internationally.

The Goodman Museum, housed in an 1859 house, displays 19th-century medical paraphernalia, antebellum artifacts and period furniture; phone (903) 531-1286.

In October, stop and smell the roses at the ◆ Texas Rose Festival. Don't miss the coronation of the Rose Queen!

**Tyler Area Convention and Visitors Bureau:** 315 N. Broadway, Tyler, TX 75710. **Phone:** (903) 592-1661 or (800) 235-5712.

**BROOKSHIRE'S WORLD OF WILDLIFE MUSEUM AND COUNTRY STORE** is on FM 2493, .5 mi. s. of jct. W.S.W. Loop 323. More than 450 mounted mammals, reptiles and fish from Africa and North America are displayed. A full-size replica of a 1920s grocery store portrays the grocery industry's development during the early 1900s; exhibits include an old-time gasoline pump and a 1926 Model T Ford delivery truck. **Time:** Allow 1 hour minimum. **Hours:** Tues.-Sat. 9-5, Mar.-Sept.; 10-4, rest of year. Closed major holidays. **Cost:** Free. **Phone:** (903) 534-2169. ⊞

**CALDWELL ZOO** is 1 blk. e. of US 69 at 2203 W. Martin Luther King Jr. Blvd. Comprising 85 acres, the zoo provides natural habitats for more than 2,000 animals from North and South America and Africa, including lions, leopards, elephants, giraffes, otters, flamingos, and a collection of ducks from around the world. Other highlights include a native Texas exhibit and two aquariums featuring fish, penguins and snapping turtles. A separate facility houses snakes and spiders. Tropical foliage, ponds and wooden walkways enhance the setting.

**Time:** Allow 1 hour, 30 minutes minimum. **Hours:** Daily 9-5, Mar. 1-Labor Day; 9-4, rest of year. Closed Jan. 1, Thanksgiving and Christmas. **Cost:** $10.50; $9.25 (ages 55+); $7 (ages 3-12). **Phone:** (903) 593-0121.

**CAMP FORD HISTORIC PARK** is at US 271 and Loop 323. During the Civil War this site acted as the largest prisoner of war compound for Union troops west of the Mississippi River. A replica of a POW cabin, numerous hiking trails and educational storyboards also are on the grounds. **Time:** Allow 30 minutes minimum. **Hours:** Daily dawn-dusk. **Cost:** Free. **Phone:** (903) 592-5993.

**DISCOVERY SCIENCE PLACE** is at 308 N. Broadway. More than 85 interactive exhibits provide children with challenges, entertainment and educational opportunities. **Time:** Allow 1 hour minimum. **Hours:** Mon.-Sat. 9-5, Sun. 1-5. Closed major holidays. **Cost:** $8; $6 (ages 2-16 and 62+); $5 (military with ID); free (ages 0-1). **Phone:** (903) 533-8011.

**HISTORIC AVIATION MEMORIAL MUSEUM** is at 150 Airport Dr. Featuring 20th-century aviation memorabilia, the museum's collection includes uniforms, pictures and historical maps. A hangar contains biplanes and fighter jets including an FJ-4 Fury, T2-C Buckeye, an F-105D Thunderchief, an F-111 Aardvark and a T-33 Shooting Star. Visitors can listen to audio of World War II veterans recounting the Bataan Death March and the Battle of Midway. **Time:** Allow 30 minutes minimum. **Hours:** Tues.-Sat. 10-5, Sun. 1-5. Closed major holidays. **Cost:** $5; $4 (ages 65+); $3 (ages 13-17); $2 (ages 6-12); free (active military with ID). **Phone:** (903) 526-1945.

**SMITH COUNTY HISTORICAL SOCIETY MUSEUM AND ARCHIVES** is at 125 S. College Ave. Exhibits pertaining to the county's history are located inside the historic 1904 Carnegie building, which was once the town's public library. A music room with antique organs and Victrolas and artifacts dating to the Caddo Indians are featured. The archives contain photographs and documents. **Time:** Allow 30 minutes minimum. **Hours:** Tues.-Sat. 10-4. Closed major holidays. **Cost:** Donations. **Phone:** (903) 592-5993.

**TIGER CREEK WILDLIFE REFUGE** is off I-20 exit 562, then 4.8 mi. n. to 17552 FM 14. The rescue and rehabilitation facility harbors more than 30 big cats, including tigers, lions and leopards, in large fenced habitats. **Time:** Allow 30 minutes minimum. **Hours:** Mon.-Sat. 10-5. Closed major holidays. **Cost:** $10; $9 (ages 55+); $6 (ages 4-12). **Phone:** (903) 858-1008.

**TYLER MUNICIPAL ROSE GARDEN** is at 420 Rose Park Dr. Some 38,000 rosebushes representing 500 varieties blossom among 14 acres of tall pines, fountains, ponds, reflection pools, gazebos and archways. The Heritage Rose and Sensory Garden has antique rose varieties dating back to 1867. Blooms peak in early May and continue through October. The Rose Museum features historical exhibits about the Texas Rose Festival and the state's rose industry.

**Hours:** Garden daily dawn-dusk. Museum Mon.-Fri. 9-4:30, Sat. 10-4:30, Sun. 1:30-4:30, Mar.-Oct.; Tues.-Fri. 9-4:30, Sat. 10-4:30, rest of year. **Cost:** Free. Museum $3.50; $2 (ages 3-11). **Phone:** (903) 531-1212 for the garden, or (903) 597-3130 for the museum.

**TYLER MUSEUM OF ART** is adjacent to Tyler Junior College at 1300 S. Mahon Ave. A permanent collection of more than 600 19th- and 20th-century works includes paintings, photographs, sculpture and prints by Texas artists Vernon Fisher, Ancel E. Nunn and Skeet McAuley. Traveling exhibitions also are featured. Guided tours are available by reservation. **Time:** Allow 30 minutes minimum. **Hours:** Tues.-Sat. 10-5, Sun. 1-5. Closed major holidays. **Cost:** Donations. A fee may be charged for special exhibitions. **Phone:** (903) 595-1001.

## BEST WESTERN PLUS SOUTHPARK INN & SUITES
(903)534-8800

 Hotel $100-$140

 **AAA Benefit:** Members save 10% or more with Best Western!

**Address:** 120 W Rieck Rd 75703 **Location:** Jct US 69 and W Rieck Rd, just w. **Facility:** 61 units. 3 stories, interior corridors. **Pool(s):** outdoor. **Activities:** exercise room. **Guest Services:** valet and coin laundry.

## CANDLEWOOD SUITES
(903)509-4131

Extended Stay Hotel $81-$119 **Address:** 315 E Rieck Rd 75703 **Location:** 1.1 mi s of jct Loop 323 and US 69 to Rieck Rd, just e. **Facility:** 64 efficiencies. 4 stories, interior corridors. **Terms:** cancellation fee imposed. **Activities:** exercise room. **Guest Services:** complimentary and valet laundry.

## COMFORT SUITES
(903)534-0999

Hotel $90-$149 **Address:** 303 E Rieck Rd 75703 **Location:** 1.1 mi s of jct Loop 323 and US 69 to E Rieck Rd, just e. **Facility:** 65 units, some efficiencies. 3 stories, interior corridors. **Pool(s):** heated indoor. **Activities:** hot tub, exercise room. **Guest Services:** valet and coin laundry.

**COUNTRY INN & SUITES BY CARLSON** (903)561-0863

WWWW Hotel $89-$139 Address: 6702 S Broadway Ave 75703 Location: On US 69, 1.6 mi s of Loop 323. Facility: 69 units. 3 stories, interior corridors. Terms: 7 day cancellation notice. Pool(s): heated indoor. Activities: hot tub, exercise room. Guest Services: valet and coin laundry.

**COURTYARD BY MARRIOTT TYLER** (903)509-4411

Hotel
$79-$169

COURTYARD
Marriott

**AAA Benefit:**
Members save 5%
or more!

Address: 7424 S Broadway Ave 75703 Location: 2.8 mi s of Loop 323 on US 69. Facility: 121 units. 4 stories, interior corridors. Pool(s): indoor. Activities: hot tub, exercise room. Guest Services: valet and coin laundry.

**FAIRFIELD INN BY MARRIOTT** (903)561-2535

WW Hotel $95-$119 Address: 1945 W SW Loop 323 75701 Location: 1.5 mi s w of S US 69. Facility: 64 units. 3 stories, interior corridors. Pool(s): heated indoor. Activities: hot tub. Guest Services: valet laundry.

**AAA Benefit:**
Members save 5%
or more!

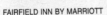

**HAMPTON INN** 903/596-7752

WWW Hotel. Rates not provided. Address: 3130 Troup Hwy 75701 Location: 0.3 mi n of jct E Loop 323 and SR 110. Facility: 77 units. 3 stories, exterior corridors. Pool(s): heated indoor. Activities: hot tub, exercise room. Guest Services: valet laundry.

**AAA Benefit:**
Members save up to
10%!

**HILTON GARDEN INN TYLER** (903)509-1166

WWWW Hotel $109-$189 Address: 220 E Grande Blvd 75703 Location: 1.7 mi s of jct Loop 323 and US 69 to Grande Blvd, just e. Facility: 125 units. 3 stories, interior corridors. Terms: 1-7 night minimum stay, cancellation fee imposed. Pool(s): heated indoor. Activities: hot tub, exercise room. Guest Services: valet and coin laundry.

**AAA Benefit:**
Members save up to
10%!

**HOLIDAY INN EXPRESS HOTEL & SUITES TYLER SOUTH** (903)566-0600

Hotel
$105-$139

Address: 2421 E Southeast Loop 323 75701 Location: 0.3 mi e of SR 110; between SR 110 and Spur 248. Facility: 88 units. 4 stories, interior corridors. Pool(s): heated indoor. Activities: sauna, hot tub, exercise room. Guest Services: valet and coin laundry. Featured Amenity: breakfast buffet.

**HOLIDAY INN SOUTH BROADWAY** (903)561-5800

WWWW Hotel $99-$129 Address: 5701 S Broadway Ave 75703 Location: 1.1 mi s of jct Loop 323 and US 69. Facility: 183 units. 8 stories, interior corridors. Pool(s): outdoor. Activities: exercise room. Guest Services: complimentary and valet laundry, area transportation.

**RESIDENCE INN BY MARRIOTT** (903)595-5188

WWW Extended Stay Hotel $92-$134 Address: 3303 Troup Hwy 75701 Location: 0.3 mi n of jct E Loop 323 and SR 110. Facility: 128 kitchen units, some two bedrooms. 2 stories (no elevator), exterior corridors. Pool(s): heated outdoor. Activities: hot tub. Guest Services: valet and coin laundry.

**AAA Benefit:**
Members save 5%
or more!

---

**WHERE TO EAT**

**CHUY'S** 903/509-2489

WW WW Tex-Mex. Casual Dining. $6-$12 AAA Inspector Notes: This Texas original serves up Mexican kitsch like no else in its décor but takes pride in its several house-made chile sauces and hand-made tortillas. Although the menu is familiar—fajitas, tacos and enchiladas—the freshness of the ingredients and chiles sets this place apart. The bar is always abuzz, but families can be just as comfortable there. Features: full bar, patio dining, happy hour. Address: 5935 S Broadway Ave 75703 Location: Jct US 69 and Loop 323, 1.5 mi s.

**CLEAR SPRINGS TEXAS SEAFOOD RESTAURANT** 903/561-0700

WW WW American. Casual Dining. $8-$18 AAA Inspector Notes: Rustic Western, nautical and hunting décor combine to provide the ambience at this small Texas chain. Steak, fish, shrimp and chicken are all provided in large portions and desserts are homemade. Features: full bar. Address: 6519 S Broadway Ave 75703 Location: Jct US 60 and Loop 323, 1.3 mi s.

**DON JUAN MEXICAN RESTAURANT** 903/526-2999

WW WW Mexican. Casual Dining. $4-$12 AAA Inspector Notes: The neighborhood may seem questionable, but the restaurant isn't. Family-owned and -operated, Don Juan sports colorful décor reflective of Mexico and offers a good selection of Tex-Mex and Mexican food. I would recommend the sopes. Not often encountered on menus on this side of the border, they are delicious bundles of freshness—lettuce, meat, tomatoes, avocados and queso fresco—built up on a thick tortilla base. Smother with salsa and enjoy. Address: 1313 E Erwin Ave 75702 Location: Jct US 271, SR 155 and 31, 0.3 mi n, then 0.5 mi e.

**GRANDY'S RESTAURANT** 903/593-8362

WW American. Quick Serve. $4-$8 AAA Inspector Notes: Fried chicken and country-fried steak are menu standbys at the restaurant, a regional franchise. They also offer a family-style dining menu. The décor is a step up from that of most quick-serve eateries and more resembles that of a conventional restaurant. Some elements of increased service include additional rolls, iced tea refills and tray removal. Address: 1226 S Beckham Ave 75701 Location: Just n of jct SR 64 and 155/110.

**JUCY'S HAMBURGERS** 903/597-0660

WW Burgers. Quick Serve. $4-$8 AAA Inspector Notes: This small east Texas chain is loved for its thick burgers and hand-cut fries. Save room for some Texas-made Blue Bell ice cream. Address: 2330 E 5th St 75701 Location: Jct SR 64 and 323, just w.

**JUMBO SEAFOOD GRILL** 903/526-9595

WW Seafood. Casual Dining. $4-$19 AAA Inspector Notes: Although no one goes for the ambience, they do go for the fresh catfish (farm grown), as well as seafood and steaks. Address: 3278 Mineola Hwy 75706 Location: Jct US 69 and Loop 323; southeast corner.

SPRING CREEK BBQ                    903/561-5695

▽▽ Barbecue. Casual Dining. $8-$13 **AAA Inspector Notes:** Expect Texas-Style barbecue at its simple, homey best. Hickory smoked ribs, beef, pork and turkey lace the air with a spicy aroma that mingles with the scent of freshly baked rolls and cold ice cream slowly melting over a dish of homemade peach cobbler. Plates often are loaded with all the coleslaw, potato salad and corn on the cob they can support. Part of a small chain, this barbecue restaurant displays a rustic décor that gives patrons the impression they are "at the ranch." **Features:** beer only. **Address:** 5810 S Broadway Ave 75703 **Location:** Jct US 69 and Loop 323, 1.1 mi s. ⃝ L ⃝ D ⃝

TEXAS BEST SMOKEHOUSE               903/877-0800

▽▽ Barbecue. Quick Serve. $5-$11 **AAA Inspector Notes:** Don't let the fact that this place is in a travel plaza bother you. The barbecue comes with a mild or spicy sauce and there are vegetables, sides and desserts to pair it up with. They have some of the nicest bathrooms on the road and a variety of goodies such as beef jerky, deli items, pastries and Texas souvenirs. Most people just stumble upon it; for others it has become a mandatory stop on their itinerary. **Address:** 16243 Hwy 271 N 75708 **Location:** I-20 exit 571A, just s. ⃝ L ⃝ D ⃝ CALL ⃝M

## UMBARGER (B-5) elev. 3,765'

**BUFFALO LAKE NATIONAL WILDLIFE REFUGE** is 1.5 mi. s. on FM 168, following signs to refuge entrance. A winter refuge for ducks and geese, the 7,664-acre refuge no longer contains the lake for which it is named. Facilities for picnicking, camping and bird-watching are available. For information write the Refuge Manager, Box 179, Umbarger, TX 79091. **Hours:** Entrance open daily 8-8, Apr.-Sept.; 8-6, rest of year. **Cost:** $2 per private vehicle per day. **Phone:** (806) 499-3382. 🏕

## UNIVERSAL CITY pop. 18,530
• Part of San Antonio area — see map p. 458

HAWTHORN SUITES BY WYNDHAM    (210)655-9491

▽▽▽▽
Extended Stay Hotel
$89-$149

**Address:** 13101 E Loop 1604 N 78233 **Location:** Loop 1604 at Pat Booker Rd; 0.8 mi e of I-35. Located in a quiet area. **Facility:** 100 kitchen units, some two bedrooms. 2 stories (no elevator), exterior corridors. **Terms:** check-in 4 pm, 3 day cancellation notice. **Pool(s):** heated outdoor. **Activities:** hot tub, exercise room. **Guest Services:** coin laundry. **Featured Amenity:** full hot breakfast. (See ad p. 510.)

⃝SAVE ⃝ ⃝ ⃝BIZ ⃝HS ⃝
⃝ ⃝ ⃝ ⃝ / SOME UNITS ⃝

### WHERE TO EAT

BILL MILLER BAR-B-Q                 210/659-5525

▽ Barbecue. Quick Serve. $6-$11 **AAA Inspector Notes:** The relaxed, family-focused barbecue restaurant prepares ribs, chicken, brisket, turkey and sausage for sandwiches or plates. **Address:** 122 Pat Booker Rd 78148 **Location:** Jct CR 78. ⃝ L ⃝ D ⃝

## UNIVERSITY PARK (H-3) pop. 23,068, elev. 548'

When Southern Methodist University opened in 1915, a small community sprang up around it to house faculty members. University Park was incorporated in 1924; the university remains its largest employer.

◥◤ **GEORGE W. BUSH PRESIDENTIAL LIBRARY AND MUSEUM** is at 2943 SMU Blvd., on the Southern Methodist University campus. Housed inside the 226,565-square-foot, LEED-certified George W. Bush Presidential Center complex, the museum features artifacts and multimedia exhibits pertaining to the 43rd U.S. president's time in office.

The Decision Points Theater offers an inside look at some of the difficult decisions Bush was faced with during his 8-year term. Using touch screens, visitors gather information about Bush-era crisis situations (think Hurricane Katrina and the 2003 invasion of Iraq) and evaluate the former president's response to those events.

Condolence letters, a damaged steel beam retrieved from the World Trade Center debris, and other poignant reminders of the 9/11 terrorist attacks are displayed in the Day of Fire exhibit. Other noteworthy exhibits focus on topics like the wars in Afghanistan and Iraq, the 2000 presidential election, the No Child Left Behind initiative, the global impact of and fight against AIDS, first lady and SMU alumna Laura Bush's travels, and the Bush family's life in the White House.

Items in the museum's collection include photos, documents, campaign memorabilia, videos, news clips, replicas, statues and gifts from admirers and heads of state. A full-size reproduction of the Oval Office opens out to a rose garden—a lovely, tranquil spot for reflection—that overlooks a hilly, 15-acre park reminiscent of a Texas prairie. With pathways and seating areas surrounded by native trees, wildflowers, grasses and plants, the park is a great place to stroll and relax after your museum tour.

**Note:** The parking lot is small and requires the use of a credit or debit card. As an alternative, park for free at the DART Mockingbird Station (5465 Mockingbird Ln.) and take the Bush Center/Meadows Museum shuttle (Route 743). A limited number of tickets is available each day; purchasing tickets in advance online is recommended. Upon arrival, visitors must pass through a metal detector.

**Time:** Allow 2 hours minimum. **Hours:** Mon.-Sat. 9-5, Sun. noon-5. Closed Jan. 1, Thanksgiving and Christmas. **Cost:** $16; $14 (ages 13-17); $13 (ages 62+ and college students with ID); $10 (ages 5-12 and retired military with ID); free (active military with ID). **Parking:** $7. **Phone:** (214) 346-1650. 🅣

**MEADOWS MUSEUM, SOUTHERN METHODIST UNIVERSITY** is at 5900 Bishop Blvd. An extensive Spanish collection spans the millennium from the 10th century to the end of the 20th century. Sculptures, paintings and works on paper include medieval objects from Islamic and Christian Spain; Renaissance and Baroque polychrome sculptures; and works by El Greco, Francisco José de Goya, Joan Miró, Pablo Picasso, José Ribera and Diego Velázquez.

(See maps & indexes p. 175, 184.)

**Tours:** Guided tours are available. **Time:** Allow 30 minutes minimum. **Hours:** Tues.-Sat. 10-5 (also Thurs. 5-9), Sun. 1-5. Guided tours Thurs. at 6:30, Sun. at 2. Closed major holidays. **Cost:** $10; $8 (ages 65+); $4 (students with ID); free (ages 0-11 and Thurs. after 5). **Phone:** (214) 768-2516.

**THE LUMEN**     214/219-2400   [30]

Hotel
Rates not provided

**Address:** 6101 Hillcrest Ave 75205 **Location:** Just n of jct Mockingbird Ln and Hillcrest Ave. **Facility:** 93 units. 3-4 stories, interior corridors. **Parking:** valet only. **Amenities:** safes. **Pool(s):** heated outdoor. **Activities:** exercise room. **Guest Services:** valet laundry, area transportation.

---

**WHERE TO EAT**

**R+D KITCHEN**     214/890-7900   [82]

American. Casual Dining. $12-$31 **AAA Inspector Notes:** They are keeping things simple here, dedicating themselves to doing a few things well rather than a lot of things so-so. The menu has sushi, a few sandwiches/burgers, and a small selection of entrées like meatloaf and pan-fried fish. As part of an established upscale neighborhood, the décor is contemporary and the people well-heeled. **Features:** full bar, Sunday brunch. **Reservations:** suggested. **Address:** 8300 Preston Center Plaza 75225 **Location:** Dallas North Tollway exit Northwest Hwy, just e, then just s. [L] [D]

## UVALDE (G-6) pop. 15,751, elev. 920'

Known as Encina 1855-56 and renamed in honor of Spanish Army general Juan de Ugalde, Uvalde once was the domain of notorious frontier sheriff and outlaw, J. King Fisher. A more respectable resident was John Nance Garner, President Franklin Delano Roosevelt's first- and second-term vice president. After serving two terms in office, Garner returned to Uvalde, where he died at age 98.

**Uvalde Convention and Visitors Bureau:** 300 E. Main St., Uvalde, TX 78801. **Phone:** (830) 278-4115 or (800) 588-2533.

**BRISCOE-GARNER MUSEUM,** .2 mi. w. at 333 N. Park St., highlights the lives of prominent Uvalde-bred politicians John Nance "Cactus Jack" Garner and Dolph Briscoe. Displays include documents, photos and other memorabilia. **Time:** Allow 1 hour minimum. **Hours:** Tues.-Sat. 9-5. Closed major holidays. **Cost:** Donations. **Phone:** (830) 278-5018.

**GRAND OPERA HOUSE** is at 104 W. North St. Built in 1891, the performing arts center accommodates community performances, professional troupes and a concert series throughout the year. A visitor center features a pictorial history of Uvalde County. **Time:** Allow 30 minutes minimum. **Hours:** Mon.-Fri. 9-5, Sat. 9:30-2:30 by appointment. Closed city holidays. **Cost:** Donations. **Phone:** (830) 278-4184.

---

**HOLIDAY INN EXPRESS UVALDE**     (830)278-7300

Hotel
$119

**Address:** 2801 E Main St 78801 **Location:** Just e of town. **Facility:** 80 units. 3 stories, interior corridors. **Pool(s):** outdoor. **Activities:** hot tub, exercise room. **Guest Services:** valet and coin laundry. **Featured Amenity: full hot breakfast.**

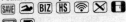

**QUALITY INN OF UVALDE**     (830)278-4511

Hotel $80-$130 **Address:** 920 E Main St 78801 **Location:** 0.5 mi e on US 90. **Facility:** 114 units. 2 stories (no elevator), exterior corridors. **Pool(s):** outdoor. **Guest Services:** valet and coin laundry.

## VANDERPOOL (F-7) elev. 1,578'

**LONE STAR MOTORCYCLE MUSEUM,** at 36517 FM 187N, showcases more than 60 antique motorcycles, including Ducatis, Nortons, Indians and Harley Davidsons. Of particular interest is a 1916 Royal Enfield with canvas front cowling. Some of the bikes have won races and are decorated with trophies and race photos. **Time:** Allow 1 hour minimum. **Hours:** Fri.-Sun. 10-5, Mar.-Nov. **Cost:** $5; $4 (ages 65-89); $3 (active military and spouse with ID); free (ages 0-14 and 90+). **Phone:** (830) 966-6103. [☎]

## VAN HORN (E-3) pop. 2,063, elev. 4,047'

**RED ROCK RANCH TOURS** is at 305 W. Broadway. Driving tours, guided hiking excursions, and rock hunts through a scenic area of wind- and water-carved sandstone canyons are available. Visitors can enjoy panoramic vistas and hike to see centuries-old Native American campsites, pictographs, an old Western movie set, an 1880 homestead and diverse plant and animal life.

**Time:** Allow 3 hours minimum. **Hours:** Daily dawn-dusk. **Cost:** Hiking tours start at $45 (fee depends on difficulty level of hike). Driving tour $40. Reservations are recommended. **Phone:** (432) 284-1284 or (800) 735-6911.

**ECONO LODGE**     (432)283-2211

Hotel
$65-$98

**Address:** 1601 W Broadway St 79855 **Location:** I-10 exit 138, 0.5 mi e on Business Rt I-10. **Facility:** 39 units. 2 stories (no elevator), exterior corridors. **Pool(s):** outdoor. **Featured Amenity: continental breakfast.**

**ECONOMY INN**     432/283-2754

Motel. Rates not provided. **Address:** 1500 W Broadway St 79855 **Location:** I-10 exit 138, 0.5 mi on US 80. **Facility:** 16 units. 1 story, exterior corridors.

## HAMPTON INN

(432)283-0088

◆◆◆ Hotel $99-$159 **Address:** 1921 SW Frontage Rd 79855 **Location:** I-10 exit 138, just w on S Frontage Rd. **Facility:** 59 units. 2 stories, interior corridors. **Terms:** 1-7 night minimum stay, cancellation fee imposed. **Pool(s):** heated indoor. **Activities:** hot tub, exercise room. **Guest Services:** coin laundry.

**AAA Benefit:** Members save up to 10%!

[icons]

## HOTEL EL CAPITAN

432/283-1220

◆◆◆ **Classic Historic Hotel.** Rates not provided. **Address:** 100 E Broadway 79855 **Location:** I-10 exit 140A; jct US 90/Van Horn St; center. **Facility:** This beautifully restored property dating from the 1930s offers wonderful public areas for relaxation. The on-site restaurant and bar complete the upgraded amenities for this hotel. 38 units. 2 stories, interior corridors. **Activities:** exercise room. **Guest Services:** coin laundry.

[icons]

### WHERE TO EAT

## CHUY'S RESTAURANT

432/283-2066

◆◆◆
Mexican
Casual Dining
$7-$16

**AAA Inspector Notes:** Fun and family-operated, the unpretentious cafe prepares requisite Mexican dishes--such as tacos and enchiladas--as well as seafood, steak and chicken selections. Juicy fajitas are served with new potatoes. **Features:** beer & wine. **Address:** 1200 W Broadway St 79855 **Location:** I-10 exit 138; center.

[B] [L] [D]

# VEGA pop. 884

## BEST WESTERN COUNTRY INN

(806)267-2131

◆◆◆
Motel
$80-$100

**AAA Benefit:** Members save 10% or more with Best Western!

**Address:** 1800 W Vega Blvd 79092 **Location:** 0.5 mi w on US 40 business loop. **Facility:** 41 units. 1 story, exterior corridors. **Pool(s):** outdoor.

[icons]

## DAYS INN VEGA

(806)267-0126

◆◆◆
Hotel
$70

**Address:** 1005 S Main St 79092 **Location:** I-40 exit 36. **Facility:** 42 units. 2 stories (no elevator), interior corridors. **Guest Services:** coin laundry. **Featured Amenity:** continental breakfast.

[icons]

# VERNON (C-7) pop. 11,002, elev. 1,205'

Originally named Eagle Flats for the birds nesting nearby, Vernon is a commercial center for farming, ranching and oil. The town was the birthplace of singer and songwriter Roy Orbison.

**RED RIVER VALLEY MUSEUM** is at 4600 College Dr. (US 70W). The history of Texas ranching and the Great Western Cattle Trail is presented through artifacts and murals. A replica of the sculpture studio of Texas artist Electra Waggonner Biggs houses one of the largest collections of her work in one location. Also displayed are 135 big-game trophies, collections of Native American and pioneer items, gems, rocks and minerals. A Jack Teagarden exhibit contains memorabilia of the jazz trombonist, who was born in Vernon. **Time:** Allow 1 hour minimum. **Hours:** Tues.-Sun. 1-5. Closed Easter, July 4, Thanksgiving and Christmas. **Cost:** $5; $3 (ages 60+); $2 (students). **Phone:** (940) 553-1848.

## BEST WESTERN VILLAGE INN

(940)552-5417

◆◆◆
Hotel
$66-$85

**AAA Benefit:** Members save 10% or more with Best Western!

**Address:** 1615 US Hwy 287 E 76384 **Location:** Jct Main St, just e. **Facility:** 47 units. 1-2 stories (no elevator), interior/exterior corridors. **Parking:** winter plug-ins. **Pool(s):** heated outdoor. **Guest Services:** coin laundry.

[icons]

## HAMPTON INN

(940)552-2100

◆◆◆ Hotel $109 **Address:** 4131 Western Trail Dr 76384 **Location:** Jct US 287 and 70; on W Frontage Rd. **Facility:** 64 units. 3 stories, interior corridors. **Terms:** 1-7 night minimum stay, cancellation fee imposed. **Pool(s):** outdoor. **Activities:** hot tub, exercise room. **Guest Services:** valet and coin laundry.

**AAA Benefit:** Members save up to 10%!

[icons]

## HOLIDAY INN EXPRESS HOTEL & SUITES

(940)552-0200

◆◆◆ Hotel $99-$114 **Address:** 700 Hillcrest Dr 76384 **Location:** Jct US 287 and 70; on W Frontage Rd. **Facility:** 60 units. 3 stories, interior corridors. **Terms:** cancellation fee imposed. **Pool(s):** heated indoor. **Activities:** hot tub, exercise room. **Guest Services:** valet and coin laundry.

[icons]

# VICTORIA (G-8) pop. 62,592, elev. 140'
- Hotels p. 560 • Restaurants p. 561

Victoria, in an area originally settled in 1685 by French explorer René-Robert Cavelier, Sieur de La Salle, was organized by the Spanish and in 1824 named for a Mexican president, Guadalupe Victoria. The first military capital of the new republic was established here after the Battle of San Jacinto. The city is now a leading cattle market and the home of several petrochemical plants.

**Victoria Convention and Visitors Bureau:** 700 Main Center, Suite 101, Victoria, TX 77901. **Phone:** (361) 485-3116 or (800) 926-5774.

**MUSEUM OF THE COASTAL BEND** is at 2200 E. Red River, on the Victoria College campus. Exhibits showcase the heritage of the mid-coastal region of Texas. Photographs and cannons from Fort St. Louis are highlights. Also displayed are relics recovered from René-Robert Cavelier, Sieur de La Salle's ship, *La Belle,* which sank in nearby Matagorda Bay. **Time:** Allow 30 minutes minimum. **Hours:** Tues.-Sat. 10-4. Closed major holidays. **Cost:** $3.50; $2.50 (ages 56+); $2 (ages 4-14). **Phone:** (361) 582-2511.

**NAVE MUSEUM** is in the Royston Nave Memorial at 306 W. Commercial. Works by Royston Nave and other contemporary North American artists are exhibited. Nave, who painted extensively in and around Victoria, achieved distinction in New York art circles during the 1920s. Exhibits in the Greco-Roman hall change every 8 weeks, with a 1-week interval for installation. **Time:** Allow 30 minutes minimum. **Hours:** Tues.-Sun. noon-4 (also Thurs. 4-7). Closed major holidays. **Cost:** $2; $1 (ages 0-12, ages 60+, and students and military with ID). **Phone:** (361) 575-8227.

**RIVERSIDE PARK** is at the end of W. Stayton Ave. The park encompasses 512 acres of woodland and gardens bordered by the Guadalupe River. Recreational activities include fishing and picnicking; hiking and walking trails, ball fields and golf are offered. A rose garden and a duck pond also are on the grounds. **Cost:** Free. **Phone:** (361) 485-3200. 🏕

**Texas Zoo** is at 110 Memorial Dr. Native and exotic animals reside in this 6-acre park. **Time:** Allow 30 minutes minimum. **Hours:** Daily 9-5. Closed Thanksgiving, Christmas Eve and Christmas. **Cost:** $7; $6 (ages 3-12 and military with ID); $5.50 (ages 65+). **Phone:** (361) 573-7681.

**BEST WESTERN PLUS VICTORIA INN & SUITES**
(361)485-2300

Hotel
$130-$170

**AAA Benefit:** Members save 10% or more with Best Western!

**Address:** 8106 NE Zac Lenz Pkwy 77904 **Location:** Jct Zac Lenz Pkwy and Invitational Dr. **Facility:** 54 units. 3 stories, interior corridors. **Pool(s):** outdoor. **Activities:** hot tub, exercise room. **Guest Services:** valet and coin laundry.

**CANDLEWOOD SUITES**                 361/578-0236

Extended Stay Hotel. Rates not provided. **Address:** 7103 N Navarro St 77904 **Location:** Jct US 77 and Navarro St, just s. **Facility:** 82 efficiencies. 3 stories, interior corridors. **Pool(s):** outdoor. **Activities:** exercise room. **Guest Services:** complimentary and valet laundry.

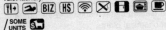

**DAYS INN**                           (361)894-8644

Hotel
$89

**Address:** 6203 Dairy Rd 77904 **Location:** US 77 and Loop 463; just e on S Frontage Rd. **Facility:** 64 units. 3 stories, interior corridors. **Activities:** exercise room. **Guest Services:** valet and coin laundry. **Featured Amenity:** full hot breakfast.

**FAIRFIELD INN BY MARRIOTT**          (361)582-0660

Hotel $100-$190 **Address:** 7502 N Navarro St 77904 **Location:** US 77 at Loop 463. **Facility:** 64 units. 3 stories, interior corridors. **Pool(s):** indoor. **Activities:** hot tub. **Guest Services:** valet laundry.

**AAA Benefit:** Members save 5% or more!

**FRIENDLY OAKS BED AND BREAKFAST**    361/575-0000

Historic Bed & Breakfast $75-$105 **Address:** 210 E Juan Linn St 77901 **Location:** Jct US 77 and Main St, 0.7 mi s on Main St, just n. Located in a quiet neighborhood. **Facility:** Individually themed rooms are featured at this B&B close to the town square. It's located in a quiet neighborhood and is close to many historic buildings. 4 units. 2 stories (no elevator), interior corridors. **Terms:** check-in 4 pm, 3 day cancellation notice-fee imposed.

**HAMPTON INN**                        (361)573-9911

Hotel $120-$165 **Address:** 7006 N Navarro St 77904 **Location:** Jct US 77 and Navarro St, just s. **Facility:** 68 units. 3 stories, interior corridors. **Terms:** 1-7 night minimum stay, cancellation fee imposed. **Amenities:** video games. **Pool(s):** outdoor. **Activities:** exercise room. **Guest Services:** valet and coin laundry.

**AAA Benefit:** Members save up to 10%!

 CALL 🛎

**HOLIDAY INN EXPRESS**                361/575-1600

Hotel. Rates not provided. **Address:** 111 Huvar St 77901 **Location:** Jct US 77 and Navarro St, just s. **Facility:** 76 units. 3 stories, interior corridors. **Pool(s):** outdoor. **Activities:** hot tub, exercise room. **Guest Services:** valet and coin laundry.

**LA QUINTA INN VICTORIA**             (361)572-3585

Hotel $109-$194 **Address:** 7603 N Navarro St (US 77 N) 77904 **Location:** 4 mi n; at Loop 463. **Facility:** 130 units. 2 stories (no elevator), exterior corridors. **Amenities:** video games. **Pool(s):** outdoor.

**LONE STAR INN & SUITES**             (361)579-0225

Hotel
$90-$170

**Address:** 1907 US 59 N 77905 **Location:** US 59 exit Bloomington (SR 185); on northeast corner. **Facility:** 69 units, some kitchens. 2 stories (no elevator), exterior corridors. **Terms:** cancellation fee imposed. **Pool(s):** outdoor. **Activities:** exercise room. **Guest Services:** coin laundry. **Featured Amenity:** full hot breakfast.

MOTEL 6 VICTORIA - #4729                    (361)573-1273
W Motel $60-$100 Address: 3716 Houston Hwy 77901 Location: On Business Rt US 59. Facility: 80 units. 2 stories (no elevator), exterior corridors. Bath: shower only. Pool(s): outdoor. Guest Services: coin laundry.

VICTORY INN                                 361/578-2030
WW Hotel. Rates not provided. Address: 3112 E Houston Hwy (Business Rt 59) 77901 Location: On Business Rt US 59, 2 mi ne. Facility: 100 units. 2 stories (no elevator), exterior corridors. Pool(s): outdoor. Guest Services: valet and coin laundry, area transportation.

## WHERE TO EAT

GRANDY'S RESTAURANT                         361/575-9563
W American. Family Dining. $4-$8 AAA Inspector Notes: Fried chicken and country-fried steak are menu standbys at the restaurant, a regional franchise. They also offer a family-style dining menu. The décor is a step up from that of most quick-serve eateries and more resembles that of a conventional restaurant. Some elements of increased service include additional rolls, iced tea refills and tray removal. Address: 4201 N Navarro St 77904 Location: Just s of jct US 77 (N Navarro St) and E Mockingbird Ln.
B L D

LOS REYES MEXICAN GRILL                     361/575-9966
WW Tex-Mex. Casual Dining. $7-$13 AAA Inspector Notes: A wide variety of Tex-Mex dishes like chile rellenos, chicken enchiladas and beef caldo are offered at this longtime city favorite by a cordial and friendly staff. Great breakfast tacos, too! Features: full bar. Address: 6908 N Navarro St 77904 Location: Jct US 77 and Navarro St, just s. B L D

MONTANA MIKE'S                              361/576-0333
WW Steak. Casual Dining. $8-$20 AAA Inspector Notes: This steakhouse offers a dining experience for the whole family. A rustic look with Western appointments characterizes the dining room. Although it's hard to go wrong with a hearty steak of USDA Choice aged beef, guests also can try smoked, fire-grilled chicken breast, chicken-fried steak, baby back ribs and other selections. Features: full bar. Address: 6409 N Navarro St 77904 Location: Jct US 77 and Loop 463, 0.5 mi s. L D

ROSEBUD FOUNTAIN & GRILL                    361/573-5111
W American. Family Dining. $6-$16 AAA Inspector Notes: Kids and adults alike enjoy dining here for the selection of classic sandwiches and home-style platters. The dining room resembles an old-time malt shop, with memorabilia lining the walls and a player piano providing entertainment. Everyone is invited up to the "bar" for a banana split or chocolate shake. It's open for dinner on Friday and Saturday. Features: full bar. Address: 102 S Main St 77901 Location: Just s of jct US 77. Parking: street only. L

TOKYO GRILL & SUSHI LOUNGE                  361/570-7228
WW Japanese. Casual Dining. $9-$46 AAA Inspector Notes: Patrons of this contemporary restaurant can dine on sushi bar offerings or opt for more traditional Japanese steakhouse selections of chicken, beef, seafood or combination dinners. Features: full bar. Address: 5006 N Navarro St 77904 Location: Jct US 77 N and Loop 465, 1.5 mi s. L D CALL

## VIDOR  pop. 10,579

HOLIDAY INN EXPRESS                         409/783-2420
WWWW Hotel. Rates not provided. Address: 260 East Frwy 77662 Location: I-10 exit 860; on eastbound frontage road. Facility: 73 units. 3 stories, interior corridors. Pool(s): outdoor. Activities: exercise room. Guest Services: valet and coin laundry.
CALL

# WACO  (E-8) pop. 124,805, elev. 427'
• Hotels p. 562 • Restaurants p. 563

Waco probably derives its name from the Hueco (WAY-co) Indians. Bisected by the Brazos River, the city has long been at the crossroads of trade and travel in central Texas. Cattle drives northward along the Chisholm Trail traversed the area. One of the city's original settlers began ferry service across the Brazos shortly after Waco was settled in 1849.

The construction of a suspension bridge in 1870 increased business and trade, and Waco joined the ranks of the rough-and-tumble cow towns. The railroad came to Waco the following year, thereby securing the town's commercial progress. Modern Waco is the largest marketing center between Dallas and Austin; its economy focuses on diversified industry, agriculture and education.

Waco Tourist Information Center: 106 Texas Ranger Tr., Waco, TX 76706. Phone: (254) 750-8696 or (800) 922-6386.

ART CENTER WACO is at 1300 College Dr. Two galleries are located inside an old house turned museum. Landscaped grounds include a sculpture path. Time: Allow 30 minutes minimum. Hours: Tues.-Sat. 10-5, Sun. 1-5. Closed major holidays. Cost: Donations. Phone: (254) 752-4371.

BAYLOR UNIVERSITY is at 1311 S. Fifth St. Established in 1845, this is the oldest university in the state and the largest Baptist university in the world. Phone: (800) 229-5678.

Armstrong Browning Library of Baylor University is at Eighth and Speight sts. The Italian Renaissance-style building has 62 stained-glass windows. The two-story McLean Foyer of Meditation hall has a gold leaf dome, a two-ton chandelier and murals. The library has one of the largest collections of books, manuscripts and artifacts relating to the Victorian poet Robert Browning and his wife, poetess Elizabeth Barrett Browning. Also featured are paintings by their son Pen Browning and manuscripts from the library's holdings.

Time: Allow 1 hour minimum. Hours: Mon.-Fri. 9-5, Sat. 10-2. Closed major holidays. Cost: Donations. Phone: (254) 710-3566.

Mayborn Museum Complex, 1300 S. University Parks Dr., includes a natural history museum with walk-in dioramas and exploration stations, 17 themed discovery rooms, and a 13-acre historic village that represents life in Texas from the 1880s to 1910. The complex also has rotating temporary exhibits and a 185-seat theater. Hours: Mon.-Sat. 10-5 (also Thurs. 5-8), Sun. 1-5. Closed Jan. 1, Good Friday-Easter, Thanksgiving, Christmas Eve and Christmas. Cost: $6; $5 (ages 65+); $4 (ages 18 months-12 years). Phone: (254) 710-1110.

CAMERON PARK ZOO is off I-35 exit 335A, then 2 mi. w. to 1701 N. Fourth St. The zoo features 52 acres of re-created natural habitats. The African savannah is home to giraffes, lions, white rhinoceroses and elephants; the herpetarium has king cobras, chameleons and alligators. Other residents are gibbons, lemurs, Galapagos tortoises and the critically endangered orangutans and Sumatran tigers. Brazos River Country includes a 50,000-gallon coral reef saltwater aquarium and a variety of habitats showcasing animals that live on the Brazos River.

Time: Allow 1 hour minimum. Hours: Mon.-Sat. 9-5, Sun. 11-5. Closed Jan. 1, last Fri. and Sat. in June, Thanksgiving and Christmas. Cost: $9; $8 (ages 60+); $6 (ages 4-12). Phone: (254) 750-8400. ⑪

DR PEPPER MUSEUM is at 300 S. Fifth St. A historical perspective of Dr Pepper and its creator Charles Alderton is explained through historic memorabilia and displays. A soda fountain serves freshly mixed drinks. The third level of the building houses the Free Enterprise Institute, which honors leaders in the world of soft drinks. Time: Allow 1 hour minimum. Hours: Mon.-Sat. 10-5, Sun. noon-5. Last ticket sold 45 minutes before closing. Closed Jan. 1, Easter, Thanksgiving and Christmas. Cost: $8; $6 (ages 65+ and military with ID); $5 (children). Phone: (254) 757-1025.

EAST TERRACE is at 100 Mill St. This restored Italianate-style villa is near the Brazos River. Highlights include Victorian furnishings, some of which belonged to John Wesley Mann, a pioneer-industrialist who began construction of the house in 1872. Time: Allow 30 minutes minimum. Hours: Tues.-Fri. 11-3, Sat.-Sun. 2-5, July-Sept.; Sun. 2-5, Jan.-June; Sat. 2-5, rest of year. Closed major holidays. Cost: $3; $2.50 (ages 50+); $2 (students with ID); free (ages 0-5 and active military with ID). Phone: (254) 753-5166.

HOMESTEAD HERITAGE TRADITIONAL CRAFTS VILLAGE is at 608 Dry Creek Rd. A working farm and craft shops include a blacksmith, gristmill, fiber craft shop, furniture shop and pottery shop that offer demonstrations. Classes are held in woodworking, pottery, blacksmithing and homesteading.

Guided and self-guiding tours are available. Time: Allow 1 hour, 30 minutes minimum. Hours: Mon.-Sat. 10-6. Closed Jan. 1 and Christmas. Cost: Free. Phone: (254) 754-9600. ⑪

TEXAS RANGER HALL OF FAME AND MUSEUM is off I-35 exit 335B at 100 Texas Ranger Tr. in Fort Fisher Park. The Rangers date from 1823, when Stephen F. Austin selected the original ten men. The complex comprises the Hall of Fame, which pays tribute to 31 Texas Rangers; and a museum, which contains such artifacts as badges and firearms.

A 45-minute film of the history of the Texas Rangers is presented every 90 minutes. Hours: Daily 9-5. Closed Jan. 1, Thanksgiving and Christmas. Cost: $7; $6 (ages 60+ and military with ID); $3 (ages 6-12). Phone: (254) 750-8631.

TEXAS SPORTS HALL OF FAME is .2 mi. e. of I-35 exit 335B at 1108 S. University Parks Dr. Notable Texas athletes, coaches and teams are lauded in exhibits that are grouped by sport—with emphasis on baseball, tennis, football and basketball—and span from high school to the professional leagues. Films of sports highlights are shown in the Tom Landry Theater. Hours: Mon.-Sat. 9-5, Sun. noon-5. Closed Jan. 1, Easter, Thanksgiving and Christmas. Cost: $7; $6 (ages 60+); $3 (ages 6-18 and students with ID); free (ages 0-5 and active military with ID). Phone: (254) 756-1633 or (800) 567-9561.

## HAMPTON INN & SUITES WACO SOUTH    (254)662-9500

Hotel
$107-$134

**AAA Benefit:** Members save up to 10%!

**Address:** 2501 Market Place Dr 76711 **Location:** I-35 exit 330B (SR 6) southbound; exit 331 (New Rd) northbound; at Central Texas Marketplace. Located behind Kohl's. **Facility:** 123 units. 4 stories, interior corridors. **Terms:** 1-7 night minimum stay, cancellation fee imposed. **Pool(s):** heated indoor. **Activities:** hot tub, exercise room. **Guest Services:** valet and coin laundry. **Featured Amenity: breakfast buffet.**

[SAVE] [CALL] [&M] [≈] [BIZ] [HS] [≈] [X] [🎬] [🛁] [🖥] [💻]

## HAMPTON INN-WACO    (254)412-1999

Hotel $110-$265 **Address:** 4259 N I-35 76705 **Location:** I-35 exit 339 (Lake Shore Dr), just s on west frontage road. **Facility:** 119 units. 4 stories, interior corridors. **Terms:** 1-7 night minimum stay, cancellation fee imposed. **Amenities:** video games. **Pool(s):** outdoor, heated indoor. **Activities:** hot tub, exercise room. **Guest Services:** valet and coin laundry.

**AAA Benefit:** Members save up to 10%!

[↗] [¶↑] [≈] [BIZ] [HS] [≈] [🛁] [🖥] [💻]

## HILTON-WACO    (254)754-8484

Hotel $99-$189 **Address:** 113 S University Parks Dr 76701 **Location:** I-35 exit 335B, 0.5 mi w. **Facility:** 195 units. 11 stories, interior corridors. **Terms:** 1-7 night minimum stay, cancellation fee imposed. **Pool(s):** outdoor. **Activities:** hot tub, exercise room. **Guest Services:** valet and coin laundry.

**AAA Benefit:** Members save 5% or more!

[↗] [¶] [Y] [CALL] [&M] [≈] [BIZ] [HS] [≈] [🖥]
[/SOME UNITS] [🐕] [🛁] [🖥]

## HOLIDAY INN HOTEL & SUITES    (254)799-9997

Hotel $99-$149 **Address:** 1801 Development Blvd 76705 **Location:** I-35 exit 339 (Lake Shore Dr), 0.7 mi n on east frontage road, then just e. **Facility:** 122 units, some two bedrooms. 5 stories, interior corridors. **Terms:** 7 day cancellation notice-fee imposed. **Pool(s):** indoor. **Activities:** hot tub, exercise room. **Guest Services:** valet and coin laundry.

[↗] [¶] [Y] [CALL] [&M] [≈] [BIZ] [HS] [≈] [X] [🛁]
[🖥] [💻]

## HOMEWOOD SUITES BY HILTON WACO-LEGENDS CROSSING    254/644-4663

Extended Stay Contemporary Hotel. Rates not provided. **Address:** 5620 Legends Lake Pkwy 76712 **Location:** I-35 exit 330, just s on west frontage road to Corporation

**AAA Benefit:** Members save up to 10%!

Dr. **Facility:** 88 efficiencies, some two bedrooms. 4 stories, interior corridors. **Pool(s):** outdoor. **Activities:** hot tub, exercise room. **Guest Services:** valet and coin laundry.

[CALL] [&M] [≈] [BIZ] [HS] [≈] [🛁] [🖥] [💻]

## LA QUINTA INN WACO UNIVERSITY    (254)752-9741

Hotel $79-$124 **Address:** 1110 S 9th St 76706 **Location:** I-35 exit 334 (17th St) southbound; exit 334A (18th St) northbound; on east frontage road. **Facility:** 101 units. 2 stories (no elevator), exterior corridors. **Pool(s):** outdoor.

[↗] [¶↑] [≈] [≈] [💻] [/SOME UNITS] [🐕] [HS] [🛁] [🖥]

## MAGNUSON HOTEL WACO    (254)752-1991

Hotel $45-$150 **Address:** 1430 I-35 S 76706 **Location:** I-35 exit 334 (17th St); on northbound frontage road. **Facility:** 54 units. 2 stories (no elevator), exterior corridors. **Terms:** cancellation fee imposed. **Pool(s):** outdoor.

[≈] [HS] [≈] [💻] [/SOME UNITS] [🐕] [🛁] [🖥]

## QUALITY INN & SUITES    (254)799-9989

Hotel $80-$100 **Address:** 1508 I-35 N 76705 **Location:** I-35 exit 338B southbound; exit 339 northbound; on southbound access road. **Facility:** 56 units, some efficiencies. 3 stories, interior corridors. **Pool(s):** outdoor. **Activities:** exercise room. **Guest Services:** valet and coin laundry.

[¶↑] [CALL] [&M] [≈] [BIZ] [HS] [≈] [🛁] [🖥] [💻]

## QUALITY INN & SUITES NEAR UNIVERSITY    (254)296-0550

Hotel $79-$190 **Address:** 2410 S New Rd 76711 **Location:** I-35 exit 331 (New Rd), just w. **Facility:** 71 units. 3 stories, interior corridors. **Pool(s):** heated indoor. **Activities:** hot tub, exercise room. **Guest Services:** valet and coin laundry.

[CALL] [&M] [≈] [BIZ] [HS] [≈] [🛁] [🖥] [💻]

## RESIDENCE INN BY MARRIOTT    (254)714-1386

Extended Stay Hotel $150-$165 **Address:** 501 S University Parks Dr 76701 **Location:** I-35 exit 335B, 0.3 mi w. **Facility:** 78 units, some two bedrooms, efficiencies and kitchens.

**AAA Benefit:** Members save 5% or more!

3 stories, interior corridors. **Pool(s):** heated indoor. **Activities:** hot tub, exercise room. **Guest Services:** valet and coin laundry.

[≈] [BIZ] [≈] [X] [🛁] [🖥] [💻] [/SOME UNITS] [🐕]

## SUPER 8-WACO    (254)754-1023

Hotel
$49-$109

**Address:** 1320 S Jack Kultgen Frwy 76706 **Location:** I-35 exit 334 (17th St), just n on east frontage road. **Facility:** 78 units. 3 stories, interior corridors. **Featured Amenity: continental breakfast.**

[SAVE] [¶↑] [♿] [≈] [🛁] [🖥]
[/SOME UNITS] [🐕] [🖥]

---

## WHERE TO EAT

## BUZZARD BILLY'S    254/753-2778

Cajun. Casual Dining. $7-$19 **AAA Inspector Notes:** The specialty is seafood, sausage, chicken and beef dishes all cooked with a Cajun flair. The restaurant sits on the banks of the Brazos River, has a roadhouse feel and has TVs on the walls. **Features:** full bar. **Address:** 100 N I-35 76704 **Location:** I-35 exit 335C, just s on west frontage road; on the river. [L] [D]

## CASA DE CASTILLO    254/772-8246

Tex-Mex. Casual Dining. $8-$12 **AAA Inspector Notes:** The family-owned-and-operated restaurant on the west side of the city offers standard Mexican favorites, such as enchiladas, chalupas, fajitas and tamales. Those who prefer American dishes will find some of those on the menu as well. **Features:** full bar. **Address:** 4820 Sanger Ave 76710 **Location:** 0.7 mi w of jct US 84 and Valley Mills Dr to Sanger Ave, just s. [L] [D]

## CHUY'S MEXICAN RESTAURANT    254/420-4242

Tex-Mex. Casual Dining. $6-$12 **AAA Inspector Notes:** This Texas original serves up Mexican kitsch like no else in its décor but takes pride in its several house-made chile sauces and handmade tortillas. Although the menu is familiar—fajitas, tacos and enchiladas—the freshness of the ingredients and chiles sets this place apart. The bar is always abuzz, but families are welcome. **Features:** full bar, patio dining, happy hour. **Address:** 5501 Legend Lake Pkwy 76712 **Location:** SR 6 exit Bagby Ave, just e on frontage road, then just s. [L] [D] [CALL] [&M]

### EL CHICO
254/662-2750

♦♦♦ ♦♦♦
Tex-Mex
Casual Dining
$6-$23

**AAA Inspector Notes:** Inside and out, the decor of the popular Mexican restaurant is inviting. The menu features traditional favorites such as enchiladas, tacos, burritos and fajitas. The broad menu also lists a few American classics. **Features:** full bar. **Address:** 2111 S Valley Mills Dr 76706 **Location:** I-35 exit 333A (Valley Mills Dr), just e on Waco Cir. L D

### ELITE CIRCLE GRILLE
254/754-4941

♦♦♦ ♦♦♦ American. Casual Dining. $8-$18 **AAA Inspector Notes:** *Classic.* Take a walk back in time to the '40s and '50s at this café. Pictures of locals on motorcycles hang in the colorful dining room. Home-style cooking features chicken-fried steak, juicy burgers, sandwiches and steak. The restaurant is located on Waco's old circle on the southeast side of town. Easy access to I-35 for those traveling through the area. **Features:** full bar, Sunday brunch. **Address:** 2132 S Valley Mills Dr 76706 **Location:** I-35 exit 333A (Valley Mills Dr), just e on Waco Cir. L D

### LA FIESTA RESTAURANT & CANTINA
254/756-4701

♦♦♦ ♦♦♦ Tex-Mex. Casual Dining. $7-$15 **AAA Inspector Notes:** The smell of sizzling onions, green peppers, grilled beef and chicken fill the air. Fajitas are a specialty here. Seafood lovers try the tasty shrimp fajitas sauteed over roasted potatoes. There is a wide selection of enchiladas, burritos, tacos and chimichangas to satisfy everyone's cravings; a selection of vegetable sides is a welcome surprise on the menu. **Features:** full bar, patio dining, happy hour. **Address:** 3815 Franklin Ave 76710 **Location:** I-35 exit 333A (Valley Mills Dr), 2.2 mi w to Franklin Ave exit; on northwest corner. L D

### LAKE BRAZOS STEAKHOUSE
254/755-7797

♦♦♦ ♦♦♦ Steak. Casual Dining. $5-$23 **AAA Inspector Notes:** The Texas-style steakhouse is right on the Brazos River near downtown. While the specialty is "hand-cut" steaks, the menu also lists seafood, chicken and pork dishes. River views are excellent. **Features:** full bar, patio dining. **Address:** 1620 N Martin Luther King Jr Blvd 76704 **Location:** I-35 exit 335C, 2 mi w. L D 🐾

### NINFA'S
254/757-2050

♦♦♦ ♦♦♦ Tex-Mex. Casual Dining. $6-$23 **AAA Inspector Notes:** The small restaurant chain, which operates in some larger Texas cities, prepares a wide range of traditional Tex-Mex fare, including fajitas, chimichangas, chiles rellenos, tacos and other south-of-the-border favorites. Menu surprises include some "heart-healthy" items not typically seen in eateries of this type. **Features:** full bar. **Address:** 220 S 3rd St 76701 **Location:** I-35 exit 335B, 0.5 mi w; in The Shops of River Center. L D

### RUDY'S COUNTRY STORE AND BAR-B-QUE
254/750-9995

♦♦♦ Barbecue. Quick Serve. $5-$14 **AAA Inspector Notes:** This small, informal barbecue chain has a twist: The tasty food is ordered by the pound. Guests can mix and match and order three-quarters of a pound of beef with a half-pound of turkey or pork, for example. Desserts and coleslaw are prepackaged, and precooked beans accompany the meat. A drive-through window is available at most locations. **Features:** beer only. **Address:** 2510 Circle Rd 76706 **Location:** I-35 exit 333A (Valley Mills Dr). B L D

### TRUJILLO'S RESTAURANT Y CANTINA
254/756-1331

♦♦♦ ♦♦♦ Tex-Mex. Casual Dining. $6-$13 **AAA Inspector Notes:** This family-owned and -operated restaurant merges the traditional Tex-Mex fare and a small selection of American food on its menu. **Features:** full bar, happy hour. **Address:** 2612 La Salle Ave 76706 **Location:** I-35 exit 333A (Valley Mills Dr); at Waco circle. L D

### UNCLE DAN'S RIB HOUSE
254/772-3532

♦♦♦ Barbecue. Quick Serve. $7-$11 **AAA Inspector Notes:** If you are in the mood for Texas-style barbecue, you have to stop by this eatery. They serve a variety of mouthwatering barbecue items made to satisfy any appetite. Place your order and then stroll down a buffet line filled with tasty side dishes. **Features:** beer only. **Address:** 1001 Lake Air Dr 76710 **Location:** I-35 exit 333A (Valley Mills Dr), 3 mi w, then just s. L D

## WASHINGTON (F-9) elev. 245'

Also known as Washington-on-the-Brazos or Old Washington, Washington was established in 1834. The town was the site of the signing of the Texas Declaration of Independence.

**WASHINGTON-ON-THE-BRAZOS STATE HISTORIC SITE** is on FM 1155 just 1 mi. s. of jct. SR 105. The 293-acre park on the site of the first capitol of the Republic of Texas includes a living history farm, a museum and Independence Hall, a replica of the building where the Texas Declaration of Independence was signed. Also on the grounds are an amphitheater, walking trails and a picnic area.

**Hours:** Daily 8-dusk. Guided tours of Independence Hall are available daily at 10, 11, 1, 2, 3 and 4. **Cost:** Park free. Independence Hall $5; $3 (students with ID). **Phone:** (936) 878-2214. 🎫

**Barrington Living History Farm** is at 23100 Barrington Ln. This living-history farm depicts Washington County life in the 1850s and features costumed interpreters carrying out everyday farm chores. The antebellum house of Anson Jones, the last president of the Republic of Texas, has been restored on the grounds. A kitchen, a barn, slave quarters and other outbuildings from the Jones cotton plantation have been reconstructed.

**Time:** Allow 1 hour minimum. **Hours:** Daily 10-5. Closed Thanksgiving and Christmas-Jan. 2. **Cost:** $5; $3 (students with ID). **Phone:** (936) 878-2214.

**Star of the Republic Museum** is off FM 1155 at 23200 Park Rd. 12. The story of Texas' struggle for independence from Mexico is told in exhibits that include army uniforms and weaponry as well as artifacts from the Republic of Texas. A Lone Star flag, thought to be the oldest in existence, is displayed. A 20-minute film describes the founding of the republic. The Showers-Brown Discovery Center is a multisensory area that offers hands-on displays exploring Texas history.

**Time:** Allow 2 hours minimum. **Hours:** Daily 10-5. Closed Jan. 1, Thanksgiving and Christmas Eve-Dec. 31. **Cost:** $5; $3 (students with ID); free (ages 0-6). **Phone:** (936) 878-2461.

### THE INN AT DOS BRISAS
979/277-7750

♦♦♦ ♦♦♦ ♦♦♦ Country Inn. Rates not provided. **Address:** 10000 Champion Dr 77880 **Location:** US 290 exit Chapel Hill to FM 1155, 6.5 mi n. **Facility:** More than 300 acres surround the upscale lodging and dining facilities at this private countryside location. 9 units. 1 story, exterior corridors. **Amenities:** safes. **Dining:** restaurant, see separate listing. **Pool(s):** heated outdoor. **Activities:** hot tub. **Guest Services:** valet laundry.

## THE INN AT DOS BRISAS
979/277-7750

Regional
American
Fine Dining
$95-$165

**AAA Inspector Notes:** Only an hour from metropolitan Houston, this elegant country retreat offers diners a respite into an elegant world of fine dining created by Chef Robinson. American cuisine intermingles with French interpretations using predominantly the freshest herbs, vegetables and fruits from their organic gardens. Rich, dense flavors are created from local Wagyu beef, Hudson River Valley foie gras and other exceptional ingredients. **Features:** full bar. **Reservations:** required. **Address:** 10000 Champion Dr 77880 **Location:** US 290 exit Chapel Hill to FM 1155, 6.5 mi n. **Parking:** on-site and valet.
D

## WAXAHACHIE (D-9) pop. 29,621, elev. 585'

Only 30 minutes from high-tech Dallas, Waxahachie is nearly a century distant, for it is a town where the gingerbread of Victorian-era buildings sates even the most jaded architectural palate. Twenty percent of the Texas buildings listed on the National Register of Historic Places are in Waxahachie. The 1895 Ellis County Courthouse, one of the most photographed structures in the state, is a red sandstone and granite edifice decorated with ornate capitals, carved by expert Italian artisans.

**Waxahachie Convention and Visitors Bureau:** 102 YMCA Dr., Waxahachie, TX 75165. **Phone:** (972) 937-2390, or (972) 938-9617 in the Metroplex area.

## SUPER 8
(972)938-9088

Hotel
$55-$125

**Address:** 400 N I-35 E 75165 **Location:** I-35E exit 401B. **Facility:** 38 units. 2 stories (no elevator), interior corridors. **Pool(s):** outdoor. **Guest Services:** coin laundry. **Featured Amenity:** continental breakfast.

WAXAHACHIE SLEEP INN & SUITES (972)938-1600
Hotel $70-$110 **Address:** 1701 US Hwy 77 N 75165 **Location:** US 287 exit US 77, just n. **Facility:** 63 units. 3 stories, interior corridors. **Pool(s):** outdoor. **Guest Services:** valet and coin laundry.

## TUSCAN SLICE
972/937-6770
Italian. Casual Dining. $9-$15 **AAA Inspector Notes:** Don't be fooled by the name; this restaurant has a number of pleasing offerings besides wood-fired pizza, including pasta, steak, hearty salads, sandwiches and seafood dishes. The lackluster shopping center it's in belies the inviting open dining room made cozy by the warmth from the brick oven and closely set tables. **Features:** full bar, Sunday brunch, happy hour. **Address:** 401 N Hwy 77, Suite 15 75165 **Location:** US 287 exit US 77, 1 mi s; in University Plaza.
L D

## WEATHERFORD pop. 25,250
• Restaurants p. 566

### BEST WESTERN PLUS CUTTING HORSE INN & SUITES
(817)599-3300

Hotel
$100-$110

**AAA Benefit:** Members save 10% or more with Best Western!

**Address:** 210 Alford Dr 76087 **Location:** I-20 exit 408, just s on SR 171, then just w. **Facility:** 57 units. 3 stories, interior corridors. **Pool(s):** heated indoor. **Activities:** hot tub, exercise room. **Guest Services:** valet and coin laundry. **Featured Amenity:** full hot breakfast.

### FAIRFIELD INN & SUITES BY MARRIOTT (817)599-4040
Hotel
$99-$149

FAIRFIELD INN & SUITES Marriott

**AAA Benefit:** Members save 5% or more!

**Address:** 175 Alford Dr 76086 **Location:** I-20 exit 408, just s. **Facility:** 86 units. 4 stories, interior corridors. **Pool(s):** heated indoor. **Activities:** hot tub, exercise room. **Guest Services:** valet and coin laundry.

### HAMPTON INN
(817)599-4800
Hotel $92-$99 **Address:** 2524 S Main St 76087 **Location:** I-20 exit 408. **Facility:** 56 units. 3 stories, interior corridors. **Terms:** 1-7 night minimum stay, cancellation fee imposed. **Amenities:** video games. **Pool(s):** outdoor. **Activities:** hot tub, exercise room. **Guest Services:** valet and coin laundry.

**AAA Benefit:** Members save up to 10%!

### QUALITY INN & SUITES
(817)599-3700
Hotel $75-$139 **Address:** 2500 S Main St 76087 **Location:** I-20 exit 408, just s. **Facility:** 64 units. 2 stories, interior/exterior corridors. **Pool(s):** outdoor. **Activities:** hot tub. **Guest Services:** valet and coin laundry.

### SLEEP INN & SUITES
(817)594-9699
Hotel $75-$160 **Address:** 1911 Wall St 76086 **Location:** I-20 exit 480, just ne. **Facility:** 50 units. 3 stories, interior corridors. **Pool(s):** heated indoor. **Activities:** hot tub, exercise room. **Guest Services:** valet and coin laundry.

### WEATHERFORD HERITAGE INN
817/594-7401
Hotel. Rates not provided. **Address:** 1927 Santa Fe Dr 76086 **Location:** I-20 exit 409 (Clear Lake Rd/FM 2552), 0.3 mi nw. Located in a semi-rural area. **Facility:** 45 units. 2 stories (no elevator), exterior corridors. **Pool(s):** outdoor. **Guest Services:** coin laundry.

Explore on-the-go travel tools at
AAA.com/mobile or CAA.ca/mobile

## WHERE TO EAT

**BAKER'S RIBS**     817/599-4229

Barbecue. Quick Serve. $6-$13 **AAA Inspector Notes:** This small chain of restaurants specializes in barbecue by the pound and also offers a takeout service. Beef, pork, sausage, ham, turkey and chicken are all offered, along with chicken-fried steak and sandwiches. A children's menu and low-carb meals also are available. Their fried pie shop sells both sweet and savory pies such as apricot, apple and peach or meat and potatoes and chicken and broccoli. **Features:** full bar, patio dining. **Address:** 1921 S Main St 76086 **Location:** I-20 exit 408, just n. L D

**MESQUITE PIT**     817/596-7046

Barbecue. Casual Dining. $8-$30 **AAA Inspector Notes:** With a definite country feel, this popular restaurant serves large portions of Texas barbecue as well as chicken, beef and pork dishes. Also on the menu are several steak choices that cater to those with hearty appetites. Barbecue places are known for their no-frills attitude, but this place does it up with a little flare. **Features:** full bar. **Address:** 1201 Fort Worth Hwy 76086 **Location:** 1.2 mi e of courthouse square; center. L D

**MONTANA RESTAURANT**     817/341-3444

American. Casual Dining. $7-$16 **AAA Inspector Notes:** Rustic décor characterizes this restaurant, which offers simply prepared American and Mexican cuisine. Off I-20 near Weatherford College, this place employs friendly college students to provide service. **Features:** full bar, happy hour. **Address:** 1910 S Main St 76086 **Location:** I-20 exit 408, just n. L D

**R & K CAFE**     817/594-7701

American. Casual Dining. $0-$19 **AAA Inspector Notes:** With a staff as friendly as the people of this small town, it's no wonder this place is a local favorite. Large servings of home-style entrées such as meatloaf, pork chops, sandwiches and catfish are provided in a Western-themed dining room. If you should find yourself here without cash, an ATM is available to help you out. **Address:** 3311 Fort Worth Hwy 76087 **Location:** I-20 exit 415, 1.2 mi w. B L D

**WEATHERFORD DOWNTOWN CAFE**     817/594-8717

American. Casual Dining. $5-$10 **AAA Inspector Notes:** In historic old downtown, the small family-owned café is directly across the street from the courthouse on the square. Simple down-home cooking is reasonably priced. Burgers, sandwiches and fried catfish are just a few sample items. It's known for its breakfast, however, lucky for you, they serve it all day. **Address:** 101 W Church St 76086 **Location:** Southwest corner of Weatherford Square; downtown. B L D

## WEBSTER pop. 10,400

- **Hotels & Restaurants map & index p. 324**
- **Part of Houston area — see map p. 301**

**COMFORT SUITES**     (281)554-5400   152

Hotel $90-$140 **Address:** 16931 N Texas Ave 77598 **Location:** I-45 exit 26 (Bay Area Blvd), 0.5 mi e to Texas Ave, then just s. **Facility:** 58 units. 3 stories, interior corridors. **Pool(s):** indoor. **Activities:** hot tub, exercise room. **Guest Services:** valet and coin laundry.

/ SOME UNITS

**EXTENDED STAY AMERICA HOUSTON NASA-BAY AREA BLVD**     (281)338-7711   151

Extended Stay Hotel $85-$100 **Address:** 720 W Bay Area Blvd 77598 **Location:** I-45 exit 26 (Bay Area Blvd), just e. **Facility:** 86 units, some efficiencies and kitchens. 3 stories, interior corridors. **Terms:** cancellation fee imposed. **Pool(s):** outdoor. **Activities:** exercise room. **Guest Services:** coin laundry.

/ SOME UNITS

**HAMPTON INN & SUITES HOUSTON CLEAR LAKE/NASA**     (281)332-7952   148

Hotel $99-$209 **Address:** 506 W Bay Area Blvd 77598 **Location:** I-45 exit 26 (Bay Area Blvd), 0.5 mi e. **Facility:** 108 units, some efficiencies. 5 stories, interior corridors. **Terms:** 1-7 night minimum stay, cancellation fee imposed. **Pool(s):** outdoor. **Activities:** hot tub, exercise room. **Guest Services:** valet and coin laundry.

**AAA Benefit:** Members save up to 10%!

**HOLIDAY INN EXPRESS HOTEL & SUITES**     (281)316-9750   153

Hotel $99-$139 **Address:** 900 Rogers Ct 77598 **Location:** I-45 exit 26 (Bay Area Blvd), just s off southbound frontage road. **Facility:** 101 units. 4 stories, interior corridors. **Terms:** cancellation fee imposed. **Pool(s):** outdoor. **Activities:** hot tub, exercise room. **Guest Services:** valet and coin laundry.

**HOLIDAY INN NASA/ WEBSTER**     281/335-6272   147

Hotel. Rates not provided. **Address:** 302 W Bay Area Blvd 77598 **Location:** I-45 exit 26 (Bay Area Blvd), 1.1 mi e. **Facility:** 109 units. 5 stories, interior corridors. **Pool(s):** heated indoor. **Activities:** hot tub, exercise room. **Guest Services:** valet and coin laundry.

**LA QUINTA INN & SUITES CLEARLAKE/WEBSTER**     (281)554-5290   149

Hotel $109-$144 **Address:** 520 W Bay Area Blvd 77598 **Location:** I-45 exit 26 (Bay Area Blvd), just e. **Facility:** 68 units. 3 stories, interior corridors. **Pool(s):** indoor. **Activities:** hot tub, exercise room. **Guest Services:** valet and coin laundry.

/ SOME UNITS

**SPRINGHILL SUITES BY MARRIOTT HOUSTON CLEAR LAKE/WEBSTER**     (281)332-2999   154

Hotel $89-$299 **Address:** 1101 Magnolia Ave 77598 **Location:** I-45 exit 25 (NASA Rd 1), just e, then 0.5 mi s on Kobayashi Rd. **Facility:** 121 units. 6 stories, interior corridors. **Pool(s):** outdoor. **Activities:** exercise room. **Guest Services:** valet and coin laundry.

**AAA Benefit:** Members save 5% or more!

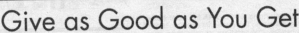

(See map & index p. 324.)

### STAYBRIDGE SUITES HOUSTON/ CLEAR LAKE
(281)338-0900   **146**

◆◆◆◆ **Extended Stay Hotel** $99-$199 **Address:** 501 W Texas Ave 77598 **Location:** I-45 exit 26 (Bay Area Blvd), right, then left at 3rd light. **Facility:** 112 efficiencies, some two bedrooms. 4 stories, interior corridors. **Pool(s):** outdoor. **Activities:** hot tub, exercise room. **Guest Services:** valet and coin laundry.

CALL 🖥️📶 BIZ HS 🛜 ✕ 🛄 🍽️ ☕
/ SOME UNITS 🛏️

### SUPER 8-HOUSTON-WEBSTER-NASA
(281)333-5385   **150**

Motel
$79-$130

**Address:** 18103 Kingsrow Rd 77058 **Location:** I-45 exit 25 (NASA Rd 1), 1.5 mi e. **Facility:** 69 units. 2 stories (no elevator), exterior corridors. **Terms:** 3 day cancellation notice-fee imposed. **Pool(s):** outdoor. **Activities:** hot tub. **Featured Amenity: continental breakfast.**

SAVE 🍴 📶 🛜 🛄 🍽️ ☕
/ SOME UNITS 🛏️ HS

---

## WHERE TO EAT

### CAFE EXPRESS
281/554-6999

◆ American. Casual Dining. $6-$13 **AAA Inspector Notes:** Even if this place does serve burgers, its American/Mediterranean menu lists plenty of more healthful options, such as pasta dishes, roasted chicken and Caesar salad. Everything is made to order and served fast for people on the go. Those with a little more time to spare may want to enjoy some wine or the classic German chocolate cake. **Features:** beer & wine, patio dining. **Address:** 19443 Gulf Way 77598 **Location:** I-45 exit 26 (Bay Area Blvd), just e; in Baybrook Passage Center. B L D

### FREEBIRDS WORLD BURRITO
281/557-2300

◆ Tex-Mex. Quick Serve. $5-$13 **AAA Inspector Notes:** Large California-style burritos are packed with your chosen fillings and salsas. In keeping with the NASA-area location, the setting resembles an airplane hangar and has a figure of a motorcycle-riding Statue of Liberty breaking out of the sky. Patrons use the aluminum foil in which burritos are served to make their own creatures (and leave them behind). **Address:** 528 W Bay Area Blvd 77598 **Location:** I-45 exit 26 (Bay Area Blvd), 0.5 mi e. L D

### LA MADELEINE COUNTRY FRENCH CAFE
281/316-6135

◆ Traditional French. Casual Dining. $7-$12 **AAA Inspector Notes:** A fireplace creates the focal point at this cozy European style café where you can always get a quiche or savory stuffed puffed pastry on the go or stick around for a chicken crêpe or French dip sandwich. Heartier entrées like rotisserie chicken are offered and every season promises menu surprises. Whatever you decide on you probably will not get out the door without enjoying one of their tempting sweet pastries. **Features:** beer & wine. **Address:** 929 W Bay Area Blvd 77598 **Location:** Jct I-45 and W Bay Area Blvd. B L D

### LUPE TORTILLA MEXICAN RESTAURANT
281/338-2711

◆◆ Mexican. Casual Dining. $8-$21 **AAA Inspector Notes:** Not every enchilada tastes the same. Here, green chicken enchiladas with tomatillo sauce have a great flavor, and the flan dessert is right on the mark. The environment is lively, sparked by cantina décor, background music and energetic service. An outdoor playground makes this place fun for the whole family. **Features:** full bar. **Address:** 891 W Bay Area Blvd 77598 **Location:** I-45 exit 26 (Bay Area Blvd), just e. L D ✎

### PAPPAS BBQ
281/332-1285   **63**

◆ Barbecue. Casual Dining. $6-$20 **AAA Inspector Notes:** The very nice selection of slow-smoked meats with all the fixins and a tasty homemade sauce really hit the spot. The turkey was moist and the sausage was very flavorful, as was the pork rib-eye. **Features:** beer only. **Address:** 20794 Gulf Frwy 77598 **Location:** I-35 exit 24 southbound; exit 25 northbound; on W Frontage Rd. L D CALL 🖥️

### PAPPASITO'S CANTINA
281/338-2885

◆◆ Tex-Mex. Casual Dining. $10-$49 **AAA Inspector Notes:** Fine traditional offerings are served in an upscale cantina atmosphere. Often crowded during peak hours, the immensely popular stop dishes up generous portions of sizzling fajitas, enchiladas and other traditional Mexican favorites, including some shrimp specialties. The terrific margaritas are guaranteed to get attention. Tables in the large dining room are closely spaced. Ice cream with cinnamon on chocolate bread pudding shouldn't be missed. **Features:** full bar, happy hour. **Address:** 20099 Gulf Frwy S 77598 **Location:** I-45 exit 25 (NASA Rd 1), just n on E Frontage Rd. L D ✎

### PAPPAS SEAFOOD HOUSE
281/332-7546

◆◆ Seafood. Casual Dining. $12-$45 **AAA Inspector Notes:** This popular local seafood chain serves a great variety of extremely fresh seafood with Louisiana-inspired entrées, raw bar items, steaks, pastas and even sushi. The service is friendly and the atmosphere relaxed. **Features:** full bar, happy hour. **Address:** 19991 I-45 S 77598 **Location:** I-45 exit 25 (NASA Rd 1), 0.7 mi n on E Frontage Rd. L D

### SALTGRASS STEAKHOUSE
281/338-9778   **62**

◆◆ Steak. Casual Dining. $9-$30 **AAA Inspector Notes:** Those looking for something different should try the comfortable steakhouse, which never says no to a special request. Born from the spirit of Texas cattle drives, the restaurant resembles a Texas lodge, with high ceilings and mounted animal heads. Baby back ribs are so tender the meat falls off the bone. Also on the menu are hearty steaks, prime rib, chicken, seafood and yummy desserts. **Features:** full bar. **Address:** 20241 Gulf Frwy S 77598 **Location:** I-45 exit 25 (NASA Rd 1), 0.3 mi n on E Frontage Rd. SAVE L D CALL 🖥️

### TRADICAO
281/557-9999   **61**

◆◆◆ Brazilian Steak. Casual Dining. $40 **AAA Inspector Notes:** A fabulous salad bar is followed up by more selections of meat dishes than you can count. Everything is perfectly prepared by the very attentive staff. I had a very entertaining evening with the folks at Tradicao. **Features:** full bar. **Address:** 201 W Bay Area Blvd 77598 **Location:** I-45 exit 26 (Bay Area Blvd), 1 mi e. D CALL 🖥️

(See map & index p. 324.)

ZIO'S ITALIAN KITCHEN                    281/338-7800

◆◆ Italian. Casual Dining. $8-$18 **AAA Inspector Notes:** The warm, comfortable atmosphere and Old World decor complement the menu. Meals are a good value, and so is the service. This small chain specializes in Italian cuisine, including oven-baked pizzas and pasta dishes. Guests are encouraged to get creative with their pizzas by mixing and matching from a list of 24 toppings. Particularly tempting dishes are Artichoke spinach pasta, chicken parmigiana, and Shrimp Limone. **Features:** full bar. **Address:** 820 W Bay Area Blvd 77598 **Location:** I-45 exit 26 (Bay Area Blvd), just e. [L] [D]

## WELLINGTON   pop. 2,189

CHEROKEE INN & RESTAURANT               (806)447-2508

◆ Motel $60-$100 **Address:** 1105 Houston St 79095 **Location:** US 83, just n of jct FM 338. **Facility:** 21 units. 1 story, exterior corridors. **Terms:** cancellation fee imposed. 🛜 🍴 🖥

## WESLACO   (I-8) pop. 35,670, elev. 79'

**ESTERO LLANO GRANDE STATE PARK** is 2.4 mi. s. on FM 1015 (International Blvd.). This 176-acre refuge within the World Birding Center network is comprised of lakes and woodlands that invite shorebirds, coastal species, endangered species and migrating waterfowl. Amenities include boardwalks, a pavilion, 3 miles of nature trails and a visitor center. **Time:** Allow 2 hours minimum. **Hours:** Daily 8-5, Oct.-Mar.; Tues.-Sun. 8-5, Apr.-June; Wed.-Sun. 8-5, rest of year. **Cost:** $5; free (ages 0-12). **Phone:** (956) 565-3919. 🍴

PALM AIRE INN & SUITES                  956/969-2411

[fyi] **Hotel.** Rates not provided. Under major renovation, scheduled to be completed July 2013. **Last Rated:** ◆◆ **Address:** 415 S International Blvd 78596 **Location:** US 83 exit International Blvd, just s. Located in a quiet area. **Facility:** 193 units. 2 stories (no elevator), exterior corridors. **Pool(s):** outdoor. **Activities:** sauna, hot tub, steamroom, tennis, exercise room, massage. **Guest Services:** valet and coin laundry.

🍴 🛋 🚗 [BIZ] 🛜 🖥 / SOME UNITS 🐕 🍴 🖥

SUPER 8                                 (956)969-9920

◆◆ Hotel $45-$65

**Address:** 1702 E Expwy 83 78596 **Location:** US 83 exit Airport Dr. **Facility:** 52 units. 2 stories (no elevator), interior corridors. **Pool(s):** outdoor. **Activities:** hot tub, exercise room. **Guest Services:** coin laundry. **Featured Amenity: continental breakfast.**

[SAVE] 🚗 [BIZ] [HS] 🛜 🖥 🍴 🖥

### WHERE TO EAT

THE BLUE ONION                          956/447-0067

◆◆ New American. Quick Serve. $5-$10 **AAA Inspector Notes:** The intriguing menu concept starts with pecan-smoked meats and grilled flatbreads for wraps, po' boys and gyros and at least 10 made-in-house dips and dressings for accompaniment. Also offered are great salads, pizzas, calzones, children's dishes and meal-in-a-bowl daily specials such as bouillabaisse, chicken and sausage gumbo or tortilla soup. Colorful local artwork decorates the casual modern setting. **Features:** full bar. **Address:** 423 S International Blvd 78596 **Location:** US 83 exit International Blvd, just s. [L] [D]

## WEST COLUMBIA   (G-9) pop. 3,905, elev. 40'

The first duly-elected Congress of the Republic of Texas met in West Columbia, the capital, on October 3, 1836. Sam Houston was inaugurated the first president of the Republic of Texas, and Stephen F. Austin was named its secretary of state in West Columbia, Texas' first capital. The provisional government was forced to move after Texans declared their independence from Mexico on March 2, 1836, at Washington on the Brazos. A replica of the first capitol is in the center of town.

**West Columbia Chamber of Commerce:** 202 E. Brazos St., P.O. Box 837, West Columbia, TX 77486. **Phone:** (979) 345-3921.

**Self-guiding tours:** Brochures outlining historical sites are available at the West Columbia Chamber of Commerce.

**VARNER-HOGG PLANTATION STATE HISTORIC SITE** is 1 mi. n.e. off SR 35 at 1702 N. 13th St. (FM 2852). The property's first owner, Martin Varner, received a land grant from Stephen F. Austin in 1824. Later a sugar plantation, the estate was purchased by Gov. James S. Hogg in 1901. The 66-acre site includes the 1836 plantation manor, outbuildings, sugar mill ruins and pecan orchards.

Guided tours of the mansion are available. **Time:** Allow 1 hour minimum. **Hours:** Tues.-Sun. 8-5. Guided tours depart at 9, 10, 11, 1:30, 2:30 and 3:30. **Cost:** Grounds $3; free (ages 0-5). Tours $6; $4 (ages 6-18 and students with ID). **Phone:** (979) 345-4656. 🏛

## WESTLAKE   pop. 992

DALLAS/FT. WORTH MARRIOTT SOLANA        (817)430-5000

◆◆◆ Hotel $98-$249 **Address:** 5 Village Cir 76262 **Location:** SR 114 exit Kirkwood Blvd, just s. **Facility:** 294 units. 7 stories, interior corridors. **Pool(s):** outdoor. **Activities:** hot tub, exercise room. **Guest Services:** complimentary and valet laundry, area transportation.

**AAA Benefit:** Members save 5% or more!

[ECO] [←] 🍴 🛋 🍸 [CALL] [M] 🚗 [BIZ] [SHS] 🛜 [✕] 🐾 🖥 🖥 / SOME UNITS 🖥

## WHARTON   (G-9) pop. 8,832, elev. 111'

Rice, corn, cotton and grain make Wharton a major agricultural producer. Established along the banks of the Colorado River, the town was the birthplace of playwright Horton Foote and journalist Dan Rather.

**WHARTON COUNTY HISTORICAL MUSEUM** is at 3615 N. Richmond Rd. (SR 60). The museum displays wildlife trophies as well as county artifacts and photographs dealing with ranching, agriculture, archeology, medicine, local sulfur mines and Wharton County's Congressional Medal of Honor recipients Roy Benavidez and Johnnie Hutchins. An extensive collection of everyday items introduced in the 1900s—including typewriters, computers, radios, kitchen appliances and arcade games—also is featured.

On the grounds is the original home of Dan Rather, TV news anchor. **Hours:** Mon.-Fri. 9:30-4:30, Sat.-Sun. 1-5. **Cost:** Free. **Phone:** (979) 532-2600.

## WICHITA FALLS (C-7) pop. 104,553, elev. 946'
• Restaurants p. 570

It is hard to believe that the waterfall that gave Wichita Falls its name could exist in this flat country. Although no Niagara, the 5-foot cascade was such a rare sight that early settlers and surveyors felt it no exaggeration to christen it "Wichita Falls." Four years after the railroad brought the town's first settlers in 1882, the falls were washed away by a flood.

The loss of the falls did not affect the new community, which grew into a marketplace for north Texas agriculture. The city restored a piece of its past when it re-established the falls; in 1987 a 54-foot-high, terraced cascade was built downstream from the original waterfall.

The oil boom in the early part of the 20th century changed the small community's fortunes dramatically. By 1920 a local business almanac listed 500 oil companies, and living space was so scarce that cots were rented on a sleeping-time rate. Modern Wichita Falls is a diversified industrial center based on its agricultural and petroleum past.

For lovers of the outdoors, nearby Lake Arrowhead, with its distinctive oil derricks, offers a variety of recreational opportunities *(see Recreation Areas Chart)*.

Wichita Falls' residents are ardent supporters of the arts. The city boasts a symphony orchestra, a ballet and theater companies.

**Wichita Falls Convention and Visitors Bureau:** 1000 Fifth St., Wichita Falls, TX 76301. **Phone:** (940) 716-5500 or (800) 799-6732.

**MUSEUM OF NORTH TEXAS HISTORY** is at 720 Indiana Ave. Exhibits focus on Native American history, the military, the oil industry, medicine and other topics. Highlights include a collection of military ship models and a collection of 500-plus cowboy hats. **Time:** Allow 30 minutes minimum. **Hours:** Tues.-Sat. 10-4. Closed Jan. 1, Thanksgiving and Christmas. **Cost:** Free. **Phone:** (940) 322-7628.

**RIVER BEND NATURE CENTER,** 2200 3rd St., features 17 acres of wetlands and forests teeming with birds and other wildlife. Visitors can explore trails, a children's garden and a conservatory housing plants, butterflies, prairie dogs and turtles. A resource library and a pavilion also are on the grounds. **Time:** Allow 30 minutes minimum. **Hours:** Mon.-Fri. 9-5, Sat. 10-4, Sun. noon-4. Closed Jan. 1, Thanksgiving and Christmas. **Cost:** $5; $4 (ages 63+); free (ages 0-1). **Phone:** (940) 767-0843.

**WICHITA FALLS MUSEUM OF ART AT MIDWESTERN STATE UNIVERSITY** is off I-281S and SR 79, then 3 mi. w. on Midwestern Pkwy. to 2 Eureka Cir., adjoining Midwestern State University. Works from the museum's permanent collection of American arts are displayed. Traveling exhibits also are available. **Time:** Allow 30 minutes minimum. **Hours:** Museum Tues.-Fri. 10-5, Sat. 1-5. Closed major holidays. **Cost:** Free. **Phone:** (940) 397-8900.

**BEST WESTERN PLUS UNIVERSITY INN & SUITES**
(940)687-2025

Hotel
$75-$110

**AAA Benefit:** Members save 10% or more with Best Western!

**Address:** 4540 Maplewood Ave 76308 **Location:** Jct Southwest Pkwy (CR 369), just n. **Facility:** 78 units. 3 stories, interior corridors. **Pool(s):** outdoor. **Activities:** exercise room. **Guest Services:** coin laundry. **Featured Amenity:** full hot breakfast.

**COURTYARD BY MARRIOTT WICHITA FALLS**
(940)696-0010

Hotel
$79-$149

COURTYARD Marriott

**AAA Benefit:** Members save 5% or more!

**Address:** 3800 Tarry St 76308 **Location:** US 82 exit Lawrence Rd, just s. **Facility:** 93 units. 4 stories, interior corridors. **Pool(s):** heated indoor. **Activities:** hot tub, exercise room. **Guest Services:** valet and coin laundry.

**FAIRFIELD INN BY MARRIOTT** (940)691-1066

Hotel $81-$125 **Address:** 4414 Westgate Dr 76308 **Location:** 1.6 mi s of jct US 82/277 and Kemp Blvd. **Facility:** 64 units. 3 stories, interior corridors. **Pool(s):** heated indoor. **Activities:** hot tub. **Guest Services:** valet laundry.

**AAA Benefit:** Members save 5% or more!

**HAMPTON INN** (940)692-1999

Hotel $104-$159 **Address:** 4217 Kemp Blvd 76308 **Location:** 1.5 mi s of jct US 82/277. **Facility:** 74 units. 3 stories, interior corridors. **Terms:** 1-7 night minimum stay, cancellation fee imposed. **Pool(s):** heated indoor. **Activities:** hot tub, exercise room. **Guest Services:** valet and coin laundry.

**AAA Benefit:** Members save up to 10%!

## HOLIDAY INN                                (940)761-6000

◆◆◆ **Hotel** $79-$149 **Address:** 100 Central Frwy 76306 **Location:** I-44 exit 1C, on west side access road. **Facility:** 167 units. 6 stories, interior corridors. **Terms:** 3 day cancellation notice-fee imposed. **Pool(s):** heated indoor. **Activities:** hot tub, exercise room. **Guest Services:** valet laundry.

[icons]

## HOMEWOOD SUITES BY HILTON              (940)691-4663

◆◆◆◆ **Extended Stay Hotel** $144 **Address:** 2675 Plaza Pkwy 76308 **Location:** Jct Maplewood Ave. **Facility:** 73 units, some efficiencies. 4 stories, interior corridors. **Terms:** 1-7 night minimum stay, cancellation fee imposed. **Amenities:** video games. **Pool(s):** heated indoor. **Activities:** hot tub, exercise room. **Guest Services:** valet and coin laundry.

**AAA Benefit:** Members save up to 10%!

[icons]

## LA QUINTA INN WICHITA FALLS AIRPORT AREA       (940)322-6971

◆◆◆ **Hotel** $69-$110 **Address:** 1128 Central Frwy N 76306 **Location:** I-44 exit 2 (Maurine St), just w. **Facility:** 139 units, some two bedrooms. 2 stories (no elevator), exterior corridors. **Pool(s):** outdoor. **Guest Services:** coin laundry.

[icons]

## RED ROOF INN- WITCHITA FALLS              (940)766-6881

◆◆◆
Hotel
$60-$80

**Address:** 1032 Central Frwy 76306 **Location:** I-44 exit 2 (Maurine St), just w. **Facility:** 111 units. 3 stories, exterior corridors. **Pool(s):** outdoor. **Activities:** hot tub, exercise room. **Guest Services:** coin laundry. **Featured Amenity: continental breakfast.**

[icons]

## SUPER 8-WICHITA FALLS                   (940)322-8880

◆◆◆
Hotel
$50-$80

**Address:** 1307 Kenley Ave 76306 **Location:** I-44 exit 2 (Maurine St), just w. **Facility:** 103 units. 3 stories, interior corridors. **Activities:** exercise room. **Guest Services:** coin laundry. **Featured Amenity: continental breakfast.**

[icons]

**WHERE TO EAT**

## EL CHICO

◆◆◆
Tex-Mex
Casual Dining
$7-$16

*For additional information, visit AAA.com*

**AAA Inspector Notes:** Inside and out, the decor of the popular Mexican restaurant is inviting. The menu features traditional favorites such as enchiladas, tacos, burritos and fajitas. The broad menu also lists a few American classics. **Bar:** full bar. [L] [D] [icon]

**LOCATIONS:**
**Address:** 1028 Central Frwy 76306 **Location:** I-44 exit 2 (Maurine St), just w. **Phone:** 940/322-1455

**Address:** 2801 Southwest Pkwy, Suite A 76308 **Location:** US 281 exit Southwest Pkwy (CR 369), 2 mi w.
**Phone:** 940/692-1415

## THE JALAPENO TREE                        940/696-7074

◆◆ **Tex-Mex. Casual Dining.** $7-$17 **AAA Inspector Notes:** A lively restaurant with interesting, authentic décor and generous portions. **Features:** full bar. **Address:** 2927 Southwest Pkwy 76309 **Location:** US 281 exit Southwest Pkwy (CR 369), 2.5 mi w. [L] [D] [icon]

## MCBRIDE LAND & CATTLE COMPANY           940/322-2516

◆◆ **American. Casual Dining.** $8-$23 **AAA Inspector Notes:** Family-owned and -operated since 1975, this restaurant sports a rustic exterior and a log cabin-like dining room with a large stone fireplace as its centerpiece. Generous portions and a good variety of offerings can be expected. **Features:** full bar. **Address:** 501 Scott St 76301 **Location:** Jct 5th St; downtown. [L] [D] CALL [M]

## MCBRIDE'S STEAKS                         940/696-0250

◆◆ **American. Casual Dining.** $7-$33 **AAA Inspector Notes:** Saddles hang from the rafters of the casual dining room. Diners with hearty appetites can sample from a wide choice of steaks, as well as ribs, chicken and seafood dishes. **Features:** full bar. **Address:** 4537 Maplewood Ave 76308 **Location:** US 281 exit Southwest Pkwy (CR 369), 2.3 mi w to Maplewood Ave, then just n. [L] [D]

## SAMURAI OF TOKYO                         940/696-2626

◆◆ **Japanese. Casual Dining.** $7-$31 **AAA Inspector Notes:** A good variety of fresh seafood is prepared and presented with flair. **Features:** full bar. **Address:** 2518 Mallard Dr 76308 **Location:** US 82 exit Kemp Blvd, 2 mi s to Elmwood Ave, just e. [L] [D]

## WILLIS  pop. 5,662
• Part of Houston area — see map p. 301

## BEST WESTERN WILLIS                      (936)856-1906

◆◆
Hotel
$73-$86

[Best Western logo] **AAA Benefit:** Members save 10% or more with Best Western!

**Address:** 12323 IH-45 N 77318 **Location:** I-45 exit 94, just s on frontage road to Old Montgomery Hwy, just sw to Western Rd, then just s. **Facility:** 47 units. 2 stories (no elevator), exterior corridors. **Pool(s):** outdoor. **Activities:** exercise room.

[icons]

## WIMBERLEY  pop. 2,626

## BLAIR HOUSE INN                          (512)847-1111

◆◆◆ **Bed & Breakfast** $158-$345 **Address:** 100 W Spoke Hill Rd 78676 **Location:** Jct SR 32 and 12, 2.4 mi n; 1.4 mi s of downtown on SR 12. **Facility:** Wildflowers, towering oak trees and a hammock make the inn's extensive grounds well suited for long walks or lounging. Very upscale accommodations and a professional ownership ensure a fabulous stay. 12 units. 1 story, interior/exterior corridors. **Terms:** 2 night minimum stay - weekends, age restrictions may apply, 30 day cancellation notice-fee imposed. **Pool(s):** outdoor. **Activities:** sauna, hot tub, bicycles, trails, spa. **Guest Services:** complimentary laundry. [icons]

## WINNIE  pop. 3,254
• Part of Houston area — see map p. 301

## COMFORT INN & SUITES                     (409)296-6200

◆◆◆ **Hotel** $89-$104 **Address:** 338 Spur 5 77665 **Location:** I-10 exit 829, just s. **Facility:** 53 units. 3 stories, interior corridors. **Pool(s):** outdoor. **Guest Services:** coin laundry.

[icons]

## DAYS INN & SUITES

Hotel
$69-$114

(409)296-2866

**Address:** 14932 FM 1663 77665 **Location:** I-10 exit 829, just n. **Facility:** 43 units, some two bedrooms and kitchens. 2 stories (no elevator), exterior corridors. **Terms:** cancellation fee imposed. **Activities:** exercise room. **Guest Services:** coin laundry. **Featured Amenity:** continental breakfast.

## WINNIE INN & SUITES

(409)296-2947

Hotel $50-$90 **Address:** 205 Spur 5, Hwy 124 77665 **Location:** I-10 exit 829, just s. **Facility:** 40 units. 1 story, exterior corridors. **Pool(s):** outdoor. **Guest Services:** coin laundry.

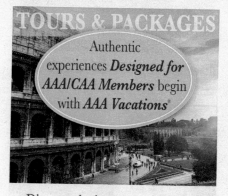

## WOODVILLE (E-10) pop. 2,586, elev. 281'

Named for George T. Wood, the second governor of Texas, Woodville is a major commercial center for lumbering and forest products.

**Tyler County Chamber of Commerce:** 717 W. Bluff, Woodville, TX 75979. **Phone:** (409) 283-2632.

**ALLAN SHIVERS MUSEUM** is 1 blk. w. of US 69 and 2 blks. n. of US 190, at 302 N. Charlton St. The museum, in a restored Victorian house, displays mementos of the family of Allan Shivers, governor of Texas 1949-57. The second floor contains historical documents pertinent to Shivers' gubernatorial service. **Time:** Allow 30 minutes minimum. **Hours:** Mon.-Fri. 9-5, Sat. 10-2. Last tour begins 30 minutes before closing. Closed major holidays. **Cost:** $3; $2 (ages 50+); $1 (ages 5-14). **Phone:** (409) 283-3709.

**HERITAGE VILLAGE MUSEUM** is 1.5 mi. w. on US 190. The village offers a glimpse of life in a rural Texas farm community. Buildings include a saloon, a railroad depot, blacksmith and apothecary shops, physician's and lawyer's offices and a schoolhouse. An East Texas model railroad and a nature trail also are on the grounds. Guided tours are available by reservation.

**Time:** Allow 30 minutes minimum. **Hours:** Daily 9-5. Closed major holidays. **Cost:** $4; $2 (ages 0-12). **Phone:** (409) 283-2272 or (800) 323-0389.

## STAGECOACH INN

(409)331-1100

Motel $77-$99 **Address:** 902 S Magnolia St 75979 **Location:** 0.5 mi s of jct US 190. **Facility:** 32 units. 1 story, exterior corridors. **Pool(s):** outdoor.

### WHERE TO EAT

## ELIJAH'S CAFE

409/331-9090

Southern. Casual Dining. $6-$13 **AAA Inspector Notes:** This is a great stop for traditional home-style Southern food and fast, friendly service. The large menu offers a range of choices with sandwiches, burgers, salads and entrées such as chicken-fried steak, grilled catfish and pot roast. **Address:** 810 Magnolia St 75979 **Location:** 0.5 mi s of jct US 190.

## THE PICKETT HOUSE

409/283-3371

American. Casual Dining. $8-$10 **AAA Inspector Notes:** *Historic.* Located inside an old restored schoolhouse, fried chicken dinners are served boardinghouse style. Warm combread and biscuits, country-style vegetables, noodles with chicken gravy and freshly made warm peach cobbler also are available. The all-you-can-eat option is a great value. Note that lunch is served daily, but dinner is served weekends only. **Address:** Hwy 190 W 75979 **Location:** 1.5 mi w; in Heritage Village.

## WOODWAY pop. 8,452

## FAIRFIELD INN BY MARRIOTT-WACO SOUTH

(254)776-7821

Hotel $109-$170 **Address:** 5805 N Woodway Dr 76712 **Location:** I-35 exit 330 (SR 6), 5 mi sw; Loop 340 exit 330 to jct SR 84. **Facility:** 64 units. 3 stories, interior corridors. **Pool(s):** heated indoor. **Activities:** hot tub. **Guest Services:** valet laundry.

**AAA Benefit:** Members save 5% or more!

## HOLIDAY INN EXPRESS HOTEL & SUITES (254)772-2227

 **Hotel** $119-$169 **Address:** 6808 Woodway Dr 76712 **Location:** On US 84, 0.3 mi w of jct SR 6 and Loop 340. **Facility:** 72 units, some efficiencies. 3 stories, interior corridors. **Terms:** cancellation fee imposed. **Amenities:** video games. *Some:* safes. **Pool(s):** heated indoor. **Activities:** hot tub, exercise room. **Guest Services:** valet and coin laundry.

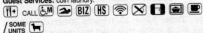

## LA QUINTA INN & SUITES (254)772-0200

 **Hotel** $119-$154 **Address:** 6003 Woodway Dr 76712 **Location:** I-35 exit 330 (SR 6), 2.5 mi w to jct US 84, then just s on N Frontage Rd. **Facility:** 99 units, some kitchens. 3 stories, interior corridors. **Pool(s):** heated indoor. **Activities:** hot tub, exercise room. **Guest Services:** coin laundry.

## SPRINGHILL SUITES BY MARRIOTT (254)732-7979

 **Hotel** $112-$154 **Address:** 200 Collonade Pkwy 76712 **Location:** I-35 exit 330, 2.5 mi nw to jct US 84, then 1 mi w on S Frontage Rd. **Facility:** 82 units. 4 stories, interior corridors. **Amenities:** safes. **Pool(s):** heated indoor. **Activities:** hot tub, picnic facilities, exercise room. **Guest Services:** valet and coin laundry.

**AAA Benefit:** Members save 5% or more!

## SUPER 8 WACO MALL (254)776-3194

 Hotel $55-$109

**Address:** 6624 Woodway Dr (Hwy 84 W) 76712 **Location:** Jct US 84 and SR 6, just w. **Facility:** 55 units. 2 stories (no elevator), exterior corridors. **Pool(s):** outdoor. **Guest Services:** valet laundry. **Featured Amenity:** continental breakfast.

## WYLIE pop. 41,427
• Part of Dallas area — see map p. 161

## BEST WESTERN PLUS WYLIE INN & SUITES (972)429-1771

Hotel $85-$159

**AAA Benefit:** Members save 10% or more with Best Western!

**Address:** 2011 Hwy 78 N 75098 **Location:** 1.8 mi ne of SR 2514 (Ballard St); downtown. **Facility:** 51 units, some kitchens. 3 stories, interior corridors. **Pool(s):** outdoor. **Activities:** exercise room. **Guest Services:** valet laundry. **Featured Amenity:** breakfast buffet.

## YOAKUM pop. 5,815

## REGENCY INN & SUITES 361/293-9595

**Motel.** Rates not provided. **Address:** 104 Ellen May Rd 77995 **Location:** On Alternate Rt US 77, at jct Alternate Business Rt US 77. **Facility:** 25 units. 1 story, exterior corridors. **Pool(s):** outdoor. **Activities:** limited exercise equipment. **Guest Services:** coin laundry.

## ZAPATA pop. 5,089

## BEST WESTERN INN BY THE LAKE (956)765-8403

 Hotel $86-$96

**AAA Benefit:** Members save 10% or more with Best Western!

**Address:** 1896 S US Hwy 83 78076 **Location:** On US 83, 0.5 mi se. Next to Falcon Lake. **Facility:** 56 units, some efficiencies. 1 story, exterior corridors. **Parking:** winter plug-ins. **Pool(s):** outdoor. **Activities:** boat dock, exercise room. **Guest Services:** coin laundry. **Featured Amenity:** full hot breakfast.

## HOLIDAY INN EXPRESS 956/765-1333

**Hotel.** Rates not provided. **Address:** 167 S Hwy 83 78076 **Location:** On US 83 southbound. Located in a quiet area on eastern edge of town. **Facility:** 70 units. 3 stories, interior corridors. **Pool(s):** outdoor. **Activities:** exercise room. **Guest Services:** coin laundry.

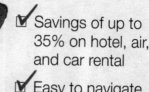

Disney's Art of Animation Resort

©Disney/Pixar

Disneyland® Resort Hotel

# ENJOY A MAGICAL DISNEY VACATION

What's the best way to experience all the enchantment of a vacation to the *Walt Disney World*® Resort in Florida or the *Disneyland*® Resort in California? How do you squeeze the most magic out of the Theme Parks and the whimsically themed *Disney Resort* hotels? And how can you enjoy great savings and exclusive rewards not available anywhere else? By booking a *AAA Vacations*® package from AAA Travel, of course!

## DISNEYLAND® RESORT, CALIFORNIA

- Stay just steps away from the magic at a *Disneyland*® Resort Hotel.

- **Now open!**
  Get ready to be floored—cruise into the amazing Cars Land at *Disney California Adventure*® Park.

## WALT DISNEY WORLD RESORT, FLORIDA

- Stay in the middle of the magic at a *Walt Disney World* Resort hotel.

- **Now open!**
  New Fantasyland™—immersing you in Disney stories like never before at *Magic Kingdom*® Park.

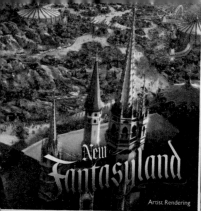

New **Fantasyland**

Artist Rendering

©Disney/Pixar

Cars Land

# WITH ENCHANTING AAA BENEFITS!

## LET AAA BE YOUR GUIDE...

With a *AAA Vacations*® package, you can create the Disney vacation that fits your family, your taste and your budget. And not only will your AAA Travel professional help put everything (like accommodations, tickets and flights) together, you'll also get to enjoy great Disney benefits on top of the exclusive AAA benefits and savings once you get there! Then all you need to do is relax and have fun.

**READY TO START MAKING MAGIC?**
Then contact your **AAA Travel professional** today!

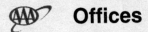 **Offices**

Cities with main offices are listed in **BOLD TYPE** and toll-free member service numbers in *ITALIC TYPE*.
All are closed Saturdays, Sundays and holidays unless otherwise indicated.
The addresses, phone numbers and hours for any AAA/CAA office are subject to change.
The type of service provided is designated below the name of the city where the office is located:

✛ Auto travel services, including books and maps, and on-demand TripTik® routings.
● Auto travel services, including selected books and maps, and on-demand TripTik® routings.
■ Books/maps only, no marked maps or on-demand TripTik® routings.
▲ Travel Agency Services; cruise, tour, air, car and rail reservations; domestic and international hotel reservations; passport photo services; international and domestic travel guides and maps; travel money products; and International Driving Permits. In addition, assistance with travel related insurance products including trip cancellation, travel accident, lost luggage, trip delay and assistance products.
❍ Insurance services provided. If only this icon appears, only insurance services are provided at that office.
C Car Care Plus Facility provides car care services.
▣ Electric vehicle charging station on premises.

**AAA NATIONAL OFFICE: 1000 AAA DRIVE, HEATHROW, FLORIDA 32746-5063, (407) 444-7000**

## TEXAS

**ALLEN**—AAA TEXAS, 190 E STACY RD STE 212, 75002.
WEEKDAYS (M-F) 9:00-6:00, SAT 9:00-1:00. (972) 912-3015
✛▲❍

**AMARILLO**—AAA TEXAS, 2607 WOLFLIN VILLAGE, 79109.
WEEKDAYS (M-F) 9:00-6:00, SAT 9:00-1:00. (806) 354-8288
✛▲❍

**ARLINGTON**—AAA TEXAS, 4634 S COOPER #176, 76017.
WEEKDAYS (M-F) 9:00-6:00, SAT 9:00-1:00. (817) 417-5636
✛▲❍

**AUSTIN**—AAA TEXAS, 13376 HWY 183 N STE 108, 78750.
WEEKDAYS (M-F) 9:00-6:00, SAT 9:00-1:00. (512) 335-5222
✛▲❍

**AUSTIN**—AAA TEXAS, 4970 HWY 290 W #310, 78735.
WEEKDAYS (M-F) 9:00-6:00, SAT 9:00-1:00. (512) 444-4757
✛▲❍

**CONROE**—AAA TEXAS, 27726 I-45 N, 77385. WEEKDAYS (M-F) 9:00-6:00, SAT 9:00-1:00. (713) 834-3200 ✛▲❍

**DALLAS**—AAA TEXAS, 5455 BELTLINE RD STE 100, 75254.
WEEKDAYS (M-F) 9:00-6:00, SAT 9:00-1:00. (214) 252-2493
✛▲❍

**DALLAS**—AAA TEXAS, 8160 PARK LN STE 305, 75231.
WEEKDAYS (M-F) 9:00-6:00, SAT 9:00-1:00. (214) 706-3000
✛▲❍

**DENTON**—AAA TEXAS, 1732 S LOOP 288 STE 100, 76205.
WEEKDAYS (M-F) 9:00-6:00, SAT 9:00-1:00. (940) 323-3240
✛▲❍

**EL PASO**—AAA TEXAS, 5867 N MESA STE A, 79912.
WEEKDAYS (M-F) 9:00-6:00, SAT 9:00-1:00. (915) 778-9521
✛▲❍

**EULESS**—AAA TEXAS, 3001 HWY 121 STE 250, 76039.
WEEKDAYS (M-F) 9:00-6:00, SAT 9:00-1:00. (817) 858-9383
✛▲❍

**FLOWER MOUND**—AAA TEXAS, 6020 LONG PRAIRIE RD #200, 75028. WEEKDAYS (M-F) 9:00-6:00, SAT 9:00-1:00.
(972) 956-9938 ✛▲❍

**FORT WORTH**—AAA TEXAS, 5431 S HULEN ST, 76132.
WEEKDAYS (M-F) 9:00-6:00, SAT 9:00-1:00. (817) 370-3000
✛▲❍

**FORT WORTH**—AAA TEXAS, 9509 SAGE MEADOW TRL, 76177.
WEEKDAYS (M-F) 9:00-6:00, SAT 9:00-1:00. (817) 750-1550
✛▲❍

**FRISCO**—AAA TEXAS, 4760 PRESTON RD STE 208, 75034.
WEEKDAYS (M-F) 9:00-6:00, SAT 9:00-1:00. (972) 712-0569
✛▲❍

**GARLAND**—AAA TEXAS, 4280 LAVON DR STE 216, 75040.
WEEKDAYS (M-F) 9:00-6:00, SAT 9:00-1:00. (972) 926-1535
✛▲❍

**HOUSTON**—AAA TEXAS, 13845 BRECK ST, 77066. WEEKDAYS
(M-F) 9:00-6:00, SAT 9:00-1:00. (713) 284-6450 ✛▲❍

**HOUSTON**—AAA TEXAS, 19604 KATY FWY, 77094.
WEEKDAYS (M-F) 9:00-6:00, SAT 9:00-1:00. (713) 284-6300
✛▲❍

**HOUSTON**—AAA TEXAS, 3307 SAGE RD, 77056. WEEKDAYS
(M-F) 9:00-6:00, SAT 9:00-1:00. (713) 284-6335 ✛▲❍

**HOUSTON**—AAA TEXAS, 8508 HWY 6 N, 77095. WEEKDAYS
(M-F) 9:00-6:00, SAT 9:00-1:00. (713) 284-6630 ✛▲❍

**HOUSTON**—AAA TEXAS, 9311 KATY FWY #E, 77024.
WEEKDAYS (M-F) 9:00-6:00, SAT 9:00-1:00. (713) 284-6489
✛▲❍

**HUMBLE**—AAA TEXAS, 9761 FM 1960 BYP, 77338. WEEKDAYS
(M-F) 9:00-6:00, SAT 9:00-1:00. (713) 834-3320 ❍

**IRVING**—AAA TEXAS, 941 MACARTHUR PK DR #100, 75063.
WEEKDAYS (M-F) 9:00-6:00, SAT 9:00-1:00. (972) 444-7800
✛▲❍

**LEWISVILLE**—AAA TEXAS, 713 HEBRON PKWY #270, 75057.
WEEKDAYS (M-F) 9:00-6:00, SAT 9:00-1:00. (972) 316-5660
✛▲❍

**MISSOURI CITY**—AAA TEXAS, 4729 HWY 6, 77459.
WEEKDAYS (M-F) 9:00-6:00, SAT 9:00-1:00. (713) 284-6494
✛▲❍

**PLANO**—AAA TEXAS, 7200 INDEPENDENCE PKY 224, 75025.
WEEKDAYS (M-F) 9:00-6:00, SAT 9:00-1:00. (214) 706-3757
✛▲❍

**ROUND ROCK**—AAA TEXAS, 201 UNIVERSITY OAKS #750,
78665. WEEKDAYS (M-F) 9:00-6:00, SAT 9:00-1:00.
(512) 248-5150 ✛▲❍

**SAN ANTONIO**—AAA TEXAS, 11075 I - H 10 W STE 309, 78230.
WEEKDAYS (M-F) 9:00-6:00, SAT 9:00-1:00. (210) 877-2222
✛▲❍

**SAN ANTONIO**—AAA TEXAS, 13415 SAN PEDRO AVE, 78216.
WEEKDAYS (M-F) 9:00-6:00, SAT 9:00-1:00. (210) 499-0222
✛▲❍

# Metric Equivalents Chart

## TEMPERATURE

To convert Fahrenheit to Celsius, subtract 32 from the Fahrenheit temperature, multiply by 5 and divide by 9. To convert Celsius to Fahrenheit, multiply by 9, divide by 5 and add 32.

## ACRES

1 acre = 0.4 hectare (ha)  |  1 hectare = 2.47 acres

## MILES AND KILOMETERS

**Note:** A kilometer is approximately 5/8 or 0.6 of a mile. To convert kilometers to miles multiply by 0.6.

| Miles/Kilometers | | Kilometers/Miles | |
|---|---|---|---|
| 15 | 24.1 | 30 | 18.6 |
| 20 | 32.2 | 35 | 21.7 |
| 25 | 40.2 | 40 | 24.8 |
| 30 | 48.3 | 45 | 27.9 |
| 35 | 56.3 | 50 | 31.0 |
| 40 | 64.4 | 55 | 34.1 |
| 45 | 72.4 | 60 | 37.2 |
| 50 | 80.5 | 65 | 40.3 |
| 55 | 88.5 | 70 | 43.4 |
| 60 | 96.6 | 75 | 46.6 |
| 65 | 104.6 | 80 | 49.7 |
| 70 | 112.7 | 85 | 52.8 |
| 75 | 120.7 | 90 | 55.9 |
| 80 | 128.7 | 95 | 59.0 |
| 85 | 136.8 | 100 | 62.1 |
| 90 | 144.8 | 105 | 65.2 |
| 95 | 152.9 | 110 | 68.3 |
| 100 | 160.9 | 115 | 71.4 |

| Celsius ° | | Fahrenheit ° |
|---|---|---|
| 100 | BOILING | 212 |
| 37 | | 100 |
| 35 | | 95 |
| 32 | | 90 |
| 29 | | 85 |
| 27 | | 80 |
| 24 | | 75 |
| 21 | | 70 |
| 18 | | 65 |
| 16 | | 60 |
| 13 | | 55 |
| 10 | | 50 |
| 7 | | 45 |
| 4 | | 40 |
| 2 | | 35 |
| 0 | FREEZING | 32 |
| -4 | | 25 |
| -7 | | 20 |
| -9 | | 15 |
| -12 | | 10 |
| -15 | | 5 |
| -18 | | 0 |
| -21 | | -5 |
| -24 | | -10 |
| -27 | | -15 |

## LINEAR MEASURE

| Customary | Metric |
|---|---|
| 1 inch = 2.54 centimeters | 1 centimeter = 0.4 inches |
| 1 foot = 30 centimeters | 1 meter = 3.3 feet |
| 1 yard = 0.91 meters | 1 meter = 1.09 yards |
| 1 mile = 1.6 kilometers | 1 kilometer = .62 miles |

## LIQUID MEASURE

| Customary | Metric |
|---|---|
| 1 fluid ounce = 30 milliliters | 1 milliliter = .03 fluid ounces |
| 1 cup = .24 liters | 1 liter = 2.1 pints |
| 1 pint = .47 liters | 1 liter = 1.06 quarts |
| 1 quart = .95 liters | 1 liter = .26 gallons |
| 1 gallon = 3.8 liters | |

## WEIGHT

| If You Know: | Multiply By: | To Find: |
|---|---|---|
| Ounces | 28 | Grams |
| Pounds | 0.45 | Kilograms |
| Grams | 0.035 | Ounces |
| Kilograms | 2.2 | Pounds |

## PRESSURE

Air pressure in automobile tires is expressed in kilopascals. Multiply pound-force per square inch (psi) by 6.89 to find kilopascals (kPa).

24 psi = 165 kPa  |  28 psi = 193 kPa
26 psi = 179 kPa  |  30 psi = 207 kPa

## GALLONS AND LITERS

| Gallons/Liters | | | | Liters/Gallons | | | |
|---|---|---|---|---|---|---|---|
| 5 | 19.0 | 12 | 45.6 | 10 | 2.6 | 40 | 10.4 |
| 6 | 22.8 | 14 | 53.2 | 15 | 3.9 | 50 | 13.0 |
| 7 | 26.6 | 16 | 60.8 | 20 | 5.2 | 60 | 15.6 |
| 8 | 30.4 | 18 | 68.4 | 25 | 6.5 | 70 | 18.2 |
| 9 | 34.2 | 20 | 76.0 | 30 | 7.8 | 80 | 20.8 |
| 10 | 38.0 | 25 | 95.0 | 35 | 9.1 | 90 | 23.4 |

578

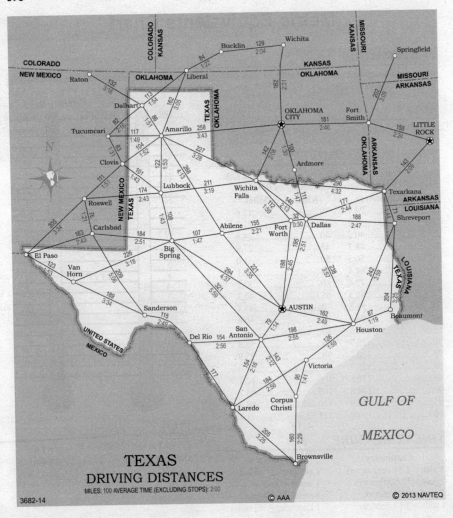

## TEXAS
### DRIVING DISTANCES
MILES: 100 AVERAGE TIME (EXCLUDING STOPS): 2:00

3682-14

© AAA

© 2013 NAVTEQ

# Border Information

## Traveling to Mexico

### FOR U.S. AND CANADIAN RESIDENTS TRAVELING TO MEXICO

**Border crossing requirements:** Travelers are required to present proper travel documents for travel to Mexico and to return to the United States.

**Air travel:** U.S. and Canadian citizens traveling between the United States and Mexico by air are required to show a valid passport.

**Land or sea travel:** A passport or passport card, or other U.S. official ID (not including a state-issued driver's license), is required to enter Mexico by land or sea. U.S. citizens returning to the United States from Mexico by land or sea are required to present proper travel documents according to the Western Hemisphere Travel Initiative. Approved documents include a passport or passport card, Enhanced Driver's License or Trusted Traveler program card; for more information refer to the U.S. Department of State's website travel.state.gov. Canadian citizens should refer to the Canada Border Services Agency website cbsa-asfc.gc.ca for requirements to re-enter Canada.

**Children:** Minors under age 18 traveling alone or with one parent are not required to present a notarized letter of consent from one or both absent parents giving permission to go on the trip, or furnish proof of parent/child relationship, such as a birth certificate or court document. This former requirement has been suspended until at least Jan. 24, 2014.

**Automobile insurance:** Full coverage from a reliable Mexican insurance company is required, including property damage and public liability. AAA offices in border states (along with offices in Nevada and Utah) can provide Mexican automobile insurance to members. U.S. or Canadian automobile insurance is not valid in Mexico.

**Tourist permits:** When traveling to Mexico as a tourist you must obtain an FMM tourist permit. You must show proof of citizenship (valid passport, birth certificate and photo ID, or voter's registration card and photo ID) to obtain a permit.

Permits are issued at Mexican consulates in the United States and Canada, immigration offices at official points of entry and at Mexican tourism offices. You must have a valid tourist permit if you remain within the border zone—the area within 20 to 30 kilometers (12 to 19 miles) of the U.S. border, depending on the Mexican state—for more than 72 hours, or if you travel beyond the border zone.

The permit costs approximately $22 (U.S.), which must be paid at a Mexican bank (see the list of banks on the back of the permit form) or at a bank window at the border. You are required to show the "Fee Paid" stamp on your tourist permit when leaving Mexico. It is recommended that you obtain your tourist permit before leaving the United States and pay the fee at the border.

If traveling by air, the permit is distributed on the flight and the fee is included in the airline ticket price. If arriving by cruise ship, the fee is collected when disembarking or is included in the cruise fare if the stay is longer than 72 hours.

**Exemptions:**
- Visitors traveling by sea, staying less than 72 hours and remaining in the seaport.
- Visitors traveling by land to destinations within the border zone and staying less than 72 hours.

- Visitors traveling by land beyond the border zone, staying less than 72 hours and limiting their visit to the following destinations/tourist corridors: Tijuana to Ensenada, Baja California; Sonoyta to Puerto Peñasco, Sonora; Ciudad Juárez to Paquime, Chihuahua; Piedras Negras to Santa Rosa, Coahuila; and Reynosa to Presa Cuchillo, Nuevo León.
- Business travelers with a business visa; students (as defined by Mexican immigration laws) with a student visa (contact a Mexican consulate for business/student visa information).

**Permit validity:**
- The permit is valid for up to 180 days.
- A multiple-entry permit allows unlimited visits into and out of Mexico within the 180-day period.
- In Baja California a tourist permit is good for a maximum of 180 days per year and 30 days per visit.
- A tourist permit not used within 90 days of issue becomes void.
- Visitors should carry their tourist permit with them at all times while in Mexico.
- If a permit is lost, obtain a duplicate from local immigration officials (write down the tourist permit number and keep it separate from the permit to expedite this process).
- Permits are required to be turned in to Mexican immigration officials at the border when you depart the country.
- If you choose to remain in Mexico beyond the permit validity period an extension must be requested from immigration authorities prior to the expiration date.
- Violation of the laws governing tourist permits may result in subsequently being refused entry into Mexico and/or incurring a substantial fine.

Vehicle travel beyond the border zone requires a government-issued temporary vehicle importation permit and a promise to return vehicle form. These two documents are not required in Baja California unless the vehicle is put on a ferry bound for the mainland. They also are not required for travel to the following destinations in the state of Sonora: Rocky Point (Puerto Peñasco), Guaymas, San Carlos, Bahía Kino and other locations west of Mex. 15, as well as cities along Mex. 15 (Magdalena, Santa Ana, Hermosillo).

An Only Sonora permit is acceptable if driving is confined within the state east of Mex. 15 as well as south of Empalme (about 350 miles south of the U.S. border). The permit can be obtained at Banjercito offices in Agua Prieta (opposite Douglas, Ariz.), Cananea (on Mex. 2 southwest of Agua Prieta) and Empalme (on Mex. 15 at Km marker 98, just south of the Guaymas bypass).

To obtain the temporary vehicle importation permit and promise to return vehicle form at an official point of entry (immigration checkpoint), the vehicle owner must have a valid (unexpired) tourist permit, a valid international major credit card and a current vehicle license/registration receipt (the original and two copies). Information on the application for temporary vehicle importation and on the promise to return form must match; the same requirements apply to both.

An administration fee plus tax must be paid with a major international credit card (American Express, Mastercard or Visa) at the official point of entry (mainland border crossing or ferry crossing from Baja California to the mainland) in order to receive a temporary importation permit windshield sticker. The credit card must be in the vehicle owner's name and issued by a U.S. or Canadian bank or lending institution. Vehicle owners who don't have a major credit card must post a bond ($200 to $400 based on vehicle value) with a Mexican bonding firm (Afianzadora) at the point of entry. Cash, checks, money orders or credit cards issued by a Mexican bank are not accepted.

**More about temporary importation permits:**
- Generally issued for 180 days, the same length as the tourist permit.
- Only one permit will be issued per person, for one motorized vehicle at a time.
- Carry the permit with you; do not leave it in the vehicle.
- Return permit, promise to return vehicle form and windshield sticker to Mexican customs officials at the Banjercito office at the border before or on the expiration date shown on the form, or be subject to a fine.
- If the permit or form is lost or stolen, Mexican customs offices can issue replacement documentation provided you obtain a certified document attesting to the loss from your homeland (U.S. or Canada) embassy or consulate.
- If you remain in Mexico beyond the authorized time period and without the

proper documentation, your car will be immediately confiscated.

**Pets:** U.S. visitors may bring a dog, cat or bird into Mexico with government approval. A pet health certificate signed not more than 15 days before the animal enters Mexico and a pet vaccination certificate showing proof of treatment for rabies, hepatitis and leptospirosis are required at the border for each animal. A pet permit fee is charged at the time of entry.

# Leaving Mexico

## FOR U.S. AND CANADIAN RESIDENTS LEAVING MEXICO

### When leaving the country:
- FMM tourist permits, temporary vehicle importation permits, promise to return vehicle forms and windshield stickers must be returned to Mexican immigration and customs officials at the departure or border checkpoint (or at an interior inspection point).
- Those entering Mexico with a motor vehicle must leave the country with the vehicle.
- At highway stations near the U.S. border, Mexican agricultural officials will inspect vehicles traveling north that are carrying any fruits, vegetables, houseplants and other plant matter.
- You must have an export certificate to take official cultural artifacts (excluding handicrafts) out of the country.

- Religious or archeological artifacts may not be taken out of the country.

### Returning to the United States or Canada:

U.S. citizens returning from Mexico by land or sea are required to present proper travel documents; refer to the U.S. Department of State website for the most current information. Canadian citizens entering the United States are subject to the rules governing entry to the U.S. by foreign nationals; refer to the Canadian Border Services Agency website for requirements to re-enter Canada.

### U.S. exemptions:
- You may bring back duty-free articles not exceeding $800 in retail value from a stay abroad of at least 48 hours.
- The exemption is allowed once every 30 days.
- A family (related persons living in the same household) may combine exemptions; i.e., a family of six would be entitled to $1,600 worth of goods duty-free on one declaration, even if the articles claimed by one member exceed that individual's $800 amount.
- Duty must be paid on all items in excess of the exemption amount.
- Payment of duty is required upon arrival.
- Gifts taken across the U.S./Mexico border are considered to be for personal use and are included in the $800 exemption.
- Articles purchased and left behind for alterations or other reasons do not qualify for the $800 exemption when shipped at a later date.
- The $800 exemption may include no more than 1 liter of alcoholic beverages and no more than 200 cigarettes and 100 cigars.

**Restricted or prohibited articles:** An agricultural quarantine bans the importation of certain fruits, vegetables, plants, livestock, poultry and meats. All food products brought into the United States must be declared. The U.S. Department of Agriculture also prohibits bringing back any type of pet. Visit the Animal and Plant Health Inspection Service (APHIS) website or U.S. Customs at cbp.gov for more information.

One foreign-made article carrying a protected U.S. trademark (i.e., camera, binoculars, musical instrument, jewelry or watch) may normally be brought into the United States under your personal exemption, provided it is for your private use and not sold within 1 year of importation. Some perfumes are limited to one bottle and others are prohibited; inquire about trademark restrictions beforehand.

The following are prohibited: narcotics and dangerous drugs, drug paraphernalia, obscene articles and publications, seditious or treasonable matter, lottery tickets, hazardous items (fireworks, dangerous toys, toxic or poisonous substances) and switchblade knives. Goods originating in the following embargoed countries are prohibited: Western Balkans, Burma, Ivory Coast, Cuba, Democratic Republic of Congo, Iran, Iraq, Liberia, Sierra Leone, Sudan, Syria and Zimbabwe.

If you plan to bring back items made of fur or whalebone, any animal skin other than cowhide leather, or any product manufactured wholly or in part from any type of wildlife, contact the U.S. Fish and Wildlife Service's Office of Law Enforcement, 4401 N. Fairfax Dr., MS-LE-3000, Arlington, VA 22203. Phone (703) 358-1949 for regulations; fws.gov/le.

**Alcoholic beverages:** Both federal and state laws apply. When regulations conflict state laws supersede; know the import limits of your state of residence and the state of entry.

U.S. residents 21 years of age or older may bring into the United States 1 liter of alcohol duty-free once every 30 days. However, if you arrive in a state that permits a lesser amount than what you have legally brought into the United States, state law prevails.

**Gifts:** Gifts in packages with a total retail value not exceeding $100 may be sent to friends or relatives in the United States free of U.S. customs duty or tax, provided no recipient receives more than one gift shipment per day. Gifts may be sent to more than one person in the same package if they are individually wrapped and labeled with each recipient's name. Perfumes valued at more than $5 retail, tobacco products or alcoholic beverages may not be included in gift packages, which should be clearly marked with the designation "Unsolicited Gift," the gift giver's name and the retail value of the contents.

**Duties:** A flat rate duty of 3 percent is applied to the first $1,000 (fair retail value) worth of merchandise in excess of the $800 customs exemption. A sales receipt constitutes proof of value. Family members

residing in one household and traveling together may group articles for application of the flat-duty rate, which may be taken once every 30 days. Articles must accompany you to the U.S. border.

**Canadian exemptions:** Citizens who have been outside Canada at least 48 hours may bring back duty- and tax-free goods not exceeding $400 (CAN) in retail value. The exemption can be claimed any number of times a year. Citizens who have been outside Canada 7 days or more may bring back duty- and tax-free goods not exceeding $750 (CAN) in retail value. The $750 exemption can be claimed regardless of any $400 exemption taken on a previous trip and requires a written declaration. The two exemptions may not be combined.

Citizens may claim duty- and tax-free entry for articles (excluding tobacco products or alcoholic beverages) not exceeding $50 (CAN) in retail value when returning from a trip abroad of at least 24 hours. Items brought into Canada under a personal exemption must be for personal or household use, souvenirs or gifts.

**Canadian limitations (on either the $400 or $750 exemption):** 50 cigars, 200 cigarettes, 200 tobacco sticks, 200 grams (6.4 ounces) of tobacco, 40 ounces (1.1 liters) of liquor, 53 imperial ounces of wine and 300 ounces (8.5 liters) of beer or ale (equivalent to 24 12-ounce bottles/cans). All exemptions are individual and may not be combined with that of another person to cover an article valued at more than the maximum exemption. You may be asked to prove the length of your visit outside Canada. Dated sales receipts for goods or services constitute valid proof.

All declared goods associated with the $400 personal exemption must accompany the purchaser to the Canadian border. Declared goods associated with the $750 personal exemption may follow the purchaser by mail.

While AAA makes every effort to provide accurate and complete information, AAA makes no warranty, express or implied, and assumes no legal liability or responsibility for the accuracy or completeness of any information contained herein.

# Points of Interest Index

 Attractions appear at the top of each category
and offer a Great Experience for Members®.

## Index Legend

| | |
|---|---|
| NB....................... national battlefield | NR....................national river |
| NBP...................national battlefield park | NS........................national seashore |
| NC.................... national cemetery | NWR..................national wildlife refuge |
| NF......................national forest | PHP...................provincial historic(al) park |
| NHM........ national historic(al) monument | PHS....................provincial historic(al) site |
| NHP.......... national historic(al) park | PP..........................provincial park |
| NHS.............national historic(al) site | SF.............................state forest |
| NL.......................national lakeshore | SHM........ state historic(al) monument |
| NME.................... national memorial | SHP..................state historic(al) park |
| NMO..................national monument | SHS............ state historic(al) site |
| NMP.............national military park | SME........................state memorial |
| NP.......................national park | SP...........................state park |
| NRA.............national recreation area | SRA.................state recreation area |

## CHILDREN'S ACTIVITIES

## EVENTS & FESTIVALS

## OUTDOORS & SCIENCE

## SHOPPING

## SPORTS & RECREATION

# Photo Credits

Page numbers are in bold type. Picture credit abbreviations are as follows:
- (i) numeric sequence from top to bottom, left to right ■ (AAA) AAA Travel library.

- (Cover) Texas State Capitol, Austin / © iStockphoto.com / nashvilledino2
- **2** (i) © Rolf Nussbaumer / DanitaDelimont.com
- **2** (ii) © SuperStock / Alamy
- **2** (iii) © Chris Howes / Wild Places Photography / Alamy
- **2** (iv) © SuperStock / age fotostock
- **7** © Monashee Frantz / age fotostock
- **13** © iStockphoto.com / Adivin
- **18** (i) © BILL HEINSOHN / age fotostock
- **18** (ii) © svenwerk / flickr
- **19** © Rolf Nussbaumer / DanitaDelimont.com
- **20** (i) © Chris Howes / Wild Places Photography / Alamy
- **20** (ii) Courtesy of Wikimedia Commons
- **23** (i) © SuperStock / age fotostock
- **23** (ii) © Claudia Uripos / eStock Photo
- **23** (iii) © TowPix / eStock Photo
- **23** (iv) Published with permission from AAA travel editor Maria White
- **23** (v) © Peter Miller / eStock Photo
- **24** (i) © Scott T. Smith / DanitaDelimont.com
- **24** (ii) © Horizons WWP / Alamy
- **24** (iii) © Chris Howes / Wild Places Photography / Alamy
- **24** (iv) © Keith Kapple / Alamy
- **160** © Richard Cummins / age fotostock
- **163** © AAA. Photo by AAA travel editor Maria White for AAA

- **164** © Witold Skrypczak / Alamy
- **165** © SuperStock / Alamy
- **166** © Ian Dagnall / Alamy
- **167** © AAA. Photo by AAA travel editor Maria White for AAA
- **168** © Mauricio Rojas / Alamy
- **171** © SuperStock / age fotostock
- **172** © SuperStock / age fotostock
- **300** © Richard Cummins / age fotostock
- **303** © Horizons WWP / Alamy
- **304** © Gabbro / Alamy
- **305** © Larry Lamsa / flickr
- **306** © Gabbro / Alamy
- **311** © Michael DeFreitas North America / Alamy
- **457** © Michael DeFreitas / age fotostock
- **460** Published with permission from AAA travel editor Greg Weekes
- **461** © Adam Jones / DanitaDelimont.com
- **462** © Stuart Seeger / flickr
- **463** © Dave Wilson / flickr
- **464** Published with permission from AAA associate Thuyvi Gates
- **465** © Don Despain / Alamy
- **466** © Nikreates / Alamy
- **471** © Bernard Friel / DanitaDelimont.com
- **475** © Dennis Cox / Alamy
- **477** Published with permission from AAA travel editor Greg Weekes
- **579** © Garry Gay / Alamy
- **581** © Danita Delimont / Alamy

# AAA Auto Buying Tools

*New Car? Simple.*

Download the free iPhone app or use AAA AutoMaker® on AAA.com

- **SEARCH** hundreds of vehicle makes and models
- **COMPARE** vehicles, get TrueCar price reports, view photo galleries, read AAA reviews
- **BUILD** your ideal car by make/model, style and price

AAA.com/mobile

# Evaluate Your Driving Ability.

# Get Home Safely.

Assess your driving skills and
make adjustments before your next trip.

 AAA.com/DrivingEvaluation

# LET'S GET SOCIAL
## Stay connected with #AAA

Visit with us on your favorite social media sites for the latest updates on hot discounts, cool destinations and handy automotive know-how.

## Talk with us!

- Plus.google.com/+AAAnews
- Twitter.com/AAA_Travel
- YouTube.com/AAA
- Facebook.com/AAAFanPage
- Pinterest.com/AAA

# Find your way: AAA/CAA Road Atlases

Plan or change your driving route with up-close, up-to-date road maps.

Enjoy exceptional features like easy-to-read map text, same-page indexing, mileage and clearly identified exit numbers on major highways. Choose the standard version or the Easy Reading edition featuring 40 percent larger type.

*Purchase at participating AAA/CAA club offices.*